The Ku Klux Klan

The Ku Klux Klan

History, Organization, Language,
Influence and Activities of America's
Most Notorious Secret Society

MICHAEL NEWTON

McFarland & Company, Inc., Publishers
Jefferson, North Carolina, and London

Library of Congress Cataloguing-in-Publication Data

Newton, Michael, 1951–
The Ku Klux Klan : history, organization, language, influence and
activities of America's most notorious secret society / Michael Newton.
p. cm.
Includes bibliographical references and index.

ISBN-13: 978-0-7864-2787-1
ISBN-10: 0-7864-2787-6
(illustrated case binding : 50# alkaline paper) ∞

1. Ku Klux Klan (1915–)—History.
2. Ku-Klux Klan (1866–1869)—History. I. Title.
HS2330.K63N494 2007 322.4'20973—dc22 2006030954

British Library cataloguing data are available

Cover photograph ©2006 PhotoSpin

Manufactured in the United States of America

*McFarland & Company, Inc., Publishers
Box 611, Jefferson, North Carolina 28640
www.mcfarlandpub.com*

For David Mark Chalmers

TABLE OF CONTENTS

PREFACE

The Ku Klux Klan was ninety-five years old when I encountered it for the first time, in June 1961. The setting was a movie theater on Fremont Street, in Las Vegas, Nevada. White-robed klansmen swarmed across the screen, larger than life, wreaking havoc before they were outwitted and corralled by G-man James Stewart in a segment of *The FBI Story*.

I was vaguely aware of the Klan by that time—one month earlier, its members had received global publicity for terrorizing Alabama freedom riders—but I generally paid no more attention to the news than any other nine-year-old. Now, Hollywood's portrayal of the KKK fired my imagination with its flaming crosses, ghostly costumes, and the narrator's description of "a secret society so powerful it didn't have to be secret." I vowed to learn more about this mysterious group, whose members trafficked in mayhem while concealing their identities beneath peaked hoods.

The information was not long in coming. Klan-watching was all the rage in the 1960s, with daily reports of racist atrocities below the Mason-Dixon Line. Bombings and beatings were routine, arrests so rare they seemed miraculous when they occurred. In June 1963, two years to the week since I had first glimpsed the Klan, one of its members murdered civil rights crusader Medgar Evers at his Mississippi home. Three months later, on the eve of my twelfth birthday, an Alabama church bombing slaughtered four girls my own age. In 1965, with more Ku Klux assassinations in the headlines, David Chalmers released his magisterial history of the Klan, *Hooded Americanism*. I found it at my high school library during my freshman year.

We learned, in those days, that police were not always our friends, and that the mighty FBI sometimes deliberately failed to get its man if he was white, his victims black. High-ranking politicians pandered to the Klan and helped conceal its crimes, accomplices after the fact. The federal government, meanwhile, seemed powerless to guarantee the safety of Americans in their own land. The litany of dead and maimed from Dixie had a numbing quality: James Chaney. Michael Schwerner. Andrew Goodman. Lemuel Penn. James Reeb. Viola Liuzzo. O'Neal Moore. Jonathan Daniels. Vernon Dahmer. Wharlest Jackson. Martin Luther King. All slain by Klansmen or in circumstances where the KKK was implicated by persuasive evidence.

For all those lessons, yet another decade passed before my father let it slip in conversation that my grandfather had been a member of the 1920s Oklahoma Klan. One memorable night, a truckload of "the boys" in full regalia had pulled into his yard, calling John Newton from the house to ask if he was coming with them to enjoy the subsequent festivities. He put them off with some excuse, but surely there were other nights when he did not refuse. By then, I knew that Oklahoma's Klan had been among the most sadistic in the nation, whipping thousands, killing an uncertain number, prior to a decree of statewide martial law in 1923.

This book, my fourth devoted to the KKK, is the product of research spanning forty-five years, but I could not have finished it alone. As with so many other projects in the past, I owe a heartfelt debt of gratitude to David Frasier, friend and researcher *par excellence* at Indiana University. Mark Potoc and his staff of the Southern Poverty Law Center provided valuable information and assistance in obtaining illustrations; they deserve a special vote of gratitude for their persistent, often hazardous, surveillance of American hate groups. Jerry Mitchell, with the Jackson *Clarion-Ledger,* supplied material on an elusive Mississippi case. Margaret Locken, likewise, provided critical material on several Mississippi crimes.

Above all else, I wish to thank my wife, Heather, for her unfailing love and support.

Every effort has been made to ensure the accuracy of information contained herein. Any factual mistakes are the author's sole responsibility, and readers are invited to submit corrections or updates of KKK activity, either through McFarland or directly to the author at his website, http://www.michaelnewton.homestead.com.

ABBREVIATIONS

ACCA—Anti-Communist Christian Association
ACLU—American Civil Liberties Union
ACMHR—Alabama Christian Movement for Human Rights
ADL—Anti-Defamation League
AFL—American Federation of Labor
AGK—Association of Georgia Klans
AIP—American Independent Party
ANP—American Nazi Party
APWR—Americans for Preservation of the White Race
ARA—Aryan Republican Army
ATF—Bureau of Alcohol, Tobacco and Firearms
AUL—American Unity League
CCC—Council of Conservative Citizens
CIA—Central Intelligence Agency
CIO—Congress of Industrial Organizations
CJJC—Church of Jesus Christ Christian
COFO—Council of Federated Organizations
COINTELPRO—counterintelligence program (FBI)
CPUSA—Communist Party, USA
CSA—Covenant, Sword and Arm of the Lord
CUG—Constitutional Union Guard
DOJ—Department of Justice
EURO—European-American Unity and Rights Organization
FBI—Federal Bureau of Investigation
FCC—Federal Communications Commission
FDLE—Florida Department of Law Enforcement
FDR—Franklin Delano Roosevelt
FEPC—Fair Employment Practices Commission
GBI—Georgia Bureau of Investigation
GOP—Republican Party (Grand Old Party)
HSCA—House Select Committee on Assassinations
HUAC—House Committee on Un-American Activities
IEKKKK—Invisible Empire Knights of the KKK
ILD—International Labor Defense
IRS—Internal Revenue Service
IWW—Industrial Workers of the World
JBS—John Birch Society
JDL—Jewish Defense League
JFK—John Fitzgerald Kennedy
KBI—Klan Bureau of Investigation
KKK—Ku Klux Klan
KKKK—Knights of the Ku Klux Klan
KoC—Knights of Columbus
KRS—Knights of the Rising Sun
KWC—Knights of the White Camellia
KYC—Klan Youth Corps

LAPD—Los Angeles Police Department
LBJ—Lyndon Baines Johnson
LDS—Latter-Day Saints (Mormons)
LOS—League of the South
LSU—Louisiana State University (Baton Rouge)
MFDP—Mississippi Freedom Democratic Party
NAACP—National Association for the Advancement of Colored People
NAAWP—National Association for the Advancement of White People
NLRB—National Labor Relations Board
NOFEAR—National Organization for European American Rights
NOI—Nation of Islam (Black Muslims)
NRA—National Rifle Association
NRP—National Renaissance Party
NSPA—National Socialist Party of America
NSRP—National States Rights Party
NSLF—National Socialist Liberation Front
NSWPP—National Socialist White People's Party
NYPD—New York City Police Department
OEO—Office of Economic Opportunity
RRRR—Royal Riders of the Red Robe
SCB—Southern Conference on Bombing
SCHW—Southern Conference on Human Welfare
SCLC—Southern Christian Leadership Conference
SCU—Share Croppers' Union
SDA—Seventh-Day Adventist Church
SDS—Students for a Democratic Society
SLED—South Carolina Law Enforcement Division
SNCC—Student Nonviolent Coordinating Committee
SNYC—Southern Negro Youth Conference
SPLC—Southern Poverty Law Center
STFU—Southern Tenant Farmers Union
SWP—Socialist Workers Party
UACG—United Americans for Conservative Government
UFKKK—United Florida Ku Klux Klan
UKA—United Klans of America
UNIA—Universal Negro Improvement Association
WAR—White Aryan Resistance
WCC—World Church of the Creator
WCTU—Women's Christian Temperance Union
WKKKKM—White Knights of the KKK of Mississippi
WKL—White Knights of Liberty
WPP—White Patriot Party
YMDC—Young Men's Democratic Club

1 A BRIEF HISTORY OF THE KU KLUX KLAN

America suffers from a recurring nightmare. For the past 140 years, the Land of Opportunity has harbored terrorists who pledge themselves to crushing any hope of progress for minorities—nonwhites, non–Christians, immigrants, or anyone who does not toe the line of fundamentalist Old Testament "morality." The punishment for nonconformity is arson, bombing, whipping, mutilation—even death. Attired in ghostly robes, their faces hidden under hoods, today these insurrectionists conspire against the U.S. government itself.

Most white Americans, if asked to sketch a terrorist, would draw a swarthy Middle Eastern figure with a turban and a beard. If pressed, they might recall that certain Irishmen have planted bombs from time to time, while sundry Africans and Eastern Europeans have indulged in genocide. Perhaps one in a thousand realizes that the oldest group of terrorists still active in the world today was spawned on U.S. soil—or that it had more than 160 active, well-armed units nationwide in May 2006.

That group has murdered thousands and injured tens of thousands more. It has destroyed or damaged property worth untold millions. It has rioted, skirmished with U.S. troops, and toppled state governments. It has infiltrated law enforcement agencies, state governments, Congress, the U.S. Supreme Court—and the White House itself.

It is the Ku Klux Klan.

Those who believe the KKK is dead and gone, consigned to ancient history, are sadly misinformed. It lives today—a shadow of its former self, perhaps, but armed and dangerous, allied with kindred groups all dedicated to a single goal: elimination of their enemies from the American landscape by any means available. To face the modern Klan and its persistent threat to the United States, however, we must understand its history.

"White Man's Country"

Every human organization has a finite point of origin, but social movements may be decades—even centuries—in the making, and the KKK is no exception. Its seed was planted in late August 1619, when the first ship carrying twenty African slaves dropped anchor off Jamestown, Virginia. Between 1641 and 1750, eleven British colonies legally recognized slavery. Between 1664 and 1725, seven colonies passed "antiamalgamation" statutes, banning interracial marriages. Thus was racism enshrined by law in North America, beginning 135 years before the Declaration of Independence.

The story of slavery's spread and later concentration in the southern states is too well known to bear repetition here. Despite the efforts of modern neo–Confederate spokesmen to paint Dixie's "peculiar institution" in a flattering light, chattel slavery in America was a daily exercise in brutality, dehumanizing both sides. Captive Africans were not always the passive "darkies" some historians pretend, however. Many fled their masters, while others fought back with the weapons at hand. On 13 September 1663, an indentured servant betrayed America's first serious slave-revolt conspiracy in Gloucester County, Virginia. Another rocked New York City in April 1712, leaving nine whites dead and twenty-one slaves condemned to death by torture. Rebellious slaves killed twenty-five whites at Stono, South Carolina, before their uprising was crushed on 9 September 1739. Between 1750 and 1860, no fewer than 400 slave revolts were reported from various points in the South.

Dixie's answer, in addition to the mass execution of convicted rebels and "incendiaries," was the institution of organized slave patrols (known to bondsmen as "patterollers"). Most slave states made patrol service mandatory for white males of a certain age, although Louisiana called for volunteers. Tennessee required "all citizens" to serve on the patrols, imposing a five-dollar fine for each instance of refusal. Mississippi, meanwhile, imposed the duty only on slave owners and men subject to state militia duty below the rank of captain. In most states, legislation notwithstanding, wealthy men avoided service by employing mercenaries. One contemporary observer described those hired recruits as "just about the worst fellows that can be found, as bad as you could pick up on the wharves. The reason is that no decent man will undertake the business." Empowered to search any place where slaves might hide, and to seize any black person found abroad at night without a pass from his or her master, the patrols became a law unto themselves.

Long before the KKK was organized, slave masters and patrollers pioneered the methods later used by klansmen. Some masters and overseers kept their slaves home at night with tales of "haunts" at large, donning ghostly costumes to frighten those who questioned the stories. Many patrollers also wore disguises, presenting themselves as ghosts, though some slaves saw through the charade. Texas bondsman Leonard Franklin recalled:

> A paterole come in one night before freedom and asked for a drink of water. He said he was thirsty. He had a rubber thing on and drank two or three buckets of water. His rubber bag swelled up and made his head or the thing that looked like his head under the hood grow taller. Instead of gettin' 'fraid, mother threw a shovelful of hot ashes on him and I'll tell you he lit out from there and never did come back no more.

Post-war klansmen used that very trick and others like it to cow superstitious freedmen, but as with the patrols, violence followed inevitably when "jokes" failed to produce submission. Frequently intoxicated, armed with arbitrary power, patrollers invaded black homes at will and "subject[ed] them to all manner of outrages." Maryland Senator Reverdy Johnson (1863–68) described the original KKK as "the legitimate offspring of the patrol," and one slave—J.T. Tims—claimed that the Klan's name was invoked even before secession. "It was before the war that I knew 'bout the Ku Klux," Tims wrote. "There wasn't no difference between the patroles and the Ku Klux that I knows of. If th'd ketch you, they all would whip you. I don't know nothin' about the Ku Klux Klan after the War." No other source describes a pre-war KKK, and Tims may well have been confused, but there is no doubt that Dixie's first klansmen either had served on slave patrols or were acquainted with their methods. John Hunnicut, who led some of the Klan's first raids around Greensboro, Alabama, in early 1868, later bragged to friends that he and other nightriders terrorized blacks "in regular old style."

While southern masters learned to fear their slaves and organized patrols to keep them off the roads at night, Americans above the Mason-Dixon Line were preoccupied with another "alien" menace, personified by the Pope and his Roman Catholic followers. Sectarian hatred preceded discovery of the New World and sparked North America's first religious massacre (French Huguenot Protestants slaughtered by Spanish Catholics) at the site of modern-day St. Augustine, Florida, in September 1565. Anti-Catholicism flourished in colonial America, resulting in attacks on convents and churches, while New York City's nineteenth-century street gangs fought pitched battles between Irish Catholics and self-styled "true Americans." The country's first bona fide nativist organization, the American Brotherhood, was launched from New York in December 1844, later changing its name to the Order of United Americans. A competing group, the Supreme Order of the Star-Spangled Banner (SSSB), warned its oath-bound members to say, "I know nothing" if questioned regarding the group, its rituals or illegal activities.

Thus was born the "Know-Nothing" movement, a loose confederation of bigots who spent a decade rioting in Kentucky, Maine, Massachusetts, Missouri, New Hampshire, New Jersey, New York, Ohio and Pennsylvania. Their victims were most often Catholics, but "true American" mobs also targeted Jews, Mormons, blacks and abolitionists who sought an end to slavery. In 1854, organized as the American Party, Know-Nothings won seats in Congress and captured various state offices. (They also stole and destroyed a block of granite contributed by Pope Pius IX for the Washington Monument.) AP votes elected Levi

Boone as Chicago's mayor in 1855, whereupon he barred all immigrants from city jobs. A year later, Know-Nothing support failed to grant Millard Fillmore a second term as president, but he polled 874,534 votes nationwide. With regard to the KKK, historian Carleton Beals notes that notes that certain early Klan oaths and "a few of the actors" were "the same as in Know-Nothingism." In fact, Beals claims, the birthplace of the Klan—Pulaski, Tennessee—was "controlled by the Know-Nothings as early as 1854." In Tennessee and Kentucky, Beals reports, local chapters of the SSSB were known as "clans" or "klans."

Hatred of Catholics was put on hold in 1861, with the eruption of the Civil War. Four years of combat over slavery produced 10,455 armed engagements, leaving a reported 623,026 persons dead on both sides, with at least 471,427 wounded. Most southern soldiers owned no slaves, but as author Robert Goldston explains, "Southern poor whites were the system's most vigorous, even fanatical defenders. They had no education—most were illiterate—and their primitive religions, backwoods Methodism or Baptism, had long since become propaganda organs for the 'divine' sanction of slavery." As stated by historian Ulrich Phillips, the "central theme" of southern history was a determination to preserve the section as "a white man's country." It was a lost cause, all the same—or so the Union victors thought in 1865—but Confederate President Jefferson Davis held a different view. With Dixie in ruins, Davis confided to a friend, "The Confederate cause is not lost, but is only sleeping."

Birth of the KKK

America's most persistent terrorist group began life as a private social club in the spring of 1866. Its founders were six young Confederate veterans, residing in Pulaski, Tennessee. All were in their twenties, the well-educated sons of good families. Their number included a judge's son, three fledgling attorneys, a future state legislator, a future Masonic Grand Master of Tennessee, and the editor-in-chief of Giles County's only newspaper. As described by one of them, years later, they were "hungering and thirsting" for amusement after four long years of war. Their only goal, at first, was to "have fun, make mischief, and play pranks on the public."

To that end, they organized a secret society. Some of them were college men, familiar with the southern collegiate fraternity Kuklos Adelphon ("circle of brothers"), founded at the University of North Carolina in 1812, which spread throughout the South in antebellum decades and dissolved during the Civil War. They chose *ku klux*—a corruption of the Greek *kuklos* ("circle") as the name of their club, adding *clan* (spelled with a "k" for uniformity). As founding officers, they made up lofty titles for themselves: Frank McCord became the Grand Cyclops, John B. Kennedy the Grand Magi, Major James Crowe the Grand Turk, and Richard Reed the Lictor, while Calvin Jones and Captain John Lester served as Night Hawks. Costumes were left to the individual member's taste, stressing a flair for the ghoulish and bizarre. As far as playing pranks, "the public" was primarily confined to superstitious former slaves, whom klansmen terrorized at will by posing as the ghosts or zombies of Confederate

Early Klan costumes were sometimes complex and unique.

Codes" passed by every southern state, which made a public mockery of the Thirteenth Amendment's ban on slavery. Under the Black Codes, freedmen were variously forbidden to own land or weapons, to break labor contracts with white employers or establish any "independent business," to make "insulting gestures" or utter "seditious speeches." South Carolina barred blacks from any occupation except "farmer or house servant." Florida prescribed thirty-nine lashes for blacks who "intruded" on white assemblies or public conveyances, while the same punishment awaited blacks caught publicly smoking cigars in Selma, Alabama. "Stubborn or refractory servants" could be fined $50 under Alabama's Black Code, or "hired out at auction for a period of six months" if unable to pay the fine. Black children over two years old could be torn from their families and "apprenticed" to whites until maturity, if their parents failed to teach them white-approved "habits of industry and honesty."

Congressional Republicans, dubbed "Radicals" by white-supremacist southern Democrats, were livid at the South's flagrant defiance. In April 1866 they passed America's first Civil Rights Bill, overriding President Johnson's veto. Two months later, a Fourteenth Amendment to the U.S. Constitution was approved—again over Johnson's veto—to guarantee freedmen full citizenship. President Johnson's third veto was overridden in January 1867, with passage of a law granting the vote to blacks in Washington, D.C. Southern whites reacted to the news from Washington as they had for generations, with violence directed toward blacks. In May 1866, Memphis police led white rioters on a pogrom that left forty-six freedmen and two white Republicans dead, more than eighty blacks wounded, with ninety black homes, twelve schools and four churches burned to the ground. Two months later, New Orleans police led another massacre, killing thirty-four blacks and wounding more than 200. Throughout Dixie, individual lynchings, murders and assaults upon freedmen increased exponentially.

war dead. Almost at once, the Klan lured new initiates and soon expanded from Giles County to surrounding districts.

Pulaski's "social club" arrived at an auspicious time in southern history. Martyred president Abraham Lincoln and his successor, Tennessee Unionist Andrew Johnson, had proposed a simple plan for readmission of the wayward Confederate states. In order to rejoin the Union, ten percent of each state's white electorate from 1860 was required to abolish slavery, repeal secession ordinances, and repudiate any Confederate war debts. Blanket amnesty was granted to any ex–Confederate (except ranking leaders of the late rebel government), who swore an oath of loyalty to the United States. By November 1865, every state except Texas had complied with those terms. Newly elected senators and representatives stood ready to take their seats on Capitol Hill when Congress reconvened on 4 December 1865.

The Republicans who dominated Congress quickly dashed those hopes. Presidential Reconstruction was too slick and easy for embittered war hawks like Charles Sumner and Thaddeus Stevens, who wanted the Old South to pay for its sins. More to the point, those sins were still ongoing, in the form of "Black

Redeeming Dixie

On 2 March 1867, Congress passed the first of several Reconstruction Acts, dividing the former Confederacy into military districts ruled by Union generals, ordering new elections for state constitutional conventions, and empowering blacks to vote for the first time in southern history. One month later, the KKK's Pulaski den called a meeting at Nashville's Maxwell House hotel, synchronized with the state's Democratic convention. The meeting's purpose was declared in secret circulars:

> To reorganize the Klan on a plan corresponding to its size and present purposes; to bind the isolated Dens together; to secure unity of purpose and concert of action; to hedge the members up by such limitations and regulations as are best adapted to restrain them within proper limits; to distribute the authority among prudent men at local centers and exact from them a close supervision of those under their charge.

The Klan's unstated "present purpose" was guerrilla warfare against blacks, Republicans, and any other groups or individuals who jeopardized the vaunted "southern way of life," embodied in the antebellum economic system and the holy creed of white supremacy. To that end, a command structure was formalized including provinces (counties), dominions (congressional districts), and realms (states). Each state would theoretically be ruled by a grand dragon, while Dixie at large—now christened the Klan's "Invisible Empire"—would be supervised by an autocratic grand wizard. In its new prescript, the Klan vowed to "recognize our relations to the United States Government and acknowledge the supremacy of its laws," while dedicating itself "To the Lovers of Law and Order, Peace and Justice."

The Klan's choice for grand wizard demonstrated the gap between stated ideals and practical reality. Forty-six-year-old Nathan Bedford Forrest was a former slave trader and Confederate cavalry leader, known in equal measure for his daring in combat and gross insubordination (including death threats) to his superiors in uniform. In April 1864 his troops had massacred black prisoners of war at Fort Pillow, Tennessee, their victims including a number of women and children. Controversy persists as to whether Forrest ordered the slaughter or simply lost control of his men, but one telling report describes his tour of the killing ground, pointing out individual corpses and remarking, "They've been in my nigger-yard in Memphis." Appointed grand wizard in May 1867, Forrest insured by his style of command that the reorganized KKK would combine the worst aspects of violence and irresponsibility.

Wherever dens were organized, a racist reign of terror ensued. Tennessee witnessed the first bloodshed by klansmen under Grand Dragon George Gordon, with Pulaski and Giles County among the state's most lawless districts. Murders were common, and floggings more so; one victim was left crippled after he received 900 lashes on a midnight raid. In Alabama, Congress documented 109 murders committed by Grand Dragon John Morgan's knights, and that number was no doubt conservative. Klansmen burned Greene County's courthouse, followed shortly by three schools for blacks. In Eutaw, Klan rioters killed four blacks and wounded fifty in October 1870. Georgia was worse yet, under Grand Dragon (later Governor and U.S. Senator) John Gordon: in the three-month period from August to October 1868, klansmen killed thirty-one persons, shot forty-three more, stabbed five, and whipped at least fifty-five, including eight floggings of 300 to 500 lashes apiece. The Klan-led riot at Camilla, in September 1868, left seven blacks dead and over thirty injured.

Virginia suffered only scattered violence before its Klan dissolved in late 1868, but Arkansas endured a replay of the Civil War in miniature, between Governor Powell Clayton's militia and klansmen led by Grand Dragon Robert Shaver (or Augustus Garland; reports vary). Columbia County saw ten blacks killed in a three-week period of August 1868, while Lafayette County logged twenty murders in the same month. When Governor Clayton purchased muskets for his troops from New York, klansmen hijacked the shipment and destroyed them. At Lewisburg, in November 1868, klansmen destroyed one-third of the town while trying to burn a Republican's store. Louisiana's terror climaxed during the presidential campaign of 1868, with an appalling 1,081 murders, 135 persons shot and wounded, and 507 otherwise assaulted. Florida klansmen mimicked their Arkansas

brethren by stealing muskets from the state militia, appropriating some for their own use. Jackson County was among the South's worst in Reconstruction, its 179 murder victims including two Republican county clerks and the Klan's first Jewish target, liberal merchant Samuel Fleishman. Mississippi klansmen, under Grand Dragon James George, conducted a vicious campaign against black schools and "carpetbag" teachers. Meridian's riot of March 1871 started in the county courthouse, klansmen killing the judge and eight black witnesses before they ran amok through the town at large.

In Texas, where klansmen competed or collaborated with Knights of the White Camellia and Knights of the Rising Sun, near anarchy prevailed throughout Reconstruction. General John Reynolds, commanding Union forces in the Lone Star State, found murders of freedmen "so common as to render it impossible to keep an accurate record of them," and no final tabulation was attempted. Kentucky and Missouri witnessed as much Ku Klux violence as any state of the old Confederacy, but it was more diverse. In addition to the usual raids on blacks and Republicans, Kentucky klansmen burned Shaker homes at Bowling Green and devoted much of their time to defending moonshine stills. At Harrodsburg alone, they murdered twenty-five victims and flogged at least one hundred. Missouri raiders also stood guard over illegal stills, and murdered enemies of klansmen from the Deep South when they managed to escape across the Mason-Dixon Line. Klansmen got a late start on their raids in North Carolina, but they made up for it in 1869 and 1870, battling Governor William Holden's militia in Alamance and Caswell Counties. More than a hundred members were arrested, but in vain; in 1871, Holden made history as the first American governor to be impeached and removed from office. The terror lasted longest in South Carolina, where the Laurens riot of October 1870 killed twelve Republicans on the eve of state elections. York County was the Klan's strongest bastion, with two-thirds of all white men enlisted; its raiders killed at least eleven persons and flogged 600, burning down five schools and churches.

Fervent denials notwithstanding, much of the Klan's violence was clearly political. Blacks were targeted more often for voting than for any real or imaginary crimes, and Republican officials of both races were constantly at risk throughout the South. In every state where klansmen rode, the terrorism had dramatic political impact. Tennessee Republicans saw their margin of victory slashed by 18,000 votes between 1867 and 1868. In Alabama, 2,000 "Radical" votes were wiped out in Greene County alone. Louisiana's Republican primary vote of April 1868 was cut in half before November's general election, while the Democratic turnout more than doubled. Terrorists disenfranchised some 3,000 Georgia Republicans in 1868, and Democrats effectively regained control of the state government two years later. Kentucky blacks voted for the first time in 1870, with passage of the Fifteenth Amendment, but renewed Ku Klux raiding soon barred them from the polls.

With southern lawmen either friendly to the KKK or driven into hiding by its threats, with state militias frequently outnumbered and outgunned by nightriders, only the federal government remained to curb Klan terrorism. Step one, in

March 1870, was the Fifteenth Amendment to the U.S. Constitution, promising the vote to former slaves. To give that pledge teeth, Congress next passed a series of Enforcement Acts. The first, in May 1870, applied stiff penalties to anyone convicted of conspiring to deprive U.S. citizens of suffrage or other civil rights. The second, nine months later, placed federal authorities in charge of voter registration and balloting in congressional elections. Finally, in April 1871, a third bill—popularly dubbed the Ku Klux Act—defined Klan violence as rebellion against the United States, permitting the president to declare martial law in troubled areas.

While southern Democrats denounced the new legislation and denied any need for federal intervention in Dixie, a joint congressional committee opened hearings on the plague of racial violence in the late Confederacy. The panel interviewed scores of victims and

Reconstruction-era klansmen often raided black homes by night (Library of Congress).

dozens of klansmen, including Grand Wizard Forrest (who later admitted to friends that he "lied like a gentleman" while testifying under oath). The net result, a 612-page report with twelve volumes of supporting testimony, documented a state of virtual anarchy across the Deep South, from Mississippi through the Carolinas.

Thus doubly armed with facts and legislation, President Ulysses Grant launched his campaign against the Ku Klux Klan. Before the program ran its course, 1,849 terrorists were indicted in South Carolina, 1,180 in North Carolina, 930 in Mississippi, and lesser numbers in four other states. Only South Carolina fell subject to the Ku Klux Act, with martial law briefly imposed in nine of the state's most violent counties. There was a world of difference, though, between arresting Klansmen and convicting them. In Tennessee, only a single raider was ever convicted. Fourteen Klansmen faced trial in Florida, again with only one conviction. Together, Alabama and Georgia saw 160 Klansmen indicted in 1871, but none went to trial. A total of 262 Mississippi knights were convicted, including twenty-eight who pled guilty to murder, but all received suspended prison terms after promising to quit the Klan. Fifty-seven klansmen were imprisoned in South Carolina's York County, but 161 of those indicted for serious crimes were never tried. By late 1872, sixty-five Klansmen were in federal prison, with several times that number confined to southern jails, but parole and pardons liberated nearly all of them by 1875.

President Ulysses Grant declared martial law to suppress Klan violence in South Carolina.

Grant's war against the KKK was superficially effective, in that it suppressed the formal order. Virginia's Klan had dissolved in December 1868, and Grand Wizard Forrest called for general disbandment a month later, but his order was widely ignored. Tennessee knights remained active until spring 1869, while Louisiana's Knights of the White Camellia apparently folded their robes in summer of that year. Klan leaders in Alabama and Georgia tried to disband their realms in 1869 and 1870, respectively, but raiding continued until federal troops began making arrests. South Carolina was the last hold-out, but most students of the Klan agree that the invisible empire formally dissolved in all states sometime between late 1871 and early 1873.

Klansmen without their robes and titles, though, were still klansmen in spirit—and they still had work to do in several states before the South was finally restored to what the Democratic Party called "Home Rule." On Easter Sunday 1873, terrorists in Colfax, Louisiana, burned the courthouse and slaughtered more than sixty blacks. Nine months later, armed Democrats seized power in Texas and abolished Reconstruction there. April 1874 saw the formation of a new, unmasked White League in Louisiana, followed by a massacre of sixty Republicans at Coushatta in August and a coup d'état that toppled the state government in September, leaving twenty-seven dead and 105 wounded in New Orleans. The same bloody season witnessed a mass lynching of sixteen Tennessee blacks on 26 August 1874. White terrorists inaugurated the "Mississippi Plan" for political domination in December 1874, with a massacre of seventy-five Republicans at Vicksburg. Subsequent slaughters at Yazoo City (July 1875) and Clinton (September 1875) paved the way for near-insurrection at November's election, thus restoring the state to "home rule" by white supremacists. The presidential campaign of 1876 sparked racist pogroms at Hamburg, Arkansas, and in several South Carolina towns, where former klansmen were reorganized as Red Shirts; the worst outbreak, at Ellenton in September, claimed forty-one lives. November's balloting was marked by violence throughout the South, climaxed by a compromise between Republican Rutherford Hayes and Democratic contender Samuel Tilden. After meeting with a Democratic delegation that included Georgia's late grand dragon, Hayes traded Dixie for the White House, ending Reconstruction in exchange for Tilden's concession of defeat. As seen by many southern whites, the KKK and allied groups had won their battle to "redeem" the prostrate South.

Winning the Peace

Congress made a last bid to insure black civil rights two years before the Hayes-Tilden compromise, with passage

A sketch of two South Carolina klansmen arrested in 1871 (Library of Congress).

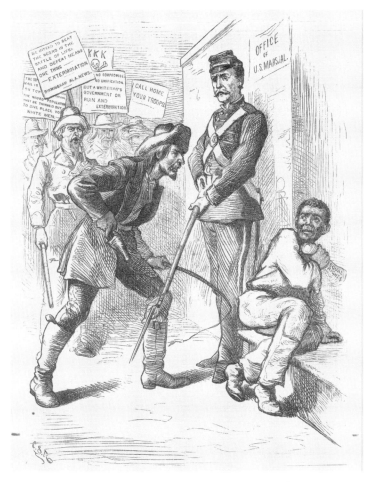

Above: Organized Klans gave way to the White League and other racist groups in the latter 1870s (Florida State Archives). *Right:* A cartoon depicts Washington's abandonment of southern blacks after the election of 1876 (Florida State Archives).

of another Civil Rights Act in March 1875. It anticipated progress of another century when it declared:

> All persons within the jurisdiction of the United States shall be entitled to the full and equal enjoyment of the accommodations, advantages, facilities, and privileges of inns, public conveyances on land or water, theaters, and other places of public amusement; subject only to the conditions and limitations established by law and applicable alike to citizens of every race and color, regardless of any previous condition of servitude.

By the time President Grant signed that law, however, the U.S. Supreme Court had already begun whittling away the rights of blacks protected under federal law. The war of attrition began in 1873 with the *Slaughter-House* cases, declaring that the Fourteenth Amendment protected only federal civil rights, not "civil rights heretofore belonging exclusively to the states." Two years later, in *Minor v. Happersett,* the court seemingly ignored the Fifteenth Amendment, ruling that the U.S. Constitution conferred suffrage on no one, and that the United States per se had no voters of its own creation. Two cases from 1876 carried the campaign further: in *United States v. Reese et al.,* the court held that while the Fifteenth Amendment barred discrimination in voting, it did not confer a right to vote; *United States v. Cruikshank,* springing from the Colfax massacre of 1873, dismissed the federal convictions of three Louisiana terrorists, permitting only federal prosecution of state officials who conspired against free exercise of civil rights. In *Hall v. de Cuir* (1877), the court held that states could not prohibit racial segregation on a common carrier. Six years later, a ruling in the collective *Civil Rights Cases* found the Civil Rights Act of 1875 unconstitutional, its various provisions unenforceable. In 1890's case of *Louisville, New*

Orleans, and Texas Railroad v. Mississippi, the court ruled that states could constitutionally require segregation on public conveyances. *Plessy v. Ferguson* affirmed that ruling in 1896, establishing the doctrine of "separate but equal" facilities for different races. *Williams v. Mississippi* accelerated disfranchisement of freedmen in 1898, approving Mississippi's literacy tests and "understanding" rules that stripped blacks of their right to vote. As late as 1903, the court's decision in *James v. Bowman* confirmed that federal legislation banning private or official interference with the right to vote was unconstitutional.

With a green light from the White House and the Supreme Court, southern states wasted no time in grinding out a paper avalanche of "Jim Crow" segregation ordinances. Railroads were first on the list, beginning in Tennessee (1881), soon followed by Florida (1887); Mississippi (1888); Texas (1889); Louisiana (1890); Alabama, Arkansas, Kentucky and Georgia (all in 1891); South Carolina (1898), North Carolina (1900); Maryland (1904); and Oklahoma (1907). Street cars were next, proceeding with North Carolina and Virginia (1901); Louisiana (1902); Arkansas, South Carolina and Tennessee (1903); Maryland and Mississippi (1904); Florida (1905); Alabama (1906); and Oklahoma (1907). Other laws filled in the gaps, segregating everything from water fountains, theaters, and public parks to residential neighborhoods. Blacks lost the power to challenge such statutes as they were stripped of the vote, state by state across Dixie, between 1890 and 1908. Wherever they turned in the South, their path to the ballot box was blocked by literacy tests, poll taxes, biased "understanding" tests that demanded strict interpretation of obscure state laws (invariably judged by whites), and "grandfather" clauses restricting suffrage to those whose (white) grandfathers had been legally enfranchised.

The need for such restrictions on "race mixing" was explained in the early twentieth century by a new wave of racist propaganda. Titles told the story for such works as Charles Carroll's *"The Negro a Beast"; or "In the Image of God"* (1900); William Calhoun's *The Caucasian and the Negro in the United States* (1902); William Smith's *The Color Line: A Brief in Behalf of the Unborn* (1905); and Robert Shufeldt's *The Negro, a Menace to American Civilization* (1907). The judgment of those tomes was buttressed by a revisionist "moonlight-and-magnolia" school of southern history, exemplified in the writings of professors William Dunning, John Ford Rhodes, John Reynolds, and future president Woodrow Wilson. These and others painted "Radical" Reconstruction as a grievous assault on white civilization, while praising the Ku Klux Klan for its efforts to "restore law and order" in Dixie. Finally, skewed history and pseudo-science merged in the popular novels of Thomas Dixon, a North Carolina native born in 1864. A classmate of Woodrow Wilson at Johns Hopkins University, Dixon was elected to the North Carolina state

President Woodrow Wilson endorsed *The Birth of a Nation*'s heroic portrayal of the KKK.

legislature before he reached voting age, later preaching a hell-fire Baptist gospel in New York City for nearly a decade, spicing his sermons with praise for white supremacy and warnings against "creeping negroidism." His popular novels, aptly described by one critic as "racist sermons in the guise of fiction," included *The Leopard's Spots: A Romance of the White Man's Burden—1865–1900* (1902), *The Clansman: An Historical Romance of the Ku Klux Klan* (1905), and *The Traitor: A Story of the Fall of the Invisible Empire* (1907).

Fueled by such venom and encouraged by legislation demeaning to blacks, a new wave of racist violence swept the South. At least 3,236 blacks were lynched by white mobs between 1883 and 1915, without a single indictment returned against killers who often posed for photographs beside the mutilated bodies of their victims. Rioting by whites was also common in this period. Four blacks died in an outbreak at Danville, Virginia, in November 1883. Twenty were killed in the Carrollton, Mississippi, riot of March 1886. Another six blacks lost their lives in a New Orleans riot, during March 1895. Wilmington, North Carolina, saw eight blacks slain by white rioters in November 1898. Rowdy New Orleans suffered another three-day outbreak in July 1900, leaving two white policemen and an unspecified number of black victims dead in its wake. White terrorists in Atlanta killed twelve blacks and provoked a declaration of martial law in September 1906. Three days of rioting at Springfield, Illinois, during August 1908, left three blacks dead and seventy-five injured before troops intervened. In Tampa, Florida, terrorists fired on a black church and killed three worshipers in July 1910; later the same month, whites murdered eighteen blacks "without any real cause at all" at Palestine, Texas. In March 1913, nightriders raided a black home at Henderson, North Carolina, killing four persons and burning the house.

With so much bigotry and racial violence in the land, the time was ripe for a revival of the Ku Klux Klan. Unknown to southern partisans who cherished fantasies of Ku Klux "heroism" in the 1860s, its revival was about to get a boost from unexpected allies in the nation's capital—and from Hollywood. In April 1914, director D.W. Griffith purchased screen rights to *The Clansman*, Thomas Dixon's best-selling novel, and began production of America's first epic motion picture. The end result, titled *The Birth of a Nation*, filled twelve reels and cost a record $110,000 to finish, premiering in Los Angeles on 8 January 1915. Blacks and liberal whites condemned the film's portrayal of brutish freedmen (played by white actors in black-face) and its glorification of the violent Ku Klux Klan. Dixon appealed to his friend Woodrow Wilson, now president of the United States, and Wilson viewed the film at a special White House screening on 18 February. Moved almost to tears, Wilson declared, "It is like writing history with lightning, and my only regret is that it is all so terribly true." Further endorsement came from Edward White, Chief Justice of the U.S. Supreme Court and a veteran of the Louisiana Klan. The movie opened in New York in March, to stern condemnation from critics including Jane Addams and Upton Sinclair. Blacks were barred from the Boston premiere in April, but they sneaked into the theater and lobbed eggs at the screen. More protests erupted at screenings in Atlantic City, Pittsburgh, Milwaukee, Spokane and Portland, Oregon.

The Klan Reborn

New York protesters picket *The Birth of a Nation* in 1915 (Library of Congress).

For all their racist zeal, the self-styled knights weren't klansmen—yet. The "honor" of a KKK revival fell to William Joseph Simmons, a defrocked Alabama minister who made his living as a recruiter and insurance salesman for fraternal lodges. In 1914 Simmons moved to Atlanta as district manager for the Woodmen of the World, which graced him with an honorary colonel's rank. While recuperating from an auto accident, Simmons claimed to have a vision of robed klansmen galloping around his room on horseback. Thus inspired, he set about revising the Klan's original prescript, expanding it into a volume he called *The Kloran*. He dreamed up new ranks, titles, passwords and codes, most starting with the mystic letters "Kl." His invisible empire embraced the whole world—but membership was nonetheless restricted to white, native-born Protestant men. The Simmons Klan would stand for "an uncompromising standard of pure Americanism untrammeled by alien influences and free from the entanglements of foreign alliances." Simmons defined klannishness as "real fraternity practically applied," supporting "the soul of chivalry and virtue's impenetrable shield." His knights, if any were recruited, would "shield the sanctity of the home and the chastity of womanhood," while vowing "to forever maintain white supremacy." Above all, klansmen were pledged "to protect the weak, the innocent, and the defenseless from the indignities, wrongs and outrages of the lawless, the violent, and the brutal; to relieve the injured and the oppressed; to succor the suffering and unfortunate, especially widows and orphans."

White southern audiences were more appreciative, cheering the celluloid klansmen and firing pistols at the first appearance of the film's black rapist. Admirers of the film urged Dixon to revive the KKK, suggesting that he call it "Sons of the Clansmen," or perhaps the "Aryan League of America."

While *The Birth of a Nation* made its way around the country, bigots found a new cause for excitement in Georgia. Thirteen-year-old Mary Phagan was murdered on 26 April 1913, at the Atlanta pencil factory where she worked for Leo Frank, a Jew originally from New York. A black employee at the plant was first suspected, but he saved himself from jail (or lynching) by incriminating Frank. Convicted and condemned in a trial marked by perjury and anti–Semitic hysteria, Frank was spared from the gallows after Georgia's governor examined the flimsy evidence and commuted his sentence to life imprisonment. The governor's "traitorous" action galvanized Georgia demagogue Thomas Watson, a Populist campaigner from the 1890s so embittered by the failure of his liberal campaigns that he embraced racism and thus won election to the U.S. Senate. In his spare time, Watson spewed venom at blacks, Jews and Catholics via two periodicals, *Watson's Magazine* and the *Weekly Jeffersonian*. His obsession with race-mixing sex and "libidinous priests" was so extreme that several issues of his magazines were banned from the U.S. mail as obscene, yet bigots from coast to coast devoured each issue. Taking up the Frank case as a personal crusade, Watson cheered Frank's August 1915 lynching by a mob whose members called themselves the Knights of Mary Phagan. On 2 September, Watson called for the creation of "another Ku Klux Klan" in Georgia "to restore HOME RULE." Six weeks later, on 16 October, the Knights of Mary Phagan climbed Stone Mountain, near Atlanta, and lit America's first fiery cross in a scene lifted straight from the pages of *The Clansman*.

Elaborate blueprints aside, Simmons let his dream lie dormant until October 1915. Ten days after the Stone Mountain cross-burning, on 26 October, Simmons and thirty-four others (including two original klansmen and several Knights of Mary Phagan) filed Georgia charter applications for the Knights of the Ku Klux Klan, described as a "purely benevolent and eleemosynary order." On Thanksgiving night, Simmons led a party up Stone Mountain, where they lit another cross. On 4 December 1915, two days before *The Birth of a Nation* opened in Atlanta, local newspapers published advertisements for the KKK, billed as "a classy order of the highest class." Black models donned robes for publicity photos, and ninety-two members enlisted over the next two weeks.

The Klan was on its way, but no one seemed to know where it was going yet. Racial violence continued in Dixie, meanwhile: fifty-six blacks were lynched in 1916, fifteen of them in Georgia, but none of the mayhem was directly traceable to Simmons or his knights. Another cause would spur the KKK to action soon, but it was sparked by bloodshed overseas.

War raged in Europe for nearly three years before the United States became officially involved, on 6 April 1917. Amer-

The Knights of Mary Phagan lynched Leo Frank in August 1915 (Georgia Department of Archives and History).

Racist agitator Thomas Watson praised Frank's lynchers and called for a Klan revival in 1915.

ica's belated declaration of hostilities was preceded, however, by long and furious debates over "preparedness," including widespread agitation against German immigrants and other supposed "enemy aliens." White Protestant America's historic fear of swarthy anarchists was further aggravated by the Russian revolution and its ominous echoes in the United States. The fledgling FBI, still small, weak and disorganized, gladly accepted help and information from members of such vigilante networks as the American Defense Society, the American Protective League, and the National Security League. Across the nation, self-appointed superpatriots kept watch on "radicals," "slackers," organized labor and "hyphenated Americans." Klansmen in Tulsa, Oklahoma—operating as the Knights of Justice—flogged, tarred and feathered alleged IWW members in November 1917. The following year, robed knights staged one of their first parades in Montgomery, Alabama, as a warning to foreign spies and saboteurs.

Unfortunately, peace in Europe brought no corresponding calm at home. Wartime inflation decimated salaries and prompted workers to demand more pay, which management indignantly refused. From coast to coast a stunning wave of strikes ensued—3,600 in 1919 alone, four million laborers leaving their jobs to walk picket lines. Some of the unions calling strikes were frankly socialistic, and a handful advocated violence. It was easy to brand all union organizers "Reds" and "Bolsheviks." The U.S. Senate convened hearings on American bolshevism in February 1919, but others preferred a more direct response. Increasingly, "radical" unions were met with brute force—from police, strike breakers, or ultra-patriotic groups like the American Legion, whose members tortured and lynched an IWW organizer at Centralia, Washington, in November 1919.

And as usual, racial violence accompanied the spread of patriotic fervor. Southern lynch mobs killed at least 129 blacks without meeting resistance in 1919 and 1920, but white rioters were no longer always so fortunate. Twenty-six race riots rocked America during the "Red Summer" of 1919, scattered from Longview, Texas, to Omaha, Chicago, and the nation's capital (six dead, more than 100 injured). Some of the outbreaks were grimly traditional, as with the massacre of twenty-five black sharecroppers in Phillips County, Arkansas, but even there five whites were killed as blacks fought back. The death toll in Chicago's riot was more nearly equal: fifteen whites and twenty-three blacks killed in fighting that raged for three days. Although the violence was invariably started by white racists, blacks and "Reds" still got the blame. Arkansas governor Charles Brough condemned a black newspaper, the *Chicago Defender,* for encouraging a "conspiracy" in his state, and the FBI curiously cited Bolshevik propaganda as a primary cause of the white riots in Chicago and Washington, D.C.

Despite its ardent war work and pursuit of radicals, and despite the flood tide of violent racism in 1919, the KKK was still pitifully small as a new decade dawned. Five years of sporadic recruiting, cross-burning and torchlight parades had lured no more than 3,000 members by spring 1920, with chartered klaverns confined to Georgia and Alabama. Imperial Wizard Simmons lived hand-to-mouth, barely making ends meet. A new approach was desperately needed if his empire was to thrive.

Paths to Power

In June 1920, Simmons struck a bargain with Edward Young Clarke and Elizabeth Tyler, proprietors of the Atlanta-based Southern Publicity Association. Tyler's son-in-law had lately joined the Klan, suggesting that the hooded knights might benefit from hiring a professional press agent. Clarke and Tyler had previously organized fund-raisers for the Anti-Saloon League, the Red Cross, the YMCA and the Theodore Roosevelt Memorial League (which sued Clarke for embezzling $5,000). The partners were impressed with Simmons—whom Tyler described as "a minister and a clean living man"—and also by the Klan's cash-cow potential. Simmons agreed to place Clarke and Tyler in charge of a new KKK propagation department, dispatching a sales force of kleagles to boost membership nationwide. The propagation department would keep eight dollars of each ten-dollar klecktoken, while the rest went to Simmons. By year's end, Clarke and Tyler had 1,100 kleagles in the field, casting their nets among fraternal lodges and fundamentalist Protestant churches, stressing issues and concerns of local interest in order to maximize sales.

And there was no shortage of such issues in 1920–21. Racism was a staple of white society, exacerbated by the migration of 750,000 blacks from southern farms to northern cities during World War I, supported by propaganda broadsides such as Madison Grant's *The Passing of the Great Race* (1916) and klansman Lothrop Stoddard's *The Rising Tide of Color Against White Supremacy* (1921). The arrival in America of 14.5 million immigrants, most of them from southern and eastern Europe, swelled urban ghettos between 1900 and 1920, while sparking a new wave of nativism unequaled since the Know-Nothing campaigns of the mid–nineteenth century. Resurgent anti–Semitism took its cue from European proto-fascists and from Henry Ford's newspaper diatribes against "The International Jew." War fever and the recent Red Scare left many Americans seething in the grip of "100-percent Americanism" that verged on paranoia. Prohibition's advent and the crime wave it produced gave hard-linc moralists carte blanche to scrutinize and judge their neighbors. Finally, as in the Reconstruction era, many young men who had come of age on battlefields found peacetime tedious. From coast to coast, wherever discontent stalked white America, the Klan's brigade of kleagles offered simple answers for a price.

By late summer 1921 the KKK was flourishing. An estimated 850,000 "aliens" had been "naturalized" as new members of the invisible empire at ten dollars per head, plus expenses for costumes, monthly dues, Klan literature and memorabilia, life insurance and sundry incidentals. William Simmons, with twenty percent of the take, banked $170,000 plus another $25,000 in back pay for the lean years, and acquired a $33,000 home in suburban Atlanta, dubbed Klan Krest. A new imperial headquarters, valued at $65,000, was established on Atlanta's Peachtree Street. Tax auditors would later estimate that the initial gold rush brought $1.5 million pouring into Klan coffers, with no end in sight.

Wherever Klansmen marched and rallied in those glory days, violence inevitably followed. Texas blacks who fraternized with white women were flogged in Bolton, branded with acid in Dallas, and castrated in Houston. A white butcher in Birmingham, Alabama, was whipped for maintaining "friendly relations" with black customers. In Miami, a black Episcopal archdeacon was tarred and feathered by Klansmen for "preaching racial equality." Blacks in Ocoee, Florida, fought back when klansmen attacked their homes on election day, in November 1920, but they still got the worst of the battle. Other communities scarred by race riots included Chicago and Waukegan, Illinois (June 1920); Springfield, Ohio (March 1921); and Augusta, Georgia (August 1921). Oklahoma, soon to rank among the Klan's most violent realms, witnessed a grim outbreak at Tulsa in June 1921, with twenty-one whites and an uncertain number of blacks (some sources claim 300) left dead in the ruins. Across Dixie, fifty-nine blacks were murdered by lynch mobs in 1921. Klansmen were not responsible for all the violence, by any means, but they claimed their share of victims while using each new incident to recruit angry or frightened whites.

Northern newspapers, meanwhile, used the expanding Klan as a tool to increase circulation. The New York *Journal-American* focused primarily on reports of financial and political chicanery in Atlanta, while the competing New York *World* ran a two-week series on Klan activities in the forty-eight states, climaxed on 19 September 1921 with a list of 152 outrages that included four murders, forty-one floggings, and twenty-seven tar-and-feather parties. Inspired by those reports, the House Rules Committee convened hearings on the KKK in October 1921, with Imperial Wizard Simmons appearing as the Klan's star witness. Waxing eloquent, Simmons described his brainchild as a vehicle of "race pride," rather than bigotry; the Klan's white hood and robe, he claimed, were "as innocent as the breath of an angel." Proving once again that even bad publicity beats none at all, Klan membership increased another twenty percent by December 1921, with more than 200 new klaverns organized. The following summer, with membership above one million and still rising, Clarke and Tyler received an average of 1,000 applications per day in Atlanta. Ten realms were chartered by 1922, spanning the South from Texas to the Carolinas, while active units thrived in at least twenty-three other states. As Simmons told the press, "Congress gave us the best publicity we ever got. Congress made us." In fact, the KKK became so profitable that greedy conspirators soon deposed Simmons, replacing him as imperial wizard in November 1922 with Dr. Hiram Evans, a Dallas dentist who would lead the Klan until 1937.

Violence followed the KKK on its march nationwide. Klan rallies sparked riots in Delaware, Indiana, Maryland, Massachusetts, New Jersey, Ohio, Pennsylvania and Texas. An epidemic of nocturnal floggings scarred more than a thousand victims each in Oklahoma and Texas; more than 100 each in Alabama, Florida and Georgia; dozens in California and the Carolinas. Two hundred Klansmen swept through Smackover, Arkansas, in November 1922, burning suspected vice dens, killing one man in the process, wounding and whipping dozens more. Pennsylvania knights shot up a black Boy Scout camp and wounded two policemen at a college campus rally. Klansmen in Niles, Ohio, bombed the mayor's home in October 1924, after he refused them a parade permit. In Talladega County, Alabama, klansmen bombed two homes and burned a third, together with a school, a church, two dance halls and several barns.

The 1920s Klan claimed fewer lives than its Reconstruction predecessor, yet it was lethal enough. At least five persons died in riots sparked by Klan activities in Pennsylvania and Texas. Those deaths were likely unintended, but the same cannot be said for other homicides around the country. Historian Kenneth Jackson counts six murders committed by southern Klansmen between 1920 and 1925, but his tally remains incomplete. In addition to the fatal Smackover skirmish and the 1922 murder of two Klan critics at Mer Rouge, Louisiana, other documented slayings from the period include an arson suspect lynched by Arkansas klansmen in 1921; Father James Coyle, a Catholic priest shot by a Birmingham Klansman in April 1921; Manolo Cabeza, lynched by Key West knights at Christmas 1921; Walter Gibbs, shot for dating black women at Nashville, Arkansas, in March 1922; Parks Banks, hanged near Yazoo Mississippi, after quarreling with Klan leaders in August 1922; two unnamed blacks tortured and burned alive by Klansmen at Beaver Falls, Pennsylvania, in 1923; William Coburn, a Klan publicist shot by one of his Atlanta komrades in 1923; a bootlegger shot at Ardmore, Oklahoma, in 1923; Joseph Zimmerman, vanished forever after Birmingham klansmen kidnapped him in March 1925; and three victims killed when a Muskegon, Michigan, Klan leader bombed the home of a political rival in 1925. No final body count is available from Rosewood, Florida, where klansmen and their allies razed a black community in January 1923, but published estimates range from eight victims to 100 or more.

Klan homicides continued through the latter 1920s. In Herrin County, Illinois, battles between bootleggers and the KKK claimed at least twenty lives during 1924–26. Herman Bigby and neighbor Walton Adams were killed when Klansmen raided Bigby's home at Royston, Georgia, in March 1926. Toombs County, Georgia, saw at least two victims whipped to death in the same period. A Colorado knight was beaten to death when he tried to leave the order, and a three-year-old Pennsylvania girl never returned after klansmen snatched her from her grandparents' home. An undercover policeman was ambushed and killed by Klan gunmen in Buffalo, New York. Outside Terrell, Texas, eight men condemned by a kangaroo court were burned alive while some 800 klansmen watched.

Such mayhem could only persist while FBI agents ignored it and local police sympathized with the terrorists. No comprehensive list of Klan cops from the 1920s is available, but a sampling proves the case. In Dallas, Police Commissioner Louis Turley was a Klansman. After three of his patrolmen were identified as Klan floggers, Turley ordered his detectives to "forget all about the charges brought against any member of the force." Other Dallas knights included Police Chief Henry Tanner, the county sheriff, his chief deputies and the district attorney. Portland, Oregon's police department commissioned 100 klansmen as auxiliary officers, hand-picked by Grand Dragon Fred Gifford. Denver's Klan roster included the mayor, city attorney, manager of public safety, the police chief, scores of policemen, four judges, two federal narcotics officers, and at least two deputy sheriffs. In Waco, Texas, the mayor and board of police commissioners signed up en masse. White knights in

Baton Rouge, Louisiana, included Sheriff Horace Lyons, a district judge and his court clerk. In Morehouse Parish, scene of at least two unpunished murders, Sheriff Fred Carpenter, his deputies, and District Attorney David Garrett were klansmen. When California's Klan rolls were revealed, members included ten percent of the public officials in every major city. Sacramento's kleagle was a deputy sheriff who recruited many other policemen and firefighters; at least twenty-five policemen and eighty-one federal employees joined the Klan in San Francisco; seven Fresno patrolmen paid dues to the invisible empire; Bakersfield's police chief and police judge were members; in Los Angeles, the list included Sheriff William Traeger, Police Chief Louis Oaks, and U.S. Attorney Joseph Burke. The Klan controlled law enforcement in Birmingham, Alabama, where knights paraded with police motorcycle escorts. Known members on the public payroll included Sheriff T.J. Shirley and Chief Deputy Henry Hill, while historian William Snell reports that most Birmingham policemen, "if not all of them," were Klansmen.

Nor can it be argued that law enforcement officers joined the Klan as a mere fraternal exercise. Seven members of the Alabama National Guard were jailed for lynching a black man in January 1921, but the charges were later dismissed. Nationwide, between 1920 and 1929, at least forty-two other blacks were lynched in circumstances suggesting police collusion. After the Smackover, Arkansas, raids of November 1922, Ouachita County's sheriff praised the KKK for driving away "undesirables." Birmingham Public Safety Commissioner W.B. Cloe likewise expressed gratitude for illegal Klan vice raids, and off-duty policemen led hooded knights against local Chinese cafés in 1926. Key West's Ku Klux sheriff, Roland Curry, surrendered Manolo Cabeza to Klan lynchers in December 1923. Police Chief B.M. Lawson was one of three Klansmen arrested for flogging two women at Lumberton, North Carolina, in April 1923. A policeman who joined the Klan's raid on a Pennsylvania Boy Scout camp was fired in July 1924, but he faced no criminal charges. The police chief of Taft, California, joined klansmen to cheer the flogging of a dentist who filed divorce papers. In Inglewood, California, Klan raiders traded shots with a patrolmen who caught them kidnapping a suspected bootlegger; klansmen killed or wounded in the battle included a town constable and a deputy sheriff.

Law enforcement was not the only target of Klan infiltration in the 1920s. Indeed, the hooded order infested every level of white American society. FBI historian Don Whitehead, estimating total membership at "almost one million in forty-six states," was wrong on both counts. In fact, the order was found in all forty-eight states and the District of Columbia, with active outposts in several foreign countries. Published estimates of total membership range from 2,028,000 to an improbably precise 8,904,887, with most tallies falling somewhere in the three-to-five million range.

Whatever the final hood count, those numbers spelled power as the Klan plunged headlong into politics. As usual, its methods were deceptive. While Imperial Wizard Simmons declared that the KKK "is not a political organization," and successor Hiram Evans vowed that the order would "take no part in politics," imperial headquarters banished St. Louis Exalted Cyclops John R. Jones for complaining about the Klan's political activities in 1924. Indeed, it now seems likely that the KKK once captured America's highest political office. Rumors of President Warren Harding's White House initiation circulated widely during 1921, and Imperial Klokard Alton Young confirmed them on his deathbed, in the 1940s. According to Young, a five-man induction team led by William Simmons ushered Harding into the invisible empire, rewarded for their service with War Department license plates that exempted them from speeding tickets. Attorney General Harry Daugherty denied that either he or Harding were Klansmen, yet the stories persisted. The Klan mourned Harding's death with public demonstrations in August 1923, and Ohio Klansmen stood guard at his tomb.

Nationwide, Klan votes elected seventy-five congressmen, sixteen U.S. senators, eleven governors and countless other officials. Georgia governor Thomas Hardwick praised the KKK, while successor Clifford Walker was himself a klansman and Richard Russell—chief justice of Georgia's supreme court—sought Klan political advice. Colorado's knights included Secretary of State Carl Milliken, Denver Mayor Ben Stapleton and city attorney Clarence Morley. Ohio Klansmen elected twelve mayors in 1923, including those of Akron, Columbus and Toledo. In Oregon, where Klansman K.K. Kubli served as speaker of the house and a fellow knight ruled the state senate, legislators banned parochial schools. Indiana knights or friends beholden to Grand Dragon David Stephenson included Governor Ed Jackson, state prohibition director Charles Orbison, congressman Harry Rowbottom, and the mayors of various cities including Indianapolis, Kokomo and Evansville. Arkansas Governor Thomas McRae practiced "friendly neutrality" toward the Klan, while appointing a knight as his personal secretary. In California, Governor Friend Richardson chose Sacramento's kludd as chaplain of the state senate. Alabama surpassed even Georgia in Klan infestation: known members in the Cotton State included Governor Bibb Graves, U.S. Senators Hugo Black and Thomas Heflin, Attorney General Charles McCall, supreme court justice John Anderson, and Birmingham Mayor Cooper Green. Governor Graves sponsored a bill imposing $25,000 fines on anyone who uttered "libelous" criticism of klansmen in office, and Birmingham attorney Irving Engle offered this assessment of the state at large: "When I say powerful, they took over the state. You couldn't be an officer, couldn't win an election unless you were a member of the Klan, that was true of [the] counties and the cities."

Decline and Fall

Klan strength peaked in 1924, then declined almost as swiftly as it had grown. More than forty thousand klansmen and women marched through Washington, D.C., on 8 August 1925, but less than half as many returned for a second parade one year later. Published estimates of declining Ku Klux membership include 321,000 in 1927; "no more than several hundred thousand" in 1928; 82,600 in 1929; and 35,000 to 45,000 in 1930. The latter counts are too conservative, since 30,000 knights remained in Florida alone, but there is no doubt that the Klan's great wave had crested and withdrawn.

Primary causes of the Klan's precipitous decline in 1926–30 included disillusionment with Ku Klux violence, extremism and rampant financial corruption. Local arrests revealed some klansmen as sadistic thugs. Time after time, Klan officers absconded with cash or indulged in luxuries the rank and file could not afford. Imperial Kleagle Edward Clarke himself was caught with bootleg liquor and pled guilty to charges of transporting women across state lines for immoral purposes. Embarrassment and plunging membership drove many politicians to desert the KKK, while some urged Klan endorsement of opponents on election day. A murder case in Indiana and a civil trial in Pennsylvania ultimately dominated reasons for the Klan's downfall.

Forty thousand Klan members paraded through Washington, D.C., in 1925 (Georgia Department of Archives and History).

No Klansman in the 1920s enjoyed more personal power than Indiana Grand Dragon David Stephenson. Alone, he hand-picked Hoosier officeholders from small towns to Congress and the governor's mansion, obtaining from each written pledges of loyalty. Stephenson liked to call himself "the law in Indiana," and he had his sights fixed on a U.S. Senate vacancy in 1928, when passion intervened and ruined everything. On 15 March 1925, Stephenson invited a schoolteacher, Madge Oberholtzer, to join him on journey to Chicago. In their train compartment, shared with a Klan bodyguard, Stephenson swilled alcohol and assaulted his date, inflicting deep bite marks all over her body. When the train stopped at Hammond, Indiana, Stephenson checked into a hotel and made the error of allowing Oberholtzer to go shopping with his gunman. She bought poison at a local pharmacy and drank it, leading to her death on 14 April. Stephenson was charged with second-degree murder and later convicted at trial. When Governor Ed Jackson failed to pardon him, Stephenson opened his files to journalists and prosecutors, resulting in scandal, impeachments and criminal trials throughout the state. Within a year, Klan membership in Indiana dropped by ninety-six percent, from 350,000 to an estimated 15,000. Historian Wyn Wade suggests that Stephenson's downfall did "more than any [other] single factor" to defeat the KKK.

In western Pennsylvania, meanwhile, klansmen complained to imperial headquarters about the high-handed style of Grand Dragon Sam Rich. Imperial Wizard Evans fired Rich, but his replacement—Rev. Herbert Shaw—proved no more popular with the unhappy Keystone knights. When their complaints resumed, Evans banished spokesman John Strayer and revoked the charters of eight dissident klaverns. The ousted klansmen continued to meet on their own, prompting Evans to file suit in 1927 for return of their regalia and $100,000 in damages. Strayer and five codefendants countered with a $15 million claim against Evans, for misuse of dues collected prior to their expulsion. The trial, in April 1928, was disastrous for Evans, facing a parade of witnesses who detailed Klan corruption and violence in open court. Klansman J.R. Ramsey described nocturnal raids, ordered by Evans and Rich, that included "burning barns, tar-and-feather parties and other ruthlessness." Two black men had been tortured and burned to death, Ramsey said, at a July 1923 "castration party" outside Beaver Falls. Other witnesses fingered Sam Rich himself in the still-unsolved kidnapping of a three-year-old Pittsburgh girl and described the ritual immolation of seven or eight men in Texas. On the witness stand, Evans grudgingly admitted that he could have stopped a riotous parade through Carnegie which left one klansman dead in 1923. In his

Less than half as many knights appeared for a second Washington march in 1925 (Library of Congress).

summation, defense attorney Van Barrickman denounced the Klan as "supreme in its rottenness," and Judge W.II.S. Thompson agreed. On 13 April 1928, Thompson dismissed both claims with a judgment that read:

> I find as a fact that the Ku Klux Klan has established and is maintaining a form of despotic rule, which is being operated in secret under the direct sanction and authority of the plaintiff's chief officers; that, in violation of the rights and liberties of the people, it has set up tribunals not known to law, before which citizens of the Commonwealth, not members of the Klan are brought, subjected to some form of trial, and, upon conviction, severe corporal punishments are imposed, painful, humiliating and often brutal in their character, and in some instances destructive of life itself.
>
> I also find as a fact that in the secret operation of the corporation's activities and in hostility to the civil authorities, military organizations are established and maintained with arms, regalia and equipment, with officers of varying rank and military titles, these officers being bound to obey without question the commands of the superior officer in authority of the plaintiff corporation. In addition to this, bands known as "night-riders," or the "black-robed gang," armed, equipped and masked, are formed and operated here and there throughout the country, both organizations being used as instruments of terror, oppression and violence, and being thus a continued menace to the public peace and destructive of the public order.
>
> I also find as a fact that Hiram Wesley Evans was present and spoke to the assembled multitude in Carnegie immediately before the riot; that he and Rich were well aware that the civil authorities of Carnegie had forbidden the parade, and that in defiance of this position and in utter disregard of the consequences which might naturally follow, he gave the order to march, which resulted in the serious riot in which men were beaten and severely injured. At least one man was wounded by gunfire and another man was shot to death. Under these circumstances, he [Evans] was directly responsible for the riot and bloodshed which ensued....
>
> In view of all the facts disclosed by the evidence, the plaintiff corporation, stigmatized as it is by its unlawful acts and conduct, could hardly hope for judicial assistance in a court of the United States which is commissioned to extend to all litigants before it, without distinction of race, creed, color or condition, those high guarantees of liberty and equality vouchsafed by the Constitution of the United States.
>
> This unlawful organization, so destructive of the rights and liberties of the people, has come in vain asking this court of equity for injunction or other relief. They come with filthy hands and can get no assistance here.

Eighteen months after Judge Thompson threw the Klan out of court, Wall Street's stock market crash rocked the nation, inaugurating the Great Depression and leaving countless klansmen either unemployed or desperately short of cash with which to pay their dues. Hiram Evans sought to revive the failing order with infusions of anti-communism, manifested in nightriding campaigns against organized labor, but while violence persisted in several states, it failed to resuscitate the invisible empire. Evans resigned as wizard in 1937, replaced by Hoosier veterinarian James Colescott, while imperial headquarters went on the auction block, purchased at last by the Catholic Church. Colescott's administration was marked by prosecution of lethal floggers in Florida and Georgia, with mixed results, while north-

ern klansmen fraternized with pro–Nazi members of the German-American Bund, the Silver Shirt Legion, and other native fascist groups. Military conscription after Pearl Harbor decimated Klan ranks, but the death blow came from Atlanta's IRS office, in the form of a bill for $685,355 in taxes unpaid from the 1920s. Strapped for cash, Colescott disbanded the national order in April 1944, plaintively telling reporters, "Maybe the government can make something out of the Klan. I never could."

Lean and Violent Years

Disbandment of the national Klan in April 1944 did not spell death for the order, as Colescott himself privately acknowledged. Active klaverns clung to life in several states, notably Georgia, Alabama, Florida and Tennessee. Dr. Samuel Green organized the Association of Georgia Klans (AGK) in May 1944, mimicked by the Ku Klux Klan of Florida four months later. Alabama's Klan formally revived on 27 March 1946, with eight crosses fired in Birmingham the next night. The same month witnessed a cross-burning in Knoxville, Tennessee, followed by similar demonstrations in New Jersey (August), Miami (October) and at Stone Mountain, Georgia (October). A Jewish merchant closed her shop in Red Bank, Tennessee, after repeated cross-burnings. Within a single week of June 1946, two crosses were burned in Los Angeles and a Hollywood synagogue was vandalized with racist graffiti. Three months later, a new Federated Ku Klux Klans filed its incorporation papers in Alabama.

The spate of post-war Klan activity provoked federal attention. In May 1946, Attorney General Tom Clark announced his intent to use every available statute against racist organizations. Two months later, Clark reported that the FBI was investigating Klan activities in California, Florida, Michigan, Mississippi, New York and Tennessee. No prosecutions resulted, but Clark listed the Klan as a subversive organization in December 1947, theoretically barring its members from federal employment in Cold War America. On a more practical level, between May and December 1946, Klan charters were revoked by state authorities in California, Georgia, Kentucky, New Jersey, New York and Wisconsin. Several states and cities passed anti-mask laws, while New York went further still, imposing six-month jail terms and $10,000 fines on would-be Klan recruiters.

Georgia, as ever since the KKK's rebirth in 1915, was the heart of postwar Klan activity. Members of Atlanta's Klavalier Klub resumed nightly floggings and bragged of killing a black cab driver in August 1945. Klan ally Eugene Talmadge, pursuing his third term as governor in July 1946, warned black voters to stay away from the polls during Georgia's Democratic primary, while FBI agents reported a "well-organized plot" to murder incumbent governor Ellis Arnall. On primary day, 17 July, Sam Green boasted that the Klan had delivered 100,000 votes for "Old Gene." Nine days later, an unmasked vigilante firing squad executed four "uppity" blacks outside Monroe. Those crimes remained officially unsolved, at least in part, due to police complicity. Sam Roper, back on the Atlanta force after his stint as chief of the GBI, doubled as a detective and the exalted cyclops of Klan Post 297. Elsewhere in Atlanta, eleven uniformed policemen attended a Klan meeting on 3 June 1946, while thirty-eight turned out for another rally ten days later. One of those compromised lawmen assured his fellow Klansmen that they would be granted leave to handle any local race riots "in their own way."

Talmadge won election in November 1946, but Klansmen were stunned by his sudden death on 21 December. They backed a hasty plan to replace Old Gene with son Herman Talmadge, but the coup lasted barely two months, until Lieutenant Governor Melvin Thompson dethroned the younger Talmadge. Terrorism resumed that summer, escalating into the 1948 primary season, as Herman Talmadge planned his first full-fledged gubernatorial bid. At Wrightsville, on primary eve, Grand Dragon Green proclaimed that "blood will flow in the streets" if Georgia blacks sought equality with whites. Klansmen circulated through the neighborhood after that rally, and none of Wrightsville's four hundred black voters cast ballots the next day. At Swainsboro, cardboard coffins marked with the initials "KKK" were left at black homes overnight, persuading two-thirds of all registered blacks to refrain from voting. One who ignored the warning was murdered at Alton, his killer acquitted on a plea of "self-defense."

Once again, the Klan was free to kill and maim where politicians and police supported it. Herman Talmadge celebrated his inauguration by naming Green as a lieutenant colonel and aide-de-camp on his staff. Talmadge later denied any knowledge of the appointment, but Green had a framed certificate to prove it. Talmadge was less bashful at Green's 1948 birthday party, where he delivered the keynote speech. Georgia and the nation were lucky, he said, to have Klansmen who "will save America for Americans," standing "ready to fight for the preservation of our American traditions against the Communists, foreign agitators, Negroes, Catholics and Jews." Others also shared the governor's view. In Atlanta, "Brother Judge" Caleb Callaway received a Ku Klux letter of commendation for his rulings "conforming with the principles of Klannishness." At a November 1948 Klan meeting, three Atlanta policemen gave speeches. One of them, Patrolman "Trigger" Nash, was honored for killing his thirteenth black victim "in the line of duty." To loud applause, Nash "said he hoped he wouldn't have the honor of killing all the niggers in the South and he hoped the people would do something about it themselves."

Georgia was not the only state plagued by Klan mayhem and official inaction during 1946–48. Senator Theodore Bilbo, campaigning for reelection in Mississippi, confessed Klan membership in August 1946. In fact, he said, Bilbo Klan No. 40 was named in his honor. Bilbo "was not in sympathy" with certain Klan activities, but he solemnly declared, "No man can ever leave the Klan. He takes an oath not to do that. Once a Ku Klux, always a Ku Klux." His message to Mississippi whites was straightforward: "If you never voted for me before, vote for me now. Let me go back to Washington. I'll represent you in the Senate so that you'll be proud and never regret it. I'll fight and fight, and I'll kill and kill." As for black voters, he suggested, "The best way to keep the nigger from the polls is to visit him the night before the election." Taking those words to heart,

whites flogged a black man to death at Lexington, on 22 July 1946. A month later, racists mobbed blacks in Magee. The floggers were acquitted by an all-white jury, while the rioters escaped indictment.

Alabama hosted several competing Klan factions in 1946–48, all of them violent. A union organizer was kidnapped from Elba and whipped in December 1946. In 1947, "Parson" Jack Johnston's Original Southern Klan stormed a Phenix City courthouse and staged a demonstration in the jury box. Other knights raided a black Girl Scout camp outside Bessemer. Birmingham Klansmen bombed the first of many black homes in August 1947. The city's public safety commissioner, Eugene "Bull" Connor, warned another black resident that his presence in a once-white neighborhood "might lead to violence and if [Connor] were in his place he would move immediately." In April 1948, soon after another black home was bombed in the district nicknamed "Dynamite Hill," Connor warned the pastor of Birmingham's Sixteenth Street Baptist Church that God—acting through the KKK—would "strike the church down" if it hosted a meeting of the Southern Conference for Human Welfare.

Sporadic violence also flared in other southern states. At Columbia, Tennessee, rioting whites swept through a black neighborhood on 26 February 1946, injuring ten persons, vandalizing homes and shops with KKK graffiti. Police responded by jailing seventy blacks and fatally shooting two of them during a jailhouse interrogation on 28 February. Two months later, Klan threats and nocturnal shootings kept all but one of Perry, Florida's 150 black voters from casting ballots in the Democratic primary. A black union activist was threatened by Miami klansmen in August 1946. On 1 November 1948, Mayor Thomas Cummings reported that black neighborhoods in Nashville, Tennessee, were "flooded" with threats against potential voters in the next day's election.

In Georgia, shortly before an August 1949 heart attack claimed his life, Sam Green boasted that FBI agents used Klansmen to collect intelligence on southern race problems. Days after Green's death, IRS agent Marion Allen slapped the AGK with a bill for $9,332, representing unpaid taxes from 1946–48, and earned more death threats in the process. Assaults and whippings were rife throughout the state, including an attack on Soperton's mayor and two raids against one-armed mayor C.L. Drake in Iron City. Lynchings with probable police complicity were recorded at Irwinton (September 1949) and Bainbridge (May 1950). Klan bombing targets included a black family in Atlanta and a newsman who exposed corruption within the Talmadge regime. In February 1949, klansmen abducted three black high-school students from Columbus, Georgia, and drove them across the state line to Phenix City, Alabama, where they were whipped, grilled about their rumored ties to the NAACP, then released with a flurry of shots to speed them on their way.

Alabama's knights kept pace with their Georgia brethren where violence was concerned. The Federated Klans, led by William Morris and Dr. E.P. Pruitt, flogged so many victims around Birmingham in early 1949 that Governor James Folsom reminded his constituents, "Your home is your castle. Defend it in any way necessary." Seventeen Klansmen were finally indicted by state authorities, but only two faced trial and both were acquitted. Morris was the only knight incarcerated, spending sixty-seven days in jail on a contempt citation for refusing to identify his klansmen. The same month he emerged from custody, Birmingham klansmen pulled down the tower of a black radio station. In Mobile, nightriders bombed three homes and burned a fourth, together with an elementary school. Other racist bombings jarred Cottonwood, Crossville and Phenix City. In "Bombingham," Bull Conner's police left seven more bombings unsolved in 1949–50. Assistant police chief Jack Warren admitted that racist bombings "would not be truly adequately investigated," yet Washington saw no cause to intervene. After blacks finally ambushed a group of Birmingham nightriders, killing one man and wounding another, police and white-owned newspapers suppressed news of the shooting, but it brought six years of relative quiet to Dynamite Hill.

Elsewhere across the south, Klansmen struck when and where they could. Virginia's knights whipped a Columbus County woman in January 1951 and bombed three Norfolk County homes in summer 1953. Authorities in Dallas, Texas, recorded seventeen racist bombings between March 1949 and January 1952, while another series of blasts rocked Houston in August 1953. One of the nation's most violent klaverns was found in Chattanooga, Tennessee, where klansman Jesse Stoner called for deportation of blacks and mass execution of Jews. Sam Green expelled the klavern from his AGK in August 1949, after reports of sixteen floggings and a bombing, but the mayhem continued with another home bombed in May 1950. In Nashville, occupancy of a new housing project was switched from blacks to whites in January 1950, after cross-burnings and a dynamite blast. Emboldened by their victory, klansmen bombed another black family's home in March 1951. Between January 1951 and June 1952, more than forty racist bombings scarred the southern states, but the worst rash of violence occurred in the Carolinas.

Atlanta wholesale grocer Thomas Hamilton moved to Leesville, South Carolina, in 1948, representing Samuel Green and the AGK. His knights liked action, and committed their first known flogging at Sandy Bottoms on 24 July 1949, when four blacks were whipped with the warning that "This is your civil rights." Four months later, Hamilton defected from the AGK to found his own Association of Carolina Klans, with strength concentrated in Horry County, South Carolina, and neighboring Columbus County, North Carolina. Nocturnal kidnappings and beatings proliferated over the next two years, scarring an uncertain number of victims. Whites and blacks alike were flogged, typically for some alleged infraction of Klan "morals." Known victims included war veterans, farmers, a pregnant woman and two disabled brothers. Hamilton's knights also set off a bomb in Wake Forest, North Carolina, and stoned the home of federal judge J. Waites Waring, who had invalidated South Carolina's white primary. On 26 August 1950, Klansmen raided Charlie Fitzgerald's nightclub at Myrtle Beach, South Carolina, firing some 300 shots and leaving one of their own dead at the scene. When the corpse was unmasked, authorities recognized an off-duty Conway policeman, recently elected magistrate. Another of Hamilton's men was killed three months later, while whipping victim Clayton Moore at Greenwood, South Carolina.

Five days after the Myrtle Beach skirmish, Sheriff C.E. Sasser charged Hamilton with conspiracy to incite mob violence, but a Horry County grand jury refused to indict him. The same result occurred, on an identical charge, after Hamilton was briefly jailed for the beating of a YWCA swim instructor who stumbled upon a Klan meeting near Bishopville, South Carolina. Emboldened, the grand dragon launched a new series of raids on both sides of the border. Most of the whippings were carried out by members of Fair Bluff, North Carolina's "Southlands Sport Club"—led by Exalted Cyclops (and former police chief) Early Brooks—but some were more public affairs. On 25 August 1951, two black men were pummeled at a Klan rally while police stood and watched. Six months later, candidate C.L.C. Glymph blamed Klan threats for his decision to quit the race for town council in Gaffney, South Carolina. Tom Hamilton's first conviction, for criminal libel, was recorded on 30 October 1951, but he escaped with a $1,000 fine.

By that time, FBI agents were on the dragon's case. Their focus was the Fair Bluff abduction of white victims Ben Grainger and Dorothy Martin, on 6 October 1951. Klansmen had driven their captives across the state line into South Carolina, thus violating the Lindbergh Law, and injuries inflicted on the couple made their kidnappers eligible for capital punishment. G-men spent four months collecting evidence, then joined Sheriff Hugh Nance for synchronized raids that bagged ten Columbus County Klansmen on 18 February 1952. The federal arrests encouraged state authorities to tackle klansmen on their own. Throughout the Carolinas, fifty-one knights faced various charges, all but eight of them finally convicted. Ten entered prison on 1 September 1952, while twenty-four others paid fines totaling $15,850. In October 1953, Tom Hamilton penned an open letter from prison, urging "my Klan friends everywhere to disband wherever you are."

Florida had been the Klan's strongest realm in 1930–44, and its knights remained violently active in the postwar era. By 1949, at least three rival Klans competed for members and money in the Sunshine State, but their core "values" of white supremacy and anti–Semitism were unchanged. Immediate postwar concerns included "radical" labor unions invading the state's citrus industry and the threat of black suffrage pursued by Harry Moore's Progressive Voters League. To hold those threats at bay, klansmen pursued their normal tactics—terrorism and alliances with racist lawmen. They beat and murdered black victim Melvin Womack at Winter Garden, in March 1951, then went on to detonate a series of bombs in Miami and Orlando. Black homes were favored targets—Miami's Carver Village housing project was bombed three times in as many months—but synagogues and a Catholic church were also included. A second murder victim, Willie Vincent, was pitched from a speeding car in Tampa. In Orlando, nightriders beat Arthur Holland and grazed his scalp with a bullet "as a lesson to other Negroes." On 25 December 1951, a powerful bomb exploded beneath Harry Moore's home in Mims, killing Moore and his wife. That crime, like the rest in Florida's long reign of terror, remains unsolved today.

The Second Reconstruction

On 1 May 1954 the U.S. Supreme Court issued its landmark ruling on school desegregation in the case of *Brown v. the Board of Education*. That unanimous judgment overturned the 1896 *Plessy* rule of "separate but equal" facilities for different races, proclaiming that segregated classrooms were "inherently unequal," and thus unconstitutional. Twelve months later, when no all-white school had admitted a single black pupil, the court demanded "a prompt and reasonable start" on integration, proceeding "with all deliberate speed."

Below the Mason-Dixon Line, *Brown* was a call to arms unrivaled since the outbreak of the Civil War. In darkest Mississippi, Judge Tom Brady scorned the ruling as "Black Monday" and called for organized resistance, while Senator James Eastland told his white constituents, "You are not required to obey any court which passes out such a ruling. In fact, you are obligated to defy it." Shrunken Klan factions found a new lease on life, while facing rampant competition. By May 1956, Dixie boasted ninety active segregationist groups, claiming 250,000 to 300,000 members. Most pledged themselves to "lawful" means of resisting integration, but actions spoke louder than words. In 1959 the Southern Regional Council published a five-year roster of 530 incidents involving "racial violence, reprisal and intimidation": the tab included six murders, forty-four nonfatal shootings, fifty-seven bombings, eleven arson attacks on homes or public buildings, and seventeen riots. Georgia klansman James Venable spoke for many "segs," in and out of the Klan, when he said of public schools, "Let's close them up. Let's burn them up, if it comes to that."

While the KKK enjoyed its most successful recruiting drive in thirty years, new organizations took the forefront in resisting integration. Chief among them were the loosely-knit Citizens' Councils, spawned by Mississippi businessmen and politicians in July 1954. The Councils expanded to Alabama, Arkansas, Florida, Louisiana, South Carolina and Texas in 1955, while Governor Herman Talmadge presided at the birth of Georgia's States' Rights Council in September of that year. Council leaders followed Tom Brady's lead in dissociating themselves from the "nefarious Ku Klux Klans." Brady himself condemned klansmen "because they hid their faces, because they did things that you and I wouldn't approve of." Still, perhaps inevitably, the Councils were branded by blacks and northern liberals as "white-collar Klans," "button-down Klans," or "the uptown KKK."

As with the Klan itself, wherever Council members gathered in the South, racist rhetoric soon gave way to violent deeds. Mississippi set the standard in May 1955, when black suffrage activist George Lee was shot and killed at Belzoni, after ignoring repeated threats from local Council members. Sheriff Isaac Shelton first declared that shotgun pellets taken from Lee's face were "fillings from his teeth"; after an FBI report identified the buckshot, Shelton blamed "some jealous nigger" for the slaying. Attorney General Herbert Brownell, Jr., ordered an FBI investigation of Lee's death, under pressure from the NAACP and American Civil Liberties Union, but the killers remained at large. Three months after Lee's assassination, black activist Lamar Smith was gunned down in broad daylight, outside the

Brookhaven courthouse. The FBI ignored that case, and while three whites were briefly detained, a grand jury refused to indict them. Another black resident of Belzoni, Gus Courts, was threatened by racists in 1955 for his voter registration efforts. That autumn, a known Council member warned Courts, "They're planning to get rid of you." Courts was wounded in a drive-by shooting on 25 November 1955, with Sheriff Shelton once again declaring that "some nigger had it in for him." Three days later, Attorney General Brownell announced that the FBI had opened a "preliminary investigation" of the incident, but the effort was perfunctory at best. Courts complained that G-men never spoke with him beyond a brief hospital interview, and when his physician presented the shotgun pellets extracted from Courts, two G-men told him to "keep them." Once again, the case remained unsolved.

While FBI Director J. Edgar Hoover dismissed the Klan as "pretty much defunct" in March 1956, the invisible empire was growing rapidly, both in membership and in the number of competing Klans. Atlanta auto worker Eldon Edwards led the country's largest faction, chartered in October 1955. His U.S. Klans had chapters in eight southern states by 1956. A year later, Edwards faced competition from at least twenty-three rival Klans, including six each in Alabama and South Carolina, four in Florida, two each in Georgia and Texas, plus one each in Louisiana, Mississippi and North Carolina. Membership estimates for the late 1950s vary widely. The ADL granted Edwards 12,000 to 15,000 knights in 1956, increasing by January 1961 to a probable 20,000. According to the same source, independent Klans claimed 7,000 to 10,500 members in 1956, versus 20,000 to 37,000 in early 1961. Historian Arnold Rice pegs the figure much higher, counting "well over 100,000" knights in "more than 500 new chapters" by mid–1958.

Next to Georgia, Alabama is the state where klansmen have enjoyed their greatest strength and closest ties to public officeholders since the 1920s. On 19 March 1958, state attorney general John Patterson launched his gubernatorial race with a mass-mailing of letters to Alabama Klansmen. The missives solicited votes in the name of "a mutual friend, Mr. R.M. (Bob) Shelton," who had recently defected from the U.S. Klans to lead the independent Alabama Knights. Rival candidate George Wallace denounced Klansmen as "pistol-toters and toughs," chastising Patterson for "rolling with the new wave of the Klan and its terrible tradition of lawlessness." On election day, Patterson trounced Wallace by a margin of 35,000 votes, and Shelton—then a salesman for the B.F. Goodrich rubber company—celebrated his candidate's victory with a million-dollar contract for new tires on state vehicles.

Alabama also set the standard for renewed Klan terrorism, with violence surrounding the Montgomery bus boycott of 1955–57. Montgomery Klansmen also murdered Willie Edwards, a black truck driver, in January 1957, though his death was dismissed as an accident until 1976. Elsewhere in the Cotton State, more than a dozen blacks were whipped by nightriders in August 1957 alone. The following month, on 2 September, members of Asa Carter's Original KKK of the Confederacy kidnapped victim Edward Aaron in Birmingham, castrating him in a Ku Klux initiation ceremony. A week after that heinous crime, other knights mobbed and chain-whipped Rev. Fred Shuttlesworth as he escorted four black children into a newly-integrated school. Bull Connor's all-white Birmingham police force recruited known klansmen, including prolific bomber "Dynamite Bob" Chambliss, as auxiliary officers to patrol black neighborhoods. Saraland's police chief and six other whites were jailed for illegal cross-burnings in September 1958. Reporters speculated that the seven might be linked to the mayor's recent murder, but no indictments were filed.

South Carolina, another traditional stronghold of klancraft, witnessed violence on a par with Alabama's in the latter 1950s. Klansmen burned the Summerton home of one black activist, Rev. Joseph Delaine, then vandalized his new home at Lake City and burned down his church. When another masked party came for him in October 1955, Delaine scattered them with gunfire. In September 1956, Clarendon County knights fired on the home of a local NAACP leader, then torched his uncle's church. Four klansmen were jailed for the July 1957 whipping of Claude Cruell, in Greenville, and six more were arrested for beating of a white high-school teacher at Camden. Elsewhere in Dixie, arsonists burned two rural schools slated for integration near Deep Creek, North Carolina, in August 1958. Another arson fire struck the home of C.G. Hall, Arkansas's secretary of state, after he criticized the Klan in June 1959. Four masked kidnappers snatched Felton Turner from Houston, Texas, in March 1960; they hung him upside down, whipped him, and carved "KKK" on his chest. Five months later, klansmen from Florida and Georgia staged three days of rioting against sit-in demonstrators at Jacksonville.

A trademark of Klan terrorism in the 1950s was an increasing reliance on explosives. Statistics on the plague of racist bombings vary: one media report from December 1954 claimed 195 bombings for that year alone, while a May 1963 article in *New South* listed 142 explosions since January 1956. Whatever the actual tally, klansmen and their allies on the neo-Nazi fringe clearly had launched an all-out war against blacks, Jews, and anyone who counseled moderation on the race issue. While no part of the country was immune to terrorism, most bombings occurred in the South, at or near flashpoints in the struggle for integration. A black boycott of segregated buses lit the fuse in Montgomery, Alabama, where ten bombings shook the city during 1956–57. Five Klansmen were charged with those crimes, two acquitted at trial despite signed confessions; charges against the other three were dropped as part of a general amnesty that also freed black boycott leaders. Terrorism continued apace in "Bombingham," where Bull Connor's police repeatedly seized weapons from blacks guarding churches and homes during 1957–58; the latter 1950s saw at least seventeen bombings in Birmingham, Bessemer and Mobile. Atlanta recorded eighteen racist bombings between 1957 and 1960, while a black activist's wife was killed in the bombing of her home at Ringgold, Georgia, in November 1957. Tennessee Klansmen were equally bomb-happy, touching off eight blasts at Clinton and thirteen in Chattanooga (where they also burned two homes).

Alabama seized the spotlight once again in May 1961, when CORE dispatched two teams of integrated "freedom riders" to test the U.S. Supreme Court's ruling in *Boynton v. Virginia*, banning segregation in bus and train terminals. Bull Connor, still defending Birmingham's reputation as America's "most segregated city," hatched a plot with Robert Shelton's Alabama Knights to greet the demonstrators with a brutal show of force. Klansmen were promised fifteen minutes with the riders, free of interference from police, in which to "beat them, bomb them, murder or kill them," as they pleased. The resultant riots—not only in Birmingham, but in Anniston and Montgomery, as well—showcased Alabama's contempt for civilized behavior, while prompting federal injunctions against three Klan factions identified as participants in the mayhem. The only klansman finally punished was one convicted of perjury for lying about his KKK membership, in order to sit on a jury that acquitted his komrades.

Alabama's knights were not entirely preoccupied by the Freedom Rides in 1961. One day before the Trailways depot riot in Birmingham, Talladega Klansmen whipped three whites who had allowed a black babysitter to discipline their children. On 16 January 1962, bombs damaged three black churches in Birmingham. Seven months later, Birmingham police conspired with klansmen to murder Rev. Fred Shuttlesworth, but an FBI tip saved the activist minister's life.

By spring 1962, eight years after the *Brown* decision, only 2,725 of Dixie's 2.5 million black students were attending integrated classes. That tally included twelve of Louisiana's 295,000 black children, eight out of 303,000 in Georgia, and none at all in Alabama, Mississippi or South Carolina. At that rate, "all deliberate speed" would see southern schools fully integrated by the year 9256. Klansmen deserved a share of credit for the slowdown, as at Athens, Georgia, during January 1961. The state university admitted its first black student on 10 January, and six hundred whites staged a riot on campus the following day; of sixteen arrested, at least eight were Klan members. A new United Klans of America (UKA) was created in July 1961, soon shifting its headquarters from traditional Atlanta to the Tuscaloosa, Alabama, home of Imperial Wizard Robert Shelton. By September 1962, its rallies drew thousands in Alabama, Florida and Georgia.

On 25 June 1962, a federal court ordered the University of Mississippi—"Ole Miss," at Oxford—to admit its first black student, Kosciusko resident James Meredith. When resistance by Governor Ross Barnett proved futile, Klan leaders issued calls for knights to man the barricades, resulting in a riot on 30 September that author William Doyle calls "the beginnings of a Ku Klux Klan rebellion." The Ole Miss melee claimed two lives, while leaving 166 U.S. marshals, 48 soldiers and 375 civilians injured. Federal officers arrested 300 rioters, but none were seriously punished. (Mississippi lawmen, predictably, made no arrests.)

The Klan's great hope in 1962 was former opponent George Wallace. After his defeat in the 1958 gubernatorial race, Wallace had vowed that "no son of a bitch will ever out-nigger me again." For the 1962 campaign, he chose ex-wizard Asa Carter as his chief speech writer and dispatched him to address Klan rallies in the hinterlands. "He'd get the crowds all churned up," Robert Shelton recalled. "He was really good at doing that." Other knights distributed Wallace campaign signs, and Shelton himself received $7,500 to "cover expenses." Wallace's inaugural speech, penned by Carter, included a promise to "stand in the schoolhouse door" against desegregation, closing with a vow cribbed from the Klan's own motto: "Segregation today! Segregation tomorrow! Segregation forever!" Birmingham's knights celebrated Wallace's election with another bombing of Rev. Shuttlesworth's church, on 14 December 1962. While the FBI vacillated between investigating the Alabama Klan and concealing its crimes, the U.S. Army chose outright collaboration. Intelligence agents from the Army's 20th Special Forces Group in Birmingham solicited Robert Shelton's help in collecting data on "subversive" civil rights groups. As revealed three decades later, by the Memphis *Commercial-Appeal*, "In return for paramilitary training at a farm in Cullman, Alabama, Klansmen soon became the 20th's intelligence network, whose information was passed on to the Pentagon." Another Birmingham Klansman from the 1960s, Martin McWhorter, later claimed the order's "primary objective" during 1961–69 "was information supply, to the CIA and the FBI."

Soon after Wallace's inauguration, Dr. Martin Luther King brought his SCLC demonstrators to Birmingham, bent on cracking Alabama's staunches bastion of segregation. Ranged against him were Bull Connor's police and fire department, Alabama state troopers under Colonel Al Lingo (introduced at Klan rallies as "a good friend of ours"), and Robert Shelton's violent UKA. When clubs, fire hoses and attack dogs failed to stem the tide of protest in Birmingham's streets, klansmen tried their hands with a new rash of bombings. The Klan's most heinous crime of the decade occurred on 15 September 1963, when dynamite shattered the Sixteenth Street Baptist Church, leaving four young girls dead in the ruins. Governor Wallace and Al Lingo conspired to frustrate prosecution of the bombers, aided by FBI headquarters in Washington, and while the culprits were soon identified, the first would not face trial until 1977. Two others were belatedly convicted in 2001, after a new generation of G-men "discovered" crucial evidence filed and forgotten since 1963.

Ironically, for all its racist fervor, Mississippi was the one Deep South state where J. Edgar Hoover's description of the "defunct" KKK seemed accurate. Despite reported Ku Klux stirrings in 1946, 1950 and 1956–57, the Klan had failed to prosper in postwar Mississippi. Its full-scale return is usually dated from autumn 1963, when kleagles from Louisiana's Original Knights recruited three hundred Mississippi converts, but no records exist to pinpoint the date. Those converts soon defected en masse to form the militant White Knights under Imperial Wizard Samuel Bowers, while Robert Shelton's UKA belatedly organized under Grand Dragon Edward McDaniel. The main target of white rage in Mississippi was Medgar Evers, state chairman of the NAACP, killed by a sniper's bullet at his Jackson home on 12 June 1963. Authorities soon identified the shooter as klansman Byron De La Beckwith, but two mistrials and three decades of official apathy delayed his conviction until February 1994.

In spring 1964, after his victory in Birmingham, Dr. King tackled St. Augustine, Florida, described by the U.S. Civil Rights Commission as a "segregated super-bomb ... [with a] short fuse." King, for his part, would call it "the most lawless city I have ever seen." Contributing to that riotous state of affairs were Holsted Manucy's nightriding Ancient City Gun Club (identified in FBI memos as a Klan front), Jesse Stoner's NSRP, Ku Klux "evangelist" Connie Lynch, and Sheriff Lawrence Davis (who recruited klansmen as "special deputies"). Together, those defenders of Jim Crow whipped St. Augustine into a racist frenzy, plagued by riots and cross-burnings, arson and shootings, flagrant police brutality toward blacks and criminal negligence in coping with white terrorists. As with the Alabama freedom rides, it would require federal injunctions to sever the Klan-police alliance and restore a semblance of order to America's oldest city.

If Florida presented stiff resistance to desegregation, Mississippi was a veritable fortress, pledged to maintenance of white supremacy at any cost. Proponents of a new civil rights offensive joined forces in January 1964 to create the Council of Federated Organizations (COFO), laying plans for a "Freedom Summer" that would radically change life in the Magnolia State. Opposing that "invasion" were Governor Paul Johnson, the State Sovereignty Commission, thousands of white lawmen, the Citizens' Council—and two factions of the Ku Klux Klan. On 24 April 1964, cross-burnings were reported in sixty-four of the state's eighty-two counties, with statewide Klan membership climbing toward 10,000 at year's end. Between May and September 1964, at least seven blacks and two white civil rights workers were murdered in Mississippi; three other activists were wounded by gunfire; another thirty-five shootings were reported; at least eighty victims were beaten; sixty-eight buildings were bombed or burned (including thirty-seven churches); and ten cars were damaged or destroyed. The year's most notorious case—the murder of COFO workers James Chaney, Andrew Goodman and Michael Schwerner in Neshoba County—threatened a replay of the Evers case until federal charges, filed under the Reconstruction-era Ku Klux Act, resulted in the 1967 conviction of Imperial Wizard Sam Bowers and six klansmen.

Louisiana witnessed its own rash of Ku Klux terrorism during 1964–66, including three known murders, seven bombings, ten arson incidents (including five black churches burned), and thirteen riots led by klansmen. Much of the mayhem occurred around Bogalusa, in Washington Parish. Although forty percent of its residents were black, Bogalusa also harbored some eight hundred Klansmen, earning the nickname "Klantown USA" because no other American city had a higher per capita number of knights. Federal injunctions failed to halt the violence, so angry victims organized a paramilitary group, the Deacons for Defense and Justice, to respond in kind. In Georgia, meanwhile, klansmen brawled with sit-in demonstrators, strafed black homes with gunfire, and on 11 July 1964 murdered Lemuel Penn, a black Army Reserve officer returning home to Washington, D.C., from summer training exercises at Fort Benning. On 6 August, G-men arrested four UKA members for conspiring to deprive Penn of his civil rights. Jurors acquitted the triggermen of murder on 4 September, prompting Klan attorney James Venable to remark, "You'll never be able to convict a white man that kills a nigger what encroaches on the white race of the South." Their prosecutor shook hands with Myers and Sims as they left the courtroom, and Madison County's sheriff attended a victory banquet for the acquitted killers. Finally, in July 1966, federal jurors convicted gunmen Cecil Myers and Joseph Sims on civil rights charges, resulting in ten-year prison terms.

North Carolina was the Klan's strongest realm in 1964–65. Robert Shelton's UKA boasted 7,500 members in 192 klaverns, while James Venable's National Knights had an active chapter in Wilson County. Two knights were arrested for trying to burn a black church at Elm City, in July 1964, and other terrorists proved more successful in their efforts. Bombers destroyed a civil rights worker's car at Charlotte, in early January 1965, then visited New Bern on 24 January to damage a church used for NAACP meetings and a mortuary owned by a black activist. On 29 January, G-men arrested three knights, who pled guilty in state court and received suspended sentences. That wrist-slap did not halt the mayhem in North Carolina. Rioting klansmen beat twenty-seven blacks in Plymouth, on 26 August 1965; when the attacks resumed on 31 August, Governor Dan Moore banned all non-resident knights from the city. Three months later, on 22 November, bombers struck the homes of four civil rights activists in Charlotte. Another bomb destroyed a black church at Ernul, on 9 April 1966. On 30 June 1967, bombs damaged property owned by five members of the Anson County school board in Wadesboro. Finally, on 18 July 1967, FBI agents arrested twelve Klansmen for participating in a two-year reign of terror that spanned three counties. Four cases were dropped before eight defendants faced trial in January 1968. Seven defendants were acquitted on 19 January, while jurors deadlocked on the eighth and no further prosecution was pursued.

The next great civil rights campaign was fought in Alabama, centering on tiny Selma. SNCC volunteers launched a voter-registration drive in Dallas County, Alabama, during 1964, augmented in early 1965 by Martin Luther King and his SCLC. SNCC volunteers launched a voter-registration drive in Dallas County, Alabama during 1964, augmented in early 1965 by Martin Luther King and his SCLC. The Alabama effort cost four lives, including three civil rights workers murdered by klansmen and one shot by Alabama state troopers under Colonel Al Lingo. Rev. James Reeb suffered a fatal beating in Selma on 9 March 1965, his killers acquitted after Sheriff Jim Clark paid an eleventh-hour visit to the jury room. On 25 July, klansmen shot Detroit volunteer Viola Liuzzo in "Bloody Lowndes" County. Despite the presence of an FBI informant at the scene, white juries acquitted three defendants of murder, leaving federal prosecutors to convict them on lesser charges under the old Ku Klux Act. But even that adulterated brand of justice proved elusive in the next Lowndes County slaying. After a klansman shot two white northern clergymen, killing one, jurors acquitted him of manslaughter and set him free.

With so much violence in the daily news, Congress decided to conduct its first full-scale investigation of the Klan since 1921. HUAC convened public hearings on 19 October 1965, grilling a total of 187 witnesses before the show folded on 24 February 1966. The first round of hearings focused chiefly on Klan organization and alleged financial improprieties, while the latter phase revealed details of Ku Klux terrorism. Most of those summoned were Klansmen, and most of them refused to answer any substantive questions. Robert Shelton and three of his grand dragons were cited for contempt of Congress, over their refusal to produce Klan records on demand. Convicted by future Watergate judge John Sirica in September 1966, Shelton received a one-year prison sentence and was fined $1,000. Dragons J.R. Jones (North Carolina) and Robert Scoggin (South Carolina) received identical terms and served nine months each, while Georgia's Calvin Craig escaped with only a fine. HUAC climaxed its inquiry with legislative hearings in July 1966 and released its final report on the Klan in December 1967. Meanwhile, Chairman Willis drafted an "Organizational Conspiracies Act" that imposed life sentences on members of vaguely-defined "clandestine organizations" who conspired in acts of violence. The bill, introduced on 19 September 1967, was so poorly drafted and so broad in scope that vocal adversaries ranged from the Klan to black activist groups and the ACLU. It died in committee as the show wound to a close.

The FBI, meanwhile, was operating on another track. Between September 1964 and April 1971, G-men waged full-scale covert war against various Klan factions and their allies on the neo–Nazi fringe, under a "counterintelligence program" (COINTELPRO) designed "to expose, disrupt and otherwise neutralize the activities of the various Klans and hate organizations, their leadership and adherents." Between 1964 and 1971, Hoover authorized 287 specific operations against racist groups, proceeding on three distinct fronts. The first (and only legitimate) effort involved field investigation of actual crimes; the second encompassed myriad "dirty tricks," many illegal and all outside the FBI's purview; while the third comprised a publicity campaign heralding the bureau's "secret war" in articles and books penned by "reliable and cooperative" authors. Phase three served the FBI's "educational purpose" of bringing Klansmen "into disrepute before the American public," while simultaneously casting Hoover and his agents as champions of the civil rights movement. The overall campaign—justified by Hoover's finding that "the KKK and supporting groups" were "essentially subversive"—included illegal bugs and wiretaps, burglaries and theft of mail, "snitch jacketing" (false branding of loyal klansmen as informers), anonymous mailings, IRS audits, and disruption of marriages by paid informants sanctioned to seduce Klan wives. On one occasion, G-men shot up a tavern patronized by klansmen. In at least two other instances, the FBI itself established Klans led by informants with criminal records. By 1966, J. Edgar Hoover estimated that one of every five dues-paying klansmen drew a paycheck from the FBI.

While COINTELPRO eventually produced a handful of convictions, it failed to put an immediate brake on Klan violence. Mississippi witnessed the most persistent mayhem. Klansmen murdered Hattiesburg NAACP officer Vernon Dahmer and burned his home on 10 January 1966. Six months later, a reputed shot James Meredith during his one-man "walk against fear." In July and September 1966, members of the UKA's Grenada klavern rioted repeatedly against civil rights protests and court-ordered school integration. Even as a group of White Knights faced federal charges for the Neshoba County murders, in 1967, Imperial Wizard Sam Bowers launched a new terror campaign, this time including Mississippi Jews among his targets. A car bomb killed Natchez NAACP secretary Wharlest

Jackson on 27 February 1967. Over the next nine months, klansmen bombed or burned eight churches, two synagogues, two homes, an all-black college, the office of a realtor who had black clients, and the car of black activist Kaley Duckworth. The attacks ended on 30 June 1968, when Meridian police ambushed two would-be bombers, killing one and gravely wounding the other (who lived to receive a thirty-year prison term). That trap, it turned out, was arranged by two paid FBI informants—including one of the Neshoba county triggermen.

Estimates of Klan membership in the latter 1960s varied widely. ADL investigators pegged the total at some 30,000 in summer 1966, increasing to 55,000 by November 1967, but HUAC counted only 16,000 active members (scattered over eighteen states and thirteen rival Klans) in December 1967. The discrepancy may have sprung from HUAC's wish to minimize Klan influence in Dixie, much as the committee had inflated communist strength for the past three decades. Still, even accepting the ADL's figures as accurate, the Klan's resurgence was short lived. If we trust FBI reports, membership had plummeted to 14,000 klansmen by spring 1968. Historian Wyn Wade goes even further, reporting drops of fifty percent in each of the next two years, for a total of 3,500 knights remaining in 1970.

New Issues, New Enemies

The KKK was in eclipse by 1973, when the ADL placed national membership around 5,000, for a crushing loss of 50,000 knights in six years' time. If accurate—and there is no clear reason to dispute it—that loss represented the Klan's worst tailspin since the late 1920s, all the worse because it had so few committed knights to lose. The ragged remnant who remained could not have known it, but their savior was already waiting in the wings.

David Ernest Duke was a Louisiana high school student when he joined the Klan in 1967, at age seventeen. Most members of his small klavern were Catholics, sharing Duke's preoccupation with the "danger" posed by blacks and Jews. A budding fascist at heart, Duke flirted with various neo–Nazi groups, calling Adolf Hitler's *Mein Kampf* "the greatest piece of literature of the twentieth century" and dubbing ANP founder George Lincoln Rockwell "the greatest American who ever lived." In January 1972, Duke teamed with real estate developer James Lindsay (alias "Ed White") to found a new Knights of the KKK in New Orleans. While welcoming Catholic recruits, the Lindsay-Duke faction reflected the Klan's most blatant flirtation with Nazism since New Jersey knights rallied with the German-American Bund in 1940. By the time of Lindsay's still-unsolved murder in June 1975, that recipe had boosted membership to 6,500 in 1975, rising to at least 8,000 (some reports said 10,500) in 1979. (The FBI, out of step as usual, counted only 1,700 klansmen in 1974 and 2,200 in 1976.) Duke took the American media by storm, appearing on numerous talk shows, granting endless interviews to journalists who found his views repugnant, but who seldom failed to comment on his eloquence, his stylish clothes and hair, even his sex appeal. Despite his adulation of Hitler, fantastic Holocaust denial and persistent violence by his klansmen, Duke's brand of "button-down racism" gave the KKK a new lease on life.

It was not all smooth sailing for Duke, however. His Klan suffered its first mass defection in August 1975, when electrician Bill Wilkinson accused Duke of embezzling Klan money. Duke's replies failed to pacify Wilkinson and others, who resigned en masse to form the new Invisible Empire Knights. When Duke branded Wilkinson "practically an illiterate who has never read anything," Wilkinson released a document which all KKKK recruits were compelled to sign, agreeing that in the event a Klan oath was breached, the KKK "is entitled to all my real estate, personal property, bank accounts, and everything of monetary or sentimental value." Duke grudgingly admitted that the pledge was legally binding, but termed it "a protection for our members."

By the late 1970s, despite his seeming omnipresence in the media, Duke found his KKKK running in third place, with membership trailing both Robert Shelton's UKA and Wilkinson IEKKKK. That lapse was due in equal parts to Duke's political preoccupations, his personal problems, and the mass defection of dissatisfied realms. When Florida Grand Dragon Jack Gregory joined the chorus of complaints concerning Duke's financial mismanagement, Duke banished him. Furious, Gregory denounced Duke as a "con artist" who looted Klan coffers to finance a jet-set life style. California Grand Dragon Tom Metzger left the KKK on his own initiative, briefly leading the rival California Knights and pronouncing the advent of "Fifth Position" racism—divorced from right- or left-wing politics—before he founded WAR and plunged full-time into the world of neo–Nazi fantasy. Unknown to his followers, Duke began to plot his exit from the KKK in early 1979, while laying the groundwork for his first abortive presidential campaign. His new vehicle, quietly organized in December 1979, was a retooled model of the NAAWP. In January 1980, Duke opened negotiations for sale of his membership list to Wilkinson (asking price, $35,000), but when the wizards met on 20 July 1980, Wilkinson brought a TV news crew instead of his checkbook. While Wilkinson branded Duke a "traitor" and "sell-out," Duke tried to take the high road. "I'm resigning," he told reporters, "because I don't think the Klan can succeed at this point."

Still, the KKK had made progress in the 1970s. Aside from its 8,000 to 10,500 dues-paying members in 1979, the ADL estimated that another 75,000 Americans supported the Klan's racist program without taking the final step toward membership. Ku Klux statements and actions also revealed an escalating militancy. In May 1978, Florida klansmen cheered John Garrell—millionaire founder of the Illinois-based Christian Patriots Defense League—when he urged them to arm against "niggers and Jews." Bill Wilkinson told journalists, "We tried the moderate approach in trying to halt the extravagant gains by blacks but it failed. No we are resorting to other methods." In the face of David Duke's prolific pamphleteering, Wilkinson observed, "You don't fight wars with words and books. You fight them with bullets and bombs." Henceforth, when weapons were displayed at his rallies, Wilkinson warned, "These guns are not for killing rabbits, they're for wasting people." Wilkinson's followers attacked black demonstrators in Decatur, Alabama, and Tupelo,

Mississippi during 1979, but the worst violence emerged from North Carolina, where members of Virgil Griffin's North Carolina Knights and Harold Covington's NSPA murdered five participants in a "Death to the Klan" demonstration at Greensboro, on 3 November 1979. Although the shootings were captured on videotape and beamed to a global audience, successive all-white juries still acquitted the gunmen of murder (in 1980) and on federal conspiracy charges (in 1984).

At War with "ZOG"

David Duke's successor as head of the KKKK, Alabama Grand Dragon Stephen Black, was a chip off the old block, obsessed with Nazism from age fifteen, affiliated with Jesse Stoner's NSRP (and shot by one of Stoner's bodyguards in still-disputed circumstances) a year later. Expelled from the University of Alabama's ROTC program for his racist activities, Black quit school altogether in 1977 to lead Duke's Klan in the Cotton State. With Duke's departure, Black moved imperial headquarters to Tuscumbia, Alabama, and did his best to carry on. His June 1981 arrest and subsequent conviction for plotting to invade the Caribbean nation of Grenada finished Black as a Klan leader, though he later pioneered racism on the Internet. Control of the KKKK thereafter passed to Christian Identity minister Thomas Robb, who presided over a tempestuous empire from headquarters in Arkansas. Bill Wilkinson faced troubles of his own, meanwhile. Exposed as a longtime FBI informant in 1981, he clung to command of the IEKKKK while members defected in droves. Lawsuits and criminal prosecutions left his Klan bankrupt by January 1983, but Wilkinson hung on as wizard until August 1984, when he finally passed the reins to Alabama klansman James Blair. After two years of futile recruiting drives, Blair in turn ceded command to James Farrands—a Connecticut Catholic whose reign as imperial wizard marked an historic departure from the KKK's southern Protestant tradition.

While those leaders struggled, and David Duke achieved marginal success with election to one term in the Louisiana state legislature, Klan ranks suffered further attrition. ADL observers counted 6,500 active knights in 1984, 7,000 in 1985, and 5,500 in 1987. While membership declined, however, Klans proliferated, with splinter factions constantly in flux from coast to coast. As Klans divided and multiplied, their attraction to the neo-Nazi fringe increased. Richard Butler's Aryan Nations compound in Idaho and the Michigan farm owned by former UKA Grand Dragon Robert Miles became rallying points on a par with Georgia's Stone Mountain, hosting "unity" rallies where fiery crosses blazed beside swastika banners, white robes mingling freely with fascist brownshirts, skinheads in black leather, and "survivalists" clad in camouflage fatigues. Anger at "ZOG"—the hated "Zionist occupation government" in Washington, D.C.—was universal, proceeding by degrees from contempt toward open declarations of war.

President Ronald Reagan, inaugurated in January 1981, displayed a pervasive blindness toward right-wing terrorism. Where they had not already done so, G-men followed Reagan's lead and gave up any pretense of investigating Klansmen, Nazis and their ilk. The handful of federal Klan prosecutions during 1981–82 were invariably initiated by ATF agents pursuing bomb and firearms violations against such groups as the Adamic Knights of the KKK (in Maryland and Pennsylvania), the Confederate Vigilantes of the KKK (in Tennessee), and the Death Knights of the KKK (in Kentucky). ATF agents also arrested and convicted a gang of Nazis who planned to bomb downtown Greensboro, North Carolina, in 1981. For their efforts, President Reagan slashed ATF's funding, then made unsuccessful efforts to disband the unit altogether. Director William Webster announcing on 4 December 1984 that bombings of abortion clinics and similar targets did not meet the Bureau's definition of "domestic terrorism." Some Klan violence in the 1980s was brutally traditional. A case in point was the abduction and lynching of black teenager Michael Donald in Mobile, Alabama, on 21 March 1981. It took local police and FBI agents two years to notice that Henry Hays, a UKA kligrapp, lived across the street from the murder scene. That "coincidence" led G-men to investigate the Mobile Klan, and so the case was finally solved. Klansman James "Tiger" Knowles pled guilty in federal court to violating Donald's civil rights, while Hays denied any knowledge of the crime. Both were charged with murder in June 1983 and subsequently convicted, Hays sentenced to die while Knowles received a sentence of ten years to life for cooperating with the prosecution. Hays was executed on 7 June 1997, and accomplice Benjamin Cox received a life sentence in May 1989. The crowning blow, however, came when SPLC attorneys filed suit against the UKA on behalf of Donald's mother, winning a $7 million judgment that forced Imperial Wizard Robert Shelton to surrender his Tuscaloosa headquarters.

The first serious attack on ZOG was launched by Robert Jay Mathews, an anti–Semite associate of the Aryan Nations and National Alliance. Mathews developed an obsession for *The Turner Diaries,* a racist novel published in 1978 by National Alliance leader William Pierce, describing an America enslaved by ZOG, wherein white patriots of "The Order" struggle to reclaim their native land. In summer 1983, Mathews decided it was time for the fictional war to begin in real life. His version of The Order, also known the Silent Brotherhood, included members from the Aryan Nations, National Alliance and other neo–Nazi groups, with a hardcore contingent of klansmen from Alabama, California, Colorado and Pennsylvania. They progressed from clumsy counterfeiting and bombing of adult theaters to murder and armed robbery in 1984, bagging $3.6 million from a single heist in California. From that haul, Mathews allegedly donated loot to Texas klansman Louis Beam ($100,000), Richard Butler ($40,000), Robert Miles ($15,500), Frazier Glenn Miller of the Carolina Knights ($200,000), Tom Metzger ($260,000 to $300,000), and William Pierce ($50,000). (All but Miller denied the allegations.) In November 1984, The Order issued a formal "declaration of war on ZOG" signed by ten members. FBI agents killed Mathews on Whidbey Island, Washington, then rounded up most of his gang over the next six months. Order member David Tate received a life sentence for the April 1985 murder of a Missouri state trooper. Fifteen other defendants pled guilty on various charges, receiving sentences that ranged from six months to sixty years. Eleven Order defendants were convicted at trial, their prison terms ranging from three years to 250 years.

In spring 1985, emboldened by his share of the Ukiah loot, klansman Glenn Miller renamed his Carolina Knights the White Patriot Party, which he dubbed "a citizens' militia." Members shed their robes in favor of camouflage army fatigues, berets and combat boots, symbolizing a new aggressive militancy. Their goal was nothing less than the creation of a "White Republic within the geographical bounds of the Southern United States." Stockpiles of weapons and training sessions led by active-duty soldiers from Fort Bragg, North Carolina, prompted Morris Dees and his SPLC to sue Miller, demanding a federal investigation of WPP ties to army personnel. That case produced a court order banning further paramilitary exercises and drove Miller to pen his own declaration of war. Miller and a comrade were found guilty of contempt on 25 July 1986, for resuming their paramilitary exercises. Two months later, several party members were charged with plotting to rob a restaurant in Fayetteville. Five more White Patriots were indicted on 8 January 1987, on federal charges of conspiring to steal weapons from Fort Bragg. Miller fled underground in March 1987, but he was captured on 30 April, slapped with a nine-count conspiracy indictment. He pled guilty to reduced charges on 4 January 1988 and received five years in prison on reduced charges, while two codefendants took their chances with a jury and received 20-year terms. In the wake of Miller's sentencing, the WPP dissolved, some of its members drifting off to join the Maryland-based National Democratic Front.

Part of Miller's plea bargain was an agreement to testify against fellow racist leaders at their impending sedition trial. That case arose in equal parts from crimes committed by the Order and another Christian Identity cult, the Missouri-based Covenant, Sword and Arm of the Lord (CSA). CSA leader James Ellison received a five-year prison term in August 1985, after he and five others pled guilty to manufacturing illegal weapons for The Order. Tired of prison by 1987, Ellison offered testimony against others in exchange for early release. Aside from his own group's activities, he revealed further details of The Order's crimes and distribution of its Brinks loot to racist leaders across the country. Those charged with sedition as a result included Louis Beam, Richard Butler and Robert Miles; CSA members Snell, David McGuire, Lambert Miller, William Wade and his son Ivan; Order members Andrew Barnhill, David Lane, Ardie McBreatry, Bruce Pierce and Richard Scutari; and Arkansas gun dealer Robert Smalley, earlier convicted for falsifying records of his sales to Order members. Indictments were issued on 24 April 1987, and Beam promptly fled to Mexico, recaptured there after his wife shot and wounded a Mexican policeman. In addition to the known crimes of the Order and the CSA, defendants charged in the indictment were accused of buying stolen weapons and explosives in Missouri and Oklahoma; planning demolition of federal buildings in Denver, Kansas City, Minneapolis, New Orleans, New York City and St. Louis; poisoning the municipal water supplies of Chicago, New York, and Washington, D.C.; and sabotaging sundry railroads, utilities and sewer lines.

Trial on the charges commenced in February 1988, before Judge Morris Arnold at Fort Smith, Arkansas. Over the next seven weeks, more than 100 witnesses testified, while prosecutors presented some 1,200 pieces of physical evidence. James Ellison described secret meetings, wherein Robert Mathews allegedly planned illegal acts with defendants Beam and Butler. In a separate incident, Ellison claimed Robert Miles delivered a thirty-gallon barrel of the deadly poison ricin, slated for use on water supplies in the nation's capital. Glenn Miller detailed his receipt of stolen cash from Mathews and his girlfriend, Zillah Craig. Craig herself confirmed the story, while Order turncoat William Soderquist described a similar payment to Robert Miles. Tom Martinez outlined the Order's bungled counterfeiting operation. Another ex-Aryan warrior, Denver Parmenter, walked jurors through the Brinks holdup itself. After both sides had rested their cases, Judge Arnold entered a directed verdict of acquittal for Robert Smalley. On 7 April 1988 jurors acquitted the other thirteen defendants on all counts. Louis Beam, emerging from the courthouse, bowed to a nearby Confederate monument and proclaimed, "The Zionist Occupation Government has suffered a terrible blow."

"Yesterday, Today, Forever"

While klansmen and their neo–Nazi allies failed to topple ZOG, they remained a persistent threat to domestic tranquility in the 1990s and the early twenty-first century. Between 1990 and 1996, fifty-seven black churches were burned by arsonists in southern states, with thirty-two of those fires recorded in 1995–96. None were listed by the FBI as acts of domestic terrorism. Congress belatedly convened a one-day hearing on the problem, and while President Bill Clinton demanded a federal investigation, his National Church Arson Task Force reported in June 1997 that it could find "no evidence of a national conspiracy" to burn black churches. That finding may have been technically accurate, but there was nonetheless ample evidence of conspiracy in individual cases. A report from the ADL, published on 20 June 1996, identified fourteen Klan factions active in nine states where churches were burned; other militant racist groups organized in the same region included the Aryan Nations, Christian Defense League, National Alliance, and David Duke's NAAWP. In South Carolina, two members of the Christian Knights of the KKK confessed to burning black churches at Bloomville and Greeleyville, on consecutive nights in June 1995. Another case was solved in July 1997, with the arrest of five Alabama teenagers who burned one church and vandalized another, two days after attending a KKK rally at Tenesaw.

Despite such incidents, an FBI survey listed only two cases of right-wing terrorism during 1992–94. Only a single case of terrorism, the Oklahoma City bombing (see below), was identified for all of 1995. As noted by author Beau Grossup, publication of those statistics "meant ignoring the fact that several major personalities and organizations who came to dominate the new and violent right-wing Patriot Movement of the 1990s had been active in FBI-documented terrorism from the 1970s through the mid–1980s. More importantly, it required ignoring or 'defining away' numerous domestic terrorist incidents." Henceforth, private watchdog groups would be left to monitor right-wing and white-supremacist mayhem, while the FBI remained aloof. Chief among those was the SPLC, led by attorney Morris Dees. While the ADL and other groups mounted surveillance on hate groups, the SPLC went further, finding legal means to punish violent extremists and bankrupt their organizations through civil litigation.

From 1994 through the turn of the millennium, many klansmen and neo–Nazis allied themselves with the heavily-armed "patriot militia" movement. John Trochmann, a frequent visitor to the Aryan Nations compound, founded the first such significant group—the Militia of Montana—on 1 January 1994. While Trochmann later split with Richard Butler, earning Butler's condemnation as an "anti–Christ," literature from the Aryan Nations, KKK, National Alliance, John Birch Society and other fringe groups circulated

"Yesterday, Today, Forever." Klansmen boast that their order is immortal (Florida State Archives).

widely among militia groups nationwide. From Florida to the Pacific Northwest, militia leadership frequently overlapped with that of the Klan and other white-supremacist groups. Timothy McVeigh, an ex-klansman and disaffected soldier obsessed with *The Turner Diaries,* bombed Oklahoma City's Alfred P. Murrah Federal Building on 19 April 1995, killing at least 168 persons (some reports say 169) and injuring 850. Jurors convicted McVeigh on 2 June 1997 and recommended a death sentence on 13 June. Accomplice Terry Nichols faced trial in Denver on 3 November 1997, but prosecutors failed to place him at the crime scene, prompting a compromise verdict. Nichols was convicted of conspiracy and eight counts of involuntary manslaughter (reduced from murder), acquitted on charges of destruction by explosives and using a weapon of mass destruction. Jurors deadlocked on penalty deliberations, and Judge Matsch settled the matter by imposing a life prison term on 4 June 1998. After appeals and delays occasioned by FBI mishandling of evidence, McVeigh was executed by lethal injection on 11 June 2001.

The decade after Oklahoma City witnessed at least fifty-nine terrorist conspiracies by identified far-right groups and individuals. Their schemes echoed The Order's plans: armed robberies, arson and bombings, attempts to poison municipal water supplies, and assassination of various government figures or law

enforcement officers. In terms of mayhem and fantastic plots, militia members competed with skinheads, Christian Identity cultists, self-styled "Phineas Priests," and a bank-robbing Aryan Republican Army. Klansmen were also represented in the carnage—stockpiling illegal weapons in Illinois, building bombs in Texas, killing one another in North Carolina. At press time for this volume, SPLC investigators counted thirty-four separate Klans nationwide, with 162 active klaverns in thirty states and the District of Columbia. Their efforts were supported by twenty neo–Nazi groups (with 158 chapters), twenty-eight racist skinhead gangs (48 chapters), and twenty-seven Christian Identity congregations.

The Klan endures because its prejudice still finds an audience and echoes with disturbing resonance. That message is the dark side of America, the nightmare lurking in the shadow of the dream, embodied in the promise penned almost a century ago:

> Yesterday, Today, Forever,
> Since Eighteen Hundred and Sixty-Six,
> the KU KLUX KLAN
> has been riding and will
> continue to do so as long as
> the WHITE MAN LIVETH.

2 KLANSPEAK

Fraternities and secret societies traditionally employ private passwords, codes and jargon to identify their members and prevent outsiders from deciphering communications. The KKK is no exception to that rule, its need for secrecy compounded by frequent involvement in conspiratorial and criminal activities.

The Reconstruction Klan's initial terminology and titles were devised by its six founders in Pulaski, Tennessee, based on familiar elements from the Kuklos Adelphon collegiate fraternity. That secret language was elaborated a year later, in the pre–script drafted at Nashville. Many accounts credit its language to ex–General Albert Pike of Arkansas, a high-ranking Mason, poet and explorer who may have been the Razorback State's first grand dragon. Despite enumeration of its ranks and rituals, the KKK was never named in the original prescript, the words "Ku Klux Klan" replaced instead by asterisks.

William Simmons clearly used the first Klan's prescript as a model for his own *Kloran*, in 1915, but he also made substantial changes. Most of the modern Klan's terms and titles beginning with "K" or "Kl" were coined by Simmons and remain in use, with minor variations, nine decades after he first set pen to paper. His Kalendar also reveals significant deviations from the Register of the original Klan, and his rituals are more detailed than those of the nineteenth-century order. Since the parent Klan's official disbandment in 1944, splinter factions have been free to coin terms of their own, reflecting personal preferences and a general drift by most Klans toward accommodation with neo–Nazi allies since the 1980s.

Action squad—A Klan unit organized for acts of violence. *See also* Wrecking Crew

Adamic/Adamite race—Descendants of Adam in the Old Testament, presumed in Identity theology to be white. *See also* Aryan race

Akia—"A Klansman I am" (password response to Ayak?).

Alarming month—June on both the 1867 Register and the Kalendar.

Alien—Any nonmember of the Invisible Empire.

Alta California—A twenty-mile buffer zone along the U.S.-Mexican border, proposed by David Duke to stop illegal immigration from Mexico.

Amber day—Wednesday on the 1868 Register.

Anno Klan—"Year of the Klan," calculated from 1866 (e.g., Anno Klan L would be 1916).

Appalling hour—(a) Eleventh hour on the 1867 Register; (b) fourth hour on the 1868 Register.

Aryan race—Non-Jewish Caucasians, principally of Nordic or western European ancestry.

Aryan Socialism *see* Third Position

Ass-tear Squad—A select unit assigned to perform acts of violence. *See also* Wrecking Crew

Appalling month—December on the Kalendar.

Awful hour—(a) Third hour on the 1867 Register; (b) ninth hour on the 1868 Register.

Ayak?—"Are you a Klansman?" (interrogatory password)

Belt Line—A gauntlet run by Klansmen convicted of various disciplinary infractions, wherein they are whipped by fellow knights.

Benevolence Committee—In the 1960s Original Knights, a panel appointed to coordinate charitable activities.

Black day—Wednesday on the 1867 Register.

Bloody hour—Sixth hour on the 1867 Register.

Bloody month—January on the Kalendar.

Blooming month—May on the 1868 Register.

Blue day—Tuesday on the 1867 Register.

Boom-stick boys—Klansmen who specialize in bombing.

Brilliant month—June on the 1868 Register.

Building Committee—In the 1960s Original Knights, a panel assigned to construction and maintenance of a klavern.

Ca Bark—"Constantly Applied by All Real Klansman" (proper password response "Clasp")

Captain of the Guard—In the 1960s Original Knights, the officer responsible for klavern security.

Capowe—"Countersign and password or written evidence" (a challenge to follow "Akia").

Carpetbagger—In Reconstruction, any northerner who moved to Dixie, presumably intent on corrupt financial dealings and subversion of all-white "home rule."

Chief Klanbursar—Supreme treasurer of the WKKKKM.

Chief Klanjustice—Head of the WKKKKM's judicial branch.

Citizen—An initiated member of the Invisible Empire.

Clasp—"Clannish Loyalty a Sacred Principle" (password).

Council of Centaurs—One of two tribunals established by the Reconstruction KKK, assigned to try Ghouls accused of violating Klan rules and regulations.

Council of Yahoos—The second tribunal theoretically created by the Reconstruction Klan, to judge ranking officers accused of misconduct. No evidence exists to suggest that the council was ever convened.

Crimson day—Saturday on both versions of the Register.

Cross lighting—A term applied to cross-burnings, as a substitute for the more negative "cross burning."

Cross-wheel—Since 1915, the circular emblem enclosing a cross, worn on many Klan robes and often printed on KKK literature. In many versions, a drop of blood surmounts the cross, representing loyalty unto death.

Cumberland—Unexplained term, appended as Part IV of the revised Register in 1868. Stanley Horn suggests that it represents a numerical code, with its letters "standing successively for the numbers 1, 2, 3, 4, 5, 6, 7, 8, 9, 0." If so, its usefulness in preparing coded correspondence was clearly limited, since it omitted 16 of the alphabet's 26 letters.

Cygnar—"Can you give number and realm?" (interrogatory password).

Dark day—Sunday on the Kalendar.

Dark month—February on the 1867 Register.

Deadly day—Monday on the Kalendar.

Degree Team—In some Klans, a committee appointed to initiate new members.

Den—In Reconstruction, the official designation for a local Klan chapter or its normal meeting place. *See also* Klavern

Deputy Klokan—In the 1960s Original Knights, an officer who assists the Klokan of a klavern.

Desolate day—Thursday on the Kalendar.

Desperate day—Saturday on the Kalendar.

Dismal day—Tuesday on the Kalendar.

Dismal month—January on both versions of the Register.

District—In the WKKKKM, five subdivisions of Mississippi, each including twelve to twenty-four counties.

Doleful day—Wednesday on the Kalendar.

Doleful hour—Seventh hour on the 1867 Register.

Domain—During 1921–22, an administrative unit consisting of several combined states.

Dominion—During Reconstruction, a subdivision of the Invisible Empire comprising one congressional district, administered by a Grand Titan. *See also* province.

Dreadful day—Friday on the Kalendar.

Dreadful hour—Eleventh hour on the 1868 Register.

Dreadful month—July on the 1867 Register.

Dying month—December on the 1867 Register.

East Mongolia—The Hawaiian Islands, proposed by David Duke as a segregated homeland for all Asians now living in the U.S.

Education Committee—In the 1960s Original Knights, a klanton-level panel assigned to public education.

88—"H.H." or "Heil Hitler" (H being the eighth letter of the alphabet), displayed as a tattoo or in graffiti by various neo–Nazi Klans and allied fascist groups.

El Magus—Title assumed by William Simmons in April 1923, during his brief leadership of Kamelia.

Elimination primary—A political process employed mainly by Arkansas and Texas klansmen, wherein klaverns were polled to choose candidates for the KKK to support in public elections.

Emerald day—Saturday on the 1868 Register.

Emperor—Honorary title created to pacify William Simmons in 1922, after he was deposed as Imperial Wizard by Hiram Evans.

Exalted Cyclops—Since 1915, the officer commanding a Klan or Klavern.

Eyes of Scrutiny—Ritual viewing of new recruits by Klansmen during an initiation ceremony.

Fading month—September on the 1868 Register.

Fearful hour—First hour on both versions of the Register.

Fearful month—April on the Kalendar.

Fifth Era—Touted by Robert Miles as a new revolutionary era of Klan history, marked by public collaboration with neo–Nazi groups. Spokesmen for Thom Robb's Knights of the KKK disagree, citing this era as the period of Klan leadership by David Duke (1975–80).

First Era—The original KKK of Reconstruction. *See also* 33/1

Fourteen Words—A slogan issued from prison by klansman David Lane: "We must secure the existence of our people and a future for white children."

Fourth Era—Variously described by Klan spokesmen as the period 1954–70 or 1961–75, including the Klans led by Robert Shelton and Sam Bowers in violent reaction to the black civil rights movement. Klanswoman Rachel Pendergraft calls the period "a propaganda fiasco," during which "the Klan wasn't a failure ... but the leaders lacked vision," failing to grasp the public impact of their racist comments on TV. *See also* 33/4

Francia—A segregated homeland for Americans of French-Canadian descent along the U.S. border with Québec, proposed by David Duke.

Frightful hour—(a) Tenth hour on the 1867 Register; (b) eighth hour on the 1868 Register.

Frightful month—November on the Kalendar.

Furies—(a) In Reconstruction, six officers appointed to help a Grand Titan administer his Dominion; (b) in the 20th century, seven officers who perform the same function for a Great Titan in his province. The modern furies include three Great Klaliffs, one Great Klabee, one Great Kligrapp, one Great Kludd, and one Great Nighthawk; (c) in the 1960s Original Knights, eleven members of the Great Titan's Kommittee.

Furious month—(a) March on the 1867 Register; (b) May on the Kalendar.

Genii—(a) In Reconstruction, ten knights serving as policy advisors to the Grand Wizard; (b) in the, fifteen officers who compose the Grand Kloncilium, advising the Imperial Wizard as necessary. Modern Genii include the Imperial Klabee, Imperial Kladd, Imperial Klaliff, Imperial Klarogo, Imperial Klexter, Imperial Kligrapp, Imperial Klokard, Imperial Klonsel, Imperial Kludd, Imperial Nighthawk, and five members of the Imperial Klokann.

Ghouls—Rank-and-file members of the Reconstruction KKK. During 1867–68, in Maury County, Tennessee, curious and confusing attempts were made to adapt the title for members of higher rank, but the change was never clarified or officially sanctioned. Published sources disagree as to whether the term is used among modern Klansmen, but it does not appear in the Kloran or in any constitution of the various competing Klans.

Giant—(a) In the UKA, a purely honorary title applied to retired officers at various levels, with a Klansman's prior rank determined by the prefix. Thus, a Giant is a retired Exalted Cyclops;

a Grand Giant is a retired Grand Dragon; and an Imperial Giant is a former Imperial Wizard; (b) in the WKKKKM, the commanding officer of a province.

Gloomy month—(a) December on the 1868 Register; (b) February on the Kalendar.

Glorious month—November on the 1868 Register.

Goblins—In the original Klan, four officers appointed as aides to the Grand Giant of each province. No corresponding rank exists among modern Klans.

Grand Banner—The official flag of the Reconstruction KKK.

Grand Chaplain—In the WKKKKM, fourth-in-command of the Invisible Empire.

Grand Council—The anonymous commanding body of the 1970s Association of South Carolina Klans.

Grand Cyclops—In Reconstruction, the officer commanding a local den, assisted by two Nighthawks. *See also* Exalted Cyclops

Grand Director of the Klan Bureau of Investigation—In the WKKKKM, chief investigator and fifth-in-command of the Invisible Empire.

Grand Dragon—(a) In most Klans, the supreme commander of a Realm. In Reconstruction, the Grand Dragon was assisted by eight Hydras, increased to nine after 1915; (b) in the AGK (1946–49), the supreme commander of the Invisible Empire; (c) in some Klans restricted to a single state, the highest-ranking officer; (d) in the WKKKKM, second-in-command of the Invisible Empire.

Grand Empress—Self-conferred title adopted by Cincinnati Klanswoman Eloise Witte in the 1960s.

Grand Ensign—(a) In Reconstruction, the officer in charge of a local den's banner; (b) in the UKA, the banner carried by a klavern's Kladd.

Grand Exchequer—In the original Klan, a title applied to KKK treasurers at all levels from the grass-roots den to imperial headquarters, without variations in title. *See also* Klabee

Grand Giant—(a) In Reconstruction and among some modern Klans, the commander of a province, advised by four Goblins; (b) in the UKA, an honorary title for retired Grand Dragons; (c) in the WKKKKM, third-in-command of the Invisible Empire.

Grand Guard—In the original KKK, sentries chosen by a den's Grand Sentinel to stand watch during meetings. *See also* Klexter

Grand Klabee—In the modern KKK, treasurer of a realm.

Grand Kladd—Since 1915, the officer responsible for a realm's ritual paraphernalia.

Grand Klaliff—In the modern Klan, vice-president of a realm.

Grand Klan—A special gathering convened in Spartanburg County, South Carolina, in spring 1871, wherein delegates from a four-county area banned further nightriding without specific orders from the Grand Klan. Penalties for disobedience were established, but the order proved unenforceable.

Grand Klarogo—Since 1915, the sergeant-at-arms of a realm.

Grand Klexter—In the modern Klan, the officer responsible for external security at statewide meetings and gatherings of realm officials.

Grand Kligrapp—The secretary of a realm.

Grand Klokan—A member of the Grand Klokann.

Grand Klokann—The advisory board of a realm, consisting of five Klokans.

Grand Klokard—A realm's designated lecturer.

Grand Kludd—The chaplain of a realm.

Grand Magi—In Reconstruction, the officer second-in-command of a den, who presides over meetings when the Grand Cyclops is absent. *See also* Klaliff

Grand Monk—In the original Klan, the officer third-in-command of a den, presiding when both the Grand Cyclops and Grand Magi are absent.

Grand Nighthawk—Since 1915, the chief courier of a realm, sometimes with additional duties involving security.

Grand Scribe—Secretaries of the Reconstruction Klan, serving at various levels from local dens to imperial headquarters without different titles. *See also* Kligrapp

Grand Sentinel—In Reconstruction, the officer responsible for den security, including selection of the Grand Guard. *See also* Klarogo; Klexter

Grand Titan—During Reconstruction, the chief officer of a Dominion, advised by six Furies.

Grand Turk—In the original KKK, the executive officer of a local den, responsible for alerting Ghouls to any extraordinary meetings ordered by the Grand Cyclops.

Grand Tycoon—The anonymous signatory of a reputed Klan circular published in Lebanon, Tennessee, in September 1868, ordering local Klansmen to disband. The order apparently ended nightriding in Wilson County, despite its irregularity.

Grand Wizard—(a) Supreme commander of the Reconstruction Klan, assisted by ten Genii; (b) in modern times, the highest officer of certain smaller Klans. *See also* Imperial Wizard

Great Giant—In the UKA, an honorary title applied to retired Great Titans.

Great Klabee—The treasurer of a province.

Great Klaliffs—Since 1915, officers of a three-member advisory board serving the Grand Titan of a province.

Great Kligrapp—The secretary of a province.

Great Klokan—A member of the Great Klokann.

Great Klokann—The advisory board of a province, consisting of three Klokans.

Great Klokard—The designated lecturer of a province.

Great Kludd—The chaplain of a province.

Great Nighthawk—The chief courier of a province, often with additional duties involving security.

Great Titan—In modern Klans, the commander of a province, assisted by seven Furies.

Green day—Monday on both versions of the Register.

Head-knockers—Klansmen appointed to perform beatings and other violent acts. *See also* Wrecking Crew

Hideous hour—(a) Ninth hour on the 1867 Register; (b) seventh hour on the 1868 Register.

Hideous month—March on the Kalendar.

Horrible hour—Tenth hour on the 1868 Register.

Horrible month—(a) September on the 1867 Register; (b) August on the Kalendar.

Horrid hour—Fifth hour on the 1867 Register.

Hydras—(a) In Reconstruction, six officers assigned to advise a Grand Dragon; (b) in the modern Klan, nine officers performing the same duty. They include the Grand Klabee, Grand Kladd, Grand Klaliff, Grand Klarogo, Grand Klexter, Grand Kligrapp, Grand Klokard, Grand Kludd, and Grand Nighthawk.

Identity—A variant sect of Christianity, regarding white European races as the lost tribes of Israel.

Imperial Commander—Title held by the 1920s leader of the Women of the KKK.

Imperial Dragon—Title assumed by Royal Young, Jr., of the 1960s Original Knights, while organizing klaverns in Mississippi.

Imperial Emperor—Redundant title claimed by Lycurgus Spinks in 1949, as leader of the Knights of the KKK of America.

Imperial Giant—In the UKA, a proposed honorary title (never used) for retired Imperial Wizards.

Imperial Klabee—Since 1915, the Klan's national treasurer and one of fifteen Genii.

Imperial Kladd—Headquarters custodian of the modern KKK's ritual paraphernalia and one of fifteen Genii.

Imperial Klaliff—Since 1915, second-in-command of the Invisible Empire and one of fifteen Genii.

Imperial Klarogo—In modern parlance, the supreme sergeant-at-arms of the Invisible Empire and one of fifteen Genii.

Imperial Klazik—In the 1920s Klan, a national officer assigned to supervise activities in various realms.

Imperial Kleagle—In the 1920s, the commander of the KKK's propagation department, responsible for appointment and supervision of traveling Kleagles.

Imperial Klexter—Since 1915, the officer responsible for external security at imperial headquarters and national gatherings, also one of fifteen Genii.

Imperial Kligrapp—Secretary of the Invisible Empire and one of fifteen Genii.

Imperial Klokann—An advisory board serving the Imperial Wizard, consisting of five Klokans who are also Genii.

Imperial Klokard—The Invisible Empire's chief designated lecturer, and one of fifteen Genii.

Imperial Kloncilium—The supreme executive council and judicial body of the 1920s Klan.

Imperial Klonvokation—The legislative body of the Invisible Empire.

Imperial Kludd—Chaplain of the Invisible Empire at large, and one of fifteen Genii.

Imperial Kloncilium—(a) A group of six high-ranking Klansmen, selected in 1923 to resolve the dispute between William Simmons and Hiram Evans concerning final ownership of the KKK, its regalia and published rituals; (b) in the UKA, a panel of fifteen Genii serving as the Imperial Wizard's general staff and supreme judicial tribunal. They include the Imperial Klabee, Imperial Kladd, Imperial Klaliff, Imperial Klarogo, Imperial Klexter, Imperial Kligrapp, Imperial Klokard, Imperial Klonsel, Imperial Kludd, Imperial Nighthawk, and the five-member Imperial Klokann.

Imperial Nighthawk—Chief courier and security officer of the Invisible Empire, also one of fifteen Genii.

Imperial Palace—KKK headquarters.

Imperial Representative—The acting Grand Dragon of a provisional realm, appointed by the Imperial Wizard to organize Klansmen in sufficient numbers to elect state officers and obtain a realm charter. In some cases, he may also be empowered to appoint Kleagles.

Imperial Tax—Periodic dues paid to the KKK by every Klansman in good standing.

Imperial Wizard—Since 1915, the supreme commander of the Invisible Empire. *See also* Grand Wizard

Invisible Empire—(a) The complete geographical jurisdiction of a Klan, or of all Klans collectively, divided by major Klans into realms, provinces and klantons for administrative purposes; (b) the collective secret knowledge of a Klan.

ITSUB—"In the Secret Unfailing Bond" (salutation or closing in formal KKK correspondence) Naturalization—Formal induction of aliens into the Invisible Empire.

Kabinet—In the 1960s Original Knights, a panel of nine Hydras who assist and advise the Grand Dragon. Members include the Grand Klabee, Grand Kleagle, Grand Kligrapp, Grand Klokan, Grand Klokard, Grand Kludd, Grand Titan and two Hydras whose titles are unspecified.

Kalendar—Since 1915, the KKK's system of naming months, weeks and days. Years may be numbered from the date of the original KKK's creation or from its revival in 1915.

Kamelia—A short-lived ladies' auxiliary to the KKK, created by William Simmons in 1922, following his ouster as Imperial Wizard by Hiram Evans. The group disbanded in 1924.

Kappa Beta Lambda—A Klan-sponsored fraternity at the University of Michigan, founded in the 1920s. Its initials represent the slogan "Klansman Be Loyal."

Kardinal Kullors—In the UKA, official colors used for banners and robes denoting Klan ranks, including white, crimson, gold and black. Secondary kullors include gray, green and blue. Only the Imperial Wizard may wear royal purple.

K-Duo—The second degree of Klankraft. *See also* Knights Kamelia

Kharter—In the WKKKKM, a synonym for "charter" (as in "khartered klavern").

KIGY—"Klansman I Greet You" (password).

King Kleagle—The chief recruiter of a realm, responsible for supervising Kleagles.

Klabee—The treasurer of a klanton.

Kladd—The custodian of a klanton's ritual paraphernalia, who also introduces candidates for naturalization.

Klaliff—The vice president of a Klan or klavern.

Klan—(a) Since 1915, the smallest unit of the Invisible Empire, administered by an Exalted Cyclops and twelve Terrors; (b) in Reconstruction, a local unit of the Constitutional Union Guard. *See also* Den; Klavern

Klanburgesses—In the WKKKKM, the "lower house" of Klongress.

Klanbursar—In the WKKKKM, a district treasurer.

Klanjustices—In the WKKKKM, five members of the Klan's judicial department, one chosen from each district.

Klankraft—Since 1915, a general term for the collective beliefs and rituals of the Invisible Empire, including all aspects of ritual, regalia and "klanishness." At various times, klankraft has been encouraged by the sale of such "official" paraphernalia as belt buckles and jewelry, T-shirts and decals, records and tapes, jackknives, watches, and miniature "fiery crosses" (either bejeweled or electric).

Klanishness—The practice, where feasible, of trading and associating only with other KKK members. Sometimes spelled *klannishness.*

Klansman—An individual member of the KKK.

Klansman-at-large—In the 1920s, a special class of membership reserved for prominent figures (such as Oklahoma's Governor John Walton) who wished their affiliation with the KKK to be kept secret.

Klanswoman—A female member of the KKK or one of its ladies' auxiliaries.

Klanton—Since 1915, a subdivision of a province, the domain of a Klan, administered by an Exalted Cyclops and his twelve Terrors. *See also* Klavern

Klarogo—The inner guard of a klanton, equivalent to a sergeant-at-arms.

Klavalcade—An official KKK parade

Klavaliers—An "elite" Klan unit, commonly entrusted with acts of violence. *See also* Wrecking Crew

Klavern—(a) The gathering place of a Klan; (b) the local Klan itself. *See also* Den; Klan

Klavern Investigators—In the WKKKKM, Klansmen assigned to conduct investigations at the klavern level.

Kleagle—Since 1915, an organizer or recruiter appointed to recruit aliens for naturalization into the Invisible Empire, generally paid on a commission basis.

Klectoken/Klecktoken/Klecktokon—The KKK initiation fee established by William Simmons in 1915, with variant spellings in different Klans. The UKA manual describes it as "a donation to its propagation and general fund and not in any sense of purchasing membership."

Klepeer—In the WKKKKM, a klavern's representative to Klongress.

Klexter—Since 1915, the outer guard of a Klan, responsible for external security during regular meetings.

Kligraph—In the WKKKKM, a klavern secretary, also second-in-command to the Province Giant. *See also* Kligrapp

Kligrapp—The secretary of a Klan. *See also* Kligraph

Klikon—The "sacred picture" (icon) of a Klan, undefined but commonly including a robed Klansman on horseback, with or without a fiery cross, incorporating the name or initials of the particular group.

Klokan—An individual member of a Klokann. Three serve at the klanton and province levels, while five are specified for a realm and imperial headquarters.

Klokann—The advisory board of a Klan, with three Klokans serving as auditors and investigators.

Klokard—The designated lecturer of a Klan.

Klokord—Klavern lecturer in the 1960s Original Knights. *See also* Klokard

Klongress—The proposed "legislative branch" of the WKKKKM, theoretically consisting of two houses, the Klaburgesses and Klonvocation.

Klonklaves—Regular weekly meetings of a Klan, held at the klavern.

Klonversation—In the modern KKK, a portion of the naturalization ceremony, wherein new Klansmen receive official passwords and countersigns.

Klonverse—(a) A monthly province meeting, with the Great Titan presiding; (b) in the 1960s Original Knights, a body including the Great Titan, his Kommittee, plus the Exalted Cyclopes, Klaliffs and Klokans of all klaverns within a province.

Klonvocation—In the WKKKKM, the upper house of Klongress.

Klonvokation—(a) A national convention held annually by large Klan organizations; (b) the legislative body of a Klan.

Kloran—The Klan bible, written by William Simmons in 1915, subsequently adapted by many later Klans.

Klorero—(a) The administrative board of a realm, including the Grand Dragon and all other grand officers, plus the Kleagles, Titans and Furies from each province; (b) in the 1960s Original Knights, a meeting of the Grand Dragon, his Kabinet, all Great Titans and all Exalted Cyclopes within a realm.

Kloxology—A quasi-religious song, sung by klansmen at the conclusion of klavern meetings.

Kludd—The chaplain of a Klan, usually a Protestant minister.

Knight—Any Klansman in good standing. No gender-specific distinguishing term exists for Klanswomen.

Knight Hawk—In the 1960s Original Knights, a keeper of the klavern, responsible for any aliens introduced to the Klan. *See also* Nighthawks

Knights Kamelia—Designated title for the second degree of Klankraft. *See also* K-Duo

Knights of the Great Forest—Designated title for the third degree of Klankraft, created in 1928 and allegedly restricted to klansmen who abandoned their masks. *See also* K-Trio

Knights Party—Alternative name for the sixth-era Klan, denoting its political focus.

Knock-off Squad—A group selected to perform murders. *See also* Wrecking Crew

Kommittee—In the 1960s Original Knights, eleven Furies who advise a Grand Titan on provincial matters. Members include the Great Klabee, Great Kleagle, Great Kligrapp, Great Klokan, Great Klokard, Great Kludd, and five others without established titles.

Konstitution—By-laws of the 1960s Original Knights.

Konvention—Among the 1960s Original Knights, a meeting convened to amend the Konstitution.

K-Quad—The fourth degree of Klankraft.

K-Trio—The third degree of Klankraft. *See also* Knights of the Great Forest

K-Uno—The first degree of Klankraft.

Last hour—Twelfth hour on both versions of the Register.

Leaderless resistance—A guerrilla tactic wherein small units operate without any higher authority, thus minimizing risks of infiltration and betrayal.

Lictor—In the original Klan, a guardian of the den. *See also* Nighthawk

Lone wolf—A violent activist operating without official sanction or supervision from any organization.

Master of Ceremonies—Performs the installation rituals for UKA officers.

Marshal of Ceremonies—Assists the Master of Ceremonies during UKA installation rituals.

Melancholy month—October on the both versions of the Register.

Membership Committee—In the 1960s Original Knights, a panel that keeps a klanton's membership records.

Minoria—The New York metropolitan area (less Manhattan and Long Island), proposed by David Duke as a homeland for "inassimilable" minorities from eastern and southern Mediterranean regions, as well as Puerto Rico.

Missionary work—Acts of violence performed by a wrecking crew.

Mournful hour—Fifth hour on the 1868 Register.

Mournful month—(a) November on the 1867 Register; (b) September on the Kalendar.

Mystic month—February on the 1868 Register.

National Adjutant—Rank assumed by Bill Hendrix during 1949–52, as the supposed second-in-command of the Northern and Southern Knights of the KKK.

Naturalization—Formal induction of aliens into the Invisible Empire.

Navahona—Proposed by David Duke as a desert homeland for all American Indians, roughly equivalent to present-day New Mexico.

New Africa—Proposed by David Duke as a segregated homeland for African Americans, including most of Florida with portions of Alabama, Georgia, Louisiana and Mississippi.

New Cuba—Dade County, Florida, proposed by David Duke as a segregated enclave for Cuban Americans.

"Nigger-knocking"—Random drive-by shootings of African Americans.

Night run—A shorter-than-average Klan robe, made from black cloth, for concealment and ease of movement on nocturnal raids.

Nighthawks—(a) In Reconstruction, two officers chosen as aides to the Grand Cyclops of a den; (b) since 1915, the couriers of a Klan, sometimes with additional guard duties. *See also* Knight Hawk

Painful month—July on the 1868 Register.

Peculiar month—April on the 1868 Register.

Political Action Committee—In the 1960s Original Knights, a panel assigned to study and report on all political activity within a klanton.

Portentious month—(a) April on the 1867 Register; (b) August on the 1868 Register.

President of the Klonvocation—In the WKKKKM, chief of the upper house of Klongress, also seventh-in-command of the Invisible Empire.

Province—(a) In Reconstruction, a county, administered by a Grand Giant; (b) since 1915, generally a congressional district commanded by Great Titan, though smaller areas are sometimes tagged with the same label; (c) in the WKKKKM, nine subdivisions of Mississippi, each containing multiple counties. *See also* Dominion

Province Chaplain—In the WKKKKM, chief religious officer of a province. *See also* Great Kludd

Province Giant—In the WKKKKM, the commander of a province.

Province Klan Bureau of Investigation—In the WKKKKM, an investigative body active at the province level.

Public Relations Committee—In the 1960s Original Knights, a klanton-level committee in charge of Klan publicity.

Purple day—(a) Saturday on the 1867 Register; (b) Thursday on the 1868 Register.

Realm—A state, administered by a Grand Dragon. In the 1920s, when individual states lacked sufficient members to constitute a realm, two or more might be merged. Maine, New Hampshire and Vermont were thus combined into a single realm.

Realm Klonvokation—The legislative body of a realm, including all state officers.

Register—A forerunner of the Kalendar, outlined in the original Klan prescript of 1867 and revised with certain alterations in 1868. Unlike the Kalendar, it lists no names for weeks of the month but does name twelve hours of the day.

Royal Order of the Purple Dog—Ritual hazing performed to test the worthiness of new imperial officers in the UKA. *See also* Yellow Dog

Sacred Symbols of the Klan—In the UKA, the hood and robe, with objects typically displayed on a klavern's altar, including a Bible, cross, flag, sword and glass of water.

San Bog—"Strangers Are Near; Be on Guard" (warning used as needed with other passwords) Sargent [*sic*] of the Guard—In the 1960s Original Knights, an officer who assists the Captain of the Guard in maintaining klavern security.

Scalawag—In Reconstruction, any native southerner who supported the Republican Party of black civil rights.

Second Era—The Klan led by Imperial Wizards Simmons, Evans and Colescott (1915–44). *See also* 33/2

Secondary Kullors *see* Kardinal Kullors

Seedline theology—A tenet of some Identity sects, holding that Jews are the literal offspring of Satan, produced by Eve's copulation with the serpent in Eden.

Secret Six—A 1960s Klan unit in Georgia, which allegedly planned acts of violence. *See also* Wrecking Crew

Sixth Era—The present Invisible Empire, variously defined as a politically focused Knights Party or as a revolutionary phase including leaderless resistance and alliance with neo–Nazi groups. Rachel Pendergrast defines the movement as "politician and very Christian," although some Klans and allied groups have abandoned Christianity entirely. *See also* 33/6

Smith & Wesson Line—Klan nickname for the Mason-Dixon Line, implying death for "outside agitators."

Sorrowful hour—Eighth hour on the 1867 Register.

Sorrowful month—October on the Kalendar.

Speaker of the Klanburgesses—In the WKKKKM, chief officer of the lower house of Klongress, also sixth-in-command of the Invisible Empire.

Startling hour—Second hour on both versions of the Register.

Stormy month—March on the 1868 Register.

Supreme Kleagle—In the UKA, a dual function of the Imperial Wizard.

Terrible month—(a) August on the 1867 Register; (b) July on the Kalendar.

Terrors—Since 1915, the twelve-member executive board of a Klan or klavern, appointed to advise the Exalted Cyclops.

Third Era—Variously defined by different Klan spokesmen as the period 1944–53, 1944–61, or 1954–61 (oddly omitting the decade after World War II). *See also* 33/3

Third Position—As defined by Tom Metzger, a rejection of both left and right, wherein racists serve as defenders of the white working class and the environment; also called Aryan Socialism.

33/1—A coded reference to the first-era KKK (the eleventh letter of the alphabet, multiplied by three).

33/2—Coded reference to the second-era Klan.

33/3—Coded reference to the third-era KKK.

33/4—Coded reference to the fourth-era Klan.

33/5—Coded reference to the fifth-era KKK.

33/6—Coded reference to the sixth-era Klan.

Tribunal of Justice—In Reconstruction, the KKK's judicial branch, subdivided into a Council of Centaurs and a Council of Yahoos.

Wailing week—Third week of a month, on the Kalendar.

Weeping week—Second week of the month, on the Kalendar.

Weird week—Fifth week of a month, on the Kalendar.

West Israel—A segregated homeland for U.S. Jews, proposed by David Duke, comprising Manhattan and Long Island, New York.

White Bastion—An Aryan homeland proposed by Robert Miles, including the present states of Idaho, Montana, Oregon, Washington and Wyoming.

White day—Sunday on both versions of the Register.

Woeful hour—Fourth hour on the 1867 Register.

Woeful week—First week of a month, on the Kalendar.

Wonderful hour—Third hour on the 1868 Register.

Wonderful week—Fourth week of a month, on the Kalendar.

Wonderful month—May on the 1867 Register.

Wrecking Crew—A secret squad assigned to commit acts of violence.

Yellow day—(a) Thursday on the 1867 Register; (b) Tuesday on the 1868 Register.

Yellow Dog—An informal hazing ritual practiced in some UKA klaverns to test the mettle of new initiates. A typical exercise involved swallowing a raw oyster tied to a string, which was then pulled back from the initiate's stomach.

3 THE KLAN KREED

The Ku Klux Klan has always claimed to stand on principle. Some of those principles have changed with time—a few more radically than others—as society evolves, and as with any other group of human beings, contradictions have arisen, leading to disputes, disunity, and sometimes violence within the Ku Klux ranks. Still, klansmen are outspoken in promoting their beliefs, and no true understanding of the KKK is possible without reviewing those tenets of faith, tracing their origins and recognizing how they reached their present state.

Fraternalism

All accounts agree that the KKK began life as a fun-loving fraternal lodge, founded by six young veterans of the Confederate army in Pulaski, Tennessee. They borrowed their new group's name from the Kuklos Adelphon collegiate fraternity, founded by four Phi Beta Kappa members at the University of North Carolina in 1812, and dissolved during the Civil War. The titles they selected for themselves—cyclops, lictor, night hawk—were no more outlandish than other lodge ranks of that time (or our own). Pulaski boasted six Masonic lodges when the KKK was organized, in 1866, and founder James Crowe was certainly a member, later serving as Masonic Grand Master for the state. General John C. Brown, Tennessee's grand dragon during Reconstruction, also served as the Volunteer State's Masonic Grand Master, while General George Gordon (one of the original Klan's first recruits) was another high-ranking Mason.

When the KKK reorganized for paramilitary action in spring 1867, it retained its fraternal trappings with a grand wizard in command of dragons, hydras, titans, giants, furies and goblins, while rank-and-file members were labeled as "ghouls." Albert Pike, named by some historians as author of the Klan's prescript and possibly grand dragon of Arkansas, had served in 1859 as Sovereign Grand Commander in the Scottish Rite Masons. While the Klan's first prescript failed to justify the order, a revised version from 1868 described the KKK as "an institution of Chivalry, Humanity, Mercy, and Patriotism; embodying in its genius and its principles all that is chivalric in conduct, noble in sentiment, generous in manhood, and patriotic in purpose." As lodges specialized in passwords, countersigns and such, so early klansmen managed to identify each other. Georgia member Walter Brooks described the system to Congress in 1871, as outlined to him by fellow ghoul Daniel Dodson.

He said that supposing we were in a crowd, or in a house where there were a great many people together, and he wanted to know whether I belonged to the organization or not, he would put his foot on top of mine and press on it, and say, "I ask your pardon." If I belonged to the order, I would remark, "It is granted." Also, if I met with a gentleman and shook hands with him, or anything of that sort, and asked him how he was, if he belonged to the organization he would say, "I am *well;* how are you?" He said "well" was the word. That is about what he told me. He said that one sign was to shut up the third and fourth fingers of the right hand, and put the thumb on them, and have the first and second fingers stretched out straight; and the answer would be the same way with the left hand.

At least one lynching by the Reconstruction-era Klan sprang from a quarrel within the Masonic lodge. In March 1869, Dr. G.W. Darden blackballed klansman Charles Wallace from the lodge in Warren County, Georgia. Wallace retaliated by publishing a notice in his newspaper, the *Georgia Clipper,* that demanded "satisfaction" from Darden, while denouncing him as a scalawag, coward and liar. Darden won the duel, but was immediately jailed, whereupon a mob of klansmen dragged him from his cell and riddled him with bullets.

Fraternalism was a major selling point for the Klan when it revived in 1915. Imperial Wizard William Simmons was a professional recruiter for the Woodmen of the World—which dubbed him "Colonel"—and a member of eleven other lodges (notably including the Knights Templar, Masons and Odd Fellows). The Klan's Georgia charter application described it as a "purely benevolent and eleemosynary [charitable] order," while newspaper advertisements billed it as "a classy order of the highest class." In the *Kloran,* his revision of the 1868 Ku Klux prescript, Simmons described his brainchild as "a standard fraternal order enforcing fraternal conduct, and not merely a 'social association.' It is a duly incorporated, legally recognized institution, honest in purpose, noble in sentiment and practical in results that commands the hearty respect of all respectable people throughout the Nation." The order's practice of clannishness (typically spelled with a "k"), Simmons defined as:

real fraternity practically applied—standing by and sticking to each other in all things honorable. Encouraging, protecting, cultivating, and exemplifying the real "fraternal human relationship" to shield and enhance each other's happiness and welfare. A devoted, unfailing loyalty to the principles, mission, and purposes of the order in promoting the highest and best interest of the community, State and Nation.

Beyond the KKK's internal rituals, practice of klannishness included barbecues and picnics, sporting events, stage plays, weddings and funerals. In Oklahoma and Texas, state fairs devoted special "Klan days" to members of the order and their families. Despite its rampant violence and high-level financial corruption, the resurrected Klan *did* practice charity, including cash donations to various groups and causes, coupled with holiday-season donations of food and other gifts to the needy (sometimes including impoverished blacks). "TWK" signs in a merchant's windows reminded fellow members to *t*rade *w*ith a *k*lansman. Simmons retained some of the original Klan's titles and jargon, while coining others that mostly began with the letters "kl"—klabee, klexter, kligrapp, and so forth. He also promoted himself from *grand* to *imperial* wizard, while his rank-and-file members were elevated from ghouls to knights. Degrees of klannishness were outlined—K-Uno, K-Duo, etc.—with each producing more income at imperial headquarters. Simmons also sold "initiation water" to his chartered klaverns at the modest rate of ten dollars per quart.

Inevitably, Simmons and successor Hiram Evans (another Mason) recruited extensively among established fraternal lodges. Those who contributed the most klansmen, despite occasional opposition from their national leaders, included the Masonic lodge and Scottish Rite Masons, the Elks and Oddfellows, the Orange Order and Knights of Pythias, the Junior Order of Mechanics, Woodmen of the World, and the Patriotic Order, Sons of America. All generally shared the Klan's view of "100-percent Americanism" and its prejudice toward immigrants (especially Catholics). Indiana, with the highest per capita fraternal membership of any state in the 1920s, also became one of the Klan's greatest strongholds, when Grand Dragon David Stephenson ordered his kleagles to infiltrate local lodges and convert their members to klannishness. Defending the KKK before Congress in October 1921, Simmons countered claims of anti-Catholicism by noting that the Knights of Columbus excluded Protestants, while every prominent American lodge barred blacks from membership. Likewise, the Klan remained boy's club, with women relegated to auxiliary units until the mid–1970s.

Fraternalism remained a part of KKK life after World War II, though picnics in the troubled 1960s and beyond were likely to include classes in bomb-making and paramilitary training exercises. Chattanooga's klavern fielded a softball team in the 1950s, and childish hazing rituals continued in conjunction with some Klan initiation ceremonies at least through the 1960s. In contrast to the 1920s, when Klan members included prominent politicians and professional men, initiates since World War II have come increasingly from America's "white ghetto"—a term coined in 1965 by sociologist Peter Young and adopted three years later by the FBI to describe disaffected, frequently impoverished whites who feel themselves abandoned by The System. For some, the KKK has graduated from being a *part* of life to become life itself. Those hard-core members rely on Klan leaders and Klan publications for news of the world, fraternize exclusively with other klansmen where they can, and thus reinforce the principles that lead to ever greater disaffection and potential violence. In its most extreme form, members of Klan-allied groups

such as the Aryan Nations, CSA and various "patriot militias" retreat into insular compounds, severing all links to the outside world insofar as possible.

White Supremacy

The original Klan prescripts of 1867 and 1868 made no mention of white supremacy, simply because none was necessary. Reconstruction-era klansmen were born and raised in a society which enslaved blacks and defended that practice with passages from the Bible. As defenders of the late Confederacy and its "peculiar institution," they took for granted that blacks were subhumans unfit for any semblance of parity with whites—much less complete equality with its ever-present specter of miscegenation and "amalgamation." Even in its "innocent" fraternal days, between spring 1866 and April 1867, the KKK maintained racist tradition by dressing as ghosts to frighten ex-slaves. As one of the Klan's founding fathers told Congress in 1871, the "impression sought to be made upon" freedmen "was that these white-robed night prowlers were the ghosts of Confederate dead, who had arisen from their graves in order to wreak vengeance on an undesirable class." The fact that those "undesirables" were nearly always black speaks volumes in regard to KKK mentality.

After reorganizing as a paramilitary movement to resist "Radical" Reconstruction, the Klan terrorized both freedmen and any whites (primarily Republicans) who sought to elevate the black man's status in society. "Redemption" of Dixie, to klansmen, meant reversal of their losses from the Civil War wherever possible, chiefly subjugation of newly freed blacks to a state approximating antebellum slavery. Draconian "Black Codes," designed to achieve that goal in 1865–66, were swiftly overturned by Congress, but a later U.S. Supreme Court approved sweeping segregation of the races from the 1880s onward. The "home rule" pursued by members of the original Klan was *white* rule in a system where blacks were disfranchised and barred from testifying against whites in court. And while klansmen claimed to reserve their worst wrath for blacks who threatened the sanctity of "white womanhood," they perpetrated equal violence against whites who taught blacks to read, and blacks who purchased land or prospered in their chosen trades. The Ku Klux victory, embodied in a "Solid South" that endured from 1877 through the 1960s, was essentially complete.

In 1915, William Simmons invited "all men who can qualify the invisible empire," while restricting membership to "native born American citizens who believe in the tenets of the Christian religion and owe no allegiance of any degree or nature to any foreign Government, nation, political institution, sect, people, or person." More specifically, he wrote: "We avow the distinction between the races of mankind as same has been decreed by the Creator, and we shall ever be true to the faithful maintenance of White Supremacy and will strenuously oppose any compromise thereof in any and all things." Elaborating further, Simmons claimed that "[w]hile membership in the Ku-Klux Klan is open only to white American citizens, the organization wages war on no individual or organization, regardless of race, color, or creed. It takes no part as an organization in any political or religious controversy, and it concedes the right of every man to think, vote, and worship God as he pleases." Klansmen soon disproved that claim with innumerable acts of violence, yet the *Kloran* pretended to take the high road in respect to racial separation. Simmons wrote:

The Anglo-Saxon race, the only race that has ever proved its ability and supremacy and demonstrated its determination to progress under any and all conditions and handicaps, owes its high place in the world to-day to the fact that this spirit has been kept alive from the foundation of the world and has never lagged in any land or clime. And if the Anglo-Saxon race is to maintain its prestige, if it is to continue as the leader in the affairs of the world and to fulfill its sacred mission it must maintain and jealously guard its purity, its power, and its dignity; and while it should aid and encourage to the limit of its ability all men of whatever race or creed, it must forever maintain its own peculiar identity as the Anglo-Saxon race and preserve the integrity of its civilization, for the shores of time hold the shipwreck of all the mongrel civilization [*sic*] of the past which is evidence that in keeping with the laws of creative justice nature has decreed that mixed civilizations, together with governments of mixed races, are doomed to destruction and oblivion.

Despite his disavowal of intent to wage war on minorities, Simmons publicly declared, "An inevitable conflict between the white race and the colored race is indicated by the present unrest. This conflict will be Armageddon, unless the Anglo-Saxon, in unity with the Latin and Teutonic nations, takes the leadership of the world and shows to all that it has and will hold the world mastery forever!"

Successor Hiram Evans reiterated that theme shortly before his own retirement as imperial wizard. He wrote: "The first essential to the success of any nation, and particularly of any democracy, is a national unity of mind. Its citizens must be *one people* ... they must have common instincts and racial and national purpose. It follows that any class, race, or group of people which is permanently unassimilable to the spirit and purpose of the nation has no place in a democracy. The negro [*sic*], so far in the future as human vision can pierce, must always remain a group *unable* to be a part of the American people. His racial inferiority has nothing to do with this fact; the unfitness applies equally to *all alien races* and justifies our attitude toward Chinese, Japanese, and Hindus. No amount of education can ever make a white man out of a man of any other color. It is a law on this earth that races never can exist together in complete peace and friendship and certainly never in a state of equality."

A later Klan, organized at the end of World War II, ignored the recent lesson of Nazism and proclaimed, in its list of "Ideals":

We must keep this a White Man's country. Only by doing this can we be faithful to the foundations laid by our forefathers. This Republic was established by White Men. It was established for White Men. Our forefathers never intended that it should fall into the hands of an inferior race. Every effort to wrest from White Men the management of its affairs in order to transfer it to the control of blacks or any other color, or to permit them to share in its control, is an invasion of our sacred Constitutional prerogatives and a violation of divinely estab-

lished laws. We would not rob the colored population of their rights, but we demand that they respect the rights of the White Race in whose country they are permitted to reside. When it comes to the point that they cannot and will not recognize and respect those rights, they must be reminded that this is a White Man's country!

Such attitudes only hardened after 1954, when the U.S Supreme Court and Congress began dismantling legal segregation in Dixie. Klansmen violently resisted the change, while reiterating their devotion to white supremacy at every opportunity. Robert Shelton's UKA declared as its primary purpose an intent "to unite white male persons, native-born Gentile citizens of the United States of America." Mississippi's White Knights pledged themselves "to promote the purity and integrity of the separate races of mankind," while Louisiana's Original Knights vowed "to maintain forever Segregation of the races and the Divinely directed and historically proven supremacy of the White Race." If there was any doubt about the Klan's intent and methods, though, Imperial Wizard Sam Bowers removed it with a pamphlet addressed to participants in Mississippi's 1964 "Freedom Summer." That flyer read: "We are not going to sit back and permit our rights to be negotiated away by a group of Jewish priests, bluegum black savages and mongrelized money worshippers. We will buy you a ticket to the Eternal if you insist."

Imperial Wizard Robert Shelton, speaking for the larger UKA in 1965, declared, "The white race of people have had a cul-ture civilization for over 2,000 years. The nigger has only been out of the savage jungles of Africa for approximately 200 years. And the niggers had the same opportunity and resources in Africa to develop himself and his race of people as our forefathers did in America. I think we can all realize that the nigger does not have the initiative, the basic intelligence, to be creative—does not have the ingenuity to devise, invent, create things that the white race does. The nigger is a diseased animal and can never be our equal. If he was forced into captivity in coming to America, what's so bad about forcing him into captivity and carrying him back to his home?"

In the 1970s, David Duke tried to repair KKK's reputation for ignorant racism, insisting that klansmen hated no one: they simply loved their own race and reflected "white pride" in the same manner as blacks who lately demanded respect after centuries of legally-enforced degradation. Those claims rang hollow, though, as Duke peddled Nazi literature, drew maps of an America divided into ethnic enclaves, and addressed Klan audiences on the topic of "shooting niggers." Since Duke alleged retirement from the KKK in 1980, no Klan leader has aspired to either eloquence or moderation. By the dawn of the twenty-first century, most were publicly allied with neo-Nazi groups and street-brawling skinhead gangs, spewing fantasies of "mud races" spawned by bestiality in Old Testament times or fabricated in bizarre prehistoric experiments conducted by Satanic mad scientists. The Klan's prescription for dealing with those enemies—brute force—remained unchanged from its first campaigns in 1867.

Patriotism

The Klan's definition of patriotism has waffled more radically over the past 140 years than any other of the order's tenets. Members of the original KKK were Confederate partisans by definition, "good ole rebels" who sang proudly that "I won't be reconstructed and I do not give a damn." They were also die-hard Democrats, blaming "radical" Republicans for secession, the destructive Civil War, and all the ills of Reconstruction. When they spoke of "redeeming" Dixie for "home rule," they invariably meant the reestablishment of state governments run by and for white Democrats, in which Republicans and other "scalawags" or "traitors" would be stripped of any significant influence.

Still, klansmen—then, as now—disguised their motives insofar as possible. The Klan's first prescript of 1867 opened with a preamble declaring that "[w]e recognize our relations to the United States Government, and acknowledge the supremacy of its laws." That was pure balderdash, revised a year later with a declaration of the KKK's intent "to protect and defend the Constitution of the United States, and all laws passed *in conformity thereto,* and to protect the States and the people thereof from all invasion from any source whatever." (Emphasis added.) As seen through Ku Klux eyes, the hated Thirteenth, Fourteenth and Fifteenth Amendments, along with various Enforcement and Reconstruction Acts passed by Congress during 1865–75, violated the spirit of America's founding fathers and the Constitution that had recognized slavery as a legal institution. The "invaders" whom klansmen were pledged to repel included U.S. troops and any "carpetbaggers" from the North who tampered with the "southern way of life" by teaching blacks to read, write, vote, or otherwise forget "their place." From that perspective, Klan murders of federal soldiers, elected officeholders and Republican candidates for office were patriotic acts in defense of antebellum American values.

William Simmons revived the KKK in 1915 with a fervent prayer: "God save our Nation! And help us to be a Nation worthy of existence on the earth. Keep ablaze in each klansman's heart the sacred fire of a devoted patriotism to our country and its Government." As presented by Simmons, the Klan "stands for America first—first in thought, first in affections, and first in the galaxy of nations. The Stars and Stripes forever above all other and every kind of government in the whole world." The order existed, he claimed, "to promote real patriotism toward our civil Government; honorable peace among men and nations; protection for and happiness in the homes of our people; ... and liberty, justice and fraternity among all mankind." In fact, Simmons declared, "No man is wanted in this order who will not or can not swear an unqualified allegiance to the Government of the United States of America, its flag, and its Constitution. No man is wanted in this order who does not esteem the Government of the United States of America above any other government, civil, political, or ecclesiastical, in the whole world." Finally, cribbing from the original KKK prescript, Simmons wrote:

> We recognize our relation to the Government of the United States of America, the supremacy of its Constitution, the Union of States thereunder, and the constitutional laws thereof, and we shall be ever devoted to the sublime principles of a pure Americanism and valiant in the defense of its ideals and institutions.

As we have seen, however, Simmons and the Klan could not abide "governments of mixed races." And like their Reconstruction-era forefathers, twentieth-century klansmen reserved for themselves the absolute right to decide which laws were constitutional. They opposed the Sixteenth and Nineteenth Amendments (respectively establishing the federal income tax and women's suffrage), while applauding the Eighteenth (prohibition of alcoholic beverages), condemned all New Deal measures of the 1930s, and violently resisted any legal efforts to expand black civil rights. That stance remained unchanged between 1945 and 1970—Robert Shelton's UKA, in 1961, quoted Simmons verbatim on the Klan's "relationship to the government of the United States of America"— while klansmen condemned and resisted an ever-growing list of civil rights laws, federal court rulings and executive orders from the White House. Through it all, Klan members viewed themselves as patriots—perhaps the last surviving in the land—while vilifying every move made by the White House and Congress.

A dramatic alteration of perspective swept the invisible empire during the latter 1970s. Klansmen who had once paid lip service to the government while condemning most of its leaders

Divided loyalties in the Great Depression (Florida State Archives).

as traitors began instead to rail against "ZOG"—the "Zionist Occupation Government" in Washington. Instead of simply being infiltrated and perverted by Reds and race-mixers, klansmen and their neo–Nazi comrades henceforth saw the federal government as beyond redemption, captured and wholly owned by Jew-Communist traitors bent on wholesale eradication of the Aryan race. In the face of such a menace, far-right racists felt obliged to resist with armed force. Some groups, like The Order and Glenn Miller's White Patriot Party (formerly the Carolina Knights of the KKK), issued formal declarations of war against Washington; others embarked on undeclared guerrilla campaigns—robbing banks, planting bombs, plotting assassinations and occasionally managing to pull one off.

Matters went from bad to worse in the 1990s, as President George H.W. Bush's stammering declaration of a "new world order" gave fascists of all kinds new bogeys to fear. Klansmen and their allies rallied to the "patriot militia" movement after 1994, training in earnest for a war that never came, although its deadly skirmishes included the bombing of Oklahoma City's federal building by ex-klansman Timothy McVeigh, claiming 168 lives. It seemed to most observers by the year 2000 that klansmen had relinquished any claim on loyalty to the United States. Where not embroiled in southern battles to "save" the Confederate flag, the commonly marched under swastika banners, brandishing Old Glory as an afterthought, where they displayed the U.S. flag at all. Their conversion to "racial nationalism" was expressed in the neo–Nazi slogan (borrowed in garbled form from Adolf Hitler's SS): "My race is my nation."

Religion

Slavery had a traumatic impact on America's Protestant churches, as upon every other aspect of society. Debate over human bondage split the Presbyterian Church in 1838, followed by rifts in the Methodist Episcopal and Baptist denominations (in 1844 and 1845, respectively). The northern faction of each sect condemned slavery, while the southern branches praised it as divinely ordained. That racist gospel was drilled into generations of white southern children, ensuring that defenders of slavery (and later segregation) would regard themselves as champions of "that Old Time Religion."

The first Klan did not cast itself in religious terms, although both versions of its prescript opened with a statement averring that all klansmen "reverently acknowledge the Majesty and Supremacy of the Divine Being, and recognize the Goodness and Providence of the Same." That "reverence," like the Klan's pledge of fealty to the U.S. Constitution, was naturally viewed through the distorting lens of racism, which made fair game of black churches, their pastors and parishioners, along with any whites who practiced "deviant" reli-

gions within the KKK's sphere of influence. In 1868, klansmen at Bowling Green, Kentucky, burned several buildings in the Shaker community causing $250,000 in damage as they fought to drive the nonconformists from their midst. Northern Methodist congregations suffered threats and raids by klansmen in Alabama and Mississippi. Nightriders also burned or demolished black churches in Alabama, Kentucky, Mississippi, North Carolina and South Carolina. In some cases, the attacks were politically motivated: the klansmen who raided a church at Tuskegee, Alabama, and killed two worshipers in summer 1870 thought they had found a Republican meeting in progress. Another Alabama church, burned in Chattooga County during 1871, had doubled as a school for freedmen. That same year, at Spartanburg, South Carolina, klansmen whipped a white Republican for leading black Sunday school classes.

William Simmons deliberately closed the gap between Klan and church in 1915. Despite the mock–Islamic title of his *Kloran*, Simmons borrowed the original Klan's pledge of reverence to God and amplified it with specific devotional prayers, while restricting membership in his order to native-born Protestants. The new Klan's hard-line stance on religion, anticipating the modern "Religious Right" by six decades, drew many fundamentalist ministers into the order. Historian Wyn Wade estimates that 40,000 Protestant clergymen belonged to the KKK in its peak years of 1923–25. Each klavern had its chaplain (kludd), and many ministers served as exalted cyclops of their local units, while clergymen rose to the rank of grand dragon in Colorado, North Dakota, Pennsylvania and Texas. Of thirty-nine klokards (national lecturers) paid by imperial headquarters, twenty-six were ordained Protestant ministers. Other evangelists—including the famed Bob Jones, Billy Sunday and "Fighting Bob" Shuler—welcomed klansmen to their rallies but apparently stopped short of joining the order itself. (Some doubt remains in Shuler's case, based on his frequent praise of the Klan

Church visits like this one were a common Klan tactic from 1920 through the early 1950s (Florida State Archives).

both in print and from his pulpit. In 1923 he declared, "Good men everywhere are coming to understand that the Klan is dangerous only to the lawless and un–American elements within their midst.") Wade rates clerical support essential for the 1920s Klan's success in Indiana, Iowa, Maine, Missouri, New Jersey, North Carolina, Ohio and Rhode Island. The same was true in parts of Canada, where clergymen joined the KKK and opened their churches for rallies when civic auditoriums rejected the Klan.

Meanwhile, Rev. Reuben Sawyer introduced Oregon klansmen to the creed of British-Israelism, later dubbed Christian Identity. The racist tenets of that doctrine proclaim that ancient European tribes (rather than Jews) were the biblical "lost tribes of Israel" and thus rightful heirs to God's Old Testament covenant. Jews posing as Jehovah's "chosen people" are therefore impostors—and worse, since some Identity sects believe the first Jews sprang from Eve's sexual coupling with Satan in the Garden of Eden (which produced the first murderer, Cain). They, in turn, performed various prehistoric experiments resulting in creation of the nonwhite "mud races" that populated Africa, Asia and the pre–Columbian Americas. A variation on that theme is the belief held by "pre–Adamite" cultists that God created inferior races—dubbed "beasts of the field" in *Genesis* 2:20—before the creation of Adam and Eve. Adam's divinely-sanctioned "dominion" over those "beasts" thus justified slavery, segregation, or even genocide. Klan allies William Dudley Pelley and Gerald L.K. Smith embraced Christian Identity in the 1930s, while klansman Wesley Swift emerged as the sect's leading spokesman after World War II, with his California-based Church of Jesus Christ Christian. The KKK's most notorious agitator of the 1960s, Charles "Connie" Lynch, was ordained in

Swift's church and spread its gospel nationwide, inciting racist riots everywhere he went.

Southern klansmen faced a religious conundrum in the 1960s. Most Klans endorsed some variation of the Reconstruction-era pledge to God as revised by William Simmons in 1915, where they did not quote it verbatim. Imperial Wizard Sam Bowers mixed religion with the U.S. Constitution in the founding document of his WKKKKM, proclaiming that the White Knights "recogniz[e] Almighty God as our Creator, our Savior, and our Inspiration, in order to form a more Christian and Effective Klan." Still, there were mavericks in their ranks. In 1966–67, some smaller Klans and neo–Nazi groups sought affiliation with Anton LaVey's California-based Church of Satan, while Imperial Wizard Robert Shelton found it necessary to announce that his UKA had not done so. (LaVey insisted to his dying day that *he* rejected overtures from Shelton's Klan.) Some of Shelton's northern officers, meanwhile, were neo–Nazis with a taste for ancient Norse religions such as Odinism. Daniel Burros, a closet Jew and veteran of several neo–Nazi groups, became grand dragon of New York after acknowledging that Jesus Christ "was cool and everything."

By the 1970s, a majority of klansmen seemed to be adherents of Christian Identity. Robert Miles, the UKA's former grand dragon of Michigan, preached its tenets from the pulpit of his Mountain Church, while Richard Butler (Wesley Swift's heir to the Church of Jesus Christ Christian) welcomed klansmen and Nazis alike to his Aryan Nations compound at Hayden Lake, Idaho. James Warner, an alumnus of George Rockwell's American Nazi Party, doubled as a spokesman for David Duke's KKKK and pastor of his own Louisiana-based New Christian Crusade Church. Duke's Texas grand dragon, Louis Beam, vowed to meet his enemies "with a Bible in one hand and a .38 in the other," but he later defected to serve as "ambassador at large" for the Aryan Nations. Throughout the United States and Canada, an estimated 350,000 Identity believers met in local groups without any recognized national body. The militant Posse Comitatus embraced Identity's anti–Semitic theology, some members retreating from mainstream society into rural "survivalist" compounds where they divided their time between worship and manufacturing illegal weapons.

Identity fanatics tapped those arsenals in the 1980s, when groups including The Order, James Ellison's CSA and Glenn Miller's White Patriot Party issued declarations of war against the federal government. A decade later, their rebellion was

Robed klansmen form a cross at a 1924 tent revival (Library of Congress).

echoed by "patriot militia" groups nationwide, many of them led or infiltrated by Identity adherents. Oklahoma City bomber Timothy McVeigh was influenced in equal parts by Christian Identity and the neo–Nazi ravings of National Alliance leader William Pierce, whose novel *The Turner Diaries* inspired a new generation of domestic terrorists. Many racist skinhead gangs also embraced Christian Identity, while leadership of David Duke's failing KKKK descended to Arkansas Identity minister Thomas Robb.

By the late 1970s, however, some racists rejected even Identity's skewed take on scripture, denouncing the Holy Bible in its entirety as a work of Hebrew propaganda. Ben Klassen's Church of the Creator offered its own *White Man's Bible,* while lampooning the King James version as "Jewish pornography." The next step in rejection of traditional religion was embodied in a return to Nordic or Germanic paganism, including the sects of Ásatrú and Odinism. The latter faith, revived in the 1960s by Else Christensen's Odinist Fellowship in America, offered a spiritual haven for latter-day racists, presenting a world view of social Darwinism described by one observer as "the most dynamic of all tendencies on the radical right." At the turn of the twenty-first century, American penal authorities called Odinism/Ásatrú the fastest-growing religion behind prison walls. In states that track such matters, a conservative census found 189 racist pagans in Texas state prisons, 120 in Kansas, 92 in Colorado, and 90 in Arizona. Converts include two notorious members of The Order, Richard Scutari and klansman David Lane (whose Fourteen Words Press offers his "wisdom" to the world at large). Phil Rodriguez, a gang investigator for the Arizona state prison system, described Ásatrú to SPLC reporters as "the new big fad" among white racist inmates, challenging the older Aryan Brotherhood. More than 100 known adherents are identified in federal lockups nationwide.

Outside prison walls, an estimated fifteen percent of all U.S. adherents of Odinism/Ásatrú profess overtly racist beliefs. Carl Raschke, a professor of religion at the University of Denver, told the SPLC's *Intelligence Report,* "Ásatrú is an effort to make religion more post–Modern, hip and appealing to a generation raised on rock music. It is romantic, a kind of Teutonic mythology that gives them a cultural and religious identity." The Arizona-based Ásatrú Alliance was founded in 1987 by Michael "Valgard" Murray, who first joined George Rockwell's ANP as a teenager in the 1960s. While Murray proclaimed that his Alliance "does not advocate any type of political or racial extremist views or affiliations," observers remain unconvinced. Stephen McNallen, a native Texan who leads the rival Ásatrú Folk Assembly, welcomes members such as Ronald "Ragnar" Schuett, head of the Assembly's teaching guild and former Colorado state leader of the SS Action Group, who posed in full Nazi regalia for reporters in 1992, telling them, "I'm a white racist and proud of it." While no prominent Klan leaders have thus far endorsed Odinism/Ásatrú, joint demonstrations staged by various Klan factions commonly include skinheads and adult neo–Nazis immersed in the pagan religions, while converts Lane and Scutari are icons of the racist right, confirming that the KKK's hard-line adherence to fundamental Christianity is a thing of the past.

Nativism

America is a nation of immigrants. Even "native" American Indians trace their lineage to Asia, when a prehistoric land bridge closed the Bering Strait between present-day Russia and Alaska. It is a common trait of immigrants, however, that upon establishing their roots in some new land—and often facing persecution there, from those who came before—they join in persecuting those who follow after them. America is not unique in that respect, nor should it come as any great surprise that settlers who came to the New World in search of freedom to pursue their deviant religions vented brutal wrath on anyone who challenged their beliefs. Jews, Anabaptists, Quakers, "witches" and a host of others were harassed, imprisoned, tortured, even executed by pilgrims whom we recognize as founding fathers of America.

American nativism—the policy and practice of defending U.S. "natives" against incursion by unwelcome immigrants—hinged both on religion and race. The first nativists were militant Protestants who condemned and attacked Roman Catholics. Disorganized at first, the "true American" movement evolved by the 1840s into a coalition of "Know-Nothing" societies, so called because their members were commanded to say, "I know nothing" if interrogated or arrested. A leading bulwark of the movement, the Supreme Order of the Star-Spangled Banner (SSSB), spread southward from New York and Pennsylvania into Kentucky and Tennessee, where its members referred to their chapters as "clans." Historian Carleton Beals reports that Know-Nothing politicians controlled Pulaski, Tennessee—the KKK's birthplace—by 1854, and the Klan's "immortal six" founders were doubtless acquainted with Know-Nothing doctrines. So was Albert Pike, named by some historians as an author of the Klan's original prescript and perhaps the first grand dragon of Arkansas. Pike joined the SSSB after serving in the Mexican-American War, rose to a post on its national council, and helped draft the order's third-degree oath based on Masonic ritual, while serving as the movement's figurehead in Arkansas.

That said, the Klan professed no animosity toward immigrants or Catholics in Reconstruction. Blacks and "radical" Republicans preoccupied nightriders in the KKK's first era, and white racists were welcome to join the Klan without religious distinction. A majority of Louisiana klansmen and KWC members were Catholics, particularly in New Orleans, and some later reports identified Father Abram J. Ryan—a wartime Catholic chaplain with the Confederate army—as the KKK's official chaplain. If so, he filled a post unmentioned in the Klan's prescripts of 1867–68, and no specific evidence exists to cast him as a member of the hooded order.

Before 1860, the vast majority of voluntary immigrants to the United States came from northern and western Europe, with nativists reviling Irish Catholics as the greatest threat to ethnic purity. After Appomattox, the complexion of American immigration changed dramatically, shifting to southern and eastern Europe, with a sizable contingent from Asia. Chinese immigrants were legally barred in 1882 and Japanese by 1907, but the flood of Italians, Slavs and Russian Jews continued apace. Long-standing racial and religious bigotry was amplified when some of those new immigrants identified themselves as socialists or anarchists. The KKK revived by William Simmons in 1915 accepted only white, native-born Protestants as members, while lumping recent immigrants together as "European 'riff-raff' ... the very scum of the earth."

Klansmen found some aliens were more repugnant than others. Florida's knights took a special dislike to Greeks, while Japanese immigrants felt the Klan's wrath in California and Mexicans faced harassment in Texas. Still, Roman Catholics remained the Klan's most frequent target between 1915 and 1930. A new generation of knights had been taught to hate "papists" by Tom Watson's *Weekly Jeffersonian* and *Watson's Magazine,* which railed so zealously against "libidinous priests" that several issues were banned from the mails as obscene. "Is there not one [priest] among them," Watson wrote in July 1911, "to point out the absurdity of wearing a garment emblematic of sexual intercourse?" In another issue, he warned: "At the confessional the priest finds out what girls and married women he can seduce. Having discovered the trail, he wouldn't be human if he did not take advantage of the opportunity." Once that end was accomplished, Watson wrote, "No man can imagine a woman who could maintain her self-respect after being compelled to act as a sewer pipe for a bachelor priest's accumulation of garbage." Black priests were the ultimate horror to Watson, causing him to declaim: *"Heavens above! Think of a Negro priest taking the vow of chastity and then being turned loose among women... It is a thing to make one shudder."* (Emphasis in the original.)

Primed by such outpourings of venom, amplified by Ku Klux orators who opined that "the only way to cure a Catholic is to kill him," klansmen throughout the U.S. and Canada boycotted Catholic merchants, flocked to lectures by alleged "escaped nuns," and called for congressional investigation of the Knights of Columbus. Some went further still, robbing, bombing and burning Catholic churches. In November 1922, suspected Klan arsonists torched St. Boniface College in Winnipeg, Canada, leaving eight students and two teachers dead in the rubble. Two years later, klansmen in Gainesville, Florida, kidnapped and castrated Father John Conoley for the "crime" of directing a collegiate drama club. In North Manchester, Indiana, a Klan orator warned gullible rubes that the Pope could arrive any day to take over their town: "He may even be on the northbound train tomorrow! He may! Watch the trains!" Thus inflamed, a mob besieged the railroad terminal next morning and nearly lynched a traveling corset salesman, who escaped with his life after showing his wares to the crowd. In 1924, klansmen claimed credit for passage of the Johnson Act, which slashed America's immigration quotas by ninety percent, from 1.5 million to 150,000 immigrants per year (while entirely excluding some Asians and Pacific islanders). In that year, and again in 1928, the KKK ardently opposed Catholic New Yorker Al Smith's.

While much of the Klan's emphasis shifted to Jews and communists in the 1930s, imperial headquarters still attacked President Franklin Roosevelt for naming a Catholic as America's Postmaster General. Future Georgia Governor Herman Talmadge, addressing the audience at Grand Dragon Samuel Green's 1948 birthday party, listed Catholics among the enemies who threatened "our American traditions." Florida klansman Bill Hendrix welcomed Catholics to join his Southern Knights in April 1957, but it brought no rush of new recruits. Three years later, the KKK dusted off its hate sheets from the 1920s to campaign against Democratic presidential candidate John Kennedy, but this time no amount of ranting against papists could prevent election of America's first Catholic president. Still, violence and intimidation continued. On 9 September 1960, nightriders burned a cross near a Catholic church in Tifton, Georgia, hours after its pastor married a black couple. One of five Klan bombs discovered in Birmingham, Alabama, on 21 March 1965—and the only one with a white target—was planted at a Catholic church. On 24 June 1966, klansmen burned a rural Catholic school for blacks near Carthage, Mississippi. Robert Shelton's UKA preserved the 1915 Simmons ban on Catholic klansmen, and even Louisiana's Original Knights demanded knights "who are not members of the Roman Catholic church."

That picture changed in the 1970s, as klansmen became increasingly preoccupied with anti–Semitism and expulsion of nonwhite "mud races" from the United States. On 15 December 1974, James Venable's National Knights dropped its ban on Catholic members, but the announcement failed to interest many more recruits than had Bill Hendrix, seventeen years ear-

Klansmen first supported, then bitterly attacked President Franklin Roosevelt's New Deal.

lier. David Duke had better luck in Louisiana, announcing in May 1975 that nearly half of his Bayou State members were Catholics. Five months later, Dale Reusch's Invisible Empire Knights welcomed Catholic klansmen to the fold. Connecticut klansman James Farrands broke the last taboo in 1986, when he became the KKK's first Catholic imperial wizard *and* the first from New England.

By then, most klansmen were more concerned with the complexion and nationality of new immigrants than their religion. In 1977, David Duke and California Grand Dragon Tom Metzger launched a half-hearted Klan Border Watch, reinforced by off-duty Marines from Camp Pendleton. Three years later, after splitting from Duke's KKK, Metzger and his California Knights sparked a riot in Oceanside, when they brandished baseball bats and chains to clear John Landes Park of Mexican-Americans. In 1981, Texas klansman Louis Beam orchestrated harassment of Vietnamese fishermen until lawsuits filed by the SPLC forced him to cease and desist. Robert Shelton's *Fiery Cross,* in an exposé of "America Invaded," warned that "illegal aliens will take even more jobs away from Americans and create more welfare for the working American to support! ... [A]nd unless our government returns to sane politics regarding illegal aliens America will soon be overrun with these coloreds from the Caribbean and Mexico." In April 1993, klansman Jesse Stoner's Crusade Against Corruption sent a petition to President Bill Clinton with the header "Who Needs AIDS Carrying Haitian Niggers?" The document called upon Clinton to "DEFEND AMERICA and our shores by SINKING THE HAITIAN BOATS and by ordering that HAITIAN INVADERS WHO LAND IN AMERICA BE SHOT ON SIGHT." AIDS aside, Stoner complained that "voodoo negroids ... take jobs away from U.S. niggeros and White workers." As recently as 2005, the so-called Minuteman Project welcomed members of the neo–Nazi National Alliance to its armed border patrols, while an SPLC lawsuit bankrupted members of another group, Ranch Rescue, who illegally detained and brutalized Mexican-American victims. In April 2005, klansman Daniel Schertz sold several pipe bombs to ATF agents with the understanding that they would be "detonated on a bus carrying Mexican workers to work in Florida." According to Schertz's indictment, he also planned to bomb Haitian immigrants in Florida. Schertz received a 14-year federal prison term on 4 November 2005.

A Jewish merchant addresses 1920s klansmen (Library of Congress).

Anti-Semitism

While Jews faced discrimination of various kinds from their first arrival in the New World, carried over from the Inquisition and massacres of Europe, U.S. anti–Semitism was not organized in any systematic until the latter nineteenth century. Klansmen of the Reconstruction era, although thoroughly indoctrinated with Know-Nothing attitudes toward "aliens," gave little thought to Jews unless an individual's behavior sparked antagonism in a local den. Thus, in 1868, klansmen in Greensboro, Alabama, harassed two Jewish shopkeepers accused of overcharging their customers, but the campaign failed to drive either merchant out of town. A year later, in Marianna, Florida, "King of the Ku Klux" James Coker accused Samuel Fleishman of encouraging local blacks to retaliate with armed force against Ku Klux nightriders. First, on 3 October 1869, Coker led a mob to Fleishman's store, looting it of arms and ammunition. Two days later, Coker and company escorted Fleishman to Bainbridge, Georgia, with orders never to return. When Fleishman came back on 6 October, he was ambushed and slain on the highway by "persons unknown."

Thomas Watson, in his racist publications, castigated Jews as "moral cripples" cursed with "an utter contempt for law and a ravenous appetite for the forbidden fruit—a lustful eagerness enhanced by the novelty of the girls of the uncircumcised." That menace was realized for Georgians in 1913, when police charged Leo Frank, a New York Jew, with the rape-murder of a girl employed at his Atlanta pencil factory. Frank's conviction, based on perjured testimony from the probable killer, might have satisfied Watson, but Georgia's governor reviewed the flimsy evidence and commuted Frank's death sentence to a term of life imprisonment. Outraged, Watson described the act of clemency as part of a Hebrew conspiracy, wherein members of the "Jewish aristocracy" decreed that "no aristocrat of their race should die for the death of a working-class Gentile girl." Watson called for "another Ku Klux Klan" to put things right, whereupon the self-styled Knights of Mary Phagan lynched Frank in August 1915. ("When mobs are no longer possible," Watson pontificated, "liberty will be dead.") Three months later, some of the lynchers joined Imperial Wizard William Simmons to revive the KKK.

That Klan specifically excluded Jews from membership, while elevating them to the status of a national menace on a par with blacks and Catholics. Klan presses cranked out new copies of *The Protocols of the Learned Elders of Zion,* long since exposed as a Tsarist forgery, while Klan orators archly noted that Karl Marx and Russia's Leon Trotsky were Jews. American icon Henry Ford joined the circus in 1920, with a long series of anti–Semitic articles in his *Dearborn Independent,* subsequently published in book form as *The International Jew.* Throughout the nation, klansmen subjected Jewish merchants to boycotts, threats, cross-burnings and occasional acts of violence. In August 1923, police in Tulsa, Oklahoma, collaborated with klansmen in the kidnapping, whipping and sexual mutilation of Nathan Hantaman, a Jewish landlord whom they suspected of selling narcotics. That outrage prompted Governor John Walton to declare martial law in Tulsa—and in turn, ultimately led to his impeachment.

Ku Klux antagonism toward Jews increased during the Great Depression, as Klan orators blamed the nation's economic catastrophe on thinly-disguised "international financiers." President Franklin Roosevelt's efforts to salvage the nation were also suspect, as imperial headquarters blamed the New Deal's "socialistic" programs on cabinet members Harold Ickes and Henry Morgenthau (both Jews). Professional anti–Semites Gerald L.K. Smith and Conde McGinley joined the rabid chorus amplified by the ravings of Father Charles Coughlin's Christian Front, Charles Lindbergh's America First Committee, William Pelley's Silver Shirt Legion, Fritz Kuhn's German-American Bund, and other groups infatuated with new German Chancellor Adolf Hitler. New Jersey klansmen took a media beating for their joint rally with the Bund in August 1940, but the KKK revival after World War II featured even stronger strains of anti–Semitism. America's first neo–Nazi group, the rag-tag Columbians, courted Klan allies in Georgia and Florida, but Chattanooga klansman Jesse Stoner found himself expelled from Dr. Sam Green's AGK for advocating an American holocaust.

Unfazed, Stoner went on to found and lead a series of Klans and neo–Nazi groups pledged to eradication of Jews from American life. His most successful project was the National States Rights Party, allied with various Klan factions from 1958 through the 1970s. Elsewhere, Christian Identity zealots preached that Jews were the literal children of Satan, spawned by Eve's dalliance with the serpent in Eden, while George Rockwell's American Nazi Party and various imitators sprinkled the landscape with goose-stepping fascists. Klansmen schooled to regard blacks as ignorant, indolent beasts needed a scapegoat for

the 1960s civil rights movement, and they found it in the "International Jew." As Imperial Wizard Robert Shelton explained, in 1965, "We all know the that the nigger ain't smart enough to manipulate the moves he's making. It's the Jews who are in back of this. Did the NAACP ever have a nigger president? No! I don't hate niggers, but I hate the Jews. The nigger's a child, but the Jews are dangerous people. All their pseudo-intellectuals from Harvard and their low moral standards. All they want is control and domination of the Gentiles through a conspiracy with the niggers." After his Mississippi klansmen murdered civil rights activist Michael Schwerner in June 1964, Imperial Wizard Sam Bowers hailed the event as "the first time in history that Christians carried out the execution of a Jew."

Louisiana klansmen David Duke and James Lindsay brought Ku Klux anti–Semitism to new heights in the 1970s, with direct infusions of Nazi propaganda. Whereas Robert Shelton made token efforts (without much success) to bar neo–Nazis from leadership posts in his UKA, Duke and Lindsay welcomed them with open arms. Duke was himself a teenage convert to the brown-shirted NSWPP and had paraded in full Nazi regalia on his college campus, carrying a copy of Rockwell's *White Power.* He revered Hitler, offered translations of Hitler's *Mein Kampf* for sale at Klan headquarters, and freely indulged in the "revisionist" mind game of Holocaust denial—in effect, an apologia for Nazi Germany. Duke's list of colleagues included aging anti–Semite John Crommelin, ANP alumnus James Warner, NSRP founder Edward Fields, and William Pierce (head of the neo–Nazi National Alliance and author of *The Turner Diaries*).

By the time Duke left the Klan in 1980, the invisible empire had drifted into a degenerating orbit with such openly fascistic groups as Richard Butler's Aryan Nations, Ben Klassen's Church of the Creator, James Ellison's CSA, and others training for the overthrow of "ZOG"—the Zionist Occupation Government in Washington, D.C. When Robert Mathews founded The Order in 1983, during a rally at Butler's Idaho compound, klansmen from several states joined the campaign of robbery, bombing and murder. In their perverse theology, Jews were to blame for every crisis from the Civil War to the 1979 seizure of American hostages in Iran. Injection of Jew baiting into every issue, coupled with frequent misidentification of Gentile enemies as Jews, marked klannishness as a sub-species of neo–Nazism at the dawn of the new millennium.

Moralism

While the original KKK had no moral mission per se, Reconstruction-era klansmen viewed their struggle for white supremacy and Democratic "home rule" as a momentous battle to preserve Anglo-Saxon civilization from ruin. The order's 1868 prescript pledged all members "[t]o aid and assist in the execution of all constitutional laws, and to protect the people from unlawful seizure, and from trial except by their peers in conformity to the laws of the land." While lynching the occasional suspected criminal, early klansmen disguised their political guerrilla war as a crusade for "law and order." They sometimes filed false charges against their political opponents, either to remove

Klan critics from office or to facilitate their murder in jail. After various assassinations, klansmen routinely mounted campaigns of character assassination, slandering their late victims with claims of corruption, alcoholism, sexual perversion or miscegenation.

Overall, first era klansmen avoided the moralistic campaigns so beloved by their descendants, although raiders in Alamance County, North Carolina, put two backwoods brothels out of business in autumn 1869. They burned the establishment run by Mary Gappins when she ignored warnings to leave the area, then raided a competing house managed by Sally Holt. In the latter raid, klansmen released Holt's male customers unharmed but forced her daughter to strip, after which they beat her genitals. Conversely, klansmen in northeastern Kentucky spent most of Reconstruction defending their moonshine stills against federal revenue agents. White County klansmen murdered one officer in November 1870, subsequently threatening and torturing members of a black family that witnessed the crime. Similar raids against black suspected informers also occurred in Walton County. In May 1871, after federal marshals arrested two bootleggers in Bollinger County, Missouri, twenty masked klansmen tried to liberate the suspects from custody, but they lacked sufficient firepower to accomplish their goal. Residents of Walton County, Georgia, freely recognized Klan leader William Felker as a prominent local moonshiner.

William Simmons ignored that shaky moral background in 1915, when he revived the order as "an enduring monument to the valor and patriotic achievements" of the first KKK. He borrowed from the 1868 prescript and embellished its language, dedicating his Klan "to aid and assist in the execution of all constitutional laws, and to preserve the honor and dignity of the State by opposing tyranny in any and every form or degree attempted from any and every source whatsoever by a fearless and faithful administration of justice, and to promptly and properly meet every behest of duty without fear and without reproach." The oath sworn by new recruits included a promise "to correct evils in my community, particularly vices tending to the destruction of the home, family, childhood and womanhood." Thus was the groundwork laid for vigilante action, regardless of any "behest" from duly constituted authorities.

What were the evils klansmen rallied to oppose? The order was (at least publicly) a staunch defender of Prohibition; liquor raids by klansmen, whether deputized or acting on their own, were logged in a majority of states where klaverns organized and sometimes led to fatal violence. Gambling was also rife in speakeasies and roadhouses, evoking condemnation from the Klan. Both drink and dice were damned for their destructive impact on the family, klansmen adding their own ethnic twist until "rum" and "Rome" were virtually synonymous in Ku Klux publications. Any breach of family honor, from adultery to wifebeating, incest or nonsupport, might earn the miscreant a visit from the hooded knights. Premarital sex and excessive dating were condemned; unmarried lovers were sometimes dragged from home or darkened cars to be whipped before a fiery cross. Pool halls and movie theaters were frequently condemned and sometimes targeted for vandalism. Deviation from the "one true faith"—or simply skipping Sunday services—might draw attention from the Klan's new Puritans. Commercial competition with a klansman could prove hazardous, and any criticism of the Klan was actionable, in and of itself. Where threats failed to resolve a problem, objects of the KKK's displeasure might be lashed or treated to a coat of tar and feathers; mutilation was performed from time to time, including branding and castration. Some victims did not survive the treatment, and deliberate murder was an option held by klansmen in reserve for special cases, where all other methods failed.

As for their chosen targets, klansmen displayed a wide range of interest. In 1921, a billboard erected in Mobile, Alabama, threatened Klan vengeance against "taxi drivers, gamblers, thieves, loafers and any street mashers, bad women, shinny dealers and all violators of the law." Birmingham klansmen whipped a man who refused to remarry his ex-wife, while knights in neighboring Bessemer flogged another who filed for legal separation. Oklahoma klansmen whipped and mutilated Jewish victim Nathan Hantaman on suspicion of selling narcotics. Klan floggers in North Carolina, including a chief of police, whipped two women for allegedly abusing their husbands.

As in Reconstruction, however, klansmen frequently failed to meet the order's high moral standards. The KKK was a cash cow to its leaders, many of whom embezzled funds from the order to pad their own wallets, sometimes absconding with their loot to parts unknown. Despite their pledge to uphold Prohibition, some klansmen drank heavily and others indulged in bootlegging. During January 1923, klansmen in Horry County, North Carolina, twice tried to murder Daniel Duncan for directing lawmen to their hidden stills. Federal agents caught Imperial Kleagle Edward Clarke with whiskey in his luggage, and Clarke subsequently pled guilty to Mann Act violations (transporting women across state lines for immoral purposes). The case of Grand Dragon David Stephenson was even worse, involving the abduction, rape and suicide of an Indiana schoolteacher that sent Stephenson to prison for life.

By 1932 the national atmosphere had changed so much that both political parties openly supported the repeal of Prohibition. With liquor legalized once more in December 1933, attacks on vendors and drinkers could no longer be excused as law enforcement once removed. Victims could (and would) be whipped for other "sins," but the rigors of the Great Depression put a damper on Ku Klux crusades against vice. One glaring exception was the March 1935 castration of Robert Cargell in St. Petersburg, Florida, where klansmen accused him of "running around with the wrong lady." Prosecutors failed to punish that crime, or most of the Klan's other moralistic excesses, but a Georgia court subsequently fined ex–Imperial Wizard Hiram Evans for his role in an illegal highway paving kickback scheme. In April 1944, the IRS turned a national spotlight on Ku Klux "morality" with the revelation that imperial headquarters owned $685,355 in unpaid taxes and penalties from the 1920s. That lien dissolved that national order, but its survivors learned nothing from the experience. In August and September 1949, Dr. Samuel Green's AGK was slapped with two more federal tax liens in the amount of $9,332 and $8,383.

While the tax man tormented Georgia's knights, William Morris and his Federated KKK issued a blanket warning to all "honky-tonk operators, common brier-patch prostitutes, and people of that type" in the state of Alabama. Two months later, in June 1949, Birmingham klansmen menaced Edna McDanal on charges of dancing nude, bedding teenage boys, and selling liquor to minors. Floggings followed, led by local deputy sheriffs, but jurors chose not to convict those accused of nightriding crimes. Florida klansmen raided gambling clubs around Miami, burned the home of an alleged child-molester, beat and shot a school janitor who allegedly entered the girls' restroom unescorted, then murdered the janitor's brother-in-law in an apparent case of mistaken identity. As in Alabama and elsewhere, their crimes went unpunished.

Klan pretensions to supreme morality continued during the 1950s and 1960s, but few outside the order bought the shopworn line. Hoots of derision greeted the 1964 revelation that Holsted Manucy a leader of riotous klansmen in St. Augustine, Florida—was also a convicted bootlegger. During 1965, HUAC investigators proved that Imperial Wizard Robert Shelton and his wife tapped the UKA's till for personal luxury items, sometimes writing checks on the Klan's account under pseudonyms. Exposure of Ku Klux corruption struck a spark at FBI headquarters, inspiring a rash of anonymous postcards as part of the Bureau's illegal COINTELPRO harassment campaign. The cards, sent to klansmen throughout Dixie, included a crude cartoon of a hooded man and woman sipping cocktails, with the caption: "Which Klan leaders are spending your money tonight?"

At the same time, G-men encouraged hired informants to disrupt Klan families by seducing the wives of their komrades. In the 1970s, David Duke followed in the footsteps of wizards Simmons, Evans and Shelton, milking his Klan for all it was worth. His profiteering prompted mass defections, and while he escaped prosecution as a klansman, Duke served prison time for fraud three decades later.

While Duke chased money and publicity, other klansmen sought to launch new moralistic campaigns in the 1970s and 1980s. As a quasireligious order dedicated to America's salvation from sin, the KKK cast about for modern causes and fastened on the "right to life" crusade, organized in response to the U.S. Supreme Court's 1973 pro-abortion ruling in *Roe v. Wade*. As always, there was a racial slang to the Klan's argument. From California, Tom Metzger declared, "Almost all abortion doctors are Jews. Abortion makes money for Jews. Almost all abortion nurses are lesbians. Abortion gives thrills to lesbians.... Jews must be punished for this holocaust and murder of white children along with their perverted lesbian nurses." Across the continent, Glenn Miller's Confederate Knights agreed, proclaiming in a printed statement: "More than ten million white babies have been murdered through Jewish-engineered legalized abortion since 1973 here in America and more than a million per year are being slaughtered this way.... The Klan understands that this is just one of many tools used to destroy the white race and we know who it is [*sic*]." In 1985, Miller's new

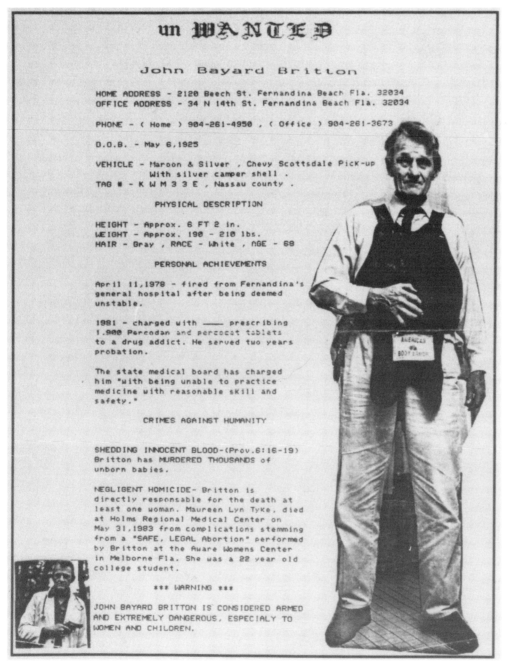

Klansmen pioneered "Wanted" posters targeting abortion providers in the 1980s.

White Patriot Party pioneered the use of "Wanted" posters to target specific abortion providers, displaying photographs of various physicians together with their home addresses and telephone numbers, pronouncing that selected individuals had been "tried, convicted, and sentenced to death."

When not attacking women's clinics, Klan moralists concerned themselves with the sex lives of their neighbors—and most particularly if those neighbors were gay or lesbian. Longtime klansman Jesse Stoner was fresh out of jail on a church-bombing charge when he launched a new Crusade Against Corruption, preaching Christian Identity tenets and bumping homosexuals to the top of his time-honored enemies list. Premiered in a *Thunderbolt* advertisement under the headline "Praise God for AIDS," Stoner's new vehicle operated on the premise that "God is intervening in early affairs with Aids [*sic*] to destroy his enemies.... Aids is a racial disease of jews [*sic*] and negroids [*sic*] that also exterminates sodomites.... Racial segregation is necessary."

As in the past, Klan moralists were rarely capable of living by the standards they applied to others. Florida Grand Dragon Tony Bastanzio's 1979 narcotics conviction scuttled his dreams of elective office and barred him from legally owning a firearm. In November 1982, officials in Broward County, Florida, seized KKK regalia, guns and cash when they jailed two brothers on charges of posing as policemen to shake down drug dealers for profit. Rubin Collinsworth, a former Klan leader in Florida's Palm Beach County, took his estranged wife hostage at gunpoint on 24 May 1984, in an ill-conceived attempt to save their marriage; jailed without bond, he faced new charges in November 1984, after offering two fellow inmates $25,000 to murder his spouse. In January 1986, jurors convicted Florida klansman Donald Spivey of sexual battery on a teenage girl. Police in Conyers, Georgia, jailed Grand Dragon Greg Walker in May 1992, for selling illegal drugs and weapons to undercover officers. Alabama klansman Gregory Garrett received a twenty-five-year prison term in February 1999, for the rape of a child he molested in 1997. Three months later, officers in Baton Rouge, Louisiana, charged klansman Greg David with aggravated rape, oral sexual battery and crimes against nature for his attack on a black man. In November 1999, police in Rutherford County, North Carolina, raided the home of Robert Guffey and his son Anthony, seizing illegal drugs, stolen property, homemade bombs and a cache of KKK literature.

Education

Most rank-and-file klansmen of the Reconstruction era were illiterate and seemed determined to remain so. Education in the antebellum South had been a privilege restricted to affluent whites, in a society where tax-supported public schools did not exist for whites and teaching blacks to read had been a criminal offense. Indeed, the quarrel over slavery prior to 1861 produced an attitude explained by a Virginia newspaper editor: "We have got to hating everything with the prefix free—from free negroes up and down through the whole catalogue—*free farms, free labor, free society ... free schools*—all belonging to the same brood of damnable isms." When various "radical" state governments established tax-supported schools in Dixie during Reconstruction, klansmen rose against them in a rage of terrorism seemingly devoted to perpetuation of universal ignorance.

Southern Democrats and the klansmen who served them opposed public schools both for the new tax burden they imposed and from fear that education would incline former slaves toward pretensions of social equality. With that in mind, the Klan harassed, threatened, whipped and sometimes murdered teachers of both races, often burning schools, churches or other buildings wherein classes were convened. Nightriders whipped teacher J.C. Dunlap at Shelbyville, Tennessee, in July 1867, but their second attempt in January 1868 was repulsed with gunfire. Whites in Warren County, Georgia, refused to let a new black school hold class unless it was privately supported. In Chattooga County, meanwhile, klansmen burned a black school and whipped its teacher, but left the white school standing. Alabama's knights were less discriminating: they burned white public schools in Blount and Calhoun Counties, along with black schools in other locations, while Tuscaloosa leader Ryland Randolph mounted a campaign of harassment that closed the state university in early 1871. Teachers were also beaten, ter-

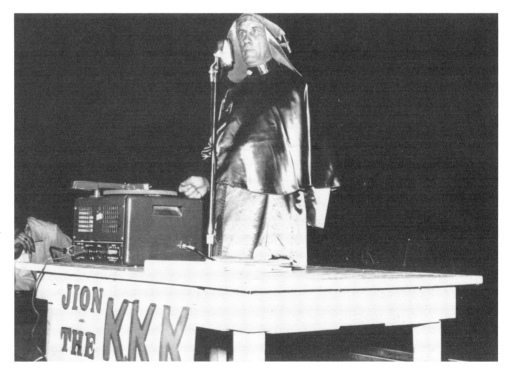

As indicated by the sign, Klan protests against school integration had nothing to do with education (Florida State Archives).

rorized, and driven out of town in Bowling Green and Lexington, Kentucky, and in Company Shops (now Burlington), North Carolina.

Mississippi klansmen carried out the most concerted crusade against public schools during Reconstruction. One of the first targets, a minister and teacher named McLachlan, was warned to leave Starkville in 1870 but remained until his near-miss with a lynch mob in spring 1871. As elsewhere in Dixie, black schools were the primary target, but some white schools also suffered violence. Winston County klansmen closed eleven schools, while Monroe County knights closed twenty-six and flogged county superintendent A.P. Huggins. Aberdeen's night-riders forced a local teacher to close his private school, but offered to help him collect tuition if he reopened it as a private academy. Robert Flournoy established sixty-four schools in Pontotoc County by May 1871, all but twelve of them for whites, and fifty-three of his sixty-four teachers were loyal Democrats, but klansmen tried to kill him anyway. They lost that battle and one of their own on 12 May 1871, but six months later county voters chose the leader of the raid—Grand Cyclops Tom Saddler—to serve as their sheriff.

Klansmen ultimately lost their battle to eliminate all public schools in Dixie, but right-wing politicians proved so miserly where education was concerned that Deep South states boasted America's highest illiteracy rates and lowest per capita expenditures for students over the next century. Black schools and students lagged even farther behind, under the pernicious "separate but equal" doctrine of segregation enshrined by the U.S. Supreme Court's 1896 ruling in *Plessy v. Ferguson.* By the time William Simmons revived the KKK in 1915, Jim Crow education was a fact of life in nineteen states and the District of Columbia.

Simmons made no reference to education in the *Kloran,* but Ku Klux spokesmen pledged themselves to uphold "100-percent Americanism" in all things, a narrow view that seldom looked beyond the Bible and *McGuffey's Reader* as sources of instruction in the hallowed "Little Red Schoolhouse." Ironically, that view—coupled with rampant nativism—prompted klansmen to reverse their hard-line view from Reconstruction and insist that only tax-supported public schools be authorized throughout America. From coast to coast, klansmen supported legislation banning parochial schools. (One such statute passed in Oregon, but it was soon declared unconstitutional.) That said, klansmen insisted on quasi-religious education for public school students, including daily helpings of scripture from King James and an air-tight ban on the pernicious taint of Darwinism. When fundamentalist Christian tenets were removed from tax-supported education, klansmen complained, "it becomes easy for the Jew then to strike a deathblow at Christianity."

In terms of higher education, imperial headquarters naturally distrusted colleges and universities where "liberal" free-thinking was encouraged. In place of such subversive institutions, KKK leaders planned to establish their own institution where klannishness reigned supreme. In 1923, when Grand Dragon David Stephenson announced plans to purchase Indiana's Valparaiso University, the scheme touched off a firestorm of protest. The Philadelphia *Ledger* worried that school spirit

would soon give way to "unprecedented savagery," while New York's *Call* asked whether the new "kurrikulum" would include classes in "horsewhipping" and "tarring and feathering." In the final event, Stephenson's rift with Imperial Wizard Hiram Evans scuttled the sale. Instead, Evans funded a Confederate memorial at Stone Mountain, Georgia, leaving Stephenson to complain that national Klan leaders "donated $100,000 to erect a monument to the memory of the rebels who once tried to destroy America, yet they refused to give a single dollar for Valparaiso University to help educate the patriots of the North who saved the Union to posterity, unsullied from the contamination of southern traitors."

Public education held no further interest for klansmen until May 1954, when the U.S. Supreme Court's *Brown v. Board of Education* banned "separate but equal" classrooms. Southern racist politicians instantly closed ranks with a pledge of "massive resistance," including legal steps in some states to dismantle public schools entirely. Mississippi Senator James Eastland told his constituents, "You are not required to obey any court which passes out such a ruling. In fact, you are obligated to defy it." Georgia Governor Herman Talmadge, long a public ally of the KKK, warned that "blood will flow in the streets" if federal authorities tried to enforce the court's order. Two years before *Brown,* Florida Klan leader Bill Hendrix had warned that his knights would "bear arms to uphold our Constitutional rights" if the Supreme Court banned school segregation. Now, with that ruling on the record, Georgia klansman James Venable said of Dixie's public schools, "Let's close them up. Let's burn them up, if it comes to that."

Thus encouraged, klansmen did their best to stem the tide of integration in America. They led or joined in riots against integrated schools in Tuscaloosa, Alabama (1956); in Clinton and Oliver Springs, Tennessee (1956); in Alvarado, Mansfield and Texarkana, Texas (1956); in Clay and Sturgis, Kentucky (1956); in Mt. Gay, West Virginia (1956); in New Orleans, Louisiana (1956, 1960) Little Rock, Arkansas (1957); in Nashville, Tennessee (1957); in Matoaka, West Virginia (1957); in Athens, Georgia (1961); in Oxford, Mississippi (1962); in Grenada, Mississippi (1966); and in Boston, Massachusetts (1974). Between 1955 and 1967, terrorists opposed to school desegregation bombed or burned schools, homes, buses and other targets in Alabama, Arkansas, Florida, Michigan, Mississippi, North Carolina, South Carolina, Tennessee, Texas and West Virginia. Imperial Wizard Robert Shelton's UKA announced plans for private "white academies" in Alabama or Georgia, but the scheme was never realized.

For modern klansmen and their allies, the threat of integrated education was much the same as that of black schools during Reconstruction. Simply stated, educated blacks were better suited to identify, demand and win their civil rights, thus challenging the vaunted "southern way of life." Mixed classes added further danger, from a racist viewpoint, by encouraging social interaction between blacks and whites. Mississippi state legislator Walter Givhan spoke for thousands of racists when he told a 1955 Citizens' Council rally, "The real purpose of the Supreme Court's decision against school segregation is to open the bedroom doors of our white women to Negro men! The

Negroes want to see to it that the nation gets a Negro Vice-President, so they can then assassinate the President and thus get a Negro President!"

Over the past quarter century, klansmen and their neo–Nazi allies have generally given up on "saving" American schools. In the 1970s, some found their way to insular rural communities, often fortified and heavily armed, where they were free to "educate" their children without interference from the state. Others pursued a similar course through home-schooling, without uprooting their families entirely. Untainted students who desired a higher education might find room at one of several private colleges like South Carolina's Bob Jones University, founded in 1927 by pro–Klan evangelist Bob Jones, Sr. Within those cloistered walls, students pursuing a variety of majors also receive daily doses of anti–Catholic propaganda virtually indistinguishable from that spewed by the nineteenth-century Know Nothing movement or the 1920s KKK. BJU barred black students until 1971, then admitted only married blacks until 1975, when a federal court ruling (*McCray v. Runyon*) outlawed racial exclusion from private schools. The university countered that setback with a ban on interracial dating and a rule mandating expulsion for students linked to "any group or organization which holds as one of its goals or advocates interracial marriage." Those policies remained in effect until 2000, when President Bob Jones III formally renounced them on *Larry King Live*.

Women and Children Last

One of the Reconstruction-era Klan's primary motives, though unstated in its prescripts, was the armed defense of "white womanhood." Centuries of slavery—wherein white men were free to rape women as they pleased, but any carnal contact between black men and white women meant brutal death for the males—had transformed Dixie by 1865 into a seething cauldron of lust, repression, and sexual paranoia. Klan historian David Chalmers explains the average klansman's attitude toward white women, unaltered to the present day:

> The woman not only stood at the core of his sense of property and chivalry, she represented the heart of the culture. By the fact that she was not accessible to the Negro, she marked the ultimate line of difference between white and black. Not only was any attack on white womanhood a blow against the whole idea of the South, but any change in the status of the Negro in the South thereby also became an attack on the cultural symbol: the white woman. Therefore, though rape was bad enough in itself, it was impossible to assault either the Southern woman or the South without having implicitly levied a carnal attack on the other.

Still, war and politics were "men's business" in the nineteenth century, relegating white women—or, at least, the most affluent of them—to their traditional place on a pedestal. The KKK's original prescripts make no allusion to gender, beyond the 1868 edition's pledge that klansmen would be "generous in manhood," but no female members were contemplated or admitted to the order. Klan wives, mothers and sisters might sew costumes and banners for their nightriding menfolk, might join in whis-

pering campaigns against the Klan's "radical" enemies, might bind wounds or offer up false alibis in court, but none participated in the daily (or nightly) workings of the order. Their exclusion was a part of "chivalry"—which did not extend to the black women frequently raped, whipped or murdered by klansmen.

A half-century later, William Simmons revived the Klan on behalf of "white American citizens," but his *Kloran* invited only "all men who can qualify" to join the order's ranks. In fairness to the wizard, all fraternities barred female members in those days, but as the KKK spread nationwide in 1920–21, thousands of women yearned for a seat on the bandwagon. Unofficial ladies' auxiliary chapters sprang up in various states, including the Ladies of the Cu Clux Clan, Ladies of the Golden Den, Ladies of the Golden Mask, and Ladies of the Invisible Eye (which counted Elizabeth Tyler, co-chairman of the KKK's national propagation department, among its members). Simmons remained aloof to the Klan's distaff side until March 1923, four months after he was muscled out of office by successor Hiram Evans. Then, in a bid to compete with his own creation, Simmons launched Kamelia, conceived as the first national women's auxiliary to the KKK. Meanwhile, Indiana Grand Dragon David Stephenson had launched his own Queens of the Golden Mask, while imperial headquarters founded the Women of the KKK to compete with both groups. A February 1924 court order scuttled Kamelia and eased Simmons into retirement, while the WKKK spread nationwide. By November 1923, thirty-six states hosted active WKKK chapters, with an estimated 250,000 members. Growth continued through 1924, with charters granted to an estimated fifty new locals per week.

All this occurred despite the Klan's provincial view of women during an "enlightened" age, when Alabama Senator (and klansman) Thomas Heflin campaigned long and hard against women's suffrage. Klanswomen generally shared the concerns of their husbands, fathers and brothers in regard to fundamentalist morality, ultra-conservative politics, and racism. Phrased another way, they were equally gullible and sometimes more ardent than klansmen themselves in the perceived defense of home and family. In Indiana, where Grand Dragon Stephenson counted some 27,500 loyal WKKK members, klanswomen served as his "poison society," quietly slandering critics and political opponents of the KKK. Sometimes disguised behind front groups, klanswomen also proved to be a potent force in civic life for many towns, demanding strict enforcement of the vice laws, boycotting "subversive" merchants, and supporting charitable projects in the name of "100-percent Americanism."

At the same time, imperial headquarters was determined to leave no stone unturned in the quest for recruits and ready cash. Late in 1923, Wizard Evans inaugurated a Junior KKK for teenage boys and a Tri-K Klub for girls below age sixteen. Both sported distinctive regalia and performed simplified rituals adapted from the adult Klan or WKKK. Fifteen states harbored Junior KKK dens by 1924, while the Tri-K Klub enjoyed similar growth. During initiation ceremonies, the Tri-K girls knelt and sang a special song to the tune of "Auld Lang Syne."

> We pledge to you our friendship true
> Through happiness and tears
> The tie that bind our hearts to you

Will hold throughout the years.
Beneath the flag that waves above
This cross that lights our way
You'll always find a sister's love
In the heart of each Tri-K.

The WKKK and junior auxiliaries suffered the same pangs of internal dissension as the Klan at large, exacerbated in most cases by the fact of long-distance domination by men (or adults). Exposure of Klan immorality, extremism and violence winnowed members from the ranks, and the remnants of all three organizations dissolved when Imperial Wizard James Colescott disbanded the national Klan in April 1944.

While various Klan factions multiplied, rose and fell during the years after World War II, women still found no active role in the KKK's ranks. The pattern of subservient auxiliary groups remained in place through the 1960s, when Robert Shelton's UKA boasted thirty-seven ladies' chapters in six states (versus 521 male klaverns in sixteen states). Klanswomen might encourage acts of violence—like those who cheered the near-murder of four black trespassers beaten at a September 1963 Klan rally outside St. Augustine, Florida—but Shelton's Klan and its major competitors still barred women from the order's inner councils. Ohio klanswoman Eloise Witte came closest to command rank in the 1960s, leading a Cincinnati auxiliary unit of James Venable's National Knights, where she dubbed herself "grand empress" and allegedly discussed assassination plans with various subordinates. Witte herself denied those charges, and the only active female Ku Klux terrorist identified during America's chaotic "Second Reconstruction" was Mississippi schoolteacher Kathryn Ainsworth, killed by Meridian police when she joined Thomas Tarrants on a bombing raid in June 1968.

David Duke was the first Klan leader to admit women as full-fledged members with access to command ranks. Under Duke, klanswomen Sandra Bergeron and "Gladys X" reigned as giants in Jefferson Parish, Louisiana, and Nashville, Tennessee, respectively, while Clara Pecoraro served as national security chief for the KKKK. Jockey Mary Bacon also sacrificed her career by unmasking herself as a member of Duke's Klan in April 1975, when she told an audience in Walker, Louisiana, "We are not just a bunch of illiterate southern nigger-killers. We are good white Christian people, hard-working people working for a white America. When one of your wives or one of your sisters gets raped by a nigger, maybe you'll get smart and join the Klan." Still, Duke's philandering and divorce from wife Chloe, paralleled by publication in 1976 of a pseudonymous sex manual for women, *Finders-Keepers* ("You must love sex for its own sake"), undercut his image as a liberator of patriotic women.

Duke himself had joined the Klan as a teenager and organized his own White Youth Alliance in college, an experience that prompted his foundation of a Klan Youth Corps for recruits under age seventeen, allegedly claiming some 3,000 members by the time Duke assumed full command of the KKKK in June 1975. Rival wizard Bill Wilkinson soon adopted the corps for his own IEKKKK, outlining a plan of action in *The Klansman* whereby KYC members would campaign within their schools "to build racial pride through a program of white racial courses." Wilkinson's five-point strategy urged KYC members to:

1. Organize White Youth in every school along racial lines.
2. [Adopt a] "Get tough" policy with arrogant non-Whites.
3. Force school administrators to drop their appeasement policy to minorities by threatening public exposure followed by possible boycotts.
4. Implement a "tit for tat" policy by demanding equal rights for White students. If minorities have a Minority Cultural Class, Whites should have a White Cultural Class.
5. [Seek] Segregation of classes, followed by eventual segregation of schools.

It is unknown how far recruiting on those lines progressed, but some inroads were clearly made by Wilkinson's Klan and others. In New Jersey, an eighteen-year-old klansman told *Junior Scholastic* that the KKK was working to "get the kids off the streets and give them something to do." At the University of Florida, a faculty adviser to the newly-organized White Students Union resigned in June 1990, to protest the WSU's alliance with Tony Bastanzio's Dixie Knights of the KKK.

Trouble followed the KYC wherever it spread. In Nashville, Tennessee, police charged the director of Wilkinson's KYC with plotting to bomb a local synagogue and various Jewish-owned business establishments. In Oklahoma City, teens claiming membership in two Klan groups wielded baseball bats against the patrons of a gay bar. Boy Scout leaders in Houston, Texas, rejected the charter application of a new Explorer post after learning that its adult sponsor was a klansman who had trained his ten young followers in hand-to-hand combat with machetes. In 1992, administrators at Gulf Middle School in Cape Coral, Florida, suspended eleven students after the KKK chapter they founded "as a joke" provoked interracial fighting on campus. By December 1992, Florida's Independent Knights of the KKK boasted an eighteen-year-old wizard, one Howard "Archie" Johnson, but its membership was slim to nonexistent. James Roesch, affiliated with the Klan from age fifteen (in 1995), proved more successful in Texas, rising to command the Knights of the White Kamellia by 1999.

The last two decades of the twentieth century found klansmen and their neo–Nazi allies deeply divided on the proper role of women in the struggle for white supremacy. Lisa Turner launched a "Women's Frontier" faction of Matt Hale's World Church of the Creator in May 1998, proclaiming on the Internet that "Everyone is starting to realize that if we are going to overcome in this struggle we are going to have to do it together—Man and Woman—side by side!" Women for Aryan Unity, a Canadian-based group of Odinists, advised "squeamish, bug-fearing females" to "lose your forest phobias and start preparing for tomorrow" with hard-core survivalist training. In 1999, media reports identified Pennsylvania's grand dragon of the American Knights as Kathryn Hedrick, AKA "Kay Ryan." Perhaps the most unusual front-line female member of a U.S. racist group was Cortney Mann, a *black* woman identified in 1997 as Philadelphia's leader of the NAAWP.

Despite such female "progress" on the racist front, other groups maintain a more traditional view of women and their place within society. Thomas Robb, speaking for the KKKK from Harrison, Arkansas, declares: "While we accept the contributions that can be offered by our women, the Klan still believes that our women find their greatest fulfillment as mothers of our children.... [N]o woman should be forced away from her home and children as is being done today by the shambled economy brought upon us by the greedy bankers of international finance." Spokesmen for the Aryan Nations echoed that sentiment, proclaiming: "Nature has ordained that man should be the guardian of the family and the protector of the community. The world of contented womanhood is made of family: husband, children and home.... Honored above all is the mother. It is a far greater love and service to be the mother of healthy Aryan children than to be a clever woman lawyer." Female members of The Order, spawned at an Aryan Nations gathering in 1983, signed the group's declaration of war against "ZOG" in November 1984, but they were largely relegated to receptacles for "white seed"—breeders for the movement, in effect. By the 1990s, some isolated racist groups advocated polygamy as a means of producing more "Aryan warriors" for combat.

Kapital and Labor

If ever proof was needed that racism and ignorance go hand in hand, that evidence is found within the history of southern poverty. In his book *The Coming of the Civil War* (1972), historian Robert Goldston explained how bigotry has long impoverished Dixie's poor whites, as well as blacks.

> It might be thought that since their economic hardships were directly traceable to the institution of slavery, the majority of Southerners would oppose it. Yet Southern poor whites were the system's most vigorous, even fanatical defenders.... The extremes of great wealth and great poverty had created a class consciousness in the South, and the average poor white could find comfort only in the fact that however low on the social scale he might be, he was, by definition, superior to a black, slave or free.... Self-hatred is, psychologically, the basis of hatred of others. The emotional investment by Southern poor whites in black slavery was even greater than the economic investment in it held by the few rich.

A century after the Civil War, that attitude still dominated the thinking of poor southern whites who filled the Klan's ranks. As one man indicted for the murder of a black victim asked author William Bradford Huie, "If I ain't better'n a goddamn, black-assed nigger, then what the hell am I better'n of?"

While the Thirteenth Amendment to the U.S. Constitution banned human bondage in 1865, many southern whites sought to replace Dixie's "peculiar institution" with a system of thinly-disguised peonage, returning blacks to a state of virtual slavery. Failing to achieve that goal with Black Codes during 1865–66, southern patricians next relied on klansmen to enforce their will. Throughout the old Confederacy, former slaves were terrorized for "laziness," for owning land or for rejecting offers to rejoin their antebellum masters as indentured servants—in short, for forgetting "their place." Mississippi klansmen drove blacks from their land in Noxubee, Tippah and Winston Counties, either claiming it themselves or (more often) watching it sold to rich planters. In Alcorn County, meanwhile, they claimed jobs vacated by fleeing black employees of the Gulf and Ohio Railroad. Nightriders in Clay County, Florida, whipped Samuel Tutson, raped his wife, crippled his infant son and demolished his house after Tutson refused a white man's offer on his three-acre farm. Six of the raiders were arrested, then acquitted by white jurors, after which the Tutsons were convicted of "swearing falsely" against their attackers. In October 1868, men led by ex-slave Doc Rountree's former master whipped Rountree, his wife, and four of their ten children, warning all concerned that they "didn't allow damned niggers to live on land of their own." Rountree's ex-owner ordered Doc and his children to report for work the next morning, resuming their lives as field hands paid with food and clothing in lieu of cash. In Florida's Orange County, after a group of "crackers" hired to clear an orchard were dismissed in favor of cheaper black labor, the sheriff led a band of klansmen to raid the black camp.

By the time William Simmons revived the KKK in 1915, conservative America was up in arms over labor unions and their "radical" demands—including the eight-hour day, living wages, and basic safety precautions on hazardous jobs. After the Russian Revolution of 1917, U.S. industrial leaders routinely denounced all unions as "communistic" and "subversive," a claim echoed from on high by various governors, FBI directors, U.S. Attorneys General and Presidents. In Alabama, Birmingham's industrial "Big Mules" endorsed the modern Klan as a sure-fire antidote to unionism and black "uppitiness," unleashing hooded knights against the "Reds" in their midst. In 1918, Birmingham klansmen defused a steel mill strike by kidnapping the union's leader. The same year witnessed Ku Klux intervention in a Mobile shipyard strike, where one union organizer firsts suffered a beating, then vanished without a trace. In 1921, Mobile klansmen dragged an AFL official from a train and whipped him unconscious. The following year, during a statewide railroad strike, klansmen flogged two white workers at Tarrant City and two blacks in Montgomery. James Bowron, an executive of the Tennessee Coal and Iron Company (TCI, owned by U.S. Steel), addressed a klavern meeting at Wahouma, Alabama, in 1927, telling the assembled knights that he "approved quite extensively of their principles." An atypical victim, elderly Ben Way, was flogged by klansmen at Sanford, Florida, in April 1925, after complaining (accurately, as it turned out) that local celery growers used pesticides unfit for human consumption.

In the 1930s, after John L. Lewis launched the CIO's "Operation Dixie," Imperial Wizard Hiram Evans warned, "The Klan will not sit idly by and allow the CIO to destroy our social order ... without swift punishment." A local Ku Klux leader told reporters, "We will fight horror with horror!" As in the 1920s, Alabama and Florida remained two of the KKK's most active battlegrounds against unionism. Klansmen in the Cotton State flogged textile strikers at Huntsville in 1934, and joined company goons in Birmingham to ambush an AFL parade the following year, killing one marcher and wounding six more. Assassins posing as sheriff's deputies kidnapped unionist Frank Norman from Lakeland, Florida, in 1934; he was never seen again, but a local klansman later told journalists that he had helped conceal the corpses of a dozen union agitators in Florida's swamps and flooded phosphate mines. In 1936, at Gadsden, Alabama, a Klan mob demolished the United Rubber Workers office and beat its occupants while police watched; afterward, the cops provided first aid and free rides out of town. Birmingham klansmen administered a near-fatal beating to CIO deputy Joe Gelders in September 1936, soon after he arrived to coordinate organizational efforts against Tennessee Coal and Iron.

James Colescott replaced Hiram Evans as imperial wizard in 1937, and while he publicly claimed that the Klan "has no fight with any labor unions," violence and intimidation continued. In 1937, klansmen fought the CIO Textile Workers Organizing Committee with threatening placards, cross-burnings, and numerous whippings. The following year, Atlanta's knights whipped wayward employees of the Scottsdale Mills (owned by the Georgia Savings Bank & Trust Company), warning their victims, "We're going to break up these damn unions." In far-off Aberdeen, Washington, on 6 December 1939, klansmen smashed windows at the AFL Central Labor Council and the local CIO office. In May 1941, an agent for Detroit's Pontiac auto company attended the Klan's imperial kloncilium in Atlanta, negotiating a plan to replace union workers with Michigan klansmen. Florida Kleagle Fred Bass, formerly indicted in the 1935 Joseph Shoemaker slaying, posed as "a boilermaker from New York" to visit Orlando's CIO Citrus Workers Union office in December 1942; two months later, he led a team of klansmen who distributed anti-union leaflets outside the Fosgate Citrus packing plant, during an NLRB election campaign.

In January 1944, Wizard Colescott devised a new strategy for breaking unions. Instead of attacking their leaders and members by night, he preferred to bore from within. First, a *Fiery Cross* editorial called upon "those [klansmen] affiliated with labor organizations to organize themselves and take over active leadership." A subsequent letter from Colescott to his knights at large read:

> My Faithful Klanspeople;
> ... [E]ach exalted cyclops shall contact immediately all members of our organization holding membership in unions of the Workers Alliance, CIO, and the AFL. Each group so represented with membership in the local unit shall be instructed to ... present themselves as a solid block within their labor organization unit for the purpose of sponsoring ... the name of a member of their labor organization whose Americanism is beyond question as president and to every other office within the labor unit....

An IRS tax lien scuttled Colescott's scheme three months later, but the link between klansmen and big business survived. In 1948, with a new spate of Klan violence terrorizing Alabama, Attorney General Albert Carmichael addressed the following message to Senator Lister Hill (uncorrected for grammar):

> That these Klan activities are handled from tall buildings THERE IS NO DOUBT,—I SAY, NONE AT ALL. ... O, how careful one must be in the Birmingham District,—one will step in the wrong place if one does not watch one's step. I had never realized just how powerful the following group is: T.C.I. and the owners of the mines ... BUT don't forget this: The Ala. Klan *IS* unquestionably and undoubtedly directed from tall buildings and, its most likely that its directed from one certain tall building.

Carmichael referred to the First Avenue office of U.S. Steel, which owned and controlled TCI. An employee at TCI's Fairfield plant was E.E. Campbell, exalted cyclops of the local Robert E. Lee Klavern—and who enjoyed free access to the files of Birmingham police commissioner Eugene "Bull" Connor. During that same period, prolific Klan bomber Robert "Dynamite Bob" Chambliss was employed by Birmingham's city government.

Klansmen also maintained an interest in the criminal activities of southern labor contractors, who enslaved black workers with fraudulent debts and then trucked them around the country to harvest various crops, working under armed guard and housed in barns while their mythical debts for transportation, food and lodging, tools and so forth always exceeded wages. When those prisoners tried to escape, they were run down by posses of corrupt lawmen and Klan members, punished with torture or slain if they tried to resist. Those who stayed "safe" in camp were likewise menaced by

Klansmen rally against "radical" labor unions in the 1930s (Florida State Archives).

robed klansmen and fiery crosses, to ensure cooperation with their slave masters.

Throughout the long campaign of terror, few rank-and-file klansmen were wise enough to realize that their support for robber barons kept them trapped in jobs that ruined their health and impoverished their families. Fewer still had the courage to defy Klan discipline and speak out against the system that degraded them along with blacks. Blinded by racism and self-destructive loyalty to the "southern way of life" that left them ignorant and penniless, klansmen shunned integrated unions that would have improved their lot, preferring poverty and violence to a new system that would have placed them on more equal footing with nonwhites.

That futile bigotry prevailed into the 1960s and beyond. In 1963, after klansman Byron De La Beckwith murdered Mississippi NAACP leader Medgar Evers, folk singer Bob Dylan penned a song titled "Only a Pawn in Their Game," about Beckwith's role as a pawn of Mississippi's ruling class. A year later, wealthy Mississippi oilman J.E. Thornhill bankrolled the UKA's McComb Unit 700 (AKA the South Pike Marksmanship Association). Author John Dittmer suggests that Thornhill also provided members of the violent "Pike County Wolf Pack" with dynamite used in its many bombings. A prominent member of Unit No. 700 was Sterling "Bubba" Gillis, son of a McComb civic leader. In 1965, Birmingham klansmen (including the slayers of civil rights worker Viola Liuzzo) waged a terrorist campaign against black workers who sought union representation at the W.S. Dickey Clay Manufacturing Company. Before the strike ended, klansmen were implicated in (but never punished for) a series beatings, shootings, and nine separate bombings at the Dickey plant.

One klansman who bucked the anti-labor tide was Claiborne Ellis, exalted cyclops of a UKA klavern in Durham, North Carolina. In the early 1970s, Ellis grew disenchanted with the Klan's war on unions, recognizing that it damaged whites as well as blacks. In October 1973 he told reporters for *The Nation* how Durham city officials used the KKK to counteract black protests. "We would show up with our guns on our belts," Ellis said, "and the next day I would see the same city official on the street and expect him to come up and thank me. And instead, he would cross to the other side of the street to keep from meeting me. I found out that we were being used to keep those folks in power. And I decided we weren't going to be used any more." That decision prompted UKA leaders to ban Ellis from state klonvokations in 1972 and 1973, but he remained in the Klan while joining the Durham Human Rights Commission, working side-by-side with black activists to relieve their shared misery.

Modern klansmen and their neo–Nazi allies are a breed apart from their forebears, inasmuch as many of them shun the conventional trappings of capitalism. Former California klansman and WAR founder Tom Metzger heralded that shift in the 1980s, with his announcement of a "Third Position," also dubbed Aryan Socialism, an alleged rejection of both right- and left-wing dogma which (thus far) has no coherent program and which sounds like Nazi doubletalk. Elsewhere, racist groups that have tried to withdraw from "Jewish" civilization and forge their own insular societies have seldom lasted long, as criminal activities result in raids, arrests and convictions. In any case, the KKK is no longer a serious threat to organized labor per se, and few industrial executives would be foolish enough to court the shrunken, increasingly marginalized invisible empire.

4 WHO'S WHO IN THE INVISIBLE EMPIRE

No comprehensive list of Klan members exists today, and with the order's fluctuating size—500,000 members during Reconstruction, three to five million in the 1920s, tens of thousands during later eras—mere presentation of the names (assuming they could ever be collected) would fill several dozen volumes larger than the work in hand. That said, despite the Klan's penchant for secrecy, most of its officers *are* known, along with many members of the rank and file whose public statements or illegal actions have propelled them into headlines. This chapter presents a representative sampling of Klan leaders (wizards and dragons), lower-ranking officers, and knights whose criminal activities have stripped away their masks.

Wizards and Dragons

Klansmen listed in this section represent the order's highest-ranking officers, commanding whole Klans or individual realms at various times in the KKK's history.

Adams, Sherman—As Kentucky grand dragon of the UKA, Adams led an unauthorized parade of 260 robed klansmen through Shepherdsville on 3 July 1976. The parade was allowed to proceed, despite lack of permits, since klansmen outnumbered the local police force. On 15 August 1976, three masked horsemen led several hundred knights on another march through the Louisville suburb of Okolona, a hotbed of white anti-busing sentiment. Adams told reporters that the march was held to demonstrate support for police and the U.S. Constitution. In March 1977, Adams was one of eleven Kentucky klansmen indicted for staging a private drug raid on a local teenage party. During the course of that raid, fifteen to twenty armed klansmen disguised in ski masks kicked in the door and herded guests into a back bedroom, warning, "If anybody comes out, you'll be sorry." The raiders, who boasted they were klansmen, then ransacked the mobile home, spraying graffiti on the ceiling and walls.

Adler, J.D.—A resident of Port St. Lucie, Florida, Adler was identified in August 1994 as leader of the United Florida KKK. His Klan's debut came on 20 August, when nine klansmen protested abortion outside a Melbourne women's clinic.

Ambrose, Rev. F. Halsey—As pastor of the First Presbyterian Church in Grand Forks, North Dakota, Ambrose was also the driving force behind the state's 1920s KKK. In January 1923 he addressed the state legislature in a futile attempt to block passage of an anti-mask law.

Anderson, Raymond—A resident of Maryville, Tennessee, Anderson was elected Tennessee grand dragon of the UKA in 1961. His efforts met with little success, recruiting a mere 225 klansmen for ten klaverns statewide by 1967.

Bailey, Walter F.—In 1958, Bailey founded the Mississippi Knights of the KKK, serving as imperial wizard. Never boasting more than twenty-five members, Bailey's Klan was reduced to a one-man operation after the White Knights emerged in early 1964. The Mississippi Knights vanished entirely with his death, in 1966.

Ballentine, Donald J.—A defector from the United Florida KKK, Ballentine emerged as imperial wizard of Jacksonville's Militant Knights, organized in spring 1965. Still active in early 1967, Ballentine's group vanished before a new ADL survey was completed in 1970.

Barefoot, Charles Robert, Jr.—On 19 July 2002, police in North Carolina, jailed Barefoot—identified in media reports as "self-styled" grand dragon of the Nation's Knights of the KKK—for allegedly plotting to bomb the Johnston County sheriff's office and the county jail. An additional count charged Barefoot with illegally owning guns and ammunition while subject to a domestic violence protective order. (The previous case involved Barefoot's alleged assault upon his wife with a deadly weapon.) Weapons seized from his home near Benson included pistols, rifles, a submachine gun, an AK-47 assault rifle, two homemade bombs, bomb-making components and 4,500 rounds of ammunition. Prior to defecting and founding his own splinter group in January 2002, Barefoot was an officer of the Indiana-based National Knights, but he deemed that group too moderate in ideology and tactics. Barefoot pled guilty to violating terms of the protective order in January 2003 and was sentenced to twenty-seven months in prison. Released in October 2004, he faced indictment with his wife and four other defendants, related to the death of victim Lawrence Arthur Pettit, whose decomposed remains were found near Clinton, North Carolina, in 2003. Prosecutors charge that Pettit was slain in 2001 because he possessed knowledge of threats issued against law enforcement officers by Grand Dragon Michael Brewer of Robeson County (also charged with murder in that case). Legal delays postponed Barefoot's federal indictment until 15 June 2005, when federal prosecutors charged him with various weapons and explosives violations. Neither that case nor the pending murder charge had gone to trial at press time for this work.

Barnard, Elmo C.—A Mobile, Alabama, klansman and gunsmith whose shop stood half a block from police headquarters, Barnard killed a black youth, 15-year-old Melvin Williams, during an alleged burglary on 26 September 1953. Barnard was later identified as leader of the Klan group that visited a Loxley, Alabama, Missionary Baptist Church on 15 October 1955, where knights received an enthusiastic welcome from the pastor after handing over a cash donation. In April 1957, Barnard emerged as leader of the Gulf KKK, proclaiming that "a little violence" might be needed to preserve southern segregation. He told reporters, "We're for free speech, free press, white supremacy, free public schools—be sure you put that white supremacy in there—just laws, the pursuit of happiness and no foreign creeds. One thing we don't like is social equality, and that's what the Supreme Court declared for. It's my information that a lot of money changed hands in that deal. All this agitation in the South is communist-inspired." Barnard's Klan dissolved before HUAC's 1965 investigation of the KKK began.

Bastanzio, Tony—Bastanzio emerged as a Florida grand dragon of the Dixie Knights in June 1991, with Tampa protests opposing passage of a gay-rights ordinance. A 1979 narcotics conviction scuttled Bastanzio's dreams of elective office, and prohibited ownership of firearms. He compensated by recruiting skinheads to inflate attendance at his rallies and forged a working alliance with the White Student Union.

Baumgardner, John—Identified in 1994 as the grand dragon of Florida's Templar Knights, Baumgardner called for demonstrations against women's clinics practicing abortion. The following year, his newsletter ran a poem lauding a warrior of "Yahweh" who kills an abortionist and blows up the U.S. Supreme Court.

Beall, Frank H.—Beall served as Maryland grand dragon of the 1920s Klan, claiming an estimated 33,000 members by 1922. He resigned four years later, declaring that some officers at imperial headquarters were "shamefully crooked" and "shockingly immoral."

Bednarsky, Joseph—Bednarsky defected from the IEKKKK's New Jersey realm in 1989,

to serve as grand dragon of the Confederate Knights. In November of that year, police in Gloucester City jailed IEKKKK Grand Dragon Richard Doak and two other Klan members for plotting to murder Bednarsky. On 23 April 1992, police in Millville charged Bednarsky and another klansman with harassing and threatening their Hispanic neighbors. Bednarsky pled guilty to that charge on 9 September 1992. In June 1996, Bednarsky shot a black woman with a slingshot, receiving a one-year jail term for that crime on 3 June 1998.

Behringer, John—An ex-policeman serving as New Jersey's grand dragon in 1968, Behringer told newsmen on 23 June of that

Grand Dragon John Baumgardner issued this poster protesting a Florida gay bar in 1991.

year that he had inducted Newark vigilante leader Anthony Imperiale into the Klan on 19 April 1967. Imperiale denied the claim, but admitted teaching karate to klansmen.

Bell, Arthur H.—An attorney from Bloomfield, New Jersey, Bell doubled as the state's grand dragon during the 1920s and 1930s, while his wife handled affairs for the Tri-K Girls. In 1928, Bell rented a hotel room in Atlantic City, inviting political candidates to stop by and prove their Americanism before the impending election, but he got no takers. In August 1940, Bell arranged a joint meeting between the KKK and the German-American Bund at Camp Nordland. Bell himself was featured as a speaker at the gathering, denouncing the song "God Bless America" as a Jewish tune fit only for brothels. Public outrage at the rally led Imperial Wizard James Colescott to remove Bell from office, citing Bell's failure "to adhere to the principles and ideals of the Klan." Called before a congressional panel investigating the Bund in October 1940, Bell said he thought the joint meeting was a good idea at the time, "but I don't now."

Berry, Jeffery—In the latter 1990s, Imperial Wizard Jeff Berry built the American Knights of the KKK into the nation's largest Klan, boasting some three dozen klaverns scattered from California to New York. Operating from headquarters in Butler, Indiana, he traveled widely and appeared on television talkshows, spouting an old-fashioned racism starkly at odds with the "button-down" image of David Duke and similar competitors. The tactic paid off in recruits, but Berry found trouble when his tough talk lapsed into action. On 17 November 1999, he held a TV reporter and cameraman hostage at gunpoint in his home, until they surrendered tapes of a just-completed interview. The SPLC filed suit on behalf of his victims in that case, and Berry lost by default on 20 April 2000, when he failed to appear for trial. On 12 August 2000, Berry quarreled with a black spectator at a Klan rally in Hazard, Kentucky, then chased the man for two miles in a van before ramming his car. While grand jurors considered charges in that case, an Indiana court convicted Berry of conspiracy to commit criminal confinement (for the hostage incident) and handed him a seven-year prison term on 4 December 2001.

Beshella, Allan—A British national, born in 1957, Beshella spent much of his early life in the United States, where he joined the IEKKKK under Imperial Wizard James Farrands. Home again in the early 1990s, Beshella emerged as grand dragon of the IEKKKK's English realm, then defected to lead his own Invisible Empire, United Klans of Europe. He resigned after *Serchlight* magazine exposed his 1972 arrest for child molestation in Los Angeles.

Betts, Rev. James L.—Identified in 1976 as the Missouri grand dragon of the New Order Knights of the KKK, Betts sported a Hitler-style haircut and mustache to match his neo-Nazi uniform with a Klan armband. His chief activity was publication of the newsletter *White Liberty!* In March 1976, Betts offered St. Louis police a team of forty klansmen to patrol the streets, but the city declined his generosity.

Bickley, James H.—Appointed as South Carolina grand dragon for the U.S. Klans in September 1956, Bickley increased the state's total of klaverns from twenty to thirty-five by January 1957. Proud of his achievement, Bickley told the press, "I ain't got nothing against niggers. I don't believe most of them would be causing any trouble if it wasn't for the NAACP and the Jews. I understand there are a lot of communists behind this thing, trying to get us to integrate with the niggers so we'll breed down the race."

Black, Barry E.—Internet postings from the American Knights of the KKK identified Black as imperial wizard in early 1997. He was subsequently replaced by Indiana klansman Jeff Berry.

Black, Stephen Donald—Don Black's anti–Semitic activities date from his high school years in Athens, Alabama, when he joined the National Socialist Youth Movement, a branch of the Virginia-based NSWPP. At the same time, he was active in supporting J.B. Stoner's unsuccessful Alabama gubernatorial campaign, a circumstance which Stoner later described as Black's deliberate attempt to infiltrate the NSRP. In 1970, NSRP member Jerry Ray shot and wounded Black during a break-in at Stoner's headquarters in Savannah, Georgia. Black went on to hold membership in the White Youth Alliance and the National Party, later forming his own klavern while enrolled at the University of Alabama (where he was dropped from the ROTC for his racist activities). Black joined David Duke's knights of the KKK in 1975, and two years later won appointment as Alabama's grand dragon. When Duke resigned his leadership of the Knights in 1980, Black assumed control of the dwindling organization. In spring 1981, with nine others, he hatched a plot to invade and conquer the Caribbean island of Dominica, a scheme resulting in a three-year prison term for violating the U.S. Neutrality Act. In 1982, before going to prison, Black was chosen to lead the new Confederation of Klans. Paroled in spring 1985, Black married Duke's ex-wife Chloe and announced formation of a 120-man Klan unit, the Nathan Bedford Forrest Brigade, organized to aid right-wing Contra terrorists in Nicaragua. Black announced that his group would conduct psychological warfare in Central America, while at the same time providing "a civil action unit to promote a stable economy." Klansmen apparently felt they had official blessings from the White House when President Ronald Reagan declared it "traditional" for American volunteers to join revolutionary movements abroad. That movement failed to prosper, but Black—resettled in Florida—broke new ground with the first dial-up bulletin board for racists, evolving into Stormfront—the Internet's best-known hate site—in March 1995. By 2005, more than 50,000 subscribers logged onto Stormfront on a regular basis.

Bolen, Aubrey E.—In the early 1960s, Bolen served as imperial wizard of the Association of South Carolina Klans, also holding a seat on the ASCK's four-man grand council. No trace of the group remained when ADL investigators surveyed the invisible empire in 1970.

Booker, Ray—A resident of Vidor, Texas, Booker was one of two Texas grand dragons identified for David Duke's Knights of the KKK in the mid–1970s. His activities included operating a Klan bookstore in Vidor, and a campaign to keep blacks out of restaurants by posting signs that read: "10% of All Our Profits Go to the KKK."

Bossert, Walter—In 1924, after a rift between Imperial Wizard Hiram Evans and Indiana Grand Dragon David Stephenson, Evans chose Bossert to take Stephenson's place. Stephenson retaliated by suing Bossert for libel, also seeking damages for a bombing that wrecked Stephenson's yacht. Bossert joined Evans to lead a sixty-man delegation to the 1924 Republican National Convention, later serving as one of five men on the Klan's strategy board at the Democratic National Convention. Retired from the KKK by 1938, Bossert was defeated that year in the Republican senatorial primary race.

Bowers, Samuel Holloway, Jr.—Born in New Orleans in 1924, Bowers was the grandson of a distinguished Mississippi lawyer who served four terms in Congress; he was also a direct descendant of the first president of the Virginia House of Burgesses. His parents divorced when Bowers was fourteen, and he followed his father around the South on business trips. Leaving high school to join the navy in early 1942, Bowers was honorably discharged in 1945. He earned his GED, then attended Tulane University before transferring to the University of Southern California School of Engineering. (FBI informant Delmar Dennis later claimed that Bowers joined the CPUSA while enrolled at USC, but no evidence for that claim was forthcoming.) After graduation, he settled in Laurel, Mississippi, and established the Sambo Amusement Company, sharing quarters behind the shop with his partner until 1970 (when Bowers entered federal prison).

In early 1964, Bowers emerged as imperial wizard of the Mississippi White Knights, personally directing his klansmen in an unprecedented campaign of terrorism against Mississippi blacks, Jews, and civil rights workers. A lapsed Catholic, Bowers showed no great interest in religion until 1966, when he joined the Southern Baptist Church in the wake of a murder indictment. (Authorities dismissed the conversion as a move to sway potential jurors.) Around his home, Bowers sometimes wore a Nazi armband and posed before a full-length mirror, clicking his heels and shouting, "Sieg heil!" Personally implicated in at least four murders, Bowers surrendered to FBI agents for the slaying of NAACP officer Vernon Dahmer on 31 March 1966, two days after G-men found a "small arsenal" at his home. On 20 October 1967, federal jurors convicted Bowers on civil rights charges in the murders of James Chaney, Andrew Goodman and Michael Schwerner, resulting in a ten-year prison term. Three weeks later, Bowers and two other klansmen were charged with kidnapping Jack Watkins,

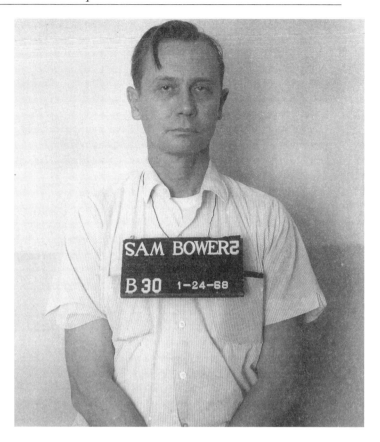

Mug shot of Imperial Wizard Samuel Bowers, taken after his arrest for the murder of Vernon Dahmer (FBI).

Masks and weapons seized from the Mississippi home of Imperial Wizard Samuel Bowers in March 1966.

a prosecution witness in the Dahmer case. On 21 December 1967, police stopped klansman Thomas Tarrants for reckless driving in Collins, Mississippi, with Bowers in the car. Both were arrested when officers found a submachine gun in the backseat, but jurors acquitted Bowers of weapons charges on 18 January 1968. Seven days later, his first trial in the Dahmer case ended with a hung jury. Three more mistrials followed in that case, before murder charges were dismissed in 1969. Bowers entered federal prison at McNeil Island, Washington, on 3 April 1970, to serve his ten-year term in the Chaney-Goodman-Schwerner case. Federal charges related to Dahmer's slaying were dismissed in 1973, and Bowers was paroled in March 1976. Mississippi sources claimed that a small, hard-core unit of White Knights revived "within two days" of his release, but no new Klan activity followed. State authorities filed new murder charges in the Dahmer case on 28 May 1998, and jurors convicted Bowers on 21 August 1998, resulting in an automatic life sentence.

Boyce, Terry—Media reports from 1992 identified North Carolina resident Terry Boyce as the imperial wizard of the Confederate Knights of America. On 8 August 1992, police conducting a routine driver's license check near an Aryan Youth concert in St. Clair County, Alabama, found three pistols in Boyce's car. They jailed Boyce—with companions Hank Scmidt (head of the New National Socialist movement) and Mack Frizzell—on charges of carrying a concealed weapon. A fourth occupant of the vehicle, skinhead Terry Sergent III, was held on an outstanding fugitive warrant from California.

Brassell, William P.—Brassell replaced Robert Creel as the UKA's Alabama grand dragon on 1 January 1966, holding that office until James Spears was elected at the state klonvokation, on 19 June 1966.

Brewer, Michael Anthony—A resident of Lumberton, North Carolina, born in 1972, Brewer served as North Carolina's grand dragon for the National Knights at the turn of the twenty-first century. In January 2003, prosecutors charged Brewer and four other defendants with murder in the 2001 slaying of Lawrence Arthur Pettit, whose decomposed remains were found in Sampson County on 2 January 2003. Others charged in that case included Charles Barefoot, Jr. (grand dragon of the rival Nation's Knights), Barefoot's estranged wife Sharon, Mark Anthony Denning and Marvin Glen Gautier (both reputed klansmen). Authorities claimed that Pettit was killed because he had knowledge of threats Brewer made against Robeson County law enforcement officers and Barefoot's alleged plot to bomb the Johnston County sheriff's office. No trial had been held on the charges at press time for this volume.

Britton, Neumann—Author Patsy Sims identified Britton as the grand dragon of Arkansas in 1977. He was also an NSRP member and served as a spokesman for the National Emancipation of Our White Seed.

Brook, Paul—Identified as Indiana's grand dragon in 1968, Brook was the target of arsonists who burned his Kokomo home on 14 September.

Brown, Jack Wilson—A klansman and gas station proprietor in Chattanooga, Tennessee, Brown arranged for the KKK to enter local softball playoffs in 1956. He was later active in the United White Party and served the NSRP as a presidential elector. In 1957, with brother Harry and several others, Brown was expelled from the U.S. Klans, moving on that October to charter his own Dixie Klans and to serve as imperial wizard, holding that post until his death in summer 1965. NSRP member Joseph Milteer named Brown as a suspect in the 1963 bombing of Birmingham's Sixteenth Street Baptist Church and implicated him in plots to kill Dr. Martin Luther King.

Brown, John C.—An ex–Confederate general from Tennessee and brother of an antebellum governor, Brown was identified as Tennessee's grand dragon during Reconstruction. On 1 August 1868, he joined Grand Wizard Nathan Forrest and eleven other ex-generals (all klansmen) at a Nashville meeting to protest Gov. William Brownlow's efforts to raise a state militia. Brown denied any knowledge of the Klan's conspiracy to topple Brownlow's government, maintaining that militia units were unnecessary. On Christmas Eve 1868, in Pulaski, Brown joined Klan founder Frank McCord to denounce mob violence, a step that effectively ended local nightriding. Elected governor in 1870, Brown also served as Masonic grand master in Tennessee and as president of the Tennessee Coal and Iron Company.

Bryant, Joseph—Following the Supreme Court's *Brown* ruling in May 1954, Bryant and his brother Arthur organized a small Klan faction in North Carolina. Both were arrested in 1955 for possession of dynamite and sending anonymous hate literature through the mail. Jurors acquitted the brothers on all charges, but the investigation had already publicized their criminal records: Joseph for juvenile rape and adult solicitation of prostitutes; Arthur for larceny and check fraud. By 1969, employed as a naturopath in Charlotte, Joseph emerged as acting grand dragon of the UKA, while James Jones served a prison term for contempt of Congress. On 4 July 1969, a shootout at Swan Quarter sent Bryant and sixteen other klansmen to jail, with several weapons seized by police. Defended by attorney Arthur Hanes, Sr., the knights were fined $1,000 each for inciting a riot, while their jail terms were suspended. Bryant subsequently accused Imperial Wizard Melvin Sexton of running scared during the shooting, and their quarrel broadened into charges of mismanagement under Sexton's administration. On 16 September 1969, Bryant led a rally where UKA members nailed their membership cards to a cross and set it afire, thereafter joining the new North Carolina Knights, organized (with covert FBI support) by Bryant and Edward Dawson. Unable to control the rank and file, Bryan was subsequently ousted by his members, replaced by Virgil Griffin.

Burros, Daniel—One of the U.S. soldiers who helped integrate Little Rock's Central High School in 1957, Dan Burros allegedly quit the army in disgust at his assignment "protecting niggers." In fact, he was judged unfit for service after attempting suicide and leaving a note signed "Heil Hitler," receiving an honorable discharge "by reasons of unsuitability, character, and behavior disorder." By December 1958 he was in touch with various neo–Nazi groups, signing his letters with a red swastika stamp and the name of a nonexistent American National Socialist Party. In June 1960 he moved to American Nazi Party headquarters in Arlington, Virginia. A month later, Burros was jailed with George Rockwell and fifteen others for a brawl during one of Rockwell's speeches in Washington, D.C. Burros was arrested again, later the same month, with John Patler for pasting Nazi stickers around ADL headquarters in Washington. In May 1961 he toured the South with Patler in the ANP's "hate bus," protesting CORE's freedom rides. Burros defected from the ANP in November 1961, joining Patler in New York to publish *Kill!*, a magazine "dedicated to the annihilation of the enemies of the white people." They named their two-man group the American National Party. In spring 1963, Burros joined the National Renaissance Party and thus met future klansman Frank Rotella. In July 1963, Burros and other NRP members were jailed for brawling with blacks at a New York City diner. Burros joined the UKA in July 1965, recruited by Roy Frankhouser, and soon won appointment to the dual roles of grand dragon and king kleagle for New York. In October 1965, the *New York Times* discovered that Burros's parents were Jewish, releasing the story on 31 October. The same day, Burros shot and killed himself at Frankhouser's home in Reading, Pennsylvania. Seven days later, klansmen burned a cross in his honor at Rising Sun, Maryland. The *NRP Bulletin* praised Burros for his willingness to "blast himself into oblivion as final proof of his loyalty."

Bush, Wilson D.—As Brooklyn, New York's exalted cyclops in the 1920s, Bush held Klan meetings after hours in the local traffic court, presiding from the judge's bench. After exposure of that practice, the district attorney upheld the Klan's right to assemble, but police soon found a cache of weapons (including hand grenades) at Bush's home. In 1946, he resurfaced as New York grand dragon for the AGK. That August, Georgia Attorney General Dan Duke announced that "a leading candidate for governor"—presumably Eugene Talmadge—had recently visited Bush in New York, seeking financial support for his Georgia campaign.

Byrd, Douglas—In autumn 1963, Byrd was named temporary grand dragon of Mississippi for the Louisiana-based Original Knights. In December, controversy erupted when Byrd and klansman Edward McDaniel accused Original Knights leader John Swenson of financial misconduct. Swenson responded with threats and charges of slander, expelling both knights. Two hundred klansmen followed Byrd into the new White Knights, but he was soon replaced by Imperial Wizard Sam Bowers, afterward fading into obscurity.

Cannon, Jack—Cannon replaced Royce McPhail as Texas grand dragon of the UKA in April 1966. His chief publicity stunt was the announcement of a rally near President Lyndon Johnson's ranch, but the effort was blocked by what he called "federal harassment."

Carr, G.E.—As Michigan's grand dragon in the 1920s, Carr once issued a Christmas message urging klansmen to "evidence

their devotion to our Lord through their activities in making this great day a bright one for all they can consistently reach." The order produced some rare good publicity, with numerous reports of klansmen giving food and clothing to needy persons of all races.

Carter, Asa Earl—An Alabama native, "Ace" Carter received radio training in the navy, followed by enrollment at the University of Colorado, where he received a "certificate of journalism" in 1949. Carter worked briefly with professional anti–Semite Gerald L.K. Smith, later holding jobs as a radio newscaster in Colorado, Mississippi and Alabama. In 1955, while employed in Birmingham, his anti–Semitic broadcasts during Brotherhood Week sparked protests from the National Conference of Christians and Jews, prompting his dismissal. An early member of the Alabama Citizens' Council, Carter soon broke with leader Sam Englehardt over Carter's insistence that "the mountain people—the real redneck—is our strength." Carter founded a competing North Alabama Citizens' Council in October 1955, excluding Jews from membership and publishing a magazine, *The Southerner,* that attacked rock-and-roll as "sensuous Negro music" eroding "all the white man has built through his devotion to God." (A sign displayed at Carter's headquarters bore the legend: "Be Bop Promotes Communism.") Englehardt countered by calling Carter a "fascist," and Carter's group soon veered into violent confrontation with blacks. Six of his members assaulted singer Nat "King" Cole during a Birmingham performance in April 1956. Carter proclaimed that Cole was "a vicious agitator for integration" and sponsored a White People's Defense Fund for the defendants. Later in April 1956, John Crommelin introduced Carter to John Kasper, and their early collaboration resulted in formation of a White Youth League, while their subsequent harassment of blacks produced seventeen arrests for contempt of court. Carter also helped Kasper organize the Seaboard White Citizens' Council in Washington, D.C., and they shared the dais at a September 1956 council rally where hooded klansmen joined the audience. That same month, Carter joined Kasper for riotous demonstrations in Clinton, Tennessee, and Charlottesville, Virginia.

Two months later, Carter formally announced the creation of his own Original KKK of the Confederacy, divided into "squads and platoons with areas of responsibility." Thirty-five knights were initiated on 15 November, before a bonfire of skulls, with Carter exhorting his recruits to "fight the enemies of Jesus Christ to the bitter end and after." In December 1956, Carter announced plans for a troop of white Minutemen to patrol city buses and enforce segregation in the face of a black boycott. On 22 January 1957, Carter shot klansmen Charles Bridges and J.P. Tillery, after they rose in a meeting to protest his "one-man rule." Police jailed Carter the following day, while three others were charged with assault in the same incident. (All charges were later dismissed.) In September 1957, four of Carter's klansmen castrated Edward Aaron, a black victim, subsequently receiving twenty-year prison terms. Carter's Klan dissolved soon afterward, but he resurfaced in 1963 as "special assistant" and chief speech-writer for governor-elect George Wallace. Carter penned Wallace's infamous "segregation forever" inauguration speech, its key phrase lifted directly from the Klan's "Yesterday, Today, Forever" motto. After years of service to Wallace and his wife Lurleen (elected governor in 1966), Carter reinvented himself once again, emerging as a successful novelist. Writing as "Forrest" Carter (in honor of Nathan Bedford Forrest), the ex-wizard published the Western novels *Gone to Texas* (1973) and *The Vengeance Trail of Josey Wales* (1976)—inspiration for a popular Clint Eastwood movie—and an "oral history" of the Apaches, *Look for Me on the Mountain* (1978). His most famous work, *The Education of Little Tree* (1986), was published posthumously, falsely advertised as the autobiography of a Cherokee orphan. Carter died in 1979, his passing usually attributed to a heart attack, although the ambulance attendant who transported his body claims that Carter aspirated vomit following a drunken brawl with his son. *Little Tree* became a cult hit in the 1990s and was filmed by Hollywood in 1997.

Chaney, William Marshall—The Kentucky-reared son of a Baptist minister and a veteran of World War II, Chaney moved to Indianapolis in 1959. Appointed as the UKA's Indiana grand dragon in January 1967, he scheduled a statewide rally for 11 August, but the meeting was banned by order of the Johnson County superior court. In 1968, Chaney addressed several rallies supporting the presidential candidacy of George Wallace. Proud of his racist views, Chaney told an interviewer in March 1973 that "people are tired of seeing our white women escorted on the street by nigger bucks." On 24 August 1974, after two shooting incidents left klansmen wounded in the midst of a Kokomo recruiting drive, Chaney advised his followers to "arm every household with shotguns." In May 1976, police jailed Chaney for firebombing an Indianapolis advertising company where he had once been employed. Despite attorney J.B. Stoner's best defense, jurors convicted Chaney on three felony counts. Chaney split with the UKA at a rally in Pulaski, Tennessee, on 31 May 1976. Wizard Robert Shelton blamed his dismissal on liquor and womanizing, while Chaney cited clashes over handling of Klan funds and Shelton's tendency to talk tough with no follow-through. As a free agent, Chaney organized his own Confederation of Independent Orders, while also serving as national coordinator for the Northern and Southern Knights of the KKK. His election to the latter post occurred on 5 June 1977, at a "unity conference" where Dale Reusch, Robert Scoggin and Bill Wilkinson lost out in their bids to control the new Klan. Chaney's appeal of his arson conviction produced a new trial, and he was convicted a second time in November 1977.

Cheney, Turner—While serving as grand dragon of Illinois, Cheney was jailed on 26 September 1966 for participation in two Milwaukee, Wisconsin bombings. Targets included a linoleum store owned by the former president of the Wisconsin Civil Rights Congress (bombed on 1 July) and the Milwaukee NAACP office (9 August). On 1 May 1967, police charged Cheney with soliciting the murder of a codefendant, klansman Robert Schmidt, to prevent Schmidt from turning state's evidence.

Chopper, Phillip—As Kentucky's grand dragon, Chopper held two joint rallies with David Duke in August 1975, shar-

ing the stage with Robert Scoggin and James Warner. Afterward, he publicly accused Duke of making off with $4,000 collected at the rallies and denounced Duke as a "fraud." Duke responded by calling Chopper a "self-appointed" dragon who lacked authority and followers. On 6 September 1975, Chopper was one of seventy-five persons jailed in a white anti-busing march through Louisville. A month later, Louisiana authorities extradited Chopper to face check-fraud charges.

Christmas, Charles—Born in Meridian, Mississippi, Christmas moved to Louisiana in 1956 and joined the Original Knights three years later. After that group split up in autumn 1964, he emerged as the grand dragon of a new splinter group in the Sixth Congressional District, which included strife-torn Bogalusa. His klansmen were among the South's most violent, largely ignoring Christmas's April 1965 agreement with Bogalusa's mayor that police should handle black demonstrations without KKK interference. At the height of local rioting in 1965, Christmas allegedly chased transient agitators Connie Lynch and J.B. Stoner out of town in an effort to restore order. Still serving as grand dragon of the shrunken Original Knights in 1976, Christmas claimed an improbable 1,500 members.

Clanton, James Holt—Named in various published sources as Alabama's grand dragon during Reconstruction, Clanton was a veteran of the Mexican War (1846–48) who later served in Alabama's state legislature prior to secession. He joined the Confederate army in the Civil War and rose to the rank of general. Aside from his KKK duties in Reconstruction, Clanton doubled as chairman of the state's Democratic Party until 27 September 1871, when he was killed by a man who picked a quarrel with him in Knoxville, Tennessee.

Clary, Johnny Lee—In the September 1998 issue of *Guideposts Magazine*, Clary identified himself as "former national leader of the Ku Klux Klan, now a world-renowned civil rights leader." A resident of Tulsa, Oklahoma, Clary once also wrestled professionally (as "Johnny Angel"), recalling that he was taught from age five by his father to shout insults at blacks on the street. Clary asserts that he joined David Duke's KKKK at age fourteen, subsequently rising to the rank of Oklahoma grand dragon at twenty, after a stint as Duke's personal bodyguard. His change of heart began with a TV debate against Rev. Wade Watts, a Tulsa NAACP official whose kindness touched Clary and moved him to break with the Klan. Bible study with Watts transformed Clary into a "born-again" evangelist who supports racial harmony. No independent source confirms Clary's assertion that he served as "national leader" of any Klan faction.

Cole, Rev. James W.—Popularly known as "Catfish," Cole was an ex-carnival barker, patent medicine salesman and Freewill Baptist preacher who emerged as a Klan celebrity in the late 1950s. (He also boasted a police record dating from 1940, with several arrests for assault.) In the latter part of 1956, Cole defected from the U.S. Klans to lead his own North Carolina Knights. His chief publicity stunt was a campaign against the Lumbee Indians in Robeson County, where a three-way segregation system separated whites, blacks and Indians. Beginning on 13 January 1958, Cole's klansmen burned several crosses on property owned by Lumbees, culminating in a rally at Lumberton on 18 January. Armed Lumbees raided the gathering that night, capturing the Klan's banner and public address system, shooting up several cars, while the knights fled on foot. State police declared Cole a fugitive on 21 January, and he failed to appear at a Burlington rally where 2,000 spectators gathered on 25 January. Extradited from South Carolina for trial, Cole was convicted on 13 March 1958 for inciting a riot. He drew a prison term of eighteen months to two years, later overturned on appeal. Following a second conviction on similar charges, he escaped with payment of a fine. In 1967, Cole joined forces with George Dorsett to found a new faction, the Confederate Knights, supported with covert funding from FBI headquarters.

Coleman, Peter—Media reports from June 1999 identified Coleman as Australia's grand dragon for the Kentucky-based Imperial Klans of America. Before joining the IKA, Coleman was deputy chief of the Australian Nationalist Movement, a group linked to various hate crimes including firebombings of Asian restaurants in Perth. Coleman reportedly did much of his KKK recruiting at One Nation rallies convened throughout Australia.

Colescott, James A.—An Ohio veterinarian and early member of the 1920s Klan, Colescott won election as Ohio's grand dragon in 1925. Promotion later took him to imperial headquarters in Atlanta, where he replaced Hiram Evans as imperial wizard in June 1939. Colescott announced that his administration would be one of action, and his tenure was marked by an increase in violence against blacks and CIO organizers throughout the South. Colescott cited his goal as "mopping up the cesspools of communism in the United States," but added that "anyone who flogs, lynches or intimidates ought to be in the penitentiary." Colescott was embarrassed by Klan flirtation with the German-American Bund in 1940, and he moved to tone down anti–Semitism after the Pearl Harbor raid, announcing withdrawal of all Klan literature "of a controversial nature." In April 1944, the IRS slapped Colescott with a $685,535 in back taxes, prompting the KKK to formally dissolve at a special klonvokation on 23 April. Retiring to Florida, Colescott told reporters, "Maybe the government can make something out of the Klan. I never could." At the same time, in private comments to Stetson Kennedy, Colescott denied that the Klan had disbanded. His name appeared as imperial wizard in 1946, when Georgia klansmen renewed their state charter, but he apparently took no active role in the Klan. Chairing a board of KKK trustees in July 1946, Colescott signed a statement asking Georgia officials to drop their charter revocation lawsuit on grounds that the Klan had "ceased to exist" in 1944.

Coley, Sandy—In spring 1965, while serving as interim Virginia grand dragon for the UKA, Coley organized several klaverns around Chesapeake and Portsmouth. His recruiting drive soon flagged, however, and by late summer Marshall Kornegay replaced him.

Comer, James C.—A judge in Little Rock and Arkansas grand dragon of the 1920s Klan, Comer was an intimate friend of Hiram Evans and played a key role in helping Evans depose Wizard William Simmons in November 1922. One of six klansmen named to the Imperial Kloncilium in 1923, he helped settle the year-long dispute over ownership of KKK regalia and ritual in favor of Evans. Comer also briefly dominated the Women of the KKK through his wife's appointment as leader of that group, but opposition to his personal style and his wife's extravagant spending sparked a virtual mutiny within the Little Rock klavern by 1924.

Comer, Robbie Gill—As wife of Arkansas Grand Dragon James Comer, and as part of her husband's payoff for helping Hiram Evans become imperial wizard, Robbie Comer was named to lead the Women of the KKK. Her imperious style and free spending provoked dissatisfaction in the ranks, verging on open rebellion by 1924.

Converse, Frank—A Texas gun dealer and UKA grand dragon of Texas in the early 1970s, Converse declined to answer a Houston grand jury's questions in 1971, concerning terrorist attacks on the local Pacifica Foundation's radio station and other targets. In June 1971, Converse announced plans to run for sheriff on a platform of "sheets and sawed-off shotguns," but voters rejected his candidacy. Interviewed by Patsy Sims in 1977, Converse claimed the CIA had approached him in 1969 to arrange the murder of an unnamed Panamanian general, but the project was allegedly sidetracked when the White House withdrew its support.

Cothran, Donald—In autumn 1964, Robert Shelton appointed Cothran as the UKA's Florida grand dragon. Cothran's efforts to recruit klansmen outside Jacksonville were generally unsuccessful, with fewer than 100 enlisted statewide by 1965. In October 1965, Broward County knights accused Cothran of "dictatorial tactics" and financial mismanagement, deserting the UKA to create the United Knights of the KKK.

Craig, Calvin Fred—Encouraged by his mother, Craig and his wife joined the Georgia realm of the U.S. Klans in 1960. In January 1961, he was among eight klansmen arrested during riots at the University of Georgia, in Athens. On 21 February 1961, Craig was second-in-command when Robert Davidson chartered his new United Klans in Fulton County. Assuming full control when Davidson resigned two months later, Craig merged his faction with Robert Shelton's Alabama Knights to create the UKA in July 1961, emerging as Georgia's grand dragon. Failing to qualify for a state senate race in 1962, he later ran (unsuccessfully) for a seat on the Fulton County Democratic executive committee. Conscious of media impact, Craig told his klansmen in 1963, "Let's be nonviolent. We've got to start fighting just like the niggers." On 4 July 1964, he shared the state with Lester Maddox and Alabama Governor George Wallace at an Atlanta racist rally where two blacks were mobbed and beaten in the audience. A year later, at Crawfordsville, Georgia, police jailed Craig for assaulting a black demonstrator. Fined $1,000 for contempt of Congress following his 1965 HUAC appearance, Craig escaped the prison time imposed on Shelton and other UKA leaders. In January 1968, he was elected to a policy-making position on Atlanta's federally-funded Model

Cities program, initially shifting seats each time a black committee member sat beside him, but his views were changing. On 28 April 1968, Craig announced his resignation from the UKA, declaring that all races "should stand shoulder-to-shoulder in a united America." Three months later, he ran unsuccessfully for sheriff in Fulton County, promising to hire black deputies and vowing "not to hesitate one minute to arrest a klansman who's committed a crime." By the launch of his 1976 campaign for a seat on the Clayton County commission, Craig had rejoined the UKA, though some klansmen considered him a "sell-out."

Creel, Robert—While serving as Alabama's UKA grand dragon, between March 1964 and January 1966, Creel told reporters, "I don't believe in segregation. I believe in slavery." Creel's resignation coincided with his 5 January 1966 arrest for drunken driving, when police found a rifle and two pistols in his car. Convicted of driving while intoxicated and carrying concealed weapons, Creel paid a $300 fine, while his sixty-day jail term was suspended.

Crodser, W.H., Jr.—A resident of Columbus, Georgia, and self-proclaimed president of the Original Southern Klans in 1949, Crodser signed the application for Bill Hendrix's appointment as the OSK's resident agent in Florida.

Davidson, Robert Lee ("Wild Bill")—Serving as Georgia grand dragon for the U.S. Klans during 1957–60, Davidson earned his nickname from the fringed leather jacket he wore in his daily employment as an insurance salesman, prior to joining his father to run a bag-salvaging plant. In January 1960, he announced plans for a private Klan school in Atlanta to help white families avoid court-ordered school integration. Assuming the title of imperial wizard when Eldon Edwards died in August 1960, Davidson said of the KKK, "I'm trying to bring it out of the darkness and make it a progressive movement, not just a protest movement." In that light, he publicly rejected Robert Shelton, John Kasper, George Rockwell and the NSRP as too extreme. "I don't get myself connected with any fanatical movement," he told the press. "I can't go around lambasting Jews, Negroes and Catholics and expect to get a national following." By November 1960, his stance became more militant, complete with warnings that klansmen would use buckshot if necessary, to prevent integration. Harassed and hamstrung by lawsuits from Eldon Edwards's widow and would-be wizard E.E. George, Davidson resigned from the U.S. Klans on 18 February 1961. Three days later, with Calvin Craig, he announced formation of a new Invisible Empire, United Klans, Knights of the KKK of America, Inc. Davidson ruled the new Klan as imperial wizard until 1 April 1961, when he resigned in the midst of a dispute over KKK involvement in riots at the University of Georgia.

Davis, Willy Ray—Media reports from May 2004 identified Davis as Indiana grand dragon for an unspecified Klan. The event propelling Davis into headlines was a clash between two groups of "German history enthusiasts" (i.e., neo–Nazi skinheads) outside a fast-food restaurant in Greensboro. Davis held a press conference to call for cessation of intra-racial violence. He told reporters, "The tragedy of this incident and so many others like it is that our fine young Aryan men are killing each other, cutting one another down in the prime of their lives when they should be working together to secure justice from our oppressors." In fact, he continued, "Most of them tell me they'd rather be out chasing foreigners out of town or harassing Catholics, but since the mill closed we really don't have any of those kinds of folks around here anymore." To fill that void, Davis proposed a midnight basketball program for skinheads and held his own "Stop the Madness" rally at Kennard, Indiana, featuring a three-legged "race for supremacy" and a "running Aryans" scavenger hunt. "We're not just about Klu [*sic*] or Klux anymore. At our core, we're here to serve the Klan. We're a family-oriented hate group now."

Deputy, Paul W., Sr.—Internet postings from early 1997 identified Deputy as Delaware's grand dragon for the American Knights of the KKK, under Imperial Wizard Barry Black.

Doak, Joseph P.—As New Jersey grand dragon of the IEKKKK, Doak conspired with his wife and Grand Nighthawk Harold Patterson, Jr., to murder defectors Joseph Bednarsky and Andy Jones in 1990. Police arrested the plotters in November 1990, and all three pled guilty in July 1992. Doak received a three-year prison term on 28 August 1992.

Dodge, William—In 1992, media reports identified Dodge as Connecticut's grand dragon for the IEKKKK. Two years later, he served as grand dragon of Connecticut's Unified KKK. On 21 January of that year, authorities arrested Dodge and four other klansmen on various weapons and explosives charges. On 26 May 1994, Dodge pled guilty to possessing a pipe bomb. He received a prison term of sixty-three months.

Doerfler, Rev. Raymond—Roy Frankhouser's replacement as grand dragon of Pennsylvania in the 1970s, Doerfler addressed Robert Scoggin's Conference of Eastern Dragons in 1976. In the same year, he was publicly associated with William Chaney's Confederation of Independent Orders, greeting klansmen at one rally as "fellow terrorists." Around the same time, Doerfler persuaded klansman Jimmy Mitchell to infiltrate the ADL, reporting back to the Klan on its activities.

Drager, Frank—A resident of Trenton, New Jersey, and the state's 1970s grand dragon, Drager was jailed in September 1973 for purchasing a gun without a permit. He received a six-month jail sentence on 6 November 1976.

Draper, Ricky—On 1 April 1992, Draper announced formation of the Alabama Invisible Empire Knights, based in Morgan, Alabama. In 1996, ADL investigators identified Draper as the leader of America's Invisible Empire Knights of the KKK.

Duke, David Ernest—Born in Tulsa, Oklahoma, on 1 July 1950, Duke attended elementary school in the Netherlands before moving on to a private academy in Georgia. His family moved to New Orleans in the 1960s, where Duke graduated from high school. Entering LSU in 1968, he organized the White Youth Alliance (later the National Party) a year later, recruiting members on several college campuses. Working in collaboration with the NSLF and NSWPP, Duke donned a Nazi uniform and carried a picket sign—"Gas the Chicago Seven"—to protest a 1969 appearance by attorney William Kunstler at Tulane University. During 1971–72, New Orleans authorities accused Duke's National Party of fomenting racial unrest at local high schools. Police jailed Duke and several followers in January 1972, for manufacturing incendiary devices, then arrested him again six months later, on charges of theft by fraud while collecting funds for George Wallace's presidential campaign.

By 1973, Duke was listed as national information director and Louisiana grand dragon for the Knights of the KKK. When white Bostonians rioted against court-ordered school integration in September 1974, Duke was on hand to harangue angry crowds, his appearance producing graffiti in South Boston reading: "This is Klan Country." Taking control of the KKKK when its founder was murdered in 1975, Duke dropped the imperial wizard title to serve as "national director." (Around the same time, Gov. Wallace named Duke an honorary colonel in the Alabama state militia, to repay his past support.) In a typical speech, Duke proclaimed, "We say give us liberty and give them [blacks] death. There's times I've felt like picking up a gun and going shooting a nigger. We've got a heritage to protect. We're going to do everything to protect our race." At the same time, he sought distance from older, established Klans, seeking to recruit "other intellectuals" for his movement, welcoming Catholics and women to full KKK membership. The new approach brought marginal success in 1975, when Duke hosted the largest Klan rally in a decade—with 2,700 attending—at Walker, Louisiana. Managing his own advertising agency on the side, Duke ran for state senate that year, polling 11,079 votes (one-third of those cast). Later in 1975, Duke journeyed to Kansas City for a strategy meeting with Robert Shelton, Robert DePugh, James Warner, and other far-right leaders. Police in Metairie, Louisiana, jailed Duke for inciting a riot on 13 July 1976, after a scuffle with deputies. He lost another race for the Louisiana state senate in 1979.

On 21 July 1980, Duke met with rival Bill Wilkinson for a secret discussion attended by Alabama Grand Dragon Don Black and others. In return for $35,000, Duke offered to resign his post as leader of the KKKK, deliver his mailing list of 3,000 names to Wilkinson, and publicly name Wilkinson as the nation's most "capable and effective" Klan leader. Wilkinson rejected the offer, then went public with it, prompting Duke's resignation from the Klan on 24 July, to lead a new NAAWP. Duke described his latest venture as "more of a racialist movement, more of a high-class thing, mainly upper-middle-class people." Still, despite his apparent divorce from the Klan, Duke joined in ceremonies at Stone Mountain, Georgia, where the Confederation of Klans was created in September 1982. In January 1989, Duke astounded his critics by winning a GOP primary race for the state legislature in Metairie. Despite renunciations from the White House and national GOP leaders, Duke won a narrow victory in the general election, but he proved to be a one-term wonder, and his subsequent campaigns for the White House proved futile.

Duke continued his international travels with a visit to Russia in 1995, where he met with far-right leaders to discuss fu-

DAVID DUKE FOR GOVERNOR
A <u>Real Choice</u> for a Change

Cut the Fat, No Tax Increases
Louisiana has the highest personal tax rate of any Southern state, higher taxes than even Teddy Kennedy's Massachusetts! Hard-working, middle class people are already taxed too much and I say **enough is enough!** Gov. Roemer has tried to raise taxes even more than "Super Taxer," Edwin Edwards. He raised sales taxes and telephone taxes, increased fees, tried to triple income taxes, and tried to destroy the Homestead Exemption; I stand firmly against tax increases on the working person or the small businessman.

Scrub the Budget -- Duke Action vs. Roemer Rhetoric
Gov. Roemer took office promising to scrub Edwards' bloated budget. Edwards' last fat budget was $6.7 billion. Roemer's proposed budget is over $9 billion, a 34% increase from Edwards' already sky-high budget -- in just one term!

A Balanced Budget
Instead of cutting the budget as he promised, Roemer's first act as Governor was to borrow one billion dollars. $500 million was used on the first year's expenditures. He has left us a crushing debt of $700 million that we and our children will pay. Borrowing is not balancing. I will not increase our state debt. I will use the line-item veto to eliminate waste.

Reduce the Size of Government
Big Government has grown by leaps and bounds under Edwards and Roemer. We have twice the number of state employees, per capita, as our neighbor, Texas. And while we have not given our current employees and retirees a fair raise, Big Government continues to expand with more boards, commissions, and employees! Government is out of control! I will implement a hiring freeze and let attrition reduce the size of our top-heavy state bureaucracy.

David Duke dominated Klan affairs in the late 1970s, while campaigning for various offices.

ture alliances. Three years later, publication of his autobiography (*My Awakening*, 1998) created a furor when Florida college professor Glayde Whitney contributed a glowing foreword. Slapped with an IRS tax lien in 1999, Duke belatedly paid up after blaming his accountant for the "mistake." A federal grand jury also questioned Duke about his finances in 1999, but he invoked the Fifth Amendment during both appearances. In January 2000 he abandoned the NAAWP to lead NOFEAR, described as a "civil rights" group created to fight the "massive discrimination" suffered by white Americans. Duke was midway through his fourth visit to Russia when FBI agents raided his Louisiana home, in November 2002, and he spent the next two years in self-imposed exile, fraternizing with neo–Nazis from Moscow to France, Italy and Germany. In June 2001, he changed NOFEAR's name to EURO, and three months later—after the terrorist attacks of 11 September—began billing himself as "one of the leading commentators in the world on the Mideast conflict."

Duke returned from Russia on 14 December 2002, and four days later he pled guilty to federal fraud charges in Washington, D.C. EURO spokesmen blamed his incarceration in "The

Gulag"—i.e., Texas—on a federal effort to suppress "the truth" about 9/11. Paroled in May 2004, Duke flew to New Orleans for a racist unity conference sponsored by EURO, the CCC, the National Alliance and Willis Carto. Addressing an audience of 300, while some 67,000 viewed a simulcast of the proceedings over EURO's website, Duke introduced his "New Orleans Protocol," a set of racist principles "pledging adherence to a pan–European outlook" and (ironically) commitment to "honorable and ethical behavior." Signatories of the protocol included Carto, Don Black, Edward Fields, plus National Alliance leaders Don Pringle and Kevin Strom. At last report, Duke was busy working on another memoir, *For Love of My People.* Longtime aide Roy Armstrong claims that another Duke opus, *Jewish Supremacism,* has sold more than 850,000 copies worldwide.

Duncan, Dr. Amos—Duncan served as North Carolina's grand dragon under Wizard James Colescott, during 1939–44.

Dutton, Jerry—Georgia native Jerry Dutton organized the Knights of the Confederacy while still in high school. He later moved to Birmingham, Alabama, and joined the NSRP, named among eight party members indicted on 23 September 1963 for violent interference with school integration. Eight years later, he resurfaced as Alabama grand dragon of the Louisiana-based Knights of the KKK. Dutton left the KKKK in 1977, after James Warner accused him of stealing Klan funds, and shifted his allegiance to Bill Wilkinson's Invisible Empire Knights.

Edwards, Eldon Lee—A resident of College Park, Georgia, Edwards worked as a paint sprayer at the General Motors Fisher Body Plant in Atlanta before devoting himself full-time to the KKK. In 1953, he gathered remnants of the old AGK into a new U.S. Klans, formally chartered in October 1955. Two months later, on 27 December, police jailed him for drunk driving, disorderly conduct, assaulting an officer and resisting arrest. Most of the charges were dismissed, leaving Edwards to pay a $50 fine. By 1958, when he testified as a character witness at the bombing trial of NSRP member George Bright, Edwards was the nation's preeminent wizard, claiming an estimated 15,000 followers in ten states. He died of a heart attack at age fifty-four, on 1 August 1960.

Edwards, James Malcolm—Elected as Louisiana grand dragon for the UKA in 1964, Edwards presided over the state's greatest period of Klan growth. In 1965, he addressed a letter to HUAC, urging Chairman Edwin Willis "to investigate the United Klans and make your findings public as soon as possible." Presumably, Edwards felt the probe would clear the Klan's reputation, but his superiors disagreed. In December 1965, shortly before his own HUAC testimony, Edwards was dismissed and replaced by former Grand Klaliff Jack Helm.

Edwards, Ronald—A resident of Dawson Springs, Kentucky, Edwards emerged as the dominant KKK leader of the early twenty-first century, Imperial Klans of American claiming thirty-four klaverns in twenty-four states at the close of 2004. That growth represented a strong comeback from 1999, when ATF and FBI agents joined Kentucky State Police in a

series of sweeping raids against the IKA, on 14 April. Striking at the homes of Edwards, his imperial knighthawk and two other klansmen, the raiders seized computers, literature and alleged bomb-making components, but no convictions were recorded as of press time for this volume. Edwards denounced the raids as a government "witch hunt," planned to disrupt a scheduled White Unity Gathering on 29 April 1999. Given the long history of federal harassment against fringe groups of both left and right, the charge may well be true.

Effinger, V.F.—An electrical contractor from Lima, Ohio, and a high-ranking klansman through 1931, Effinger took command of the rival Black Legion when that group expanded beyond its original base in Detroit, Michigan.

Ellington, Doyle—A resident of Brownsville, Texas, Ellington was identified in 1968 as Texas grand dragon for the UKA.

Ellis, Dr. A.D.—An Episcopal minister in Beaumont, Texas, Ellis was also the first grand dragon of the modern Texas realm, elected in 1922. His klavern was also the first in Texas to make headlines with floggings and other terroristic acts. That

Eldon Edwards led the dominant Klan of the late 1950s (Florida State Archives).

publicity soon forced imperial headquarters to lift the Beaumont klavern's charter.

Esdale, James—Alabama's grand dragon in the 1920s, Esdale was attacked by Birmingham newspapers for his speeches advocating flogging of Klan opponents. Nonetheless, despite pervasive violence in his realm, Esdale's friendship with Governor (and klansman) Bibb Graves made him legally untouchable. Esdale's political efforts ranged far afield, including circulation of anti–Catholic literature published in an effort to defeat Virginia state treasurer John Purcell.

Evans, Dr. Hiram Wesley—A Dallas dentist and exalted cyclops of the largest Texas klavern after World War I, Evans later served as grand titan of Province No. 2. Congressional testimony linked him personally to the flogging and acid-branding of a black Dallas bellhop. In 1921, Edward Clarke summoned Evans to Atlanta, elevating him to the rank of imperial kligrapp in charge of the Klan's thirteen chartered realms. Evans traveled widely, plotting with Indiana's David Stephenson and others to advance himself over Klan founder William Simmons. In November 1922, his allies muscled Simmons out of power, with Evans assuming the throne, but disputes over cash and KKK regalia dragged on into 1924. The following year, with an estimated four million klansmen under his nominal control, Evans marched with 40,000 members through Washington, D.C. In 1927, he was invited to sit on the dais at Georgia Governor Charles McCall's inauguration, as a gesture of gratitude for KKK electoral support. Unable to reverse the Klan's eventual decline, Evans ordered his knights to unmask in summer 1928. Eight years later, he announced that the Klan was deemphasizing "racial and religious matters" to focus on "communism and the CIO." Late in 1936, an insurance company bought the Klan's headquarters in Atlanta, then embarrassed Evans by selling it to the Catholic Church. Hard-core klansmen were furious in 1939, when Evans accepted an invitation to the grand opening of a new rectory for the Cathedral of Christ the King, but Evans considered the outing "a good exit." Retiring from the KKK in June 1939, he was replaced by James Colescott. When Dr. Samuel Green sought to revive the Klan in 1946, Evans wistfully declared, "You can't start a fire in wet ashes."

Farnsworth, Eugene—An ex-member of a Salvation Army band, Farnsworth emerged as the 1920s grand dragon of Maine, with additional responsibility for klansmen in New Hampshire and Vermont. Operating from his tri-state headquarters in Bangor, Farnsworth drew attention in 1924 with the announcement that he would personally select Maine's next governor. When he failed to deliver, imperial headquarters replaced Farnsworth with Dr. E.W. Gayer.

Farrands, James Wilfred—Connecticut Catholic James Farrands replaced Bill Wilkinson as imperial wizard of the IEKKKK in 1986, subsequently moving Klan headquarters from his home state to North Carolina. He succeeded in recouping Wilkinson's losses to some extent, including sponsorship of Maine's first Klan rally in half a century (1987), and in 1989 he visited England to recruit international members (including Ian Donaldson, leader of the racist band Skrewdriver). A side trip to Wales included meetings with like-minded bigots from Wales, Scotland and West Germany. Around the same time, Farrands also announced a recruitment campaign in Australia. Farrands boasted klaverns in seventeen states by 1993, when disaster struck in the form of a federal lawsuit filed by the SPLC on behalf of Georgia blacks beaten by klansmen in 1987. A court order in that case disbanded the IEKKKK nationwide, while Farrands retreated to Connecticut, then disbanded his unit in 1999.

Fields, Edward Reed—Introduced to Nazi philosophy at age fourteen, when he attended an Atlanta meeting of the Columbians, Fields later worked with George Van Horn Moseley's Free Emory Burke Committee, attempting to liberate the Columbians' leader from prison. In October 1950, when Atlanta's first desegregation lawsuit was filed, Fields responded by distributing pamphlets headlined: "Jewish Communists Behind Atlanta's School Segregation Suit." While attending law school in Atlanta during 1952, Fields teamed with J.B. Stoner to found the Christian Anti-Jewish Party. An Iowa chiropractic school distracted Fields during 1953–56, and by 1957 he had settled in Louisville, Kentucky, using his spare time to recruit members for the Citizens' Council and the United White Party (renamed the NSRP in 1958). Fields copied the NSRP's thunderbolt insignia from the Columbians (who stole it from Hitler's SS), and sponsored an "Anti-Jew Week," plastering windows of Jewish-owned shops with anti–Semitic posters. In 1958, he testified at George Bright's Atlanta bombing trial, and three years later Fields was cited for contempt of court after proceeding with a banned racist rally at Fairfield, Alabama. (The U.S. Supreme Court reversed that conviction on 16 December 1963.) In September 1963, Fields was one of eight NSRP members indicted for violent interference with school integration in Birmingham,

Hiram Evans (left) replaced Simmons as imperial wizard in November 1922. Here, he poses with a member of the original KKK (Georgia Department of Archives and History).

Alabama. When state attorney general Bill Baxley reopened investigations of a fatal Birmingham church bombing in 1976, Fields fired off a letter of protest. (Baxley replied: "My response to your letter of February 19, 1976, is—kiss my ass.") In 1980, Fields attended the first national conference of Don Black's KKKK in Alabama, and in 1981 he hosted a banquet in Marietta, Georgia, honoring klansmen and neo–Nazis who murdered five persons in Greensboro, North Carolina. In 1982–83, representing both the NSRP and his own Georgia-based New Order Knights of the KKK, Fields attended rallies that produced a new Confederation of Klans.

Flinn, Darrell—In 1996, ADL investigators named Flinn as head of the Louisiana-based Invisible Knights of the KKK.

Fogel, Richard—In June 1988, Fogel was identified as Pennsylvania's grand dragon.

Ford, Richard—Identified as leader of Florida's Fraternal White Knights in 1990, Ford actively recruited neo–Nazi skinheads for his short-lived order.

Ford, William—Media reports from 2002 identified Ford as Virginia's grand dragon for the Mystic knights of the KKK.

Foreman, Gene—In 1966, HUAC identified Foreman as grand dragon of the Jacksonville, Florida, Militant Knights, serving as second-in-command to Imperial Wizard Donald Ballentine.

Forman, Wilbur—Named in media reports as the Illinois grand dragon of an unspecified Klan, Forman attended Robert Scoggin's Conference of Eastern Dragons in 1976.

Forney, William Henry—Several historians name William Forney as Alabama's grand dragon during Reconstruction, either as the lone occupant of that office or as successor to John T. Morgan. An attorney, veteran of the Mexican War (1846–48) and trustee of the University of Alabama (1851–60), Forney also served in the state legislature (1859–60). During the Civil War, he joined the Confederate army as a captain and advanced to the rank of brigadier general. After "redemption," he served eight terms in Congress (1875–93) and died in January 1894.

Forrest, Nathan Bedford—A wealthy slave trader and cotton planter before the Civil War, Forrest served as a general in the Confederate army and left his mark on history as a cavalry leader who offered opponents the choice of unconditional surrender or annihilation. On 12 April 1864, his troops captured the Union garrison at Fort Pillow, Tennessee, proceeding to massacre some 250 black soldiers (including some who were burned or buried alive). His semiliterate report of that engagement read, in part: "We bust the fort at ninerclock and scattered the niggers. The men are still a killenem in the woods." Later, with ample time to clean up his grammar, Forrest wrote, "The river was dyed with the blood of the slaughtered for two hundred yards. It is hoped that these facts will demonstrate to the Northern people that Negro soldiers cannot cope with Southerners." A pardon from President Andrew Johnson spared Forrest from prosecution as a war criminal, and in 1867 he was named grand wizard of the Reconstruction Klan. Traveling through the South as a railroad insurance representative, Forrest was "coincidentally" present when Klan dens were organized in Alabama, Arkansas, Georgia, Mississippi and North Carolina. Interviewed in August 1868, he claimed a following of 40,000 klansmen in Tennessee and 500,000 throughout Dixie. Staunchly denying any racist motives, Forrest told the interviewer, "I have no powder to burn killing Negroes. I intend to kill the radicals. There is not a radical leader in this town but is a marked man, and if trouble should break out, none of them would be left alive." Despite such statements, Forrest denied Klan membership, but granted that he was "in sympathy and will cooperate with them." Five months later, forgetting his denials, Forrest issued "General Order Number One" on 25 January 1869, ordering all Ku Klux disguises "entirely abolished and destroyed" in the presence of local Klan leaders. Unfortunately for Klan victims, his order had no apparent effect outside Tennessee.

By 1870, as an apostle of the "New South," Forrest traveled on railroad business with Alabama Republican William Blackford, a circumstance that die-hard klansmen found "disgraceful and disgusting." Nonetheless, North Carolina klans-

General Nathan Bedford Forrest, slave trader and war criminal, was the Klan's first national leader (Library of Congress).

men held Forrest's business by discouraging black competitors from recruiting railroad workers. A year later, testifying before Congress, Forrest still denied Klan membership (though he admitted joining the Order of Pale Faces), yet he spoke with seeming authority on the KKK's origin and purpose. According to Forrest, the Klan grew out of "insecurity felt by many Southern people. Many Northern men were coming down there, forming Leagues all over the country. The Negroes were holding night meetings; were going about; were becoming very insolent; and the Southern people were very much alarmed. Parties organized themselves so as to be ready in case they were attacked. Ladies were ravished by some of those Negroes. There was a great deal of insecurity. This organization was got up to protect the weak, with no political intention at all." Stopped by a reporter as he left that hearing, Forrest smiled and quipped that he had "lied like a gentleman" while under oath.

Forrest, Nathan Bedford III—A grandson of the Klan's original grand wizard, Forrest was also a high school classmate of James Venable and an aide to William Simmons in the 1915 KKK revival. Launching his career in Atlanta as exalted cyclops of Nathan Bedford Forrest Klan No. 1, he later rose to serve as Georgia's grand dragon. One of six klansmen chosen for the imperial kloncilium to settle financial disputes between Simmons and Hiram Evans in 1923, Forrest moved on a year later to serve on the Klan's strategy board at the Democratic National Convention. A moderate as klansmen go, Forrest once complained of getting twenty calls a week from persons hoping that the KKK would flog their enemies; one woman even asked him to arrange a lynching. Forrest's death, near the end of the Great Depression, marked a day of mourning for klansmen nationwide.

Foster, C. Edward—A Pennsylvania truck driver, born in 1950, Foster served as grand dragon for the American Knights of the KKK in 1997. That April, he led forty-seven klansmen and six skinheads in an hour-long "hate opera" at Pittsburgh's City-County Building, while 1,000 hecklers jeered and lobbed stones from beyond a chain-link fence. "The gloves are off," Foster told his audience. "It's all-out white revolution. Right now we are building an army that will liberate every city in America."

Fox, Dale—Media reports in 2001–02 identified Fox as Illinois grand dragon for the Imperial Klans of America. Wizard Ron Edwards reportedly expelled Fox in March 2002, "for reasons unknown."

Frankhouser, Roy E.—The product of a bitter parental custody fight and three years in a state children's home, Frankhouser pursued his search for "family" as a young adult into the ANP, NRP, NSRP, Minutemen and the UKA. With more than sixty arrests on various charges, he earned the nickname "Riot Roy" from fellow klansmen, for displays of aggressive violence. A typical case occurred on 1 September 1961, when Frankhouser was jailed for disturbing the peace and assaulting a policeman at a UKA rally in Atlanta. In hometown Reading, Pennsylvania, he lost one eye in a 1965 tavern brawl. That summer, Wizard Robert Shelton named Frankhouser grand dragon of Pennsylvania, with additional recruiting duties in New York, New Jersey, Maryland and Delaware. With widespread contacts

on the neo–Nazi fringe, Frankhouser enlisted many brownshirts as klansmen (including future New York Grand Dragon Dan Burros), sometimes arranging joint rallies to pad the turnout. Shelton was initially reluctant to accept fascists, but he soon realized that the northern Klan would have to draw its membership from like-minded groups.

On 4 October 1965, Frankhouser reported an attempt on his life, but police identified no suspects. Six months later, Delaware's attorney general claimed that Frankhouser controlled that state's UKA organization, with Grand Titan Bennie Sartin "just a puppet goose-stepping along behind Frankhouser." To gain publicity, Frankhouser announced a June 1966 march from Gettysburg to Washington, D.C., protesting James Meredith's "walk against fear" in Mississippi. On 8 October 1966, police jailed Frankhouser and two other klansmen for disorderly conduct during an NAACP demonstration at Philadelphia's Girard College. In spring 1972, when New York City banned public display of Nazi uniforms, Frankhouser and fourteen NRP members marched on Rhodesia's National Tourist Board in full regalia, to test the law's constitutionality. Two years later, on 1 March 1974, a Philadelphia grand jury indicted Frankhouser and two others on charges of receiving and selling stolen explosives (specifically, 240 pounds of TNT delivered to a former bodyguard of Robert Miles). That indictment ended Frankhouser's long, covert career as a federal informant, including an alleged assignment with White House approval, to infiltrate a Canadian cell of the Black September terrorist group.

Acquitted of the explosives charges at trial, and despite his exposure as an FBI "rat," Frankhouser remained active in the UKA through the early 1980s, describing himself as the Klan's "counterintelligence and informational officer." At the same time, he lead a Reading congregation of the Mountain Church of Jesus Christ, founded by Robert Miles. In February 1983, Frankhouser raised eyebrows by collaborating with black community activists in a drive to reduce unemployment and crime. When journalists questioned his "credibility and sincerity in working with blacks," Frankhouser replied, "Make no mistake about it, I don't renounce my past associations or affiliations. I was dedicated to them when I belonged, and I still belong to them in one way or another." In 1985, Frankhouser joined Tom Metzger and other neo–Nazis at a Michigan meeting with Black Muslim leaders. In December 1987, while serving as an aide to extremist presidential candidate Lyndon LaRouche, Frankhouser was convicted in Boston of plotting to obstruct a federal investigation of LaRouche's purported credit card frauds. Seven years after that conviction, in November 1994, FBI agents charged Frankhouser with obstructing their investigation of a Massachusetts skinhead gang by persuading the relative of one criminal suspect to destroy evidence. Jurors convicted Frankhouser in that case on 16 February 1995. He was free again by August 1998, to face a lawsuit filed against himself and other neo–Nazis faced a harassment lawsuit by Reading fair-housing activists and the SPLC. The final judgment cost defendant Ryan Wilson and his ALPHA HQ group $1 million, while Frankhouser was ordered to attend eighty hours of sensitivity training and perform 1,000 hours of community service. In regard to the classes, Frankhouser told reporters, "Hey, if the taxpayers want to foot the bill, God bless 'em. If they don't give me lunch, I won't go." In September 2001, Frankhouser led a tiny demonstration with nine other robed klansmen of uncertain affiliation, in Lancaster County, Pennsylvania.

Gaile, Gordon—In 1976, Gaile served as Mississippi grand dragon for Bill Wilkinson's IEKKKK.

Gamble, Tony—Media reports identified Gamble as imperial wizard of the Tri-State Knight Riders of the KKK in 1997. On 25 August of that year, police in Cincinnati, Ohio, charged him with rape and sodomy, related to his alleged molestation of a thirteen-year-old girl. Gamble's sexual assaults on that child supposedly spanned eighteen months.

Garcia, George—In the 1930s, Garcia served as Florida's grand dragon under Wizard Hiram Evans.

Garland, Augustus Hill—A Tennessee native who later settled in Arkansas, Garland was a delegate to the Razorback State's secession convention in 1861 and later served in the Confederate Congress (1861–65). Some historians name him as grand dragon of Arkansas during Reconstruction. He subsequently served as governor of Arkansas (1874–77), then moved on to the U.S. Senate (1877–85), before serving as U.S. Attorney General under President Grover Cleveland (1885–89). Garland died on 26 January 1899, while arguing a case before the U.S. Supreme Court.

Augustus Garland, named in some accounts as grand dragon of Arkansas, later served as U.S. Attorney General.

Gayer, Dr. E.W.—As the 1920s successor to Eugene Farnsworth, controlling the tri-state realm of Maine, New Hampshire and Vermont, Farnsworth moved Klan headquarters from Bangor to Rochester, New Hampshire, there presiding over the realm's swift decline.

George, Rev. E.E.—Backed by the widow of Eldon Edwards, George challenged Robert Davidson for control of the U.S. Klans in winter 1960, assuming command when Davidson resigned in February 1961. On 26 October 1963, klansmen in College Park, Georgia, advised George that a secret klonvokation had voted his removal from office, based on financial irregularities. George responded by leading most of the group's membership into a new faction, the Improved Order of U.S. Klans, based at Lithonia, Georgia. HUAC estimated total membership around 100 in 1967.

George, James Zacariah—A Georgia native who later settled in Mississippi, George was a veteran of the Mexican War (1846–48) and an attorney who served as reporter of the Mississippi Supreme Court in 1854. Seven years later, he was a delegate to Mississippi's secession convention, then joined the Confederate army and rose to the rank of brigadier general. Several historians name him as Mississippi's Reconstruction–era grand dragon. After "redemption," he was appointed to the state supreme court (1879) and later elected chief justice. He later served in the U.S. Senate (1881–97) and died in office on 14 August 1897.

Giddens, Ira W.—A resident of Hartselle, Alabama, Giddens replaced Bill McGlocklin as grand dragon of the Alabama Knights on 30 March 1992.

Gifford, Fred—A Portland, Oregon, power company employee, Gifford became Oregon's grand dragon in 1921 and soon emerged as the top Klan leader west of the Rockies. As his power increased, he won election to the board of Oregon's Federation of Patriotic Societies, created to endorse "American" candidates for office. Gifford's authoritarian style and mishandling of cash drove Salem's klansmen to leave the order en masse. In one notorious case, Gifford swindled klansmen out of their investments in Skyline Corporation, founded to build a Klan skyscraper that never materialized, while similar schemes included a nonexistent WCTU children's camp near Corvallis. Further criticized for dominating the Ladies of the Invisible Empire, Gifford refused to surrender his post, creating internal dissension that eventually doomed the Oregon Klan.

Gilliam, Harry—A resident of Spartanburg, South Carolina and next-door neighbor of UKA Grand Dragon Robert Scoggin, Grand Klaliff Harry Gilliam replaced Scoggin when Scoggin was imprisoned during 1969, for contempt of Congress. His refusal to step down after Scoggin's release sparked a bitter power struggle, resulting in Scoggin's banishment from the UKA. Gilliam, in turn, was soon replaced by Dean Williams.

Gollub, Jordan—Raised in Pennsylvania and identified in 1989 as imperial wizard of the Mississippi Christian Knights of the KKK, Poplarville resident Jordan Gollub was deposed in May of that year, after klansmen discovered his parents were Jewish. Gollub staunchly proclaimed his commitment to Christianity and blamed his ouster on rival Klan leader Virgil Griffin, who allegedly disliked Gollub's "background and the fact that I'm against Catholics joining the Klan." In parting, Gollub announced plans to found a new KKK faction, but it never materialized.

Gordon, George Washington—Born in 1836, an

ex–Confederate general and one of the Tennessee Klan's earliest recruits in Reconstruction, Gordon is widely credited with drafting the order's original prescript in 1867. He was also the chief organizer of the April 1867 conference in Nashville, which reorganized the KKK as an instrument of political terrorism. While serving as Tennessee's grand dragon, in July 1868, Gordon sent R.J. Brunson to organize dens in South Carolina, but the Klan's increasing violence soon repulsed him. Gordon joined Grand Wizard Forrest and others in pleading with Gov. William Brownlow to disband the state militia, citing black troops as an irritant bound to provoke further mayhem. On 3 August 1868, Gordon addressed a crowd in Pulaski, pleading for an end to nightriding, and his influence soon helped to curb local terror. Memphis voters elected Gordon to Congress in 1907, and he served until his death in 1911.

Gordon, John Brown—A Georgia native, born in Feb-

ruary 1832, Gordon served the Confederacy as a general, then maintained his taste for military action as Georgia's grand dragon during Reconstruction. Black votes prevented his election as governor in 1868, but following Georgia's "redemption" for

John B. Gordon was Georgia's first grand dragon, later a governor and U.S. Senator.

"home rule," white Democrats sent him to the U.S. Senate (1873–80, 1891–97) and also granted him one term in the state house (1886–90). During his first Senate term, Gordon was a member of the Democratic delegation that negotiated delivery of the White House to GOP candidate Rutherford Hayes in 1877, extracting as his price the end of southern Reconstruction and Washington's de facto abandonment of black citizens in Dixie. After his second Senate term, Gordon retired to Florida and died in Miami on 9 January 1904.

Grady, Henry A.—A superior court judge and North Car-

olina's grand dragon during 1922–27, Grady was a member of the court-appointed board that supervised the transfer of imperial power from William Simmons to Hiram Evans in 1923. Three years later, he clashed with Evans over masked demonstrations and Klan involvement in politics. Evans finally banished Grady for refusing to support a package of "silly, unseemly, and unconstitutional" bills sponsored by imperial headquarters, targeting blacks and Catholics. Still occupying his judicial bench at New Bern in February 1952, Grady personally announced the mass arrest of KKK floggers, declaring, "There is no place in North Carolina for the Ku Klux Klan."

Green, Dr. Samuel, Sr.—An Atlanta obstetrician, Green

joined the KKK in the early 1920s and worked his way up to serve as Georgia's grand dragon in the 1930s, acting as Wizard James Colescott's right-hand man. A month after Colescott's April 1944 disbandment order, Green organized the AGK, holding together a loose network of klaverns in Georgia, Alabama, Florida, South Carolina and Tennessee. The AGK's existence was formally announced in October 1945, with a cross-burning at Stone Mountain, and Green presided over the Klan's greatest period of growth in the late 1940s. In Georgia politics, he maintained close ties to the Talmadge family, and Green was treated to a lively ovation by Gov. Strom Thurmond's South Carolina state legislature in 1948. The tide began to turn in 1949, as "bolshevik Klans" competed with the AGK for mem-

Grand Dragon Samuel Green (with sword) initiates new members in 1946.

bers and money, while journalists and politicians increasingly condemned Klan violence. In July 1949, Green told a black interviewer, "If God wanted us all to be equal, He would have made all people white men." A special klonkave elevated Green to imperial wizard in early August 1949, but his glory was fleeting. A heart attack claimed his life on 18 August, and Samuel Roper replaced Green at the AGK's helm nine days later.

Greene, Jerry—After serving briefly as grand dragon of New Jersey, Greene moved to South Carolina in 1976 and launched an abortive congressional race.

Griffin, Virgil—A high school dropout and textile mill worker who joined the KKK at age eighteen, Griffin succeeded Joseph Bryant as grand dragon of the North Carolina Knights of the KKK, later emerging as imperial wizard of the Christian Knights. He attended Robert Scoggin's Conference of Eastern Dragons in 1976, and two years later met with Greensboro members of the NSPA to create a United Racist Front. Griffin's klansmen accepted a public challenge from the Communist Workers' Party to attend an anti–Klan rally at Greensboro on 3 November 1979, resulting in five deaths. After jurors acquitted the gunmen, Griffin declared, "I don't see any difference between killing communists in Vietnam and killing them here." A separate jury held Griffin civilly liable for the slayings, but that judgment failed to put him out of business. In 1988, his Klan supported David Duke's presidential campaign. Griffin led two demonstrations in Washington, D.C., in 1990, and his Klan conducted weekly demonstrations throughout the Carolinas, Georgia, and Virginia during 1991–92. Shrunken to a single klavern, operating from Griffin's home at Holly Springs, the Christian Knights finally dissolved in 2000.

Griffin, William J.—Griffin founded the Association of Florida Ku Klux Klans in July 1953 and reportedly disbanded the group two years later. By 1960, however, he was competing with Bill Hendrix for dominance of the Florida realm. His public endorsement of Richard Nixon for president became an embarrassing public issue during Nixon's televised debates with JFK in October 1960. On 13 October, in their crucial third debate, Kennedy was asked about a statement from his publicist that "all bigots will vote for Nixon." Kennedy replied, "Well, Mr. Griffin, I believe, who is the head of the Klan, who lives in Tampa, Florida, indicated in a statement, I think, two or three weeks ago, that he was not going to vote for me, and that he was going to vote for Mr. Nixon. I do not suggest in any way—nor have I ever—that that indicates that Mr. Nixon has the slightest sympathy in regard to the Ku Klux Klan." Nixon echoed that rejection, but in an election where black votes made a vital difference, the disavowal was too little and too late. In Tampa, Griffin told reporters, "I don't give a damn what Nixon said. I'm still voting for him."

Hamby, Boyd Lee, Sr.—A North Carolina native, Hamby served as grand nighthawk for the UKA under Grand Dragon James Jones until late 1965. In September of that year, after Rev. Roy Woodle quit the UKA and offered embarrassing testimony before HUAC, Hamby reportedly visited Woodle's home and told Woodle he had been given "the authority to do away with me." A few weeks later, Wizard Robert Shelton sent Hamby and George Dorsett to recruit klansmen in Florida. Hamby emerged as grand dragon of the Florida realm, with headquarters at Titusville.

Hamilton, Thomas L.—An Atlanta wholesale grocer and onetime aide to Samuel Green in the AGK, Hamilton moved to Leesville, South Carolina, in 1948, there dividing his time between the grocery business and the invisible empire. Within a year, Hamilton Association of Carolina Klans demanded his full attention, with klansmen kicking off a two-year reign of terror that spanned two states, including dozens of kidnappings and floggings. On 31 August 1950, ACK members raided Charlie Fitzgerald's dance hall at Myrtle Beach, South Carolina, resulting in one death (a klansman) and several injuries (including Fitzgerald, who was beaten and had both ears severed). Police jailed Hamilton for conspiracy to incite mob violence in that case, but prosecutors declined to proceed with a trial. On 18 September, Hamilton was jailed again on identical charges, this time related to an August 1950 whipping. A new state law against cross-burning prompted Hamilton's third arrest, on 19 May 1951, after he led a motorcade through Conway, South Carolina, with an electric cross mounted on his car. Five months later, on 30 October 1951, jurors convicted Hamilton of criminal libel for his attacks on a newsman in Anderson, South Carolina. Hamilton paid a $1,000 fine in that case, then went back to jail on conspiracy charges, for two North Carolina whippings, on 24 May 1952. Indictments issued on 19 June charged Hamilton and twenty-three others with kidnapping, conspiracy, and assault in the flogging of seven victims. In July 1952, Hamilton pled no contest in one case and received a four-year prison term. In custody, he formally renounced his Klan membership, urging his followers to disband on 22 October 1953. Few remained by that time, as the Greensboro *Daily News* reported that the "Tarhellias *Führer* of the meat counter and vegetable bins" had received his comeuppance. Paroled in February 1954, Hamilton apparently made good on his promise to avoid the KKK.

Hampton, Wade—A South Carolina native, born in March 1818, Hampton served in the state legislature (1852–56, 1858–61) and joined the Confederate army after secession, wounded three times in the Civil War while he rose to the rank of lieutenant general. Stetson Kennedy names Hampton as South Carolina's grand dragon during Reconstruction, and while other historians question that claim, Hampton indisputably raised a private (and illegal) company to terrorize blacks in 1870. Six years later, with the KKK presumably defunct, Hampton led "Red Shirt" terrorists to "redeem" South Carolina and install himself as governor (1876–79). At the outset of that campaign, Hampton told his thugs: "In speeches to negroes you must remember that argument has no effect upon them. They can only be influenced by their fears, superstition and cupidity. Do not attempt to flatter and persuade them.... Treat them so as to show them you are the superior race, and that their natural position is that of subordination to the white man." As governor, in 1877, Hampton persuaded President Rutherford Hayes to dismiss out-

Wade Hampton, named in several accounts as South Carolina's first grand dragon, later used "Red Shirt" terrorists to win election as governor and U.S. Senator.

standing charges against fugitive klansman J. Rufus Bratton, permitting Bratton to return from exile in Canada. Hampton subsequently served in the U.S. Senate (1879–91) and as U.S. railroad commissioner (1893–97). He died on 11 April 1902.

Handley, Roger—In 1979, Handley served as Alabama grand dragon for Bill Wilkinson's IEKKKK. Active in fomenting violent rallies around Decatur, in connection with the rape trial of black defendant Tommy Lee Hines, Handley also donated forty-seven acres of land near Cullman for establishment of a paramilitary training center dubbed Camp My Lai (after the site of a U.S. Army massacre of unarmed civilians in Vietnam). In statements to the press, Handley described the camp as one of several facilities in Alabama, claiming that locations were frequently changed to ensure tight security. In 1989, as losers in a federal lawsuit filed by the SPLC, Handley and nine other klansmen were ordered to pay $11,500 each to blacks injured in the Decatur riots. They were also ordered to attend classes in race relations, taught by members of the SPLC, a verdict which Imperial Wizard James Farrands denounced as "cruel and unusual punishment."

Harcus, William—A resident of Winnipeg, Canada, born in 1970, Harcus dabbled in Satanism before converting to Christian Identity as a teenager and joining the SS Action Group. In October 1989, while corresponding with the Missouri Knights of the KKK, he joined Dennis Godin to publish a neo–Nazi magazine, *Maximum National Socialism.* In April 1990 Harcus founded the Manitoba Knights of the KKK, serving as grand dragon. Authorities jailed him on 18 December 1991, for advocating genocide, but the charges were dismissed at trial based on evidence of police perjury.

Harper, Julius—In 1964, Harper served as grand dragon for the WKKKKM, acting as second-in-command to Imperial Wizard Sam Bowers. In October of that year, after FBI agents jailed several Klan bombers around McComb, Harper warned other klansmen to bury any explosives they might have on hand, thus preserving them for future use.

Harris, David—Identified as Wisconsin's grand dragon in 1966, Harris was the target of gunmen who fired into his Waukesha home on 8 October. Denouncing the subsequent police investigation as a "whitewash," while vowing retaliation, Harris posted armed guards (including bombing suspect Robert Long) around his house. The attack was not repeated.

Harris, Jim—Cincinnati resident Jim Harris replaced Flynn Harvey as Ohio grand dragon of the UKA in late 1965. On 11 September 1972, he announced Wizard Robert Shelton's order for all klansmen to undergo polygraph tests, in an effort to weed out government informants. According to Harris, the UKA had already purchased several lie detectors, and operators were being trained to administer the tests.

Harris, Roger—In 1996, ADL investigators named Harris the leader of Louisiana's Bayou Knights of the KKK.

Harrison, Andrew Jackson—In 1976, the ADL identified Harrison as the teenaged leader of the Junior Order, United Klans of America.

Harrison, McCord—A resident of Phoenix, Arizona, Harrison served as king kleagle and editor of *Arizona Klankraft* in the early 1920s. He was elected as Arizona's grand dragon in summer 1923.

Harvey, Flynn—Harvey served briefly as Ohio's grand dragon for the UKA, during 1964–65.

Harwood, Brown—In 1922, Harwood replaced Dr. A.D. Ellis as grand dragon of Texas.

Helm, Jack—Appointed as Louisiana grand klaliff of the UKA in 1965, Helm replaced James Edwards as grand dragon early the following year. His reign was short-lived, and internal dissension drove him to resign in March 1967. Helm then led most of the UKA's southern Louisiana provinces into a new Universal Klans (also known as The South). On 23 February 1967, a few days before his break with the UKA, Helm and klansman Jack Kimble reportedly visited the New Orleans apartment of JFK assassination suspect David Ferrie—an associate of Lee Harvey Oswald and Mafia boss Carlos Marcello, who died of a purported stroke on 22 February. According to Kimble's later testimony, Helm removed a valise filled with documents from Ferrie's apartment and took it to a local bank, where it was stored in a safe-deposit box.

Hendrix, William—A plumbing contractor from Tallahassee, Florida, Bill Hendrix founded the Southern Knights of the KKK in January 1949, with an estimated 200 members. In April, he published his first and only issue of *The Klansman*, then emerged a month later as Florida grand dragon for Evall Johnston's Original Southern Klans. When the Georgia home office folded, Hendrix took charge, hosting an 11 June ceremony that drew 1,000 knights from Florida, Alabama and Georgia, with 250 new members initiated. Hendrix soon changed his group's name to the more expansive Northern and Southern Knights, with a Jacksonville mailing address. On 28 August 1949, after a secret klonvokation in Jacksonville, Hendrix announced his election as "national adjutant," serving under an unnamed (perhaps nonexistent) "Permanent Emperor Samuel II." Permanence notwithstanding, the faceless emperor was soon replaced with an equally anonymous imperial wizard, whom Hendrix designated "Number 4-006800." Speaking from parts unknown, said wizard issued an edict advising all klansmen to await orders on how they could best preserve "the American way of life," since "a state of emergency exists in the Invisible Empire." A prime Hendrix target was the "communist-inspired income tax," but he also mailed thousands of letters in 1949 supporting a bill sponsored by Mississippi Rep. John Rankin, imposing a one-year prison term and $1,000 fine on anyone who joined the ADL. The August 1949 riots at Peekskill, New York, allowed Hendrix to claim members north of the Mason-Dixon Line, but his public call for a week of nationwide cross-burnings "to light up the skies of America in protest of communism" produced only six crosses in Florida and Georgia. Visiting Montgomery, Alabama, in December 1949, Hendrix met with William Morris and Thomas Hamilton to form the "governing body" of an alleged national Klan, pointedly excluding Sam Roper's AGK. Tallahassee police arrested Hendrix on 12 February 1952, for mailing material "too libelous" to appear in court records, attacking Gov. Fuller Warren, columnist Drew Pearson and others. While denouncing his trial as "a case of outright persecution," Hendrix was convicted of obscene mailings on 20 February, ordered to pay a $700 fine, with one year's jail time suspended on his promise to refrain from similar pursuits. Five months later, Hendrix announced the formation of a new American Confederate Army, kicking off a gubernatorial campaign that won him 11,200 votes in November. General apathy led to disbandment of his Klan in 1953, but "Black Monday" revitalized Hendrix, sparking a new recruiting drive in autumn 1956. Undaunted when the competing Florida KKK denounced him as a "swindler" using the KKK "for personal gain only," Hendrix sought to compensate for his lack of members with diversity of organizations, including at various times the Knights of the White Camellia, the Order of the Rattlesnake, and the Konsolidated Ku Klux Klans of the Invisible Empire. In August 1958, Hendrix joined J.B. Stoner for an NSRP convention in Louisville, Kentucky. Two years later, on 29 December 1960, he resigned from the KKK, declaring integration inevitable and declaring that "I cannot agree to go outside the law to maintain segregation." Hendrix apparently changed his mind on 24 July 1964, announcing creation of an American Underground that would cooperate with klansmen and other racists to defy the new Civil Rights Act. As Hendrix told the press, "We will fight legally so far as we can, and violently when necessary." In 1967, HUAC investigators linked Hendrix to the tiny Knights of the KKK, Florida, which boasted ten active members in Oldsmar. By 1970, the KKKKF and Hendrix had faded from sight, apparently for the last time.

Henson, Don—Identified in 1977 as the grand dragon of Tennessee, Henson drew attention that September, when he visited Indiana to support a statewide Klan recruiting drive.

Higgins, George, Jr.—Mississippi's grand dragon of the UKA made headlines in 1976, when his wife's election as a delegate to the National Women's Conference outraged liberal supporters of the Equal Rights Amendment.

Holland, David W.—As founder and Georgia grand dragon of the Southern White Knights, Holland stood among eleven klansmen indicted for assaulting black civil rights marchers at Cumming, in 1987. The court's verdict, delivered in October 1988, required the SWK to pay $400,000 in damages, divided among fifty victims. Holland's personal fine was fixed at $50,000. In June 1992, Holland was convicted of further offenses, receiving a sentence of two years' probation, six months' home detention, 250 hours of community service and $921.50 restitution to the court.

Horn, Rev. Alvin—Horn joined Alabama's Federated KKK in 1948, rising to the post of kleagle and a seat on the Klan's board of directors that same year. A resident of Talladega, where he owned substantial property, Horn divided his time between the KKK and three churches which he served as pastor. In February 1950, he was implicated in the Klan slaying of victim Charlie Hurst, at Pell City, but murder charges against Horn were dismissed in October 1952. By that time, Horn had quarreled with leader William Morris and defected to Sam Roper's AGK, then defected once more to join the U.S. Klans in summer 1956. Horn soon emerged as the new Klan's most effective Alabama organizer, increasing its number of klaverns from two to 100 by early 1957. In January 1957, he told a Birmingham rally of 235 klansmen that the KKK would "not give another inch or another concession" toward desegregation. A short time later, his personal life intruded on Klan affairs, to Horn's detriment. His wife committed suicide, leaving Horn with six children to manage, and he soon eloped with a fifteen-year-old girl, whom he had impregnated. The resultant scandal destroyed Horn's standing in the U.S. Klans, allowing Robert Shelton to replace him as grand dragon, but Horn was persistent. Shelton soon left the fold to found the Alabama Knights, while Imperial Wizard Eldon Edwards died from a heart attack in August 1960. New Wizard Robert Davidson named Horn his Alabama grand dragon, and while the realm kept losing members to Shelton's faction, Horn retained enough followers to rate inclusion in Judge Frank Johnson's May 1961 injunction, banning Klan attacks on integrated freedom riders.

Howard, John—Once a member of James Venable's National Knights, Howard joined the September 1975 exodus led by Dale Reusch, to create a new Invisible Empire, Knights of the

KKK. Howard soon emerged as South Carolina's grand dragon, serving during the late 1970s.

Hudgins, Robert Eugene—As the UKA's imperial kladd in the 1960s, Hudgins refused to furnish Klan records to HUAC in 1965. That stance earned him a citation for contempt of Congress, but criminal charges were later dismissed. In September 1969, Hudgins moved from North Carolina to Richmond, Virginia, and replaced Grand Dragon Marshal Kornegay. The statewide KKK revival included a ban on drinking by klansmen, with Hudgins reminding his troops, "This is a Christian organization." In September 1970, Hudgins made headlines with his futile attempt to have federal judge Robert Merhige, Jr., arrested for ordering busing to achieve integration of Richmond's public schools.

Jessup, Cletus—Internet postings from 2001 identified Jessup as grand dragon of an unspecified "Mississippi KKK." No further information was available at press time for this volume.

Johnston, Rev. Evall G. ("Parson Jack")—A leader of the AGK in Columbus, Georgia, Johnston tried to organize a White Protestant Christian Party in August 1947, his membership applications urging recruits to prevent America from becoming "a mixed and mingled mass of -isms." Quarreling with Grand Dragon Samuel Green over money a few months later, Johnston resigned in June 1948 to lead his own Original Southern Klans. Poor health was cited as grounds for his departure in February 1949, replaced by Alton Pate. By 1952, editorials in Johnston's *Georgia Tribune* questioned the Klan's ability to preserve segregation, and he sold the paper in January 1953, to pursue his racist ministry full-time. Typical sermons suggested that southern blacks should be "encouraged" to move north, but Johnston also addressed broader issues. Hosting an "anti–United Nations" convention at his Columbus Baptist Tabernacle, he invited Klan leaders Tom Hamilton and Bill Hendrix as guest speakers, but the high point was his reading of a telegram from Gen. Douglas MacArthur, expressing regret at his inability to attend. The conference accomplished nothing, but it drew a round of praise from spokesmen for the fledgling NAAWP.

Jones, H.H.—On 29 February 1960, H.H. Jones announced his election as imperial wizard of the Knights of the KKK, based in Jonesboro, Georgia. According to Jones, klansmen from seventeen southeastern and southwestern states had convened over the weekend to form the new Klan, with recruiting drives planned for the North. Despite extravagant claims of 42,000 members, the group vanished before HUAC investigators began their survey of the invisible empire in March 1965.

Jones, H.J.—Once the exalted cyclops of Klavern No. 297 in College Park, Georgia, Jones was elected imperial wizard of the U.S. Klans on 26 October 1963, thereby unseating incumbent E.E. George. Jones remained in office as of January 1967, when HUAC estimated his total membership at fifty klansmen, but he and the U.S. Klans dropped from sight by the end of the decade.

Jones, Hamilton Chamberlain, Sr.—A resident of Reconstruction-era Charlotte, North Carolina, Jones joined the KKK in 1867 and was later identified as a high-ranking state officer. Some accounts name him as North Carolina's grand dragon. At the same time, he was also a leader in the state senate, representing Mecklenburg County. His son, Hamilton Jr., subsequently served as a judge, state senator, and in the U.S. House of Representatives (1947–53).

Jones, James Robertson—A second-generation klansman, Jones had trouble in the U.S. Navy when he refused to salute black officers. Back in civilian life, he worked as a lightning rod salesman until June 1963, when he met with former members of the U.S. Klans and decided to petition Imperial Wizard Robert Shelton for affiliation with the UKA. Shelton sent Grand Dragon Robert Scoggin from South Carolina to coordinate an organizational meeting in mid–July, and eighty members were swiftly recruited for the new realm. Jones was named acting grand dragon for ninety days, then won election to a three-year term on 17 August, with the UKA's first statewide rally staged on 21 August 1963. A dynamic salesman, Jones initiated mass recruiting drives that soon transformed North Carolina into the UKA's largest realm. Though theoretically opposed to violence, Jones twice visited a black church in Elm City, warning its elders against letting integrated workers paint the building. His thinly-veiled threats were ignored, and on 17 July 1964 police jailed two klansmen for trying to burn the church. Summoned before HUAC in October 1965, Jones faced accusations of financial irregularities, including falsification of UKA corporate income reports and "coercing" klansmen into buying him a new Cadillac. (His biggest money-making item was Klan regalia, manufactured for $3.20 and sold to the faithful for $15.) Cited for contempt of Congress after he ignored subpoenas for various UKA documents, Jones appealed his conviction and spent the intervening months on new recruitment. In September 1968, Rowan County's sheriff named Jones a "special deputy" to help maintain order at an impending Klan rally, but adverse publicity forced cancellation of the appointment. The contempt charge caught up with Jones in March 1969, resulting in a one-year prison term. By the time Jones emerged, nine months later, his realm was in chaos, with dissident leaders and splinter groups vying for power, while the bulk of Klan membership dissipated.

Kelly, Roger—Identified as Pennsylvania's grand dragon in 1988, Kelly was convicted of illegal cross-burning in February of that year and received sentence of six months' probation.

Kersey, Jason E.—A resident of Samsula, Florida, Kersey won election as grand dragon of the United Florida KKK in June 1961. He held the office through early 1967, although declining health left subordinates effectively in charge of the Klan after 1965.

King, Horace—A resident of Pelion, South Carolina, King served as grand dragon of the Christian Knights in 1995, when members of his realm burned the Macedonia Baptist Church in Clarendon County. SPLC attorneys filed suit against the Klan and various members on behalf of the church's black parishioners, winning an historic $37.8 million judgment in July 1998. Jurors assessed King's personal share of that judgment at $15 million, while the South Carolina realm owed another $7 million.

Kornegay, Marshal Robert—A former Raleigh, North Carolina, insurance salesman with a record of "questionable business practices," Kornegay served as grand titan and grand klokard of the UKA's North Carolina realm before he transferred to Virginia as grand dragon in August 1965. Establishing his headquarters at South Hill, Kornegay focused recruiting efforts on southern Virginia, establishing 32 klaverns with 1,250 members by January 1967. Summoned before HUAC in October 1965, he kept silent as investigators dredged up his past, including suggestions that his move to Virginia was encouraged by exposure of insurance scams in North Carolina. Outside the hearing room, Kornegay regained his voice, telling reporters, "We need more mass killings in Selma, Alabama." Despite the tough talk, however, Kornegay seemed to draw a line where violence was concerned. When nightriders bombed a black Richmond church on 5 October 1965, Kornegay denounced the event as a "dastardly crime," offering Klan money and labor to help rebuild the chapel. In January 1967, Kornegay complained to Virginia's governor about ongoing FBI surveillance and harassment, but the governor was unmoved, dismissing the Klan as "obnoxious."

LaRicci, Tony—Born in Norfolk, Virginia, LaRicci lived in New Jersey until age ten, when his family moved to Baltimore. He joined the UKA in 1965, soon winning promotion to exalted cyclops of his own klavern. Within a year, LaRicci replaced Vernon Naimaster as Maryland's imperial representative. He sold his house at a loss when blacks moved into the neighborhood, and his turbulent UKA career included LaRicci's arrest with four others for trying to kidnap an undercover police officer whom they mistook for a drug dealer. Internal bickering prompted LaRicci to leave the UKA in 1966, following Xavier Edwards into the new Maryland Knights. By 1969, LaRicci commanded the groups, and he followed Robert Scoggin's advice by affiliating with James Venable's National Knights. In October 1975, LaRicci was one of five grand dragons who resigned (or were banished by Venable), soon creating the Invisible Empire Knights under Imperial Wizard Dale Reusch. Never satisfied with any arrangement for long, LaRicci briefed reporters in 1976 on a new, unnamed coalition of right-wing groups in Maryland, including the KKK. With action in mind, he organized the paramilitary Klan Beret, and defeated a bid by Grand Klaliff Will Minton to seize control of the realm in early 1977. September 1977 found LaRicci affiliated with William Chaney's Confederation of Independent Orders. LaRicci last made headlines in July 1978, when prosecutors convicted three of his knights for attempting to bomb a Lochearn, Maryland, synagogue.

Larocque, Michel—A Canadian skinhead and ex-convict, Larocque emerged in May 1990 as Québec grand dragon of the IEKKKK, under Imperial Wizard James Farrands. Larocque subsequently broke with Farrands to lead his own Longitude 74 KKK in Montreal, then dissolved that group in 1991 to head the *Mouvement des Revendications des Droits de la Majorité*, affiliated with Thomas Robb's KKKK. He also published and distributed a Klan newspaper, *The White Patriot*.

Lee, Charles—In 1996, ADL investigators and spokesmen for the Texas Commission on Human Rights named Lee as leader of the Knights of the White Camellia. TCHR attorneys filed suit against Lee and rival Klan leader Michael Lowe that same year, for harassing minorities in Vidor. Ben Roesch subsequently replaced Lee as head of the KWC.

Leland, Bobby—Leland was named Texas grand dragon of James Venable's National Knights in October 1975, after incumbent Dan Smithers defected to join Dale Reusch's Invisible Empire Knights.

Lewis, Charles B.—A Klan troubleshooter in the 1920s, Lewis served as grand dragon of Michigan before moving on to found a new realm in Wisconsin. In 1927, Wizard Hiram Evans placed him in charge of the troubled New York realm, but Lewis was unable to reverse the damage done by scandal, violence, and passage of the Walker Law.

Lindsay, Jim—A prosperous New Orleans realtor and man of many pseudonyms, Lindsay was also known as "James Lawrence" and "Ed White"—the name he used to found and lead the Knights of the KKK in the 1960s. Following Lindsay's still-unsolved murder in June 1975, Louisiana Grand Dragon David Duke assumed control of the KKKK. Lindsay's widow faced trial for his murder but won acquittal by blaming his Klan connections, allegedly unknown to her before his death.

Locke, Dr. John Galen—A Colorado physician denied membership in the Denver County Medical Association, Locke went on to practice in his own small hospital. An early member and kleagle of the 1920s Colorado Klan, he became the state's grand dragon in late 1923. The following year, he occupied a private box at Denver's civic auditorium, where he supervised the GOP state convention. Soon after November's election, Locke ordered the abduction of a Denver hotel owner's son, threatening the boy with castration if he refused to marry his pregnant girlfriend. (The boy chose marriage, which was performed on the spot.) When the groom's parents complained, Locke found himself in children's court before Judge Ben Lindsey, charged with conspiracy and kidnapping. IRS agents compounded Locke's problems in spring 1925, charging him with income tax evasion spanning thirteen years. Locke claimed that his financial records were "lost," whereupon a judge fined him $1,500 and gave him ten days in jail to reconsider. More bad publicity followed when Governor-elect (and klansman) Clarence Morley appointed Locke as his aide-de-camp, a public relations officer for the National Guard, and as a colonel in the Guard's medical corps. Revelations that Locke had handpicked Denver's police chief in 1925 made new headlines, along with reports that Locke had ordered Colorado klansmen to refrain from violence while he was in jail. Imperial headquarters demanded Locke's resignation on 1 July 1925, and while 20,000 klansmen rallied to support him, he grudgingly complied, announcing the creation of a new Minutemen organization for his loyal disciples.

Lowe, Michael—In 1996, ADL investigators identified Lowe as Texas grand dragon for Thom Robb's Knights of the KKK. Lowe's klansmen and members of the rival KWC were linked to acts of racial intimidation around Vidor, prompting the Texas Commission on Human Rights to file suit against Lowe and KWC leader Charles Lee.

Loy, Richard—In July 2003, Indiana's *South Bend Tribune* identified Loy as Hoosier grand dragon of an unspecified Klan. His message of the moment featured opposition to a new "hate activities" ordinance passed by St. Joseph's city council, banning cross-burning and other actions motivated by a desire to "intimidate or threaten another because of his or her actual or perceived race, religion, disability, or nationality." Loy warned reporters that he would continue cross-burnings on his property at will, and would stop anyone who tried to interfere "by any means necessary."

Lumpkin, James—An Alabama native and third-generation klansman, Lumpkin joined the U.S. Klans at age eighteen, then briefly dallied with Robert Shelton's Alabama Knights, before moving to Georgia and joining James Venable's National Knights in the mid–1960s. Employed as a textile mill foreman in Thomaston while serving as Georgia's grand dragon, Lumpkin issued a controversial eleventh-hour endorsement of Lester Maddox in the 1974 gubernatorial primary. (Anxious to divorce himself from Klan support, Maddox blamed the endorsement on "dirty tricks" contrived by his opponent.) Lumpkin later won promotion to imperial klaliff, serving as Venable's second-in-command.

Lutterman, Harry—Newspaper accounts named Lutterman as the 1920s grand dragon of Connecticut.

Lynch, Woodrow W.—The proprietor of Lynch Chemical Company in Shelby, North Carolina, Lynch doubled as grand dragon for the Ancient Order, Invisible Knights of the KKK. Unknown bombers struck his plant on 19 August 1967, apparently in retaliation for his Klan activities.

Macpherson, Ian Verner—A resident of Alberta, Canada, Macpherson founded the Confederate Knights of Alberta in 1972. On 12 September 1974 he shot and killed a Mexican man at his home in Calgary. Authorities dissolved Macpherson's Klan in 1975, while he awaited trial on those charges, but jury accepted his claim of an accidental shooting in July 1975, and Macpherson escaped with a $2,000 fine for negligent use of a firearm. In February 1980, after changing his name to Teàrlach Barra Eoin Ros Dunsford Mac a'Phearsoin, he launched the Invisible Empire Association of Alberta, Knights of the KKK. That group disbanded in February 1989, after three of Macphearson's klansmen pled guilty on charges of conspiring to bomb the Calgary Jewish Centre.

Maddox, Charles Homer—A member of the U.S. Klans, in 1960 Maddox led dissatisfied klansmen into a new Association of Georgia Klans, emerging as the group's imperial wizard. In September 1964, his group affiliated with James Venable's National Association of Ku Klux Klan, and Maddox was named klokard for the NAKKK. By 1965, media reports identified him as Georgia grand dragon of Venable's National Knights, telling one Klan audience, "We need to do a lot to stop these national politicians. A boy down in Texas did a lot already, remember?" His allusion to the JFK assassination of November 1963 drew cheers from the assembled knights.

Martin, Murray H.—With klansman Billy Skipper, Martin took command of Louisiana's Original Knights in early 1964, after leaders John Swenson and Royal Young were banished for misappropriating Klan funds. By autumn 1964, the Klan suffered a three-way rift in membership, with knights in the Shreveport-Bossier City area remaining loyal to Martin and conducting business as the Christian Constitutional Crusaders. Leading his faction into affiliation with James Venable's National Association of Ku Klux Klan by year's end, Martin emerged as klokann chief for the NAKKK.

McCorkle, Albert—As Missouri's grand dragon, McCorkle attended Robert Scoggin's Conference of Eastern Dragons in 1976.

McGlocklin, Bill—McGlocklin served as grand dragon of the Alabama Knights in the early 1990s, until Ira Giddens replaced him on 30 March 1992.

McKinney, James—Identified as the grand dragon of Illinois, McKinney was arrested at Centralia on 1 September 1980, held for questioning in a series of burglaries spanning seven counties. Police seized stolen guns, dynamite, plastic explosives, furniture and stereo equipment from the home McKinney shared with klansman Robert Hansen (who was named as codefendant in the case). Jurors convicted McKinney of burglary and theft, resulting in two concurrent three-year prison terms. Hansen drew a six-month sentence and four years' probation, paying a $4,000 fine.

McNaught, Dr. C.E.—An avid fraternalist and member of at least a dozen organizations besides the KKK, McNaught variously held officer as regimental surgeon of the Patriarchs Militant and as Minnesota grand master of the International Order of Odd Fellows. In July 1930, while serving his second term as mayor of St. James, Minnesota, he was elected grand dragon of the tri-state realm including Minnesota, North and South Dakota.

McNeely, George—In 1965, McNeely served as Arkansas grand dragon for the UKA.

McPhail, Royce—Chosen as the UKA's Texas grand dragon in December 1965, McPhail was barred from speaking at the University of Texas a month later. His tenure was short-lived, ending with his resignation in autumn 1966.

McQueeney, Michael—Media reports from January 1998 identified McQueeney as Wisconsin's grand dragon for an unspecified Klan.

Metzger, Tom—Raised a Catholic in his native Indiana, Metzger moved to Los Angeles in 1961 and found work as a television repairman. Affiliated with the John Birch Society in the early 1960s, he eventually broke with that group because, as he explained, "I soon found out you could not criticize the Jews." In search of a new movement, Metzger briefly led his own White

Brotherhood prior to joining David Duke's Knights of the KKK in 1975. A move to San Diego coincided with Metzger's appointment as grand dragon of California, and in summer 1979 he organized Klan patrols of the Mexican border, searching for illegal aliens. Metzger's Klan security guards dressed in black uniforms and helmets, carrying clubs, chemical Mace and black-lacquered plywood shields in public demonstrations, clashing with hecklers and police on several occasions. Defecting from the KKKK in summer 1980, Metzger formed his own California Knights and launched a series of protests against Vietnamese refugees living in San Diego. That autumn, he entered politics as a Democratic congressional candidate, his radio spots urging voters to "Let me raise a little hell for you." The appeal produced a surprise primacy victory for Metzger, polling 33,000 votes, but November's election saw little improvement on that total: the GOP opponent's 245,000 votes overwhelmed Metzger's 35,000. Two years later, after publicly renouncing his Klan connection, Metzger launched a U.S. Senate race that earned him 75,593 votes (2.8 percent of all ballots cast).

After retiring from the KKK and politics, Metzger organized the White American Political Association, later renamed White Aryan Resistance (WAR), while son John led the White Aryan Resistance Youth (WARY). Both groups were based in Fallbrook, California, focused on recruitment of neo–Nazi skinheads throughout the United States. Federal prosecutors allege that Metzger received loot from bank holdups carried out by The Order in 1983, but he was not among the right-wing leaders indicted (and later acquitted) in sedition charges stemming from that crime spree. In December 1983, Metzger was among fifteen persons (including Aryan Nations leader Richard Butler) arrested for illegal cross-burnings in the Lakeview Terrace district of Los Angeles. According to Metzger, the twenty-foot crosses were burned in honor of a white policeman killed by blacks six months earlier. In November 1988, a gang of skinheads affiliated with WAR murdered Mulugeta Seraw, an Ethiopian student in Portland, Oregon. The SPLC filed suit against WAR, and in October 1990 jurors found the Metzgers liable for Seraw's death, awarding the victim's family $12.5 million in damages. That judgment cost Metzger his home, truck and tools, with $800 monthly payments continuing into the twenty-first century, but WAR survives today, pursuing Metzger's post-trial vow to put "blood on the streets like you've never seen." Described by SPLC spokesmen as "one of the grand old men of organized hate," Metzger inspired the character portrayed by Stacy Keach in the film *American History X* (1998).

Miles, Robert Edward—A New York City native and self-proclaimed racist, Miles settled at Cohoctah, Michigan, in 1953, employed as a traffic safety engineer and manager of an insurance company. Appointed as Michigan grand dragon of the UKA in 1969, Miles left his insurance job the following year, claiming political harassment by his employers. In 1970, Miles launched a race for Michigan secretary of state, but voters rejected his appeals to racial animosity. On 30 August 1971, bombs destroyed ten buses scheduled for use in court-ordered school desegregation in Pontiac, Michigan. Ten days later, FBI agents arrested Miles and five other klansmen on conspiracy charges,

alleging that the plot was hatched during a July Klan meeting at Lake Odessa. Those arrests, based on testimony from an informant, preempted plans to bomb a local power station, scheduled as a diversion for a mortar attack on Pontiac's remaining school buses. A federal grand jury indicted Miles and four others in October 1971, with all five convicted at trial in May 1973. Miles was also convicted for his role in tarring and feathering a high school principal, receiving a sentence of nine years in prison.

While his case wound its way through the courts, Miles served briefly as the UKA's imperial kludd, resigning that post in 1972. Soon afterward, he founded his own racist group, the Mountain Church of Jesus Christ, while assuring the faithful that "I am still, always was, and always will be a klansman." The church was forced to do without its pastor until 1979, when Miles won parole, but Sunday services featured armed guards and fiery crosses in the KKK tradition. Upon his release, Miles organized a front group called Unity Now, promoting Michigan appearances by Klan leaders Don Black, Edward Fields and Robert Shelton. Another "church" affiliate, the Free Association Forum, imported speakers such as J.B. Stoner and leaders of the neo–Nazi American Nationalist Party. In summer 1982, Miles addressed members of the Aryan Nations in Idaho and graced a KKK unity rally at Stone Mountain, Georgia. His persistent affiliation with militant racists (and his alleged receipt of bank loot from The Order during 1983) prompted a federal sedition indictment in 1987, but white jurors acquitted Miles and his twelve codefendants at Fort Smith, Arkansas, in April 1988. In June 1989, Miles announced his retirement from racist activity to care for his ailing wife. He left his disciples with instructions that "the torches now must be lighted everywhere. New hands, younger hands, more merciless and totally fanatical holders of the torches will appear. Instead of merely raising the torches as guideposts atop the walls, the new hands will turn the prairies and fields into beacons of flame and firestorm. My work is done. After us, the true wildfire of the raging barbarian!" Miles died in 1992, with his vision for a war-torn nation unfulfilled.

Miller, Frazier Glenn, Jr.—Born in 1940, Miller spent twenty years in the U.S. Army, rising to a sergeant's rank in the Special Forces before his discharge for distributing neo–Nazi literature to an undercover intelligence officer. Affiliated with the NSPA in the 1970s, he subsequently founded and led the Carolina Knights of the KKK (later renamed the Confederate Knights), based at Angier, North Carolina. In November 1979, Miller was present (but did not participate) when klansmen and neo–Nazis murdered five anti–Klan demonstrators in Greensboro. Afterward, he told reporters, "I was more proud to have been in Greensboro for eighty-eight seconds in 1979 than twenty years in the U.S. Army. It was the only armed victory over communism in this country." In April 1980, Miller's Klan and the National Socialist Party celebrated "Hitlerfest," honoring Adolf Hitler's birthday, on property owned by Miller at Benson, North Carolina. In September 1982, Miller attended a KKK unity rally at Stone Mountain, Georgia. During 1983–84, he collaborated with The Order and received $75,000 in bank loot stolen by

Order guerrillas. In 1985, Miller transformed his Klan once more, into the White Patriot Party, but the SPLC spoiled his fun with a lawsuit filed under North Carolina statutes banning private armies. A court ordered Miller to cease paramilitary training, then slapped him with contempt charges when he persisted. Fleeing underground, Miller issued a declaration of war against "ZOG," but after his arrest in May 1987, Miller pled guilty to mailing threats and received a six-month jail term with three years' probation. Indicted with other neo–Nazi leaders for his part in The Order's conspiracy, Miller turned state's evidence and testified against his former comrades at their 1988 trial in Arkansas, but jurors refused to convict them. Miller, for his part, returned the remainder of his bank loot and received another five-year prison term.

Miller, Horace Sherman—A disabled veteran of World War I and self-styled grand dragon of the Aryan Knights of the KKK, based in Waco, Texas, Miller compensated for his nonexistent stateside membership by mailing literature to neo–Nazi groups around the world. At various times in the late 1950s, authorities linked him to Klan cells in Austria, Chile and Sweden. Closer to home, Miller called for boycotts against Ford Motor Company and the makers of Marlboro and Phillip Morris cigarettes, based on their corporate donations to the National Urban League.

Mills, Roger Quarles—A Kentucky native, born in 1832, Mills moved to Texas in 1849 and was admitted to the bar in 1852. He served in the state legislature during 1859–60, then joined the Confederate army and rose to the rank of colonel during the Civil War. Several sources name him as grand dragon of the chaotic Texas realm during Reconstruction. Following "redemption," Mills served in the House of Representatives (1873–92) and in the U.S. Senate (1892–99). He died in Texas on 2 September 1911.

Morgan, John T.—A former Confederate general, Morgan is identified in some published accounts as the grand dragon of Reconstruction-era Alabama.

Morris, Houston—Launching his Klan career as an officer of the Louisiana-based Original Knights, Morris lost his bid for internal promotion in autumn 1964, then defected to launch his own Original KKK of America in January 1965. Three months later, he presided at a rally in Hamburg, Arkansas, where black-robed klansmen threatened a police officer and pursued a carload of journalists who took "unauthorized" photos. (Morris dubbed the black-clad gang "our political action committee.") Following that incident, Morris withdrew from the OKKKA, leading several Arkansas and Louisiana klaverns into the UKA.

Morris, William Hugh—A Birmingham, Alabama, roofing contractor and Klan member since 1924, Morris emerged in June 1946 as grand wizard of his own Federated Ku Klux Klans. By 1949, he claimed 30,000 klansmen in sixty-five klaverns, an assertion which rival Lycurgus Spinks conceded was correct—if Morris counted each of his knights fifteen times. A rash of floggings in spring 1949 prompted Alabama Attorney General A.A. Carmichael to denounced the Federated Klans as "bums, hoodlums, and cutthroats." State legislators passed an anti-mask law in June, and a grand jury jailed Morris in July for refusing to give up his membership list. Morris spent sixty-seven days in custody, first claiming that the list was stolen, then "recreating" an abbreviated roster from memory. In December 1949, Morris met with Bill Hendrix and Thomas Hamilton to forge a national Klan, but the movement never took hold. In February 1952, Morris was arraigned for mailing "obscene, lewd, lascivious, filthy and indecent" pamphlets. In 1958, police commissioner Bull Connor used Morris in a "sting" operation against J.B. Stoner, but the bungled plan resulted in NSRP members bombing Rev. Fred Shuttlesworth's church, while police failed to intervene. By 1963, Morris was settled in Georgia and affiliated with James Venable's National Knights. Selected as imperial klaliff and a member of the Klan's imperial kloncilium in 1965, he was also the alleged target of an assassination plot by Ohio Grand Empress Eloise Witte. Police informants accused Morris of hiring New Orleans gangsters to murder Dr. Martin Luther King in 1968, but the HSCA found no evidence to substantiate those claims.

Murphy, Robert Patrick—Identified as Delaware's grand dragon in 1965, Murphy was arrested by state police that November, in connection with a shooting incident at Hartley. Prosecutors filed additional charges when police found weapons in his car, at the time of Murphy's arrest.

Murray, Harold—Klansman Harold Murphy lost his job as clerk of Charlotte's city building inspection department in 1970, when he was elected to serve as North Carolina's grand dragon. In December 1971, a federal court ruled that the city had violated Murray's civil rights by firing him for his KKK membership.

Naimaster, Vernon—Identified in 1965 as acting Maryland grand dragon for the UKA, Naimaster lost his job as a Baltimore bus driver after Maryland's NAACP president called for his dismissal and the drivers' union (66 percent black) threatened a wildcat strike. Naimaster's lawsuit against the NAACP failed, but he remained active in the KKK and emerged as Maryland's grand titan in 1966. Addressing a small rally near Baltimore, that May, he declared: "Before [blacks] take over this country, there's going to be an awful lot of bloodshed. I hope to God this won't happen. But I'm gonna keep fighting. The only thing that is gonna stop me is a bullet." In fact, sluggish recruiting did the trick, and before year's end Naimaster was replaced by Tony LaRicci.

Nelson, Scott Monroe—A resident of Houston, Texas, Nelson was identified in 1974 as the imperial wizard of the Texas Fiery Knights. He sparked controversy that April, announcing his political support for Jack Terry, a black candidate running for justice of the peace. Seven months later, Nelson spoke for the Klan's radical fringe in withdrawing support from the future political aspirations of Alabama's George Wallace, declaring, "He is not as white as he was in 1968. His mind has deteriorated, I'm sorry to say, along with his body." In January 1975, Nelson adopted "White" as a second middle name, announcing, "I want to include the most beautiful word in the English language in my name." In 1976, James Venable's National Knights chose

Nelson as their vice-presidential candidate, running with Ohio Grand Dragon Dale Reusch.

Novak, Ed—Chicago resident Edward Melkonian adopted the pseudonym "Ed Novak" while active in the NSPA, and retained it when he joined the Klan. Until early 1995, he served as Illinois grand dragon for the KKKK under Wizard Thom Robb, with additional duties as national knighthawk and as a member of the Klan's grand council. In April 1995, Novak defected from Robb's order to lead his own Federation of Klans, including former KKKK members in Alabama, Colorado, Illinois and Kentucky. ADL investigators described Novak as a well-armed "advocate of secrecy."

Osborn, Clyde W.—A Youngstown, Ohio, attorney and 1920s klansmen, Osborn became grand dragon when the Ohio realm was chartered in 1924. By his own admission, he saw the KKK primarily as a means of electing a Republican president, while making money on the side. Before year's end, he was replaced by Gilbert Taylor.

Page, Hubert A.—Appointed in 1961 as the UKA's first Alabama grand dragon, Page served until March 1964, when he was replaced by Robert Creel. In 1963, he sat for FBI polygraph tests concerning his possible involvement in the fatal bombing of Birmingham's Sixteenth Street Baptist Church.

Palmer, David—An electrician residing in Sydney, Australia, Palmer joined the neo–Nazi group National Action in the 1980s, then resigned on 20 April 1990 (Adolf Hitler's birthday) to lead his own National Security Defending Australian People, also known as Australian National Socialist Defence of Aryan People. In June 1999, Palmer announced formation of the Australian Knights of the KKK, which he led as imperial wizard. That declaration earned him expulsion from Australia's far-right One Nation party, but Palmer remained defiant. By 2002, he led three separate organizations, adding a new Australian Strikeforce Guards for Aryan Resistance and Defence to his existing AKKKK and NSDAP.

Parker, C.L.—Identified as Florida's grand dragon in 1953, Parker issued an announcement that October, proclaiming that his Klan had abandoned robes and rituals, opening its ranks to "all races, creeds or colors" on a strictly segregated basis.

Pate, Alton E.—Named as imperial wizard of the Original Southern Klans in June 1948, Pate held office as a nominal leader, reportedly controlled by Evall Johnston and Fred New.

Perkins, Deforest—Appointed grand dragon of Maine in 1926, Perkins was subsequently implicated with Gov. Owen Brewster and Imperial Wizard Hiram Evans in a plot to swing a special election in favor of the Klan's candidate by accusing his opponent of illegal overspending in the state primary.

Perry, J.W.—While doubling as grand dragon of Connecticut and Rhode Island in the 1920s, Perry faced charges of perjury before a 1927 Rhode Island state legislative committee investigating Klan involvement in politics. Jurors acquitted him in a trial, in winter 1928.

Peterson, Kenneth N.—Media reports from 1992 identified Peterson as imperial wizard of the Wisconsin-based National Knights. That same year witnessed bitter struggles for control of the organization, with Ohio klansman Stephen Anderson trying to unseat Peterson. On 23 June 1992, police in Janesville jailed Peterson for disorderly conduct, after an argument over the sale of a car. Two months later, on 26 August, Peterson announced that he was disbanding the National Knights and leaving Janesville. Before departing, in October 1992, Peterson surrendered all his files and other Klan materials to a Wisconsin social justice organization.

Pierce, Ernest G.—In 1992, media reports identified Pierce as grand dragon of the Kentucky Knights. On 8 June of that year, police charged him with ordering klansmen to burn a church at Bowling Green, whose pastor had criticized the KKK. Jurors subsequently convicted Pierce of conspiracy, whereupon he received a prison term of four years and four months.

Pierce, John—Media reports from 2002 identified Pierce as Michigan grand dragon for the Mystic Knights of the KKK.

Pike, Albert—A Boston native, born in 1809 and raised in Massachusetts, Pike toured the West as a trapper and explorer in 1831–33, then settled in Arkansas, where he taught school, published a newspaper, and studied law. He fought in the Mexican War (1846–48), then joined the nativist Know Nothing movement, while rising to the rank of Sovereign Grand Commander in the Scottish Rite Masons (1859). Pike opposed seces-

Some historians name Albert Pike as author of the Klan's original prescript and grand dragon of Arkansas.

sion, but joined the Confederate as a brigadier general in 1861, subsequently deserting after his Native American troops were accused of scalping enemies at the battle of Pea Ridge (March 1862). Treason charges were filed, despite his written resignation from the army (July 1862), then were dismissed in November 1862, whereupon Pike returned to Arkansas. Some authors name Pike as the Reconstruction-era grand dragon of Arkansas, further suggesting that fascination with Masonic ritual made him a likely author of the Klan's original prescript. Pardoned by President Andrew Johnson in August 1865, Pike served on the state supreme court, then moved to Memphis and finally settled in Washington, D.C., in 1870. There, he focused his attentions on poetry and Masonic activities, while publishing another newspaper, *The Patriot.* Pike died on 2 April 1891. He is the only Confederate office honored by a statue in the nation's capital.

Pruitt, Dr. E.P.—A Birmingham, Alabama, physician, Pruitt was named president of the Federated Klans when that group incorporated in July 1946. Three years later, with Wizard William Morris in jail, Pruitt ordered the Klan to unmask in compliance with state law. Enraged, Morris declared that Pruitt had "overstepped his authority" and "accepted" the doctor's resignation.

Pryor, Ralph—An ex-policeman in Wilmington, Delaware, Pryor was appointed to serve as Delaware's grand dragon of the UKA on 31 July 1965. By mid–November, he was voicing his dissatisfaction with the Klan to journalists, citing mismanagement of funds and prevalence of neo–Nazis in the northern membership. Prior initially agreed to testify before HUAC in 1965, then reneged, telling reporters: "If I testify, someday they are going to find me in Selma, Alabama, with thirty bullet holes in me, and that killer is going to get off Scot free." Pryor formally resigned from the UKA in January 1966, replaced by Bennie Sartin.

Reusch, Dale—An auto worker in Lodi, Ohio, and grand dragon for the National Knights, Reusch ran for sheriff in Medina County in 1968 and 1972. Defeated in those campaigns, he next ran as a write-in candidate for governor, in 1974, but lost again. In September 1974, spokesmen for the National Knights announced that Reusch would be the Klan's presidential candidate in 1976, with running mate Scott Nelson. Early 1975 found Reusch involved in a campaign to rescue Ohio textbooks from the taint of "government indoctrination and nationalized education." Quarreling with Wizard James Venable that October, Reusch led four other dissident dragons into the new Invisible Empire Knights, proclaiming that Catholics and naturalized Americans would be welcome as members. In February 1976, Reusch filed as a vice presidential candidate in West Virginia's Democratic primary, voicing hopes for the number-two spot on a ticket headed by Alabama's George Wallace. Despite his claim of control over Klan votes in eighteen states, Reusch was resoundingly defeated in 1976, and again in his 1978 bid to become Ohio's lieutenant governor. By 1980, his Klan was defunct, its title usurped by Bill Wilkinson's more militant organization.

Reynolds, Edwin—An unemployed machinist and UKA kleagle in New Jersey, Reynolds was fired by Pennsylvania's grand dragon on charges of adultery, drug abuse, misusing Klan funds, and for "being a member of an anti–Christian cult." UKA spokesmen charged that Reynolds had "set aside our oath and substituted his own, requiring everyone to swear allegiance to Hitler." In retaliation, Reynolds founded his own White Knights of the KKK in New Jersey, maintaining friendly relations with the American Nazi Party, but his membership dwindled into single digits after his 1980 arrest for rape, on charges filed by a female JDL member. Prior to trial, Reynolds announced the Klan's disbandment, urging his handful of loyalists to join David Duke's Knights of the KKK. Pressed for comments on the case, he replied, "I will only say that I am innocent. Heil Hitler!" Jurors ultimately agreed, acquitting Reynolds of all charges.

Riccio, Bill—A member of the Aryan Nations, Riccio once served as Alabama grand dragon for Bill Wilkinson's IEKKKK and was also identified as an officer of the White Knights of Alabama. In 1979, during protests surrounding the rape trial of black defendant Tommy Hines, Riccio was among the klansmen charged with assaulting black demonstrators in Decatur, Alabama. He fought that case in court for a decade, finally receiving a two-year prison term in January 1989 for obstructing justice. Meanwhile, a separate 1979 conviction on weapons charges sent him to prison, then came back to haunt him in April 1985, when he was caught in possession of firearms once again, thus violating terms of his parole. That indiscretion earned Riccio another two-year sentence, interrupting his recruitment of neo–Nazi skinheads for a future race war. Following his 1989 conviction, Riccio appeared repentant, telling the judge: "I guess I was hardheaded for a long time. I will not let the court down if given the opportunity to prove I am a changed person." He ultimately served one year, then was released.

Riddlehoover, Charles B. ("Rip")—A klansman in Fort Lauderdale, Florida, Riddlehoover quarreled with Grand Dragon Donald Cothran in October 1965 and led other dissident into a new United Knights of the KKK, with Riddlehoover serving as grand dragon. He was barely installed in office when Miami police arrested him for a traffic violation, adding concealed weapons charges when they found a pistol in Riddlehoover's car.

Robb, Thomas Arthur—A self-styled Christian Identity "pastor" from Harrison, Arkansas, Robb earned national notoriety in 1980–81, as national chaplain for Don Black's Knights of the KKK. Following Black's conviction on charges of conspiring to invade Dominica, Robb emerged as national director of the KKKK, a post he retained at press time for this volume. He traveled nationwide to address Klan rallies, including a November 1982 excursion to Washington, D.C., that sparked two hours of rioting by Klan opponents. Robb was a driving force behind a September 1983 unity rally at Stone Mountain, Georgia, but his best efforts failed to forge a cohesive invisible empire. Closely affiliated with Robert Miles and the Aryan Nations, Robb raised defense funds when Miles, Richard Butler and others faced trial for sedition in 1988. Klan membership has fluctuated wildly under Robb's leadership, but 2005 found the KKKK shrunken to five klaverns in Arkansas, Florida, North Carolina and Tennessee.

Roberts, Charles Macon—A longtime klansman from Chattanooga, Tennessee, Roberts assumed control of the Dixie Klans when Imperial Wizard Jack Brown died in 1965.

Roesch, James—Ohio native James Roesch made his first contact with the KKK in 1995, at age fifteen. A year later, with best friend Logan Hofferbert, he founded a high school racist group called the New White Order. Ranked as the nation's youngest grand dragon (for Ohio) in 1998, Roesch met his future wife on a field trip to Jasper, Texas, where he joined in a cross-burning ceremony after the funeral of Klan murder victim James Byrd. Love and opportunity combined to make him pull up stakes and move to Jasper, where he emerged in 2000 as imperial wizard for the Knights of the White Kamelia. Within a year, some reports described the KWK as America's largest Klan faction, but its apparent success was a flash in the pan, declining from seven active klaverns in 2001 to three in 2002. By 2003, headquarters had vanished from Jasper, leaving only one klavern in Ohio. That, in turn, dissolved during 2004.

Rogers, John Paul—As Florida grand dragon of the UKA, Rogers ran for a seat on the Polk County school board in 1972, polling 7,000 votes to his opponent's 12,000. In May 1976, when local Boy Scouts withdrew from their own Memorial Parade to protest Klan involvement, Rogers accused the them of "prejudice and bigotry." A month later, in Lake Wales, Rogers paid $1,000 to a black man for his role in helping police crack a ring of home invaders who preyed on white families. Rogers was last heard from in autumn 1976, when he launched an abortive congressional campaign.

Roper, Samuel W.—An Atlanta policeman and member of the 1920s Klan, Roper headed the GBI during 1941–42, under Gov. Eugene Talmadge. In 1946, he emerged as second-in-command of the AGK, doubling as nighthawk for Grand Dragon Sam Green and as exalted cyclops of Oakland City Post No. 297 in Atlanta. When Green died in August 1949, Roper assumed control of the AGK, which he described as "an educational outfit." While de-emphasizing violence, Roper saw his Klan dwindle in size, retreating into a two-room headquarters above a poultry market. Before year's end, he joined forces with Lycurgus Spinks, thus serving both as grand dragon of the AGK and imperial wizard of the new Associated Klans of America. Roper and both splinter groups vanished into obscurity before "Black Monday," in May 1954.

Rossiter, Leo—Media reports from 1990 identified Rossiter as Grand Dragon of the Maryland Knights. He was perhaps best known for his collaboration with youthful neo–Nazi skinhead gangs, including Baltimore's American Resistance and BASH (*B*altimore *A*rea *S*kin*h*eads), as well as Philadelphia's White Justice group. American Resistance members joined Rossiter in picketing Baltimore's NAACP office on 1 January 1990, and again four months later in a brawl with opponents from the International Committee Against Racism.

Sartin, Bennie—A resident of Elkton, Maryland, Sartin replaced Ralph Pryor as Delaware grand dragon of the UKA in early 1966. That April, Delaware Attorney General David Buckson described Sartin as "just a puppet goose-stepping along behind [Pennsylvania Grand Dragon Roy] Frankhouser."

Saunders, William L.—A native of Wake County, North Carolina, Saunders served as a colonel in the Confederate army, then returned to publish the Wilmington *Journal,* a Democratic newspaper that praised the KKK and published many Ku Klux notices. Several sources name him as the state's grand dragon, either as successor or alternative to Hamilton C. Jones. Of all the reputed klansmen questioned by Congress in 1871, Saunders was the only witness who invoked the Fifth Amendment and refused to answer any questions. A recognized scholar who published a ten-volume history of colonial North Carolina, Saunders subsequently served as the state's secretary of state (1879–91).

Schoonmaker, Earl—While employed as a teacher at the medium-security Eastern New York Correctional Facility in Napanock, Schoonmaker also served as grand dragon of the Northern Independent KKK of New York. His superiors suspended him in December 1974, based on charges filed by Nancy Loorie, head of prison vocational services, who claimed that klansmen had threatened her life, vandalized her car and office, and set fires in the cells of black inmates. Superintendent Jerome Peterson denied the charge of office vandalism, further declaring that only one of six prison fires reported since September 1974 was deemed suspicious—and that was blamed on prisoners. Not even inmates blamed the Klan, which made its first appearance at the prison that September. Loorie claimed to have seen a membership list naming 15–20 klansmen among 400 prison personnel, but Charles Krom—spokesman for a council representing 284 correctional officers—called that allegation irresponsible. Nonetheless, administrators fired Schoonmaker on 23 December 1974, while members of the Pine Bush school board demanded wife Janice's resignation from her post as director of that body. (She refused to step down.) In 1976, Schoonmaker attended Robert Scoggin's Conference of Eastern Dragons, and in 1977 he resurfaced as imperial klokard of William Chaney's Confederation of Independent Orders.

Scoggin, Robert Echols—As a member of the U.S. Klans in South Carolina, Scoggin worked his way up from exalted cyclops to grand titan and grand dragon of the realm, before defecting to the UKA in July 1961. As a charter officer of the UKA, he was named to serve as imperial kladd while retaining his post as South Carolina's grand dragon and presiding over North Carolina klansmen until James Jones became that state's grand dragon in 1963. Under Scoggin, the UKA enjoyed steady growth in South Carolina, increasing from twenty klaverns in 1964 to fifty by late 1966. At the same time, Scoggin also managed to line his pockets, depositing $15,690 to personal bank accounts in one year, while declaring only $574 income to the IRS. A tough-talking leader, Scoggin condoned formation of a paramilitary Underground organization, designed to train klansmen for violent action, but his realm was relatively pacific. In October 1965, HUAC exposed his record of drunk driving convictions and fraudulent billing of the Veterans Administration for exaggerated war injuries, but Scoggin stood firm on the Fifth Amendment, drawing a one-year prison sentence for contempt of Congress in March 1968. Paroled in December 1969, he returned to find statewide Klan membership shrunken by forty percent under acting Grand Dragon Harry Gilliam. Public quarrels with Gilliam and Wizard Robert Shelton soon forced Scoggin out of the UKA, and in 1970 he founded his own Invisible Empire Knights of the KKK, Realm of South Carolina. In September 1970, police jailed Scoggin for conspiracy to commit robbery and as an accomplice after the fact to murder, following the death of klansman Willie Odom at a rally near Sumter. Prosecutors dismissed those charges in time for Scoggin to serve as a middleman, coordinating a merger between UKA defector Tony LaRicci's Maryland Knights and James Venable's National Knights. In August 1975, Scoggin visited Louisville, Kentucky, during a school busing controversy, sharing the dais at joint rallies with David Duke, James Warner and Phillip Chopper. In spring 1976 he hosted a Conference of Eastern Dragons in South Carolina, while his three-way struggle with Dale Reusch and Bill Wilkinson for control of various independent Klans led to a curious unity conference in June 1977. When the smoke cleared, all three contestants lost out to Hoosier klansman William Chaney, chosen to command the new Confederation of Independent Orders.

Sexton, Melvin—An Alabama member of the UKA and next-door neighbor of Wizard Robert Shelton in Tuscaloosa, Sexton was named to serve as imperial kligrapp in summer 1965. Four years later, he filled in for Shelton as acting imperial wizard, while Shelton served a prison term for contempt of Congress. His performance in that role sparked a major revolt in North Carolina, where klansmen accused Sexton of pocketing money collected for the legal defense of knights jailed in a July 1969 shootout at Swan Quarter. Sexton dismissed the complaints and moved to chastise his accusers, thereby prompting Joseph Bryant and Edward Dawson to defect and form their own rival Klan (with covert FBI backing).

Shaver, Robert Glenn—A former Confederate general and resident of Jackson County, Arkansas, Shaver granted a press interview in 1911, wherein he claimed service as the state's Reconstruction-era grand dragon. No documentary proof was forthcoming, and some historians reject Shaver's claim.

Shaw, Rev. Herbert—A Tennessee native and virulent anti–Catholic, Shaw served as a Baptist minister in Erie, Pennsylvania, during the 1920s. In 1925, Wizard Hiram Evans named him Pennsylvania's grand dragon, overruling protests from local klansmen who wanted to choose their own leader. Shaw embarrassed many knights with his violent tirades against Catholics and blacks, but he retained staunch support from imperial headquarters. In autumn 1926, Evans responded to new complaints from the ranks by banishing one dissident klansman and revoking the charters of eight Pennsylvania klaverns, filing suit to block further use of the Klan's name and regalia. The Keystone knights fought back in court, aware that plaintiffs in equity lawsuits must come to court with "clean hands." Testimony from ex–Wizard William Simmons and others documented the sordid tale of Klan violence and corruption, ending with dismissal of the imperial lawsuit.

Sheeley, James—Media reports from 2001 identified Sheeley as New York grand dragon for Jeff Berry's American Knights of the KKK. Following Berry's imprisonment in December 2001, Sheeley defected to serve as grand titan for the Imperial Klans of America, taking most of his New York klansmen with him into the new organization.

Shelton, Jimmy Ray—Media reports from 1998–99 identified Shelton as the imperial wizard of the Confederate Ghost Knights, based in North Carolina. Lexington police arrested him on 8 August 1998, for carrying a concealed weapon at a Klan rally, but Shelton failed to get the message. Seven months later, on 29 March 1999, he exchanged shots with police officers during a high-speed car chase outside Austin, Texas. Prosecutors charged Shelton and companion Eddie Melvin Bradley with attempted capital murder on 13 April, and jurors convicted him on 17 September 1999, resulting in a 99-year prison term.

Shelton, Robert Marvin—The son of a Tuscaloosa, Alabama, grocer and klansman, Shelton briefly enrolled at the state university, but lack of funds forced him to drop out and abandon his dream of attending law school. He joined the U.S. Air Force in 1947 and served in Germany, where he was outraged by the spectacle of black servicemen dating white women. Back in Tuscaloosa, Shelton found work at the B.F. Goodrich tire plant and joined the U.S. Klans, rising through the ranks until personal conflict with Grand Dragon Alvin Horn prompted him to defect and found his own Alabama Knights. In 1958, Shelton's support for winning gubernatorial candidate John Patterson landed Goodrich a $1.6 million state contract, and Shelton was promoted to a traveling sales job that spanned Dixie, but he was fired in 1961 for devoting too much time to the Klan. In May 1961, he was one of four Klan leaders named in Judge Frank Johnson's federal injunction barring violence against the integrated freedom rides.

In July 1961, Shelton merged his Alabama Knights with Georgia klansmen led by Calvin Craig and South Carolina units under Robert Scoggin, creating the UKA with headquarters in Tuscaloosa. Within a month, demolition courses were offered to UKA members in Georgia, as Shelton collaborated with the ultra-violent Nacirema Inc. In 1962, Shelton backed another political winner in Alabama Gov. George Wallace, and the following year saw Shelton's father named as a colonel on Wallace's staff. By 1964, Shelton's UKA was the nation's dominant Klan, with klaverns in every southern state. Called before HUAC in 1965, Shelton refused to produce Klan records, citing the Fifth Amendment as he declined to answer 158 questions. Independent evidence showed that Shelton had drawn money from a UKA front, the Alabama Rescue Service—including checks forged under fictitious names—and used the cash for personal expenses, including diamond rings. Charged with contempt of Congress, Shelton was convicted before future Watergate judge

Robert Shelton's UKA was the dominant Klan of the 1960s, allied closely with George Wallace in Alabama (Southern Poverty Law Center).

John Sirica in September 1966, drawing the maximum penalty of one year in prison and a $1,000 fine.

Paroled in November 1969, Shelton promised a new drive to rid America of "the infected black carcass that's dragging us down to the low morals and disruption that's in this nation today," but the UKA had withered in his absence, under the inept handling of acting imperial wizard Melvin Sexton. Shelton's national speaking tour in November 1970 failed to revitalize the order, although Shelton claimed recruits in Michigan and Pennsylvania. The speeches were vintage Shelton, including a remark to an audience in Forest City, Arkansas, that "Negroid is like hemorrhoid: they're both a pain." Despite a drop in Klan membership nationwide, Shelton's UKA remained one of the largest factions, with some 4,000 members in 1983. Still relatively strong, with 1,500 knights in 1987, the UKA was crippled by an SPLC lawsuit in the lynching death of black teenager Michael Donald at Mobile, Alabama, resulting in forfeiture of imperial headquarters to settle the jury's $7 million award to Donald's mother.

Sickles, Charles William—As the head of Maryland's militant Adamic Knights, Sickles was one of ten klansmen jailed

by ATF agents in May 1981, charged with federal firearms violations and conspiracy to firebomb Baltimore's NAACP office. His June indictment listed twenty separate felony counts, and Sickles received a five-year prison term upon conviction in October 1981.

Simmons, William Joseph—An Alabama native born in 1880, Simmons claimed (perhaps falsely) that his father was a member of the Reconstruction Klan. He joined the U.S. Army at eighteen and saw action in the Spanish-American War, then entered the Methodist ministry in 1900, as a circuit-riding preacher in rural Alabama and Florida. In 1912, Alabama's Methodist Conference defrocked Simmons on grounds of inefficiency and "moral impairment," after which he briefly worked as a salesman before finding his niche as a fraternal organizer and recruiter. Simmons soon became the youngest "colonel" in the Woodmen of the World—a title he used for the rest of his life—and within two years he earned $15,000 annually from the lodge. He also joined numerous other lodges and at least two different churches, while nurturing dreams of reviving the KKK. (That aspiration, Simmons said, sprang from a vision he experienced while bedridden after a car accident.) In October 1915, a Georgia cross-burning by the Knights of Mary Phagan and publicity surrounding the Atlanta premiere of *The Birth of a Nation* inspired Simmons to make his dream a reality. After applying for a state charter, he led two dozen charter klansmen up Stone Mountain on Thanksgiving night, to burn a giant cross and herald the Klan's reincarnation.

His brainchild got off to a sluggish start, but Simmons turned the corner on success in 1920, when he hired publicists Edward Clarke and Elizabeth Tyler to promote the Klan nationwide. Media exposure of Klan violence in September 1921, followed by congressional hearings a month later, ensured the KKK's success. Simmons was the star of hearings held before the House Rules Committee, urging the assembled congressmen, "If this organization is unworthy, then let me know and I

Simmons (in mask) leads an early Georgia Klan rally (Southern Poverty Law Center).

Imperial Wizard William Simmons testifies before Congress in October 1921 (Library of Congress).

will destroy it, but if it is not, let it stand." Turning to the gallery of spectators, he asked them "to call upon the Father to forgive those who have persecuted the Klan," the collapsed to the floor in a faint. Membership applications flooded imperial headquarters after that performance, prompting Simmons to declare that "Congress made us." By November 1922, ambitious subordinates had their eyes on the imperial throne, and Dallas dentist Hiram Evans executed a bloodless coup, emerging as "temporary" imperial wizard while Simmons became "emperor for life." Perusing the new constitution, approved by klonvokation delegates, Simmons found himself relegated to the status of an impotent figurehead. He retaliated by organizing Kamelia, a ladies' auxiliary, but its membership never matched that of the Klan. An April 1923 court order granted Simmons control of the KKK, but Evans loyalists absconded with crucial documents and $107,000 in cash before he could resume control. The power struggle dragged on until February 1924, when a final settlement gave Simmons $90,000 in return for disbandment of Kamelia and his promise to refrain from further competition with the KKK. He died in poverty at Luverne, Alabama, in May 1945.

Skipper, Billy—With Murray Martin, Skipper assumed control of the Louisiana-based Original Knights in early 1964, operating publicly as the Christian Constitutional Crusaders. Skipper remained loyal to Martin when a three-way rift shattered the Klan that autumn, with most of their dwindling membership drawn from Bossier City and Shreveport.

Smithers, Dan—Smithers served as Texas grand dragon of James Venable's National Knights until October 1975, when he left to join the Invisible Empire Knights under Imperial Wizard Dale Reusch.

Snellings, Dennis—For a time in the 1980s, Snellings served as Virginia's grand dragon of the IEKKKK. He was apparently retired from that post by 12 August 1991, when Charlottesville police jailed him for assaulting a black student.

Snelson, Earl—A resident of Long Beach, California, Snelson served as California's grand dragon in the late 1930s, under Wizard James Colescott.

Spears, Rev. James—Spears was elected to serve as the UKA's Alabama grand dragon in June 1966, replacing William Brassell. Three years later, in July 1969, he was one of seventeen klansmen arrested after a shootout with blacks at Swan Quarter, North Carolina. In 1976, Wizard Robert Shelton elevated Spears to the rank of imperial kludd.

Spinks, Lycurgus—After ten years of preaching in Arkansas and the Carolinas, Spinks dubbed himself "Doctor" and switched to lectures on sexology, offering presentations "For Men Only," with special matinees "For Women Only." He also once toured Dixie on a lecture tour wherein he billed himself as a reincarnation of George Washington. In 1947, Spinks ran for governor in Mississippi, receiving 4,344 of the 350,000 votes cast, and he did just as poorly in two later races for state tax collector. He was associated with the Federated KKK in 1948–49, until flogging prosecutions began to fragment that group. On 8 August 1949, klansmen from six states met in Montgomery, Alabama, to elect Spinks as "imperial emperor" of a new Knights of the KKK of America. Spinks promptly claimed a membership of 650,000, while a rival leader insisted that Spinks was wizard "over himself and one other guy." In fact, Spinks claimed to represent *all* klansmen, whether they knew it or not. In October 1949, he appeared on NBC's *Meet the Press* for what turned out to be an unintentionally hilarious performance: Spinks said that he thought Jesus Christ was a klansman, and later stated that blacks in Dixie "know that the best friend they've got on earth is the Knights of the Ku Klux Klan." South Carolina sought to extradite Spinks for banking irregularities occurring while he served as a receiver there, but Mississippi Gov. Theodore Bilbo refused to honor the request. On 17 September 1950, Spinks announced that he was severing all KKK ties, since his dream of a national Klan had "turned into a nightmare."

Stephens, Ed—Stephens participated in Klan assaults on black demonstrators at Cumming, Georgia, in January 1987, and was named as a defendant in a federal lawsuit filed by the SPLC. By 1989, when the case went to trial, media reports named him as Georgia grand dragon of the IEKKKK. In October 1989, jurors ordered Stephens to pay his victims $30,000 in damages, while attending race-relations classes taught by members of the SCLC.

Stephenson, David Clarke—A Texas native and elementary school dropout, born in 1891, Stephenson was working as a printer in Oklahoma when he joined the National Guard to serve in World War I. Discharged as a lieutenant, he moved to Evansville, Indiana, in 1920, selling coal and recruiting members for veterans organizations. Indian's first klavern was organized at Evansville that same year, and Stephenson soon succeeded Joe Huffington as its exalted cyclops. His program for Klan-building included appeals to Protestant clergymen, appeals to vigilantism, and creation of an all-female "poison society," the Queens of the Golden Mask. By early 1922, membership had topped 5,000 and Stephenson was chosen for a key role in Hiram Evans's plot to depose Wizard William Simmons. The coup was successful, and Evans rewarded Stephenson with command of a sub-empire spanning twenty-three northern and Midwestern states. With more than a half-million knights in Indiana alone, Stephenson soon emerged as the "old man" of Hoosier politics, relying for support on the apparatus he called his "Military Machine." Confirmed as grand dragon in 1923, Stephenson formally resigned his Klan titles that September, then convened a special convention in May 1924, where klansmen elected him grand dragon of a new Independent Klans of America. Evans retaliated by backing Joe Huffington's move to depose Stephenson, and a bomb destroyed Stephenson's yacht at its mooring in Ohio.

Stephenson, meanwhile, maintained his focus on politics, dreaming of a personal Senate race in 1926 and a White House campaign in 1928. Meanwhile, in 1924, he helped elect Indiana's governor, the mayor of Indianapolis, plus many other state and local officials. A split in the state legislature stalled most proposed legislation, but Stephenson remained confident of final victory until March 1925, when jurors convicted him kidnapping, raping and murdering schoolteacher Madge Oberholtzer. That conviction carried a life sentence, but Stephenson clung to hopes of a pardon from Gov. Ed Jackson. When it failed to materialize, he released documents linking various respected politicians to the Klan, resulting in multiple resignations, impeachments, and bribery convictions. Friends of the KKK who escaped indictment soon found themselves purged from office by voters disgusted with Ku Klux corruption, while the ongoing scandal prompted thousands of members to quit the KKK. Paroled to the custody of Oklahoma relatives in March 1950, Stephenson vanished five months later, traced to Minneapolis where FBI agents found him working as a printer. A year of legal wrangling ended with his return to Indiana's state prison in 1951, but he was paroled once again in December 1954. Settled in Seymour, Indiana, Stephenson married for the third time in 1958, then disappeared until 1961, when he was jailed for molesting a teenage girl at Independence, Missouri. Prosecutors dropped those charges on condition that he leave the state, and Stephenson became a drifter, finally settling in Jonesboro, Tennessee. At his death, in June 1966, his fourth wife professed shock upon learning of Stephenson's notorious past.

Stoner, Jesse Benjamin

—Born in 1924, Georgia native J.B. Stoner endured a grim childhood, losing his father at age five, crippled by polio a few years later, orphaned by his mother's death at sixteen. Exempted by his limp from military service during World War II, he joined a Chattanooga klavern in 1942 and soon won promotion to kleagle. Obsessive anti–Semitism had become the keystone of his life, revealed in 1944 by a petition urging passage of a congressional resolution that "Jews are the children of the Devil." In 1945, he organized the Stoner Anti-Jewish Party, advocating legislation that would "make being a Jew a crime punishable by death." Interviewed in 1946, Stoner described Adolf Hitler as "too moderate," declaring that his own neo–Nazi party would eradicate Jews via gas chambers, electric chairs, firing squads, or "whatever seems appropriate." At the same time, Stoner remained active in the Klan, joining Sam

J.B. Stoner (with microphone) harangues a 1964 Klan rally in St. Augustine, Florida. Grand Dragon Don Cothran stands behind him on stage (Florida State Archives).

Green's AGK in 1947. Klan-watcher Stetson Kennedy listened to one of Stoner's near-hysterical speeches before an Atlanta klavern, calling for annihilation of the Jews, and branded him "stark raving crazy." In 1948, Stoner campaigned for a Tennessee congressional seat, polling 541 votes out of 30,000 cast. Sam Roper expelled him from the Associated Klans of America in January 1950, after Stoner urged members of Klavern No. 317 to drive all Jewish residents from Chattanooga.

Moving to Atlanta, Stoner finished law school and teamed with Edward Fields, once a member of the Columbians, to organize the Christian Anti-Jewish Party in 1952. In 1954, Stoner and four party members picketed the White House with anti–Semitic placards. Sharing law offices with klansman James Venable in the late 1950s, Stoner rallied with like-minded racists to create the NSRP in May 1958. Two charter members were indicted for the October 1958 bombing of an Atlanta synagogue, while police named Stoner as the probable source of dynamite used in the blast. In July 1959, Stoner proclaimed himself "archleader" of the Christian Knights of the KKK, based in Louisville, Kentucky. During August and September 1959, Stoner and Fields joined forces to protest integration of Miami's Orchard Villa School, and Stoner made headlines again in October, denouncing the rival U.S. Klans as "Jew-dominated." By June 1960, the Christian Knights were based in Atlanta, using the same post office box as Stoner's former Christian Anti-Jewish Party.

Wherever Stoner traveled in the South, bombings occurred. Birmingham police commissioner Bull Connor collaborated with Klan leader William Morris in 1958, to entrap Stoner with a bomb plot concocted by authorities, but two of Stoner's men escaped scot-free after bombing Rev. Fred Shuttlesworth's church, while Connor buried the case to avoid personal embarrassment. Journalists named Stoner as a member or associate of Nacirema in summer 1963, noting his July lecture on bomb-making to an NSRP audience in Birmingham. Two months later, he returned in time for the fatal bombing of Birmingham's Sixteenth Street Baptist Church. During 1963–64, Stoner teamed with klansmen Charles "Connie" Lynch and Holsted "Hoss" Manucy to incite riots and nightriding violence against black protesters in St. Augustine, Florida. Nominated as the NSRP's vice-presidential candidate in 1964, Stoner (with running mate John Kasper) polled 6,957 votes nationwide. He traveled widely with Lynch through 1965 agitating klansmen in Bogalusa, Louisiana, and NSRP members in Anniston, Alabama (where nightriders murdered black victim Willie Brewster following a Stoner tirade). Summoned before HUAC in February 1966, Stoner refused to answer any questions but enraged the committee with an editorial branding Chairman Edwin Willis "part ape."

In 1970, Stoner ran for governor of Georgia on the NSRP ticket, but won less than three percent of the registered electorate. Two years later, he polled a surprising 40,600 votes in a campaign for the U.S. Senate, while 71,000 Georgians endorsed his 1974 bid to become lieutenant governor. A Birmingham grand jury indicted Stoner in September 1977 for the 1958 church bombing, prompting a new gubernatorial campaign which, if successful, would have permitted Stoner to deny his own extradition from Georgia. He failed to win election, but scored a minor victory when the FCC barred Georgia television stations from censoring Stoner's political ads. Thereafter, viewers were subjected to Stoner's prime-time denunciation of integration as "a nigger plot" to seduce white women, coupled with proclamations that "You can't have law and order and niggers, too." Stone ran third in the final election and was extradited to Alabama in January 1980. At his trial, Bull Connor and ex-policeman Tom Cook (named in FBI files as a Klan ally) testified for the state. Jurors convicted Stoner on 14 May, and he received the maximum ten-year sentence, informing the court: "This confirms my conviction that this is a Jew-dominated country with no freedom for white Christians." A month later, Stoner sued the Georgia Democratic party over its ruling that his felony conviction and impending prison term barred him from opposing incumbent Sen. Herman Talmadge in August's primary. A federal judge upheld his right to appear on the ballot, but Stoner ran fifth among six candidates, with fewer than 20,000 votes statewide. An appellate court upheld his bombing conviction in April 1982, and he formally resigned from the NSRP nine months later, forfeiting $20,000 bond when he went underground as a fugitive. Captured in May 1983, Stoner served barely one-third of his sentence and won parole in November 1986. He immediately resumed his racist activities, and emerged in 1989 as the head of a new Crusade Against Corruption, based in Marietta, Georgia. The group's slogan: "Thank God for AIDS."

Strickland, Rev. Perry E. — A resident of Baton Rouge, Louisiana, and founder of the Central Baptist Mission, Strickland joined the U.S. Klans in 1955, then left a year later, in a financial dispute. The quarrel began at a rally in Atlanta, where Strickland challenged the accounting practices of Wizard Eldon Edwards. ("They just told us the Klan had a balance of $300.") Before year's end, Strickland chartered his own Louisiana Knights, telling journalists: "The NAACP is backed by Jew money. Catholic Archbishop [Joseph] Rummel came out for integration, but most Catholics don't go along with him. Some Catholics tried to join us, but we turned them down. We need a white, Protestant group based on American principles."

Swenson, John D. — A resident of Bossier City, Louisiana, described by HUAC investigators as the "modern father of the Klan" in his state, Swenson served as grand dragon and national kleagle for the Original Knights of the KKK. Assisted by Royal Young, Swenson recruited new members in Mississippi and Arkansas, but charges of financial chicanery surfaced in late 1963, with Swenson and Young accused of hiding Klan assets in the name of the Louisiana Rifle Association. Before surrendering control in early 1964, Swenson burned Klan records, allegedly to prevent their falling "into the hands of the enemy—the communists." Authorities countered with suggestions that he hoped to hide the evidence of profits earned from sale of Klan robes, but Swenson refused to answer questions when he appeared before HUAC in January 1966.

Taylor, Edgar — A Baton Rouge welder and gas station attendant, Taylor served as Louisiana grand dragon of the U.S. Klans in 1957. In spring of that year he told reporters, "The niggers are the main thing with us now. We are not fighting Jews and Catholics except where they help the niggers."

Taylor, Gilbert — An ex-congressman from Huron County, Ohio, Taylor succeeded Clyde Osborn as Ohio's grand dragon in 1924.

Taylor, Kenneth — Imperial Wizard James Farrands dismissed Taylor as Indiana's grand dragon of the IEKKKK in September 1988, but a special tribunal of dragons reinstated him a month later. With that meager victory in hand, Taylor resigned in a bid to disassociate himself and Hoosier knights from Farrands's "cult" of neo–Nazis and skinhead recruitment. In November 1988, he ran for coroner of Montgomery County, with the prediction "I can't lose." Voters proved him wrong, and a year later there was still no sign of the "new constitution" he promised to Indiana klansmen in 1988.

Terwillinger, Lewis — Terwillinger served as Montana's grand dragon in the 1920s.

Thompson, H. Roswell — Identified in 1971 as imperial wizard of Louisiana's Universal Klan (also known as the Fraternal Order of the Klan), Thompson was injured by three brick-wielding Black Panthers in January 1972, while marching in a birthday parade for Gen. Robert E. Lee. Prior to his death in 1976, Thompson launched four unsuccessful gubernatorial campaigns, also running for mayor in New Orleans and various lesser positions.

Tucker, Bobby — As grand dragon of Tennessee, Tucker attended Robert Scoggin's Conference of Eastern Dragons in 1976.

Tuttle, Douglas — Tuttle identified himself as Indiana's grand dragon in October 1989, after New York State Police jailed him on weapons charges following a routine traffic stop. Tuttle was held in lieu of $10,000 bond, while Ken Taylor denied his leadership role in the Hoosier KKK.

Upchurch, William — Identified as the imperial wizard of the Justice Knights of the KKK, Upchurch was charged with shooting four black women (some accounts claim five victims) in Chattanooga, Tennessee, in April 1980. Jurors acquitted him three months later, in a verdict that sparked black riots. In November 1982, police jailed Upchurch for the rape of a seven year-old white girl in Amelia County, Virginia.

Vachon, Eric—Canadian klansman Vachon replaced Michel Larocque as Québec grand dragon of the IEKKKK in autumn 1990. He also distributed a newspaper, *The Klansman,* which landed three of his members in jail during November 1991 for smuggling illegal hate literature.

Vail, Vernon—Vail defected from the Maryland Knights in autumn 1976, to serve as grand dragon of his own splinter faction. Established Klan leaders dismissed his thirty followers as "misfits," and Vail himself left the group in March 1977, complaining that the recent arrest of klansman William Aitcheson had "set the Klan back fifty years."

Vance, Zebulon Baird—Prior to secession, Vance served in the North Carolina state legislature (1854) and represented his state in Congress (1858–61). During the Civil War, he served briefly as a colonel in the Confederate Army, then won election as North Carolina's governor (1862–65). Several historians name him as the state's grand dragon during Reconstruction. Following "redemption," he served once more as governor (1877–79) and in the U.S. Senate (1879–94). Vance died in office on 14 April 1894. Vance County, North Carolina, is named in his honor.

Venable, James R.—The quintessential klansman, Venable was the product of a true Klan family, with members including his father and several uncles. In 1915, the Venable Brothers granite company—then owners of Stone Mountain, Georgia—allowed William Simmons to use their property for the modern Klan's first public ceremony. Years later, when state authorities took over Stone Mountain, Venable's family retained a pasture at its base, ideal for rallies and cross-burnings. Venable himself joined the KKK in 1924, three years before he graduated from Georgia Tech engineering school. In 1930, he completed law school in Atlanta and entered private practice, always ready to defend klansmen or other racists when they broke the law. Friendly with a succession of imperial wizards from Hiram Evans to Eldon Edwards, Venable also served three terms as mayor of Stone Mountain. In 1946, he joined Sam Green's AGK, and ten years later Venable surfaced as imperial klonsel for the U.S. Klans. Sharing offices with J.B. Stoner in the late 1950s, Venable scored national headlines for his defense of accused synagogue bomber George Bright in 1958.

When dissension split the U.S. Klans in 1961, Venable retained membership in that group and simultaneously joined its successor, serving as imperial klonsel for the new UKA. In 1962, Venable organized his own Defensive League of Registered Americans, retaining his post with the UKA until 1963, when he left to found the National Knights. That group, in turn, was one of eight independent factions loosely united under Venable's umbrella organization, the National Association of Ku Klux Klan. His other diverse organizations included the Committee of One Million Caucasians to March on Washington and the Christian Voters and Buyers League (created with UKA defec-

tor Wallace Butterworth). Apparently more militant than his competitors, Venable told a 1964 audience that if southern schools were integrated, "We'll close them up. We'll burn them up, if it comes to that." In May 1965, he attended a Klan meeting in Montgomery, Alabama, where attendees agreed "not to participate in castration, but if it was necessary to liquidate someone to prove the Klan was not kidding, this would be done." That same year, the National Knights created a hard-core "elite" branch, the Black Shirts, which welcomed klansmen expelled from the UKA after their arrest on murder charges. Appearing before HUAC in February 1966, Venable said he would "like to retract" and "apologize" for earlier pamphlets attacking manufacturers of kosher foods.

In 1975, five of Venable's grand dragons accused him of mismanagement and senility, defecting en masse to create the Invisible Empire Knights under Dale Reusch. Klan-watchers viewed the National Knights as moribund by 1978, except for annual cross-burning picnics on Venable's land near Stone Mountain, but Venable made a new bid for leadership in 1982–83, hosting successive Labor Day unity meetings attended by leaders of seven rival Klans. The result was a loose-knit Confederation of Klans, with Venable listed as an imperial officer, but continued dissension prevented the group from attaining real strength. No trace of the Confederation or the National Knights remained by 1987, though Venable remained active, allegedly meeting with leaders of the IEKKKK and Southern White Knights before their members assaulted black marchers in Forsyth County, Georgia. Venable's relative status in the movement by that time was reflected in his omission from the list of

Zebulon Vance, North Carolina's governor during the Civil War, was also probably the state's first grand dragon.

defendants sued in that case, by SPLC attorneys. Venable died in 1993.

Vitter, Rob—Identified in 2005 as the imperial wizard of the Empire Knights of the KKK, Vitter also ran the Konfederation of Klans website, serving members of his own group, the Mississippi White Knights, the United Knights, and several other factions.

Walker, Douglas—Media reports in 2002 identified Walker as imperial wizard of the Mystic Knights of the KKK, headquartered in Dayton, Ohio.

Walton, Dale—Once exalted cyclops of a UKA klavern in Tupelo, Mississippi, Walton emerged as imperial wizard of the Knights of the Green Forest in 1966. Three years later, in September 1969, he was arrested with other klansmen for conspiring to murder black gubernatorial candidate Charles Evers. A search of Walton's car revealed six guns and produced additional charges of illegally carrying concealed weapons.

Warner, James Konrad—As an early member of the American Nazi Party, Warner was jailed with George Rockwell, Daniel Burros and fourteen others when a July 1960 demonstration in Washington, D.C., degenerated into street fighting. Three years later, Warner was among eight NSRP members indicted for violent interference with school integration in Birmingham, Alabama. Following Rockwell's 1967 assassination, Warner served for a time as editor of the *National Socialist Bulletin,* published by the NSWPP. In 1968, he organized southern California's neo–Nazi Sons of Liberty, later moving its headquarters to Metairie, Louisiana, where the group survived to the late 1980s. Along the way, Warner's antics gained him a place on a U.S. Secret Service list of persons deemed dangerous to the president. In September 1976, while serving as Louisiana grand dragon and national information director of David Duke's KKKK, Warner was jailed with Duke during a New Orleans demonstration. Early the following year, he left the Klan to work full-time for his own New Christian Crusade Church, a branch of the Christian Identity movement. Closely affiliated with the "church" was Warner's Christian Defense League, organized in 1977 for whites desirous of "fighting back" against the "satanic Jewish conspiracy." Warner remains active on the neo–Nazi fringe today, figuring prominently in Holocaust-denial circles. He made headlines again in December 2000, when late Boston millionaire Richard Cotter, Jr., bequeathed $500,000 to Warner's church, then based in Chalmette, Louisiana.

Waters, John—In 1997 SPLC investigators identified Waters as Florida's grand dragon of the Bayou Knights.

West, Gene—Identified in press releases as a former Texas grand dragon, West was jailed at San Antonio in May 1985, on charges of manufacturing and possessing illegal drugs. His son Joe and accomplice James Cornelius were also charged by federal prosecutors. Another son, Michael West, subsequently faced charges in an unrelated arson case.

West, John—Media reports from 2002 identified West as Ohio's grand dragon for the Mystic Knights of the KKK.

Wilkinson, Elbert Claude ("Bill")—A native of Galvez, Louisiana, Wilkinson graduated from high school at age sixteen and immediately joined the U.S. Navy, serving as a cryptographer aboard the submarine USS *Simon Bolivar.* He retired from the service after eight years and settled at Denham Springs, where he joined David Duke's KKKK as Louisiana grand dragon and editor of *The Crusader.* In 1975, Wilkinson quarreled with Duke over disposition of Klan funds and defected to lead his own IEKKKK. In spring 1976, he was a featured speaker at Robert Scoggin's Conference of Eastern Dragons in South Carolina. A year later, he view with Scoggin and Dale Reusch for control of various independent Klans at a special unity conference, but William Chaney emerged as leaser of the new Confederation of Independent Orders. Wilkinson soon earned a reputation for "ambulance chasing," gaining new members in areas where racial tension made headlines. His hottest case involved the 1979 rape trial of black defendant Tommy Hines, in Decatur, Alabama, climaxed with a riot that left four persons wounded by gunfire. In spring 1979, Wilkinson scored another media coup by recreating the 1965 civil rights march from Selma to Montgomery, Alabama, with klansmen trooping over highways where black marchers had risked their lives for voting rights. Another recruiting gimmick was Wilkinson's Klan Youth Corps, which offered paramilitary training to teenagers before media exposés drove the operation underground.

By 1980, Wilkinson's following outnumbered Duke's, and he finished off his rival that summer by exposing Duke's offer to sell his membership list for $35,000. Still, the wizard's glory days were numbered. In 1981, journalists revealed that Wilkinson had served as a paid FBI informant since 1974, a betrayal that led many klansmen to desert. In January 1983, harassed by an IRS lien for back taxes and an SPLC lawsuit stemming from the Decatur riot, Wilkinson declared the IEKKKK bankrupt. Two months later, jurors in Hammond, Louisiana, convicted Wilkinson and six klansmen of disturbing the peace during a protest in December 1982. Wilkinson finally resigned, ceding his office to

Bill Wilkinson (in suit) led America's dominant Klan in the early 1980s (Southern Poverty Law Center).

Connecticut Catholic James Farrands, and disappeared from Klan affairs.

Williams, Bill—Once grand dragon for the Association of Arkansas Klans, Williams later stepped down to serve as exalted cyclops of the group's Pine Bluff klavern in 1957.

Williams, Dean—In 1970, Williams replaced Harry Gilliam as UKA grand dragon of South Carolina.

Winder, Alan—A former newsagent, born in 1963, Winder took command of the Invisible Empire, United Klans of Europe in the 1990s, after *Searchlight* magazine revealed Grand Dragon Allab Beshella's prior arrest for child molestation. Winder soon established a new corporation—No. 03409828, the Invisible Empire (Europe) Ltd.—in what observers called an effort to shield his Klan from prosecution for distributing illegal hate literature. "I intend to make us a success," he told reporters in June 1998. "By a 'success,' I mean nothing short of being the leading group throughout Europe for the fight for the preservation of our race and exile of the Jewish and mud races."

Witte, Eloise—Ohio resident Eloise Witte proclaimed herself "grand empress" of the KKK in the mid–1960s, simultaneously presiding over the ladies' auxiliary of James Venable's National Knights and a Cincinnati chapter of the NSRP. In 1966, HUAC witness Daniel Wagner named Witte as the instigator of abortive murder plots against President Lyndon Johnson, Vice President Hubert Humphrey, Dr. Martin Luther King, Klan leader William Morris, and her own husband. Witte allegedly furnished Wagner with firearms, telling him to "practice on Negroes as a sniper, to prove yourself and to help the white race." King's assassination was scheduled to occur at Antioch College, with Wagner ordered "to shoot King and make sure he was dead." As far as killing politicians was concerned, Wagner suggested that "blowing up the White House would be appropriate, and she agreed." Witte testified before HUAC in February 1966, calling Wagner a "psychopath" and a "mentally disturbed loudmouth." She pled the Fifth Amendment when it came to naming other klansmen, but admitted that her home had been "like Grand Central Station" for "at least fifteen Klan groups" seeking footholds in Ohio.

Woodley, Robert "Woody"—In 1997 SPLC investigators identified Woodley as grand dragon of Pennsylvania's Keystone Knights.

Young, Royal Virgin, Sr.—An early member of the Louisiana-based Original Knights, Young served as "imperial dragon" in 1963, helping John Swenson expand the order into neighboring Mississippi. Ousted from the Klan in early 1964, on charges of financial irregularity, Young drifted into the Original KKK of America and was briefly named imperial wizard of that group before resigning in April 1965, to work with ex-general Edwin Walker in Texas. Summoned by HUAC three months later, Young was generally cooperative but used the Fifth Amendment to avoid discussion of his ties to a Louisiana Klan faction known as the American Royal Rangers.

Middle Management

This section profiles Ku Klux officers of lower ranks, ranging from secondary imperial officials to exalted cyclopes of various noteworthy klaverns.

Allen, Rev. Keith K.—An Oregon klansman and chief investigator for the 1920s grand dragon, Allen left the United States for Vancouver, B.C., in 1924, to form a chapter of the RRRR.

Annable, Robert—An Ohio klansman and leader of the Cleveland-based National Christian Conservative Society, Annable testified before HUAC in 1965, calling the KKK "a good organization." In 1968, he led the North American Alliance of White People and the George Wallace Christian Conservative Party of Ohio. The latter group's platform called for racial segregation and immediate repeal of Ohio's fair-housing laws.

Asher, Court—A Prohibition-era bootlegger and chief lieutenant to Grand Dragon David Stephenson in the 1920s Indiana Klan, Asher remained active during and after World War II, publishing the racist newsletter *X-Ray* from his base in Muncie. He was among twenty-eight defendants charged with sedition in July 1942.

Avery, James W.—A Reconstruction-era planter and KKK leader in York County, South Carolina, Avery presided over an area of unrivaled violence. Between November 1870 and September 1871, his district witnessed at least eleven murders and more than 600 whippings, in addition to the destruction of five black schools and churches. (One structure was rebuilt and demolished by the Klan four times.) In May 1871, Avery issued a statement condemning violence, but he could not control his ghouls. Refusing to appear before congressional investigators, he later fled to Canada and found refuge there with other Carolina expatriates.

Babington, Robert—A Reconstruction officer of the KWC in Washington Parish, Louisiana, Babington was also a merchant, postmaster, and chairman of the Democratic Party's central committee. Those divided loyalties still left time for him to serve as secretary of the local KKK, in which capacity he issued "protection papers" for blacks who voted Democratic in the 1868 elections. Prior to the final vote, Babington was identified as a member of the hooded gang that rode through Franklinton on five successive nights, intimidating would-be Republican voters.

Beam, Louis Ray, Jr.—As a child growing up in Lake Jackson, Texas, Louis Beam attended an all-white school, where classmates recall that he was "very much against blacks." Military service in Vietnam did nothing to change his views, and he returned home to join the Texas realm of the UKA, then led by Grand Dragon Frank Converse. By 1971, Beam was a member of the KBI, serving as a self-styled public relations agent. On 11 June 1971, Beam was one of four klansmen indicted on charges of mounting a terrorist campaign against the local Pacifica Foundation radio station and other targets in Houston. Avoiding conviction on those charges, he shifted allegiance to David Duke's KKKK in 1976, emerging as grand dragon for Texas. When Duke and Beam addressed a rally at Euless, in summer 1979, their "honor guard" consisted of new recruits from Fort Hood, dressed in paramilitary uniforms complete with rifles, bayonets and pistols. Known for his extremism of word and deed, Beam ranted at one Texas Klan rally, "I've got news for you, nigger. I'm not going to be in front of my television set, I'm gonna be hunting you. I don't need any of the three Jewish-owned networks to tell me what I've got to do. I've got the Bible in one hand and a .38 in the other hand and I know what to do."

One step toward the ultimate hunt was Beam's creation of the Texas Emergency Reserve for paramilitary training of adults—and, in the case of one facility near Houston, teenage members of the Civil Air Patrol and the Boy Scouts Explorer program. In early 1981, Beam's klansmen targeted a Texas community of Vietnamese refugees, prompting a federal lawsuit by the SPLC and the Vietnamese Fishermen's Association that April. In May, Beam and his knights were slapped with an injunction barring further harassment, while a second lawsuit closed his training camps forever in June 1982. (Beam subsequently challenged SPLC leader Morris Dees to a duel.) Fresh from his defeats in court, Beam became a self-styled "ambassador at large" for the Aryan Nations, launching its Internet bulletin board and devising a point system for qualification of "Aryan warriors." In Beam's calculation, killing a congressman was worth one-fifth of a point, judges one-sixth, federal agents one-tenth, and journalists or local politicians one-twelfth, while instant qualification (with one point) could be gained by murdering the President of the United States.

In April 1987, Beam was one of fourteen neo–Nazis indicted on federal sedition charges, for allegedly accepting $100,000 in bank loot from terrorists of The Order during 1983–84. He fled into hiding and was added to the FBI's "Ten Most Wanted" list on 14 July 1987. Traced to Guadalajara, Mexico, he was captured on 6 November 1987, after his wife engaged in a shootout with Mexican police. After white jurors at Fort Smith, Arkansas, acquitted all fourteen defendants in April 1988, Beam emerged from the courtroom to tell reporters, "There are over 150 other political prisoners held in ZOG's jails that need to be freed. I think ZOG has suffered a terrible defeat here today. I think everyone saw through the charade and saw that I was simply being punished for being a vociferous and outspoken opponent of ZOG."

Encouraged by the Fort Smith verdict, Beam remained active with the Aryan Nations, published *Essays of a Klansman,* and proudly declared himself "a seditionist," expounding the concept of "leaderless resistance." On 22 October 1992, he appeared as a keynote speaker at a Christian Identity meeting in Estes Park, Colorado—hailed as the "Rocky Mountain Rendezvous"—which laid the groundwork for the 1990s "patriot militia" movement. He remained a fixture at Richard Butler's annual Aryan World Congress through the 1990s, and attended the militia-sponsored "Jubilation 96" in April 1996. Thus far, in the twenty-first century, Beam has apparently limited his activity to Internet website postings.

Bellesen, Paul L.—A black Catholic from Nampa, Idaho, Bellesen joined the National Knights of the KKK by mail, as a prank, in 1965. Sight-unseen, Wizard James Venable named him grand titan of Idaho, resulting in predictable embarrassment when Bellesen went public.

Bergeron, Sandra—While serving as a giant for David Duke's KKKK, Bergeron was frequently cited as living proof of women's opportunities in the "new" Klan. Her husband once bailed Duke out of jail in New Orleans, following Duke's arrest for inciting a riot.

Bonner, George—A resident of Monroe, Louisiana, Bonner served as klaliff when the Original KKK of America was chartered in Ouachita Parish, on 26 January 1965.

Borglum, John Gutzon de la Mothe—The son of a Mormon polygamist, born in 1867, sculptor Gutzon Borglum carved Mt. Rushmore and the Confederate memorial on Stone Mountain, Georgia. He was also a high-ranking klansman in the 1920s, a participant in strategy meetings between Hiram Evans and David Stephenson, prior to the Evans coup against Wizard William Simmons in November 1922. One of six knights chosen for the Imperial Kloncilium of 1923, Borglum tried to settle the Evans-Simmons dispute over ownership of KKK funds, regalia and ritual. He once described the Klan as a movement expressing the "minds of the villagers and agrarians" in America, without resort to foreign creeds. Borglum died in 1941.

Gutzon Borglum, sculptor of Mt. Rushmore, was a high-ranking klansman in the 1920s.

Brock, John L.—While serving as grand klaliff of the UKA in Georgia, Brock was jailed with thirty-nine others (including ten children) during a wild party at the DeKalb County klavern. Identified as a member of Nacirema, Brock also joined Grand Dragon Calvin Craig in assaulting black demonstrators at Crawfordsville, in October 1965.

Buckles, Billy—As grand giant of the WKKKKM, Buckles addressed a Jackson, Mississippi, Klan rally following the triple-murder of civil rights workers in Neshoba County, telling assembled klansmen, "Now they know what we will do. We have shown them what we can do, and we will do it again if necessary."

Burton, Benjamin F.—While serving as grand titan of the Essex-Middle River Knights, Burton was convicted of illegal cross-burning and received a one-year prison term on 20 November 1964. At the time of his conviction, Burton and another klansman were awaiting trial on charges of attempted murder, stemming from their knife attack on two black patrons in a bar.

Butterworth, Wallace—A former "vox pop" radio announcer, Butterworth served as public relations director and an imperial board member of the UKA in 1961. He befriended imperial klonsel James Venable, and in April 1962 helped Venable organize the Defensive Legion of Registered Americans and its subsidiary, the Christian Voters and Buyers League. Over the next two years, Butterworth coordinated anti–Semitic radio broadcasts in Atlanta, Georgia, and in November 1963 he left the UKA to serve as an incorporating officer of Venable's National Knights. Three months later, he joined Venable in founding the Committee of One Million Americans to March on Washington, but the planned 4 July protest failed to materialize, and Butterworth retired from Klan affairs soon afterward.

Clarke, Edward Young—A partner with Elizabeth Tyler in the Atlanta-based Southern Publicity Association, Clark was arrested with Tyler in a local bawdy house, drunk and semi-nude, in October 1919. He paid a five-dollar fine and later contrived to destroy the official report of his arrest, but the event came back to haunt him years later, after Clarke rose to power in the KKK. Hired by Wizard William Simmons to promote the Klan in June 1920, Clarke became the first imperial kleagle. His propagation department received eight dollars from each new klansman's ten-dollar klecktoken, with four dollars paid to local kleagles, one dollar reserved for the realm's king kleagle, fifty cents for the resident grand goblin, and $2.50 split by Clarke and Tyler (while the last two dollars went to Simmons). In less than a year, Clarke had 1,100 kleagles active nationwide, obeying his directives to stress nativism and religious prejudice in their appeals outside the South. On the side, Clarke owned a real estate company, created to manipulate Klan holdings for personal profit. In September 1921, the *New York World* exposed his 1919 arrest, producing widespread calls for dismissal of Clarke and Tyler. Simmons resisted, and named Clarke imperial wizard *pro tem* during an extended vacation in 1922. In March 1923, following Clarke's indictment on federal Mann Act charges in Texas, Wizard Hiram Evans canceled his contract "for the good of the order." A panel of grand dragons confirmed his banishment on

11 January 1924, prompting Clarke to contact President Calvin Coolidge, calling for federal action against the KKK as "a cheap political machine." Two months later, on 10 March, Clarke pled guilty to the Mann Act charge (transporting women across state lines for immoral purposes) and paid a $5,000 fine.

Coburn, William S.—When Los Angeles police raided local Klan headquarters in 1922, Grand Goblin William Coburn slipped past them to put the order's membership list in a mailbox, safe from confiscation. Briefly jailed for that escapade, he later served as personal attorney for Wizard William Simmons in Atlanta, Georgia. In 1923, Philip Fox—a supporter and speechwriter for rival Hiram Evans, shot Coburn to death. The murder prompted Simmons to abandon imperial headquarters, telling reporters, "I didn't want to fight men who could kill that way."

Coker, James P.—A wealthy shopkeeper in Marianna, Florida, Coker also served as chief of the Reconstruction KKK in Jackson County. Rated as Florida's most violent county and one of the worst in the south, Jackson County was described by a black minister as the place "where Satan has his seat." An estimated 179 murders, mostly of black and Republican victims, occurred by late 1871, while a Klan intimidation campaign forced the sheriff to resign in March of that year. A month later, klansmen murdered John Dickinson, the only GOP officeholder left in the county. Federal authorities jailed Coker on 11 December 1871 and took him to Tallahassee for trial, then dismissed his case after a year of legal delays.

Cooper, Jock—An Australian knife and gun dealer, Cooper was identified in 2002 as exalted cyclops for the Imperial Klans of America in Coonabarabran, New South Wales. Although presumably subordinate to Grand Dragon Peter Coleman, Cooper promoted his klavern primarily as a vigilante organization whose members were "fed up with insane policies relating to reconciliation, multiculturalism and homosexuality." Cooper actively recruited local bikers, but at last report his Klan had not committed any acts of violence. As for racial matters, Cooper told reporters, "Yes I'm a racist. I'm the first to admit it, otherwise I wouldn't be in the KKK, but this is for the kids."

Crowe, James R.—One of the KKK's "immortal six" founders in Pulaski, Tennessee, Crowe is often credited with naming the order. He served as the Klan's first grand turk and attended the April 1867 reorganization conference in Nashville. After Reconstruction, Crowe served as Masonic grand master of Tennessee.

Cummins, Eli—An ex–Confederate army officer and attorney in Wilkinson County, Georgia, Cummins also served as leader of the local KKK in Reconstruction. In August 1871, he contrived the false arrest of black Republican Henry Lowther, followed by Lowther's abduction from jail and castration by klansmen.

Deese, Charles Douglas ("Bud")—North Carolina native Bud Deese came to the KKK with a record of felony convictions for breaking and entering, larceny, robbery and assaulting a woman. In January 1964, less than two years after the latter conviction, he became North Carolina's grand kligrapp for the UKA. A month later, police jailed Deese for carrying concealed weapons at a civil rights demonstration, and jurors later convicted him. (Additional charges at his booking included causing a riot, interfering with a police officer, and using indecent language.) In June 1965, jurors convicted Deese of assaulting another woman. Summoned before HUAC four months later, he stood silent behind the Fifth Amendment.

Demarest, Horace A.—One of New York state's original klansmen, Demarest chartered the KKK as the Alpha Pi Sigma fraternity in 1923, finally dropping the front two years later. In 1946, while serving as deputy state motor vehicle commissioner and a Republican leader in Queens, Demarest suffered embarrassment from exposure of his Klan background. Despite his denials of any surviving Klan ties, he was dismissed on 5 May 1946, his supervisors citing "discrepancies" in statements on his job application.

Dibrell, C.G.—A Tennessee native and former Confederate general, Dibrell was a delegate to the KKK's April 1867 convention in Nashville. Elected grand titan of the new order, he assumed responsibility for Klan recruiting in eastern Tennessee. Dibrell was one of thirteen ranking klansmen who met in Nashville on 1 August 1868, to protest formation of a state militia and assure Republicans (falsely) that the KKK had no plans to depose the state government.

DiSalvo, Louis Anthony—A barber and licensed firearms dealer in Waveland, Mississippi, DiSalvo joined the WKKKKM in 1964 and served as exalted cyclops of a Hancock County klavern. In his professional capacity, he supplied firearms to fellow klansmen, including knights later arrested for bombings around McComb. His efforts to recruit a Klan firing squad at Poplarville, approved by Wizard Sam Bowers, prompted several White Knights to defect and join the UKA. In September 1964, DiSalvo tried without success to interest other klansmen in his plot to bomb LBJ's campaign train on its passage through Mississippi. He also conducted seminars on use of venomous snakes as lethal weapons. In July 1965, DiSalvo appeared on the dais at a UKA rally in Poplarville, and three months later he served as master of ceremonies for a UKA rally at Bay St. Louis. At the time, he claimed simultaneous membership in the UKA and WKKKKM.

Dorsett, George Franklin—A Greensboro, North Carolina house painter, Dorsett served the UKA as imperial kludd during 1964–65, while doubling as North Carolina's grand titan and chaplain of the UKA's security guards. He often told parishioners that the "message of Christian love is a tool in communist hands." In 1965, Wizard Robert Shelton sent Dorsett to Florida, where he helped Kleagle Boyd Hamby establish a new realm based at Titusville. Shelton later banished Dorsett, on 4 April 1966, for disclosing "secret information" to HUAC, but Dorsett attended a UKA rally days later, where klansmen rocked his car and pelted it with stones. A secret FBI informant, Dorsett secured Bureau backing in 1967, when he and James Cole founded the Confederate Knights of the KKK. Moving on from

Imperial Kludd George Dorsett collects donations at an August 1965 UKA rally in Landis, North Carolina (HUAC).

there to join the North Carolina Knights, Dorsett was finally exposed as a traitor in 1975. On 12 January 1976, the UKA's North Carolina state board issued a notice of exile on Dorsett, its members voting nine-to-one to banish him "forever."

Droege, Walter Wolfgang—A German native, born in 1949, Droege emigrated to Canada with his family in 1952. He joined the neo–Nazi Western Guard in 1974, and spent two weeks in jail the following year, for painting racist graffiti along the route of an African Liberation Day parade in Toronto. In the same year, 1975, Droege befriended James McQuirter and soon emerged as a spokesman for the Canadian KKK. Convicted of assaulting a reporter in 1976, he got out of jail in time to attend David Duke's "International Patriotic Congress" in New Orleans. Soon affiliated with Duke's KKKK, Droege organized a Canadian speaking tour for Duke in 1979. In April 1981, he was among ten men arrested for plotting to invade Grenada. Convicted with Don Black and other klansmen for violating the U.S. Neutrality Act, Droege received a three-year prison term. In 1985, Alabama authorities jailed him as an illegal alien, found in possession of cocaine and concealed weapons. Droege served four years of a thirteen-year sentence in that case, then left for Libya in September 1989. Later that year, after his fourth deportation from the U.S., Droege helped found the Heritage Front in Canada, serving as one of the racist group's seven directors.

A brawl in 1993 sent him back to jail for possession of deadly weapons, followed by a three-month jail term for contempt of court in 1994. In 1998, Droege pled guilty to possession of a stolen car. Police found him shot to death in his Toronto apartment on 14 April 2005, subsequently charging a friend of Droege's with second-degree murder spawned by a romantic triangle. Droege's remains were cremated and shipped to Germany.

DuBois, Joseph G.—While serving as klabee of a Goldsboro, North Carolina klavern, DuBois appeared as the first cooperative witness in HUAC's 1965–66 KKK investigation. Testifying on 22 October 1965, he resigned from the UKA on the witness stand and delivered Klan records to the committee. Disillusioned by the refusal of UKA leaders to answer HUAC's questions, DuBois proclaimed, "Anyone who takes the Fifth Amendment either has something to hide or is a communist." Following his testimony, DuBois received several anonymous death threats.

Durham, Plato—An ex–Confederate officer in the Civil War, Durham also served as a ranking Klan leader in Reconstruction-era Cleveland County, North Carolina. In March 1871, he secretly conferred with Democratic leaders in violence-plagued Rutherford County, seeking unsuccessfully to reduce Klan nightriding.

Earle, Joshua F.—An ex–Confederate army officer and prominent Democrat in Crittenden County, Arkansas, Earle also led the local KKK. When Gov. Powell Clayton declared martial law in November 1868, Earle fled to Memphis, but Tennessee's governor approved his extradition in February 1869. At his arrest, police found Earle in possession of a letter addressed to Crittenden County klansmen, ordering them to disband.

Edwards, Xavier—As a kleagle for the UKA, Edwards began recruiting for a Maryland realm in August 1965. Early the following year, he launched a harassment campaign against Robert Lee's New Era Bookshop in Laurel, telling reporters, "Wherever the store goes, they can expect to find the Ku Klux Klan." If Lee closed his shop, Edwards said, he planned boycotts of local Jewish merchants. On 27 March 1966, after a weekend of cross-burning ceremonies, Edwards announced his resignation from the UKA, saying he feared the Klan had turned to violence and he wanted no part of criminal activity. UKA leaders responded with charges that Edwards was banished for recruiting ANP members into the Klan. In either case, his defection split the small Maryland realm, with Edwards leading his own Maryland Knights (also known as the Interstate Knights) from headquarters in Laurel. By the time Patsy Sims interviews leaders of that faction in 1977, Edwards had long since departed.

Ellis, Claiborne P.—As exalted cyclops of the UKA in Durham, North Carolina, C.P. Ellis was a study in contradictions. Soon after his election in the early 1970s, he began to resent the Klan's role as a tool of wealthy whites, used by the establishment to counteract black progress. "We would show up with out guns in out belts," he said, "and the next day I would see the same city official on the street and expect him to come up and thank me. And instead, he would cross the street to keep from meeting me. I found out we were being used to keep those folks in power. And I decided we weren't going to be used any more." Ellis encouraged klansmen to participate openly in politics, presenting a Klan position on public issues. Convinced that black and poor white children faced identical discrimination from "liberal" teachers in Durham's schools, Ellis won success from several influential blacks in his unsuccessful 1972 campaign for a seat on the school board. Excluded from UKA state klonvokations in 1972–73, the rebellious cyclops clung to his office with support from klansmen who shared his view of wealthy white merchants as the chief enemies of both blacks and blue-collar whites. Late in 1972, Ellis was invited to join the Durham Human Relations Commission, a move that he described as an attempt to co-opt his leadership, while using the KKK to neutralize blacks on the panel, but Ellis confounded his critics by siding with blacks to oppose housing discrimination. "I turned on them that put me there," he said, "and now they don't know what to do with me." By 1973, still holding both his Klan office and seat on the commission, Ellis emerged as a leader of the International Union of Operating Engineers, representing service workers at Duke University.

Etheridge, Paul S.—A longtime member of the Fulton County commission in Atlanta, Georgia, Etheridge was one of the modern Klan's first recruits in November 1915. While holding public office, he doubled as imperial klonsel and later served as the Klan's chief of staff. In 1923, he was one of six klansmen chosen for the imperial kloncilium to resolve the power struggle between William Simmons and Hiram Evans. In 1932, Etheridge briefly headed the Roosevelt Southern Clubs, before imperial headquarters denounced FDR's New Deal.

Farmer, Saxon—A resident of Bogalusa, Louisiana, Farmer served as grand titan of the Original Knights before a three-way rift shattered the group in autumn 1964. Remaining active in the Sixth Congressional District, he joined Grand Dragon Charles Christmas to found a new front group, the ACCA, in January 1965. Active in violent opposition to civil rights marchers that year, Farmer was named as a defendant when the DOJ filed suit to enjoin klansmen from terrorizing local blacks. Called to testify in New Orleans that summer, Farmer swore that the KKK had disbanded in Bogalusa, but federal judges disbelieved him, granting a permanent injunction against further acts of violence. Farmer subsequently shifted his allegiance to the UKA, luring his fellow knights into the new group that soon became Washington Parish's dominant Klan.

Fraser, J.E. ("Frog")—A nursery owner in MacClenny, Florida, Fraser emerged in 1957 as a spokesman for the Florida KKK, although he denied being the group's imperial wizard. A klansman since 1923 and a self-described "cracker," he told reporters, "We're for segregation and white supremacy and upholding the law. There's plenty of ways to do things within the law and sometimes we have to straighten up officials. Fellow sells his house to a nigger in a white neighborhood and we just spread the word. He loses his business and his friends. That ol' boy better just get out of this state."

Gholson, Samuel J.—An attorney and ex–Confederate general, Gholson led the Reconstruction-era KKK in Monroe County, Mississippi, and environs. In June 1871, he defended twenty klansmen charged with murdering black victim Alec Page.

Gilbert, Ernest S.—When the WKKKKM was incorporated in April 1964, Gilbert served as the chief of the group's KBI.

Girgenti, Gladys—Identified as co-founder of Tennessee's Confederate Vigilantes, Knights of the KKK, Girgenti was one of six persons jailed after a bungled Nashville synagogue bombing, in May 1981. The defendants also faced charges of plotting to bomb a local television tower and several Jewish-owned stores.

Green, Samuel, Jr.—The son of AGK Grand Dragon Samuel Green, Sr., and a loyal klansman, Green served as attorney for Eldon Edwards when he incorporated the U.S. Klans in October 1955.

Hays, Bennie Jack—As grand titan of the UKA in Mobile, Alabama, Hays was convicted (with his wife) of mail fraud, wire fraud, and conspiracy in October 1984. Three years later, police charged him as an accomplice in the 1981 lynching of Michael Donald, a case that saw both Hays's son and son-in-law convicted of first-degree murder. Hays faced trial on that charge in February 1988, but his failing health aborted the proceedings. Hays died in August 1993, before a second trial could be convened.

Head, Daniel—A leader of the Reconstruction-era KKK in Haralson County, Georgia, Head was also father of a Democratic candidate for the state legislature in 1871.

Hodges, Robert E.—New York native Robert Hodges was attending Columbia (South Carolina) Commercial College in 1957, when newspaper identified him as exalted cyclops for the local Association of South Carolina Klans. Promoted to grand kligrapp three years later, he actively opposed JFK's presidential candidacy on religious grounds, telling journalists, "You cannot afford to support or vote for anyone or group [*sic*] that represents the Roman Catholic Church. Heaven help your soul if you vote away your religious liberty." In 1967, HUAC identified Hodges as a grand council member for the ASCK, serving simultaneously as a nighthawk for James Venable's National Knights. He remained active in the KKK as late as 1976, while employed as a postal worker.

Hoff, William—Appointed in 1965 as the UKA's king kleagle for New York, Hoff served concurrently as state director for the NSRP. During the April 1968 race riots in Newark, New Jersey, Hoff threw a concussion grenade into a bar patronized by blacks, wounding two persons. Arrested in New York City four months later, after giving an undercover officer dynamite to bomb the home of a local draft resistance leader, Hoff faced charges of conspiring to murder 158 leftists and civil rights activists. Investigation of those charges revealed his ongoing links to the KKK, NSRP, ANP and the Minutemen. On 21 August 1969, Hoff pled guilty on two of nine felony counts filed against him. In 1992, media reports identified Hoff as New York grand dragon of the IEKKKK. Exposure of that role cost him his job on 21 May 1992, when his black employer dismissed him.

Jones, Calvin E.—A Confederate veteran and one of the KKK's "immortal six" in Pulaski, Tennessee, Jones convened the order's first meeting at the office of his father, Judge Thomas M. Jones. Later an attorney, Jones served the Reconstruction-era Klan as a nighthawk.

Kennedy, John B.—A Confederate army captain, wounded three times and captured by Union forces during the Civil War, Kennedy was another of the KKK's "immortal six" founders in Pulaski, Tennessee. Tradition credits him with suggesting addition of "Klan" to "Ku Klux," for purposed of alliteration. As the Klan's first grand magi, he participated in a January 1869 race riot in Pulaski that left one black man dead and several wounded.

Long, Jacob A.—A young attorney in Reconstruction-era Guilford County, North Carolina, Long was also a klansman, county leader of the White Brotherhood, and a commander of the local CUG. In late 1869, he served as secretary for a Klan-dominated Conservative-Democratic conference that protested efforts to suppress nightriding. Long was among those jailed when Gov. William Holden imposed martial law in 1870. In December 1871, he was indicted with seventeen others for the February 1870 murder of Wyatt Outlaw at Graham, North Carolina.

Manucy, Holsted R. ("Hoss")—A convicted bootlegger and outspoken segregationist in St. Augustine, Florida, Manucy led the Ancient City Gun (or Hunting) Club and an informal group of racists locally known as Manucy's Raiders. Questioned about his open fraternization with klansmen, Manucy told reporters, "I'm not a member of the Klan—I'm Catholic—but I'm not knocking it, either. I think the Klan is a very good organization." In fact, various Florida Klans began admitting Catholics in the 1950s, and HUAC identified the ACGC as a front for Klavern No. 519 of the UFKKK, while FBI files named Manucy as the klavern's exalted cyclops. J.B. Stoner also admitted "some overlap" between the Klan and the ACGC. Manucy, meanwhile, declared that his primary occupations were "raisin' hogs and shootin' niggers." Employed by Sheriff L.O. Davis as a "special" deputy until Judge Bryan Simpson banned official recruitment of klansmen, Manucy embarrassed himself in March 1964 be betraying klansmen William Rosecrans, bomber of a black home in Jacksonville. Manucy mistakenly believed Rosecrans had bombed the strike-bound Florida East Coast Railway and turned him in for the outstanding reward. Throughout 1963–64, Manucy's ACGC members participated enthusiastically in riots and nightriding against blacks.

Mars, Grady—Passed over for promotion in favor of a black soldier, Mars quit the U.S. Army and returned to his native North Carolina, where he joined the Klan and served as grand klaliff for the UKA in the early 1960s. In 1965, he was named custodian of the Raymond Mills defense fund, established to aid klansmen accused of bombings around New Bern. Mars refused to answer HUAC's questions in October 1965, and the experience left him despondent. He committed suicide at home on 12 December 1965.

McCord, Frank O.—Another of the KKK's "immortal six" founders in Pulaski, Tennessee, McCord served simultaneously as grand cyclops and editor of the Pulaski *Citizen*. He published the first KKK notice on 29 March 1867, and attended the Klan's reorganization conference in Nashville two weeks later. On 19 April 1867, he published an account of the grand turk (James Crowe) invading his newspaper office. "Awed into submission," McCord ran a notice of the Klan's next Pulaski den meeting. He briefly fled the area in 1869, when Gov. William Brownlow deployed militia units against the KKK, then returned to business as usual when the troops were withdrawn.

McGhee, Rev. Charles D.—A Methodist minister and klansman in St. Louis, Missouri, McGhee earned a reprimand from Bishop W.B. McMurray for his KKK activities in September 1923. McMurray said, "If he wants to parade in a mask, that's his business, but I don't believe it will help his work as a disciple of Christ." McGhee countered by telling reporters, "If it comes to a choice between the Methodist Church and the Klan, I shall choose the Klan." Removed from his pulpit a short time later, McGhee raged, "The Klan has your number, Bishop! We have had it for months. We know where to find you and will attend to your case!" Despite the public threats, klansmen staged no attacks upon McMurray.

McKoin, Dr. B.M.—As exalted cyclops of the Mer Rouge, Louisiana, klavern, McKoin declared a private war on crime in 1922, staging a bogus attempt on his life to dramatize the problem of local bootleg gangs. Implicated in a double murder in August 1922, he initially entered Johns Hopkins Hospital in Baltimore, in order to evade arrest, then later waived extradition and returned to face a grand jury (which failed to indict him).

McRae, Dandridge—An ex–Confederate general, McRae served during Reconstruction as grand titan of the congressional district including Independence, Jackson and White Counties, Arkansas. He fled to Canada in 1868, to escape murder charges, but returned for trial in 1871. Jurors acquitted McRae and his co-defendants despite the eyewitness testimony of turncoat klansman John McCauley.

Milam, Dennis—In 1974–75, official reports identified Milam as one of three pioneer klansmen promoting the UKA's expansion in Illinois. An April 1975 clash with fellow klansman Wilburn Foreman escalated into verbal warfare with UKA imperial headquarters after Milam described Wizard Robert Shelton as "stupid" and "out of his mind" for appointing Foreman imperial representative from Illinois. Ostracized by UKA leaders, Milam launched a one-man recruiting drive around Chicago, Cicero and Kankakee, with negligible results. Shelton grudgingly named Milam a kleagle in August 1975, with orders to avoid adverse publicity, then banished him three months later, following a Danville speech in which Milam labeled blacks subhuman deserving of treatment as animals.

Miner, Roy—A salesman of fraternal regalia and exalted cyclops of the 1920s Minneapolis Klan, Miner ran for mayor in 1923. As part of his campaign, the KKK recruited a female jail inmate to claim she had been intimate with the incumbent. A grand jury deemed the story criminally libelous, resulting in jail time for Miner and three other knights.

Muldrow, Henry Lowndes—An attorney in Starkville, Mississippi, during Reconstruction, Muldrow founded and led the local KKK. In his professional capacity, he defended klansmen charged in a series of attacks that drove a Methodist minister named McLachlen from the area in 1871. Repeated postponements ultimately scuttled the case, and local Klan supporters showed their gratitude by electing Muldrow to Congress.

Murphy, Matthew Hobson, Jr.—Named imperial klonsel of the UKA after James Venable resigned in 1963, Murphy achieved national notoriety two years later, for his defense of the klansmen who murdered Viola Liuzzo. He secured a mistrial for triggerman Collie Wilkins in May 1965, then toured the South with his clients for triumphant UKA rallies where the killers posed for photos and signed autographs. On 21 August 1965, Murphy died in an auto accident north of Tuscaloosa, Alabama. Legal representation of indicted UKA members then passed to attorney and ex-mayor of Birmingham Arthur Hanes, Sr.

Newberry, James Douglas—In 1965, HUAC accused Newberry—then Georgia's grand klabee for the UKA—of withdrawing money from the Klan's Atlanta bank account and using it for personal expenses. Three years later, Newberry was elected (with Grand Dragon Calvin Craig) to a seat on Atlanta's model cities program. At the time, both klansmen stressed their desire for racial harmony and cooperation.

Nix, Deavours—A ranking member of the WKKKKM under Wizard Sam Bowers, Nix was named in June 1965 to head that faction's KBI. Nine months later, authorities seized a cache of weapons from his home and charged him with participation in the Vernon Dahmer arson-slaying. Federal prosecutors indicted him in February 1967, for violating Dahmer's civil rights, while Mississippi jailed him again in November 1967, for kidnapping Dahmer prosecution witness Jack Watkins. Jurors deadlocked in his federal case, in May 1969. In 1978, the HSCA probed alleged links between Nix, the WKKKKM and the 1968 murder of Martin Luther King, but the panel found no evidence substantiating a connection. State prosecutors charged him with arson (in the Dahmer case) on 28 May 1998, but Nix died five months later, before facing trial. Nix's wife, Sybil, served as secretary-treasurer for the 1960s APWR, and in 1968 doubled as Mississippi treasurer for the AIP during George Wallace's presidential campaign.

Overton, Harold—A klansman since 1922, based in Wilkinson, Indiana, Overton emerged in October 1946 as Indiana king kleagle for Samuel Green's AGK. In an interview dated 8 November 1946, he claimed to lead a secret council of five, including a banker, a businessman, a labor leader, a farmer and a city councilman—all left anonymous. Overton also alleged that the AGK was active in sixty of Indiana's ninety-two counties, stressing a program of "no rough stuff" and minimal cross-burning, with robes worn only at rallies.

Pecoraro, Clara—A New Orleans native and reputed kung fu expert, Pecoraro joined Jim Lindsay's KKKK in 1973, rising to the rank of Klan security chief under successor David Duke.

Pettus, Edmund Winston—An Alabama native, born in Limestone County during 1821 and later resident in Selma, Pettus served as a lieutenant in the Mexican War (1846–48), then tried his luck in the California gold rush (1849) before returning to serve in Alabama as a solicitor (1853–55) and circuit court judge (1855–58). After secession, Pettus served as Alabama's envoy to Mississippi, then joined the Confederate army as a major, rising to the rank of brigadier general in the Civil War. After Appomattox, he returned to Selma as a lawyer, chairman of the Democratic Party, and a leader of the KKK in Dallas County. Congressional investigators questioned Pettus in July 1871, and while he acknowledged certain local acts of violence, he failed to mention his own Klan membership. He served as an Alabama delegate to the Democratic National Convention in 1876. Three years later, voters sent him to the U.S. Senate, where he remained until his death in office, on 27 July 1907. A bridge in Selma, named in his honor, was the scene of 1965's "Bloody Sunday" confrontation between Al Lingo's state troopers, Sheriff Jim Clark's "special" posse, and black protesters seeking suffrage.

Pottle, E.H.—A prominent Reconstruction-era attorney in Warrenton, Georgia, Pottle represented the local KKK and was recognized as having influence over the order. In 1870, he was a prime mover behind the false bribery prosecution of anti–Klan Sheriff John Norris.

Powell, Luther—Powell was the Klan's pioneer in Oregon in 1921, recruiting 100 Jackson County members during his first week of operation, later serving as king kleagle for Washington and Idaho. From his office in Spokane, he published a Klan newspaper, *The Watcher on the Tower,* and helped found the RRRR. In the late 1920s, Powell moved to Alaska, where his recruiting efforts had little success.

Prins, Jacob—A Dutch native, Prins initially resisted German invaders in 1940, then turned collaborator, working on guidance systems for Adolf Hitler's V-1 and V-2 rockets. After V-E Day, he emigrated to Canada, filled with remorse for his brief opposition to Nazism. "I betrayed myself and my country," Prins later declared. "I had killed Germans. I regretted it ever since and maybe that's why subconsciously I try to make up for it." Convinced that "we would have had a much better world" under Hitler, Prins attached himself to various neo–Nazi groups and the KKK, paying a fine in 1969 for his operation of an anti–Semitic telephone "hotline." Other criminal charges filed against Prins over time include assault, theft, and breaking and entering. In 1975, he emerged as Canadian grand dragon for Dale Reusch's Invisible Empire Knights, while simultaneously leading the White Confederacy of Understanding and playing an active role in the Toronto-based Western Front. In a 1976 inter-

view, Prins opined that "the root of all evil is the Jew." Not surprisingly, Prins is also known as an active spokesman for Holocaust denial.

Ramsey, H.C.—In November 1922, while serving as a klaliff in Louisiana, Ramsey joined in the campaign to replace Wizard William Simmons with Hiram Evans. In the wake of that successful coup, Evans rewarded Ramsey with a transfer to Atlanta as imperial klaliff.

Randolph, Ryland—A bitter racist, Randolph moved to Tuscaloosa, Alabama, in 1867 and purchased the *Independent Monitor,* publishing his newspaper under the masthead: "White Man—Right or Wrong—Still the White Man!" In December 1867, he penned an editorial calling for armed resistance to Reconstruction, and local klansmen made their first appearance on 30 December, carrying Randolph off into mock captivity. Widely acknowledged as Tuscaloosa's cyclops, Randolph began printing regular Ku Klux notices in March 1868, his ghouls quickly resorting to violence when simple threats failed. Years later, in 1901, Randolph fondly recalled how blacks were "thrashed in the regular antebellum style, until their unnatural nigger-pride had a tumble, and humbleness to the white man reigned supreme." Never one to stand on the sidelines of a fight, Randolph once waded into a brawl between a white man and two blacks, stabbing one of the freedmen "in self-defense." On another occasion, he allegedly confronted a mob of 100 blacks and scattered them by brandishing a pistol. His penchant for street brawls led Democratic leaders to shun Randolph by mid–1868, but klansmen remained fiercely loyal, and a gang of them joined him to break up a GOP rally in autumn 1868. Despite his extremism and distance from the party, Ryland served two terms in the state legislature (1869–73), while pursuing his Klan duties at home. His crowning "achievement" was a campaign of intimidation targeting GOP staffers and students at the University of Alabama in Tuscaloosa, which briefly closed the school in 1870. In April 1870, armed with a Bowie knife and pistol, Randolph carried his fight to the streets once again, stalking Prof. Vernon Vaughn. He met student William Smith (a nephew of Alabama's governor) instead, and Smith proved quicker on the draw, wounding Randolph in the leg and killing an elderly bystander. Amputation of his injured leg dampened Randolph's zest for battle, and a June 1870 editorial declared: "It is now time, we are free to announce, for murders and assassinations to cease." A year later, testifying before Congress, Randolph lamented that the once-honorable KKK had fallen into low and violent hands.

Reavis, Henry—An ex-judge and practicing attorney in Gainesville, Alabama, Reavis served as cyclops and chief counsel for the local KKK, enrolling members at his law office.

Reed, Richard—One of the KKK's "immortal six" founders in Pulaski, Tennessee, Reed served as the order's first lictor.

Ridley, Rev. Caleb—An Atlanta minister and imperial kludd of the 1920s KKK, Ridley brought the Klan unfortunate publicity when he was jailed for drunk driving in 1921. Two years later, he served as a member of the imperial kloncilium appointed to mediate the power struggle between William Simmons and Hiram Evans.

Rotella, Frank—Wizard Robert Shelton chose Rotella, a Catholic graduate of New York's Hofstra University, to serve as New Jersey king kleagle for the UKA in July 1965. Rotella simultaneously served as state director for the NSRP, while active in the ANP and the National Socialist American Party. Rotella's superiors at the New York City Welfare Department suspended him in October 1965, when his Klan ties went public, and fired him a month later. In December 1965, a grand jury subpoenaed Rotella concerning KKK activities in Paterson. Four months later, when Rotella announced plans for a rally near Bridgeton, a police informant told reporters Klan ranks were so thin they "could meet in a telephone booth." In fact, only six of Rotella's ninety-odd estimated members could afford robes for the rally on 13 May, where Rotella and his half-dozen disciples were jailed for violating state fire laws and carrying concealed weapons. Rotella quit the UKA without explanation in June 1966, resurfacing on 5 November to lead a cross-burning ceremony for his new splinter faction, the White Crusaders of the North.

Roton, Ralph—An Alabama high-school dropout, Roton joined the Alabama Knights in 1959 and later followed Robert Shelton into the UKA, emerging as head of that group's KBI. Shelton used Roton to infiltrate various civil rights groups, which led in turn to Roton's employment by Alabama's Legislative Commission to Preserve the Peace under Gov. George Wallace. In that capacity, he reported both to Shelton and state legislators on the "communist roots" of the black revolution. He also played an active role in the investigation of Birmingham's fatal church bombing on 15 September 1963, arriving within moments of the blast to photograph bystanders at the crime scene.

Rowley, Ewell—While serving as principal of a Slidell, Louisiana high school in 1963, Rowley doubled as exalted cyclops of the Original Knights' Pearl River klavern. Summoned by HUAC in January 1966, he refused to answer any questions.

Savage, Fred—An ex-detective and professional strikebreaker from New York City, Savage served as chief investigator for Wizard William Simmons during 1920–22. In November 1922, he turned on his employer and joined in the conspiracy to dethrone Simmons, in favor of Hiram Evans. Savage approached Simmons on the eve of the imperial klonvokation, claiming that his "sources" had uncovered a plan to "attack Simmons's character" at the convention, vowing that his men had orders to kill any klansman who insulted Simmons publicly. That threat of mayhem prompted Simmons to accept "temporary" replacement by Evans, whereupon Evans named Savage the Klan's chief of staff.

Shaffer, H.F.—A disciple of veteran anti–Semite Gerald L.K. Smith, Shaffer served as exalted cyclops of a Chambersburg, Pennsylvania klavern in 1952–53, filling the mail with "open letters" inviting "white Gentile Protestants" to join the KKK. One such flier, titled *America for Americans,* read in part: "It is and always will be the earnest endeavor of the Knights of the Ku Klux Klan to preserve this great Nation for its native born through Christ Jesus our Criterion of Character."

Shaw, Ian—An engineering inspector in London, England, Shaw was identified as a Klan recruiter in May 1957. He told reporters, "We aim at putting down subversives. We fight social evils like the vile prostitution in London's west end." When klansmen were blamed for the dismissal of Trinidadian laborer Dick Henderson, fired from his job after whites refused to work with him, Shaw called the incident "a hoax to frighten communists."

Shotwell, Randolph A.—A young Confederate veteran and son of a Presbyterian minister, Shotwell joined the KKK soon after it was organized in Reconstruction-era Rutherford County, North Carolina. He briefly published the Democratic *Vindicator* in Rutherfordton, during 1868, them moved to Asheville, where he drove another paper into bankruptcy. A bitter racist and alcoholic, Shotwell was restless for action after his Civil War adventures, and his Asheville sojourn saw him wounded in a street fight with a U.S. district attorney, whom Shotwell sought to punish for prosecuting klansmen. Back in Rutherford County, between drinking binges, he was elected chief of the county's Klan when it organized in spring 1871. Shotwell's drinking and self-imposed distance from his 300 ghouls made him an ineffective leader, although local klansmen managed to rape several women and whip numerous blacks. The den's biggest raid, targeting white Unionist Aaron Biggerstaff, occurred two week's after Shotwell's election as cyclops but apparently took place without his knowledge. Klansmen later testified that Shotwell organized a June 1871 raid that vandalized a Republican newspaper, the Rutherford *Star*. In September 1871, federal authorities convicted Shotwell, his brother, and ten other klansmen for that crime, sending all of them to prison. From his cell, while filling his diary with tirades against the "traitors" who turned state's evidence against him Shotwell volunteered to testify against other klansmen. Years later, he blamed local nightriding on "reckless young country boys" whom he could never control.

Simkins, W.S.—A Reconstruction leader of the KKK and YMDC in Jackson County, Florida, Simkins later served as a professor of law at the University of Texas. In his twilight years, he published memoirs declaring that his Florida klansmen played on black superstition without resulting to violence, a claim belied by Jackson County's 179 racist murders committed during 1868–71.

Skipworth, J.K.—A Confederate veteran and mayor of Bastrop, Louisiana, before World War I, Skipworth emerged as exalted cyclops of Bastrop's Klan in the early 1920s. Unable to control his members, he was effectively dominated by Dr. B.M. McKoin, with unrestrained violence producing a notorious 1922 double-murder at Mer Rouge. Investigation of that crime failed to implicate Skipworth, but he was fined ten dollars for raiding an illegal still without authority. In 1923, he led a delegation to Atlanta, supporting William Simmons in his power struggle against Hiram Evans.

Stoddard, Lothrop—The 1920s exalted cyclops of Massachusetts Provisional Klan No. 1, Stoddard also published a seminal racist text, *The Rising Tide of Color Against White Supremacy* (1920), which warned that "the white race will be absorbed and fused with those of darker color, unless precautionary measures are taken" by barring immigration from southern and eastern Europe.

Swift, Rev. Wesley A.—An ex-chauffeur and bodyguard for Gerald L.K. Smith, Swift also served as a KKK rifle team instructor in the 1940s, before founding his own Church of Jesus Christ Christian in 1946. Claiming an improbable 1.6 million members in the United States and another 1 million abroad, Swift preached Christian Identity tenets and regaled his congregation with the message that "all Jews must be destroyed." (Until passage of time proved him wrong, he was fond of telling the faithful, "I prophesy that before November 1953, there will not be a Jew in the United States, and by that I mean a Jew that will be able to walk or talk.") In October 1950, Swift traveled to Utah with Smith to aid in a smear campaign against Sen. Elbert Thomas, who lost his bid for a fourth term. While in Salt Lake City, Swift and Smith visited Gov. J. Bracken Lee, emerging to claim that Lee supported their anti–Semitic campaigns. Over the next two months, Swift and Smith marshaled opposition to Anita Rosenberg's appointment as assistant secretary of defense, presenting the Senate Armed Services Committee with "proof" of her alleged communist ties on 5 December. Back home in Lancaster, California, Swift fabricated a baffling network of paper organizations, considered by some as the west coast's strongest neo–Nazi element in 1953. Over the years, members KKK, NSRP, Minutemen and California Rangers were named to leading positions in Swift's "church," lending their talents to such diverse enterprises as the Christian Defense League, the Southern California Freedom Councils, the Friends of Rhodesia, the California Anti-Communist League, and the Christian Nationalist Alliance. Swift "ordained" a list of Identity ministers including Connie Lynch, Dennis Mower and Oren Potito to spread his gospel of anti–Semitism and white supremacy. Following Swift's death in 1970, Richard Butler took command of the "church," added Aryan Nations to its title, and in 1976 moved its headquarters to Idaho.

Taylor, John Ross—A Canadian anti–Semite, Taylor toured Europe in the late 1920s and returned with a boundless admiration for Nazism. In 1937, he ran unsuccessfully for public office on a Jew-baiting platform, then found himself interned as a Nazi sympathizer during World War II. He resurfaced in 1965 as head of the National Order Party (disbanded by government order for disseminating hate literature). The year 1972 found him active in the neo–Nazi Western Guard and serving as an organizer for a Michigan KKK banquet. He addressed the NSRP's convention in 1973, ran unsuccessfully for the House of Commons in 1974 (102 votes), and in 1976 attended David Duke's "international congress" in New Orleans. Taylor gained control of the Western Guard in 1976, and four years later received a one-year prison term for broadcasting racist messages via a telephone "hotline." He spent two months in hiding, then surrendered to serve his time in October 1981. Paroled in March 1982, he was

subsequently jailed again for violating the Canadian Human Rights Act, with that verdict upheld by Canada's Supreme Court in 1990. Following his latest parole, Taylor moved to Calgary, Alberta, where he managed affairs for the Aryan Nations. He died at a Calgary boarding house on 6 November 1994.

Thomas, Robert—Named by FBI informant Gary Rowe as Alabama's grand titan for the UKA, Thomas allegedly relayed orders from Wizard Robert Shelton that sent a Klan hit team to Selma on 25 March 1965—the day UKA members murdered Viola Liuzzo. HUAC investigators described him in 1967 as "one of the most influential members of the United Klans of America in Alabama."

Tracy, R.N.—A prominent Reconstruction-era planter and KKK leader in Fulton County, Arkansas, Tracy was a prime suspect in the September 1868 ambush-murder of militia Capt. Simpson Mason. He fled the county to avoid arrest, while his farm was occupied by troops, fortified against Klan assaults.

Tyler, Elizabeth—Edward Clarke's partner in the Atlanta-based Southern Publicity Association, Tyler was arrested with Clarke in October 1919, semi-nude and intoxicated in a local bawdy house. Each paid a five-dollar fine for disorderly conduct, and while the original police records later disappeared, copies found their way to the *New York World* in 1921. Meanwhile, Tyler's son-in-law joined the KKK in 1920, introducing her to Wizard William Simmons, and in June of that year Simmons hired the SPA to manage Klan recruiting nationwide. Tapped for interviews as membership climbed past the 100,000 mark, Tyler told reporters that Jews feared the KKK because klannishness "teaches the wisdom of spending American money with American men." Exposure of the 1919 arrest in 1921 sparked dissension in the ranks of an order pledged to defend chastity, morality and temperance. Clarke responded by commissioning a bogus attempt on Tyler's life, thus portraying his partner as a victim of "un–American" persecution. Still, many klansmen resented Tyler's prominent role in the order (which barred women from membership), and she was pressured to resign in 1922, citing her daughter's illness and a need for rest. She married a prominent Atlanta businessman in 1923, around the same time Wizard Hiram Evans fired Clarke "for the good of the order."

Walraven, Gerald—A Texas spokesman for the UKA, Walraven was interviewed by Houston radio station KTRH in 1965. The station paid for his appearance on the program, and the check came back endorsed by ANP leader George Lincoln Rockwell, complete with a swastika stamp.

Wheat, G. Clinton—A California klansman, Wheat hosted a series of meetings at his Los Angeles home in 1963–64, where members of the Christian Defense League plotted illegal raids against Cuba. Moving to northern California in 1965, Wheat vanished two years later, when New Orleans District Attorney Jim Garrison issued warrants for his arrest as a material witness in the JFK assassination.

Wilkins, Fred—An Alabama native who migrated to Lakewood, Colorado, Wilkins was briefly suspended from his job as a firefighter in 1979, after publicly threatening radio host Alan Berg. That incident sent Wilkins to jail on a charge of felony menacing, while exposing his role as a local Klan leader. Proud of the fact that his father and grandfather were Alabama knights, Wilkins told reporters in 1980 that "the Klan tries to teach racial pride. If you define a racist as someone who loves his race, then I am one. But I'm not against the other races."

Williams, Joseph John—A prominent planter from Tallahassee, Florida, Williams led Leon County's vigilante slave patrols before the Civil War, while serving nine terms in the state legislature. As speaker of the house in 1866, he played a prominent role in drafting Florida's repressive Black Codes, later stricken down by Congress. During 1867–68, he emerged as founder and admitted leader of three YMDC chapters in Leon County, commanding an estimated 400 gunmen (roughly equivalent to half the county's registered Democratic voters). While Williams denied any statewide office in the YMDC, he admitted to congressional investigators in 1871 that he sometimes threatened violence against "radicals" who were "exciting the [black] voters to riot." In December 1870, Williams chaired the grand jury that dismissed Gov. Harrison Reed's complaint of Klan threats against his life. In 1872, Williams was elected president of the state Democratic convention. He denied any role in the Klan, but other YMDC members told Congress the two groups were "one and the same."

Wilson, Fred Lee—A convicted gambler with arrests dating from 1949, Lee served as the UKA's grand klabee for North Carolina in 1964.

Winter, Paul—A leader of the 1920s Klan in Philadelphia, Pennsylvania, Winter alienated members with his pompous attitude and seamy private life, including an adulterous love affair with the wife of a Triple-S Super Secret Society leader. Dissident knights filed charges against him in 1925, but Wizard Hiram Evans supported Winter, while his opponents lacked the three-fourths majority needed to remove him from office. Winter retaliated by banishing his accusers and disbanding the Warren G. Harding Klan, whereupon other klaverns resigned en masse. Evans finally transferred Winter to Queens, New York, in a bid to salvage the Philadelphia Klan, but his efforts proved too little and too late.

Woodle, Roy—A bricklayer and self-ordained minister, Woodle served as grand kludd for the UKA's North Carolina realm until 1965, when he resigned to appear as a cooperative witness before HUAC. While Woodle still supported the Klan's racist doctrines, he had grown disgusted at the personal enrichment of UKA officers, including use of shills to stimulate generous donations at public rallies. Woodle told the committee, "The way I see it, they come into town this month, have a rally, get all the money you can get, and get out, and say, 'Now you folks work hard, get all the members you can. We will be back next year for another rally.' And then on other occasions, I saw poor men on the side, can't hardly pay their bills, supporting it, and [Klan leaders] promising you, 'We are going to give you the victory. We are going to stand. We are going to stand,' but ain't nobody found out what they are going to stand for."

Young, S. Glenn—Dismissed from the U.S. Prohibition Bureau after killing an unarmed suspect, Young took command of the crusading klavern in Herrin, Illinois, during 1923. Sporting a paramilitary uniform, twin .45-caliber pistols on his belt, and often carrying a submachine gun, Young led his raiders into private homes and Catholic churches, berating and frequently beating the occupants in his war against bootleggers and other "undesirables." In 1923–24, Young's klansmen closed more than 100 speakeasies and arrested hundreds of prisoners, including so many French and Italian immigrants that both nations filed formal protests with Washington. Facing trial for assault and battery in one case, Young packed the court with armed klansmen and secured a hasty verdict of acquittal. Illinois gangsters responded violently, ambushing Young's car in May 1924, wounding Young and blinding his wife. Grieving klansmen killed the supposed triggermen, thus sparking open war in "Bloody Williamson" County. National Guardsmen were deployed eight times over the next four years, as violence between klansmen and anti–Klan forces claimed at least twenty lives. Imperial headquarters expelled Young from the KKK in 1924, but his knights remained loyal and the battle continued. Young and a leading anti–Klan gunman, lately commissioned as a sheriff's deputy, killed each other (and two bystanders) on 24 January 1925, but sporadic fighting continued for another fifteen months. A cease-fire was finally negotiated in April 1926, following a battle on election day that left several men dead or wounded.

The Wrecking Crew

Klansmen listed in this section have been charged and/or convicted with various crimes, from Reconstruction to the twenty-first century. Details of their cases are derived from media reports, official documents, and from reports published by such watchdog agencies as the ADL and SPLC.

Adams, Ellis—A member of the Reconstruction KKK in Warren County, Georgia, Adams was linked to the stabbing of a black man and various other crimes in 1868. On 10 May 1869, witnesses identified him as the gunman who murdered GOP state senator Joseph Adkins, near Dearing. Adams evaded arrest for that crime, but died in a December 1869 shootout with authorities.

Adams, Kenneth—A resident of Anniston, Alabama, and a longtime klansman, Adams was one of the North Alabama Citizens' Council members who assaulted singer Nat "King" Cole during a 1956 performance in Birmingham. Five years later, in May 1961, he was subpoenaed by federal prosecutors investigating attacks on CORE's freedom riders at Anniston. Represented by attorney J.B. Stoner, Adams pled the Fifth Amendment. Indicted with eight others in that case, Adams won a directed verdict of acquittal on 3 November 1961. In November 1963, NSRP member Joseph Milteer described Adams as "a mean damn man" and "one of the hard-core of the underground," desired as a recruit for Milteer's Constitutional American Party of the United States. After quitting the Klan, Adams led NSRP's chapter in Anniston. On 15 July 1965, Adams shared the stage with Stoner and Connie Lynch at an Anniston rally, after which rally participants murdered black victim Willie Brewster. One defendant in that case was a friend and employee of Adams. Later in 1965, federal prosecutors charged Adams with receiving explosives stolen from nearby Fort McClellan. Jurors acquitted him on 21 January 1966.

Ainsworth, Kathryn Madlyn

—A Mississippi housewife and fifth-grade teacher who once angrily protested the enrollment of a black girl in her class, Ainsworth also led a secret life as a nightriding KKK terrorist. Police in Meridian shot and killed her on 30 June 1968, when she accompanied klansman Thomas Tarrants to bomb the home of a Jewish businessman. Officers found a pistol in Ainsworth's purse, with membership cards for the UKA and the Louisiana-based Original Knights. A search of her home revealed membership documents for the WKKKKM and APWR, along with literature from the Minutemen and the NSRP. Ainsworth's husband admitted knowledge of her Klan membership, but claimed ignorance of her involvement in terrorism. Tarrants, from his prison cell, described her as "a real worthwhile human being who was just misguided."

Beckwith, Byron De La

—California born in 1920, the son of Mississippi natives, Beckwith returned to the Magnolia

Klansman Byron De La Beckwith murdered Medgar Evers in June 1963 but avoided prison until 1994 (Library of Congress).

State with his family at age five. He graduated from high school in 1940 and subsequently served with the U.S. Marines in World War II. In 1954, "Black Monday" propelled Beckwith into the Citizens' Council, whose leader Robert Patterson he worshipped "like a god." Three years later, he wrote to a Jackson newspaper: "I believe in segregation like I believe in God. I shall combat the evils of integration and I shall bend every effort to rid the U.S.A. of the integrationist whoever and wherever he may be." When the national council of the Protestant Episcopal Church announced a policy of nondiscrimination in its churches, Beckwith printed and distributed leaflets attacking the decision. (He also carried a pistol to church, in case blacks tried to enter.) In a January 1963 letter to the NRA, he wrote: "Gentlemen, for the next 15 years we here in Mississippi are going to have to do a lot of shooting to protect our wives, children and ourselves from bad niggers."

Various sources differ on when and where Beckwith first joined the KKK. FBI informant Delmar Dennis told this author in 1968 that he believed Beckwith joined the UKA in early 1963, while other evidence an close relationship with the WKKKKM during 1964–67. In any case, Beckwith was clearly thinking like a klansman when he ambushed and murdered Mississippi NAACP leader Medgar Evers in Jackson, on 12 June 1963. Police found Beckwith's rifle at the murder scene, allegedly bearing his fingerprints (Beckwith claimed it was stolen), and two taxi drivers fingered Beckwith as the fare who had asked them for directions to Evers's home, remarking, "I've got to find him in a couple of days." (After Beckwith's arrest, the Jackson *Clarion-Ledger* headlined: "Californian is Charged with Murder of Medgar Evers.") FBI agents learned that Beckwith and two other men attended a meeting addressed by Evers on 11 June, leaving when an NAACP secretary asked their business. Held in the Rankin County jail after his murder indictment, Beckwith received a hero's treatment, including permission to keep his own TV set and gun collection in his cell. Hinds County's sheriff barred the guns when Beckwith transferred in November 1963, despite Beckwith's plea that he might need them "mighty bad when I get out."

An ad hoc White Citizens Legal Fund, chaired by fourteen prominent business and professional men, paid Beckwith's trial expenses, while his battery of lawyers included a former district attorney, a leader of the Citizens' Council, and a partner in Gov. Ross Barnett's law firm. (Barnett himself appeared in court to shake Beckwith's hand, in full view of the jury.) At his first trial, a businessman and two policemen swore they had seen Beckwith in Greenwood (sixty miles from Jackson) at the time Evers was shot. On 7 February 1964, jurors deadlocked seven-to-five for acquittal, and the judge declared a mistrial, whereupon ex–General Edwin Walker appeared to congratulate Beckwith. Klansmen turned out in force for Beckwith's second trial, burning crosses statewide on 10 April 1964, with seventy-five knights packing the courtroom next morning. A key prosecution witness, cabbie H.R. Speight, retreated under oath from his early identification of Beckwith, then admitted receiving death threats. A second mistrial was declared on 17 April, with jurors deadlocked eight-to-four for acquittal.

Beckwith returned to a triumphant hero's welcome in

Greenwood, sparking further controversy when the U.S. Post Office purchased land from him for $25,000. Free on bond pending a third trial that failed to materialize, Beckwith joined other klansmen in harassing patrons of a local desegregated theater. He also joined in joined in violence seminars convened by the WKKKKM, telling klansmen at one 1965 gathering, "Killing that nigger gave me no more inner discomfort than our wives endure when they give birth to our children. We ask them to do that for us. We should do just as much. So, let's get in there and kill those enemies, including the president, from the top down!" In May 1965, Beckwith helped klansman Gordon Lackey paint a black ring around the home of a man who hired "the wrong nigger" to paint his house. In 1966, Beckwith emerged as part-owner of a pro–Klan newspaper, *The Southern Review*. He ran for lieutenant governor in 1967, billing himself as "a straight-shooter," declaring that the campaign "will provide me with the opportunity to repay the many kindnesses which I have received from my fellow Mississippians by offering myself as a candidate whose political position has already been clearly established."

Voters rejected Beckwith at the polls, but he remained active in racist circles. In 1973, he was a featured speaker at the NSRP's annual convention. On 1 October 1973, police and FBI agents tracked him from Jackson to New Orleans, carrying a small arsenal of firearms and a Klan-made bomb allegedly intended for the home of ADL director Adolph Blotnick. Klansmen rallied to support Beckwith, with UKA members collecting cash while David Duke proclaimed: "This penniless victim of government illegality and crime must be defended." After a five-day trial, federal jurors acquitted Beckwith of all counts, on 19 January 1974. New Orleans authorities filed state charges on 31 January, resulting in a second trial where jurors convicted Beckwith (on 15 March 1975) of illegally carrying explosives across the state line. On 1 August 1975, Beckwith received the maximum sentence of five years in prison and a $1,000 fine.

Paroled on 13 January 1980, Beckwith continued his association with Klan and neo–Nazi groups, moving to Tennessee in 1983. Largely forgotten by the outside world, Beckwith made headlines again in November 1991, when Mississippi authorities announced their intent to retry him for the Evers slaying. Beckwith fought extradition, but was finally returned for trial, commencing in January 1994. Jurors convicted him of first-degree murder on 4 February, and Beckwith received a life sentence. He died in prison on 21 January 2001, with his conviction still on appeal.

Bratton, Dr. J. Rufus—A Reconstruction-era klansman in York County, South Carolina, Bratton led the gang that lynched ex-militia Capt. Jim Williams on 6 March 1871. He also helped organize black political meetings in the area, manipulating selection of "Uncle Tom" spokesmen who called on Republican officials to resign from office. In May 1871, Bratton publicly renounced further nightriding, but his ban proved ineffective. One of 200 klansmen who fled the state to avoid prosecution, he was extradited from Canada in June 1872 but managed to escape a second time, remaining in Ontario until Wade Hampton negotiated his safe return with President Rutherford Hayes in 1877.

Brooks, Early L.—Brooks served as police chief of Fair Bluff, North Carolina, in the 1940s, until he was charged with shooting a fellow officer in 1947. Despite acquittal on that charge, public opinion forced his resignation, whereupon he became a lightning rod salesman, moonlighting as a local constable. Brooks also served as exalted cyclops in Fair Bluff for the Association of Carolina Klans. FBI agents jailed him on 16 February 1952, for the October 1951 kidnap-flogging of victims Ben Grainger and Dorothy Martin. Eleven days later, Brooks faced charges (with ten other knights) in the case of Esther Floyd, abducted and whipped in November 1951. On 8 May 1952, Brooks pled no contest and received a two-year prison sentence for the December 1951 whipping of Woodrow Johnson. Five days later, jurors convicted him on two counts in the Grainger-Martin case, resulting in two concurrent five-year prison terms.

Buckley, Travis—A Mississippi lawyer and member of the WKKKKM, Buckley represented various klansmen summoned by HUAC in 1965–66, also serving as chief defense counsel for various White Knights indicted for murder, bombing and other crimes in the same period. On 9 March 1967, authorities in Pascagoula charged Buckley with kidnapping Jack Watkins, a prosecution witness in the Vernon Dahmer murder case. Ten months later, on 25 January 1968, a judge in Hattiesburg ordered Buckley's arrest on arson charges in the same case. Jurors convicted Buckley of the Watkins kidnapping in March 1968, while Pascagoula authorities filed additional charges of jury-tampering. District Attorney Donald Cumbest told reporters, "These people have been terrorizing, kidnapping and murdering, and I'm damn sick of it." Buckley's conviction resulted in disbarment, but his license to practice law was later restored. Buckley defended Wizard Sam Bowers (unsuccessfully) at his 1996 trial for the Dahmer slaying.

Chambliss, Robert Edward—A native of Pratt City, Alabama, born in 1904, Chambliss joined the KKK in 1924. Eleven years later, he logged his first arrest (for a liquor violation), and in 1936 he faced charges of desertion and nonsupport of his first wife and children. Chambliss committed his first known bombing in August 1947, at the home of black attorney Arthur Shores (whose recent lawsuit had dismantled Birmingham's zoning segregation laws). Over the next few years, he bombed so many homes that fellow klansmen nicknamed him "Dynamite Bob," while Birmingham's black district became known as "Dynamite Hill" and the city was dubbed "Bombingham." Once suspended from his city job for threatening a black resident whose home he later bombed, Chambliss was fired in 1949 after arrests for flogging (July) and assaulting a reporter with a hammer (24 September) at a Klan rally at Warrior, Alabama. In February 1956, Chambliss participated (and was jailed again) in the riot protesting black coed Autherine Lucy's enrollment at the University of Alabama. Soon after his arrest, Chambliss and three other klansmen sued Lucy and the NAACP for $4 million, for "damages" to their dubious reputations. While a member of Asa Carter's Original KKK of the Confederacy, then Robert Shelton's Alabama Knights and UKA, Chambliss resumed his bombing campaign against black homes and churches. Police Commissioner Bull Connor protected Chambliss, but Connor's removal from office in 1963 coincided with a rift in the UKA, wherein Chambliss and other violence-prone klansmen defected to form the Cahaba River Group.

That breakaway klavern came under scrutiny after the 15 September 1963 bombing of Birmingham's Sixteenth Street Baptist Church, which killed four young girls. Forces including Gov. George Wallace, Col. Al Lingo's state troopers, and UKA Wizard Robert Shelton collaborated to blame Chambliss and company for the slaughter, although they stopped short of filing murder charges. In fact, Chambliss and two other klansmen—Charles Cagle and John "Nigger" Hall—faced only misdemeanor charges of illegally possessing dynamite, escaping with the payment of $100 fines. Another fourteen years passed before state authorities charged Chambliss with murder, on 24 September 1977. A relative testified for the prosecution at trial, in November 1977, recalling comments by Chambliss (suppressed by the FBI since 1963) that linked him to the bombing. Before the blast, he remarked, "You just wait until after Sunday morning, and they will beg us to let them segregate." Hours later, he complained, "It wasn't supposed to hurt anybody. It didn't go off when it was supposed to." Attorney Arthur Hanes, Sr., argued that "everybody talked tough back then," but jurors disagreed, convicting Chambliss of first-degree murder on 17 November. He received a life sentence and died in prison on 19 October 1985.

Cody James—Authorities identified Cody and his two brothers as the klansmen who ambushed Sheriff John Norris in Warren County, Georgia, in December 1868. He also led the mob that lynched Dr. G.W. Darden in March 1869. Despite arrests in both cases, all-white grand juries refused to indict him.

Coker, William—The son of Reconstruction-era Klan leader James Coker, William (or "Billy") was identified as the ringleader in numerous murders and other racist crimes in Jackson County, Florida, including the 1870 assassination of black constable Calvin Rogers at Marianna. His crimes went unpunished.

Coleman, Tom Lemuel—Born in 1911, the alcoholic son of a former Alabama state legislator, Coleman was a state highway department employee and "special" deputy in Lowndes County, Alabama, where acquaintances described him as "maddened by the prospect of Negroes voting." In August 1959, he shot and killed a black inmate who allegedly assaulted a guard at the Greenville prison camp. (Coleman was not a guard, but he was in the neighborhood and armed; he was cleared at a hasty inquest on his plea of self-defense.) Coleman's son was a state trooper and bodyguard for Col. Al Lingo, who numbered Tom Coleman among his good friends. Although Coleman denied membership in the Klan, he confronted Alabama Attorney General Richmond Flowers on 10 August 1965, warning Flowers, "If you don't get off this Klan investigation, we'll get you off."

Ten days later, on 20 August, Coleman shot two white civil rights workers in Hayneville, killing seminary student Jonathan Daniels and critically wounding Rev. Richard Morrisroe. After the shooting, he telephoned Al Lingo to report, "I just shot two preachers. You'd better get on down here." Lingo, with Coleman's son at the wheel, rushed to Hayneville with a bail bondsman linked to the Klan. Taking personal charge of the investigation, Lingo raged at reporters, "It's none of your damn business. I'm not giving you or the damn attorney general or the damn FBI or anybody any information until I'm good and ready." Sheriff Frank Ryals initially claimed Coleman had been acting as a deputy, responding to reports of "a disturbance" at the store where the shooting occurred, then backpedaled to deny that Coleman had ever been deputized. Initially charged with murder and attempted murder on 21 August, Coleman saw the charges reduced on 13 September by a grand jury that indicted him for manslaughter (Daniels) and assault and battery (Morrisroe). An all-white jury acquitted him of manslaughter, while the lesser charges were later dismissed. Coleman remained with the highway department until 1977 and died in Hayneville on 13 June 1997.

Collier, Clarence—A Reconstruction-era klansman in Crittenden County, Arkansas, Collier fled the area when Gov. Powell Clayton declared martial law in 1868, then returned when the decree was lifted. In July 1869, he murdered militia Capt. A.J. Haynes on the main street of Marion, shooting Haynes first in the back, then emptying a pistol into his prostrate form before casually riding out of town. Thrilled by that act of "heroism," the Memphis *Public Ledger* gushed: "Gallant Clarence Collier! The blessings of an oppressed people go with you, and wherever the clouds lift you shall be known and honored throughout the land as the William Tell of Crittenden County, Arkansas."

Cox, Gary Christopher—With fellow klansman Timothy Adron Welch, Cox burned two black churches at Bloomville and Greeleyville, South Carolina, on 20–21 June 1995. Combined state and federal investigations of those crimes, along with the stabbing of a black male victim, produced confessions from Cox and Welch in summer 1996. Both defendants pled guilty to federal arson and civil rights charges on 14 August 1996, facing maximum terms of fifty-five years in prison. State authorities announced that Cox and Welch would also plead guilty in the stabbing case. On 16 August 1996, DOJ spokesmen announced the indictment of two more klansmen Arthur Allen Haley and Hubert Lavon Rowell, for conspiracy in the same arson incidents, plus fires at a local labor camp and the blaze that destroyed a black man's car. The SPLC and parishioners of the Macedonia Baptist Church later filed suit against the defendants and their Klan, the Christian Knights, winning a $37.8 million judgment on 24 July 1998.

Eaton, William Orville—A former steelworker and member of the UKA's Klavern No. 20 in Bessemer, Alabama, Eaton was a member of the hit team that killed civil rights worker Viola Liuzzo on 25 March 1965. With codefendants Eugene Thomas and Collie Wilkins, Eaton was also linked to bombings and other acts of violence during a 1965 strike at the W.S. Dickey Clay Manufacturing Company, where klansmen harassed black coworkers. In September 1965, Eaton withdrew his son from Bessemer's newly integrated high school. Three months later, on 3 December, federal jurors convicted him of violating Liuzzo's civil rights. He received a ten-year prison term but died from a heart attack on 10 March 1966, while the verdict was still on appeal.

Felker, William—A Reconstruction-era storekeeper and moonshiner in Walton County, Georgia, Felker was also repeatedly named as the leader of nightriding KKK raids. In 1871, one of Felker's black employees related Felker's advice on peaceful coexistence with whites to congressional investigators: "He told me how to do. He said if I always raised my hat to the people when I passed and was always polite to them, I would not be bothered."

Fox, Philip—A former editor of the Dallas *Times-Herald,* Fox moved from Texas to Atlanta, Georgia, when Hiram Evans replaced William Simmons as imperial wizard in November 1922. He soon advanced from imperial speechwriter to editor of *The Knight Hawk* and the national Klan's chief publicity agent. In 1923, Fox murdered William Coburn, Simmons's attorney, then escaped the death penalty with an insanity plea. Sentenced to life imprisonment, Fox served ten years before winning parole under Gov. Eugene Talmadge, followed by a pardon from Gov. E.D. Rivers. (Both governors were past or present klansmen.) Fox returned to Texas and managed publicity for LBJ's 1948 Senate race. Eight years later, he produced a TV documentary, *The Port Arthur Story,* alleging communist support for gubernatorial candidate Ralph Yarborough.

Franklin, Joseph Paul—Born James Clayton Vaughn, Jr., in Mobile, Alabama, Franklin was the eldest son of an alcoholic drifter who often abandoned his family for months or years at a time. Siblings recall that James Vaughn, Sr., celebrated his homecomings with violent domestic abuse, while James Jr. absorbed the worst punishment. As a youth, Franklin sampled dietary fads and fringe religions, dropping out of high school when an accident left him nearly blind in one eye. He married in 1968, his bride reporting a change "like night and day" soon after the wedding. He turned abusive, emulating the father he hated, and at other times wept inexplicably. Around the same time, their all-white neighborhood desegregated, and Franklin veered into pathological racism. Ugly incidents and sporadic arrests marked the next few years, while Franklin joined the KKK, NSRP and ANP. Migrating to Atlanta, he began harassing interracial couples on the street, spraying one couple with chemical Mace in September 1976. Soon afterward, Vaughn/Franklin legally changed his name, shedding the last links to his former life. (He chose "Joseph Paul" in honor of Third Reich propagandist Paul Joseph Goebbels, and "Franklin" for America's Benjamin Franklin.) During 1977–80 he roamed aimlessly across the country, murdering at least twenty persons as he waged a one-man war against blacks, "race-mixers" and Jews.

The first known incident of Franklin's rampage occurred on 29 July 1977, when he bombed a synagogue on Chattanooga, Tennessee. Nine days later, he shot and killed an interracial couple (Alphonse Manning and Toni Schewnn) in Madison, Wisconsin. On 8 October, he killed Gerald Gordon and wounded two other male victims at a bar mitzvah in Richmond Heights, Missouri. On 6 March 1978, Franklin wounded Larry Flynt (publisher of *Hustler* magazine) and Flynt's attorney Gene Reaves outside a courthouse in Gwinnett County, Georgia. On 28 July 1978, Franklin murdered a black man and wounded his white girlfriend in Chattanooga, Tennessee. Sniper fire killed Harold McIver, a black restaurant manager, in Doraville, Georgia, on 22 July 1979. On 18 August, Franklin murdered a black man outside a fast-food restaurant. On 21 October 1979, he killed another interracial couple (Jesse Taylor and Marian Bresette) in Oklahoma City. On 5 December 1979, Franklin killed Mercedes Master, a teenaged prostitute who lived with Franklin for a time after he met her hitchhiking. Franklin struck twice in Indianapolis during January 1980, killing black victims Larry Reese (8 January) and Lee Watkins (14 January). On 3 May 1980, he killed white victim Rebecca Bergstrom and dumped her corpse near Tomah, Wisconsin. On May 29, Franklin wounded National Urban League director Vernon Jordan in Fort Wayne, Indiana, while Jordan sat with a white female companion outside a motel. Franklin surfaced again on 8 June 1980, in Cincinnati, killing black joggers Dante Brown and Darrell Lane. On 15 June, he slew another interracial couple (Arthur Smothers and Kathleen Mikula) in Johnstown, Pennsylvania. On 25 June, Franklin picked up two white female hitchhikers, murdering both in Pocahontas County, Virginia. Black joggers Ted Fields and David Martin died from Franklin's gunfire in Salt Lake City, Utah, on 20 August 1980.

Police finally captured Franklin in September 1980, but he escaped and fled to Florida, to be recaptured a month later. In custody, he confessed twenty murders, six attempted murders, sixteen bank robberies and two bombings. His convictions include two life sentences for the Manning-Schewnn murders in Wisconsin, a death sentence in Missouri for killing Gerald Gordon, two life terms for murder and one for robbery in Tennessee, and two life terms for murder in Utah. Neo-Nazi leader William Pierce, founder and head of the National Alliance, published a novel based on Franklin's crimes (*Hunter,* 1984), which was also dedicated to Franklin. Franklin deemed it "an honor."

Fuller, Edward Willard—Between 1947 and 1958, Louisiana police arrested Fuller nine times on charges of drunkenness, fighting and disorderly conduct, gambling, carrying concealed weapons, reckless driving and suspicion of rape. In 1964, Fuller joined the WKKKKM, serving as exalted cyclops of a Louisiana klavern near the Mississippi border. Simultaneously, he managed a roadhouse specializing in gambling and prostitution. In April 1964, Fuller used a shotgun to assault a black man. He reportedly beat up two other victims in early 1965, firing a gun into one victim's car, and later that same year police jailed him again, for aggravated assault. Summoned by HUAC in January 1966, he refused to answer any questions about his past.

Hall, John Wesley ("Nigger")—Nicknamed for his dark complexion by fellow UKA members in Birmingham, Alabama, Hall once volunteered to murder Rev. Fred Shuttlesworth, but a leak from FBI informant Gary Rowe robbed him of the opportunity. By 1963, as a member of the rogue Cahaba River Group, Hall himself had turned informant—with a twist. After the fatal bombing of Birmingham's Sixteenth Street Baptist Church, on 15 September 1963, Hall led G-men to a field where Klan terrorists allegedly stashed their explosives. The agents found nothing, Hall led Birmingham police and Col. Al Lingo's state troopers back to the same site days later, this time recovering a case of dynamite. Authorities used that evidence to charge Hall, Charles Cagle and Robert Chambliss with illegal possession of explosives, resulting in $100 fines (later overturned on appeal). Alabama Attorney General Richmond Flowers complained that the premature arrests, orchestrated by Lingo and UKA Wizard Robert Shelton, had ruined any chance of trying the suspects for murder. Despite Hall's failure of an FBI polygraph test related to the church bombing, G-men kept him on their payroll as an informant and Director J. Edgar Hoover vetoed prosecution of the known church bombers, on grounds that indictments would compromise Hall as a source. In 1977, Attorney General Bill Baxley named Hall as the man who built the church bomb, but Hall was already dead and beyond the law's reach.

Hawkins, Joe Daniel ("Danny Joe")—A second-generation Mississippi klansman whose father doubled as a director of the APWR, Hawkins ranked among the WKKKKM's most violent members. In 1967, authorities indicted him on three counts of assault and battery with intent to kill, for beating and shooting black civil rights workers. Tried twice on one count, he escaped with mistrials when the juries deadlocked. On 18 September 1967, Hawkins and his father rammed a carload of FBI agents with their own vehicle in Jackson, Mississippi, facing charges of assaulting federal agents. During 1967–68, Hawkins participated in a series of bombings with Thomas Tarrants and others, but FBI scrutiny caused him to decline the Meridian bombing of 30 June 1968, where police captured Tarrants and killed Kathy Ainsworth. Nonetheless, prosecutors charged Hawkins with conspiracy in that case, prompting him to flee underground as a fugitive. Still at large in April 1981, he was jailed with Don Black and seven others for plotting to invade Dominica. Convicted of violating the U.S. Neutrality Act, Hawkins received a three-year prison term.

Hays, Henry—A member of the UKA in Mobile, Alabama, and the son of southern Alabama's grand titan, Henry Hays led the lynching party that killed teenager Michael Donald in March 1981. Jurors convicted Hays of first-degree murder in February 1984, whereupon he was sentenced to death. After exhausting his appeals, Hays died in the electric chair on 6 June 1997.

Holder, James—A sergeant in Glenn Miller's Confederate Knights of the KKK, Holder shot and killed fellow klansman David Wallace in November 1983, during an argument at a Klan rally. Convicted of murder in June 1984, he received an eighteen-year prison term.

Hunnicutt, John L.—As a teenage student in Greensboro, Alabama, Hunnicutt led the area's first Klan raid in early 1868, threatening the white teacher of a black school and terrorizing three black families "in regular old style." Local Democratic Party leaders supplied horses for the raid, which succeeded in driving the teacher our of Hale County. Witnesses identified the klansmen, and a grand jury convened to indict them, but its foreman was a sponsor of the raid and no charges were forthcom-

ing. Soon afterward, Hunnicutt organized a formal den with support from "some of the best citizens" in Greensboro, publishing his first Ku Klux notices in March 1868.

Killen, Edgar Ray ("Preacher")—A Philadelphia, Mississippi, sawmill operator, Baptist minister and kleagle for the WKKKKM in 1964, Killen was instrumental in establishing klaverns in Lauderdale and Neshoba Counties. FBI informants described Killen as the leader of a wrecking crew that assaulted black parishioners and burned the Mt. Zion Methodist Church on 16 June 1964, and as the mastermind of a plot to murder COFO activist Michael Schwerner five days later. Killen was among the klansmen tried on federal conspiracy charges in 1967, but jurors deadlocked on his case (eleven-to-one for conviction) and prosecutors dismissed the charges in 1973. Three years later, in an interview with Patsy Sims, Killen denied Klan membership but admitted joining the APWR. Mississippi prosecutors belatedly filed murder charges against Killen in 2005, and jurors convicted Killen on 21 June. He received a sixty-year prison term on 23 June 2005.

Kimble, Jules Rocco—An admitted klansman from New Orleans, Kimble was also a key witness in District Attorney Jim Garrison's 1967 probe of the JFK assassination. Kimble testified that he and UKA Grand Dragon Jack Helm visited the home of assassination suspect David Ferrie on 23 February 1967—one day after Ferrie's mysterious death—and removed a valise filled with papers, which they transported to a bank safety-deposit vault. Helm also described trips to Montreal, Québec, undertaken on behalf of the Minutemen and CIA. After giving Garrison his statement, Kimble vanished briefly, then resurfaced in Tampa, Florida, after visits to Montreal and Atlanta, Georgia. Canadian journalists speculated on possible links between Kimble and James Earl Ray in the 1968 slaying of Dr. Martin Luther King. (Ray also traveled widely, spending time in Atlanta, Montreal and New Orleans before King's assassination.) In 1978, the HSCA confirmed Kimble's KKK connections and his "extensive criminal record," but found no link to King's murder.

Kinard, William—A member of the Ancient City Gun Club in St. Augustine, Florida, Kinard was shot and killed on 25 October 1963, while riding in an armed procession through a black neighborhood. (Dying, he fired a shotgun blast through the door of his own car.) Police initially charged five NAACP members with the slaying, but none were convicted. Three days after Kinard's death, nightriders retaliated by firing into two black homes, two nightclubs, and a grocery store. A hand grenade thrown at one of the taverns failed to explode. HUAC subsequently identified the ACGC as Klavern No. 519 of the UFKKK. Klansman Charles "Connie" Lynch officiated at Kinard's funeral, while pallbearers included three exalted cyclops and a Jacksonville klansman who doubled as head of the local NSRP.

Knowles, James ("Tiger")—As a member of the UKA in Mobile, Alabama, Knowles participated in the March 1981 lynching of black teenager Michael Donald. Arrested in 1983, he turned state's evidence and accepted a life prison sentence in return for testimony against his accomplices.

Lane, David Eden—A resident of Denver, Colorado, Lane earned his living as a golf hustler and part-time real estate agent before he discovered anti–Semitism and Christian Identity in the 1970s. Accounts of his departure from the real estate profession vary: some claim his license was revoked for refusal to serve nonwhite clients, while others state that he came to view property sales as part of a global Jewish conspiracy. In any case, he joined the KKK and became an aggressive kleagle, until banished by Exalted Cyclops Fred Wilkins for mixing neo–Nazi literature with the Klan literature Lane was assigned to distribute. In 1981, police arrested Lane for passing out his own crude pamphlet (*The Death of the White Race*) on public streets without a permit. Publicity surrounding that arrest prompted radio host Alan Berg to book Lane as a guest on his talk-show, and their verbal sparring sparked a hatred on Lane's part that led to Berg's murder three years later. In the meantime, Lane moved to Idaho and served as a spokesman for the Aryan Nations, emerging as propaganda minister for The Order in 1983. Lane avoided participation in The Order's armed robberies, but tried his hand at counterfeiting and drove the getaway car when members murdered Alan Berg in June 1984. Conviction in Berg's slaying earned Lane a 150 prison term, while forty years were added on a federal racketeering charge. Lane was also among the conspirators charged with sedition in 1987, but jurors acquitted them all in April 1988. Though jailed for the rest of his life, Lane remains an icon and revered spokesman for the white-supremacist movement. In 1986, his latest pamphlet (*Identity: Under This Sign You Shall Conquer*) was distributed at Richard Butler's World Aryan Congress. Lane maintains contact with free-world racists via Internet websites, and is credited with authoring The Fourteen Words: "We must secure the existence of our people and a future for white children." Fourteen Words Press, a racist publishing house in St. Maries, Idaho, exists solely to publish Lane's screeds.

Lea, John G.—A founder of the Reconstruction-era Klan in Caswell County, North Carolina, Lea admitted planning the 1870 murder of state senator John Stephens and personally leading the assassination party. Arrested shortly after the slaying, Lea was released for lack of evidence, then penned a detailed confession in 1919, which was released after his death in 1935.

Livingston, William Kyle, Jr. ("Sonny")—A Montgomery, Alabama, klansman, Livingston confessed to bombing the home of Rev. Ralph Abernathy in 1957, but authorities released him as part of a general amnesty including other klansmen and black boycott leaders. In 1961, while on "street patrol" with other knights, he used a baseball bat to beat a black woman in plain view of several policemen (who ignored the assault). In January 1976, officers arrested Livingston for forcing his way into a police impound lot, armed with a pistol, to capture a bail-jumper, but prosecutors declined to press charges. Alabama Attorney General Bill Baxley later observed, in a classic understatement, that "Livingston's got a bunch of buddies on the police department." Friendship failed him on 21 February 1976, when prosecutors charged him with the 1957 murder of black victim Willie Edwards, but a judge dismissed the charges two months later, when authorities failed to docu-

ment the victim's cause of death and key witness Raymond Britt recanted his identification of Livingston. On 11 August 1979, when more than 100 members of Bill Wilkinson's IEKKKK were jailed after a march from Selma to Montgomery, Livingston helped them post bond.

Llewallyn, Cecil—Investigators named Alabama klansman Cecil Llewallyn as one of those who burned a Greyhound bus outside Anniston during the May 1961 freedom rides. Questioned by Judge Frank Johnson on 30 May, Llewallyn claimed his Fifth Amendment privilege but spent two hours in jail for refusing to say who advised him not to testify. Back in court a second time, Llewallyn again refused to speak, this time represented by attorney J.B. Stoner.

Lollar, Coleman A. ("Brownie")—A member of the Federated KKK in Birmingham, Alabama, Lollar was identified in 1949 as a ringleader of local terrorism. Once commissioned as a "special deputy" for Jefferson County, Lollar was stripped of his badge by the sheriff after standing guard at an Adamsville KKK rally in June 1949. Witnesses identified Lollar and his brother Richard as members of the flogging party that whipped Jack Alexander, Mary Henderson, Mrs. Hugh McDanal and William Stevens in June 1949. Lollar's trial in that case convened on 26 October 1949, and jurors acquitted him three days later, to rousing applause from the spectator gallery.

Lutterloh, Dr. Thomas—A physician and klansman in Reconstruction-era Alamance County, North Carolina, Lutterloh privately admitted joining in a December 1869 raid, during which he personally whipped a black victim to death.

Lynch, Charles Conley ("Connie")—Born in 1913, Lynch served as an army cook in World War II, then joined Wesley Swift's Church of Jesus Christ Christian upon his return to civilian life. His talent for inflammatory speeches quickly won him ordination as a minister of hate, and he served the sect in California for ten years before taking his show on the road. From 1957 onward, Lynch toured the country in a pink Cadil-

Rev. Connie Lynch (in rebel vest) addresses a St. Augustine Klan rally, flanked by rival Grand Dragons Bart Griffin (left) and Don Cothran (Florida State Archives).

lac, sporting a vest sewn from a Confederate battle flag, haranguing crowds from coast to coast, working as an itinerant plasterer between racial crises. An early member of the Minutemen, he doubled as California state organizer for the NSRP in 1962, launching a friendship with J.B. Stoner that endured for the rest of his life. As a member of multiple Klans, Lynch performed impartially for various factions, including UFKKK, the UKA, and the Original Knights. On 13 October 1962, he shared the stage with Wizard Robert Shelton at a UKA rally in Bessemer, Alabama. Five months later, on 21 March 1963, Lynch and two other NSRP members were convicted of battery and disturbing the peace in California, after they assaulted several teenagers and shot one with a pellet gun. Released after paying a $1,200 fine, Lynch rolled on to log arrests before year's end in Memphis, Little Rock, and Gadsden, Alabama. He teamed with Shelton again at Spartanburg, South Carolina, on 17 August 1963, then moved on to address a St. Augustine, Florida, rally on 18 September, where he said of Birmingham's recent deadly church bombing: "If there's four less niggers tonight, then I say good for whoever planted the bomb. We're all better off."

St. Augustine marked the pinnacle of Lynch's career as a wandering salesman of hate. In spring 1964, he returned with Stoner to harangue white mobs and send them off to riot in the streets against black protesters. "There's gonna be a bloody race riot all over this nation," he told one crowd at the city's historic slave market. "The stage is being set for the earth to get a bloodbath. When the smoke clears, there ain't gonna be nothin' left except white faces." On 24 July 1964, Lynch and Stoner were jailed with three local klansmen for illegal cross-burning. A year later, the pair teamed to address KKK/NSRP rallies in Bogalusa, Louisiana, and Anniston, Alabama. At the latter gathering, Lynch declared, "If it takes killing to get the Negroes out of the white man's streets and to protect our constitutional rights, I say, 'Yes, kill them!'" Following that rally, members of the crowd (including a friend of klansman Kenneth Adams) murdered black victim Willie Brewster.

In 1966, Lynch made an east coast tour for the NSRP, appearing in Baltimore on 28 July, where he denounced Mayor Theodore McKeldin as a "super-pompous jackassie niggerlover." Lynch told his cheering audience of 1,000, "To hell with the niggers, and those who don't like it, they can get the hell out of here." Rioting erupted, and authorities obtained an emergency injunction to ban Lynch's next speech, scheduled for the following day. On 21 November 1966, jurors convicted Lynch of inciting a riot, conspiracy to riot, disorderly conduct and violation of city park rules. (A federal appeals court later overturned the conviction, accepting the free-speech arguments raised by Lynch's black ACLU attorney.) On 1 September 1968, Lynch was one of thirteen persons held on murder charges after a shootout left two men dead at an NSRP rally in Berea, Kentucky. Prosecutors never tried that case, and Lynch made numerous speeches in 1968 on behalf of presidential candidate George Wallace. Heart disease claimed his life in 1972, leaving J.B. Stoner to tell reporters, "Connie and I had a lot of fun."

Mabry, Jesse—As a member of Asa Carter's North Alabama Citizen's Council, Mabry assaulted black singer Nat "King" Cole during an April 1956 performance at Birmingham's municipal auditorium. The following year, as a klabee in Carter's Original KKK of the Confederacy, he joined the party that kidnapped and castrated victim Edward Aaron on 2 September 1957. Police charged four klansmen in that case, and jurors convicted all four of mayhem, resulting in twenty-year prison terms. Mabry exhausted his appeals and entered custody in 1959, followed by a 1960 ruling from the state parole board that he must serve at least two-thirds of his term—six years and eight months—before he was considered for parole. Notwithstanding that judgment, Gov. George Wallace (who employed "Ace" Carter as a personal advisor) released Mabry in February 1964, two years ahead of schedule.

Miller, Emmett E.—A founder and onetime president of the Citizens' Council in Little Rock, Arkansas, Miller also served as a kleagle in the late 1950s. On 12 July 1960, FBI agents caught Miller and klansman Robert Parks in the act of planting a bomb at Philander Smith College, in Little Rock. A third accomplice, Hugh Adams, was jailed later the same day. Prosecutors filed charges under the 1960 Civil Rights Act, then dropped their case in October 1960, based on lack of evidence that the explosives had been moved across state lines. Three months later, a local grand jury indicted Miller on the misdemeanor charge of conspiring to commit a felony. Adams and Parks were not indicted, thereby invalidating the conspiracy charge (which requires at least two participants). In May 1961, the DOJ requested dismissal of federal charges against Miller and company, based on the FBI's refusal to identify local Klan informants. A year later, in May 1962, Miller emerged as the leader of NSRP cells in Little Rock and West Memphis, Arkansas.

Mills, Raymond Duguid—While serving as the UKA's exalted cyclops in New Bern, North Carolina, Mills was jailed on 29 January 1965 for bombing two cars and a black-owned funeral home. Mills and two codefendants later pled guilty to bombing Oscar Dove's mortuary and received suspended jail terms. Grand Dragon James Jones issued a banishment order on Mills, but HUAC investigators learned that Mills was never cut from the UKA's membership rolls.

Morrison, Aaron—A onetime kleagle in New Jersey, Morrison faced charges in 1980 for firing rifle shots into a black family's home in Barnegat Township. He pled guilty in January 1981, with two accomplices, then reneged and demanded a trial. Jurors convicted Morrison in March 1983, but the judge suspended his three-month jail term.

Myers, Cecil William—A yarn-plucker by trade and militant racist by choice, Myers was a member of the UKA's Georgia realm in August 1964, when FBI agents charged him with murdering black Lt. Col. Lemuel Penn. Grand Dragon Calvin Craig suspended Myers at his arrest, pending dismissal if indicted. Jurors acquitted Myers and codefendant Joseph Sims of murder charges on 4 September 1964, and both subsequently joined James Venable's National Knights, spearheading activities of that Klan's militant Black Shirts. On 13 October 1965, police jailed Myers for assaulting a black photographer at Crawfordsville. Five days later, they arrested him again (with seven other Black Shirts) for attacking black victims in the same town. On 8 July 1966, federal jurors convicted Myers and Sims of violating Penn's civil rights, whereupon both received the maximum ten-year sentence. Myers served his prison time in Pennsylvania.

Nalls, Rev. L.A.—A Baptist minister and 1920s klansman in Crenshaw County, Alabama, Nalls supervised the whipping of a divorced farmer and the divorcée with two children whom he married. After the beating, Nalls told the female victim, "Sister, you were not punished in anger this evening; you were punished in a spirit of kindness and correction, to set your feet aright and to show your children how a good mother should go." Nalls then collected $3.50 from the floggers, handing the cash to his victim with a jar of Vaseline for her wounds. Nalls later fled to Texas when the state attorney general (himself a klansman) launched an investigation of recent whippings.

Oxford, James—A klansman in Reconstruction-era Georgia, Oxford was jailed at Sparta on murder charges, but a masked gang liberated him from custody. Convicted of another murder in 1871, he received a death sentence in Washington County. Klansmen declined to intervene on his behalf a second time.

Pickett, A.C.—An ex–Confederate army officer and Reconstruction klansman in Woodruff County, Arkansas, Pickett led a force of 200 insurgents who threatened to attack state militiamen at Augusta in December 1868. Militia officers broke up the group by seizing hostages and vowing to destroy the town in the event of an assault. Pickett later led a delegation to visit Gov. Powell Clayton and denied any KKK activity in Woodruff County, but Clayton countered by producing a list of known members, with Pickett's name at the top. Back home, Pickett convened a public meeting on 18 December 1868, at which 400 whites signed a pledge to help state authorities curb terrorism.

Pitts, Billy Roy—A Mississippi high school dropout and member of the WKKKKM, Pitts joined the raiding party that burned NAACP activist Vernon Dahmer's home and store on 10 January 1966, leaving Dahmer fatally injured. Pitts also left his pistol at the crime scene, leading FBI agents to his door in March 1966. Hoping to sabotage the case, Pitts joined in the January 1967 kidnapping of prosecution witness Jack Watkins, only to find himself charged with additional crimes on 10 March 1967. On 8 March 1968, Pitts pled guilty to state charges of arson and murder, receiving a life prison term. In the Watkins case, he pled guilty to kidnapping and assault, receiving a five-year sentence, accompanied by a concurrent five-year term for his guilty plea on federal civil rights charges. Released after serving a portion of his five-year terms, Pitts dropped from sight and was never compelled to serve his life sentence—an apparent payback for his testimony against fellow klansmen at their murder trials. On 17 January 1998, after the Jackson *Clarion Ledger* revealed that Pitts had never served a day in prison for his crimes, authorities issued a new arrest warrant. That move induced Pitts to collaborate with prosecutors once again, this time as a witness at the 1998 murder trial of former WKKKKM Imperial Wizard Sam Bowers.

Pritchett, Joseph—As an exalted cyclops in Asa Carter's Original KKK of the Confederacy, Pritchett led the team that kidnapped black victim Edward Aaron from a Birmingham, Alabama, street on 2 September 1957, afterward castrating him as part of a grisly initiation ritual. Jurors convicted Pritchett and three codefendants of mayhem in that case, whereupon all four received the maximum twenty-year sentence. Their appeals ran out in 1959, whereupon the four entered prison. Alabama law required inmates to serve ten years or one-third of their sentence (whichever was shorter) before release, and in 1960 the state parole board decreed that Aaron's assailants must spend at least six years and eight months in custody. Gov. George Wallace subsequently reversed that decision, releasing Pritchett a year ahead of schedule.

Redwine, Clifford—In July 1980, police in Muncie, Indiana, jailed klansman Clifford Redwine for firebombing a black family's home. Redwine boasted to friends that he had "killed eight niggers" in the fire, but in fact no one died. With his son and another klansman, Redwine received a six-year prison term but seemingly learned nothing. Upon his return to Muncie, he murdered two gun shop employees and received a 100-year prison term.

Reed, John C.—In April 1868, Reed served as grand giant of a Ku Klux den in Oglethorpe County, Georgia, pledged to save the South from "Africanization." He led demonstrations to discourage black voting in 1868's presidential election, and again during state elections in 1870. His subsequent testimony dated local KKK disbandment from late 1870, though masked nightriding continued well into 1871.

Roberts, Alton Wayne—A Golden Gloves boxer and nightclub bouncer, Roberts joined the WKKKKM in 1964 and participated in the conspiracy to murder COFO activist Michael Schwerner that spring. On 21 June, he personally shot and killed Schwerner and victim Andrew Goodman, afterward helping to hide their corpses (with that of James Chaney) on a farm owned by klansman Olen Burrage. At trial, in October 1967, Roberts was one of six klansmen convicted on federal civil rights charges, receiving a ten-year prison term. He was still free on appeal in 1968, when a new wave of anti–Semitic terrorism rocked Mississippi. With brother Raymond, Roberts agreed to betray fellow klansmen for cash, receiving an uncertain amount (published estimates range from $10,000 to $30,000) from Jewish businessmen and the FBI. In return, Roberts arranged for White Knights to bomb the Meridian home of a prominent Jew, where police lay in wait on 30 June 1968, killing Kathy Ainsworth and capturing Thomas Tarrants. Roberts exhausted his appeals and entered prison in 1970. He died in September 1999, at age sixty-one.

Rosecrans, William Sterling—An Indiana native, Rosecrans moved to Florida in 1963 and joined the UFKKK "to fight niggers." He participated in the February 1964 theft of dynamite from two Jacksonville construction sites, using the stolen explosives on 16 February to bomb the home of George Gilliam, a black resident whose grandson attended a newly-integrated school. After the bombing, Rosecrans fled to St. Augustine, where Sheriff L.O. Davis helped klansmen and members of the Ancient City Gun Club conceal him from FBI agents, while Rosecrans found work under a pseudonym. Ironically, ACGC leader Holsted Manucy betrayed Rosecrans to G-men on 4 March 1964, believing him responsible for bombing the strike-bound Florida East Coast Railroad (and hoping to collect a large reward.) A polygraph test cleared Rosecrans in that case, but he confessed the Gilliam bombing and pled guilty to civil rights charges on 13 March, receiving a seven-year prison term. His confession implicated five other klansmen in the bombing, but death threats induced him to recant, and the others won acquittal at trial.

Rowe, Gary Thomas, Jr.—A Georgia native, born in 1932, Rowe quit school in eighth grade, Rowe lied about his age to join the National Guard, then faced arrest in Savannah at age eighteen for carrying a concealed weapon (after accidentally shooting himself with his own pistol). He later drifted to Birmingham, Alabama, where he found work at a dairy plant. A heavy-drinking, self-styled barroom brawler, Rowe also idolized law enforcement officers and paid a $30 fine in 1956 for impersonating a policeman. By April 1960, he was impersonating an FBI agent, but G-men waived criminal charges, instead hiring Rowe to infiltrate Robert Shelton's Alabama Knights. Formally initiated on 23 June, Rowe won promotion to Nighthawk of Eastview Klavern No. 13 on 18 August 1960. Over the next five years, he earned an estimated $20,000 from the FBI, which concealed his involvement in numerous crimes. Rowe's reports exposed collusion between Birmingham police and the KKK during 1961's freedom rides, but G-men filed no charges and Rowe enthusiastically participated in the riots of 14 May, suffering a slashed throat when one black victim defended himself with a knife. (The FBI paid Rowe's medical bills and added a $125 bonus for his "services" in the riot.)

In July 1961, Rowe followed Shelton into the new UKA and maintained his reputation as a zealous participant in violent "missionary work." After Birmingham's fatal church bombing of 15 September 1963, Rowe failed a polygraph test wherein he denied involvement in that crime. He was also a suspect in the bombing of black businessman A.G. Gaston's home, and in the fatal shooting of a black man during a 1963 race riot. (Rowe confessed that slaying to state authorities, claiming that his FBI contact told him to "just sit tight and don't say anything about it." FBI headquarters dismissed that claim as an "absolute falsehood.") When G-men launched their COINTELPRO campaign against the KKK in September 1964, Rowe got orders to spread dissension by bedding the wives of fellow klansmen—a duty he cheerfully pursued. On 25 March 1965, Rowe was present when UKA members murdered Viola Liuzzo in Lowndes County, Alabama, discarding his cover at last to testify against defendants William Eaton, Eugene Thomas and Collie Wilkins.

Death threats in that case drove Rowe into hiding, as "Thomas Neal Moore" in the federal witness protection program, but Rowe resurfaced in 1975 to testify before the U.S. Senate's Church Committee, describing the FBI's COINTELPRO crimes. A year later, Bantam Books paid Rowe $25,000 for

his autobiography, *My Undercover Years with the Ku Klux Klan* (1976), while Columbia Pictures paid another $25,000 for screen rights to his story (aired by NBC television as *Undercover with the KKK* in 1979). Rowe worked the talk-show circuit, appearing in a mask to promote his book, but the publicity backfired. Alabama Attorney General Bill Baxley considered using Rowe as a witness against church bomber Robert Chambliss in 1977, then rejected him when polygraph tests implicated Rowe in the fatal blast and several other bombings. DOJ spokesmen announced a review of Rowe's federal service in July 1978, officially "clearing" the FBI of any misconduct, but Lowndes County prosecutors indicted Rowe for Liuzzo's murder two months later. Georgia's governor approved Rowe's extradition to Alabama in February 1979, but the charge was dropped prior to trial. In March 1983, in the Liuzzo family's wrongful-death action against the FBI, Gene Thomas and Collie Wilkins claimed that Rowe shot Liuzzo. Two Birmingham policemen also testified that Rowe confessed the crime to them, while Grand Dragon Robert Creel's ex-wife put the blame back on Wilkins. Gary Rowe, "bankrupt and $60,000 in debt," died from a heart attack in 1998.

Seale, James Ford—On 2 May 1964, members of the WKKKKM kidnapped black students Henry Dee and Charlie Moore, seeking information on a rumored plot by Black Muslims to foment an "insurrection" in Mississippi. Two months later, the victims' corpses were dragged from a river near Tallulah, Louisiana. FBI agents arrested klansmen James Seale and Charles Edwards, obtaining an admission from Edwards that Dee and Moore were beaten to death in the Homochitto National Forest. State prosecutors charged Seale and Edwards with murder, then dismissed the case on 11 January 1965. The DOJ likewise declined to prosecute, although Dee and Moore were killed on federal land. Prosecutors reopened the case in January 2000, with much fanfare about belated justice, but still no prosecution was forthcoming. Ex-agent Bill Dukes, now a lawyer in Gulfport, told reporters, "It's a closed era in Mississippi, and I don't want to be a part of its resurrection." Seal toured the murder site with FBI agents but remained confident of his invincibility, reminding journalists, "I ain't in jail, am I?"

Sessum, Cecil Victor—As an exalted cyclops of the WKKKKM in Jones County, Mississippi, Sessum participated in the January 1966 murder of NAACP activist Vernon Dahmer at Hattiesburg. FBI agents arrested Sessum and twelve other klansmen on 28 March 1966. Eight months later, state authorities charged Sessum with the kidnapping of Dahmer prosecution witness Jack Watkins. A federal grand jury indicted Sessum and twelve others in February 1967, for conspiring to violate Dahmer's civil rights. Jurors convicted him of state murder charges in March 1968, resulting in a life prison term.

Silva, Frank Lee—A recognized leader of the 1980s California Klan, Silva joined The Order in late 1983 or early 1984, operating a message center that helped the neo–Nazi guerrillas communicate with one another. In April 1985, FBI agents arrested Silva at Bentonville, Arkansas, seizing an arsenal of weapons from his car. Five months later, convicted with nine other defendants in a federal racketeering trial in Seattle, Washington, Silva received a forty-year prison term. Despite incarceration and dismal prospects for parole, Silva was chosen to lead the shattered Order and reportedly continues to solicit new members from his cell, nurturing futile dreams of an Aryan rebellion against "ZOG."

Sims, Joseph Howard—A Georgia member of the UKA, Sims traveled the South in 1963–64, participating in violent Klan demonstrations from Birmingham, Alabama, to St. Augustine, Florida. Police confiscated a pistol from Sims in March 1964, after he threatened an elderly black man in an Athens, Georgia, café. Four months later, he was one of the klansmen who shot and killed black Lt. Col. Lemuel Penn. Grand Dragon Calvin Craig suspended Sims and codefendant Cecil Myers from the UKA, prompting both to join James Venable's National Knights. Jurors acquitted both klansmen of murder on 4 September 1964, and they soon emerged as charter members of Venable's militant Black Shirts. Police in Crawfordsville, Georgia, arrested Sims and Myers twice in October 1965, for assaulting blacks on public highways. Federal jurors convicted Sims and Myers in July 1966, on charges of violating Penn's civil rights, and both received the maximum ten-year sentence. Sims drew an additional ten years with a guilty plea to shooting his own wife in May 1966.

Smith, Jerry Paul—One of six defendants charged with murdering five anti–Klan demonstrators at Greensboro, North Carolina, in November 1979, Smith won acquittal from an all-white jury in November 1980. Das later, he reported an attempt on his life, allegedly trading shots with unknown gunmen while driving near Maiden, North Carolina. Honored at a 1981 NSRP banquet, Smith ran (unsuccessfully) for sheriff in Lincoln County the following year. In August 1984, police jailed him for assaulting a referee at a high school sporting event.

Stokes, Wilda Ira—A resident of Enterprise, Alabama, Stokes accosted two youths at a local shopping center in July 1984, raving about his KKK connections and his plan to "burn out" the home of Judge Warren Rowe. The incident climaxed with Stokes assaulting both boys, clubbing them with a beer bottle. Ironically, Judge Rowe was assigned to try his case. Upon conviction, Stokes received a one-year jail term.

Tackett, Elmer—A Michigan security guard for the UKA, diagnosed as terminally ill in March 1974, Tackett had two weeks to live when he issued a statement designed to "clear my conscience" in the August 1971 bombing of ten school buses at Pontiac. Tackett claimed to be the only person involved in the bombing, although Grand Dragon Robert Miles and four other klansmen were already serving time for conspiracy in that case. Authorities were unimpressed with Tackett's deathbed attempt to liberate his friends.

Tarrants, Thomas Albert III—A native of Mobile, Alabama, Tarrants was a precocious anti–Semite and bombmaker, known to local police as "a thorn in our side ever since he was seventeen years old." His first foray into far-right politics occurred in 1964, with exposure to John Birch Society literature during Barry Goldwater's presidential campaign. That summer, Tarrants began making regular trips to NSRP headquarters in Birmingham, where chief Edward Fields mistrusted his rabid racism. At home in Mobile, Tarrants carried a sawed-off shotgun and spent time with local NSRP leader Bob Smith, forging ties to the Klan while he harassed local blacks and Jews. In 1967, he joined the WKKKKM as a self-styled "guerrilla for God," bombing synagogues, churches and homes at the direction of Imperial Wizard Sam Bowers. Bowers was riding with Tarrants in December 1967, when police in Collins, Mississippi, stopped Tarrants for reckless driving and found a submachine gun in his car. Typically paired with Joe Daniel Hawkins on nocturnal bombing raids, Tarrants also welcomed Kathy Ainsworth's help when Hawkins was forced to hide from FBI agents. Turncoat klansmen Alton and Raymond Roberts arranged a trap for Tarrants in June 1968, resulting in a Meridian ambush that killed Ainsworth and critically wounded Tarrants (along with a policeman and a bystander) on 30 June. Indicted with fugitive Hawkins for conspiracy on 14 November 1968, Tarrants faced trial two weeks later and upon conviction drew a thirty-year prison term. No other charges were filed, but Meridian Police Chief Roy Gunn named Tarrants as the prime suspect in at least seven other bombings, occurring between 18 September 1967 and 6 June 1968. Tarrants briefly escaped from prison, assisted by other White Knights, but he was quickly recaptured and later "found Jesus" in custody, renouncing his past in favor of theology. State authorities paroled him in December 1976, to attend the University of Mississippi. His memoir, *The Conversion of a Klansman* (1979), describes the odyssey from Aryan warrior to "born-again" Christian.

Terbeck, Donald—Police jailed Terbeck in December 1982, for wounding a black man with rifle shots outside a restaurant in DeKalb County, Georgia. Terbeck denied Klan membership, but witnesses recalled him passing out "Klan calling cards" at the same café before the shooting, and Wizard James Venable served as his defense attorney.

Thomas, Eugene—A steelworker from Fairfield, Alabama, and a member of the UKA's Bessemer Klavern No. 20, Thomas drove the car from which fellow klansmen shot and killed Viola Liuzzo on 25 March 1965. FBI agents confiscated an illegal sawed-off shotgun from Thomas at his arrest, but he soon posted bail and joined his codefendants at a series of UKA rallies where klansmen besieged him for autographs. On 3 December 1965, federal jurors convicted him of violating Liuzzo's civil rights, whereupon Thomas received the maximum ten-year sentence. In February 1966, he received a consecutive two-year term on federal weapons charges (for the shotgun). Despite those verdicts, a local jury consisting of eight blacks and four whites acquitted Thomas of Liuzzo's murder in September 1966. Federal authorities denied his first bid for parole in April 1973.

Thrash, Marshall—A member of the Justice Knights in Chattanooga, Tennessee, Thrash was jailed with two other knights in April 1980, on charges of wounding four black women in a drive-by shooting. At trial in July 1980, jurors convicted Thrash of simple assault and battery (reduced from assault with intent to kill), while acquitting his two codefendants. Thrash received an eight-month jail term and a $225, while announcement of the acquittals and lenient sentence sparked black riots in Chattanooga.

Tucker, Gary A.—A retired bus driver and member of the Cahaba River Group in Birmingham, Alabama, Tucker approached FBI agents in October 1988 to confess his role in the fatal church bombing of 15 September 1963. Klansman Robert Chambliss had been convicted of murder in that case eleven years earlier (and died in prison during 1985), but Tucker kept silent until he was diagnosed as terminally ill. In his final interview, he expressed a desire to clear his conscience before he died.

Vittur, Cliff—A Georgia klansman in the 1940s, Vittur was identified by Stetson Kennedy and Drew Pearson as the "chief ass tearer" for AGK Klavern No. 1, in Atlanta. Following his public exposure in Pearson's newspaper column, arsonists burned several vehicles at Vittur's trucking company.

Wagner, Daniel—An Ohio member of James Venable's National Knights, Wagner testified before HUAC in February 1966, while free on bond from an armed robbery charge. He told the panel that Columbus Klan leader Vernon Gilliam (also charged with robbery) transported dynamite from Georgia to Ohio with the aim of launching a "civil war" in 1965. Suppliers of the TNT allegedly included Cecil Myers and Joseph Sims. Wagner also recounted conversations with Klan "empress" Eloise Witte, concerning plots to murder LBJ, Vice President Hubert Humphrey, Dr. Martin Luther King, and others. Wagner claimed that Witte gave him a rifle and pistol, ordering him to "practice on Negroes as a sniper to prove yourself and help the white race." Witte later denied the accusations under oath, branding Wagner a "psychopath" and a "mentally disturbed loudmouth."

White, Robert L.—As a Maryland member of William Chaney's Confederation of Independent Orders, White organized a special unit of action-hungry klansmen in 1977. State police charged that the group was formed "with the intent and purpose of engaging in illegal violent acts aimed primarily at religious and ethnic targets." In July 1978, jurors convicted White and two other klansmen of plotting to bomb a Lochearn synagogue. Police also charged that White planned to bomb the home of Rep. Parren Mitchell.

Wilkins, Collie Leroy, Jr.—An auto mechanic and member of the UKA from Fairfield, Alabama, Wilkins logged his first arrest at Hueytown in 1964, for carrying an illegal sawed-off shotgun. His guilty plea on federal firearms charges earned him a one-year suspended prison term and two years' probation, conditional on his promise to remain within the judicial district at all times. In early 1965 he joined in a campaign of violence at Bessemer's W.S. Dickey Clay Manufacturing Company, where klansmen harassed black employees. On 25 March 1965, he was part of the UKA hit team that murdered civil rights worker Viola Liuzzo in Lowndes County. His first murder trial, in May 1965, ended with the jury deadlocked, but a second panel acquitted Wilkins in October. Two months later, in December 1965, federal jurors convicted Wilkins of violating Liuzzo's civil rights, whereupon he received the maximum ten-year sentence. With his appeal of that verdict pending, a judge jailed Wilkins for his previous conviction, ruling that the trip from Birmingham to Lowndes County (where Liuzzo died) violated terms of the klansman's probation. Federal authorities denied his first bid for parole in April 1973.

Williams, Furman Dean—As a member of the UKA in Gaffney, South Carolina, Williams organized a covert action squad known as The Underground. HUAC testimony indicated that the unit was created and trained for violence with the approval of Grand Dragon Robert Scoggin. Summoned before the committee in February 1966, Williams declined to answer questions on grounds of possible self-incrimination.

Wilson, Charles Clifford—A member of the WKKKKM, Wilson received a distinguished service award from the Junior Chamber of Commerce in 1968, three days before his indictment for murdering NAACP activist Vernon Dahmer in January 1966. Convicted and sentenced to life imprisonment in January 1969, Wilson sparked new controversy in 1972, when Gov. William Waller—Wilson's former appellate attorney—granted him a work-release from prison. Wilson's assignment was particularly strange: he was dispatched to Southern Mississippi State Hospital in Laurel (former headquarters of the WKKKKM and home of Wizard Sam Bowers), where he worked primarily with indigent blacks. Further investigation revealed that Wilson had spent only a short time in prison, thanks to long furloughs granted by Gov. John Bell Williams and his successor. Immediately prior to placing Wilson in the work-release program, Gov. Waller had granted his former client two consecutive ninety-day furloughs.

Wilson, Paul Dewey—A Mississippi UKA member and head of its front group, the South Pike Marksmanship Association, Wilson led the "Pike County Wolf Pack," believed responsible for numerous bombings around McComb in 1964. Wilson and his cousin Billy Earl were among nine klansmen arrested by FBI agents in September 1964 and convicted the following month (whereupon a friendly judge suspended their jail terms, opining that the terrorists were "provoked" by civil rights workers). Summoned by HUAC in January 1966, Billy Earl Wilson described his recruitment by cousin Paul, and the manner in which Pike County klansmen drew lots for targets on their bombing raids.

5 A Gathering of Klans

While the KKK presented a more or less monolithic façade in Reconstruction and the early 1920s, splinter factions have existed for nearly seven decades, proliferating after World War II until no group could claim to be *The* Klan. The list below identifies various Klans active throughout the order's history, presented alphabetically. The chapter's second segment lists known front groups of the KKK.

Adamic Knights of the KKK—Maryland-based faction, led by Charles Sickles, exposed for the first time in May 1981, when ATF agents raided Klan hangouts in Delaware, Maryland, New Jersey and Pennsylvania. Sickles and nine others were jailed for weapons violations, linked to an alleged conspiracy to bomb a Baltimore NAACP office. The group was apparently defunct by 1983, when the ADL published a new list of active Klans.

Alabama Empire Knights of the KKK—Founded by Steve Hugh Stone in 1990, the AEKKKK ran afoul of the law on 24 March 1991, when several members burned a cross at the home of a black family in Albertville. Federal agents arrested Stone, Klabee Christopher Daniel, and four other on charges of intimidation, violating federal housing laws, and using fire in the commission of a felony. Jurors convicted Stone, Daniel and Dennis Stewart in 1992. Stone received a sentence of 106 months in prison, while Daniel and Stewart got 90 months each. Three other knights—Lynn Gibson, Thomas Murphee and Clarence Whitlock, Jr.—pled guilty to reduced charges, each receiving sentences of four months in jail, four months of house arrest, 200 hours of community service, and a $1,000 fine. Those convictions effectively dissolved the AEKKKK.

Alabama Invisible Knights of the KKK—Founded by self-proclaimed Grand Dragon Ricky Draper in early 1992, the AIKKKK claimed an estimated forty members in Morgan by April. It disappeared before SPLC investigators completed their census of Klans for 1997.

Alabama Knights of the KKK—Formed by Robert Shelton in 1958, after his break with the U.S. Klans. In July 1961 it merged with other factions to create the UKA.

Alabama Knights of the KKK—Founded at Decatur in 1991, this splinter group was run by Grand Dragon Bill McGlocklin until 30 March 1992, when he ceded control to Ira Giddens of Hartselle. It disbanded sometime before the SPLC completed its national census of hate groups for 1997.

Alabama Ku Klux Klan, Inc.—Organized in 1957, one of seven Alabama factions active following "Black Monday."

Alabama White Knights of the KKK—Founded in 1997, with headquarters at Semmes and a second klavern in Little River, this faction grew to a peak strength of thirteen klaverns in 1999. Headquarters transferred to Satsuma that year, then to Clanton in 2001, while membership steadily declined. By 2003, only chapters in Clanton and Birmingham remained. The group vanished entirely before the SPLC completed its survey of active Klans in 2004.

Alabama's White Pride—This small faction was organized at Jasper, Alabama, in 1999, but disappeared before SPLC's next survey of active Klans in 2000.

Allied Klans—A small faction of uncertain venue, publicized for the first time in August 1949, when its unnamed leaders joined the Knights of the KKK of America, led by Lycurgus Spinks.

American Klan, Knights of the KKK—Formerly the American Knights, led by Bill Albers in Modesto, California, this group changed its name in 1991 and passed from the scene shortly thereafter.

American Knights of the KKK (California)—Led by Bill Albers of Modesto and closely linked to the Aryan Nations, this group was accused of harassing black residents of Livermore in 1985. It claimed fewer than 100 members by 1987, and Albers renamed it the American Klan in 1991, shortly before the group disbanded.

American Knights of the KKK (Indiana)—Founded in the mid–1990s by Jeff Berry, of Butler, this Klan rapidly expanded to claim twenty-six additional klaverns in thirteen states by 1998. At its peak in 1998–2000, the AKKKK had active units in Arkansas, California, Colorado, Delaware, Florida, Georgia, Illinois, Indiana, Louisiana, Maryland, Mississippi, Missouri, New Hampshire, New York, North Carolina, Ohio, Oklahoma, Pennsylvania, Tennessee, Texas and Wisconsin. Membership declined from 2000 onward, due in large part to Berry's repeated arrests, and the group had only three klaverns aside from its headquarters unit (in Arkansas and Oklahoma) by 2003. A year later, SPLC investigators failed to find any active klaverns remaining.

American Krusaders—A Klan-affiliated order active in Washington state during the 1920s, this group recruited naturalized U.S. citizens who otherwise met all requirements for KKK membership. Over time, it absorbed local units of a similar group, the Royal Riders of the Red Robe.

American Order of Clansmen—Short-lived San Francisco group created after the 1915 California premiere of *The Birth of a Nation*. Although billed as "a nation-wide, patriotic, social and benevolent secret society" created for the purpose of "uniting all loyal, white American citizens," it apparently never spread beyond California and was quickly upstaged by the Georgia-based Knights of the KKK.

American White Knights of the KKK—Based at Munford, Alabama, this faction emerged in 2002 with four additional klaverns in Alabama, Georgia, Mississippi and Texas. Internal dissension shattered the group in 2003, leaving only one klavern (in Cordele, Georgia), but a minor comeback in 2004 saw a second unit active in San Angelo, Texas.

America's Invisible Empire Knights of the KKK—Launched in the late 1990s, this faction based at Hartselle, Alabama, in 1997 this faction claimed six additional units in Alabama, Georgia, Louisiana and Oklahoma. It lost two Alabama chapters in 1998, but gained new members in Kentucky. The Georgia and Oklahoma realms dissolved in 1999, while the AIEKKKK planted two new klaverns in Alabama and one in New Jersey. A year later, headquarters shifted to Eva, Alabama, while the overall Klan shrank to four klaverns in Alabama and Louisiana. Shrinkage continued in 2001, with headquarters back in Hartselle and the only other active klavern planted in Pulaski, Tennessee. A short-lived renaissance in 2002–03 saw new klaverns established in Alabama and Louisiana, but the Klan disbanded in 2004.

Ameriklan—This small faction, created in 2004, has its headquarters (and its only klavern) in Heber Springs, Arkansas.

Ancient Order, Invisible Knights of the KKK—A North Carolina faction, based in Shelby and led by Grand Dragon Woodrow Lynch, reported active during 1968–70.

Aryan Christian Knights of the KKK—Led by Imperial Wizard Clyde Jones from Browns Summit, North Carolina, this faction expanded to Virginia in 1990, under Grand Dragon Ron Lackey. Few Virginians answered the call, however, and Browns Summit hosted the ACK's only klavern between 1998 and 2001, when the group dissolved.

Aryan Knights of the Confederacy KKK—Founded at Bellefontaine, Ohio, in 2000, the AKCKKK maintained its only klavern there through 2001, then dropped from sight in 2002–03. It reappeared in 2004, with new headquarters in Springfield, Ohio.

Aryan Knights of the KKK—Based in Waco, Texas, and led by Horace Miller, this tiny 1950s Klan mailed literature to racists in Austria, Chile and England.

Aryan Nations Knights of the KKK—Launched dramatically from headquarters at Munford, Alabama, in 2003, this neo–Nazi Klan claimed fourteen active klaverns in Con-

necticut, Florida, Georgia, Louisiana, Michigan, Mississippi, Montana, New York, North Carolina, Ohio, Pennsylvania, Tennessee and Texas. Headquarters moved to Thorsby, Alabama, in 2004, while nine realms and ten klaverns fell away, leaving individual units in Florida, Louisiana, Ohio and Texas.

Aryan Reformation Knights of the KKK—This Klan established one small klavern in Indianapolis, Indiana, during 2003, but it disappeared the following year.

Aryan White Knights of the KKK—A short-lived faction, established at Jasper, Alabama, in 1997, the AWK disbanded before the turn of the millennium.

Associated Klans of America (1949)—An insubstantial umbrella Klan, created (at least on paper) when Sam Roper's AGK merged with the Knights of the KKK of America, led by Lycurgus Spinks.

Associated Klans of America—ADL investigators found this small Klan operating from Stephens City, Virginia, in 1996. No trace of it remained when the SPLC surveyed active hate groups in 1999.

Association of Alabama Knights of the KKK—A short-lived faction created in 1957, in response to "Black Monday." Its range included several small klaverns in Mississippi.

Association of Arkansas Klans—One of three Arkansas factions active in summer 1959. Its chief activity involved printing of posters proclaiming the virtues of racial segregation.

Association of Carolina Klans—Founded in November 1949 by Thomas Hamilton, consolidating various independent Klans in North and South Carolina, operating from headquarters at Leesville, S.C. During 1951–52, Hamilton and 112 of his Klansmen were jailed on various state and federal charges for their involvement in numerous abductions and floggings. Sixty-three (including Hamilton) were convicted during summer 1952, drawing prison terms from eighteen months to six years.

Association of Florida Ku Klux Klan—Organized by Tampa klansman William Griffin in July 1953, disbanded in August 1955.

Association of Georgia Klans—Founded by Dr. Samuel Green, Sr., on 21 May 1944, the AGK was a direct descendant of the Knights of the KKK (1915–44). By 1948 it had at least one klavern in each of Georgia's 159 counties, while a rally at Stone Mountain on July 23 of that year drew 10,000 people. Despite its name and lack of a national charter, the AGK also had scattered klaverns in Alabama and Florida, while several breakaway rivals—dubbed "Bolshevik Klans" by Dr. Green—challenged its supremacy. A key element in the AGK's early success was its close relationship with Georgia governors Eugene and Herman Talmadge. After Green's death in August 1949, Atlanta policeman Sam Roper assumed control of the AGK, and its decline accelerated with two IRS liens for back taxes, filed in August ($9,322.40) and October 1948 ($8,383.72). In 1952, Roper's second-in-command was charged with bomb-

Dr. Green leads a rally at Wrightsville, Georgia, to intimidate black voters in 1948 (Library of Congress).

ing a black family's home in Atlanta, and the AGK apparently dissolved before "Black Monday," in 1954.

Association of South Carolina Klans (1955–67)—One of seven Klans active in South Carolina after "Black Monday," this group was founded in autumn 1955 by alumni of Tom Hamilton's Association of Carolina Klans, with R.E. Hodges serving as its primary spokesman from Columbia. By April 1957, Klan-watchers called it the third-largest faction in Dixie, and three members were charged with flogging a black victim at Greenville. In the early 1960s the ASCK affiliated with James Venable's National Association of Ku Klux Klan. In 1965, congressional investigators identified 250 active members, divided among eight klaverns in six of South Carolina's forty-six counties.

Association of South Carolina Klans (1970s)—A splinter group reported active in 1976, so secretive that professed member John Howard told author Patsy Sims, "The members don't even know who their grand dragon is." Orders supposedly issued from an anonymous Grand Council, but no specific actions were confirmed.

Australian Knights of the KKK—Robert Leys announced formation of this Klan in June 1999, distinguishing his faction from other Australian Klans by acceptance of non–Christian members. Some accounts describe the AKKKK as a "pagan" Klan, but Leys called it an "anything" group, with membership open to all comers "as long as they're white."

Bayou Knights of the KKK—ADL investigators reported this Louisiana faction active in 1996, headquartered at Choudrant under Roger Harris. No trace of it remained during the SPLC's 1999 survey of hate groups, but it resurfaced in 2000, with klaverns in Homer, Louisiana, and Brookhaven, Mississippi. In 2002, the Mississippi klavern moved to Fulton, followed by addition of a new Louisiana chapter in 2003. Modest

growth continued through 2004, with nine klaverns active in Arkansas, Louisiana and Mississippi. All remained active in 2005.

Bayou Patriots Knights of the KKK—Established at Choudrant, Louisiana, in 1997, this faction claimed an addition klavern in McDavid, Florida. A year later, SPLC researchers found the sole active chapter in Walker, Louisiana, and the Klan dissolved before year's end.

Bedford Forrest Brigade—Named for the KKK's original grand wizard, this faction was active in Gainesville, Florida during 1997–98, then faded from the scene.

Bell Kounty Koon Klub—A small Klan active in Kentucky's Bell County during 1997–98, this faction apparently disbanded by early 1999.

Black Shirts (1950s) see Chessmen

Black Shirts (1964–66)—A secretive, violence-prone unit of James Venable's National Knights, the Black Shirts organized (as the Vigilantes) at Barnesville, Georgia, in the latter half of 1964. Leaders were identified as Earl Holcombe (an ex-member of the U.S. Klans who participated in a 1961 riot at the University of Georgia) and Colbert McGriff (expelled from the UKA after a shooting incident in Griffin). Prominent members included ex–UKA members Cecil Myers and Joseph Sims, both charged with the 1964 murder of Lemuel Penn. Black Shirts assaulted civil rights demonstrators around Crawfordsville, Georgia, in October 1965, but the group apparently dissolved after Myers and Sims were convicted on federal civil rights charges in 1966.

Bonnie Blue Knights of the KKK—Founded at Hiawassee, Georgia, in 2002, this Klan with a light-hearted name failed to survive its first year.

British Knights of the KKK see Invisible Empire, United Klans of Europe

Brotherhood of Klans, Knights of the KKK—Founded in Prospect Heights, Illinois, during 2002, this faction claimed three additional klaverns in Illinois, Nebraska, and Wisconsin. Steady growth saw it increase to seventeen klaverns by 2004, with active units in Alabama, California, Illinois, Michigan, Missouri, Nebraska, Ohio, Oklahoma, Tennessee and Wisconsin. All remained active in 2005.

Cahaba River Group—A violent splinter group composed of defectors from the UKA's Eastview Klavern No. 13 in Bessemer, Alabama. Members, including "Dynamite Bob" Chambliss, participated in many Birmingham bombings, and three (including Chambliss) were convicted of planting the bomb that killed four young girls in the Sixteenth Street Baptist Church, on September 15, 1963. FBI reports declassified in 1988 revealed that Imperial Wizard Robert Shelton and other UKA leaders actively collaborated with Col. Al Lingo's state troopers to implicate Cahaba River Klansmen in that case.

California Knights of the KKK—Organized by Tom Metzger in summer 1980, after he resigned as California grand

dragon for David Duke's Knights of the KKK, this faction remained active until late 1982, when Metzger founded his neo--Nazi vehicle, White Aryan Resistance. Reports of its survival beyond Metzger's defection are ambiguous. Police informants linked Metzger's Klan to violent harassment of Hispanics around San Pablo, reporting that Klansmen boasted of beheading an unnamed Mexican victim.

Calvary White Knights of the KKK—Founder Jordan Gollub renamed his Poplarville, Mississippi, White Sons of the Confederacy in early 1990, soon claiming a second klavern in Rome, Georgia, during 1987. By 1991, the Georgia realm had folded, but klaverns had emerged in Virginia and West Virginia. None survived to the end of the decade.

Camellia White Knights of the KKK—An independent Texas splinter group, the CWK reportedly claimed fewer than 100 members in 1987.

Canadian Knights of the KKK—Organized in the 1970s and based in British Columbia, led by neo–Nazi Wolfgang Droege, the Canadian Knights were affiliated with David Duke's Knights of the KKK in the U.S. A major Toronto recruiting drive was announced in June 1980.

Carolina Knights of the KKK (1980s)—In 1980, following a series of trials resulting from the KKK's murder of five unarmed protesters in Greensboro, North Carolina, Glenn Miller replaced Virgil Griffin as head of the North Carolina Knights of the KKK, changing its name to the Carolina Knights in a cosmetic publicity move. In January 1983, four members sought to bail out a black man jailed for rape in Iredell County, but the prisoner declined their generosity. Federal prosecutors alleged (and Miller subsequently confessed) that the group received donations from leaders of The Order, consisting of cash stolen from banks and armored cars in 1984. Miller's subsequent indictment and conviction on various charges prompted the Klan to seek cover under various alternate names, including the Confederate Knights, the White Patriot Party, and the Southern National Front. Membership declined to an estimated 300 in 1987, and the group apparently dissolved before year's end.

Carolina Knights of the KKK (2000)—Founded at Spartanburg, South Carolina, this small faction disbanded during its first year.

Carolina White Knights of the KKK—Founded in 2003, with klaverns in Charleston and Lexington, South Carolina, the CWKKKK lost its Lexington unit in 2004, while Charleston headquarters struggled to remain solvent.

Celtic Knights of the KKK—This short-lived Texas faction was founded in Austin, in 2001, and disbanded before year's end.

Charles Knights of the KKK—This La Plata, Maryland, unit was affiliated in 1991 with the larger Invisible Empire Knights, led by James Farrands. It dissolved, with the rest of the IEKKKK, by 1993.

Chessmen—A violent faction, also known as Black Shirts after the black masks and garb of their standard uniforms, ac-

tive in North Carolina during the late 1950s. Chessmen were implicated in at least one residential bombing, during 1958, and in spring 1959 they protested hiring of blacks at a sawmill in Richfield by pouring sand and sugar into the gas tank of an expensive engine.

Christian Knights of the KKK (1959–61)—Based in Atlanta, Georgia, this faction was founded and led by J.B. Stoner. In August 1959 he wrote to NYPD, offering 5,000 Klansmen to "clean up Harlem," but his letter was ignored. Stoner's group was excluded from a February 1960 meeting in Atlanta that created the Knights of the KKK, Inc. By early 1961, the Christian Knights had been reduced to a paper organization, as recruiting failed and Stoner devoted most of his time to the NSRP.

Christian Knights of the KKK (1980s–2000)—Based at Mount Holly, North Carolina, and led by Virgil Griffin, the CKKKK enjoyed sporadic success in recruiting outside the Tarheel State. ADL investigators estimated its total membership at 200–500 klansmen in 1989, with active klaverns in Kentucky, Mississippi, South Carolina, Virginia, and West Virginia. Size remained static in 1990, but the Mississippi and West Virginia realms dissolved in 1991, replaced by a klavern in Missouri. Shrinkage continued through 1997, when the SPLC found five active klaverns in Illinois, Kentucky, and the Carolinas. A year later, headquarters struggled on with only two satellite chapters, one each in North Carolina and South Carolina. That year (1998) brought a crushing lawsuit from the SPLC, winning $37.8 million in damages against the CKKKK and various individual klansmen for a church burned by two members in June 1995. Mount Holly headquarters stood alone in 2000, and the CKKKK dissolved that same year.

Members of the Christian Knights rally at Parkersburg, West Virginia, in October 1987 (Southern Poverty Law Center).

The Parkersburg rally continues after nightfall (Southern Poverty Law Center).

Christian White Knights of the KKK—Founded in Gainesville, Florida, in 1997, the CWKKKK boasted a second klavern in Chesterfield, Virginia, but neither survived to the turn of the millennium.

Cleveland Knights of the KKK—Created at Lawndale, North Carolina, in 2003, this Klan moved its headquarters to Mount Holly the following year, while opening two additional klaverns in North Carolina and Tennessee.

Confederate Crusaders—A small Louisiana faction, active in Homer from 2000 to 2003, when it disbanded.

Confederate Forces Knights of the KKK—A short-lived Klan, established at Conyers, Georgia, in 1991, which failed to survive the mid–1990s.

Confederate Ghost Knights of the KKK—Briefly active in North Carolina during 1998–99, this splinter group suffered from the violent tendencies of Imperial Wizard Jimmy Ray Shelton and dissolved entirely after his March 1999 arrest for attempting to murder police officers outside Austin, Texas. By the time Shelton received his 99-year prison term in September 1999, the CGKKKK was already a fading memory.

Confederate Independent Order Knights of the KKK—A Maryland splinter group reported active in 1987, this short-lived faction claimed fewer than 100 members and apparently disbanded in 1990.

Confederate Knights of Alberta—Canadian klansman Ian Macpherson organized this group in 1972. Alberta authorities dissolved it three years later, while Macpherson awaited trial for killing a Mexican man at his Calgary home.

Confederate Knights of America—Founded in 1989, this North Carolina faction was jointly run from Huntersville by Terry Boyce and neo–Nazi activist Harold Covington, with satellite klaverns in Kentucky and Virginia. The Virginia realm disbanded by 1990, but new chapters were added in Alabama

and South Carolina. The following year, operations expanded to include one klavern each in Mississippi, New Jersey, North Carolina, South Carolina, and Virginia, but the growth spurt proved to be a dying gasp, and the CKA disbanded by mid-decade.

Confederate Knights of the KKK (1967–69)—A curious North Carolina faction, created and secretly funded by the FBI as part of J. Edgar Hoover's COINTELPRO campaign. The group was led by James Cole and George Dorsett (an FBI informant and former imperial kludd for the UKA). Based in Greensboro, the group was supported by G-men (who drafted its first recruiting letter) as a means of increasing dissension between other Carolina Klans.

Confederate Knights of the KKK (1980s) *see* Carolina Knights of the KKK

Confederate Knights of the KKK (1990–2005)—In 1990, this faction claimed active klaverns in Mississippi, New Jersey, and North Carolina. The New Jersey realm dissolved in 1991, while a new klavern opened in Texas. By 1997, operating from headquarters in Henderson, North Carolina, the CKKKKK nurtured three satellite klaverns in Kentucky and Virginia, with a new North Carolina chapter added in 2000. Its growth soon petered out, however, leaving Henderson's klavern the only active unit in 2003–05.

Confederate Vigilantes, Knights of the KKK—A short-lived Tennessee splinter group, dissolved in May 1981, after cofounder Gladys Girgenti and five other members were jailed on charges of plotting to bomb a synagogue. The defendants were also charged with conspiracy to dynamite a TV tower and several businesses owned by Jews. Upon conviction, Girgenti received a fifteen-year prison term.

Confederate White Knights of the KKK (Alabama)—Created at Clanton in 1997, this small unit failed to survive the decade.

Confederate White Knights of the KKK (Georgia)—Led by Lewis Baxter, of Sylvania, in 1990, the CWKKKK disbanded before the SCLC conducted its next survey of active Klans in 1991.

Confederate White Knights of the KKK (South Carolina)—Founded and led by Imperial Wizard Dewayne Goins, of Newberry, during 1990–91, this Klan dissolved by mid-decade.

Confederation of Independent Orders—Invisible Empire—Knights of the KKK—An umbrella group led by William Chaney, this loose confederation of twenty-six Klans emerged from a "unity conference" held on July 5, 1977. Further divided into northern and southern sections, the confederation charged each member Klan $100 per year, regardless of size. In July 1978, three members of Grand Dragon Tony LaRicci's Maryland faction were jailed for plotting to bomb a synagogue at Lochearn. In 1983, an ADL survey reported that the confederation was still active, but dwindling in

size due to traditional rivalries between competing Klans. It disappeared before the next Klan census, in 1985.

Confederation of Klans—A loose alliance of seven independent factions, forged during a meeting at Stone Mountain, Georgia, in September 1982. Participants included "ex"-klansman David Duke, representing the NAAWP; Stephen Black, Duke's successor as head of the Knights of the KKK; Edward Fields, of the New Order Knights; convicted bomber Robert Miles, founder of the Mountain Church in Michigan; James Venable, leader of the National Knights; and North Carolina's Glenn Miller. Black was elected to lead the confederation, retaining his office when the group met again in September 1983. According to Black, Bill Wilkinson's Invisible Empire Knights were deliberately excluded to avoid "bad publicity."

Conference of Eastern Dragons—Convened by Robert Scoggin in 1976, at Spartanburg, South Carolina, this one-time meeting was meant to bring order from the chaos then pervading the Invisible Empire. Known participants included Neuman Britton (Arkansas), Raymond Doerfler (Pennsylvania), Wilbur Forman (Illinois); Virgil Griffin (North Carolina), Tony LaRicci (Maryland), Albert McCorkle (Missouri), Earl Schoonmaker (New York), Dan Smithers (Texas), Buddy Tucker (Tennessee), and Bill Wilkinson (of the Invisible Empire Knights). While unity remained elusive, a highlight of the gathering was the auction sale of Roy Frankhouser's glass eye, purchased by Schoonmaker for five dollars.

Covenant Knights of the KKK—Founded in Jacksonville, Florida, in 1997, the CKKKK was briefly active but dissolved before the turn of the millennium.

Der Deutsche Orden des Fuerigen Kreuzes—Three naturalized Americans of German descent founded the German Order of Fiery Crosses in Berlin, in early 1921. All were expelled from the order in 1925, but the group survived until 1934, when Adolf Hitler's Nazi Party banned all competing racist groups. The order's members wore standard KKK regalia and pledged themselves to "ridding the country of undesirables by fighting the Jews."

Dixie Klans, Knights of the KKK, Inc.—This faction was chartered in Chattanooga, Tennessee, on October 13, 1957, by Klansmen recently expelled from Klavern No. 1 of the U.S. Klans. Brothers Harry and Jack Brown were the new Klan's driving force, campaigning beyond Chattanooga to plant small klaverns in Anniston, Alabama, and in northwestern Georgia (at Chatsworth and Dalton). In 1962, the Dixie Klans joined seven other independent groups to create the National Association of Ku Klux Klan, chaired by James Venable. Jack Brown served as imperial wizard until his death in summer 1965. Within a year, successor Charles Roberts suggested a merger of his remaining 150 members with the UKA. Congressional investigators found the Dixie Klans so small by 1966 that none of its members were subpoenaed to appear at HUAC hearings on Klan violence, and the group disbanded a short time later.

Dixie Knights of the KKK (1990–97)—Initially led by Tony Bastanzio from Apopka, Florida, the DKKKK claimed an additional klavern in Belpre, Ohio, during 1990. It expanded dramatically the following year, with units launched in Arizona, Iowa, New Jersey, North Carolina, Tennessee and West Virginia, but the growth was not sustained, and the Klan dissolved entirely by 1997.

Dixie Knights of the KKK (2002)—Organized at Elizabethtown, North Carolina, in 2002, this small Klan failed to endure through its first year of life.

Dixie Protestant Women's Political League—A white-supremacist women's organization based in Atlanta, which paraded publicly in regalia closely resembling the Klan's.

Dixieland White Knights of the KKK—Founded at Burleson, Texas, in 1998, this splinter group disbanded by the end of the decade.

Essex–Middle River Knights of the KKK—A small New Jersey splinter group, exposed in 1984, when Grand Titan Benjamin Butler and five other Klansmen were sent to prison for illegal cross-burnings and attempted murder of a black man.

Federated Knights of the KKK—In 1983, the ADL identified this group as a splinter faction active on a small scale in North and South Carolina.

Federated Ku Klux Klans, Inc.—Founded by William Hugh Morris in Birmingham, Alabama, on June 21, 1946, this Klan was Alabama's largest and most active faction between World War II and "Black Monday." Still, its claim of 30,000 members in 1949 was greatly inflated, and its newspaper (*Uxtra*) published only one issue before it folded that same year. In July 1949, seventeen Birmingham members were indicted on criminal charges including twenty-eight floggings, eight illegal boycotts, six burglaries, one count of carnal knowledge, and two misdemeanors. Morris was jailed for contempt of court on July 14, when he refused to produce a list of his members. The next day, grand jury hearings were briefly delayed when panel member Alexander Brewis was identified as a klansman, and several others were found to have criminal records. On July 18, presiding judge George Bailes admitted Klan membership in the 1920s, declaring that he had resigned from the order in 1925. Morris won release from jail in August, "recreating" an abbreviated membership roster from memory to replace the master list stolen (he claimed) from his home by unknown burglars. Despite sporadic activity through early 1950, the Federated KKK was moribund by year's end. Morris revived it in 1959, recruiting a few small units in neighboring Georgia, and he mustered enough Alabama members to rate inclusion in a 1961 federal injunction barring interference with CORE's integrated "freedom rides." Testimony before Congress in 1979 revealed that Morris was an FBI informant in the latter 1950s.

Federation of Klans, Knights of the KKK—This Chicago-based faction was founded in April 1995, when Illinois Grand Dragon Ed Novak left Thom Robb's KKKK to lead his own order. Units in Alabama, Colorado, Illinois and Ken-

tucky joined the FKKKKK, but it failed to prosper, disbanding before the SPLC conducted its survey of hate groups in 1999.

Fiery Cross Knights of the KKK—Founded in Richmond, Virginia, during 1998, this faction disbanded the following year.

Flaming Sword Knights of the KKK—Reported active in South Vineland, New Jersey, during 2003, this small faction apparently reincarnated the Flaming Sword KKK reported by SPLC investigators during 1990–92. No evidence of further activity has been exposed since 2003.

Flaming Sword Ku Klux Klan—Launched by klansmen in South Vineland, New Jersey, in 1990, this faction gained a small klavern at Stroudsburg, Pennsylvania the next year, then apparently disbanded. No trace of it was found by SPLC researchers prior to 2003, when a "new" Flaming Sword Knights of the KKK briefly surfaced in South Vineland, then disbanded.

Florida Biker Klan—This short-lived klavern on wheels was reported from Daytona, Florida, in 1991, but it apparently disbanded by year's end.

Florida Black Knights of the KKK—Based in Micanopy, this small faction first appeared in 1997 and failed to survive the close of the decade.

Florida Klans, Inc.—A short-lived spin-off from the AGK, this faction was created in 1948 by Klansmen whom Samuel Green described as "three sharp fellows" bent on fleecing the faithful.

Florida Ku Klux Klan—Organized in 1955, this was one of five Klans active in Florida after "Black Monday." Members raided the Wildwood jail in October 1956, to "punish" a black man who requested confinement for his own protection. Led by J.E. Fraser in 1957, the group ranked second in statewide membership, after the U.S. Klans, but claims of 30,000 dues-paying members clearly were inflated for publicity's sake. On June 25, 1961, Florida KKK leaders met with officers of the rival United KKK, merging to form the United Florida KKK.

Florida White Knights of the KKK—An independent splinter group active in 1987–90, led by Imperial Wizard Richard Ford from West Palm Beach, this Klan never had more than 100 members. according to ADL investigators.

Fraternal Order of Georgia—Based at Cartersville in 1991, this single-klavern operation dissolved before mid-decade.

Fraternal White Knights of the KKK—Richard Ford led this small faction, based in Lantana, Florida, during 1990. It apparently disbanded the following year.

Free Knights of the KKK—A small but relatively durable faction, based in Hiram, Georgia, the FKKKK was founded in 2002 with satellite klaverns in New York and North Carolina. It gained another Georgia chapter in 2003 and moved its headquarters to Buchanan in 2004, while nurturing three other klaverns in Georgia, New York, and North Carolina. All four units remained active in 2005.

Georgia Konfederate Knights of the KKK—Founded at Thomasville in 2000, this tiny faction disbanded before SPLC investigators conducted their next census of active Klans in 2001.

Georgia White Knights of the KKK—A single-klavern faction based in Rossville, the GWKKKK was organized in 2002 and failed to survive its first year.

Ghost Riders of the KKK—Another Florida faction, based at Lake Helen, the GRKKK emerged in 1999 and dissolved by early 1991.

Great Tennessee Knights of the KKK—A small faction based in Telford, briefly active during 2003.

Green Mountain Knights of the KKK—Active in Poultney, Vermont, during 1998–99, this Klan vanished by the turn of the millennium.

Greenville County Klan—A small and ineffective splinter group, identified as one of seven South Carolina factions competing after "Black Monday."

Gulf Coast Ku Klux Klan—Based in Mobile, Alabama, and led by gun dealer Elmo Bernard, this group was one of six Klans active in the Cotton State after "Black Monday." While smaller than some of its rivals, with an estimated 1,000 members in 1957, the GCKKK cherished a reputation for aggressive action. Bernard maintained a loose alliance with the Association of South Carolina Klans, but it failed to sustain him, and his faction disbanded by the early 1960s.

Heartland White Knights of the KKK—Led by Imperial Wizard John Clary, the HWKKKK claimed a single klavern in Tulsa, Oklahoma, during 1989–90, but disbanded thereafter.

Hooded Ladies of the Mystic Den—Early 1920s ladies' auxiliary, absorbed after June 1923 by the Women of the KKK.

Imperial Empire Knights of the KKK—SPLC investigators identified this Indianapolis faction in 1999, but found no trace of it the following year.

Imperial Guard Ku Klux Klan—Based at Sparta, Missouri, this small Klan was briefly active during 2003.

Imperial Klans of America—The early twenty-first century's most successful Klan was founded at Powderly, Kentucky, in 1997, with two satellite klaverns in Kentucky and Illinois. A year later, only headquarters and a small Adams, Wisconsin, unit remained, but the IKA experienced dramatic growth in 2000, claiming eighteen additional units in thirteen states. Three more realms were added in 2001, and the Klan's strength peaked in 2002, with thirty-six klaverns identified in Alabama, Arkansas, California, Florida, Georgia, Illinois, Indiana, Iowa, Kansas, Kentucky, Louisiana, Maryland, Michigan, Missouri, New York, North Carolina, Ohio, Pennsylvania, Tennessee,

Texas, Virginia, Washington and West Virginia. Headquarters moved to Dawson Springs, Kentucky, in 2003, with a net loss of one klavern for the year, but the IKA retained most of its strength in 2004, with thirty-three active klaverns, including new realms in Oklahoma and the District of Columbia. An additional klavern joined the list in 2005.

Imperial Knights of the KKK—Launched in 1991, with headquarters in York, Pennsylvania, this small Klan disappeared by mid-decade.

Imperial White Knights of the KKK—Led by Imperial Wizard Charles Murphy in Cross Anchor, South Carolina, this group was active during 1989–90 but dissolved in early 1991.

Improved Order of the U.S. Klans, Knights of the KKK, Inc.—Chartered in Georgia on November 7, 1963, this Klan was organized by Lithonia resident E.E. George, after his removal from leadership of the U.S. Klans. Rival Klan leader James Venable served as counsel for the group's incorporating officers, and representatives of the new faction attended gatherings of Venable's National Association of Ku Klux Klan. At its peak strength, the group boasted two klaverns in Georgia (Lithonia and Tallapoosa), two in Alabama (Heilberger and Union Springs), and three in Florida (two in Jacksonville, and one in Ocala). The Jacksonville units disbanded in December 1964, followed by those in Alabama. By January 1967, an estimated 100 members remained in Georgia.

Independent Invisible Knights of the KKK—In 1983, this splinter group was identified as one of two active Ohio Klans.

Independent Klan of America—Indiana's D.C. Stephenson organized this group in May 1924, following his break with the Atlanta-based Knights of the KKK, but the move backfired when most Indiana klansman remained loyal to the parent order. In 1925, the Independent Klan solicited members without much success in Ulster County, New York, and its efforts were finally doomed by Stephenson's conviction in the Madge Oberholtzer rape-murder case.

Independent Klans—A small faction of uncertain venue, publicized for the first time in August 1949, when its unnamed leaders joined the Knights of the KKK of America, led by Lycurgus Spinks.

Independent Knights of the KKK—One of seven KKK factions active in South Carolina after "Black Monday."

Independent Mississippi Klan—Organized in 1957, this splinter group included defecting klaverns earlier established by the Association of Alabama Knights. The group disbanded sometime before kleagles from Louisiana's Original Knights invaded Mississippi, in autumn 1963.

Independent Northern Klans, Inc.—Based at Pine Bush, New York, this faction drew attention in 1976, when Grand Dragon Earl Schoonmaker and several other members were identified as state prison guards. New York Attorney General Louis Lefkowitz demanded the group's membership list under a 1920s anti-Klan statute requiring public registration of members in oath-bound societies, but Schoonmaker resisted. On January 15, 1976, the state supreme court ruled in Schoonmaker's favor, finding that the Klan's membership pledge was not an "oath" within the statute's definition. The controversy stirred public interest, but the Klan's fame was fleeting, and it disbanded during 1979.

Independent Order Knights of the KKK—A Maryland splinter group, active in 1987–89, this Klan claimed fewer than 100 members by the time it disbanded in 1990.

International Association of the Knights of the KKK—Despite its ambitious title, this small Klan consisted of a single klavern at Enoree, South Carolina, active during 2000–01.

International Keystone Knights of the KKK—Established at Johnstown, Pennsylvania, in 1997, the IKKKKK claimed satellite klaverns in Florida, Pennsylvania and South Carolina. A year later, SPLC investigators found active units in Arkansas, Florida, Indiana, Pennsylvania, South Carolina, Tennessee and Washington. By 1999, five realms had dissolved, leaving only headquarters, with single klaverns in Arkansas and South Carolina. The see-saw pattern continued in 2000, with establishment of new units in Delaware, Indiana, Pennsylvania, Tennessee and Virginia, while 2001 witnessed disbandment of all klaverns except imperial headquarters and one unit in Bayse, Virginia. The latter klavern folded in 2002, replaced by a small unit at Parkin, Arkansas. In 2003, the IKKKKK gained another Arkansas klavern, plus one in Ohio, but the growth was not sustained. By 2004, headquarters claimed a chapter in Louisville, Kentucky, as its only satellite klavern.

International White Knights of the KKK—This small faction was founded at Elizabethtown, North Carolina, in 2004, surviving with a single klavern into 2005.

Interstate Klans, Knights of the KKK—Based in Laurel, Maryland, this faction was created in 1966, after UKA Grand Dragon Vernon Naimaster chastised Exalted Cyclops Xavier Edwards for recruiting members of the American Nazi Party. Edwards then defected, creating his own Klan with a loose affiliation to the ANP. On occasion, Edwards referred to his group as the Maryland Knights of the KKK (unrelated to a Klan of the same name, organized by Tony LaRicci in 1969). Edwards sought help from New York Governor Nelson Rockefeller, to repeal New York's anti-Klan legislation and permit a Klan march through Harlem, but neither effort was successful, and his faction faded from the scene by 1970.

Invincible Empire Knights of the KKK—Organized at Rocky Ridge, Maryland, in 1997, the IEKKKK claimed a second klavern that year, in Chambersburg, Pennsylvania. In 1998, headquarters moved to Hancock, Maryland, with one additional Maryland klavern and two in West Virginia. The year 2000 brought dramatic changes, with transfer of imperial headquarters to Piney Flats, Tennessee, while ten addition klaverns were identified in Maryland, Pennsylvania, Virginia, and West

Virginia. Despite that sudden growth, SPLC researchers found no surviving traces of the group in 2001.

Invincible Empire, Knights of the White Rose—
A tiny California faction, identified as one of three Klans active in the state during 1983.

Invincible Realm Knights of the KKK—The small Lakeland, Florida, group emerged in 1997 and disbanded before the turn of the century.

Invisible Empire Association of Alberta, Knights of the KKK—Canadian klansman Ian Macpherson organized this group in February 1980, as a successor to his defunct Confederate Klans of Alberta. The IEAAKKKK dissolved in February 1989, after three members pled guilty to a bombing plot in Calgary.

Invisible Empire, Indiana KKK—Based at Knox, Indiana, in 1998, this tiny faction disappeared sometime before 2000.

Invisible Empire, Knights of the KKK (1975–93)—Founded in August 1975 by Bill Wilkinson, based in Denham Springs, Louisiana, this faction emerged as the dominant Klan of the early 1980s. Born of a rift with David Duke's Knights of the KKK, Wilkinson's order claimed one-fifth to one-third of all identified Klansmen by 1979, and remained dominant until 1983. At its peak, the IEKKKK engaged in violent confrontations with blacks at Oklona and Tupelo, Mississippi; at Decatur, Alabama; and in Forsyth County, Georgia. Total membership was estimated at 2,000 to 2,500 Klansmen in 1980, but autumn forays into Connecticut and Pennsylvania met lukewarm responses. Wilkinson's control of the Klan began unraveling in 1981, when the media revealed his role as an FBI informant, and he declared bankruptcy in January 1983. James Farrands, a Connecticut Catholic, replaced Wilkinson as imperial wizard and infused the Klan with new vitality, claiming active klaverns in twelve states by 1989. The following year, Farrands moved his headquarters to Gulf, North Carolina, and widespread recruiting continued. By 1991 the IEKKKK had units in Alabama, California, Connecticut, Florida, Georgia, Indiana, Kentucky, Louisiana, Maine, Nebraska, New Hampshire, New Jersey, New York, Oklahoma, Pennsylvania, South Carolina and Virginia. Disaster struck in 1993, in the form of a federal lawsuit filed by the SPLC on behalf of Georgia blacks beaten by klansmen in 1987. A punitive court order in that case disbanded the IEKKKK nationwide in May 1992, and while two small units clung stubbornly to life in 1998, at Forestville, Connecticut, and Louisville, Kentucky, none remained at the turn of the century.

Invisible Empire, Knights of the KKK (1975–83)—Unrelated to Bill Wilkinson's group of the same name, but founded in the same year, this faction was created on 13 October 1975, when five grand dragons deserted the National Knights, charging Imperial Wizard James Venable with mismanagement and senility. Venable responded by banishing the five and revoking their commissions as dragons, saying, "They been runnin' over states creatin' trouble and getting' in undesirable members, takin' in anybody who had fifteen dollars." Ohio's Dale Reusch was elected imperial wizard of the new Klan, supported by Grand Dragons Raymond Doerfler (Pennsylvania), John Howard (South Carolina), Tony LaRicci (Maryland), and W.B. Miller II (West Virginia). In a bid for new members, the IEK opened its ranks to women, children, Catholics and naturalized citizens. Jacob Prins was named as the group's Canadian dragon in mid–1976, but the IEK failed to thrive and disappeared entirely by 1983.

Invisible Empire Knights of the KKK (New Jersey)—An independent splinter group reported active in 1990, this faction claimed fewer than 100 members when it disbanded the following year.

Invisible Empire Knights of the KKK (Texas)—Active in Conroe during 2002–03, this small Klan disbanded before SPLC investigators completed their annual survey of hate groups for 2004.

Invisible Empire, Knights of the KKK, Realm of South Carolina—Founded in 1969 or 1970 by Robert Scoggin, following his banishment as South Carolina's grand dragon for the UKA, this group had no ties to the other two groups using similar names in the 1970s. Based at Spartanburg, the Klan gained its first known recruits outside South Carolina in May 1975, when Indiana klansman Wilburn Foreman brought thirty UKA defectors into the fold. A year later, Scoggin hosted the Conference of Eastern Dragons, hoping to promote the illusion of a far-flung organization. A 1983 ADL survey of active Klans revealed no trace of Scoggin's group remaining.

Invisible Empire Ku Klux Klan, Inc.—Led by Ken Taylor from Crawfordsville, Indiana, in 1990, this Hoosier Klan apparently disbanded the following year.

Invisible Empire, KKK of Pennsylvania and New Jersey—Led by Grand Dragons Raymond Doerfler (Pennsylvania) and Edwin Reynolds (New Jersey), this faction was affiliated with the Confederation of Independent Orders.

The Invisible Empire Knights march through Crawfordsville, Indiana, in July 1986 (Southern Poverty Law Center).

It had an estimated 150–200 members in 1978, but none remained when the ADL surveyed active Klans in 1979.

Invisible Empire National Knights of the KKK

—SPLC investigators reported this small Klan active in Luxora, Arkansas, in 2000. No trace of it remained the following year.

Invisible Empire of the International Knights of the KKK

—Hope springs eternal for this tiny faction based in Enoree, South Carolina during 2004. It was formerly known as the International Association of Knights of the KKK (2000–01) and the Invisible Empire of National Knights (2003).

Invisible Empire of the National Knights

—This small faction, based at Enoree, South Carolina, was known in 2000–01 as the International Association of Knights of the KKK. In 2004 its leaders changed the name again, to the even more grandiose Invisible Empire of International Knights.

Invisible Empire, Pennsylvania KKK

—Based at Punxsutawney, this single-klavern faction was active during 1997–2000 but disbanded in 2001.

Invisible Empire, United Klans of Europe

—Despite its expansive title, this 1990s faction (also called the British Knights of the KKK) was restricted to England, where founder Allan Beshella created it after defecting from the U.S.-based IEKKKK. The group disbanded after *Searchlight* magazine revealed Beshella's 1972 arrest for child molestation.

Invisible Empire White Knights of the KKK

—SPLC observers found this Klan operating at Oaks, Pennsylvania, in 2002. It moved to Washington, Pennsylvania, the next year, and dissolved in early 2004.

Invisible Empire, United Klans, Knights of the KKK of America, Inc.

—A spin-off from the U.S. Klans, chartered in Georgia on 21 February 1961, with Robert Davidson as imperial wizard and Calvin Craig as grand dragon of Georgia. Most of the early members were U.S Klan defectors in Georgia and Alabama, where Rev. Alvin Horn led the neighboring realm. Davidson's public opposition to violence dissatisfied many members, prompting his resignation on 1 April 1961. Craig immediately opened negotiations with Robert Shelton, leader of the militant Alabama Knights, and a merger was formalized on 8 July 1961, with Klan headquarters shifted to Tuscaloosa, Alabama. While Davidson's original title was used in the new group's incorporation papers, the Shelton-Craig operation was henceforth known as the United Klans of America, Inc., Knights of the KKK.

Invisible Knights of the KKK (1990s)

—ADL investigators found the IKKKK active in 1996, promoting its views over public access cable television from its base in Lafayette, Louisiana.

Invisible Knights of the KKK (2003)

—Based in Fort Wayne, Indiana, this splinter group was briefly active during 2003.

Iron Riders Motorcycle Club

—SPLC investigators identified this Greenville, Tennessee, group as a Klan unit active during 1991. It apparently dissolved the following year.

Junior Ku Klux Klan

—Established in 1924 to recruit boys between the ages of twelve and eighteen.

Justice Knights of the KKK

—A splinter group based in Chattanooga, Tennessee, this faction was led by Imperial Wizard Bill Church in 1980. On 20 April of that year, Church and two other Klansmen were jailed for shooting several black women on the street. Church and Larry Payne were acquitted, while Marshall Thrash was convicted on reduced charges, the verdicts sparking riots in Chattanooga's ghetto.

JWS Militant Knights of the KKK

—Based at Valley Head, Alabama, in 1997, this faction (named for deceased Georgia klansman James W. Spivey) moved its headquarters (and only klavern) to Georgia in 1998, then disbanded before year's end.

Kamelia

—A short-lived organization created by William Simmons in 1922, after Hiram Evans replaced him as imperial wizard, to serve as the "official" KKK ladies' auxiliary. Members infiltrated Oklahoma's White American Protestant Study Club and soon took control of that group, but Kamelia failed to prosper. Evans retaliated by forbidding Klansmen to associate with Kamelia members, and Simmons finally agreed to disband the group in 1924, as part of his final settlement with Evans.

Kentucky Knights of the KKK

—This short-lived faction of the early 1990s disbanded shortly after 8 June 1992, when Grand Dragon Ernest Pierce and three of his klansmen faced charges of burning a church in Bowling Green. All of the defendants were convicted and sentenced to prison in 1994. The pastor of the church had criticized the KKK.

KKK #87

—Led in 1989 by Imperial Wizard Tony Bastanzio, of Apopka, Florida, this group also claimed a small klavern in Belpre, Ohio. Only headquarters remained in 1991, and the group disbanded by mid-decade.

Klan of the North

—Apparently an alternate name for D.C. Stephenson's Independent Klan of America, defunct after his murder conviction in 1926. Still, Indiana Governor Ralf Gates moved to formally revoke the group's charter in November 1946.

Klan Youth Corps

—Conceived by David Duke to recruit young members for his Knights of the KKK, the KYC concept was soon adopted by competing factions (without credit to Duke). In 1980–81, the IEKKKK's KYC operation included Camp My Lai, in Louisiana, where youngsters received paramilitary training and indoctrination into klannishness. A teenaged New Jersey klansman told *Junior Scholastic* that the KKK was trying to "get kids off the street and give them something to do," but an SPLC lawsuit finally closed the camp. In May 1981, Bill Wilkinson's KYC director was one of six persons arrested for plotting to bomb a synagogue and Jewish businesses in Nashville, Tennessee. In Decatur, Alabama, teens wearing Klan T-shirts staged a public demonstration, burning a derelict bus to register their protest against school integration. Other students in Oklahoma City, claiming membership in two Klan groups, assaulted patrons at a gay bar, beating them with baseball bats.

Klansman's Klean-up Kommittee—A reform group founded by Tulsa klansmen in September 1924, to "purify" the KKK of abuses allegedly committed by Grand Dragon N. Clay Jewett. While it failed to depose Jewett, the group, led by State Senator Wash Hudson, won a concession from Hiram Evans that future appointments of grand dragons would include approval from the state's rank-and-file klansmen.

Klavalier Klub—Identified by infiltrator Stetson Kennedy as the Atlanta wrecking crew of the 1940s AGK, the Klavalier Klub was implicated in the fatal 1945 stabbing of Porter Turner and the February 1946 flogging of a black hotel bellboy. State Attorney General Dan Duke reported that the group had fifty members, chosen for their brawn and sadism. Kennedy, himself a member of the squad, was ordered to buy a pistol and was told, "We Klavaliers serve as the secret police of the KKK and are trusted with carrying out all 'direct-line' activity." Klavaliers took turns flogging each victim, so that none could implicate the others without condemning himself.

Klavaliers—A paramilitary arm of the 1920s Wisconsin Klan, which infiltrated Madison's police force and employed spies in minority neighborhoods to direct vice raids.

Klay Kounty Klavern—SPLC investigators identified this small faction in Grandin, Florida, during 1997. It disbanded before the end of the decade.

Klinton Kounty Knights of the KKK—Active in Centralia, Illinois, during 1998, the KKKKKK dissolved before 2000.

Knight Riders of the KKK (Virginia)—Organized in Winchester, Virginia, during 2000, this faction disappeared the following year.

Knight Riders of the KKK (West Virginia)—Possibly spawned by a faction of the same name in neighboring Virginia, the KRKKK was active in Daniels during 2002–05.

Knights Kamelia—The "second degree" of 1920s klannishness, also known as K-Duo.

Knights of American Protestantism—A splinter group active in Wisconsin's Fox River Valley, the short-lived KAP broke away from D.C. Stephenson's Independent Klan of America in late 1924 or early 1925.

Knights of the Air—Conceived as a 1920s Klan air force, led by C. Anderson Wright, this abortive program collapsed when imperial headquarters withheld financial support.

Knights of the Apocalypse—Active in Valrico, Florida, during 1997, this small Klan disbanded sometime before 1999. A similarly named organization appeared in Kathleen, Florida, during 2002.

Knights of Bedford Forest of the KKK—Operating in Greenville, Tennessee, during 2003–05, this faction assumed its title by misspelling the name of the Klan's original grand wizard.

Knights of the Black Cross—A white-supremacist group active in Franklin County, Mississippi, during early 1868, whose overlapping membership with the local KKK made the groups essentially indistinguishable.

Knights of the Flaming Sword—ADL investigators identified this small Mississippi group as a Klan faction active in 1996. It disbanded sometime before the SPLC's survey of hate groups in 1999.

Knights of the Forest—SPLC researchers found this Klan faction operating in Silver Springs, Florida, during 1997. It disbanded before the decade's end.

Knights of the Golden Eagle—A black-robed "action" unit, which made its one and only public appearance with J.B. Stoner and representatives of the United Florida KKK at a May 1964 rally in Jacksonville.

Knights of the Great Forest—The "third degree" of klannishness, created by imperial headquarters in 1928 for klansmen who had (in theory) discarded their masks. The order was also known as K-Trio.

Knights of the Green Forest—Organized in 1966, this militant splinter group was led by Imperial Wizard Dale Watson, composed of defectors from the UKA's Mississippi realm. It apparently dissolved after September 1969, when Watson was jailed for plotting to murder civil rights activist Charles Evers.

Knights of the KKK (1955–?)—Identified as one of five Florida Klans organized after "Black Monday," this short-lived group soon vanished in the general hysteria of the period.

Knights of the KKK (1955–?)—One of seven splinter groups active in South Carolina after "Black Monday," this Klan apparently dissolved by 1960, leaving no trace of itself behind.

Knights of the KKK (1956)—Chartered in Louisiana, this Klan led an uneventful life and vanished by 1960.

Knights of the KKK (1964)—An alternative name for the United Florida KKK, sometimes employed by leader Eunice Fallaw.

Knights of the KKK (1997–98)—An offshoot of Thom Robb's KKKK, this Klan was established in 1997, with headquarters in Huntsville, Missouri, and satellite klaverns in California, Florida, Georgia, Illinois, Indiana, Kentucky, Louisiana, Massachusetts, Michigan, New York, Ohio, Oklahoma, Oregon and Virginia. A year later, imperial headquarters moved to Duson, Louisiana, with nineteen klaverns active in fifteen states. A fatal schism during 1998 shattered the group into small, independent splinter factions.

Knights of the KKK (Arkansas)—Unrelated to Thom Robb's Klan of the same name, in Harrison, this Luxora-based faction was briefly active during 1998.

Knights of the KKK (Missouri)—Founded at Humansville in 1999, this Klan also boasted a klavern in Rosman, North Carolina. Both units disbanded by year's end.

Knights of the KKK, Florida—Founded by Bill Hendrix in 1962, with headquarters at Oldsmar. Congressional investigators identified ten dues-paying members in 1967, reporting that the Klan's "only activity in the past five years has been its infrequent meetings." By decade's end, it had dissolved entirely.

Knights of the KKK (Florida)—Founded at New Port Richey in 1997, this independent group moved to Kathleen in 1998 and disbanded early in 1999.

Knights of the KKK (Kansas)—A short-lived faction, active in Salina during 1997, this group vanished before SPLC investigators surveyed national hate groups in 1998.

Knights of the KKK (North Carolina)—Based at Pisgah Forest, the KKKK was briefly active in 1998.

Knights of the KKK (Ohio)—Founded at Lodi in 1997, this group disbanded early the following year.

Knights of the KKK (Pennsylvania)—Active in Reading during 1998–2001, this independent Klan disappeared before SPLC researchers completed their census of U.S. hate groups for 2002.

Knights of the KKK (Tennessee)—Another independent faction, the KKKK maintained klaverns in London and Memphis during 1989–90.

Knights of the KKK (Virginia)—A splinter group active in Stephens City during 1998.

Knights of the KKK, Inc. (1915–44)—The "second era" KKK, organized by William Simmons in November 1915 and headquartered in Atlanta, Georgia. After a slow start, the group recruited 100,000 members in 1921 and moved on from there to plant klaverns in each of the forty-eight states. Peak membership estimates for 1924–26 range from two million to an implausibly precise 8,904,887, with most estimates falling in the three-to-five million range. Texas dentist Hiram Evans supplanted Simmons as imperial wizard in 1922 and ruled the Invisible Empire until his resignation in 1939. Successor James Colescott supervised the declining organization until an IRS lien for $685,305 in back taxes from the 1920s forced its disbandment on 23 April 1944. Colescott left Dr. Samuel Green, Sr., in charge of the surviving Georgia Klan, and while he warned journalists that the KKK might revive after World War II, Colescott had no part in its subsequent resurrection.

Knights of the KKK, Inc. (1960)—Imperial Wizard H.H. Jones announced the formation of this Klan on 29 February 1960, following a weekend meeting in Atlanta reportedly attended by Klansmen from seventeen southeastern and southwestern states. Jones claimed 42,000 members at the outset, with a recruiting drive planned for the North, but no more was heard from the group.

Knights of the KKK, Inc. (1975–)—Originally founded in New Orleans, this Klan was led by realtor Jim Lindsay (alias "Ed White") until his murder in June 1975. Louisiana Grand Dragon David Duke then took charge and filed state incorporation papers that granted him, as a "founding member," the absolute right to determine Klan policy. By year's end, Duke had organized the largest KKK rally in a decade, luring an estimated 2,700 spectators to Walker, Louisiana. Operating from headquarters at Metairie, Duke built the Knights into the dominant Klan of the 1970s, but dissatisfaction with his leadership (and alleged profiteering) prompted Grand Dragons Tom Metzger and Bill Wilkinson to defect. By 1979, Wilkinson's Invisible Empire Knights claimed more members, while Duke focused increasingly on mainstream politics. Meeting with Wilkinson in July 1980, Duke offered to sell his membership list for $35,000, but Wilkinson rejected the deal and publicized Duke's "betrayal." Resigning to found the "new" NAAWP, Duke left Alabama Grand Dragon Stephen Black in charge of the Knights, with headquarters at Tuscumbia. Black's subsequent imprisonment for plotting to invade Dominica left a power vacuum at the top, with Stanley McCollum (in Alabama) and Thomas Robb (Louisiana) each claiming control of the Klan. Members of the Knights joined in a seven-Klan unity conference at Stone Mountain, Georgia, in September 1982, but the meeting failed to unify. Robb emerged triumphant at a second Georgia gathering, in 1983, and transferred Klan headquarters to Harrison, Arkansas. By 1991, energetic recruiting had established klaverns in Alabama, California, Colorado, Florida, Iowa, Illinois, Kentucky, Maryland, Missouri, New Jersey, Ohio, Tennessee and Texas. Over the next seven years, attrition and dissension struck at the heart of the KKKK, until headquarters alone remained during 1999–2003. Klanwatchers were surprised in 2004, when a new growth spurt added individual klaverns in Florida, North Carolina and Tennessee. The group retained five klaverns in 2005.

Knights of the KKK/Knights of the Apocalypse—A Florida faction, presumably related to Valrico's Knights of the Apocalypse (1997), this Klan was active in the town of Kathleen during 2002.

Knights of the KKK of America—On 23 August 1949, fifty Klansmen from six southern states gathered in Montgomery, Alabama, to merge their local groups into a stronger, more dynamic Klan. Participants included leaders of such obscure groups as the Allied Klans, Independent Klans, Ozark Klans, River Valley Klans, Seashore Klans and Star Klans. Delegates elected Lycurgus Spinks as their "imperial emperor," and he immediately claimed an incredible 650,000 members spanning Alabama, Mississippi, Missouri and Louisiana. Following a peculiar appearance on *Meet the Press,* Spinks announced relocation of his headquarters from Montgomery to Jackson, Mississippi, in March 1950, but nothing more was heard of the group.

Knights of the KKK of the Confederacy—Founded in Alabama during 1957, this splinter group apparently had no connection to Asa Carter's Original KKK of the Confederacy. No details of its short-lived operations are presently available.

Knights of the KKK, Southern Brotherhood—Active in Atlanta, Georgia, during 1998, the KKKKSB disbanded before the turn of the new century.

Knights of Liberty—A black-robed vigilante group active against the IWW in Tulsa, Oklahoma, during 1917, described in the *Tulsa World* as the "modern Ku Klux Klan."

Knights of the True Cross—This single-klavern Georgia faction was briefly active during 2003.

Knights of the White Camellia (1950s)—A short-lived group founded by Florida Klan leader Bill Hendrix after "Black Monday."

Knights of the White Camellia (1980s)—The Texas-based Original Knights of the KKK adopted this name in 1982, in a failed attempt to improve its public image, but the group soon dissolved.

Knights of the White Camellia of the KKK—A Texas faction led by Grand Dragon Charles Lee, this group had an estimated 300 members when Lee staged a write-in gubernatorial campaign in 1990. He failed to win election, and the KWCKKK soon disbanded.

Knights of the White Kamellia—Originally based in Lafayette, Louisiana, the KWK boasted eleven klaverns in six states during 1997. Headquarters moved to Vidor, Texas, in 1998, under teenage Imperial Wizard James Roesch, with twenty-two klaverns in Alabama, Florida, Georgia, Louisiana, Michigan, Missouri, Ohio, Oklahoma, Texas, Virginia and West Virginia. Strength declined to eight klaverns in four states by 2000, when Roesch moved his base to Jasper, Texas (site of the 1998 James Byrd lynching). That provocative move briefly boosted KWK operations, expanding to eight klaverns in seven states, but rapid attrition left the group with only two satellite klaverns (in North Carolina and Ohio) by 2002. A final shakeup transferred headquarters (and the sole surviving klavern) to Germantown, Ohio, in 2003, and the KWC disbanded before year's end.

Knights of Yahweh—A Tennessee faction, this Klan was active in Dandridge and Morristown during 2001–05.

Knights Party—SPLC investigators identified this small faction in January 2005, after fliers bearing its logo were scattered on lawns in Westwood, Massachusetts. No further information on its size or structure is available.

Konsolidated Ku Klux Klans of the Invisible Empire—Yet another of the short-lived Florida factions created by Bill Hendrix during the 1950s.

Kountry Knights of the KKK—This small faction was active in Jennings, Louisiana, during 2000.

Ku Klux Klan (1866–187?)—The original Reconstruction Klan was founded at Pulaski, Tennessee, in spring 1866 and held its first anniversary parade on 5 June 1867. By that time, the Klan had already passed from its first presumed function as a social club for Confederate veterans, reorganized along paramilitary lines at a meeting in Nashville, convened in April 1867. With Nathan Bedford Forrest installed as its first and only grand wizard, the KKK planted dens in thirteen states, including all states of the former Confederacy (Alabama, Arkansas, Florida, Georgia, Louisiana, Mississippi, North Carolina, South Car-olina, Tennessee, Texas and Virginia) plus the "loyal" former slave states of Kentucky and Missouri. Interviewed in 1868, Forrest claimed 40,000 members in Tennessee and 500,000 across the South (although he later denied any affiliation with or special knowledge of the Klan). Flourishing terrorism prompted Forrest to officially disband the order on 25 January 1869, but his order had no apparent effect outside Tennessee. Between May 1870 and April 1871, Congress enacted legislation aimed at curbing Klan violence, and most activity had ceased in five southern states by the time congressional investigators probed Ku Klux crimes, in a series of hearings held between May and December 1871. Still, it remained for martial law and wholesale indictments to quell nightriding in the Carolinas, Florida, and Mississippi. Debate continues regarding the final date of KKK disbandment. Most sources place its dissolution sometime during 1872–73, but Florida victim Jonathan Gibbs reported Klan threats before his sudden death in 1874, and N.C. Cochran, a witness in the federal Ku Klux trials, was murdered in Missouri as late as 1877. Klan-style terrorism was pervasive during the 1876 presidential election, and former Georgia Grand Dragon John Gordon was among the Democratic Party spokesmen who negotiated recognition of Rutherford Hayes at the winner of that fiercely-contested campaign. There is no doubt that former Klansmen participated in nightriding violence by the Red Shirts, White Caps, and similar groups throughout the remainder of the nineteenth century.

Ku Klux Klan (2002–05)—Founded at Compton, Arkansas, in 2002, this faction remained a one-klavern unit until 2004, when it gained a second chapter in Beaverton, Alabama.

Ku Klux Klan of America—This title was found on KKK literature seized by Austrian police from neo-Nazis in Vienna, during February 1960. It was ultimately traced to Horace Miller's Aryan Knights of the KKK, based in Waco, Texas.

Ku Klux Klan of Florida, Inc.—Chartered on 7 September 1944, with headquarters in Orlando, this faction was led by A.F. Gilliam, H.F. McCormack, and A.B. Taylor. Its strength was concentrated in central Florida, where it operated as an affiliate of Samuel Green's AGK. Members were involved in acts of terrorism during 1945–53, but the group apparently dissolved before "Black Monday," during federal investigations of the Harry Moore assassination.

Ku Klux Klan of the Confederacy—Alternate title sometimes used in media reports for Asa Carter's Original KKK of the Confederacy. It may represent a variant name used by Klansmen themselves, or a garbled version created by the press.

Ku Klux Rangers—A Reconstruction-era group active around Sulphur Springs, Texas, which maintained affiliation with the local Democratic Party.

Ladies of the Cu Clux Clan—A 1920s women's auxiliary, absorbed after June 1923 by the Women of the KKK.

Ladies of the Golden Den—Ladies' auxiliary of the 1920s Klan, absorbed in 1923 by the Women of the KKK.

Ladies of the Golden Mask—Ladies' auxiliary of the 1920s Indiana Klan.

Ladies of the Invisible Empire—Nationwide ladies' auxiliary (nicknamed LOTIES), superseded in June 1923 by the Women of the KKK.

Ladies of the Invisible Eye—A 1920s women's group closely affiliated with the Klan, which disappeared after June 1923, presumably absorbed by the Women of the KKK.

Liberty Knights of the KKK—Founded at Boonville, Indiana, in 1999, the LKKKK also claimed one Illinois klavern and two in Louisiana. Only headquarters remained in 2000, and the group disbanded by year's end.

Longitude 74 Ku Klux Klan—Founded by Canadian klansman Michel Larocque in autumn 1990, this faction draws its name from Montreal's map coordinates.

Lookout Mountain Knights of the KKK—Founded and led by Imperial Wizard Don Marshall, this Klan was active at Lookout Mountain, Tennessee, during 1989–91.

Louisiana Knights of the KKK—A short-lived faction based at Baton Rouge, created by Rev. Perry Strickland after his defection from the U.S. Klans in 1956. It disbanded prior to creation of the Original Knights in 1960.

Louisiana White Knights of the KKK—An independent faction, active in Walker during 2003–05.

Loyal Order of White Knights, KKK—Founded at Hinesville, Georgia, in 1991, this Klan survived for roughly a year.

Manitoba Knights of the KKK—Canadian klansman Bill Harcus founded this Klan in spring 1990. Authorities charged Harcus and colleague Theron Skyrba with advocating genocide in December 1991, but the charges were dismissed at trial on grounds of apparent police perjury.

Maryland Knights of the KKK (1966–67)—Also known as the Interstate Knights, this splinter group was created by Xavier Edwards after his expulsion from the UKA. It maintained close ties to the American Nazi Party and apparently dissolved soon after ANP leader George Lincoln Rockwell's murder in August 1967.

Maryland Knights of the KKK (1969–80)—Grand Dragon Tony LaRicci left the UKA to lead his own Maryland faction in 1969, affiliated with the National Knights until October 1975, when Imperial Wizard James Venable banished LaRicci and four other dissident dragons. Imperial Klaliff Will Minton failed in his 1977 bid to seize power from LaRicci, and the Maryland Knights joined the Confederation of Independent Orders in June of that year. Membership declined sharply after July 1978, when three of LaRicci's Klansmen were convicted of plotting to bomb a Lochearn synagogue.

Maryland Knights of the KKK (1989–90)—Grand Dragon Robert White led this single-klavern faction, in Thurmont.

Michigan Ku Klux Klan—One of three small factions reported active during 1983, in the Wolverine State.

Militant Knights of the KKK—Organized by former UFKKK members in spring 1965, this Klan maintained a single klavern in Jacksonville, Florida, with redundant leadership from Imperial Wizard Donald Ballentine and Grand Dragon Gene Foreman. Congressional investigators estimated its total membership at twenty-five in January 1967, and the group apparently disbanded by year's end.

Mississippi Christian Knights of the KKK—A short-lived faction of the latter 1980s, based in Poplarville, the MCKKKK faded away after May 1989, when Imperial Wizard Jordan Gollub was identified as a closet Jew.

Mississippi Royal Confederate Knights of the KKK—SPLC investigators reported this Jackson-based Klan active in 2000.

Mississippi White Knights of the KKK—Unrelated to the violent White Knights faction that terrorized Mississippi blacks and Jews in 1964–68, this Klan consisted of a single klavern in Petal during 2000–02. Two more Mississippi klaverns were established in 2003, and while both dissolved before year's end, the MWKKKK boasted five chapters in Arkansas, Florida, Texas and Vermont during 2004. No word was available at press time for this volume, as to whether the expansion beyond Mississippi would include a change of name.

Missouri Federation of Klans, Inc.—SPLC researchers found this faction active in St. Louis during 1997–99.

Missouri Knights of the KKK—A splinter group active in the late 1980s, which sparked controversy in Kansas during February 1988, after a klansman was invited to speak on a student radio station at the state university at Lawrence. School administrators postponed the broadcast, while Klan leaders announced plans to buy time on public-access TV.

Mountaineer Knights of the KKK—Observers reported this small faction active in Stroudsburg, Pennsylvania, during 1991–92.

Mouvement des Revendications des Droits de la Majorité—Québec klansman Michel Larocque organized this Klan faction as a successor to his Longitude 74 KKK, in 1991. The group was affiliated with Thomas Robb's Arkansas-based KKKK and briefly published a newspaper, *The White Patriot.*

Mystic Knights Ku Klux Klan—Founded at Dayton, Ohio, in 1999, the MKKKK added a klavern at Delaplane, Virginia, in 2000, followed by two more in Michigan and Virginia the following year. One Virginia klavern folded in 2002, but headquarters claimed a new Ohio unit in 2003. By 2004, the Klan had expanded to include six satellite klaverns in Georgia, Indiana, Michigan, Ohio, Tennessee and Virginia.

Mystic Knights of Arkansas—A splinter group formed in November 1925 by klansmen defecting from Little Rock Klan No. 1, in Arkansas.

Nacirema, Inc.—Organized in Cobb County, Georgia, during 1960, Nacirema ("American" spelled backwards) was a group composed of Klansmen and NSRP members disappointed by the lack of violent action in their various organizations. Atlanta police first learned of the organization after a local prostitute told detectives that her boyfriend had asked her to wash his black robe, remarking, "I thought the Klan boys wore white ones." (In fact, KKK robes are color-coded by rank.) Subsequent investigation revealed Nacirema's hard-core membership as a group of sixty fanatics linked to 138 bombings in eleven states since "Black Monday." Police infiltrated an October 1961 training session near Macon, where twenty-six racists were instructed in the manufacture of bombs and booby traps. UKA Imperial Wizard Robert Shelton attended the class, with Georgia Grand Dragon Calvin Craig. Leaders of Nacirema were identified as UKA members William Anderson and William Crowe (both boasting long arrest records). Two alleged Nacirema members were also seen in Birmingham, Alabama, on 14 September 1963, the day before a bomb killed four girls in the Sixteenth Street Baptist Church. Atlanta police captain Everett Little said of the group, "These fellas were the real hoods of the whole racist movement, guys who would take a contract to blow up a place, just like an underworld hood would take a contract to kill a man."

Nathan Bedford Forrest Brigade—Organized by Don Black in 1985, described as a 120-member Klan unit created to aid the right-wing Contra terrorists in Nicaragua.

National Association of Ku Klux Klan—Organized by James Venable after his split from the UKA in late 1962 or early 1963, the NAKKK was a loosely-knit collection of independent Klans, with Venable serving as chairman, assisted by ranking officers from the other groups in various capacities. Affiliated groups included the Association of Arkansas Klans, the Association of Georgia Klans, the Association of South Carolina Klans, the Dixie Klans, Venable's own National Knights, the Original Knights (Louisiana), the U.S. Klans, and the United Florida KKK. Ranking officers included Flynn Harvey, of the Original Knights (klarogo); H.G. Hill, of the Original Knights (kludd); Robert Hodges, of the ASCK (nighthawk); Charles Maddox, of the AGK (klokard); Murray Martin, of the Original Knights (klokann chief); P.L. Morgan, of the Original Knights (klaliff); Walter Rogers, of the UFKKK (kladd); and I.T. Shearhouse, of the AGK (doubling as klabee and kligrapp). Congressional investigators pegged the association's total membership below 1,200 in early 1967.

National Christian Knights of the KKK—Founded in North Carolina in 1957, the NCK met legal difficulties in February 1958, when Grand Wizard Lester Caldwell and two subordinates were imprisoned for bombing a school near Charlotte. Two other Klansmen were acquitted in that case, but the group did not long survive its public exposure.

National Confederation of the Knights of the KKK—Based at Clarkton, Missouri, in 1992, this group tried to expand in May of that year by absorbing the members of Southern Justice, a racist group in the Pacific Northwest. What-

ever the benefits of that alliance, neither group survived to rate a listing in the SPLC's 1997 census of American hate groups.

National Knights of the KKK (1963–91)—This faction was chartered in DeKalb County, Georgia, on 1 November 1963, with its incorporating officers listed as James Venable, William Hugh Morris, Wally Butterworth and H.G. Hill. Longtime klansman Venable served as the group's first and only imperial wizard, operating from headquarters in Tucker. Morris was the former leader of the Federated Ku Klux Klans in Alabama, later identified as an FBI informant. In September 1964, the National Knights merged with seven smaller Klans to form the National Association of Ku Klux Klan, with Venable serving as chairman. At various times, Venable's Klan claimed klaverns in Alabama, Georgia, Louisiana, Maryland, North Carolina and Ohio, but congressional investigators estimated its total membership at 100 in January 1967. In October 1975, Venable banished five of his grand dragons who accused him of mismanagement and senility. The move cost him most of his members, and while the National Knights maintained a small Stone Mountain klavern through the 1980s, it dissolved in early 1991.

National Knights of the KKK (1991–92)—A remnant of James Venable's organization, this splinter of the parent order clung briefly to life in the Midwest, led by Imperial Wizard Ken Peterson of Janesville, Wisconsin. Early 1992 found Peterson embroiled in a power struggle with Ohio klansman Stephen Anderson, exacerbated by Peterson's arrest for disorderly conduct in June 1992. Two months later on 26 August, Peterson announced the disbandment of his Klan. In October he surrendered all its files and other materials to a Wisconsin-based social justice organization.

National Knights of the KKK (1997–2005)—Founded at South Bend, Indiana, in 1997, the NKKKK established a second klavern the following year, in Littleton, Colorado. That unit soon disbanded, but another was active in Mercer, Wisconsin, during 1999–2000. In 2001, the Klan claimed three active satellite klaverns in Iowa, Ohio and Texas. A year later, SPLC investigators reported four klaverns in California, Florida, Pennsylvania and Wisconsin, expanding in 2003 to add units in Alabama, Michigan, Tennessee and Texas. Steady growth continued through 2004, with sixteen active klaverns reported in Alabama, Colorado, Florida, Illinois, Indiana, Kentucky, Michigan, New Jersey, New York, Ohio, Oklahoma, Tennessee, Texas and Wisconsin. All sixteen units remained active in 2005.

National Knights of the KKK Youth—Apparently unrelated to any parent Klan, the NKKKKY was active in Muncie, Indiana, during 2001.

National Ku Klux Klan—This short-lived faction was one of seven Klans active in South Carolina after "Black Monday."

National Order of Knights of the KKK, Inc.—A Georgia splinter group organized after World War II, the NOKKKK surrendered its state charter in June 1947, in exchange for dismissal of outstanding felony charges.

Nation's Knights of the KKK—Founded at Benson, North Carolina, in 2002, the NKKKK was disrupted in July of that year when police arrested leader Charles Barefoot with a cache of illegal weapons and explosives. Barefoot pled guilty on those charges in January 2003, but further trouble lay in store. Upon his release from prison in October 2004, Barefoot was indicted (with his wife and four other klansmen) on murder charges. The victim in that case allegedly possessed knowledge of threats made by Grand Dragon Anthony Brewer against police in Robeson County. The combined indictments resulted in disbandment of the NKKKK in 2003.

National Service Corporation—A commercial branch of the 1920s KKK promoting "vocational klannishness," whose members pledged to do business only with fellow klansmen wherever possible. Klan-owned business paid $35 each for listings in a National Service Directory that was never published, though many klaverns kept their own local directories.

Negro Knights of the KKK—Announced by C.L. Parker in October 1953, as a segregated branch of the United Klan for blacks. None applied, and the group never evolved beyond the planning stage.

Nevada Ku Klux Klan—Publicized in the early 1980s, this "group" proved to be a one-man operation, seeking to recruit teenagers by scattering leaflets at local high schools.

New Empire Ku Klux Klan—Identified in 1983 as one of three active factions in North Carolina, the NEKKK disappeared before the next ADL census of Klans in 1987.

New Jersey Invisible Empire—Led by Grand Wizard Richard Bondira, the NJIE was active in Oxford during 1989–90.

New Knights of the KKK (Florida)—SPLC investigators reported this faction active in Sanford, during 1998–99.

New Knights of the KKK (Washington)—Apparently unrelated to a Florida Klan of the same name, this group was briefly active in Tacoma during 1999.

New Order, Knights of the KKK (Georgia)—Organized in 1980 by veteran neo–Nazi Edward Fields, the NOKKKK was active in harassing Polk County's Hispanic residents that November. In 1982 and 1983, Fields joined rival Klan leaders in unity conferences held at Stone Mountain, Georgia, but no trace of his group remained when the ADL surveyed active Klans in 1987.

New Order Knights of the KKK (Missouri)—Founded and led by James Betts in Overland, the NOKKKK remained a one-klavern Klan until 1997, when it gained a second unit in Garden Grove, California. That klavern soon disbanded, but 1998 saw three more established in Ohio, Texas and Virginia, with an Arkansas klavern chartered in 1999. The new units failed to endure, however, and headquarters stood along during 2000 and 2001, when the group finally dissolved.

New Order of Knights of the KKK—A St. Louis, Missouri, splinter group, organized and led by Rev. James Betts in 1976, the New Order reaped local publicity that March, when police rejected Betts's offer of forty Klansmen to patrol city streets against crime. The group remained active in 1992, with a single klavern at Overton, then expanded by 1998 to include chapters in Ohio, Texas and Virginia (plus active Internet websites). The Ohio and Virginia klaverns folded in 1999, and the Texas chapter dissolved in 2000. The last Missouri klavern finally disbanded in 2002.

New Orleans Ku Klux Klan—A local splinter group active in 1971–72, the NOKKK was led throughout its brief tenure by Imperial Wizard H. Boswell Thompson.

Night Riders—An elite band of black-robed Klansmen recruited for violent action around Bellaire, Ohio, in the 1920s, led by Dr. William Shepard. The group's uniforms reportedly sparked envy among other knights at the Klan's Ohio Konklave in 1925.

North Carolina Knights of the KKK (1956–58)—A spin-off from the U.S. Klans, organized and led by James Cole, this faction reaped its primary—and final—publicity from a confrontation with Lumbee Indians in Robeson County, on 18 January 1958. Cole's prosecution for inciting a riot finished the group, though he resurfaced as an active KKK leader in the latter 1960s.

North Carolina Knights of the KKK (1969–80)—Joseph Bryant and Edward Dawson organized this splinter group in September 1969, after Bryant quarreled with acting Imperial Wizard Melvin Sexton, of the UKA. On 16 September, Bryant led his followers in a public demonstration, nailing their UKA membership cards to a cross which they then set afire. Bryant was soon deposed by militant Virgil Griffin, who led the NCKKKK into an alliance with the National Socialist Party of America, creating the United Racist Front. Members of both groups were involved in the shooting that claimed five lives at Greensboro, on 3 November 1979. While Griffin escaped conviction in that case, he resigned from leadership of the Klan. His successor, Glenn Miller, subsequently tried to expand his influence by renaming the group the Carolina Knights of the KKK.

North Eastern Klans—Despite its plural name, thc NEK consisted of a single klavern, active in Waterbury, Connecticut during 1991.

North Florida Klan—An alternative name for the United Florida KKK, sometimes employed by leader Eunice Fallaw.

North Georgia White Knights of the KKK—Founded at Rossville, Georgia, in 1996, the NGWKKKK expanded to include a Hogansville klavern in 1998. Only headquarters has survived since then, continuing at Rossville during 1999, then at Fort Oglethorpe in 2000–05.

Northern and Southern Knights of the KKK (1949–52)—An outgrowth of the disintegrating Original Southern Klans, this faction was created by Bill Hendrix in June 1949, at a Florida rally that drew 1,000 Klansmen, including delegations from Alabama and Georgia. The group was based in

Jacksonville, where an August 1949 klonvokation installed Hendrix as "national adjutant," serving under an anonymous "Permanent Emperor Samuel II"—soon replaced by an imperial wizard known only as "Number 4–006800." (There seems little doubt that both officers were figments of Hendrix's active imagination.) The Klan's unofficial newspaper, *The Southern Gospel*, was published by A.C. Shuler in River Junction, Florida.

Northern and Southern Knights of the KKK
(1977–78)—Created and led by William Chaney, in affiliation with his Confederation of Independent Orders, this group was described by its spokesmen as a loosely-knit alliance of independent Klans in twenty-six states, each paying $100 per year for the privilege of membership. Regardless of its actual size, the resultant combination was too relaxed to survive, and no trace of it remained when the ADL surveyed active Klans in 1979.

Northern Independent Ku Klux Klan of New York
—A splinter group led by Earl Schoonmaker and his wife Janice, based in Pine Bush, New York, this group reaped national publicity in 1975, when Schoonmaker was fired from his job as a state prison guard. Journalists lost interest as his appeal wound its way through the courts, and the Klan dissolved sometime before the ADL's census of active factions in 1979.

Northwest Knights of the KKK
—Founded by King Kleagle K.A. Badynski, of Tacoma, Washington, in 1990, the NKKKK moved its headquarters to Spokane in 1991, and to Coeur d'Alene, Idaho, in 1998. That year found five active satellite klaverns in Montana, Oregon, Washington and Wyoming, but most soon disbanded. Only chapters in Seattle and Tacoma survived during 1999–2000, after which the group dissolved.

Northwest Territory Knights of the KKK
—Joe Gosciniak led this group's single klavern in Brookville, Indiana, during 1990. Headquarters moved to Vevay, Indiana, in 1991, and the Klan soon disbanded.

Nutmeg Knights of the KKK
—SPLC investigators reported this small faction active in Meriden, Connecticut, during 1998–99.

Ohio Knights of the KKK
—Reported active in the 1980s, led from Hamilton by Imperial Wizard Pete Collins, this small faction boasted fewer than 100 members when it disbanded in early 1991.

Oklahoma White Man's Association
—Joe Grego, of Catoosa, led this small faction during its brief life in 1989–90.

Order of American Women
—A 1920s ladies' auxiliary of the Klan in Houston, Texas, absorbed after June 1923 by the Women of the KKK.

Order of the KKK
—SPCL researchers found this Klan based at Rockville, Indiana, in 1997, with a satellite klavern in California. Only headquarters remained by 1999, and the OKKK dissolved that same year.

Original Knights of the KKK
—This Louisiana faction was created in 1962, after a rift with the Texas-based Original

KKK. J.D. Swenson initially led the group, serving in a dual capacity as grand dragon and national kleagle. Royal Young, Jr., was named imperial dragon in early 1963, and recruiting expanded into that autumn into Arkansas and Mississippi. While small klaverns were planted at Crockett and El Dorado, Arkansas, the OKKKK enjoyed greater success in Mississippi, under Douglas Byrd and Edward McDaniel. Swenson expelled both in December 1963, amid mutual charges of embezzlement, and the Mississippi rejects went on to found the White Knights of the KKK with Samuel Bowers. Meanwhile, dissension within the Louisiana realm produced a grass-roots rebellion in early 1964, climaxing with the ouster of Swenson and Young for alleged financial malfeasance. Murray Martin and Billy Skipper then seized control of the OKKKK, but dissension continued. Disgruntled subordinate Houston Morris withdrew in autumn 1964 to lead the Original KKK of America, based in Monroe, Louisiana, while another dissident faction defected in the Amite-Bogalusa region, operating as the Anti-Communist Christian Association under Grand Dragon Charles Christmas and Grand Titan Saxon Farmer. Murray Martin's loyalists, concentrated in the Shreveport–Bossier City area, soon faced incursions by the rival UKA, operating under cover of the Christian Constitutional Crusaders. Murray's faction of the OKKKK subsequently joined in creation of James Venable's National Association of Ku Klux Klan. OKKKK members were primarily responsible for racist terrorism around Bogalusa in 1964–65, including the murder of black deputy sheriff O'Neal Moore. A federal injunction, issued on 1 December 1965, barred the OKKKK, the ACCA, and thirty-eight specific Klansmen from further violence against blacks in Washington Parish, but sporadic mayhem continued through 1966. Congressional investigators estimated total membership at 250 in January 1967, and the OKKKK disbanded before the decade's end.

Original Ku Klux Klan
—Organized and led from Dallas by Imperial Wizard Roy Davis in 1959, the Original KKK expanded into Arkansas that summer and planted klaverns in Louisiana during 1960. The Louisiana realm defected *en masse* in 1962, to become the Original Knights of the KKK. The Texas realm clung to tenuous life over the next two decades, under various leaders, and changed its name in 1982 to become the Knights of the White Camellia. The bid to refurbish its image failed, and the Klan disbanded sometime before 1990.

Original Ku Klux Klan of America
—A product of dissension in the Louisiana-based Original Knights, the OKKKA was created in autumn 1964 by Houston Morris, based in Monroe, Louisiana. Morris obtained a state charter on 26 January 1965, but internal dissent continued, and he resigned as imperial wizard in late April, leading most of his Klansmen into the UKA during June 1965. The OKKKA survived through autumn 1965, but congressional investigators found no active units remaining by January 1967.

Original Ku Klux Klan of the Confederacy
—This violent Klan was an outgrowth of Asa Carter's North Alabama Citizens' Council, founded by carter in 1956 or early 1957. It was noted for its strident anti–Semitism and Nazi-style brownshirt uniforms. Carter's Klansmen participated in the February

1956 riot against black coed Autherine Lucy's admission to the University of Alabama, and assaulted singer Nat "King" Cole during a performance at Birmingham's municipal auditorium. On 2 September 1957, four members abducted a black victim, Edward Aaron, and castrated him as part of a Klan initiation ceremony. That episode resulted in twenty-year prison terms, and the group was further damaged when Carter shot and wounded two of his followers in a dispute over disposition of Klan funds. The group apparently dissolved sometime in early 1958.

Original Southern Klans, Inc.—A product of dissension in the AGK, this Klan was chartered in Muscogee County, Georgia, during June 1948. Members of two AGK klaverns in Columbus and Manchester defected *en masse* to rally behind new Grand Wizard Alton Pate, supported by Rev. Evall Johnston and Fred New. The group's grandiose aims included establishment of a Klan radio station, a newspaper printing plant and a robe factory, but none were ever realized. Only two issues of a KKK newspaper, *The Klansman,* were issued, and meetings drew minuscule crowds. Expansion into Alabama was marked by an incident in Phenix City, where fifteen robed knights invaded a courtroom and staged a demonstration in the jury box. AGK leader Samuel Green called the OSK a "bolshevik Klan," and the group was included on the U.S. attorney general's list of subversive organizations in 1949. A Florida klavern, led by Bill Hendrix, emerged after the demise of Georgia imperial headquarters, soon renamed the Northern and Southern Knights of the KKK.

Orion Knights of the KKK—Founded at Grand Bay, Alabama, in 2003, the OKKKK claimed seven additional klaverns in Alabama, Arkansas, Florida, Mississippi and Tennessee. The Florida and Tennessee realms evaporated in 2004, leaving three klaverns active.

Ozark Klans—A small Missouri faction, publicized for the first time in August 1949, when it merged with the Knights of the KKK of America, led by Lycurgus Spinks.

Palmetto Knights of the KKK—Founded in the late 1950s, the PKKKK was one of seven Klans active in South Carolina after "Black Monday."

Puritan Daughters of America—Early 1920s women's auxiliary, absorbed after June 1923 by the Women of the KKK.

Queens of the Golden Mask—Created by Grand Dragon D.C. Stephenson in 1922, as the official ladies' auxiliary and "poison squad" whispering society of the Indiana KKK. Stephenson once boasted that the QGM could transmit a rumor the length of the state, from Evansville to Gary, within twenty-four hours.

Racial Covenant Knights KKK—SPLC investigators found the RCKKKK briefly active in Ogallala, Nebraska, in 2001.

Rangers of the Cross—An independent splinter faction, briefly active in Deland, Florida, during 1997–98.

Rangers of the Cross, Knights of the KKK—Apparently unrelated to Florida's short-lived Rangers of the Cross,

the RCKKKK appeared in Watkins, Colorado, during 1998 and remained active through the following year.

Rebel Brigade Knights of the KKK—Observers found this small faction active in Martinsville, Virginia, during 2003–05. It presumably evolved from another local faction, the Rebel Knights, active in 1998–2001.

Rebel Knights of the KKK—Founded at Woolwine, Virginia, in 1998, the RKKKK claimed a second klavern that year in Martinsville. Only the latter unit survived during 1999–2001, when it apparently disbanded. A "new" Klan, the Rebel Brigade Knights, was organized in Martinsville during 2003.

Righteous Knights Klan—SPLC investigators reported this small faction active in Fayetteville, North Carolina, during 1991–92.

River Valley Klans—A small faction of uncertain venue, publicized for the first time in August 1949, when its unnamed leaders joined the Knights of the KKK of America, led by Lycurgus Spinks.

Royal Confederate Knights of the KKK (Georgia)—Active in Lindale during 1991–92, the RCKKKK disbanded before mid-decade.

Royal Confederate Knights of the KKK (Mississippi)—Klanwatchers reported this small faction active in Jackson during 2002.

Royal Knights of the KKK—Deltona, Florida, hosted this single-klavern Klan during 1997–98.

Royal Riders of the Red Robe—Based in Portland, Oregon, this affiliate of the 1920s KKK was created to serve naturalized citizens who qualified for Klan membership in all other respects. Organized by kleagle Luther Powell and Dr. M.W. Rose (himself a naturalized citizen from Canada), the RRRR had its own grand dragon, in charge of a program offering "a real patriotic organization to all Canadians, Englishmen, and other white, gentile Protestants." Rev. Keith Allen launched a Vancouver chapter in 1924, and the group was also reported active in Colorado, later merging with the American Krusaders.

Seashore Klans—A small faction of uncertain venue, publicized for the first time in August 1949, when its unnamed leaders joined the Knights of the KKK of America, led by Lycurgus Spinks.

Secret Six—This action squad of the Georgia Klan reportedly planned a series of murders in 1965, its targets including Atlanta Vice-Mayor Sam Massel, Morris Abrams (head of the American Jewish Committee), and an unnamed white southern clergyman. FBI agents warned the prospective victims, and none of the slayings were attempted.

Silver Dollar Group—Similar in concept to Nacirema, this splinter group was composed of Klansmen from various factions who sought more violent action than their Klans provided. Members included knights from Adams County, Mississippi, and neighboring Concordia Parish, Louisiana, various drawn from the Original Knights, UKA, and White Knights. Its formation followed a moratorium on nightriding declared by Imperial Wizard Sam Bowers, after the Neshoba County murders of three COFO activists in June 1964. Members of the group identified themselves with silver dollars minted in the years of their respective births, and rural "family picnics" were combined with demolition seminars, including practice in techniques of wiring explosives to the ignition switch of a car. At its peak, the group included an estimated twenty members, who prided themselves on being "the toughest Klansmen in Mississippi or Louisiana." According to FBI agents, the group's first victim was Frank Morris, fatally burned in an arson attack on 10 December 1964. Silver Dollar knights were also suspected (but never charged) in the August 1965 car bombing that crippled Natchez NAACP leader George Metcalfe, and another Natchez blast that killed his successor, Wharlest Jackson, in February 1967. Those unpunished crimes prompted an unnamed G-man to tell author Don Whitehead, "Perhaps the perfect crime is one in which the killers are known, but you can't reach them for lack of substantive evidence."

Sipsey Swampers—A faction of the Reconstruction-era Klan, active in western Tuscaloosa County, Alabama, named for the local swamp where members held their den meetings. The group was blamed for numerous acts of terrorism in Tuscaloosa and adjacent counties, and lost two of its own men in April 1869, during a three-day "nigger hunt" that left two blacks dead, several others wounded, and a number of black homes burned to the ground.

South Arkansas Knights of the KKK—Active in Smackover during 2000–03, the SAKKKK disbanded in early 2004.

South Carolina Knights of the KKK—A 1950s splinter group, identified as one of seven Klans active in South Carolina after "Black Monday."

Southern Confederate Knights of the KKK—This small Klan was active in Palmetto, Florida, during 1991–92.

Southern Cross Militant Knights of the KKK—Descended from the JWS Militant Knights (1997), this Klan was founded at Valley Head, Alabama, in 1997. It remained an isolated klavern until 2000, when two additional units were chartered in Alabama. One of those folded in 2001, and headquarters followed suit in 2002, leaving active klaverns at Ider and Red Bay. None remained when the SPLC completed its survey of Klans in 2003.

Southern Knights of the KKK (1950s)—Yet another faction led by Florida klansman Bill Hendrix, the SKKKK met in January 1950 with spokesmen for the Federated Klans and the Association of Carolina Klans, issuing a joint declaration of war on "hate groups" such as B'nai B'rith and the NAACP. Unlike its two allies, the groups survived into the late 1950s, recognized as one of six Florida factions active after "Black Monday."

Southern Knights of the KKK (1997–98)—This small faction was confined during its brief life to Monticello, Florida.

Top and above: **Southern White Knights rally in Gainesville, Georgia, in September 1989 (both photographs: Southern Poverty Law Center).**

Southern Mississippi Knights of the KKK—A single-klavern faction based in Petal, the SMKKKK competed with another local Klan, the Mississippi White Knights, during 1999–2002, when it disbanded.

Southern Patriot Organized Order of Knights, KKK—SPLC investigators found this Klan active in Wynnewood, Oklahoma, during 2004–05.

Southern Realm Invisible Knights of the KKK—A small North Carolina faction, the SRIKKKK was founded at Lincolnton in 2004. It remained active in 2005.

Southern White Knights of the KKK (1985–93)—A Georgia-based Klan, organized in 1985 by former National Knights Grand Dragon Dave Holland, who described his faction as "the most militant white racist organization in the South." In January 1987 the group joined members of the Invisible Empire Knights to assault black protesters in Forsyth County, Georgia, a move that backfired with a lawsuit filed by the SPLC. That case ended with a $940,000 damage judgment against the two Klans and various individual members, including a $50,000 personal judgment against Holland. The court also required convicted Klansmen to attend classes on race relations, taught by members of the SCLC. ADL observers identified Grand Dragon Randall Smith as the group's leader in 1989, but Holland apparently regained control in 1990 and maintained the SWKKKK's top post until the group dissolved.

Southern White Knights of the KKK (2001–05)—More successful than its Georgia namesake, this Klan was founded at Denham Springs, Louisiana, with four additional klaverns in Alabama, Connecticut, Louisiana and South Carolina. A Georgia klavern was added in 2002, and headquarters shifted to Savannah the following year, while new units appeared in Florida and Ohio. In 2004, the SWKKKK's headquarters moved again, this time to Watson, Louisiana, and SPLC investigators found nineteen satellite klaverns in Alabama, Arkansas, Florida, Georgia, Maryland, Michigan, Mississippi, New Jersey, North Carolina, Ohio, Pennsylvania, South Carolina, Tennessee, Texas and Virginia. All units remained active in 2005.

SS Knights of the KKK—A neo–Nazi faction, founded in Louisville, Kentucky, during 2001, the SS Knights gained a second klavern at Liberty, Kentucky, in 2002, then abruptly disbanded.

Star Klans—A small faction of uncertain venue, publicized for the first time in August 1949, when its unnamed leaders joined the Knights of the KKK of America, led by Lycurgus Spinks.

Templar Knights of the KKK—Organized in Port St. Lucie, Florida, during 1997, the Templar Knights added an Owensburg, Kentucky, klavern in 1999, then apparently disbanded. It resurfaced at Fort McCoy, Florida, during 2002–03, then once again dissolved.

Texas Fiery Knights of the KKK—Based in Houston and led Scott Nelson in the early 1970s, the TFKKKK created a minor sensation in April 1974, with its endorsement of a black candidate for justice of the peace in Precinct Six. The Klan was loosely affiliated with James Venable's National Knights, and Nelson was named as a prospective vice presidential candidate for that group in 1976.

Texas Knights of the KKK—In 2002, SPLC investigators reported one klavern of this new Klan active in each of eight Texas counties. A year later, eighteen counties harbored klaverns, with headquarters located in San Antonio, but the TKKKK disbanded in early 2004.

Texas Knights of the Invisible Empire Inc.—The appearance of this Klan in San Antonio, during 2004, coincided with disbandment of the Texas Knights of the KKK. Unlike its predecessor, the "new" group claimed no additional klaverns.

Third State Empire—This short-lived group maintained a single klavern in Deland, Florida, during 1998–99.

Tri-County White Knights of the KKK—A Missouri Klan, based in Mt. Grove, the TCWKKKK was briefly active during 1997–98.

Tri-K Club—The distaff equivalent of the 1920s Junior KKK, created for girls aged twelve to eighteen, as an auxiliary to the Women of the KKK.

Tri-State Knight Riders of the KKK—Despite its name, membership in this faction was apparently confined to Ohio and Kentucky during its short life in 1997–99. Cincinnati police jailed Imperial Wizard Tony Gamble on rape and sodomy charges in August 1997, relating to his alleged molestation of an adolescent girl, and while the Klan struggled on for a time in his absence, it never truly recovered.

Tri-State Ku Klux Klan—Reported active in 1970, this Klan drew members from Delaware, Maryland and Pennsylvania. It was allegedly responsible for a December 1970 raid on Phoenix Center, a controversial students' enclave at the University of Delaware, whose occupants were active in civil rights and anti-war protests. With their faces darkened like commandos, klansmen ransacked the house, smashing telephones and appliances, then fled after burning a cross on the lawn.

True Knights of the KKK—SPLC investigators found this small faction operating in Boyd, Texas, during 1997–98.

The Underground—Organized by klansman Furman Williams of Gaffney, South Carolina, this group served as a secret action squad within the UKA's South Carolina realm. Tacitly encouraged by Grand Dragon Robert Scoggin, members stockpiled weapons and practiced marksmanship through the mid–1960s, but no evidence exists linking the group to specific acts of violence.

Unified Ku Klux Klan—A Connecticut splinter group active in the early 1990s, the UKKK apparently disbanded after leader and three others were jailed by police in Wallingford, on 21 January 1994, on various weapons and explosives charges.

Union Knights of the KKK—Founded at Butler, Pennsylvania, in 1998, the UKKKK disbanded early the following year.

United Confederate Knights of the KKK—Launched as a Texas Klan in 1998, with klaverns in Dallas and Odessa, this faction abandoned its home state entirely in 1999. Headquarters shifted to Merritt Island, Florida, while a second klavern operated in Oklahoma. A year later, only the Oklahoma klavern remained, and it disbanded by early 2001.

United Empire, Knights of the KKK—A Tennessee splinter group led by Imperial Wizard Rocky Coker, this faction was linked to racial disturbances in Chattanooga, in July 1980. Coker and two other klansmen were arrested that month for rioting and illegal possession of explosives. The group apparently disbanded after Coker's 1984 arrest and subsequent conviction on murder charges in Dunlap, resulting in a death sentence.

United Klan—An early 1950s faction led by C.L. Parker from River Junction, Florida. In October 1953, Parker announced that his group would abandon robes and rituals, opening its ranks to "all races, creeds or colors" on a strictly segregated basis.

United Klan of Florida—This small faction, led by J.D. Adler, emerged in August 1994 to protest Florida abortion clinics. No trace of it remained when the SPLC surveyed active hate groups in 1999.

United Klans of America, Inc., Knights of the KKK—On 8 July 1961, five hundred klansmen from seven states gathered at Indian Springs, Georgia, with the majority representing Robert Shelton's Alabama Knights and Calvin Craig's Georgia-based Invisible Empire, United Klans, Knights of the KKK. Shelton's forceful personality and uniformed eight-man security team were so impressive that he was named imperial wizard by acclamation, presiding over a new Klan that retained Craig's Fulton County charter. The group's headquarters soon shifted to Shelton's home in Tuscaloosa, Alabama, and Shelton set about building the nation's dominant Klan, with klaverns found in sixteen states by 1966. Shelton professed distaste for the neo–Nazi movement, but at least five of his grand dragons—in Delaware, Maryland, New Jersey, New York and Pennsylvania—were acknowledged members of the American Nazi Party. Imperial headquarters likewise adopted an ambiguous attitude toward violence, urging klansmen to adopt the tactics of civil disobedience while Shelton and Craig attended demolition seminars sponsored by Nacirema, Inc., in 1961, and Shelton shared the stage with violent rabble-rouser Connie Lynch at rallies during 1962–63. UKA members accused of murder were banished from the Klan in 1964, but others charged with an identical slaying in 1965 were hailed as heroes, furnished with legal support for their trials. In fact, a review of the UKA's record clearly links its members to at least eight murders, plus dozens of bombings, shootings, and beatings. One such crime, the 1981 lynching of Michael Donald in Mobile, Alabama, finally finished the UKA. Several members were convicted of that crime, with one executed, and the SPLC slapped Shelton with a civil suit for wrongful death, proving in court that UKA publications and statements encouraged the murder of blacks. A $7 million judgment against the UKA, rendered in 1987, forced Shelton sell his headquarters and formally disband the Klan.

United Knights of the KKK (Florida)—This short-lived splinter group emerged from a rift in the UKA's Florida realm, during autumn 1965. Its existence was exposed on 29 October, when Miami police jailed Grand Dragon Charles Riddlehoover for reckless driving and found Klan documents in his car. No evidence exists of the UKKK's survival beyond that episode.

United Knights of the KKK (Indiana)—SPLC investigators reported this small faction active in Indianapolis during 2003.

United Knights of the KKK (Texas)—Based in Fort Worth, the UKKKK was briefly active during 1997–98.

United White Klans—Founded in 2000, with headquarters in Philadelphia, Mississippi, the UWK boasted six more klaverns in the Magnolia State, plus one in Pennsylvania and two in South Carolina. The Pennsylvania realm and three Mississippi klaverns disbanded in 2001. Only Philadelphia's klavern survived by 2002, and the Klan dissolved before year's end.

Universal Klans—Also sometimes called "The South," this Louisiana splinter group was formed by Jack Helm in March 1967, when he left his post as UKA grand dragon for the state. Its membership consisted of UKA defectors and affiliated Minutemen, with the two groups maintaining a joint guerrilla training camp in St. Bernard Parish, fifty miles outside New Orleans. A small train, purchased from an amusement park, carried trainees from a farmhouse stocked with Nazi art and literature, through the woods to a hidden rifle range. Led by Roswell Thompson in 1972, the group also maintained a fortified storehouse, containing what one investigator called an "enormous" supply of weapons, ammunition and explosives. No trace of the Klan remained when the ADL surveyed active factions in 1978.

U.S. Klans (1990s)—ADL investigators found this small group active in Mississippi during 1996. No further details are presently available.

U.S. Klans (2000s)—National pretensions notwithstanding, this faction was restricted to a Jonesboro, Georgia, klavern at its founding in 2002. A second Georgia units appeared in 2003, but both disbanded by early 2004.

U.S. Klans, KKK Inc.—This short-lived Klan was active in Coalmont, Indiana, during 2000.

U.S. Klans, Knights of the KKK (1997–98)—SPLC reports describe this faction as active in Camden, Tennessee, during 1997–99.

U.S. Klans, Knights of the KKK (2001–05)—Launched at Big Sandy, Tennessee, the USKKKK was a one-klavern operation until 2004, when its headquarters shifted to Leitchfield, Kentucky, with three additional units active in Missouri, Ohio and Tennessee. All units remained active in 2005.

U.S. Klans, Knights of the KKK, Inc.—Eldon Edwards chartered this Klan in Atlanta on 24 October 1955, after revising and copyrighting the 1915 rituals of William Simmons to preserve a "direct link" with the 1920s KKK. Competitors were thereby branded "outlaws and counterfeiters." Samuel Green, Jr., served as klonsel for the group, with klansmen William Daniel and M. Wesley Morgan listed as incorporating officers. In September 1956, Edwards presided over the largest Klan rally since World War II, at Stone Mountain, and by 1959 he had an estimated 15,000 members in ten states, with his greatest strength concentrated in Alabama, Georgia, Louisiana and South Carolina. When Edwards died in August 1965, his widow named E.E. George to replace him, but the membership rebelled in favor of Robert Davidson, and a bitter power struggle ensued. Davidson and Georgia Grand Dragon Calvin Craig defected in February 1961, leading a majority of their members into the new UKA. E.E. George presided over the U.S. Klans until October 1963, when dissident members of Georgia's College Park Klavern No. 297 accused him of financial irregularities, holding a special klonvokation to elect H.J. Jones as the new imperial wizard. It proved a Pyrrhic victory, with Klavern No. 297 abandoned as George and the Klan's remaining units created a new Improved Order of the U.S. Klans. Congressional investigators counted fifty members of the U.S. Klans in January 1967, and the group disappeared entirely by 1969.

U.S. Klans of America—Founded in 1991, Keith Smith's USKA never expanded beyond its base in Stockbridge, Georgia, and it vanished entirely during 1992.

U.S. Klans of Georgia—Organized in September 1953 by Eldon Edwards, this group consisted chiefly of remnants from the old AGK. Edwards went national after "Black Monday," renaming his group the U.S. Klans, Knights of the KKK, Inc.

U.S. Knights of the KKK—Founded by Pete Collins of Hamilton, Ohio, in 1990, the USKKKK gained new klaverns in Georgia and Kentucky the following year. Still, it failed to prosper, and all units vanished by mid-decade.

White Camelia Knights of the KKK—Led by Imperial Wizard Allen Miller, of Pasadena, Texas, during 1989–90, the WCKKKK moved its headquarters to Cleveland, Texas, in 1992. It remained a single-klavern group until 1998, when a second unit opened in Midland, Texas. That klavern folded by year's end, but a new one replaced it in Sulphur Springs during 1998–99. Cleveland headquarters remained as the group's sole klavern in 2000–05.

White Christian Knights of the KKK—SPLC observers found this small faction active in Slidell, Louisiana, during 1999.

White Imperial Knights of the KKK—ADL investigators found this faction active in Alabama during 1996, with members in several towns.

White Knight Coalition of the KKK—Founded in 2002, this coalition consisted of headquarters in Starke, Florida, and a satellite klavern in Morristown, Tennessee. Neither survived into 2003.

White Knights of the KKK—Organized in Kansas City, Missouri, during 1989, the WKKKK was jointly led by Dennis Mahon, J. Allen Moran, and Ed Stephens. Moran disappeared from the command roster in 1990, while the Klan expanded to plant klaverns in Indiana, Kansas, Nebraska, Oklahoma, Tennessee and Wisconsin. Only the Kansas, Nebraska and Oklahoma realms remained in 1991, and all disbanded by the mid–1990s.

White Knights of the KKK (Iowa)—An independent faction active in 1983, it disbanded prior to an ADL survey of Klans conducted in 1984.

White Knights of the KKK (Michigan)—Yet another independent faction claiming this popular title, reported active during 1983 but absent from the ADL's census of surviving Klans in 1984.

White Knights of the KKK (Pennsylvania, 1983)—A splinter group active in 1983, which disappeared by the following year.

White Knights of the KKK (Pennsylvania, 1999)—This small splinter faction was briefly active in Houston, over the course of a year.

White Knights of the KKK (Virginia)—SPLC investigators reported this small faction active in Colonial Heights, during 2001.

White Knights of the KKK of the Sovereign Realm of Mississippi—A product of dissension in the Louisiana-based Original Knights, this militant faction was formally organized by Natchez klansman Edward McDaniel at Brookhaven, Mississippi, in February 1964. The Klan allegedly claimed its first victim on 29 February, murdering a black man accused of romantic involvement with a white woman in Centreville. A brief power struggle in April 1964 left Samuel Bowers in charge of the WKKKK, while McDaniel moved on to recruit for the rival UKA. In a dramatic show of strength, the WKKKK burned crosses in sixty-four of Mississippi's eighty-two counties on the night of 24 April, and members gathered near Raleigh on 7 June to plot their strategy for the upcoming COFO "Freedom Summer." A leaflet warned civil rights workers: "We are not going to sit back and permit our rights to be negotiated away by a group of Jewish priests, bluegum black savages and mongrelized money worshippers. We will buy you a ticket to the Eternal if you insist." To that end, over the next two years, WKKKK members participated in an estimated eighty beatings and thirty-five shootings in 1964, while bombing or burning thirty-seven churches and thirty-one other buildings. Another twenty-six churches were destroyed during 1965–68, while the Klan was linked to at least eight more murders. Membership peaked around 5,000 in mid–1965, then declined to an estimated 1,500 by January 1966, as federal arrests began to decimate the ranks. The only modern Klan whose imperial wizard sought to direct and control violence personally, the WKKKK was uniquely vulnerable to conspiracy prosecutions. By 1966, FBI agents reported that 488 members had turned informant, providing inside information on the Klan, and in February 1967, eighteen klansmen were indicted on federal charges related to a triple murder in Neshoba County. Bowers and six others were convicted in that case, while state authorities imprisoned several klansmen for the 1966 slaying of NAACP activist Vernon Dahmer. In November 1968, a federal court in Vicksburg awarded $1,021,500 in damages to relatives of Ben White, murdered by the WKKKK in 1966. December 1968 saw another member jailed for shooting at a black man's home in Monroe, Louisiana, but a legal technicality freed that suspect in February 1969. Considered defunct with Bowers in prison, the WKKKK was allegedly revived within days of his March 1976 parole, but informed sourced pegged the total membership around one dozen. Bowers was convicted of the Dahmer slaying in August 1998, and received a life prison term. Edgar Killen, former exalted cyclops of the Meridian klavern, was convicted in June 2005 on three manslaughter counts, related to the 1964 Neshoba County murders.

White Knights of Liberty—Led by Joe Grady in Greensboro, North Carolina, this faction ignored a challenge from the Communist Workers Party that resulted in a local massacre of five CWP members on 3 November 1979, but its members were not averse to occasional violence. In July 1985, on klansman pled guilty to harassing blacks in Alexander and Iredell Counties, turning state's evidence to convict several comrades. Eleven months later, another member was jailed in Nash County for brandishing firearms at participants in a NAACP parade. Grady remained in charge of the group during 1989–90, from headquarters in Winston-Salem, but the WKL vanished thereafter.

White Knights of the New Jersey KKK—Organized by Edwin Reynolds in 1978, following his dismissal as Pennsylvania's grand dragon on charges of adultery, misuse of Klan funds, and membership in an "anti-Christian cult," this faction held joint rallies with local neo-Nazis. Its small membership shrank to an estimated nine klansmen in 1980, after Reynolds was charged with raping a Jewish informant, and Reynolds soon announced its disbandment. Reynolds urged his followers to join David Duke's Knights of the KKK, which he described as "the future of the Klan and the white race," but some apparently stood fast. ADL observers listed the group in 1983 but found it "largely inactive" the following year. No trace of it remained by 1990, but a new White Unity Party had sprung up in its place.

White Knights of Pennsylvania—SPLC investigators found this small group active during 1991–92. It then vanished until 2001, when a klavern briefly opened in Oaks, disbanding in 2002.

White Knights of the Sovereign State of Mississippi—A minuscule klavern, reported from Jackson in 2002, the WKSSM disbanded by early 2003.

White Knights of West Virginia—Founded at Masontown in 1991, this Klan dissolved sometime during 1992–93.

White Knights of Wisconsin—Observers reported the WKW's headquarters and only klavern in Madison, during 1991–92.

White Shield Knights of the KKK—Founded at Parkersburg, West Virginia, in 1997, the WSKKKK claimed seven additional klaverns in Ohio and West Virginia by 1998. None remained active during 1999–2003, but a small unit reopened at Mineral Wells, West Virginia, in 2004 and remained active in 2005.

White Sons of the Confederacy—Jordan Gollub founded this group at Poplarville, Mississippi, in 1989, then changed its name to the Calvary White Knights of the KKK in 1990.

White Unity Party—ADL investigators identified this group as a Pennsylvania faction of the KKK, with klaverns operating in Shrewsbury and York during 1990–91.

Winder Knights of the KKK—Named for its hometown of Winder, Georgia, this independent Klan was founded in 1991 and survived until the latter months of 1998.

Women of the KKK—Founded on 10 June 1923, this ladies' auxiliary was legally separate from the national Klan but was "sanctioned" by imperial headquarters. It maintained headquarters in Little Rock and was led by Robbie Comer, wife of the Arkansas grand dragon. By year's end it absorbed most other women's auxiliary units nationwide. State Klan leaders retained a portion of the dues and fattened their wallets by naming their wives as kleagles. Sexism and rigid control from headquarters, coupled with various scandals and the KKK's nationwide decline after 1925, ultimately doomed the organization.

World Knights of the KKK—Founded in 2003, this faction maintained headquarters in Sharpsburg, Maryland, with a second klavern in New Castle, Pennsylvania. A year later, SPLC investigators identified three new klaverns in Alabama, North Carolina and Tennessee. All five units remained active in 2005.

Wyoming Knights of the KKK—State Officer John Abarr led this small Klan in Casper, during 1989–90.

York County Klan—One of seven Klans active in South Carolina after "Black Monday," this faction disbanded prior to 1960.

Front Groups

Whenever possible, the KKK prefers to travel in disguise. This section lists "front" groups created by various Klans to disguise KKK activity, identified in government and media reports from Reconstruction to the present day. Listings include the front group's name, together with the Klan or klavern it represents and the approximate time frame of operation. (Spelling and grammar have not been corrected.)

Action—1960s Galveston, Texas, klavern of the UKA.

Adams County Civic & Betterment Association—Natchez, Mississippi, Unit No. 719 of the UKA, 1960s.

Alabama Rescue Service—A 1960s front for the UKA imperial treasury.

Altamaha Men's Club No. 72—1960s Baxley, Georgia, klavern of the UKA.

American Confederate Army—Southern Knights of the KKK, organized at Orlando, Florida, in July 1952.

American Fellowship Club—A front for the KKK in Des Moines, Iowa, during World War II.

American Keystone Foundation (or Society)—Identified by Walter Winchell in April 1944 as a new front for the recently dissolved KKK. Wizard James Colescott denied its existence, while simultaneously denying that the Klan had disbanded.

American Vigilant Intelligence Federation—Shared an office with Illinois Klan leader Gale Carter during 1940–41.

Americans for Preservation of the White Race—1960s front for the White Knights of the KKK in Mississippi.

Ancient City Gun Club—St. Augustine Klavern No. 519 of the United Florida KKK, also called the Ancient City Hunting Club in some published reports.

Anson Sportsman Club—Peachland, North Carolina, klavern of the UKA.

Anti-Communist Christian Association—Statewide front for the 1960s Original Knights in Louisiana.

Apex Ladies League—Apex, North Carolina, ladies' auxiliary of the UKA.

Apex Restoration Association—Apex, North Carolina, klavern of the UKA.

Arcadia Sportsman Club—Arcadia, Louisiana, klavern of the 1960s Original Knights.

Assembly of Christian Soldiers, Inc.—A "church" founded by former leaders of the Original Knights of the KKK of the Confederacy in 1972, claiming 3,000 members in Alabama, Georgia and Mississippi.

Auburndale Fisherman's Club—1960s Auburndale klavern of the United Florida KKK.

Ayden Christian Fellowship Club—Ayden, North Carolina, klavern of the UKA.

Ayden Garden Club—Ayden, North Carolina, UKA ladies' auxiliary.

B & H Sporting Club—Lewiston, North Carolina, klavern of the UKA.

Back Swamp Hunting Club—Chinquapin, North Carolina, klavern of the UKA.

Baker Hunting & Fishing Club—Baker, Louisiana, klavern of the 1960s Original Knights.

Bassett Creek Hunting Club—Wagarville, Alabama, klavern of the UKA.

Beaufort County Hunting Club—Beaufort, South Carolina, klavern of the UKA (also known as Hunting Club No. 18).

Beaver Creek Men's Fellowship Club—Kinston, North Carolina, klavern of the UKA.

Benevolent Association—Winterville, North Carolina, klavern of the UKA.

Benevolent Association Unit No. 53—Greenville, North Carolina, klavern of the UKA.

Bernice Sportsman's Club—Bernice, Louisiana, klavern of the UKA.

Better Business Builders—A front for the KKK in Aberdeen, Washington, active in December 1939.

Better Citizens Club—Mount Olive, North Carolina, klavern of the UKA.

Black River Club—Kingstree, South Carolina, Unit No. 17 of the UKA.

Black River Improvement Club—Used simultaneously by UKA klaverns in Angier and Wendell, North Carolina.

Blount County Hunters Club—Maryville, Tennessee, Klavern No. 1 of the UKA.

Bogue Homa Hunting & Rifle Club—Jones County Unit No. 1 of the 1960s White Knights, based in Laurel, Mississippi.

Brotherhood of Jasper County—Ridgeland, South Carolina, klavern of the UKA.

Broward Club—Fort Lauderdale, Florida, klavern of the UKA.

Broward Fellowship Club—Davie, Florida, klavern of the UKA, whose members defected in 1965 to the United Knights of the KKK.

Broward Rod & Reel Club—A second Fort Lauderdale, Florida, klavern of the UKA.

Brunswick Sportsman—Lawrenceville, Virginia, klavern of the UKA.

Bunn Saddle Club—Bunn, North Carolina, klavern of the UKA.

Burke County Improvement Society—Morganton, North Carolina klavern of the UKA.

Bush Hunting & Fishing Club No. 1055—Bush, Louisiana, klavern of the 1960s Original Knights.

Cairo Hunting Lodge—Eldorado, Arkansas, Unit No. 2 of the UKA.

Caldwell Improvement Association—Whitnel, North Carolina, klavern of the UKA.

Calhoun Businessmen's Association—Choudrant, Louisiana, klavern of the UKA.

California Anti-Communist League—Founded at Lancaster, California, by Wesley Swift and Dennis Mower in 1971.

Camp Creek Club—Lancaster, South Carolina, klavern of the 1960s Association of South Carolina Klans.

Cane River Hunting & Fishing Club—Natchitoches, Louisiana, klavern of the 1960s Original Knights.

Cape Fear Fishing Club—Wallace, North Carolina, klavern of the UKA.

Capitol City Sportsman's Club—Columbia, South Carolina, Unit No. 9 of the UKA.

Cash Sportsman Club—Unit No. 16 of the UKA, in Society Hill, South Carolina.

Catahoula Sportsman Club—Catahoula Parish, Louisiana, klavern of the 1960s Original Knights.

Catarrah Sports Club—Jefferson, South Carolina, klavern of the UKA.

Catawba Improvement Association—Unit No. 83 of the UKA, in Hickory, North Carolina.

Caucasian Clubs—Cover for several Louisiana chapters of the KWC after January 1869.

Central Carolina Ladies League—UKA ladies' auxiliary in Goldston, North Carolina.

Central Dekalb Civic Club—Decatur, Georgia, klavern of the UKA.

Central Improvement Association of Lillington—Lillington, North Carolina, klavern of the UKA.

Central Sportsmans Club No. 101—Haines City, Florida, klavern of the UKA.

Charlotte County Anonymous Club—Charlotte County, Virginia, klavern of the UKA.

Chase City Fellowship Club—Chase City, Virginia, klavern of the UKA.

Chatham Citizens Club—Unit No. 19 of the UKA, drawing members from Bynum and Pittsboro, North Carolina.

Chatham Hunting & Fishing Club—Chatham, Louisiana, klavern of the 1960s Original Knights.

Cherokee 92 Men's Club—Roswell, Georgia, klavern of the UKA.

Cherokee Sportsmans Club—Gaffney, South Carolina, klavern of the UKA.

Chesapeake Bar-B-Q Club—Chesapeake, Virginia, klavern of the UKA.

Chessmen—A 1950s action squad in the Carolinas.

Chester Conservative Clan—Organized in Chester County, South Carolina, in spring 1868, spreading to York County in June.

Chesterfield County Sportsmans Club—Cheraw, South Carolina, klavern of the UKA.

Choudrant Rod & Gun Club—Choudrant, Louisiana, klavern of the 1960s Original Knights.

Chowan Boat Club—Edenton, North Carolina, klavern of the UKA.

Christian Constitutional Crusaders—Organized in 1964 after a rift in Louisiana's 1960s Original Knights, drawing members from Bossier City and Shreveport.

Christian Voters and Buyers League—Founded by James Venable in the early 1960s to expose the "kosher food racket."

Chula Men's Club—Amelia, Virginia, klavern of the UKA.

Circle Club—A front for the 1940s Klan in New York.

Clark-Washington Hunting & Fishing Club—Jackson, Alabama, klavern of the UKA.

Clark's Game Bird Farm—Beulaville, North Carolina, klavern of the UKA.

Clayton Civic Club—Klavern No. 52 of the UKA, in Jonesboro, Georgia.

Clinton Hunting & Fishing Club—Clinton, Louisiana, klavern of the 1960s Original Knights.

Club No. 50—Cuba, Alabama, klavern of the UKA.

Columbus County Sportsman Club—Whiteville, North Carolina, klavern of the UKA.

Committee of One Million Caucasians to March on Washington—Created by James Venable and Wally Butterworth in 1964 to "wrest control of the U.S. government from the Communist hands of foreign Asiatic Jews and African Negroes."

Community Improvement Association—Jacksonville, North Carolina, klavern of the UKA.

Confederate Club No. 38—Dade City klavern of the United Florida KKK.

Confederate Lodge No. 11—Bessemer, Alabama, klavern of the UKA.

Confederate Lodge No. 304—Gadsden, Alabama, klavern of the UKA.

Confederate No. 14—Tarrant City, Alabama, klavern of the UKA.

Conservative Clubs—Organized in Alabama during early 1869, with an active unit also reported from Marion County, Texas.

Constitutional Union Guard—Reconstruction-era all or front group for the North Carolina KKK, whose local units were called "klans."

Continental League for Christian Freedom—Led by Millard Grubbs in Louisville, Kentucky, described by Georgia Attorney General Dan Duke in November 1946 as a Klan front.

Coolidge Fishing Club—Coolidge, Georgia, klavern of the UKA.

Coon Hunters Club—Rutherfordton, North Carolina, klavern of the UKA.

Copiah Rod & Gun Club—Crystal Springs, Mississippi, klavern of the 1960s White Knights.

Council of Safety—Created in Columbia, South Carolina, in December 1870, ostensibly to combat "Negro uprisings." Membership included known Klansmen.

Cove City Hunting Club—Cove City, North Carolina, klavern of the UKA.

Covington Hunting & Fishing Club—Covington, Louisiana, klavern of the 1960s Original Knights.

Craven County Improvement Association—Klavern No. 33 of the UKA in New Bern, North Carolina.

Craven County Ladies Auxiliary—Ladies' auxiliary of UKA Klavern No. 13 in New Bern, North Carolina.

Craven Fellowship Club No. 1—Vanceboro, North Carolina, klavern of the UKA.

Craven Fellowship Club No. 2—A second Vanceboro, North Carolina, klavern of the UKA.

Crusaders of the North—Launched by former UKA Grand Dragon Frank Rotella with a cross-burning at Cedarville, New Jersey, on November 5, 1966.

Cumberland County Patriots—Klavern No. 89 of the UKA in Fayetteville, North Carolina.

Davidson County Rescue Service—Nashville, Tennessee, klavern of the UKA.

Davidson County Sportsman Club—Lexington, North Carolina, klavern of the UKA.

Defensive Legion of Registered Americans—Led by James Venable, chartered in Georgia on April 11, 1962.

DeLand Sportsmans Club—Samsula klavern of the United Florida Knights of the KKK.

Delaware Birdwatchers—Statewide front for the Delaware realm of the UKA.

Delhi Sportsman Club—Delhi, Louisiana, klavern of the 1960s Original Knights.

Delta Sportsman Club—Delta, Louisiana, klavern of the 1960s Original Knights.

Democratic Clubs—Reconstruction-era paramilitary groups linked to the KKK, appearing first in South Carolina during February 1868, later reported in Arkansas, Florida and Louisiana.

Deville Hunting & Fishing Club—Deville, Louisiana, klavern of the 1960s Original Knights.

Dixie Belle Ladies Club—Ladies' auxiliary of the UKA in Sophia, North Carolina.

Dixie Travel Club—Mount Holly, North Carolina, klavern of the UKA.

Donalsonville Lodge No. 3—Donalsonville, Georgia, klavern of the UKA.

Douglas Sportsman Club—Unit 34 of the UKA in Clarendon County, South Carolina.

Dover Community Club—Dover, North Carolina, klavern of the UKA.

Draper Hunting Club—Leadsville, North Carolina, klavern of the UKA.

Dreamland Club—A front for the 1940s Klan in Detroit.

Dubach Hunting & Fishing Club—Dubach, Louisiana, klavern of the UKA.

Dudgemonce Hunting Club—Jonesboro, Louisiana, klavern of the UKA.

Duval Fellowship Club—Jacksonville Klavern No. 502 of the United Florida KKK.

Early Lodge No. 35—Blakely, Georgia, klavern of the UKA.

East Hillsborough Sportsman's Club—Plant City klavern of the United Florida KKK.

East Side Fellowship Club—Fayetteville, North Carolina, klavern of the UKA.

Eastern Triangle Ladies League—Raleigh, North Carolina, ladies' auxiliary of the UKA.

Echo Valley Club—Oconee, South Carolina, klavern of the UKA.

Enterprise Club—Unit No. 46 of the UKA in Clinton, North Carolina.

Etowah Rescue Service—Unit No. 4 of the UKA in Etowah, Tennessee.

Family Improvement Club—Henderson, North Carolina, ladies' auxiliary of the UKA.

Fayette S.A. Club—Fayette, Alabama, klavern of the UKA.

Federation of Community Clubs—A 1920s front for the KKK in Indianapolis. Members called for segregated schools with mandatory New Testament instruction.

Fellowship Club—Mount Olive, North Carolina, klavern of the UKA.

51 Club—Columbia, Alabama, klavern of the UKA.

Fine Fellows Club—Reidsville, North Carolina, klavern of the UKA.

Flint River Men's Club No. 8—Albany, Georgia, klavern of the UKA.

Flint River Men's Group No. 30—Bainbridge, Georgia, klavern of the UKA.

Flint River Sportsman's Club—Alternate front for Bainbridge, Georgia, klavern of the UKA.

Folsom Sportsman's Club—Folsom, Louisiana, klavern of the 1960s Original Knights.

Forrest Club No. 11—Lakeland klavern of the United Florida KKK.

Franklin County Improvement Association—Unit 121 of the UKA in Louisburg, North Carolina.

Fraternal Order of Rangers—A cover for the 1920s Indiana Klan.

Free Association Forum—Robert Miles created this paper organization in the 1980s, inviting various KKK and neo-Nazi speakers to address his Mountain Church of Jesus Christ in Cohocta, Michigan.

Friendly Circle—UKA ladies' auxiliary in Durham, North Carolina.

Friendship Club—Women's auxiliary of UKA Klavern No. 2 in Jacksonville, Florida.

Garden City Club—Orangeburg, South Carolina, klavern of the UKA.

Garner Improvement Association—Garner, North Carolina, klavern of the UKA.

Gaston County Sportsman Club—Unit 34 of the UKA in Cherryville, North Carolina.

Georgetown Tidewater Club—Georgetown, South Carolina, klavern of the UKA.

Graham Game Club—Unit No. 50 of the UKA in Graham, North Carolina.

Grand Empire Club—Beecher, Illinois, klavern of the Invisible Empire Knights, identified by SPLC investigators in 1991.

Grand League of Protestant Women—Organized in Houston, Texas, during 1922, combining social work with demands for "white supremacy, protection of womanhood, [and] defense of the flag."

Gravel Ridge Hunters Lodge—Hermitage, Arkansas, klavern of the UKA.

Green Thumb Garden Club—UKA Ladies Auxiliary No. 4 in Monroe, Louisiana.

Greene County Improvement Association—Snow Hill, North Carolina klavern of the UKA.

Grifton Christian Society—Grifton, North Carolina, klavern of the UKA.

Guilford County Boosters Club—Greensboro, North Carolina, klavern of the UKA.

Halifax County Ladies Club—UKA ladies' auxiliary for klaverns in Enfield and Weldon, North Carolina.

Hamburg Sportsman Club—Hamburg, Arkansas, klavern of the UKA.

Hannah Hawks Club—Florence, South Carolina, klavern of the UKA.

Harmony Club—Unit No. 46 of the UKA in Clinton, North Carolina.

Harnett County Improvement Association—Unit No. 22 of the UKA in Dunn, North Carolina.

Harnett County Ladies League—UKA ladies' auxiliary in Dunn, North Carolina.

Harriman Volunteer Club—Unit No. 2 of the UKA in Harriman, Tennessee.

Hartsville Sportsmans Club—Unit No. 24 of the UKA in Hartsville, South Carolina.

Haw River Fishing Club—Greensboro, North Carolina klavern of the UKA.

Hemingway Sportsmans Club—Unit No. 17 of the UKA in Hemingway, South Carolina.

Henry County No. 49 Club—Abbeville, Alabama, klavern of the UKA.

Heritage Enterprises—Corporate front for the UKA, founded by Robert Shelton, with subsidiaries including Heritage Garment Works (in Columbia, South Carolina) and Heritage Insurance Company (in Bessemer, Alabama).

High Point Brotherhood Club—High Point, North Carolina, klavern of the UKA.

Highway 14 Hunting Club—Unit No. 47 of the UKA in Eutaw, Alabama.

Hineston Hunting & Fishing Club—Hineston, Louisiana, klavern of the 1960s Original Knights.

Homer Hunting & Fishing Club—Homer, Louisiana, klavern of the 1960s Original Knights.

Horse Thief Detective Society—Indiana vigilante group founded in 1908, revived to serve as the Indiana KKK's 1920s "police force."

House of Prayer for All People—White-supremacist "church" founded by Denver, Colorado, klansman William Blessing in the early 1950s.

Houston County Committee for Law and Order—Crockett, Texas, klavern of the UKA.

Hunters Club—Shelby, North Carolina, klavern of the UKA.

Hunting Club—Roseboro, North Carolina, klavern of the UKA.

Impala No. 42—Jackson, Georgia, klavern of the UKA.

Imperial Club No. 27–1—Sebring klavern of the United Florida KKK.

Indian River Hunt Club—Virginia Beach, Virginia, klavern of the UKA.

Jacinto City Citizens Committee for Law and Order—Houston, Texas, klavern of the UKA.

Jack Robinsons—Founded in 1871 by Sheriff Tom Saddler, a known klansman in Pontotoc County, Mississippi.

Jacksonville Sports Club—Jacksonville, North Carolina, klavern of the UKA.

Jena Hunting & Fishing Club—Jena, Louisiana, klavern of the 1960s Original Knights

Joseph E. Johnson Club No. 61—Marietta, Georgia, klavern of the UKA.

Junction City Sportsman's Club—Junction City, Louisiana, klavern of the UKA.

Junior Citizens Club—Created in March 1923 to recruit underage prospective klansmen in Portland, Oregon.

Kappa Beta Lambda—1920s fraternity at the University of Michigan; its initials stand for "klansman be loyal."

Kay-Bee Adsign Company—A 1920s front for the KKK in Buffalo, New York.

Kemper Fishing Lodge—Lake View, South Carolina, klavern of the UKA.

Keystone Club—Henderson, North Carolina, klavern of the UKA.

Keystone Patriotic Society—Identified by Stetson Kennedy as a 1940s front for the Pittsburgh, Pennsylvania, Klan.

Kingsville Hunt Club—Farmville, Virginia, klavern of the UKA.

Knights of American Protestantism—Klan splinter group in Wisconsin's Fox River Valley, created in late 1924 or early 1925.

Kon Klave Klub—Quitman, Mississippi, klavern of the UKA.

Ladies Auxiliary of the Surf Club—UKA ladies' auxiliary in Holly Ridge, North Carolina.

Ladies Confederate Dixons Mills Unit—UKA ladies' auxiliary in Dixons Mill, Alabama.

Ladies Confederates—UKA ladies' auxiliary in Linden, Alabama.

Ladies of Savannah—UKA ladies' auxiliary in Savannah, Georgia.

Lake Wales Pioneer Club No. 5–4—Lake Wales klavern of the United Florida KKK.

Lakeview Men's Club—Locust Grove, Georgia, klavern of the UKA.

Lee County Improvement Association—Unit No. 23 of the UKA in Sanford, North Carolina.

Lenoir Fellowship Club—Kinston, North Carolina, klavern of the UKA.

Lilburn Men's Club No. 229—Dacula, Georgia, klavern of the UKA.

Limestone Debating Club—Wilmington, Delaware, klavern of the UKA.

Lincoln County W.P. Lodge—Lincolnton, North Carolina, klavern of the UKA.

Lithonia No. 57 Club—Lithonia, Georgia, klavern of the UKA.

Little Cohaire Improvement Association—Salemburg, North Carolina klavern of the UKA.

Little River Club No. 27—Biscoe, North Carolina, klavern of the UKA.

Little River Rod & Gun Club—Dry Prong, Louisiana, klavern of the 1960s Original Knights.

Louisiana-Arkansas Law Enforcement League—KKK border patrol group created in 1922.

Louisiana Rifle Association—Cover for banks accounts of the Original Knights during 1960–64.

Louisiana Taxpayers Association—Created in 1974 as a front for David Duke's Knights of the KKK.

Loyal Liberty League—A front for the 1920s Indiana Klan.

Lynches River Hunting Club—Lamar, South Carolina, klavern of the UKA.

M. Murphy Club—Union, South Carolina, klavern of the UKA.

Magic City Lodge—Florence, South Carolina klavern of the UKA.

Magnolia Sportsman Club No. 10—Macon, Georgia, klavern of the UKA.

Mantle Club—A 1940s front for the KKK in Knoxville, Tennessee.

Many Hunting & Fishing Club—Many, Louisiana, klavern of the 1960s Original Knights.

Marion County Catfish Club—Marion, South Carolina, klavern of the UKA.

Marion Hunting & Fishing Club—Marion, Louisiana, klavern of the UKA.

Martin County Ladies Improvement Club—UKA ladies' auxiliary in Williamston, North Carolina.

Martin County Sportsman Club—Unit No. 4 of the UKA in Williamston, North Carolina.

Meadow Improvement Association—UKA klavern serving Benson and Dunn, North Carolina.

Mecklenburg Sportsman Club—Charlotte, North Carolina, klavern of the UKA.

Men's Club of Strong Community—Strong, Arkansas, klavern of the UKA.

Midway Club—Unit No. 5 of the UKA in West Columbia, South Carolina.

Minutemen—Splinter group created by Colorado Grand Dragon John Locke following his rift with the national Klan in 1925.

Mississippi Constitution Party—Created by the White Knights in 1965.

Mississippi White Caps—A cover for the 1960s White Knights.

Modern Minute Men—A front group for the 1920s Indiana KKK.

Monroe Hunting & Fishing Club—Monroe, Louisiana, klavern of the UKA.

Monticello Men's Club—Monticello, Arkansas, klavern of the UKA.

Morehouse Hunt and Gun Club—Bastrop, Louisiana, training facility shared by 1960s Klansmen and Minutemen.

Mountain Church of Jesus Christ—Splinter group founded by Robert Miles at Cohoctah, Michigan, after his release from prison in the 1970s (also known as the Mountain Kirk).

Nacirema, Inc.—1960s faction devoted to bombing, whose name is "American" spelled backwards.

Nansemond & Suffolk Hunt Club—UKA klavern drawing members from Holland and Suffolk, Virginia.

Nash County Charter Service—Unit No. 1 of the UKA in Nash County, North Carolina.

National Christian Church—Created by Bill Hendrix in 1960, sharing an Oldsmar, Florida, address with his Knights of the White Camellia.

National Christian Democratic Party—Founded in 1978 by Lansing, Michigan, KKK/NSRP member Gerald Carlson to serve as his personal political vehicle.

National Christian Party—An Oklahoma Klan front active in 1973–74.

National Research Bureau—A front for the Michigan KKK in the early 1920s.

Native Americans Club—A front for the 1920s Indiana Klan.

Native Sons of the South—White-supremacist group with known Klansmen in its ranks, active during 1871 in Lowndes and Noxubee Counties, Mississippi.

Neuse Hunting Club—Kinston, North Carolina, klavern of the UKA.

Neuse Rescue Service—Second Kinston, North Carolina, klavern of the UKA.

Never Club—Smithfield, Virginia, klavern of the UKA.

New Hanover County Improvement Association, Inc.—Wilmington, North Carolina, klavern of the UKA.

New River Fishing Club—Beulaville, North Carolina, klavern of the UKA.

New River Rifle Club—New River, Louisiana, klavern of the 1960s Original Knights.

Newport Fellowship Club—Morehead City, North Carolina, klavern of the UKA.

Northeast Gun Club—Monroe, Louisiana, klavern of the 1960s Original Knights.

Nottoway Club—Emporia, Virginia, klavern of the UKA.

Oakville Outdoor Sports Club—Chesapeake, Virginia, klavern of the UKA.

Ocala Hunt Club—Ocala, Florida, klavern of the Improved Order of the U.S. Klans.

Odd Brothers Club No. 16—Dillon, South Carolina, klavern of the UKA.

Odd Brothers Club No. 33—Second Dillon, South Carolina, klavern of the UKA.

Okaloosa Hunting & Fishing Club—Monroe, Louisiana, klavern of the 1960s Original Knights.

Old Dominion Club—Danville, Virginia, klavern of the UKA.

Old Hickory Club—Klavern No. 1 of the Dixie Klans, in Chattanooga, Tennessee.

Onslow County Improvement Association—Jacksonville, North Carolina, klavern of the UKA.

Order of American Patriots—A 1940s front for the KKK in Texas.

Order of the Rattlesnake—Created by Florida KKK leader Bill Hendrix in the late 1950s, inactive by 1961.

Ormandsville Loyal Fellowship Association—Ormandsville, North Carolina, klavern of the UKA.

Ouachita Parish Hunting & Fishing Club—Monroe, Louisiana, klavern of the UKA.

Our Fishing Club—Baltimore, Maryland, klavern of the UKA.

Pactolus Hunting Club—Unit No. 162 of the UKA, in Pactolus, North Carolina.

Paradise No. 115—Winder, Georgia, klavern of the UKA.

Patriots Interorganizational Communications Center—Established at an August 1975 UKA klonvokation in Lakeland, Florida, jointly led by Robert Shelton and Minutemen founder Robert DePugh, with headquarters in Norbonne, Missouri.

Paul Revere Historical Society—Jacksonville Klavern No. 502 of the United Florida KKK.

Pearl River Gun & Rod Club—Crossroads Community, Mississippi, klavern of the 1960s White Knights.

Pearl River Hunting & Fishing Lodge No. 1028—Pearl River, Louisiana, klavern of the 1960s Original Knights.

Pee Dee Gun Club—Darlington, South Carolina, klavern of the UKA.

Pender County Improvement Association—UKA klavern drawing members from Atkinson and Currie, North Carolina.

Pichett Club—Lawrenceville, Virginia, klavern of the UKA.

Pin Hook Improvement Association—Wallace, North Carolina, klavern of the UKA.

Pine Grove Hunting & Fishing Club—Pine Grove, Louisiana, klavern of the 1960s Original Knights.

Pine Valley Lodge—Buford, Georgia, klavern of the UKA.

Pinedale Saddle Club—Unit No. 10 of the UKA, including members from Greensboro and Pleasant Garden, North Carolina.

Pioneer Sportsman Club—Covington, Georgia, klavern of the UKA.

Pitt County Christian Fellowship Club—Greenville, North Carolina, klavern of the UKA.

Pitt County Improvement Association—Unit No. 37 of the UKA in Farmville, North Carolina.

Poinsettia Unit 101—Originally a Jacksonville, Florida, klavern of the Improved Order of the U.S. Klans, disbanded in December 1964, subsequently revived by the UKA.

Pollock Hunting & Fishing Club—Dry Prong, Louisiana, klavern of the 1960s Original Knights (later renamed the Little River Rod & Gun Club).

Portland Police Vigilantes—The armed branch of Portland, Oregon's, Klan No. 1 in the 1920s.

Pride Sportsman League—Pride, Louisiana, klavern of the 1960s Original Knights.

Protestant War Veterans of America—Founded by Edward Smythe in 1946, named by Georgia Attorney General Dan Duke as a Klan front.

Quilting Club—UKA ladies' auxiliary in Roxboro, North Carolina.

R.H. Volunteers of America—Rock Hill, South Carolina, klavern of the UKA.

Rainbow Club—UKA ladies' auxiliary in Pink Hill, North Carolina.

Ranch Gun Club—Clayton, North Carolina, klavern of the UKA.

Red Bluff Hunting Club—Bennettsville, South Carolina, klavern of the UKA.

Red River Club—Unit No. 19 of the UKA in Bennettsville, South Carolina.

Red Wood League—Unit No. 35 of the UKA in Kings Mountain, North Carolina.

Richburg Sportsman Club—Unit No. 32 of the UKA in Chester, South Carolina.

Riverside Sportsman Club—Wendell, North Carolina, klavern of the UKA.

Robinson Family—Alternate name for the Jack Robinsons, founded in 1871 by Sheriff Tom Saddler, a klansman in Pontotoc county, Mississippi.

Rock of Freedom—Yet another front for the 1920s Indiana Klan.

Roseland Hunting Club—Roseland, Louisiana, klavern of the 1960s Original Knights.

Round Hill Fishing Club—Landrum, South Carolina, klavern of the UKA.

Rowan Sportsman's Club—Unit No. 1 of the UKA in North Carolina, drawing members from Salisbury and Spencer.

Roxboro Fishing Club—Roxboro, North Carolina, klavern of the UKA.

Sand Hill Hunting Club—Mount Olive, North Carolina, klavern of the UKA.

Sandhill Stag Club—Unit 32 of the UKA in Rockingham, North Carolina.

Santee Sportsman Club—St. Stephen, South Carolina, klavern of the UKA.

7–11 Sportsman Club—Americus, Georgia, klavern of the UKA.

7–1 Club—Orlando klavern of the United Florida KKK.

772 Club—UKA klavern in Mecklenburg County, Virginia, drawing members from Boydton and South Hill.

Sneads Ferry Fellowship Club—UKA Unit No. 154 in Sneads Ferry, North Carolina.

Sons of Democracy—Plymouth, North Carolina, klavern of the UKA.

Sophia Rebels Club—Sophia, North Carolina, klavern of the UKA.

South Hill "85" Club—UKA klavern in Mecklenburg County, Virginia, drawing members from La Cross and South Hill.

South Pike Marksmanship Association—Unit 700 of the UKA in McComb, Mississippi.

South Rowan Gun Club—Landis, North Carolina, klavern of the UKA.

Southern Justice—Despite its name, this white supremacist group operated in the Pacific Northwest, with headquarters in Vancouver, Washington. It also claimed members in Boise, Idaho, and in Portland, Oregon. In May 1992, leader Shannon LaRue announced that the group had been "certified as a local chapter" of the Missouri-based National Confederacy of the KKKK. No trace of either group remained when the SPLC completed its national census of hate groups for 1997.

Southern National Front—Alternate name for Glenn Miller's Carolina Knights of the KKK in the mid–1980s. The group claimed 250–300 members in 1987, when it merged with the larger National Democratic Front.

Southern Publicity Bureau—The Klan's first Chicago klavern, organized in 1921.

Southlands Sport Club of Fair Bluff—1950s Columbia County, North Carolina, klavern of Tom Hamilton's Association of Carolina Klans.

Southside Beagle Club—Burkeville, Virginia, klavern of the UKA.

Southside Handcraft Club—Richmond, Virginia, klavern of the UKA.

Southside Sportsman Club No. 39—UKA klavern in Mecklenburg County, Virginia, drawing members from Boydton and South Hill.

Spencer Club—Goochland, Virginia klavern of the UKA.

Sports, Inc.—Front for a Miami, Florida, klavern active during 1950–51.

Sportsman Club—Rosehill, North Carolina, klavern of the UKA.

Sportsmans Club—Unit 4 of the UKA in Pickens, South Carolina.

Sportsman's Club No. 3—Ocala, Florida, klavern of the Improved Order of the U.S. Klans.

Sportsman's Lakeside Lodge—Hillsboro, North Carolina, klavern of the UKA.

Stanly Improvement Association—Albemarle, North Carolina, klavern of the UKA.

Sterlington Hunting & Fishing Club—Sterlington, Louisiana, klavern of the 1960s Original Knights.

Stonewall Jackson No. 1—Jacksonville, Florida, klavern of the Improved Order of the U.S. Klans, disbanded in late 1964, then revived by the UKA.

Stork Club—Canton, Mississippi, klavern of the UKA.

Straight Arrow No. 17—Cumming, Georgia, klavern of the UKA.

Summerfield Fellowship Club—Belleview, Florida, klavern of the UKA.

Summerfield Sewing Auxiliary—UKA ladies' auxiliary in Belleview, Florida.

Sumter Sportsmans Club—Unit No. 10 of the UKA in Sumter, South Carolina.

Supply Improvement Association—Unit No. 28 of the UKA in Supply, North Carolina.

Surry County Sportsman Club—Mount Airy, North Carolina, klavern of the UKA.

Swansboro–White Oak Fishing Club—Swansboro, North Carolina, klavern of the UKA.

Swartz Hunting & Fishing Club—Swartz, Louisiana, klavern of the 1960s Original Knights.

Tar Heel Development Association, Sampson County—Salemburg, North Carolina, klavern of the UKA.

Taylor Town Hunting Club—Bernice, Louisiana, klavern of the UKA.

Tensas Sportsman Club—Tensas Parish, Louisiana, klavern of the 1960s Original Knights.

Texas Emergency Service—Created in the late 1970s by Louis Beam, Texas grand dragon for David Duke's Knights of the KKK.

Thomasville Brotherhood Club—Thomasville, North Carolina, klavern of the UKA.

Tipton County Community Center—Covington, Tennessee, klavern of the UKA.

Top Sail Fishing Association—Holly Ridge, North Carolina, klavern of the UKA.

Town & Country Sportsman Club—Durham, North Carolina, klavern of the UKA.

Trent Community Club—Kinston, North Carolina, klavern of the UKA.

Tri-City Lodge—Dinwiddie County, Virginia, klavern of the UKA, drawing members from Ettrick and Petersburg.

Tri-County Sportsman Club—Unit No. 24 of the UKA in Rocky Mount, North Carolina.

Tri-Valley Sportsman Club—Vero Beach, Florida, klavern of the UKA.

Triple Ace Club—Faison, North Carolina, klavern of the UKA.

Triple-S Super Secret Society—Cover for the 1920s Pennsylvania Klan.

Tulls Mill Recreation Club—Deep Run, North Carolina, klavern of the UKA.

Tulsa Benevolent Association—A front for the 1920s Klan in Tulsa, Oklahoma, this group operated the Beno Hall at the corner of Main Street and Easton Avenue. While "Beno" allegedly derived from "Benevolent," local klansmen boasted that it stood for "Be No Nigger, Be No Catholic, Be No Jew."

Turkey Creek Rod & Gun Club—Turkey Creek, Louisiana, klavern of the 1960s Original Knights.

211 Pointers Club—Unit No. 63 of the UKA in Southern Pines, North Carolina.

Tyrell County Men's Club—Columbia, North Carolina, klavern of the UKA.

United Americans for Conservative Government—The UKA's primary front group in 1960s Alabama politics.

United Conservatives of Mississippi, Inc., No. 1—Unit No. 702 of the UKA, drawing members from Crossroads Community and Poplarville, Mississippi.

United Ladies Club—UKA ladies' auxiliary in Amelia, Virginia.

United Social Club—Savannah, Georgia, klavern of the UKA.

Unity Now—Another creation of Robert Miles, this paper organization invited leaders of various rival Klans to address the Mountain Church of Jesus Christ at Cohoctah, Michigan, thereby presumably fostering "unity" throughout the invisible empire.

Varnado Sportsmans Club—Varnado, Louisiana, klavern of the 1960s Original Knights.

Venus Rescue Service—Venus, Florida, klavern of the UKA.

Victoria Hunt Club—Victoria, Virginia, klavern of the UKA.

Vidalia Sportsman's Club—Vidalia, Louisiana, klavern of the 1960s Original Knights.

Vigilantes—A Barnesville, Georgia, splinter group formed in May 1964 by former UKA members who switched their allegiance to the National Knights.

Virginia Hunting Club No. 1039—South Boston, Virginia, klavern of the UKA.

Virginia Rod & Gun Club—Richmond, Virginia, klavern of the UKA.

Wade Hampton Club—Unit No. 1 of the UKA in Greenville, South Carolina.

Wake Forest Restoration Service—Wake Forest, North Carolina, klavern of the UKA.

Wa-lin-da Beach Club—Andrews, South Carolina, klavcrn of the UKA.

Wallace Fellowship Club—Wallace, North Carolina, klavern of the UKA.

W-A-M-B-A—Morganton, North Carolina, klavern of the UKA.

Ward 10 Hunting Club—Winfield, Louisiana, klavern of the UKA.

Warren County Improvement Association—Unit No. 30 of the UKA, drawing members from Norlina and Warrenton, North Carolina.

Warren Women's Improvement Association—UKA ladies' auxiliary in Norlina, North Carolina.

Warsaw Fellowship Club—Warsaw, North Carolina, klavern of the UKA.

Warwick Men's Club—UKA klavern in Southampton County, Virginia, drawing members from Franklin and Newport News.

Washington County Fellowship Club—Creswell, North Carolina, klavern of the UKA.

WASP Inc.—A cover for the 1960s White Knights in Mississippi.

Watson Hunting Club—Watson, Louisiana, klavern of the 1960s Original Knights.

Wayne County Improvement Association—Unit No. 38 of the UKA in Goldsboro, North Carolina.

Wayne County Rifle and Pistol Club—A front for the 1930s Black Legion in Detroit, Michigan.

Wayne County Sewing Circle—UKA ladies' auxiliary in Pikeville, North Carolina.

West Carroll Rifleman Club—West Carroll Parish, Louisiana, klavern of the 1960s Original Knights.

West Columbia Club—Klavern No. 335, Association of South Carolina Klans, in West Columbia.

West Duplin Boating & Fishing Club—Unit No. 46 of the UKA in Clinton, North Carolina.

West Melbourne Fellowship Club—Melbourne, Florida, klavern of the UKA.

West Orange Sportsman's Lodge No. 7–3—Apopka klavern of the United Florida KKK.

White American Protestants—A 1920s chain of Texas "study clubs" led by oilman and reputed klansman E.F. Keith.

White Band—Paramilitary action squad created by Exalted Cyclops Robert Bing of UKA Klavern No. 52, in Clayton County, Georgia.

White Caps—Organized in 1965 as a front for the White Knights of Mississippi, also reported active around Ferriday, Louisiana.

White Christian Protective and Legal Defense Fund—Created by Imperial Wizard Sam Bowers in 1965 to defray legal expenses of White Knights charged with criminal offenses in Mississippi.

White Citizens of Randolph—Asheboro, North Carolina, klavern of the UKA.

White Citizens of Whitsett—Randolph County, North Carolina, klavern of the UKA, drawing members from Julian and Whitsett.

White Crusaders for God and Country—Led by former UKA Grand Dragon Frank Rotella, linked to cross-burnings around Salem, New Jersey, in 1966–67.

White Crusaders of the North—Another creation of former UKA Grand Dragon Frank Rotella, unveiled at a 1966 cross-burning outside Cedarville, New Jersey.

White Patriot Party—The final incarnation of Glenn Miller's Confederate Knights of the KKK, created in 1985.

Members of the White Patriot Party protest the Martin Luther King holiday in Raleigh, North Carolina, January 1986 (Southern Poverty Law Center).

White Patriots—Brantley, Alabama, klavern of the UKA.

White People's Committee to Restore God's Laws—Launched by Arkansas klansman Thomas Robb in 1983.

White People's Defense Fund—Created by Asa Carter in April 1956, after his Klansmen attacked singer Nat "King" Cole in Birmingham, Alabama.

White People's March Toward Freedom—Ashland, Mississippi, klavern of the UKA.

White Power Canada—Founded in 1990 by Canadian klansmen Michel Larocque and Alain Roy, the WPC was conceived as a "junior Klan" for Québec skinheads who could do the Klan's dirty work. On various occasions, WPC members attacked opponents from the World Anti-Fascist League and SHARP (Skinheads Against Racial Prejudice). On 29 November 1990, four WPC members bludgeoned and robbed victim Yves Lalone, mistakenly presuming that he was gay. Police arrested the killers on 3 December, and all four pled guilty to second-degree murder in April 1993.

White Protestant Christian Party—Founded in 1947 by Rev. Evall Johnston, officer of the AGK in Columbus.

White Supremacy League—A front for the 1920s Indiana KKK, with individual chapters led by klansmen.

Whiteman's Defense Fund—Created by Imperial Wizard Robert Shelton in March 1965, to defray legal expenses of UKA members charged with murdering Viola Liuzzo.

Wilder's Golf Club—Selma, North Carolina, klavern of the UKA.

Wildwood Sewing Auxiliary—UKA ladies' auxiliary in Wildwood, Florida.

Wilkes County Club No. 301—Washington, Georgia, klavern of the UKA.

Willow Springs Restoration Association—Willow Springs, North Carolina, klavern of the UKA.

Wills Valley Hunting Club—Fort Payne, Alabama, klavern of the UKA.

Wilson County Improvement Association—Unit No. 31 of the UKA in Wilson County, North Carolina, serving members from Lucama and Wilson.

Winfield Hunting & Fishing Club—Winnfield, Louisiana, klavern of the 1960s Original Knights.

Wolverine Republican Club—1930s front for the Black Legion in Michigan.

Women's Activity Club—UKA ladies' auxiliary in Portsmouth, Virginia.

Young Men's Democratic Clubs—Reconstruction-era fronts for the Florida Klan, described by a member in sworn testimony as "one and the same."

Young Men's Social Club—Simultaneously used as cover for UKA klaverns in Bessemer and Dora, Alabama.

6 KOMRADES IN ARMS

The Invisible Empire has never consisted solely of Klans and Klan front groups. From the beginning, various affiliated groups and individual supporters have provided aid and comfort to the cause. ADL analysts estimate that ideological allies of the KKK outnumber dues-paying knights by roughly three-to-one at any given time. Some supporters are "former" klansmen whose formal membership has lapsed, while they remain in touch (or, at the very least, in sympathy) with active members of the order. Others are members of alternate fringe groups, ranging from "respectable" racist cliques (which welcome klansmen as associates but hide the fact) to hard-core neo–Nazi groups that rally with the KKK in public. "Closet" supporters come from all strata of society, including pillars of society and the professions. This chapter examines individuals and organizations that have allied themselves with the KKK at various times, either proudly or covertly, in pursuit of common goals.

Individuals

Allen, Wallace—An early member of the NSRP in Atlanta, Georgia, Allen was one of six neo–Nazis jailed without bond in October 1958, on suspicion of bombing a local synagogue. When police searched his home, they found literature from an Anniston, Alabama, KKK faction and Bill Hendrix's KWC. George Lincoln Rockwell, founder of the ANP and National Committee to Free America from Jewish Domination, admitted writing a letter to Allen including references to a "big blast," but Rockwell denied any knowledge of the bombing. Prosecutors dropped all charges against Allen after jurors acquitted co-defendant George Bright in January 1959.

Andrew, Dr. John S.—A resident of Stone Mountain, Georgia, Andrew led Atlanta's Emory chapter of the JBS until he resigned to run for the state legislature in 1965. Despite his resignation, he remained an active member of the JBS, which continued to hold meetings at his home. After losing the primary election, Andrew addressed a UKA rally in Atlanta, on 23 August 1965, telling klansmen that he was defeated by an "international banking conspiracy." On 13 September 1965, Andrew escorted the parents of John Birch to a JBS rally in Atlanta's Henry Grady Hotel, where Edwin Walker told the audience, "There will be a KKK in the USA longer than there will be an LBJ!"

Andrews, Don—A native Serb, born Vilim Zlomislic in 1942, Andrews is the son of an anti–Nazi partisan who died fighting German invaders during World War II. A Red Cross worker brought him to Canada in 1952, and he was raised in Toronto. Zlomislic later assumed the name "Don Andrews" (allegedly in honor of the Red Cross worker) and then inexplicably launched himself into neo–Nazi politics. In 1967, he co-founded the Edmund Burke Society with Paul Fromm, renaming it the Western Guard in 1972. Andrews was the first person charged by Canadian authorities with "willfully promoting hatred." In 1975, he received a two-year prison term on weapons and conspiracy charges, for plotting to bomb an Israeli soccer team. Upon release, in 1977, Andrews was barred from association with the Western Guard. He compensated by founding the Nationalist Party and running several times for mayor of Toronto. At last report, he owned a string of downtown rooming houses catering to neo–Nazi skinheads.

Barrett, Richard—A native Yankee, born in 1943, raised in New York City and East Orange, New Jersey. He attended Rutgers University, then served in Vietnam before migrating to Mississippi in 1966, where an early strain of racism took root and flourished. ("Mississippians," he wrote, "were endowed with an unconquerable anti-communist spirit because they had to perennially guard against a takeover by Negroes.") While promoting various "patriotic" and "white heritage" causes, Barrett earned a law degree from Tennessee's Memphis State University and won admission to the Mississippi bar. He subsequently founded the Nationalist Movement and ran for governor in 1979, placing last in a field of six candidates with only two percent of the vote. Barrett's autobiography, *The Commission* (1982), was immodestly billed in dust-jacket blurbs as "the most important book of our time," while Barrett rated praise as "a man whose name will be written in lightning across the pages of American history." The text called for "resettlement" of "those who were once citizens" to "Puerto Rico, Mexico, Israel, the Orient and Africa," coupled with sterilization and compulsory abortions for the "unfit."

In 1984, Barrett placed second in a Mississippi congressional race, winning 9,500 votes in a campaign which he characterized as a contest between "the cotton boll and three lumps of coal." Three years later, he served as lead attorney for the Forsyth County Defense League, created to defend klansmen indicted after riots around Cummings, Georgia. In January 1988,

Barrett led a parade of sixty-five protesters (including forty robed klansmen) through Cummings, proudly affixing his signature to "The Forsyth County Covenant," a racist document proclaiming that "America's heritage as a free, white, Christian, English-speaking democracy ... must be advanced," while "all efforts to make us a bi-lingual, bi-sexual or bi-racial society must be defeated." Summer 1988 found Barrett back in Georgia, picketing the Democratic National Convention with Edward Fields and J.B. Stoner. December 1988 saw him recruiting neo–Nazi skinheads for a "Warrior Weekend" of paramilitary training at Barrett's home, where photos of Martin Luther King were used as rifle targets. In 1994, Barrett collected 4,000 signatures on a petition to Gov. Kirk Fordyce to pardon Klan assassin Byron De La Beckwith, and when that bid was rejected, he led demonstrations that included klansmen marching in support of Beckwith's freedom. Other far-flung protests in Los Angeles (supporting policemen who beat Rodney King) and in Morristown, New Jersey ("Independence from Affirmative Action Day") found Barrett's supporters outnumbered by hecklers. His main legal activity of late consists of threats to sue websites which describe his disciples as "haters," a campaign which at last count had removed more than two dozen pages from the Internet.

Bishop, Ann—An active NSRP member in Little Rock, Arkansas, Bishop helped gather 29,552 petition signatures needed to put the party on state ballots in 1962. (On election day, the NSRP polled 28,952 votes statewide.) In 1962, media reports identified Bishop as the NSRP's executive secretary.

Bowles, Bryant—A Baltimore, Maryland, resident and notorious anti–Semite, Bowles addressed several KKK rallies as a guest speaker before founding his own NAAWP in 1959. That group dissolved, and Bowles disappeared from the racist scene, after Texas prosecutors imprisoned him for murdering his brother-in-law.

Bowling, Richard—An early member of the NSRP in Atlanta, Georgia, Bowling visited Birmingham, Alabama, to bomb Rev. Fred Shuttlesworth's church on 29 June 1958. That bombing was arranged by Birmingham police, as part of a bungled "sting" operation against J.B. Stoner, but Bowling was never arrested. Four months later, Atlanta police jailed him as a suspect in a 12 October synagogue bombing. Charges against Bowling, his brother Robert, and three other NSRP members were dropped in 1959, after jurors acquitted defendant George Bright in the same case.

Branham, Billy—A member of the NSRP in Atlanta, Georgia, Branham accompanied George Bright and Leslie Rogers to greet John Kasper on his emergence from federal prison, in 1957.

Brannen, Robert—Media reports identified Brannen as an ex-klansman and associate of George Lincoln Rockwell's ANP, who joined Cincinnati's National Socialist Movement in the 1970s and later replaced founder James Mason at the helm, when Mason left to form the competing NSLF.

Bright, George Michael—A member of the NSRP in Atlanta, Georgia, Bright was one of four neo–Nazis jailed in July 1958 while picketing the Atlanta *Journal and Constitution* with anti–Semitic placards. Three months later, police jailed Bright and five other NSRP members (Wallace Allen, Richard Bright, Robert Bright, Luther Crowley, and Kenneth Griffin) for bombing an Atlanta synagogue on 12 October. Prosecutors denied bail to the defendants after members of a grand jury received threatening phone calls from the Confederate Underground. Bright faced trial on 1 December 1958, defended by KKK attorney James Venable. Prosecutors produced a threatening note found in Bright's home, addressed to the synagogue's rabbi ("You are going to experience the most terrifying thing in your life."), while state witnesses included an FBI informant in the U.S. Klans and a cellmate of Bright's who detailed his confession to the bombing. Venable countered with character witnesses including U.S. Klans Imperial Wizard Eldon Edwards, NSRP chairman Arthur Cole, Edward Fields, ANP member Matt Koehl, and an inmate from the state asylum (testifying during a moment of "temporary lucidity"). Jurors deadlocked nine-to-three for conviction on 10 December, whereupon the judge declared a mistrial. A second panel acquitted Bright in January 1959, after which prosecutors dismissed all charges against his codefendants. Bright subsequently joined John Crommelin, John Hamilton, Bill Hendrix and other racist leaders for a party celebrating John Kasper's release from federal prison.

Brown, Robert Kenneth—An army captain stationed at Fort Benning, Georgia, Brown told FBI agents in December 1963 that he had been active for several years in covert campaigns against Cuba's Fidel Castro. Brown's travels in that cause included a visit to the NSRP's Los Angeles office, where party members discussed the need to eliminate "[President John] Kennedy, the Cabinet, all the members of the Americans for Democratic Action, and maybe 10,000 other people."

Bruce, Melvin—U.S. marshals arrested Bruce, once a chauffeur for ANP founder George Rockwell, during the 30 September 1962 riot against James Meredith's admission to the University of Mississippi, at Oxford. At the time of his arrest, Bruce carried a rifle with a JBS sticker affixed to its stock. At trial, defended by attorney J.B. Stoner, Bruce won acquittal after a National Guardsman claimed he had seen federal marshals beat Bruce.

Burford, James—In 1982, Burford replaced Michael Allen as head of the NSPA, formally renaming that group the American Nazi Party. Media reports claimed a split in the group during 1983, ex-klansman Dennis Milam replaced Burford as leader, but SPLC investigators found Burford in charge of the ANP during 1989–91.

Burt, John—Florida resident John Burt was a self-described ex-klansman, reformed alcoholic and ex-drug addict who discovered "pro-life" activism in the early 1980s, billing himself as the Sunshine State's spokesman for Rescue America. When not harassing patients and staffers at Pensacola's Ladies' Center, Burt also served as pastor for the Whitfield Assembly of God and ran Our Father's House, a home for wayward girls endowed with state permission to inflict corporal punishment and compel Sunday church attendance by its teenage inmates. About the KKK, Burt told reporters, "Fundamentalist Christians and those people [klansmen] are close, scary close, fighting for God and country. Some day we may all be in the trenches together in the fight against the slaughter of unborn children."

Burt's war included intimate association with Pensacola "pro-life" terrorists John Brockhoeft (jailed by ATF agents for clinic bombings in 1988), Michael Griffin (sentenced to life imprisonment for the 1993 murder of Dr. David Gunn), and Paul Hill (executed on 3 September 2004 for the 1994 murders of Dr. Lawrence Britton and his bodyguard). The SPLC filed suit against Burt in March 1995, charging him with wrongful death in Dr. Gunn's slaying, and Burt settled the claim out of court in July 1996. Eight years later, police charged Burt with molesting a fifteen-year-old girl at Our Father's House. Jurors convicted him in April 2004, resulting in an eighteen-year prison term.

Butler, Richard Girnt—A native of Bennett, Colorado, born 23 February 1918, Butler studied aeronautical engineering in Los Angeles during the 1930s, while holding membership in William Pelley's Silver Shirt Legion of America. After Pearl Harbor, he joined the Army Air Corps but never saw combat. Back in civilian life, Butler spent the McCarthy era of the 1950s fraternizing with William Potter Gale and future ANP leader George Lincoln Rockwell. In 1961, he joined Wesley Swift's Anglo-Saxon Christian Congregation, later the Church of Jesus Christ Christian. Two years later, Butler served as director of Swift's Christian Defense League. In 1968, Butler joined Lockheed Aircraft as a senior marketing engineer, but any pretense of normal employment ended with Swift's death in 1970. Butler then assumed command of Swift's church, while drifting ever further toward the paramilitary neo–Nazi fringe. In 1974, Butler pulled up stakes and moved the church to a twenty-acre compound at Hayden Lake, Idaho, leaving James Warner behind to command the Christian Defense League. The impetus for Butler's move came from two arrests in California, one on weapons charges and the other for lewd conduct near a school playground. A decade later, in 1982, Butler issued an open letter to his followers, claiming that he was "set up" on the latter charge, insisting that he was "not a homosexual child molester." A strange addendum to that note claimed that his great-grandfather had wed a "Nigerian Princess," an act which Butler described as "marrying 'up' into a royal family." Having delivered that startling news, Butler reassured the faithful that his "royal Nigerian blood ... hardly shows."

Once established in Idaho, Butler formed his own chapter of the Christian Posse Comitatus (1975) and created the Aryan Nations as the political arm of his church (1977). He hosted his first Aryan World Congress in 1978, welcoming klansmen and neo–Nazis from around the nation and the world. That gathering became an annual event, maintained each year except for 1984, when Butler's involvement with guerrillas of The Order intervened. His receipt of stolen bank loot from The Order prompted a federal sedition indictment in 1987, but jurors acquitted Butler and his thirteen codefendants at their trial in Arkansas, in April 1988. Although victorious in court, Butler emerged to find his order under siege. Dissension in the ranks

produced defections, rival groups competing for attention and recruits. The SPLC filed suit against Butler in 1998, on behalf of a mother and son assaulted by guards at his compound, and jurors found Butler culpably negligent in September 2000, assessing damages of $6.3 million. That verdict left him bankrupt, and he formally retired as leader of the sect in July 2002, leaving younger fascists to squabble over its remnants. Butler died on 8 September 2004.

Carlson, Gerald Russell—A neo–Nazi activist in Lansing, Michigan, Carlson held membership in the KKK, NSRP, AIP and JBS before he professed "disenchantment" in 1978 and founded his own National Christian Democratic Party. He soon established a "White Power Hot Line," broadcasting racist telephone messages, until Michigan Bell demanded inclusion of his personal address in each tirade. In August 1980, Carlson won the GOP's Fifteenth Congressional District primary with 3,759 votes, defeating his opponent by more than 700 votes. Republican leaders instantly withdrew their support from Carlson and he lost the November election, but his total of 53,570 votes led ADL spokesmen to voice "deep concern." In February 1981, Carlson lost another congressional race, this time in Michigan's Fourth District. Shifting to Pennsylvania for a special congressional race four months later, he was scratched from the ballot when election officials discovered his false claims of residency in Philadelphia. In August 1982, Carlson tried his luck again in Michigan's Fifteenth Congressional District, but he polled only 7,486 votes.

Carroll, Joseph—A spokesman for the NSRP, Carroll joined party members Connie Lynch and Richard Norton to address a Baltimore, Maryland, rally on 29 July 1966, sparking a race riot by 1,000 whites. On 21 November 1966, Carroll received a jail sentence for inciting a riot, conspiracy to riot, and violating city park regulations.

Carto, Willis Alison—An Indiana native, born in 1926 and raised in Ohio, Carto served in the U.S. Army during World War II, then returned to study at Ohio's Dennison University and spent one semester at the University of Cincinnati's law school. In the early 1950s, he moved to San Francisco and immersed himself in right-wing politics, heavily influenced by the writings of neo–Nazi Francis Parker Yockey. After Yockey's suicide, Carto wrote, "Hitler's defeat was the defeat of Europe. And of America. How could we have been so blind? The blame, it seems, must be laid at the door of the international Jews." With that in mind, the reclusive anti–Semite spent the next half-century organizing, leading and/or supporting myriad right-wing racist groups and publications, including his own Liberty and Property, Western Destiny, Noontide Press, *American Mercury*, National Youth Alliance, Institute for Historical Review, Populist Party and Liberty Lobby. While Carto steadfastly denied any taint of bigotry, he summarized his core philosophy as follows: "If Satan himself, with all of his super-human genius and diabolical ingenuity at his command, had tried to create a permanent disintegration and force for the destruction of the nations, he could have done no better than to invent the Jews." The issue of Carto's racism was officially decided in 1988, when a federal appeals court dismissed his libel suit against the *Washington Post* for calling him "anti Semitic." Judge Robert Bork declared, "We tend to agree with a district court that if the term 'anti–Semitic' has a core, factual meaning, then the truth of the description was proved here."

Carto's personality and management style produced many rifts with his associates and subordinates, prompting various defections and creation of spin-off groups. A case in point is the Institute for Historical Review, founded by Carto in 1979 as a vehicle for Holocaust-denial propaganda. Leaders of the IHR severed their ties to Carto in September 1993, announcing that he had been "fired" for general mismanagement and tapping the IHR's till to buy his wife a new car. Litigation ensued, as Carto grappled with the insurgent IHR staff for control of $10 million in stock certificates bequeathed to the IHR's parent organization (the Legion for the Survival of Freedom) by a wealthy heir of Thomas Edison. Carto lost that case on 15 November 1996, with Judge Runston Maino declaring, "I found that much of his testimony made no sense; much of his testimony in court was different from his previous testimony; much of his testimony was contradicted by other witnesses or by documents. By the end of the trial I was of the opinion that Mr. Carto lacked candor, lacked memory, and lacked the ability to be forthright about what he did honestly remember." In the wake of that verdict, Carto and Liberty Lobby filed for bankruptcy. A series of verdicts in Federal Bankruptcy Court, delivered in June and July 2001, forced Carto to relinquish control over the Liberty Lobby and its primary publication, *The Spotlight.* He rebounded in August 2001, launching the new *American Free Press,* and Carto remained active in far-right racist circles at press time for this volume, including co-sponsorship of a New Orleans white-supremacist rally convened on 29 May 2004. On that occasion, Carto joined David Duke, Stephen Black and others in signing Duke's "New Orleans Protocol," pledging unity among American racist groups against their common enemies.

Chase, Rev. William Sheafe

—While serving as the Episcopal Canon for Brooklyn, New York, in the 1920s, Chase praised the KKK as a group "organized to resist the corruption of politics and the lawlessness of our times."

Cole, Arthur

—Media reports described Cole as chairman of the NSRP in 1958. That winter, he was summoned from his home in LaFollette, Tennessee, to testify as a character witness for party member and accused synagogue bomber George Bright in Atlanta, Georgia.

Collin, Frank

—Leaders of the NSWPP expelled Collin in 1970, after discovering his Jewish ancestry. (FBI agents later claimed credit for the leak, as part of their COINTELPRO campaign against white-supremacist groups.) Collin founded his own NSPA in Chicago before year's end, largely ignored until 1977, when he sought permission to march through suburban Skokie, a neighborhood populated by Holocaust survivors. Court orders banned the march, but Collin still reaped international publicity, including a made-for-TV movie starring Danny Kaye. A 1980 conviction for child-molestation finally removed Collin from the neo–Nazi movement.

Corley, Luther King

—An early member of the NSRP in Atlanta, Georgia, Corley was jailed in July 1958 while picketing the Atlanta *Journal and Constitution,* and again three months later on suspicion of bombing a local synagogue. The latter charge was dismissed after jurors acquitted co-defendant George Bright, in January 1959.

Cotter, Richard J.

—The racist fringe draws support from some unusual benefactors, but none more surprising than Harvard-educated lawyer Richard Cotter, once a friend of JFK and assistant attorney general of Massachusetts. When Cotter died a millionaire in 1999, his will included bequests of $500,000 to James Warner's New Christian Crusade Church, $100,000 to imprisoned Canadian Holocaust–denial spokesman Ernst Zundel, $25,000 to William Pierce's National Alliance, and $25,000 to a group of Massachusetts anti–Semites, the Polish Freedom Fighters. Executor Donald Smith, who challenged the bequests, told reporters, "I always knew [Cotter] was a conservative guy, but not someone who thought the world would have been a better place had Hitler won the war."

Coughlin, Charles

—Born 25 October 1891, Father Charles Coughlin served throughout the 1920s and 1930s as pastor of a Catholic church, the Shrine of the Little Flower, in Royal Oak, Michigan. Klansmen burned a cross outside his church in 1926, prompting Coughlin's first radio broadcast with a plea for religious tolerance. He proved so popular on-air that many other stations soon picked up his program, but the nature of Coughlin's message changed radically during the Great Depression. After endorsing FDR for president in 1932, with the slogan "Roosevelt or ruin," Coughlin turned against the New Deal with a vengeance three years later. By 1936, Coughlin praised Adolf Hitler and Benito Mussolini as the fascist antidote to Bolshevism, seasoning his rants with strong doses of anti–Semitism. In addition to his radio broadcasts, Coughlin published a newspaper (*Social Justice*) that headlined excerpts from the fraudulent *Protocols of the Elders of Zion* and other anti–Semitic broadsides. At the same time, Coughlin supported a paramilitary Christian Front which claimed him as an inspiration (while admitting klansmen and Nazi admirers to its ranks). On 18 December 1938, 2,000 CF members marched through New York City, protesting new political asylum legislation and demanding that the government "send Jews back where they came from in leaky boats." In January 1940, FBI agents jailed CF leaders on sedition charges, claiming that they planned to overthrow the U.S. government and establish "a dictatorship similar to the Hitler dictatorship in Germany." After the raids, Coughlin defiantly addressed the nation and FBI Director J. Edgar Hoover, proclaiming that "the real Christians of this nation will not beat a retreat." In 1942, Catholic officials ordered Coughlin to cease his radio tirades and focus on his duties as a parish priest. At the same time, the U.S. Postmaster-General banned *Social Justice* from the mails. Thus effectively silenced, Coughlin faded from public view and died in obscurity on 27 October 1979.

Covington, Harold

—A resident of Raleigh, North Carolina, affiliated with the NSPA, Covington identified several of his members as participants in the deadly Greensboro shooting of 3 November 1979. In 1980, he replaced convicted child-molester Frank Collin as head of the NSPA and in April of that year he sponsored a joint KKK/NSPA "Hitlerfest" at Benson, North Carolina, celebrating the late Führer's birthday. The same year witnesses Covington's campaign for the state attorney general's office, polling 5,400 votes in November. Covington resigned from the NSPA in April 1981, was replaced by Michael Allen, then resurfaced in 1994 to lead a new organization, borrowing its NSWPP title from Matt Koehl's defunct group. By 1996, Covington had an active Internet website, broadcasting hate worldwide, and while the NSWPP disbanded in 1999, Covington remained active in cyberspace at press time for this book.

Cowan, Frederick—A resident of New Rochelle, New York, and member of the NSRP, Cowan was an ardent body-builder and gun collector who decorated his apartment with Nazi posters, once telling a friend, "I should have been born forty years ago, so that I could have been in the SS." Employed at a local moving company, Cowan quarreled with his Jewish supervisor and was suspended from work in February 1977. On 14 February he came to work with a rifle and two pistols, intent on killing the foreman, but his target was absent that day. Instead, Cowan murdered three black employees and an Indian immigrant, then wounded a policeman as officers rushed to the scene. Surrounded by 300 officers and FBI agents, Cowan then shot himself. From NSRP headquarters, J.B. Stoner told reporters, "The FBI caused niggers to start harassing Cowan on the job. Apparently the FBI's to blame for the whole incident."

Crommelin, John—One of five brothers who served the U.S. Navy with distinction during World War II, Crommelin rose to the rank of rear admiral before he was forced to resign in 1950, following public disputes with the Air Force leaders. Thereafter, he retired to Montgomery, Alabama, and devoted his life to racist causes, including long-term collaboration with professional anti–Semites Conde McGinley and Gerald L.K. Smith. Defeated in four campaigns for the U.S. Senate (1950, 1954, 1956 and 1960), Crommelin also ran for mayor of Montgomery (1959), for governor of Alabama (1958 and 1962), and for Vice President of the United States (on the NSRP ticket, in 1960). His campaign speeches consisted primarily of tirades against blacks and Jews, including the observation that "ninety percent of Jews are Mongoloids; that's why they're particular to Asiatic communism." (Crommelin also coined the term "Jew-latto," in support of his belief that Jews are really black.) In 1955, Crommelin launched a petition drive seeking ten million signatures to protest the censure of Sen. Joseph McCarthy. A year later, while addressing Asa Carter's North Alabama Citizens' Council, Crommelin met John Kasper and welcomed the New Yorker aboard for his latest senatorial campaign. Crommelin accompanied Kasper several times to Clinton, Tennessee, and later appeared as a defense witness at Kasper's trial for inciting race riots there. His testimony failed to sway jurors, but Crommelin was on hand to welcome Kasper on his release from federal prison, in 1957. FBI agents questioned Crommelin as a potential suspect in October 1958, after NSRP members bombed an Atlanta synagogue. Crommelin's 1962 campaign manager, Oren

Potito, later served as an NSRP recruiter in Florida. In September 1963, shortly before a Klan church bombing killed four girls in Birmingham, Crommelin visited that city for a covert meeting with KKK associates Sidney Barnes and William Potter Gale (himself a "closet" Jew). Undaunted by age, Crommelin emerged as regional director of James Warner's Christian Defense League in 1971, then resurfaced in 1977 as an editor of David Duke's Klan newspaper, *The Crusader*. In the 1980s, Crommelin fielded correspondence for Duke's various political campaigns, assuring concerned anti–Semites that Duke was "O.K." on the "Jewish question," despite his public façade of moderation. During the same period, Crommelin served on the advisory board of William Pierce's neo–Nazi National Alliance. Crommelin died in 1997.

Croom, Henry—A member of the CUG in Reconstruction-era Alamance County, North Carolina, Croom traded whiskey to his fellow racists in return for raw corn and armed protection for his still. In August 1869, prosecutors indicted Croom and twenty-four other CUG terrorists for murder.

Crump, Richard P.—A prominent resident of Reconstruction-era Jefferson County, Texas, Crump was also an early member of the Knights of the Rising Sun. He led the party that tried to murder George Smith on 3 October 1868, then had Smith arrested for assault when Smith fired back at the mob in self-defense. After Smith's subsequent lynching, prosecutors charged Crump and three other KRS members with murder, but jurors acquitted all four.

Culbert, James J.—An associate of the Pennsylvania Klan from St. Claire, Culbert faced criminal charges on 1 March 1974 for receiving, selling and disposing of stolen explosives. Co-defendants in that case included Grand Dragon Roy Frankhouser and Thomas Kanger.

Cutler, Bud—Cutler served as security chief of the Aryan Nations at Hayden Lake, Idaho, until August 1985, when he offered an undercover policeman $1,800 to arrange the decapitation-slaying of suspected FBI informant Thomas Martinez (a member of The Order). David Dorr filled Cutler's post after Cutler's conviction.

Daniels, H.E. ("Dan")—Daniels served as a colonel in the U.S. Army's military police and saw action in the Korean War before retiring to civilian law enforcement. He served as sheriff of Polk County, Florida, in 1985–87, but his elective four-year term ended abruptly after a grand jury aired various misconduct charges. Daniels escaped prosecution and soon "came out swinging" for the white-supremacist cause, publishing a monthly tabloid (*The Eagle*) that vilified blacks, gays, Jews and mainstream politicians. In the 1990s, Daniels emerged as second-in-command (behind Paul Allen) of David Duke's NAAWP in Florida. That group denied links to the KKK, but Daniels sank that lie in 1997, when he hosted a joint meeting of klansmen, neo–Nazis and NAAWP members at his ranch near Auburndale. Attendees included Don Black, Thom Robb, Hans Schmidt of the German-American Political Action Committee, and a contingent from the National Alliance. ABC's *Prime Time Live* documented the rally, producing a rancorous split in the ranks of the NAAWP. Undaunted by the exposure, Daniels later told a *Wall Street Journal* reporter: "Americans had better get used to Trade Center–like bombing and Okie City.... They're only the tip of the iceberg. People are fighting back against government." Daniels died in 2003 and was honored with a full-dress police funeral, including a twenty-one-gun salute.

Davis, Philip—A Tulsa, Oklahoma, attorney and associate of Gerald L.K. Smith, Davis visited Atlanta in 1946 to defend indicted members of the Columbians.

Deatherage, George—A resident of St. Albans, West Virginia, and an engineer by profession, Deatherage was a klansman prior to 1934, when he left to revive the KWC. A proponent of "constitutional fascism," Deatherage openly affiliated his KWC with Nazi propagandists from Germany and Britain, suggesting a switch from burning crosses to fiery swastikas that would strike "terror and fear into the hearts of many." (Deatherage also claimed that Adolf Hitler's Nazis had copied their anti–Semitic beliefs and stiff-armed salute from the KKK.) By 1936, as founder of the American Nationalist Foundation, Deatherage entertained U.S. Army officers at his home, touting the virtues of a fascist revolution, and writing speeches for Georgia anti–Semite George Van Horn Moseley. In 1937, Deatherage and his military cohorts corresponded directly with German agents, a circumstance that prompted his sedition indictment in January 1943. That case, involving thirty-three alleged conspirators, ended with a mistrial in November 1943. Deatherage maintained his Klan ties as late as 1960, appearing as a guest speaker before the UFKKK's Duval Fellowship Club in Jacksonville.

DeBlanc, Alcibiade—A veteran of the Confederate army, DeBlanc was founding member of the KWC in St. Mary's Parish, Louisiana, in May 1867. Historians also regard him as the order's probable grand commander, although he never publicly acknowledged service in that role.

DePugh, Robert Bolivar—A native of Independence, Missouri, born in 1923, DePugh graduated from high school in 1941, then served in the U.S. Army until 1944, when he was discharged on medical grounds. In 1952, he ran for Congress in Missouri, finishing fourth in a field of five candidates. Turning from politics to chemistry, DePugh then founded Biolab Corporation, a drug manufacturing firm, and moved his home-office to Norborne, Missouri, in 1960. Around that same time, he organized the Minutemen, a paramilitary anti-communist group that prefigured the "patriot militias" of the 1990s. The group made its first headlines in October 1961, with a guerrilla warfare seminar conducted at Shiloh, Illinois. In the mid–1960s, DePugh met several times with UKA Wizard Robert Shelton to discuss formation of a right-wing underground network, but nothing came of the plan. In 1966, DePugh publicly opened his ranks to klansmen; American Nazis were also welcome, provided they acknowledged the ANP's "ideological errors." (ANP founder George Rockwell complained that DePugh had "stolen" three of his party's chief financial backers.) DePugh himself fled underground in February 1968, following his indictment with

seven other Minutemen on federal charges of plotting to rob banks in Seattle, Washington. Prior to his June 1969 capture in New Mexico, DePugh issued political appeals on behalf of presidential candidate George Wallace. In July 1969, DePugh received an eleven-year prison term for bail-jumping and violating federal firearms laws.

While imprisoned, DePugh lent his name to the National Association to Keep and Bear Arms, a right-wing consortium of gun-control opponents that included Robert Shelton on its board of directors. Paroled in May 1973, DePugh replaced the defunct Minutemen with a new Patriots Inter-Organizational Communications Center staffed by members of various far-right groups, serving as a national information clearinghouse for the political fringe. In 1975, at one of DePugh's annual Patriot's Leadership Conferences in Kansas City, he met with Shelton, David Duke, James Warner and others to plot strategies for the future. One result was DePugh's Committee of Ten Million, created in 1978 and headquartered at Independence, Missouri, with nationwide chapters financially supporting appearances by Shelton and DePugh. In December 1980, DePugh came full-circle with announcements of plans for a paramilitary training seminar.

Dixon, Thomas, Jr.—A native of North Carolina, born in 1864, Dixon was a classmate of future President Woodrow Wil-

Thomas Dixon's racist novels, filmed as *The Birth of a Nation*, inspired the 1915 Klan revival.

son at Johns Hopkins University. Elected to the North Carolina state legislature before he reached voting age, Dixon soon resigned his post to enter the Baptist ministry with financial backing from oil tycoon John D. Rockefeller. He subsequently published three novels about Reconstruction—*The Leopard's Spots* (1902), *The Clansman* (1905) and *The Traitor* (1907)—which idealized the original Klan (and introduced the practice of cross-burning, unknown to real-life klansmen before 1915). The novels proved so popular that Dixon turned *The Clansman* into a traveling stage play, starring in the production himself. In April 1914, he sold screen rights to *The Clansman* for $2,500 and one-fourth of the movie's profits. Director D.W. Griffith filmed the story in 1915 and released it as *The Birth of a Nation*, a title suggested by Dixon after a preview screening in New York City. When critics panned the film, Dixon persuaded President Wilson and Chief Justice Edward White of the U.S. Supreme Court to offer public endorsements, thus clearing the way for its national release. Initially proud of the new Klan chartered by William Simmons in 1915, Dixon changed his tune after media reports exposed KKK corruption and violence in 1922. Disillusioned, he told an interviewer, "There can be but one end to a secret order of disguised men. It will grow eventually into a reign of terror which only martial law will be able to put down."

Dorr, David—Ben Cutler's replacement as security chief of the Aryan Nations in 1985, Dorr received prison time of his own a year later, convicted in a series of bombings around Coeur d'Alene, Idaho.

Drennan, Dr. Stanley L.—Identified as a 1960s leader of the NSRP in North Hollywood, California, Drennan was active with Capt. Robert Brown and others in covert campaigns against Cuba's Fidel Castro. According to FBI files, Drennan told Brown that "what the organization needed was a group of young men to get rid of [President John] Kennedy, the Cabinet, and all the members of the Americans for Democratic Action, and maybe 10,000 other people." Brown told G-men that he had "gained the impression that Drennan may have been propositioning him on this matter." Members of the Warren Commission ignored this and other leads to the racist right in their investigation of the JFK assassination.

Dunn, Edward—Identified in media reports as co-chairman of Michigan's S.S. Action Group, Dunn collaborated with the KKK in demonstrations around Detroit and elsewhere. With other SSAG members, he also attended cross-burning ceremonies at the Mountain Church of Jesus Christ, run by klansman Robert Miles at Cohoctah, Michigan.

Dupes, Ned—Media reports from 1962 identified Dupes as secretary-treasurer of the NSRP, residing in Knoxville, Tennessee.

Ellison, James—A Texas native, born in 1940, Ellison moved to Arkansas in 1971, establishing a religious retreat called Zarephaph-Horeb in Marion County. Dubbed the "King James of the Ozarks," Ellison was a leading spokesman of the Christian Identity movement in the 1970s and early 1980s. He founded the CSA in 1976 and kept two wives at the group's

fortified compound, where machine shops churned out illegal automatic weapons and explosive devices for various extremist allies. (Ellison termed his encampment "an arms depot and paramilitary training ground for Aryan Warriors.") Inspired by his association with The Order in 1983, Ellison launched a guerrilla war of his own on 9 August 1983, when he drove to Springfield, Missouri, with accomplice William Thomas and burned a church that ministered to gays. Six days later, acting on Ellison's orders to "rob something," Thomas and three other members firebombed a Jewish community center in Bloomington, Indiana. Other raids included the bungled bombing of a natural gas pipeline near Fulton, Arkansas (2 November), and the robbery of a Texarkana pawn shop (11 November) where CSA gunman Richard Snell killed the proprietor, after mistaking him for a Jew. Federal agents tracking members of The Order raided Ellison's compound in April 1985, slapping Ellison and five disciples with a twenty-count indictment. All six pled guilty in August 1985, with Ellison receiving a five-year prison term. Additional indictments persuaded Ellison to turn state's evidence against his comrades, appearing as a prosecution witness when fourteen white-supremacist leaders faced trial for sedition in 1988. Jurors acquitted all fourteen, leaving Ellison to serve his time alone, divorced by his two wives. Paroled in 1991, he settled at Elohim City, Oklahoma, and married one of patriarch Robert Millar's granddaughters.

Emry, Sheldon—A native of Minneapolis, Minnesota, Emry first drew public attention in 1962, as chairman of the Twin Cities Committee to Warn of the Arrival of Communist Merchandise on the Local Business Scene. Transplanted to Arizona in the mid–1960s, Emry founded the Lord's Covenant Church, considered an integral part of the Christian Identity movement. In addition to his church activities and broadcasts of the *America's Promise* radio program, Emry also linked with the Citizens Emergency Defense System, created by John Harrell, co-founder of the Christian-Patriots Defense League.

Euliss, Eli—A leader of the CUG in Reconstruction-era Alamance County, North Carolina, Euliss retained his friendship with Republican state senator T.M. Shoffner when Shoffner became a target for racist assassins. In December 1869, Euliss learned of a Klan plot against Shoffner's life, helping Shoffner escape from the county alive.

Forbes, Ralph P.—As a member of George Rockwell's ANP, Forbes picketed screenings of *Exodus* in 1961 and had his nose bloodied a year later, while marching outside the White House with anti–Semitic placards. Moving to California in 1963, he won promotion to the rank of captain, but his recruiting efforts proved ineffectual. Two decades later, Forbes emerged as a prime mover behind the Sword of Christ, a racist group based in London, Arkansas. His front group, the Shamrock Society, urged patriots to "Kick the Jew Habit" at Christmas by spending their money on anti–Semitic literature, tapes, and membership in "God's White Army"—led, of course, by Forbes. In 1988, Forbes served as manager for David Duke's presidential campaign. Two years later, Forbes himself was on the ballot, winning a surprise upset victory in the Arkansas lieutenant governor's primary race (but losing the November general election).

Fry, Leslie—Mystery surrounds Leslie Fry (née Paquita de Shishmareff), a conspiracy theorist and anti-Semite of uncertain nationality who allegedly helped Henry Ford produce *The International Jew*. Emerging as a major Nazi propagandist during the Great Depression, Fry once offered Wizard Hiram Evans $75,000 for ownership of the KKK. (Evans declined.) After Pearl Harbor, Fry escaped to Germany before prosecutors could place her on trial for sedition. No record of her fate survives.

Gale, William Potter—Born to Jewish parents in St. Paul, Minnesota, on 20 November 1916, Gale moved with his family to Monterey, California, in 1922. He joined the U.S. Army after high school, in 1934, was discharged in June 1937, then rejoined in 1941 and was medically discharged as a lieutenant colonel in 1949. Gale subsequently lied about his final rank (describing himself as a full colonel) and about his nonexistent combat wounds (his discharge indicates disability due to hepatitis). In 1953, Gale embraced the racist tenants of Christian Identity, converted by klansmen Wesley Swift and San Jacinto Capt, with help from an anti-Semitic Catholic priest known only as Father Eustace. In 1960, recruiting from veterans' groups, Gale founded the paramilitary California Rangers, instructing his troops that communists were tools of "the international Jewish conspiracy. You got your nigger Jews, you got your Asiatic Jews, and you got your white Jews. They're all Jews, and they're all the offspring of the devil. Turn a nigger inside out and you've got a Jew."

During 1960–61, Gale was allegedly involved with members of the KKK and NSRP in CIA-sponsored guerrilla activities against Fidel Castro in Cuba. In September 1963, shortly before the deadly bombing of Birmingham's Sixteenth Street Baptist Church, Gale visited that embattled Alabama city for meetings with longtime anti-Semite John Crommelin and klansman Sidney Barnes. A month later, on 15 October, he addressed a private gathering at the William Penn Hotel in Whittier, California, where the audience included Klan agitator Charles "Connie" Lynch and at least two police informants. Gale diversified in 1964, founding the Ministry of Christ Church with a paramilitary arm he called the Christian Defense League. That same year, Gale's son reported finding a Klan robe in his father's closet. Gale ran for governor of California in 1966, but won only a handful of votes. In 1969, Gale launched his best-known vehicle, the United Christian Posse Association, which in turn served as the model for nationwide chapters of the militant Posse Comitatus. A typical "sermon" to Posse members included this warning: "If the Jews ever fool around with us, or try to harm us in any way, every rabbi in Los Angeles will die within twenty-four hours. Let 'em start."

In April 1972, Gale addressed a Los Angeles rally of James Warner's New Christian Crusade Church on the topic of "How to Survive the Coming Anti-Christian Bloodbath." Eight years later, the Aryan Nations newsletter named Gale one of "our Aryan Racial Comrades in the battle for the Resurrection of our Nation." In March 1982, Gale served as an instructor at a Posse Comitatus training camp near Weskan, Kansas, afterward

founding a new Committee of the States to promote his radical philosophy. In 1984, Gale's latest group issued a fifteen-point "Declaration of Alteration and Reform" (signed by Richard Butler and several members of the Arizona Patriots), demanding immediate repeal of the federal income tax, followed by mass resignation of all U.S. legislators. On 23 October 1986, federal prosecutors indicted Gale and seven others on charges of conspiracy, interfering with federal tax laws, and mailing death threats to IRS agents. Three defendants turned state's evidence against their comrades, while jurors convicted Gale and four others on 2 October 1987. Gale received three concurrent one-year sentences and died in prison on 28 April 1988.

Garland, William H.—A member of Wesley Swift's Christian Defense League in Cucamonga, California, Garland was jailed in 1964 when police raided his home, seizing eight machine guns, plus several incendiary bombs and blasting caps. Garland told authorities he had stockpiled the illegal weapons to repel "invaders."

Garvey, Marcus—An early black separatist and founder of the Universal Negro Improvement Association, Garvey drew praise from 1920s Klan leaders for his attempts to repatriate American blacks to Africa. Garvey took advantage of the KKK's support, fraternizing with Edward Clarke and other klansmen in a tenuous alliance, while simultaneously citing Klan violence as a reason why blacks should leave the United States. Black historian W.E.B. DuBois explains: "Garvey's motives were clear. The triumph of the Klan would drive Negroes to his program in despair." When black leaders pressured President Calvin Coolidge to denounce the KKK, Garvey wired Coolidge a promise of "the full sympathy of 4 million of our organization in your refusal to be drawn into the Ku Klux controversy." In 1923, federal prosecutors convicted Garvey of mail fraud, resulting in a five-year prison term. Coolidge pardoned Garvey in 1927, whereupon he was deported to his native Jamaica as an undesirable alien.

Gayman, Daniel—Born in 1937, Gayman served as a high school principal before deserting public education to join the family business, publicly known as the Church of Israel. Founded by Gayman's father and other dissident Mormons in the 1930s, relocated to Missouri in 1941, the church evolved into a pillar of the Christian Identity movement by the early 1970s, with Klan leader Thom Robb on its board of directors. During 1973–76, Gayman served as a spokesman for Buddy Tucker's National Emancipation of Our White Seed, assisting with publication of Tucker's newsletter, *The Battle Axe News*. During the same period, Gayman appeared as a featured speaker for Aryan Nations rallies at Hayden Lake, Idaho. In the early 1980s, he collaborated with neo-Nazi leaders Richard Butler (Aryan Nations), John Harrell (Christian-Patriots Defense League) and Gordon Mohr (Citizens Emergency Defense System) to establish a network of far-right paramilitary training centers throughout the United States. In 1987, a federal grand jury named Gayman as the recipient of $10,000 in bank loot stolen by The Order, but he escaped indictment on sedition charges by turning state's evidence against his racist colleagues (all of whom were acquitted in April 1988). Gayman subsequently denounced violence as incompatible with the tenants of Christian Identity, a stand which placed him at odds with most spokesmen for the cult. SPLC investigators found his church active at Schell City, Missouri, through 2003, but it failed to appear on the 2004 census of U.S. hate groups.

Gibson, Leroy—A twenty-year veteran of the U.S. Marine Corps, Gibson was identified in October 1971 as leader of a militant racist group, the Rights of White People, in Wilmington, North Carolina. A resident of Jacksonville, some fifty miles distant, Gibson told reporters that his RWP was prepared to deal forcefully with the "communist-inspired black revolutionaries" he blamed for recent race riots. He further explained, "Our organization is growing, and not just in the South. If necessary, we'll eliminate the black race. What are we supposed to do while these animals run loose in the streets? They'll either abide by the law, or we'll wipe them out." In May 1973, Wilmington police jailed Gibson for bombing a bookstore.

Gilbert, Keith—Born in 1939, Keith Gilbert served prison time for threatening to murder Dr. Martin Luther King in the 1960s, then resurfaced in Idaho as an aide to Aryan Nations chief Richard Butler before founding his own Social Nationalist Aryan People's Party in 1979. In 1982, he launched a year-long campaign of harassment against the children of Kootenai County resident Connie Fort, whose ex-husbands were black and Native American. The war of nerves included hate mail, death threats, personal confrontations, and one attempt by Gilbert to strike the children with his car. In 1983, when Cleveland serial killer Frank Spisak murdered two blacks and a man his mistook for a Jew, Gilbert claimed Spisak was "acting under direct orders from the party." Gilbert served more time for his attack on Fort's children, but it taught him nothing. In 2004, Gilbert and cohort William Heinrich allegedly sold automatic rifles to an ATF informant, prompting their arrest on 15 February 2005. Both men were charged as convicted felons illegally possessing firearms. Trial in that case was pending at press time for this volume.

Gliebe, Erich J.—A resident of Cleveland, Ohio, born in 1963, Gliebe once boxed professionally as "the Aryan Barbarian." He subsequently joined William Pierce's National Alliance, staging "European-American cultural festivals" to lure new recruits, while boosting sales of white-power music through the NA's Resistance Records. Six days after Pierce's death, in July 2002, the NA board chose Gliebe to take his place as leader. He soon fired energetic spokesman Billy Roper and moved on to alienate other racist leaders, whom he dubbed "morons," "hobbyists," and dwellers in "the make-believe world otherwise known as 'the movement.'"

Goff, Oliver Kenneth—An active member of the CPUSA during the 1930s, Goff recanted his communist ties before HUAC in 1939 and later claimed that his testimony "aided in removing 169 communists from the federal payrolls." An instant convert to right-wing extremism, Goff added anti-Semitism to his repertoire in 1944, when he served as national chairman of Gerald L.K. Smith's Christian Youth for America.

In later years, he claimed authorship of twenty-eight books, countless tracts, and two extremist periodicals: *The Pilgrim Torch* (1962–67) and *Christian Battle Cry* (1966–71). In *Hitler and the Twentieth Century Hoax* (1954), Goff argued that Der Führer was a closet communist (and probably a Jew) who launched World War II to benefit the Kremlin. In later life, Goff ran the Soldiers of the Cross Training Institute, a seminary of sorts for would-be Christian Identity ministers (including graduate Dan Gayman), also linked in police reports to Robert DePugh's Minutemen.

Griffin, Kenneth Chester—Identified as Georgia state chairman of the NSRP in 1958, Griffin was one of four party members jailed for picketing the *Atlanta Journal and Constitution* in July of that year. Three months later, authorities indicted him as a suspect in the bombing of an Atlanta synagogue. Charges in that case were dismissed after jurors acquitted codefendant George Bright in January 1959.

Grimstad, William N.—A professional anti–Semite who once registered as a foreign agent for Saudi Arabia, Grimstad launched his career on the lunatic fringe by joining the NSWPP in 1971. Within a year, he rose to serve as managing editor for the party's *White Power* newspaper. By 1977, Grimstad had published numerous anti–Semitic books and articles, including one detailing the "Zionist myth" of the Holocaust. In 1979, he joined David Duke's KKKK as corresponding editor for *The Crusader*.

Hale, Matthew F.—A native of East Peoria, Illinois, born 27 July 1971, Hale describes himself as a committed racist since age twelve, when he felt repulsed by the sight of an interracial couple kissing. Study of *Mein Kampf* expanded his prejudice to include anti–Semitism, prompting Hale to attempt creation of a "New Reich" gang in high school. That effort and his bid to organize a White Student Union at East Peoria's Bradley University proved futile, but Hale logged his first arrest at age nineteen, for burning an Israeli flag in violation of a local ordinance. A year later, he was fined for littering after he dumped piles of racist literature at a shopping mall. In 1990, Hale organized the American White Supremacist Party. A year later, he switched allegiance to the NAAWP, led by David Duke (whom Hale described as "the greatest politician that this country may have ever seen.") In May 1991, Hale and his brother allegedly threatened three blacks with a gun. Police jailed him for mob action, then added a charge of obstructing justice when Hale refused to name his accomplice. Hale was convicted at trial, but won reversal of the verdict on appeal. In 1992, Hale named himself "national leader" of a new hate group, the National Socialist White Americans Party, and faced new criminal charges for attacking a mall security guard. Convicted in that case, he received a sentence of six months house arrest and thirty months "intensive" probation.

The year 1993 brought Hale's first success, in the form of graduation from Bradley University (B.A. in political science). Two years later, while studying at Southern Illinois Law School, he ran for a seat on East Peoria's city council as an avowed white supremacist, receiving fourteen percent of the vote. Before year's end, Hale took command of Ben Klassen's neo–Nazi Church of the Creator, using his authority as "Pontifex Maximus" to transfer cult headquarters from North Carolina to East Peoria. In 1996, he changed the sect's name to World Church of the Creator, using the Internet and public demonstrations to establish ninety-two chapters in thirty states by 2001. In 1997, Hale married Terra Herron, a sixteen-year-old WCOTC member, but they separated three months later. Hale earned his LL.B. in May 1998 and passed the bar exam two months later, but the Illinois Bar Committee on Character and Fitness rejected his application to practice law on 16 December 1998, citing "gross deficiency in moral character." Hale's appeal of that decision was rejected on 30 June 1999, making him a martyr of sorts for the neo–Nazi movement. Infuriated by that ruling, "Creator of the Year" Benjamin Smith launched a shooting spree on 4 July 1999, killing two persons and wounding nine others in Illinois and Indiana, then committing suicide. (The Montana state bar subsequently rejected Hale's application, in 2001.)

More legal problems in 2000, when members of the Te-Ta-Ma Truth Foundation sued Hale and the WCOTC for trademark infringement. The plaintiffs won that case, persuading Judge Joan Lefkow that they had registered the "Church of the Creator" name years earlier. In November 2002, Lefkow ordered Hale to change his cult's name, give up its Web address, and surrender all printed material bearing the illicit name. Hale refused to comply, and approached an FBI informant with a plan to kill Judge Lefkow. In January 2003, when Hale appeared in court for a contempt hearing, G-men arrested him for soliciting the murder of a federal judge. Jurors convicted him at trial, and he received a forty-year prison term on 6 April 2005. In his absence, the renamed Creativity Movement operates from headquarters in Springfield, Missouri, claiming fifteen satellite chapters in thirteen states.

Hand, Karl, Jr.—A member of David Duke's KKKK, Hand was one of three knights indicted in February 1980, for firing shots into the home of Joseph and Shirley Sanders, a black couple in Barnegat Township, New Jersey. Hand pled innocent to the charges in March, then fled underground to avoid prosecution. While hiding from the law, he attempted suicide by drinking antifreeze, thereafter spending several months in various hospitals. In January 1981, Hand pled guilty to attempted bodily harm, with sentencing deferred until April. In the meantime, he quit the Klan and joined the NSPA, planning a neo-Nazi rally in Buffalo, New York, on 15 January 1981, to "celebrate" Martin Luther King's birthday. In February 1981, Hand switched allegiance once more, defecting from the NSPA to lead the NSLF, after current chief David Russ was imprisoned on firearms charges. Two months later, Hand received a six-month jail term for the New Jersey shooting, with three months suspended and two years' probation. Free on bond pending appeal, Hand moved to Metairie, Louisiana, proclaiming the NSLF "a revolutionary movement that has repudiated mass tactics and has instead embraced armed struggle and political terrorism." An appellate court rejected Hand's appeal in October 1982, and he surrendered to begin serving his three-month sentence in April 1983. A subsequent conviction for attempted murder and weapons charges sent him back to prison for fifteen years, effectively ending Hand's career in the neo–Nazi movement.

Hanes, Arthur J., Sr.—A native of Birmingham, Alabama, and son of a Methodist minister, born 19 October 1916, Hanes played semi-pro baseball and studied law before joining the FBI in the 1940s. He served the Bureau in Chicago and in Washington, D.C., before a hometown offer brought him back to Birmingham as security chief for Hayes Aircraft Corporation. Following "Black Monday," Hanes filled his spare time with speaking engagements for Asa Carter's North Alabama Citizens' Council and tirelessly supported Bull Connor's effort to regain office as Birmingham's commissioner of public safety in 1957. Connor repaid that favor in early 1961, hand-picking Hanes to run for mayor when incumbent Jimmy Morgan retired. On 2 May 1961, Hanes trailed primary opponent Tom King by 1,500 ballots, immediately buying TV time to inform local whites that King had carried most of Birmingham's black votes. Behind the scenes, Connor enlisted Klan support for Hanes, with the result that Hanes beat King by 3,748 on their 30 May runoff. Between those contests, on 14 May, Birmingham was rocked by Ku Klux riots against CORE's integrated freedom riders, organized with Connor's complicity. When a civic group approached mayor-elect Hanes, seeking his assurance that no further violence would occur, Hanes replied, "Well, before I can promise you anything, I've got to check with Bull."

Indeed, Klan violence escalated during Hanes's tenure as mayor (1961–63), and declassified FBI files describe Hanes as "a very strong supporter" of Connor's brutality against SPLC demonstrators. When Birmingham moderates negotiated a desegregation agreement in 1963, Hanes complained, "These traitors have sold their birthright to negotiate with these niggers." In August 1965, after UKA Imperial Klonsel Matt Murphy died in a car crash, Hanes served as one of Murphy's pallbearers, then assumed the legal defense of three klansmen who murdered civil rights worker Viola Liuzzo. In his summation at the trial of Collie Wilkins, Hanes told jurors, "Maybe the murderer is from the Watts area of Los Angeles or over in Crawfordville, Georgia, trying to produce a body to raise money for their nefarious schemes." Hanes publicly denied any link to the KKK, telling reporters, "I was hired by these boys, but as far as I know, the Klan has nothing to do with paying me." FBI headquarters, meanwhile, felt differently. A memo from J. Edgar Hoover, dated 20 June 1968, described Hanes as "no good" and "a fellow who certainly has a very strong smell of the Klan about him."

By the time Hoover penned that memo, Hanes had been hired to represent James Earl Ray, the alleged assassin of Dr. Martin Luther King, Jr. Midwestern Klan leader George Wilson later claimed that Hanes received a $10,000 retainer from the UKA in that case, though no evidence survives to support the allegation. Congressional investigators documented two meetings between Hanes and UKA Wizard Robert Shelton in June and August 1968, but their topics of discussion remain uncertain. In 1969, Hanes attended a meeting of the UKA's imperial board, led by acting wizard Melvin Sexton, where Klan leaders discussed his $12,500 fee for defending klansmen jailed in North Carolina. In 1977, Hanes (and son Arthur Jr.) defended klansman Robert Chambliss at his murder trial, for the September 1963 bombing of Birmingham's Sixteenth Street Baptist Church. Hanes died on 8 May 1997.

Harrell, John R.—As leader of the Christian-Patriot Defense League, Harrell participated in May 1978 UKA rallies in Orlando and Plant City, Florida.

Hensley, Don—Media reports from 1958 identified Hensley as Tennessee state chairman of the NSRP.

Hunt, Harold Wheeler—An elderly anti–Semite associated with the Aryan Nations at Hayden Lake, Idaho, Hunt publicly advocated violence to rid America of Jews. In 1980, as publisher of the twice-weekly *National Chronicle,* he told an interviewer that his 1,400 subscribers "don't want a single sign of Jews or scum that's along with them on the earth. Everything buried."

Imperiale, Anthony—A native of Newark, New Jersey, born in 1931, Imperiale founded and led the vigilante North Ward Citizens' Committee during 1967–69. In June 1967, New Jersey's grand dragon told reporters that he had initiated Imperiale as a klansman on 19 April. Imperiale denied the assertion, but admitted teaching karate to various local klansmen. Imperiale ran unsuccessfully for mayor of Newark in 1970 and 1974, but enjoyed better success in legislative races. He served as a member of the New Jersey state assembly in 1972–74 and 1980–82, and spent one year in the state senate (1976) before voters turned him out. Imperiale's bid for governor failed in 1981. He died in Newark on 26 December 1999.

Jackson, Helen—A prime attraction on the 1920s lecture circuit, Jackson was one of several "escaped nuns" who delivered anti–Catholic speeches to klansmen and other credulous listeners. She had in fact escaped from a Catholic *reformatory* in Detroit, and her quest for revenge coupled with greed inspired Jackson's sermonettes on priestly debauchery. Jackson's "autobiography," *Convent Cruelties or My Life in the Convent: Awful Revelations* (1919), was a best-seller among klansmen, while her lectures were usually segregated by gender. Jackson regaled female audiences with details of a papal plot to brainwash their children in parochial schools, while men heard a more prurient version, complete with a display of small leather bags allegedly used for illegitimate newborns en route to a convent furnace. Not always well received, Jackson touched off riots in 1922, when her appearance at Brooklyn's First Baptist Church sparked the anger of neighborhood Catholics.

Jones, Robert Reynolds, Sr.—Alabama native Bob Jones, Sr., born in 1883, became a Sunday-school superintendent at age twelve and won ordination as a Methodist minister three years later. Jones never joined the modern KKK, but as a traveling evangelist in the 1920s he fraternized with klansmen, accepted their public cash donations, and endorsed Klan principles from his pulpit. On one occasion, at Andalusia, Alabama, hooded knights delivered $1,568 to Jones before a cheering audience. Later, at a revival in Dallas, Texas, klansmen circulated through his congregation with the following pamphlet:

> I am a Searchlight on a high tower.
> I run my relentless eye to and fro throughout the land; my piercing glance penetrates the brooding places of Iniquity. I plant my eyes and ears in the whispering Corridors of Crime.

> Whenever men gather furtively together, there am I, an austere and invisible Presence. I am the Recording Angel's Proxy.
> When I invade the fetid dens of Infamy there is a sudden scampering and squeaking as of rats forsaking a doomed ship.
> I am the haunting dread of the depraved and the hated Nemesis of the vicious.
> The foe of Vice, the friend of Innocence, the rod and staff of Law.
> I am—
> THE KU KLUX KLAN.

In 1927, Jones founded Bob Jones University at Greenville, South Carolina, long recognized as a stronghold of fundamentalist religion, far-right politics, and white-supremacist attitudes. Jones died in 1968, the same year grandson Bob Jones III published an interview describing blacks as Biblical descendants of Ham, ordained by God to fill the niche of a "servant's servant." As Jones explained, "a Negro is best when he serves at the table. When he does that, he's doing what he knows how to do best. And the Negroes who have ascended to positions in government, in education, that sort of thing, I think you'll find, by and large, have a strong strain of white blood in them." BJU's ban on black students and interracial dating cost the school its tax-exempt status before Bob Jones III reluctantly lifted the racist policies in March 2000. Even then, the university (which lacked accreditation as of press time for this volume) was renowned for its link to anti–Catholic organizations, including extremist fringe groups in Ireland. Stephen Jones, son of Bob III, assumed office as BJU's president in May 2005.

Kahl, Gordon—A North Dakota farmer, born in 1919, Kahl was decorated and twice wounded during World War II. Falling wheat prices left him bankrupt in the late 1960s, whereupon he blamed Jews for his losses and joined the radical Posse Comitatus, refusing to pay income taxes after a 1970 "religious conversion" convinced him that the IRS was "sinful." For nearly a decade, Kahl traveled the Midwest, lecturing right-wing audiences on the fine points of tax evasion and nuisance lawsuits against the federal government, taking time off for occasional guerrilla warfare training courses sponsored by the Posse. On 13 February 1983, federal marshals sought to arrest Kahl at his home near Medina, North Dakota, for violating probation on a tax-evasion conviction. The resultant shootout left two marshals dead and four persons wounded, while Kahl's son and another Posse member faced prison time on murder charges. Kahl escaped and fled to the fortified home of Posse members Leon and Norma Ginter, near Smithville, Arkansas. From that hideout, Kahl penned letters to the Aryan Nations, describing himself as a "Christian patriot." Authorities traced him to Smithville on 3 June 1983, sparking another battle wherein Kahl murdered Sheriff Gene Matthews. A smoke grenade hurled by one of the raiders detonated ammunition stored in the bunker, and Kahl died in the blast, thereby becoming an instant martyr for the right-wing lunatic fringe.

Kasper, Frederick John—A native of Camden, New Jersey, born in 1929, Kasper fell in love with the poetry of Ezra Pound while studying at New York's Columbia University. He absorbed Pound's anti–Semitism and convinced himself that Pound's commitment to a mental hospital constituted political martyrdom. ("I think it is important to realize," Kasper once told reporters, "that almost one hundred percent of psychiatric therapy is Jewish and that eighty percent of psychiatrists are Jewish.") Kasper met Alabama klansman Asa Carter in April 1956, while managing John Crommelin's unsuccessful race for the U.S. Senate. A month later, Kasper founded the Seaboard White Citizens' Council in Washington, D.C., distributing literature that embarrassed many "legitimate" Council leaders with its strident racism. On 23 August 1956, Kasper disrupted a meeting of the Virginia Council on Human Relations in Charlottesville, denouncing the panel members as "flat-chested highbrows" and warning them, "We of the Citizens' Council have declared war on you people. We're going to run you out of town." Meanwhile, supporters burned a cross outside the meeting hall, while Kasper logged his first arrest for distributing leaflets without a permit.

Leaving Virginia after his arrest, Kasper arrived in Clinton, Tennessee, on 25 August 1956. Local schools faced court-ordered integration, but Kasper sought to prevent it by fiery speeches calling for violent resistance. Jailed again on 27 August, he made bail the following day. Riots erupted on 29 August, with National Guardsmen and tanks dispatched to restore order. Jailed yet again for inciting the outbreak, Kasper remained in custody until 6 September. Upon release, he addressed a rally of Carter's North Alabama Citizens' Council, welcoming robed klansmen to the audience with the comment: "We need all the rabble rousers we can get. We want trouble and we want it everywhere we can get it." In that vein, Kasper called for "roving bands of fearless patriots" to stand alert, descending on any town threatened by imminent desegregation. Addressing a Warrior, Alabama, Klan rally on 6 October, Kasper shared the stage with Carter and klansman Kenneth Adams (jailed in April for assaulting singer Nat "King" Cole in Birmingham).

After a two-week trial in Clinton, jurors acquitted Kasper on 20 November 1956, to thunderous applause from the gallery. Two weeks later, police in Fairfax, Virginia, jailed Kasper for reckless driving. His January 1957 appearance in Florida, complete with cross-burnings and rumors of dynamite caches around Miami, spurred state legislators into action. Summoned before a special investigative committee in March, Kasper ruefully admitted dating black women when he lived in New York City. Still undaunted, he addressed a March 1957 Klan rally at Chiefland, Florida, urging the knights to support his "segregation gospel." Members of an audience at Inverness heard Kasper say, "God stamped ugliness on the face of the Jew for the same reason that He put rattlers on the snake." Kasper's antidote to liberal U.S. Supreme Court decisions included pleas to "hang the nine swine."

The Florida investigation soon produced a backlash, however. On 16 March 1957, speakers at a Cleveland, Tennessee, Klan rally branded Kasper a "troublemaker" for his actions at Clinton. Ace Carter told reporters that confessions of interracial dating "will about fix Kasper in the South," adding that he had warned Kasper "we didn't want him back in Alabama." Another segregationist declared: "When John Kasper crossed the Mason-Dixon Line, it set the cause of white supremacy back twenty years." John Crommelin bucked the tide when he told a Clin-

ton audience, "You may not see it, and I may not see it, but someday a statue will be erected on this courthouse lawn to John Kasper." The KKK disagreed, its members physically ejecting Kasper from a Clinton rally on 11 May 1957. Two months later, jurors convicted Kasper and six other defendants of violating a federal injunction against interference with school integration in Clinton. Nashville klansmen distributed pamphlets for Kasper on 4 August 1957, but police interrupted his speech for lack of proper permits. Kasper surfaced again on 28 August, to announce a campaign of harassment against thirteen black families whose children had enrolled in "white" schools, including a boast to reporters that targets were threatened with bombing and death. After bombers struck the Hattie Cotton School on 10 September, Nashville police jailed Kasper and twenty-six other suspects. Subsequent conviction on those charges earned him further jail time, and Kasper departed for prison in Florida that November, carrying a copy of *Mein Kampf.*

Paroled in August 1958, Kasper found a reception committee waiting for him at the prison gates, including Crommelin, Florida klansman Bill Hendrix, and future synagogue-bombing defendant George Bright. Integration was still a hot topic in Dixie, but Kasper had lost his edge. Hecklers outnumbered supporters at the Charlotte, North Carolina, courthouse on 1 September, and Kasper needed a police escort to escape in one piece. Belated riot charges from Nashville sent Kasper back to jail for six months in 1960, but he emerged from the lockup on 15 July with an NSRP escort, in a car festooned with "Kasper for President" stickers. Still, his White House race was put on hold while the party tried its luck with Orval Faubus and John Crommelin. In 1964, it was Kasper's turn, nominated for president with J.B. Stoner as his running mate, but the slate polled only 6,953 votes nationwide.

Kennedy, Jesse C.—A prosperous mill owner and leader of the CUG in Reconstruction-era Lenoir County, North Carolina, Kennedy was one of twenty-five terrorists indicted on murder and other charges in August 1869.

Kerr, Martin—A native of New Jersey, Kerr began his neo-Nazi career in high school, after reading a published interview with George Lincoln Rockwell. In the late 1960s and early 1970s, he served as a group leader for James Madole's NRP and edited the party's newsletter. While studying at Hofstra University on Long Island, Kerr received media coverage for displaying a Nazi flag in his dormitory window. Around the same time, he shifted allegiance from the NRP to Matt Koehl's NSWPP, inserting ads for both groups in the Hofstra campus newspaper. By 1976, Kerr served as an organizer for the NSWPP in Washington, D.C. Six years later, his distribution of neo–Nazi literature in Maryland prompted state legislators to consider a bill punishing purveyors of "defamatory material" with one year in jail and a $1,000 fine. (It failed to pass.) The attendant publicity earned Kerr a promotion to serve as national spokesman for the NSWPP, announcing Koehl's 1982 decision to relocate in Wisconsin.

King, L.J.—After serving as a 1920s Klan evangelist, King founded the Book and Bible House in Decatur, Georgia, widely recognized as the nation's leading source of anti–Catholic literature through the early 1950s. Harking back to the tales of "escaped nuns," King specialized in such titles as *Abolish the Nunneries and Save the Girls.* Shortly before death in 1952, King proclaimed: "God has specially sent me after the nunneries and the confessional box. Destroy these two institutions and Romanism is ended."

Koehl, Matthias, Jr.—Milwaukee native Matt Koehl first

professed his admiration for Adolf Hitler at age thirteen, adopting a stance he has never abandoned. He distributed anti–Semitic literature to classmates at Washington High School, serving as spokesman for a one-man neo–Nazi youth group, the American Action Army. Upon graduating in 1952, Koehl moved to New York City and joined James Madole's NRP. A 1953 HUAC report identified Koehl as leader of the NRP's young elite guard in Manhattan, but Koehl subsequently moved to Chicago, there attending college while he corresponded with various fascist groups. Koehl joined the NRSP in 1957 and was named the party's national organizer in 1958. Later that year, he served as a character witness at George Bright's bombing trial in Atlanta, Georgia. By 1959, Koehl was affiliated with the Fighting American Nationalists, widely recognized as a front for George Rockwell's ANP. In 1962, Koehl resigned from the NSRP to head the ANP's Chicago chapter, earning himself a 1963 promotion to party secretary at ANP headquarters in Arlington, Virginia. Koehl opposed Rockwell's change of the party name (to NSWPP) in 1966, but he nonetheless kept the new name after Rockwell was murdered in August 1967. (Despite the conviction of gunman John Patler in Rockwell's death, dissident fascists circulated posters proclaiming that Koehl was "Wanted for Murder.") In 1982, the IRS slapped Koehl and the NSWPP with a lien for $37,000 in unpaid taxes. Foreclosure on headquarters followed, prompting Koehl's relocation to Wisconsin as leader of a reconstructed group he called the New Order. That faction survived until 1999, when it (and Koehl) vanished from the SPLC's list of active hate groups in America.

Kuhn, Fritz Julius—Born in Munich, Germany, in 1896,

Kuhn fought for the Kaiser in World War I and was wounded three times, winning an Iron Cross for bravery. After the war, he earned a master's degree in chemical engineering from the University of Munich. A devoted follower of Adolf Hitler, Kuhn falsely claimed participation in the Munich *putsch* of 1923. In fact, a theft indictment prompted him to flee Bavaria in 1927, settling first in Mexico, then moving on to Detroit in 1928, where he worked as a chemist at Henry Ford Hospital, then in the chemical division of Ford's Rouge River automobile factory. Kuhn felt at home on Ford's payroll, given the millionaire's long campaign against Jews, and he became a naturalized U.S. citizen in 1934. Two years later, in March 1936, he rose to command a pro–Nazi group, the Association of Friends of the New Germany, and renamed it the German-American Bund. Proclaiming the Bund "as American as apple pie," Kuhn led a delegation to Munich for the 1936 Olympic games, then returned to seek alliances with various native American groups, ranging from unresponsive Indian tribes to the KKK. Since Southern klansmen were generally hostile to Nazis in those days, Kuhn got

a warmer reception in New Jersey, where Grand Dragon Arthur Bell agreed to a joint KKK–GAB rally in August 1940, at the Bund's Camp Nordland. Kuhn missed that gathering, however, since a New York jury had convicted him in 1939 of embezzling $14,000 from the Bund's treasury. He served two and a half years at Sing Sing, then spent the remainder of World War II at an internment camp in Texas. Deported to Germany in 1946, Kuhn died there on 14 December 1951.

Kurts, Daniel—A resident of Dayton, Ohio, Kurts led a

faction of the NAAWP in the early 1950s. His publications included a 1953 article praising a rally of the Southern Klans at Columbus, Georgia. "You klansmen have a great organization," he wrote. "You have a right to be proud of it."

Lauck, Gary Rex ("Gerhard")—Born in Milwaukee

and raised in Lincoln, Nebraska, Lauck became fascinated with Nazism at age thirteen, after a reading of *Mein Kampf* persuaded him that "Adolf Hitler was the greatest man who ever lived." (Hitler's only defect, Lauck opined, was being "too humane.") Enrolling at the University of Nebraska after high school, Lauck studied philosophy and German for two years before dropping out to pursue fascist politics full-time. After holding membership in Matt Koehl's NSWPP and Frank Collin's NSPA, Lauck founded his own tiny NSDAP/AO. Pursuing his fascination with all things German, Lauck not only named his group in German, but also changed his name to "Gerhard," while affecting a Hitlerian haircut and toothbrush mustache. Uniquely among American-born fascists, he also published neo–Nazi literature primarily for a foreign audience, traveling repeatedly to Germany and other European nations between the 1970s and early 1990s. (Observers nicknamed Lauck "the Farm Belt Führer.") West German police detained Lauck in 1972, for distributing banned Nazi materials. Two years later, German authorities expelled him following a speech entitled "Why Hitler is still so popular in the United States." In 1976, German police caught him again, with a cache of 20,000 Nazi posters. Conviction in that case earned Lauck four months in jail and a permanent ban from the Fatherland. Granted immunity from prosecution in 1979, he returned long enough to testify as a defense witness at the trial of six neo–Nazis charged with acts of terrorism. Danish police arrested Lauck in March 1995 and extradited him to Germany, where a court convicted him on 22 August 1996 of inciting racial hatred and disseminating illegal Nazi propaganda. Upon receipt of a four-year jail term, Lauck raged at his judge, "The fight will go on!" Released from custody on 23 March 1999, Lauck hurried home and told reporters from the *Lincoln Journal Star,* "If anything, I'm even more convinced, determined and fanatical than before."

Lauderdale, E.A.—As a director of the Citizens' Council

in Little Rock, Arkansas, Lauderdale theoretically pledged himself to resist integration by lawful and nonviolent means. Nonetheless, on 10 September 1959, FBI agents arrested him and two other suspects (Jessie Perry and J.B. Sims) in connection with local bombings that targeted the school board's office, a construction firm owned by Little Rock's mayor, and a car belonging to the fire chief (whose men had dispersed white rioters with high-pressure hoses). Agents jailed two more suspects, Gradon Beavers and John Coggins, after another blast on 11 September. Sims pled guilty on 18 September, drawing a five-year prison term and a $500 fine. Jurors convicted Perry on 28 October, resulting in a three-year sentence. Another panel convicted Lauderdale on 28 November 1959, recommending five years in prison and a $500 fine. Beavers pled guilty on 13 October 1960, receiving the same penalty as Lauderdale and Sims. Testimony at Lauderdale's trial established that the Little Rock bombings were planned at a KKK meeting. Lauderdale served six months in jail before Gov. Orval Faubus reduced his sentence, making him eligible for immediate parole. Faubus also refunded Lauderdale's fine.

Linderman, Frank—An author and hotel proprietor from Flathead Lake, Montana, Linderman once led the anti–Catholic American Protective Association. With Klan support, he won the 1924 GOP nomination for a U.S. Senate race against incumbent Thomas Walsh. Klansmen mounted a smear campaign against the Catholic Walsh, implying a conspiratorial connection to the Vatican, but Linderman still trailed Walsh by 8,000 votes on election day.

Lyons, Kirk D.—A Texas native, born in 1956, Lyons graduated from the University of Texas and earned his LL.B. from the University of Houston, where he met Grand Dragon Louis Beam. After passing the bar exam on his second attempt, Lyons found work handling personal injury claims for a small Houston law firm. Beam renewed their acquaintance in 1985, seeking advice on pending charges related to Beam's affiliation with The Order. In 1987, after federal prosecutors indicted Beam and thirteen other suspects for sedition, Lyons quit his job to defend Beam at trial in Fort Smith, Arkansas. Victory in that case made Lyons a celebrity of sorts on the neo–Nazi fringe, a position reinforced when he created the Patriots Defense Foundation in 1989. A year later, Lyons married the daughter of Charles Tate, then second-in-command of Richard Butler's Aryan Nations compound in Idaho, with Beam serving as best man. In 1991, he changed the PDF's name to CAUSE, standing for *C*anada, *A*ustralia/New Zealand, the *U*nited States, *S*outh Africa and *E*urope (where he deems the rights of white people endangered). In 1992, Lyons moved his office to Black Mountain, North Carolina, and later changed his group's name once again, in 1996, to the Southern Legal Resource Center.

While Lyons claims to specialize in "southern heritage" cases (chiefly involving "persecution" of those who display Confederate flags), his racist opinions are well known. In 1992, Lyons joined Edward Fields in launching a "National Campaign to Expose the Holocaust." The same year saw him on tour in Europe, speaking to various Holocaust-denial groups. In the course of that journey, he granted an interview to *Voklstreue*, a neo–Nazi skinhead magazine, concerning his opinion of the KKK. Lyons declared: "I have great respect for the Klan historically, but, sadly the Klan today is ineffective and sometimes even destructive. There are many spies in it and most of its best leaders have left the Klan to do more effective work within the movement. It would be good if the Klan followed the advice of former Klansman Robert Miles: 'Become invisible. Hang the robes and hoods

in the cupboard and become an underground organization.' This would make the Klan stronger than ever." (The same interview included Lyons's observation that "democracy is a fraud and a failure.") In 1993, Lyons joined Klan leaders William Hoff and Thomas Robb to demonstrate against the Holocaust Museum in Washington, D.C. Speaking of Lyons in 1990, Texas Klan leader William Latham declared, "He's like a Klan lawyer. He understands our beliefs. He shares them." Sam Dickson, a Georgia attorney and board member of CAUSE, has also represented David Duke and other klansmen through the years.

Lyons does not restrict his services to Klan members. In 1988 he addressed Richard Butler's Aryan World Congress and defended Posse Comitatus leader James Wickstrom on counterfeiting charges. In 1990, he "advised" Tom Metzger on his Oregon lawsuit filed by the SPLC, then defended Aryan Nations member Stephen Nelson, charged with plotting to bomb a Seattle synagogue. In 1992, addressing Willis Carto's Populist Party (which ran David Duke for president in 1988), he declared: "This is a global struggle that European people will not perish from the face of the earth, [and] if we are going to succeed in a worldwide movement, for that of white rights and a white future … we must encourage professionalism." In the same year, Lyons joined Louis Beam to address the "Rocky Mountain Rendezvous" which laid the foundation for America's "patriot militia" movement. A year later, advertising in Tom Metzger's WAR newsletter, Lyons billed CAUSE as "America's only pro–White law firm." During 1994, Lyons helped client Andreas Strassmeir (later a suspect in the Oklahoma City bombing) find work as a security guard at Elohim City, a Christian Identity compound in Oklahoma. The same year saw Lyons affiliated with the CCC, appearing as a keynote speaker at the group's April convention in Arkansas. Lieutenant Governor Mike Huckabee refused to share the stage with Lyons, but CCC leader Gordon Baum shrugged off complaints about his choice of speakers, insisting, "We're not the thought police." Elsewhere, Lyons proclaimed The Order's murderous bank robbers "prisoners of conscience," while describing Adolf Hitler as "probably the most misunderstood man in German history." In April 2003, Lyons delivered a "fine speech" to the American Friends of the British National Party on the subject of "how we as racial Nationalists should be making alliances when and wherever we can."

Mabry, H.P.—A retired judge and former Confederate general, Mabry emerged as a leader of the KRS in Reconstruction-era Texas. In spring 1869, he served as defense attorney for KRS members charged with murder, but Mabry later fled to Canada when one defendant turned state's evidence, naming Mabry as the leader of a mob that lynched George Smith at Jefferson, in October 1868.

Madole, James Hartung—Born in 1927, Madole found Nazism through the backdoor of science fiction, rising to command the NRP in 1949, from offices in New York City. While anti–Semitic to the core, Madole also borrowed heavily from Theosophy and tales of elite "hidden masters" directing mankind. Such esoterica did not distract the NRP from gutter-level racism, however, as witnessed by the July 1963 brawl with blacks that sent Madole, Dan Burros and another party member to jail for ten days. (Police found several knives, an axe, and a crossbow in their truck.) In 1968, Madole led the NRP into a formal alliance with the NSWPP, the Minutemen, and Roy Frankhouser's Pennsylvania Klan. At the same time, however, Madole socialized with Anton LaVey, pursuing an alliance with LaVey's Church of Satan and a competing satanic cult, the Order of the Black Ram. In the 1970s, Madole penned series of "New Atlantis" articles for the *National Renaissance Bulletin*, touting reorganization of American society along Hindu caste lines. Simultaneously, and without apparent contradiction in his own mind, he allied the NRP with the pro–Islamic Greenshirt movement, rejecting both capitalism and communism in a manner that anticipated Tom Metzger's "Third Position" doctrine. Madole's party died with him in 1979, but his curious writings remain influential in some quarters of the neo–Nazi movement.

Mann, F. Allen—Media reports from 1958 named Mann as Illinois state chairman for the NSRP.

Manness, David V.—A militant anti–Semite, Manness was jailed on 1 February 1969 for bombing a synagogue in Prince Georges County, Maryland. A police raid on his home revealed Minutemen literature, twenty rifles, twenty-five pistols, several bombs, and thousands of rounds of ammunition.

Mason, James—A native of Chillicothe, Ohio, born in 1952, Mason became enthralled with fascism in adolescence, after viewing TV coverage of a 1966 ANP demonstration in Chicago. Correspondence with Allen Vincent in California led Mason in turn to George Rockwell's headquarters in Arlington, Virginia, and Mason became the party's youngest dues-paying member at age fourteen. A chronic truant by age sixteen, Mason quit school and accepted William Pierce's invitation to Virginia, where he served on Matt Koehl's headquarters staff. When dissension split the NSWPP and Koehl decamped for Wisconsin, Mason followed Joseph Tomassi into the spin-off NSLF. That group died with Tomassi in 1975, but Mason had already found a new guru in convicted serial killer Charles Manson. At Manson's urging, Mason quit the NSLF to found his own Universal Order, touting Manson as the spiritual guru of National Socialism. Emulation of Manson proved risky, however, and Mason's romance with a fourteen-year-old girl sent him to Ohio's state prison in the 1990s. Briefly paroled in 1997, he went back inside when authorities found him in possession of pornography and pistol ammunition. Released again in March 1998, Mason spent five months with an ankle monitor before discharging his parole. Another conviction in 1999 sent him briefly back to jail, but the new millennium found Mason free once more, reportedly working on several books with "prophetic and apocalyptic themes."

McGinley, Conde—A longtime ally of Gerald L.K. Smith and John Crommelin, McGinley published the newsletter *Common Sense* from his home in New Jersey, providing klansmen and neo–Nazis with much of their anti–Semitic propaganda in the 1950s and early 1960s.

McMichael, Obed—As a leader of the White Brotherhood in Guilford County, North Carolina, McMichael introduced the order into neighboring Alamance County in 1868.

Mohr, Gordon ("Jack")—A retired lieutenant colonel of the U.S. Army, Mohr was a native of Bay St. Louis, Mississippi, whose ardent anti-communism sprang from his capture by Red Chinese in the Korean War. Mohr traveled nationwide as an orator with the JBS's American Speakers Bureau during 1969–80, until his strident anti–Semitism produced complaints. Mohr then joined John Harrell's extremist Citizens' Emergency Defense System and the Christian Patriots Defense League (ranked as a CPDL brigadier general), teaching firearms classes at a "Freedom Festival" convened on Harrell's estate at Louisville, Illinois. On the side, Mohr emerged as a prominent Christian Identity spokesman, publishing remarks such as the following:

> No matter how you feel about Adolf Hitler—and I volunteered to go to war against him—he was right when he stated in 1939: "Only when the Jewish influence that splits the nations apart has been eliminated, will it be possible to bring about the international cooperation based on a lasting understanding." Because Hitler understood the plans of International Jewry and what they were trying to do to Western Christian civilization, he was marked for destruction by any means, even the murder of countless millions by a World War.

Despite that seeming admiration for *Der Führer*, author Jeffrey Kaplan claims that Mohr "outspokenly opposed the increasing inroads of National Socialism and violent rhetoric into the Identity world." If so, Mohr's reticence did not prevent him from participating in Richard Butler's Aryan World Congress, where Mohr joined klansman Louis Beam to teach classes in urban guerrilla warfare. Mohr died on 17 July 2003, at age eighty-seven, in North Little Rock, Arkansas.

Moseley, George Van Horn—A native of Evanston, Illinois, born 28 September 1874, Moseley graduated from West Point in 1899, seeing combat in the Philippines and during World War I. He ultimately held the rank of major general, serving at various times as executive for the assistant secretary of war (1929–30), deputy chief of staff for the army (1930–33), commanding general of the Fifth Corps (1933–34), commanding general of the Fourth Corps (1934–36), and as commanding general of the Third U.S. Army (1936–38). Somewhere along the way, Moseley developed a deep-seated strain of racism and anti–Semitism, recalling: "[W]hen I was a Cadet [at West Point], there was one Jew in my class, a very undesirable creature, who was soon eliminated." He suggested that "governmental measures should be considered" to bar miscegenation by "imported manpower of an inferior kind." Testimony implicated Moseley in an abortive plot to depose President Franklin Roosevelt, but he escaped indictment for sedition with other supposed conspirators. Instead, he was forced to resign after delivering an anti–Semitic speech to Army reservists at Tulane University in 1938. For the remainder of the Great Depression, Moseley fraternized with Gerald L.K. Smith, various Klans and pro–Nazi groups from his suite in Atlanta's Biltmore Hotel. Still active in neo–Nazi politics after World War II, Moseley collaborated with Edward Fields on a 1946 campaign to liberate imprisoned Columbians leader Emory Burke. Moseley died in Atlanta on 7 November 1960.

Mower, Dennis—A member of the paramilitary Minutemen, ordained minister of Wesley Swift's Church of Jesus Christ Christian, and a close friend of WKKKKM Wizard Sam Bowers, Mower faced trial at Springfield, Missouri, in 1967, for possessing and transporting unlicensed machine guns. Mower's defense attorney, Bertrand Comparet, was best known for defending NSRP members on various felony charges. In June 1968, after a deadly shootout in Meridian, Mississippi, police found one of Mower's business cards on klansman Thomas Tarrants. (It read: "The wages of sin is death.") During 1968–70, Mower collaborated with Wesley Swift in creating such groups as the California Anti-Communist League, the Christian Nationalist Alliance, Friends of Rhodesia, and the Southern California Freedom Councils. By 1971, authorities described Mower as second-in-command of California's Minutemen.

Munroe, A.—An attorney in Reconstruction-era Kinston, North Carolina, Munroe also served as a member of Lenoir County's CUG, joining the mob that lynched five black prisoners in January 1869. In August 1869, he was one of twenty-five CUG members indicted on various felony charges, their prosecution effectively ending terrorism in Lenoir County.

Norton, Richard—A spokesman for the NSRP, Norton was banned from Baltimore, Maryland, with fellow agitators Connie Lynch and Joseph Carroll, after their rallies sparked white riots in July 1966. At trial four months later, Norton received a jail term for inciting a riot, conspiracy to riot, disorderly conduct and violating city park regulations. A decade later, in Los Angeles, he resurfaced as an organizer for James Warner's New Christian Crusade Church.

Patler, John C.—As a member of George Rockwell's ANP, Patler (né John Patsalos) traveled the South with Dan Burros in May 1961, protesting CORE's integrated freedom rides with a Nazi "hate bus." That autumn, he defected with Burros to found the two-man American National Party in New York City, publishing a magazine entitled *Kill!* In 1964, Patler mocked the MFDP by invading the House of Representatives in blackface makeup, dressed in a leopard skin, shouting, "I's de Mississippi delegation!" Back in the ANP fold two years later, Patler joined Rockwell and robed klansmen for an August 1966 rally in Chicago's Marquette Park. In March 1967, Rockwell fired Patler for spreading dissent between light- and dark-skinned Nazis at ANP headquarters in Arlington, Virginia. Five months later, on 25 August, Patler shot Rockwell to death at a local laundromat, subsequently receiving a twenty-year prison term in December 1967.

Patterson, James A.J.—A resident of Alamance County, North Carolina, during Reconstruction, Patterson organized the CUG's first "klan" in September 1868, later serving as county chief of the order.

Pelley, William Dudley—A Massachusetts native, born 12 March 1890, Pelley was the son of an impoverished Methodist minister. Mainly self-educated, he became a freelance journalist and foreign correspondent, traveling widely through Russia during the revolution of 1917–18. That experience left him with a deep hatred of communism and Jews, whom he believed were plotting to control the world. Back in the United States by 1920, Pelley prospered as a Hollywood screenwriter, but the onset of the Great Depression in 1929 drove him ever deeper into far-right, racist politics. An early proponent of Christian Identity, Pelley settled in Asheville, North Carolina, where in 1932 he founded Galahad College (a correspondence school specializing in "Christian economics" and "social metaphysics"). On 31 January 1933, the day after Adolf Hitler took power in Germany, Pelley founded the Silver Shirt Legion of America, recruiting anti–Semites such as Gerald L.K. Smith to spread the movement nationwide. A die-hard enemy of FDR's New Deal, Pelley also formed the Christian Party to pursue a futile presidential race in 1936. His campaign slogan, "Christ or Chaos," was illuminated when he told a Seattle gathering of the German-American Folk Union that "the time has come for an American Hitler and a pogrom." Recognized as a friend of prominent klansmen, Pelley was instrumental in persuading Michigan Klan leaders to enter politics, while his publishing house furnished anti–Semitic literature for klansmen and Nazis alike.

Persistent agitation during 1936–40 prompted federal raids, a HUAC summons, and IRS charges of tax evasion. Pelley weathered those trials, aligning himself with Charles Lindbergh's America First Committee. After Pearl Harbor, Pelley accused FDR and company of hiding the truth about U.S. losses in Hawaii. Sedition charges followed, and while prosecutors later dismissed the most serious counts against Pelley, he still faced a fifteen-year sentence on conviction of lesser offenses. Impoverished by legal expenses, Pelley sat in prison until 1950, when relatives raised the cash to appeal his conviction. Parole followed before year's end, on condition that he abstain from politics for life. Retired to Noblesville, Indiana, Pelley founded Soulcraft Press, producing right-wing texts and books on metaphysics while dodging pre-war charges of securities fraud. Until his death in 1965, Pelley remained an ardent enemy of Jews, desegregation, and the United Nations.

Phelps, Coy Ray—A neo–Nazi activist in San Francisco, California, Phelps planted bombs at two synagogues, a rabbi's home, and two other targets in 1985. Only one of the bombs exploded, and forensic evidence led police to Phelps's home, where raiders seized explosives plus racist literature from the KKK and Aryan Nations. Phelps's van bore a bumper sticker issued by Bill Wilkinson's IEKKKK.

Pierce, William Luther—A native of Atlanta, Georgia, born 11 September 1933, Pierce earned his B.A. in physics from Rice University in 1951, then worked at Los Alamos Scientific Laboratory while working toward his Ph.D. (received in 1962). With doctorate in hand, Pierce joined a Connecticut aerospace firm as a senior research scientist, but his interests were already drifting toward far-right politics. Dissatisfied with the John Birch Society, Pierce quit his job in 1966 to join George Rockwell's ANP, headquartered in Arlington, Virginia. He bought a printing press, publishing the party's *National Socialist World,* and emerged as a leader of the renamed NSWPP after Rockwell's

August 1967 assassination. A year later, he joined Willis Carto's Youth for Wallace movement, promoting the presidential dreams of Alabama's racist governor George Wallace. In 1970, Pierce and Carto renamed that thirty-member group the National Youth Alliance. Over the next three years, increasingly bitter relations between Pierce and Carto kept the NYA from anything resembling success. At last, in 1974, Pierce cut the ties completely to lead his own revamped National Alliance, with headquarters in Arlington.

Adopting slogans such as "Free Men Are Not Equal" and "Equal Men Are Not Free," Pierce built his neo–Nazi faction as a monument to Adolf Hitler, whom he called "The Great One." In 1978, as "Andrew Macdonald," Pierce published *The Turner Diaries,* a futuristic racist novel credited with inspiring neo–Nazi terrorism throughout the U.S. and Britain during 1983–2000. Robert Mathews, Pacific Northwest leader of the NA, used the novel as his blueprint for The Order in 1983, and subsequently furnished Pierce with cash from that group's armed robberies. Various accounts (including testimony under oath) claim that Pierce received between $50,000 and $642,000 from Mathews in 1983–84, but he nonetheless escaped indictment with other loot recipients when the Justice Department filed sedition charges in 1987. Meanwhile, in 1984, Pierce paid $95,000 in cash for a 346-acre farm at Mill Point, West Virginia, relocating his headquarters and founding the Cosmotheist Community Church ("all is within God and God is within all"), while diversifying on the business front with such enterprises as National Vanguard Books and Resistance Records. In 1989, "Andrew Macdonald" published *Hunter,* a novel of a lone "Aryan warrior" based on (and dedicated to) racist serial killer Joseph Franklin.

In 1994, Pierce began making annual trips to Europe, forging ties with various neo–Nazi groups abroad. The following year, after several phone calls to Pierce's headquarters, ex-klansman Timothy McVeigh bombed Oklahoma City's federal building, killing 168 persons. At McVeigh's arrest, police found a copy of *The Turner Diaries* in his car, one chapter depicting a near-identical truck-bomb attack. Ten days after the bombing, Pierce predicted that white resentment of Jews and minorities in America would soon produce terror "on a scale the world has never seen before." In 1996, authorities alleged that Pierce received at least $2,000 from bank-robbing NA member Todd Vanbiber, but again Pierce escaped indictment. In May of that year, SPLC attorneys won an $85,000 judgment against Pierce for his part in a scheme to conceal assets of another racist group, the Church of the Creator. In his declining years, Pierce became a semi-recluse, amusing himself with a series of mail-order brides from Eastern Europe, avoiding the limelight whenever possible. He delivered his last public speech on 20 April 2002 (Hitler's birthday), by which time SPLC observers pegged his income at more than $1 million per year. Cancer claimed Pierce's life on 23 July 2002.

Pires, Robert—A member of the Aryan Nations indicted for bombings in Idaho, Pires also shot and killed white-supremacist Kenneth Shray near Baltimore, Maryland, in August 1986. Pires later pled guilty and received a long prison term.

Potito, Oren—A member of the NSRP in St. Petersburg, Florida, Potito traveled to Alabama in 1962 as campaign manager for John Crommelin's U.S. Senate race. In October 1962, police jailed him in Oxford, Mississippi, where Potito had organized protests against desegregation of the state university. Officers seized a small arsenal of firearms from his car on that occasion. By 1962, "Reverend" Potito led the eastern conference of Wesley Swift's Church of Jesus Christ Christian, announcing that his church had formed guerrilla warfare teams to "defend the country in case of a takeover." Potito remained active in racist causes at press time for this volume. His most recent publication is *Germany & the True Story of the Third Reich.*

Pyle, Harry William—A retired house painter and ex-klansman in Memphis, Tennessee, Pyle served as chairman of the segregationist Pro-Southerners until March 1956, when internal policy disputes split the group and he resigned at age seventy-five.

Ray, Gerald—A brother of alleged assassin James Earl Ray, Gerald attached himself to NSRP headquarters in Savannah, Georgia, while J.B. Stoner appealed James's conviction for killing Dr. Martin Luther King, Jr. Serving as Stoner's chauffeur and personal bodyguard, Ray spent his free time selling copies of *The Thunderbolt,* later emerging as campaign manager for Stoner's 1970 gubernatorial race. In July 1970, Ray shot and wounded future Klan leader Stephen Black during an alleged burglary at NSRP headquarters. Jurors acquitted Ray of attempted murder charges in November 1970.

Roberts, James W.—In 1965, Roberts pled guilty to stealing military explosives from Fort McClellan, Alabama, and passing them to klansman Kenneth Adams. In January 1966, jurors acquitted Adams on charges of receiving stolen government property.

Robinson, James—Police in Selma, Alabama, jailed NSRP member Robinson for assaulting Martin Luther King in January 1965. A sixty-day jail term and $100 fine failed to keep him out of trouble, however. In March 1965, FBI agents arrested Robinson for attacking them on Highway 80, east of Selma, while the G-men photographed a group of whites beating a black man. A judge fined Robinson $27 for punching one agent and stealing his camera.

Rockwell, George Lincoln—The son of famous vaudeville comedians, born in Bloomington, Illinois, on 9 March 1918, Rockwell graduated from Brown University before joining the U.S. Navy as a pilot. He served in World War II and the Korean War without seeing combat, meanwhile devouring Adolf Hitler's *Mein Kampf* and the writings of native anti–Semites Conde McGinley and Gerald L.K. Smith. In 1952, Rockwell spent his honeymoon at Berchtesgaden, Germany, the site of Hitler's "Eagle's Nest" retreat. In 1958, Rockwell founded a National Committee to Free America from Jewish Domination, replaced by the American Nazi Party in November 1958 or March 1959 (reports differ). Operating from headquarters in Arlington, Virginia, Rockwell also led the American Party of the World Union of Free Enterprise Socialists, visiting Chicago in 1959 for joint meetings with the black-separatist Joint Council on Repatriation. In July 1960, police arrested Rockwell, Dan Burros, James Warner, and fourteen other party members, after an ANP rally degenerated into brawling on The Mall in Washington, D.C.

Dissension on the racist fringe barred Rockwell from the NSRP's 1964 presidential convention, with Edward Fields branding Rockwell "a known leftist." Not to be outdone, Rockwell entered Wisconsin's 1964 presidential primary, but the only state resident who volunteered to represent the ANP found himself disqualified on grounds that he had never registered to vote. A year later, Rockwell ran for governor of Virginia as a candidate of the White Majority Party, and he was a spectator at HUAC hearings on the KKK. Robed klansmen joined Rockwell for riotous demonstrations in Chicago, in July 1966, but his own party—lately renamed the NSWPP—was torn by internal conflict. Rockwell fired lieutenant John Patler for inciting feuds between dark- and light-skinned members, but Patler had the last word. On 25 August 1967, he ambushed Rockwell at a local laundromat, killing Rockwell with a semiautomatic pistol. Party members cremated Rockwell's remains in a secret ceremony on 31 August. During his tenure at ANP headquarters, known Nazis doubled as ranking members of the UKA in California, Delaware, Maryland, New Jersey, New York and Pennsylvania.

Roeder, Manfred Richard Kurt—Born in 1929, a

German attorney who proudly claimed membership in the Hitler Youth, Roeder remained loyal to Nazi precepts after World War II. Austrian officials found his politics so offensive that they banned Roeder from entering their nation during 1974–79. Undaunted, he founded the Liberation Movement of the German Reich and an affiliated group, the German Citizens' Initiative, with offices in both West Germany and the United States. On 27 July 1976, a judge in Heilbronn fined Roeder DM5,000 and sentenced him to seven months in jail (suspended) for publishing *The Auschwitz Lie,* a piece of Holocaust-denial propaganda. Days later, Roeder embarked on a five-week tour in the U.S., including an appearance at the World Conference of National Socialists, sponsored by James Warner's New Christian Crusade Church. In November 1977, German indictments for resisting arrest and causing great bodily harm to police officers sent Roeder into globe-trotting exile during 1978–80, with stops in Austria, Brazil, Britain, Canada, South Africa, and the United States. William Pierce welcomed Roeder at National Alliance headquarters, and the footloose fascist moved on to Hayden Lake, Idaho, for an extended sojourn with the Aryan Nations. Before returning to Germany, Roeder also met with Klan leaders David Duke and Bill Wilkinson, picking up speaker's fees for lectures at several KKK rallies. As 1980 ended, West German police linked Roeder to a series of bombing attacks perpetrated by the German Action Groups, including strikes at Holocaust memorials, a home for Ethiopian refugees in Loerrach, and a Hamburg shelter for Vietnamese "boat people." Two Vietnamese died in one firebombing, while two Ethiopians were seriously injured in a separate attack. Upon conviction in that case, Roeder received a thirteen-year prison term and was disbarred from practicing law. Paroled in 1990, Roeder resumed his racist activities and found more trouble

waiting. In June 1996, he paid a DM4,500 fine in Erfurt for another anti–Semitic tirade. A year later, he ran for a seat in the Bundestag as "a man that Germany loves," but voters proved him wrong. December 1999 brought Roeder another fine of DM4,500 for pro–Nazi pronouncements, and he received a prison term of twenty-seven months on 29 June 2001 for advocating armed revolution. An appellate court shaved six months off that sentence on 2 July 2002, leaving Roeder unrepentant and ready for action upon his release.

Rogers, Louis J.—A resident of Lisbon, Connecticut,

Rogers chaired a local committee supporting George Wallace's presidential campaign in 1968. In August of that year, he joined a group of Minutemen who raided a pacifist camp outside Voluntown, leaving four raiders, one female camper, and one state trooper wounded by gunfire. Prosecutors indicted Rogers and five other defendants for assault with intent to kill and conspiracy to commit arson.

Roper, Billy Joe, III—A resident of Russellville, Arkan-

sas, once ranked as deputy membership coordinator for the neo-Nazi National Alliance, Roper also joined the CCC in the late 1990s and found a warm reception before its Arkansas chapters. After William Pierce died in July 2002, successor Erich Gliebe expelled Roper for fraternizing with other racist groups. Roper promptly formed his own White Revolution clique, competing with the NA in sales of white-power music and other fascist paraphernalia. On 25 January 2003, he organized a protest at SPLC headquarters in Montgomery, Alabama, including members of the KKK, Aryan Nations, and Church of the Creator.

Rucker, Elza—An officer of the NSRP, Rucker died in a

shootout with blacks at a rally outside Berea, Kentucky, on 1 September 1968.

Russell, Katherine—A Miami, Florida, resident and vice

president of the Edison Center Civic Association, Russell allegedly conspired with klansmen in 1951 to prevent blacks from moving into the Carver Village housing project. In October 1952, a federal grand jury declared that Russell helped organize Klan motorcades and a robed demonstration outside the complex (which also suffered multiple bombings). The panel indicted Russell for perjury in December 1952, but KKK attorney Edgar Waybright later won dismissal of the charges.

Rust, David C.—Following Joseph Tomassi's murder by a

rival neo–Nazi in 1975, Rust assumed command of the NSLF. He, in turn, was replaced by Karl Hand after prosecutors convicted Rust of federal firearms violations.

Saufley, William P.—Elected leader of the KRS on 19

September 1868, Saufley led the mob that lynched Capt. George Smith at Jefferson, Texas, two weeks later. He left town "on business" in early December, a day before federal authorities started arresting the lynchers, and escaped through Indian Territory, making his way to New York, thereby avoiding trial for murder.

Scaife, Dorothy—Identified as a staff sergeant in the Veterans for Victory Over Communism, Scaife participated in guer-

rilla training exercises at Camp Puller, near Houston, Texas, before an SPLC lawsuit closed that facility in December 1980. While admitting that any klansmen were welcome in camp, she told journalists, "We make it very clear he's not to wear his insignia or talk about it."

Shuler, Rev. Allen C.—As pastor of Jacksonville, Florida's Calvary Baptist Church, Shuler became an early convert to the 1920s KKK. In 1921, he launched *The Crusader,* a racist tabloid that survived into the early 1950s. Two years later, klansmen visited Shuler in the midst of a tent revival and "expressed appreciation on the part of the order" for his ongoing work. In 1946, after police in Atlanta jailed members of the neo–Nazi Columbians for terrorist activity, Shuler invited the group to meet at his Jacksonville church. In 1950, media reports identified Shuler as the imperial kludd of Sam Roper's AGK, briefly doubling as publisher of the *American Klansman* newsletter, and he appeared as the keynote speaker at a rally atop Georgia's Stone Mountain. He also briefly published a monthly newsletter for Bill Northern and Southern Knights. In January 1951, Shuler announced his retirement from the KKK to work full-time on *The Crusader.* A year later, after presidential candidate Dwight Eisenhower voiced his opposition to federal civil rights laws, Shuler told Stetson Kennedy that he was "packing my bags to hit the sawdust trail" as a GOP campaigner. "Of course the KKK likes Ike!" Shuler declared. "All things considered, the Republican Party has what it takes to save America." After "Black Monday," Shuler emerged as an active member of the Florida Citizens' Councils.

Shuler, Rev. Robert Pierce—A backwoods Virginia native, born in 1880, "Fighting Bob" Shuler bypassed formal education as a child, spending three months with *McGuffey's Readers* before enrolling at Emory and Henry College as a "subfreshman" in 1903. Two years later, he entered service as a Methodist minister. In 1920, Shuler became the pastor of Trinity Methodist Church in Los Angeles, California. His appointment coincided with the Klan's arrival in the Golden State, and Shuler welcomed klansmen as adjuncts to his endless moralistic crusade. Once, after winning a ham on the wheel-of-fortune at a Shriners' charity bazaar, Shuler charged the lodge with running a "gambling ring." On another occasion, he sat all night outside a brothel, waiting for the county sheriff to emerge, then hounded the lawman from office and ruined his career. When not hiring private investigators to root out vice in L.A., Shuler freely praised klansmen for their own vigilante efforts. He told his congregation, "Good men everywhere are coming to understand that the Klan is dangerous only to the lawless and un–American elements within [our] midst." In fact, he said, Christians should "love the Klan for the enemies she has made." Grateful klansmen responded in kind, rallying behind Shuler in his feud with rival evangelist Aimee Semple McPherson, helping Shuler increase his congregation fivefold in the space of three years. In 1929, he expanded his audience via radio, and in 1932 campaigned for the U.S. Senate on the Prohibition Party ticket (trailing his competitor by 50,000 votes). In later years, Shuler praised dictator Francisco Franco's fascist government in Spain and backed maverick Gen. Douglas MacArthur for president.

Shuler retired in 1953, leaving the pulpit to his sons, and died in 1965.

Smith, Bob—Identified in media reports as leader of the NSRP in Mobile, Alabama, Smith was jailed in summer 1964 with teenage colleague Thomas Tarrants. A search of their car revealed a sawed-off shotgun, resulting in criminal charges against Tarrants.

Smith, Gerald Lyman Kenneth—A native of Pardeeville, Wisconsin, born 27 February 1898, Smith was ordained in 1916 as a minister for the Disciples of Christ. He launched his career as a professional anti–Semite in 1933, when he joined William Dudley Pelley's Silver Shirt Legion of America. Smith briefly toured the Midwest with a "storm troop" of Silver Shirt bodyguards, but he soon quarreled with Pelley and migrated to Shreveport, Louisiana, as pastor of the King's Highway Church. Ever alert to opportunity, Smith soon attached himself to "Kingfish" Huey Long, encouraging Long's presidential ambitions, but an assassin killed that dream in 1935. Smith's bid to seize control of Long's political machine was foiled by cronies closer to the throne, but he rebounded in 1936, supporting Father Charles Coughlin's National Union for Social Justice and Francis Townsend's Share-the-Wealth plan. By summer 1936, Smith billed himself as a "contact man for the Union Party, director of the Townsend organization, a keynote speaker for Father Coughlin and supporter of [Coughlin candidate William] Lemke for president." Smith also found time to share the campaign for Georgia Gov. Eugene Talmadge and to organize a Committee of One Million as a "nationalist front against communism" (interpreted by mainstream journalists as a bid to "seize the government of the United States").

In the latter 1930s, Smith tried to purchase *X-Ray* magazine from klansman Court Asher, but Asher rejected his offer. In 1940, Detroit voters likewise rejected Smith's bid for a U.S. Senate seat with the America First Party (although he polled 130,000 votes). Four years later, he won only 1,781 votes in his bid for the GOP presidential nomination. In November 1946, Georgia Attorney General Dan Duke declared that Smith and his associates were forging ties with the post-war KKK. Notorious klansman Wesley Swift served as Smith's chauffeur, prior to striking off on his own with the Christian Defense League and Church of Jesus Christ Christian. Smith attended the States Rights Party's founding convention in 1948, but leader Strom Thurmond found Smith's Jew-baiting embarrassing and kept him at arm's length. Settling in Arkansas, Smith launched his own Christian Nationalist Crusade at the turn of the decade, using its political arm—the Christian Nationalist Party—to run for president in 1952 and 1956. (On the first attempt, he polled 13,883 votes; the second campaign failed to score double digits.)

Throughout the 1960s and early 1970s, editorials in Smith's monthly magazine (*The Cross and the Flag*) supported the KKK and Citizens' Councils in their resistance to court-ordered desegregation, and his anti–Semitic literature was a staple of far-right distributors, from the Klan and NSRP to the John Birch Society. In 1964, Smith began construction of a religious theme park at Eureka, Arkansas, completing his giant Christ of the

Ozarks statue two years later. (Sculptor Emmet Sullivan had previously worked with klansman Gutzon Borglum on Mt. Rushmore.) Smith's plans for a life-sized recreation of ancient Jerusalem were never realized, but he consoled himself with yearly stagings of a gruesome "passion play." Meanwhile, the Jew-baiting continued unabated. One of Smith's associates, W. Henry McFarland, Jr., was linked to James Madole's NRP in the early 1960s, and ex-lieutenant Kenneth Goff campaigned on behalf of Robert DePugh's Patriotic Party in 1966. Smith died of pneumonia on 15 April 1976, passing the torch of hate to other eager hands.

Smythe, Edward James—As founder of the Protestant War Veterans and an associate of the German-American Bund, Smythe helped organize a joint rally between the Bund and KKK in August 1940, at Camp Nordland, New Jersey. He shared the stage on that occasion with Grand Dragon Arthur Bell and various Bund leaders. On the side, Smythe also wrote a weekly column for the *X-Ray*, published by klansman Court Asher. Indicted for sedition in July 1942, with twenty-eight other defendants, Smythe escaped conviction when a mistrial was declared in 1944 and prosecutors dropped the case. Following the 1946 election of Eugene Talmadge as Georgia's governor, Smythe announced plans to open an Atlanta office of his Protestant War Veterans. Georgia Attorney General Dan Duke immediately launched an investigation of the PWV, declaring it a front group for the KKK.

Snell, Richard Wayne—A militant member of James Ellison's CSA, Snell joined two other members to bomb a natural gas pipeline near Fulton, Arkansas, on 2 November 1983. The blast caused only minor damage, and their subsequent attempt to blast electric power lines in Fort Smith failed completely. On 11 November, Snell and two compatriots robbed a pawn shop in Texarkana, where Snell murdered proprietor William Stumpp. (He mistook Stumpp for a Jew, later telling CSA comrades that his victim "needed to die.") On 30 June 1984, during a routine traffic stop, Snell shot and killed a black state trooper, Louis Bryant, near DeQueen, Arkansas. Police wounded and captured Snell later that day, outside Broken Bow, Oklahoma. In separate trials, he received a life sentence for Bryant's murder and was sentenced to die for Stumpp's slaying. Indicted for sedition with thirteen other white supremacists in 1987, Snell won acquittal at Fort Smith, Arkansas, in 1988. He died by lethal injection on 19 April 1995, shortly after ex-klansman Timothy McVeigh bombed Oklahoma City's federal building. Watching televised reports of that attack, Snell smiled and told his guards, "Justice is coming." Racist colleagues buried Snell at Oklahoma's Elohim City compound, a stronghold of Christian Identity cultists.

Stanley, David—A Canadian member of the NSRP, Stanley was one of eight racists indicted in September 1963, for violent interference with school integration in Birmingham, Alabama. Two years later, while addressing a Canadian government panel that denied him mailing privileges for neo-Nazi literature, Stanley denied membership in the NSRP but admitted serving as its Canadian representative.

Tate, David—A member of the Aryan Nations and The Order, Tate was a fugitive from federal racketeering charges in April 1985, when Missouri highway patrolmen stopped him for a minor traffic violation outside Branson. Tate fired on the officers with a submachine gun, killing Patrolman Jimmie Linegar and wounding Patrolman Allen Hines. FBI agents captured Tate a week later, at the CSA's Arkansas compound, and he subsequently received a life sentence for murder. Federal charges related to his actions with The Order were dismissed.

Tomassi, Joseph—Born in 1951, Tomassi emerged as a precocious California leader of George Rockwell's NSWPP at age sixteen. In 1969, encouraged by fellow fascist William Pierce, Tomassi founded the rival NSLF, although his formal break with the NSWPP did not occur until 1973, when Matt Koehl dismissed Tomassi for misusing party funds and smoking marijuana at NSWPP headquarters. Promoting the NSLF full-time during 1973–74, Tomassi proclaimed that "the future belongs to the few of us willing to get our hands dirty." His violent rhetoric attracted followers from coast to coast, including Louisiana college student David Duke. Tomassi's ongoing feud with the NSWPP climaxed in August 1975, when NSWPP member Jerry Jones shot and killed Tomassi in El Monte, California.

Tucker, Rev. Buddy—A Christian Identity minister from Knoxville, Tennessee, Tucker shared the stage with Klan assassin Byron De La Beckwith at a 1973 NSRP convention. Three years later, as leader of the Louisiana-based National Emancipation of Our White Seed, Tucker addressed Robert Scoggin's Conference of Eastern Dragons. In the 1980s, Tucker also collaborated with Dan Gayman's anti–Semitic Church of Israel.

Veh, Russell Raymond—A native of Toledo, Ohio, Veh founded the one-man Ohio Nationalist Party in 1970, renamed the American White Nationalist Party a year later. In July 1971, prosecutors indicted Veh for using false names in an ill-conceived plot to swindle the Book-of-the-Month Club and various magazine publishers. Convicted of mail fraud in August 1972, Veh received three years' probation. He subsequently moved to Los Angeles, where in 1974 he founded the National Socialist League for openly gay neo–Nazis. When the NSL failed to prosper in L.A., Veh moved to San Diego for another try in 1982, then faded from the racist scene.

Vincent, Allen—A resident of San Francisco, California, Vincent organized the National Socialist White Workers Party in the mid–1970s, gaining publicity in April 1977 when he opened his Rudolph Hess bookshop in a Jewish neighborhood. Later that year, he was embroiled in further controversy when journalists revealed that city officials had rented the NSWWP a clubhouse in a public park. In February 1978, Vincent filed a $28 million lawsuit against San Francisco's mayor and various other defendants, charging abridgment of his civil rights, but a judge dismissed the action eight months later.

Walker, Edwin A.—A Texas native, born 10 November 1909, Walker graduated from New Mexico Military Institute in 1927 and from West Point in 1931. After combat service in World War II and the Korean War, Col. Walker commanded the

U.S. Army Reserve district in Little Rock, Arkansas. President Dwight Eisenhower mobilized his troops to enforce court-ordered school integration in 1957–58. (One of his soldiers on the scene was future klansman Dan Burros.) In 1959, as a major general, Walker commanded the Twenty-fourth Infantry Division in Germany. Two years later, Walker's superiors admonished him for distributing JBS extremist literature to his troops. Walker resigned in protest and retired to Texas as a right-wing "martyr," flying a Rhodesian flag outside his Dallas home to protest the advance of civil rights. A favorite speaker before JBS and Citizens' Council assemblies, Walker leaped from words to action in September 1962, issuing a national call to arms in defiance of court-ordered integration at the University of Mississippi in Oxford. Walker personally supervised (some say led) the riot at "Ole Miss" on 30 September, and while U.S. marshals arrested him, federal prosecutors declined to indict him.

On 10 April 1963, Walker survived an apparent murder attempt at his home, later blamed on alleged presidential assassin Lee Harvey Oswald. Ten months later, he appeared in a Jackson, Mississippi, courtroom to shake hands with Byron De La Beckwith, facing trial for the murder of NAACP leader Medgar Evers. By 1965, when he shared the dais with Georgia segregationist Lester Maddox and JBS founder Robert Welch at a Chicago "Congress of Conservatives," Walker was collaborating full-time with Royal Young, founder of the Louisiana-based Original Knights of the KKK. In fact, Walker told the Chicago audience, there were "more good Americans in the Ku Klux Klan" than in the liberal Americans for Democratic Action. In September 1965, speaking at the Henry Grady Hotel in Atlanta, Walker promised another cheering crowd, "There will be a KKK in the USA longer than there will be an LBJ." For all his bombast, though, Walker had passed his peak of influence. He died in Dallas, largely forgotten, on 31 October 1993.

Warthen, Perry ("Red")—A self-described pen pal of serial killer Charles Manson, Warthen led California's Chico Area National Socialists in the early 1980s, recruiting young members for acts of harassment and vandalism, nocturnal shootings, and stockpiling of weapons. In September 1982, police charged Warthen in the death of teenage neo–Nazi Joseph Hoover, shot eight times in the head after giving authorities information about the CANS. Conviction on murder charges sent Warthen to prison for life without parole.

Weber, Mark—A freelance writer and German translator, Weber traveled widely in Europe and Africa before settling in Washington, D.C., in 1977. By May 1978, he was employed as editor of the *National Vanguard,* published by William Pierce's National Alliance. In 1979, collaborating with Willis Carto's Liberty Lobby, Weber emerged as a major voice of Holocaust denial in America. A typical editorial, from December 1979, declared: "A careful examination of the origins of the 'holocaust' legend in the famous Nuremberg Trials and other 'war crimes' trials reveals just how fraudulent the entire story really is." In June 1981, Weber took up the cause of convicted German terrorist Manfred Roeder, imprisoned for participation in a series of bombings that killed two persons and wounded several others. As Weber viewed the case: "His violations of the law are purely political in nature. In America his actions would be considered completely legal expressions of opinion protected by the Constitution. Not crimes. Men and women sentenced for such 'crimes' in the Soviet Union are praised by American politicians and newspapers as courageous 'dissidents.' Roeder's case is no different." At press time for this volume, Weber served as director of America's leading Holocaust-denial vehicle, the Institute for Historical Review.

White, Mollie Alma Bridwell—The most active and prolific fundamentalist minister of the 1920s, born in Kentucky in 1862, White founded the Pillar of Fire Church with headquarters at Zarephath, New Jersey, and established forty-nine active branches nationwide. She also openly endorsed the KKK as an ally in her sect's crusade against "modernism" and sin, publishing a magazine (*The Good Citizen*) which denounced Catholics as "toe kissers" and "wafer worshipers." In a typical editorial, White wrote: "We hail the KKK in the great movement that is now on foot, as the army divinely appointed to set the forces in operation to rescue Americanism and save our Protestant institutions from the designs of the 'Scarlet Mother.'" When Klan orators visited White's church at Bound Brook, New Jersey, for a widely publicized meeting in May 1923, hundreds of angry townspeople surrounded the chapel and showered it with stones, smashing windows and furniture, and damaging parked cars before a small detachment of police cleared an escape route. Despite the setback and continuing opposition, White remained the only leader of a Protestant denomination to openly praise the KKK. She died in New Jersey on 26 June 1946.

Wickstrom, James P.—A native of Munising, Michigan, born in 1942, Wickstrom emerged in his thirties as a spokesman for the militant Posse Comitatus and self-proclaimed "national director of counterinsurgency for the United Posses of America." By 1981, his extreme anti–Semitism prompted him to hold joint rallies with Richard Butler's Aryan Nations. Wickstrom served his first prison term following a 1983 conviction for impersonating a federal officer, with parole contingent on his agreement to refrain from further political activity. That promise was illusory, however, and Wickstrom renewed his radical activity by 1988, when he conspired to distribute counterfeit money at Butler's yearly Aryan World Congress. His first trial on those charges ended with a deadlocked jury, but a second panel convicted Wickstrom on 14 June 1990. Upon release in 1995, Wickstrom returned to his hometown and established a small Christian Identity congregation, running a Posse website and selling survivalist gear on the side. In the late 1990s, he frequently addressed the Dayton Township congregation led by Scott Woodring (killed by authorities in July 2003, after he murdered a policeman). In June 2003, Wickstrom announced another move, this time to Tennessee. A year later, he told a racist audience: "I have a dream! If that goddamn nigger [Dr. Martin Luther King] can have a dream, I can have a dream too. I have a dream that in the days to come there won't be anybody who isn't white that's gonna be in America!" Before year's end, that sentiment won him appointment as "Chaplin" of Charles Juba's Pennsylvania-based Tabernacle of the Phineas Priesthood (motto: "No Jew left alive in 2005").

Williams, Londell—A Missouri carpenter and member of the CSA, Williams was jailed with his wife at Belleville, Illinois, in May 1988 for allegedly plotting to murder black presidential candidate Jesse Jackson. In custody, Williams boasted of his militant connections, telling police that fellow CSA members gave him an automatic rifle before he started stalking Jackson on the campaign trail.

Winrod, Gerald—A fundamentalist minister from Kansas, born in 1900, Winrod discovered anti–Semitism in the 1920s and embarked on a career that earned him recognition as the "Jayhawk Nazi." In 1926 he launched the *Defender,* an extremist magazine published by members of his family over the next half-century. Convinced of a Jewish world conspiracy by *The Protocols of the Learned Elders of Zion* and Henry Ford's *The International Jew,* Winrod saw his worst nightmares realized under FDR's New Deal. Winrod's outspoken support for Adolf Hitler in the *Defender* and another publication, the *Revealer* (1934–37), earned him a federal sedition indictment in 1942, but the charges were dropped two years later. Winrod died in 1957, leaving son Gordon to carry on his work. Missouri's Synod of the Lutheran Church expelled Rev. Gordon Winrod in 1960, for his anti–Semitic statements, but he soon found employment as national chaplain of the NSRP. In 1963, Winrod established Our Savior's Church in Gainesville, Missouri, using its pulpit as a form from which he advocated "killing all Jews" in the United States. In 1994–95, Winrod orchestrated the abduction of his six grandchildren from their fathers in Missouri, concealing them at his farm while he "home schooled" them in neo–Nazi doctrine. Police finally cracked the case four years later, indicting Winrod and his two daughters (mothers of the children, who divorced their respective husbands in 1992) on kidnapping charges. Jurors convicted Gordon Winrod in 2001, resulting in a thirty-year prison sentence for the septuagenarian fascist.

Yockey, Francis Parker—A Chicago native, born in 1917, Yockey graduated with honors from Notre Dame University's law school in 1938. Although opposed to American involvement in World War II, he joined the U.S. Army and served until mid–1942, when he was discharged on grounds of "gross mental instability," specifically "dementia praecox, paranoid type." Despite that diagnosis, U.S. authorities chose Yockey as a staffer for the Nuremberg War Crimes Tribunal in 1946. In Germany, his obvious pro–Nazi sentiments rendered him useless as a member of the prosecution team, and Yockey resigned in early 1947. Traveling through Europe, he fraternized with surviving fascists, helped found the neo–Nazi European Liberation Front in 1949, and penned the fascist screed *Imperium* as "Ulrick Varange." Settled in San Francisco by 1952, with his passport officially revoked, Yockey met budding anti–Semite Willis Carto and sold him the American rights to *Imperium.* Authorities jailed Yockey for a passport violation in 1959, holding him in lieu of $50,000 bail. After a last visit from Carto, Yockey killed himself with cyanide on 16 June 1960. Carto subsequently republished *Imperium* and organized a secretive Francis Parker Yockey Society in his hero's honor.

Organizations

Adolf Hitler Free Corps—A handful of neo–Nazis in Kirkwood, Pennsylvania, organized the AHFC in 1997, then disbanded the following year.

America First Committee (1982–93)—A neo–Nazi splinter group founded in 1982 by ANP defectors, led by Arthur Jones of Chicago, the AFC remained on friendly terms with its parent organization and other racist groups. In 1983, ads promoting the AFC appeared in the ANP's *Bulletin.* The AFC survived through 1991, but apparently disbanded the following year.

American Conservative Party—Based in St. Louis, Missouri, the ACP shared a mailing address with the local Workers for [George] Wallace organization in 1967–68. Leader Floyd Kitchen doubled as president of the St. Louis Property Owners Association, which sponsored an appearance by J.B. Stoner in 1968. Another ACP officer, James Kernodle, was a member of Robert DePugh's Minutemen.

American National Socialist Party—The neo–Nazi ANSP established chapters in Cowarts, Alabama, and Yukon, Pennsylvania, during 1998, but neither survived the following year.

American National Socialist Resistance—Active in Bellevue, Illinois, during 1997, the ANSR dissolved in early 1998.

American Nationalist Confederation—Founded in 1936 by West Virginia klansman George Deatherage, the ANC billed itself as a coalition of seventy-two pro–Nazi fringe groups. It shared a mailing address with Deatherage's Knights of the White Camellia, and dissolved following his 1942 sedition indictment.

American Nationalist Federation—SPLC investigators found this neo–Nazi splinter group active in Lawrenceville, Georgia, during 1990, but it disbanded the following year.

American Nationalist Party—This neo–Nazi group operated from Portage, Michigan, in 1999, then disbanded in early 2000.

American Nazi Party (1958–67)—The most visible neo–Nazi movement in America was founded by George Lincoln Rockwell in November 1958 or March 1959 (reports vary), with headquarters at Arlington, Virginia. In his autobiography, *This Time the World* (1962), Rockwell described his followers thusly: "The anti–Jewish movement abounds with cowards, jerks, queers and fanatics. Many of the characters who were attracted to us were pretty sorry." In 1959, Rockwell sold ANP headquarters to Floyd Fleming, former supporter of John Kasper. Two years later, in May 1961, the party's "hate bus" toured Dixie in protest against CORE's integrated freedom rides. Virginia authorities revoked the ANP's charter on 6 April 1962, but Rockwell remained in business. He sent a three-man delegation to counter SPLC demonstrations in Albany, Georgia, and Rockwell himself was on hand for joint demonstrations with robed klansmen in Chicago's Marquette Park, in July 1966.

Members of the American Nazi Party were closely allied to various KKK factions (Library of Congress).

That same month, his followers joined klansmen and NSRP members for a joint rally in Cambridge, Maryland. UKA Wizard Robert Shelton initially disdained collaboration with the ANP, but various UKA officers from Texas to California, Delaware, New Jersey, New York and Pennsylvania held joint membership in both groups. In 1966, over opposition from key aide Matt Koehl, Rockwell renamed his party the NSWPP. After Rockwell's August 1967 assassination, Koehl took the helm, but his personality clashes with subordinates produced numerous defections, leaving the party in shambles.

American Nazi Party (1982–93)—"Colonel" James Burford of Chicago commanded the NSPA in 1982, renaming it in honor of George Rockwell's original ANP. Some media reports from 1983 claim that dissension split the group a few months later, with ex-klansman Dennis Milam taking the helm,

but SPLC investigators found Burford still leading the ANP in 1989. By that time, satellite chapters existed in Indianapolis, Milwaukee, and San Antonio, Texas. A year later, the Texas and Wisconsin chapters vanished, replaced by outposts in California and New Jersey. Chicago headquarters stood alone by 1991, and the ANP disbanded sometime before the SPLC's survey of active hate groups in 1997.

American States Rights Association—One of Alabama's first resistance groups organized in 1954, the ASRA was founded by Birmingham insurance salesman Olin Horton (also a favored speaker at Citizens' Council rallies). Asa Carter joined the ASRA before moving on to found his own North Alabama Citizens' Council in 1955.

American Vanguard—This neo–Nazi clique operated briefly from Tewsbury, Massachusetts, during 1991–92.

American White Separatist—Despite its title, which appears to describe a single individual, this neo–Nazi group had chapters in Glendale, California, and Bremerton, Washington, in 1991. It disbanded sometime during 1992–93.

American Workers Party—Based in Bethlehem, Pennsylvania, this neo–Nazi group was briefly active during 1991–92.

Anglo-Saxon Christian Congregation—Klansman Wesley Swift founded this Christian Identity group in Los Angeles, in 1945, and led it through the early 1950s. ADL investigators pegged its membership around 300, marking it as California's strongest anti–Semitic group of the era.

Aryan Brotherhood—Founded at California's San Quentin prison in 1967, this criminal gang with neo–Nazi roots has spread through prisons nationwide over the past four decades, while members in the "free world" pursue careers in auto theft, drug-dealing, prostitution and contract murder. The AB evolved from a 1950s gang called the Bluebirds, also dubbed the Nazi Gang, adopting a strange mixture of Norse/Viking and occult/satanic symbolism. Its "blood in-blood out" philosophy mandates murder as an initiation rite and assures that gang members may never retire short of death. After a brief flirtation with Charles Manson's "family" in the early 1970s, AB members found marginally more stable allies in the Aryan Nations and the Hells Angels motorcycle gang. Law enforcement spokesmen contend that a central "Commission" rules AB affairs. Many AB members now regard *The Turner Diaries* (written by National Alliance leader William Pierce) as their "Bible." The three racists who murdered James Byrd at Jasper, Texas, in June 1998 all claimed membership in the AB, as well as a small Ku Klux faction.

Aryan Free Press—A neo–Nazi propaganda mill, based in Champaign, Illinois, the AFP operated briefly during 1997.

Aryan Mothers Inspiring Something Hopeful—Hope fell short for this neo–Nazi sorority, briefly active in New Holland, Pennsylvania, during 1998.

Aryan Nations—In 1974, veteran neo–Nazi Richard Butler transplanted klansman Wesley Swift's Church of Jesus Christ Christian from Lancaster, California, to Hayden Lake, Idaho.

Guards screen new arrivals to the Aryan World Congress at Hayden Lake, Idaho, in July 1988 (Southern Poverty Law Center).

Approximately three years later, he announced creation of a new hate group, the Aryan Nations, as the "political arm" of his cult. Shortly thereafter, Butler's annual Aryan World Congress became a rallying point for anti–Semites and white supremacists of every description, including members of various Klans and affiliated paramilitary groups. Cross-burnings were a frequent sight at the Aryan Nations compound, and Butler kept a small sculpture of a robed klansman on his desk, along with busts of Adolf Hitler. During 1982–83, members of Butler's group, the National Alliance, and several Klan factions met at Hayden Lake to organize their own private army, called The Order after a guerrilla band in William Pierce's racist novel *The Turner Diaries*. When the group became successful at armed robbery, Butler received a share of their loot—and subsequently found himself indicted for sedition with other alleged participants in the conspiracy. Trial on those charges ended with acquittal for all concerned, but trouble persisted in Idaho, where AN members faced charges of plotting contract murder (1985), threatening federal officers (1986), and detonating a series of bombs around Coeur d'Alene (1986).

On 7 October 1989, Aryan Nations staged their first-ever public parade in Pulaski, Tennessee (the KKK's birthplace), and there established its first chapter outside of Idaho. A decade later, Butler's expanding group claimed fourteen chapters in as many states. In 2000, when Butler announced creation of a short-lived Aryan National Alliance, SPLC investigators found twenty-four chapters active in nineteen states, but the tide was turning. Success inspired defectors to compete with Butler for members and headlines. One splinter group, the Church of True Israel, left Butler's fold in 1996 to follow racist guru Charles Mangels. Two years later, SPLC attorneys sued Butler on behalf of victims assaulted by his security guards, and a $6.3 million damage award in September 2000 left the cult bankrupt. Butler retired as "pastor" in 2002, and presided over his last parade through Coeur d'Alene in July 2003, succeeded by a four-man ruling council that included former Alabama klansman Clark "Laslo" Patterson. After Butler's death, in September 2004, Patterson announced the relocation of AN "World Headquarters"

to Lincoln, Alabama. By year's end, Patterson's group claimed fifteen chapters in fourteen states, while rival groups in Pennsylvania and Louisiana claimed rightful ownership of Butler's legacy.

Aryan Nations (offshoot)—Organized by Posse Comitatus veteran August Kreis in 2002, this splinter group headquartered at Ulysses, Pennsylvania, claimed twelve chapters in eleven states. A year later, SPLC investigators found only two chapters remaining (both in Pennsylvania), but the group expanded slightly in 2004, claiming satellite chapters in Florida and Michigan. The group draws occasional support from ex-convict James Wickstrom, who also promotes ex–Klansman Charles Juba's Tabernacle of the Phineas Priesthood.

Aryan Racial Loyalist Party—Another neo–Nazi splinter faction of the early 1990s, the ARLP operated in Zanesville, Ohio, during 1991–92. A hiatus then ensued, until the group resurfaced briefly at Lakewood, Ohio, during 1998. No trace of it remained in 1999.

Aryan Resistance Society—First reported active in 2002, with chapters in Livingston, New Jersey, and Fort Worth, Texas, the ARS lost its Lone Star chapter in 2003, while gaining outposts in Missouri and New York. SPLC investigators found no active units surviving in 2004.

Aryan Werwulfe Brotherhood—SPLC investigators found this neo–Nazi clique active in Palm Beach, Florida, during 2002. No trace of it remained the following year.

Aryan Workers Organization—Based at Science Hill, Kentucky, the AWO was briefly active during 1991–92.

Assembly of Christian Soldiers, Inc.—A racist "church" active in 1972–74, the ACS claimed 3,000 members in Alabama, Georgia and Mississippi. Journalist Albert Foley described the group's leader as a former imperial wizard of the "Original Knights of the KKK of the Confederacy," but Foley provided no name. A front group, dubbed The Southerners, issued sporadic bulletins and maintained telephone dial-a-message services. Denied religious tax exemption by the IRS, the ACS borrowed $35,000 from a Birmingham physician to open a grocery store. When that venture failed, the doctor foreclosed and hauled off the produce to settle the debt. Another ACS project, mimicking the Klan, was a drive for private white "academies," permitting racist parents to transfer their children from integrated public schools. A widow in Mobile donated a twenty-acre former stockyard for ACS headquarters, and public rallies on the site drew an average of 300 persons. At one such gathering, ACS members mistook reporter Foley for an FBI agent, attacking him with hammers, but he escaped with only minor injuries. An estimated 1,200 workers from three states volunteered to erect ACS headquarters, but the sect was evicted for nonpayment of rent before they broke ground.

Black Cavalry—This group of racist "regulators" organized in Tallapoosa County, Alabama, soon after the Civil War. Its nightriding members "disciplined" freedmen and drove some from the county, later merging with the local KKK.

Black Legion—The modern Klan's most significant spin-off organization began life in the 1920s as the Black Guards, a black-robed security unit of the Ohio KKK. Klansman Arthur Lupp founded a Michigan regiment of the Black Guards in 1931, serving as its "major general" while subordinates organized into brigades, regiments, battalions and companies. By the time his unit formally broke with the Klan, operating as the Black Legion, Lupp claimed a million members in the Wolverine State, but realistic estimates placed the group's peak total somewhere between 20,000 and 30,000 (one-third of whom lived in Detroit). Like its parent organization, the Black Legion worked behind front groups, including the Wolverine Republican Club and the Wayne County Rifle and Pistol Club. Its stated goals were to "fight political Romanism, Judaism, Communism, and all 'isms' which our forefathers came to this country to avoid." The order recruited numerous Detroit policemen, including Commissioner Heinrich Pickert, thus securing a measure of immunity for its campaign of floggings, bombings and murders. Labor organizers suffered the Legion's wrath, while Lupp (and inspector for Detroit's Department of Public Health) investigated means of spreading typhoid fever through the city's "undesirable" neighborhoods. Exposure followed the May 1936 murder of Charles Poole, an organizer for the Works Progress Administration, whom legionnaires accused of wife-beating. (In fact, his wife was hospitalized for complications related to pregnancy.) Triggerman Dayton Dean, an employee of Detroit's Public Lighting Department, confessed and named his cohorts in custody, prompting a series of wide-ranging scandals and investigations through 1936–37. Twelve members faced trial for Poole's murder, with eleven convicted and sentenced to life imprisonment before year's end. Broader indictments ultimately sent thirty-seven more legionnaires to prison on various charges. When Hollywood released *The Black Legion* in 1937, Georgia Klan sued for unauthorized use of KKK regalia and symbols.

Black Muslims *see* Nation of Islam

California Anti-Communist League—An anti-Semitic group run by Wesley Swift and Dennis Mower, the CACL operated from Lancaster, California, in 1971.

California Rangers—Founded by William Potter Gale in 1960, this paramilitary group recruited most of its members from veterans' organizations, arming to defend the Golden State from a mythical Red invasion. In 1963, journalists exposed Gale's bid to control an American Legion post in Signal Hill, California, and police jailed one of Gale's rangers for selling automatic weapons to an undercover officer. A 1965 report from the state legislature declared that the California Rangers "have intimate connections with the Ku Klux Klan, the National States Rights Party, the Christian Defense League, and the Church of Jesus Christ Christian."

Caucasian Clubs—This alternate name was applied to some KWC "councils" around New Orleans after January 1869.

Caucasian League—Organized in Miami, Florida, after "Black Monday," this short-lived group devoted itself to opposing school integration.

Cavalcade of White Americans—Founded by ex-policeman Henry Brooks in Savannah, Georgia, the CWA armed in preparation for black riots during 1962 and staged a raucous motorcade in protest against a black boycott led by the Chatham County Crusade for Voters.

Central New York White Pride—Based in Syracuse, this neo–Nazi group operated from 1998–2001, then disbanded.

Chicago White Vikings—An ambitious neo–Nazi clique with little follow-through, the CWV appeared in 1990 and disbanded the following year.

Christian Defense League—Another brainchild of California klansman Wesley Swift and retired Lt. Col. William Gale, the CDL maintained close ties with other racist groups nationwide. Klan orator Connie Lynch was a leading CDL member in the 1960s, while director Bertrand Comparet served as attorney for the Minutemen and the NSRP in San Diego. In 1964, police raided a CDL member's home in Cucamonga, California, seizing eight machine guns, incendiary bombs, and blasting caps. Police informants reported that the CDL welcomed klansmen and other extremists into its ranks, making it "the central group, the reporting group, for all these organizations. The very sister and co-worker in this, of the CDL on the West Coast, is the National States Rights Party." In June 1964, CDL leaders met with ANP founder George Rockwell to share information on police infiltrators. During 1963–64, the CDL held meetings at the Los Angeles home of klansman G. Clinton Wheat, and California Attorney General Thomas McDonald announced a "real coalescence" between the CDL, the NSRP, and other racist groups. Aging anti–Semite John Crommelin served as the CDL's eastern coordinator in 1971, but the seat of operations soon shifted to Louisiana, with offices at Arabi and Baton Rouge. Ex-klansman James Warner led the CDL as late as 1983, combining the group's operation with that of his New Christian Crusade Church. The group remained active, albeit shrunken and marginalized, at press time for this volume.

Christian Freedom Council—Organized by Michigan Rep. Mark Siljander in 1979, the CFC was created to purge "obscene" books from public libraries in Niles and Three Rivers. Leaders were embarrassed when klansmen flocked to the effort, one CFC spokesman branding the KKK as "disgustingly more immoral than any pornographic book or magazine could ever be."

Christian Nationalist Alliance—Another short-lived creation of klansman Wesley Swift and Dennis Mower, the CNA shared Swift's home address in Lancaster, California, during 1971.

Christian Nationalist Crusade—Launched by professional anti–Semite Gerald L.K. Smith in 1947, the CNC welcomed klansmen into membership and positions of authority (e.g., Wesley Swift). Based in Eureka, Arkansas, the CNC served as a racist propaganda mill, providing literature to various Klans, Citizens' Councils and the John Birch Society, among others. In that capacity, it served as an early bridge between white-supremacist groups and the anti-communist fringe of the post–World War II era. Smith's magazine, *The Cross and the Flag*, supported Klan terrorists through the 1960s, decrying their "persecution" by FBI agents and the DOJ. After Smith's death in 1976, successor R.L. Morgan moved the CNC's headquarters to Glendale, California, but the group soon collapsed when deprived of its founder's energy and guiding hand.

Christian-Patriots Defense League—John Harrell
founded this anti–Semitic survivalist group at Flora, Illinois, in 1977. Members freely mingled with klansmen, while CPDL spokesmen predicted "an almost certain and inescapable collapse of the present [U.S.] structure," caused by insidious agents of "the Pharisaical anti–Christ system." In 1979, Harrell announced his intent to train whites for a coming race war against the "Christ-hating International Jewish Conspiracy." Throughout the early 1980s, CPDL members gathered for semi-annual "Freedom Festivals" at Harrell's fifty-acre estate outside Louisville, Illinois, incorporating conferences of Harrell's Citizens Emergency Defense System. The CEDS, in turn, published a list of approved "Christian-patriotic" groups that included Robert Shelton's UKA. At the 1980 summer festival, more than 1,000 persons joined in seminars on firearms, archery and knife-fighting. The same year saw Harrell announce plans for a 232-acre "permanent base" in Missouri's Ozark region, some twenty-five miles from Fort Leonard Wood, with a second base located in West Virginia. The CPDL's ultimate goal was creation of a white "survival area" in the American heartland, spanning parts of twenty states, with its four corners at Pittsburgh, Pennsylvania; Atlanta, Georgia; Lubbock, Texas; and Scottsbluff, Nebraska. Harrell's grandiose plans did not survive the 1980s, and the CPDL vanished before SPLC investigators surveyed active hate groups in 1990.

Church of Jesus Christ—SPLC investigators listed
KKKK leader Thom Robb as pastor of this racist church, based in Harrison, Arkansas, from 1989 through 1998. The sect added "Christian" to its name in 1997—thereby apparently claiming kinship to late klansman Wesley Swift and his spin-off "religion," the Aryan Nations—but the suffix vanished in 1998. Church headquarters shifted to Bergman, Arkansas, in 1999 (while the KKKK's imperial office remained in Harrison), suggesting a change in leadership. No trace of the CJC remained when the SPLC surveyed active hate groups in 2000.

Church of Jesus Christ Christian—Founded by
klansman Wesley Swift in 1946, as the Anglo-Saxon Christian Congregation, the CJCC served as a major outlet for Christian Identity doctrines in the United States. By the early 1960s, a string of "parishes" in California and a small-station radio network carried Swift's message to an estimated one million listeners. Swift's ordained ministers included klansman Connie Lynch and Dennis Mower, an NSRP member and close friend of WKKKKM Wizard Sam Bowers. Oren Potito, head of the CJCC's "eastern conference" in St. Petersburg, Florida, was another NSRP recruiter and former campaign manager for anti-Semite John Crommelin. In 1965, California state legislators found CJCC leaders working closely with the Klan, NSRP, Minutemen and California Rangers. After Swift's death in 1970,

successor Richard Butler moved the sect's headquarters to Hayden Lake, Idaho, appending the name "Aryan Nations" to its former title. In its new guise, the CJCC remained a keystone of the neo–Nazi movement through the remainder of the twentieth century.

Church of the Avenger—Neo–Nazis in Tampa, Florida,
created this "church" in 1997, then dissolved it in early 1998.

Church of the Creator *see* World Church of the Creator

Church of the Sons of Yahweh—This Christian Identity splinter sect was founded in 2002 by Aryan Nations defectors Morris Gullett and Harold "Ray" Redfeairn. Both hailed from Dayton, Ohio, where Redfeairn was imprisoned for shooting a police officer in 1979. Paroled in 1991, he collected more convictions for drunk driving and carrying concealed weapons, while serving first as an Ohio Klan leader, then (in 1997) as the state's top-ranking Aryan Nations member, operating from his former KKK headquarters in New Vienna. Gullett was jailed in March 1997 for separate assaults on a park ranger and a Dayton policeman, but he pled guilty on reduced charges and served only one year of a potential twenty-year prison term. After Redfeairn's death from a heart attack in October 2003, Gullett transferred church headquarters to Calhoun, Louisiana, and changed its name to the Church of the Sons of YHVH/Legion of Saints. ADL observers deem it "the most disturbing" of several Aryan Nations splinter groups still active in America.

Church of the Swastika—A thinly-veiled neo–Nazi group in Monterey, California, this "church" was briefly active during 1991–92.

Citizens' Council(s)—Launched in July 1954 to oppose the U.S. Supreme Court's "Black Monday" ruling on school integration, the Citizens' Council advertised itself as a peaceable and law-abiding organization, pledged to defend "the southern way of life" by all legal means. Its founders prided themselves on respectability, bristling when critics dubbed their group the "uptown Klan," "white-collar Klan," or even *White* Citizens' Council. (Patriotic blacks were always free to join, spokesmen declared, as long as they supported segregation.) Florida klansman Bill Hendrix quickly denounced the Councils as "full of Jews," but many CC chapters distributed anti–Semitic literature from Gerald Smith's Christian Nationalist Crusade and other sources, along with their other racist, far-right publications. Favored CC pressure techniques included dismissal of "radical" blacks from their jobs, termination of credit at various stores, foreclosure of mortgages, publication of names when blacks registered to vote, and "reverse freedom rides" that dispatched indigent southern blacks on one-way trips to "liberal" northern cities. Politicians in thrall to the Councils simultaneously launched investigations of "subversive" civil rights groups, threatened "nullification" of Supreme Court rulings in Dixie, and passed dozens of unconstitutional statutes supporting Jim Crow.

Still, some southern observers were skeptical about the CC's ability to preserve segregation. One racist spokesman declared that the Councils were "watchdogs of segregation in the

Deep South, but when the going gets tough and they need bull-dogs with that instinct for the jugular, the Klan will be there to step in." And in fact, some Councils were secretly (or openly) allied with the KKK from their earliest days. The membership of Asa Carter's North Alabama Citizens' Council, established in October 1955, was virtually interchangeable with that of his Original KKK of the Confederacy, created a year later. Carter's men joined in February 1956 riot against black coed Autherine Lucy's admission to the University of Alabama, assaulted singer Nat "King" Cole during a Birmingham performance in April 1956, and castrated another black victim, Edward Aaron, in September 1957. In 1956, in the midst of a bus boycott let by Dr. Martin Luther King, CC leaders in Montgomery, Alabama, invited Mississippi Senator James Eastland to address a cheering crowd of 12,000 racists. Pamphlets circulated through the audience read:

> When in the course of human events it becomes necessary to abolish the Negro race, proper methods should be used. Among these are guns, bows and arrows, sling shots and knives. We hold these truths to be self-evident, that all whites are created equal with certain rights, among these are life, liberty and the pursuit of dead niggers.
>
> In every stage of the bus boycott, we have been oppressed and degraded because of black, slimy, juicy unbearably stinking niggers. Their conduct should not be dwelt upon because behind them they have an ancestral background of Pygmies, Head Hunters and snot suckers. My friends, it is time we wised up to these black devils. I tell you they are a group of two-legged agitators who persist in walking up and down our streets protruding their black lips. If we don't stop helping these African flesh eaters, we will soon wake up and find Reverend King in the White House.
> LET'S GET ON THE BALL WHITE CITIZENS.

Council-Klan collaboration was common wherever both groups existed side-by-side. In June 1956, racist agitator John Kasper organized his own Seaboard White Citizens' Council in Washington, D.C., moving on to incite riots and terrorist bombings (with help from Asa Carter) in Clinton, Tennessee. A year later, in Louisville, Kentucky, Edward Fields served the local CC, before graduating to the United White Party and its successor, the NSRP. In winter 1958–59, CC leaders in South Carolina charged that klansmen had infiltrated the Council by subterfuge, seeking to advance their own "cowardly, secretive" ends. In 1959, Homer Barrs served as secretary-treasurer of Florida's Association of Citizens' Councils, describing Klan leader J.E. Fraser as a friend and "fine, right-thinking boy." (In media interviews, Barrs stressed that klansmen were not barred from joining the ACC.) At a June 1963 Council meeting in Birmingham, Alabama, Klan leaflets circulated through the audience and speakers announced a forthcoming UKA rally. A month later, klansmen joined CC members to picket Birmingham's new biracial commission on 13 July 1963. In September 1970, CC members again joined klansmen to protest new "awareness" programs in Memphis, Tennessee, grade schools.

Even when not collaborating with klansmen, "respectable" CC members and supporters were capable of deadly violence. In 1955, gunmen in Belzoni, Mississippi, murdered NAACP leader George Lee and wounded colleague Gus Courts, after both targets ignored threats from known CC members. In September 1959, police in Little Rock, Arkansas, jailed E.A. Lauderdale—a director of the local CC—for bombing the school board office and other targets linked to school integration. Ten months later, FBI agents caught Emmett Miller—founder of the Crittenden County Citizens' Council in Little Rock—planting a bomb at Philander Smith College. After his release from prison, Smith went on to serve as a kleagle and NSRP officer. November 1960 witnessed white riots in New Orleans, after racist politician Leander Perez told an audience of 5,000 CC members, "These Congolese rape your daughters." After a sniper killed Mississippi NAACP leader Medgar Evers, in June 1963, FBI agents traced the murder weapon to CC member Byron De La Beckwith, whereupon CC members organized a White Citizens' Defense Fund to cover Beckwith's legal bills.

By mid–1964, with a new civil rights act passed by Congress and Mississippi's "Freedom Summer" in full swing, most observers agreed that the Councils had failed in their bid to preserve segregation. In Mississippi, klansmen and APWR members infiltrated the Councils, further undermining their tarnished "respectable" image. The movement's last hope was embodied in Alabama Governor George Wallace, a proud CC member with presidential ambitions. Council members zealously supported Wallace's third-party movement in 1968, remaining steadfast when his near-assassination passed the torch to California congressman (and JBS spokesman) John Schmitz in 1972. Doomed by attrition after that defeat, the Councils withered and dissolved—then rose again in 1985, as the Council of Conservative Citizens.

Citizens' Council of America—Despite its name, this short-lived group was actually a branch of the paramilitary Posse Comitatus, operating from Camden, Arkansas, during 1989–90 under "Colonel" John Warnock. It dissolved in early 1991.

Citizens' Segregation Committee—A forerunner of Alabama's various Citizens' Councils, this group was organized in Birmingham to resist school integration after "Black Monday."

Civilian Materiel Assistance—Organized by Alabama residents in 1983, to provide "humanitarian" aid for the far-right Contra terrorists in Nicaragua, CMA was transformed by 1986 into an extralegal paramilitary group dedicated to stalking illegal immigrants along the U.S.–Mexican border. In July 1986, Hispanic civil rights groups filed formal complaints against CMA, alleging that its members set lethal booby traps along the border and detained suspected aliens at gunpoint, without authority. Texas state officials announced plans to file criminal charges against CMA, while national director Tommy Posey declared that patrols would continue. A policy rift split CMA's first national convention, held in Memphis, Tennessee, during July 1986, when Texas state coordinator D.L. "Pappy" Hicks announced immediate suspension of vigilante patrols, while denying reported links between CMA and the Texas Klan. Hicks told reporters, "Most of us believe that we've distracted [*sic*] from what we were set up for: to give aid to the freedom fighters in Nicaragua."

Columbians, Inc.

Columbians, Inc.—America's first neo–Nazi group was chartered in Georgia on 17 August 1946. According to official documents, the organization's purpose was "to encourage people to think in terms of race, nation and faith and to work for a national moral reawakening in order to build a progressive white community that is bound together by a deep spiritual consciousness of a common past and determination to share a common future." In practice, potential Columbians were asked three questions: "Do you hate Jews? Do you hate Negroes? Do you have three dollars?" Leading Columbians included architect Emory Burke (self-styled "sole authority" on policy decisions), Homer Loomis, Jr., and John Zimmerlee, Jr. Burke's prior experience included work on *The Storm*, a 1930s racist paper published in New York, while a fake British accent masked his Alabama roots. Loomis, a New Yorker, claimed to be a graduate of Princeton University, but his credentials were invisible. Attorney Vester Ownby came to the Columbians via a Georgia group called We the People, briefly active during World War II. Columbian recruits wore khaki uniforms emblazoned with lightning-bolt insignia borrowed from Adolf Hitler's SS. Organizational guidelines came straight from a book titled *Klan Building*, published by a Midwestern realm in 1937–38. Small wonder, then, that Georgia Attorney General Dan Duke would later describe Burke's crew as "the juvenile delinquents of the Klan."

By autumn 1946, out-of-state chapters were planted in Indianapolis and Gary, Indiana, in Minneapolis, Philadelphia, and New York City, with still more authorized in Florida, Tennessee, Texas and Wisconsin. October 1946 found the Columbians patrolling Atlanta's streets, assaulting blacks at random, and bombing a black-owned home on Halloween. On 2 November, police raided a Columbian picket line outside another black home, jailing Loomis and three others for inciting a riot. State authorities moved to revoke the group's charter on 5 November, then slapped Burke and Loomis with charges of usurping police powers on 10 November. Dan Duke told reporters that Burke's name had graced the masthead of "nearly every fascist organization in the country prior to World War II." On 23 November, Duke punched Burke during a confrontation in judge's chambers, thereby earning himself a place on the Columbians' "lynch list" (revealed by infiltrators from the Anti-Nazi League). On 13 December 1946, prosecutors indicted Burke, Loomis and Ira Jett for illegal possession of dynamite, alleging a conspiracy to bomb police headquarters, Atlanta's civic auditorium, and two newspaper offices. Jurors convicted Loomis of inciting a riot on 16 February 1947, while a second panel convicted him of usurping police powers on 27 March, resulting in a thirty-month prison term. In a separate trial, on 21 February 1947, jurors convicted Burke on three misdemeanor counts, sending him to jail for three years. Stripped of their Georgia charter on 27 June 1947, the Columbians joined Sam Green's AGK and the CPUSA on the U.S. Attorney General's list of subversive organizations. A decade later, Edward Fields and J.B. Stoner copied the group's uniforms, insignia and title of its newspaper (*The Thunderbolt*) for their own NSRP.

Committee of the States

Committee of the States—Another Posse Comitatus chapter with a deceptive title, this group surfaced briefly in 1989, under leader Lee Luttrell. SPLC investigators could not locate its headquarters, but the search proved irrelevant with the faction's disbandment in 1990.

Confederate Society of America

Confederate Society of America—Billing itself as the "FIRST southern nationalist organization," led by Craig Maus from Warrensburg, Missouri, the CSA is closely linked to the racist CCC and League of the South. CSA founder Jim Bitzer was a member of the CCC's executive board, while Maus was a League member and former head of the CCC's Virginia branch, and vice president Kenny Ashford was chairman of the CCC in Baton Rouge, Louisiana.

Confederate States of America

Confederate States of America—Seeking to revive the rebel government which lost the Civil War, the CSA is led by ex-"militia" members Rick Ainsworth and Bill Cox from headquarters in Tallahassee, Florida. The group also seeks repeal of U.S. Constitutional Amendments 11 through 26, thus effectively negating black citizenship, women's suffrage and the federal income tax. Confederate battle flags, CSA spokesmen suggest, "should be held in reserve until hostilities begin."

Constitutional Union Guard

Constitutional Union Guard—Organized in North Carolina during winter 1867–68, the CUG collaborated with the KKK and White Brotherhood in defense of white supremacy and the Democratic Party during Reconstruction. There is no doubt that klansmen joined the CUG; in fact, its local units were called "klans." Primarily restricted to the Tarheel State, CUG members terrorized Republicans during the 1868 presidential campaign and lynched five black prisoners at Kinston in January 1869. Four months later, klansmen teamed with the CUG to murder Jones County Sheriff O.R. Cosgrove, subsequently driving his brother—state legislator D.D. Cosgrove—out of the state. In August 1869, CUG gunmen assassinated GOP leader M.L. Shepard. Investigators persuaded three members to turn state's evidence in that case, whereupon twenty-five suspects were indicted and held for trial in October 1869. The CUG dissolved in 1870, after Klan leader James Boyd persuaded its officers to join him in renouncing violence.

Council of Conservative Citizens

Council of Conservative Citizens—On 7 March 1985, thirty aging white men met in Atlanta, Georgia, to share their anger at federal "giveaway programs, special preferences and quotas, crack-related crime and single mothers and third generation welfare mothers dependent on government checks and food stamps." Most of those assembled were ex-members of the defunct Citizens' Council, including 1950s CC founder Robert "Tut" Patterson, Mississippian William Lord (former CC regional organizer), and St. Louis attorney Gordon Lee Baum (formerly Midwestern field organizer for the 1960s Councils). The men founded a new Council of Conservative Citizens in Atlanta, named Baum as its leader, and used old CC membership lists to solicit recruits nationwide. The SPLC estimated CCC membership at 15,000 in 1999. By press time for this volume, the CCC claimed fifty-one chapters in eighteen states, although its heaviest concentration (thirty-five chapters) lay below the Mason-Dixon Line.

Like its parent organization, the CCC affects a mantle of respectability while filling its newsletter (the *Citizen Informer*) and the pages of its Internet website with blatant racist propaganda. Typical CCC rants include articles branding Abraham Lincoln a homosexual and warnings that nonwhite immigration may reduce America to "a slimy brown mass of glop." Also prominently featured are lurid stories of black-on-white crime and pseudo-scientific treatises "proving" nonwhites genetically inferior. On the group's California website, contributor Peter Anthony wrote: "Just as breeds of dogs are different, races of people are different as well. And just as no two cultures created by different Races are even remotely alike, no two races have the same destiny in the eyes of God." Anthony also voiced nostalgia for simpler times "when the Klan could 'march on Washington' to the cheers of an adoring public, when race-mixing and homosexuality were taboo, when racial separation was the norm." The *Citizens Informer* carries ads for other racist groups, such as the Ohio-based Heritage Lost Ministries (purveyors of neo–Nazi literature), while managing editor Christ Temple calls himself a "very close personal friend" of Aryan Nations founder Richard Butler.

Despite such flagrant bigotry, the CCC has drawn many right-wing politicians to its fold, as honored speakers (if not dues-paying members). The most notorious example was Sen. Trent Lott, who frequently addressed CCC gatherings before his racist comments cost him his post as Senate majority leader. In 1992, Lott told a Greenwood, Mississippi, CCC audience, "We need more meetings like this. The people in this room stand for the right principles and the right philosophy. Let's take it in the right direction and our children will be the beneficiaries." When his affiliation with the CCC was finally exposed in 1998, Lott falsely claimed that he had "no first-hand knowledge" of the group. (Lott also wrote a column for the *Citizen Informer*, while his uncle served on the CCC's executive board, and CCC leaders dubbed Lott an "honorary member" of their group.) Likewise, Georgia's Rep. Bob Barr (keynote speaker at the CCC's June 1998 convention) later told reporters he had "no idea" what leaders of the group believe and preach. Other political allies include ex-governor Lester Maddox (Georgia), ex-congressman John Rarick (named in FBI files as an active Louisiana klansman in the early 1970s), Sen. Jesse Helms (North Carolina), ex–Gov. Guy Hunt (Alabama), ex–Gov. Kirk Fordyce (Mississippi), Gov. Haley Barbour (Mississippi), and Rep. Webb Franklin (Mississippi), and Kay Cobb (presiding justice of Mississippi's supreme court). In 2004, SPLC researchers identified fifty politicians aligned with the CCC, including twenty-six state legislators (twenty-three in Mississippi) and twelve local officials. Nearly all were "conservative" Republicans.

Pleas of ignorance from such figures, concerning the CCC's extremism, appear disingenuous. Mississippi state senator (and CCC) member Mike Gunn once received $9,500 with his wife, for preparing David Duke's political campaign literature. Baum and two other CCC leaders urged members to support Duke's campaigns in the early 1990s, and Duke himself addressed the CCC's South Carolina chapter in 1995. Three years later, in November 1998, Duke attended a CCC rally in Jackson, Mississippi, where Baum permitted sale of Duke's hate literature until Gov. Fordyce and other dignitaries arrived to address the assembly. (British neo–Nazi leader Mark Cotterill also claims

Duke was invited to address a CCC meeting in Washington, D.C.; Baum denies it.) Prof. Glayde Whitney, a CCC member in Florida, wrote the foreword for Duke's autobiography (*My Awakening*) in 1998.

Nor is Duke the only fringe spokesman linked to the CCC in recent years. At the turn of the millennium, SPLC investigators found a significant number of CCC members carried Klan-Nazi baggage of their own. Vince Reed, security chief of the Aryan Nations and a covert police informant, stayed as a guest in Baum's home during 1995. Reed says Baum offered him a post on the CCC's executive board, while remarking, "The Jews are going to fall from the inside, not the outside, and the niggers will be puppets on a string for us." (Baum calls Reed's tale a "total lie.") Three years later, after South Carolina CCC member Marshal Catterton shot a black teenager who tore a picture of the Confederate flag, Baum told reporters he might do "just as Catterton did" in the same situation. Billy Roper, founder of the neo–Nazi group White Revolution, joined the CCC in the late 1990s and addressed its Arkansas chapter in 2000 on the subject of racial evolution. In January 1999, Baum publicly admitted that his group drew criticism because "we were just being too dang candid" on matters of race. Nonetheless, within weeks, the CCC's Washington chapter welcomed DeWest Hooker (self-described "best friend" of ANP founder George Rockwell) as a guest speaker. His prescription for success: "Be a Nazi, but don't use the word." Delegates to the CCC's 2005 convention in Montgomery, Alabama, included former Imperial Wizard Stephen Donald Black (founder of the racist Stormfront website), Edward Fields (perennial klansman and founder of the NSRP), Jamie Kelso (David Duke's former Louisiana roommate and longtime aide-de-camp), and Alabama CCC leader Leonard "Flagpole" Wilson (a leader of the 1956 riot that drove black coed Autherine Lucy from the University of Alabama).

Covenant, Sword and Arm of the Lord—Christian Identity minister James Ellison founded the CSA in 1976, with headquarters in Marion County, Arkansas, at the commune he dubbed Zarephath-Horeb. Spokesman Kerry Noble described the group as a collection of "Christian survivalists who believe in preparing for the ultimate holocaust." To that end, Ellison established an "Endtime Overcomer Survival Training School," which offered CSA members and selected outsiders classes in marksmanship, survival techniques, and "Christian martial arts." Later, as Ellison fraternized increasingly with the Aryan Nations and other neo–Nazi groups, he characterized Zarephath-Horeb as "an arms depot and paramilitary training ground for Aryan Warriors." In 1981–82, CSA members served as security guards for "Freedom Festivals" sponsored by the Christian-Patriots Defense League in Louisville, Illinois. By August 1983, inspired by members of The Order, Ellison launched his own guerrilla campaign against "ZOG," including acts of arson, bombing, and at least two murders committed by CSA member Richard Snell. An FBI raid in April 1985 left Ellison and other CSA members facing federal prison time, while fewer than thirty full-time residents remained at Zarephath-Horeb. The CSA dissolved in 1988, after Ellison turned state's evidence against other far-right leaders charged with sedition at Fort Smith, Arkansas.

Crusade Against Corruption—J.B. Stoner founded this group after his release from prison and ran it from headquarters in Marietta, Georgia, until it dissolved in early 2001. Throughout that period, Stoner traveled through the South as usual, staging joint rallies with klansmen and like-minded racists, while brandishing placards that read "Praise God for AIDS!" It may be mere coincidence that longtime Stoner ally Edward Fields also published his latest tabloid, *The Truth at Last*, from Marietta during 1989–2001.

After his release from prison in the 1980s, J.B. Stoner (with microphone) led a new Crusade Against Corruption (Southern Poverty Law Center).

Defenders of State Sovereignty and Individual Rights—A racist group organized in October 1954, with membership concentrated in Virginia's Fourth Congressional District, the DSSIR was created to obstruct school integration. Its leader, Robert Crawford, was a dry-cleaner from Farmville. Membership peaked around 15,000 before the group merged with the Citizens' Council.

Democratic Clubs—A network of paramilitary groups with numerous links to the KKK, the Democratic Clubs first surfaced in South Carolina during February 1868, when ex-governor Benjamin Perry called on whites to organize against Reconstruction. (The South Carolina Klan announced its first meeting a month later.) An Abbeville County klansman later told congressional investigators that the Klan and Democratic Clubs were identical. By autumn 1868, the clubs were widely organized in Louisiana, issuing "protection papers" to blacks who agreed to vote Democratic in November. In New Orleans, DC members focused on disruption of the Republican-dominated police force. Most residents of Fulton County, Arkansas, where a Democratic Club emerged in September 1868, regarded it as a front for the Klan. Similar opinions prevailed in northern Florida, when the clubs appeared in 1869–70.

Devil's Advocates—A Kankakee, Illinois, motorcycle gang notorious for its racist views, the Devil's Advocates participated in a May 1975 UKA organizational meeting, convened at the Kankakee Ramada Inn. Of twenty-five persons present (including three police informants), ten were gang members.

Euro-American Alliance—Founded in 1976 by neo-Nazi propagandist Donald Clerkin, the Milwaukee-based EAA was conceived as a "nationalist front" for "Christian soldiers." In April 1982, EAA members attended racist gatherings at the Mountain Church of Jesus Christ in Cohoctah, Michigan, run by klansman Robert Miles. Other groups represented included Don Black's KKKK, the Aryan Nations, the NSWPP and the National Alliance. The EAA remained active through 1999, but disbanded sometime in 2000.

European-American Educational Association—This neo-Nazi faction operated in Eastpointe, Michigan, during 1997–99, but dissolved on the eve of the new millennium.

European-American Unity and Rights Organization—At press time for this volume, EURO was the latest in a series of racist groups founded and led by former klansman David Duke. It is, in fact, a continuation of Duke's earlier National Organization for European American Rights, renamed in June 2001 (or 2003, accounts differ), after threats of trademark litigation surrounding the "NOFEAR" logo. EURO's message remains identical to that of NOFEAR and its predecessor, the NAAWP.

Fascist Action Group—A small neo-Nazi group, active in Boca Raton, Florida, during 1997–98, the FAG disbanded in early 1999.

Florida National Socialist Party—SPLC investigators reported this neo-Nazi group briefly active during 1991–92, but they failed to locate its headquarters or identify its leader.

Florida States Rights, Inc.—Organized in Miami after "Black Monday," this short-lived group opposed school integration.

Forsyth County Defense League—Mark Watts led this white-supremacist group based in Cumming, Georgia, during 1989–90. While not a Klan chapter per se, its emergence at the scene of so much Ku Klux violence during 1987 strains the limits of coincidence.

Georgians Unwilling to Surrender—A segregationist group founded by Atlanta restaurateur (and future Georgia governor) Lester Maddox in 1960, GUTS reportedly maintained friendly relations with Grand Dragon Calvin Craig of the U.S. Klans and UKA.

German-American Bund—Organized in July 1933 as the Association of Friends of the New Germany, the Bund was one of several pro-Nazi factions active in America during the Great Depression. Reorganized and renamed after chemist Fritz Kuhn took the helm in March 1936, the GAB was essentially a foreign arm of Adolf Hitler's Third Reich, receiving financial

Members of the German-American Bund parade in New Jersey, ca. 1940 (Library of Congress).

support and marching orders directly from Berlin. (Millionaire anti–Semite Henry Ford also supported the Bund, keeping many members on his payroll in Detroit as strikebreakers.) By November 1938, the Bund claimed an estimated 100,000 members nationwide. Klansmen were bitterly divided on the Nazi question, with southern and Midwestern members generally opposed to collaboration, while the Bund found support among KKK leaders in New Jersey, New York, and along the west coast. Negotiations with the New Jersey Klan bore fruit on 18 August 1940, when several hundred knights turned out for a joint rally at Camp Nordland, near Andover. Grand Dragon Arthur Bell and middleman Edward Smythe shared the stage with Deputy *Bundesführer* August Klapprott, beaming as Klapprott proclaimed, "The principles of the Bund and the principles of the Klan are the same." Adverse publicity moved Wizard James Colescott to dismiss Bell and New Jersey Kligrapp A.M. Young, but his effort at damage control came too late. With Kuhn imprisoned on a larceny charge, the Bund's days were numbered, finished at last by America's declaration of war against Germany, in December 1941.

German-American Nationalist Political Action Committee

—Founded at Pensacola, Florida, in 1997, the neo–Nazi GANPAC group remained marginally active at press time for this volume.

German-American Political Action Committee

—Hans Schmidt led this neo–Nazi clique in Santa Monica, California, during 1990, but it disbanded the following year.

Golden Mean Team

—Peggy Christiansen led this tiny splinter of the Posse Comitatus from Missoula, Montana, during 1989–91. No trace of it remains today.

Grass Roots League

—Yet another post–*Brown* racist group, the GRL opposed school integration in Charleston, South Carolina, during 1954–55.

Heggie's Scouts

—A Reconstruction-era white-supremacist group with ties to the KKK (if they were not, in fact, identical), Heggie's Scouts were active during 1867–68 in Carroll, Holmes, and Montgomery Counties, Mississippi.

Heritage Enterprises, Inc.

—Imperial Wizard Robert Shelton founded this corporation in the 1960s, with fifty-one percent of its stock owned by the UKA and forty-nine percent held by Shelton's personal friends. Subsidiaries included the Heritage Garment Works (which produced Klan regalia) in Columbia, South Carolina, and Heritage Insurance Company in Bessemer, Alabama. In 1965, HUAC discovered that Shelton received a commission on robe sales from Heritage Garment Works, in addition to a share of the company's profits. Trouble arose when Shelton accused Heritage manager Younger Newton of furnishing robe-buyers' names to the FBI. Newton also continued business dealings with South Carolina Grand Dragon Robert Scoggin after Shelton banished Scoggin from the UKA. Henceforth, production of robes was relegated to individual realms.

Heritage Library

—Despite its lofty title, SPLC investigators listed the Heritage Library as a neo–Nazi group, briefly active in Velma, Oklahoma, during 1990.

Heritage Preservation Association

—Based in Atlanta, Georgia, this nonprofit organization was founded to "fight political correctness and cultural bigotry against the South." Despite a proclamation that "We do not foster hatred, nor do we tolerate those who do," HPA leaders openly associate with members of the Klan, the CCC, and certain neo–Nazi groups. Known for its close ties to former Alabama governors Fob James and George Wallace, in January 2000 the HPA declared "Total War" on the NAACP, SCLC, and other groups which oppose public display of Confederate flags. On 25 January 2003, Linda Sewell (then president of the HPA's Alabama branch) and her husband (a CCC member) joined klansmen, members of the Aryan Nations and Church of the Creator to picket the SPLC in Montgomery, Alabama. (Sewell wore a scarf and sunglasses to hide her face.) After that demonstration, the Sewells attended a banquet in Clanton, Alabama, where Linda received a "certificate of appreciation" from Imperial Wizard Bradley Jenkins, representing the Aryan Knights of the KKK. The presentation, which followed a rant against "Jews, the niggers, the Mexicans and the mud race," featured a plaque bearing the Klan's cross-wheel symbol and other KKK symbols. Jenkins declared, "This certificate of appreciation is presented to Linda Sewell in appreciation of all her hard work and dedication to our cause." Questioned by reporters in April 2003, after SPLC investigators publicized the banquet, Sewell first denied attending the ceremony, then changed her story to claim that the plaque bore no Klan symbols. (Published photographs debunked that claim.) On 22 April, HPA spokesman Ben George announced from Mobile, Alabama, that Sewell had left the organization. National president P. Charles Lunsford (earlier expelled from the Sons of Confederate Veterans after giving a speech to the CCC), contradicted that announcement, declaring that Sewell "has done nothing to deserve to be removed." Lunsford also claimed that Sewell "had no idea" klansmen would attend the award banquet (meanwhile ignoring the previous protest, where neo–Nazi flags were openly displayed). At press time for this work, the HPA claimed members in forty-nine states and six unspecified foreign countries.

Howard Allen Enterprises—Named for its founder and editor-in-chief, this racist publishing house in Cape Canaveral, Florida, furnished propaganda for a broad spectrum of white-supremacist and anti–Semitic groups through the latter 1980s. SPLC investigators pronounced it defunct in 1991.

Innocents Club—A militant white-supremacist group active in Louisiana during the 1868 presidential campaign, this group collaborated with KKK and KWC members to intimidate or murder black voters. While membership in the three groups apparently overlapped, IC members focused narrowly on politics, generally ignoring black schools, interracial affairs, and other issues that mobilized klansmen.

Institute for Historical Review—North America's primary source of Holocaust-denial propaganda was founded by veteran anti–Semite Willis Carto in 1978, with headquarters in Los Angeles, California. The IHR's first "Revisionist Convention," in September 1979, featured an international cast of speakers, while the group's *Journal of Historical Review* boasted an initial mailing list of 12,000. Legitimate historians panned the IHR's efforts to rewrite history in Adolf Hitler's favor, though a few academics (including Florida professor and CCC member Glayde Whitney) signed on to promote the effort. Generally, the IHR's "Holohoax" message found a warmer reception among klansmen and neo–Nazis, epitomized by David Duke. At its first conference in 1979, the IHR offered $50,000 to anyone "who could prove that the Nazis operated gas-chambers to exterminate Jews during World War II." Auschwitz survivor Mel Mermelstein accepted the challenge, sparking a protracted lawsuit when the IHR reneged on its reward offer. In 1985, Mermelstein won the $50,000 plus another $40,000 and a letter of apology for anti–Semitic harassment he suffered from IHR members and fans. Carto and the IHR then counter sued Mermelstein for libel, but dropped their case in 1988. IHR leaders, in turn, severed their embarrassing link to Carto in October 1993, prompting another round of complex litigation. In November 1996, a California court decreed that Carto owed the IHR $6.43 million, apparently siphoned from a $10 million gift of stock certificates from Jean Farrel (an heir of Thomas Edison). At press time for this book, the full amount had not been paid. Any pretense of scholarship or objectivity the IHR might claim was swept away on 24 April 2004, when the group held a joint rally with the neo–Nazi National Alliance in Sacramento, California. On that occasion, IHR director Mark Weber told the audience, "....[W]hether you are a conservative, or a liberal, whether your primary loyalties are to your religion, to your ethnic group, to your country, to your heritage in whatever form, you will come up inevitably against this great Jewish Zionist power... [W]hat we are involved in, is a global struggle ... and what is important is to come out of this conference today ... not merely more aware, with greater understanding, but more determined to act, to do something, to be active, in a struggle that is not merely for ... abstractions like justice or truth, but it's truly a struggle for the interests of us all and the interests of humanity."

International Brotherhood of Teamsters—While best known for its ties to organized crime and the corruption charges filed against its various officers, the IBT also has a KKK connection. In November 1961, IBT officers met with leaders of the UKA in Tennessee for a strategy session concerning president Jimmy Hoffa's upcoming criminal trial. According to DOJ reports, klansmen agreed to help intimidate jurors and witnesses, in exchange for Teamster "muscle" to be used suppressing rival Klans. Hoffa's trial ended with a deadlocked jury in December 1962, but prosecutors subsequently convicted him of jury-tampering in that case.

Jimmy Hoffa's International Brotherhood of Teamsters collaborated with klansmen in the early 1960s (Library of Congress).

Iowa Society for Educated Citizens—The "education" was debatable for members of this Posse Comitatus chapter, based in Iowa City during 1989–90.

Jackson County Citizens Emergency Unit—Based in Pascagoula, Mississippi, the JCCEU was founded in October 1962 by Sheriff James Grimsley, with its first recruits including participants in the 30 September "Ole Miss" riot at Ox-

ford. Grimsley himself participated in that melee, protesting black student James Meredith's enrollment at the University of Mississippi, and FBI files state that "the purpose of the Unit was to secretly go to the University of Mississippi … 'to get' or kidnap Meredith." While that plan never materialized, JCCEU members spent considerable time menacing Ira Harkey, Jr., "liberal" editor of the Pascagoula *Chronicle*. Membership peaked around 400, then declined sharply when FBI agents arrived to investigate attempts on Harkey's life. Opposition from the AFL-CIO also prompted union members to desert the JCCEU's ranks. Grimsley resigned as leader to run for state office in 1963, while his replacement as JCCEU chief ran ninth in a field of eleven candidates for sheriff that same year.

Knights of the Black Cross—This nightriding terrorist group preceded the KKK in Franklin County, Mississippi, during 1867. Its members later merged with the larger, more powerful Klan.

Knights of Freedom—Investigators found this neo–Nazi group active in Spartanburg, South Carolina, in 1999, claiming fourteen additional chapters in eleven states. Only an Internet website remained when the SPLC surveyed active hate groups in 2000.

Knights of Mary Phagan—This short-lived group took its name from a twelve-year-old girl murdered at Leo Frank's pencil factory in Atlanta, Georgia, on 26 April 1913. Jurors convicted Frank in August 1913, but Gov. John Slaton commuted Frank's death sentence in June 1915. Soon afterward, incited by anti–Semitic editorials from Thomas Watson's *Jeffersonian* magazine, the KMP met at Phagan's grave to swear vengeance on Frank. On 16 August 1915, a gang of twenty-five men snatched Frank from the state prison farm and lynched him at Marietta, afterward posing for snapshots with his dangling corpse. Watson's subsequent editorials applauded the murder and called for a new KKK to restore "home rule" in Georgia. On 16 October 1915, KMP members scaled Stone Mountain and burned a huge cross, visible for miles. William Simmons filed a charter application for his new Klan ten days later, with leaders of the KMP among his earliest recruits. Following the KMP's example, Simmons conducted the Klan's first-ever cross-burning atop Stone Mountain at Thanksgiving 1915.

Knights of the Flaming Sword—Not to be confused with a the identically-named Klan faction of the late twentieth century, this KFS was a short-lived Klan competitor, founded by William Simmons in 1924, following his ouster as imperial wizard of the KKK. Chartered in Florida and funded with most of Simmons's $90,000 settlement from rival Hiram Evans, the KFS catered (without much success) to dissatisfied, dissident klansmen. A band of KKK defectors in Hoboken, New Jersey, considered joining Simmons, then reneged upon learning that they would have to pay new initiation fees. The KFS disbanded while Simmons convalesced from a February 1925 auto accident.

Knights of the Rising Sun—A Klan-like group with overlapping membership, the KRS was active in Jefferson and Marion counties, Texas, during 1867–69. An audience of 1,500 (including members of the Seymour Knights in full regalia) gathered on 19 September 1868 to witness installation of the group's grand officers. William Saufley, chairman of the Democratic Party in Marion County, served as grand commander, while guest speakers at the gathering include a rare black Democrat and several party regulars. Historians credit the KRS with lynching two black prisoners at Jefferson, on 4 October 1868, plus various attacks on blacks and Republicans during that year's presidential campaign. The resultant federal investigation prompted many members to flee Texas, some running as far as New York and Canada to find refuge. KRS violence declined in early 1869, although sporadic nightriding continued for several years thereafter.

Knights of the White Camellia (1867–69)—Organized in St. Mary Parish, Louisiana, in May 1867, this friendly rival of the Reconstruction-era Klan claimed Col. Alcibiade DeBlanc as its founding father. The KWC's heaviest concentration of members and activity centered on the French Creole region west of New Orleans, but chapters spread to Alabama and Arkansas during 1868. Generally, members were drawn from the upper classes, and displayed more discipline than klansmen, but the two groups shared identical goals, and membership sometimes overlapped. In Louisiana, KWC members were more numerous—and marginally less violent—than klansmen, while Arkansas residents generally regarded the KWC and KKK as identical. The KWC's charge to initiates proclaimed that the organization's "main and fundamental goal is the MAINTENANCE OF THE SUPREMACY OF THE WHITE RACE in this Republic." A New Orleans convention formalized the KWC's constitution in June 1868, dividing the order into councils administered by commanders, lieutenant commanders, guards, secretaries and treasurers. Where sufficient members were enrolled, each council was further subdivided into circles of fifty men and groups of ten. The constitution allowed for a supreme council once the KWC spread to five states, but it never reached that goal. By November 1868, a majority of white men had joined the KWC in some southern Louisiana parishes, with 15,000 estimated in New Orleans alone (out of 32,000 white male residents). For all its apparent strength, the KWC's activity declined sharply after the carnage attending the 1868 presidential campaign, assisted by newspaper publication of the group's secrets in December 1868. After the January 1869 state convention, some councils began calling themselves Caucasian Clubs, and the KWC apparently disbanded by early summer 1869.

Knights of the White Camellia (1934–42)—Founded by klansman George Deatherage in St. Albans, West Virginia, this thinly-veiled fascist group shared quarters with another Deatherage creation, the American Nationalist Confederation, after 1936. Deatherage proposed burning swastikas in place of crosses, but the notion never caught on, and the KWC apparently dissolved after his 1942 sedition indictment. In 1949, long after its practical demise, the KWC was posted to the U.S. Attorney General's subversive list.

Knights of the White Camellia (1950s)—One of
many Klan look-alikes founded by Florida klansman Bill Hendrix, the 1950s KWC sometimes billed itself as the National Christian Church. Hendrix announced formation of the KWC after a Klan unity conference in Montgomery, Alabama, setting the group's tone when he told an early gathering: "Now, I don't want you good people to go around blowin' up buildings or temples, but the next time somebody does blow up a temple, I sure hope it is filled with Jews." Georgia police seized KWC literature in October 1958, when they raided the home of suspected NSRP synagogue bomber Wallace Allen. When Atlanta officers jailed NSRP bombing suspect Richard Bowling on 18 October 1958, they found him in possession of a letter from the "National Commander of the White Camillia [*sic*]." Journalists reported the group's last gasp in summer 1960, when anonymous flyers urged Florida residents to withhold income taxes as a means to "get the chains of the bureaucrats off their necks." Reporters traced the pamphlets to an Oldsmar address used by Hendrix—who, by then, faced federal prosecution for tax evasion. A typical notice mailed from KWC headquarters proclaimed: "We intend to fight fire with fire. Smear with smear. We hope it does not take violence to win our country back from the U.S. Extreme Court."

Knights of the White Carnation—Organized at
Tuskegee, Alabama, soon after the Civil War, the KWC anticipated the Reconstruction-era Klan's vigilante campaign against black "lawbreakers." Its leader, ex–Confederate general Cullen Battle, may have been affiliated with the Louisiana-based Knights of the White Camellia. Apparently absorbed by the KKK in 1868, Battle's nightriders remained active through 1870, at least. In June of that year, Battle's raiders drove black state legislator James Alston (once a slave owned by Battle) from Tuskegee under threat of death.

Knights of White Christians—A short-lived, Klan-like
group in New Orleans, the KWC was founded by Alvin Cobb in response to "Black Monday." It dissolved sometime prior to 1960, leaving no records behind.

Ku Klux Rangers—While taking its name from the Klan,
this group of brigands based in Clarksville, Texas, during 1868 was not part of the KKK led by Grand Wizard Nathan Forrest. Its members were considered little more than outlaws by most locals, but they espoused common racist beliefs and terrorized blacks on occasion, thus proving their loyalty to Dixie.

League of American Workers—Founded in Seattle,
Washington, during 1990, the neo–Nazi LAW disbanded early the following year. Perhaps coincidentally, a League of Aryan Workers appeared in Poulsbo—across Puget Sound, in Kitsap County—during 1991.

League of Aryan Workers—A probable successor to
Seattle's League of American Workers, this neo–Nazi faction operated briefly from Poulsbo, Washington, in 1991–92.

League of St. George—A European neo–Nazi group active in the 1970s, the League sent representatives to New Orleans in September 1976, for a joint demonstration with David Duke's KKKK.

League of the South—The LOS was founded in Tuscaloosa, Alabama, in 1994, with a call for the South to secede from the Union. The group's all-white founding fathers included president J. Michael Hill (then a history professor at historically black Stillman College), G. David Cooksey (formerly linked to an Alabama "militia" group, currently an officer of the racist CCC), Michael Grissom (national advisor to the CCC), and Jack Kershaw (a Tennessee CCC member, formerly active in the 1960s Citizens' Council). In 1998, the LOS claimed 4,000 members, increasing by 2000 to 9,000 members in ninety-six chapters spanning twenty states. Headquarters shifted to Monroe, Louisiana, during 2001–02, then moved to Killen, Alabama in 2003 and remained there at press time for this volume (with ninety-six chapters in sixteen states).

The LOS makes no pretense of moderation in its defense of southern "heritage" and Confederate symbols. In March 2000, LOS leaders welcomed Klan-allied lawyer Kirk Lyons to a rally in Montgomery, Alabama, to sign a declaration of "Southern Cultural Independence" from the United States. Reminded that Lyons frequently represents violent klansmen and neo–Nazis, LOS spokesman Michael Grissom replied, "What would worry me more is if he defended some communist, socialist terrorist." In fact, as LOS leaders make clear, their group shares Lyons's racism. In 2000, Phil Beverly, president of the League's Birmingham chapter, posted *Webster's* definition of racism on an Internet website, then wrote: "I fail to see why anyone would shrink from the application of the term.... Why should we be afraid of telling the truth?" President Hill responded, "Let us not flinch when our enemies call us 'racists'; rather, just reply with, 'So, what's your point?'" Cooksey was even more extreme, following news of a rape in New York with a posting that read: "You see the day is coming when we NEED a new type of Klan. Yes I said Klan!! If push comes to shove I'm for it! ... Time has come to stop this crap now! Or would you all like to see your daughters raped???" Jack Kershaw, who erected a Nashville monument to KKK Grand Wizard Nathan Bedford Forrest with LOS backing, declared in 1998 that "[s]omeone needs to say a good word for slavery. Where in the world are the Negroes better off than in America?" Hill agreed, but longed for a return to segregation, writing: "The destruction of states rights in the South was the first necessity leading to forced policies undermining the cultural dominance of the Anglo-Celtic people and its institutions. [Klan-allied Alabama Governor George] Wallace rightly identified the enemy and fought it until the attempt on his life in 1972." William Cawthon, head of the Northeast Georgia LOS chapter, agreed that segregation "is not evil or wrong," but rather a question of racial "integrity."

Liberty Bell Publications—This clearinghouse for
racist, anti–Semitic literature operated from Reedy, West Virginia, during 2000–02, then moved to York, South Carolina, in 2003. SPLC investigators found no trace of it remaining in 2004.

Liberty Lobby—Willis Carto conceived the notion of "a
lobby for patriotism" in 1955, realizing his dream three years later when he founded the Liberty Lobby in Washington, D.C. By 1965, at least a half-dozen right-wing congressmen were

publicly affiliated with the group, which reported income exceeding $500,000. Retired Air Force colonel Curtis Dall (ex-son-in-law of FDR) served as the lobby's first chairman, while Carto ran the show as "treasurer." Despite an initial façade of legitimacy, the group and its weekly tabloid publication (*The Searchlight*) were soon exposed as vehicles of anti–Semitic and white-supremacist propaganda, fueled by the writings of late neo–Nazi Francis Parker Yockey. One spin-off group, the National Youth Alliance (formerly Youth for Wallace), became the neo–Nazi National Alliance under William Pierce. Another affiliated group, the Populist Party, ran ex-klansman David Duke for president under the management of ANP member Ralph Forbes. Following a round of bitter litigation with yet another of his satellite groups—the Institute for Historical Review—Carto and the Liberty Lobby filed for bankruptcy in 1996. Five years later, a series of judgments in Federal Bankruptcy Court forced Carto to vacate his Washington office, relinquishing control of the Liberty Lobby and *The Spotlight*.

Men of Justice—A Reconstruction-era vigilante group, organized in Alabama during 1867, the Men of Justice merged with the KKK in 1868.

Minnesota White Man's Association—Based in East St. Paul, this neo–Nazi group was briefly active during 1991–92.

Minutemen—A paramilitary anti-communist organization founded by Robert DePugh in 1959, at Norborne, Missouri, the Minutemen prefigured the 1990s "patriot militia" movement. Members stockpiled weapons in preparation for a Red invasion of America, soon turning their wrath against the established leaders when the foreign threat failed to materialize. DePugh welcomed members from the KKK and neo–Nazi groups, distributing racist and anti–Semitic literature along with standard anti-communist fare from the John Birch Society and other outlets. Some members participated in training Cuban guerrillas for the 1961 Bay of Pigs invasion, and several Minutemen were named by New Orleans District Attorney Jim Garrison as suspects in the 1963 JFK assassination. In October 1966, police jailed nineteen Minutemen for conspiracy on the eve of scheduled raids against various "leftist targets" in New York. Two years later, official reports linked the Minutemen to William Hoff and Paul Dommer, UKA–NSRP members accused of plotting race war in New Jersey. Dennis Mower, California's number-two Minuteman, was a close friend of WKKKKM Wizard Sam Bowers and an ordained minister of Wesley Swift's Church of Jesus Christ Christian; one of his business cards was found on klansman Thomas Tarrants after a June 1968 shootout with police in Meridian, Mississippi. DePugh founded the Patriotic Part on 4 July 1966, as the Minutemen's political arm, backing KKK–NSRP member Robert Bagwell as a New York congressional candidate in 1970. In 1971, police revealed a membership overlap between the Minutemen and Louisiana's Universal Klans, including shared guerrilla-warfare training facilities. As one Klan spokesman declared, "We won't need the National Guard if a race riot breaks out around here. We'll wipe them out with the Minutemen." Pennsylvania Grand Dragon

Roy Frankhouser combined membership in the Minutemen and the UKA, stating: "We work independently, but we also complement each other, and the lines of communication are always open between us. We've got the same enemies, the same friends, and the same goals. We're fighting under different leadership, but we're fighting together just the same." (Frankhouser also proudly called the Minutemen a "terrorist organization.") The group disbanded after DePugh was imprisoned in 1969, on federal conspiracy charges. Upon his release in 1973, DePugh announced formation of a new Patriots' Inter-Organizational Communications Center designed to unite far-right groups. As late as 1980, the "new" groups still distributed stickers bearing the old Minutemen cross-hairs logo.

Nation of Islam ("Black Muslims")—The NOI was founded in Detroit, around 1933, by a wandering "prophet" named Wallace D. Fard (AKA Professor Ford, Wali Farrad, Farrad Mohammad, etc.). Fard variously posed as an African or Arab, while one Detroit newspaper later called him "a Turkish-born Nazi agent [who] worked for Hitler during World War II." Before his mysterious disappearance in June 1934, Fard converted local blacks to a bastardized form of Islam, touting the fable of a mad scientist named Yakub who "grafted" Caucasian "devils" from black "Original Man" in 4712 B.C. Fard's disappearance left Elijah Muhammad (né Poole) in command of the cult, later expanding nationwide despite Muhammad's 1942 conviction for conspiring with Japanese agents to overthrow the U.S. government.

As Marcus Garvey's UNIA pursued negotiations with the 1920s Klan, so the black-separatist NOI found strange bedfellows forty years later. In 1961, Elijah Muhammad met with Klan leaders at Magnolia Hall, in Atlanta, Georgia. George Lincoln Rockwell and other members of his ANP attended NOI rallies in Chicago, during June 1961 and again the following year. On the latter occasion, Rockwell told an audience of 5,000 Muslims that he was "proud to stand here before black men.... Elijah Muhammad is the Adolf Hitler of the black man." In 1964, Grand Dragon Calvin Craig introduced NOI minister Jeremiah

Black Muslims joined the KKK in calling for racial segregation (Library of Congress).

X to klansmen gathered in Atlanta's Hurd Park. The relationship soured in November 1969, when NOI members bought a farm near Ashville, Alabama, from its white owner. Local klansmen opposed the sale, killing several cows on the farm with nocturnal sniper fire, then torching the former owner's auto dealership in Pell City. UKA Wizard Robert Shelton announced plans to purchase land surrounding the farm, to "keep an eye on things," and sporadic attacks continued until March 1970, when the Muslims sold out and moved on.

Peaceful relations were restored after Louis Farrakhan succeeded the late Elijah Muhammad as head of the NOI. In September 1985, following one of Farrakhan's anti–Semitic tirades in Los Angeles, WAR founder Tom Metzger donated $100 to the NOI. A month later, on 12 October, Metzger addressed 200 white supremacists (including klansman Roy Frankhouser) in Michigan, proclaiming, "The enemy of my enemy is my friend. I salute Louis Farrakhan and anyone else who stands up against the Jews. America is like a rotting carcass. The Jews are living off the carcass like the parasites they are. Farrakhan understands this." In May 1990, Farrakhan's *Final Call* published articles favorable to extremist presidential candidate Lyndon LaRouche (who employed Frankhouser as his security chief), and two months later Farrakhan granted an exclusive interview to Willis Carto's *Spotlight* magazine, whose editors described the NOI as "based on the cultivation of spiritual, education, and family values, as well as racial separation."

National Alliance

National Alliance—America's premier neo–Nazi group of the latter twentieth century began life in 1968, as Willis Carto's Youth for Wallace group, supporting the presidential ambitions of Klan-allied Alabama Governor George Wallace. With his defeat in November 1968, Carto renamed his group the National Youth Alliance, recruiting on college campuses nationwide. William Pierce, an ANP/NSWPP alumnus, joined the NYA in 1970 and led a mass defection from Carto's leadership four years later, creating his own National Alliance with headquarters in Arlington, Virginia. Pierce lost his appeal for a federal tax exemption in 1978, with that judgment upheld on appeal in 1981 and 1983. Cash from armed robberies committed by The Order (led by NA member Robert Mathews) helped finance the group, though Pierce escaped indictment with other racist leaders on sedition charges resulting from that crime spree. In 1985, Pierce moved his base of operations to a 346-acre farm at Mill Point, West Virginia, where he founded a new racist religion ("Cosmotheism") and diversified with businesses including National Vanguard Books, Cymophone Records, and Resistance Records. By 2002, the NA claimed fifty chapters in twenty-six states (including one in Alaska). Its members engaged in various racially motivated crimes, including the murder of a black couple in North Carolina (1995), a sniping incident in Mississippi (1996), armed robberies in Connecticut and Florida (1996), attempted bombings in Florida (1997), stockpiling illegal weapons in New York City (2000), and a deadly shootout with Illinois State Police (2001). Extremist groups affiliated with the NA at various times include various factions of the KKK, the Aryan Nations, the Mountain Church of Jesus Christ (founded by klansman Robert Miles), David Duke's

NOFEAR and EURO, and the Council of Conservative Citizens. Overseas, the NA forged ties to Holocaust-denial author David Irving, the British National Party, the German National Democratic Party, and assorted racist groups in the Czech Republic, France, the Netherlands, Russia, Scandinavia, and South Africa. While spokesmen for the ADL and SPLC reported declining NA membership after Pierce's death in July 2002, successor Shaun Walker claimed fifty-nine active chapters in thirty states during 2004.

National American Socialist Renaissance Party

National American Socialist Renaissance Party—A small neo–Nazi clique based in Queens, New York, the NASRP was exposed in January 1960, when police jailed three members (perhaps its entire membership) for plotting to attack Jews in Fresh Meadows. Defendants Hugh Barlow, Richard Phelps and John Wallace initially faced treason charges, carrying a possible death penalty, but they later plea-bargained for reduced felonies.

National Association for the Advancement of White People (1951)

National Association for the Advancement of White People (1951)—Daniel Kurts organized the first NAAWP in Dayton, Ohio, expressing his public admiration for the KKK. "You klansmen have a great organization," he declared. "You have a right to be proud of it." No record of any substantial activity remains.

National Association for the Advancement of White People (1954–55)

National Association for the Advancement of White People (1954–55)—No details survive concerning this short-lived faction, reported active in Washington, D.C., after "Black Monday."

National Association for the Advancement of White People (1955–56)

National Association for the Advancement of White People (1955–56)—Apparently unrelated to the group in Washington, D.C., this short-lived organization appeared in South Carolina as a response to the Supreme Court's *Brown* decision on school integration.

National Association for the Advancement of White People (1957)

National Association for the Advancement of White People (1957)—Created to resist school integration in Milford, Delaware, the NAAWP gathered enough support to briefly reverse the local school board's resolution of compliance with a federal desegregation order.

National Association for the Advancement of White People (1959)

National Association for the Advancement of White People (1959)—Founded in Baltimore by veteran anti–Semite Bryant Bowles, this version of the NAAWP dissolved after Bowles was imprisoned in Texas, for killing his brother-in-law.

National Association for the Advancement of White People (1980–)

National Association for the Advancement of White People (1980–)—The NAAWP's latest incarnation was founded in 1980 by David Duke, following his resignation from the KKKK. Headquartered in Metairie, Louisiana, the group attained its peak strength in 1997, with seventy-eight chapters active in twenty-nine states (including Hawaii). A steady decline then ensued, accelerated by Duke's departure to lead a new National Organization For European American Rights (NOFEAR) in January 2000. By year's end, NAAWP headquarters had relocated to Tampa, Florida, while sixteen satellite chapters survived in fifteen states. By 2004, only

NAAWP Principles

EQUAL RIGHTS FOR WHITES

We demand an immediate end to racial discrimination and quotas against white people in employment, promotions, scholarships, and in union and college admittance. We want American government, military, education and business to make excellence the sole criterion for advancement.

AN END TO FORCED BUSING

We want an end to busing and forced integration. We believe that forcing the races together has resulted in a marked decline in educational quality and increased racial tension and violence. Additionally, busing constitutes a tremendous waste of tax money and precious energy resources.

TOTAL WELFARE REFORM

We believe that the present welfare system is taking advantage of productive and hard-working Americans and that instead of alleviating poverty, it is only increasing it. We see two fundamental solutions to the growing welfare problem:

1) Workfare instead of welfare. Under this program, able-bodied welfare recipients would have to perform work for the community in order to receive their welfare benefits.

2) Welfare family planning. A vigorous promotion of family planning must be instituted for welfare recipients in which they would be given financial incentives to have smaller families. Such a program would be humanitarian by bringing fewer children into intolerable conditions, and it would allow more money to be applied to training and guidance programs for the poor. Thus, such a program would be beneficial to the indigent, while progressively reducing the number of poor each generation, and thus lessening the tax burden shouldered by productive Americans.

CRACKDOWN ON VIOLENT CRIME

We want swift and sure punishment of violent criminals and an end to special consideration for rioters and other violent criminals who are black. We believe that local police should be given more community support in their defense of the potential victim.

NO MORE IMMIGRATION

We believe that America, Canada, and Europe already have the maximum population for the maintenance of good economic health. Legal and illegal aliens are increasing unemployment among citizens, adding to already overburdened welfare rolls, and contributing to violent crime. The time has come to demand enforcement of our laws concerning illegal immigration and to severely limit legal immigration.

AN END TO RACE HATRED IN MEDIA

We want an end to the chronic portrayal of white people as exploiters and oppressors of blacks and other minorities. Such portrayals instill guilt in white children and hatred in young blacks that often manifests itself in violent crime against white people.

PRESERVATION OF THE WHITE RACE AND ITS HERITAGE

We believe that all peoples on this planet must have the right to life, that is, the right to exist and preserve their cultural integrity. We do not object to black groups having black beauty contests, black radio stations, black colleges, or black scholarships. Nor do we object to blacks teaching their young about black heritage and instilling black pride in them, but we do demand the same rights for our own people, for we deeply love the beauty, culture, and heritage of the white race, and want to preserve them.

EXCELLENCE IN ALL THINGS

We believe in a society where the young are educated to the best of their ability, a society in which the best qualified, hardest working, and most talented are rewarded commensurate with their contribution to the nation. We believe in equal justice under the law, equal opportunity, and equal rights as the fairest means of determining the best in any field. True equality in opportunity will enable the men and women of quality to step forward and serve the ideal of a higher humanity.

After resigning from the Klan in 1980, Duke led a new racist group, the NAAWP.

headquarters and two outlying chapters remained, although the group maintains an active website with the motto "Equal Rights for All—Special Privileges for None." (A Florida offshoot using the same name also appeared in 2000 and remained marginally active at press time for this work.)

National Association for the Preservation of the Races—Founded in Memphis, Tennessee, during 1954, the NAPR opposed school integration as a first step toward "race-mixing."

National Association for the Preservation of the White Race—Based in Augusta, Georgia, this forerunner of the Citizens' Councils opposed school desegregation during 1954–55.

National Christian Conservative Society—Founded in Cleveland, Ohio, by ex-klansman Robert Annable, the NCCS worked closely with Ohio's knights during spring 1967.

National Committee to Free America from Jewish Domination—George Lincoln Rockwell formed this group in 1957, as a forerunner of the ANP. In 1958, police investigating an Atlanta synagogue bombing uncovered lengthy correspondence between Rockwell and Georgia NSRP member Wallace Allen.

National Democratic Front—Run by Gary Gallo from Gaithersburg, Maryland, this neo–Nazi splinter group appeared in 1989 and followed its founder to Knoxville, Tennessee, the following year. It survived through 1991 at the new location, then apparently disbanded.

National Emancipation of Our White Seed—Missouri anti–Semite Dan Gayman founded this group in the early 1970s, as a conglomerate of right-wing racist groups, then passed the torch of leadership to Tennessee klansman Buddy Tucker in 1976. Tucker moved NEOWS headquarters to Knoxville, then to Louisiana in the 1980s. It disbanded prior to the SPLC's survey of active hate groups in 1989.

National Organization For European American Rights—David Duke announced the creation of NOFEAR in January 2000, after severing relations with the NAAWP. Its stated purpose was to "defend the civil rights of European Americans," though in fact NOFEAR served as a vehicle for the same racist and anti–Semitic propaganda Duke had peddled since his college neo–Nazi days and throughout his leadership of the KKKK. Throughout NOFEAR's brief life, Duke continued his longstanding fraternization with neo–Nazis at home and abroad. Threats of litigation for trademark infringement forced Duke to drop the NOFEAR logo in June 2001 (or 2003, reports differ), whereupon he renamed his group the European-American Unity and Rights Organization (EURO).

National Party (Canada)—Members of this neo–Nazi group joined klansmen in 1980, for a joint rally with the NSPA at Raleigh, North Carolina.

National Party (U.S.)—Created by then-student David Duke at Louisiana State University, the NP was an outgrowth of Duke's previous White Youth Alliance. New Orleans police blamed brown-shirted NP members for sparking violence at two racially-troubled high schools during the 1971–72 school year. In a 1976 interview with Patsy Sims, Duke described the NP as "a Klan that wasn't called a Klan."

National Renaissance Party—A small neo–Nazi group founded in 1949 by New Yorker James Madole, the NRP actively recruited klansmen, including Dan Burros, Roy Frankhouser and Frank Rotella. Madole, Burros and another NRP member served ten days in jail for brawling with blacks outside a New York restaurant, in July 1963; a search of their truck revealed a crossbow, an axe, and several knives. Madole suffered embarrassment in 1965, when newspaper reports identified members Dan Burros and Robert Burros (no relation) as Jews. In July 1967, an NRP rally at Newburgh, New York, touched off two days of black rioting with seventy persons arrested. In 1968, the *NRP Bulletin* headlines the party's formal alliance with the Minutemen, the NSWPP and Frankhouser's Pennsylvania Klan. New York City police jailed Frankhouser and fourteen other members after a rowdy demonstration in April 1971. The NRP finally dissolved after Madole's death, in 1979.

National Socialist German Workers Party-Overseas Organization—Longtime neo–Nazi propagandist Gary Lauck's obsession with the Third Reich translates

(literally) into German through his *National Sozialistische Deutsche Arbeiter Partei—Auslands Organization* (NSDAP–AO), established in the late 1970s. Most observers consider this "group" a one-man operation, churning out hate literature from Lauck's home in Lincoln, Nebraska, for distribution worldwide. Lauck's propaganda mill remained active at press time for this book.

National Socialist Irish Workers Party—Despite its limited appeal, this neo–Nazi group for Irish-Americans survived in Bethlehem, Pennsylvania, during 1997–99, then disbanded in early 2000.

National Socialist Kindred—Active in Nevada City, California, during 1990, the NSK was founded by a Vietnam-war veteran known only as "Jost." The group disbanded in early 1991, replaced by a system of meditation dubbed Arya Kriya, merging National Socialism and Odinism. Jost later wrote to a colleague in Sweden, "Yes, we had some problems with Nazis. They destroyed years of hard work.... Most were psychopaths and dangerous." Jost died of a heart attack in 1996.

National Socialist League—Founded in 1974 by defectors from the NSWPP, the San Diego–based NSL was unique in restricting its membership to homosexual neo–Nazis. Led by veteran anti–Semite Russell Veh, the group distributed membership applications declaring the NSL's "determination to seek sexual, social, and political freedom." No trace of it remained when the SPLC surveyed U.S. hate groups in 1989.

National Socialist Liberation Front—Founded in 1969 by former west coast ANP leader Joseph Tomassi, with support and inspiration from William Pierce, the NSLF earned a reputation as one of America's most violent neo–Nazi groups. Prior to his 1975 murder by a member of the rival NSWPP, Tomassi claimed that the NSLF was responsible for bombing a California SWP office. David Rust assumed control of the NSLF until his conviction on federal firearms charges. In March 1981, ex-klansman Karl Hand defected from the NSPA to take charge of the NSLF, calling it "a revolutionary movement that has repudiated mass tactics and has instead embraced armed struggle and political terrorism." Despite relocation of its headquarters to Metairie, Louisiana, the NSLF retained a strong California flavor. In June 1985, a phone call claimed credit for anti–Semitic vandalism at the Studio City home of actor Ed Asner. The NSLF disbanded sometime prior to 1989.

National Socialist Movement—Founded by ANP veterans Robert Brannen and Cliff Herrington in 1974, the NSM began life as the National Socialist American Workers Freedom Movement, arousing little interest beyond its home base in St. Paul, Minnesota. Multiple strokes soon left Brannen disabled, but Herrington established chapters in Detroit, Michigan, and Ashton, Rhode Island, distributing swastika stickers bearing the slogan: "Off the Jew-Capitalist Pigs." A typical NSM pamphlet was emblazoned with swastikas and a hand clutching a cocked revolver, with a message reading: "The future belongs to the few of us still willing to get our hands dirty. POLITICAL TERROR ... It's the only thing they understand. Build the Na-

tional Socialist Revolution through Armed Struggle." Violence erupted at a Detroit city council meeting in June 1980, when local NSM spokesman William Russell joined klansman Seth Klipoth in requesting a parade permit; ten persons were arrested after members of the Detroit Anti-Klan Coalition and the Revolutionary Socialist League assaulted the assembled racists. In November 1982, the NSM's McKenzie, Tennessee, chapter filed a $3.2 million lawsuit against Carroll County officials, claiming its members had been "arrested and railroaded" as part of a conspiracy "to stop all Nazi activity in the state." (Those arrests included charges of parole violation, illegal possession of a sawed-off shotgun, and malicious mischief.)

Despite such antics, the mainstream press—and even the SPLC—ignored the NSM until 1993, when Herrington and another member appeared at a Minnesota legislative committee hearing in full Nazi regalia, protesting gay-rights legislation. A year later, Herrington (age forty-seven) ceded leadership of the NSM to twenty-one-year-old Jeff Schoep, whose appeal to racist skinheads helped the group expand. In 1998, Schoep won endorsements for the NSM and his "great bloodlines" from veteran neo–Nazis Tom Metzger and Allen Vincent. Reorganized on paramilitary lines, with weapons training offered to its members, the NSM expanded steadily from its Twin Cities headquarters, claiming sixteen chapters in ten states by 2000, twenty-seven in fourteen states by 2001, forty-two in twenty-three states by 2002, and forty-four in twenty-nine states by 2003. Estimates of its present strength range from forty chapters in twenty-four states (SPLC) to forty in thirty-one states (ADL).

While the NSM appeals primarily to younger neo–Nazis, it still welcomes aging veterans as well—including William Hoff, the UKA's former king kleagle for New York. Ranked as the second-largest neo–Nazi group in America (after the National Alliance), the NSM freely collaborates with other racist groups, including various KKK factions and Billy Roper's White Revolution. Schoep has held numerous "unity rallies" over the past dozen years, once briefly claiming leadership of an illusory United Patriot Front. Members of a dozen different white-supremacist groups joined one such NSM rally in 2002, at Topeka, Kansas. The group's political program includes denial of U.S. citizenship to Jews, nonwhites and homosexuals.

National Socialist Party—Another short-lived neo–Nazi splinter group, the NSP was active in Denver, Colorado, during 1989–90, then vanished in 1991.

National Socialist Party of America—Frank Colin founded the NSPA in Chicago, during 1970, soon after NSWPP expelled him as a closet Jew. Claiming an average membership of 100 over the next decade, the NSPA drew national attention in 1977–78 for its threats to stage marches through Skokie, a Chicago suburb occupied by Holocaust survivors. A year of legal wrangling finally permitted the group to hold a "monster rally" in Chicago's Marquette Park, where twenty-five demonstrators found themselves outnumbered by hecklers and police. Elsewhere during summer 1978, the NSPA staged marches in St. Louis and Florisant, Missouri. Leadership passed to Harold Covington in 1980, after Colin's conviction for child-molestation, and Covington transferred the NSPA's headquarters to

North Carolina. There, in April 1980, NSPA members joined klansmen for a "Hitlerfest" to celebrate the late Führer's birthday. Later in 1980, the NSPA courted Canadian racist groups, including the National Party, the Western Guard, and the Canadian KKK. Upon Covington's resignation in April 1981, Michael Allen assumed command and moved party headquarters back to Chicago. A few months later, Nebraska neo–Nazi Gary Lauck announced the NSPA's merger with his own Lincoln-based splinter group, the NSDAP–AO, and Lauck's *New Order* tabloid functioned as the NSPA's official newsletter through 1983. James Buford took command in 1982 and renamed the NSPA the American Nazi Party.

National Socialist Party of Florida—Another short-lived neo–Nazi group, the NSPF operated briefly during 1991–92.

National Socialist Resistance—Resistance was brief for this neo–Nazi clique in Lake Worth, Florida, founded in 1997 and disbanded the following year.

National Socialist Vanguard—Rick Cooper founded this neo–Nazi faction at Salinas, California, in January 1983, subsequently moving its headquarters to Goldendale, Washington (1985) and The Dalles, Oregon (1989). An Omaha chapter joined the fold in 1991, but disbanded sometime before the SPLC's survey of active hate groups in 1997. Headquarters moved to Goldendale, Washington, in 1998, then backtracked to The Dalles a year later, where it remained marginally active at press time for this volume.

National Socialist Viking Front—Chapters of the NSVF operated briefly in Chicago and Worcester, Massachusetts, during 1991–92.

National Socialist White Action Party—First reported from Pacific Palisades, California, in 1997, the NSWAP claimed five chapters in five other states by year's end. None remained when the SPLC completed its survey of active hate groups in 1997.

National Socialist White America Party—This short-lived neo–Nazi group surfaced in Pacific Palisades, California, during 1989–90, then disbanded in early 1991. It resurfaced in 1997 as the National Socialist White Action Party.

National Socialist White People's Party (1966–82)—In 1966, George Lincoln Rockwell changed the name of his ANP to imitate the NAACP's successful logo. Matt Koehl took command of the party after Rockwell's August 1967 murder, alienating many key aides with leadership style. Struggling through the early 1980s with 100 hard-core members and a somewhat larger pool of dues-paying "official supporters," the NSWPP maintained headquarters in Arlington, Virginia, while operating small chapters in California, Illinois, Minnesota, Ohio and Wisconsin. The party's official publishing house, Arlington Place Books, produced most of the titles published by klansman James Warner in the 1970s. In 1982, the IRS hit Koehl and the NSWPP with a lien for $37,000 in back taxes, subsequently foreclosing on party headquarters. Accordingly, in November of that year, Koehl renamed his organization the New Order, transferring headquarters to New Berlin, Wisconsin.

National Socialist White People's Party (1994–)—Veteran neo–Nazi Harold Covington lifted the name of Matt Koehl's former group for his own latest venture in 1994, operating from Charleston, South Carolina, and claiming ten other chapters in as many states by 1997. Headquarters moved to San Antonio, Texas, in 1998, while the NSWPP expanded to twenty-one chapters in fifteen states. That phenomenal growth was short-lived, however, and by 1999 only a single chapter remained (in Salt Lake City, Utah). Even that had vanished by the time SPLC investigators surveyed active hate groups in 2000.

National Socialist White Workers Party (California)—Founded in the mid–1970s by San Francisco neo–Nazi Allen Vincent, the NSWWP got national publicity in 1977, by opening its Rudolph Hess Bookstore in a heavily–Jewish neighborhood. Local controversy and sporadic nuisance litigation continued through the end of the decade, culminating in the April 1980 police revocation of an "incomplete" permit granting NSWWP members permission to rally at the San Francisco Civic Center.

National Socialist White Workers Party (Florida)—Presumably unrelated to California's NSWWP of the 1970s, this neo–Nazi clique operated briefly from Nokomis, Florida, during 1991–92.

National Socialists for Anglo Aryans—This group's name symbolized its confusion. It operated briefly in Gwinnett County, Georgia, during 1991–92, then disappeared without a trace.

National States Rights Party—An "ideal" merger of KKK and neo–Nazi philosophies, the NSRP was founded at Knoxville, Tennessee, in 1957, by twenty veterans of the United White Party. Founder Edward Fields borrowed the group's lightning-flash insignia (and title of its newspaper, *The Thunderbolt*) from the defunct Columbians, who in turn had lifted it from Adolf Hitler's SS. In October 1958, Atlanta police charged NSRP members with bombing a synagogue, but jurors acquitted the first defendant and all other charges were then dismissed. In March 1960, NSRP delegates convened in Dayton, Ohio, to nominate Arkansas Gov. Orval Faubus for president with running mate John Crommelin. Despite Faubus's public rejection of the NSRP, its slate polled 214,195 votes in November. Two years later, an NSRP congressional candidate received 65,000 votes in Alabama (more than half of them from Birmingham, where party headquarters resided).

In 1963, the NSRP launched a "Fire Your Nigger" campaign, designed to drive blacks from the South. On 15 September 1963, during a riot sparked by Birmingham's fatal church bombing, two white teenagers well-known at NSRP headquarters shot and killed a black youth, Virgil Ware. One of three klansmen jailed for illegal dynamite possession after that bombing was also an NSRP member. Eight more—including Fields, J.B. Stoner, and James Warner—were indicted on 22 September

1963 for stoning a newly integrated school in Birmingham. (The presiding judge also reported attempts to intimidate the grand jury.) A report from the California state legislature, issued in 1963, called the NSRP "more potentially dangerous than any of the American Nazi groups, as it is interested in activities that are far more vigorous and direct." In 1964, the NSRP held joint rallies with klansmen at Selma, Alabama. In March of that year, delegates convened in Louisville, Kentucky to nominate John Kasper and J.B. Stoner for the party's presidential slate. (With a paltry 6,957 votes in November, it was the NSRP's last national campaign.) Active in racial violence around St. Augustine, Florida (1964), and Bogalusa, Alabama (1965), NSRP members were ironically denounced as communist *provocateurs* by spokesmen for the John Birch Society. Willie Brewster, a black man, was murdered in July 1965 by participants in an NSRP rally at Anniston, Alabama. A year later, NSRP members joined klansmen and American Nazis for a rally in Cambridge, Maryland, but police dispersed their motorcade. Baltimore police banned NSRP rallies in summer 1966, after speeches by Connie Lynch (the party's "official policy speaker") touched off white riots. In August 1966, Chicago police jailed an NSRP officer and an Ohio Klan leader at an unauthorized rally, while ANP leader George Rockwell escaped in the confusion.

Gunfire erupted during an NSRP rally at Berea, Kentucky, in September 1968, with one party member and one black man killed in the exchange of shots. Connie Lynch and twelve others were jailed in that incident, then later released without charges. Named as national chairman of the NSRP in 1969, J.B. Stoner moved party headquarters to Marietta, Georgia, in 1971, after thirteen years of housing "beneath the proper dignity needed to present us in a highly professional light to the public." Stoner remained as chairman of the NSRP until 1983, when he was imprisoned on church-bombing charges. Rev. R.B. Montgomery succeeded Stoner, but was soon replaced by chairman W. Eugene Wilson. In February 1986, klansmen and NSRP members assaulted civil rights marchers in Cobb County, Georgia. With membership estimated at 1,000 in the latter 1980s, some 15,000 readers subscribed to *The Thunderbolt*. Still, it was not enough to sustain the NSRP, which disbanded prior to the SPLC's survey of active hate groups in 1989.

National White Americans Party—This short-lived neo–Nazi group joined klansmen and James Venable's Defensive Legion of Registered Americans for a joint rally at Stone Mountain, Georgia, on 4 July 1962.

National White Resistance—Based in Metairie, Louisiana, during 1991–92, the NWR drew its tiny membership from the same pool of racists that earlier supported David Duke's KKKK and the various neo–Nazi factions led by James Warner.

National Youth Alliance—Organized by longtime anti-Semite Willis Carto in 1969, this outgrowth of the recently defunct Youth for Wallace movement was designed as "a fighting movement" intended to "liquidate the enemies of the American people." Mutinous ANP veterans led by William Pierce broke with Carto in 1970, renaming their group the National Alliance.

Nationalist Movement—Mississippi lawyer Richard Barrett founded this white-supremacist group in Jackson during the 1980s, subsequently moving its headquarters to Learned, where it remained active at press time for this volume. The group claimed three Nebraska chapters during 1999, but SPLC investigators found none remaining in 2000. Aside from well-publicized rallies, Barrett's activities include legal defense of klansmen charged with violent crimes in Georgia, petitions supporting Byron De La Beckwith during his 1994 murder trial, and various actions against websites that describe his followers as "haters."

Nazi Party USA—SPLC investigators found this small neo-fascist group active in Memphis, Tennessee, during 1998–99. It apparently disbanded in 2000.

New Christian Crusade Church—Closely affiliated with the Christian Defense League, this Christian Identity group was founded by James Warner in 1975, while Warner doubled as Louisiana grand dragon for David Duke's KKKK. In spring 1976, Warner left the Klan to handle church affairs full-time, while former Maryland NSRP leader Richard Norton led supervised a Los Angeles congregation. By 1989, control of the church passed to Craig Dermott, while Warner devoted more time to the CDL. The NCCC disbanded during 1991.

New Nation U.S.A.—S.A. Freeman led this short-lived racist group from Morongo Valley, California, in 1989. It disbanded prior to the SPLC's survey of active hate cliques in 1990.

New National Socialists—Hank Schmidt of Melrose, Florida, led this neo–Nazi clique at its foundation, in 1989. He gained a distant chapter in Astoria, New York, the following year, then lost it in 1991 while shifting headquarters to Tampa. The NNS disbanded soon thereafter, no trace remaining for the SPLC's census of American hate groups in 1997.

New Order—Veteran neo–Nazi Matt Koehl created the New Order in 1982, renaming his NSWPP and moving headquarters from Arlington, Virginia, to New Berlin, Wisconsin (later Milwaukee). Some nostalgia must have lingered, though, for SPLC investigators found an Arlington chapter clinging to life in 1989–90. The group remained marginally active through 1997, but apparently disbanded prior to the SPLC's survey of American hate groups in 1999 (although a website by the same title survived). Koehl's group should not be confused with Gary Lauck's *New Order* tabloid, published in Lincoln, Nebraska, from 1983 through the mid–1990s.

New South Freedom Fighters—In March 1987, this group sent letters to journalists in San Antonio, Texas, claiming credit for the alleged murder of two illegal immigrants near Ozona. No evidence was found to support the claim, and the NSFF has not been heard from since.

New White Working Youth—Work took a backseat to neo–Nazi propaganda with this tiny faction, active in Jacksonville, Florida, during 1991–92.

North Alabama Citizens' Council—Organized by Birmingham's Asa Carter in October 1955, this radical splinter group drew criticism from "mainstream" Citizens' Councils for excluding Jews. NACC members (including klansman Robert Chambliss) joined in the February 1956 riot against Autherine Lucy's admission to the University of Alabama, and three Council officers defected after Carter demanded the university president's resignation. Several NACC members assaulted black singer Nat "King" Cole during a Birmingham performance, in April 1956, and Carter promptly organized a White People's Defense Fund to cover their legal expenses. Within a year, NACC membership was indistinguishable from that of Carters Original KKK of the Confederacy.

North American Alliance for White People—
An Ohio white-supremacist group active in spring 1967, the NAAWP collaborated with Ohio klansmen.

North Carolina Association for the Preservation of the White Race—
This Durham-based group was a predecessor of the Citizens' Council, opposing school integration as a first step toward "mongrelization."

North Carolina Defenders of States Rights—
Organized in 1958, the NCDSR absorbed various defectors from the Patriots of North Carolina. In its turn, the group later merged with a larger movement led by I. Beverly Lake, a white-supremacist law professor and assistant state attorney general.

Odinist Religion and Nordic Faith Movement—
A California fringe group led by NSRP member and future klansman James Warner, this neo–Nazi group served as a forerunner of Warner's New Christian Crusade Church.

Ohio White Nationalist Party—
Russell Veh founded this one-man outlet for neo–Nazi propaganda in 1970, operating from his home in Toledo. Its disappearance coincided with Veh's 1974 move to California, where he founded the National Socialist League for gay fascists.

Oklahoma White Man's Association—
Based in Catoosa, this white-supremacist group surfaced in 1991 and disbanded early the following year.

The Order—
Conceived and outlined by National Alliance leader William Pierce in *The Turner Diaries* (1978), The Order came to life five years later under the command of National Alliance member Robert Jay Mathews. Founded at the Aryan Nations compound in Idaho, the paramilitary group—also called *Brüder Schweigen* ("Silent Brotherhood") included klansmen James Dye (Pennsylvania), Randy Evans (California), Mark Jones (Alabama), David Lane (Colorado), Thomas Martinez (Pennsylvania), Michael Norris (Alabama), and Frank Silva (California) among its charter members. When not plotting war against "ZOG," Order members relaxed by watching *The Birth of a Nation* on videotape.

The group first turned to crime with an amateurish counterfeiting operation, then graduated to bombings and armed robbery. Its first successful heist, in Seattle, claimed $524,000 in April 1984. The group's first murder, of loose-lipped Aryan Nations member Walter West, occurred a month later. In June 1984, an Order hit team murdered Denver talk-show host Alan

Richard Scutari was a member of The Order and a participant in its various crimes (FBI).

Berg. One month later, the guerrillas stole $3.6 million from an armored truck outside Ukiah, California. From that score, Mathews allegedly donated cash to Texas klansman Louis Beam ($100,000), Richard Butler of Aryan Nations ($40,000), Michigan klansman Robert Miles ($15,500), Frazier Miller of the Carolina Knights ($200,000), Tom Metzger of White Aryan Resistance ($260,000 to $300,000, accounts vary) and William Pierce of the National Alliance ($50,000 to $642,000, reported by various sources). All but Miller denied accepting the loot, and none were convicted of receiving stolen property. On 26 November 1984, with FBI agents closing in on the gang, Mathews and nine other members signed a formal "declaration of war on ZOG." G-men traced Mathews to Whidbey Island, Washington, and killed him in a shootout on 7 December 1984. Subsequent state and federal trials sent twenty-one Order members to prison for terms ranging from six months to 250 years. Klan members in the group drew terms of 190 years (Lane), 40 years (Evans and Silva), 20 years (Dye) and five years (Norris). Martinez turned state's evidence against his comrades and received $25,000 from the FBI in return. Jones also testified against his former friends and disappeared into the federal witness protection program.

Order of Pale Faces—
A white-supremacist group organized at Columbia, Tennessee, in 1867, the OPF quickly spread statewide. Thirty-four local "camps" were reported active by October 1868, when the first Grand Camp (state convention) met in Columbia. Spokesmen for the OPF denied any Klan

affiliation in letters to the press, but KKK Grand Wizard Nathan Bedford Forrest later admitted membership in the order. After another OPF member, John Bicknell, was robbed and murdered by a black highwayman in Maury County, in February 1868, klansmen and Pale Faces marched together in his funeral procession. A masked gang subsequently lynched Bicknell's slayer in Columbia. Some historians now regard the OPF and KKK as identical.

Patriotic Legal Fund—Organized in 1969 by J.B. Stoner, this group solicited funds for the legal defense of James Earl Ray, then appealed his conviction in the murder of Dr. Martin Luther King, Jr.

Patriotic Party of Iowa—Despite its name, this short-lived splinter group, headquartered at Okoboji, was in fact a neo–Nazi cell.

Patriots Defense Foundation—Texas attorney Kirk Lyons founded the PDF in December 1989, as "an ACLU–type organization to serve the needs and concerns of the 'Patriotic Movement.'" He solicited donations of office equipment and other material assistance from the Aryan Nations, the Mountain Church of Jesus Christ, and other white-supremacist groups, while serving primarily as a defense attorney for indicted klansmen, neo–Nazis and Christian Identity cultists. In 1991, SPLC investigators ranked Lyons as one of America's top-ten racist figures. A year later, Lyons moved from Houston to North Carolina, renaming his firm the CAUSE Foundation (for *C*anada, *A*ustralia, *U*nited States, *S*outh Africa, and *E*urope).

Patriots of North Carolina, Inc.—Yet another racist group organized in the wake of "Black Monday," the PNCI was chartered in August 1955 by prominent whites from fifty-nine North Carolina counties, with headquarters in Greensboro. President Wesley George served as a professor at the University of North Carolina Medical School, while executive secretary A. Allison James was a Winston-Salem pharmacist. Despite its relatively "high tone," the group failed to attract a mass following and faded from the racist scene in 1957.

Patriots Organizational Communications Center—Established at the August 1975 UKA klonvokation in Lakeland, Florida, this ambitious coalition of far-right groups was jointly led by UKA Wizard Robert Shelton and Minutemen founder Robert DePugh. Despite establishment of headquarters at DePugh's home in Norborne, Missouri, the POCC existed chiefly on paper, its goal of uniting the racist right still unrealized.

People's Movement—A West German neo–Nazi organization, the People's Movement sent delegates to New Orleans for joint demonstrations with David Duke's KKKK in September 1976.

Phineas Priesthood—The Biblical story of Phinehas (Numbers 25:7–8) depicts the execution of a mixed-race couple, killed on God's orders, to avert a plague from Israel. American white supremacists adopted the story sometime in the 1970s (while misspelling the main character's name), and Christian Identity spokesman Richard Hopkins offered an alleged history of the "Phineas Priesthood" in his book *Vigilantes of Christendom* (1990). Since then, various neo–Nazi splinter groups have claimed the title for themselves, and a *New York Times* report (30 October 1991) described the order as "God's executioners." Klan assassin Byron De La Beckwith claimed knowledge of the movement (if not active membership), while an unnamed resident of Tennessee told author Reed Massengill: "They target anybody who threatens the movement.... If you let out these secrets, they are not just going to kill you. They are going to kill your family."

Self-identified Phineas Priests include Walter Thody (imprisoned in 1991 for armed robberies in Oklahoma) and a quartet of extremists—Charles Barbee, Robert Berry, Verne Merrel and Brian Ratigan—who robbed banks and bombed abortion clinics around Spokane, Washington, in 1995–96. In 2002, Pennsylvania Aryan Nations leaders August Kreis and Joshua Sutter praised Palestinian suicide bombers, while calling for "Phineas Priests and Priestesses" to execute similar attacks in the United States. Sutter, who declared himself a member of the sect, proclaimed that the "Phineas Priesthood is alive and well in this state and we will be coming soon to a church near you!" Another Aryan Nations defector, Pennsylvania's Charles Juba, subsequently founded his own Tabernacle of the Phineas Priesthood, adopting Posse Comitatus veteran James Wickstrom as the group's "chaplin." Juba's motto at the time: "No Jew left alive in 2005."

Posse Comitatus—A volatile blend of survivalism, neo–Nazi politics and Christian Identity religion, the racist Posse Comitatus ("power of the county," in Latin) drew its inspiration from the post–Civil War Posse Comitatus Act, forbidding use of federal troops to enforce local laws. As interpreted by Posse founder William Potter Gale, that law invalidated any form of government above the county sheriff's office—and even that authority was disregarded if a sheriff supported the edicts of "ZOG" (the "Zionist Occupation Government" in Washington, D.C.). Gale founded his United Christian Posse Association in 1969, headquartered at Glendale, California, while veteran fascist Henry Lamont Beach (a Silver Shirt Legion alumnus) plagiarized Gale's handbook and launched his own chapter in Portland, Oregon, the same year. Scattered Posse units attracted klansmen, neo–Nazis, Identity cultists, tax-dodgers and disaffected farmers in at least a dozen states, resisting foreclosures and threatening officials who investigated the movement. Klan leader David Duke told reporters, "We work with the Posses whenever we can. We get their material and funnel it to our groups." By the mid–1970s, Posse members were active enough to prompt creation of a special IRS Illegal Tax Protester Program. In 1980, federal agents identified 17,222 dedicated tax protesters, that number increasing to 49,213 in 1982 and 57,754 in 1983.

Angry and well armed, the Posses soon turned to crime. In May 1982, Colorado police jailed eight Posse members (including one known klansman) for plotting to kill a federal judge and bomb Denver's IRS office. In February 1983, North Dakota member Gordon Kahl murdered a U.S. marshal, then fled to Arkansas, where he killed a sheriff in the June shootout that claimed his life. September 1983 saw a Hiawatha, Kansas, informant describe the recent "accidental" death of Sheriff David Nigus as a Posse execution. In October 1984, Nebraska farmer Arthur Kirk died in a battle with sheriff's SWAT officers, after declaring his land a sovereign county under Posse dictates. In 1985, federal agents raided Posse "barter centers" in Colorado, Iowa, Minnesota and South Dakota, seizing ten tons of silver bullion collected from 20,000 participants in an illegal pyramid scheme. In July 1986, Colorado jurors convicted Posse member Roderick Elliott of embezzling funds "donated" by Midwestern farmers in a similar barter arrangement. James Wickstrom, self-described "national director of counterinsurgency for the United Posses of America," drew prison time in 1991 for circulating counterfeit money among members of the Aryan Nations. While most observers consider the Posse Comitatus defunct, Wickstrom and others maintain an active presence on the Internet, promoting racist views and agitating for revolt against "the enemy" in Washington.

Pro-Southerners—Harry Pyle, an ex-klansman from Memphis, Tennessee, led this Georgia-based white-supremacist group from headquarters in Ft. Pierce, until it dissolved in March 1956.

Pro-Southerners League—Not to be confused with Harry Pyle's Pro-Southerners in Tennessee, the PSL opposed school integration in Fort Pierce, Florida, during 1954–55.

Racial Nationalist Party of America—SPLC investigators found this neo-fascist group active in Lockport, New York, during 1998–99. No trace of it remained in 2000.

Red Caps—This racist group was active in Humphreys County, Tennessee, during 1868. Its members sometimes operated in conjunction with another group, the Yellow Jackets.

Reichsfolk—Based in Auburn, Indiana, this neo–Nazi faction operated during 1998–99, but vanished in 2000. During its brief lifetime, it served primarily as an outlet for the writings of David Myatt, a British neo–Nazi who collaborated with leaders of a Satanist sect, the Order of the Nine Angles.

Rights of White People—Police described this North Carolina racist group, led by ex-marine Leroy Gibson, as "more dangerous than the Klan." RWP members patrolled Wilmington's streets during black riots in October 1971,with Gibson telling journalists: "We're going where the trouble is and do some shooting if we have to. We'll destroy them all if necessary." Gibson's rallies drew several hundred armed whites, and the RWP's motorcades through black neighborhoods prompted a legal ban on public display of firearms. Wilmington police chief H.E. Williamson complained that half of his seventy-six-man department was kept busy trailing the RWP around town, to prevent acts of random violence. Gibson responded by offering paramilitary training courses to white high school students, announcing: "We have as many as 2,000 white men in Wilmington who are willing to settle the trouble right now. If it weren't for the Wilmington police, the blacks in there would have been destroyed by now."

Seaboard White Citizens' Council—Racist firebrand John Kasper founded the SWCC in May 1956, with headquarters in Washington, D.C. His extremist literature and public behavior—including speeches at KKK rallies and calls for violent resistance to school integration—embarrassed many "legitimate" Council leaders, prompting them to shun Kasper and the SWCC. Kasper's support thus came primarily from known klansmen (e.g., Asa Carter and Kenneth Adams) and from professional anti–Semites, including John Crommelin and future leaders of the NSRP.

Seventy-Six Society—A racist group allied with local Klans, the SSS was active during 1871 in Kemper, Lowndes, and Monroe Counties, Mississippi.

Seymour Knights—A Louisiana terrorist group, organized in 1868, the Seymour Knights operated in those parishes between New Orleans and the Arkansas state line. Members collaborated with the KKK and KWC, including occasional joint demonstrations. On 28 September 1868, three members raided a black school in Opelousas and beat its teenage white teacher, Emerson Bentley. Local blacks sought to retaliate, but Bentley dissuaded them and they were soon disarmed by white vigilantes.

Sieg Heil—Huntsville, Alabama, hosted this tiny neo–Nazi splinter group in 1991–92.

Silver Shirt Legion of America—Organized by William Dudley Pelley the day after Adolf Hitler seized power in Germany (31 January 1933), the SSL was bankrolled by wealthy anti–Semites and sales of racist literature from Pelley's Fellowship Press in Asheville, North Carolina. (Congressional investigators established that Pelley received more than $166,000 in private donations between September 1937 and July 1939.) Gerald L.K. Smith was an early recruit, conducting street rallies and traveling under guard from a self-styled "Silver Shirt storm troop." Pelley's Midwestern membership overlapped with that of the Klan and Black Legion, while Pelley himself consulted Michigan KKK leaders on points of political strategy. Pelley's presidential campaign in 1936 failed to put him in the White House, but it reaped national publicity for the Silver Shirts, attracting members who included Rev. W.D. Riley (founder of the World's Christian Fundamentals Association in Minneapolis, director of the Northwestern Bible Seminary) and Joseph Jeffers (pastor of the Kingdom Temple in Los Angeles, who toured Germany and Italy in 1938, for personal visits with Josef Goebbels and Benito Mussolini). In 1939, Jeffers screened a Silver Shirt promotional film at his church, narrated by recruiter Ron Zachary, who boasted of his willingness to kill President Franklin Roosevelt "if nobody else will." That spring, Jeffers and his bride of nine months were scandalized by press reports of sex orgies at their home, involving "unconventional practices while naked for the entertainment of house guests." Elsewhere, recruiter Walter Bailey Bishop fraternized with Father Charles Coughlin's anti–Semitic Christian Front, while Montana Rep. Jacob Thorkelson appeared frequently as a guest speaker at Silver Shirt rallies. The order dissolved after Pelley's sedition indictment, during World War II, but aging alumnus

Henry Beach later emerged as a spokesman for the militant Posse Comitatus. Another Pelley follower, Richard Girnt Butler, teamed with klansman Wesley Swift after the war, to found the Church of Jesus Christ Christian (later the Aryan Nations).

Skinheads—Described by one observer as "the children of the Klan," neo–Nazi skinheads actually trace their roots to England in the 1960s. They evolved from British "hard Mods," known for their shaved scalps, steel-toed boots and drunken brawls at soccer matches. By the early 1970s, gay-bashing and random assaults on nonwhite victims had been added to the skinhead repertoire, influenced and encouraged by older members of England's neo-fascist National Front. America's first recognized skinhead gang, Romantic Violence from Chicago, surfaced in 1985 at a gathering of hate groups in Michigan. By 1989, ADL investigators estimated that the nation harbored some 3,000 racist skinheads, dispersed among 154 gangs in thirty-four states. The highest skinhead concentrations were found in California (with at least thirty-three gangs), New Jersey (with fifteen), and Michigan (ten gangs). Impulsive, disaffected and frequently intoxicated, the skinheads turned quickly to violence, committing at least seventeen known murders between 1988 and 1992. Skinhead assaults and incidents of vandalism numbered in the hundreds.

As with Ku Klux factions nationwide, the number of known skinhead gangs and their affiliation with older, larger groups constantly fluctuates. SPLC investigators counted 79 skinhead gangs in 1989, 69 in 1990, 104 in 1991, 108 in 1992, 42 in 1997, 48 in 1998, 40 in 1999, 39 in 2000, 43 in 2001, 18 in 2002, 39 in 2003, 48 in 2004, and 28 in 2005. At press time for this volume, skinhead groups were active in twenty states, with New Jersey boasting the heaviest concentration (twelve chapters of eight competing gangs). The largest skinhead gang was Pennsylvania's Keystone State Skinheads, with headquarters at Harrisburg and satellite chapters in nine other cities. Gangs with chapters in more than one state included the Confederate Hammerskins (Florida, Georgia and Tennessee), the TCB Hate Crew (Illinois, Missouri and Texas), The Hated (Florida and New Jer-

Some skinheads openly display Klan insignia with their Nazi regalia (Southern Poverty Law Center).

sey), and the White Power Liberation Front (New Jersey and Texas).

Wherever gangs of any size exist, they have been linked to factions of the KKK and neo–Nazi groups through joint rallies,

Neo-Nazi skinheads have joined many Klan demonstrations since 1985 (Southern Poverty Law Center).

Racist vandalism is a common skinhead activity (Florida State Archives).

correspondence, shared literature and occasional acts of violence. Some adult fascists shave their heads in a display of solidarity with skinhead youth, while skinheads often now display Klan insignias on their clothing. A few examples of that interaction include the following:

October 1987: **Modesto, California**—Leaders of the American Knights publicly initiated three skinheads.

November 1988: **Philadelphia, Pennsylvania**—After heckling prompted klansmen to cancel a scheduled rally at Independence Hall, skinheads brawled with some of the anti–Klan protesters.

April 1989: **Hayden Lake, Idaho**—Aryan Nations leader Richard Butler hosted a three-day skinhead gathering with past and present Klan leaders Kim Badynski, Louis Beam and Thomas Robb.

September 1989: **Stone Mountain, Georgia**—100 skinheads joined in a Klan rally, upsetting some klansmen with their raucous style of music.

October 1989: **Detroit, Michigan**—Skinheads staged a joint rally with the SS Action Group, distributing literature from the Church of the Creator, David Duke's NAAWP and Tom Metzger's WAR.

1989–90: **San Antonio, Texas**—Members of the San Antonio Area Skinheads (SMASH) corresponded extensively with various KKK factions.

1990: **Kansas City, Missouri**—ADL reports identified two local skinheads as regular participants in White Knights rallies and other Klan activities.

1990: **Casper, Wyoming**—Members of the Casper Area Skinheads (CASH) adopted the alternative name of Wyoming Knights of the KKK, but ADL investigators found no actual link to any functional Klan.

1 January 1990: **Baltimore, Maryland**—Maryland Knights Grand Dragon Leo Rossiter and members of the skinhead gang Aryan Resistance demonstrated outside the city's NAACP office.

April 1990: **New Jersey**—Police arrested Pieter Van Gulden, head of the New Orleans skinhead gang National White Resistance, for disorderly conduct at a KKK rally.

7 April 1990: **Baltimore, Maryland**—Grand Dragon Leo Rossiter and Aryan Resistance skinheads brawled with opponents from the leftist International Committee Against Racism.

9 April 1990: **Oxford, Ohio**—Indianapolis skinhead leader Matthew Myers and two skinheads from Columbus, Ohio, appeared as honored guests at a Klan rally.

Spring 1992: **Indianapolis, Indiana**—Skinheads brawled with hecklers during a rally of Thom Robb's KKKK at the state capitol.

18 April 1992: **Birmingham, Alabama**—Hours after attending a rally led by former klansman Bill Riccio, three skinheads fatally stabbed a homeless black man.

1995: The Confederate Knights of America established a skinhead affiliate, the SS of America, whose members donned black uniforms and served as security guards at Klan rallies.

15 November 1997: **Fresno, California**—After 500 Klan opponents heckled a KKK rally on the California State University campus, skinheads assaulted four of the protesters.

19 January 2002: **Newport, Tennessee**—While hecklers jeered a Klan rally, skinheads waving Nazi flags attempted to incite the protesters to violence.

2004: **Fountain Hills, Arizona**—Klansmen, skinheads and members of other racist groups held an "international" Aryanfest at McDowell Regional Mountain Park.

Past and present Klan leaders who have displayed a particular affinity for skinhead youths include:

John Baumgardner—Identified as Florida's grand dragon for the IEKKKK during 1988–90, Baumgardner forged an alliance with Orlando's Florida Corps Skinheads. Members of that gang displayed the KKK's "cross-wheel" design on their jackets and commonly appeared at IEKKKK rallies.

Tony Bastanzio—A competitor of Baumgardner's, as leader of the rival Dixie Knights in Florida, Bastanzio welcomed members of Orlando's skinhead Youth Corps 87 to his public rallies. The Dixie Knights also had ties to skinhead leader David Lynch and his American Front, with chapters in Fort Pierce, Jensen Beach and Treasure Coast.

Tom Metzger—Once David Duke's California grand dragon for the KKKK, later head of his own California Knights, Metzger has relied extensively on skinhead members and support since launching his neo–Nazi WAR in the mid–1980s. Son John Metzger helped organize the affiliated War Skins, while WAR forged alliances with various other skinhead gangs on the west coast and nationwide. In 1988, WAR recruiters supplied the baseball bats that young members of East Side White Pride used to murder an Ethiopian student in Portland, Oregon. That slaying rebounded against WAR in October 1989, when a lawsuit filed by the SPLC cost the Metzgers $12.5 million in damages. The group disbanded after Riccio went back to prison on a weapons charge and Handley was jailed for sex crimes.

Bill Riccio—A former Alabama klansman and four-time convicted felon, Riccio joined Klan leader William Handley to lead the Aryan Defense League (also known as the Aryan National Front) in the early 1990s. That affiliation gained Riccio national publicity in 1993, when HBO's program *Skinheads USA: Soldiers of the Race War* focused on that group exclusively, portraying Riccio as a combination Führer and father figure to a group of disaffected misfits.

Leo Rossiter—A former grand dragon of the 1980s Maryland Knights, Rossiter allied his Klan with several skinhead gangs including Baltimore's American Resistance and BASH (*B*altimore *A*rea *S*kin*h*eads), as well as White Justice, based in Philadelphia, Pennsylvania.

Skrewdriver Services—SPLC investigators found this small neo–Nazi group (named for an infamous white-power rock band) active in Aurora, Colorado, during 1991–92.

Social Nationalist Aryan People's Party— Neo-Nazi Keith Gilbert organized the SNAPP in 1979, after spending five years in California prisons for shooting a black man and plotting to murder Dr. Martin Luther King, Jr. In August 1983, after transvestite serial killer Frank Spisak, Jr., murdered two blacks and a suspected Jew in Cleveland, Ohio, Gilbert claimed that Spisak was a SNAPP lieutenant "acting under direct orders from the party." Those orders, according to Gilbert: "Kill niggers until the last one is dead." Prosecutors found no evidence supporting that claim, and Gilbert's group dissolved before SPLC investigators completed their census of hate groups in 1989.

Society for the Preservation of State Government and Racial Integrity—New Orleans resident Harry Gamble, Sr., organized this group to resist school integration in 1955. Gamble later moved on to the more profitable Citizens' Council.

Sons of Confederate Veterans—Founded in 1896, the SCV allegedly restricts its membership to direct male descendants of Confederate military veterans and claims no interest beyond Civil War memorial projects. In pursuit of legitimacy, the group passed a 1990 resolution condemning hate groups, but has nonetheless drifted into a neo–Confederate posture since then, including espousal of frankly racist messages and members. In 1996, then-leader Peter Orlebeke offered a Biblical defense of slavery while contending that enslavement was beneficial to blacks. "There have been many times," he said, "that I wish someone had said to me, 'I'll give you a job for the rest of your life.'" In April 2000, the SCV's *Alabama Confederate* featured an editorial condemning Abraham Lincoln's Emancipation Proclamation as unconstitutional, plus articles penned by members of the racist League of the South (LOS). Prominent SCV members identified by the SPLC include Michael Grissom (a CCC and LOS member), Donald and Walter Kennedy (charter LOS members), white-supremacist attorney Kirk Lyons, and Jared Taylor (editor of the racist *American Renaissance* magazine). Concerning Lyons, long affiliated with the KKK and neo–Nazi groups, SCV Commander-in-Chief Patrick Griffin told the SPLC, "If Kirk has become controversial outside the SCV, I would just view that as part of his personal life." In 1998, LOS leaders praised the SCV's apparent shift in policy, noting that the anti-racist "old guard" was losing influence and that "the organization appears to be ready to work with us as a fellow pro–South group."

Sons of Liberty—A California affiliate of the ANP, led by future klansman James Warner in the late 1960s, the Sons of Liberty staged occasional joint demonstrations with other neo–Nazis in Los Angeles. Transplanted to Louisiana with Warner in the 1970s, the group survived as an adjunct of his New Christian Crusade Church through the mid–1980s, but disbanded prior to the SPLC's survey of active hate groups in 1989. After an eleven-year hiatus, it then resurfaced on the SPLC's roster in 2002–04.

South Florida Aryan Alliance—The SFAA claimed chapters in Pompano Beach and Sunrise during 2001, but both disbanded in early 2002.

Southern Gentlemen, Inc.—A semi-secret racist group based in Baton Rouge, Louisiana, the SGI was briefly active in the wake of "Black Monday," opposing school integration.

The Southerners *see* Assembly of Christian Soldiers, Inc.

SS Action Group—Also known as the Security Services Action Group, this neo–Nazi group began life in 1979 as the Detroit chapter of the National Socialist Movement. Leaders Edward James Dunn and John Moriarty split from the NSM later that year, recruiting an estimated fifty members for pugnacious demonstrations during 1980–81. In August 1981, the Klan and SSAG obtained permits for a joint rally at Detroit's Kennedy Square, prompting creation of a left-wing Committee Against Klan/Nazi Terror. The resultant confrontation sent eight persons to jail, as hecklers broke police lines to assault KKK/SSAG demonstrators. By 1982, violence was a staple of SSAG rallies, with its members on the receiving end of eggs, stones and bricks in Ann Arbor, Detroit, and Birmingham, Michigan. Similar outbreaks occurred in March 1983 at Ann Arbor, and a month later in Cleveland, Ohio, where eight SSAG members staged a joint rally with the United White Party. SSAG members also attended cross-burning rites in Cohoctah, Michigan, on the farm owned by klansman Robert Miles and his Mountain Church of Jesus Christ. Dunn ran the SSAG from Dearborn Heights, Michigan, in 1989–91, planting far-flung chapters in six other states from Arizona to New York, but it disbanded sometime before the SPLC's survey of active hate groups in 1997.

SS Enterprises—SPLC investigators found this neo–Nazi splinter group active in Fresno, California, during 1997. Subsequent hate-group surveys in 1998–2000 failed to confirm its survival, but it resurfaced at its old location during 2001–04. The lapse may indicate a hiatus in operations or a simple oversight by SPLC auditors.

SS Regalia—Based in Edgewater, Maryland, this outlet for Nazi paraphernalia catered to neo-fascists nationwide in 2001–04.

States Rights Council—Roy V. Harris, onetime speaker of the house in Georgia's state legislature and a founder of the Peach State's Citizens' Council, organized this racist group in December 1954. Its crowning achievement, in July 1955, was cancellation of Augusta's soapbox derby to prevent two black boys from competing in a field of eighty racers (described by SRC spokesmen as an "attack on our white civilization"). Membership peaked around 10,000 in 1955–56.

Texas Emergency Reserve—Organized by Grand Dragon Louis Beam to provide paramilitary training for klansmen and like-minded racists, this group maintained camps outside Galveston and at several other locations in the Lone Star State. In 1980, it operated Camp Puller, where students were required to read *The Turner Diaries* as part of their training. Beam dissolved the TER in June 1982, after SPLC attorneys filed suit under an obscure Texas statute banning private armies. That defeat drove Beam to Idaho, where he joined the Aryan Nations and decreed "two death sentences" against SPLC chief counsel Morris Dees.

Texas White Man's Association—Based in Austin, this white-supremacist group was sporadically active during 1990–92.

United Nordic Confederation—A neo–Nazi splinter group dedicated to "unifying and purifying the Nordic people,"

the UNC made headlines on 18 January 1958, when New York City police jailed leader George Leggett and six of his disciples on weapons charges. According to authorities, the seven fascists planned to finance their *putsch* by robbing a bank in Kew Gardens. At age twenty-one, Leggett was the UNC's oldest member. His teenage followers included Brian Casey, Bryan Colgan, Jap Page, William Schultz, Joseph Wagner, and George Zack.

United Protestant Alliance—A 1920s anti–Catholic group in Queens, New York, the UPA held meetings at the Klan-owned Triangle Ballroom in Richmond Hill, where speakers including Sen. Tom Heflin regaled the faithful with tales of papist perfidy. In retrospect, the UPA may have been a simple front for the New York KKK.

United Racist Front—Organized in Greensboro, North Carolina, in 1978, the URF sought to merge local klansmen and neo–Nazis. Some of its members participated in the November 1979 murders of five unarmed protesters in Greensboro.

United Southern Aryans—Based in Bossier City, Louisiana, this neo–Nazi group appeared in 1997 and vanished early the following year.

United White Party—A forerunner of the NSRP, founded in 1957, this neo–Nazi group counted Tennessee klansman Jack Brown and future ANP founder George Lincoln Rockwell among its supporters.

United White Workers—This small neo–Nazi faction operated in Salt Lake City, Utah, during 1991–92.

Uptown Rebels—A Chicago street gang linked to the 1980s ANP, the Uptown Rebels were linked to the separate murders of victims Henry Hampton and Kevin Zornes in 1985.

Vigilantes, Inc.—Organized by Georgia's ex-governor Eugene Talmadge after his electoral defeat, in October 1942, this group was billed by its supporters as a "secret, patriotic white man's organization." With Talmadge as the figurehead and guiding light, actual leadership fell to Maj. John Goodwin of the Georgia Highway Patrol, based in Atlanta. Investigator John Carlson had trouble obtaining the group's address, until he finally asked a local klavern of the KKK, reporting afterward that the Klan and Vigilantes cooperated closely in their "patriotic" work. Stetson Kennedy reports that Goodwin shared the stage with Talmadge at a 1943 Klan rally in Porterdale, Georgia.

Volksfront—Oregon skinhead Randall Krager founded this neo–Nazi group in 1994, after serving two years in prison for assaulting a black victim chosen at random. Krager's inspiration was ex-klansman Tom Metzger of WAR, whom he described as "one of the nicest guys you'd ever meet." Volksfront's stated goals were "to protect and advise skinheads entering the prison system, oppose drug use and traffic amongst White inmates, promote Odinic Religious education and have Odinism/Asatru recognized by the Dept. of Corrections, to enforce a unified course of action and standards in the Portland Racialist movement, to educate young Whites on pro–White politics, to provide an alternate means of activism to Whites that would prevent their in-carceration and to oppose red action and expansion on Portland streets." Death threats to an anti–Nazi skinhead sent Krager back to prison in 1995, where he served another fourteen months. Meanwhile, the group launched a website and Thule Publications, expanding with chapters in Eugene and Salem, plus a short-lived group in Minnesota. By 2003, Volksfront claimed chapters in seven states plus Australia, British Columbia and Germany. Featured speakers at Volksfront rallies included Metzger, Richard Butler and Billy Roper. When three Tacoma, Washington, members murdered homeless victim David Pillatos in 2002, Volksfront's website disowned the defendants, striking a pose of nonviolence, but the group's rallies still feature inflammatory racist rhetoric, embodied in the motto "Race Over All!"

Washington Brothers—Organized in Leake County, Mississippi, during 1867, this violent white-supremacist group later merged with the KKK.

Western Front—Founded in 1965 by Walter White, Jr., husband of notorious 1940s anti–Semite Opal Tanner White, the Western Front worked closely with Gerald L.K. Smith until his death in 1979. It remained active in Hollywood, California, through the mid–1980s, publishing tracts that exposed the "Jewish conspiracy," but no trace of it remained when SPLC investigators surveyed active hate groups in 1989.

Western Guard—A Canadian neo–Nazi group based in Toronto, founded as the Edmund Burke Society in 1967, the WG was renamed by co-founder Don Andrews in 1972. It maintains close ties with Klan groups on both sides of the border, with officers including klansmen Wolfgang Droege, James McQuirter, Jacob Prins, and John Ross Taylor. The WG also fraternized with NSRP members, welcoming J.B. Stoner as guest speaker at a 1974 banquet. Members joined David Duke's KKKK for protests in New Orleans, during September 1976, and in 1980 traveled to Raleigh, North Carolina, for the NSPA's first annual convention. Arrests, schisms and public condemnation further marginalized the Western Guard in the 1990s.

White America, Inc.—An Arkansas racist group, based in Pine Bluff and organized with aid from the Mississippi Citizens' Council, White America mounted a series of demonstrations that closed Hoxie's schools for three weeks in August 1955.

White American Freedom Fighters—Rev. James Betts ran this neo–Nazi fringe group at Overland, Missouri, during 1989–91, but it dissolved sometime before the SPLC's survey of active American hate groups in 1997.

White American Political Association—Organized by California klansman Tom Metzger after he lost a 1980 congressional race, the WAPA was created to promote "pro-white" candidates for public office. Describing its restricted membership, Metzger told reporters, "I wouldn't knowingly allow a Jew to belong. Judaism is a conspiracy against all races." In 1983, the WAPA was supplanted by Metzger's WAR.

White Aryan Legion—SPLC investigators found this neo–Nazi splinter group active in Louisville, Kentucky, during 1998. It disbanded early the following year.

White Aryan Resistance—Ex-klansman Tom Metzger founded WAR in 1983, as "an association dedicated to the struggle of the white working people." Critics charge that Metzger received $250,000 in stolen bank loot from members of The Order during 1984, but Metzger escaped indictment with other neo-Nazi leaders for sedition in April 1987, and he still denies involvement in any criminal conspiracy. Son John Metzger managed affairs for the White Students Union, also known as the Aryan Youth Movement, WAR Youth, and WAR Skins, recruiting skinhead thugs when not appearing with his father on various TV talk-shows. In the late 1980s, Metzger's *Race and Reason* television show aired on more than fifty cable systems in at least a dozen states, and he maintains an active Internet website. In October 1989, ADL and SPLC attorneys sued the Metzgers for complicity in the death of a Nigerian student murdered by Oregon skinheads in November 1988. At trial, lead counsel Morris Dees proved that a WAR recruiter not only encouraged such violence, but also furnished the baseball bats used in the slaying. (Metzger himself proclaimed that the killers had done "their civic duty.") The resultant $12.5 million damage award cost Metzger his house, truck, and TV-repair tools, but he remained unrepentant, vowing to "put blood on the streets like you've never seen." The trial verdict initially seemed to boost WAR's membership, with twenty-one active chapters reported from eleven states and Washington, D.C., during 1990, but that number fell to six chapters in 1991. By 1997, only headquarters (in Fallbrook, California) and a lone Oklahoma chapter remained. Metzger's home chapter stood alone after 2001, clinging to life primarily on paper at press time for this volume. While WAR's membership is impossible to estimate, Metzger's website survives and his *WAR* tabloid continues to promote crude racism.

White Brotherhood (1868–70)—A Reconstruction-era terrorist group, organized in 1868, the White Brotherhood operated chiefly in North Carolina, where it shared space and members with the KKK and CUG. Local units were designated as camps, administered by captains, but no evidence exists of any officers above the county chiefs, who also served as captains of "grand camps." The Brotherhood was strongest in Alamance County, where its members included the sheriff, his deputies, and all of the county's state legislators. Ranking officers joined CUG leaders and a few Klan spokesmen to call for disbandment in 1870, during Gov. William Holden's war against terrorists, and the WB apparently dissolved before year's end.

White Brotherhood (1954–55)—Based in Atlanta, Georgia, this group opposed school integration after "Black Monday," then disappeared as the Citizens' Councils assumed responsibility for "legitimate" resistance.

White Caps—First organized in Crawford and Harrison Counties, Indiana, where settlers from Tennessee (including veterans of the Reconstruction-era KKK) had put down roots, the White Caps quickly spread as disconnected bands with purely local operations and objectives. In Indiana and Ohio, White Caps served primarily as vigilante "regulators," while the Georgia faction spent its time protecting moonshine stills. In Sevier County, Tennessee, the White Caps focused primarily on ridding their district of "lewd and adulterous" women. (That moralistic campaign climaxed with the murder of Laura and William Whaley before the eyes of their infant child, in December 1896.) In Texas, White Cap victims were mostly black or Hispanic, hounded from their land on behalf of wealthy Anglo ranchers. Republicans and nonwhites bore the brunt of White Cap violence in New Mexico, until Juan José Herrera organized an Hispanic chapter to defend his people from racist aggression in 1890–92. Mississippi's first White Caps appeared in 1892–93, then returned a decade later, driving black tenants off land seized from whites in bank foreclosures. By 1905, scattered White Cap bands rode throughout the Midwest and Border South, serving as vigilance committees, recruiting whites whose income and political influence were steadily declining. Many historians regard the White Caps as a "bridge" between the first and second Klans, tilling soil for the modern KKK in regions untouched by the Reconstruction-era order.

White Christian Crusaders—A Pennsylvania splinter group organized by Steven White and his wife in March 1971, the WCC consisted primarily of defectors from the UKA. Explaining his unit's paramilitary garb, White said, "We designed a uniform to look like the stormtroopers of Germany thirty years ago, to wake people up." White publicly disavowed violence, but police jailed four WCC members on weapons charges in Hightstown, New Jersey, after a street brawl with JDL activists. Politically, White's troopers supported Philadelphia's racist mayor Frank Rizzo and the second presidential bid of Alabama's George Wallace.

White Confederacy of Understanding—Canadian klansman and neo-Nazi Jacob Prins founded this short-lived group in 1976.

White Front—William Blanchard founded this pro-Nazi group in Miami, Florida, during the 1930s. Many local klansmen joined the WF, perhaps seeking a change of regalia in its gray-shirted uniforms, and while Blanchard praised the KKK extravagantly in his *Race and Nation* newsletter, most of the WF's literature came directly from Adolf Hitler's Welt Dienst agency in Germany. Blanchard joined the German-American Bund and Silver Shirt Legion in promoting legislation to segregate Jews and make miscegenation a felony. White Fronters liked to boast that "[w]hen Hitler has killed all the Jews in Europe, he's going to help us drive all the Jews on Miami Beach into the sea," but battle-hardened members of the Jewish War Veterans had other ideas, forming quick-response teams to pummel and humiliate WF members wherever they surfaced to harass Jewish merchants.

White House Network—SPLC investigators reported this neo-Nazi splinter group active in Harrisburg, Pennsylvania, during 1997. It disbanded early in 1998.

White League—A paramilitary racist group, including many former klansmen in its ranks, the White League staged a bloody coup d'état against Louisiana's Republican state government in September 1874, leaving 27 dead and 105 wounded in the streets of New Orleans. Federal troops suppressed the rebellion, but it marked the effective end of Reconstruction in Louisiana, and white-supremacist Democrats restored "home rule" two years later.

White Man's League—Conceived by Emory Burke in November 1949, this one-man effort to revive the Columbians failed to entice white residents of Atlanta, Georgia.

White Race Party—Based at Merritt Island, Florida, this neo–Nazi splinter group appeared in 1990 and disbanded the following year.

White Revolution—Billy Roper defected from the National Alliance to found this competing neo–Nazi group in 2002. Headquartered in Russellville, Arkansas, White Revolution boasted nine chapters in as many states by 2003, while holding joint rallies with the National Socialist Movement and allied racist groups. A net loss of two chapters (and states) in 2004 failed to dampen Roper's enthusiasm for Jew-baiting.

White Rose Society—A racist vigilante group that predated the Reconstruction-era Klan in Noxubee County, Mississippi, the WRS remained active into 1871, raiding alongside the KKK and apparently sharing certain members.

White Students Union—Initially led by John Metzger, son of ex-klansman and neo–Nazi Tom Metzger, the WSU served as an adjunct to White Aryan Resistance. At various times, it has also been known as the Aryan Youth Movement, WAR Skins, and WAR Youth. In 1989, John Metzger and his skinhead followers staged a minor riot on the set of Geraldo Rivera's TV talk-show, leaving Rivera with a broken nose. The following year, SPLC investigators listed Mark Wright as the WSU's chairman, operating from Gainesville, Florida, with chapters in Chicago, New Orleans and Philadelphia. No trace of the group remained in 1991.

White Unity Coalition—Unity (and members) remained elusive for this racist splinter group in Warren, Michigan. Led by Rocky Suhayda in 1990, it disbanded in early 1991.

Wide Awake Club—A Louisiana white-supremacist group, organized during the 1868 presidential campaign, the WAC collaborated with the KKK, KWC and the Innocents Club to terrorize blacks and Republicans. On 25 October 1868, WAC members joined the KWC to murder seven blacks at Algiers.

Women for Aryan Unity—Launched in 2003 with headquarters at Eagle River, Alaska, and chapters in three other states, the WAU expanded to five chapters in five states by 2001. The year 2002 saw headquarters shift to Costa Mesa, California, while two active chapters disbanded. Another change of headquarters—to Brooklyn, New York—revitalized the group in 2003, expanding slightly to claim six chapters in six states by 2004.

World Aryan Party—Its grandiose title notwithstanding, the WAP consisted of a single chapter in Athens, Tennessee, briefly active during 2000.

World Church of the Creator—Prior to founding his Church of the Creator in 1973, Benhardt Klassen served as a Florida state legislator and as state chairman of George Wallace's 1968 presidential campaign. In his book *Nature's Eternal Religion* (1973), Klassen described his "Creativity" movement as driven by "our sacred goal to populate the lands of this earth with White people exclusively." To that end, Klassen published *The White Man's Bible* in 1981, and moved his headquarters in 1982 to a farm outside Otto, North Carolina. In June 1983, he launched publication of a monthly newsletter, *Racial Loyalty,* and adopted "RAHOWA!" (*Racial Holy War*) as the COTC's motto. In 1988, at age seventy, Klassen began his search for a successor as "Pontifex Maximus." California neo–Nazi John Metzger rejected the offer that year, followed by Klassen's selection of Rudy Stanko (serving prison time for selling tainted meat) in 1990. Following the death of Klassen's wife in January 1992, he canceled Stanko's appointment, naming first Charles Altvater, then Mark Wilson, and finally Richard McCarty as his successor. Confronted with an SPLC lawsuit after one of his followers murdered a black Gulf War veteran in Florida, Klassen sold most of his North Carolina compound to neo–Nazi William Pierce in 1992, then killed himself on 7 August 1993.

McCarty moved COTC headquarters back to Florida in 1993, then yielded control of the cult to Illinois fascist Matthew Hale in 1995. Hale transferred headquarters to his East Peoria home and renamed his group the World Church of the Creator in December 1995, with Klassen loyalist Jonathan Viktor serving as "Hasta Primus" (vice president). Hale's virulent extremism, broadcast via the Internet, produced an escalating wave of violence by his members, climaxed by Hale's own April 2004 conviction for soliciting the murder of federal judge Joan Lefkow. (The impetus for that conspiracy was Lefkow's ruling in a trademark lawsuit, lost by Hale, that required him to change his cult's name. It became the Creativity Movement.) Other crimes associated with the WCOTC include the following:

June 1986: COTC security chief Carl Messick fires nineteen shots at the car of a Georgia couple who inadvertently entered the cult's property. He later receives a seven-year prison term.

May 1989: Milwaukee police jail two COTC members for brawling with anti–Nazi activists.

August 1990: Ohio authorities arrest COTC state leader Matthew Hayhow for robbing two banks. He receives a twenty-five year prison term.

17 May 1991: COTC "minister" George Loeb shoots and kills Harold Mansfield, a black U.S. Navy veteran, after a traffic altercation in Jacksonville, Florida. Mansfield receives a life prison term on 12 August 1992, while his case inspires the SPLC's subsequent lawsuit against the COTC, precipitating Klassen's suicide.

17 May 1993: Canadian COTC member Richard Manley pleads guilty to illegally possessing weapons (including an Uzi submachine gun) and 1,000 rounds of ammunition in Toronto.

July 1993: Washington state COTC leader Jeremiah Knesal and two other members bomb an NAACP meeting hall in Tacoma and a gay bar in Seattle. Pleading guilty at trial, Knesal admits conspiring in other attacks against blacks and Jews. He receives a prison term of six years and six months. Accomplice Wayne Wooten, Jr., receives a five year prison term on 28 September 1994. Codefendant Mark Kowalski receives a twelve-year sentence for the NAACP bombing.

July 1993: Los Angeles police arrest COTC member Geremy von Rineman and his girlfriend, Jill Scarborough, for plotting to bomb the city's largest black church. The defendants receive probation on weapons charges in 1994.

1994: Illinois COTC member John McLaughlin receives two and a half years probation on charges of stockpiling illegal weapons for the "ultimate race war."

4 January 1994: Baltimore COTC leader Charles Altvater pleads guilty in the 1992 bombing of a police officer's home. He receives a twenty-five-year prison term.

August 1997: Police in Sunrise, Florida, jail WCOTC members Jules Fettu, Donald Hansard and Raymond Leone for assaulting two black men at a concert. Hansard and Leone plead guilty to aggravated assault, resulting in eight-year prison terms, while jurors convict Fettu at trial in 1999. (He receives a two-year sentence.) In June 1998, authorities charge WCOTC "White Beret" commander Guy Lombardi with threatening witnesses in the same case. He subsequently pleads guilty and receives four years' probation. Matt Hale subsequently expels Lombardi for "insubordination," while calling his arrest "a badge of honor."

November 1997: California police jail WCOTC member William Johnson on charges of attempted murder, for stabbing a critic of the church.

March 1998: In a scenario drawn from *The Turner Diaries,* WCOTC members Donald Hansard, Jr., Angela King, Ray Leone and Dawn Witherspoon rob a video store in Hollywood, Florida, to help finance their cult. All four plead guilty to the robbery and beating of the shop's Jewish proprietor. Leone receives a six-year prison term; Hansard receives four and a half years; King receives eighteen months; and Witherspoon receives thirteen months.

4 July 1999: WCOTC member and "Creator of the Year" Benjamin Smith launches a shooting spree in Illinois and Indiana, killing two victims and wounding nine others before he commits suicide. His rampage is triggered by the Illinois bar's refusal to admit Matt Hale as an attorney.

4 October 1999: WCOTC member Jody Mathis pleads guilty to selling a stolen shotgun in Fort Lauderdale, Florida. His case marks the seventh local conviction of WCOTC members on various criminal charges in two years.

August 2000: Police in Saratoga County, New York, stop Connecticut ex-convict Bruce Silvernail for a routine traffic violation, then discover a cache of illegal weapons and WCOTC literature in his car. On 13 March 2001, Silvernail pleads guilty to illegal firearms possession.

3 July 2001: WCOTC member Joshua Gilmore pleads guilty on multiple charges, including attempted murder, from his 1997 attack on two members of an anti–Nazi skinhead group. He receives a life prison term.

11 December 2001: Police in New Haven, Connecticut, raid the home of WCOTC member Charles Cornelius, seizing an arsenal of weapons and illegal explosives purchased with false identification. In 2004, Cornelius pleads guilty to federal charges of identity theft and unlawful interstate transportation of firearms, as well as state weapons and explosives charges.

29 April 2002: WCOTC member Trevor Thompson pleads guilty to attempted murder in Indianapolis, Indiana, stemming from his shooting of a teenage black girl in 2001. He receives a thirty-year prison term.

8 July 2002: Massachusetts authorities revoke the parole of state WCOTC leader Tony Menear, previously convicted and imprisoned for armed robbery. His violation involves consorting with ex-convicts.

August 2002: Jurors in Melbourne, Victoria, convict Australian WCOTC leader Patrick O'Sullivan of assaulting and stabbing another church member in 1999.

13 March 2003: Massachusetts WCOTC member Erica Chase receives a prison term of four years and nine months for her part in a 2001 conspiracy to bomb black and Jewish landmarks. Boyfriend Leo Felton, a member of the White Order of Thule, received a twenty-two-year prison term in December 2002.

1 March 2004: Jurors in Las Vegas, Nevada, convict WCOTC member Anthony Prentice of killing and mutilating his driving instructor. Prentice receives a prison term of life without parole.

3 August 2004: Hardy Lloyd, former leader of the WCOTC in Pittsburgh, Pennsylvania, fatally shoots girlfriend Lori Fann. Police arrest Lloyd three days later. No trial had been scheduled at press time for this work.

Confusion surrounds the fate of the renamed Creativity Movement since Hale's imprisonment in April 2004. At press time for this volume, ADL observers reported that "Hasta Primus" Thomas Kroenke led a remnant loyal to Hale, with headquarters in Wyoming. The SPLC, meanwhile, placed Creativity headquarters in Springfield, Missouri, with fifteen satellite chapters in thirteen other states. At the same time, a website for the Church of Creativity advertised "No Membership Lists ... No Paperwork ... No Bureaucracy ... No Leaders ... No Rules ... Nothing between you and the Faith. The Church of Creativity is the Church for the Lone Wolf Creator!"

Yellow Jackets—A Klan-like group with apparent overlapping membership, the Yellow Jackets terrorized blacks and Republicans in Humphreys County, Tennessee, in spring 1868.

7 MAPPING THE EMPIRE

While the Invisible Empire theoretically encompasses all of Planet Earth—or, at least, all nations inhabited by whites eligible for Klan membership—the KKK in fact has never enjoyed such widespread distribution. During Reconstruction, the order planted dens in all eleven states of the former Confederacy, plus the "loyal" former slave states of Kentucky and Missouri (and a supposed chapter of dubious legitimacy in New York). The 1920s KKK had klaverns in all of the forty-eight states, with outposts in at least two foreign countries. More recently, splinter factions and Klan-allied groups have again spread nationwide, while enjoying broader international distribution. This chapter reviews the KKK's geographic expansion in three sections: (A) the United States, (B) foreign countries, and (C) subdivisions of America proposed by modern klansmen in their fantasies of ultimate conquest. Entries within each section are arranged alphabetically.

The United States

Alabama—Alabama witnessed the first Reconstruction Klan activity outside Tennessee, with a den founded in Tuscaloosa County during autumn 1867. Newspaper editor Ryland Randolph was the Cotton State's most visible and volatile klansman, and Ku Klux violence was a constant fact of life around Tuscaloosa through early 1871. Klansmen issued their first public warnings in Blount County during November 1867, and by spring 1868 dens were organized throughout northern Alabama's Tennessee Valley, where Klan goals and membership overlapped those of the KWC. Green County knights burned their county courthouse on 20 March 1868, to destroy criminal records, while Hale County authorities foiled a similar effort the following day. Alabama's northern and eastern counties witnessed the worst mayhem during 1868's elections, with Tuscaloosa County ranked among the most dangerous venues for blacks and Republicans. There, Ryland Randolph's campaign against "radicals" and "carpetbaggers" at the state university compelled faculty resignations and briefly closed the school. During 1869–70, Klan violence in Alabama was more virulent and widespread than in any other state except chaotic North Carolina. No precise casualty figures are available, but congressional investigators estimated that Alabama's klansmen murdered at least 109 victims between 1868 and 1871, with many times that number whipped, raped, mutilated, or otherwise abused. Two major areas of KKK activity were the western counties (Fayette, Greene, Sumter and

Tuscaloosa) and a southern tier including the mountain counties around Birmingham. Authorities noted a decline in nightriding after Democrats swept the November 1870 elections, but scattered violence continued well into 1871. In that year, Democrats and Republicans joined forces in denouncing klansmen as "the lowest-down, meanest characters that we have got among us." Public disapproval brought a marked decrease in violence by summer 1871, though raiding continued in Choctaw County through early 1872.

With the Klan's revival in 1915, fond memories were kindled in the hearts of Alabama racists. Imperial Wizard William Simmons sent a kleagle to till the fertile soil in 1916, and Alabama soon harbored the only klaverns chartered outside Georgia prior to 1920. Klansmen were active throughout World War I, watching for saboteurs and spies, but the realm's real growth occurred from 1920 onward. By 1926, the Invisible Empire boasted some 50,000 members in Alabama, and their strength was felt at the ballot box. Hundreds of klansmen won public office in that year's elections, including Bibb Graves (governor), Charles McCall (attorney general), and Hugo Black (U.S. Senator). Graves—the exalted cyclops of Montgomery Klavern No. 3—seated Wizard Hiram Evans and Grand Dragon James Esdale on the stage at his inauguration, but McCall (a member of the same klavern) raised a storm of public protest when he named Esdale as an assistant attorney general, quickly rescinding the appointment. For all of Montgomery's prominence in state politics, the KKK was most firmly entrenched among blue-collar workers in Birmingham, where the order controlled some 18,000 of the city's 32,000 votes. Senator Oscar Underwood opposed the order at his peril, thereby dooming his hopes for a presidential nod in 1924, later withdrawing rather than face Ku Klux opposition in his 1927 reelection race. Senator Thomas Heflin, meanwhile, became a staple on Klan lecture circuits, inciting klansmen—and some Klan opponents—to violent outbursts with rants against Catholics. Inevitably, violence followed the Klan's march to power, with at least twenty victims flogged in Birmingham during 1921–22 and over 100 beatings recorded statewide during 1924–26. Bloodshed and blatant political cronyism produced a backlash by 1928, and statewide membership shriveled to an estimated 6,000 in 1930.

Alabama klansmen continued to ride through the 1930s and 1940s, primarily targeting blacks and CIO unionists, but their future lay in diversity. William Morris chartered his Federated KKK in September 1946, its members linked to a rash of Birmingham floggings in 1949–50. (Dynamite was also popular around "Bombingham," where some forty-nine blasts were linked to the KKK between 1947 and summer 1963.) Governor James Folsom opposed the post-war Klan, urging citizens to defend their homes "by any means necessary," but Alabama governors were barred by law from succeeding themselves, and the KKK survived Folsom's tenure, chafing at restrictions imposed by an anti-mask law. Splinter groups proliferated after the U.S. Supreme Court's "Black Monday" decision of May 1954, with the U.S. Klans, Dixie Klans, Robert Shelton's Alabama Knights, Asa Carter's Original KKK of the Confederacy, and Mobile's Gulf Coast KKK campaigning against school integration. Tuscaloosa witnessed rioting in 1956, after black coed Autherine Lucy enrolled at the state university, and mayhem increased after 1958, with the election of Governor John Patterson. A friend of the Klan, indebted to Robert Shelton for his election, Patterson favored the Alabama Knights with financial rewards and political patronage, publicly siding with terrorists when they rioted against CORE's integrated "freedom rides" in 1961. The Klan counted on friends in law enforcement—including Selma's Sheriff Jim Clark and Birmingham's "Bull" Connor—to ignore nightriding and to cover the KKK's tracks after bombings and murders. Shelton's new United Klans, based at Tuscaloosa, worked hard for gubernatorial candidate George Wallace in 1962 and reaped traditional rewards from his victory (including appointment of "good friend" Al Lingo to lead the state police). By 1964, the UKA had 1,200 members in Alabama, dispersed among forty klaverns, and they bore responsibility for at least three murders during 1965. Congressional investigations and public reaction to unbridled violence reduced the Klan's strength by 1970, but the order clung to life, undaunted, as the new decade began.

The 1970s and 1980s produced mixed blessings for Alabama klansmen. George Wallace remained faithful through his 1968 and 1972 presidential campaigns, but his near-assassination in the latter race wrought changes, prompting a Texas Klan leader to complain that Wallace "isn't as white as he used to be." Still, the KKK had other friends in office, including U.S. Senator James Allen (who sent a congratulatory telegram to the UKA's 1970 klonvokation) and Lieutenant Governor Jere Beasley (who graced the same gathering as a keynote speaker). The reverse side of that coin was Attorney General Bill Baxley, a die-hard opponent of the Klan who secured the first murder conviction in Birmingham's most notorious bombing and also sent longtime terrorist J.B. Stoner to prison for blasting another church in 1958. (Those prosecutions doomed Baxley's gubernatorial bid.) Sporadic violence continued, as always, with Klan riots at Decatur in 1979, shootings in Lauderdale and Talladega Counties the same year, and the 1980 Michael Donald lynching in Mobile. Police were still sluggish to move against klansmen in most cases, but new opposition arose from Montgomery's Southern Poverty Law Center and its dedicated Klanwatch project. SPCLC attorneys filed lawsuits against Klans and klansmen in the most notorious cases, sending Decatur's rioters to school for racial-sensitivity classes and bankrupting Robert Shelton's UKA with a $7 million judgment in the Donald lynching (while one of the killers was finally sent to death row).

Despite such pressures, the KKK and its affiliated groups endure in Alabama. At press time for this work, eight Klans had active klaverns in the Cotton State. They include the Aryan Nations Knights (headquartered at Thorsley), the Brotherhood of Klans, the Imperial Klans of America, the Ku Klux Klan, the National Knights, the Orion Knights, the Southern White Knights, and the World Knights (headquartered at Sharpsburg). Groups affiliated with the KKK or which share its philosophies, sometimes welcoming klansmen as members include the Aryan Nations (headquartered at Lincoln), the Aryan Raiders, the CCC (with five chapters), the League of the South (headquartered at Killen, with three additional chapters statewide), Birmingham's Lebensraum Assembly Church, and the National Alliance.

Alaska—Luther Powell, the Klan's pioneer kleagle in Oregon during the 1920s, abandoned the Beaver State sometime in 1927–28 to try his luck recruiting in the Territory of Alaska. Author David Chalmers reports that Powell succeeded in establishing one active klavern, but no details of its progress now survive. Racism undoubtedly exists in the Land of the Midnight Sun, as witnessed by a chapter of the neo–Nazi National Alliance active in Anchorage since 2001, but the KKK never regained its foothold in the frozen north.

Arizona—The modern Klan reached Arizona in 1922, but its recruiting drive stalled early on, with some 4,000 to 5,000 knights enlisted statewide. The Grand Canyon State's most visible klansman was Tom Akers, exalted cyclops of Kamelback Klan No. 6 in Phoenix and former editor of the local *Gazette*. Violence sputtered during 1922–23, with three floggings reported and a school principal scarred with acid. Akers fled to Atlanta after authorities indicted him for beating a black janitor, and Governor George Hunt announced discovery of a list naming 900 Arizona klansmen. The implied threat of publication sparked mass resignations, but the shrunken KKK endured. Tom Akers returned from his new job with the Klan's intelligence branch to witness Grand Dragon McCord Harrison's 1923 inauguration. Harrison soon divided the state into two districts, with dual headquarters at Tempe and Winslow, but the move signaled no rise in membership. The Arizona Klan made its one and only political foray in 1924, surfacing as a key issue in the gubernatorial primary, but anti–Klan incumbent Hunt easily retained his office, while the KKK's candidate ran a distant third. Few members remained to the order by 1926, and it faded from the Arizona scene entirely before the advent of the Great Depression.

Organized racism was slow to revive in Arizona after World War II. Phoenix Jews received threats from the Aryan Brotherhood in 1980, and members of the Arizona Patriots signed William Potter Gale's "Declaration of Alteration and Reform" four years later. On 15 December 1986, FBI agents arrested eight Arizona Patriots, seizing large quantities of weapons and explosives, ultimately charging four defendants with conspiracy to rob an armored car and bomb diverse targets including a Phoenix synagogue, an IRS office in Utah, three dams, an ADL office and the Simon Wiesenthal Center. On 9 October 1995, still-unidentified "Sons of Gestapo" claimed credit for sabotaging an Amtrak railroad line outside Hyder, killing one person and injuring dozens more. In April 2005, the vigilante "Minuteman Project" brought 150 armed racists (including self-identified members of the neo–Nazi National Alliance) to Cochise County, posing as "undocumented border patrol agents" to harass suspected illegal immigrants. At press time for this volume, the Imperial Klans of America claimed a small klavern in Mesa. Other active Arizona groups of a similar mind included the Aryan Nations, National Alliance and Volksfront.

Arkansas—The Reconstruction Klan invaded Arkansas in March 1868, competing for members with the KWC around Little Rock and in the state's southern counties. By May 1868, nightriding in Crittenden County produced calls for federal troops, and that summer the state legislature granted Governor Powell Clayton's plea for twelve militia companies (two of which were black) to be ready for action by August. Widespread violence continued through September and October, concentrated in the southern and northeastern counties; by contrast, raids were rare in the northern part of the Razorback State, where blacks were less plentiful and white Unionists held a solid majority. As in other states, no precise body count is available for Reconstruction, but Arkansas klansmen scored their most famous murder with the October 1868 assassination of Rep. James Hinds in Little Rock. That same month, klansmen hijacked the steamboat *Hesper* on the Mississippi River, routing her crew and destroying a shipment of weapons earmarked for the state militia. In November 1868, Governor Clayton declared martial law over ten of the state's most lawless counties, extending military rule to Conway County a month later. That move ignited a storm of controversy, but brutal violence gradually swayed public opinion against the Klan (as in Lewisburg, where arsonists who torched a Republican's store destroyed most of the town). Powell's militia campaign proved remarkably effective, driving many klansmen from the state, and martial law was lifted in March 1869, while new legislation passed on 13 March specifically banned the KKK and KWC. Although few prosecutions resulted, racist violence declined, leaving Crittenden County (eight percent black) as the last scene of sporadic nightriding.

The 1920s Klan flourished in Arkansas, with an estimated 40,000 members enlisted by late 1922. That year's elections saw klansmen win most of Little Rock's public offices, and violence swiftly followed their ascension to power, with vigilante raids around Hot Springs and a pitched battle at Smackover routing some 2,000 "undesirables" from the region's oilfields. Soon, however, internal conflict doomed the Arkansas Klan. Thousands of klansmen resigned to protest the imperious rule of Grand Dragon James Comer, while members of the ladies' auxiliary did likewise to avoid his haughty wife, Robbie Gill. State elections in 1924 proved disastrous for Klan-endorsed candidates, and statewide membership declined to 10,000 in 1925, with desertions ongoing until the final order of national disbandment in April 1944.

Largely quiescent during World War II and its immediate aftermath, the Arkansas Klan revived in 1954, with the U.S. Supreme Court's "Black Monday" decision. The Georgia-based U.S. Klans won converts in the state, competing with a new Association of Arkansas Klans, and knights from both factions saw action around Little Rock during the school integration crisis of 1957–59. Governor Orval Faubus had a soft spot in his heart for racist bombers, standing by with pardons if they faced jail time, but he drew the line at running for president on the neo–Nazi NSRP ticket. In the 1960s, Robert Shelton's UKA boasted ten klaverns in six Arkansas counties, with an estimated 150 members overall, while the tiny AAK clung to life with twenty-five klansmen in Pine Bluff and Texarkana. Two alleged knights faced trial for killing a black newspaper delivery boy in 1965, but most of the decade's civil rights battles were waged farther south.

Those who remained loyal to the KKK through the 1970s sought their leaders out of state, generally following Louisiana klansmen David Duke or Bill Wilkinson, but homegrown Christian Identity minister Thomas Robb assumed the mantle of Duke's KKKK in the early 1980s, operating (as he does today) from the Harrison headquarters of his Kingdom Identity Ministries. James Ellison's CSA provided arms and comfort to fugitive right-wing guerrillas in the mid–1980s, until Ellison himself was imprisoned and turned state's evidence against his comrades at their 1988 sedition trial in Fort Smith. Active Klans in Arkansas, at press time for this book, included Ameriklan (headquartered at Heber Springs), the Bayou Knights, the Imperial Klans of America, the Ku Klux Klan (headquartered at Compton), the Mississippi White Knights, the Orion Knights, and the Southern White Knights. Klan-allied or sympathetic groups active within the state include Aryan Nations, the CCC, Bergman's Church of Jesus Christ, League of the South (three chapters), National Alliance, National Socialist Movement, and Billy Roper's White Revolution (headquartered at Russellville).

California—The Golden State was a fertile recruiting ground for kleagles in the 1920s, with dual headquarters located in Los Angeles and San Francisco. California klansmen viewed infiltration of law enforcement as a top priority, and a deputy sheriff doubled as Sacramento's kleagle. At least a score of San Francisco policemen joined the KKK, and recruiters in Los Angeles had similar success. Bakersfield's police chief was a klansman, as were most of the officers in nearby Taft, where uniformed patrolmen attended public floggings at the local ballpark. Thus protected, nightriders felt free to enforce their brand of morality on Californians at large. In June 1922, the Elduayan kidnapping case left one Klan policeman dead and prompted indictments of thirty-seven other knights, but a friendly judge directed verdicts of acquittal for all concerned. Still, exposure of Klan violence and financial chicanery weakened the order, and membership was dropping by 1924, when state legislators passed a strict anti-mask law.

Despite that inconvenience, klansmen hung on through the Great Depression, making California one of thirteen states in which the order retained significant strength through the 1930s. Official disbandment in April 1944 left California klansmen at loose ends, but they rallied in summer 1945 to harass Jewish merchants with cross-burnings in Los Angeles. A year later, when the AGK announced its revival from Atlanta, stirrings in southern California brought Attorney General Robert

California klansmen rally in 1940 (Library of Congress).

joint rally of the KKK, ANP and Minutemen in 1965 drew only 250 persons—but an energetic right-wing bombing campaign rocked Los Angeles in the mid–1970s, ignored for the most part by LAPD and the FBI. David Duke's KKKK made California inroads in the latter 1970s, recruiting Marines at Camp Pendleton and achieving somewhat greater success in San Diego, where Grand Dragon Tom Metzger ran repeatedly (and unsuccessfully) for public office. Metzger soon abandoned Duke to form the California Knights, then left the Klan entirely to lead his own neo–Nazi WAR, while the KKK's shrunken realm foundered in disarray.

As this volume went to press, California harbored five active klaverns, two representing the Brotherhood of Klans, and three for the Imperial Klans of America. Allied or like-minded organizations include the Aryan Nations and Aryan Nations Youth Action Corps, the CCC (in Bakersfield, a former Citizens' Council outpost), League of the South (badly misplaced in San Jose), National Alliance, National Socialist Movement, Northern California Aryan Volk, Fresno's SS Enterprises, Volksfront (four chapters), and Tom Metzger's WAR (headquartered at Fallbrook).

Colorado—Colorado witnessed brutal riots against Chinese immigrants in the 1880s, and enough of that racism survived to support a successful Klan realm in the 1920s. Denver hosted the state's first klavern in 1921, and four years later, one in every seven residents had joined the KKK or its ladies' auxiliary. A series of threatening letters

Kenney into court with a motion to revoke the Klan's charter. Ex-kleagle Ray Snyder, testifying in October 1946, declared that klansmen had simply gone underground in the guise of "card clubs," with one of the state's largest klaverns still thriving in Compton. Around the same time, klansman Wesley Swift founded his racist Church of Jesus Christ Christian, operating from Lancaster until Swift's death in 1970.

Swift's church was only one of several racist paramilitary groups soliciting converts in post–World War II California. The Georgia-based NSRP shared members and meetings with Robert DePugh's Minutemen, William Gale's California Rangers and Christian Defense League, George Rockwell's ANP and the Sons of Liberty. Membership was marginal—a

prompted Denver's grand jury to investigate, exposing the Denver Doers Club as a Ku Klux front. By that time, klansman Ben Stapleton occupied the mayor's office, using his appointive powers to fill city offices with brother knights. Grand Dragon John Locke had a private box at the state Republican convention in 1924, and klansmen swept the year's elections statewide. Victorious klansmen included Governor Clarence Morley, Secretary of State Carl Milliken, U.S. Senator Rice Means, and a majority of the state legislature's lower house. A month later, police jailed Locke for kidnapping a local youth and using threats of castration to make the boy marry his pregnant girlfriend. Further controversy followed Locke's appointment as an officer in the Colorado National Guard, and IRS agents closely scrutinized his tax returns. Investigation revealed that Locke had hand-picked Denver's police chief, with his choice rubber-stamped by Mayor Stapleton. Imperial Wizard Hiram Evans sought to cut his losses by replacing Locke, but the defiant dragon took his case to the grass roots, exhorting an audience of 30,000 klansmen on 1 July 1925. Many of them followed Locke into his new, short-lived Minutemen organization, leaving the Colorado Klan with only one-third of its former membership in 1926, unable to carry a single election campaign that November.

Moribund for the next half-century, Colorado's Klan showed signs of life in the late 1970s. Fred Wilkins organized a small Denver klavern, then lost his job for threatening Jewish talk-show host Alan Berg in 1979. Five years later, Denver klansman David Lane drove the getaway car when members of The Order killed Berg at his home. In 1992, klansmen joined neo–Nazis and Christian Identity cultists for a "Rocky Mountain Rendezvous" at Estes Park, laying the foundation for the 1990s "patriot militia" movement. Still, the Centennial State saw little action as that movement rose and fell, its violence in the main enacted farther south and west. At press time for this book, the National Knights of the KKK claimed a lonely klavern in Olathe, while the League of the South had a misplaced chapter in Louisville and National Alliance was represented by small groups in Denver and Colorado Springs.

Connecticut—Led by Grand Dragon Harry Lutterman from Darien, the Connecticut Klan boasted 18,000 members in 1925, when internal dissension began to thin its ranks. Klansmen in the Nutmeg State were already suspicious of imperial headquarters, which ceased providing financial reports to the various realms in 1924, and their protests fell on deaf ears in Atlanta. In January 1926, members of the state's premier New Haven klavern voted to disband, while Exalted Cyclops Arthur Mann publicly condemned the order's corruption. Mass resignations followed, and the Wall Street crash of 1929 found Connecticut's realm already defunct.

Bill Wilkinson sparked a Klan renaissance of sorts in September 1980, when his IEKKKK rallied at Scotland, in Windham County. Three days of cross-burnings and scuffles with hecklers left six persons injured and eight more in jail, while winning the Klan an estimated 500 members and supporters. One of those recruited was James Farrands, a Catholic who found acceptance in a Klan preoccupied with hating blacks and Jews. When Wilkinson returned for more rallies in August 1982, policemen outnumbered the assembled klansmen, and their wizard retreated behind charges of "police harassment." Farrands rose to command the IEKKKK in 1986, making history as the order's first Catholic wizard, and while he subsequently moved his headquarters to Klan-friendly North Carolina, violence and lawsuits forced him home again in the late 1990s, disbanding his unit in 1999. No active Klan remained in Connecticut as this work went to press, although a neo–Nazi skinhead gang, the Connecticut White Wolves, maintained a presence in Stratford.

Delaware—By late 1922, the KKK claimed substantial membership around Laurel, in southwestern Delaware, but opposition swiftly followed. In summer 1923, protesters stormed a Klan initiation ceremony near New Castle, sparking a riot that saw three men shot and fifty others injured. Klansmen remained active through the late 1920s, their strength concentrated in rural Kent and Sussex Counties, but the hooded order disappeared with the advent of the Great Depression. UKA Grand Dragon Ralph Pryor tried to rekindle the flame in 1965, but his recruiting efforts floundered amid charges of fraternization with American Nazis. At its peak, the Delaware UKA claimed barely 100 members, scattered among five klaverns, and it soon disappeared entirely. No active Klan remained in the Diamond State at press time for this volume, though a chapter of the National Socialist Movement/Skinhead Division clung to tenuous life in Newark.

District of Columbia—Although a southern city at heart, Washington, D.C., was untouched by the Reconstruction-era KKK, reviled by klansmen as the seat of power ruled by "radical" Republicans. When the modern Klan plunged into politics, Wizard Hiram Evans moved his administrative office from Atlanta to Massachusetts Avenue in the nation's capital, in 1923. Kleagles were active in the District of Columbia, but an estimate of 15,133 local members published by the *Washington Post* in 1930 seems both inflated and impossibly precise. Nonetheless, Washington hosted the KKK's single greatest show of strength on 8 August 1925, as 40,000 klansmen and -women marched down Pennsylvania Avenue in full regalia. When the march was repeated in 1926, less than half as many knights participated, their shrunken ranks a testimony to the order's dwindling membership. From the 1930s to the present day, Washington remains a hostile city to the KKK, reviled by southern knights as "Hersheytown" ("ninety percent chocolate and ten percent nuts"). From FDR's "Jew Deal" to the Warren Court, JFK's New Frontier and LBJ's Great Society to the fable of "ZOG," klansmen mostly view Washington as an enemy capital, targeted by some (including The Order and Glenn Miller's White Patriot Party) with formal declarations of war. At press time for this work, Washington harbored one small klavern of the Imperial Klans of America.

Florida—The Reconstruction Klan breached Florida's borders on 30 November 1867, posing as the Constitutional League of Florida, with headquarters at Welatka. The League soon disappeared, absorbed by the KKK that surfaced in its own right (or as the Young Men's Democratic Club) during April and May 1868. Little violence occurred in those early days, but nightriding flourished in autumn, with the approach of 1868's presidential election. State legislators authorized a militia to combat white terrorism in August 1868, but the law proved difficult to implement. Governor Harrison Reed purchased muskets and ammunition from New York, but klansmen were ready when the shipment arrived on 5 November, stealing the cargo from its moving train between Jacksonville and Tallahassee. Raiders terrorized ten Florida counties during 1869–70, with 179 murders logged in Jackson County alone. Statewide, authorities listed 235 Klan slayings in 1868–71, and their tabulation was certainly conservative. Congressional investigation and federal intervention combined to suppress the worst violence by December 1871, when Jackson County's black majority elected two Republican officers without criminal opposition, but Florida's subsequent

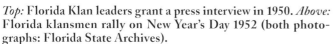

Top: Florida Klan leaders grant a press interview in 1950. *Above:* Florida klansmen rally on New Year's Day 1952 (both photographs: Florida State Archives).

Top: Klansmen parade through Tallahassee, Florida, in 1977. *Above:* Members of the Southern Knights prepare for a 1949 motorcade through Tallahassee, Florida (both photographs: Florida State Archives).

"redemption" for white "home rule" followed the same pattern seen in other states. Friends of black state legislator Jonathan Gibbs blamed his mysterious 1873 death on klansmen, and terrorists murdered Republican official Elisha Johnson at Lake City, on 21 July 1875.

Anti-Catholic candidate Sidney Catts rallied Klan-type sentiment to win Florida's gubernatorial race in 1915, while the first chartered klavern appeared in Jacksonville five years later. Sunshine State klansmen entered politics in 1922, scoring a clean sweep in Volusia County's June primary elections. As elsewhere, violence flourished with the KKK's expansion. Klansmen lynched saloonkeeper Manolo Cabeza at Key West in December 1921, joined the mob that burned Rosewood's black community in January 1923, hanged two black murder suspects in Miami six months later, and castrated Father John Conoley in February 1924. (Prime suspects in that case included Gainesville's mayor and chief of police.) Flogging squads kept busy throughout the state, with sixty-three whippings reported from Putnam County alone in 1926. Unlike the residents of other

states, however, Floridians were remarkably blasé toward racist violence. Their state claimed America's highest per-capita lynching rate, and Florida ranked as the Klan's strongest realm in the 1930s, with an estimated 30,000 members. Union organizers suffered the worst Depression-era violence, exemplified by Joseph Shoemaker's unpunished 1935 torture-slaying by klansmen acting with police support. Five months after the national order disbanded, in April 1944, a new KKK of Florida was chartered to preserve the Klan's brutal tradition.

Post-war Governor Fuller Warren (himself a former klansman) proved ambiguous in dealing with the KKK: he signed an anti-mask law while branding current knights "hooded hoodlums and sheeted jerks," then appointed a Georgia klansman to investigate the order's crimes. Encouraged by the state's repeated failure to arrest known terrorists, inspired by the violent rhetoric of Grand Dragon Bill Hendrix, Klansmen raided Groveland's black community in July 1949 and launched a two-year bombing campaign that flattened targets from Miami to Orlando. On 25 December 1951, bombers killed NAACP leader Harry Moore

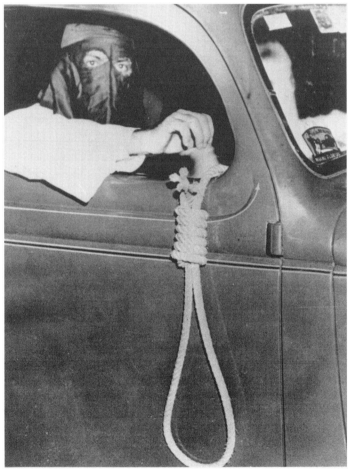

Top: **St. Augustine klansmen burned this car in a black family's garage in 1964 (Florida State Archives).** *Above:* **Florida klansmen warn blacks against voting in 1939 (Library of Congress).**

and his wife in their home, at Mims, in a crime that remains officially unsolved today. Federal investigators subsequently indicted a handful of klansmen on minor charges, but all the counts were dismissed prior to trial.

The U.S. Supreme Court's *Brown* decision of May 1954

Top: **Klansmen rally near Gibsonton, Florida, in the 1970s (Florida State Archives).** *Above:* **Rioting klansmen burned the home of a black rape suspect's father near Groveland, Florida, in July 1949 (Library of Congress).**

gave the Florida Klans a new lease on life, with at least five splinter groups active through the late 1950s. Jacksonville's knights made headlines in August 1960, rioting against black demonstrators on "Axe-handle Saturday," and the United Florida KKK was born ten months later, merging two rival groups into a unit that would dominate Florida's realm for the next three years. In autumn 1963, itinerant racists Connie Lynch and Jesse Stoner began recruiting members for "a rough and tough Klan, looking for action" around Jacksonville and St. Augustine. By spring 1964, local knights had been reshuffled into a regional unit dubbed "Providence No. 41," which claimed 1,000 members by the time race riots rocked St. Augustine in June. Recruiters for the UKA followed the action, organizing twenty-seven klaverns in the Sunshine State by autumn 1964, but bitter schisms were a fact of life in the Florida Klan. Quarrels over money and policy split the UKA and UFKKK in 1965, spawning Jacksonville's Militant Knights and Melbourne's United Knights of the KKK, but the realm had already passed its prime, with membership sharply declining.

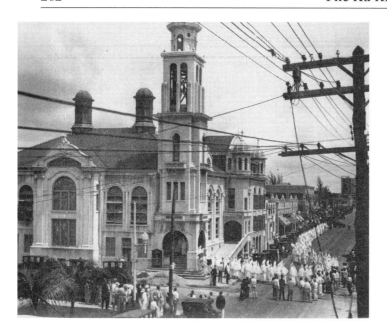

WE ARE WHITE, TRIED AND TRUE, 100% AMERICAN. WHAT ABOUT YOU? WE ARE WILLING TO FIGHT, SUFFER AND DIE THAT AMERICA SHALL STAND. THAT'S WHY WE ARE CALLED KNIGHTS

KKK

TO-DAY'S DEFENSE IS TO-MORROW'S SECURITY. BUY DEFENSE BONDS NOW!!

APPLICATION FOR CITIZENSHIP OR RE-INSTATEMENT

NAME

BUSINESS ADDRESS   PHONE

RESIDENCE ADDRESS   PHONE

MY MEMBERSHIP WAS IN

KLAN NO.   REALM OF
REFERENCES:

NAME   ADDRESS

UNITED WE STAND — SEVEN MILLION STRONG

PLEASE ENCLOSE IN ENVELOPE AND MAIL TO JOHN B. GORDON, KLAN NO. 24
P. O. BOX 3272, MIAMI, FLORIDA

Top: Florida klansmen dedicate a White Temple in the 1920s. *Above:* A membership application for Miami's Klan, circa 1940 (both photographs: Florida State Archives).

Still, as in prior decades, the Florida Klan refused to die. David Duke won recruits for his KKKK in the 1970s, while scattered UKA klaverns survived until an Alabama lawsuit broke imperial headquarters in 1987. At press time for this volume, Florida harbored at least six active Klans: the Aryan Nations

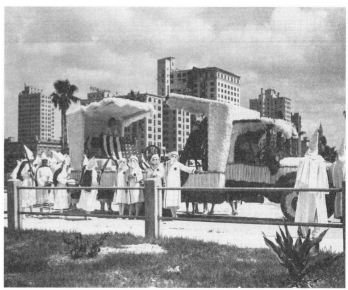

Florida klansmen entered this float in a 1927 Independence Day parade (Florida State Archives).

Knights, Imperial Klans of America, the KKKK, Mississippi White Knights, National Knights, and Southern White Knights. Ocala's Klan Store enjoyed steady trade in the new millennium, while former Alabama klansman Stephen Black operates his Stormfront website from West Palm Beach. Other Florida groups with strong affiliations to the KKK or sympathy with its objectives include the Aryan Nations, two chapters of the CCC, the Creativity Movement, David Duke's EURO, the League of the South (thirteen chapters), the German American Nationalist PAC, the National Alliance, three chapters of the NAAWP, Lake Worth's Nordwave, White Revolution, and Women for Aryan Unity.

Georgia—Georgia's first Ku Klux den was established at Columbus in March 1868, and the order spread swiftly thereafter, with the approach of November's presidential election. No part of the state was immune to Klan violence that year, though a majority of bloodshed occurred in eastern counties, adjacent to Alabama and Florida. Between August and October 1868, leaders of the Freedmen's Bureau recorded thirty-one racist murders, forty-three nonfatal shootings, five stabbings, fifty-five beatings, and eight whippings. Klansmen committed countless other crimes through 1871, and a published estimate of seventy-four Ku Klux murders during 1868–71 doubtless falls short of the actual mark. Whether they rode by night or rallied in daylight—as for the Camilla riot of September 1868—klansmen were largely successful in their primary goal of intimidating Republican voters. Throughout the Peach State, GOP victory margins fell sharply in 1868, and eleven counties recorded no Republican votes in November. Warren County was the Reconstruction-era Klan's primary stronghold, where Sheriff John Norris dodged assassins and waged a two-year war against the KKK until its members framed him on a bribery charge and removed him from office in 1870. Democrats captured the state legislature that December, but sporadic nightriding continued into 1871, with klansmen in Chattoga and Floyd Counties enlisting

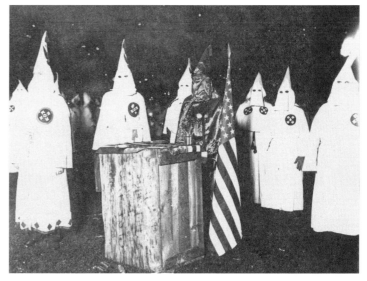

Top: Weapons and other items seized from UKA members in Griffin, Georgia in April 1964 (HUAC). *Above:* Klansmen demonstrate in Georgia during the 1940s (Library of Congress).

Top: Georgia klansmen stage a rally in 1920 (Library of Congress). *Above:* Klansmen rally at Stone Mountain, Georgia, ca. 1921. (Southern Poverty Law Center).

aid from dens in neighboring Alabama. Grand Dragon John B. Gordon subsequently served as a U.S. Senator (1873–80, 1891–97) and as governor (1886–90). In 1876, he played a key role in negotiations that placed Rutherford Hayes in the White House and effectively "redeemed" the South for white-supremacist "home rule."

For all its activity during 1868–71, the Georgia Klan never played the preeminent role in Reconstruction that it did in the twentieth century. Stone Mountain witnessed the first American cross-burning in October 1915, and Georgia officials soon chartered the reborn KKK under Imperial Wizard William Simmons. Atlanta remained the citadel of Klan power for most of the next half-century, while Georgia led the nation in lynchings. Klansmen quickly adopted a vigilante role in 1920s Georgia, though the realms of Alabama, Louisiana, Oklahoma and

Texas ultimately proved more violent. Sweeping the polls in 1922's elections, Georgia knights gloried in the election of klansman Clifford Walker as governor. Two more klansmen, Eugene Talmadge and E.D. Rivers, would occupy the governor's mansion before World War II, while the KKK also maintained a close relationship with Richard Russell, chief justice of the state supreme court (1923–38).

Disbandment of the national Klan in April 1944 was a fleeting inconvenience, as Dr. Samuel Green held the Georgia legions together, formally announcing the birth of his own AGK in May 1946. "Old Gene" Talmadge staged a comeback at the ballot box that year, aided by Klan intimidation of black voters, but when death preempted his inauguration klansmen switched allegiance to son Herman, who surpassed his father's political achievements with service both as governor (1948–55) and in the U.S. Senate (1957–81). Although stripped of its charter in

Klansmen rally in Burke County, Georgia, in 1962 (Georgia Department of Archives and History).

1946, the Georgia Klan endured, fraternizing with the neo–Nazi Columbians, reviving its Klavalier Klub flogging squad, and retaining its friendly relationship with Atlanta's police department. Detective Samuel Roper rose to command the AGK in August 1949, following Dr. Green's untimely death, but his ineffective leadership encouraged defectors to form their own "Bolshevik Klans."

Eldon Edwards of Atlanta was the order's next significant leader, founding his U.S. Klans in 1953 and securing a state charter in October 1955. Fired by the threat of school integration, an estimated 15,000 klansmen in ten states rallied to Edwards over the next four years. He publicly discouraged violence, but testified as a character witness on behalf of accused NSRP synagogue bombers in 1958, while Klan attorney James Venable handled their defense. When Edwards died in August 1960, successor Robert Davidson proved unequal to the task of replacing him. A schism in the U.S. Klans spawned a new United Klans of America, and national headquarters left Georgia for the first time in fifty years, transferring to Tuscaloosa, Alabama, under Wizard Robert Shelton. UKA Grand Dragon Calvin Craig, a veteran of riots at Georgia's state university in early 1961, managed the realm from Atlanta and cultivated friendship with future governor Lester Maddox, while his knights learned bombing techniques from Nacirema instructors and fraternized with Jesse Stoner's NSRP. James Venable left the UKA in 1963, to lead his own National Knights, and while he never rivaled Shelton's strength, Venable's Klan gladly accepted knights expelled from the UKA for acts of criminal violence. While Craig urged his klansmen to "be nonviolent, just like the niggers," Venable recruited paramilitary Black Shirts with proven histories of mayhem. Congressional investigations and federal prosecutions winnowed the Georgia ranks during 1966–69, but once again the KKK endured, nurtured by politicians and a population that had grown accustomed to its presence in their midst.

The 1970s were lean times for the Klan in general, and election of a Georgian to the White House in 1976 failed to benefit Peach State klansmen. Jimmy Carter was liberal even by north-

Top: Klansmen rally outside Valdosta, Georgia, in October 1922 (Georgia Department of Archives and History). *Above:* Atlanta klansmen picket an integrated restaurant in 1964 (Library of Congress).

ern standards, and klansmen accomplished little by circulating tales that branded him an illegitimate brother of the Massachusetts Kennedys. Longtime klansman Jesse Stoner ran for governor in 1980, hoping for a chance to deny his own extradition on Alabama bombing charges, but voters rejected his message. KKK "unity rallies" convened at Stone Mountain in 1982–83 failed to forge the hoped-for national alliance, even as they gave the lie to David Duke's insistent claim that he had left the Klan. Black demonstrations in Forsyth County gave white knights a chance to lash out at their traditional enemies in 1987, but the outburst proved costly in court. Even Stoner's brown-shirted NSRP, headquartered in Georgia for thirty years, was replaced after his release from prison by a half-hearted Crusade Against Corruption.

Still, the Klan's roots run too deep in Georgia soil to be expunged. At press time for this work, nearly four decades since its last great wizard died in Atlanta, the Peach State nurtured six active Klans: the American White Knights (headquartered in

Cordele), the Free Knights (based in Buchanan), the Imperial Klans of America, the Mystic Knights, the North Georgia White Knights (headquartered at Ft. Oglethorpe), and the Southern White Knights (two klaverns). Other Klan-allied or sympathetic groups include the Aryan Nations, the CCC (two chapters), EURO, the League of the South (seven chapters), the National Alliance, the National Socialist Movement, two racist skinhead gangs (in Atlanta and Marietta), and White Revolution.

Hawaii—Rumors of KKK activity on the Hawaiian Islands surfaced in the 1920s, but no hard proof ever emerged to support the claims. The Klan has never returned to Hawaii, although two far-right "patriot" groups—the Constitution Party and the Cornerstone of Freedom Research Foundation—briefly colonized the islands in 1999, and the Klan-minded NAAWP boasted a chapter in Honolulu during 2001.

Idaho—Kleagles infiltrated Idaho from neighboring Washington in the early 1920s, spreading their gospel of "100-percent Americanism" along the Snake River Valley. Recruiters operated out of Boise and Lewiston, with active klaverns identified in five other cities. The masked invasion of a black family's home in Lewiston prompted shoot-to-kill orders against nightriders, but Idaho klansmen were generally more pacific. In one small town, the only Jewish family routinely joined in KKK picnics and other fraternal activities. A fading memory by the early 1930s, the KKK resurfaced briefly—and embarrassingly—in 1965, when Wizard James Venable announced the appointment of a new grand titan for his National Knights. The fledgling klansman had applied by mail and was accepted, sight-unseen, to build a new realm in the Gem State. Sadly for Venable, his latest member was a black Catholic who wasted no time in airing his charade for the media.

Richard Butler brought organized hatred back to Idaho in 1973, when he transplanted his Church of Jesus Christ Christian from California to a rural compound at Hayden Lake and created the Aryan Nations as his sect's "political arm." The retreat served as a magnet for klansmen and neo–Nazis nationwide, gathered for Butler's annual Aryan World Congress and sundry other celebrations that included fiery crosses side-by-side with swastikas. The compound bred violence, concealing at least one murder in 1983 and spawning a rash of bombings around Coeur d'Alene. Guerrillas of The Order founded their movement at Butler's compound and later favored him with gifts of cash procured via armed robbery. Federal prosecutors failed to take the aging Nazi out of circulation with sedition charges filed in 1987, but dissension in the ranks and lawsuits filed by the SPLC fractured Butler's empire at the turn of the millennium. At press time for this work, only a tiny remnant of the Aryan Nations remained in Coeur d'Alene, competing for money and members with a local chapter of David Duke's EURO.

Illinois—The modern KKK was well established in Chicago by 1921, where it posed as the Southern Publicity Bureau and prospered despite official condemnation. Eighteen klaverns operated in the Windy City during 1922, with 287 more throughout the state by 1923. Estimates of statewide membership ranged upward from 95,000, while the Chicago-based American Unity League fought to stem the tide by publishing names of known (or suspected) klansmen. Opposition in southern Illinois was more direct, where a virtual state of civil war prevailed in "Bloody Williamson" County. There, pitched battles between Glenn Young's klansmen and "anti–Kluckers" allied with the Shelton bootlegging gang claimed at least twenty lives during 1923–26. National Guardsmen were dispatched to Herrin and environs on eight separate occasions, to restore public order, until the death of leaders on both sides produced a cease-fire. Elsewhere in the Prairie State, klansmen chose sides in the power struggle between William Simmons and Hiram Evans, or fell out in quarrels over politics. Klan membership declined after 1926, but the realm remained one of thirteen where significant strength lingered during the Great Depression, until formal disbandment in April 1944 left the faithful adrift.

Georgia klansman James Venable tried to rekindle the old fires in 1967, but he received unwelcome publicity a year later, when eight klansmen on the Chicago police force were fired and jailed for plotting to kill Mayor Richard Daley. Robert Shelton's UKA made the next concerted bid for Illinois members, in March 1975, prompting a full-scale investigation by state legislators. Investigators learned that Aurora klansman Wilburn Foreman had struggled for eight years to launch a viable klavern, succeeding only after he sought help from knights in neighboring Indiana. Foreman finally recruited 100 klansmen

Bikers join the Christian Knights at Parkersburg in October 1987 (Southern Poverty Law Center).

statewide, including members of a scruffy motorcycle gang, and thirty of those followed Foreman into Robert Scoggin's Invisible Empire Knights, after Foreman broke with Shelton in May 1975. By October 1976, no more than fifteen Illinoisans claimed the hooded order as their own.

Still, efforts have persisted to revive organized bigotry in Illinois. Lifelong neo–Nazi Matthew Hale took control of the neo–Nazi Church of the Creator in 1995, moving its headquarters from North Carolina to the home he shared with his father in East Peoria. The movement soon spread nationwide, its members frequently marching with klansmen in racist parades, but state authorities refused to let Hale practice law in Illinois (despite his passage of the bar exam), and a lawsuit for trademark infringement forced Hale to rename his "church" the Creativity Movement. That crowning indignity provoked Hale to solicit the murder of a federal judge, which in turn earned him a twenty-year prison term. In February 1998, three members of the KKK's New Order were jailed on weapons charges in East St. Louis, while plotting a far-flung guerrilla war against their sundry enemies. At press time for this book, three Klans were marginally active in Illinois: the Brotherhood of Klans (two klaverns), the Imperial Klans of America, and the National Knights. Groups friendly to the Klan or its beliefs include American Renaissance, the Aryan Nations Youth Action Corps, the CCC (three chapters), the Creativity Movement (two chapters), the National Alliance, and the National Socialist Movement (two chapters).

Indiana—Indiana was the great success story of the 1920s Klan, and that success was due in large part to a single man—Grand Dragon David Stephenson. A super-salesman long before he joined the KKK, Stephenson ruled his realm with an iron hand, ultimately dooming the Hoosier Klan—and, some say, the national order as well—when personal failings led to his downfall. Indiana's first klavern was chartered at Evansville, in 1920, and Stephenson's salesmanship pumped statewide membership to an estimated 5,000 by early 1922. A year later, some 300,000 Hoosiers belonged to the Klan, with 40,000 knights in Indianapolis alone. Stephenson's backstage role in the 1922 palace coup that deposed Wizard William Simmons earned him a powerful friend in successor Hiram Evans, and his reward was command of a sub-empire spanning twenty-three northern states. Evans traveled to Kokomo in July 1923, for Stephenson's inauguration as grand dragon, but titanic egos put the two men constantly at odds. They quarreled bitterly in May 1924, prompting Stephenson to resign and organize his own Independent Klan of America. His "military machine" swept the state elections that year, electing friendly Governor Ed Jackson and a majority of the state legislature, plus countless mayors and lesser officials. In Indianapolis, Stephenson's hand-picked mayor signed a pledge to clear all civic appointments with the dragon in advance. Still, for all his local power, Stephenson's war with Evans divided Indiana klansmen, city officials and senators generally backing Stephenson, while klansmen in the legislature's lower house followed dictates from Evans in Atlanta. The end came swiftly, after Stephenson kidnapped and raped Madge Oberholtzer, afterward withholding medical aid when she swallowed poison. Convicted of murder and sentenced to life im-

prisonment, Stephenson waited in vain for a gubernatorial pardon, then began leaking details of Hoosier political corruption that scandalized state and Klan alike. Thousands of members nationwide quit the Klan after Stephenson's conviction, leaving fewer than 7,000 dues-paying knights in Indiana by 1927.

The Indiana Klan never recovered from Stephenson's fall, and Grand Dragon Walter Bossert was ridiculed when he sought a U.S. Senate seat in 1938. Eight years later, rumbles of an Indianapolis Klan revival sent the state's attorney general to court, filing suit to revoke the KKK's charter, along with those of such front groups as the Fraternal Order of Rangers, the Horse Thief Detective Society, the Loyal Liberty League, the Modern Minutemen, the Native Americans Club, and the Rock of Freedom. In January 1967, Robert Shelton announced William Chaney's appointment as Indiana grand dragon of the UKA, but congressional investigators found only a handful of klansmen statewide, with no chartered klaverns. Robed klansmen paraded through Martinsville in July 1967, and Klan involvement is still suspected in the September 1968 murder of black victim Carol Jenkins. For the most part, however, the new breed of knights kept to themselves and caused few disturbances.

Grand Dragon Chaney broke with Shelton and the UKA in May 1976, winning election in June 1977 to the dual posts of imperial wizard for a new Confederation of Independent Orders and as national coordinator for the ambitious-sounding Northern and Southern Knights, but conviction on bombing charges sent Chaney to prison in November 1977. Bill Wilkinson's IEKKKK recruited a few knights in the early 1980s, but state leadership was torn by personal rivalry. Grand Dragon Ken Taylor quarreled with Wilkinson's successor, Catholic Wizard James Farrands, and was banished from the IEKKKK in October 1988. He later won reinstatement, only to resign and launch his own Klan, billing himself in August 1989 as imperial wizard, with his "national office" in Crawfordsville. The 1990s brought Jeff Berry's American Knights to the fore, ruling a ten-state empire from Butler, Indiana, in 2003, but Berry's propensity for impulsive violence sent him to prison in 2004. At press time for this volume, Indiana harbored klaverns of three splinter groups: the Imperial Klans of America, the Mystic Knights, and the National Knights. Like-minded groups within the Hoosier State include the CCC (two chapters), the National Socialist Movement (two chapters), Muncie's Southern European Aryans League Army, and White Revolution.

Iowa—The 1920s Iowa Klan appeared first in Des Moines, then rapidly spread despite early and determined opposition from various groups, enrolling some 30,000 members statewide. Numerous Protestant ministers joined the KKK to serve as kludds and kleagles. Passage of an anti-mask law in 1923 inconvenienced Hawkeye State klansmen, but their sweeping victory in 1924's school board elections made it difficult for Catholic teachers to find work in Iowa. Two years later, Klan opponents mounted a concerted drive to purge the hooded order. In Des Moines, a mob armed with crowbars and pitchforks menaced assembled klansmen, retreating only when threatened with military force. By the end of the decade, the Iowa Klan was no more.

Hard times and farm foreclosures in the 1970s made Iowa a prime recruiting ground for Posse Comitatus extremists, but residents were spared the outbursts of violence that scarred Nebraska and the Dakotas during that era. Two decades later, the "patriot militia" movement found a few recruits in Iowa, enlisting members for the extremist U.S. Taxpayers Party (later the Constitution Party) around Story City. At press time for this work, Iowa klansmen rallied to a single klavern of the Imperial Klans of America.

Kansas—The Klan's first kleagles reached Kansas in 1922, planting klaverns along the Oklahoma border, and by 1924 they had enrolled an estimated 100,000 members statewide. Klansmen played an active vigilante role in the Sunflower State, stopping cars on rural highways to search for contraband liquor, raiding homes around Emporia to catch "sinners" playing cards on Sunday. Nightriders kidnapped and flogged Liberty's mayor, after he denied the KKK permission to meet in City Hall, and Ku Klux candidates scored municipal victories in at least seven cities (including Wichita and Kansas City) during 1923. William Allen White, editor of the Emporia *Gazette,* was the Kansas Klan's most vocal and persistent enemy. In 1924, he launched a shoestring gubernatorial campaign to publicize Klan corruption and violence, stumping the state despite constant death threats. White failed to capture the governor's mansion, but his primary goal was achieved as thousands of Kansans turned against the KKK, leaving the realm in ruins by 1927.

As elsewhere in the Midwest, economic setbacks in the 1970s and early 1980s brought Kansas recruits to the Posse Comitatus movement, followed in the 1990s by such far-right "patriot" groups as Abilene's Christian Court, Baldwin's Constitutionist Networking Center, Wichita's branch of the U.S. Taxpayers Party, and kangaroo "common-law courts" in Rice, Sedgwick and Shawnee Counties. At press time for this book, no Klan units were active in the state, although the Klan-allied League of the South maintained one misplaced chapter and the National Socialist Movement boasted a small cell in Hutchinson.

Kentucky—The Bluegrass State was one of two "loyal" Union states whose antebellum support for slavery provided KKK recruiters with ample opportunities in Reconstruction. The Kentucky Klan was not concerned with politics per se, since blacks were barred from voting in the state until 1870 and could not testify in court against whites until 1872. Instead, Kentucky klansmen served most often in a vigilante capacity, employing brutal terrorism to enforce white supremacy and the KKK's version of "community values." (Ironically, another major function of the Klan was guarding the illegal moonshine stills its members ran for profit, thereby circumventing taxes.) Organized in 1868, klansmen rode most often in the state's Bluegrass region, tormenting blacks and Unionists in southwestern Kentucky, from Bowling Green to the Mississippi River. In July 1869, newspapers reported that twenty-five men had been lynched, with 100 more severely whipped or otherwise abused, within a twenty-mile radius of Harrodsburg. Near Stanford, a black man who defended himself and killed three klansmen in the process faced trial for murder. By early 1870, most of the nightriding

action centered on Madison and Richmond Counties, where klansmen resisted the Fifteenth Amendment's imposition of black suffrage. Black postal agents were a favored target of Kentucky's Klan, but no one was immune. In March 1871, a published list detailed 116 Ku Klux outrages during the past three years, culminating with a jailbreak at the state capital. August's election sparked a race riot in Frankfort, followed by two months of sporadic disorder.

Against that background, kleagles were delighted with their 1920s progress in Kentucky, claiming 30,000 members by the most conservative estimate. The modern Klan invaded Louisville in 1921, when an Oklahoma kleagle operated briefly in the face of opposition from the mayor and his police force. Harassment drove the Klan's pioneer out of town, until a federal appellate court confirmed his right to preach the Ku Klux gospel, but that drama distracted Klanwatchers from the order's steady progress in the Ohio River valley, spreading eastward from Covington. Klan strength in Kentucky peaked during 1924, when hooded knights clashed with unionized miners in the state's coalfields. Internal disputes over money and politics soon split the realm, and membership faded in the 1930s, leaving small klaverns in Ashland and Lexington.

Rumors of a post-war KKK revival mobilized Kentucky's attorney general in July 1946, seeking revocation of state charters for the group he described as a "lawless, seditious one of Nazi tendency, whose sole purpose is to create division and dissension in the United States." The order lost its charter in September 1946, and Kentucky did without a Klan for twenty years, until anger over busing to achieve school integration brought a small klavern to Louisville. As always, legal problems drained the KKK's resources, while its violent rhetoric appealed primarily to outcasts from society. Still, interest remains, and as this volume went to press the Bluegrass State harbored three active splinter groups: the Imperial Klans of America (three klaverns), the Keystone Knights, and the National Knights. Kentucky klansmen also find comrades in Mount Washington's chapter of the Aryan Nations.

Louisiana—Louisiana pioneered armed resistance to Reconstruction with the Knights of the White Camellia, organized in May 1867. The Bayou State's first Ku Klux dens appeared in spring 1868, after which the two groups shared members and worked in concert to terrorize blacks and white Republicans. Most of the violence was politically inspired, accelerating in the final weeks before November's presidential election. In Alexandria, the sheriff and 200 blacks armed with clubs routed a Klan raiding party, but the outcome of most such engagements reflected the armed superiority of racist whites. Shreveport residents counted thirty dead blacks floating in the river past their homes in October 1868, and the same month saw forty-two slaughtered in Caddo Parish. Whites rioted in New Orleans before the election, while white gunmen in Bossier Parish murdered 162 freedmen. Congressional investigators subsequently published a roster of terrorist acts committed in Louisiana between April and November 1868: 1,081 murders, 135 persons wounded by gunfire, and 507 whipped or otherwise assaulted. Republican margins dropped sharply in the affected parishes, and Democratic victories generally signaled an end to nightriding. The KWC officially dissolved in early 1869, followed by the KKK a short time later, but Louisiana whites continued their war to "redeem" the state for "home rule." An unmasked White League staged a bloody coup d'état in New Orleans during September 1874, leaving twenty-seven dead and 105 wounded. Federal troops restored order in the Crescent City after five days of battle, but white supremacists carried their war to the backcountry, regaining control of the state two years later.

In 1922, another outburst of violence made Louisiana the modern Klan's most notorious realm. By that time, more than 50,000 klansmen and -women had pledged allegiance to the invisible empire, infiltrating law enforcement and state government so thoroughly that Governor John Parker asked Washington for help. FBI agents investigated a double murder committed by klansmen at Mer Rouge, but the G-men found no violations of federal law and the killers went free after paying small fines on misdemeanor charges. Still, publicity surrounding that case cost the KKK prestige and members, both within Louisiana and across the country. State legislators passed an anti-mask law in 1924, supported by some Klan leaders who hoped the statute would spruce up their image. Instead, they watched realm membership decline through the late 1920s and early 1930s, when opposition from "Kingfish" Huey Long's political machine made life doubly difficult for the Louisiana Klan.

Sporadic cross-burnings and lynchings kept the Klan spirit alive after World War II, but it remained for the U.S. Supreme Court's "Black Monday" decision on school integration to revitalize the order in 1954. A homegrown Knights of the KKK appeared in 1956, competing with the Georgia-based U.S. Klans for members and cash. Louisiana's most successful faction since the 1920s organized as the Original Knights in 1960, expanding into Mississippi three years later. The Original Knights dominated Louisiana until autumn 1964, when a three-way split in the ranks permitted Robert Shelton's UKA to gain a foothold in the state. Endemic violence, including the murder of a black sheriff's deputy, rocked Bogalusa during 1965, but state legislators ignored the carnage. In July 1965, Louisiana's Joint Legislative Committee on Un-American Activities called the KKK a "political action group" with "a certain Halloween spirit." The panel pegged state membership at 19,000 and uncovered no illegal acts, suggesting merely that the Klan existed to express "frustration with the current national administration." Federal authorities disagreed, obtaining broad injunctions in December 1965 that theoretically barred the KKK from further terrorism around Bogalusa. By early 1967, observers estimated the combined membership of the UKA and Original Knights around 950.

The 1970s and early 1980s witnessed a revival of Louisiana's Klan, first in the media-savvy hands of David Duke, and after his departure to the realm of politics, under the crude and visceral regime of Bill Wilkinson. Briefly recognized as the nation's premier klansman, Wilkinson fell from grace with revelation of his double life as an FBI informant, a scandal that left the KKK deeply wounded. Still, the Ku Klux spirit never truly dies out in Louisiana. At press time for this work, active splinter groups in the Bayou State included the Aryan Nations Knights,

the Bayou Knights (headquartered at Homer), the Imperial Klans of America, and the Louisiana White Knights (headquartered in Walker). Allied or sympathetic groups include the Christian Defense League (based in Arabi), the CCC (two chapters), David Duke's EURO (headquartered at Mandeville), the League of the South, and the National Alliance (two chapters).

Maine—The Pine Tree State's first klavern organized at Bangor, where Grand Dragon Eugene Farnsworth maintained a $60,000 estate and supervised a tri-state realm (also including New Hampshire and Vermont). By 1923, with some 15,000 members, the order had sufficient strength to carry elections in Rockland and Sacco, but political factionalism split the state organization along party lines in 1924 and 1928, resulting in mass resignations and a general decline in influence. In 1929, Portland's mayor denied the Klan use of city hall for a speech by visiting Alabama Senator Tom Heflin, and no serious KKK activity has been recorded since that time. As this work went to press, Maine harbored small chapters of the Klan-allied Creativity Movement and National Socialist Movement, but no trace of the hooded order itself remained in the state.

Maryland—Kleagles found their way to Maryland in 1920, but Atlanta headquarters withheld a charter from the realm until 1923, when membership reached 33,000. Klansmen were not idle in the meantime. They whipped and branded a philandering husband at Hagerstown, in 1922, but when they tarred and feathered several railroad workers, jurors sent four of the raiders to prison for seven years each. Baltimore residents rioted when one of the Klan's "escaped nuns" addressed the faithful at the First Baptist Church, and arsonists tried to destroy a former Presbyterian church where the Thomas Dixon Klan held its weekly meetings. Grand Dragon Frank Beall claimed seventy-two klaverns statewide, but the order never made its presence felt in politics. Beall's resignation in 1926, accompanied by angry blasts at imperial headquarters, precipitated mass resignations and eventual dissolution of the realm.

Grand Dragon Vernon Naimaster brought Robert Shelton's UKA to Maryland in August 1965, but his recruiting efforts had borne little fruit by the following summer, when dissident klansman Xavier Edwards and his followers earned banishment for their flirtation with George Rockwell's ANP. Edwards soon organized his own Maryland Knights, leaving Naimaster with an estimated twenty-five klansmen split between four tiny klaverns. The original Maryland Knights disappeared prior to 1969, when UKA Grand Dragon Tony LaRicci quarreled with Shelton and adopted the name for his own fledgling order. Sporadic cross-burnings and local acts of violence kept LaRicci in the news through the late 1970s, but notoriety signaled no significant membership growth. In May 1981, Baltimore jurors convicted three members of the Adamic Knights of plotting to bomb the local NAACP office, sending leader Richard Savina to prison for fifteen years. A 1983 survey by the ADL found no active klaverns in Maryland, but sporadic recruiting efforts continued over the next two decades. At press time for this volume, the state hosted three Klans, including the Imperial Klans of America, the Southern White Knights, and the World Knights (headquar-

Another Klan initiation ceremony, this one outside New Brunswick, Maryland, in June 1922 (Southern Poverty Law Center).

tered at Sharpsburg). Edgewater's SS Regalia supplies paraphernalia to Free State neo–Nazis, including a chapter of the National Alliance.

Massachusetts

—The modern KKK has a traumatic history in Massachusetts, where its first appearance in the early 1920s met opposition from Freemasons, most elected officials, and Catholics who used the Klan's own violent tactics to defeat the hooded order. Klansmen enjoyed their warmest reception in Worcester, where they rallied at the local Shriner's hall and furnished guest speakers for the Exchange Club. The rest of the Bay State proved less hospitable, although klansmen finally numbered 12,000 or more. In 1923, the Massachusetts House of Representatives issued a resolution condemning the KKK as a threat to American freedom, and the 1924 state Democratic convention adopted a plank denouncing the order by name. During 1924–25, a series of bloody anti–Klan riots rocked Worcester County, where the white knights found themselves habitually outnumbered. Similar outbreaks occurred in Essex, Middlesex and Norfolk. At Westwood, twenty klansmen suffered injuries from a stone-throwing mob. Framingham police jailed seventy-nine Kluxers and seized an arsenal of weapons after gunfire at a Klan rally left five men wounded. By 1928, when the Democratic Party nominated Catholic Al Smith for president, the Massachusetts Klan had disappeared.

Stirrings of a KKK revival occurred a half-century later, when white opposition to court-ordered school integration sparked angry demonstrations in South Boston. Louisiana klansman David Duke arrived in search of converts, while the mob attacked school buses bearing black children to class, and locals erected signs proclaiming "This is Klan Country." Still, hot tempers did not translate into long-term Klan success. No klaverns remained in the state as this work went to press, although active Klan-allied groups included the Creativity Movement (two chapters), the National Alliance (two chapters), the National Socialist Movement, Volksfront and White Revolution.

Michigan

—The Wolverine State's late-blooming KKK did not reach its peak membership until the mid–1920s, with an estimated 80,000 klansmen and -women enrolled. Pioneer kleagles posed as spokesmen for the "National Research Bureau" until their realm was chartered from Atlanta, and organized opposition soon followed the Klan's coming-out party. State legislators passed an anti-mask law in 1923, but klansmen were their own worst enemies, quarreling endlessly over policy and control of the realm's treasury. In 1926, Muskegon's exalted cyclops killed three persons with a bomb mailed to a political opponent's home, and his conviction prompted mass resignations statewide. Within three years, the Klan had nearly disappeared from Michigan, but its replacement—the spin-off Black Legion—proved every bit as secretive and brutal as the parent order. Concentrated in Detroit, where it counted the city's police commissioner and many officers among its members, the Legion specialized in strike-breaking until a 1936 murder exposed its operations and outraged public opinion.

In the late 1960s, UKA kleagles tried to rekindle interest with a brisk recruiting drive, and congressional investigators found three klaverns active in 1967, boasting some 200 members. A year later, Michigan klansmen were active on behalf of George Wallace's AIP. Alabama headquarters supervised the realm until 1969, when Robert Miles won the nod as UKA grand dragon. Indicted in 1971 for bombing school buses and flogging a high school principal, Miles resigned from the UKA in 1972 to lead the Mountain Church of Jesus Christ at Cohoctah, but he maintained close ties to the Klan and allied groups for the remainder of his life. Aside from Miles's cult, two other Klans—the Michigan KKK and the White Knights—claimed scattered members in the 1980s. At press time for this work, their number had increased to five: the Brotherhood of Klans, the Imperial Klans of America, the Mystic Knights, the National Knights, and the Southern White Knights. Neo-fascist groups active in Michigan include Westland's American Nazi Party, an Aryan Nations offshoot, the Creativity Movement, the National Alliance (five chapters), and the National Socialist Movement.

Minnesota

—Kleagles in the North Star State enjoyed less success than their other Midwestern brethren in the 1920s. Peak membership undoubtedly fell short of the 65,000 estimated by the *Washington Post* in November 1930, but author Kenneth Jackson's 5,000 klansmen statewide is likely too conservative. The order's banner year in Minnesota was 1923, marked by klansman Roy Miner's mayoral campaign in Minneapolis and his subsequent conviction on charges of criminal libel. Thereafter, membership declined precipitously. By July 1930, only 500 knights remained to elect a new grand dragon, named to rule a consolidated tri-state realm including Minnesota and the Dakotas. Largely ignored by Klan recruiters since the Great Depression, Minnesota harbored no active klaverns at press time for this volume, though its neo–Nazi groups included the Aryan Nations Youth Action Corps, the National Alliance, and the National Socialist Movement.

Mississippi

—The Reconstruction-era Klan invaded Mississippi in spring 1868 but restrained itself from significant violence until a new "radical" state constitution was ratified in November 1869. Contemporary racist groups—including Heggie's Scouts, Knights of the Black Cross, and the Washington Brothers—subsequently disbanded or merged with the KKK as mayhem escalated through 1870. In Lauderdale County, klansmen murdered two black county supervisors in separate attacks, also whipping several black women on charges that they "entertained" white lovers. Ku Klux violence was generally concentrated along Mississippi's eastern border, where Alabama reinforcements were readily available to their brethren in Chickasaw, Kemper, Lauderdale, Lowndes, Monroe, Noxubee and Winston Counties. Violence peaked in spring 1871, with a concerted purge of "carpetbag" teachers from black schools and a vicious pogrom at Meridian, declining after federal arrests began in June. Still, few of the Magnolia State's indicted klansmen were convicted, and five years later the terroristic "Mississippi Plan" (or "Shotgun Plan") assured "redemption" of the state for white "home rule."

In the 1920s, kleagles recruited more than 15,000 Mississippi klansmen, but they proved less militant than their forefathers. The state still took pride in its lynch mobs, but the Klan displayed no political strength above the precinct level, and even that was on the wane by 1924. Klansman Theodore Bilbo served as governor (1916–20, 1928–32) and later in the U.S. Senate (1935–47), but his personal advancement failed to save the KKK. When state legislators proposed an anti-mask law in 1928, Jack-

Governor Adelbert Ames was unable to suppress Klan violence in Reconstruction-era Mississippi.

son's *Daily News* advised, "Don't kick the corpse." Vague stirrings were reported through the late 1940s, and Imperial Emperor Lycurgus Spinks transferred his Alabama headquarters to Mississippi in March 1950, but his following was minuscule at best. The Supreme Court's *Brown* ruling sparked creation of the first "respectable" Citizens' Councils in 1954, and klansmen also organized in the Magnolia State. Journalist Ira Harkey reported KKK activity around Pascagoula in September 1954, and

The Christian Knights prepare for a rally at Philadelphia, Mississippi, in March 1989 (Southern Poverty Law Center).

Christian Knights sell souvenirs at their Philadelphia rally, March 1989 (Southern Poverty Law Center).

Members of the Christian Knights pose for photographs at their Mississippi rally, March 1989 (Southern Poverty Law Center).

the Association of Alabama Klans launched several Mississippi klaverns in 1956. Those knights deserted the parent order a year later, reorganized as the Independent Mississippi Klan, but the movement failed to produce a dynamic leader and faded from the scene by 1960.

Members of the Citizens' Council (AKA the "white-collar Klan") generally handled Mississippi's resistance to integration through summer 1962, when a federal court ordered admission of black student James Meredith to the University of Mississippi at Oxford. When Governor Ross Barnett failed to block Meredith's admission, klansmen from surrounding states answered a call from firebrand Edwin Walker, staging a riot that left two men dead and hundreds more injured. A year later, the Louisiana-based Original Knights recruited some 300 members in Mississippi, but the new recruits soon separated from the parent order, following Douglas Byrd and Edward McDaniel into the new, more militant White Knights. Samuel Bowers assumed control of the WKKKKM in early 1964, launching a guerrilla war through 1964–68 that included at least ten murders, plus scores of bombings and arson attacks. Membership in the WKKKKM peaked around 6,000 in late 1964, while the competing UKA claimed 750 members statewide. Active fronts and splinter groups included the APWR, Knights of the Green Forest, and the Silver Dollar Group (trained specialists in bombing). State and federal prosecutions thinned the ranks in 1967–68, although it took another thirty years to jail klansman Byron De La Beckwith for the 1963 slaying of state NAACP leader Medgar Evers.

Rival leaders David Duke and Bill Wilkinson competed for members in Mississippi during the late 1970s, each recruiting small numbers of klansmen. Burnsville knights were linked to a murder and four nonfatal shootings in 1980, while Jackson klansmen twice shot up the office of a newspaper that criticized their group in 1981–82. Meridian police suspected klansmen in the July 1982 murder of black teenager Beverly Parnell, but the case remains officially unsolved. Racist vandalism at DeSoto County's New Hope Missionary Baptist Church, in January 1986, previewed a new wave of arson attacks on black churches in the 1990s. At press time for this book, four Klans survived in Mississippi, including the Bayou Knights (two klaverns), the

Mississippi White Knights (headquartered at Petal), the Orion Knights, and the Southern White Knights (two klaverns). Like-minded groups include the CCC (nine chapters), the Creativity Movement, David Duke's EURO (two chapters), the League of the South, and the National Alliance.

Missouri—Habitually overlooked in histories of the KKK, Missouri was the second Union state (with Kentucky) to host an active Klan after the Civil War. Boonville witnessed the first display of Klan recruiting posters, in April 1868, and violence soon followed, mimicking the Show-Me State's five years of bloody turmoil over slavery during 1856–61. Republicans were the Missouri Klan's primary targets, but klansmen crossed the state line from Howell County in September 1868, to murder Capt. Simpson Mason in neighboring Arkansas. An armed response from Mason's friends discouraged violence for a time, but nightriding resumed with the approach of 1872's presidential election. As in the Deep South proper, Democrats persistently denied the Klan's existence in Missouri, even when its members flaunted their regalia in Stoddard County, in May 1871. As in Kentucky, Reconstruction-era klansmen in Missouri also took up arms to guard illegal whiskey stills and liberate moonshiners jailed by state authorities. When William Jeffers, a former Confederate colonel and post-war peace officer, raided illegal saloons in Conklin, Klan threats drove him out of town. In October 1871, state investigators in Dunklin and Stoddard County's pronounced local klansmen "nothing but a band of horse thieves, robbers and murderers ... opposed to all who are in favor of enforcing the laws." Violence declined in Dunklin County after a sheriff's posse killed four klansmen, but Governor B. Gratz Brown still raised a 200-man militia company to patrol Dunklin and Stoddard. Klansmen killed two Stoddard County Republicans in March 1872, while launching a parallel reign of terror in Butler and Ripley Counties. Others assassinated Marion Weeks, a deputy postmaster, en route from St. Louis to Reynolds. As late as 1877, unknown gunman ambushed and murdered a prosecution witness from the Deep South's federal Ku Klux trials.

The Klan returned to Missouri in force in the 1920s, with published membership estimates ranging from 45,000 to 165,000. St. Louis served as headquarters for kleagles recruiting throughout the Mississippi Valley, and they prospered in the Missouri, with collaboration from the state's Protestant clergy. (At least one KKK evangelistic service was conducted in the Missouri's House of Representatives.) Klansmen whipped their first known victim at Warrensburg, in 1921, and made some inconclusive political maneuvers the following year. One Missouri resident who paid his klecktoken in 1922 was judicial candidate Harry Truman, but he soon quit the Klan in disgust (some say before his formal initiation) and later found his way to the White House despite Klan opposition. Membership began to wane in 1924, although some klaverns persevered into the early 1930s.

Organized racism languished in Missouri until 1971, when James Ellison's CSA established its fortified compound near the Arkansas border, arming for war against "ZOG." Affiliated with The Order, Ellison's raiders burned a gay church at Springfield in August 1983, then launched a bush-league guerrilla campaign that sent member Richard Snell to death row for killing a pawn broker whom he presumed (incorrectly) was Jewish. FBI agents raided Ellison's compound in April 1985, and later "turned" him as a prosecution witness against his former comrades. Meanwhile, the Klan's New Order Knights scrabbled to survive in Missouri, claiming fewer than 100 members by 1987, while the rival Missouri Knights made abortive recruiting forays into Kansas. In the 1990s, Missouri harbored nine separate "patriot militia" groups, most of them espousing racist and anti–Semitic philosophies. Jeff Berry's Indiana-based American Knights of the KKK claimed one Missouri klavern in 2000–01, before Berry's imprisonment dissolved the group. At press time for this book, active Missouri factions included the Brotherhood of Klans, the Imperial Klans of America, and the U.S. Klans. Likeminded organizations include the CCC (three chapters), League of the South (five chapters), the National Alliance, and Women for Aryan Unity.

Montana

Montana klansmen tried their hands at violence in the early 1920s, flogging one victim at Warland and issuing dire threats elsewhere, but they soon got the "rough stuff" out of their systems. Imperial headquarters chartered the Treasure State realm in September 1923, with published estimates of total membership ranging from 5,000 to 40,000. The Billings klavern bought newspaper ads in 1923, denying any prejudice against blacks, Jews or Catholics, but klansmen still opposed Catholic Senator Thomas Walsh based on his religion, when he sought reelection in 1924. Montana voters granted Walsh another six years in Washington, but the final count was close enough to encourage eager kleagles. Grand Dragon Lewis Terwilliger persuaded the Billings Chamber of Commerce to hold a banquet for visiting Wizard Hiram Evans in 1924, but the fete was not indicative of broad support. Within a year, Klan membership was falling rapidly, and the order vanished from Montana by 1930.

Klansmen are few and far between in modern Montana, but the state still harbors its share of racists. Threats and cross-burnings dogged a female resident of Troy who dated black men during 1983, while the White Student Union distributed pamphlets at three Billings high schools in 1986. Noxon's well-armed Militia of Montana was the most notorious of five "patriot" groups active through the 1990s, with leader John Trochmann well known for his ties to the Aryan Nations. A Klan splinter group, the Aryan Nations Knights, claimed a small Montana klavern during 2003, but no trace of it remained as this book went to press. A neo–Confederate organization, the Klan-friendly League of the South, boasts a small chapter in Big Fork, far from its Dixie heartland.

Nebraska

The 1920s KKK established its first Nebraska klavern in Omaha and soon expanded statewide, enrolling more than 40,000 converts to the invisible empire. Five thousand klansmen inhabited Lincoln alone, but their presence in the state capital did not forestall opposition. Omaha's mayor banned Ku Klux parades, and the Klan's great political drive in 1926 saw most of its candidates defeated. Scattered klaverns survived to 1930, but the order's marginal influence within the Cornhusker State had already evaporated. Forgotten by kleagles after World War II, Nebraska saw its next wave of organized hatred arise from the Posse Comitatus and affiliated groups such as the anti–Semitic National Agricultural Press Association. NAPA member Arthur Kirk died in a shootout with sheriff's deputies at Cairo, in 1984. A year later, police raided a Posse compound outside Rulo, charging member Michael Ryan with the torture slayings of a man and a five-year-old boy. A 1986 cross-burning at Norfolk left residents more confused than frightened, and another eighteen years elapsed before the Brotherhood of Klans planted a small klavern in Omaha. Two chapters of the neo–Nazi National Alliance offer aid and comfort to the small Cornhusker Klan, while Gary Lauck's one-man National Socialist German Worker's Party specialized in shipping neo–Nazi literature to comrades abroad.

Nevada

Nevada's sparse population discouraged kleagles in the 1920s, though they finally recruited some 2,000 knights statewide. (The *Washington Post*'s November 1930 estimate for once fell short of the mark, claiming 1,003 Nevada klansmen.) Most of the Silver State's knights were in Reno, then the state's largest city, but while Reno's klavern claimed 1,800 members on paper—fifteen percent of the city's adult male population—only 200 marched in the order's one-and-only public demonstration. Sixty years later, police identified the new Nevada KKK as a one-man effort, seeking teenage members via leaflets left on high school campuses. No active Klans existed in the state at press time for this work, although Nevada harbored one chapter of the Aryan Nations and two of the National Socialist Movement.

New Hampshire

The 1920s New Hampshire Klan was strongest around Rochester, where Dr. E.W. Gayer established his regional headquarters after replacing Grand Dragon Eugene Farnsworth. Estimates of New Hampshire's total Klan membership range from 2,000 to 75,000, but the latter figure (proposed by the *Washington Post* in November 1930) is clearly preposterous. New Hampshire's inclusion in a tri-state realm with Maine and Vermont highlights the state's poor prospects, and most of Gayer's attention focused on neighboring Maine. Even the 1980s advent of Connecticut-born James Farrands as the Klan's first Catholic wizard could not spark a revival in the Granite State. At press time for the work in hand, no active klaverns remained, and the state's sole racist group was a Manchester chapter of the National Socialist Movement.

New Jersey

The modern KKK invaded New Jersey from neighboring New York and Pennsylvania during 1921, establishing its first strongholds in Bergen, Essex, Morris, Passaic and Union Counties, with outposts at Camden and Trenton. Grand Dragon Arthur Bell hailed from Bloomfield, but his greatest concentration of klansmen lay farther south, in Monmouth County. Estimates of peak membership in the Garden State range from 60,000 to a ridiculous 720,220 (from the *Washington Post*). Early opposition came from merchants in Asbury Park, after klansmen tried to dam the flow of Catholic and Jewish tourists from New York, but Protestant ministers staunchly supported the New Jersey Klan. At Zarephath, congregants from the Pillar of Fire Church signed up en masse, and in May 1923 they came close to martyrdom while besieged and stoned by Klan opponents at Bound Brook. Three months later, a series of anti–Klan riots rocked Perth Amboy, but adversity only made New Jersey klansmen more tenacious. A divisive element in state politics, the KKK failed to elect any brethren to office, and membership was dropping by 1927, when Wizard Hiram Evans paid a visit to inspire the faithful. One of thirteen states where the Klan retained significant strength through the 1930s, New Jersey suffered embarrassment when Bell's knights rallied with the pro–Nazi German-American Bund in August 1940. The realm finally folded when a federal tax lien closed imperial headquarters in 1944.

Two years later, with new stirring in Dixie, the Garden State Klan tried a comeback, but the attorney general moved to lift its charter in July 1946, and the state supreme court filed an official judgment of ouster three months later. Two decades elapsed before the UKA attempted to revive New Jersey's realm under Grand Dragon Frank Rotella, but a rally scheduled for May 1966 was scuttled by last minute cancellation of its keynote speaker, South Carolina Grand Dragon Robert Scoggin. Rotella quit the UKA in June 1966, moving on to lead his own neo–Nazi organization, and by 1967 congressional investigators dismissed New Jersey's membership as "negligible," with no active klaverns surviving.

In 1981, New Jersey klansmen went to jail for firing shots into a black family's home at Tom's River. A flurry of cross-burnings in 1983–84 announced formation of a new White Knights faction, succeeded by the Invisible Empire Knights in 1987. The 1990s saw three "patriot militia" groups founded in New Jersey, but their outbursts were restricted to strong rhetoric. At press time for this book, two Klans were active in New Jersey: the National Knights and the Southern White Knights. Affiliated or sympathetic racist groups include the Aryan Nations, the CCC, the National Alliance (two chapters), the National Socialist Movement (two chapters), White Revolution, and seven neo–Nazi skinhead gangs.

New Mexico

—The 1920s Klan endured a lackluster existence in New Mexico, with estimates of its peak membership ranging from 1,000 to 5,311 members. (The latter figure, published by the *Washington Post*, is both inflated and suspiciously precise.) In 1924, the state Democratic convention adopted a plank that denounced the KKK for doing violence to the spirit of American institutions, and Republicans were no more eager to embrace the order. By 1931, only scattered klaverns clung to life in the Land of Enchantment, languishing in a realm whose governor was Jewish and where eighty percent of the population consisted of Hispanic Catholics. The Klan has never returned to New Mexico, and while the state harbored a dozen "patriot militia" groups during the 1990s, SPLC investigators found no active hate groups present at press time for this book.

New York

—While New York—or "Jew York," to klansmen—is commonly viewed as a hotbed of liberalism, the Empire State also nurtures a dark strain of racism dating back to colonial times. In 1863, Irish immigrants angered by military conscription for the Civil War rioted in New York City, killing dozens (some say hundreds) of blacks before troops restored order. Seven

"Division 289" of the KKK in Watertown, New York, circa 1870 (Library of Congress).

years later, while klansmen terrorized the former Confederacy, ten residents of Watertown posed for a group photograph in hats marked "KKK," styling themselves as "Division 289" of the Klan. No other record survives of that group, and the order did not resurface in the Empire State until autumn 1922, when klansmen created a furor by distributing leaflets at Manhattan's largest Baptist church. Brooklyn's knights convened in city traffic court after hours, with Exalted Cyclops Wilson Bush presiding from the judge's bench, and the district attorney affirmed their right to meet on city property. Klan parades sparked brawling in Elmira during summer 1923, but recruitment proceeded, and by early 1924 one in every seven residents of Suffolk County was a member. As the Klan expanded, growing toward a peak membership above 90,000 (300,426 in the *Washington Post*'s inflated estimate), members first tried to incorporate as a fraternity called Alpha Pi Sigma. That effort failed, but the knights were undaunted. They patrolled Long Island highways, raided bootleg stills, drove a Jewish merchant from Hicksville, and burned crosses on campus after Columbia University admitted its first black student. In 1926, state legislators passed the Walker Law of 1926, outlawing masks and requiring publication of membership lists for oath-bound secret societies. Klanwatchers soon observed declining membership throughout New York, a trend accelerated by 1927's anti–Klan riots in Manhattan, leaving two persons dead, and by a 1928 U.S. Supreme Court ruling that upheld the Walker Law. Still, the invisible empire survived in New York through the 1930s, with twelve active klaverns in New York City alone. When imperial headquarters folded in April 1944, the local membership consolidated into four klaverns—one each for Brooklyn, Queens, the Bronx and Staten Island.

Klansmen were quick to surface after World War II, but official resistance continued, and the order lost its state charter in July 1946, while new statutes imposed six-month jail terms and $10,000 fines on any person who espoused racist beliefs. A First Amendment challenge doomed that legislation, but the state attorney general soon produced a list of 1,100 New York klansmen, now affiliated with Samuel Green's Atlanta-based AGK. Identified leaders included publicist and politician Wilson Bush, Grand Titan Clarence Herlth from Richmond Hill, and Brooklyn Kligrapp James Wagner. Klansman Horace Demarest, who doubled as the Republican Party's leader in Queens, lost his job as a deputy state motor vehicle inspector, while Governor Tom Dewey caught flack for appointing him in the first place. By year's end, state authorities pronounced the New York Klan officially extinct.

Two decades later, veteran neo–Nazi Daniel Burros assumed office as New York king kleagle for Robert Shelton's UKA, presiding over two Manhattan klaverns. Burros killed himself in October 1965, after the *New York Times* revealed his Jewish ancestry, and was replaced by yet another Nazi stalwart, William Hoff (supervised by Pennsylvania Grand Dragon Roy Frankhouser). By 1967, congressional investigators found one small klavern struggling to survive in Queens, with an estimated twenty-five hard-core members. A new splinter group, the Independent Northern Klans, surfaced at Pine Bush in the early 1970s, with Grand Dragon Earl Schoonmaker and most of his followers employed as state prison guards. Exposure of that faction spelled its doom, and while racist violence continued in New York throughout the 1980s, no organized klansmen were linked to the crimes.

New York harbored a half-dozen "patriot militia" groups during the 1990s, some of them affiliated with known white supremacists, and Jeff Berry's American Knights of the KKK claimed a small klavern at Newburgh during 2000–01, before Berry himself went to prison. At press time for this book, New York hosted three Klan factions: the Free Knights, the Imperial Klans of America and the National Knights. Allied or sympathetic groups within the state include the CCC (two chapters), the League of the South, the National Alliance, Volksfront, and Women for Aryan Unity.

North Carolina

North Carolina—A haven for the KKK throughout the order's history, North Carolina welcomed its first Ku Klux dens between December 1867 and March 1868. Observers at the time described three overlapping paramilitary groups active within the Tarheel State, including the Constitutional Union Guard, the White Brotherhood, and the Invisible Empire (understood to be a formal designation for the KKK, with ex-governor Zebulon Vance serving as grand dragon). Republican victories in the November 1868 elections produced a sharp increase in nightriding violence, with members of the CUG dominating the action in Duplin, Jones and Lenoir Counties. Governor William Holden's policy of appeasement and conciliation generally defused CUG violence by early 1870, but Ku Klux terrorism escalated in other parts of the state. Alamance County, where membership in the KKK and White Brotherhood were virtually identical, suffered the worst reign of terror. Faced with ever mounting violence, Republican newspapers called for a stern vigilante response, whereupon scattered groups of freedmen retaliated for nocturnal raids with strategic acts of arson, torching the barns of known or suspected klansmen. In March 1870, Governor Holden proclaimed martial law in Alamance County, but subsequent expansion of military rule produced a Democratic revolt, earning

Holden dubious distinction as the first U.S. governor impeached and removed from office (in March 1871). Klan violence continued during and after Holden's trial before the state legislature, reaching its peak in Cleveland, Gaston, Lincoln and Rutherford Counties, adjacent to the most chaotic districts of South Carolina. Interaction between Tarheel and Palmetto klansmen was commonplace, with hit teams trading off to frustrate witnesses. Federal troops and new legislation finally suppressed the KKK in North Carolina, in a hard-fought campaign waged between October 1871 and February 1872. The terrorists who finally "redeemed" their state for white "home rule" seldom wore masks, but there is little doubt that most of them were former klansmen.

The modern KKK spread quietly and quickly through the state in 1921, with membership estimates ranging from 25,000 to 129,410. Henry Grady, a judge from superior court, served as grand dragon when Atlanta chartered the realm in 1922. A year later, the hooded order had enough strength to defeat a proposed anti-mask law in the state legislature. Sporadic violence occurred throughout the state—Lumberton's police chief led the gang that whipped two women accused of abusing their sickly husbands—but Grady generally managed to restrain his knights, channeling their energy into politics and public rallies. In January 1927, imperial headquarters decided that Grady was exercising *too much* restraint over the rank and file. Presented with a package of proposed anti-black and anti–Catholic legislation, Grady refused to support it, denouncing the bills as "silly, unseemly, and unconstitutional." Imperial Wizard Hiram Evans promptly banished Grady, but the move backfired, as sixty-six of North Carolina's eighty-six klaverns disbanded in protest. Scattered units survived through the Great Depression, but national disbandment finished the order in April 1944.

Five years later, wholesale grocer Thomas Hamilton represented Samuel Green's AGK as grand dragon of North Carolina, then defected to lead his own bi-state Association of Carolina Klans. Nightriding violence began almost immediately, with several flogging victims carried across state lines in violation of the Lindbergh Law. In February 1952, FBI agents arrested Hamilton and eleven of his klansmen—including the police chief of Tabor City, North Carolina, and former police chief of Fair Bluff—on federal kidnapping charges. Ten of the eleven were convicted at trial, but Hamilton's problems had only begun. In July 1952, state authorities slapped seventy-one klansmen with 180 felony charges related to twelve flogging cases. Hamilton was among the sixty-three convicted, receiving a four-year prison term.

The U.S. Supreme Court's *Brown* ruling on school integration helped resuscitate the KKK in 1954, and North Carolina witnessed a proliferation of competing splinter groups over the next five years. The Georgia-based U.S. Klans claimed more members than its rivals, but local factions compensated with militant action in defense of segregation. Police jailed brothers Arthur and Joseph Bryant in 1955, for illegal possession of dynamite, before their fledgling Klan could establish itself. A year later, U.S. Klans defector James Cole founded his own North Carolina Knights and earned national humiliation in January 1958 when his klansmen were routed by Lumbee Indians in

"Carpetbagger" Albion Tourgée described his encounters with the North Carolina Klan in the novel *A Fool's Errand*.

Robeson County. The National Christian Knights, organized in 1957, disbanded in February 1958 after jurors convicted three members of bombing a school in Charlotte. Meanwhile, the black-shirted Chessmen harassed Richfield merchants who hired black employees.

Greensboro witnessed the first well-publicized black sit-in protests, in February 1960, but Tarheel klansmen lagged behind their brethren elsewhere in responding to the threat. The death of Wizard Eldon Edwards crippled the U.S. Klans in August 1960, and Robert Shelton's UKA only began consolidating Carolina klaverns during 1962–63. James Jones emerged as grand dragon in 1964, and within a year his realm boasted the nation's highest hood count, with an estimated 7,500 klansmen organized in 192 klaverns—more than double the number for any other state. (James Venable's National Knights ran a distant second, with one small klavern in Wilson.) Violence flared during 1965, with Exalted Cyclops Raymond Mills and two other klansmen arrested for bombings at New Bern, while August's Klan-inspired riots at Plymouth forced Governor Dan Moore to mobilize the National Guard. Exposure of the UKA's corruption during HUAC's hearing in 1965–66 drove some knights to quit the Klan entirely, while others defected into "pure" splinter groups. In 1967, George Dorsett joined James Cole to lead the new Confederate Knights, with covert backing from the FBI, but their effort was short-lived. Grand Dragon Jones received a one-year prison sentence for contempt of Congress in 1969, and his choice of Joseph Bryant as acting grand dragon suggested the low quality of talent available. A July 1969 shootout at Swan Quarter sent Bryant and sixteen others to jail, and Bryant deserted the UKA two months later, leading most of his followers into a new splinter faction, the North Carolina Knights. Unable to control the rank and file, Bryant was soon deposed by Virgil Griffin, who would dominate the Tarheel Klan over the next decade.

In the 1970s, Griffin faced competition from Joe Grady's White Knights of Liberty, seeking strength through an alliance with the neo–Nazi NSPA to create a bold United Racist Front. Their most surprising challenge came from Greensboro, where members of the tiny Communist Workers Party captured and

Robed UKA members and uniformed security guards march through Salisbury, North Carolina, on 21 August 1965 (HUAC).

Klan leaders pose at an August 1964 UKA rally near Salisbury, North Carolina. From left to right (standing): North Carolina Grand Dragon James Jones, Grand Klabee Fred Wilson, and South Carolina Grand Dragon Robert Scoggin.

burned a Klan banner, then celebrated their victory with announcement of a "Death to the Klan" rally on 3 November 1979. Klansmen and Nazis responded as they always have, with gunfire that left five victims dead and several more wounded. A series of state and federal trials failed to punish the killers, convincing some observers that the "New South" was a myth concocted by the media. Cross-burnings and violence continued through the 1980s, including an attempted lynching in Lincoln County (1981); shootings in Alexander, Cumberland, Durham and Iredell Counties (1982–83); and the rape-slaying of black victim Joyce Sinclair near a Klan rally site in Robeson County (1985). One member of the White Knights of Liberty pled guilty to terrorist violence in July 1985, accusing several of his komrades, while the Christian Knights were linked to cross-burnings in Charlotte and members of the White Patriot Party faced jail time for a 1986 robbery in Cumberland County.

The 1990s brought eight separate "patriot militias" to North Carolina, while anti-abortion terrorist Eric Rudolph chose the state as a hideout during 1997–2004, after bombings in Alabama and Georgia. Grand Dragon Charles Barefoot Jr., of the Nations Knights, pled guilty to weapons charges in January 2003, while police charged rival Dragon Anthony Brewer with plotting a murder. At press time for this volume, the Tarheel State harbored no less than eight active Klans: the Cleveland Knights (headquartered at Mt. Holly), the Confederate Knights (based at Henderson), the Free Knights, the Imperial Klans of America, the International White Knights (headquartered at Elizabethtown), the KKKK, the Southern White Knights, and the World Knights. Klan-allied or sympathetic groups are equally prolific, including the CCC (two chapters), League of the South (eight chapters), the National Alliance (six chapters), the National Socialist Movement, Wilmington's White Power Warehouse, White Revolution, and Women for Aryan Unity.

North Dakota—North Dakota seems an unlikely venue for the KKK, but kleagles still tried their hands in the Sioux State during the 1920s, recruiting at least 3,000 klansmen (50,000 in the *Washington Post*'s inflated estimate of November 1930). Those knights abstained from violence, but reports of bloodshed in other realms prompted passage of a 1923 anti-mask law applicable to any citizen over the age of fifteen. A state senator from Richland County spoke for most of his colleagues when he declared, "We don't want conditions in North Dakota to become such that a man must carry a pistol to be safe." The state's highest-ranking klansman, Rev. Halsey Ambrose, delivered a two-hour speech denouncing the law, but his effort backfired, producing a landslide vote in favor of the ban. Even unmasked, the KKK endured and took an active role in politics. Klan candidates did well throughout the state in 1924, and two years later the order won a clean sweep of municipal offices in Grand Forks (home of Rev. Ambrose). Despite such victories, however, klansmen found no enemies of any consequence to challenge them in North Dakota's overwhelmingly white Protestant population. Membership waned during the 1930s, then vanished entirely with national disbandment of the KKK in April 1944.

Hard times and racist propaganda brought some North Dakota dissidents into the Posse Comitatus fold during the 1970s and early 1980s. One of the most volatile was Gordon Kahl, a stubborn tax-evader and virulent anti–Semite who killed two U.S. marshals near Medina in February 1983, then fled to face a fiery death in Arkansas. The militant U.S. Taxpayers Party planted a chapter in Omaha during the 1990s, mixing calls for a "patriot militia" with praise for "pro-life" terrorism targeting abortion clinics, but the KKK was gone for good. Whatever prejudice may linger in the hearts and minds of individuals, at press time for this book SPLC investigators found no active hate groups in the state.

Ohio—Although perpetually overshadowed by the action in neighboring Indiana, Ohio may have been the Klan's most populous realm in the 1920s. Kleagles launched their great recruiting drive from Cincinnati in 1920, enlisting at least 240,000 members by 1923. (The *Washington Post* estimated 400,000, while historian David Chalmers pegged peak membership at half a million.) Akron and Columbus boasted 50,000 klansmen each, and imperial headquarters was pleased to charter the Buckeye realm in 1924, under Grand Dragon Clyde Osborn. Still, despite the massive turnout for Klan rallies and parades, opposition simmered, waiting to erupt. In Steubenville, rival Knights of the Flaming Circle dragged klansmen from their cars and beat them, while kleagles used the riots as another recruiting device. For all its numerical strength, the Ohio Klan's forays into politics produced only a handful of lackluster victories. Membership began declining in 1925, but the order had spread too far to die quickly. Hanging on as one of the KKK's top thirteen realms during the Great Depression, the Ohio KKK survived until national disbandment pulled the plug in April 1944.

In 1964–65, Wizard James Venable brought his National Knights to Ohio, planting small klaverns in Cincinnati, Columbus and Oregonia. Volatile members imported dynamite from Georgia and debated political assassinations, but they never followed through. Robert Shelton's UKA offered Venable some competition during 1966–67, establishing four klaverns with an estimated 100 members among them, while Venable fired back with an April 1967 campaign to ban "integrationist" textbooks from public schools in Akron, Canton and Cleveland. The National Knights remained active (albeit with few members) through 1975, when Grand Dragon Dale Reusch led defectors from several states into his new Invisible Empire Knights. Opponents in Columbus rioted against the fledgling Klan in July 1977, and it vanished by 1980, with dissident splinters remaining as the Independent Invisible Knights and the Ohio Knights. By 1987, the Ohio Knights stood alone, claiming fewer than 100 members.

In the 1990s, Ohio harbored no less than twenty-two separate "patriot militia" groups, some with ties to known white-supremacist organizations. Peter Langan, head of the bank-robbing Aryan Republican Army, was captured in Ohio after a January 1996 shootout with FBI agents. Klansmen returned to Ohio in the twenty-first century, and the state boasted seven active splinter groups at press time for this work. They include the Aryan Knights of the Confederacy (headquartered at Springfield), the Brotherhood of Klans (two klaverns), the Imperial

Klans of America (three klaverns), the Mystic Knights, the National Knights, the Southern White Knights and the U.S. Klans. Klan-friendly groups within the state include the CCC, the Creativity Movement, David Duke's EURO, the National Alliance (three chapters), and the National Socialist Movement (four chapters).

Oklahoma—Kleagles carried the Klan gospel into Oklahoma soon after William Simmons revived the order in 1915, and while no klaverns were formally chartered before 1920, Tulsa had a vigilante unit active three years earlier. The black-robed nightriders who whipped, tarred and feathered seventeen alleged IWW members on 9 November 1917 called themselves the Knights of Liberty, but an editorial in the *Tulsa World* described them as the "modern Ku Klux Klan." Victims of that attack reported that Tulsa's police chief and his officers donned hoods and robes themselves, after delivering their captives to the mob. Four years later, known klansmen participated in Tulsa's bloody race riot, killing at least thirty blacks (some reports say hundreds), while the vice president of Oklahoma's state university won appointment as grand dragon of the realm. Published estimates of the Sooner State's peak membership range from 95,000 to 239,500 klansmen and -women. Nightriders continued their early tradition of flogging labor unionists at Atoka and Bald Knob, also attacking blacks and Jews from time to time, but most of the state's flogging victims were whites selected for their failure to conform with Ku Klux standards of morality. Opposition to the order coalesced in 1922, when Governor John Walton was elected with support from unions and Klan-fearing Catholics. Fresh outbreaks of violence in summer 1923 prompted Walton to impose martial law, but he went too far by using troops to bar hostile state legislators from convening to consider his impeachment. After the courts upheld the legislature's right to meet, Walton's impeachment was a foregone conclusion, and he joined North Carolina's William Holden in the ranks of those who sacrificed political careers to fight the KKK. Despite that victory, the Klan was its own worst enemy in Oklahoma. By 1928, statewide membership had declined to some 20,000 and neither party welcomed Klan support in that year's elections. Whatever strength remained to the Klan blew away with Oklahoma's topsoil in the early 1930s and was lost beyond recall.

While Oklahoma's schools faced integration by court order after 1954, klansmen were busy elsewhere with the fight to stop race-mixing at the schoolhouse door. The troubled 1960s passed without a Klan revival in the Sooner State, and kleagles seemed to have no better fortune in the 1970s. A small Klan unit clashed with black protesters in the streets of Idabel, in early 1980, and Tullahassee's Mount Bethel Baptist Church was scarred with KKK graffiti in May 1985, but Oklahoma's handful of resident knights generally kept a low profile. The 1990s brought four "patriot militia" groups to Oklahoma, while self-styled members of the Phineas Priesthood staged armed robberies in Muskogee during 1991. Oklahoma City witnessed the decade's worst act of domestic terrorism on 19 April 1995, when former klansman Timothy McVeigh bombed the Alfred P. Murrah Federal Building, killing 168 persons. Six months later, police jailed leaders of the Oklahoma Constitutional Militia for plotting to bomb abortion clinics, gay bars, welfare offices, and the SPLC's headquarters in Montgomery, Alabama. At press time for this work, the Sooner State harbored four Ku Klux splinter groups: the Brotherhood of Klans (three klaverns), the Imperial Klans of America, the National Knights, and the Southern Patriot Organized Order of Knights (headquartered in Wynnewood). Tulsa also hosted two Klan-allied groups, David Duke's EURO and the neo–Nazi National Alliance.

Oregon—Kleagles entered Oregon from California in spring 1921, stressing nativism in their recruiting pitches, despite the Beaver State's small population of Catholics and Jews. By 1922, at least 50,000 Oregonians had joined the invisible empire (150,000 in the *Washington Post*'s estimate), and they enjoyed widespread success in state politics. Governor Ben Olcott told that year's conference of governors, "We woke up one morning and found the Klan had about gained political control of the state. Practically not a word had been raised against them." Portland was the epicenter of Klan influence and headquarters for Grand Dragon Fred Gifford, where klansmen included Mayor George Baker and K.K. Kubli, speaker of the state House of Representatives. In 1923, Oregon klansmen promoted a bill banning parochial schools, opposed by Catholics and hostile Seventh-Day Adventists alike. The bill was passed, mandating public school attendance by all Oregon children, but the U.S. Supreme Court declared it unconstitutional in 1925. By that time, Ku Klux membership was on the wane, and Oregon's knights could only help their 1926 senatorial candidate by publicly endorsing his opponent.

No Klan has breached Oregon's borders since the 1920s, but an equally virulent form of organized racism persists on the neo–Nazi fringe. Portland skinheads, inspired and encouraged by former California klansman Tom Metzger's White Aryan Resistance, murdered Ethiopian student Mulugeta Seraw on 13 November 1988, but the outburst cost them—and Metzger—dearly. While the slayers went to prison, a lawsuit filed by the SPLC cost Metzger and WAR $12.5 million in October 1990. Over the next decade, Oregonians rallied to the call of eight separate "patriot militia" groups. At press time for this book, active neo–Nazi groups in Oregon included the Aryan Nations (at North Bend) and the National Socialist Movement (in Eugene).

Pennsylvania—The KKK invaded Pennsylvania in late summer 1921, recruiting its first knights in Chester and Philadelphia Counties before Kleagle F.W. Atkins absconded with the realm's treasury and membership records. The order survived that early setback, enlisting at least 150,000 members by 1923 (twice that number in the *Washington Post*'s estimate), but the same year witnessed stiff opposition at Carnegie, where rioters blocked a Klan parade and killed one klansman as the hooded throng retreated. Violence continued through 1924, with floggings, riots, torture-slayings of at least two blacks, and the still-unsolved abduction of a three-year-old Pittsburgh girl whom klansmen allegedly snatched from her home. Two policemen suffered gunshot wounds during a chaotic Klan rally at Haverford College, but klansmen were their own worst enemies in the

The Pennsylvania Klan initiates new members in 1922 (Library of Congress).

latter 1920s. Keystone knights grew suspicious of Grand Dragon Samuel Rich's bookkeeping in 1925, and the quarrel soon spread to imperial headquarters. Wizard Hiram Evans fired Rich, but his replacement—Rev. Herbert Shaw—proved equally unpopular with klansmen in western Pennsylvania. Banishment and lawsuits followed, climaxed in April 1928 when Judge W.H.S. Thompson dismissed Atlanta's claims against the Keystone rebels, finding that the KKK came into court with "filthy hands" and was unworthy of relief. Despite all that, Pennsylvania remained one of the order's thirteen strongest realms during the 1930s, but its glory days were past and national disbandment broke the realm in April 1944.

Two years later, in August 1946, Governor Edward Martin sought FBI assistance in probing rumors of a statewide Klan revival, but no active klaverns were revealed. Another two decades elapsed before Robert Shelton's UKA raised the Klan banner in Pennsylvania, establishing a fifty-man klavern at Reading under Grand Dragon Roy Frankhouser. A dedicated anti–Semite who recruited his knights from the Minutemen and neo–Nazi groups, Frankhouser clung to his position through the early 1980s despite numerous arrests and his exposure as an FBI informant. In 1983, Klan-watchers reported marginal activity by the independent White Knights, replaced four years later by a White Unity Party (boasting fewer than 100 members). Pennsylvania hosted seven "patriot militia" groups during the 1990s, while guerrillas of the Aryan Republican Army robbed several banks in 1994–96. Jeff Berry's American Knights of the KKK maintained klaverns at Cokeburg and Prospect in 2000–02, briefly supplanted by the Aryan Nations Knights in 2003. At press time for this work, four Klans survived in Pennsylvania: the Imperial Klans of America, the Keystone Knights (headquartered in Johnstown), the Southern White Knights, and the World Knights. Klan-allied or sympathetic groups include the Aryan Nations, the CCC (three chapters), the Creativity Movement, the Keystone State Skinheads (nine chapters), the National Alliance (two chapters), the National Socialist Movement (four chapters), Volksfront, and Women for Aryan Unity.

Rhode Island—Kleagles scored a surprising success in the Ocean State during the 1920s, although published estimates of total membership vary widely, from 5,000 (Kenneth Jackson) to 15,000 (David Chalmers) or 21,321 (the *Washington Post*). Whatever the ultimate number, klansmen never found their political voice in Rhode Island, and membership apparently slipped to a hard-core 1,000 by early 1926. Two years later, the Providence *Journal* reported that klansmen had infiltrated three companies of the state militia, packing the ranks and funding acquisition of new weapons that included a machine gun. With Ku Klux officers in charge, all new militiamen were forced to join the Klan (at fifteen dollars per head) before receiving their uniforms. State legislators summoned Grand Dragon J.W. Perry to explain the situation, while Governor Norman Case disarmed the Klan-infested units. By 1930, statewide membership had plunged below 100, and the Rhode Island Klan soon vanished entirely. No effort has thus far been made to revive it, although a chapter of the militia-style U.S. Taxpayers Party met in Narragansett through the 1990s.

South Carolina—Klansmen in the Palmetto State trace their roots to February 1868, when Governor Benjamin Perry issued a call for white men to organize armed Democratic Clubs in defense of white supremacy. The KKK made its first public appearance a month later, in York County, with pranks and threats escalating into violence as November's presidential election drew closer. By autumn 1868, nightriding was reported from twelve northeastern counties, with the epicenter in Abbeville. Terrorists in Abbeville County murdered two state legislators that season, while barring some eighty percent of the county's black voters from casting their ballots on election day. (By comparison, roughly half of the registered freedmen voted in nearby Anderson and Laurens Counties.) Republicans still carried the state, with Governor-elect Robert Scott warning that any further terrorism might provoke another civil war. Klansmen generally kept a low profile over the next two years, with South Carolina reporting less racist violence than any other southern state except Virginia. The mayhem resumed in 1870, however, typified by the bloody pogrom in Laurens County, as Democrats launched a drive to recapture the state government. In York County, where an estimated 1,800 of the region's 2,300 white men were Klan members, authorities recorded eleven murders and more than 600 assaults between November 1870 and September 1871. Martial law, federal troops and sweeping prosecutions combined to suppress the official Klan during 1872–73, but its spirit (and members) survived in Wade Hampton's militant Red Shirt movement to "redeem" South Carolina at gunpoint for white supremacy and one-party rule. Hampton, named by some historians as the state's grand dragon, subsequently served as governor (1876–79) and in the U.S. Senate (1879–91).

After the Klan's rebirth, South Carolina was the last of ten realms chartered by Imperial Wizard William Simmons before Hiram Evans deposed him in 1922. By then, kleagles had scoured the state, faring best in piedmont districts, while enduring rejection on the coastal plains. Charleston was hostile enough that a 1923 mayoral candidate based his campaign on claims that he had suffered Klan harassment. Kenneth Jackson's estimate of 5,000 klansmen statewide is almost certainly too low, whereas the *Washington Post*'s 1930 estimate of 200,641 remains unsupported. Whatever the total, klansmen indulged in little nightriding and scored their only significant political victory with election of a brother as Columbia's mayor, in 1926. In 1939, Anderson and Greenville Counties emerged as strongholds of Klan opposition to organized labor, while Greenville County's sheriff joined klansmen to intimidate black voters in 1940. Several knights served prison time for flogging a white man in Anderson County, while their Greenville County brethren twice raided a black Youth Administration camp at Fountain Inn, whipping its occupants and posting signs that read: "Niggers, Your Place is in the Cotton Patch."

Disbandment of the parent Klan in April 1944 left local units at loose ends until Samuel Green's AGK took up the slack in 1946. Grand Dragon Thomas Hamilton defected three years later, creating his own militant Association of Carolina Klans with headquarters in Horry County and pockets of strength in neighboring Columbus County, North Carolina. Hamilton's klansmen raided a black nightclub at Myrtle Beach, severing the proprietor's ears and losing one of their own in an exchange of gunfire, but they avoided indictment until arrogant floggers lost sight of the Lindbergh Law's ban on interstate kidnapping. Border crossing raids prompted FBI arrests in February 1952, while state authorities weighed in with felony charges of their own. Hamilton and nine other knights subsequently received federal prison terms, while local juries convicted sixty-two of their komrades.

In May 1954, the U.S. Supreme Court's "Black Monday" ruling mobilized Klan resistance to school integration. The Georgia-based U.S. Klans faced spirited competition in South Carolina from splinter groups including the Association of South Carolina Klans, the Independent Knights, the National KKK, the Palmetto Knights, and the South Carolina Knights. In July 1961, Grand Dragon Robert Scoggin defected from the U.S. Klans to join Robert Shelton's new UKA, recruiting an estimated 800 members in fifty klaverns by 1966. Another 250 klansmen belonged to the dwindling ASCK, affiliated with James Venable's National Association of Ku Klux Klan. Despite tough talk, rumors of bombing seminars, and Scoggin's support for a hard-core militant Underground faction, the Palmetto State witnessed little actual violence before Scoggin drew a one-year prison sentence for contempt of Congress, in 1969.

Scoggin returned to find his membership shrunken by forty percent under the inept management of acting grand dragon Harry Gilliam. Banished from the UKA after quarrels with Wizard Shelton, Scoggin founded his own Invisible Empire Knights in 1970, and he briefly faced murder charges that July, after a UKA member was killed at a rally near Sumter. In 1976, Scoggin convened a Conference of Eastern Dragons in South Carolina, but the rally did not presage any widespread Klan revival. An independent faction, the Federated Knights, operated in both Carolinas through the early 1980s, but by 1987 only a small UKA contingent remained in the Palmetto State. Four "patriot militia" groups flourished statewide during the 1990s, while klansmen struggled to maintain their own identity. At press time for this work, active Klans in South Carolina included the Carolina White Knights (headquartered in Charleston), the Invisible Empire of the International Knights (based at Enoree), and the Southern White Knights. Other racist groups included the Aryan Nations, the CCC (three chapters), David Duke's EURO, the League of the South (thirty-three chapters), and the National Socialist Movement.

South Dakota—North Dakota klansman F. Halsey Ambrose tried to colonize the Mount Rushmore State in the 1920s, but he met with limited success. Nothing supports the *Washington Post*'s 1930 tabulation of 54,329 members, and most estimates peak below one-tenth of that number. In 1928, Alabama Senator (and klansman) Thomas Heflin canceled a South Dakota speaking engagement, when local knights could not provide him with an audience. Sparsely colonized by the Posse Comitatus in the 1970s, South Dakota hosted one chapter of the militant U.S. Taxpayers Party twenty years later, but SPLC observers found no active hate groups in the state at press time for this book.

Tennessee—Tennessee gave birth to the KKK, at Pulaski, in spring 1866 and witnessed the order's reorganization as a paramilitary resistance group to Congressional Reconstruction in April 1867. Grand Wizard Nathan Forrest conducted both his Klan and railroad business from Memphis, sharing state administrative duties with Grand Dragon (and Pulaski native) George Gordon. Phenomenal expansion followed the Klan's first public demonstrations, and Forrest claimed 40,000 members statewide by March 1868. Membership overlapped with the Pale Faces and other like-minded groups, but the bona fide KKK found its greatest strength in central and western Tennessee. Maury County was the center of Ku Klux violence, with klansmen raiding black homes and confiscating 400 guns in February 1868 alone, killing several persons and whipping many others (including one man who received 900 lashes). With Unionist "scalawag" William Brownlow as governor, the Volunteer State escaped military occupation during Reconstruction, but klansmen still vented their rage against freedmen and Republicans. In July 1868, the state legislature responded by authorizing a militia, thereby prompting Forrest and Gordon to form a committee of thirteen ex–Confederate generals (all klansmen) who pledged to maintain law and order if state troops were restrained. It seemed to work, briefly, but violence flared again on the eve of November's presidential election. Republicans carried the state, but President Grant's margin of victory fell 18,000 votes short of Governor Brownlow's in 1867, and klansmen in several western counties escalated their nightriding after the election. By 1869, even Klan-allied Democrats were fed up with the bloodshed, and Forrest issued his only proclamation as grand wizard on 25 January, banning any further Ku Klux demonstrations without direct orders from a grand giant or superior officer, further commanding that all Klan disguises be "entirely abolished and destroyed." Brownlow was unconvinced, declaring martial law in nine counties on 24 February 1869, but he left Tennessee for the U.S. Senate the same day, and his successor canceled the decree on 27 February. Democrats recaptured the state legislature in August 1869, and Tennessee klansmen retired to the status of southern folk heroes.

Racist leaders rally at the Klan's birthplace, Pulaski, Tennessee, in October 1989. From left to right: Louis Beam (in white suit), Aryan Nations chief Richard Butler (with bullhorn), and Jesse Stoner (with sign) (Southern Poverty Law Center).

Tennessee Governor William Brownlow raised militia companies to fight the KKK in Reconstruction.

The KKK returned to Tennessee in 1920, recruiting an estimated 35,000 members statewide (163,980 by the *Washington Post*'s tabulation) over the next three years. Klansmen made their great political push in 1923, seeking municipal offices in Chattanooga and Memphis, but the order's candidates met defeat in both cities. Membership declined thereafter, except in Chattanooga, where stubborn units clung to life through the Depression and World War II. Nightriders carried out sporadic floggings in the late 1940s, and cross-burnings drove a Jewish merchant out of Chattanooga, while Kleagle Jesse Stoner aggravated his superiors with calls for an American Holocaust. "Black Monday" revitalized the KKK to some extend in 1954, but the leaders who sparked violent resistance to school integration at Clinton in 1956 were outsiders Asa Carter and John Kasper. Kasper's efforts landed him in prison for contempt of court, while Chattanooga's klavern of the Georgia-based U.S. Klans defected in 1957 to become the rival Dixie Klans. Members made national headlines by joining in a statewide softball tournament, but nocturnal bombings conveyed the true sense of the order.

The turbulent 1960s failed to elicit the same response from Tennessee klansmen as from their brethren in neighboring states, but the realm was by no means inactive. Grand Dragon Raymond Anderson represented Robert Shelton's UKA from 1961 onward, with an estimated 225 members split among ten klaverns, while the Dixie Klans survived until 1970 with 150 members, loosely affiliated with James Venable's National Association of Ku Klux Klan. Chattanooga remained the Klan's stronghold through the 1980s, with local knights split between the Justice Knights and the United Empire Knights. Imperial Wizard Rocky Coker and another klansman were acquitted of wounding five black women in 1980, a verdict that sparked rioting in Chattanooga, but Coker's 1986 murder conviction sent him to death row. Meanwhile, UKA members burned a Knoxville home in July 1982 and scattered cross-burnings continued throughout the decade.

Tennessee welcomed the 1990s "patriot" movement, harboring three "militia" groups and ten chapters of the extremist U.S.

Taxpayers Party. Jeff Berry's American Knights of the KKK claimed isolated klaverns in 2000–02, then folded its robes when Berry went to prison. At press time for this book, the Ku Klux spirit was alive and well in Tennessee, represented by eleven splinter groups: the Brotherhood of Klans (two klaverns), the Cleveland Knights, the Imperial Klans of America, the Knights of Bedford Forrest (headquartered at Greenville), the KKKK, the Knights of Yahweh (headquartered at Dendridge), the Mystic Knights, the National Knights, the Southern White Knights, the U.S. Klans, and the World Knights. Like-minded groups include the CCC (six chapters), League of the South, the National Alliance (two chapters), and the National Socialist Movement.

Texas—Freewheeling violence was an established tradition in Texas long before the Civil War, and it only grew worse with the advent of Reconstruction. General Philip Sheridan, summarizing conditions in the Lone Star State in 1867, told friends that if he owned both Hell and Texas, he would rent out Texas and move to Hell. Authorities logged 1,035 murders statewide between April 1865 and July 1868, one-third of them committed in the latter year. Although whites outnumbered blacks in Texas three-to-one, nearly half the known victims were black. Whites committed at least 833 of the cataloged murders, versus 58 committed by blacks. The Klan made its first appearance at Marshall in April 1868, then spread quickly through eastern

The Texas Knights parade in Waco, September 1989 (Southern Poverty Law Center).

Texas, skirting Indian country and the eastern horn (where Hispanics lived in large numbers). The order announced its presence in Clarksville by attacking a black school party, but the worst violence occurred in counties bordering Arkansas and Louisiana. In the Red River counties, federal officers noted that whites had begun to massacre blacks "for the pure love of killing." Klansmen were not solely responsible, but they contributed their share to the carnage, assisted after autumn 1868 by the Knights of the Rising Sun. Jefferson and Marion Counties were the heart of operations for both groups, boasting rabid Democratic newspapers that included the *Ultra Ku Klux.* Military courts tried thirty-seven accused lynchers in early 1869, and while only six were convicted, the prospect of arrest drove the KRS to disband. By September 1869, another twenty-nine convictions before courts-martial led most KKK dens to follow suit.

Texas was the modern Klan's first self-governing realm, chartered in 1920, but the quality of its recruits declined over the next two years as membership peaked around 200,000 (450,000 in the *Washington Post*'s estimation), with more than 500 violent acts attributed to klansmen by 1922. From its launching pad in Houston, the order spread statewide, administered by Grand Dragon A.D. Ellis and Grand Titan Hiram Evans in Dallas. By the time Evans moved to Atlanta and muscled Wizard William Simmons out of office in November 1922, Lone Star knights were ready for a change. Politics was the answer, and the invisible empire scored some local victories—including capture of the sheriff's offices in Jefferson and Travis Counties—but a backlash soon developed. The KKK became a major political issue in 1924, when Miriam Ferguson won election as America's first female governor on an anti–Klan platform. By 1926, sporadic prosecutions and incessant bad publicity (including reports of eight men burned alive after kangaroo trials) cost the Texas Klan thousands of members. In Dallas alone, the ranks thinned from 16,000 to an estimated 1,200, while fewer than 18,000 knights remained statewide. Disbandment, when it came at last in April 1944, may have been viewed by most as a relief.

Surviving Texas klansmen faced a challenge in the decade after World War II. Residential integration sparked a series of bombings in Dallas during 1949, but Lone Star knights were relatively silent after the U.S. Supreme Court's "Black Monday" ruling five years later. Horace Miller's Aryan Knights established contact with neo–Nazis in Europe and Latin America, but it was still a two-man operation run from Miller's home in Waco. Dallas klansman Roy Davis made a more ambitious effort with his Original KKK in 1960, but his faction failed to thrive. Even Robert Shelton's UKA had difficulty tilling Texas soil, with three successive grand dragons appointed between summer 1965 and early 1966, all in pursuit of a paltry 200 members.

Texas knights saw a bit more action in the early 1970s, with future luminary Louis Beam leading the Houston faithful in a terrorist campaign against local leftists, pornography outlets, and the Pacifica network's radio stations. Affiliated with David Duke's KKKK by the end of the decade, Beam was also a prime mover in Klan harassment of Vietnamese refugees during 1980–81, until lawsuits filed by the SPLC forcibly restrained his klansmen. A year later, further lawsuits and injunctions closed Beam's paramilitary training camps, and he pulled up stakes to join the Aryan Nations as a racist "ambassador at large." In the vacuum created by his passing, the independent Original Knights sought protection in diverse identities, renaming their group the Knights of the White Camellia in 1983, then the Camellia White Knights in 1987. Still, Texas klansmen maintained their potential for violence. A bomb killed Dallas police informant Ward Keeton in January 1984, after he provided information on the local KKK and its ties to the American Nazi Party.

The 1990s brought the "patriot" movement to Texas, including ten well-armed "militia" units, five kangaroo "common-law courts," and the ill-conceived Republic of Texas (whose twenty chapters claimed that Texas was not and had never been a part of the United States). In April 1997, FBI agents jailed four klansmen for plotting to bomb a natural gas refinery outside Fort Worth, thereby endangering the lives of 30,000 residents. (All four pled guilty to conspiracy and were packed off to federal prison.) Jeff Berry's American Knights of the KKK claimed five Texas klaverns during 2000–02, then dissolved with its wizard's conviction on felony charges. At press time for this volume, active Texas Klans included the American White Knights, the Aryan Nations Knights, the Imperial Klans of America, the Mississippi White Knights, the National Knights (two klaverns), the Southern White Knights,, the Texas Knights of the Invisible Empire (headquartered in San Antonio), and the White Camelia Knights. Allied or sympathetic groups include the Creativity Movement, David Duke's EURO, the League of the South (nine chapters), the TCB Hate Crew (a Dallas skinhead gang), and Women for Aryan Unity.

Utah—The 1920s Klan in Utah focused its anger on Catholics, wisely avoiding conflict with the Beehive State's Mormon majority, but diplomacy produced no glut of members. Estimates of statewide membership range from 5,000 to an inflated 20,000 (by the *Washington Post*), and there is no evidence of nightriding. "Success" for Utah's knights meant retaliating for passage of an anti-mask law with legal action that barred Santa Claus (for his beard) from Salt Lake City's 1925 Christmas parade. Several thousand klansmen rallied in Provo that year, but interest and membership soon declined, leaving the KKK's political potential unrealized. California klansman Wesley Swift and anti-Semite Gerald L.K. Smith maintained friendly relations with Governor J. Bracken Lee in the early 1950s, but the flirtation signaled no access to power.

The Klan returned to Utah in summer 1975, recruiting seven members for a small Riverton klavern of David Duke's KKKK by August. Nearly four years passed before the group announced itself with a nocturnal cross-burning at Riverton City Park, on 9 June 1979. Four months later, klansmen hanged two black effigies at a local cemetery and posted racist signs. By early 1980, the Klan claimed four more klaverns (in Kearns, Murray, Sandy and Salt Lake City) plus a unit of the KYC for young prospects. The group's first public demonstration, at Weber State College in Ogden, on 14 May 1980, preceded a rift in the ranks. Some 225 members defected to form a new Utah KKK, while something less than 100 remained loyal to the KKKK in Salt Lake City. Both groups recruited from the Aryan Nations and local motorcycle gangs, but neither endured. The UKKKK "went underground" in May 1981, while the KKKK simply faded away. A Davis County corrections officer donned Klan regalia to frighten a black prisoner in April 1983, but no evidence linked him to either known faction. Organized hate groups were scarce at press time for this volume, with a single chapter of the National Alliance reported from Salt Lake City.

Vermont—As in most other realms, published reports conflict as to the progress made by 1920s kleagles in the Green Mountain State. Scholar Kenneth Jackson estimates peak membership at 2,000, while the *Washington Post* granted an overly generous 80,301 in November 1930. Vermont's relative importance to the invisible empire may be judged by the fact that it constituted one-third of a special New England realm, sharing officers with Maine and New Hampshire. Grand Dragon Eugene Farnsworth ruled that mini-kingdom in the early 1920s, drawing most of his Vermont recruits from the state's northern sector, producing some impressive rallies at Montpelier and Morrisville. Klan pride and membership suffered thereafter, when a kleagle was jailed for robbing St. Mary's Cathedral in Burlington, and the realm apparently dissolved before the onset of the Great Depression.

A half-century of inactivity ended in June 1982, with a cross-burning at Concord and telephone threats to black residents of Burlington. The Klan's latest spokesman denied any link between his group and criminal activity. "It is," he told reporters, "in some cases, young people doing what they think the Klan would approve of." In the 1990s, Vermont was generally immune to "militia" fever, though it harbored one small chapter of the extremist U.S. Taxpayers Party in Burlington. At press time for this work, the Mississippi White Knights claimed members in Vermont, but SPLC investigators could not pinpoint the klavern's location.

Virginia—The original Klan reached Virginia in spring 1868, its public notices published in Democratic newspapers over several weeks in March and April. No evidence exists of any widespread organization, and while sporadic nightriding occurred in

Top: Virginia klansmen enjoy an outing in 1920 (Southern Poverty Law Center). *Above:* Virginia klansmen stage a parade in 1922 (Library of Congress).

Lee County between June and December 1868, klansmen elsewhere generally refrained from violence, doubtless thankful that their state was exempted from military Reconstruction. "Redemption" for white "home rule" could be won at the ballot box, without sweeping resort to terrorism in the countryside.

Kleagles returned to the Old Dominion State in the 1920s, and they met concerted opposition from the start. Virginia's established political leaders were uniformly hostile to the Klan, but some local success was achieved in the state's southeastern quadrant, where authorities reported scattered raids and whippings. Estimates of total membership range from 20,000 (with 2,500 klansmen dwelling in Richmond) to the *Washington Post*'s inflated estimate of 169,630. Perhaps because Virginia klansmen seldom ventured into politics or nightriding, their realm was one of thirteen listed by imperial headquarters as retaining a substantial membership during the 1930s. National disbandment finished off Virginia's KKK in April 1944, and two decades elapsed before a new generation of knights tried their hands one more time.

Virginia politicians coined the term "massive resistance" for the South's response to court-ordered school integration in 1954, but native racists were content to let the "respectable" Citizens' Councils fight their battles without turning to the vulgar KKK. A striking exception to the rule was George Rockwell's American Nazi Party, launched from headquarters in Arlington in 1958. Grand Dragon Sandy Coley supervised the Old Dominion realm of Robert Shelton's UKA in spring 1965, but it took another year and the appointment of Grand Dragon Marshal Kornegay to secure an estimated 1,250 knights in thirty-two klaverns. Elected officials remained hostile to the order, and a spate of 1966 cross-burnings prompted Governor Mills Goodwin to post rewards for the arrest of those responsible. Police jailed five cross-burners in January 1967, including one woman and a state prison guard, and Kornegay's complaints of harassment fell on deaf ears, with Governor Goodwin calling the Klan "obnoxious."

Still, the KKK endured into the 1980s, with fiery crosses planted at the homes of blacks and Jews throughout the decade. William Upchurch, a leader of the Justice Knights acquitted in 1980 of shooting black women in Chattanooga, Tennessee, drew prison time for raping a seven-year-old Amelia County girl in November 1982. (His victim was white.) The Virginia Citizens Militia drilled at Roanoke in the 1990s, while "pro-life" zealots rallied to the U.S. Taxpayers Party and authorities recorded sporadic hate crimes statewide. Jeff Berry's Indiana-based American Knights colonized Woodbridge during 2001–02, then disbanded when its leader went to prison. At press time for this volume, Virginia hosted four Klans: the Imperial Klans of America, the Mystic Knights, the Rebel Brigade Knights (headquartered in Martinsville), and the Southern White Knights. Klan-friendly groups include the CCC (two chapters), David Duke's EURO, the League of the South (five chapters), the National Alliance (two chapters), and the National Socialist Movement.

Washington

Washington—After scoring significant success in Oregon, klansman Luther Powell moved to Seattle in early 1923, serving as king kleagle for Washington and Idaho. Again, he found no shortage of recruits, although estimates of the Evergreen State's peak membership vary widely from 25,000 (Kenneth Jackson) to 40,000 (David Chalmers) or 150,000 (*Washington Post,* November 1930). By early 1924, Powell claimed forty-two active klaverns statewide, with the largest found in Seattle, Spokane, Tacoma and Walla Walla. A Canadian immigrant, Dr. M.W. Rose, commanded the state's RRRR for naturalized citizens (later merged with the national American Krusaders). When Imperial Wizard Hiram Evans visited Washington in 1924, he was welcomed in Moose halls, honored with banquets by the Seattle Chamber of Commerce, and Scottish Rites Masons, and cheered by his legions in Seattle, Spokane and Tacoma. Klaverns in Bellingham and Seattle welcomed seamen from visiting naval vessels, and Powell claimed that U.S. Navy Klan No. 1 (provisional) was active aboard the battleship *Tennessee.* Be that as it may, the Washington realm never mustered enough political strength to elect candidates or secure passage of its mandatory public schooling bill. The KKK survived into the early 1930s, but its presence, while apparent, had no significant impact.

Kleagles generally ignored the Pacific Northwest after World War II, until Richard Butler moved his Church of Jesus Christ Christian from California to Idaho and founded the Aryan Nations as the cult's political arm. Michigan guru Robert Miles envisioned Washington as part of a future "White Bastion," and younger militants took his dream to heart in the 1980s. Guerrillas of The Order, including several klansmen, staged their first bombing and bank robbery in Seattle, in 1983. The following year, leader Robert Mathews died in a shootout with FBI agents on Whidbey Island, in Puget Sound. In December 1985, lone-wolf psychotic David Rice killed four members of Seattle's Goldmark family, proclaiming the slaughter a blow against "the Jewish-Communist conspiracy." Sporadic cross-burnings and hate crimes continued over the next two decades, while a Yakima County Militia trained for war in the 1990s. In October 1996, four self-styled Phineas Priests mimicked The Order in Spokane, robbing two banks and bombing various targets including more banks, a newspaper, and the local Planned Parenthood office. No Klans remained in Washington at press time for this book, but like-minded groups include the Creativity Movement, the Aryan Nations, and the National Alliance (two chapters).

West Virginia

West Virginia—Severed from its parent state before the Civil War, West Virginia was loyal to the Union in that conflict and harbored no Klan during Reconstruction. Kleagles worked the Mountain State industriously in the early 1920s, recruiting at least 18,000 members (75,903 by the *Washington Post*'s calculation). Klansmen dabbled in the affairs of both political parties, scoring some local success on both sides, and they allegedly comprised more than half of the state's delegation to the 1924 Democratic National Convention. Mine owners used klansmen as coalfield strikebreakers, but members of the growing United Mine Workers generally held their own in those rough-and-tumble confrontations. Mingo County's knights threatened violence to prevent black champion Jack Johnson from boxing locally, but bad publicity ensued when hooded raiders accidentally killed a white woman in Logan County. William Conley, owner of the pro–Klan *Fellowship Forum,* won election as governor in 1928, while Klan votes dashed the hopes of Catholic presidential candidate Al Smith. Several active klaverns survived into the Great Depression, finally dissolving when the KKK disbanded nationwide, in April 1944.

The post-war years proved barren for the West Virginia Klan, although kleagle (later Senator) Robert Byrd lobbied Samuel Green for an AGK charter in 1946. The bombing of a newly-integrated school in 1958 signaled no Klan revival, and none of America's eighteen active Klans claimed any West Virginia klaverns in the 1960s. A flurry of fifteen cross-burnings startled residents of Beckley and Clarksburg in 1980, and hooded knights hounded Rev. Michael Curry from his Smithburg home in June, after he refused to let a klansman speak from the pulpit of his church. Subsequent cross-burnings occurred in Wheeling (March 1983) and Princeton (autumn 1985), but the knights who lit them were seldom seen. At press time for this work, active West Virginia Ku Klux factions included the Imperial Klans of America, the Knight Riders of the KKK (headquartered at Daniels), and the White Shield Knights (based at Mineral Springs). Collaborating groups include the National Socialist Movement and White Revolution.

Wisconsin—The 1920s Klan gained its first Badger State converts among Milwaukee's businessmen and professionals, holding its first formal meeting aboard a U.S. Coast Guard cutter. Masons flocked to the order, despite protests from their Grand Master, and a surprising number of Socialists also joined the order. Estimates of Wisconsin's peak membership range from a very conservative 15,000 to the *Washington Post*'s laughable 220,850. Whatever the true figure, klansmen did well in local elections in Chippewa County, as well as Kenosha, Oshkosh and Racine. Madison's mayor deputized klansmen for a special liquor-raiding squad, unleashing them in Little Italy. Klansman Dan Woodward polled 40,000 votes in his 1924 Senate race, but he still lost out to popular Progressive incumbent Robert La Follette. Internal quarrels led to schisms in the late 1920s, with splinter group's draining off most of the realm's membership, and observers found no active klaverns remaining in early 1932.

No significant Ku Klux activity was recorded in Wisconsin between World War II and the advent of the new millennium, but the anti–Semitic Posse Comitatus found favor with some of the state's hard-pressed farmers in the 1970s. James Wickstrom, self-proclaimed "counterinsurgency director" for the Midwestern Posses, served prison time for counterfeiting in the early 1990s, while Wisconsin super-patriots pledged allegiance to the militant U.S. Taxpayers Party. At press time for this volume, Wisconsin harbored two competing Klan factions—the Brotherhood of Klans (two klaverns) and the National Knights. Sympathetic groups include the Aryan Nations, the Creativity Movement, and the National Socialist Movement (two chapters).

Wyoming—Residents of the Equality State largely ignored the 1920s Klan, although the *Washington Post*'s inflated membership estimate from November 1930 counted 24,989 members. Kenneth Jackson's figure of 1,000 may be nearer the mark. Imperial Wizard Hiram Evans suffered embarrassment when he included Wyoming on the itinerary of his national tour in 1924. First, Casper klansmen could not fill the rented meeting hall, and when deacons of the First Christian Church identified Evans, they canceled the date entirely. Six decades later, in June 1986, three masked white men threatened a black traveler passing through Rock Springs and fired a shot into his car, but investigators found no evidence of any organized Ku Klux activity. The state's sole active hate group, at press time for this work, was a small chapter of the neo–Nazi National Alliance in Douglas.

The Klan International

Australia—The spirit of the KKK infected Australia during World War II, when thousands of American servicemen were stationed Down Under. In the 1950s, neo–Nazi Graeme Royce of New South Wales corresponded with various U.S. Klan leaders, and several spokesmen later claimed to represent the order on Australian soil. In 1978, David Callahan of Katherine, Northern Territory, proclaimed himself the Australian national director and coordinator for David Duke's KKKK, convening several rallies that drew sizable crowds. The same year saw one of

Callahan's knights, policeman David Jennings, jailed for wounding three Aborigines with shotgun fire and chaining nine others together as a "work gang." In the mid–1980s, Kevin Bourke of Murumbeena, Victoria, served as kleagle for the U.S.–based IEKKKK. (Like then–Wizard James Farrands, Bourke was a staunch Catholic.) The latter 1980s brought reports of men in Klan regalia terrorizing Aborigines at Mareeba and Rockhampton, Queensland, while threatening letters and hangman's nooses were mailed to other targets in Queensland and Western Australia.

Peter Coleman, a founder of Australia's far-right One Nation party, announced the KKK's revival Down Under on 1 June 1999, proclaiming that the Kentucky-based Imperial Klans of America (which he served as grand dragon) had already enlisted seventy members. "I'm happy to shout it from the rooftops," Coleman told reporters. "Our aim is for a white Australia, a fair Australia." One Nation instantly expelled Coleman, but executive director David Etteridge proclaimed Klan infiltration of his party inevitable, "because the media kept telling extremists that we were an extremist organization." A second party member, Robert Leys, was expelled one week later, after declaring himself grand titan of the rival Australian Knights. (Aborigine spokesman Gatjil Djerrkura observed: "One Nation party officials can talk until they're blue in the face about expelling people such as Peter Coleman but they know and we know they are responsible for giving them legitimacy.") The IKA claimed klaverns in New South Wales, Queensland and Victoria, while the AKKKK initially boasted eleven chapters in New South Wales alone (later scaled back to five nationwide). Meanwhile, the Missouri-based New Order Knights announced plans for its own Aussie invasion. Grand Titan Leys soon confused matters further, by denying Klan membership and claiming affiliation with Matt Held's World Church of the Creator. David Palmer, imperial wizard of the AKKKK, responded by confirming Leys's link to the Klan and praising the "excellent work he has done in getting people organized."

Immigration Minister Phillip Ruddock banned visits by IKA Imperial Wizard Ronald Edwards and other American klansmen, but the KKK expanded nonetheless. In January 2000, persons unknown murdered a schoolteacher at Brewarrina, New South Wales, and scrawled "KKK" on his body, but police dismissed the graffiti as a false lead. In April 2001, IKA officer Colin Houston donned black robes and brandished a club while "patrolling" outside an Aboriginal housing project in Casino, New South Wales. The AKKKK announced its presence in South Australia during January 2002, while Matt Hale's racist "church" (subsequently renamed the Creativity Movement) also claimed a chapter in Unley, South Australia, but the cult apparently disbanded with Hale's imprisonment in 2004. On 28 December 2004, thirty self-declared klansmen in full regalia raided an Aboriginal shanty town near Townsville, Queensland, threatening to "bash the lot of you" unless the residents moved on. Five months later, Internet postings from the IKA's anonymous chaplain claimed the Aussie Klan receives three membership inquiries daily, "on a good day."

Austria—On 21 February 1960, police in Vienna announced their discovery of a neo–Nazi cell with links to the KKK. Confiscated propaganda, inscribed "Ku Klux Klan of America," was subsequently traced to Horace Miller's Aryan Knights in Waco, Texas. Four decades later, in 2001, fugitive ex-klansman David Duke visited Austria to fraternize with modern fascist leaders who presumably share his views on "racial nationalism."

Canada—Canada has endured more KKK activity than any other country outside the United States. Montreal witnessed the first newspaper announcement of Canadian Klan recruiting on 1 October 1921, and local knights held their first meeting two nights later, in an abandoned quarry. For whatever reason, Atlanta headquarters responded on 19 October with flat denials of any interest in a Canadian realm, and the Montreal klavern apparently disbanded. In 1922, Klan threats preceded a series of arson attacks on Catholic churches; a Catholic rest home in Oka, Québec; and St. Boniface College in Winnipeg (claiming the lives of ten victims). Wizard William Simmons denied Klan involvement in the fires, but the imperial attitude toward Canada clearly had changed.

The *Cranbrook Courier* published British Columbia's first KKK advertisement on 17 November 1922, while American kleagles Eugene Farnsworth and W.L. Higgett reached Toronto in autumn 1923. November saw thirty-two knights initiated at Hamilton, and Toronto claimed 8,000 klansmen by June 1925. Meanwhile, three Oregon kleagles launched a Vancouver recruiting drive in 1924, enrolling some 8,000 members over the next three years. Klan spokesmen claimed 13,000 members in British Columbia by 1927, but only 200 of a predicted 5,000 turned out for that year's great parade in Vancouver. Alberta welcomed its first kleagles in 1925, boasting eleven active klaverns by 1930 and forty the following year. Klan membership in Alberta peaked around 7,000, but its provincial newspaper (*The Liberator*) reached an estimated 100,000 readers. New Brunswick hosted a half-dozen klaverns by August 1925. Kleagles Hugh Emmons, Harold Scott and L.A. Scott (Harold's father) began colonizing Saskatchewan in late 1926. The following year, they claimed eleven thriving klaverns, drawing 8,000 faithful to a rally at Moose Jaw in June 1927, but police jailed Emmons and L.A. Scott near year's end, for absconding with $100,000 from the Klan's treasury. Ironically, their trial boosted recruiting, and Kleagle J.J. Maloney claimed more than 100 klaverns in the province before authorities deported him in summer 1928. After its violent debut in 1922, Winnipeg's Klan did not formally organize until June 1928. Nationwide, membership estimates range upward from 25,000, while wishful-thinking klansmen claimed 50,000 in Saskatchewan alone.

Wherever they rallied, Canadian klansmen imitated their role models in the United States. Orators railed against immigrants and minorities, adjusting their message to suit local audiences—attacking Chinese in British Columbia, Eastern Europeans in Alberta, French Canadians in Ontario and Saskatchewan. In the latter province, members of the anti–Catholic Orange Order made eager recruits, and Protestant ministers flocked to the KKK's banner (at least twenty-six in Saskatchewan alone). Klansmen tarred and feathered a promiscuous black-

smith at Lacombe, Alberta, in May 1930. Two years later, they joined company strikebreakers to attack the Red-affiliated Mine Workers Union at Crowsnest Pass. Politically, Canadian knights favored the Conservative Part. Saskatchewan's kligrapp was a Tory, and the realm's klabee served as Regina's M.P. during 1917–21. By 1928, Saskatchewan's Klan claimed the allegiance of eight mayors, eleven village clerks, seven reeves, twelve secretary-treasurers, thirty-seven councilors and several police chiefs. David Mullin, Alberta's minister of agriculture, was a klansman, and some historians maintain that John Diefenbaker joined the KKK thirty years before his election as Canada's prime minister (1957–63).

As in America, the Great Depression winnowed Ku Klux ranks in Canada. Klansmen and prospective members found it difficult to pay their dues, and many drifted off to join pro–Nazi groups such as Manitoba's Canadian Nationalist Party, the Canadian Union of Fascists, Québec's National Socialist Christian Party, or Ontario's Swastika Club. Tory leaders funneled $18,000 to the NSCP in 1930, followed by another $27,000 in 1936, while Ku Klux klaverns withered on the vine. Saskatchewan's realm held its last annual klonvokation in 1930. Seven years later, only 250 Alberta klansmen appeared for the realm's final picnic. By the start of World War II in 1939, no trace of the invisible empire remained.

The next stirring occurred at Amherstburg, Ontario, where nocturnal prowlers lit a cross on 9 August 1965 and scrawled "Niggers Beware" on a nearby church. Before year's end, William Beattie's Canadian Nazi Party sparked a riot by 5,000 opponents at Toronto's Allan Gardens. German immigrant Martin Weide seized control of the group in 1967, renaming it the Canadian National Socialist Party, but it soon dissolved despite his best efforts. In 1968, future klansmen Donald Andrews and Paul Fromm founded the neo–Nazi Edmund Burke Society, renamed the Western Guard in 1972. Michigan klansman Robert Miles addressed a Western Guard banquet in Toronto on 1 May 1972. Later that month, Ian Macpherson and four friends incorporated the Confederate Klan of Alberta, claiming eleven active klaverns by August. In 1974, Western Guard member Armand Siksna opened correspondence with KKKK leader David Duke, although three years elapsed before Duke visited Toronto to inaugurate a klavern under Siksna's leadership. Alberta officials, meanwhile, dissolved Ian Macpherson's Klan in 1975, while Macpherson awaited trial for the September 1974 killing of a Mexican man at his Calgary home. (Macpherson claimed the shooting was an accident, escaping with a $2,000 fine for negligent use of a firearm.) John Ross Taylor, a veteran Nazi from the 1930s, fraternized with Midwestern knights and attended David Duke's 1976 "international congress" in New Orleans, two years before he replaced Don Andrews as chief of the Western Guard. Another Western Guard member, Jacob Prins, declared himself Canadian grand dragon for Dale Reusch's Invisible Empire Knights in 1976.

The 1980s brought confusion to Canadian Klanwatchers. Ian Macpherson (alias Teàrlach Barra Eoin Ros Dunsford Mac a'Phearsoin) registered his new Invisible Empire Association of Alberta in February 1980, while Western Guard veterans James McQuirter, Armand Siksna, Wolfgang Droege and Jacob Prins launched the Canadian Knights in Toronto. The November 1980 announcement of KKK recruiting in Halifax, Nova Scotia, prompted creation of a local Coalition Organizing to Oppose the Klan. Al Hooper served as McQuirter's kleagle in British Columbia, claiming 200 members there by 1982, while McQuirter boasted of 7,500 recruits nationwide. Other estimates were more modest, as with author Stanley Barrett's 1987 tabulation of 221 klansmen for all of Canada. The Klan's largest single rally, in summer 1981, drew forty-five members in British Columbia, where Al Hooper admitted recruiting "a lot of bikers." On 3 June 1988, police jailed three IEA members for plotting to bomb the Calgary Jewish Center and the home of a Jewish businessman. Prosecutors named Wizard Macpherson as the plot's mastermind, and while they failed to indict him, Macpherson's Klan dissolved in February 1989, after his knights filed guilty pleas in court. Eight months later, Winnipeg teenager Bill Harcus—an ex–Satanist convert to Christian Identity, affiliated with the SS Action Group and several skinhead gangs—corresponded with the Missouri Knights, praising their order in his magazine *Maximum National Socialism.*

The 1990s brought a new flurry of Ku Klux activity in Canada. Spring 1990 saw Bill Harcus inaugurated as grand dragon of the Manitoba Knights, while skinhead ex-convict Michel Larocque revived Québec's realm in collaboration with Imperial Wizard James Farrands of the IEKKKK (buying his robes from Harcus). Larocque also teamed with Exalted Cyclops Alain Roy to found White Power Canada as a "junior Klan" for skinheads who could do the order's dirty work. (Four WPC members killed Yves Lalonde in November 1990, after mistaking him for a homosexual. All four pled guilty to second-degree murder in April 1993.) By autumn 1990, Eric Vachon had replaced Larocque as grand dragon of the IEKKKK, while Larocque moved on to organize the Longitude 74 KKK (named for Montreal's map coordinates). That venture lasted a year, replaced by Larocque's *Mouvement des Revendictations des Droits de la Majorité* in alliance with Thomas Robb's Arkansas-based KKKK. Canadian authorities responded with a flurry of charges in 1991. November saw three of Michel Larocque's klansmen arrested for smuggling hate literature, while Manitoba police jailed Bill Harcus and klansman Theron Skyrba in December, for advocating genocide. Allegations of police perjury scuttled the case against Harcus and Skyrba, but the Québec knights were fined $500 apiece in April 1992. Three months later, Alain Roy led his WPC skinheads to Ste-Anne-de-Sorrel for an "Aryan Fest" celebration, joined by Wolfang Droege, Holocaust-denial spokesman Ernst Zundel, and Church of the Creator members led by George Burdi. Canadian klansmen still make news from time to time, as when arsonists torched the Carlsbad Springs, Ontario, home of Ian Macdonald—a former diplomat, known in the 1980s for his ties to the Canadian Knights and various neo–Nazi groups—on 16 March 2005.

Chile—On 24 May 1958, police in Santiago jailed several members of a local KKK chapter whom they accused of terrorizing local Jewish merchants. Investigators said the Chilean knights obtained their literature and inspiration from Horace Miller's Aryan Knights in Waco, Texas.

China—In the early 1920s, foreign reports suggested that one or more klaverns may have been organized among Americans residing in Shanghai. While it is not impossible, no evidence supports those claims today.

Cuba—Rumors of Klan activity emerged from this Caribbean island during April 1924, but no detailed reports or other evidence exist to validate the vague rumors.

Czechoslovakia—On 30 November 1924, the *New York Times* reported that KKK propaganda leaflets had been distributed throughout Czechoslovakia, announcing creation of a foreign realm opposed to "Germans, Jews, Clericals and Communists." No other evidence supports the claim, but real-life klansmen surfaced seven decades later. In 1991, young neo–Nazi skinheads in the Czech Republic rallied to a fledgling KKK and other racist groups, including the *Bílá Liga* (White Brotherhood). On 24 November 1991, 1,000 right-wing thugs from several collaborating groups staged a demonstration in Prague's Wenceslas Square, brawling with hecklers and chanting, "Gypsies to the gas chambers!"

Dominica—The Caribbean island of Dominica (not to be confused with the Dominican Republic) fell under KKK scrutiny in 1980, when deposed Prime Minister Patrick John sought mercenary warriors to unseat successor Mary Charles. In return for that service, John offered $150,000 in cash and various future rewards to the victors. Ex-convict Michael Perdue took the bait, recruiting KKKK Imperial Wizard Stephen Black to furnish men, weapons and explosives for the mission. Canadian klansman and smuggler Wolfgang Droege signed on in hopes that "free" Dominica might become his new base of operations. Soldiers enlisted for the putsch included an ex-police chief from Kansas plus various klansmen and neo–Nazis, Mississippi fugitive Joe Daniel Hawkins among them. Their plan, fueled by visions of slavery and limitless wealth, involved a ten-man amphibious invasion and conquest of the capital (Roseau), wherein Klan shock troops would defeat local police and clear the way for John's triumphant return. To that end, Black and Perdue chartered a boat from Mike Howe of New Orleans and prepared to launch their strike from a marina on Lake Ponchartrain. The plan fizzled when Howe betrayed the plotters to ATF agents, who arrested Black and company with their cache of weapons on 27 April 1981. Federal prosecutors charged all ten conspirators with weapons violations and breach of the Neutrality Act. Seven defendants pled guilty, while Black, Hawkins, and Michael Norris stood for trial. Jurors convicted Black and Hawkins on 27 April 1981, acquitting Norris on his plea that he believed he had been working for the CIA. The rest received three-year prison terms, augmented in Droege's case by thirteen years on unrelated drug, immigration and weapons charges. Bemused ATF agents christened Black's great adventure the "Bayou of Pigs."

England—Klansmen have always cited their Anglo-Celtic roots, even belatedly adopting the ritual of cross-burning from medieval Scottish clans. Still, the KKK made no appearance in Great Britain until April 1957, when rumors of pamphleteering and recruitment campaigns prompted an investigation by Scotland Yard's detectives. Within a month, investigators announced their discovery of active klaverns in Birmingham, Bishop's Castle, Fleetwood, Liverpool, Southend, and the London working-class suburbs of Brixton and Kilburn. Police estimated British Klan membership around 1,000, affiliated with Horace Miller's Aryan Knights in Waco, Texas. Alarmed by the yearly influx of 30,000 nonwhite immigrants, English klansmen threatened landlords of minority tenants and called for boycotts of nonwhite merchants.

The movement had virtually disappeared by April 1965, when UKA Imperial Wizard Robert Shelton visited London to predict a KKK resurgence. On 7 June 1965, nightriders lit a cross at the Birmingham home of an Indian immigrant, and klansmen held their first public meeting six days later, cut short by a Birmingham pub owner who regretted renting them his upstairs room. Before the gathering was interrupted, spokesman George Newey addressed the gathering of thirteen men and three women, promising that the KKK would "rid this country of filthy niggers." That same day witnessed several cross-burnings in London, and at the homes of nonwhite residents. A similar incident on 14 June marked England's sixth cross-burning in a week, while police announced discovery of active klaverns in Birmingham, Leicester, Liverpool, London and Manchester. On 15 June, British authorities banned further visits by Shelton, but sporadic KKK activity continued through mid–August, when 100 West Indians from Birmingham and London convened to organize an anti–Klan resistance movement.

England's Klan had vanished again by the mid–1970s, but race remained a volatile issue. Race riots injured hundreds in London, during 1976–77, while the neo–Nazi National Front claimed 10,000 members by September 1977. The temptation proved too much for Louisiana klansman David Duke. Arriving in March 1978, Duke recruited "several dozen" knights and blitzed the media with hit-and-run interviews before authorities could capture and deport him. Over several weeks, Duke led police on a merry chase, once posing in full regalia outside the Tower of London, until he was finally bagged and expelled. Rival Bill Wilkinson was likewise banned from England, but he still claimed a handful of British recruits prior to his exposure as a longtime FBI informant.

Klansman Dennis Mahon slipped past British authorities in 1991, counting Derbyshire's Ian Donaldson (lead singer of the racist rock band Skrewdriver) among his handful of recruits. In the early 1990s, Wizard James Farrands picked up where predecessor Bill Wilkinson left off, organizing several klaverns under Allan Beshella before Beshella defected to lead his own Invisible Empire, United Klans of Europe (also called the British Knights). Beshella dominated the British Klan scene until *Searchlight* magazine exposed his 1972 arrest on charges of child molestation, whereupon he ceded power to newsagent Alan Winder. Winder, in turn, established a new front group—No. 03409828, the Invisible Empire (Europe) Ltd.—to insulate his Klan from charges of peddling illegal racist literature. British Klan membership peaked around 400 in the 1990s, then swiftly declined as internal quarrels wracked the order. White supremacist attorney Kirk Lyons and William Pierce, founder of the neo–Nazi National Alliance, addressed rallies of the British National Party during 1995–96, while the National Socialist Irish Workers Party and the National Socialist Party of the United Kingdom shared a post office box in Bethlehem, Pennsylvania. By 1998, *Searchlight* editor Gerry Gable estimated total Klan membership in the United Kingdom at 200, but he warned that "[t]he new Klan is attracting the worst kind of racists. A lot of people here see it as the group that has stayed the course, despite its ups and downs. There's that kind of admiration. Today, if you look at the movement in Europe, the street movement of violent activists, the inspiration definitely comes from the States. It's Louis Beam and Bob Mathews [of The Order]. Mathews is everyone's martyr over here. They name their kids after Bob Mathews."

France—Parisian authorities banned screenings of *The Birth of a Nation* in 1923, insisting that scenes of the Klan lynching blacks be deleted, but fascist groups flourished in France a decade later, and some Frenchmen welcomed the Nazi occupation of 1940–45. In 2002, Jean-Marie Le Pen's Front National entertained American fugitive David Duke, Le Pen posing for photos with his arm around Duke's shoulders. That summer, Duke's EURO announced plans to host the website of Radical Unity, a racist group banned by French officials after one of its members tried to assassinate President Jacques Chirac.

Germany—Inspired by the Klan's financial and political success in America, naturalized U.S. citizens Rev. Otto Strohschein and his son Gotthard returned to their native Berlin in February 1921 and there founded *Der Deutsche Orden des Fuerigen Kreuzes* (the German Order of Fiery Crosses). Donald Gray, an American employed at the Siemens Electrical Works, assisted in formation of the order, cribbed its membership oath from Masonic texts, and later emerged as the group's supreme leader (or "Wotan"). Within a year, the group claimed 400 members in three Berlin klaverns (dubbed Germania, Heimdal and Viking), while another 600 joined provincial chapters. Each unit was governed by a "Senate" of fourteen elected officers, while members wore white hoods and robes in imitation of the parent Klan, pledging their commitment to "ridding the country of undesirables by fighting the Jews." One newspaper proclaimed the DOFK "silly rather than dangerous," noting that Germany was "full of such groups of ill-balanced and romantic youths," but others disagreed. In 1924, after the American Klan's klonvokation, a Leipzig paper declared: "Thus, then we greet the gallant men of the Ku Klux Klan with our warmest sympathies and cherish the hope to find such cordial expressions of feeling with them in the accomplishment of our mutual aims, as are necessary to achieve victory over the powerful enemy." Dissension split the DOFK in 1925, resulting in expulsion of its founders. Gray returned to the United States, while the Strohscheins moved on to recruit new followers in Silesia. The order survived until early 1934, when Adolf Hitler's Nazi Party banned competing racist groups.

Nearly four decades later, in spring 1970, New York Rep. Seymour Halpern received a complaint that one of his constituents, U.S. Army Spec. 4 Edward Kaneta, had been beaten by fellow soldiers for crossing the color line to befriend black servicemen in Frankfurt. Kaneta named his assailants as four white sergeants, members of an on-base klavern said to have forty-seven members. A subsequent army report, issued on 3

June 1970, denied any evidence of Klan activity in West Germany, but the furor prompted UKA Wizard Robert Shelton to claim extensive infiltration of the military, both at home and abroad. No evidence emerged to support Shelton's boast, however, and the German Klan remained invisible for another twenty years.

In winter 1991, American klansman Dennis Mahon collaborated with Germany's Nationalist Front to launch a KKK recruiting drive in reunified Germany. Crosses blazed in Berlin, and a young skinhead convert in Dresden told reporters, "The Klan takes the strongest stand against the niggers and the fidschies, those who take away our jobs and flats—and of course against the lefties, too." Members of the neo–Nazi Nationalistic Front, banned by law in 1992, sometimes joined forces with the German KKK for raids and cross-burnings. Another link between the KKK and Germany was Andreas Strassmeir, a German national who visited America in the early 1990s and retained white-supremacist attorney Kirk Lyons in an abortive bid to obtain U.S. citizenship. Strassmeir befriended Dennis Mahon while residing at Elohim City, a Christian Identity compound on the Arkansas-Oklahoma border, where he also reportedly fraternized with ex-klansman Timothy McVeigh. McVeigh allegedly placed several telephone calls to Strassmeir in the days before he (McVeigh) bombed Oklahoma City's Alfred P. Murrah Federal Building on 19 April 1995, killing 168 persons. Strassmeir denies any link to that crime, and while the FBI declined to question him, State Department documents once listed him as a suspect in the bombing.

Italy—On 9 October 1947, the Italian newspaper *Unita* printed a denial of rumors that KKK klaverns existed in post-war Italy. Despite the attraction of some U.S. klansmen to fascism, and the documented existence of neo-fascist groups in Italy from 1947 to the present day, no evidence exists to substantiate Klan activity in the heavily–Catholic country. A half-century later, fugitive ex-klansman David Duke resided briefly in northern Italy, during 2001–02, consulting with neo-fascist leaders and reportedly arranging publication in Italian of his latest book.

Lithuania—On 14 July 1928 the Catholic newspaper *Kovno* reported that a unit of the KKK was active in Lithuania "with the avowed purpose of undermining the work of the Catholic church." The report alluded to a cross-burning ceremony with klansmen in full white-robed regalia, but no other newspapers carried the story and no evidence presently supports it.

Mexico—In July and August 1922, the Mexican newspaper *Excelsior* published a series of articles denouncing the Klan in America and denying rumors that the order had klaverns in Mexico. On 27 August, a band of masked men snatched editor José Campos from the street outside his home, in a suburb of Mexico City, and held him captive until he agreed to print an article confirming the Mexican Klan's existence. According to the kidnappers, their group was formed "for the purpose of enforcing justice, since the government police were inactive." No other evidence supports the KKK's presence in Mexico, and its appeal in a country dominated by the Catholic Church would have been marginal, at best.

New Zealand—On 28 August 1923, an Australian newspaper, the Melbourne *Argus*, reported that a chapter of the KKK had organized in Auckland, New Zealand, "to combat Asiatic labor and traders." The report claimed that 1,000 klansmen stood prepared to bar the Yellow Peril from their shores, but no other evidence exists to support the story. Eight decades later, in February 2001, transplanted Oklahoma klansman Johnny Lee Clary told reporters that active klaverns existed in Auckland and Christchurch. Himself a repentant ex-bigot, Clary said, "I know what these people think and I know what they're all about. They're very serious about getting their agenda pushed forward and it's sickening that they want to come into New Zealand and take advantage of people. But they're going after the youth because the youth of today will decide the kind of nation you have tomorrow. They go get these kids that feel down and out, who have been involved in gangs and that activity and take advantage of them." Rajen Prasad, New Zealand's race relations conciliator, admitted knowledge of active Klan groups but maintained that the nation's Human Rights Act contained provisions for prosecution of any persons found inciting racism.

Panama—In September 1926, the *New York Times* reported that a klavern had been organized by American residents of the U.S.–owned Canal Zone. No evidence emerged to support the claim, but Panamanian officials denied banning the order from their soil.

Romania—Since the collapse of its communist government in March 1990, Romania has witnessed a dramatic increase in neo–Nazi activity and violence against minorities by groups such as the National Salvation Front. No Klans are represented, but ex–grand wizard David Duke visited the country in 2001–02, while residing in Italy (and dodging federal indictments in Louisiana).

Russia—Russia's revolution of 1917–18 forestalled any growth of far-right groups in that vast nation, where rampant anti–Semitism might otherwise have provided fertile soil for KKK recruiters. Over the next half-century, klansmen saw Russia as the seat of a global conspiracy to destroy "white Christian civilization," but that view changed radically with the collapse of Soviet communism in 1991. Overnight, extreme nationalist and racist groups surfaced throughout the country, claiming a legitimacy denied to them in most of post-war Europe. Former klansman David Duke visited Russia for the first time in September 1995, meeting with neofascist leader Vladimir "Vlad the Mad" Zhirinovsky, who proclaims: "We must deal with minorities as America did with the Indians and Germany did with the Jews." Zhirinovsky's misnamed Liberal Party captured twenty-three percent of the popular vote in Russia's next parliamentary elections, prompting Duke to declare that "white Mother Russia" had "a greater sense of racial understanding among its population than does any other predominantly white nation." In fact, on his return to the United States, Duke claimed that Russia held the "key to white survival" on Earth.

With federal indictments looming in the States, Duke returned to Russia in August 1999, huddling in Moscow with Gen. Albert Makashov, a Red ultranationalist member of the Duma (parliament) who urged his followers to "[r]ound up the Yids and send them to the next world!" On that visit, Duke arranged for publication of a "new" book (actually a condensed version of his 1998 autobiography) titled *The Jewish Question Through the Eyes of an American,* sold on the streets of Moscow for an average price of fifty rubles ($1.80). Young racist skinheads from the People's National Party provided the sales force, while endorsements poured in from Russian anti–Semites. Federal agents raided Duke's Louisiana home in November 2000, but their quarry was far out of reach, in the midst of his fourth Russian tour. His protracted lecture tour soon turned into an odyssey of Europe, climaxed by his ultimate return to the U.S. and prison in 2004. Meanwhile, the seeds of hatred sown by Duke and others bloomed. While ADL activists urged prosecution of Duke and others under Russian laws banning ethnic, racial or religious incitement, an "extremely suspicious" fire swept a foreign student dormitory at Moscow's Russian University of People's Friendship, killing thirty-six persons and injuring 127 more.

Sweden—In May 1956, police in Stockholm jailed a neo–Nazi activist whom they described as a "Texas Klan member." As in most other foreign cases from the 1950s, literature seized from the prisoner's home issued from Horace Miller's Aryan Knights, headquartered in Waco.

Switzerland—Ex-Klansman David Duke spent time with Swiss neo–Nazi spokesmen in 2001–02, while traveling through Europe to avoid fraud charges pending in America, but no active KKK chapters existed in the country at press time for this work.

America Redrawn

Since the latter 1970s, some klansmen and their neo–Nazi allies have abandoned the longstanding dream of an America purged of all Jews and nonwhites. Michigan klansman Robert Miles and his colleagues from the Idaho-based Aryan Nations once recommended consolidation of all loyal Aryans in a "White Bastion" carved from the Pacific Northwest, including the states of Idaho, Montana, Oregon, Washington and Wyoming. Members of The Order kept that plan in mind when they launched their guerrilla war against "ZOG" in 1983–84, and several neo–Nazi groups were active in the region at press time for this work, including the Aryan Nations, the Creativity Movement, the National Alliance, and the National Socialist Movement.

Former wizard David Duke was more ambitious—and more generous to his disciples—when he sketched a new map of the United States in the December 1984 issue of his *NAAWP News.* In Duke's scheme, some eighty percent of the present United States would be reserved for Aryans only, while various minorities would be confined to the following regions:

Alta California—Stretching from San Diego, California, to the horn of Texas, including southern portions of Arizona and New Mexico, this region is reserved for documented Mexican-Americans and all illegal immigrants from Mexico. Once established, Alta California would be separated from adjoining states by a twenty-mile-wide "no man's land," patrolled by U.S. troops. As Duke explains: "To stop the creeping Mexican invasion once and for all, anyone who crossed into this buffer zone without permission from both countries will be shot on sight." Duke's Spanish (or perhaps his geography) is faulty, since Alta California should literally be located *north* of the existing state that shares its name.

East Mongolia—In Duke's ideal future, the Hawaiian Islands would become the final stop for all Americans of Asian descent. His article neglects to mention whether native Hawaiians would be permitted to stay in their homes.

Francia—Following the U.S.–Canadian border from northern Maine to the vicinity of Watertown, New York, including portions of New Hampshire and Vermont, Francia is Duke's proposed home for "America's 3 million French-Canadians who, although assimilable in a physical and cultural sense, will probably never be able to escape the emotional pull of their homeland." Unlike Alta California, Francia would not be circumscribed by a military free-fire zone.

Minoria—After designating Manhattan and Long Island as West Israel, Duke reserves the rest of the New York City metropolitan area (including part of New Jersey) for Puerto Ricans, Greeks, southern Italians and all other "unassimilable minorities" traceable to the eastern and southern Mediterranean region. Duke assumes that once Minoria is established, each ethnic group will inhabit its own discrete enclave.

Navahona—Encompassing the northern two-thirds of New Mexico, Navahona is Duke's vision of the ultimate Indian reservation, wherein all Native Americans from the continental U.S. would be relocated and thereafter left to their own devices. Duke freely admits that the desert region "is not rich or fertile," but he maintains that "there is no reason why Indians ... will not have enough elbow room, once the whites have decamped."

New Africa—Duke's proposed reservation for African Americans includes the present states of Florida (minus Dade County) and Louisiana, with those portions of Alabama, Georgia and Mississippi located below 32° latitude. As a longtime Louisiana resident himself, intimately familiar with the racial passions of Klan country, Duke admits that "Whites ... will probably not give up their homes peacefully." Military force may be required to uproot southern whites, but Duke regards it as a worthwhile effort. "In Florida, however," he writes, "where hardly anyone has roots, population transfers will be easier."

New Cuba—Duke's plan for America surrenders Dade County, Florida, to Cuban-Americans. Those who have dispersed beyond Miami and environs would be forcibly relocated to join their fellow countrymen. The plan works, in Duke's estimation, because "[o]nly Negroes, Jews and a few aged Majority members will have to vacate" Dade County.

West Israel—Duke cedes Manhattan and Long Island, New York, to America's Jews, thus conforming to the Klan's historic prejudice against "Jew York." One virtue of the scheme, he writes, is that "Jews from the Bronx, Westchester and other New York suburbs will only have a short move ... as will those from Boston, Philadelphia, and Washington, D.C." As with New Africa, Duke recognizes the danger and hardship of dispossessing four million Gentiles, but he considers it a small price to pay for the achievement of Jew-free America.

8 FRIENDS AND FOES OF THE KLAN IN POLITICS

Periodic denials notwithstanding, the Ku Klux Klan is a political organization. It has been immersed in U.S. politics since 1867, and has dabbled in affairs of government wherever else its members rallied, from Canada to Chile, Europe, or Australia and New Zealand. Klan political activity is seldom "mainstream" in the modern world, though it once dominated portions of both major parties in America. More often, since the 1960s, it supports fringe candidates and parties that espouse the KKK's racist philosophies and mirror its paranoid view of society at large. Throughout its 140 years of fervent, often feverish activity in politics, the Klan has always been a negative force. It *opposes* candidates and movements, rather than suggesting any constructive alternative. When all else fails, klansmen sometimes endorse their enemies, knowing the order's sullied reputation makes it poison at the polls.

This chapter examines KKK political involvement at various levels, beginning with a survey of Klan-affected parties, then proceeding through various levels of government from the top downward. In that hierarchy, White House occupants and contenders appear first, followed by members of Congress, U.S. Supreme Court justices, one U.S. Attorney General, state governors, lesser state officials, and finally officers of county and municipal government. Within each subsection below, parties and individuals are listed alphabetically. Individuals who held office at various levels while members of the Klan or supported by the order are described under the highest office they achieved, with cross-referencing from other levels. In cases where KKK support or opposition was irrelevant to part of an individual's career, he or she is listed under the highest office attained while involved with the Klan.

Parties

American Independent Party—Created in 1968 as the vehicle for Alabama Governor George Wallace's presidential campaigns, the AIP drew heavily on the support and membership of racist/far-right groups. In Florida, the KKK and the John Birch Society cooperated to organize the AIP at a precinct level, financed by wealthy citrus growers working quietly to avoid publicity. The Florida AIP's dominant figure was Cecil King, a wealthy farmer and longtime klansman from Parrish. In 1968,

the party's Los Angeles central committee was chaired by Kenneth Waite, who had attended secret Minutemen training camps. Georgia's AIP leader in 1968 was Roy Harris, a founding officer of the Citizens' Councils, who told journalists: "When you get right down to it, there's really only going to be one issue, and you spell it n-i-g-g-e-r." Members of the Citizens' Council also controlled the AIP in Bakersfield, California, where Rev. Alvin Mayall and William Shearer led two rival factions. On election day, Wallace and running mate Curtis LeMay (who advocated bombing Vietnam "back to the Stone Age") polled 9,446,167 popular votes nationwide, securing forty-six electoral votes from Alabama, Arkansas, Georgia, Louisiana, Mississippi and North Carolina.

While Wallace ran for governor again in 1970, supported by the UKA, Michigan's AIP nominated UKA Grand Dragon Robert Miles as secretary of state. Another Michigan klansman ran on the party's slate for a seat on Pontiac's city commission, but withdrew from the race after threats to his life. The AIP nominated Wallace for president again in 1972, and violence erupted when the candidate failed to appear at a rally in Farmington, Michigan, on 8 May. (A klansman in the audience assaulted a Democratic Party volunteer, shouting, "I'll make a vegetable out of you!") One week later, on 15 May, would-be assassin Arthur Bremer ended Wallace's run with a crippling burst of gunfire in Laurel, Maryland. In early August 1972, a "new" American Party convened in Louisville, Kentucky, to nominate California congressman John Schmitz for president, with Tennessee's Thomas Jefferson Anderson as his running mate. (Both candidates were prominent JBS members.) The AP slate ran third in 1972, with 993,199 votes, and its decline has been inexorable since that time. The party split in 1976, with Tom Anderson and Florida's Rufus Shackleford nominated by the American Party (polling 160,773 votes), while Georgia segregationist Lester Maddox and William Dyke of Wisconsin won 170,531 votes for the reconstituted AIP. The American Party dropped from sight in 1980, while the AIP nominated Louisiana Rep. John Rarick (named in FBI reports as a former Klan cyclops) for president, with running mate Eileen Shearer of California (41,268 votes). In 1984, it was the AIP's turn to vanish, while Delmar Dennis—a former Mississippi klansman, FBI informant and JBS spokesman—ran for president on the American Party ticket, with Traves Brownlee of Delaware (13,149 votes). Both groups resurfaced in 1988, Delmar Dennis polling a meager 3,476 votes for the American Party, while AIP candidates Warren Griffin of Alabama and James Burnett of Florida claimed 27,818 ballots. Neither party fielded a presidential candidate in 1992, but the American Party rebounded in 1996 to win 1,847 votes for California attorney Diane Beall Templin. Two years later, running unsuccessfully for state attorney general, Templin wore the AIP label, but Don Moore reverted to the AP banner for his presidential run in 2000 (winning no votes, according to the *U.S. Election Atlas*). Diane Templin kept the AIP logo during her subsequent campaigns for the U.S. Senate (2000), state attorney general (2002) and governor of California (2003), but reverted to the AP ticket for her second hopeless presidential bid (2004). At press time for this volume, the AIP apparently survived only in California, as an adjunct to the larger Constitution Party. While its website described the AIP as California's "third largest" and "fastest-growing" party, its leadership is distinctly parochial, including Citizens' Council alumnus William Shearer as "parliamentarian," his daughter Nancy Shearer Spirkoff as chairperson, Harold and Nada Crabtree of Palm Desert, Jim and Rayna King of San Bernardino. In 2005, the AIP's candidate for Congress was Jim Gilchrist, co-founder of the Minuteman Project whose extralegal border patrols included members of the neo–Nazi National Alliance.

Christian Nationalist Party

—Anti-Semite Gerald L.K. Smith created the CNP as his personal political vehicle, sometime in 1947 or 1948 (reports vary). He ran for president on the party's ticket in 1948, 1952 and 1956, espousing platforms that included white supremacy, deportation of blacks and Zionist Jews, and construction of ghettos for any Jews remaining after the purge. In 1957, Smith sued California's secretary of state for barring the CNP from the Golden State's gubernatorial ballot. Despite assistance from ACLU lawyers (whom he commonly reviled as Jews and communists), Smith lost that case in 1958 and the party effectively ceased to exist.

Commoner Party

—A front group for the Georgia-based Columbians, founded in 1946, the Commoner Party was organized in a futile effort to create a "gigantic powerhouse" of anti-Semitic votes. Attempts to solicit support from recognized "nationalist leaders" such as Gerald L.K. Smith and Tulsa attorney Phil Davis proved fruitless, and the party died with its parent organization.

Constitution Party

—Founded in 1952, the Constitution Party nominated ex–General Douglas MacArthur as its presidential candidate that year. By 1957, the party had been transformed from an ultra-conservative group to a racist/anti–Semitic confederation led by William Potter Gale, founder of the anti–Semitic California Rangers (and himself a secret Jew). The party welcomed members of various Klans, the NSRP, and the paramilitary Minutemen to its ranks, nominating Gale as its candidate for governor of California in 1958. Scattered outposts of the party survived into the 1980s, loosely affiliated with Gale's Posse Comitatus. Wisconsin anti–Semite James Wickstrom was the party's U.S. Senate candidate in 1980, then rebounded from that loss with an unsuccessful gubernatorial race in 1982. The modern Constitution Party, organized in 1999, bears no relation to Gale's group but maintains a corresponding far-right stance, inherited from its parent body, the U.S. Taxpayers Party (1992–99). Its stance on various issues including abortion, gun control, religion and "states' rights" conforms in all respects to those of the 1990s "patriot militia" movement.

Constitutional American Party of the United States

—In 1963, leaders of the Constitution Party (see above) reprimanded Georgia klansman and NSRP member Joseph Milteer for misrepresenting himself as a regional director of their group. Milteer retaliated in October of that year by founding his own party, the CAPUS. Veering away from conventional politics toward more direct action, Milteer envisioned his group (in the words of a declassified FBI report) as "a front to form a hard-core underground for possible violence in combating integration." The CAPUS fielded no candidates, nor was it linked to any other known activity.

Democratic Party

—Public denials notwithstanding, after April 1867 the Reconstruction-era Ku Klux Klan was a de facto arm of the southern Democratic (or "Conservative") Party, achieving by threats and violence what party leaders could not accomplish through normal political channels. Everywhere throughout the former Confederate states, klansmen supported Democratic candidates and policies, attacking Republican officials and any voters (white or black) who supported the GOP. Many Republican officials and candidates for office were assassinated by the KKK and allied groups, while countless others fled their homes or lived in mortal fear. Black voters—presumed to support the party of Lincoln—were terrorized en masse from Texas to Florida and the Carolinas, except where klansmen issued "protection papers" to those who endorsed the Democratic Party. Most Democratic newspapers and party spokesmen either supported the Klan or pretended to believe that it did not exist. When a joint committee of Congress investigated Ku Klux terrorism in 1871, the panel's Democratic members issued a minority report ignoring Klan violence while focusing on alleged corruption in various Republican state governments below the Mason-Dixon Line. After "redemption" of the South for white "home rule" in 1877, Dixie became a virtual one-party state, where Republicans (if they existed) were marginalized and victory in all-white Democratic primaries effectively chose most public officials.

The modern KKK remained primarily a Democratic organ in the South, while northern realms supported either party that offered access to power and wealth. In June 1924, with Klan membership and influence at its peak nationwide, Republican leaders followed the example of President Calvin ("Silent Cal") Coolidge, ignoring the KKK issue at their national convention in Cleveland, Ohio. Democrats proved less canny and more combative when they convened at New York City's Madison Square Garden twelve days later. There, anti–Klan delegates fought for a plank denouncing the hooded order by name, while pro-Klan party members fought the move tenaciously. (Observers later estimated that the convention's 1,090 delegates included at least 343 dues-paying knights.) After much heated argument and some physical violence, the anti–Klan plank lost by a margin of 542 to 541. Selection of a presidential candidate was likewise hampered by that rift, as Klan supporters cast their votes for William Gibbs McAdoo, while opponents of the order backed Oscar Underwood. Finally, on the 103rd ballot, the exhausted delegates nominated John William Davis—who trailed Coolidge by 7.3 million votes in November. Four years later, while the Klan had lost much of its former strength, the order and its allied nativists still had sufficient influence to defeat Democratic presidential hopeful Al Smith in a campaign marked by ugly attacks on Smith as the candidate of "Rome, rum and rebellion." Klansmen briefly supported Franklin Roosevelt in 1932, founding a string of southern Roosevelt Clubs, but they withdrew from the campaign before election day and spent the rest of the Great Depression attacking FDR's "Jew Deal."

The "Solid South" remained an exclusively Democratic preserve until 1948, when racist delegates from Alabama and Mississippi bolted from the Democratic National Convention in protest against President Harry Truman's civil rights initiatives. The resultant States Rights Democratic Party (or "Dixiecrats") polled more than nine million votes for presidential candidate Strom Thurmond, who subsequently led a southern exodus into the rightward-drifting GOP. Klansmen and other Dixie racists thereafter increasingly split their votes in presidential years, supporting state and local Democratic candidates, while casting their presidential votes for Dwight Eisenhower (1952, 1956), Richard Nixon (1960) and Barry Goldwater (1964). Nixon made the shift explicit with his "Southern Strategy" in 1968 and 1972, promising a future of "benign neglect" on civil rights in exchange for support from traditional white-supremacist Democrats. Presidents Ronald Reagan and George H.W. Bush consolidated that position in the 1980s, virtually reversing southern voting patterns from the first half of the twentieth century. As for the KKK, its members have increasingly abandoned both major political parties, supporting extremist fringe movements or shunning the polls altogether in pursuit of "third-position" lone-wolf politics.

National States Rights Party—This Klan-allied neo–Nazi group fielded presidential slates in 1960 and 1964. In the former year, NSRP delegates nominated Arkansas Governor Orval Faubus for president (against his wishes), with veteran anti–Semite John Crommelin as his running mate. The candidates polled an impressive (and disturbing) 214,195 votes on election day, despite the fact that one refused to participate in the charade and the other was an outspoken Jew-baiter. Four years later, the NSRP tried its luck with convicted agitator Frederick John Kasper and party founder Jesse Stoner. The pair received a total of 6,957 votes.

Populist Party (1984–92)—Veteran anti–Semite Willis Carto founded the Populist Party in 1984, operating from his own Liberty Lobby headquarters in Washington, D.C. Party spokesmen claimed that its platform fostered "respect for racial and cultural diversity," but Carto's literature declared: "The Populist Party will not permit any racial minority, through control of the media, culture distortion or revolutionary activity, to divide or factionalize the majority of the society-nation in which the minority lives." Populist spokesmen adopted various causes long championed by right-wing Republicans (opposition to the

Equal Rights Amendment, opposition to busing for school integration), while adding new planks of their own: a ban on future immigration, abolition of the federal income tax, and dissolution of the Federal Reserve (owned and run by "international bankers"—i.e., Jews). Carto initially served on the party's executive committee, with several known klansmen and neo–Nazi figures, while ex-klansman Robert Weems was its first national chairman. The party's first national ticket offered Olympic pole-vault gold medalist Bob Richards for president and Californian Maureen Kennedy Salaman ("first lady of nutrition") for vice president. Richards quit the campaign in mid-stream, after personal disputes with Carto, leaving Salaman to soldier on alone. The ticket polled 66,168 votes nationwide, while Carto sued Richards and various party officials to recover alleged campaign debts. Dissension left the party shattered and in ruins.

Carto tried again in 1987, joining forces with Pennsylvania activist Don Wassall to create a new Populist Party, with leaders including Illinois neo–Nazi Art Jones and former ANP member Ralph Forbes of Arkansas. A new addition to the team, Jerry Pope of Kentucky, was a former NSRP member and associate of convicted church bomber Jesse Stoner. Wassall, as national chairman, managed the party from his Pittsburgh headquarters, while Carto maintained his seat on the executive committee. In 1988, the party nominated former klansman David Duke for president, with ex–Green Beret James "Bo" Gritz as his running mate. In a reversal of 1984's events, Gritz soon abandoned the ticket to run for local office while Duke floundered on to election day, polling less than 50,000 votes nationwide. Carto thereafter withdrew from the party, leaving it wracked with debt. Two years later, Wassall established the Populist Action Committee, with neo–Nazis Forbes and Jones still on board, while Carto started sniping at the new group from the pages of his *Searchlight* magazine. Wassall's team sued for libel and eventually won, but that long-delayed victory did nothing to enhance the party's prestige. While that case wound its tortuous way through the courts, the Populist Party nominated "Bo" Gritz as its 1992 presidential candidate (sans running mate). By that time, Gritz—a convert to Christian Identity's racist tenets who played a minor role in the Randall Weaver siege at Ruby Ridge, Idaho—had abandoned his longtime search for missing U.S. servicemen in Vietnam, in favor of anti–Semitic conspiracy theories. (His 1991 publication, *Called to Serve: Profiles in Conspiracy from John F. Kennedy to George Bush,* declares that "eight jewish [*sic*] families control the FED.") Gritz's prescription for success, a call for "right, left, conservative, liberal, et. al., to UNITE AS POPULISTS," failed to lure liberals but succeeded in alienating some right-wing support. Gritz polled 98,918 votes in November 1992, and despite some sensational Internet claims, the Populist Party is now effectively defunct.

Republican Party—Founded to oppose slavery in 1856, the GOP elected its first president—Abraham Lincoln—four years later, and thereby precipitated secession of eleven slave states from the Union. After the ensuing Civil War, Republicans controlled Congress and barred readmission of states that refused to recognize ex-slaves as citizens with full political rights.

That "radical" stance inflamed southern racists and prompted the Ku Klux Klan's reorganization from a frivolous social club to a guerrilla army fighting on behalf of the southern Democratic Party. Henceforth, until "redemption" of the South for white Democratic "home rule" a decade later, klansmen and members of allied terrorist groups declared open season on Republican officials and voters, regardless of race. Frequent assassinations, pogroms and armed demonstrations made Republicans an endangered species in many parts of Dixie, where klansmen and supporting Democratic spokesmen made no secret of their intent to capture the reigns of government by any possible means. Republican President Ulysses Grant used federal troops and legislation to suppress the KKK in 1873, but his work was soon undone by Mississippi's "Shotgun Plan," Louisiana's White League, and South Carolina's Red Shirts. In the chaotic election of 1876, GOP candidate Rutherford Hayes lost the election to Democrat Samuel Tilden by 264,292 popular ballots and twenty electoral votes, yet he secured the White House through a bargain with Democratic leaders (including the former grand dragon of Georgia), pledging an end to Reconstruction in return for certification of his victory.

While stripped of all influence in the "Solid South" after 1877, the GOP remained a power to be reckoned with above the Mason-Dixon Line. From 1920 onward, as the Ku Klux Klan expanded nationwide, its northern members maintained their longstanding party affiliations and Klan strategists peddled the order's votes to whichever party proved most accommodating (or, if nothing else, least critical). Southern klansmen soon learned to split their ballots, electing traditional Democrats at home while voting for GOP presidential contenders who opposed civil rights initiatives and kept mum on Klan violence. That trend began with "Silent Cal" Coolidge in 1924, accelerated when the Democrats nominated Catholic New Yorker Al Smith for president in 1928, and continued throughout Franklin Roosevelt's "Jew Deal." Klansmen generally lacked the influence and numbers to place southern states in the GOP presidential column between 1924 and 1948, but war hero Dwight Eisenhower cracked the Solid South in 1952 and 1956. Half of Alabama's electors broke with tradition to oppose Catholic John Kennedy in 1960, mimicked by electors from Florida, Mississippi, Tennessee and Virginia. Ultra-conservative Senator Barry Goldwater carried five southern states in 1964, with KKK support, but it remained for Richard Nixon to perfect the GOP's "Southern Strategy" in 1968 and 1972, promising "benign neglect" on civil rights in exchange for white votes from Dixie. Since 1976, the only Democratic presidents elected in America have been southerners—Georgia's Jimmy Carter and Bill Clinton from Arkansas—but both proved far too liberal for klansmen and their allies to support. Ex-wizard David Duke won election to the Louisiana state legislature as a Republican in 1989, but the universal condemnation heaped upon him by mainstream GOP spokesmen encouraged Duke to seek third-party vehicles thereafter. At the same time, many conservative southern Republicans saw no contradiction in their own involvement with the racist CCC, a group that welcomed Duke and other Klan or neo-Nazi zealots to its ranks. Embarrassment at the exposure of the CCC's racism prompted Republican leaders to brand the group off-limits in 1999, but various GOP officeholders were still involved with the CCC at press time for this book.

States Rights Democratic Party—This third-party movement, popularly known as the Dixiecrats, sprang from southern revulsion against President Harry Truman's civil rights initiatives after World War II. In June 1948, after Minnesota Senator Hubert Humphrey urged the Democratic National Convention to adopt a plank condemning racial segregation, thirty-five delegates from Mississippi and Alabama (including Birmingham police commissioner "Bull" Connor) walked out in protest. Four days later, they convened in Birmingham to organize the States Rights Democratic Party with the official slogan "Segregation Forever!" Known klansmen including Jesse Stoner circulated on the convention floor, accompanied by veteran anti–Semite Gerald L.K. Smith, while the new party nominated South Carolina Governor Strom Thurmond for president, with Mississippi Governor Fielding Wright as his running mate. Thurmond recently had welcomed AGK Grand Dragon Samuel Green as a guest speaker before his state legislature, while Wright, in April 1948, warned all blacks desirous of equal rights to "make your home in some state other than Mississippi). Dixiecrat spokesmen worked hard to have their slate declared the "official" Democratic ticket in southern states, succeeding in Alabama, Louisiana, Mississippi and South Carolina. Arkansas Governor Ben Laney supported the Dixiecrat ticket, despite opposition from "turncoats" including Rep. Brooks Hays. In campaign speeches, Thurmond blamed Truman's civil rights program on "demands of the parlor pinks and the subversives," while describing Truman's FEPC as "hatched in the brains of communists." Local klansmen did their best for the Dixiecrat effort, harassing loyal Democrats and members of the leftist Progressive Party at every opportunity, but Thurmond still ran third in November, with 1,169,021 votes nationwide. Despite loyalist fears that the Dixiecrat and Progressive splinter parties would sap Democratic strength on election day, tipping the balance to Republican Thomas Dewey, Truman surprised the doomsayers with a victory margin of 2,136,525 votes. The Dixiecrat movement officially dissolved after 1948, with some of its leaders switching to the GOP, but the name is still loosely applied to certain racist southern Democrats.

White House Occupants and Contenders

Carter, James Earl—Georgia native Jimmy Carter served two terms in the state legislature (1963–66) and one term as governor (1971–75) before his election to the White House in 1976. Klansmen despised him for his liberal policies and demonstrated outside his family's church in Plains on 14 November 1976, after the congregation voted to lift its long-standing ban on black members. During the 1976 presidential campaign, literature distributed by the KKK and NSRP branded Carter as an illegitimate son of Massachusetts millionaire Joseph Kennedy.

Cleveland, Grover—As president, New Jersey Democrat Cleveland favored several klansmen with high-ranking federal appointments. During his first term (1885–89), Cleveland appointed the former grand dragon of Arkansas, Augustus Hill, to serve as the U.S. Attorney General; named prominent Mississippi klansman Henry Muldrow First Assistant Secretary of the Interior; and appointed former Louisiana klansman Edward White to a seat on the U.S. Supreme Court. In his second White House term (1893–97), Cleveland named reputed South Carolina Grand Dragon Wade Hampton to serve as U.S. railroad commissioner.

Coolidge, Calvin—Vice President Calvin Coolidge succeeded President Warren Harding after Harding's sudden death in August 1923, subsequently winning election to his own four-year term in 1924. He refrained from any public comments on the KKK during its heyday, even when assembled klansmen marched through Washington, D.C., in 1925 and 1926. "Silent Cal's" circumspection served him well in the 1924 presidential election, as the GOP rolled to easy victory over a Democratic Party torn between pro-Klan and anti-Klan voters. Coolidge declined to seek reelection in 1928. He died in Massachusetts on 5 January 1933.

Dennis, Delmar—In 1964, while serving as a kludd in the WKKKKM, Dennis found himself repulsed by Klan violence and agreed to work as an informant for the FBI. He subsequently provided critical testimony at the 1967 trial of klansmen charged with killing three civil rights workers, and in the 1994 prosecution of Byron De La Beckwith for assassinating NAACP official Medgar Evers. In 1968, Dennis joined the JBS lecture circuit, telling listeners that the Klan had been infiltrated by communists, who committed acts of racial violence to blacken the reputation of "legitimate" segregationists. In 1984 and 1988, he was the presidential candidate of the American Party (formerly the AIP). Dennis polled 13,149 votes in 1984, and only 3,476 four years later.

Duke, David Ernest *see State Officials*

Eisenhower, Dwight David—Twice elected president on his reputation as a hero of World War II, "Ike" occupied the White House from 1953 to January 1961. His tenure encompassed the U.S. Supreme Court's "Black Monday" ruling on school integration, a dramatic revival of the KKK, the birth of the Citizens' Councils, and numerous crises throughout the Deep South. Klansmen endorsed Eisenhower in 1952, urging southern whites to split their ballots and support a Republican president for the first time in history. That effort was successful in Florida, Louisiana, Tennessee, Texas and Virginia, but the other Deep South states remained solidly Democratic. The same states followed Eisenhower in 1956, while voters in Alabama, Arkansas, Georgia, Mississippi and the Carolinas remained loyal to the party of their forefathers. Eisenhower opposed civil rights legislation, but reluctantly signed the Civil Rights Acts of 1957 and 1960, which expanded FBI jurisdiction in cases of racial terrorism. (FBI headquarters largely ignored its new mandate.) In 1957, Ike destroyed whatever good will he had accumulated among southern racists by dispatching U.S. troops to enforce court-ordered integration at Little Rock's Central High School. That event created a crisis for klansmen in 1960, when the De-

mocratic Party nominated Massachusetts Catholic John Kennedy to oppose Eisenhower's vice president, Richard Nixon.

Forbes, Ralph P.—As a member of George Rockwell's ANP, Forbes picketed screenings of *Exodus* in 1961 and had his nose bloodied a year later, while marching outside the White House with anti–Semitic placards. Moving to California in 1963, he won promotion to the rank of captain in the party, but his recruiting efforts won few converts for the Nazi cause. Forbes subsequently moved again—to London, Arkansas—where he established the Sword of Christ and its front group, the Shamrock Society, urging patriots to "kick the Jew habit" at Christmas by spending their money on anti–Semitic literature, audio tapes, and membership dues for "God's White Army" (also led by Forbes). In 1982, Forbes lost his first political bid, for a Democratic congressional nomination. Four years later, as a Republican, he failed to capture the nomination for lieutenant governor, then rebounded with a losing campaign for a U.S. Senate seat. (Shortly before election day in 1986, he also filed a lawsuit to enjoin local schools from "observing the rites of Satan" by permitting Halloween costumes on campus.) Forbes soon switched allegiance once more, this time to Willis Carto's Populist Party, and in 1988 served as national coordinator for ex-klansman David Duke's presidential campaign on the Populist ticket. With that disaster behind him, Forbes ran once more for lieutenant governor (1990), then for a seat in Congress (1992). The latter campaign spawned another lawsuit, when the Arkansas Educational Television Commission barred Forbes from a candidates' debate, but the U.S. Supreme ruled in 1998 that Forbes was not a victim of discrimination. (Meanwhile, a correspondent for Carto's *Spotlight* magazine claimed inside knowledge that state GOP leaders "had illicitly stolen the 1986 nomination from Forbes.") In 1996, Forbes ran for president as an independent candidate against longtime political enemy Bill Clinton, polling a paltry 932 votes nationwide. Two years later, he attached himself to billionaire Ross Perot's Reform Party and made yet another unsuccessful bid for a seat in the U.S. House of Representatives.

Goldwater, Barry Morris—A Phoenix, Arizona, native, born in 1909, Goldwater represented his home state in the U.S. Senate during 1953–65 and 1969–87. As the Republican Party's presidential candidate in 1964, he did not seek reelection to the Senate that year. Klansmen rallied to Goldwater after Alabama Governor George Wallace dropped his White House race that spring, ignoring the facts that Goldwater's father was Jewish and that his running mate, William Miller, was a Roman Catholic. The knights appreciated Goldwater's ultra-conservative political stance, including opposition to federal civil rights laws, advocacy of nuclear strikes in Vietnam, and public statements that "extremism in defense of liberty is no vice." Georgia Grand Dragon Calvin Craig was the first Klan leader to endorse Goldwater, followed closely by UKA Imperial Wizard Robert Shelton and Alabama Grand Dragon Robert Creel. When Goldwater repudiated KKK support, Shelton told journalists, "That's his privilege." Despite the Klan's best efforts, President Lyndon Johnson carried the 1964 election by a landslide, polling 42,825,463 votes to Goldwater's 27,175,770. On election day,

Top: **Demonstrators protest KKK support for Barry Goldwater in the 1964 presidential election.** *Above:* **Goldwater left his running mate to repudiate KKK support (both photographs: Library of Congress).**

Goldwater won a majority in only six states—his own, plus the Klan strongholds of Alabama, Georgia, Louisiana, Mississippi and South Carolina. After three more terms in the Senate, during which he aired increasingly liberal views, Goldwater retired from politics and died in Arizona on 29 May 1998.

Grant, Ulysses Simpson—Union war hero U.S. Grant won election to the White House as a Republican in 1868, despite widespread terrorism by the KKK, KWC and other groups throughout the South. Political violence escalated four years later, but Grant still carried the election with 3,597,132 votes to Democrat Horace Greeley's 834,079. By that time, Klan terrorism in South Carolina had reached a state requiring special legislation to suppress it, and Grant used the new Force Bill (or Ku Klux Act) to declare martial law in several counties, permitting federal arrests of klansmen where local authorities were unable or unwilling to act. Most accounts credit Grant's action with dissolving the KKK, although few of its members suffered any real punishment and most continued their terrorist activities through groups such as Louisiana's White League and South Carolina's Red Shirts. After leaving office, Grant spent three years traveling the world, then made an unsuccessful bid for the GOP presidential nomination in 1880. Illness and financial setbacks plagued his final years, before he died in New York on 23 July 1885.

Harding, Warren Gamaliel—Another product of corrupt machine politics, Ohio Senator Warren Harding won the GOP's 1920 presidential nomination with a promise to restore "normalcy" in the wake of World War I and the Red Scare of 1919–20. He defeated fellow Ohioan James Cox on election day,

William Simmons and other Klan leaders claimed that President Warren Harding was a KKK member (Library of Congress).

despite Klan threats and riots that prevented black Republicans from voting in the South. By 1921, when Harding took his oath of office, the KKK was a force to reckon with in Ohio, and stories persist that Harding was initiated to the order by a special five-man induction team from imperial headquarters (led by Imperial Wizard William Simmons), taking his Klan oath in the Green Room of the White House. Evidence supporting that story includes the 1940s deathbed testimony of Imperial Klokard Alton Young (an alleged member of the induction team), and the fact that all five members of the team received special license plates from the U.S. War Department, permitting them to flaunt traffic laws with impunity. Harding died in San Francisco on 2 August 1923, while returning from a visit to Alaska. Klansmen nationwide staged mourning demonstrations, and historian David Chalmers reports that armed Ohio knights stood guard at Harding's tomb. Rumors of Harding's Klan membership leaked for the first time in 1924, along with claims that Attorney General Harry Daugherty was also a klansman. (Daugherty denied it.) In a 1976 interview with journalist Patsy Sims, Imperial Wizard James Venable claimed to possess—but never produced—photographs of a Klan funeral ceremony conducted for Harding in Marion, Ohio.

Hayes, Rutherford Birchard—In June 1876, the GOP nominated Ohio Governor Rutherford Hayes to succeed Ulysses Grant as president. The election campaign witnessed unparalleled terrorism in Dixie, as racists in various states adopted Mississippi's "Shotgun Plan" from 1875. On election day, Democratic contender Samuel Tilden received 4,300,590 votes, while Hayes trailed with 4,036,298. Neither had the 185 electoral votes required for victory: Tilden fell one vote short, at 184, while Hayes claimed 165. Totals were disputed in three former Klan strongholds—Florida, Louisiana, and South Carolina—but a last minute conference between Hayes and high-ranking democrats (including Georgia's former grand dragon, then a U.S. senator) tipped the balance to Hayes. In return for certification as president, Hayes agreed to end Reconstruction wherever whites had not recaptured state governments by armed force. True to his word, after Hayes was inaugurated on 5 March 1877, he withdrew federal troops from South Carolina on 10 April and from New Orleans ten days later. Hayes declined to seek a second term as president in 1880 and retired to Ohio, where he died on 17 January 1893.

Johnson, Andrew—The KKK was organized roughly one year after Johnson took office as president, succeeding Abraham Lincoln, but he never confronted the issue. A North Carolina Democrat, raised in Tennessee, he openly sympathized with the defeated Confederacy and vetoed every piece of Reconstruction legislation passed by Congress during his White House tenure. (A Republican majority overrode his veto in each case.) Congress impeached Johnson in February 1868, but the Senate's verdict failed to remove him from office. He failed to capture the Democratic presidential nomination in 1868, but he was elected to the U.S. Senate in 1874 and served four months before his death on 31 July 1875.

Johnson, Lyndon Baines—Many historians report that Johnson's father "fought the Klan" in Texas during the 1920s, but published descriptions of that fight are vague at best, describing only verbal criticism of the order. In 1948, LBJ hired Philip Fox as chief publicist for his first U.S. Senate campaign, presumably in full awareness that Fox was a 1920s klansman who served prison time in Georgia for the murder of a rival at imperial headquarters. As president (1963–69), Johnson denounced the KKK as a "hooded society of bigots" and compelled reluctant FBI Director J. Edgar Hoover to investigate Klan murders of civil rights workers in Mississippi (1964) and Alabama (1965). Johnson also secured passage of the 1964 Civil Rights Act and the 1965 Voting Rights Act. Those actions prompted Ohio klansmen to debate Johnson's assassination, but the effort apparently stopped at tough talk and collection of weapons. Protests against the war in Vietnam persuaded Johnson to decline renomination in 1968. He died in Texas on 22 January 1973.

Kennedy, John Fitzgerald—While Florida klansman Bill Hendrix dropped the order's ban on Catholics in 1957, most Klans still preached anti–Catholicism in 1960, and some members recalled first-hand the order's campaign against Catholic presidential contender Al Smith in 1928. The Democratic Party's nomination of John Kennedy was thus a double insult to southern knights—a Catholic *and* a New England liberal outspoken in support of black civil rights. Florida Klan leader William Griffin publicly endorsed GOP contender Richard Nixon, while nativist publications spewed out floods of anti–Catholic literature. In August 1960, Senator Estes Kefauver identified the KKK as a major source of anti–Catholic propaganda opposing Kennedy's election. The NSRP offered an alternative, drafting Arkansas Governor Orval Faubus for president and polling 214,195 votes nationwide. Despite the KKK's best efforts, Kennedy carried Alabama, Arkansas, Georgia, Louisiana, the Carolinas and Texas. The worst fears of anti–JFK klansmen were later realized with federal intervention to protect "free-

While endorsing Nixon, klansmen opposed candidate John Kennedy (left) because he was a Catholic (Library of Congress). The president is pictured with CIA Director John McCone.

dom riders" (1961) and Mississippi's first black college student (1962), while Kennedy proposed the most dramatic civil rights legislation since Reconstruction. Few knights mourned Kennedy's assassination on 22 November 1963, and Georgia Grand Dragon Charles Maddox publicly praised alleged assassin Lee Harvey Oswald. Conspiracy researchers note that certain klansmen were also involved in events that followed JFK's murder. Dallas police lieutenant George Butler (an outspoken klansman) was in charge of Oswald's jailhouse transfer on 24 November 1963, when gangster Jack Ruby murdered Oswald in the basement of police headquarters. In February 1967, after Oswald acquaintance and JFK conspiracy suspect David Ferrie died in New Orleans, Louisiana klansmen Jack Helm and Jules Kimble visited Ferrie's apartment, removing a valise filled with documents before District Attorney Jim Garrison could subpoena them for his ongoing investigation of the Kennedy murder.

Maddox, Lester *see Governors*

McAdoo, William Gibbs—A Georgia native, born in 1863 and raised in Tennessee, McAdoo graduated from the University of Tennessee (Knoxville) and served as clerk for the U.S. district court in eastern Tennessee (1882), then studied law and won admittance to the state bar in 1885. Seven years later, he moved to New York City, where he helped design the rapid-transit tunnels linking New York with New Jersey beneath the Hudson River, then served as president of the company which built and operated them (1902–13). At the same time, McAdoo served as chairman of the Democratic National Committee (1912), then as Secretary of the Treasury under President Woodrow Wilson (1913–18). After failing to secure the Democratic Party's 1920 presidential nomination, McAdoo moved to Los Angeles and opened a new legal practice. While not a klansman, he secured the KKK's backing for another presidential bid in 1924, after delivering a timely speech in Macon, Georgia. When a local Klan leader asked McAdoo's opinion of religious freedom, McAdoo avoided any mention of the Klan's attacks on Catholics while replying that he "stood four-square on the Constitution." That answer satisfied imperial headquarters, and rumors of closer Klan ties surfaced after McAdoo and Imperial Wizard Hiram Evans "coincidentally" appeared together at the French Lick Springs resort, in Indiana. At the 1924 Democratic National Convention, McAdoo's primary competitors were Catholic New Yorker Alfred Smith and Oscar Underwood, an outspoken critic of the KKK. Klan delegates naturally threw their votes to McAdoo, but their numbers were insufficient to secure his nomination. After 103 ballots, the convention chose compromise candidate John W. Davis, thereby ensuring victory for Republican incumbent Calvin Coolidge. McAdoo subsequently won election to the U.S. Senate from California, in 1932, but he lost his reelection bid in 1938, when his Republican opponent produced an alleged lifetime membership card in the KKK bearing McAdoo's name. McAdoo died on 1 February 1941, while visiting Washington, D.C.

Nixon, Richard Milhous—Californian Richard Nixon established his political reputation as "Tricky Dick" long before his election as vice president under Dwight Eisenhower (1953–

Richard Nixon's presidential hopes suffered damage from a Klan endorsement in 1960 (Library of Congress).

61). In 1960, with Ike barred by constitutional amendment from succeeding himself, the GOP nominated Nixon as its presidential standard bearer. Soon after that selection was made, in August 1960, Florida klansman William Griffin endorsed Nixon over Catholic Democrat John Kennedy. That endorsement became an embarrassing national issue on 13 October, in the third televised debate between Nixon and JFK. When asked about a Democratic publicist's statement that "all bigots will vote for Nixon," Kennedy replied, "Well, Mr. Griffin, I believe, who is the head of the Klan, who lives in Tampa, Florida, indicated in a statement, I think, two or three weeks ago, that he was not going to vote for me, and that he was going to vote for Mr. Nixon. I do not suggest in any way—nor have I ever—that that indicates that Mr. Nixon has the slightest sympathy in regard to the Ku Klux Klan." Nixon echoed that rejection, but Griffin stood firm, telling reporters, "I don't give a damn what Nixon said. I'm still voting for him." Some analysts suggest that the KKK endorsement may have been a crucial factor in swinging black votes to Kennedy that year, when JFK carried the nation by only 119,450 votes out of 68,836,385 cast. In his 1968 presidential campaign, Nixon devised a GOP "Southern Strategy" to lure white votes from the Democratic column and from George Wallace's AIP, promising a federal program of "benign neglect" toward blacks if Nixon was elected to the White House. That bid made the difference in Florida, the Carolinas, Tennessee and Virginia where a majority of voters deserted the Democratic Party to support Nixon. Four years later, every southern state joined Nixon's landslide, crushing liberal Democrat George McGovern. Criminal activity forced Nixon's resignation in August 1974, but he enjoyed a curious public rehabilitation prior to his death on 22 April 1994.

Rarick, John *see Congress*

Roosevelt, Franklin Delano—New York native
Franklin Roosevelt served as assistant secretary of war under President Woodrow Wilson (1913–20) and won the Democratic Party's vice-presidential nomination in 1920. In 1924, at the Democratic National Convention where quarrels over the KKK created bitter dissension, Roosevelt nominated Catholic New Yorker Alfred Smith for president. He supported Smith again in 1928, then won election to succeed Smith as New York's governor (1929–33). Klansmen should "logically" have hated FDR, both for his liberal politics and his support of Smith, but they seemed to hold no grudge against him when he ran for president in 1932. Klan historian David Chalmers suggests that Roosevelt's frequent visits to Warm Springs, Georgia, may have earned him support at imperial headquarters. In any case, klansmen organized Roosevelt Clubs throughout Dixie in early 1932, led by Atlanta klonsel Paul Etheridge. A rift developed when Democratic leaders ordered club leaders to raise money for FDR's campaign, instead of skimming cash for themselves, and Klan spokesmen suddenly "discovered" that Roosevelt campaign manager James Farley was a Catholic. Thereafter, Klan spokesmen pilloried FDR in print and from their podiums, typified by the following bulletin.

> Don't be fooled. Farley is ROOSEVELT; Tammany Hall, Catholic controlled, is ROOSEVELT.... EVERY PROMINENT ROMAN CATHOLIC YOU CAN FIND IS FOR ROOSEVELT.... The Underworld is a unit for Roosevelt. The gangsters of Chicago, St. Louis ... and New York are for Roosevelt.... Roosevelt, their subservient tool, will turn our country over to Tammany and thus we will have CATHOLIC CONTROL OF AMERICAN GOVERNMENT AND LIFE, if he is elected.... BEWARE THE 8th OF NOVEMBER!

Roosevelt's inauguration realized the Klan's worst fears. Farley became Postmaster General, while Henry Morgenthau (a Jew) took charge of the Treasury Department and Harold Ickes III (also branded a Jew by the Klan) became Secretary of the Interior. Rumors circulated on the Klan grapevine that Roosevelt's "real name" was Rosenfeld, while Ku Klux orators complained that the New Deal (or "Jew Deal") had brought "too many Jews and Catholics to Washington." Klan speakers in Virginia complained that FDR had "honeycombed Washington with communists," while knights in Westchester New York praised Adolf Hitler and condemned the "communism of FDR and the Jews." By 1934, Imperial Wizard Hiram Evans had declared a "crusade" against the New Deal, manifested primarily in attacks on organized labor. As Evans saw it, "Public-spirited people, Klansmen and non-members alike, realize that this nation is in great danger. Because of its record of heroic achievement, the Klan has been called upon by them to mobilize and co-ordinate those who are interested in preserving our Constitutional Government set up by our forefathers."

It made no difference when FDR named Alabama Senator Hugo Black to the U.S. Supreme Court in 1937, since Black had long since abandoned the KKK and its racist viewpoints. Some klansmen even lamented America's entry into World War II. As Fritz Kuhn, imprisoned leader of the German-American Bund explained, "We all approved of what Hitler was doing. Had Roosevelt not brought us into the war we would have got together against the Jews and Negroes." Although the KKK would not find a spot on the U.S. Attorney General's list until 1947, FDR took note of its activities in 1944, during his third reelection campaign. That year found Klan propagandists circulating cartoons of Roosevelt advising his wife, "You kiss the niggers, and I'll kiss the Jews, and we'll stay in the White House as long as we choose." It may be sheer coincidence that the IRS slapped imperial headquarters with a crushing tax lien in April 1944, but FDR was well known for using federal agencies against his political enemies. The order disbanded in lieu of paying its tax bill, but klansmen consoled themselves with news of Roosevelt's death, from a stroke, on 12 April 1945.

Smith, Alfred Emanuel—Al Smith, AKA "The Happy Warrior" and "The Brown Derby," was a New York City native, born 30 December 1873. He served in the state legislature (1904–15) and completed two terms as governor of New York (1919–21, 1923–29). Smith—a Roman Catholic, outspoken in his criticism of Prohibition—sought but failed to capture the Democratic Party's presidential nomination in 1920 and 1924. His second effort drew concerted opposition from the Ku Klux Klan, which raised the dual threats of "rum and Rome" to defeat his candidacy at the riotous Democratic National Convention in Smith's hometown. By 1928, Klan strength had declined to the point where Smith was unbeatable in his third bid for the presidential nod, winning nomination on the convention's first ballot. Even some klansmen had changed their minds about Smith, and several Atlanta knights were banished for refusing to pledge their votes against him. In Alabama, Senator (and klansman) Hugo Black openly campaigned for Smith, and Cotton State voters gave Smith a narrow majority on election day. Alabama's other Klan senator, Tom Heflin, stood fast in opposition to Smith's candidacy, warning New York knights of Smith's plan to tie American to "the tail of the Roman Catholic kite." In the Dakotas, Klan literature carried the slogan "Swat Smith and put Heflin in the White House," while a Methodist minister in Paterson, New Jersey, was jailed for illegally distributing Klan posters that read: "Men and Women, Keep the Roman Menace Out." The importance of Smith's religion in the final balloting—21,392,190 votes for Republican Herbert Hoover versus Smith's 15,016,443—is difficult to judge, but the KKK was relegated to a marginal role in the national campaign (although its spokesmen claimed full credit for Smith's defeat). Smith sought the Democratic presidential nomination once more, in 1932, but critical supporters in the New York underworld (including mobsters Meyer Lansky and "Lucky" Luciano) threw their weight to Franklin Roosevelt. Smith retired from public life thereafter, and died on 4 October 1944.

Thurmond, James Strom *see* *Congress*

Truman, Harry S—A product of Missouri machine politics, haberdasher Harry Truman launched his first race for office (as a Jackson County judge) in 1922. All sources, including Truman himself, agree that he paid his klecktoken to join the KKK that year, but stories differ wildly as to what happened next. Truman claimed that he changed his mind prior to initiation and got his money back, after local Klan leaders tried to dictate his postelection patronage appointments (barring selection of Jews and Catholics). Klan spokesmen later claimed that Truman was initiated as a klansman, but some historians believe that tale was concocted to embarrass him as president (1945–53). In any case, while some sources describe Truman as a lifelong racist (one website maintaining that he "used the word 'nigger' until the day he died"), Truman sparked the hooded order's wrath by integrating the U.S. armed forces after World War II and by creating the Fair Employment Practices Commission to fight job discrimination. Those civil rights initiatives prompted the "Dixiecrat" walkout at 1948's Democratic National Convention, whereupon most klansmen supported the fledgling States Rights Party and presidential candidate Strom Thurmond of South Carolina. Truman retired from politics after 1953 and died in Missouri on 26 December 1972. A subsequent one-man stage play and film, *Give 'Em Hell, Harry,* featured actor James Whitmore as Truman, his monologue including a brief vignette of Truman's alleged showdown with the KKK in 1922.

Underwood, Oscar *see* *Congress*

Wallace, George Corley *see* *Governors*

Wallace, Henry Agard—An Iowa native, born in 1888, Wallace graduated from the University of Iowa (Ames) in 1910, then spent the next twenty years as editor of a Des Moines newspaper, *Wallace's Farmer* (1910–29), while conducting various agricultural experiments and writing extensively in the field. He served as Secretary of Agriculture under President Franklin Roosevelt (1933–40), then as FDR's vice president (1941–45) and as President Harry Truman's Secretary of Commerce (1945–46). In 1948, Wallace accepted the left-wing Progressive Party's presidential nomination, while segregationist Democrats backed the States Rights ("Dixiecrat") Party. Southern racists, including KKK spokesmen, raged against Wallace when he refused to address racially segregated meetings in Dixie. Klansmen in Knoxville, Tennessee, timed their own rally to coincide with Wallace's speech at a local black church, while hecklers in North Carolina pelted Wallace with fruit. On election day, Wallace polled 1,156,013 votes nationwide, running 23,000 behind Dixiecrat candidate Strom Thurmond, while Harry Truman secured a surprise victory over Republican contender Thomas Dewey. Wallace subsequently settled in New York and resumed his agricultural interests. He died in Connecticut on 16 November 1965.

Watson, Thomas *see* *Congress*

Wilson, Thomas Woodrow—A Virginia native, born in 1856, Wilson moved to Georgia with his family as an infant, then moved again, this time to South Carolina, at age fourteen. His southern roots ran deep, including graduation from the University of Virginia's law school (1881), although he later taught at New Jersey's Princeton University (1890–1902) and served as its president (1902–10), then spent one term as governor of the Garden State (1911–13). A quarter-century in New Jersey did nothing to temper Wilson's southern sympathies. In his epic *History of the American People* (1902), he described Reconstruction klansmen as valiant saviors of Dixie, and his presidential administration (1913–21) brought full-scale racial segregation to the federal government and Washington, D.C. When former college classmate Thomas Dixon approached Wilson in 1915, seeking an endorsement for *The Birth of a Nation,* Wilson viewed the pro–Klan film and declared, "It is like writing history with lightning, and my only regret is that it is all so terribly true." Some websites name Wilson as a member of the modern KKK, but no supporting evidence exists. Wilson may well have sympathized with the order, but the strokes that incapacitated him in autumn 1919 left him an invalid. He died in Washington, D.C., on 3 February 1924.

Congress

Aiken, David Wyatt—A native of Fairfield County, South Carolina, born in 1828, Aiken graduated from the state university in 1849 and joined the Confederate army as a private in 1861, rising to the rank of colonel before battle wounds left him sidelined in September 1862. He subsequently served in the state legislature (1864–66), and remained active in the Democratic Party during Reconstruction. At the same time, he openly advocated Klan violence, issuing public calls for the murder of Republican state legislators. In 1876, Aiken served as a delegate to the Democratic National Convention. Voters elected him to the House of Representatives in 1876, where he served from 1877–87. Illness rendered him an invalid during his final term (1885–87), and Aiken declined to seek reelection in 1886. He died on 6 April 1887, one month after the conclusion of his final term in Congress.

Allen, James Browning—Born at Gadsden, Alabama, in March 1912, Allen graduated from the University of Alabama and received his LL.B. from the university's law school, entering private practice in 1938. He served in the state legislature from 1939 to 1942, when he resigned to join the U.S. Navy. Discharged in 1946, Allen served in the state senate (1946–50) and completed two terms as lieutenant governor under Governors James Folsom (1951–55) and George Wallace (1963–67). Voters elected him to the U.S. Senate in 1968, where he served until his death on 1 June 1978. In August 1968, Allen sent an autographed photo of himself to the UKA's imperial wizard in Tuscaloosa, signed: "With sincerest best wishes to my good friend Robert M. Shelton." Allen also sent a friendly telegram to the UKA's klonvokation in 1970.

Arnell, Samuel Mayes—A Tennessee native, born in 1833, Mayes attended Amherst College in Massachusetts and studied law before the Civil War. In 1865, he was a Republican delegate to Tennessee's constitutional convention. He subsequently served in the state legislature (1865–66) and in the House of Representatives (1866–71). Tennessee klansmen marked Arnell for death in June 1868, boarding a Maury County train with ropes and pistols in an effort to kill him, but Arnell eluded his would-be assassins. When Arnell asked Governor William Brownlow for troops to fight Klan violence in his district, Brownlow replied that none were available. Arnell declined to seek reelection in 1870, subsequently serving as postmaster in Columbia, Tennessee (1879–84) and as the city's superintendent of schools (1884–86). He died in Tennessee on 20 July 1903.

Bilbo, Theodore Gilmore—Ranked among America's most notorious racist politicians, Bilbo was a Mississippi native, born near Poplarville in October 1877. He attended college and law school in Nashville, Tennessee, with a brief stint at the University of Michigan. After five years as a schoolteacher, Bilbo moved on to politics, serving in the state legislature (1908–12), as lieutenant governor (1912–16), governor (1916–20, 1928–32), and in the U.S. Senate (1935–47). At some point in the 1920s, Bilbo joined the KKK, and while he subsequently denied any Klan activity in Mississippi after 1924, he told reporters during 1946, "I am a member of the Ku Klux Klan, Bilbo Klan No. 40, Mississippi." Opponents accused Bilbo of "clowning" on the Klan issue, but his racism was clearly sincere. In 1947, he published a book titled *Take Your Choice: Separation or Mongrelization,* which advocated deportation of all American blacks to Africa. That same year, he advised Mississippi whites: "You know and I know what's the best way to keep the nigger from voting. You do it the night before the election. I don't have to tell you any more than that. Red-blooded men know what I mean." Such antics prompted an investigation of his final election campaign, and the Senate refused to seat Bilbo in 1947. He died from mouth cancer (some say appropriately) on 21 August 1947.

Black, Hugo *see U.S. Supreme Court*

Brewster, Ralph *see Governors*

Byrd, Robert Carlyle—Born in North Carolina, in November 1917, Byrd was raised in West Virginia and graduated from Marshall College before studying law at George Washington University, in Washington, D.C. During World War II, while working as a shipyard worker, he joined the KKK and served the order as a kleagle. Byrd later claimed that he was only a klansmen during 1942–43, claiming, "Those were my dues-paying years, and after that I lost interest." Still, in 1946 he penned a letter to AGK Grand Dragon Samuel Green in Atlanta, stating: "I am a former kleagle of the Ku Klux Klan in Raleigh County.... The Klan is needed today as never before and I am anxious to see its rebirth in West Virginia. It is necessary that the order be promoted immediately and in every state in the union." Asked about that correspondence later, Byrd replied, "I had completely forgotten that letter." Soon after writing to Green, Byrd won election to the state legislature, where he served from 1947 to 1952. He then moved on to the House of Representatives (1953–59), and won election to the U.S. Senate in 1958 (where he remained at press time for this volume). President Richard Nixon briefly considered Byrd for a U.S. Supreme Court appointment in October 1971, then rejected him on

grounds that he had only earned his law degree in 1963 and faced stiff opposition from civil rights groups. Byrd's previous involvement with the KKK still surfaces in media reports from time to time, evoking apologies for his "young and foolish" behavior. Contrary to certain accounts, Byrd never served as West Virginia's grand dragon.

Clanton, James Holt—Several sources name Clanton as Alabama's Reconstruction-era grand dragon. Voters elected him to the House of Representatives in 1870, and he subsequently served as a minority (Democratic) member of the congressional panel assigned to investigate Klan violence in the South. On 27 September 1871, Clanton was murdered by a man who provoked a fight with him in Knoxville, Tennessee.

DuBose, Dudley McIver—A Tennessee native, born in 1834, DuBose attended the University of Mississippi and graduated from Tennessee's Lebanon Law School in 1856. He practiced law in Memphis before moving to Georgia in 1860, then joined the Confederate army as a colonel, rising to the rank of brigadier general during the Civil War. During Reconstruction, DuBose served as the KKK's grand titan in Georgia's Fifth Congressional District, one of the state's most violent regions. DuBose won election to the House of Representatives in 1870, with support from his fellow klansmen, but served only a single term (1871–73). He died at Washington, Georgia, on 2 March 1883.

Forney, William Henry—Several published accounts name Forney as Alabama's grand dragon during Reconstruction. Voters elected him to the House of Representatives in 1874 and he served eight terms, declining to seek reelection in 1892. President Grover Cleveland appointed Forney to the Gettysburg Battlefield Commission, where he served until his death on 16 January 1894.

Garland, Augustus *see U.S. Attorney General*

Gause, Lucien Coatsworth—Born on 25 December 1836 to affluent parents in North Carolina, Gause was educated by private tutors until he entered the University of Virginia, subsequently studying law at Tennessee's Cumberland University. He then settled in Arkansas, practicing law from 1859 until the outbreak of the Civil War. Gause joined the Confederate army as a lieutenant and rose to the rank of colonel by war's end. During Reconstruction, he served briefly in the Arkansas state legislature (1866) and was an active member of the KKK in Woodruff County. Gause subsequently served in the House of Representatives (1875–79), but declined to seek a third term in 1878. He died in Arkansas on 5 November 1880.

George, James Zacariah—Named in various accounts as Mississippi's grand dragon during Reconstruction, George was appointed to the state supreme court in 1879 and soon became its chief justice. Voters elected George to the U.S. Senate in 1880, and he served from 1881 until his death, on 14 August 1897. During that period, he also served as a member of Mississippi's constitutional convention (1890).

George, Walter Franklin—A Georgia native, born in January 1878, George graduated from Macon's Mercer University in 1900 and from the same school's law department in 1901. After seven years in private legal practice, he served as solicitor general in Cordele (1907–12), as a judge in superior court (1912–17), and on the state court of appeals (January to October 1917). By the time he resigned that position to become a justice of the state supreme court (1917–22), George had joined the KKK under Imperial Wizard William Simmons. Klan membership helped him win a U.S. Senate seat in November 1922, replacing the late Thomas Watson, and George held that office until January 1957. In 1926, after George supported establishment of the World Court, imperial headquarters backed candidate Richard Russell, Sr., in an abortive bid to unseat him. Two years later, George sought the Democratic presidential nomination, but it went instead to New York Catholic Alfred Smith. By 1946, Russell was back in the KKK's favor, receiving Klan donations to support his campaign against black civil rights. Poor health prevented George from seeking reelection in 1956, and he died in Georgia on 4 August 1957.

Gordon, George Washington—After serving as Tennessee's first grand dragon, under Grand Wizard Nathan Forrest, Gordon held various political offices, including railroad commissioner (1883), special Indian agent in Arizona and Nevada (1885–89), and superintendent of schools in Memphis (1889–1907). Voters elected him to the House of Representatives in 1906, and Gordon died in office on 9 August 1911.

Gordon, John Brown—Gordon lost his first gubernatorial race in 1868, while serving as Georgia's grand dragon. Five years later, with the state "redeemed" for white "home rule," he won election to the U.S. Senate, where he served until May 1880. In 1876, he helped negotiate the compromise that placed Rutherford Hayes in the White House and ended Reconstruction in the South. Gordon resigned from the Senate in 1880 to promote the Georgia Pacific Railroad, and subsequently realized his dream of being Georgia's governor (1886–90). A second Senate term (1891–97) was his last, and he declined to stand for reelection in 1896. Gordon retired to Miami, Florida, where he died on 9 January 1904.

Hampton, Wade—Published accounts name Hampton as South Carolina's probable grand dragon during Reconstruction. Voters rejected his bid for the governor's mansion in 1865, but elected him in 1876 after a campaign of "Red Shirt" terrorism orchestrated by Hampton. As governor, in 1877, he interceded with President Rutherford Hayes to quash murder charges filed against klansman J. Rufus Bratton. Hampton won election to the U.S. Senate in 1879 and served until 1891. He subsequently served as U.S. railroad commissioner under President Grover Cleveland (1893–97).

Harris, William Julius—A native of Polk County, Georgia, born in 1868, Harris graduated from the University of Georgia in 1890. He worked as a banker, insurance salesman and secretary to Senator Alexander Clay (1904–09), before winning election to the state legislature (1911–12) and serving as the state Democratic Party chairman (1912–13). Harris subsequently served as director of the U.S. Census Bureau (1913–15), then resigned to serve as acting Secretary of Commerce (1913–15) and

as a member of the Federal Trade Commission (1915–18). He won election to the U.S. Senate in 1918, but faced a serious challenge when he stood for reelection in 1924. His first opponent, state supreme court Chief Justice Richard Russell, Sr., dropped out of the race in July 1924, after a KKK delegation informed him that the Klan had pledged $500,000 to Harris's reelection campaign. Governor Thomas Hardwick, himself a former U.S. Senator, ignored similar warnings and challenged Harris for his seat in Washington, charging that Harris was a member of the KKK. Harris ignored those jibes until September 1924, when Hardwick produced a letter from former Klan publicist Elizabeth Tyler, dated 16 March 1922, addressed to "Hon. W.J. Harris, AKIA." Most Georgians knew by then that AKIA meant "A Klansman I Am," but Harris fired back with denials of joining the order, expressing dismay that Hardwick would "stoop so low" as to use an "alleged letter upon which he deliberately places a false interpretation." Klan votes returned Harris to the Senate in November 1924, and no candidates bothered to oppose his 1930 reelection bid. Harris died in office on 18 April 1932.

Hays, Lawrence Brooks—An Arkansas native, born at London in 1898, Hays served in the U.S. Army during 1918, then graduated from the University of Arkansas in 1919 and secured his LL.B. from George Washington Law School in 1922. He subsequently served as assistant state attorney general (1925–27) and as a member of the Democratic National Committee (1932–39). Arkansas voters elected Hays to the House of Representatives in 1942, where he served until 1959 and earned a reputation as a "moderate" on civil rights. Defeated by a hard-line segregationist candidate in 1958, Hays moved on to serve as a director of the Tennessee Valley Authority (1959–61), as an assistant secretary of state (1961), and as special assistant to the President of the United States (1961–64). In January 1965, while teaching government at the University of Massachusetts, Hays received an invitation to speak in strife-torn Bogalusa, Louisiana. Klansmen distributed 6,000 pamphlets advising locals that Hays was coming "to convince you that you should help integration by sitting in church with the black man, hiring more of them in your businesses, serving and eating with them in your cafes, and allowing your children to sit by filthy, runny-nosed, ragged, ugly little niggers in your public schools." The Klan also warned that anyone who attended Hays's speech would be "tagged as integrationists and will be dealt with accordingly." The event was canceled after a series of bomb threats and a cross-burning near the church where Hays was scheduled to speak. After a failed congressional campaign in North Carolina (1972), Hays retired to Chevy Chase, Maryland, where he died on 11 October 1981.

Heflin, James Thomas—Alabama's leading anti–Catholic orator of the 1920s was born in Randolph County on 6 April 1869. He graduated from Greensboro's Southern University and the Alabama Agricultural and Mechanical College (later Auburn University), then studied law and won admittance to the bar in 1893. Heflin subsequently served as mayor of Lafayette (1893–94), as a registrar of chancery (1894–96), in the state legislature (1896–1900), and as Alabama's secretary of state (1902–04). In May 1904, voters chose him to fill a vacancy in the U.S. House of Representatives, where he remained until 1920. After arguing against women's suffrage in the House, he won election to fill a U.S. Senate vacancy in 1920 and was reelected to a full term of his own in 1924. By that time, Heflin was well established as a favorite draw on the Klan lecture circuit, blasting Catholics in general and New York presidential candidate Al Smith in particular. (South Dakota klansmen printed pamphlets in 1928 reading: "Swat Smith and put Heflin in the White House.") Nor was his bigotry limited to Catholics: Heflin once shot a black man who boarded a whites-only streetcar in Washington, D.C. His extremism wore thin for most listeners by 1926, when Imperial Wizard Hiram Evans surprised klansmen by criticizing Heflin at Alabama's annual klorero. Public quarrels with his fellow senators in Washington turned much of the Alabama press against Heflin from 1928 onward, and Montgomery's mayor refused Heflin use of the city's auditorium that year. Crowds from Massachusetts to his home state pelted Heflin with eggs and rotten fruit, while Alabama's State Democratic Executive Committee formally condemned him. The state's "Big Mules" combined to defeat Heflin's reelection bid in 1930, and the state legislature formally condemned him in 1931 for besmirching Alabama's reputation. Heflin later served as special representative of the Federal Housing Administration (1935–36, 1939–42) and as special assistant to the U.S. Attorney General in Alabama (1936–37). He died at Lafayette on 22 April 1951.

Henry, Robert Lee

—Robert Henry presents the example of a politician who enjoyed some success before joining the KKK, then tried unsuccessfully to expand his horizons with Klan support. Born at Linden, Texas, in 1864, a great-grandson of Revolutionary hero Patrick Henry, Henry graduated from Georgetown's Southwestern University in 1885, then studied law and was admitted to the bar in 1886. He practiced briefly in Texarkana, won election as that city's mayor in 1890, but resigned a year later to serve as first assistant to the state attorney general (1891–93), then as assistant attorney general (1893–96). Voters elected Henry to nine terms in the House of Representatives (1897–1917), and by the time he left that post he was a member of the KKK. He sought nomination as a U.S. Senate candidate in 1922, but the Klan quietly backed rival Earl Mayfield instead, leaving Henry to draw critical fire from Klan critics. Henry likewise lost his Senate bid in 1928. On 9 July 1931, he suffered a fatal gunshot wound in Houston. Authorities ruled his death accidental.

Howard, Everette Burgess

—A Kentucky native, born at Morgantown in 1873, Howard worked as a journalist in several states before settling in Tulsa, Oklahoma, in 1905. There, after dabbling in the oil and gas business, he won election to the state board of public affairs (1911–15) and served as state auditor (1915–19) before winning election to the U.S. House of Representatives (1919–21). After losing his 1920 reelection bid, Howard returned to Tulsa and joined the KKK, using the order as a springboard to political success. Klansmen supported Howard as a gubernatorial candidate in 1922, but he quit that race in May to seek another term in Congress. Klan votes returned him to the House, while "klansman at large" John Walton captured the governor's mansion. Walton's high-profile feud

with the KKK and the state legislature climaxed with his impeachment in November 1923, but he rebounded with a run for the U.S. Senate in 1924. Encouraged by his fellow knights, Howard sacrificed his House reelection hopes to oppose Walton in the Democratic senatorial primary. Tulsa Klan leaders endorsed him in July, but Grand Dragon Clay Jewett scrubbed that vote of confidence, promising the order's votes to Tulsa oilman Charles Wrightsman. Then, on the eve of the primary, Jewett reversed himself with a flurry of telegrams, commanding all knights to vote for Howard. The resultant confusion gave Walton the Democratic nomination, and thus ensured victory for the GOP's candidate, oilman William Pine. Suspicious klansmen accused Jewett of deliberately sabotaging Howard's candidacy, their subsequent revolt gravely wounding the Oklahoma realm. Howard, meanwhile, won a third House term in 1926, then retired from politics in 1929. He returned to the petroleum business and died at Midland, Texas, on 3 April 1950.

Jarvis, Thomas Jordan

—A native of Jarvisburg, North Carolina, born in 1836, Jarvis studied law before secession, then served in the Confederate army during the Civil War. In 1865, he was a delegate to the state constitutional convention. When Congress imposed military Reconstruction, Jarvis joined the KKK and plunged headlong into racist Democratic politics. He was elected to the state house of representatives in 1868 and served as its speaker. After "redemption" of the Tarheel State for white "home rule," Jarvis served as lieutenant governor (1877–79), governor (1879–85), U.S. Minister to Brazil (1885–88), and briefly in the U.S. Senate, filling a vacancy left by fellow ex-klansman Zebulon Vance (1894–95). In 1896, Jarvis was a delegate to the Democratic National Convention. He then retired to private legal practice in Greenville and died there on 17 June 1915.

Mayfield, Earl Bradford

—Born at Overton, Texas, in 1881, Mayfield graduated from Georgetown's Southwestern University in 1900, then studied law at Austin's University of Texas (1900–01). Despite completion of his studies, he was not admitted to the state bar until 1907, the same year he won election to the state senate (1907–13). From that post, Mayfield moved on to spend a decade as the state's railroad commissioner (1913–23). He joined the KKK soon after it was organized in Texas, and used the invisible empire to further his political ambitions. In 1922, a choice of two rival klansmen seeking one U.S. Senate seat divided the Texas Klan. Imperial headquarters backed Robert Henry, but Mayfield secured victory in the crucial Democratic primary by appealing to state KKK leaders. While Henry ran openly as a klansman, drawing heavy criticism from the order's opponents, Mayfield's "stealth" campaign carried him to victory. In November's general election, Republicans tried to have Mayfield stricken from the ballot on grounds that his KKK oath meant he was not actually a Democrat. That effort failed, and Mayfield defeated his GOP opponent by a margin of 264,000 votes to 130,000. A last-ditch Republican effort failed to prevent Mayfield from taking his Senate seat in 1923, and a year later he joined the Klan's strategy board for the 1924 Democratic National Convention. In 1925, Mayfield was a featured guest of honor at the Dyersburg, Tennessee, wedding of Klan lobbyist

W.F. Zumbrunn. Three years later, with sentiment running high against the KKK in Texas, Mayfield sought reelection by publicly condemning the order and supporting Catholic Al Smith for president, but the effort was wasted. Defeated, he retired to private legal practice in Tyler, where he died on 23 June 1964.

McKellar, Kenneth Douglas

—An Alabama native, born in 1869, McKellar was home-schooled prior to his enrollment at the University of Alabama, where he earned his B.A. in 1891 and his LL.B. in 1892. He then moved to Memphis, Tennessee, and won admission to the bar in 1892. McKellar entered politics as a presidential elector for Tennessee (1904) and a delegate to the Democratic National Convention (1908), then won election to fill a congressional vacancy in 1911. After three terms in the House of Representatives (1911–17), he was elected to the U.S. Senate, where he served from 1917 to 1953. McKellar's membership in the KKK was revealed in early 1925, when he attended the Dyersburg, Tennessee, wedding of W.F. Zumbrunn, the Klan's chief lobbyist in Washington, D.C. That revelation did not impede his reelection bids in 1928, 1934, 1940, or 1946. In 1936, McKellar criticized the FBI and lampooned Director J. Edgar Hoover for the fact that he had never made an arrest. Hoover promptly arranged the "personal" capture of bank robber Alvin Karpis, while mounting surveillance on McKellar. Faced with Bureau blackmail threats, McKellar changed his tune and in 1943 attended graduation ceremonies at the FBI Academy, where he praised "this great instrument of law and order that has been built up by the grand man who is your director." McKellar failed to win renomination in 1952 and retired from public life thereafter. He died in Memphis on 25 October 1957.

Means, Rice William

—A Missouri native, born in 1877, Means moved to Denver, Colorado, with his parents at age twelve. He graduated from Denver's Sacred Heart College, then served with the U.S. Army in the Spanish American War and commanded a team of scouts in the Philippine campaign of 1899. Means graduated from the University of Michigan's law school in 1901 and commenced private practice in Denver, prior to serving as a judge in Adams County (1902–04). He failed to win a congressional seat in 1908, and resumed legal practice until World War I, when he returned to active military service as a colonel. Back in civilian life, Means joined the KKK soon after its arrival in Denver and used the Klan as his vehicle to a political career. Means served as Denver's city attorney during 1923–24, then won election in November 1924 to fill a U.S. Senate vacancy. At the start of that campaign, Means and other Ku Klux candidates were told by Grand Dragon John Locke that "the Klan will support no man in the coming election unless he signs his name on the dotted line to all the pledges and promises the Klan demands." Means agreed, but Locke briefly suspended him from the Klan in July 1925, for siding with imperial headquarters in the dispute that drove Locke from office. In 1926, seeking a full Senate term of his own, Means led the Klan's slate of candidates in the Republican primary, but voters rejected him. He subsequently moved to Washington, D.C., where he served as commander-in-chief of the United Spanish War Veterans (1926–27) and published two newspapers, the *National Tribune*

and *Stars and Stripes* (1927–37). Means died in Denver on 30 January 1949.

Mills, Roger Quarles

—Named in various reports as the Reconstruction-era grand dragon of Texas, Mills subsequently won election to the House of Representatives (1873–92) and the U.S. Senate (1892–99). He declined to seek reelection in 1898.

Morgan, John Tyler

—Several historians name Morgan as Alabama's grand dragon during Reconstruction. In 1876, he served as a delegate to the Democratic National Convention and also won election to the U.S. Senate, where he served from 1877 until his death in office, on 11 June 1897.

Muldrow, Henry Lowndes

—A native of Clay County, Mississippi, born in 1837, Muldrow graduated from the University of Mississippi in 1857 and from its law department in 1858, gaining admittance to the bar in 1859. After secession, he joined the Confederate army as a private and rose to the rank of colonel by war's end. In Reconstruction, Muldrow was a founder of the KKK in Starkville. His appointment as district attorney for Mississippi's sixth judicial district (1869–71) allowed him to sidetrack prosecution of violent klansmen, and he also defended those who drove a "carpetbag" Methodist minister from the region in 1871, winning repeated postponements that scuttled the case. Muldrow subsequently served in the state legislature (1875), in the House of Representatives (1877–85), and as First Assistant Secretary of the Interior under President Grover Cleveland (1885–89). In 1890, Muldrow was a delegate to Mississippi's constitutional convention, helping to draft the document that disenfranchised blacks throughout the state. He later served as chancellor for the first district of Mississippi (1899–1905) and died in Starkville on 1 March 1905.

Phipps, Lawrence Cowle

—A Pennsylvania native, born in 1862, Phipps retired from the Carnegie Steel Company as a vice president in 1901, then moved to Denver, Colorado, and enhanced his already substantial fortune through various investments. His wealth, in addition to high-profile work with the Red Cross and the Colorado Taxpayers' Protective League, helped Phipps win election to the U.S. Senate in 1918. He never joined the KKK, but sealed a bargain with the Klan as he prepared to seek reelection in 1924. In return for Klan votes, Phipps promised Grand Dragon John Locke that he (Phipps) would cover most of the year's Republican campaign expenses, including those of Klan candidates for governor (Clarence Morley) and Colorado's second Senate seat (Rice Means). Every GOP candidate except Phipps vowed to "sign his name on the dotted line to all the pledges and promises the Klan demands." The Phipps-Klan slate swept Colorado, but Phipps declined to seek a third term in 1930. Instead, he moved on to California, prospering in railroad and electrical power investments, and died there on 1 March 1958.

Ramspeck, Robert C. Word

—A native of Decatur, Georgia, born in 1890, Ramspeck obtained his highest formal education from that city's Donald Fraser School. He subsequently served as deputy clerk of the state superior court (1907–11), chief postal clerk for the U.S. House of Representatives (1911), as a congressional secretary (1912), and as a deputy U.S. marshal for the northern district of Georgia (1914–16). While thus employed, in 1915, Ramspeck joined William Simmons and ten others in applying for the KKK's original state charter. Two years after helping to launch the Klan, Ramspeck won promotion to chief deputy U.S. marshal (1917–19), then pursued the insurance and real estate trades while attending the Atlanta Law School and winning admission to the state bar in 1920. His career blossomed with the KKK, including service as a court solicitor in Decatur (1923–27), as Decatur's city attorney (1927–29), and as a member of the state legislature (1929). In October 1929, Ramspeck won election to fill a vacancy in the House of Representatives, where he remained through 1945. On 31 December 1945, he resigned from Congress to become executive vice president of the Air Transport Association. Ramspeck later served as chairman of the U.S. Civil Service Commission (1951–52), and vice president of Eastern Air Lines (1953–61). He remained as a consultant to Eastern until his final retirement in 1966. Ramspeck died while visiting Castor, Louisiana, on 10 September 1972.

Rarick, John Richard—An Indiana native, born in 1924, Rarick served in the U.S. Army during World War II, winning a Bronze Star and a Purple Heart for his escape from a Nazi prison camp. He subsequently graduated from Indiana's Ball State Teacher's College and from Louisiana's Tulane University School of Law. Admitted to Louisiana's state bar in 1949, Rarick served as a district judge (1961–66) and sought election to the U.S. House of Representatives in 1966. His opponent in that contest, twelve-term incumbent James Morrison, accused Rarick of being a klansman, whereupon Rarick filed a $500,000 libel suit. Rarick defeated Morrison in November 1966, and Morrison later settled the libel case out of court. The *New York Times* later reported that Morrison's charges had prompted an FBI investigation of Rarick, and Bureau documents released in 1973 confirmed Rarick's service as exalted cyclops of a klavern in St. Francisville, Louisiana. In Congress, Rarick maintained his reputation as a strict segregationist, and FBI headquarters used him in June 1969 to mount a posthumous smear campaign against Dr. Martin Luther King, Jr. Rarick lost his reelection bid in 1974 and returned to private legal practice in St. Francisville. In 1980, he polled 41,628 votes nationwide as the far-right American Independent Party's presidential candidate.

Rowbottom, Harry Emerson—Born at Aurora, Indiana, in 1884, Rowbottom attended Kentucky State College at Lexington (1902–04), then spent three years as an oil salesman before enrolling at Cincinnati Business College, where he obtained a degree in accountancy (1907). He subsequently worked as an auditor in Cincinnati (1907–10) and Chicago (1910–12), then moved to Indiana as chief clerk of Evansville's Indiana Refining Company (1913–18). Rowbottom subsequently served in the state legislature (1919–24), and joined the KKK while he was thus employed. In 1924, he obtained Klan support for a congressional race by pledging to let Grand Dragon David Stephenson make all of his (Rowbottom's) patronage appointments. Rowbottom avoided the worst fallout from Stephenson's 1926 murder conviction and the ensuing political scandals. After three terms in Congress, he declined to seek reelection in 1930, instead finding employment as a commercial agent for a trucking line. Rowbottom died in Evansville on 22 March 1934.

Steck, Daniel Frederic—A native of Ottumwa, Iowa, born in 1881, Steck earned his LL.B. from the University of Iowa (Iowa City) in 1906 and was admitted to the bar that same year. He served in World War I as a U.S. Army captain, then returned to private legal practice in Ottumwa. In 1925, with Klan support, Steck won election to the U.S. Senate. Opponent Smith Brookhart challenged the election, and a Senate panel convened to investigate. In testimony at those hearings, Steck denied any link to the KKK, but he was represented by W.F. Zumbrunn, the same Ku Klux attorney-lobbyist who earlier defeated a similar challenge against Texas Senator (and klansman) Earl Mayfield. Steck served one term in Washington, then lost his reelection bid in 1930. He briefly resumed private practice, then joined the U.S. Justice Department as a special assistant to the Attorney General under President's Franklin Roosevelt and Harry Truman (1933–47). Steck died in his hometown on 31 December 1950.

Talmadge, Herman Eugene—The son of Klan-allied Georgia Governor Eugene Talmadge, born in Telfair County on 9 August 1913, Herman Talmadge received his LL.B. from the University of Georgia in 1936 and entered private practice in Atlanta. He joined the U.S. Navy in 1941 and saw action in the Pacific theater, rising to the rank of lieutenant commander before his discharge in November 1945. When his father died before inauguration for his third term as governor, state legislators elected Herman to serve in his place. Talmadge occupied the governor's mansion for sixty-seven days, before the state supreme court rendered judgment in favor of Lieutenant Governor Melvin Thompson. Talmadge used his free time to cultivate relations with the KKK, including an appearance as guest speaker at Grand Dragon Samuel Green's birthday party in 1948. Talmadge told that audience that Georgia was fortunate to have klansmen "ready to fight for the preservation of our American traditions against the communists, foreign agitators, Negroes, Catholics and Jews." Green returned the favor in that year's gubernatorial campaign, promoting Talmadge as "the man who will put Georgia back in the white man's column." A statewide campaign of cross-burnings, demonstrations and death threats discouraged blacks from voting in the spring primary elections, and Green's AGK formally endorsed Talmadge in August 1948, with a promise of 100,000 white votes. Duly elected one month later, Talmadge rewarded Green on 17 November with an appointment to serve as lieutenant colonel and aide-de-camp on the governor's staff. Klan support for Talmadge became a major issue in the 1950 gubernatorial race, with opponent Melvin Thompson calling for a statewide anti-mask law, blaming recent acts of racial terrorism on "allies of the Talmadge machine who specialize in violence and use fear as their weapon." Talmadge fired back by branding Thompson "a friend of the Negroes, a friend of civil rights, and a friend of the FEPC," a broadside that ensured Talmadge's reelection in November 1950. In 1951, with Dr. Green dead and the Klan losing strength under Grand Dragon Samuel Roper, Talmadge demonstrated his adaptability by supporting passage of the anti-mask law his

cronies had killed in the state legislature a year earlier. At the same time, he anticipated the U.S. Supreme Court's "Black Monday" decision on school integration, introducing a state constitutional amendment placing Georgia's school system under private control, thus protecting it from federal interference. Talmadge received one electoral vote for vice president in 1956, but he was fully satisfied that year with his election to the U.S. Senate, where he served until 1981. A steadfast opponent of civil rights throughout his tenure in the Senate, Talmadge lost his bid for a fifth term in 1980, following exposure of his chronic alcoholism. He thereafter retired to private legal practice and died in Hampton, Georgia, on 21 March 2002.

Thurmond, James Strom—Born at Edgefield, South Carolina, in 1902, Strom Thurmond graduated from Clemson College in 1923, then taught school (1923–29) and served as Edgefield County's superintendent of education (1929–33) while studying law. With admission to the state bar in 1930, Thurmond doubled as a city and county attorney (1930–38) while serving in the state senate (1933–38). A circuit judge's duties occupied his time in 1938–42, and he retained that title while serving in the U.S. Army (1942–46), discharged with the rank of major general in the reserves. Thurmond next served a term as South Carolina's governor (1947–51), and in 1948 welcomed AGK Grand Dragon Samuel Green to address the state legislature. Klansmen rewarded that gesture at the polls in November 1948, when Thurmond received 1,169,021 as the Dixiecrat candidate for president. Thurmond also lost his U.S. Senate race in 1950, but finally made it to Washington in December 1954, appointed to fill the Senate vacancy left by Charles Daniel's resignation. South Carolina voters returned Thurmond to the Senate in November 1956 and kept him there until his death on 26 June 2003, at age 100. In the meantime, he had switched allegiance to the GOP, in protest against Democratic civil rights initiatives, and used all of his influence to obstruct civil rights legislation throughout the 1960s. Six months after Thurmond died, in December 2003, his family acknowledged the paternity claims of Essie Mae Washington-Williams, whom Thurmond fathered with his black teenage housekeeper in 1925.

Underwood, Oscar Wilder—A native of Louisville, Kentucky, born in 1862, Underwood was the grandson of an Alabama congressman (Joseph Underwood) who spent twenty years in Washington, D.C. He graduated from the University of Virginia, then studied law and settled in Birmingham to practice. In March 1895, Underwood presented credentials as a member-elect to the House of Representatives and served until June 1896, when rival Truman Aldrich challenged his election and replaced Underwood. Voters elected Underwood to the House once again in November 1896, and this time he remained, serving until March 1915, when he graduated to the U.S. Senate. Underwood's tenure in the House was interrupted by an abortive bid for the 1912 Democratic presidential nomination, but the snub did not discourage him. In 1924, he tried again, and this time ran headlong into the Alabama KKK. Unlike most politicians in and from his state, Underwood despised the Klan, publicly branding it "a national menace." In campaign speeches, he declared, "It is either the Ku Klux Klan or the United States

of America. Both cannot survive. Between the two, I choose my country." That anti-Klan stance was a major issue at the 1924 Democratic National Convention, where New York Catholic Al Smith was Underwood's chief competition. Ku Klux delegates threw their weight behind Californian William Gibbs McAdoo in an acrimonious battle that split the convention and resulted in the nomination of West Virginian John W. Davis on the 103rd ballot. Two years later, faced with near-certain defeat at home, Underwood declined to seek reelection. In 1928, he represented the U.S. in Havana, at the Sixth International Conference of American States. Thereafter, Underwood retired to an estate in Virginia, where he died on 25 January 1929.

Upshaw, William David—Born outside Newnan, Georgia, in 1866, Upshaw graduated from Macon's Mercer College, then pursued a business career until an accident left him incapacitated, whereupon he founded *The Golden Age* magazine (February 1906). His self-promotion in that forum secured Upshaw's election to the House of Representatives in 1919, where he served until March 1927. When the House Rules Committee convened its investigation of the KKK in October 1920, the chairman declared that Imperial Wizard William Simmons required no introduction. Upshaw provided one nonetheless, presenting Simmons as "my long-time personal friend," extolling "his sterling character," praising "his every utterance as the truth of an honest, patriotic man." Upshaw deemed Simmons "a sturdy and inspiring personality ... incapable of an unworthy unpatriotic motive, word or deed." As for the Klan itself, Upshaw admitted that he always felt "a sort of wounded pride" when it was criticized. He once wrote to Klan publicist Elizabeth Tyler, on House stationery, concerning a forthcoming article in the Klan's *Searchlight* newspaper: "I hope you, the Wizard and the Near Wizard will like it. If I can serve you and the *Searchlight* further please do not hesitate to command me." No member of the House received more laudatory attention in 1920s Klan publications than Upshaw, including a glowing profile in the 11 April 1925 issue of James Vance's *Fellowship Forum*. Small wonder, then, that critics branded Upshaw a "Kluxer in good standing" and "a klansman who had been elected by Klan votes." Upshaw declined to seek reelection in 1926, turning his talents to the fundamentalist lecture circuit. In 1932, he was the Prohibition Party's presidential candidate, polling 81,869 votes nationwide. After losing his bid for nomination at the 1942 Democratic National Convention, Upshaw returned to his traveling pulpit, later emerging as vice president of the Linda Vista Baptist Bible College and Seminary in San Diego, California. The Baptist Church ordained him as a minister in 1938, at age seventy-two. Upshaw died in California on 21 November 1952.

Vance, Zebulon Baird—Prior to secession, Vance served in the North Carolina state legislature (1854) and represented his state in Congress (1858–61). During the Civil War, he won election as North Carolina's governor (1862–65). Several historians name him as the state's grand dragon during Reconstruction. Following "redemption," he served once more as governor (1877–79) and in the U.S. Senate (1879–94). Vance died in office on 14 April 1894.

Watson, Thomas Edward—Few American politicians have undergone transformations as dramatic (or bizarre) as that of Tom Watson. A Georgia native, born 5 September 1856, Watson graduated from Macon's Mercer University, then taught school while studying law, winning admittance to the state bar in 1875. He served in the state legislature (1882–83) and as a Democratic presidential elector in 1888, before shifting to the People's Party and winning election to the House of Representatives (1891–93). Voters rejected Watson's 1892 reelection bid, and he lost another congressional race in 1894, then returned to private legal practice. In 1896, he was the Populist vice-presidential candidate, followed by unsuccessful presidential bids in 1904 and 1908. In those campaigns, he called for brotherhood among all workers, black and white, to overcome the tyranny of wealthy interests. After his national defeats, however, Watson learned to sing a very different tune.

Midway between his presidential campaigns, in 1906, Watson founded two magazines—the weekly *Jeffersonian* and the monthly *Watson's Magazine*—which soon enjoyed national circulation. By the time voters rejected him in 1908, Watson had amassed a personal fortune of $250,000, which he invested in a Georgia plantation run by tenants. At the same time, he shifted the editorial thrust of his two magazines from Populist themes to virulent attacks on blacks, Catholics and Jews. So vicious were his editorials, in fact, that both of Watson's magazines were ultimately banned from distribution through the U.S. mails as "obscene" literature. His obsession with the supposed sexual hijinx of blacks and Catholic priests drove Watson to the edge of madness. "No man," he once wrote, "can imagine a woman who could maintain her self-respect after being compelled to act as a sewer pipe for a bachelor priest's accumulation of garbage." In another issue, he ranted: "Heavens above! Think of a Negro priest taking the vow of chastity and then being turned loose among women.... It is a thing to make one shudder." A short time later, when defendant Leo Frank faced trial for killing Mary Phagan in Atlanta, Watson wrote: "Our Little Girl—ours by the Eternal God—has been pursued to a hideous death and bloody grave by this filthy perverted Jew of New York." When Georgia's governor commuted Frank's death sentence, Watson blamed a vast Jewish conspiracy, exhorting his readers: "RISE! PEOPLE OF GEORGIA!" After the Knights of Mary Phagan lynched Frank, in August 1915, Watson praised their action and declared, "When mobs are no longer possible, liberty will be dead." In fact, the *Jeffersonian* opined (2 September 1915) what Georgia needed was "another Ku Klux Klan to restore HOME RULE."

It may be sheer coincidence that William Simmons filed his application charter for the KKK one month later. No evidence has yet emerged naming Watson as a member of the modern Klan, but he certainly shared its views in all particulars concerning race and religion. The order lacked sufficient strength to elect Watson in 1918, when he ran for Congress, but the votes were there in 1920, when he sought a U.S. Senate seat. In October 1921, when the House Rules Committee opened its investigation of the KKK, Watson dropped in from the Senate to shake hands with Imperial Wizard William Simmons. On another occasion, he boasted to fellow senators that he was called "the King of the Ku Klux in Georgia." Klansmen mourned the news of Watson's death on 26 September 1922, and estimates of the throng at his funeral ranged from 10,000 to 20,000. Biographer C. Vann Woodward observes that, while no record of Watson's Klan membership exists, "if any mortal man be credited ... with releasing the forces of human malice and ignorance and prejudice, which the Klan merely mobilized, that man was Thomas E. Watson."

The U.S. Supreme Court

Black, Hugo Lafayette—Alabama native Hugo Black was born in Clay County on 27 February 1886. He attended Ashland College there and graduated from the University of Alabama's law school in 1906, winning admission to the bar before year's end. Black moved to Birmingham in 1907, serving there as a police court judge (1911–12) and prosecuting attorney (1914–17) before he joined the U.S. Army as a captain during World War I (1917–19). Back in civilian life, Black resumed private practice and joined the Birmingham Klan. In October 1921, he defended a fellow klansman, Rev. E.R. Stephenson, on charges of killing a Catholic priest in broad daylight, before multiple witnesses. Black argued that the slaying had been self-defense, and further justified because the victim had performed the wedding of Stephenson's daughter to a Puerto Rican laborer. Dimming the courtroom lights to accent the Puerto Rican's swarthy looks, Black dismissed the witness's claim of white Spanish roots with the observation that he had "descended a long way." Jurors acquitted Black's client in that case, but another panel convicted the Chinese café proprietors whom Black defended after klansmen jailed them in a series of vigilante bootleg raids. (Ironically, attorneys on both sides of that case were klansmen, and the order held no grudge against Black.)

Despite his occasional lapse in accepting nonwhite clients, the KKK still rallied behind Black in 1926, securing his election to the U.S. Senate. Black displayed proper gratitude at the Klan's September 1926 klorero in Birmingham, sharing the stage with Imperial Wizard Hiram Evans, Grand Dragon James Esdale, and Governor-elect Bibb Graves. On that occasion, Black told the audience of 2,000 klansmen, "I realize I was elected by men who believe in the principles I have sought to advocate, the real Anglo-Saxon sentiment that must and will control the destiny of the Stars and Stripes. I want your counsel ... I crave your counsel ... [and] the Anglo-Saxon spirit." Although the proud possessor of a lifetime passport to the invisible empire, Black broke with imperial headquarters in 1928 to support Catholic presidential candidate Al Smith. By August 1937, when President Franklin Roosevelt named Black to a seat on the U.S. Supreme Court, the Klan was a shadow of its former self and Black had transformed himself into a New Deal liberal. Despite heated controversy surrounding Black's appointment, the Senate confirmed him and he served with distinction on the court until failing health forced his resignation on 17 September 1971. Black died eight days later, in Bethesda, Maryland.

White, Edward Douglass—A Catholic native of Thibodaux, Louisiana, born in 1845, White attended Maryland's

Former klansman Edward White, later Chief Justice of the U.S. Supreme Court, also endorsed *The Birth of a Nation* (Library of Congress).

Mount St. Mary College and Jesuit College in New Orleans. After secession, he joined the Confederate army, then studied law at war's end and won admission to the Louisiana state bar in 1868. That same year, White joined the New Orleans Klan (which had no ban on Catholics in Reconstruction) and spent his free time on armed "patrols" of the Crescent City. After the Bayou State's "redemption" for white-supremacist "home rule," White served in the state legislature (1874), as a justice of the state supreme court (1879–80), and in the U.S. Senate (1891–94). In 1894, President Grover Cleveland named White to the U.S. Supreme Court, and President Howard Taft promoted him to chief justice in 1910. In 1915, after conversations with author Thomas Dixon, White viewed and endorsed D.W. Griffith's pro–Klan film, *The Birth of a Nation*, thus undermining criticism of the movie's racist content. Later, when violence greeted the film's premiere in Boston and New York City, White tried to rewrite history, curtly denying "rumors" of his endorsement. White died in Washington, D.C., on 19 May 1921.

U.S. Attorney General

Garland, Augustus Hill—Various published accounts name Garland as the KKK's grand dragon for Reconstruction-era Arkansas. Subsequently, he served as governor (1874–75) and in the U.S. Senate (1877–85), before resigning to serve as Attorney General under President Grover Cleveland. After Cleveland's departure from office, Garland returned to private legal practice. He died in Washington, D.C., on 26 January 1899, while arguing a case before the U.S. Supreme Court.

Governors

Allen, Henry Justin—Born in Pennsylvania, Allen moved to Kansas with his family at age two, in 1870. He graduated from Baker University (Kansas) in 1890 and entered the field of journalism, first as a reporter, later as editor of the *Wichita Beacon*. As governor of Kansas (1919–23), Allen opposed the KKK and ordered his attorney general to prosecute nightriding klansmen. In public speeches, he denounced the KKK as the "greatest curse that comes to a civilized people" and a "travesty upon Americanism." After service as special commissioner for Near East relief (1923–24) and director of publicity for the Republican National Committee (1928), Allen was appointed to fill a U.S. Senate vacancy in 1928. Voters rejected him when he stood for election to a full term in November 1930. Allen died in Wichita on 17 January 1950.

Arnall, Ellis Gibbs—A native of Newnan, Georgia, born in 1907, Arnall served in the state legislature (1933–37) and as the state's attorney general (1939–43). In the latter capacity, during 1940, he prosecuted Imperial Wizard Hiram Evans and a former purchasing agent for the state highway department on charges of price-fixing and violating the Sherman Anti-Trust Act. (Governor E.D. Rivers had permitted Evans to sell asphalt and paving materials to the state without competitive bids, as a reward for Klan support in the 1936 gubernatorial contest.) Upon conviction, Evans was forced to reimburse the state $15,000. Arnall subsequently served as governor (1943–47), his tenure in the state house coinciding with the KKK's revival after World War II. On 30 May 1946, he ordered legal action to revoke the Klan's charter in Georgia. On 21 June 1946, Arnall announced that the FBI had uncovered "a well-organized plot" against his life, hatched by Atlanta klansmen. The conspiracy called for five prospects to be chosen from each klavern, after which Grand Dragon Samuel Green would hand-pick two assassins from the finalists. No prosecutions resulted, but the Klan retaliated by issuing claims that Arnall had joined the order as a "lifetime member" in 1942. Arnall died in Georgia on 13 December 1992.

Barnett, Ross Robert—A native of Mississippi's Leake County, born in 1898, Barnett studied law before serving in the U.S. Army during World War I. Back in civilian life, he returned to build a successful law practice in Jackson. After the U.S. Supreme Court's "Black Monday" decision on school integration, Barnett affiliated himself with the racist Citizens' Councils. In 1957, he defended Klan-allied agitator John Kasper against charges of inciting racist violence in Clinton and Nashville, Tennessee. Jurors convicted Kasper in that case, but the mere attempt to free him satisfied Mississippi's white voters, who chose Barnett as their next governor in 1959. Barnet faced his own segregation crisis in 1962, after federal courts ordered the University of Mississippi (Oxford) to admit black student James Meredith. Barnett's resistance to those orders set the stage for a bloody riot on the night of 30 September, leaving two men dead and several hundred persons injured. Barnett escaped prosecution for contempt of court in that case, and continued his racist affiliations. After klansman Byron De La Beckwith murdered Mississippi NAACP leader Medgar Evers, a member of Barnett's law firm (Hugh Cunningham) joined Beckwith's defense team. Barnett himself, only a few days out of office in January 1964, visited the courtroom to shake Beckwith's hand in full view of jurors, while the trial was in progress. State law barred Barnett from succeeding himself in office, but he made another run for the governor's mansion in 1967. Beckwith ran for lieutenant governor that same year, approaching Barnett to plead for a $20,000 campaign contribution. Barnett reportedly dismissed him with the observation, "If I had twenty thousand dollars, I'd use it on my own campaign." When reporters asked Barnett if he would welcome Klan support to his campaign, he coyly responded, "What Klan?" Despite his former popularity, voters rejected Barnett in favor of John Bell Williams. Barnett died on 6 November 1987.

Bilbo, Theodore *see Congress*

Brewster, Ralph Owen—A descendant of *Mayflower* pilgrims, Brewster was born at Dexter, Maine, in 1888. He graduated from Maine's Bowdoin College and obtained his LL.B. from Harvard University in 1913, winning admittance to Maine's state bar before year's end. Brewster practiced briefly in Portland, then served in the state legislature (1917–18, 1921–25). He forged an alliance with the KKK when Portland's Catholic bishop lobbied for municipal support of parochial schools. Brewster fired back with a constitutional amendment banning such expenditures, and grateful klansmen helped elect him governor in 1924. Brewster served one term in the state house (1925–29), then sought to fill an unexpected U.S. Senate vacancy in 1926, occasioned by the retirement of incumbent William Patangall. To secure that post, Brewster met with Imperial Wizard Hiram Evans and Grand Dragon DeForest Perkins, concocting a smear campaign that accused rival Arthur Gould of illegal spending in the primary election. That effort backfired with exposure of Brewster's Klan ties, and Gould easily carried the election. Brewster tried for the Senate again in 1928, but lost the primary election. Likewise defeated in his 1932 congressional bid, Brewster nonetheless won election to the U.S. House of Representatives in 1932 and served three terms (1935–41). In 1940, he finally achieved his crowning ambition with election to the U.S. Senate, serving until his resignation in December 1952. Brewster died in Boston on Christmas Day 1961.

Brownlow, William Gannaway—Born near Wytheville, Tennessee, in 1805, Brownlow entered the Methodist ministry at age twenty-one. From 1839 onward, he aired his Republican sentiments on the pages of his own newspaper, the *Whig,* and earned a reputation as "the fighting parson" for his fierce refusal to back down in the face of Democratic opposition. In 1850, President Millard Fillmore appointed Brownlow to the Tennessee River Commission for the Improvement of Navigation. Brownlow opposed secession and remained loyal to the Union throughout the Civil War, serving as a delegate to occupied Tennessee's state constitutional convention in 1864. His postwar election as governor (1865–69) spared Tennessee from military Reconstruction, but the KKK still flourished violently in its home state, opposing Brownlow's GOP regime at every turn. Brownlow's 1868 militia campaign against the Klan bore mixed results: no klansmen were imprisoned, but the order's violence prompted Grand Wizard Nathan Bedford Forrest to order disbandment in January 1869. Unconvinced that the Klan was sincere, Brownlow declared martial law in nine counties on 24 February, then resigned the next day to fill a seat in the U.S. Senate, where he served until March 1875. Instead of seeking reelection to a second term, Brownlow returned to run his newspaper in Knoxville and died there on 29 April 1877.

Burns, William Haydon—A Chicago native, born in 1912, Burns subsequently moved to Florida with his family and served four terms as mayor of Jacksonville (1949–65). In that post, he proved himself a staunch segregationist and curried favor with the Klan by granting special permits for its public demonstrations while ordering the arrest of black civil rights protesters. In 1958, Burns overcame his passion for "massive resistance" long enough to found the Southern Conference on Bombing, but with Burns and Birmingham's "Bull" Connor directing the SCB, it solved none of Dixie's myriad hate crimes. Two years later, the inaction of Burns and his all-white police force contributed to Klan riots on "Axe-handle Saturday," in August 1960. That, and subsequent acts of unpunished mayhem around Jacksonville, encouraged the KKK and NSRP to support Burns's gubernatorial campaign in 1964. In May of that year, klansmen lounging outside Burns's campaign office in strife-torn St. Augustine jeered at black marchers, "If out man's in, you niggers have had it." Burns carried the election and served one term as governor (1965–67), then retired from politics. He died in 1987.

Byrnes, James Francis—A native of Charleston, South Carolina, born in 1882, Byrnes served as court reporter for the state's second circuit (1900–08) while simultaneously editing Aiken's *Journal and Review* (1903–07) and studying law. Admitted to the state bar in 1903, he next served as the second circuit's solicitor (1908–10) and was elected to the U.S. House of Representatives in 1910, where he served until 1925. Voters elected Byrnes to the U.S. Senate in 1930, and he served until 1941, when President Franklin Roosevelt appointed him to the U.S. Supreme Court. Byrnes resigned from the court on 3 October 1942, to head FDR's wartime Office of Economic Stabilization, then shifted to the Office of War Mobilization (1943–45) before serving as President Harry Truman's Secretary of State (1945–47). In 1950, Byrnes won election as governor of South Carolina, presiding through the initial furor over the U.S. Supreme Court's "Black Monday" decision on school integration

(1951–55). Author Stetson Kennedy claims that Byrnes appeared as the keynote speaker at a Jacksonville, Florida, KKK rally in 1951, while local Klan leader (and local Democratic Party chairman) Edgar Waybright "lurked in the background." Byrnes retired from office in 1955, but retained a voice in state politics. Five years later, while klansmen circulated anti–Catholic propaganda against Democratic presidential candidate John Kennedy, Byrnes announced his support for GOP contender Richard Nixon, denouncing his old party's civil rights platform. Byrnes died in Columbia, South Carolina, on 9 April 1972.

Clayton, Powell—A native of Bethel, Pennsylvania, born in 1833, Clayton graduated from Partridge Military Academy and studied engineering in Delaware before moving to Leavenworth, Kansas, where he served as city engineer (1857). With commencement of the Civil War, he joined the Union army and rose to the rank of brigadier general. At war's end, Clayton settled in Arkansas as a "carpetbag" planter, winning election as governor in 1868. Razorback klansmen opposed his Republican administration with guerrilla warfare, burning most of Lewisburg in November 1868 and capturing a shipment of muskets purchased for Clayton's state militia the following month. Clayton replied in kind, with a campaign that evoked complaints of confessions extracted by torture and klansmen killed in custody while "trying to escape." Democratic leaders sued for peace in early 1869 and used their own influence to suppress Klan violence thereafter. Clayton subsequently won election to the U.S. Senate (1871–77) and served as U.S. minister to Mexico (1897–98). He died in Washington, D.C., on 25 August 1914.

Faubus, Orval Eugene—A native of Madison County, Arkansas, born in 1910, Faubus served as a U.S. Army major during World War II and won election as governor of Arkansas in 1954. Prior to his election, the NAACP hailed Arkansas as "the bright spot for the South" where school desegregation was concerned, but Faubus soon changed that. His tenure in office (1955–67) encompassed the civil rights era, marked by violence after Faubus defied court orders to integrate Little Rock's Central High School in 1957. Riots ensued, and President Dwight Eisenhower dispatched federal troops to enforce the court's order. Members of the KKK and the Citizens' Council conspired in a bombing campaign around Little Rock, in 1959–60, and Governor Faubus appeared to favor the terrorists. After convicted bomber E.A. Lauderdale received a three-year prison term in November 1959, Faubus commuted the term to six months (thus making Lauderdale eligible for immediate release) and personally refunded his $500 fine. Under the circumstances, it was no surprise when the neo–Nazi NSRP nominated Faubus as its presidential candidate in 1960, with running mate John Crommelin. Faubus publicly rejected the endorsement, but racists in four states (Alabama, Arkansas, Delaware and Tennessee) still cast 214,195 votes for the NSRP ticket. After leaving office, Faubus ran for governor three more times (1970, 1974, 1986), but voters rejected him in each case. Prostate cancer claimed his life on 14 December 1994.

Folsom, James Elisha, Sr.—Alabama native "Big Jim" Folsom, born in Coffee County in October 1908, served two terms as the Cotton State's governor. During his first term (1947–51), violence by the Federated KKK in Birmingham and elsewhere forced Folsom to take a stand against the hooded order, advising potential Ku Klux victims, "Your home is your castle. Defend it in any way necessary." Investigation of the Klan sent Imperial Wizard William Morris to jail for contempt of court in Birmingham, but all-white juries acquitted the few knights who faced flogging charges. State law barred Folsom from succeeding himself, and by the time he returned to the governor's mansion (1955–59), the U.S. Supreme Court's "Black Monday" decision on school integration had kindled fresh violence throughout Alabama. Unpunished bombings followed the Montgomery bus boycott (1955–56), and "Bombingham" witnessed a new wave of nightriding terrorism. Four klansmen received prison terms for castrating black victim Edward Aaron in 1957, but they were later released by Governor George Wallace (Folsom's nephew by marriage) after serving a fraction of their prison terms. Alcoholism and its resultant erratic behavior doomed Folsom's later gubernatorial campaigns, in 1962 and 1966. He died from a heart attack on 21 November 1987.

Garland, Augustus *see U.S. Attorney General*

Gordon, John Brown *see Congress*

Graves, David Bibb—Born on 1 April 1873, Alabama native Bibb Graves served as a colonel in the U.S. Army during World War I, then returned home to join the rapidly-growing Ku Klux Klan. By 1926, when he won election as governor, Graves was the exalted cyclops of Montgomery's largest klavern. That September, at the state klorero, Graves and newly-elected Senator Hugo Black received lifetime memberships in the KKK from Imperial Wizard Hiram Evans. Montgomery's Mayor William Gunter barred klansmen from the governor's inaugural parade, whereupon KKK spokesman Horace Wilkinson (a prominent lawyer and close friend of Graves) suggested that the Klan hold its own inauguration ceremony. "We have a great victory," Wilkinson wrote. "Why should we be barred from all privileges because we are Klansmen? Can a 2x4 mayor of a Jew-owned town prevent 50,000 100-percent Americans from jubilating in our great victory? We say no." Klan nightriding flourished during Graves's first term as governor, and while he issued weak objections to some of the terrorism in 1927 ("Flogging in Alabama must cease"), prosecutions were rare and convictions rarer still. Horace Wilkinson himself defended a group of indicted klansmen in September 1927, thus persuading some observers that Graves sympathized with the floggers. Critics also noted that ninety-five percent of his political appointments went to members of the KKK, with klavern leaders specifying which candidates for office should be chosen or rejected. State law barred Graves from succeeding himself in 1930, but he captured the governor's mansion again in 1934, for a second term (1935–39) fraught with violence and controversy. After Birmingham klansmen whipped CPUSA activist Joseph Gelders in September 1926, a grand jury refused to charge them and Graves barred "outside lawyers" from investigating the case. By the time he left office the second time, Klan influence had waned in Alabama and Graves retired to Florida. He died in Sarasota on 14 March 1942.

Hampton, Wade *see Congress*

Hardwick, Thomas William—Born at Thomasville, Georgia, in 1872, Hardwick graduated from Macon's Mercer University and received his LL.B. from the University of Georgia (Athens) in 1893, winning admittance to the state bar that same year. After two years in private practice, he served as Washington County's prosecutor (1895–97), in the state legislature (1898–1902), and in the U.S. House of Representatives (1903–14). In November 1914, Hardwick won election to fill a U.S. Senate vacancy created by the death of Augustus Bacon, but voters denied his reelection bid in 1918. Elected as governor in 1920, Hardwick displayed rare courage for a Georgia politician in those days, by refusing favors to the swiftly-growing Ku Klux Klan. As a result, he was defeated when he stood for reelection two years later, but Hardwick refused to stay silent. In 1924, he entered the Democratic senatorial primary, opposing incumbent William Harris and contender Richard Russell, Sr. When Russell quit the race in July, Hardwick charged that he did so on orders from KKK headquarters, after high-ranking klansmen informed Russell of their commitment to Harris. A month later, Hardwick named Harris himself as a klansman, releasing copies of a letter from Klan publicist Elizabeth Tyler addressed to Harris as "AKIA" (*A K*lansman *I A*m). Harris denied membership in the order and won the election in a landslide, whereupon Hardwick retired to private legal practice with offices in Georgia and in Washington, D.C. He died in Sandersville, Georgia, on 31 January 1944.

Holden, William Woods—A North Carolina native, born in 1818, Holden earned his living as a Raleigh newspaper editor. He attended the Democratic National Convention in 1860, and a year later served as a delegate to North Carolina's secession convention. After the Civil War, Holden served briefly as governor (1865) before ceding the office to Jonathan Worth. While marking time as president of the state university (1865–68), Holden switched allegiance to the GOP (thus becoming a "scalawag") and thereby positioned himself for election as governor in 1868, under congressional Reconstruction. North Carolina klansmen—40,000 strong by Holden's estimate, in early 1869—opposed him in conjunction with terrorists of the CUG and other groups, preventing sheriffs and grand juries from punishing crimes committed against blacks and Republicans. In August 1869, Holden hired a private detective to gather evidence that secured indictment of several CUG leaders. He also organized a state militia to fight the Klan on its own terms, supported by the Shoffner Act of January 1870, permitting Holden to declare martial law in lawless counties. Sadly, tactical blunders and the public excesses of some militia officers sparked a political backlash, enabling white-supremacist Democrats to sweep the 1870 elections. Holden complained to Washington that the Klan's "organized conspiracy is in existence in every county of the state. And its aim is to obtain control of the government. It is believed that its leaders now direct the movements of the present legislature." In effect, he was right. The new Democratic

majority in Raleigh voted to impeach Holden in November 1870, on charges of corruption. His trial before the state senate began in December, ending with his conviction and removal from office in February 1871. The KKK thus claims credit for America's first gubernatorial impeachment. Holden retired from politics and died in Raleigh on 1 March 1892.

Jackson, Edward L.—A native of Howard County, Indiana, born in 1873, Jackson served as a state circuit judge in 1905, and as Indiana's secretary of state in 1917, before joining the U.S. Army to fight in World War I. Back in civilian life at war's end, he joined the growing Ku Klux Klan and won election to another term as secretary of state (1921–25). In 1924, Grand Dragon David Stephenson hand-picked Jackson as the Klan's candidate for governor, thereby ensuring his election in a year when klansmen virtually controlled state politics. Like many other candidates that year, Jackson signed a pledge of loyalty to Stephenson, and the American Unity League intercepted a telegram from Stephenson to Jackson after the resignation of Indiana's Republican Party chairman, reading: "Permit no selection to be made and permit no one to be named until I have had an opportunity to confer with you." Following his 1926 murder conviction, Stephenson expected clemency from Jackson. When it was not forthcoming, the imprisoned klansman released his files on Jackson and other Hoosier politicians. Jackson's claim that a $2,500 check from Stephenson constituted payment for a horse did not prevent his indictment on bribery charges. The statute of limitations saved him from conviction at trial, but Jackson's political career ended in disgrace. He left office in 1929 and faded into obscurity, dying on 18 November 1954.

Jarvis, Thomas *see Congress*

Johnson, Paul Burney, Jr.—A native of Hattiesburg, Mississippi, born in 1916, Johnson studied law and gained admission to the state bar before joining the U.S. Marine Corps in World War II. His father served as governor while Paul was overseas, and died in office (1943). Johnson lost a bid for the U.S. Senate in 1947, then returned to private practice until 1959, when he was elected to serve as Mississippi's lieutenant governor under Ross Barnett. An ardent segregationist, Johnson flirted with federal contempt citations in 1962, to keep black student James Meredith out of the state university, and that effort made him the gubernatorial front-runner in 1963. He won election that year with Klan support, in a hard-line racist campaign that included descriptions of the NAACP as a collection of "Niggers, Apes, Alligators, Coons and Possums." Adverse publicity from FBI headquarters forced Johnson to fire several klansmen from the Mississippi Highway Patrol in 1964, but he was generally more cordial to the order. After klansmen kidnapped and murdered three civil rights workers in Neshoba County, Johnson told reporters, "Governor [George] Wallace of Alabama and I are the only two people who know where they are, and we're not telling." Years later, after several knights were convicted for violating the three victims' civil rights, Johnson claimed inside knowledge of the crime. He alleged that black victim James Chaney died accidentally, struck with a chain for "acting kind of smart-aleck and talking back," whereupon the knights shot his

companions to ensure their silence. Following the expiration of his term in January 1968, Johnson returned to private legal practice.

McRae, Thomas Chipman—An Arkansas native, born at Mt. Holly in 1851, McRae graduated from Soule Business College in New Orleans (1869) and earned his LL.B. from Virginia's Washington and Lee University (1872), winning admission to the Arkansas state bar in 1873. He subsequently served as the state's election commissioner (1874), as a state legislator (1877), and as state chairman of the Democratic Party (1884, 1902). In 1885, voters elected McRae to fill a vacancy in the U.S. House of Representatives, where he remained until March 1903. He then resumed private practice with a side career in banking, serving as president of the Arkansas Bar Association (1917–18) and as a member of the state constitutional convention (1918). McRae never joined the KKK, but he maintained a policy of "friendly neutrality" toward the order and secured Klan votes for his 1920 gubernatorial campaign by appointing a klansman to serve as his personal secretary. He served one term as governor (1921–25) and died in Prescott, Arkansas, on 2 June 1929.

Maddox, Lester Garfield—A native of Atlanta, Georgia, born 30 September 1915, Maddox was raised as an ardent segregationist in a Klan-dominated state. He prospered quietly as an Atlanta restaurateur, then made headlines in 1960 as the founder of GUTS (*G*eorgians *U*nwilling *to* *S*urrender), a white-supremacist group that maintained friendly relations with the U.S. Klans under Grand Dragon Calvin Craig. A typical newspaper advertisement for GUTS proclaimed: "The mess we have this town in, it's a wonder that many more people are not going on an African hunt.... And like a customer suggested, 'Why go to Africa for hunting when Atlanta could use considerable hunting?'" On one highly-publicized occasion, Maddox drove a group of black would-be diners from his restaurant with a pistol and axe-handle. As a candidate for lieutenant governor in 1962, Maddox reportedly arranged for klansman James Venable to endorse opponent Peter Geer, but the plan backfired in victory for Geer. (Maddox later denied the story, while Venable confirmed it.) On 4 July 1964, Maddox shared the stage with Calvin Craig and Alabama Governor George Wallace at a racist rally in Atlanta, where several blacks in the audience were mobbed and beaten with metal chairs. The following year, Maddox led a parade of some 2,000 whites—including Craig and other identified klansmen—down Atlanta's Peachtree Street. Elected governor in 1966, Maddox named several Klan associates to appointive offices, but he also displayed a surprising generosity toward blacks. Maddox served one term as governor (1967–71), and another as lieutenant governor (1971–75). Analysts listed him as a front-runner in the 1974 gubernatorial race, until reporters intercepted a telegram sent to Maddox by James Lumpkin, Georgia grand dragon of Venable's National Knights. That telegram, dated 11 August 1966, offered the Klan's endorsement to Maddox and Jesse Stoner (running for lieutenant governor as an avowed neo–Nazi), calling them the "best candidates who will fight for the return of true Americanism." When the telegram was published on election eve, Maddox branded it a case of "dirty tricks," but Venable vouched for its authenticity.

Maddox failed to win a clear majority on election day, and subsequently lost the September runoff. In the 1980s, he resurfaced as a member of the racist CCC. The combined effects of cancer and a fall claimed Maddox's life on 25 June 2003.

Morley, Clarence J.—Born in February 1869, Colorado native Clarence Morley studied law and subsequently served as a criminal court judge in Denver. He joined the Klan soon after it was organized in Colorado, thereafter taking pains to stack his juries with klansmen. Elected governor with KKK support in 1924, Morley used his inauguration address to call for a ban on sacramental wine and "undesirable" immigrants. He soon appointed Grand Dragon John Locke as his aide-de-camp and named Locke a colonel in the National Guard. Morley also tried to install fifty-two klansmen as unsalaried state Prohibition agents, but that move was blocked by Colorado's civil service commission. Klan lobbyists retaliated with an unsuccessful bid to abolish civil service. Scandals surrounding Dragon Locke tarred Morley by association, and he found no popular support for a second two-year term as governor in 1926. Morley died on 15 November 1948.

Patterson, John Malcolm—A native of Goldville, Alabama, born in 1921, Patterson served in the U.S. Army during World War II and returned to study law in his home state. He subsequently served as state attorney general (1955–59) and entered the 1958 gubernatorial race as one of thirteen candidates vying for popular support. School integration was the hot topic that year, after the U.S. Supreme Court's "Black Monday" decision, and Patterson courted Klan votes via letters written on his official stationery, seeking support in the name of "a mutual friend, Mr. R.M. (Bob) Shelton"—then Alabama's grand dragon for the Georgia-based U.S. Klans. During the campaign, klansmen ripped down posters for Patterson's rivals and assaulted volunteers employed by other candidates, including one man whose scalp they tattooed with a staple gun. Patterson won the election, and Shelton (then a salesman for the B.F. Goodrich Company) received a $1 million contract from the state as his reward. Soon after Patterson's inauguration, state legislators introduced a bill to expand Alabama's mental health facilities, a move opposed by Shelton on grounds that the National Mental Health Association was "linked with the communists." Patterson echoed Shelton's sentiment from the state house, and the bill died on the assembly floor.

A rift developed between Patterson and the Shelton's Alabama Knights in August 1959, over Patterson's support for the presidential candidacy of liberal Catholic John Kennedy. On 10 August, a delegation of thirty-two klansmen visited the governor's mansion, led by an imperial kladd from Prattville, warning Patterson against collaboration with "communist–Jewish integrators." Patterson allayed their fears with a promise that "if a school in Alabama is integrated, it will be over my dead body." In December 1960, he told journalists, "You're going to have rioting on your hands if they try forced integration here. I'll be one of the first ones stirring up trouble, any way I can." In May 1961, when integrated "freedom riders" entered Alabama, Patterson promised an escort of police cars and helicopters, then abruptly withdrew security at the last moment. Blithely dismissing the subsequent Klan riots—"I can't guarantee the safety of fools"—Patterson ordered his state police to terminate all contact with the FBI, followed by a 16 June announcement that any trooper found cooperating the G-men on investigations of racial violence would be fired. Patterson finally broke with the Klan after President Kennedy named Charles Merriwether (Patterson's 1958 campaign manager) to head the Export and Import Bank, thereby drawing more criticism from Shelton for his "liberal" associations. Barred by law from succeeding himself in 1962, Patterson had no further need of KKK electoral support, and he retired from politics in January 1963 with his segregationist record intact.

Paulen, Benjamin Sanford

—A native of Fredonia, Kansas, born in 1869, Paulen served briefly in the state senate (1913) before setting his sights on higher office. He joined the KKK soon after its kleagles reached Kansas, trusting Klan votes to secure his election as lieutenant governor in 1922. Two years later, after securing the Republican nomination for governor, Paulen used his influence to kill debate on a GOP anti–Klan plank. When reporters questioned his ties to the hooded order, Paulen replied that he was not a member "at this time." Klansmen supported him nonetheless, and counted him a friend during his tenure in the state house (1925–29). Klan strength evaporated prior to Paulen's unsuccessful U.S. Senate bid, in 1932, and he subsequently retired from politics. Paulen died on 11 July 1961.

Pierce, Walter Marcus

—Born near Morris, Illinois, in 1861, Pierce subsequently moved to Oregon and entered Democratic Party politics. He served briefly in the state senate (1903), but failed to make a name for himself until the 1920s Ku Klux Klan provided a vehicle for his personal bigotry. After joining the Klan in LaGrange, Pierce campaigned for governor in 1922 on a promise to keep "America as a land for Americans." To that end, he supported Klan-proposed bans on parochial schools, sacramental garb, and sale of real estate to aliens. Pierce's campaign speeches emphasized the "dangers of allowing the Mongolian races to gain a foothold on the soil of our state," while emphasizing his own status as a ninth-generation American Protestant. Furthermore, he told klansmen, "my wife and all her relatives are Protestants." As governor, Pierce signed the Klan's compulsory public schooling bill (later deemed unconstitutional) and appointed a klansmen as customs collector for Portland. When Portland's Chamber of Commerce threw a birthday party for Grand Dragon Fred Gifford on 3 March 1923, Pierce joined Mayor George Baker as an honored guest speaker. The Klan's decline in Oregon prevented Pierce from winning a second gubernatorial term in 1926, but spent a decade in the U.S. House of Representatives (1933–43). He died in Oregon on 27 March 1954.

Richardson, Friend William

—A Michigan Quaker, born in 1865, Friend Richardson later settled in northern California and published the *Berkley Gazette* before he entered Republican politics. He served two terms as state treasurer (1915–23), then secured the GOP's nomination for governor in 1922. The California Klan supported Richardson against his Democratic rival, Los Angeles District Attorney Lee Woolwine, who branded the order "an un–American band of hooded cowards and outlaws." Richardson dodged the question of personal Klan membership, and spokesmen for the KKK helped him preserve the air of mystery. When Sacramento klansmen pressed their exalted cyclops on the matter, he replied, "I just don't like to say as to that, boys. I can say this: Richardson is all right." Richardson carried the election, and after his inauguration he appointed Sacramento's kludd to serve as the state senate's chaplain. Voters denied him a second term in 1926, and he returned to his journalistic trade in Berkeley, where he died from heart disease on 5 September 1943.

Rivers, Eurith Dickinson

—E.D. Rivers was born at Valdosta, Georgia, on 1 December 1895. He joined the modern Klan soon after its revival in 1915, and subsequently served as klokard for Atlanta's Grand Klan No. 285, under Exalted Cyclops Nathan Bedford Forrest III. Rivers subsequently served two terms as Georgia's governor (1937–41), during which Imperial Hiram Evans was named a "lieutenant colonel" on the governor's staff. That reward for Klan votes was less important to Evans than a state contract for asphalt and other paving materials, signed without solicitation of competing bids required by law. That covert deal produced federal prosecutions in 1940, and Rivers drew further criticism for his pardon of klansman Philip Fox, jailed since 1923 for the murder of William Simmons's attorney in legal disputes with Wizard Evans. After leaving office, Rivers served as a member of the Democratic National Committee (1947). He died in Georgia on 11 June 1967.

Talmadge, Eugene

—A classic demagogue, born 23 September 1884, Talmadge made no secret of his virulent racism during his three terms as governor of Georgia (1933–37, 1941–43). He railed against blacks and FDR's New Deal with equal zeal, welcoming support from klansmen in his various campaigns. The question of his Ku Klux membership is unresolved,

Daniel Duke (with whip) challenges Governor Eugene Talmadge (seated) for pardoning Klan floggers in 1941 (Library of Congress).

but Talmadge publicly confessed involvement in at least one whipping of a black man in his younger days. ("I wasn't in such bad company," he opined. "The Apostle Paul was a flogger in his life.") "Ol' Gene" cherished brief presidential hopes in 1936, sharing the stage with anti–Semite Gerald L.K. Smith at a grass-roots convention of Southern Democrats in Macon, but an un-seasonable snowfall and lukewarm public response doomed that effort. In his third term as governor, Talmadge named Atlanta klansman Samuel Roper to head the Georgia Bureau of Inves-tigation and pardoned Klan floggers convicted under predeces-sor E.D. Rivers. Defeated by protégé Ellis Arnall in 1942, Tal-madge teamed with Major John Goodwin of the state highway patrol to organize Vigilantes, Inc., a secret "patriotic" society closely allied with the Georgia Klan. In 1946, Talmadge placed his comeback campaign strategy in the hands of Roy Harris, speaker of the Georgia House, later an officer of the 1950s Cit-izens' Council and supporter of Alabama's George Wallace. To-gether, Talmadge and Harris campaigned on a vow to restore white supremacy, including a plan to "put inspectors at the state line to look into every sleeping car and see that there's no mix-ing of the races." When Sam Roper asked Talmadge's opinion on the best means for preventing black votes, Talmadge wrote a one-word answer: "Pistols." After Talmadge spoke at Soper-ton that spring, his audience rushed off to burn a black church. Branded a klansman by columnist Drew Pearson, Talmadge de-nied the charge, describing himself as the "only candidate in Georgia who wasn't a klansman." Still, he had no personal ob-jection to KKK, telling journalists that he "approved of any good order if it is handled right." Talmadge ran second in September's popular vote, but he carried the election thanks to Georgia's ar-chaic county-unit system, which guaranteed each county two electoral votes regardless of population. Stricken by a liver ail-ment prior to his inauguration, Talmadge died on 21 December 1946. Son Herman, raised in his father's likeness, subsequently served as Georgia's governor and in the U.S. Senate.

Talmadge, Herman *see* Congress

Thurmond, James Strom *see* Congress

Vance, Zebulon *see* Congress

Walker, Clifford Mitchell—A native of Monroe, Geor-gia, born 4 July 1877, Walker practiced law before winning elec-tion as the state's attorney general (1915–20). While ensconced in that office, he joined the KKK and received the order's sup-port against incumbent Caleb Ridley in 1922's gubernatorial pri-mary. With victory in the general election thus guaranteed, Walker promised klansmen his cooperation in suppressing any news of Ku Klux violence. "I'm not going to denounce anybody," he promised. "I am coming right here to your leaders and talk to you." Controversy erupted in 1924, after reporters broke the news of Walker's secret trip to address a Kansas City Klan meet-ing on the topic of "Americanism." (He lamented America's in-vasion by "the lower type of foreigners" and claimed that 1924's Democratic National Convention was controlled by a "gang of Roman Catholic priests.") Walker made matters worse for him-self in that year's election, with an open letter to Georgia's female voters, soliciting support for the judgeship of klansman Gus

Howard in Fulton County. Rebecca Felton of Cartersville, America's first woman in the U.S. Senate (1922–23), charged that the KKK had ordered Walker's support for Howard. "It is said he is a klansmen," Felton told the press. "I do not know, but it happens he hangs his 'hood and nightie' in the capitol of Geor-gia." Walker refused comment on the controversy, prompting journalists to dub him "Kautious Kleagle Kliff." He secured re-election for a second two-year term in 1924, then retired from public life after leaving office in January 1927. Walker died in Monroe, Georgia, on 9 November 1954.

Wallace, George Corley—A native of Barbour County, Alabama, born 25 August 1919, Wallace served in the U.S. Army Air Force during World War II, followed by election to the state legislature (1947–53) and service as a circuit judge (1953–58). In his first year as a judge, Wallace issued an injunction barring removal of Jim Crow signs from public railway terminals (thereby defying a U.S. Supreme Court ruling that required full integration of interstate carriers and their terminal facilities). Such antics, coupled with his diminutive stature, soon earned Wallace a reputation as "the fightin' little judge," but he was first and foremost a political opportunist. In 1958, Wallace ran for governor with support from the NAACP, attacking rival John Patterson for his ties to the Robert Shelton's Alabama Knights of the KKK. In a typical speech, Wallace warned voters that "[i]f the Klan should now succeed in electing Patterson gover-nor, the triumph might well lead to a revival of the Klan as the controlling political force in Alabama. Patterson chatters about the gangster ghosts in Phenix City, while he himself is rolling with the new wave of the Klan and its terrible tradition of law-lessness." Appearing on stage with a bed, Wallace entertained crowds by lifting the covers and asking, "Who is down there between the sheets with you, John? Are you in bed with the Ku Klux Klan?" Patterson won easily on election day, prompting Wallace to remark: "They out-niggered me that time, but they'll never do it again."

Wallace subsequently spared no effort to establish his cre-dentials as a hard-line white supremacist. When the U.S. Civil Rights Commission demanded voter rolls from his county, Wal-lace refused to comply and cheerfully pled guilty to contempt, but Judge Frank Johnson later revealed that Wallace had secretly delivered the records, staging his own contempt trial as a pub-licity stunt. With Patterson barred by law from succeeding him-self in 1962, Wallace courted Robert Shelton (then imperial wiz-ard of the UKA) and hired ex-wizard Asa Carter as his chief aide and speechwriter. Carter served as Wallace's covert liaison to the KKK, NSRP and other extremist groups, while penning speeches that cast Wallace as a champion of segregation. Sweep-ing easily to victory on election day, Wallace delivered an inau-gural address cribbed by Carter from the KKK's own motto, promising "segregation today, segregation tomorrow, segrega-tion forever." After the election, Wallace named Shelton's fa-ther a "colonel" on the governor's staff, granted state textbook contracts to the Southern Publishing Company (which also printed the UKA's *Fiery Cross* newsletter), and named two Klan-allied extremists to the state's textbook selection committee, screening authors for "possible connections with communist-

Left: Alabama Governor George Wallace was a longtime ally of the KKK (Florida State Archives). *Right:* A political cartoon from 1968 highlights George Wallace's links to the KKK (Library of Congress).

front organizations." (When journalists reminded Wallace that the KKK was also on the U.S. Attorney General's subversive list, he replied that his only concern was with authors who "front for commies.") Wallace appointed Ralph Roton, head of Shelton's KBI, to investigate civil rights groups (later calling the appointment "an accident"), and named Albert Lingo to lead the state police. Soon after his appointment, Lingo appeared at a KKK rally, where the presiding officer described him as "a good friend of ours."

Despite his evident commitment to white supremacy, Wallace could not preserve the color line indefinitely. In September 1962 he sent Al Lingo to observe racist riots at the University of Mississippi, but when integration came to Alabama's university in June 1963, Wallace barred klansmen from campus and blocked admission of black students only long enough to keep his campaign vow of "standing in the schoolhouse door." Working through Lingo and Ace Carter, Wallace organized NSRP protests against school integration in Birmingham, and he sometimes appeared to condone terrorism. Violent segregationists, he once declared, "are not thugs—they are good working people who get mad when they see something like this [integration]

happen." In September 1963, nine days before klansmen bombed a Birmingham church and killed four young girls, Wallace told a cheering audience: "What this country needs is a few first-rate funerals, and some political funerals too." After the bombing, he first blamed "unknown black perpetrators," then collaborated with Lingo and Shelton to jail three members of a Klan splinter group on misdemeanor dynamite-possession charges. After those arrests, Wallace crowed, "We beat the Kennedy crowd to the punch." Wallace cronies in the state legislature subsequently killed a bill that tightened restrictions on the purchase of dynamite.

Through all the mayhem, Wallace remained a political operator. In 1964's congressional election, the United Conservative Coalition of Alabama (including members of the KKK, the Citizens' Council and the John Birch Society) distributed 500,000 sample ballots omitting the name of moderate Rep. Carl Elliott. By the time Elliott learned of the trick, he had already lost the election. That July, Wallace shared a stage in Atlanta with Georgia Grand Dragon Calvin Craig and segregationist icon Lester Maddox, denouncing new civil rights legislation and raising no protest while racists beat black members of the audience with metal chairs. Wallace launched his first presidential campaign in 1964, securing the UKA vote when he forced an Alabama engineering firm to pay Robert Shelton $4,000 as a do-nothing "agent," thus granting the firm clearance to bid on state contracts. Mississippi's White Knights donated money to Wallace's primary campaign in Wisconsin, but Wallace later rejected a third-party race in favor of GOP candidate Barry Goldwater, furnishing Al Lingo as Goldwater's chauffeur during visits to Alabama. In 1965, the UKA launched a campaign to amend the state constitution, thereby permitting Wallace to succeed himself in office, but the effort failed and Wallace ran his wife Lurleen for governor instead. Questioned about KKK solicitation of funds for her campaign, Wallace replied, "I'm glad to get support from anyone except gangsters and communists."

In early 1967, the UKA began distributing matchbooks printed with the slogan "Draft George Wallace for President." Later that year, when Wallace visited Pennsylvania, Grand Dragon Roy Frankhouser provided his security detail. Back in Tuscaloosa, Shelton told his knights, "We made him governor and we must make him president." The *Fiery Cross* was more reserved, editorializing that "Governor Wallace may never be president, but the psychological impact upon our enemies of this possibility is our greatest word weapon, and we dare not let this great man fade from the national scene." Xavier Edwards, head of the Maryland-based Interstate Klans, cabled Wallace his "100-percent support," while Georgia's Jesse Stoner declared, "Our slogan is the same as in 1964: Governor George C. Wallace—Last Chance for the White Vote!" ANP founder George Rockwell chimed in with the observation that "Wallace, while not a Nazi, is close enough that, as president, he would probably preserve our nation and race." Plainclothes klansmen often served as security guards when Wallace hit the campaign trail in 1968, and their leaders were busy behind the scenes in the American Independent Party. In California, two rival committees supported the Wallace campaign: one led by William Shearer, head of the state's Citizens' Council, and another chaired by veteran anti–Semite Opal Tanner White. In Lisburn and Norwalk, Connecticut, Wallace's campaign was run by members of the paramilitary Minutemen facing charges of attempted murder. Attorney Richard Ryn, the AIP's chairman in Memphis, later represented James Earl Ray in an appeal of his conviction for killing Dr. Martin Luther King, Jr. In Eutaw, Alabama, after ABC photographers caught Wallace shaking hands with Robert Shelton at a party fundraiser, klansmen in mufti seized the film. Wallace failed to win the White House in November, but his total of 9,446,167 votes revealed surprising nationwide support for the "politics of rage."

That showing also paved the way for Wallace's reelection as governor in 1970. Brother Jack Wallace sponsored a twenty-four-page profile in the *Fiery Cross,* while George's official campaign newsletter headlined an ominous threat: "Unless Whites Vote on June 2, Blacks Will Control the State." Wallace won by a landslide, now empowered by amendment of Alabama's constitution to succeed himself in 1974. His main priority was still the White House, however, and he launched another AIP presidential race in 1972, cut short when would-be assassin Arthur Bremer shot Wallace on 15 May, in Laurel, Maryland.

That near-death experience mellowed Wallace, but he still named Louisiana klansman David Duke an honorary state militia colonel in 1975. Shelton's UKA mounted a half-hearted presidential draft movement for Wallace the following year, and Imperial Wizard Dale Reusch volunteered his endorsement, but national support for the wheelchair-bound candidate failed to materialize. Meanwhile, Texas klansman Scott Nelson panned Wallace as a spent force, complaining that Alabama's governor was "not as white as was in 1968. His mind has deteriorated, I'm sorry to say, along with his body." Elected to a fourth and final term as governor in 1982, Wallace declined in health thereafter and died in Montgomery on 13 September 1998.

Waller, William L.—A Mississippi native, born in 1926, Waller studied law before joining the U.S. Army to fight in the Korean War. Returning to civilian life, he built a successful legal practice in the Magnolia State. One of his clients in the latter 1960s was klansman Charles Wilson, who retained Waller to fight his conviction and life sentence for the January 1966 murder of Hattiesburg NAACP leader Vernon Dahmer. Taking a fling at politics in 1971, Waller won election as Mississippi's governor. A year later, in December 1972, a KKK informant told reporters that he had campaign for Waller's primary opponent the previous year, based on that candidate's promise to free all imprisoned klansmen within one year of his inauguration. Waller, the informant said, had countered with a promise of freedom in six months, and thus secured the Klan's support for his campaign. No such blanket pardons occurred, but Waller *did* grant former client Wilson two back-to-back ninety-day furloughs from prison in 1972, before finally admitting him to a full-time work release program at the Southern Mississippi State Hospital. Waller ignored the resultant controversy and finished out his term as governor, then returned to private practice in 1976.

Walton, John Calloway—An Indiana native, born in 1881, Walton studied engineering and worked on a railroad construction crew in the Oklahoma Territory before settling in Oklahoma as a salesman, then forming a small utilities company in 1906. In 1917, local voters chose him as their commissioner of public works, then promoted him to mayor in 1919. By February 1922, when the Farmer-Labor Reconstruction League drafted Walton as its reform candidate for governor, Oklahoma had elected four chief executives. Three of them (and one lieutenant governor) had faced impeachment threats from combative state legislators, but none had thus far been removed from office. Jack Walton soon would change that, with assistance from the Ku Klux Klan.

After klansman E.B. Howard withdrew from the gubernatorial race to seek a congressional seat in May 1922, Grand Dragon Edwin DeBarr initially pledged the Klan's 75,000 votes to candidate Robert Wilson (another klansman and state superintendent of education), but Walton led Wilson by some 35,000 votes in the Democratic primary, whereupon Wilson threw his support to Walton in the general election. Thus securing victory, Walton adopted a curious two-faced attitude toward Oklahoma's violent Klan. While ordering investigation of Klan floggings soon after his inauguration, Walton also joined the order as a special "klansman at large"—a title created by Imperial Wizard William Simmons, to oblige "Public officials whose membership is for the good of the order to remain a secret." Nonetheless, by summer 1923 Klan violence in the Sooner State had reached a level that alarmed even imperial headquarters. On 13 August, Walton declared martial law in Tulsa and dispatched the National Guard to arrest Klan nightriders. While spokesmen for the order claimed that Walton's "failure to enforce the simplest laws ... gives the Klan an excuse for existing in Oklahoma," Walton fired back with offers of "a pardon in advance" for anyone who killed masked raiders. On 7 September, Walton announced that Klan parades were "banned in Oklahoma from now until the termination of my administration." Expansion of martial law to Oklahoma City alienated most state legislators, but Walton posted soldiers to prevent a vote on his impeachment. A subsequent special election, held on 2 October despite Walton's threats and continued military rule in five Oklahoma counties, approved a constitutional amendment authorizing state legislators to meet without a summons from the governor. From that point on, Walton's impeachment was a foregone conclusion, and he found himself removed from office after ten months and ten days as governor. Successor Martin Trapp lifted the ban on KKK parades, but signed a statewide anti-mask law on 15 January 1924. Walton ran for the U.S. Senate that same year, blaming his impeachment on the KKK, but voters rejected his last bid for office. He died in Oklahoma City on 25 November 1949.

Warren, Fuller—Born in 1905, Fuller Warren was a native of Jackson County, Florida, which witnessed the state's worst Ku Klux violence during Reconstruction. Raised in that environment, it is no surprise that he joined the 1930s KKK, but military service in World War II allegedly changed Warren's attitude after he "helped fight a war to destroy the Nazis—first cousins of klansmen." Elected governor of Florida in 1948, Warren announced plans to outlaw the order in January 1949, following media coverage of a Klan motorcade through Tallahassee. While admitting his own former membership, Warren denounced the post-war Klan as a collection of "hooded hoodlums, sheeted jerks, and covered cowards." Strong words aside, however, he did nothing to curb violence under his administration (1949–53), during an era when Klan bombings, floggings and murders were commonplace. Critics noted that Warren's hand-picked investigator of racist crimes, Jefferson Elliott, had himself joined the Klan while employed with the Georgia Bureau of Investigation. Elliott claimed that he had quit the order, but Stetson Kennedy reports that Elliott responded to secret Klan hand-signals during his investigations of the 1949 Groveland rape case and the 1951 murder of NAACP leader Harry Moore. Fuller Warren retired from politics in 1953 and died in Miami on 23 September 1973.

State Officials

No definitive tabulation of klansmen or ex-klansmen who have held state offices between 1868 and the present day exists. Several hundred, at least, have certainly served in various state legislatures, while lower elective posts and appointive offices have doubtless seen thousands of knights come and go on both sides of the Mason-Dixon Line. At various times in history, most state politicians in Alabama, Georgia, Indiana and Texas were members of the KKK, and those eras spawned a near-equal number of ardent opponents. The individuals listed below were identified from various published accounts and official reports.

Adams, Dr. Clifford Leroy—A klansman and prominent physician in Suwannee County, Florida, Adams won election to the state senate in 1952, with promises of patronage appointments to his fellow knights. Before his inauguration, however, Adams was shot and killed at his office on 3 August 1952. His assailant, Ruby McCollum, was a black woman who identified herself as the doctor's secret lover and mother of his illegitimate child. Klansmen were enraged by Adams's murder, but "moderate" leaders of the order patrolled the streets in mufti to "keep things quiet" and forestall lynching.

Anderson, John C.—A 1920s Alabama klansman, Anderson served on the state supreme court, ultimately rising to the office of chief justice.

Angell, R.H.—A resident of Roanoke, Virginia, Angell was part-owner of the *Fellowship Forum*, a pro–Klan and bitterly anti–Catholic periodical. He served as a delegate to the Republican National Conventions of 1928 and 1932, stridently opposing Catholic presidential candidate Alfred Smith in the former year. Angell also served as the GOP's Virginia state chairman in 1931.

Babington, Robert—While serving as an officer of the KWC in Reconstruction-era Washington Parish, Louisiana, Babington was also a successful merchant, the local postmaster, and chairman of the Democratic Party's central committee. Those divided loyalties did not prevent him from simultaneously serving the KKK, on whose behalf he issued "protection papers" to black Democratic voters in the 1868 election (thereby exempting them from attacks by KKK–KWC nightriders). Prior to election day, Babington led a gang of hooded horsemen who rode through Franklinton on five successive nights, intimidating would-be Republican voters.

Bassett, John David—In 1925, Virginia Republican John Bassett challenged Catholic incumbent John Purcell for the office of state treasurer. Klansmen endorsed Bassett as the "100-percent candidate," but he hedged on the question of personal KKK membership. Anti-Catholic propaganda flourished during the campaign, and a Democratic Party investigation traced one shipment of hate literature to Alabama Grand Dragon James Esdale. Bassett lost the election by a narrow margin, but three years later served as a delegate to the Republican National Convention.

Baxley, William J.—The son of a prominent judge in Dothan, Alabama, born 27 June 1941, Baxley was a student at the state university in Tuscaloosa when klansmen bombed Birmingham's Sixteenth Street Baptist Church on 15 September 1963, killing four young girls. Baxley was sickened by the news and did not eat that day. In 1970, his law school classmates helped Baxley campaign successfully for the state attorney general's office. After his election, Baxley wrote the names of the Birmingham bomb victims on his state telephone card, to keep them forever in mind. His investigation of the case made no progress by 1974, when he was reelected without opposition, but Baxley finally broke through the wall of FBI obstructionism to indict and convict klansman Robert Chambliss in 1977. He also secured indictments against Georgia klansman Jesse Stoner for a 1958 church bombing and charged several Montgomery knights in the 1957 murder of black truck driver Willie Edwards. (Stoner was convicted in 1980, but the Edwards charges were later dismissed when a key witness recanted his testimony.) Prosecution of Klan terrorists was still controversial in Alabama, and it cost Baxley his gubernatorial bid in 1978. Voters reconsidered in 1982, electing Baxley as lieutenant governor (1983–87), but he never occupied the governor's mansion. Baxley continued his political involvement as a delegate to the Democratic National Conventions of 1996 and 2000.

Beasley, Jere Locke—Born at Tyler, Texas, in December 1935, Beasley moved to Barbour County, Alabama, with his family as an infant. He earned his B.S. from Auburn University in 1959 and received his J.D. from the University of Alabama in 1962, winning admittance to the state bar that same year. In 1970, he won election as lieutenant governor after a campaign that included his keynote speech to the UKA's annual klonvokation. Beasley served two terms under Governor George Wallace (1971–79), and spent one month in summer 1972 as acting governor, after would-be assassin Arthur Bremer shot Wallace in Maryland. In 1979, Beasley returned to private legal practice and built one of Alabama's premier law firms. In 2003 he secured a record $11.9 billion judgment in punitive damages against ExxonMobil Corporation, on behalf of the state.

Brower, Walter S.—An attorney and klansman in Birmingham, Alabama, Brower was also a ranking member of the local KKK. In early 1925 he joined in a Klan campaign of harassment against bankrupt automobile dealer A.P. Rich, threatening Rich with violence if he failed to pay his debts to various klansmen. Nightriders whipped Rich in March 1925, and Rich committed suicide one month later, leaving a note that described harassment by Brower up to one hour before his death. Brower subsequently blamed that accusation on his "political enemies." When asked about his Klan membership, Brower called it "an insulting question [that] ... had no bearing on the case."

Brown, J.J.—While serving as Georgia's state commissioner of agriculture in the early 1920s, Brown joined the KKK and accompanied Governor Clifford Walker to the order's 1924 klonvokation in Kansas City, Missouri.

Brownell, Cyril—Oregon klansman Cyril Brownell served in the state house of representatives in the early 1920s. Fellow legislators recognized him as a leader of the Klan block led by Speaker of the House K.K. Kubli, otherwise known as the "Kubli Klan."

Crawford, John—An ex–Confederate army officer, Crawford was jailed in November 1868 following a militia raid on Klan headquarters at Center Point, Arkansas. He escaped conviction in that case and subsequently served as state auditor, but soon defaulted and resigned from office amid charges of embezzlement.

Duke, Daniel—Dan Duke never rose high in Georgia politics, but during his terms as assistant solicitor general (1939–41) and assistant attorney general (1944–46) he had a striking impact on the KKK. It was Duke who prosecuted members of Atlanta's Klavalier Klub for their flogging spree in 1939–40, sending several klansmen to prison, and he clashed publicly with Governor Eugene Talmadge in December 1941, when Talmadge pardoned those defendants. Days later, Pearl Harbor distracted Duke and sent him off to join the U.S. Marine Corps. In 1946, when Samuel Green went public with his AGK, Duke stood ready to revoke the order's Georgia charter, telling reporters, "The Klan contains the germs of an American Gestapo." Duke also prosecuted the neo–Nazi Columbians in 1946, for a series of terrorist acts in Atlanta, describing them as "the juvenile delinquents of the Klan." On 23 November 1946, during a conference in judge's chambers, Duke flattened Columbians leader Emory Burke with a punch to the jaw. Such rugged opposition to organized racism could not survive the advent of Herman Talmadge in state government, and Duke retired to private practice after 1946.

Duke, David Ernest—Duke launched his first political campaign (for a Louisiana state senate seat) in 1975, while serving as national director of the KKKK. He lost that contest, but made a respectable showing with 11,079 votes (one-third of all ballots cast in his district). In 1988, Duke was the far-right Populist Party's presidential candidate, but on election day polled only 48,000 votes out of 91 million cast nationwide. Two months later, in January 1989, he astounded critics by rebounding to win the GOP primary race for a seat in the state house of representatives. Despite public condemnation from the White House and various Republican leaders, Duke won a narrow victory in the general election, but voters subsequently denied him a second term. In 1990, Duke lost a bid for the U.S. Senate. The following year, he campaigned for the governor's post against two-time ex-governor Edwin Edwards. Despite pervasive scandal in his prior administrations (1972–80, 1984–88), Edwards won support from anti-racist forces statewide, complete with bumper stickers reading: "Vote for the Crook. It's Important." Duke lost that race as well, but claimed 680,000 votes, including fifty-five percent of all ballots cast by white Louisianans.

Flowers, Richmond McDavid—A native of Dothan, Alabama, born 11 November 1918, Flowers attended Auburn University and studied law at the University of Alabama before the U.S. Army drafted him in November 1942. Discharged as a captain in April 1946, Flowers completed studies for his LL.B. and practiced law in Dothan until 1954, when he won election to the state senate. Elected as the state's attorney general in 1962, Flowers served during modern Alabama's worst era of racial turmoil (1963–67). In 1965, he asked Klan-allied Governor George Wallace to join him in a probe of KKK terrorism, ironically suggesting that communists had infiltrated the Klan to pervert its "patriotic" ideals. Wallace predictably refused, and in June 1965

Flowers announced that his investigation was stalled by obstruction from FBI headquarters. Two months later, Lowndes County klansman Tom Coleman confronted Flowers and told him, "If you don't get off this Klan investigation, we'll get you off." Wallace chimed in a short time later, calling on state legislators to impeach Flowers for "collaborating with the federal government." Frustrated in his efforts to convict the Klan killers of Viola Liuzzo and Jonathan Daniels (shot by Tom Coleman in Hayneville, days after Coleman threatened Flowers), Flowers still managed to collect substantial information on the KKK. His final report, issued in October 1965, linked klansmen to forty of Birmingham's forty-five racist bombings since World War II, plus twelve out of seventeen civil rights murders recorded in Dixie since 1963. As a sideline of his probe, Flowers also learned that Mississippi's White Knights had huddled with Alabama UKA leaders to discuss assassinating him. Two racists assaulted Flowers at a Montgomery football game on 30 October 1965, and public antipathy toward Flowers—once described as "the most hated public official in Alabama"—drove his star-athlete son to pursue his college education out of state. In 1966, relying on support from newly-registered black voters, Flowers ran for governor but lost to Lurleen Wallace (running in place of husband George, who could not legally succeed himself). In August 1968, a federal grand jury indicted Flowers for violating the Hobbs Act (attempting "to obstruct or affect interstate commerce by committing or conspiring to commit extortion"), and jurors convicted him on 27 February 1969. Flowers described the prosecution as a Wallace-Klan vendetta and appealed his eight-year prison sentence, but appellate courts upheld the verdict. Paroled in 1974, after serving two years of his sentence, Flowers received a full pardon from President Jimmy Carter in 1978.

Frey, George—Birmingham attorney George Frey joined the modern KKK soon after it was organized in Alabama. He defended Klan floggers in 1923, and again in 1926, after sweeping Ku Klux raids on local Chinese cafés. Elected to the state legislature with Klan support that same year, Frey introduced a bill imposing $25,000 on any newspaper that criticized state officials or damaged Alabama's public reputation. The bill failed to pass.

George, James Z. *see Congress*

Green, W. Cooper—A member of the 1920s Klan in Birmingham, Alabama, Green won election to the state senate with Klan support in 1926. He later served as mayor of Birmingham (1952–53) and threatened klansman Robert Chambliss with dismissal from his city job for threatening a black insurance agent. Chambliss countered with a threat to sue the city and retained his position until criminal charges finally forced his dismissal.

Hall, Claris G.—Long-serving Arkansas Secretary of State C.G. "Crip" Hall (1937–61) angered klansmen on 8 June 1959 with the announcement that he would use all legal means at his disposal to block the filing of KKK incorporation papers. Arsonists set fire to the porch of Hall's home one day later, but rain extinguished the flames. Grand Dragon A.C. Hightower denied Klan involvement in the crime, telling reporters, "We don't have

people who would do such a thing as that." Hall served as secretary of state until his death in 1961, at which time his wife Nancy succeeded him.

Johnson, Rivers Dunn—A native of Wilson, North Carolina, born in 1885, Johnson practiced law in Duplin County, interrupting his personal business with six one-year terms in the state senate (1911, 1915, 1923, 1927, 1931, 1935). During his third term, Johnson led the fight against an anti-mask law, speaking on behalf of "25,000 red-blooded North Carolinians who are members of the Ku Klux Klan." He told his fellow senators that "invisibility is the force of the empire," claiming that the KKK stood for "Protestant Americanism, free speech, free press, white supremacy, and the support of law." Four years later, Johnson underwent a change of heart, joining Rev. Oscar Haywood to introduce a bill outlawing masks and membership in secret societies. North Carolina's senate passed the Haywood-Johnson bill, but Klan supporters killed it in the lower house.

Kubli, Koepke Knudsen—Few historical details survive concerning the life of K.K. Kubli, a Harvard-educated businessman who settled in Portland, Oregon, and turned his hand to Republican politics during World War I. Kubli lost his race for a seat on Portland's public service commission in 1917, but rebounded with election to the state house of representatives that same year. When the KKK invaded Oregon, Kubli's initials earned him free membership in Portland's Klan No. 1, and fellow knights provided many of the 23,018 votes that returned him to the legislature for a fourth term in 1922. The following year, as speaker of the house, he led a "Kubli Klan" team of legislators to sponsor various nativistic bills drafted by imperial headquarters. The only real success was passage of a bill mandating public school education for all Oregon children, thereby effectively banning parochial schools. (The law was later stricken down as unconstitutional.) Grand Dragon Fred Gifford's political maneuvers alienated Kubli and other Oregon klansmen during 1924, by which time Kubli had left office, and so Kubli abandoned the order that shared his initials. In 1940, he served as a delegate to the Republican National Convention.

Lyle, J. Banks—An ex–Confederate military officer, South Carolina state legislator, and principal of Limestone College, Lyle led a covert life as leader of Spartanburg County's Reconstruction-era KKK during a period of unparalleled terrorism. In October 1871, immediately prior to state elections, klansmen (including one Limestone College teacher who wore his academic gown without further disguise) closed local polls to prevent freedmen from voting. Acts of violence, including several murders, were commonplace throughout the county, and Lyle later fled the state to avoid arrest. He was never prosecuted for his crimes.

Lyons, Robert W.—Indiana millionaire and chain-store lobbyist Robert Lyons joined the 1920s KKK to promote his personal career. In 1940, and again in 1944, he was elected to serve as a delegate to the Republican National Convention. On the latter occasion, a rival GOP member challenged his selection on grounds of former Klan membership. After two weeks of heated criticism, Lyons resigned as a delegate.

McAfee, Leroy—A state legislator from Cleveland County, North Carolina, McAfee also served as grand titan for his district during Reconstruction. He played a leading role in the 1870 impeachment of Governor William Holden, following Holden's attempt to crush the Tarheel Klan with armed force. In March 1871, McAfee conferred with top klansmen from Rutherford County on means of curbing the region's chaotic violence. His efforts proved fruitless, and federal authorities jailed McAfee himself in October 1871. Thirty years later, a nephew of McAfee's—Thomas Dixon—penned three novels that paved the way for a twentieth-century KKK revival.

McCall, Charles C.—McCall joined the Alabama KKK in a quest for political support, and won election as state attorney general with Klan votes in 1926. Before he was inaugurated, McCall announced a plan to name Grand Dragon James Esdale as assistant attorney general, but Esdale declined the nomination after protests from the state Public Service Commission. Thereafter, McCall's relationship to the invisible empire was a study in contradictions. He pursued Klan floggers and convicted a few, but joined Esdale in a libel suit against the Birmingham *Age-Herald* after that newspaper quoted Esdale's call for whipping of Klan opponents. (Esdale and McCall dropped the lawsuit when attorneys for the *Age-Herald* began calling Birmingham klansmen as witnesses in court.) In 1927, after McCall charged several Crenshaw County floggers, he obtained a copy of a letter dated 17 September, written by Esdale to Exalted Cyclops Ira Thompson of Luverne. In that letter, Esdale assured his subordinate that he (Esdale) would persuade Governor Bibb Graves to block McCall's prosecution of klansmen. McCall quit the Klan a month later, on 19 October, while Governor Graves slashed funding for trials of Klan terrorists. McCall lost his bid for the governor's mansion in 1930.

Milliken, Carl S.—Milliken already held office as Colorado's secretary of state when he joined the KKK in 1921 or early 1922. By the time he sought reelection in 1924, Milliken also served as klaliff of Denver's largest klavern. He won reelection with KKK support, after Grand Dragon John Locke proclaimed that "the Klan will support no man in the coming election unless he signs his name on the dotted line to all the pledges and promises the Klan demands." Milliken subsequently embarrassed the order by resigning from its ranks during the bitter quarrel between Locke and imperial headquarters.

Moore, Dr. John A.—A physician and active Democrat in Alamance County, North Carolina, Moore served one term in the state legislature immediately following the Civil War (1865). With the onset of military Reconstruction, he joined the local KKK, publicly promoting the order as "a good thing for poor men" that would "protect their families from the darkies." Klan votes secured another state legislative term for Moore in 1868.

Orbison, Charles J.—A Hoosier klansman and judge of the Indianapolis Superior Court in the 1920s, Orbison also served briefly as the state's Prohibition director. In 1927, Mayor-elect (and klansman) John Duvall named Orbison to a seat on the city's Park Board, along with Exalted Cyclops George Elliott of Klan No. 3. Imperial Wizard Hiram Evans considered Orbison as a replacement for Grand Dragon David Stephenson in 1926, then named him grand klaliff instead. A year later, with the Klan in decline after Stephenson's murder conviction, Orbison remained loyal, addressing a rally of 300 knights at the Palmer House hotel. Indiana klansmen tried to nominate him for a U.S. Senate seat in 1928, but imperial headquarters threw its support to a friendly non-klansman, James Watson.

Purl, George Clark—Dallas klansman George Purl won election to the state house of representatives with Klan support in 1922, then marched in a triumphant KKK victory parade through the heart of the city. In the early 1930s, Purl won a seat in the state senate, then retired to serve as a lobbyist for the American Retail Federation. In 1940, he was a delegate to the Democratic National Convention.

Ray, Ben F.—Birmingham klansman Ben Ray won election to the Democratic Party's state executive committee for Alabama in 1926. Three years later, he opposed (but failed to prevent) the party's expulsion of klansmen Thomas Heflin and Hugh Locke. In 1940, Ray served as a delegate to the Democratic National Convention.

Russell, Richard Brevard, Sr.—A Georgia native, born in 1861, Russell served as chief justice of the state supreme court from 1923 until his death on 3 December 1938. He was also a member of the Klan who frequently advised imperial headquarters on matters of state policy. In 1924, Russell sought Klan support for a U.S. Senate race, but Imperial Wizard Hiram Evans persuaded Russell to withdraw from the race, while the order supported incumbent William Harris. Two years later, Governor (and fellow klansman) Clifford Walker nominated Russell to serve as a chancellor of the state university, but angry student protests reversed that decision. Klan leaders next tapped Russell to oppose Senator Walter George in 1926, as punishment for George endorsing the World Court, but stubborn voters returned George to Washington for another term. Russell's son, Richard Jr., subsequently served in the House of Representatives (1927–31), as governor of Georgia (1931–33), and in the U.S. Senate (1933–71), where he consistently opposed anti-lynching and pro–civil rights legislation.

Saunders, William L.—Named in several accounts as North Carolina's grand dragon during Reconstruction, Saunders subsequently served as the secretary of state (1879–91).

Twitty, Peter S.—Georgia klansman Peter Twitty served as his state's commissioner of fish and game in the early 1920s. In September 1924, he accompanied Governor Clifford Walker to the Klan's klonvokation in Kansas City, Missouri.

Wallace, George C., Jr.—The son of Alabama's Klan-allied Governor George Corley Wallace, George C. Wallace, Jr., was born at Eufaula on 17 October 1951. He earned a B.A. from Huntingdon College in 1976 and pursued graduate studies at Auburn University, in Montgomery. After college, Wallace served as director of financial aid and alumni affairs at Montgomery's Troy State University (1978–82), advancing to vice president of the same department in 1983. In 1986, he was elected to his first term as Alabama's state treasurer, winning a second four-year term in 1990. Wallace lost his bid for a congressional seat in 1992, and his 1995 race to become lieutenant governor, but voters granted him a seat on Alabama's public service commission in 1998 (a post he retained at press time for this volume). Although his résumé includes a Freedom Award from the NAACP, Wallace still consorts with the white-supremacist CCC. According to SPLC reports, Wallace addressed the group once in 1998 and twice in 1999, before delivering the keynote speech when the CCC's national convention opened in Montgomery on 3 June 2005. Wallace, a Republican, was presumably aware of the GOP National Committee's 1999 warning, asking all party members to avoid contact with the CCC after its racist activities were exposed. Nonetheless, Wallace presented his remarks in 2005 to an audience including former Imperial Wizard Stephen Black, Jamie Kelso (an aide to David Duke who once shared rooms with Duke in Louisiana), Edward Fields (aging klansman and founder of the neo–Nazi NSRP), and Leonard "Flagpole" Wilson (a leader of the 1956 riot that drove black coed Autherine Lucy from the University of Alabama). When reporters questioned his presence at the CCC convention, Wallace replied, "There is nothing hateful about those people I've seen."

Woodward, William F.—In the early 1920s, Woodward served both as a board of education member in Portland, Oregon, and as a member of the state legislature. He was a klansman, known to fellow lawmakers in the state house of representatives as a leading member of Speaker K.K. Kubli's "Kubli Klan" faction.

Local Officials

Hundreds of active and former klansmen held various local offices during 1868–1900, while hundreds (or thousands) more won election to various minor posts during the modern Klan's gold rush days of 1915–44. No comprehensive list of Klan officeholders exists, and the order's secrecy renders compilation of any such roster impossible. The relative handful of officials listed below have been identified as klansmen or significant Klan opponents in various published reports over the past half-century.

Arnold, Luke—While serving as a judge in Atlanta, Georgia, during 1946, Arnold was also popular on the AGK lecture circuit.

Bain, Edgar H.—As the 1920s mayor of Goldsboro, North Carolina, Bain collaborated with the KKK and praised its local vigilante activities. When word circulated that Goldsboro klansmen planned a violent reception for two black residents returning from a visit to New York, historian Arnold Rice reports that Bain announced his support for the order "in terms as glowing as those a Kleagle might have used in recruiting members."

Baker, George L.—Baker was serving his second term as mayor of Portland, Oregon, when the Klan established itself in that city. He soon joined the order to corral its votes. In May 1922, when Catholic spokesmen protested a Klan demonstration held at Portland's civic auditorium, Baker replied that his police force was too small to control the hooded order's estimated 8,000 to 10,000 local members. A year later, on 3 March 1923, Baker appeared as a guest speaker when Portland's Chamber of Commerce held a birthday banquet for Grand Dragon Fred Gifford. In early 1924, Baker and state legislator K.K. Kubli both sought the Klan's endorsement for a U.S. Senate seat. Gifford initially backed Baker, then switched to candidate George Kelly, and finally gave his last-minute endorsement to incumbent Charles McNary. Baker quit the Klan as a result, while seeking an unprecedented third mayoral term in November 1924. Dragon Gifford supported klansman John Rankin in that contest, but Baker's main competition came from former circuit judge W.N. Gatens, a Catholic defeated by Klan votes in 1922. Gatens attacked Baker on his KKK affiliations, charging that Baker had surrendered to "secret societies and clandestine influence," but the argument failed to sway voters. On election day, Baker carried the contest with 41,810 ballots, while Gatens got 21,579 and Rankin trailed the field with only 1,600.

Baker, William T.—When William Baker ran for mayor of Louisville, Kentucky, as a Democrat in 1925, the GOP's campaign committee offered him $1,000 if he could prove that he was not and had never been a member of the KKK. Two days before the scheduled election, Baker acknowledged being a klansman "at one time," and withdrew from the race, forcing Democratic leaders to nominate Judge Joseph O'Neil as a last-minute replacement. Republican candidate Arthur Will won that election, but Baker weathered the storm and subsequently won election to the state legislature (1936–39).

Blaylock, Louis—Historian Kenneth Jackson reports that Texas resident Louis Blaylock was "a friend, if not a member" of local Klan No. 66 when he ran for mayor of Dallas in April 1923. Fewer than 20,000 persons voted in that contest, and Blaylock received 13,500 of the ballots cast, winning a landslide victory while other klansmen controlled the city commission.

Bowles, Charles E.—A native of Yale, Michigan, born in 1884, Bowles studied law at the state university and established his practice in Detroit. When Mayor Frank Doremus fell critically ill in summer 1924, and a special primary was scheduled for 9 September to fill the last year of his term, Bowles entered the race against rivals Joseph Martin and John Smith. He ran third in that race, but declined to bow out of the contest, announcing himself as a write-in candidate for the November run-off election. As the only Protestant seeking the office, campaigning on a promise of "strict law enforcement," Bowles won the KKK's endorsement. His opponents quickly fastened on that fact, and an anti–Klan rally was scheduled for 21 October, to "expose" Bowles as the invisible empire's candidate. Hours before that gathering, a mob of 6,000 men and boys surrounded Detroit's Arena Gardens, chanting Bowles's name and blocking access to the box office for half and hour while police fought to clear the street.

Bowles's opponents were delighted by the outburst. Martin told supporters that the "Klan accidentally tore the night shirt and pillow case from its hero and revealed to the entire citizenship that Charles Bowles was the Ku Klux candidate for mayor and general manager of Detroit," adding that in its "riotous demonstration to prevent an anti-Klan lecture, the Ku Klux Klan of Detroit pasted the symbols of the Klan and the symbols of the Bowles campaign side by side." Smith dismissed Bowles supporters as "ignorant hillbillies," reminding a Catholic audience that klansmen "have robbed Catholic churches and have attempted to burn them. They have tortured and slain Negroes and Jews." One day before the election, Smith branded the KKK an ugly monster from Dixie "which is going to the polls tomorrow to put over the parochial school amendment and its candidate for mayor." Bowles carefully avoided mention of the Klan, meanwhile, prompting Martin to challenge him: "If Charles Bowles is not the candidate of the Ku Klux Klan, as I have repeatedly charged, why does he not publicly give the Klan that condemnation which it so richly deserves?" On election day, Smith received 116,807 votes, while Bowles got 106,679 and Martin trailed with 84,929. A subsequent canvass revealed that 17,563 ballots had been disqualified, some of them for variant spellings of Bowles's name, but a recount still left Bowles second-best by some 14,000 votes. In 1925, Bowles won election to the state recorder's court, where he served until 1929. Resigning that year to run for mayor a second time, he captured the office but could not hold it. In 1930, Bowles was recalled by a coalition of opponents who charged that he took orders from the KKK *and* from Detroit's predominantly Jewish Purple Gang. Bowles subsequently sought a congressional seat (1932, 1934) and a place on the circuit court bench (1941), but victory eluded him. He died on 30 July 1957.

Burns, Haydon *see Governors*

Callaway, Caleb—An Atlanta judge and member of Grand Dragon Samuel Green's AGK in the late 1940s, Callaway once received a letter of commendation from the Klan, praising his habit of rendering judgments "conforming with the principles of Klannishness."

Cox, Shelby S.—Dallas klansman Shelby Cox won election as district attorney in 1922, after the Texas KKK pledged $10,000 to support his campaign, along with those of judicial candidate Felix Robertson and incumbent Sheriff Dan Harston. Cox addressed several Klan rallies during the campaign, and after his election admitted membership in the order, insisting that the KKK required no public defense.

Davis, Clifford—A 1920s klansman in Memphis, Tennessee, Davis ran for city judge in 1923, addressing several KKK rallies during the course of his campaign. Anti-Klan forces marshaled to defeat him, but Davis outwitted them by appealing to non-KKK elements, promising to dispense justice from the bench "without regard to influence, station, faction or creed." On election day, he polled 2,700 votes more than any other Klan candidate, coasting to an easy victory.

Davis, James Wayne—Davis won election as the recorder of deeds in Rowan County, North Carolina, in 1966, while serving as an active member of the UKA. Eight months later, in July 1967, he was one of twelve klansmen jailed on charges of mounting a terrorist campaign to prevent school integration. Davis and seven other defendants pled guilty at trial, in January 1968.

Drake, C.L.—As mayor of Iron City, Georgia, in the late 1940s, Drake was a staunch opponent of the Ku Klux Klan. On 17 July 1949, eight carloads of armed klansmen approached his home, but they were driven off by gunfire. Grand Dragon Samuel Green denied responsibility for the attack, blaming a rival Klan faction based in Columbus, Georgia. On the night of 6 August 1949, Drake and a posse of friends exchanged shots with a caravan of sixteen Klan vehicles, wounding one of the raiders. Florida klansman Bill Hendrix visited a local judge to file charges against Drake for disturbing the peace, but he fled across the Alabama border when Drake and company arrived, seeking protection in the Dothan, Alabama, police station. Undaunted, Drake followed Hendrix across the state line and had him arrested, publicly identifying Hendrix as the leader of the latest motorcade.

Duvall, John—Hoosier klansman John Duvall secured the order's support in his 1925 bid to become mayor of Indianapolis after signing a pledge that read: "In return for the political support of [Grand Dragon] D.C. Stephenson, in the event I am elected mayor of Indianapolis, I promise not to appoint any person as a member of the Board of Public Works without [*sic*] they first have the endorsement of Stephenson. I fully agree and promise to appoint Claude Worley as Chief of Police and Earl Klinck as a Captain." Ex-mayor John Holtzman complained that Duvall's election would succeed in "nourishing and strengthening of the D.C. Stephenson brand of politics," but voters ignored him (and the murder charge pending against Stephenson). On election day, Duvall beat his opponent by a margin of 9,974 votes, while all five members of the KKK's United Protestant School Board ticket likewise won their races. On 1 January 1926, Duvall traveled to Washington, D.C., at Klan expense, for a strategy meeting with Imperial Wizard Hiram Evans. He balked at Evans's choice for city corporation council, but named the candidate to the public works board and otherwise used his patronage powers in conformity with orders from imperial headquarters. The *Indianapolis News* reported that Duvall's regime "gives promise of being a Klan administration to a considerable extent." Jurors convicted Stephenson of murder two weeks later, and while Duvall avoided recall following exposure of his pledge to the imprisoned dragon, any hope of re-election was forever lost.

Etheridge, Paul—Georgia attorney Paul Etheridge was a member of Atlanta's Fulton County Board of Commissioners of Roads and Revenues when he joined the KKK in 1915, and he continued in that post long afterward, while performing legal services for the Klan. In early 1932, he led the Klan-organized Roosevelt Clubs, supporting FDR as the Democratic presidential candidate. That support evaporated after Democratic leaders reminded Etheridge that the clubs were supposed to raise money for Roosevelt, not bank it for themselves.

Glymph, C.L.C.—A black grocer in Gaffney, South Carolina, Glymph entered the Democratic primary as a candidate for city council in January 1952. He withdrew on 11 February, after he received a letter on stationery of the Association of Carolina Klans, which read: "It is not customary, as you know, for the colored race of South Carolina to hold public office. Now is the time you should realize your defeat and let your withdrawal before Feb. 12 be your protection for now and hereafter."

Graham, Royal Reed—Denver judge and klansman Royal Graham challenged incumbent Judge Benjamin Lindsey for his seat on the city's juvenile court in 1924. KKK leaders despised Lindsey for his opposition to their order, and also craved access to his files as a goldmine of potential ammunition for blackmail against various Denver residents. The *Denver Post* branded Graham as unfit "for any job, no matter how small," but Klan votes were numerous in Colorado's capital. On election day, the results were too close to call, both candidates claiming fraud by their opponents. Graham filed a lawsuit (with KKK support) claiming that ballots from the predominantly Jewish West Colfax precinct had been fraudulently marked for Lindsey. The case dragged on in court for two years, while Graham's attorney sued to recover his fee and Colorado's state bar association launched an investigation of Graham's ties to the Klan. Graham committed suicide in the face of that probe, and thus missed an appellate court's 1926 verdict disqualifying the West Colfax ballots, awarding Graham posthumous victory. Judge Lindsey burned his files and moved to California, while Colorado's grand dragon boasted, "But for the splendid work of Denver Klan No. 1, in all probability Judge Lindsey would still be sitting arrogantly on his little juvenile throne."

Holcomb, Oscar J.—While serving as mayor of Houston, Texas, Holcomb joined the KKK's Lone Star klavern in 1920. He soon grew disenchanted with the order, and quit the Klan in 1921.

Howard, Gus H.—In 1923, Georgia Governor Clifford Walker named klansman Gus Howard to fill a vacancy on the Fulton County (Atlanta) Superior Court. In 1924, when Howard sought election to a full term of his own, Walker created controversy via distribution of a letter to Atlanta's female voters, seeking their support for Howard. That move sparked complaints from Rebecca Felton of Cartersville, the first woman ever to hold a U.S. Senate seat, while rival candidate L.F. McClelland declared that the Klan's "recent entry into the political arena removes it from the realm of fraternal organizations to that of a political party." On election day, Howard defeated McClelland by a margin of 585 votes out of 14,871 cast.

Jones, Clayton—While serving as a municipal judge in Albany, Georgia, Jones addressed a local UKA rally on 7 July 1963, urging klansmen to "hurl back the black tide" in America. Striking a morbid note, Jones declared that he did not have long to live, adding, "But I hope that God will grant me the power to come back. And when I do, may I still see white faces in the positions of trust, not black faces."

Jones, Murray B.—While serving as a judge in Houston, Texas, Jones entered the 1923 mayoral race with open support from the KKK. He opposed incumbent Oscar Holcombe, also understood to be a klansman, but Holcombe retained the office.

Nosser, John—A Lebanese immigrant, born in 1900, Nosser settled in Natchez, Mississippi, as a storekeeper and served as the city's mayor in the 1960s. As a moderate in troubled times, Nosser faced condemnation from both sides. Black civil rights activists boycotted his small chain of dry-goods stores for maintaining segregation, while local klansmen hated Nosser for condemning terrorism. Nightriders detonated a bomb in Nosser's front yard on 25 September 1964, then burned his grocery store on 31 December 1965. In February 1967, after a car bomb killed Natchez NAACP leader Wharlest Jackson, Nosser appeared at a black protest rally with Sheriff Odell Anders and Police Chief J.T. Robinson, linking arms with demonstrators to sing "We Shall Overcome."

Peterson, Jim—As mayor of Soperton, Georgia, in the late 1940s, Peterson was an outspoken enemy of the KKK. Alerted by reports of robed men prowling the streets on 21 May 1949, Peterson accosted klansmen Malcolm Brady and Joe Greene near his home, ripping off their masks in a scuffle that sent the two knights to jail. Continuing his rounds, Peterson surprised three more klansmen, unmasking state highway department night watchman John Edge before Edge's companions escaped in a hail of police gunfire. President Harry Truman praised Peterson's actions, while Grand Dragon Samuel Green threatened litigation. Disorderly conduct charges were filed against the three arrested klansmen, then dismissed on 13 June 1949. A judge also dismissed their loitering charges on 28 July.

Rankin, John H.—In 1922, klansman John Rankin won election (with komrade Dolph Walker) to the public service commission in Portland, Oregon. In early 1924, both commissioners faced a recall election, charged with graft related to construction of two bridges, which produced a hike in public utility rates. Klan spokesmen blamed the Catholic Church, with headlines in the *Western American* declaring "Recall Movement Papal Drive," but voters stripped both klansmen of their offices. Rankin tried his luck with a mayoral race that fall, against incumbent George Baker, but he gathered only 1,600 votes against Baker's 41,810.

Rawls, Louis—While serving as mayor of Bogalusa, Louisiana (1971–79), Rawls accepted the KKK's endorsement for his 1974 reelection campaign, informing reporters, "The blacks won't vote for me anyway." When the IEKKKK opened a local klavern on Good Friday 1976, Rawls participated in the ribbon-cutting ceremony, accepting a Klan hood and certificate of honorary membership from Imperial Wizard Bill Wilkinson.

Rester, Robert T.—HUAC investigators identified Rester as a member of the Original Knights and its front group, the ACCA, during 1964–65. At the same time, he also served as city attorney for Bogalusa, Louisiana. Frequent acquittals of violent klansmen, coupled with vigorous prosecution of black civil rights activists in Bogalusa, raised questions concerning Rester's fitness for office during 1965, precipitating federal litigation to restrain the local KKK.

Robertson, Felix D.—Robertson was one of three political candidates to whom the Dallas, Texas, KKK pledged

$10,000 in 1922. With Ku Klux votes and money behind him, Robertson easily won election as judge of the city's criminal court. He subsequently marched in a victory parade with local Klan leaders through the heart of downtown Dallas.

Rose, John E., Jr.—In 1920, Rose was a member of Richmond, Virginia's city council and a recognized member of the KKK. The following year, with Klan support, he was elected to serve as Richmond's commissioner of revenue.

Sims, Walter A.—Sims joined the KKK in Atlanta while serving as a member of the city council. In 1922, he ran for mayor as an acknowledged klansman, voicing concerns over the "Catholic question" and calling for investigations of the Knights of Columbus. One of five opponents in that race, Police Chief James Beavers, vowed that as mayor he would "fight any improper influence the Klan may seek to exert in politics, or any hand it may seek to take in the affairs of this city." Sims led the field, supported by Klan votes, and easily won reelection in 1924.

Stapleton, Benjamin F.—Denver klansman Ben Stapleton campaigned for mayor in 1922 as a reform candidate, opposing incumbent Dewey Bailey. He concealed his KKK affiliation during that campaign, advising audiences that "true Americanism needs no disguise," and defeated Bailey by 6,363 votes. Observers initially ranked Stapleton as a capable mayor, then noticed that his appointments for city attorney, public safety manager and chief of police were all klansmen. In March 1924, soon after Stapleton named klansman William Candlish as police chief, opponents filed a recall petition against the mayor. Grand Dragon John Locke managed Stapleton's campaign for the special election scheduled on 21 August, and Stapleton won the day with 55,635 votes against Dewey Bailey's 24,277. Klansmen celebrated his victory with a motorcade through Denver on election night.

Vernado, Devan—A member of the KKK in Bogalusa, Louisiana, Vernado was twice appointed to sit on the town's housing authority in 1965, despite strenuous protests from the local black community.

Walker, Dolph—In 1922, Oregon klansman Dolph Walker won election to Portland's public service commission. By spring 1924 he faced a recall movement, with two other Klan officials, on charges of graft and inefficiency that produced higher public utility rates. Klan spokesmen blamed the recall drive on the "great Catholic machine," but voters removed all three klansmen from office.

Waybright, Edgar—Jacksonville, Florida, attorney Edgar Waybright doubled as chairman of Duval County's Democratic Executive Committee in the early 1950s. He was also a member of the KKK, presumed by some observers (including Klan infiltrator Stetson Kennedy) to be the anonymous "Permanent Emperor Samuel II" behind Bill Hendrix's Northern and Southern Knights of the KKK, founded in August 1949. Kennedy reports that Waybright "lurked in the background" while South Carolina Governor James Byrnes addressed a Jacksonville Klan rally in 1951. In the 1952 presidential election, Waybright orchestrated a shift in Klan ballots from the traditional Democratic ticket to GOP contender Dwight Eisenhower. As part of that campaign, Waybright printed 100,000 copies of a flyer with a photograph of Democratic vice-presidential candidate John Sparkman talking to three black men. The caption read: "Good Democrats and real Southerners will have no alternative but to vote for Eisenhower and Nixon to maintain our individual freedoms and way of life!" In January 1954, Waybright defended several Florida klansmen indicted on perjury charges by a federal grand jury investigating Klan terrorism in the Sunshine State. He won dismissal of all charges with an argument that federal authorities had no jurisdiction over the crimes in question.

Williams, L.C.—Klan political historian Arnold Rice identifies Mayor L.C. Williams of Ahoskie, North Carolina, as a collaborator with—if not an actual member of—the 1920s KKK. Whenever klansmen sought permission for parades or other demonstrations in the small coastal town, Williams "promptly" granted their wishes and thus guaranteed himself the order's votes at reelection time.

9 REIGN OF TERROR

Intimidation

Many klansmen are bullies by nature. From the earliest days of the order, even before it reorganized as a guerrilla army in spring 1867, the Klan's stock in trade was harassment of innocent freedmen with "practical jokes" that included posing as ghosts or zombies of Confederate war dead. After Klan leaders committed themselves to the overthrow of Reconstruction and "redemption" of the South for white-supremacist "home rule," their fabled sense of humor quickly vanished and their "jokes" became threats of whipping or worse, directed at Republicans and any blacks who dared to rise above "their place" in time-honored southern society.

While violence would be the first and last resort for some klansmen, others tried intimidation first, before taking up their whips and guns. A common form of threat during the Reconstruction era was the Ku Klux notice, either posted near a would-be victim's home or published in the pages of a Democratic newspaper. While some such notices were cryptic to the point of being indecipherable, others were perfectly clear. The following threat against Riley Kinman—the Republican sheriff-elect of Jackson County, Arkansas—appeared in the Little Rock *Morning Republican* on 13 May 1868:

> We have come! We are here! Beware! Take heed! When the black cat is gliding under the shadows of darkness, and the death watch ticks at the lone hour of night, then we, the pale riders, are abroad. Speak in whispers and we hear you. Dream as you sleep in the inmost recesses of your house, and, hovering over your beds, we gather your sleeping thoughts, while our daggers are at your throat. Ravisher of liberties of the people for whom we died and yet live, begone ere it is too late[.] Unholy blacks, cursed of God, take warning and fly. Twice has the Sacred Serpent hissed. When again his voice is heard your doom is sealed. Beware! Take heed! ... To be executed by White Death and Rattling Skeleton, at 10 to-night. K.K.K.

In April 1868, Louisiana Governor Henry Clay Warmouth received the following threat by mail, from a klansman who could not spell the name of his own order:

> Head Quarters "Klu Klux"
> *Blood! Blood!! Blood!!!*
> First Quarter *Bloody* Moon
> April 27[,] 1868
> H.C. Warmouth
> Villain beware[.] Your doom is sealed[.] Death now awaits you. The *midnight owl screams, Revenge! Revenge!! Revenge!!!*

> *Klu Klux Klan*
> By order of Grand Giant
> Bloody Knights Klu Klux Klan
> Prepare[.] *Death* now awaits *you.*

In 1915, the revived Ku Klux Klan adopted fiery crosses as its symbol, borrowed from Scottish Highland clansmen via the pages of Thomas Dixon's racist novels. Early cross-burnings were conducted at formal Klan rallies, but local klaverns and klansmen soon expanded the practice to include smaller crosses burned as warnings to various groups or individuals marked for retribution by the KKK. Ministers who criticized the Klan on Sunday morning could expect a fiery cross outside their church or rectory. Others blazed on the lawns of anti–Klan politicians, Jewish or Catholic merchants, and blacks who dared to cross the color line. Often, a cross-burning preceded acts of violence: arson, bombing, flogging, a midnight drive-by shooting. While no tabulation of intimidatory cross-burnings exists, thousands of incidents have been recorded since the Klan spread nationwide and they continue to the present day. SPLC investigators counted 226 cross-burnings during the years 1994–98. As recently as 21 February 2005, a cross was burned outside a church in Boston, Massachusetts.

Klansmen keep up with the times, at least where tactics of harassment are concerned. Over the decades, they have made countless threatening telephone calls, warning their enemies of imminent death, evacuating public buildings with bomb threats, sometimes merely spewing filth with no coherent message. In the 1970s, some Klans established "hate lines" with recorded messages, while former Imperial Wizard Stephen Black pioneered the first white-supremacist Internet bulletin board in 1985. Since then, hate messages and threats have become routine in cyberspace, with racists such as Louis Beam offering "points" to any "Aryan warrior" who will murder particular targets (the U.S. President, federal judges, SPLC founder Morris Dees, etc.).

Vandalism is often the next step in harassment, where threats fail to intimidate Klan enemies. Smashed windows and racist graffiti are so common in America that they often fail to rate mention in daily newspapers. In the 1920s, a group of Indiana klansmen known as the Venango Gang expressed their resentment by smearing buildings with cow dung. Forty years later, Mississippi klansman Byron De La Beckwith painted a black ring around the home of a white man who hired "the wrong nigger" to paint the house. Around that same time, WKKKKM Imperial Wizard Sam Bowers enjoined his "Happy Warriors" to harass civil rights workers and FBI agents with a variety of "humorous" weapons including fireworks, snakes and lizards, mad dogs, itching powder, stink bombs and tear gas, sugar and molasses (placed in fuel tanks), paint and lacquer thinner, slingshots and crossbows. KKK graffiti, commonly accompanied by swastikas and racial epithets, is still commonplace. While this chapter was in preparation, such incidents occurred in Danville, Virginia (4 February 2005); Centereach, New York (10 February 2005); Rock Hill, South Carolina (10 February 2005); and Elk Grove, California (21 March 2005).

Flogging

From Reconstruction through the early 1980s, klansmen whipped untold numbers of victims throughout the United States. Reconstruction-era victims were typically freedmen, Republicans or teachers in black schools, "warned" by flogging to desist from various activities opposed by members of the KKK. Some victims received hundreds of lashes, leaving them mortally injured or crippled for life. After 1915, Ku Klux flogging victims frequently included whites accused of some "immoral" activity—an ever-changing list that ranged from drinking and sexual promiscuity to skipping church, joining labor unions, opposing Klan political candidates, or speaking out against the KKK itself. Historically, few of the Klan's floggers were ever prosecuted and most of those hauled into court were acquitted by sympathetic (or terrified) juries; some of those convicted were subsequently pardoned by friendly politicians, such as Georgia Governor Eugene Talmadge. No classic Klan whippings have been reported since 1982, when the KKK largely abandoned moralistic crusades, joining its neo–Nazi allies in guerrilla warfare against the established U.S. government. A random sampling of Klan victims, drawn from among countless thousands, are listed below alphabetically.

Alexander, Jack—One of three known victims whipped by Alabama klansmen on the night of 19 May 1949, Alexander pressed charges against his attackers and thus secured the Cotton State's first flogging conviction in two decades. A. Byrd Carradine, an officer of the Federated KKK's Stonewall Jackson klavern, faced trial before year's end, winning a mistrial on 12 December when jurors deadlocked eight-to-four for acquittal. State authorities refused to try him a second time, but federal jurors convicted Carradine of conspiracy on 6 October 1950, resulting in a six-month prison sentence.

Biggerstaff, Aaron—An elderly Unionist and resident of Reconstruction-era Rutherford County, North Carolina, Biggerstaff was despised as a "scalawag" by most of his white neighbors. They accused him of helping Yankee troops seize Confederate horses during the Civil War, and Biggerstaff made things worse by opposing Ku Klux terrorism against freedmen and Republicans. In early 1870, he helped track a party of nightriders to the home of his own half-brother, Samuel Biggerstaff. That affair resulted in Aaron's conviction on trespassing charges, after he and others fired on Samuel's house. Forty klansmen raided Aaron's home on 8 April 1871, whipping him and his daughter. Biggerstaff recognized some of the raiders and had them arrested.

While en route to a pretrial hearing in Shelby, Biggerstaff was ambushed and suffered a second whipping. Still he persevered, and several klansmen ultimately served prison time for the assaults.

Billups, Rev. Charles—Billups won a Congressional Medal of Honor in the Korean War, then returned home to serve as a minister and Boy Scout leader in Birmingham, Alabama. In the late 1950s, he also helped Rev. Fred Shuttlesworth found the Alabama Christian Movement for Human Rights. On 10 April 1959, a group of klansmen kidnapped Billups, blindfolded him, and drove him to a wooded area where they whipped him with tire chains, demanding information about ACMHR activities. When Billups prayed instead of squealing, the knights bound him to a tree and branded the letters "KKK" on his stomach. Billups remained active in the civil rights movement, but later moved to Chicago, where he served as director of human relations for the National Food Stores. Police found him bludgeoned to death in his car, on 7 November 1968.

Brownlee, R. Wiley—As principal of Willow Run High School in Ypsilanti, Michigan, Brownlee did everything within his power to promote racial harmony on campus through the late 1960s and early 1970s. On 2 April 1971, six armed members of the UKA waylaid Brownlee on the highway outside Plymouth, dragged him from his car, then tarred and feathered him. Federal prosecutors indicted Grand Dragon Robert Miles and four other klansmen for that crime on 22 June 1972. Jurors convicted Miles, resulting in a prison term concurrent with his sentence for bombing school buses in Pontiac, Michigan.

Champion, William—A Unionist "scalawag" in pre–Civil War Spartanburg County, South Carolina, Champion emerged as a Republican activist during Reconstruction. He served as a local election commissioner and further outraged white supremacists by erecting a school for blacks on his property. The final insult came when Champion condemned the Ku Klux Klan by name, declaring publicly that "no Christian-hearted or civilized man" could belong to the order. Fifty klansmen raided Champion's home in October 1871, wounding a male visitor with bullets, then binding Champion and his friend before marching them into the woods. There, another Klan party waited with two elderly blacks, Clem Bowden and his wife. The klansmen severely whipped Champion and the Bowdens, afterward forcing Champion to perform various "degrading acts" for their amusement. In parting, the raiders warned all four victims to refrain from voting Republican in the future. Champion informed authorities of the attack and soon received a letter reading: "We have been told that our visit to you was not a sufficient hint. We now notify you to leave the country within thirty days from the reception of this notice, or abide the consequences. KKK." Champion and the Bowdens moved to Spartanburg, abandoning their lands and thus escaping further injury from the Klan.

Clay, Mamie—Mamie Clay was a problem for white supremacists in Dade County, Georgia. A resourceful black landowner who rejected lowball offers on her property, Clay soon became a target of harassment by police and klansmen alike. First, sheriff's deputies raided her home and accused her of running a brothel. When that charge failed to stick, a series of cross-burnings caused Clay to fear for her life. She invited friends to share her home, but Georgia blacks found no safety in numbers. On the night of 2 April 1949, another cross blazed on a nearby hilltop. Moments later, Sheriff John Lynch and three of his deputies arrived at Clay's house with a mob of masked klansmen. Lynch arrested seven of the blacks on false drunk-and-disorderly charges, then delivered them to the Klan. Driven to a nearby schoolyard, the seven were whipped, then ordered to "Get on over that hill and get out of here."

Clay complained to Washington, and Attorney General Tom Clark ordered an FBI investigation of the case. A federal grand jury convened at Rome, Georgia, on 3 August 1949, prompting Grand Dragon Samuel Green to banish the Trenton klavern from his AGK five days later. Twelve defendants were indicted on civil rights charges, including Sheriff Lynch, three deputies and eight civilian knights. When their trial opened on 22 November, five past or present klansmen were excluded from the jury pool, but one acknowledged knight was seated as an alternate juror. FBI agents testified that Sheriff Lynch admitted working with the KKK "to get this thing cleaned up," and that the morning after the assaults he said, "I don't think we'll be bothered about anything that happened last night." Lynch claimed his presence at Clay's home on the night of the whippings was "a coincidence," and that he tried to save her guests but had been "too slow on the draw." Deputy William Hartline confessed to helping build and deliver the cross that was burned near Clay's home, but he denied any knowledge of the floggings. Klan witnesses for the defense included Grand Dragon Sam Roper (who denied the existence of a Dade County klavern), Walter Arp (acknowledging the presence of a provisional unit), and Katherine Rogers (Sam Green's former secretary, detailing robe sales in the county).

Judge Frank Hooper directed acquittal of two defendants, L.C. Spears and Trenton city recorder John Wilkins, on 1 December 1949, then declared a mistrial on 17 December, when jurors deadlocked on the other ten defendants. Victory celebrations were premature, however, as the DOJ scheduled a new trial for March 1950. A second jury convicted Lynch and Hartline on 9 March, while acquitting their eight codefendants. Both lawmen received the maximum sentence of twelve months in prison and a $1,000 fine, with the verdicts upheld on appeal.

Colby, Abram—White residents of Reconstruction-era Warren County, Georgia, offered black legislator Abram Colby a $5,000 bribe to resign his post in 1868. When he refused, a Klan flogging party snatched him from home in October, delivering an estimated 1,000 lashes that left Colby permanently crippled. Colby identified several of his assailants, including several prominent men and others "not worth the bread they eat," but local authorities refused to prosecute the suspects. Colby later purchased a small plantation and retired to private life, but ongoing harassment forced him to spend most of his time in Atlanta.

Cruell, Claude—A black resident of Greenville, South Carolina, Cruell owned a 100-acre farm and rented a house on his land to white tenants. On 21 July 1957, the male tenant left his seven children with Cruell and Cruell's wife, while visiting his own wife in the hospital. Klansmen raided Cruell's home that night and beat him severely for "associating with white people." Jurors subsequently convicted four klansmen of participating in the raid. Greenville Exalted Cyclops Marshall Rochester received a six-year prison term, Wade Howard drew a three year sentence, while Jack Bentley and Robert Waldrop received one year each.

Dunlap, J.C.—The "carpetbag" teacher at a black school in Reconstruction-era Shelbyville, Tennessee, Dunlap received 200 lashes from Klan floggers on 4 July 1868. The klansmen threatened to return and burn him at the stake if he did not leave town, but he refused. In early January 1869, a gang of twenty-five to thirty mounted klansmen rode into Shelbyville, calling for "Dunlap and fried nigger meat," but they retreated when Dunlap and friends opened fire, killing one of the raiders. Local Unionists threatened dire reprisals against Democrats if Dunlap was further troubled, and the KKK thereafter left him in peace.

Flowers, Evergreen—A black resident of Chadbourn, North Carolina, Flowers was beaten by klansmen who invaded her home on 18 January 1950. Investigators traced the crime to Grand Dragon Thomas Hamilton's Association of Carolina Klans, and a grand jury convened to investigate the case. In May 1952, the panel indicted eleven klansmen, including Hamilton, Troy Bennett, Roy Carter, T.L. Enzor, Russell Hammacher, Jenrick Hammonds, Ernest Hardee, Joe Hardee, J.D. Nealey, Jule Richardson and Sid Scott. All pled guilty or no contest at trial, in July 1952, and received varying prison terms.

Ford, Benton—Benton was parked with girlfriend Sarah Rawls on a lover's lane outside Atlanta, Georgia, when klansmen surprised the couple one night in March 1939. The moralistic knights whipped them both so severely that neither survived. Subsequent investigation by Assistant Attorney General Dan Duke identified the floggers as members of the local Klavalier Klub, including three Fulton County deputy sheriffs. Several klansmen were convicted and sentenced to prison, but Governor Eugene Talmadge released them all soon after his 1941 inauguration.

French, Peggy Jo—A white resident of Waco, Texas, French suffered a Klan whipping in November 1982, for the "offense" of having black friends. Jurors subsequently convicted four knights in that case, which ranks as the last documented Klan flogging on record.

Gaston, Isaac—A black barber in Atlanta, Georgia, Gaston was kidnapped and whipped by local klansmen in March 1939. They left him naked and unconscious in the woods, resulting in Gaston's death from hypothermia. Investigation of this case and several others at the time sent a handful of klansmen to prison, but Georgia Governor Eugene Talmadge subsequently pardoned and released the defendants.

Gore, J.C.—A disabled white veteran of World War II, Gore was visiting his crippled uncle Sam in Conway, South Carolina, when klansmen struck on the night of 17 January 1950. The knights abducted both men, whipping them on accusations of neglecting their respective families. Four days after the beatings, police arrested nine members of Grand Dragon Thomas Hamilton's Association of Carolina Klans. All were subsequently convicted and sentenced to prison.

Griffin, Spencer—A black resident of Reconstruction-era Spencer County, Tennessee, Griffin received 150 lashes from klansmen seeking to teach blacks "that they had to do what they were told."

Harvey, Joseph—A black resident of Alamance County, North Carolina, Harvey angered local klansmen by supporting the Republican party and failing to grovel in front of white racists. Nightriders raided his home in March 1869, inflicting 150 lashes on Harvey and fatally beating his infant child.

Huggins, Allen P.—The "carpetbag" superintendent of schools for Reconstruction-era Monroe County, Mississippi, Huggins suffered a Klan flogging on 9 March 1871. He survived the attack and refused Ku Klux orders to leave the county, instead filing charges against two assailants. Their confessions landed twenty-six other klansmen in jail, while a U.S. Army officer presented Huggins's torn and bloodied shirt to Massachusetts Representative Ben Butler. Butler subsequently displayed it in Congress while calling for passage of the Ku Klux Act, thus giving rise to the phrase "waving the bloody shirt."

Hutchins, Guy—During winter 1956, klansmen in Camden, South Carolina, falsely accused high-school band director Guy Hutchins of delivering an integrationist speech to a local civic club. In fact, he had denounced Klan violence but had not spoken out against school segregation. On 28 December, while returning from a band concert in Charlotte, North Carolina, Hutchins stopped to change a flat tire on his car. Klansmen surrounded him, pulled a bag over his head, and drove him to a nearby wooded area where they tied him to a tree and beat him with a board, inflicting wounds that required hospitalization. Police jailed six knights for the crime on 3 January 1957.

Johnson, Woodrow—Klansmen lured Whiteville, North Carolina, mechanic Woodrow Johnson from his home with a phony distress call on 8 December 1951, then abducted him and whipped him on an accusation of "drinking too much." A grand jury subsequently indicted thirteen members of the Association of Carolina Klans, including Harvey Barfield, Early Brooks, Rex Connor, Steve Edmond, Henry Edwards (the victim's stepfather), John Honeycutt, Jr., Leroy Honeycutt, Ray Kelly, Frank Lewis, Lawrence Nivens, Brock Norris, Ernest Ward and George White. At trial, in May 1952, eight defendants (Brooks, Connor, Edmond, both Honeycutts, Kelly, Lewis and White) pled no contest and received two-year jail terms. Jurors Barfield, Edwards and Ward (who received identical sentences), while acquitting Nivens and Norris.

Kent, Rev. Grady—Georgia klansmen whipped Rev. Kent in 1940, after complaints that his Ben Hill congregation was "making too much noise" on Sunday.

Shoemaker, Joseph—A socialist repulsed by corrupt machine politics in Depression-era Tampa, Florida, Shoemaker founded the Modern Democrats as an alternative party in 1934. Local police infiltrated the group and conspired with members of the Ku Klux Klan to punish Shoemaker and company for their "subversive" activities. On 30 November 1935, Tampa police raided a meeting of the Modern Democrats, arresting six persons (including one paid infiltrator) and transporting them to headquarters. Two of the other five were soon released, but officers delivered Shoemaker, Eugene Poulnot and Dr. Samuel Rogers to a Klan flogging party in Brandon Woods, fourteen miles outside town. There, the three men were stripped, bound to logs, pistol-whipped, and flogged with a variety of instruments including leather straps and chains. All three were then tarred and feathered from necks to knees, while klansmen plunged one of Shoemaker's legs into the boiling tar bucket for good measure. (Historian Wyn Wade claims the floggers also seared Shoemaker's genitals with a hot iron, but other sources dispute that aspect of the torture.) Despite amputation of his charred leg below the knee, Shoemaker was beyond help. He died on 9 December, after nine days of excruciating pain.

The public outcry was immediate, sustained, and international. ACLU leaders offered $1,000 for capture of the floggers, while AFL president William Green canceled his union's 1936 convention in Tampa. The *Miami Herald* termed the Klan mob "as venomous as a mad dog, and its leaders should be dealt with just as dispassionately as we would a rabid animal." While Chief of Police R.G. Tittsworth and his Klan-infested department sought to obstruct the county sheriff's investigation, a grand jury convened to examine the case on 16 December 1935. That panel indicted five Tampa policemen on charges of murder, kidnapping, conspiracy, and assault with intent to kill (for victims Poulnot and Rogers); Chief Tittsworth and a police stenographer were also charged as accessories after the fact, while Sheriff J.R. McLeod added three klansmen (including Kleagle Arlie Gilliam) to the defendants' list. Tittsworth and four policemen faced trial for assaulting Poulnot in April 1936; jurors convicted all five, resulting in four-year prison terms (overturned on appeal by the state supreme court on 1 July 1937). Judge Robert Dewell subsequently directed verdicts of acquittal for all accused in Shoemaker's slaying, and prosecutors declined to conduct a trial in the case of Dr. Rogers. Questioned about the verdicts while visiting New York City, Governor Fred Cone told reporters, "I'm ashamed of Florida myself."

Toney, Pierce—An Atlanta union organizer active in the CIO, Toney became a target for Klan harassment in 1937, when he tried to unionize workers at the Scottdale Mill, owned by the powerful Georgia Savings Bank & Trust Company. When threats failed to frighten him off, klansmen kidnapped and whipped Toney, one of them afterward telling him: "Now I guess you'll let that damned union alone. We're going to break up all these damned unions."

Arson and Bombing

Klansmen have always liked to play with fire. A half-century before they adopted burning crosses as the symbol of their order, they burned homes, schools, and business establishments owned by political rivals. From 1915 onward, as the Klan's list of causes and enemies grew, they also torched churches, roadhouses and brothels. Dynamite held a similar fascination for Ku Klux terrorists from the 1920s onward, although the Klan's most famous bombing campaigns occurred between World War II and the end of the civil rights era. Today, arson and bombing remain the tactics of choice for many klansmen and their neo–Nazi allies. Their modern list of targets includes all the old stand-bys, plus such recent additions as women's clinics and U.S. government offices from coast to coast. The examples treated below are listed in chronological order.

1868—Lewisburg, Arkansas: The KKK's single most destructive arson attack was also one of its first. A Ku Klux raiding party invaded Lewisburg, Arkansas, one night in late November 1868, gunning down a former slave and setting fire to a white Republican's store. The blaze soon flared out of control, destroying one-third of the town. The sheriff teamed with local militiamen to arrest three klansmen, one of whom confessed to a series of local terrorist attacks before he was killed "while attempting to escape." Democratic Party spokesmen called the shooting murder, while a Lewisburg justice of the peace advised Governor Powell Clayton, "Lawlessness, with all its horrors, reign[s] supreme here…. I do not try to maintain the authority and majesty of the law, for I am very well convinced that at least half of the people here are of the Ku-Klux order." Powell imposed martial law on 8 December 1868 and dispatched 200 soldiers, but klansmen still murdered another Republican merchant the following week, burning his store as well.

1922—St. Boniface College: In 1921–22, Catholic institutions throughout Canada received a series of anonymous threats purporting to come from the Ku Klux Klan. On 25 November 1922, a fire of "suspicious" origin swept through St. Boniface College in Winnipeg, Manitoba, killing ten persons and leaving eighteen others injured. Several Catholic churches were also damaged by fire around the same time, prompting government spokesmen to publicly blame the Klan on 5 December 1922. Imperial headquarters denied any link to the arson attacks, and no culprits were ever charged in those crimes. When another church was bombed in June 1926, however, police jailed a Canadian klansman and jurors convicted him on 15 October 1926. The other crimes remain officially unsolved.

1947–65—Birmingham, Alabama: Birmingham once advertised itself as America's "most segregated city." Every aspect of life from cradle to grave was governed by strict Jim Crow laws, rigidly enforced by police and klansmen under the watchful eye of Public Safety Commissioner Eugene "Bull" Connor. While violence was a constant fact of life in Birmingham, its plague of racist bombings began in summer 1947, after a federal judge invalidated the city's 1926 ordinance establishing separate residential neighborhoods for blacks and whites. That ruling was issued on 31 July, and klansmen bombed the lawsuit plaintiff's home on 18 August. By spring 1948, racist bombings were so common that locals nicknamed the College Hills ghetto "Dynamite Hill," while Birmingham was dubbed "Bombingham." In April of that year, Bull Connor warned various black ministers in Birmingham that they risked "damage to church property" by hosting meetings of the Southern Conference for Human Welfare. In particular, Connor told leaders of the prestigious Sixteenth Street Baptist Church that God—acting through the KKK—might "strike the church down" if they welcomed SCHW members into their congregation.

After twenty-odd bombing and arson attacks during 1947–51, terrorists went on hiatus in Birmingham until 1956, when the combined threats of school integration and a black boycott of segregated city buses caused new agitation within the Klan's ranks. (Some sources claim that armed blacks killed one Ku Klux arsonist and wounded another in 1951, in a shootout suppressed by Bull Connor's police and never reported by the media.) In the seventeen months between December 1956 and April 1958, at least seven racist bombings rocked the city, several of them in the newly integrated neighborhood of Fountain Heights. In addition to the charges that exploded, police also found a defective bomb outside the Temple Beth El, on 28 April 1958. Local klansman Robert Chambliss planned and carried out nearly all of Birmingham's bombings from 1947 onward, but Bull Connor hatched a plan in May 1958 to "sting" Georgia terrorist Jesse Stoner and thus salvage Birmingham's soiled reputation. Using klansman (and FBI informant) William Morris as a go-between, two undercover policemen hired Stoner to bomb the Bethel Baptist Church, where Rev. Fred Shuttlesworth preached a "radical" message or racial equality. Stoner accepted the contract, but Connor's cops somehow failed to catch the bombers when they struck on 29 June 1958. Thus incriminated, Birmingham police resumed their time-honored habit of burying the evidence. On 17 July 1958, after yet another bombing, blacks captured and pummeled two slow-footed klansmen, thereby forcing police to file charges against the city's only identified terrorists to date.

That fiasco and the bungled Stoner sting produced another temporary cease-fire in "Bombingham." The terror resumed with a vengeance on 16 January 1962, when bombers struck three churches in a single night. The pace accelerated during 1963, as Dr. Martin Luther King's SCLC launched a historic civil rights campaign in Birmingham, capturing international headlines with images of rampant police brutality and vigilante mayhem. On 12 May 1963, following a large UKA rally in nearby Bessemer, bombs exploded at the home of King's brother and at the Gaston Motel, a black-owned establishment where Dr. King had rented rooms. Black witness Roosevelt Tatum told FBI agents that a uniformed patrolman driving squad car number 22 had planted the bomb on Rev. A.D. King's porch. On 28 June, U.S. Attorney Macon Weaver convened a federal grand jury to indict Tatum for "lying" to FBI agents, but the DOJ refused to press charges. The mood in Washington changed two months later, and Tatum was indicted on 26 August, the first federal defendant charged in Birmingham's sixteen years of terror. Jurors convicted him on 18 November 1963, and he received a sentence of 366 days in prison.

Meanwhile, klansmen executed their most infamous bombing of all time on 15 September 1963, when a blast at the Sixteenth Street Baptist Church killed four black girls aged eleven to fourteen and left fourteen other persons injured. Governor George Wallace attributed the blast to "communists or other Negroes who had a lot to gain by the ensuing publicity." In fact, the bombing was carried out by members of the Cahaba River Group, a dissident Klan faction organized by Robert Chambliss and others in August 1963. Informant Gary Rowe allegedly learned of the blast moments after it happened, from a girlfriend on the Birmingham Police Department, and then favored his FBI handlers with their first report of the crime. Still, Rowe unaccountably waited seven months to tell agents that two Klan terrorists, John Hall and Ross Keith, had missed an appointment with Rowe the same morning. Chambliss later claimed that Rowe confessed to the crime, complaining that "we" had used an insufficient charge, when he should have "put out enough to level the damn thing." Birmingham detective Red Self testified that Rowe said, "I'll tell you one thing: they will never solve the Sixteenth Street bombing because me and another guy handled it." On yet another occasion, Rowe floated the ludicrous story that black singer Harry Belafonte had financed the bombing. Various sources report that Rowe failed two polygraph tests, in which he denied bombing the church.

Birmingham police initially jailed the church's black janitor as a "suspect," then released him. On 26 September, klansman Charles Cagle led FBI agents to a field where stolen dynamite had once been hidden, but the stash was gone. Meanwhile, Governor Wallace and Col. Al Lingo of the state police schemed to "solve" the case without FBI help. On 29 September, Lingo met twice with a group of klansmen including Imperial Wizard

Mourners gather for the funeral of Carol Robertson, killed in a Birmingham church bombing on 15 September 1963 (Library of Congress).

Shelton, Hubert Page, John Hall, Robert Thomas, Bobby Cherry and UACG president Bill Morgan; the second gathering also included Arthur Hanes and attorney Wade Wallace (a UACG member and cousin of the governor). That night, state troopers accompanied by two Klansmen arrested Bob Chambliss at home. John Hall and Charles Cagle soon joined him in jail, charged with misdemeanor counts of illegally possessing dynamite. Gary Rowe, warned in advance by Red Self, neglected to inform his bureau handlers of the impending arrests. While George Wallace gloated over "beating the Kennedy crowd to the punch," DOJ officials scrambled to make sense of the arrests. Lingo's predecessor, Floyd Mann, told Washington that the charges were filed to scuttle the FBI's investigation and take the leading suspects "out of circulation." Bob Chambliss, seemingly unconcerned, fell asleep during his polygraph test and left jail with his cohorts on 1 October, after posting $300 bond.

After another stunned hiatus, Birmingham klansmen resumed their bombing campaign once more in early 1965. On 21–22 March of that year, police defused six bombs at various points around the city. Ten days later, on 1 April, bombers struck a black home, while two more time-bombs were defused at the homes of Birmingham's mayor and a city council member. The long reign of terror finally ended in February 1966, when authorities discovered a rural "bomb factory" in the woods outside town. One of the timing devices found there was identical to those used on the bombs defused in 1965. Still, no one was arrested for those crimes, or any of Birmingham's other bombings.

The Sixteenth Street bombing remained officially unsolved until 1977, when Alabama Attorney General William Baxley reopened the state's investigation. Elected in 1970 with support from Governor Wallace, Baxley sought to prosecute the church bombers in 1971,

Klan bombers demolished Birmingham's A.G. Gaston Motel in 1963 (Library of Congress).

but FBI Director J. Edgar Hoover refused to cooperate. After Hoover's death in May 1972, Baxley tackled the case, but obstacles remained. Suspects John Hall, Troy Ingram and Ross Keith died before Baxley could quiz them, while Gary Rowe and Herman Cash reportedly passed state polygraph tests. New requests for FBI assistance were blocked by "stonewalling," until Baxley threatened a Washington press conference with parents of the four murdered girls. At last, the Bureau budged, providing Baxley with sufficient evidence to indict Bob Chambliss in September 1977. Two months later, on 17 November, an integrated jury convicted Chambliss of murdering victim Denise McNair and he received a life sentence. On the same day Chambliss was convicted, Baxley served subpoenas on suspects Tom Blanton, Jr., and Bobby Cherry, but both knights stood silent behind their lawyers and no further charges were filed. Chambliss died in prison on 19 October 1985.

There matters rested for another decade, until a county grand jury convened to review the case in November 1998, culminating in the May 2000 murder indictments of Blanton and Cherry. Blanton was convicted of murder on 1 May 2001, receiving one life prison term for each of his four victims. A judge initially excused Bobby Cherry from trial on grounds of dementia, then reversed his ruling and found Cherry competent in January 2002. Four months later, jurors convicted Cherry of murder and he drew four terms of life imprisonment.

1951—Moore, Harry Tyson

From the 1930s until his death, Harry Moore campaigned for black civil rights in Florida. As a member of the NAACP and leader of the Progressive Voters League, Moore sacrificed his teaching career—and finally his life—to register black voters, while campaigning tirelessly against police brutality and lynching. On 25 December 1951, a powerful bomb exploded beneath Moore's home in Mims, Florida. Moore died instantly, while his wife lingered for nine days in the hospital. Governor Fuller Warren assigned "former" klansman Jefferson Elliott to investigate the crime, while U.S. Attorney General Howard McGrath told reporters that "every facility of the FBI ... is being used to the fullest extent" in pursuit of the bombers. Agents collected soil and other evidence from Moore's home for scientific analysis, interviewed his dying wife three times, and monitored his funeral for signs of radical fervor. Finally, in June 1952, the NAACP issued a statement condemning the "failure of the county, state, and Federal officials who, after more than six months, have proceeded no further than an investigation of the crime." J. Edgar Hoover's agents were making *some* progress, however. They learned that Orange County law enforcement was riddled with klansmen, while one informant estimated that three-fourths of Apopka's white male population was linked to the Klan "in one way or another." Joseph Cox, kligrapp of the Orlando klavern, committed suicide after his second FBI interview, in March 1952. G-men tapped the telephones of two early suspects, "renegade" klansmen Tillman Belvin and Earl Brooklyn, but neither was charged and both died within a year of Moore's murder. On 28 April 1952, Hoover told his superiors at Justice, "Our hope is that some Klan members will begin to talk if subpoenaed before a Federal Grand Jury." In fact, while federal grand juries indicted eleven klans-

Florida civil rights activist Harry Moore was a longtime Ku Klux target (Florida State Archives).

Klansmen killed Moore and his wife by bombing their home at Christmas 1951 (Florida State Archives).

men for perjury during 1952–53, all those charges were dropped prior to trial. Author Stetson Kennedy sparked new interest in the case a quarter-century later, quoting a self-described participant in the Moore bombing to "prove" that Lake County Sheriff Willis McCall planned and financed Moore's slaying, but crucial claims failed to jibe with known facts and the case remains officially unsolved today.

1956–57—Montgomery, Alabama:

Between January 1956 and January 1957, klansmen in Alabama's capital responded to a black boycott of segregated city buses with a reign of terror including cross-burnings, beating, sniper attacks, one murder and no less than eleven bombings. Starting with the home of Dr. Martin Luther King, Jr., on 30 January 1956, nightriders bombed a total of six houses, four churches and one taxi stand. On the hectic night of 9 January 1957, bombs struck four churches and two homes. A twelfth bomb, tossed at Dr. King's home on 27 January 1957, failed to explode. The following day, police jailed five klansmen for the attacks, including Henry Alexander, Raymond Britt, William "Sonny" Livingston and James York. Livingston and York faced capital charges for bombing an occupied home (owned by Rev. Ralph Abernathy) on 10 January 1957, but they faced no true risk of execution. De-

spite signed confessions from both defendants, white jurors acquitted them of all charges, accepting a defense lawyer's plea that their crimes were "provoked" by the boycott. Prosecutors subsequently dropped all charges against Alexander and Britt, in a general amnesty which also liberated various blacks charged with supporting an illegal boycott. Thus, Alabama's "justice" system equated nonviolent civil disobedience with bombing and attempted murder.

1963–68—Mississippi:

The KKK returned to Mississippi with a vengeance in 1963, inaugurating a reign of terror unprecedented in America since the days of Reconstruction. By 1964, the ultra-militant WKKKKM led by Samuel Bowers faced competition from Robert Shelton's UKA and several spin-off factions, including the Cottonmouth Moccasin Gang and the Silver Dollar Group (which conducted secret bombing seminars

Bombings like this one were a favorite Klan tactic from the 1940s through the early 1970s (Library of Congress).

Top: Pipe bombs and grenades seized from the home of a Mississippi klansman in October 1964. *Above:* Aylene Quinn's home was one of many targets bombed by klansmen around McComb, Mississippi, in 1964 (both photographs: HUAC).

for its members). Arson and bombing were favorite activities of Mississippi klansmen in those years, as they compiled a staggering toll of targets damaged or destroyed. While no definitive tally is available, Klan targets damaged by fire or explosives certainly included 63 homes, 44 churches and 2 synagogues, 10 civil rights headquarters, 9 stores, 5 vehicles, 3 restaurants, 3 newspaper offices, 2 Head Start offices, 2 recreation centers, a doctor's office, a barbershop, a fraternal hall, a community center, a nightclub, a pool hall, a school, a gas station, a motel, a barn, a tool shed, and a baseball park. Remarkably, despite the frenzied pace of violence in Mississippi, the raids claimed only two innocent lives. Six other attacks were foiled by careless preparation, while the last—in Meridian, on 28 June 1968—ended with a police ambush, killing terrorist Kathy Ainsworth and leaving klansman Thomas Tarrants III gravely wounded. That shootout effectively ended the Klan's grip of terror on the Magnolia State for a decade, until a new generation of klansmen returned to foment fresh disorders.

1970–71—Houston, Texas: Launched in August 1948, the California-based Pacifica Radio Foundation prides itself on airing unpopular viewpoints. Pacifica radio station KPFT began operating in Houston, Texas, during February 1970, and its left-of-center politics prompted a violent reaction from the local Ku Klux Klan. Nightriders bombed KPFT's transmitter in May, but the station's operators constructed a new facility fortified with sandbags. Undeterred, klansmen struck again, blasting KPFT off the air on 6 October 1970. On 21 January 1971, Texas police arrested Houston resident Jimmy Dale Hutto with a carload of weapons and Klan literature, en route to California, where he allegedly planned to bomb more Pacifica stations. Authorities charged Hutto and fellow klansman Paul Moratto with conspiracy in that case, but the arrests failed to halt Houston's bombing spree. Terrorists blasted the local SWP office on 12 March 1971, followed by the "hippie"-owned Family Hand restaurant, a motorcycle shop, and a "liberal" architect's office. On 12 June 1971, a grand jury indicted four knights—Hutto, Moratto, Louis Beam and Peter Lout, Jr.—in connection with the recent bombings. For reasons still unclear, none of the four was ever brought to trial.

1971—Pontiac, Michigan: In 1971, a federal court ordered busing of white and black students to achieve school integration in Pontiac, Michigan. Shortly before the start of school, on 30 August, explosive charges destroyed ten school buses scheduled for use in that plan. Ten days later, FBI agents arrested UKA Grand Dragon Robert Miles and five other klansmen on federal conspiracy charges, alleging that they hatched the bomb plot at a July 1971 Klan meeting at Lake Odessa. Prosecutors claimed that the arrests, based on testimony from an FBI informant, prevented the bombing a local power station, planned as a diversion for a mortar attack on Pontiac's remaining school buses. A federal grand jury indicted Miles and four others in October 1971. Jurors convicted Miles and Dennis Ramsey in May 1973, whereupon Miles received a nine-year prison term. Klansman Elmer Tackett, dying of leukemia, confessed to the Pontiac bombing on 1 March 1974, proclaiming the other defendants innocent, but prosecutors dismissed his statement. Au-

thorities dismissed outstanding charges against the untried defendants on 22 October 1974, after a key prosecution witness suffered brain damage from a beating in prison. Miles received a nine-year prison term, serving six years before he was paroled to rejoin the racist movement.

1990–96—Southern Church Arsons: Between 1990 and 1996, fifty-seven black churches were burned by arsonists in southern states, with thirty-two of those fires recorded in 1995–96. None were listed by the FBI as acts of domestic terrorism; indeed, G-men ran true to form in the handful of cases they investigated, demanding church records and polygraph tests for church leaders, suggesting that the victims themselves were guilty of arson. Congress belatedly convened a one-day hearing on the problem, and while President Clinton demanded a federal investigation, his National Church Arson Task Force reported in June 1997 that it could find "no evidence of a national conspiracy" to burn black churches.

That finding may have been technically accurate, but there was nonetheless ample evidence of conspiracy in individual cases. An ADL report, published on 20 June 1996, identified fourteen Klan factions active in nine states where churches were burned; other militant racist groups organized in the same region included the Aryan Nations, Christian Defense League, National Alliance, and David Duke's National Association for the Advancement of White People. In South Carolina, two members of the Christian Knights faced state arson charges for burning black churches at Bloomville and Greeleyville, on consecutive nights in June 1995. Federal charges were filed against the two suspects, Gary Cox and Timothy Welch, in July 1996. Both pled guilty the following month and agreed to help ATF agents with their ongoing investigation of various church fires. On 16 August 1996, two days after Cox and Welch filed their guilty pleas, federal prosecutors indicted Christian Knights leader Arthur Haley and klansman Hubert Rowell on twenty felony counts, including conspiracy to instigate the South Carolina church fires. Other charges claimed that members of the Klan plotted to burn a black man's car and to destroy a Hispanic migrant labor camp. From Washington, Deval Patrick, assistant attorney general for civil rights, told CNN, "We believe that we have proof of a conspiracy here. We have admissions by two of the defendants ... about a conspiracy that seems to be in furtherance of this particular Klan group." Defendant Rowell not only burned one of the churches in question, prosecutors alleged, but then threatened to "burn the son of a bitch down" again if it was rebuilt. Haley and Rowell eventually pled guilty, earning prison terms of twenty-one and fifteen years, respectively; Cox and Welch received sentences of nineteen and eighteen years, each reduced by five years for their cooperation with the government. In July 1998 jurors in a civil lawsuit filed against the Christian Knights by the SPLC awarded Klan victims $37.8 million dollars in damages.

Yet another arson case was solved in July 1997, when FBI agents arrested five white teenagers for burning one black church and vandalizing a second near Little River, Alabama on 30 June. The attacks followed a public rally held by the White Knights of Alabama at Tenesaw, ten miles from the scene of the attacks, on 28 June 1997. Three defendants were convicted at trial, including Alan Odom (sentenced to 180 months in prison on three felony counts), Brandy Boone and Kenneth Cumbie (41 months each on charges of conspiracy). No actual klansmen were charged in that case, which marked the FBI's only arrests in the 1990s spate of church arsons in Dixie.

1995 — Oklahoma City, Oklahoma:

On 19 April 1995, a powerful truck bomb exploded outside Oklahoma City's Alfred P. Murrah Federal Building, demolishing the structure and killing at least 168 persons. Ninety minutes later, an Oklahoma highway patrolman made a routine traffic stop in Noble County, sixty miles north of Oklahoma City. The car he stopped had no license plates, and its driver carried a poorly-concealed pistol. In custody at Perry, Oklahoma, the driver identified himself as Timothy McVeigh, age twenty-six. His name meant nothing at the time, but FBI agents soon linked him to the rented truck that had contained the fatal homemade bomb. They learned that he had joined the KKK while still on active duty with the U.S. Army, during 1990–91, and that he wore "White Power" T-shirts at Fort Riley, Kansas. McVeigh later left the Klan, branding its literature "manipulative to young people," and gravitated toward "patriot" groups including the Michigan Militia and the Arizona Patriots. He was "very upset" when he failed Green Beret training on psychological grounds, in April 1991, and afterward became "fanatical and loved to collect guns, and ... always had a gun with him." Upon leaving the army, McVeigh became a fixture at gun shows nationwide, where he bought and sold weapons, hawking countless copies of *The Turner Diaries* on the side. McVeigh had telephoned National Alliance headquarters at least seven times, and shortly before the Oklahoma City bombing he conducted a long conversation with someone at author William Pierce's unlisted phone number in West Virginia. Michigan Militia leaders claimed they had expelled McVeigh from one group meeting, but Florida militiamen told police that a man matching McVeigh's description had toured the Sunshine State with Michigan activist Mark Koernke, on a recruiting mission.

Investigation of McVeigh led agents to a fellow veteran, Terry Nichols, who shared McVeigh's contacts and anti-government views. On 11 August 1995, a federal grand jury indicted McVeigh and Nichols for conspiracy and for the murder of eight federal agents killed in the April blast. Massive publicity prompted Judge Richard Matsch to grant a change of venue in February 1996, moving the trial to Denver, Colorado. Eight months later, Matsch granted a motion that McVeigh and Nichols should be tried separately. McVeigh's trial opened on 24 April 1997, two days after his twenty-ninth birthday. Prosecutors presented 137 witnesses and reviewed 7,000 pounds of physical evidence over eighteen days. Michael and Lori Fortier, called as key witnesses for the government, were habitual drug users who had lied repeatedly to FBI agents after the bombing. In media interviews, they denied any knowledge of the crime and proclaimed McVeigh innocent. Their story only changed after Michael was charged with transporting stolen weapons and with failure to report the bomb plot in advance. A plea bargain on those counts (and a grant of full immunity for Lori) turned the Fortiers into cooperative witnesses against McVeigh, who had served as best man at their wedding. Michael told his brother, recorded for posterity on an FBI wiretap, "I can tell a fable. I can tell stories all day long.... The less I say now, the bigger the price will be later."

McVeigh's battery of fourteen court-appointed lawyers presented a more modest case, calling twenty-five witnesses in four days. Jurors convicted McVeigh on 2 June 1997 and recommended a death sentence on 13 June. Terry Nichols faced trial in Denver on 3 November 1997, but prosecutors failed to place him at the crime scene, prompting a compromise verdict. Nichols was convicted of conspiracy and eight counts of involuntary manslaughter (reduced from murder), acquitted on charges of destruction by explosives and using a weapon of mass destruction. Jurors deadlocked on penalty deliberations, and Judge Matsch settled the matter by imposing a life prison term on 4 June 1998. (A subsequent trial for Nichols on state murder charges produced 161 additional terms of life without parole in August 2004.) On 10 May 2001, six days before McVeigh's scheduled execution, FBI headquarters announced that certain files on his case had been "inadvertently" withheld from defense attorneys. The dribble soon became a flood, with 4,500 documents retrieved from forty-six bureau field offices. Agent Danny Defenbaugh, lead investigator on the case, blamed the problem on "archaic" FBI computers, then admitted knowing of the "misplaced" files for several months before headquarters broke the news. The announcement was delayed, Defenbaugh said, because he "wanted to ascertain the magnitude of the problem." Attorney General John Ashcroft granted McVeigh a 30-day stay of execution, but the documents were soon deemed immaterial to his defense and McVeigh was executed by lethal injection on 11 June 2001.

Assuming that McVeigh and Terry Nichols were guilty as charged, a nagging question remains: Do any other conspirators in the Oklahoma City bombing remain at large and unpunished? McVeigh reportedly failed a polygraph test, administered by his own defense team, in which he claimed that he and Terry Nichols were alone in the conspiracy. All sides agree that a still-unknown man, the elusive "John Doe No. 2," accompanied McVeigh to rent the Ryder truck in Kansas, but no further efforts have been made to locate him.

1997 — Fort Worth, Texas:

On 22 April 1997, FBI agents arrested Klan members Shawn Adams, his wife Catherine, and Carl Jay Wakstrom for conspiring to bomb a local natural gas refinery as a diversion for an armored car robbery. A short time later, G-men jailed a fourth suspect, Edward Taylor, Jr. According to court documents and media reports, local KKK leader Robert Spence betrayed his comrades after he developed personal misgivings, which threatened the lives of 30,000 persons living near the refinery. Jurors convicted all four defendants, resulting in twenty-year maximum prison terms, while Spence vanished into the federal witness protection program. Carl Waskom won parole in 2004. The Adamses are eligible for parole in 2006, Taylor in 2007.

Mutilation

Branding, ear-cropping, castration and other forms of mutilation were traditional punishments employed by antebellum slave owners and members of vigilante slave patrols prior to 1865. Klansmen continued the tradition during Reconstruction and beyond, with an incident of branding reported as recently as 1982. As with other Klan crimes, no definitive tally of mutilations exists, but three cases of castration (all involving blacks) emerged from Wilkinson County, North Carolina, during Reconstruction. One victim died from his injuries, but the other two survived and described their ordeals to congressional investigators in 1871. A half-century later, in August 1983, the sexual mutilation of a Jewish victim prompted Oklahoma Governor John Walton to declare martial law in Tulsa. The same year saw Colorado Grand Dragon John Locke accused of forcing a "shotgun" wedding with threats of castration against a Denver youth. Florida klansmen castrated a Catholic priest in 1924 and a suspected "playboy" in 1935. The most notorious case on record emerged from Birmingham, Alabama, in September 1957, where black victim Edward Aaron was chosen at random, kidnapped and mutilated as part of a KKK initiation ritual.

Aaron, Edward—A black resident of Birmingham, Alabama, Edward "Judge" Aaron made his living as a handyman in the 1950s, remaining aloof from any form of civil rights activity. Nonetheless, six members of Asa Carter's Original KKK of the Confederacy snatched Aaron from a street corner on 2 September 1957, driving him to their local klavern. There, the kidnappers—Exalted Cyclops Joe Pritchett, Klabee Jesse Mabry, "Captain" William Miller, Bart Floyd, John Griffin and Grover McCullough—interrogated Aaron, beat him, and finally castrated him with a razor blade, afterward pouring turpentine over his wound. Dumped beside a rural highway, Aaron nearly died from loss of blood before a motorist stopped and drove him to a hospital. In custody, Griffin and Miller turned state's evidence against their fellow knights and escaped with terms of probation. Jurors convicted Floyd, Mabry, McCullough and Pritchett of mayhem, resulting in twenty-year prison terms. Appeals left the four klansmen at liberty until 1959, when they began serving their time. Alabama law at that time required each felon to serve ten years or one-third of his sentence, whichever is shorter, and in 1960 the state parole board ordered all four klansmen to serve one-third of their time (six years and eight months) before they were considered for parole. By that standard, none of the four would be freed before mid–1966. Nonetheless, with the inauguration of Klan-allied Governor George Wallace in January 1963, the castrators soon received special treatment. Two weeks after Wallace's first appointee joined the parole board, in 1963, the board reversed its previous ruling on Floyd, Mabry, McCullough and Pritchett. Mabry won parole in February 1964, more than two years ahead of schedule, while his three cohorts were freed in 1965.

Brigan, Bill—A black resident of Reconstruction-era Wilkinson County, Georgia, Brigan was kidnapped from home by klansmen who tied him to a log and beat his genitals with a buggy trace, resulting in the loss of one testicle.

Cargell, Robert—An unmarried attorney in St. Petersburg, Florida, who retired from the practice of law in 1934 to manage his mother's hotel, Cargell angered local klansmen by "running around with the wrong lady." On 20 March 1935, an acquaintance known to Cargell as a klansman called at the hotel, inviting Cargell to join him that night at a local park, where they were supposed to be met by a couple of girls. Cargell arrived on time but found himself alone. About to leave the park, he was distracted by a stranger asking for directions to the local dog track. Before Cargell could answer, he was struck from behind, a canvas sack forced over his head, then he was pummeled and shoved into a car with five men. They drove him to an isolated spot and dragged him from the car, four of them pinning Cargell down while the fifth drew a knife and severed his scrotum. While the klansmen fled, Cargell staggered to a nearby home and caught a ride to the hospital, where doctors saved his life despite massive blood loss. Police jailed the man who lured Cargell to the park, but Tampa klansmen posted his bond and grand jurors refused to indict him. In April 1935, Cargell filed charges against one of his assailants, glimpsed through a slit in his makeshift hood. The suspect, Arthur Peacock, was a former Tampa policeman and onetime deputy sheriff for Hillsborough County. Peacock surrendered on 11 April, was released to his attorney's custody, and died six days later from an apparent stroke. Cargell's request for an autopsy was denied and the case was closed. Another suspect charged but never tried in Cargell's case was klansman F.W. Switzer, subsequently indicted for the flogging murder of Joseph Shoemaker.

Conoley, Rev. John—A Catholic priest in Gainesville, Florida, Conoley first irritated local bigots in June 1917, when he summarized "The Present Condition of Catholics in Florida" for the *Catholic Mind:* "It stinks." He freely criticized nativist Governor Sidney Catts (1916–19), condemned Protestant ministers for parroting anti–Catholic propaganda, and fueled Klan fears of creeping papism by organizing a drama club at the University of Florida. The university's president, Dr. Albert Mur-

Father John Conoley named Gainesville Police Chief Lewis Fennell as one of the klansmen who castrated him in 1924 (Florida State Archives).

phree, ordered Conoley's club off campus in response to Klan complaints, but Gainesville's knights were still unsatisfied. One night in February 1924, three klansmen in full regalia kidnapped Conoley from the rectory at St. Patrick's Church, beat him severely, castrated him, and left him near death on the steps of a church in Palatka. Conoley and another witness identified two of his attackers as Gainesville Mayor George Waldo and Chief of Police Lewis Fennell (Waldo's father-in-law). Conoley's ordeal went unreported, and Chief Fennell's Klan-ridden department conducted no investigation. As soon as he could travel, Conoley fled Gainesville, spending a year in Washington hospitals and two years in a monastery, before he relocated to a diocese in Maine.

Fitzgerald, Charlie—A black resident of Myrtle Beach, South Carolina, Fitzgerald ran a dance hall on the outskirts of town. In 1950, he became a target of Ku Klux terrorism, though various sources disagree on the Klan's motives: some say Fitzgerald was targeted for "immorality"; others say the Klan wanted to drive blacks away from desirable beachfront property; still others claim that klansmen mistook Fitzgerald's light-skinned wife for a white woman. In any case, 150 members of Grand Dragon Thomas Hamilton's Association of Carolina Klans struck Fitzgerald's club on the night of 26 August 1950, beating Fitzgerald and tossing him into one of their cars before patrons of the club opened fire. An estimated 300 shots were exchanged, one bullet killing klansman (and police officer) James Johnston before the raiders left with Fitzgerald. They drove him into the woods, there whipping him and severing both ears before they dumped him on the shoulder of a rural highway. Police jailed Hamilton and eight other klansmen on 31 August, for conspiracy to foment mob violence, and while Constable T.M. Floyd lost his job for participating in the raid, a grand jury refused to indict the klansmen.

Hantaman, Nathan—As a Jew, Hantaman automatically rated animosity from 1920s klansmen, but Tulsa's white knights also suspected him of bootlegging and selling narcotics. On 9 August 1923, six unmasked knights snatched Hantaman from the street outside Tulsa's Wonderland Theater and drove him to a rural site where they whipped him severely, then "beat his genitals to a pulp." Four days later, Governor John Walton used the attack as his basis for declaring martial law in Tulsa—a move that ultimately backfired with his own impeachment and removal from office.

Lowther, Henry—A black Republican in Reconstruction-era Wilkinson County, Georgia, Lowther outraged local racists with his politics and by suing whites who owed him money. Rumors also spread that Lowther was romancing a local white woman. Klansmen visited his home in August 1871, and while they missed their target, they warned Lowther's wife to leave the area within five days. Freedmen armed and organized to defend Lowther, but Klan leader Eli Cummins fabricated assault charges against Lowther and fifteen of his most vocal supporters, accusing them all of assaulting another black man. Police soon freed all the prisoners except Lowther, holding him until Cummins arrived with a party of 180 klansmen. Given a choice between castration and death, Lowther chose the former. The klansmen carried him from jail to a nearby swamp, where they performed the operation and released him. Lowther survived and fled to Macon, where he filed charges against his assailants. The Klan sent five men to kill Lowther, but he escaped once again, this time to Atlanta, while charges against his attackers were dropped. In Lowther's absence, the KKK spread new rumors, accusing him of fornicating with his stepdaughter.

McGrone, Frank—A black Job Corps supervisor in Edinburgh, Indiana, McGrone became a target for racist violence in September 1982, when Klan arsonists torched his car and home in separate attacks. Later that month, klansmen lured McGrone from home to some nearby woods, where they overpowered and bound him, then branded "KKK" on his chest, with a single "K" on his forehead.

Starling, Jacob—A Republican and member of the Union League in Reconstruction-era Moore County, North Carolina, Starling was kidnapped in autumn 1869 by klansmen who branded various parts of his body with the letters "UL."

Van Loon, Rev. Oren—A resident of Berkeley, Michigan, Rev. Van Loon was snatched from his home by klansmen on 30 June 1924. Twelve days later, authorities found him outside Battle Creek, delirious and disoriented, with the letters "KKK" branded on his back.

Murder

Homicide came easily to Reconstruction-era klansmen, most of whom were recently discharged from Confederate military service in the Civil War, and the KKK's guerrilla war against blacks and Republicans produced many deaths. Passage of time, inadequate records and partisan law enforcement render accurate tabulation of the final body count impossible, but well-documented cases from 1867–71 include at least 109 murders in Alabama, 90-plus in Arkansas, 235 in Florida, 74 in Georgia, 86 in Kentucky and 40-plus in Tennessee. Klansmen in the Carolinas were credited with an average of one murder per month during Reconstruction, but they frequently outdid themselves: authorities recorded thirty-five slayings in South Carolina during the first six months of 1871 alone. No general tally exists for Mississippi, but Kemper County klansmen killed thirty-five victims between 1869 and 1871. Louisiana and Texas, meanwhile, were abandoned to virtual anarchy. In the Bayou State, 1,081 persons were slain during the 1868 presidential election, and no accurate records were kept thereafter. Of 1,035 murders reported in Texas between late 1865 and July 1868, 977 were committed by whites and nearly half involved black victims.

The modern Klan has been relatively nonviolent, when compared to its "first era" ancestor, but homicide remains a standard aspect of KKK activity. Between the order's 1915 revival and its national disbandment in 1944, at least 100 persons died in violent incidents related to the Klan. Nearly one-quarter of those were killed in Illinois, where klansmen fought pitched battles with bootleggers in "Bloody Williamson" County. To that grim total we must also add the body counts for riots and pogroms inspired or assisted by klansmen in Tulsa, Oklahoma; Ocoee and Rosewood, Florida; and elsewhere. The decade after World War II was fairly peaceful, with only four well-publicized Klan murders between 1946 and 1953, but other slayings undoubtedly escaped detection, while homicides committed by Klan-allied policemen (such as Atlanta's "Trigger" Nash, acknowledged killer of thirteen black victims) indicate that the official tally may be seriously understated.

The black civil rights movement sparked a new wave of mayhem in Dixie, with eighty-six racist murders recorded by the Southern Regional Council between 1954 and 1968. At least thirty of those slayings (and several not included on the list) were directly linked to various Klans or the NSRP, and lethal violence among Klan-allied racists continues to the present day. A few selected victims of the KKK are listed below, alphabetically. They represent only a tiny fraction of those murdered by klansmen over the past 140 years.

Ashburn, George W.—As a white Republican leader in Reconstruction-era Georgia, Ashburn was a natural target for the original KKK. Shortly after midnight on 31 March 1868, a party of thirty to forty masked klansmen invaded his home at Columbus and shot him to death. A few days later, militia officers arrested thirteen suspects, including three freedmen. Local whites raised their bail by popular subscription, and none ever faced trial. Ashburn's murder marked the first known incident of Ku Klux violence outside of Tennessee.

Barmore, Seymour—A former treasury agent, hired by Tennessee Governor William Brownlow to gather information on the original KKK, Barmore never had a chance to fulfill his mission. Klansmen snatched him from a train at Columbia, after midnight on 12 January 1869, and executed him in some nearby woods. Locals retrieved his corpse from the Duck River several weeks later. The crime remains officially unsolved.

Berg, Alan—A controversial Jewish talk-show host in Denver, Colorado, Berg frequently used his radio program to ridicule right-wing extremists, including members of the Colorado Ku Klux Klan. Klansmen and neo–Nazis threatened his life on various occasions in the early 1980s, but Berg took it in stride. Members of The Order finally decided to execute Berg in 1984, spraying him with machine-gun fire in his own driveway on 18 June. Defendants charged in that case included klansman David Lane, Jean Craig, Bruce Pierce and Richard Scutari. Jurors convicted Lane and Pierce of Berg's murder on 17 November 1987, while acquitting Craig and Scutari. Lane and Pierce each received a 150-year prison term.

Cauce, Cesar *see* **Nathan, Michael**

Chaney, James *see* **Schwerner, Michael**

Dahmer, Vernon—Vernon Dahmer, an NAACP member active in voter-registration work around Hattiesburg, was marked for death by the WKKKKM in December 1965. A month later, on 10 January 1966, klansmen attacked Dahmer's rural home and store, lobbing firebombs through the windows and trading shots with Dahmer while his family escaped through a rear exit. Dahmer suffered fatal burns in the assault, but his killers left numerous clues at the scene. Nervous knights shot up one of their own cars in the heat of battle, then abandoned it nearby, also dropping a gun, spent cartridges, and a Halloween mask as they fled. The day after Dahmer's murder, informants told FBI agents that Imperial Wizard Samuel Bowers was boasting of the crime. Members of his Jones County klavern had "scored a big one," Bowers said. The crime surpassed Neshoba County's triple murder of June 1964 because "these men won't talk."

In fact, one of them did. G-men traced the bullet-riddled car to klansman Travis Giles, who had reported it stolen. Further investigation led agents to Klan "senator" Lawrence Byrd, who cracked under interrogation and confessed his part in the raid, naming Bowers and others as conspirators. The pistol found at Dahmer's home belonged to klansman Billy Pitts, Byrd said. On 27 March 1966, the DOJ filed conspiracy charges against Bowers and thirteen other knights. All but Bowers were arrested the next day; he surrendered on 31 March with two lawyers, Charles Blackwell and Travis Buckley, who had represented klansmen at recent HUAC hearings. A federal grand jury indicted fifteen suspects on 22 June 1966, but their attorneys challenged racial composition of the all-white panel and the charges were dismissed. A second grand jury, including black members, indicted twelve of the fifteen Klansmen once more on 27 February 1967. Byrd was among those dropped from the list, as a potential prosecution witness.

Six days later, G-men learned of a plot to discredit Byrd and the FBI's case. Ex-convict Jack Watkins told agents that he had been kidnapped by defendant Billy Pitts and lawyer Buckley, driven to the woods where they had threatened him with death if he did not collaborate in defense of Buckley's clients. Specifically, they ordered Watkins to claim that FBI agents had hired him to beat Lawrence Byrd and extract his confession by force. State authorities indicted Pitts and Buckley for kidnapping and conspiracy. Pitts pled guilty and received a five-year prison term, while Buckley was convicted at trial and sentenced to ten years. Buckley's verdict was later overturned on appeal by the state supreme court.

In Dahmer's case, Sam Bowers twice faced murder charges, but two juries deadlocked on the evidence and thereby set him free. Four other knights (including Billy Pitts) were convicted of murder and sentenced to life imprisonment, while Byrd received a lenient ten-year term as a reward for his cooperation. In federal court, one defendant saw his case dismissed, while three more were acquitted and a fifth's case was postponed indefinitely on grounds of poor health. Bowers and seven others were released when jurors found themselves unable to agree on verdicts. Only Billy Pitts was finally convicted of conspiracy, receiving another five-year sentence. Thirty years later, in May 1998, state authorities filed new murder indictments against Bowers. An integrated jury convicted him on 21 August 1998, and he was sentenced to life in prison.

Daniels, Jonathan Myrick—Jon Daniels was enrolled at an Episcopal seminary in Cambridge, Massachusetts, on 7 March 1965, when Dr. Martin Luther King, Jr., issued his call for volunteers to register black voters in Alabama. One day later, he landed in Montgomery aboard the same plane that carried Rev. James Reeb to his death in Selma. Daniels was assigned to "Bloody" Lowndes County, scene of the Viola Liuzzo murder on 25 March. Five months later, on 14 August, Daniels was among demonstrators arrested for picketing segregated establishments in Fort Deposit. After six days in custody, they were released without bail on 20 August, by a jailer who refused them protection and ordered them all out of town. With other demonstrators, including several blacks and a white Catholic priest, Rev. Richard Morrisroe, Daniels walked to a nearby grocery store that welcomed blacks as customers. Inside, they were confronted by klansman and part-time deputy sheriff Tom Coleman, who brandished a shotgun, ordered them to leave, then opened fire at close range, killing Daniels instantly and gravely wounding Morrisroe.

After the shooting, Coleman walked to the nearby courthouse called Col. Al Lingo, head of the state police, and told him, "I just shot two preachers. You better get on down here." Lingo raced to the scene with a Ku Klux bail bondsman, driven by Coleman's son (a state trooper and Lingo's personal chauffeur). Prosecutor Carlton Perdue arraigned Coleman Sr. on 21 August, charging him with murder (Daniels) and assault with intent to kill (Morrisroe). Coleman's defense attorney, state senator Vaughan Robison, objected to his client's $12,500 bail as "excessive," but Perdue stood firm. According to Perdue's press statement, the victims had approached the grocery store "to do some picketing and singing, and the man just let them have it, so to speak." (In fact, there was no demonstration at the store.) Still, Purdue seemed to blame the victims, remarking: "If they had been tending to their own business, like I was tending to mine, they'd be living and enjoying themselves." Rumors quickly spread that Coleman had fired in self-defense, after Daniels and Morrisroe threatened him with weapons. State Attorney General Richmond Flowers rejected that claim, calling the case "another Ku Klux Klan murder."

Alabama had suffered so much bad publicity by August 1965 that an ad hoc committee of Concerned White Citizens organized to press for justice in the latest atrocity. The group urged Flowers to relieve Perdue as prosecutor, charging that Perdue's public condemnation of the victims proved that he "could not possibly execute justice impartially." Committee spokesmen told Flowers, "There is no doubt about the immaturity and incapability of a county solicitor who implies that emotional outrage is justification for killing." Flowers initially resisted, then changed his mind on 13 September, after a grand jury indicted Coleman on reduced charges of manslaughter and assault and battery. "If this is not murder," Flowers told the press, "it is no case at all." On 15 September, Flowers moved to impanel a new grand jury, declaring that "[i]f this case was presented properly ... the members of that grand jury are as guilty as the man who pulled the trigger." When Perdue refused to call a new hearing, Flowers took charge of the case.

Coleman's manslaughter trial opened on 27 September 1965, before Judge T. Werth Thagard. Flowers arrived with an armed escort, to request postponement of the case until his key witness—Rev. Morrisroe—was fit to leave the hospital. Coleman's defenders opposed delay on such "frivolous grounds," insisting on their client's right to speedy trial, while questioning the attorney general's "sincerity" and "honesty with this court." Judge Thagard agreed, dismissing the state's motions and scheduling trial to begin the next day. Flowers stayed home on 28 September, reportedly fearing for his life, while assistant Joseph Gantt renewed objections to trying the case without Morrisroe present. Judge Thagard censured Gantt for "trifling with the court" and returned control of the case to Perdue. From Montgomery, Flowers predicted that Coleman would "walk out of court a free man."

And so it was, as Thagard's court upheld the Cotton State's tradition of exonerating racial terrorists. The dark comedy began when Coleman's name appeared on the prospective juror's list, followed by Perdue's inquiry as to whether any other jurors had a "fixed opinion" on the case. "I do," one venireman replied. "Not guilty!" He was removed from the panel, but those who remained were scarcely better. Viola Liuzzo's killers appeared as spectators in court on 28 September, when an all-white jury was seated and testimony began. Deputy Joe Jackson testified under oath that Coleman had frequently aided the sheriff's department. On the day of the shooting, in fact, he was sent to retrieve riot gear from Montgomery "to maintain peace and order" in Hayneville. Jackson also claimed that he had seen Daniels kiss a "nigger" girl "right in the mouth" at his release from jail, the day he died. (All demonstrators present fervently denied the charge.) If that was not bad enough, evidence displayed in court revealed that Daniels wore shoes "such as no man of God in Lowndes County ever wears," and carried a "subversive" paperback book—*The Fanatic*, by Meyer Levin—in his pocket. Worst of all, the victim wore red underpants that "smelled of urine" after he was shot at point-blank range.

UKA Imperial Wizard Robert Shelton appeared in court on 29 September, accompanied by KBI chief Ralph Roton. The defense produced three witnesses, all longtime friends of Coleman, who swore that Daniels was armed with a knife, while Morrisroe carried a pistol on 20 August. Both weapons had vanished, presumably taken by blacks who were glimpsed by the same defense witnesses, stuffing unknown objects into their pockets before they fled the scene. Morrisroe's affidavit, denying that either he or Daniels carried weapons, was read to the court in his absence. Defense attorney Joseph Phelps, in his summation, told jurors that Coleman was "protecting all of us" when he shot the two "false prophets." Lowndes County was the true victim, Phelps said, plagued by "agitators and terrorists" who "hide their evil motives behind the cloth of the church." Prosecutor Arthur Gamble, Jr., told jurors that the defense "would have produced these weapons if they were actually there," then seemed to concede the case with repeated mention of "that knife" in Daniels's hand. "There is no evidence here at all," Gamble said, "that Jonathan Daniels was making any attempt to actually cut [Coleman] with that knife." Vaughan Robison closed the proceedings with a classic line: "You can believe that knife was there or not. I believe it was there whether it was or not."

The jurors recognized their duty. Leaving court to deliberate on 30 September, the last man out paused long enough to wink at Coleman. The panel returned with a verdict of acquittal, and Coleman resumed his job with the state highway department. In September 1966, Richmond Flowers asked a new grand jury (including seven whites and eleven blacks) to indict Coleman for assault with intent to kill Morrisroe. Morrisroe testified in person, but the panel took only five minutes to reject the plea. Flowers next asked Judge Thagard to drop the assault charge on 26 September, thus enabling some future grand jury to reconsider it, but Thagard filed a dismissal "with prejudice," thereby effectively prohibiting another trial. No federal charge was ever filed.

Dee, Henry Hezekiah—In May 1964, klansmen around Meadville, Mississippi, were inflamed by rumors of Black Muslims smuggling guns to local activists, in preparation for a "black uprising" against whites. On 2 May 1964, they kidnapped two black Meadville students, Henry Dee and Charles Moore, to question them concerning those unfounded allegations. Unsatisfied when Dee and Moore could not reveal some grand conspiracy, the knights beat their two victims unconscious, then drove them across the border to Louisiana and dropped their weighted bodies in the Mississippi River near Tallulah. Moore's mother reported her son missing on 4 May, whereupon the Franklin County sheriff informed her that both young men were staying with a relative of Dee's in Louisiana. That lie collapsed on 12 July 1964, when a fisherman found part of a decomposed corpse in the river. More remains were discovered that day and the next, in the midst of a search for three Klan victims murdered in Neshoba County. G-men arrested two White Knights from Meadville, Charles Edwards and James Seale, on 6 November 1964. Edwards signed a confession, implicating Seale and other suspects, but state murder charges were quickly dismissed. FBI agents did not pursue the case, although they had clear jurisdiction. If Dee and Moore were killed in Louisiana, their slayers should have been tried under the Lindbergh Law; if the victims died in Mississippi, it was *still* a federal case, since they were beaten on U.S. government land in the Homochitto National Forest. More than thirty-five years later, in January 2000, FBI spokesmen announced a reopening of the case, but no charges had been filed when this volume went to press in 2005.

Edwards, Willie—A black resident of Montgomery, Alabama, Edwards vanished from his job as a grocery delivery-man on 22 January 1957. Three months later, police pulled his body from the Alabama River, twenty miles downstream. Authorities initially listed the cause of death as accidental drowning, but a new version surfaced in February 1976, when state attorney general Bill Baxley charged three local klansmen with murdering Edwards. As reconstructed by ex-klansman Raymond Britt, members of Montgomery's klavern suspected Edwards of "annoying" white women. They snatched him from his delivery route at gunpoint, "interrogated" and beat him, then finally forced Edwards to jump from a bridge when he persistently denied their allegations. Britt named the killers as Henry Alexander, William "Sonny" Livingston and Raymond York—all previously indicted for bombing black homes and churches during Montgomery's historic bus boycott (1955–57). A local judge found the indictments defective, since they stated no cause of death, and dismissed the charges on 14 April 1976. Baxley

planned to seek new indictments, but the case collapsed on 1 June 1976, when Britt recanted his identification of Livingston.

Evers, Medgar Wylie—The main target of white rage in Mississippi during 1954–63 was Medgar Evers, state chairman of the NAACP. Terrorists firebombed the carport of his Jackson home on 27 May 1963, and two weeks later, on 12 June, a sniper killed Evers at home with one shot through the back. Jackson police found a rifle at the scene, and while FBI headquarters offered assistance with the evidence or any out-of-state leads, Assistant Director Alex Rosen claimed that DOJ attorney Burke Marshall "indicated he desired no further action taken by the FBI." Rosen further claimed that Director J. Edger Hoover defied that order with a memo to all bureau field offices, commanding agents "to immediately alert racial informants and other sources to our interest in this matter, and if these offices obtain any information which might have a bearing on the Evers killing, we want to be immediately advised."

When Jackson police removed the murder rifle's scope to process it for fingerprints on 12 June, Hoover penned a note reading: "Well at least they are not using our facilities." That changed, however, with a police request for FBI examination of the crime scene evidence. The Bureau's lab in Washington received the rifle, ammunition from its magazine, the telescopic sight, a partial fingerprint from the scope, and a bullet that had passed through Evers's body before striking his house. A photo of the rifle, published nationwide on 13 June, brought a call to Jackson police from Innes McIntyre in Itta Bena, Mississippi, who had recently sold the gun to a Greenwood "segregation fanatic" named Byron De La Beckwith, Jr. Detectives filed the name but kept it from the FBI, while G-men tried in vain to match the partial fingerprint to subjects in the bureau's files. A parallel line of investigation tracked the imported telescopic sight from its entry port (Chicago) to a gun shop in Grenada, Mississippi, where it had been sold to Byron De La Beckwith.

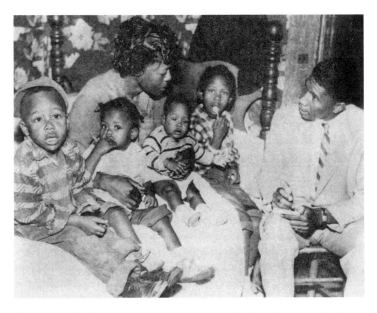

Eight years before his own assassination, Medgar Evers (right) comforts the family of racist murder victim Clinton Melton (Library of Congress).

In another triumph for the FBI, comparison of Beckwith's military records to the Jackson fingerprint then identified him as the sniper.

Or, did it?

Hoover biographer Curt Gentry notes that identity cannot be proved from a partial fingerprint. Instead, Gentry and others contend, the bureau found Beckwith via less orthodox methods. First, bribes and informants allegedly identified several Mississippians involved in a plot to kill Evers, but the triggerman remained anonymous. Then, according to retired G-man Anthony Villano, agents forged a devil's pact to solve the case. After singling out a Jackson Citizens' Council member involved in the murder conspiracy, FBI agents contacted New York mobster Gregory Scarpa, offering leniency on an outstanding federal case if he helped them crack the Evers murder. Scarpa agreed and flew to Miami with a girlfriend, to establish an alibi, then drove from Florida to Jackson and kidnapped the Council suspect. Followed by G-men, Scarpa allegedly took his captive to a remote cabin in Louisiana's bayou country, there torturing the suspect until he confessed his role in the plot and named Beckwith as the sniper. Agents crouched outside an open window, taking notes, then flashed Beckwith's name to Washington, where the fingerprint "match" was contrived. Villano paid Scarpa $1,500 for his services, preserving a receipt, and Scarpa escaped prosecution on the pending charge. When the story broke, years later, Scarpa refused to comment on the case.

Beckwith refused to speak with G-men when they first approached him, on 21 June 1963. The next day, federal prosecutors charged Beckwith with conspiracy under the 1957 Civil Rights Act dismissing that case after a local grand jury indicted him for murder on 2 July 1963. Beckwith enjoyed full support from the Citizens' Council, which established a White Citizens' Legal Fund to pay his expenses. His defense team included Hardy Lott and Hugh Cunningham, a partner in the Jackson legal firm whose members included Governor Ross Barnett. During the trial, in January 1964, Barnett himself visited the courtroom, shaking hands with Beckwith while the jury watched. FBI agents testified for the state, building the circumstantial case against Beckwith, but two policemen surprised prosecutors with claims that they had seen Beckwith in Greenwood, sixty-odd miles from Jackson, at the time of the shooting. (Neither could explain why the sightings went unreported until Beckwith's trial.) Judge Leon Hendricks declared a mistrial on 7 February 1964, with jurors deadlocked seven-to-five for acquittal. A second trial ended the same way on 17 April 1964, with the panel deadlocked eight to four in Beckwith's favor.

Soon after Evers was shot, Klan fliers circulated throughout Mississippi, bearing photos of Evers, James Meredith, John Salter, Bob Moses, lynching victim Emmett Till and other blacks, with the pictures of Evers and Till crossed out. Author Reed Massengill contends that Evers "was on a Ku Klux Klan hit list, even though the Klan was not formally organized in Mississippi," concluding that the murder "may have marked the Klan's unofficial launch in Mississippi." After Beckwith's second mistrial, fiery crosses blazed in several Jackson neighborhoods. Eight months later, on 6 December 1964, informant Delmar Dennis reported the comments of Neshoba County's exalted

cyclops, Edgar Killen, to his FBI contacts. According to Dennis, Killen "boasted that the Klan could infiltrate every jury selected in Mississippi. As an example, he cited the slaying of Medgar Evers. He said that this murder was a Klan project and that the Klan protected Beckwith by arranging to have Klansmen on the jury." In December 1990, a member of Beckwith's original jury confirmed rumors that another panel member "was in the pocket of the Klan." FBI files declassified around the same time claimed that "the murder was a Klan hit, with the Citizens' Council implicated as well."

Beckwith himself was certainly a Klansman, though dates and details of his enlistment remain obscure. On 26 June 1963, during a police interrogation, Beckwith told detectives "that we definitely needed a Ku Klux Klan at this time, that it could do a lot of good." (The officers noted that Beckwith was "also way overboard when Masonry is mentioned.") A letter penned from jail, in early 1964, declared: "When the KKK needs me enough, then I will be happy to serve them—they've asked me and I haven't said no." Most accounts agree that Beckwith was recruited by kleagle Gordon Lackey, of the Mississippi White Knights, but some versions place his initiation as late as August 1965. Beckwith and Lackey appeared before HUAC on 12 January 1966, both represented by attorney and WKKKKM member Travis Buckley. Curiously, Beckwith's subpoena demanded documents from both the White Knights and from Robert Shelton's rival United Klans of America. HUAC sources also linked Beckwith to acts of Klan violence committed in March and May 1965, well before his supposed August initiation.

By the time he went to Washington, Beckwith had been promoted to serve the White Knights as a kleagle. Delmar Dennis recalled that "Beckwith was a recruiting man. He was out getting members all over the state." At one rally, on 8 August 1965, Beckwith told his fellow knights, "Killing that nigger gave me no more inner discomfort than our wives endure when they give birth to our children. We ask them to do that for us. We should do just as much. So, let's get in there and kill those enemies, including the President, from the top down!" After his speech, Beckwith signed autographs for the faithful—including one obtained by Dennis and delivered to his FBI handlers with a report of Beckwith's self-incriminating comments. Agent Tom Van Riper remembered that report years later, and Beckwith's FBI file listed "several different sources" who described the speech. At another meeting, in Laurel, Beckwith told Klansmen that he had sworn "a Shriner's oath" to kill Charles Evers, as well.

It was doubly curious, then, that G-men kept silent on 19 June 1966, when D.A. William Waller informed the bureau that he could not try Beckwith for murder again unless he received substantial new evidence. A public confession should have done the trick, but Hoover and company suppressed the 1965 reports. On 13 July 1966, a memo from Jackson to FBI headquarters revealed more startling evidence from a "reliable" informant in the Mississippi Klan. That source described a conversation with Gordon Lackey, in which Lackey boasted of helping Beckwith murder Evers. According to the memo, Lackey claimed "that he and Beckwith made two or three trips to the [Evers] residence in order to determine his actions and activities and to make necessary plans. In each instance they used a white or light colored Valiant, which was also used on the night of the shooting." Lackey further "stated that he and Beckwith were hiding in some bushes near Evers's home and shot him when he returned to his residence late one night." Finally, the informant claimed, "Lackey stated, 'They got the wrong man. Beckwith did not do the shooting.'" The same memo noted that G-men had questioned Lackey as a suspect in June 1963, then dismissed him after two National Guardsmen claimed they were drinking with Lackey, in Hattiesburg, on the night of the murder.

J. Edgar Hoover was impressed with the 13 July report. Eight days later, he sent Jackson agent-in-charge Roy Moore a cable that read: "In view of the importance of this case and the importance of the information furnished by this informant, it is felt that every effort should be made to induce him to become a willing witness at this time." Moore offered cash, but no amount of money could persuade the still-unnamed informant to testify. He rejected each new bid with the remark that he "loved life" and would not risk it on a public move against the Klan or Beckwith. G-men kept the secret from state prosecutors, and the Evers case was not reopened for another quarter-century.

State authorities reopened the Evers case in autumn 1989, by which time Beckwith had moved to southeastern Tennessee. After three years of delay, the FBI delivered various heavily-censored documents containing further admission that Beckwith had murdered Evers. A May 1966 report from Delmar Dennis declared that "Beckwith wants people to know he is a member of the Klan and furthermore he wants people to know that he got away with murder." Mary Adams, an IRS employee, met Beckwith in 1967 and recalled that "he openly bragged that he had killed Medgar Evers." Another FBI informant recalled Beckwith's statement that "it had taken him about five weeks to get lined up on Medgar Evers.... Beckwith claimed that he hid the gun ... and that he probably would have been all right if the previous owner of the gun had not gone to the prosecuting attorney's office and reported that he had sold it to Beckwith."

Beckwith's third murder trial began on 27 January 1994, thirty years to the day from the commencement of his first. Bailiffs ejected a lone Klansman who came to honor Beckwith, and the case proceeded without further incident. New evidence included the testimony from six witnesses describing Beckwith's murder boasts. Delmar Dennis appeared for the state, followed by his former FBI handler. Ex-agent Tom Van Riper explained why the bureau had concealed Beckwith's 1965 confession, saving Dennis for a triple-murder case in Neshoba County. "That was the most important thing going at the time," Van Riper said. "The FBI would never have blown an informer as important" as Dennis on the Evers case. Mark Reiley, a Louisiana correctional officer, recounted Beckwith's confrontation with a black prison nurse. "If I could get rid of an uppity nigger like Medgar Evers," Beckwith told her, "I can get rid of a no-account nigger like you." Beckwith had often boasted to the prison staff about his powerful connections, once telling Reiley that "if he was lying and didn't have the power and connections he said he had, he would be serving time in prison for getting rid of that nigger Medgar Evers."

After ninety minutes of deliberation, the jury convicted Beckwith on 5 February 1994. Judge Breland Hilburn sentenced him to a life term in state prison, where he died on 19 January 2001.

Fleishman, Samuel—One of the KKK's first Jewish victims, Fleishman was a merchant and twenty-year resident of Marianna, Florida, whom Klan apologists nonetheless described as "a carpetbagger ... [who] catered to the black trade." In September 1869, a rumor spread that Fleishman had encouraged local blacks to arm and kill two whites for every member of their own race slain by terrorists. Klansmen James Coker led a crowd that invaded Fleishman's store on 3 October, seizing without payment his whole stock of guns and ammunition. Two days later, Coker returned with thirty men and ordered Fleishman to leave Jackson County forever. Escorted under guard to Bainbridge, Georgia, Fleishman returned on 6 October but never made it home. Ambushed on the highway east of Marianna, he was shot and killed by the usual "persons unknown."

Goodman, Andrew *see* **Schwerner, Michael**

Greensboro (N.C.) Massacre *see* **Nathan, Michael**

Henson, Everett—California klansman Everett Henson was murdered at Lakeside on 27 April 1978. Prosecutors charged another Klan member, Terry Martin, with killing Henson for revenge, after Henson tipped police to Martin's illegal drug transactions. Jurors convicted Martin at trial, and he received a life prison term on 15 June 1979.

Hurst, Charles—Alabama klansmen intended to whip retired storekeeper Charles Hurst for some infraction of Ku Klux "morality" when they raided his Pell City home on 22 February 1950, but Hurst resisted his kidnappers and they shot him dead, also wounding his son in the exchange of gunfire. In their haste to flee the murder scene, the raiders left sufficient evidence behind to identify several members of their party. Police named a Methodist minister from Talladega, Rev. Roy Heath, as the murder party's getaway driver, but Heath killed himself before detectives could question him. Heath's sons declared that Grand Dragon Alvin Horn, himself a minister, had warned them not to reveal incriminating comments made by Rev. Heath on the day of his suicide. Other suspects included klansmen Charles Carlisle, C.M. Hunter, Claude Lukes, and Louis Harrison (exalted cyclops of the Pell City klavern and athletic director for the Avondale textile mills). Jurors convicted Carlisle of manslaughter on 28 June 1950, whereupon he received a five-year prison term. Unknown assailants stabbed defendant Hunter to death at a local carnival, on 1 September 1950. Prosecutors delayed prosecution of Rev. Horn, then finally dismissed his murder charge on 13 October 1952.

Jackson, Wharlest—A black resident of Natchez, Mississippi, Jackson worked at the local Armstrong Rubber plant and doubled as treasurer of the Natchez NAACP, defying Klan threats at home and on the job. In early 1967, Jackson received a promotion to work as a chemical mixer, a post formerly held by whites only. Although initially afraid to take the job, Jackson decided that his family deserved the extra $6.80 per week to make ends meet. Former coworker and NAACP colleague George Metcalfe, crippled by a Klan car-bomb in August 1965, warned Jackson to check beneath his pickup's hood for bombs each time he used the vehicle, but caution failed Jackson in his third week on the job. He left work at 8:01 p.m. on 27 February 1967, and died ten minutes later in the blast of a time-delayed bomb attached to the pickup's chassis. Governor Paul Johnson called the bombing an "act of savagery which stains the honor of our state," and while the Natchez board of aldermen offered a $10,000 reward for arrest of the killers, civil rights activist Charles Evers insists to this day that local police "never even investigated" the slaying. Author Don Whitehead, meanwhile, claims that FBI agents quickly solved the bombing, along with Metcalfe's and the arson-murder of Frank Morris, linking all three crimes to the spin-off Silver Dollar Group. In 1970 Whitehead wrote, "The FBI is certain that it knows the klansmen responsible for the murders and the attempted murder." Agents had collected "important bits and pieces of information," but all in vain, since no witnesses agreed to testify in court. At four decades and counting, the crimes remain officially unsolved.

Jeffers, Perry—A black farmer in Reconstruction-era Warren County, Georgia, Jeffers ignored Klan warnings to vote Democratic in the 1868 presidential election, publicly declaring his report for GOP candidate Ulysses Grant. Six klansmen raided his home on the night of 1 November 1868, but Jeffers and his sons returned their gunfire, killing one klansman and wounding at least three others. Retaliation came on 5 November, when a band of 50 to 100 nightriders stormed the rural cabin. Jeffers and four of his sons hid in the woods nearby, while klansmen seized a fifth boy—crippled from infancy—and shot him eleven times, burning his corpse on a bonfire built from the family's furniture. The raiders also hanged Jeffers's wife from a nearby tree, but Jeffers cut her down after the raiders left and she survived. Jeffers identified the lynch mob's leader as Charles Wallace, editor of the Warrenton *Georgia Clipper* and a prominent Democratic Party spokesman. In the face of such opposition, Jeffers and his sons spent several nights hiding in Warrenton, then decided to flee the county. They boarded a train bound for South Carolina, but klansmen stopped it at Dearing, removing Jeffers and his sons. One boy escaped, but klansmen murdered Jeffers and the other three. Witnesses identified several of the gunmen—including notorious gunman Ellis Adams and the father of a klansman killed in the first raid on Jeffers's home—but police made no effort to arrest them.

King, Dr. Martin Luther, Jr.—From the moment he emerged as leader of the historic Montgomery, Alabama, bus boycott in 1955, various Klan factions plotted to kill Dr. Martin Luther King, Jr. Each new civil rights campaign pursued by King's SCLC intensified Klan hatred of King and the movement he led. On 4 April 1968, a sniper killed King at the Lorraine Motel in Memphis, Tennessee, where he had gone to lead protests for striking garbage workers. Much has been written since that day about King's life and death, his harassment by FBI agents, and the evidence suggesting a conspiracy behind

Top: **Dr. Martin Luther King, seen here removing a burned cross from his yard in Montgomery, Alabama, was murdered by a sniper in April 1968 (Library of Congress).** *Above:* **Klansmen rallied to defend King's alleged assassin, James Earl Ray (left, with the author at a prison interview).**

his murder. Our purpose here is to examine any links between King's death and members of the Ku Klux Klan.

Soon after his June 1968 arrest in England, alleged assassin James Earl Ray retained defense attorney Arthur Hanes, Sr., former mayor of Birmingham, Alabama, and a perennial counsel for klansmen accused of various crimes. Hanes rejected an offer of cash from Jesse Stoner and the NSRP to bankroll Ray's defense, while signing a literary contract with Alabama journalist William Bradford Huie.

FBI files reveal that Hanes also met twice with UKA Imperial Wizard Robert Shelton, in June and August 1968. Their conversations were not recorded, but informants provided details. George Wilson, a Midwestern leader of the UKA, claimed that the Klan contributed $10,000 to Ray's defense, under the guise of supporting defendants in North Carolina. Grand Dragon Furman Williams allegedly mentioned the deal at a rally in South Carolina, and other informants confirmed it. One source claimed that Shelton had arranged with Hanes to preview a list of prospective jurors for Ray's trial. Another informant reported that Shelton solicited Klansmen for donations to Ray's cause in August 1968. In any case, whatever deals may have existed with the UKA, they were dissolved when Ray fired Hanes and hired a new attorney on 10 November 1968.

The replacement was Percy Foreman, a Texas headliner who often boasted that his fee alone was punishment enough for any crime. Foreman preserved the book deal with Huie, then went to work on Ray, selling the prospect of a guilty plea. Between threats of execution and strategic loans to Ray's family, all contingent on a guilty plea with "no unseemly conduct" in court, Foreman achieved his goal after three months on the job. Ray pled guilty to murder in Memphis on 10 March 1969, accepting a ninety-nine-year prison term. Huie, meanwhile, was waffling in print on the subject of conspiracy, first telling readers of *Look* magazine that wealthy Louisiana racists had issued a contract on King, then revising his story to name Ray as the lone trigger-man—or perhaps the brains behind an insignificant "little conspiracy" involving persons unknown.

The House Select Committee on Assassinations took a closer look at King's death in the latter 1970s. FBI files subpoenaed by the panel revealed "approximately 25 Klan-related leads to potential conspiracies in the assassination of Dr. King," yet committee members deemed that only four "warranted the attention of the committee."

The first emerged from testimony of an FBI informant in Mobile, Alabama, who advised G-men of a meeting held in Birmingham sometime before the Klan's fatal church bombing of 15 September 1963. Participants included Sidney Barnes (known for his "close associates" in several Klans, including the WKKKKM), John Crommelin (an anti–Semite whose friends included Asa Carter and John Kasper), William Potter Gale (a closet Jew who led the California Rangers and the neo–Nazi Posse Comitatus), and Noah Carden (otherwise unidentified). Discussion at the meeting allegedly included plans to murder Dr. King, but agents failed to make a solid link in 1968.

A second lead surfaced on 22 April 1968, when Myrtis Hendricks—a waitress at John's Restaurant in Laurel, Mississippi—reported conversations overheard at work. Her employer, Deavours Nix, was a notorious Klansman and KBI chief for the WKKKKM. On 2 April, Hendricks said, Nix had received "a call on King" from persons unknown. The next day, she saw two men remove a rifle with a telescopic sight from Nix's office and place it in a car parked outside. On 4 April, Nix allegedly received a call reporting King's death before it made national news. Imperial Wizard Sam Bowers stopped at John's on 5 April, Hendricks said, and made comments that "raised the possibility" of his involvement in the murder. Hendricks subsequently left her job, hiding out with a boyfriend in Texas before she called the FBI. Agents found "no corroboration" for her story at the time, and Hendricks refused to confirm it for the House committee.

On 15 June 1968, one week after Ray's arrest in London, a long-distance telephone operator in Racine, Wisconsin, con-

tacted G-men with information on the King assassination. Four days earlier, she had placed three calls for an unnamed Wisconsin resident to different numbers in North Carolina. Eavesdropping on one conversation, she heard the caller identify himself as "Robert," demanding money to finance a trip abroad. Robert alluded to payment from the KKK and voiced fears that Ray would "spill his guts" when he returned to the United States. Agents traced the phone numbers, assigned to three brothers in North Carolina. One was a used-car dealer, while local police identified another as a car thief and forger of checks. All were interviewed, and each denied involvement in the King assassination. House investigators later claimed the "operator" never actually worked for the telephone company—a fact strangely missing from FBI reports on the incident. Committee spokesmen decided that "the lead was not based on credible evidence and not worthy of further investigation."

The committee's "most significant Klan-related lead" concerned attorney Arthur Hanes. The panel reviewed FBI files and questioned informants, collecting tales of sundry meetings between Hanes and leaders of the UKA. A bureau spy known only as "Source B" claimed knowledge of a meeting held in 1969, between Hanes and acting imperial wizard Melvin Sexton, where Klansmen approved paying Hanes $12,500 to defend knights charged with various crimes in North Carolina. After Hanes left the room, Sexton allegedly remarked that he had "a piece of paper for Hanes pertaining to the Ray case," but its significance is doubtful, since Ray had fired Hanes in November 1968. Before the committee, Hanes "vigorously denied" any Klan support of Ray's defense, a claim echoed under oath by Sexton, Robert Shelton, ex–Grand Dragon J.R. Jones and others. The committee noted that Hanes and Shelton "disagreed substantially regarding the duration of their friendship and whether Hanes helped establish the Klan's national defense fund," while both Hanes and the Klansmen "attempted to minimize their association." Those discrepancies were finally attributed to faulty memories or "an attempt by Hanes to minimize his relationship with Sexton and the legal work he did for him." Committee spokesmen left the matter unresolved, while finding "no indications of an agreement between the UKA and James Earl Ray prior to Dr. King's assassination."

Before abandoning the KKK entirely, committee members also questioned FBI informant William Morris and longtime klansman Jesse Stoner. G-men had eliminated Stoner as a suspect after King was killed, reporting that he addressed an NSRP rally in Meridian, Mississippi on 4 April 1968. That alibi did not preclude involvement in the crime, however, and a link was forged in 1969, when Stoner replaced Percy Foreman as counsel of record for Ray and Ray's brothers. Stoner himself blamed the FBI for King's murder, claiming that Morris approached him in the 1950s with a $25,000 contract on King's life. Convinced even then that Morris served the bureau, Stoner admitted offering to bomb King for $5,000, but he claimed that Morris had been adamant: the contract's sponsors wanted King shot with a rifle. Stoner then declined the job, while claiming that Morris had tried to solicit Asa Carter. Morris "vehemently denied" such discussions with Stoner, Carter, or anyone else, but the committee found an FBI report from 1961, wherein Morris told fellow klansmen that King's death would solve all the South's racial problems. He knew a mobster in New Orleans, Morris said, who would be glad to do the job. Morris denied that claim as well, professing total innocence.

The House committee finally announced a "likelihood" that King was slain "as a result of a conspiracy," then ruled out every racist group in the U.S. as active plotters. In that scenario, Ray was the lone gunman, assisted and financed at times by his brothers, John and Jerry. The Rays allegedly acted in hope of collecting a five-figure "bounty" on King, offered by St. Louis businessmen John Kauffmann and John Sutherland. Both were dead when the committee held its hearings, but other testimony indicated that the pair had sponsored an "open" contract on King, with a blanket offer of payment to anyone who killed him. No link to the Rays was established, though John Ray lived in St. Louis. The verdict was, in effect, a new version of Huie's "little conspiracy" from 1969.

Liuzzo, Viola Gregg — A middle-aged mother of five

from Detroit, Michigan, Liuzzo answered Dr. Martin Luther King's call for volunteers to register black Alabama voters in March 1965. She joined in King's historic march from Selma to Montgomery, and at the protest's end, on 25 March, she used her car to ferry groups of demonstrators back to Selma. On her last trip from the capital, she reported that a carload of white

Liuzzo's killers signed autographs at Klan rallies after their murder indictments. From left to right: William Eaton, Eugene Thomas and Collie Wilkins, Jr. (Southern Poverty Law Center).

men had given chase, nudging her bumper several times. Undaunted, Liuzzo left for Montgomery again at 7:34 p.m., accompanied by a black teenager, Leroy Moton. At 8:00 p.m., while traveling along Highway 80 in Lowndes County, Liuzzo was fatally wounded by gunshots from another car, and her vehicle crashed into a barbed-wire fence. Moton, uninjured but spattered with Liuzzo's blood, staggered to the highway and flagged down a passing truck filled with marchers returning to Selma.

Those facts are simply stated, but confusion still surrounds Liuzzo's murder four decades after the fact. Indeed, the riddles began hours prior to the shooting, when the morning edition of Montgomery's *Alabama Journal* ran a short article refuting "persistent rumors that a white female civil rights demonstrator had died here or in Selma." Author Mary Stanton suggests that the article contained "some sort of encoded message" anticipating Liuzzo's murder, but that riddle and others remain unanswered. One FBI report claimed six shots were fired into Liuzzo's car from two different pistols, one .38 caliber and the other .22 caliber. John Doar, representing the DOJ in Selma, was told the fatal shots came from a rifle. Leroy Moton agreed that a high-powered rifle was used, but he heard no gunfire and believed the weapon must have been equipped with a silencer. Meanwhile, state police commander Al Lingo told reporters that only *two* shots were fired, insisting that no one could determine whether Liuzzo was shot from a passing car or by a roadside sniper. A revolver found discarded on the highway's shoulder was never dusted for fingerprints by G-men or police. Moton's description of the chase and shooting further confused matters. He swore that two cars had pursued the vehicle: a black Ford tried to force her off the road soon after leaving Selma, while the fatal gunshots issued from a different car. After the shooting, Moton said, a carload of men returned to the scene and shined flashlights into Liuzzo's car, where he lay covered in the victim's blood. FBI files noted statements from three other witnesses who described a dark-colored Ford cruising near the murder scene on 25 March. *Newsweek* magazine reported the pursuit with two chase cars in its issue of 5 April 1965.

Soon after initial reports of the shooting, President Lyn-

Detroit volunteer Viola Liuzzo was murdered by Alabama klansmen on 25 March 1965 (Southern Poverty Law Center).

don Johnson ordered FBI Director J. Edgar Hoover to "find the perpetrators of this heinous crime" and "do everything possible around the clock" to solve the case. Johnson and Hoover spoke repeatedly throughout that night, continuing sporadic conversations until 6:00 a.m. on 26 March. Hoover immediately launched a smear campaign against Liuzzo and her family, telling Johnson in their first conversation that Liuzzo's husband "doesn't have too good a background and the woman had indications of needle marks in her arms." Furthermore, he said, Liuzzo "was sitting very, very close to the Negro in the car. It had the appearance of a necking party." When LBJ called back a short time later, Hoover amended his assessment of Anthony Liuzzo: "I don't say the man has a bad character but he is well known as a Teamster strongarm man." Hoover quickly added, "On the woman's body we found numerous needle marks indicating she had been taking dope, although we can't say definitely, because she's dead."

Although Liuzzo's husband *was* a Teamster, every other statement made by Hoover in his conversations with the president was false. Published reports differ on the source of his malicious information, alternately crediting "agents in Mississippi" or Agent Spencer Robb in Birmingham, who allegedly penned a memo falsely claiming that Viola Liuzzo "had puncture marks in her arms indicating recent use of a hypodermic needle." No such needle marks existed, and the memo was suppressed for two decades, but its false contents quickly leaked to right-wing journalists and to the Klan. Hoover biographer Curt Gentry claims that Hoover, a bitter racist, "wanted to believe this lie" which validated claims of civil rights activity as a prelude to "race-mixing." (The first test performed on Liuzzo's corpse by state investigators was an examination for signs of recent sexual intercourse. The results were negative.) The director also had another motive, for by sunrise on 26 March he knew that FBI informant Gary Rowe had been a member of the Ku Klux murder team.

Accounts differ as to when Rowe informed his bureau handlers of his presence at the crime scene. Author Don Whitehead claims that Rowe met an agent in Birmingham at 11:15 p.m. on 25 March, while Mary Stanton places his first call to the FBI some three hours later. In fact, as Rowe himself later admitted, his FBI contact had approved Rowe's participation in the latest "missionary work" sometime "early in the morning" of 25 March—a fact long suppressed by the Bureau. As Rowe described the shooting, he was riding in the backseat of a red-and-white Chevrolet Impala driven by klansman Eugene Thomas, accompanied by UKA members William Eaton and Collie Wilkins, Jr. They had followed Liuzzo's car through Lowndes County, debating the best method of attack. Thomas wanted to ram the Oldsmobile, but Wilkins warned him that the FBI could trace paint chips and thus identify them. Finally, Rowe said, during a high-speed chase, Eaton and Wilkins "emptied their guns" into Liuzzo's Oldsmobile. Rowe denied firing at Liuzzo, but admitted aiming his gun out the window, pretending to shoot.

The case was officially solved by 8:00 a.m. on 26 March, when President Johnson got word from Attorney General Nicholas Katzenbach. At 12:40 p.m., Johnson appeared on televi-

sion, flanked by Katzenbach and Hoover, to announce the arrest of four klansmen. Johnson named Rowe with the rest, but Rowe was not identified as an FBI informant. After branding the KKK "a hooded society of bigots," Johnson urged all knights within the sound of his voice "to get out of the Ku Klux Klan now and return to a decent society before it is too late." From Tuscaloosa, Robert Shelton called LBJ a "damn liar," describing Liuzzo's murder as a "trumped-up plot" by "Communists and sex perverts" to "frame the Ku Klux Klan." UKA headquarters posted $150,000 bond for the accused, following their arraignment on murder charges.

Sheriff Jim Clark, in Selma, sparked new controversy with his own press conference on 27 March 1965. Specifically, Clark charged that the FBI could have saved Liuzzo's life. "They had a carload of Ku Klux Klansmen under surveillance," Clark said, yet agents failed to share that information with state or local police. At 6:20 p.m. on 25 March, Clark revealed, state troopers had given Eugene Thomas a warning ticket for excessive speed. His car was stopped within ten miles of the Liuzzo murder site, but no further action was taken because of the FBI blackout. "The FBI agents have always worked closely with us in the past," Clark declared, "but this time for some reason they didn't. If we had known about it, we would have tried to keep that car under surveillance. The shooting didn't happen in my county. I regret that it happened, but I've been getting telegrams from all over the country blaming me for it. We had a march today on the courthouse and the demonstrators indicated that I was to blame for what happened. If they want to blame anybody, they ought to march on the federal building."

FBI headquarters responded furiously on 28 March, calling Clark a "malicious liar" whose public statements were "typical of his weakness in handling his responsibilities." Bureau spokesmen admitted seeing Thomas's car in a Klan motorcade in Montgomery, on 21 March, and claimed the FBI had provided a list of license plate numbers to Alabama law enforcement agencies over the next four days. Headquarters also claimed that shortly after Thomas and his "wrecking crew" left Bessemer for Montgomery on 25 March, "[a]n all-points bulletin was put out immediately by police notifying the U.S. Army and the Alabama Department of Public Safety." Two decades later, *Washington Post* columnist Jack Anderson captured the Hoover's true role in the case. "Evidently aware of the embarrassment the FBI would suffer from the presence of its undercover informer in the murderer's car," Anderson wrote, "J. Edgar Hoover marshaled the Bureau's resources to blacken the dead woman's reputation."

UKA Imperial Wizard Robert Shelton collaborated in that effort. On 28 March, Shelton told reporters that Liuzzo was "set up to become a martyr and another rallying point for the civil rights movement. If this woman was at home with the children where she belonged, she wouldn't have been in jeopardy." Shelton also claimed to possess inside information on Liuzzo's "police record"—she was fined $50 in 1964 for home schooling her children—and of her "liberated relationship" with husband Anthony. Klansmen claimed that Liuzzo had engaged in sex with Selma blacks, but the promised witnesses never appeared.

Teamster president James Hoffa flew Liuzzo's body home from Selma on a union plane, prompting Hoover to renew his false charges that Anthony Liuzzo was a "strong-arm extortionist" with Mafia ties. When Liuzzo sought to recover his late wife's personal effects, the FBI ignored him. A letter to the White House, seeking return of her wedding ring, was routed to bureau headquarters, where it sat unanswered for a decade. As noted by historian Wyn Wade, "In less than a month, the national topic changed from the willful murder of Liuzzo to her moral character." In April 1965, Hoover told northern journalists, "White citizens [in Alabama] are primarily decent, but frightened for their lives. The colored people are quite ignorant, mostly uneducated."

A federal grand jury indicted all four klansmen on 6 April 1965, for conspiracy to violate Liuzzo's rights, then corrected its error on 15 April by dismissing charges against Gary Rowe. A Lowndes County grand jury indicted Eaton, Thomas and Wilkins for first-degree murder on 22 April. UKA Imperial Klonsel Matt Murphy defended the three, while filing suit to recover $6,000 in fees from the Gary Rowe. G-men in Mobile, Alabama, countered that move with a memo to Hoover on 4 May 1965, proposing a leak to HUAC concerning "the role of a subversive lawyer in promulgating the aims of the KKK."

Collie Wilson was first to face trial for Liuzzo's murder, in May 1965. Expert testimony linked the fatal slug and several cartridges discarded along Highway 80 to a .38-caliber revolver seized at the home of Eugene Thomas. Gary Rowe appeared for the state, describing the murder and Thomas's loan of his pistol to Wilkins. Murphy attacked Rowe for breaking his "sacred" Klan secrecy oath, then capped his performance with an hysterical rant against "niggers," Communists and the United Nations. Ten white jurors voted to convict Wilkins on a reduced charge of manslaughter, but two held out for acquittal and the judge declared a mistrial on 7 May 1965. A second trial was scheduled for October, while Wilkins rushed off to sign autographs at Klan rallies.

Matt Murphy missed the second Wilkins trial, killed on 20 August 1965 when a truck hit his car on the highway between Birmingham and Tuscaloosa. In his place, the KKK retained Birmingham ex-mayor and former G-man Arthur Hanes, Sr. The state prosecution team changed in late summer as well, with Attorney General Richmond Flowers replacing county solicitor Arthur Gamble, Jr. The new jury included eight past or present Citizens' Council members, yet Flowers remained confident, declaring his case "the strongest ... I've ever had, complete with the eyewitness testimony of an FBI agent [sic]." Still, the all-white panel acquitted Wilkins on 22 October 1965, and he left court to a hero's reception. Another jury, including eight blacks and four whites, acquitted Eugene Thomas of murder on 27 September 1966. William Eaton died of a heart attack on 10 March 1966, before his case could be tried in state court.

Liuzzo's killers did not escape justice entirely, however. The federal conspiracy charges remained, and all three defendants were convicted on 3 December 1965, receiving the maximum ten-year sentence for their crime. Soon after their release, in summer of 1978, Thomas and Wilkins agreed to interviews with the ABC television program *20/20*. Both named Gary Rowe as Liuzzo's killer and passed polygraph tests in support of their story, while Rowe's test results indicated deception. That episode sparked a new grand jury hearing in Lowndes County, where Thomas and Wilkins repeated their tale under oath. The panel indicted Rowe for murder in September 1978, but while the Governor of Georgia (where Rowe then lived as "Thomas Moore") approved extradition in February 1979, the case was subsequently dropped. Liuzzo's children filed a claim of negligence against the FBI in 1977. Bureau headquarters refused to negotiate, so a formal lawsuit followed in July 1979, seeking $2 million in damages. The trial opened on 21 March 1983, before federal judge Charles Joiner. Attorney Dean Robb charged that G-men were negligent in recruiting, training and supervising Rowe, and thus were liable for Liuzzo's death. Thomas and Wilkins repeated their claim that Rowe shot Liuzzo with a pistol borrowed from Thomas, while two Birmingham detectives claimed Rowe had confessed the shooting to them on 26 March 1965. Judge Joiner rejected the plaintiffs' case on 27 May 1983, ordering Liuzzo's children to pay $80,000 in court costs for the FBI. They refused, preferring jail time for contempt, but the bill was cancelled in November 1983, after public outrage sparked a U.S. Senate resolution asking Justice to drop the vendetta.

Mallard, Robert—A prosperous black salesman and owner of a thirty-two-acre farm near Lyons, Georgia, Mallard was despised by the 1940s Klan for acting "too big." Gunmen ambushed him on 20 November 1948, as Mallard returned home from church with his wife and two friends, killing him with a gunshot through the windshield of his car. Sheriff R.E. Gray acknowledged that the killers wore "white stuff," identified by Mallard's widow and the other two survivors as Klan robes. Governor Herman Talmadge ordered a GBI investigation of the slaying, while Grand Dragon Samuel Green announced that his AGK planned an independent review of the case. Sheriff Gray blamed the shooting on Mallard, telling reporters, "This Negro was a bad Negro, as I have had dealings with him. I further know that this Negro was hated by all who knew him." On 27 November, GBI agents arrested Mallard's widow at her husband's funeral, detaining her on murder charges while two other blacks and a white reporter were jailed as material witnesses. GBI Lieutenant W.E. McDuffie told the press, "I think the Ku Klux Klan has been wrongfully accused in this case." Police subsequently released Mrs. Mallard and arrested five white suspects on 4 December 1948. Two of those jailed were formally indicted on 10 December, but prosecutors never tried them and the case remains officially unsolved.

Moore, Charlie Eddie *see* **Dee, Henry**

Morris, Frank—Author Don Whitehead, working from FBI files still closed to the general public, reported in 1970 on the Bureau's investigation of a Klan faction known to its members as the Silver Dollar Group. As described by Whitehead, the group was organized in late 1964, by klansmen from Louisiana and Mississippi who bemoaned the "lack of guts" displayed by their respective Klans, including a ninety-day moratorium on violence recently declared by WKKKKM Imperial Wizard Sam Bowers. Calling themselves the "toughest Klansmen in Mississippi or Louisiana," Silver Dollar knights prepared for action in a series of covert training sessions. Once, Whitehead reports, their wives served picnic lunches on a bayou farm while their menfolk practiced blowing stumps with dynamite and wiring bombs to a car's ignition switch. That practice paid off for the first time, Whitehead claims, in the murder of Frank Morris, a black resident of Ferriday, Louisiana. Aside from running the town's only shoe repair shop, Morris also hosted a Sunday-morning radio program featuring gospel music and sermons from local clergymen. His life seemed blameless, until Silver Dollar knights heard rumors that Morris was "flirting" with white female patrons, perhaps taking some to the small apartment behind his shop. In the predawn hours of 10 December 1964, Morris woke to sounds of smashing glass and found a white man pouring gasoline through a broken window. A second man, armed with a shotgun, ordered Morris back inside as his companion struck a match and lit the fuel. Engulfed in flames, Morris struggled to free himself. Across the street, a gas station attendant watched a dark sedan speed off toward Vidalia, before Morris staggered into the street. Two FBI agents questioned Morris that morning, accompanied by Police Chief R.W. Warren and Fire Chief Noland Mouelle. Morris told his visitors he recognized the nightriders, but did not know their names. "I think they might work at Johns Manville or something like that over in Natchez," he explained. Four days later, Morris died in excruciating pain.

Nathan, Dr. Michael—Members of the Workers Viewpoint Organization—a small bi-racial labor union in Greensboro, North Carolina—enjoyed little success in organizing local textile mill workers in 1978–79, prompting leaders of the group to seek a new, more militant image and thus reap free publicity. In summer 1979 they renamed their group the Communist Workers Party (CWP), waving a literal red flag before Greensboro's ultra-conservative establishment. Where proselytizing of workers had failed, the CWP switched to public confrontation with the local Klan. On 8 July 1979, CWP members disrupted a Klan rally at China Grove, North Carolina and publicly burned the KKK's banner. Three months later, CWP spokesmen announced plans for a "Death to the Klan" rally in Greensboro. On 19 October, civic leaders authorized a parade for 3 November, contingent on a promise that marchers would carry no weapons "open or concealed."

By that time, Grand Dragon Virgil Griffin's North Carolina Knights were hungry for payback. The NCK, originally founded by FBI informants, had recently closed ranks Frank Collin's NSPA to create a new United Racist Front (URF). On 1 November 1979, klansman and police informant Ed Dawson obtained a copy of the CWP's parade permit, including the assembly point, starting time and route of march. (Later, the same police who paid his secret salary would claim they mistook Dawson for a CWP member. When that excuse failed, they explained that the parade permit was a matter of public record, readily available to anyone.) With the permit in hand, Dawson embarked on a campaign of agitation to ensure that klansmen would be out in force to meet the unarmed marchers. Incessantly, he urged them to avenge the China Grove insult. One knight who joined the rush to combat later told the *Greensboro*

Daily News, "We'd never have come to Greensboro if it wasn't for Ed Dawson berating us." Another informant, Cleveland ATF agent Bernard Butkovich, worked within the NSPA at Winston-Salem, playing a key role in formation of the URF and its violent response to the CWP. Aside from urging Nazis to meet the Red marchers head-on, Butkovich offered illegal explosives (including hand grenades) and special kits that would convert semiautomatic weapons into illegal machine guns. Both Dawson and Butkovich attended planning sessions for the URF–CWP confrontation on 3 November 1979. Dawson twice warned Greensboro police (on 31 October and 3 November) that Klansmen would be heavily armed when they met the parade. Butkovich allegedly issued a similar warning to his ATF superiors on 3 November.

Greensboro police were strangely lethargic on 3 November 1979. Despite plans to cover the parade with a crack tactical unit, local officers began assembling at 11:30 a.m., a full hour *after* the starting time clearly printed on the CWP's parade permit. Department spokesmen called it a "logistical error," while critics accused them of acting in concert with klansmen and Nazis. In either case, the end result was tragedy. Ed Dawson admits leading a motorcade of armed URF members to intercept the CWP march, but claims he fled the scene before mayhem erupted. The racists opened fire on their defenseless targets at 11:23 a.m., killing five persons and wounding nine or ten (reports vary). The murdered victims—Cesar Cauce, Dr. Michael Nathan, William Sampson, Sandra Smith and Dr. James Waller—were a stark contrast to their semiliterate killers: their number included two physicians, a computer operator from Duke University, and the student body president of Bennett College.

President Jimmy Carter ordered a federal investigation of the massacre, code-named "GREENKILL" by the FBI (for "*Green*sboro *Kill*ings"). Video cameras had captured the killers in action, while a city patrolman had followed the Klan motorcade and witnessed the shooting. Ed Dawson met with G-men on 9 November, blaming his police employers for the massacre. "I think it was handled stinky," he complained. "With all the advance notice they had—and I told them about some of the people—I expected when I turned that corner to see nothing but helmets, just a wall of city police." CWP spokesmen agreed, accusing police of complicity in the murders. Of forty URF gunmen present at the murder scene, only sixteen were arrested, and only six of those (four klansmen and two NSPA members) were charged by state authorities with any criminal offense. No charges were filed against Dawson, Virgil Griffin, or Kleagle Mark Sherer (who admitted firing shots "into the air" during the murders). Both Griffin and Sherer were ex-convicts, banned by law from owning firearms, but state prosecutors ignored their possession of weapons on 3 November and during their flight from Greensboro. Neither Dawson nor ATF agent Butkovich were called to testify at trial, prosecutors explaining that the informants "didn't witness anything that would have helped us." They *could* have described the URF conspiracy to murder CWP members, a fact corroborated by one Nazi who admitted photos of the five slain victims were passed out to racists a week in advance, but District Attorney Michael Schlosser dismissed all conspiracy counts before trial. The killers caught on film would not be tried for plotting their crime, merely for pulling the triggers. As CWP member Nelson Johnson told author Elizabeth Wheaton, "By dismissing the possibility of a planned assault with a flippant observation such as 'The Klan always carries guns,' Schlosser gave the defense attorneys the opening they needed: self-defense."

And so it was, at trial in autumn 1980. The state called 2,200 prospective jurors, some of whom were frankly sympathetic toward the killers. One told the court, "The only thing the Klan is guilty of is poor shooting." Another opined, "I don't think we are out a lot because those people aren't with us anymore. I think we are better off without them." While those veniremen were dismissed, the final all-white panel proved little better. They were seemingly blind to videotapes of the murders in progress, deaf to testimony from eyewitnesses. One defense attorney told the jury that if Griffin's knights "had taken a machine gun and mowed the crowd down, it would have been justified," since the marchers "were attacking the very society that gives them the right to be out on the street." Jurors accepted the strange logic that those with rights should be killed for exercising them, and all defendants were acquitted on 17 November 1980.

The Greensboro verdict, strongly reminiscent of Ku Klux trials from the mid–1960s, provoked a groundswell of national outrage. In May 1982, the ACLU helped survivors of the massacre draft a complaint against Dawson, Butkovich and other defendants, including the Justice Department, for negligence in failing to prevent the murders. That lawsuit prompted federal prosecutors to move against the URF. On 21 April 1983, nine racists were indicted on charges of conspiracy to violate their victims' civil rights and to violate federal statutes, plus interference with interstate commerce (for wounding a television photographer). This time, the defendants included Dawson and Griffin, while klansmen Chris Bensen and Max Hayes received immunity in return for testimony against their fellow knights. The trial opened on 9 January 1984, before another all-white jury. As before, the jury found all nine defendants innocent. Ed Dawson, stunned, told journalists, "For once in my life, I can't think of anything to say." A smiling Virgil Griffin said, "I feel like I died and went to heaven. Now I can go to a Klan rally again."

Nothing remained of GREENKILL but the civil lawsuit filed in 1982, lumping Klansmen and Nazis together with Greensboro police, the FBI and ATF. Plaintiffs sought $48 million in damages for their injuries or loss of loved ones, while the Klan joined ranks with civic leaders and federal agents in denial of any wrongdoing. Jurors dismissed all claims of conspiracy but found eight defendants (Ed Dawson, five shooters and two Greensboro policemen) liable for various injuries. Damages were fixed at $294,959.55—including $351,500 for the death of victim Michael Nathan, another $3,600 for assault and battery on Nathan, $38,359.55 for assault and battery on survivor Paul Bermanzhon, and $1,500 for assault and battery on survivor Tom Clark. Spokesmen for the city of Greensboro announced plans to appeal the verdict, then settled the case with a payment of $351,500 to Michael Nathan's estate. None of the killers spent a day in prison for their crimes; no law enforcement agents were dismissed, suspended or reprimanded for their handling of the incident.

Oberholtzer, Madge—No single incident caused greater damage to the 1920s Klan than the Indiana death of Hagerstown schoolteacher Madge Oberholtzer, in 1925. Oberholtzer met Grand Dragon David Stephenson in January of that year, at the inaugural party of Governor Edward Jackson. While living with her parents, a few blocks from Stephenson's mansion in Irvington, she agreed to several dates but firmly rebuffed the dragon's pleas for a more intimate relationship. On the night of 15 March 1925, Stephenson called Madge at home to arrange an "urgent" meeting, dispatching bodyguard (and ex-policeman) Earl Gentry to fetch her from home. Oberholtzer's parents did not see her again until 17 March, when a stranger carried her into their house, claiming that Madge had been hurt in a car accident. A physician found bruises and bite marks all over her body, with deep lacerations on her breasts and chunks of flesh missing from her genitals.

As described by Madge, Stephenson and Gentry had plied her with liquor at Stephenson's home, then forced her aboard a train bound for Chicago. Once on board, in Stephenson's private compartment, the grand dragon had stripped Madge, then raped her and gnawed her flesh in a drunken frenzy. Rising early on 16 March, as the train stopped in Hammond, Indiana, the trio disembarked and registered at a local hotel. There, Madge tried to shoot herself with Stephenson's pistol, but he disarmed her and ordered Gentry to clean her wounds. After breakfast, Stephenson's chauffeur took Madge shopping in Hammond, where she bought deadly mercury chloride tablets instead of makeup. Back at the hotel, she gulped the poison and soon began vomiting blood. Stephenson panicked, driving her back to his Irvington home, but he refused to call a doctor, telling his aides, "I've been in worse messes than this before and got out of it." Madge dictated a sworn statement to authorities on 28 March 1925, then finally died from kidney failure on 14 April. Indicted for murder, Stephenson claimed an elaborate frame-up, while his lawyers sought to dismiss Madge's death as simple suicide. Jurors disagreed and convicted Stephenson of second-degree murder, resulting in a life prison term. Publicity surrounding the case, including revelation of Stephenson's alcoholism, sexual perversity and extensive ties to corrupt politicians, shattered the Indiana Klan and cost the order thousands of members nationwide.

Pace, Rev. Edward—In 1973, Pace was the pastor of the Oak Grove Baptist Church in Gadsden, Alabama. That November, following a Christmas parade through nearby streets, an unknown gunman killed Pace at his home. Police soon arrested UKA member Bruce Botsford for killing the black minister, reporting that Botsford confessed to "acting under the sanction of the United Klans of America" when he shot Rev. Pace. In his statement, Botsford denied knowing Pace, but claimed that he was told the minister's home served as local headquarters for the Black Panther Party. At trial, Botsford recanted his statement, claiming that detectives threatened to put him in a "cell full of niggers" unless he confessed. Prosecution witness Charles Battles testified that he and other klansmen, including Botsford,

Aubrey Arledge and his son Ricky, were standing outside their Gadsden klavern—located across the street from Pace's home—when Botsford and Ricky Arledge crossed the street, knocked on the door, and shot Pace when he answered. Ricky Arledge subsequently claimed to be an FBI informant, naming his father as the mastermind of Pace's murder. In April 1974, jurors deadlocked over murder charges filed against Aubrey Arledge, voting seven-to-five for conviction, and the judge declared a mistrial.

Page, Alec

—A former slave in Monroe County, Mississippi, Page was murdered by nightriding klansmen in 1871. Police jailed twenty-eight suspects, who received a heroes' welcome (complete with booming cannons) upon posting bail. All twenty-eight defendants pled guilty at trial, in December 1871, whereupon the judge released them with suspended jail terms.

Penn, Lemuel

—At 4:45 a.m. on 11 July 1964, unknown gunmen fired shotgun blasts into a car occupied by three black men, near Colbert, Georgia. The driver died instantly, while his passengers escaped injury. The three were officers in the U.S. Army Reserve, returning home to Washington, D.C., from summer training at Fort Benning, Georgia. The murdered victim, Lt. Col. Lemuel Penn, served in civilian life as the director of adult and vocational education for Washington's public schools. Soon after the shooting, President Lyndon Johnson telephoned Governor Carl Sanders to request federal-state cooperation in the manhunt, and Sanders—who had vowed that he would "not rest easy" while Penn's slayers were at large—agreed. Later that day, Attorney General Robert Kennedy ordered a full-scale FBI investigation of the crime. On 6 August 1964, G-men arrested four Clarke County UKA members—Herbert Guest, James Lackey, Cecil Myers and Joseph Sims—on charges of conspiring to violate Penn's civil rights.

Lackey and Guest confessed in custody, describing events of the fatal morning. Lackey admitted driving the murder car, with Myers and Sims as passengers. They had seen Penn's car at a stoplight in Athens, at 4:10 a.m., and assumed from its Washington license plates that the black occupants must be "some of President Johnson's boys." As Lackey explained, "The original reason for our following the colored men was because we heard Martin Luther King might make Georgia a testing ground for the civil rights bill. We thought some out-of-town niggers might stir up some trouble in Athens." As they overtook Penn's vehicle, Sims declared, "I'm going to kill me a nigger," then he and Myers opened fire with sawed-off shotguns. One of their weapons belonged to Herbert Guest and regularly hung on the wall of his garage, described by Lackey as "a frequent gathering place" for klansmen. Another UKA member, Thomas "Horsefly" Follendore, admitted seeing Myers and Sims return the guns to Guest's garage at 5:00 a.m. on 11 July. Guest, meanwhile, allegedly heard Myers and Sims boast of Penn's murder for the first time on 13 July, granting that Myers had taken guns from his garage on several occasions without Guest's permission.

Adverse publicity prompted confused reactions from the UKA's leadership. First, imperial headquarters dissolved Clarke County Klavern No. 244 was dissolved following the arrests, its members dispersed between Oglethorpe County Klavern No.

244 and Walton County's Vinegar Hill Klavern No. 53, where Myers and Sims appeared on the membership roll. Next, a special meeting of the Georgia realm convened on 18 August 1964, to arrange defense funding. Imperial Wizard Robert Shelton sent a letter to all klaverns in seven southern states, requesting each knight to donate at least one dollar toward support of the Georgia defendants. By such means, Exalted Cyclops Tom Whitehead in Athens collected some $3,000 for defense of Myers and Sims. A local grand jury indicted Lackey, Myers and Sims for murder on 25 August 1964, while naming Guest as an unindicted accessory after the fact.

By the time Myers and Sims faced trial on 2 September 1964, Lackey had recanted his confession, accusing G-men of unlawful arrest and coercion, extracting his statement "under fears and threats." Judge William Skelton admitted the confession, while defense attorney James Hudson cited Lackey's low IQ (90) and Agent Jack Simpson's comment to Lackey that the bureau might pay $3,000 for testimony in "complicated cases such as this." Hudson asked jurors, "What do you think this meant to James Lackey, a mentally ill person working in a filling station?" Herbert Guest also withdrew his statement to the FBI, claiming, "I don't know what they got in it. I blacked out or something happened to me.... I don't remember nothing about it.... I really don't know what went on the last three or four hours." The defense capped its case with a parade of witnesses (including one black woman) who allegedly saw Myers and Sims at a café in Athens, at 5:00 a.m. on 11 July. Jurors acquitted both defendants on 4 September, prompting Klan attorney James Venable to remark, "You'll never be able to convict a white man that kills a nigger what encroaches on the white race of the South." Prosecutor Clete Johnson shook hands with Myers and Sims as they left the courtroom, and Madison County's sheriff attended a victory banquet for the Klan triggermen at Lawrenceville.

Prosecutors dropped James Lackey's murder charge after his codefendants were acquitted. Myers and Sims remained active in the Vinegar Hill klavern following their trial, then left (or were expelled from) the UKA to join James Venable's National Knights. They soon enlisted with a violent faction known as the Black Shirts or Black Knights, led by Klansmen Earl Holcombe (who participated as a member of the U.S. Klans in a 1961 riot at Athens, Georgia) and Colbert McGriff (expelled from the UKA after a shooting incident at Griffin). On 16 October 1964, a federal grand jury indicted six Klansmen—Guest, Lackey, Myers, Sims, Denver Phillips and George Turner—for conspiring to violate Penn's civil rights. Federal judge William Bootle dismissed those charges on 19 December 1964, claiming lack of federal jurisdiction in the case. The U.S. Supreme Court reversed Bootle's ruling on 28 March 1966, reinstating the federal indictments and clearing the way for a summer trial.

Prosecutors split their case, trying defendants Myers, Sims and Turner together, while Guest, Lackey and Phillips faced a separate jury. Both cases were tried between 28 June and 7 July 1966, with confessions from Lackey and Guest produced and disputed once more. Defense counsel admitted that his clients "may be guilty of a little violence, even a little bad violence," but said they were simply trying to "help out" by "letting the colored people of Athens know that somebody else other than the police was watching them." Verdicts from the first trial were sealed until the second jury finished its deliberations. On 8 July, Judge Bootle announced that Myers and Sims had been convicted, while their codefendants were acquitted. The next day, Bootle sentenced Myers and Sims to the maximum ten-year sentence permitted under federal law. Sims got another ten years on 13 August 1966, after pleading guilty to attempted murder of his wife.

Randolph, Rev. B.F.—In 1864, after serving as a chaplain in the Union Army, Randolph settled in Orangeburg, South Carolina. After the Civil War ended, he joined the Republican Party and won election to the state senate from Abbeville County. Aside from being one of the Palmetto State's first black legislators, Randolph helped established chapters of the Union League and schools for freedmen, emerging as one of South Carolina's most prominent Republicans. On 1 October 1868, three klansmen shot Randolph at a railroad depot near Cokesbury, South Carolina. One of the killers later confessed, but none ever faced trial.

Reeb, Rev. James—After Col. Al Lingo's state troopers and Sheriff Jim Clark's mounted "posse" routed protest marchers in Selma, Alabama, on "Bloody Sunday"—7 March 1965—Dr. Martin Luther King issued a nationwide call for volunteers to join in the next demonstration. One of those who responded was Rev. James Reeb, a Unitarian minister from Washington, D.C. Reeb flew to Montgomery on 8 March and reached Selma that night, in time to join a protest march the following day. Police stopped that demonstration as well, though without the customary beatings. Later on 9 March, Reeb joined fellow demonstrators for dinner at Walker's Café. Around 7:30 p.m., he left the restaurant with two other white Unitarian ministers, Rev. Orloff Miller and Rev. Clark Olsen. Disoriented on the unfamiliar streets, they mistakenly walked into a tough white neighborhood, soon passing a Klan hangout, the Silver Moon Café. Across the street, four white men suddenly emerged from the C & C Novelty Company, rushing across the street and shouting, "Hey, you niggers!" One hammered Reeb's skull with a club, while the others assaulted Miller and Olsen with bare fists. In parting, they kicked the fallen ministers, one thug declaring, "Here's how it feels to be a nigger down here."

The three victims hobbled to a black-owned business, where an ambulance was summoned for Reeb. He was initially examined at Selma's black hospital, where doctors lacked proper facilities to treat his fractured skull. The ambulance transported Reeb to Birmingham University Hospital, where physicians diagnosed a blood clot in his brain. Life support machinery kept Reeb alive for two days, until he finally expired at 6:55 p.m. on 11 March. By that time, his presumed killers had already posted bond on an assault charge. They were identified as Elmer Cook (owner of C & C Novelty), R.B. Kelly, and brothers Namon and William Hoggle. Selma's city attorney released the four on modest bail, over strenuous protests from Police Chief Wilson Baker, but their charges were upgraded with Reeb's death. A grand jury indicted Cook and the Hoggles for murder on 13 April, excusing Kelly after he provided evidence against the other three. Local journalists regarded the indictments as a

minor miracle, since Judge James Hare had first treated the panel to a fifty-minute lecture on the plague of civil rights, claiming that U.S. leaders had "selected Selma for assassination back in the fall of 1963." Hare opined that whites had shown "unbelievable restraint" in the face of "fantastic and terroristic" acts by blacks and "self-appointed saints" drawn from the northern clergy. Still the panel recognized its duty. The indictments stood.

Klan involvement in Reeb's murder was never widely publicized, but UKA Imperial Wizard Robert Shelton took the lead in a posthumous propaganda campaign, declaring falsely on 27 March 1965 that Reeb "had been dying of cancer before he ever came to Alabama." Six weeks later, on 5 May, Grand Dragon Robert Creel told klansmen gathered at Bladen Springs that Reeb's corpse had been cremated because it was "rotten with cancer and syphilis." One of Lingo's state troopers, Capt. Lionel Freeman, appeared to justify the killing when he claimed that he saw "two men dressed as priests and four young Negro girls cross U.S. 80" in Selma on 9 March. "The priests were holding hands with two Negro girls each," Freeman said, adding that "[t]he Rev. Reeb was beaten about two or three hours later." FBI informant Gary Rowe provided another Klan link in his description of Viola Liuzzo's murder. Shortly before that shooting on 25 March, he claimed, his "wrecking crew" stopped at the Silver Moon Café for drinks. There, Eugene Thomas saw the Reeb defendants at a nearby table and allegedly introduced them to Rowe as brother klansmen. In parting, Elmer Cook remarked, "God bless you boys. You boys go do your job. I already did mine."

Cook and the Hoggles faced trial in Selma on 7 December 1965, before Judge L.S. Moore. Prosecutor Blanchard McLeod warned reporters in advance that "I don't have a very strong case," but it scarcely mattered. When McLeod questioned prospective jurors en masse, asking whether racial prejudice would hamper their impartial judgment, all but three stood mute. Judge Moore deemed their silence tantamount to a negative answer, and so they were seated, without any questions concerning their ties to the Klan or the Citizens' Council. One witness to the beating was absent from court, having fled to Mississippi, and Judge Moore barred another from testifying on grounds of "mental incompetence." Victims Miller and Olsen identified Elmer Cook as Reeb's club-wielding assailant, while defense attorneys claimed none of their clients were present at the assault. Furthermore, they alleged, Reeb's injuries as diagnosed in Selma were not lethal. By that theory, Reeb's death remained a mystery when jurors retired to deliberate on 10 December. Sheriff Clark dropped by the jury room while the deliberations were in progress, but no record of his comments was preserved. The panel returned after ninety minutes, greeted with applause in court when all three defendants were acquitted.

Authors Harry and Bonaro Overstreet, writing in 1969, claimed that FBI agents arrested the Reeb defendants in Selma for conspiracy to violate their victim's civil rights under the Reconstruction-era Ku Klux Act. While noting that "there were abundant precedents to justify the use of this law," they made no further mention of the case, leaving their readers with a false impression that Reeb's killers were sentenced to federal prison. In fact, there is no record of a federal arrest in Reeb's case. All published sources agree that his attackers were jailed and charged by Selma police, and their only trial—resulting in acquittal—occurred in local court. They never spent a night in jail. Officially, the crime remains unsolved.

Sampson, William *see* Nathan, Michael

Schwerner, Michael

—Michael Schwerner was every klansman's *bête noire,* a liberal Jewish New Yorker whose beard earned him the nickname "Goatee," immersed in Mississippi's "Freedom Summer" campaign of 1964. Already marked for death by leaders of the WKKKKM as the full-scale "invasion" began, Schwerner drove black colleague James Chaney to Oxford, Ohio for a COFO training seminar on 14 June 1964. There, they met volunteer Andrew Goodman, an anthropology student from Queens College in New York City. The trio returned to Meridian, Mississippi, on 20 June, and there learned of the latest Klan atrocity. Four days earlier, a hooded raiding party had attacked the all-black congregation of Mt. Zion Church at Longdale, beating several worshipers before they burned the church. Schwerner, Chaney and Goodman drove to Longdale on 21 June, but they never made it back. Arrested by Deputy Cecil Price in Neshoba County, they were held in jail at Philadelphia while a Klan lynching party gathered. Price released the prisoners after nightfall, then stopped them again outside town and delivered them to his fellow knights. The three were shot, then buried in an earthen dam on a farm owned by klansman Olen Burrage.

President Lyndon Johnson dispatched former CIA boss Allen Dulles to Jackson on 23 June, while the FBI sent an inspector and five more agents to join in the search, code-named "MIBURN" (for "Mississippi Burning"). That same afternoon, Schwerner's burned-out car was found in Neshoba County's Bogue Chitto Swamp. Soon afterward, UKA Imperial Wizard Robert Shelton dropped in for a personal "inspection tour," assuring journalists that "my people will continue the investigation." Meanwhile, FBI headquarters offered rewards ranging from $5,000 to $30,000 for recovery of the three missing men. That bid paid off on 4 August 1964, when G-men equipped with heavy machinery invaded the Burrage farm and unearthed the hidden corpses. FBI technicians soon discovered that Goodman and Schwerner both died from one pistol shot to the chest, while Chaney had been shot three times with a different weapon. Chaney had also suffered other injuries, consistent either with a savage beating or with damage from the bulldozer that uncovered his corpse.

Neshoba County judge O.H. Barnett—a cousin of arch-segregationist ex–Governor Ross Barnett—convened a grand jury to investigate the triple murder in September 1964. FBI agents refused to participate, for reasons explained in a memo of 3 December 1964: "A Klansman judge is unlikely to disqualify himself or to eliminate Klan members as an impediment to service on a grand jury or petit jury." At the same time, a federal grand jury convened in Biloxi. It named no killers, but on 2 October 1964 the panel indicted five lawmen Neshoba County lawmen for brutalizing black prisoners between October 1962 and January 1964. Meanwhile, G-men obtained confessions from two members of the murder party itself. James Jordan cracked in October 1964, claiming he heard but did not see the shoot-

ings. Horace Barnette told a different story, naming Jordan as James Chaney's killer. The other triggerman, he said, was klansman Alton Roberts. Ballistics evidence confirmed the accusation against Jordan. When state authorities refused to indict the killers, federal prosecutors filed conspiracy charges under the Reconstruction-era Ku Klux Act. On 4 December 1964, G-men arrested twenty-one klansmen: ten of those jailed, including Deputy Price, were named as members of the lynching party; the rest were accused of peripheral roles in planning or concealing the crime. U.S. Commissioner Esther Carter set bail for the defendants, then dismissed all charges against them on 12 December, branding Horace Barnette's confession inadmissible "hearsay." A new grand jury in Jackson indicted eighteen defendants on 15 January 1965, but Judge Harold Cox—a Kennedy appointee to the federal bench who once compared black voters in his state to chimpanzees—dismissed the latest felony indictments on 24 February. In a second ruling, issued the following day, Cox held that the defendants should be tried only on misdemeanor charges of inflicting "summary punishment" on the three murder victims "without due process of law." There the matter rested until March 1966, when the U.S. Supreme Court reversed Cox's ruling. A third grand jury reissued conspiracy indictments against nineteen White Knights on 27 February 1967, this time including Sam Bowers among the defendants.

The Neshoba County klansmen finally faced trial in October 1967, with Judge Cox presiding. He ruled that signed confessions from defendants Jordan and Barnette must have all other names removed before they could be read aloud in court. The rude surprise for klansmen came when FBI informants Delmar Dennis and Wallace Miller testified for the prosecution, describing the Klan's plot to kill Michael Schwerner. Turncoat James Jordan also told his version of the murders, while admitting that the FBI had paid $8,000 for his testimony. On 20 October, an all-white jury convicted seven knights (including Imperial Wizard Samuel Bowers, Price and Alton Roberts), acquitted eight, and deadlocked on three. At sentencing, Bowers and Roberts received ten-year prison terms, Price and plotter Billy Posey got six years apiece, while three others received three-year terms. Jordan pled guilty in separate proceedings and was sentenced to four years. The three deadlocked cases were never retried.

Even with convictions on record, Mississippi whites still made excuses for the Klan. Ex-governor Paul Johnson, interviewed in 1970, claimed that Klansmen "did not actually intend to kill those people." He explained:

> What happened was that they had been taken from jail and brought to this particular spot. There were a good many people in the group besides the sheriff and the deputy sheriff and that group. What they were going to do, they were going to hang those three persons up in a big cotton sack and leave them hanging in a tree for about a day and a half, then come out there at night and turn them loose. They thought that they'd more or less scare them off. While they were talking this Negro, the Negro boy from over at Meridian—he seemed to be the ringleader of the three—he was acting kind of smart-aleck, and talking pretty big, and one of the Klansmen walked up behind him and hit him over the head with a trace chain.... The chain came across his head and hit him on the bridge of the

nose and killed him as dead as a nit. After this boy had been killed, then is when they determined, "Well, we've got to dispose of the other two."

Another thirty-five years passed before Mississippi prosecutors filed their first (and only) murder charge in the Neshoba County triple-slaying. In 2005, authorities indicted self-ordained minister Edgar Ray Killen—once exalted cyclops of the White Knights in Meridian and one of three defendants for whom the 1967 jury could reach no verdict—for the murders of Chaney, Goodman and Schwerner. Testimony portrayed "Preacher" Killen as the crime's mastermind, although he was not present at the slayings. On 22 June 2005, jurors convicted Killen on three counts of manslaughter. At sentencing, he received three consecutive twenty-year terms.

Smith, Sandra *see* Nathan, Michael

Waller, Dr. James *see* Nathan, Michael

White, Ben Chester—In April 1966, a handful of klansmen in Adams County, Mississippi, organized a new splinter faction called the Cottonmouth Moccasin Gang. Their purpose was to murder Dr. Martin Luther King, drawn to Mississippi in June 1966, after James Meredith was shot and wounded on his one-man "Walk Against Fear." King vowed to continue the march, while members of the Cottonmouth Moccasin Gang devised a scheme to lure him to Adams County and his death. Their bait was Ben White, an elderly black caretaker on the Carter plantation, near Natchez. On 10 June 1966, Klansmen Ernest Avants, Claude Fuller and James Jones lured White from home, promising payment if he helped them find a missing dog. They drove him into the Homochitto National Forest, then shot him at close range with an automatic rifle and a shotgun. In the process, Fuller shot so many holes in Jones's car that the killers decided to ditch it and set it on fire while Jones told police that it was stolen.

The clumsy ruse failed. White's mangled, nearly headless corpse was pulled from Pretty Creek on 12 June, his many wounds prompting Sheriff Odell Anders to draw a connection to Jones's burned-out, bullet-riddled car. Questioned by deputies on 13 June, Jones failed a polygraph test and spent the night in jail, wracked by pangs of guilt that he was "deep in sin" for his role in the murder. Early next morning, he confessed and named the triggermen. Avants and Fuller were jailed on 14 June, all three defendants charged with first-degree murder. At a preliminary hearing on 17 June, Jones claimed that Fuller had told him White was active in the civil rights movement (a lie) and spoke of "orders from higher ups that the old darky had to go." Jones faced trial first, but despite his confession the jury deadlocked on 10 April 1967, producing a mistrial. Avants was next, in December 1967. Defense attorney Travis Buckley granted that his client fired a shotgun blast into White's head, but argued that the victim was already dead from wounds inflicted by Fuller. Jurors bought the argument and acquitted Avants. Fuller and Jones avoided further prosecution by pleading illness. A quarter-century after the fact, prosecutor Edwin Benoist recalled White's case as "the most atrocious murder and the greatest occurrence of injustice" he had ever seen.

While Avants could not be tried a second time, and state authorities refused to try his two accomplices, there was another avenue of prosecution. White was killed on land owned by the U.S. government, and thus the charges could be tried in federal court without invoking rules of double jeopardy. That fact was known to leaders of the DOJ and FBI, who had jailed many killers on similar charges since the 1920s, yet they ignored White's case for nearly four decades. In the meantime, Jesse White filed suit against his father's killers and the White Knights of the KKK in federal court, seeking monetary damages for wrongful death. Judge Harold Cox ruled in White's favor on 13 November 1968, and a jury awarded the plaintiffs $1,021,500 which they would never collect from the bankrupt defendants. Federal prosecutors finally reopened the White murder case in November 1999, claiming they had no idea the crime had occurred on government land until they were alerted by a broadcast of ABC's popular *20/20* news program, describing unsolved murders from the civil rights era. Reporters accepted that incredible assertion as a new grand jury convened to review the case in February 2000. Klansmen Fuller and Jones were long dead by that time, but the panel indicted Avants on a fresh murder charge. Legal delays postponed his trial until February 2003, when Avants was finally convicted and sentenced to life imprisonment. He died in custody on 14 June 2004.

Womack, Melvin—A black resident of Winter Garden, Florida, Womack was dragged from his home by klansmen who beat and fatally shot him on 31 March 1951. While the slaying was never explained, it followed a pattern of Klan terrorism throughout Florida in the years 1949–51, including several other murders and numerous bombings.

Lynching

Lynching is broadly defined as the extralegal slaying of persons who violate the customs, laws or mores of a particular so-

More than 5,000 blacks died at the hands of lynch mobs like this one between 1882 and 1951. Klansmen often participated in the murders (Library of Congress).

ciety. Most definitions require participation by a "mob" of three or more killers. Reconstruction-era klansmen frequently lynched blacks accused of criminal activity, as well as those who tried to vote or otherwise exercise their newfound civil rights. Some white Republicans, "scalawags" and "carpetbaggers" also suffered lynching, though prominent figures were more likely to be ambushed by lone klansmen or small groups of assassins. It is not true, as some sources suggest, that Klan members committed all (or even most) of the 5,000-plus lynchings recorded in America between 1882 and 1951. "Former" klansmen almost certainly participated in many of the mob scenes recorded between 1873 and 1915, and the August 1915 lynching of Leo Frank in Georgia (described below) was a pivotal event in the modern Klan's revival. Even as the KKK found new modes of violent expression in the twentieth century, however, a latent fondness for lynching remained, demonstrated in cases recorded as recently as 1980 and 1998.

Banks, Parks—A black resident of Yazoo City, Mississippi, Banks quarreled with local klansmen in summer 1922 and ignored subsequent warnings to leave the area. On 22 August, local residents found him hanging from a tree outside of town. A perfunctory police investigation identified no suspects, and the crime remains "unsolved" today.

Byrd, James, Jr.—A black resident of Jasper, Texas, Byrd was walking home from a bridal shower on 7 June 1998 when three white men in a pickup truck offered him a ride. They subsequently beat Byrd and chained him to the truck's rear bumper, then dragged him for some 3,000 yards along a rural road, until his body struck a culvert and was thus beheaded. Three days later, police jailed suspects Shawn Allen Berry, Lawrence Russell Brewer and John William King, all described as ex-convicts with prison ties to the Klan and the Aryan Brotherhood. King and Brewer both displayed racist tattoos, and one media report suggested that the lynching was intended as a KKK initiation ritual. Sheriff Billy Rowles raised hoots of derision from local blacks when he told reporters, "We have no Aryan Nation or KKK in Jasper County." National politicians and civil rights leaders condemned the slaying, while Byrd's family lobbied for passage of new bias-crime legislation, but Republican state legislators rejected the James Byrd, Jr. Hate Crimes Bill because it protected gays and bisexuals, as well as racial and religious minorities. Meanwhile, jurors convicted John King of Byrd's murder on 23 February 1999, and he received a death sentence two days later. Russell Brewer, convicted on 20 September 1999, was likewise sentenced to die. A third jury convicted Shawn Berry on 18 November 1999, but Berry escaped the death penalty, instead receiving a life prison term with no parole for at least forty years.

Cabeza, Manolo—In December 1921, klansmen in Key West, Florida, ran afoul of Manolo Cabeza, a Canary Islander and decorated World War veteran who owned and operated the Red Rooster, a waterfront coffee shop that may also have been a speakeasy. That in itself did not provoke the KKK, since illicit saloons proliferated in Key West. Cabeza went too far, though, when he moved his mistress—a mulatto prostitute—into his

quarters behind the café. On the night of 23 December, five carloads of klansmen dragged Cabeza from home, first beating him with baseball bats when he resisted (unmasking Exalted Cyclops Walter Decker and a Key West policeman), then driving him to the city outskirts where Cabeza was stripped, flogged, tarred and feathered, left with a ruptured kidney and warnings to leave town or die. When interviewed by Sheriff Roland Curry—himself widely regarded as a klansman—Cabeza denied recognizing his assailants. On Christmas Eve, armed with a pistol, he commandeered a taxi and sped off in search of revenge, killing Decker on a public street. Cornered in a downtown building, Cabeza held a Klan posse at bay until Sheriff Curry summoned U.S. Marines from the Key West naval base, finally persuading Cabeza to surrender. The marines stood guard outside Curry's jail until 1:00 a.m., when the sheriff dismissed them. No guards were present when fifteen klansmen entered Cabeza's cell, clubbing him senseless with blackjacks and dragging him behind their car to the nearest palm tree, where he was hanged and riddled with bullets. A grand jury blamed Cabeza for his own lynching, citing his "very bad character" and the "affront to society" he had committed by "living with a Negro woman."

Clarke, Charles—Georgia klansmen removed black rape suspect Charles Clarke from the Morgan County jail and lynched him in 1871.

Darden, Dr. G.O.—Darden was a physician and active Republican in Reconstruction-era Warren County, Georgia. In March 1869, he shot and killed Democratic newspaper editor Charles Wallace in a personal quarrel. Authorities jailed Darden on a murder charge, whereupon masked men dragged him from jail and lynched him. When police jailed six suspects in June 1869, they included klansmen James Cody and his two brothers, John Raley, and A.I. Hartley (Wallace's successor as editor of the racist *Georgia Clipper*). A judge who lacked authority to hear such cases subsequently released all six defendants on a writ of habeas corpus, and none were ever brought to trial.

Dennis, William—A Republican activist in Mississippi during Reconstruction, Dennis survived one Ku Klux attempt on his life before Democrats had him jailed at Meridian in early 1871, for making "incendiary" speeches. Wounded by gunshots at a preliminary court hearing on 6 March, Dennis was held in "protective custody" at the local jail, but his guards withdrew that night, leaving no opposition to klansmen who entered the jail and killed Dennis in his cell.

Donald, Michael—The UKA's most heinous crime since 1965 was the abduction and lynching of nineteen-year-old Michael Donald on 21 March 1981. Donald, a black youth, was kidnapped, beaten and hanged from a tree in downtown Mobile, Alabama, one-half mile from the spot where black prisoner Glenn Diamond suffered a "mock lynching" at the hands of Mobile policemen in 1976. Five years later, following the mistrial of another black defendant charged with killing a policeman in Mobile, agitated klansmen decided to "show Klan strength in Alabama" with a random act of murder. Plucking their victim off the street, the knights questioned Donald concerning his supposed knowledge of the ongoing Atlanta child murders, then beat, strangled and hanged him, leaving their victim with a boot print on his forehead. A cross was burned at Mobile's courthouse the same night, as a Klan "signature" for the lynching.

The crime went unsolved for two years, while local police ignored the Klan and pursued innocent black suspects. Next, District Attorney Chris Galanos sought FBI assistance, but G-men spent their time retracing the same false leads and produced no arrests. Finally, in early 1983, U.S. Attorney Thomas Figueres ordered a new FBI investigation, and agents belatedly noticed the obvious: Donald had been hanged directly opposite a house owned by Bennie Hays, a convicted cattle rustler and grand titan for the UKA in southern Alabama. The tenant was his son, Henry Hays, kligrapp of the Mobile klavern. That "coincidence" led agents to investigate the Mobile Klan, and so the case was broken at long last. Klansman James "Tiger" Knowles pled guilty in federal court to violating Donald's civil rights, while Henry Hays denied any knowledge of the crime. Both were charged with murder on 16 June 1983, while Justice dismissed the federal charge against Hays. Both were convicted at trial, Knowles receiving a sentence of ten years to life for cooperating with the prosecution. Jurors also voted life imprisonment for Hays, but Judge Braxton Kittrell, Jr., took the unusual step of ignoring that recommendation when he sentenced Hays to die. In August 1987, Bennie Hays and klansman Benjamin Cox were indicted as accomplices in Donald's murder. Poor health spared Bennie Hays from trial, but Cox was convicted and sentenced to life in May 1989. With his appeals exhausted, Henry Hays was executed on 7 June 1997.

The case might have ended there, but leaders of the SPLC filed a wrongful-death lawsuit against the UKA, on behalf of grieving mother Beulah Mae Donald. That trial convened on 9 February 1987, with retired FBI informant Gary Rowe on hand to describe the UKA's violent history. Imperial Wizard Robert Shelton and his UKA hierarchy branded the Mobile klavern a violent rogue faction, but SPLC lead attorney Morris Dees produced a 1979 issue of the *Fiery Cross* including a cartoon of a white man advising the reader: "It's terrible the way blacks are being treated! All whites should work to give the blacks what they deserve!" The next page bore a drawing of a black man dangling with a rope around his neck, just as Donald had died. Shelton denied foreknowledge of the cartoon, blaming the magazine's Louisiana editor, then confessed under oath that he had never ordered a retraction. An all-white jury found the UKA responsible for Donald's murder and awarded his mother $7 million in damages. Unable to pay the tab, Shelton surrendered his national headquarters building in lieu of cash.

Fitzpatrick, Henry—A black resident of Tennessee, suspected of burning two barns in 1868, Fitzpatrick received 200 lashes from a gang of klansmen at his home. Apparently unsatisfied with that punishment, the raiders subsequently returned and hanged him.

Frank, Leo—While Leo Frank's lynching occurred before the KKK's rebirth in 1915, it remains a pivotal event in Ku Klux history and paved the way for William Simmons to revive the order with headquarters in Atlanta. Born in Texas (1884) and raised in New York City, Frank was a member of Atlanta's Jewish community who ran a local pencil factory. Mary Phagan joined the factory workforce in 1909, at age nine, and remained on the job four years later. On 26 April 1913 (Confederate Memorial Day), she visited the factory to claim her weekly paycheck and never returned home. Newt Lee, the plant's black night watchman, called police to report discovery of her body at 3:00 a.m. on 27 April. She had been strangled with a length of cord, and genital bleeding suggested rape. Clumsy detectives ruined vital bits of evidence, including bloody fingerprints, and discounted a bloody shirt found at Newt Lee's apartment, along with two notes at the crime scene allegedly written by Phagan, accusing a "Negro" of the crime. Instead of jailing Lee, as might have been expected from the all-white force, officers soon focused on Frank instead.

The "evidence" against him was weak, to say the least. Detectives deemed Frank "nervous" when they called at his home before dawn on 27 April and took him to view Phagan's corpse at the plant. A teenage friend of Phagan's claimed that Frank had frightened her by "flirting" with her, while brothel madam Nina Formby told police that Frank had called her on 26 April, seeking a place to dispose of Phagan's body. (She later fled to New York and recanted, accusing Atlanta police of plying her with cash and liquor to obtain false statements.) When Frank hired Pinkerton detectives to prove him innocent, local bigots called the action "sinister." On 1 May 1913, factory watchman E.F. Holloway found black janitor Jim Conley washing a shirt at the plant, and told police when Conley tried to hide it. Conley subsequently lied to police about his criminal record (including the attempted murder of his common-law wife), prompting Holloway to state that he was "thoroughly convinced" that Conley "strangled Mary Phagan while about half drunk." When that news hit front pages in Atlanta, Conley hastily accused Frank of coaching him to write the notes police had found near Phagan's corpse, further claiming that Frank paid him $200 to hide a bloody shirt in Newt Lee's flat. (When police asked where the money was, Conley said Frank had changed his mind and "took it back.") Meanwhile, two independent witnesses cast doubt on Conley's statements. Carnival worker Will Green had played craps with Conley on 26 April, but fled when Conley voiced his intent to rob a white girl passing by. Insurance salesman William Mincey met Conley drunk on the street, that afternoon, and heard him say, "I have killed one today and do not wish to kill another."

Frank subsequently refused to confront Conley without his lawyer present, a circumstance which only aggravated police suspicions. A grand jury indicted Frank for Phagan's murder on 23 May 1913, and his trial began on 28 July. Frank produced numerous alibi witnesses in court, while Conley revised his ever-changing story once again, adding lurid tales of Frank's alleged sexcapades at the factory. Outside the courtroom, demagogue (and future U.S. Senator) Tom Watson whipped white Atlanta into an anti–Semitic frenzy with editorials describing a vast Jewish conspiracy to rape Gentile females. Even Frank's defense attorney, in his closing arguments, lapsed into racism, denouncing Conley as "a plain, beastly, drunken, filthy, lying nigger with a spreading nose through which probably tons of cocaine has been sniffed." Jurors convicted Frank of murder, and the judge condemned him to hang. Georgia's supreme court rejected Frank's appeal in November 1913, and the U.S. Supremc Court likewise dcnied his appeal in April 1915, by a vote of seven to two.

Tom Watson, meanwhile was busily at work in Georgia, warning via his *Jeffersonian* magazine that "[i] f Frank's rich connections keep on lying about this case, SOMETHING BAD WILL HAPPEN." When Jim Conley's lawyer, William Smith, cast doubt on his own client's innocence, a *Jefferson* headline warned: "LET W.M. SMITH BE CAREFUL!" After Governor John Slaton commuted Frank's sentence to life imprisonment, Watson wrote: "Our grand old Empire State HAS BEEN RAPED! ... Jew money has debased us, bought us, and sold us—and laughs at us ... Hereafter, let no man reproach the South with Lynch law: let him remember the unendurable provocation; and let him say whether Lynch law is not better than no law at all." Armed mobs attacked Slaton's mansion three times, repelled by state militia forces, but no soldiers were present when self-styled Knights of Mary Phagan removed Frank from a rural prison farm and lynched him on 17 August 1915. Watson subsequently praised the lynchers and called for "another Ku Klux Klan ... to restore HOME RULE." Two months later, Frank's lynchers staged the first American cross-burning atop Stone Mountain, outside Atlanta, and most of them subsequently joined the newly-chartered Klan under Imperial Wizard William Simmons.

New doubts concerning Frank's guilt surfaced in 1982, when Alonzo Mann, Frank's former office boy, accused John Conley of the murder. According to Mann's statement, he saw Conley carrying Phagan's body to the factory basement on 26 April 1915, but Conley had threatened to kill him if he told police. Thus terrified, Mann kept his story secret even after Conley died in 1962. Georgia's Board of Pardons and Paroles denied Frank a posthumous pardon in 1983, then reversed itself and pardoned him in 1986 (a year after Mann himself died).

High, Zeke—A black resident of Reconstruction-era Livingston, Alabama, High killed a white man who invaded his home during the Klan-led riots of October 1870. Charged with murder, he spent nearly a year in jail before klansmen lynched him in September 1871.

Luke, William C.—A "carpetbag" member of the American Missionary Association and schoolmaster at Cross Plains, Alabama, during Reconstruction, Luke became a target for klansmen who opposed black education. In early 1871, local police jailed Luke and four black teacher's aides on trumped-up charges, holding them in jail until a Ku Klux lynching party arrived and murdered all four prisoners. Before his death, Luke was allowed to write a letter to his wife and six children, later read before Congress in support of the new Ku Klux Act.

Outlaw, Wyatt—A black resident of Reconstruction-era Alamance County, North Carolina, Outlaw led the local Union League and won election to the Graham town council as a Republican. Local klansmen marked him for death, snatching Outlaw from his home on the night of 26 February 1870 and hanging him from a tree near the county courthouse. A note left by the lynchers at the home of Graham's mayor threatened him

with a similar fate. Federal authorities indicted eighteen klansmen for Outlaw's murder, including county chief Jacob Long, but none were ever brought to trial.

Smith, George W.—A New York native and former officer in the Union Army, Smith settled in Jefferson, Texas, after the Civil War. He befriended local blacks, recruiting them for the Republican Party, and with their support was chosen as a delegate to the 1868 state constitutional convention. Smith's political activities marked him as a target for the Klan-allied KRS, and police jailed him in Jefferson on 3 October 1868, after Smith traded shots with would-be assassins. KRS members invaded the jail on 4 October, intent on lynching Smith, but he killed one attacker and frightened the others enough that they compromised by riddling him with bullets in his cell.

Williams, James—A black militia captain in Reconstruction-era York County, South Carolina, Williams resigned from his post in early 1871, but the move came too late to save him from Ku Klux assassins. A party of klansmen snatched Williams from his home on 6 March and hanged him from a nearby tree, sparking a riot by members of his former militia company. Those soldiers initially threatened to massacre local whites in retaliation for the lynching, but their officers restrained them short of further bloodshed.

Pogroms and Riots

Mob violence in the form of riots is a staple part of American history. In many such cases, two hostile groups clash and do battle over issues that inflame both sides. Prior to the 1940s, however, most racially motivated riots in the United States were primarily white massacres of nonwhite victims, including Asians, blacks, Hispanics and Native Americans. The term *pogrom*—Russian for "devastation"—initially applied to state-sponsored slaughter of Jews under Russia's nineteenth-century tsars, but it is equally appropriate for many of the mob outbursts against nonwhites that stain the fabric of U.S. history. Klansmen have joined in many riots and pogroms since the order was reorganized in 1867. Indeed, riots by white Democrats against blacks and Republicans were a standard feature of southern elections between 1868 and 1876. In October 1919, vigilantes at Elaine, Arkansas, slaughtered more than 100 blacks who had the temerity to "meddle" in politics. A representative sampling of Klan-led pogroms and riots is offered below, with the events listed chronologically.

1868—Camilla, Georgia: On 19 September 1868, a Republican rally in this small southwestern Georgia town—the seat of Mitchell County—drew a large crowd of freedmen to hear political speeches. That, in turn, caused alarm among some local whites. Klansmen and their sympathizers quickly organized a "posse" with the county sheriff at its head and launched a day-long "nigger hunt," claiming the lives of at least seven blacks and leaving thirty to forty others wounded. Six whites reportedly suffered minor injuries during the pogrom.

1870—Eutaw, Alabama: On 24 October 1870, some 2,000 freedmen turned out for a Republican rally in Eutaw, the seat of Greene County. Klansmen and other racists gathered to heckle the speakers, then opened fire into the crowd without provocation, killing four blacks and wounding fifty more. Two whites reportedly suffered minor injuries when their victims struck back in self defense.

1871—Meridian, Mississippi: On 4 March 1871, police in Meridian jailed three Republicans for making "incendiary" speeches to local blacks. The prisoners included GOP activist William Dennis, Aaron Moore (a black state legislator), and Warren Tyler (a white teacher at a school for blacks). Klansmen, including some from nearby Alabama, packed the courtroom for their preliminary hearing on 6 March. When Tyler's attorney called on him to refute the testimony of white prosecution witness James Brantley, Brantley rushed Tyler with a raised walking stick and gunshots rang out in the court. The first volley killed Judge Bramlette and two black spectators, while wounding Tyler, Dennis, and several others. Friends of Tyler carried him from court and tried to hide him at a nearby home, but klansmen tracked him down and riddled him with bullets. Police placed William Dennis in "protective custody," but his guards withdrew at nightfall, thus permitting klansmen to invade the jail and kill him in his cell. Mobs roamed Meridian for several days, killing and mutilating blacks at random. They failed to capture Aaron Moore, who had escaped from court and town unharmed, but burned his home instead. In April 1871, a grand jury indicted six defendants on charges of unlawful assembly and assault with intent to kill. White jurors acquitted all six, but one Alabama klansman was convicted of raping a black woman during the riot. Subsequent state and federal investigations failed to produce further charges.

1871—Clinton, South Carolina: Racial tension simmered in Laurens County throughout summer and early autumn 1871, as klansmen terrorized blacks to prevent them from voting in state elections on 19 October. Authorities in Laurensville, the county seat, were braced for trouble on election day, but white marauders staged their assault on the polls at Clinton, ten miles to the east. They drove off a state constable, stationed there as an observer, and while he mustered a company of black militia to restore order, those troops withdrew on the morning of 20 October. Their departure was the signal for a general massacre of freedmen and "radicals." By 22 October, an estimated 2,500 armed whites had joined in scouring Clinton and environs. The official casualty report listed a dozen dead, including black state legislator Wade Perrin and a newly elected (white) probate judge.

1873—Colfax, Louisiana: After the Reconstruction-era Klan and KWC officially disbanded in Louisiana, a paramilitary White League arose in their place, plotting to recapture the state government for white-supremacist "home rule." On 13 April 1873, members of the White League ambushed a black militia company, killing at least 100 men. Fully half of those were executed after they surrendered, in a brutal massacre. Three members of the White League lost their lives in the lop-sided "battle," which local Democrats proclaimed a heroic victory. Several whites were subsequently convicted and sentenced to

prison under provisions of the Ku Klux Act, but the U.S. Supreme Court reversed their convictions in 1876. The ruling in that case (*United States v. Cruikshank*) decreed that only state officials could be charged with conspiring to deny freedmen their civil rights. Private terrorists, acting without official sanction, were henceforth immune to prosecution under federal law. That rule remained in force until 1965, when it was reversed to punish a new generation of nightriders.

1921—Tulsa, Oklahoma: Klansmen were organized in Tulsa by 1917, as the Knights of Liberty, and the city harbored at least 6,000 knights during the early 1920s. Many of those enthusiastically joined in Tulsa's "race war" of 31 May to 1 June 1921. Violence erupted after Dick Rowland, a black shoe-shiner, was jailed on charges of assaulting Sarah Page, a white woman. White mobs subsequently invaded the Greenwood ghetto—locally known as the "Black Wall Street"—killing blacks at random, while arsonists burned 1,256 homes, 31 restaurants, 24 grocery stores, 12 churches, 8 doctors' offices, 5 hotels, 4 pharmacies, a hospital, a public library, and the new Dunbar School. During the course of the pogrom, raiders also fired gunshots and dropped explosive charges from airplanes circling overhead. Governor James Robertson declared martial law and dispatched National Guard units, which apparently arrested only blacks, herding their captives into a baseball stadium. Estimates of the final body count range from thirty-six (the official tally: nine whites and twenty-six blacks) to 250 or more. Red Cross physicians treated 531 injured persons during the pogrom, of whom only 48 were white. No whites were ever charged with any crimes related to the rioting; a grand jury indicted fifty-seven blacks, but only one was tried, receiving a thirty-day sentence for carrying a concealed weapon. Police Chief John Gustafson—himself described by one historian as a probable klansman—was later suspended from office, then convicted on charges of negligence and corruption. Fifty years after the fact, two ex-klansmen publicly lamented their part in the massacre. Another told historian Ed Wheeler, ""If it hadn't been for the soldiers, we would have killed every goddamn nigger in the city." If necessary, the aging klansman declared, "I would do it again."

1923—Rosewood, Florida: In the early 1920s, few white Floridians were consciously aware of Rosewood, a mostly-black community in Levy County, located three miles from all-white Sumner. The two towns coexisted peacefully for some three-quarters of a century, but all that changed on New Year's morning 1923, when Fannie Taylor (a white Sumner resident) alleged that she had been assaulted by an unknown black man. Mrs. Taylor never said that her assailant hailed from Rosewood and she made no claim of rape, although she likewise never contradicted others who embellished her report with allegations of a sexual assault. Sheriff Robert Walker, alerted on New Year's Eve to the escape of black convict Jesse Hunter, leaped to the conclusion that the fugitive must be responsible for Mrs. Taylor's injuries. Bloodhounds led a hastily assembled posse to the Rosewood home of Aaron Carrier, a black war veteran whom the mob abducted and tortured until he blamed local blacksmith Sam Carter for the attack on Mrs. Taylor. Sheriff Walker then transported Carrier to jail, while his posse went on to lynch Carter.

Thus far, Ku Klux involvement in the violence remains conjectural. One published report described the original mob as Klan-led, and a participant in the mayhem later recalled that the KKK was "big in Cedar Key," one of four nearby towns whose white men were summoned to join Sheriff Walker's posse. In any case, whether klansmen joined in Sam Carter's lynching or not, most accounts agree that they were actively involved in what transpired over the next six days, some driving all the way from Georgia to "protect white womanhood."

Sumner was quiet on Tuesday, 2 January, but Wednesday brought rumors that Rosewood's blacks were hiding Jesse Hunter and threatening retaliation for Carter's lynching. The stories focused on Sylvester Carrier, cousin of Aaron, who had a history of defying local racists. After nightfall on 4 January, a white mob surrounded Carrier's home, demanding his surrender. When Sylvester refused, the mob opened fire, killing his mother and wounding two others inside the house. Two whites were killed by gunfire as they rushed the house, and at least four others were wounded before the mob fell back in disarray, torching a church and several empty houses as they fled. A call went out from Sumner, seeking reinforcements to suppress the "black rebellion." Racists from around the state answered the summons, but Sheriff Walker rejected Governor Cary Hardee's offer of National Guardsmen, claiming that he "feared no further disorder." On 5 January, a mob of some 250 stormed Sylvester Carrier's home, now abandoned, and burned it to the ground. From there, the hunters fanned out, torching more homes and churches, shooting widow Lexie Gordon as she fled her burning house. While most of Rosewood's population hid in nearby woods and swamps, no black was safe in Levy County. Most of Rosewood was burned by 6 January, while random acts of violence continued over the next two weeks.

Rosewood's final death toll is disputed to the present day. In 1994, state investigators tabulated eight fatalities, six of them black, but there is reason to mistrust their calculation. A black survivor from the 5 January shootout recalled stepping over "a pile of white bodies" when she fled the Carrier home, and while that may have been wishful thinking, reports of a higher death toll among blacks are less easily dismissed. One riot participant from Cedar Key claimed that twenty-seven blacks were killed, and the *St. Petersburg Times* quoted another white witness who saw "nearly twenty" black corpses (including several infants) buried in a single mass grave. Rosewood survivors, for their part, referred to forty dead or more, one report claiming that "close to a hundred" died in the pogrom.

1956—Tuscaloosa, Alabama: After a three-year court
battle, black coed Autherine Lucy was finally admitted to the University of Alabama at Tuscaloosa on 1 February 1956. Klansmen burned four crosses on campus that night, but no violence erupted until 3 February, after Lucy's first day of classes. That night, white students led by sophomore Leonard Wilson joined adult members of the KKK and Citizens' Council on campus, chanting racist rhymes while they pelted Lucy's dormitory with eggs and stones. Police arrested four rioters, including Birmingham klansman Robert Chambliss (later sentenced to life imprisonment for a fatal church bombing). Their charges were later

Klansmen and students rioted against Autherine Lucy's admission to the University of Alabama in 1956 (Library of Congress).

dismissed, while Chambliss and company filed a $4 million lawsuit against Lucy and the NAACP (likewise dismissed). Encouraged by Klan leader Asa Carter, Leonard Wilson subsequently founded a Citizens' Council chapter in Tuscaloosa, including many of the campus rioters among its members. Forty years later, Wilson resurfaced as a national director of the racist CCC.

1960—Jacksonville, Florida: After six months of sit-
in demonstrations in various southern cities, black protesters brought their movement to Jacksonville in mid–August 1960. Klansmen met on 23 August to plan their response, then turned out en masse on Saturday, 27 August to meet demonstrators with force. An estimated 3,000 white men crowded downtown Jacksonville that morning, purchasing every baseball bat and axe handle available for sale in local stores. Police Chief Luther Reynolds withdrew his officers from the area, while klansmen assaulted black protesters, injuring fifty and driving the rest back to "Niggertown." (Reporters dubbed the riot "Axe-handle Saturday.") By sundown, two dozen klansmen and sixty-odd blacks were in jail. Mayor Haydon Burns blamed the violence on outsiders, while Chief Reynolds insisted that "all the fellows we arrested were local boys." White rioters left jail after paying fines as low as ten dollars, while the stiffest punishment—ninety days, after a jailhouse beating by white inmates—was reserved for a black college student who planned the sit-ins.

1961—Athens, Georgia: Located seventy miles north-
west of Atlanta, Athens is the seat of Georgia's largest state university, and so made a natural target for black activists during the civil rights era. On 11 January 1961, a riotous crowd formed on campus to block the court-ordered enrollment of two black students. Grand Dragon Calvin Craig and other klansmen distributed literature to the mob, then remained to join in the ensuing riot. Eight of the sixteen rioters jailed by police that day were self-acknowledged klansmen. As at the University of Alabama five years earlier, the violence prompted university administrators to suspend their new black students "for their physical safety," but incidents continued. On 15 January, an armed man roamed the campus, asking for one of the black students by name, until

security guards disarmed him. Four days later, a grand jury indicted two students and eight adults from Atlanta (including the eight klansmen previously arrested) on riot-related charges. None served jail time, but thirteen students were expelled or suspended for participating in the violence. The two black students were subsequently reinstated by court order.

1961—Alabama Freedom Rides:

The "freedom ride" concept did not originate in 1961. Fifteen years earlier, on 3 June 1946, the U.S. Supreme Court's ruling in *Morgan v. Virginia* had banned segregated seating on interstate buses and trains. The Congress of Racial Equality (CORE) dispatched sixteen volunteers on an integrated "Journey of Reconciliation" in April 1947, but the effort drew little attention. In June 1950, the court's judgment in *Henderson v. the United States* ordered desegregation of railway dining cars, but Presidents Truman and Eisenhower balked at supporting federal legislation to enforce the rulings, and segregation remained firmly in place below the Mason-Dixon Line. Protests were belatedly triggered on 5 December 1960, when ex-klansman Hugo Black announced the court's ruling in *Boynton v. Virginia*. That decision expanded the *Morgan* rule to bus and train terminals, barring segregation in waiting rooms, restaurants and restrooms. By New Year's Day, CORE leaders were planning a fresh wave of demonstrations to test the court's latest decision.

In Birmingham, Alabama, police commissioner Eugene "Bull" Connor and his allies in the Klan stood ready to defend the color line. On 4 May 1961, as thirteen freedom riders boarded their buses in Washington, D.C., klansman (and FBI informant) Gary Rowe was summoned to a meeting with Sgt. Tom Cook and Birmingham detective W.W. "Red" Self. The officers warned Rowe of "a group of niggers and whites coming into the state of Alabama on what was to be a so-called Freedom Ride." Cook wanted klansmen to waylay the riders on arrival. Rowe quoted Cook as saying, "I don't give a damn if you beat them, bomb them, murder or kill them. I don't give a shit. We don't ever want to see another nigger ride on the bus into Birmingham again." That evening, the klansmen were told to stay alert and

John Lewis (left) and James Zwerg were among the freedom riders beaten by Alabama klansmen in May 1961 (Library of Congress).

"remain in close touch with their telephones." Rowe later testified that he arranged other meetings between Connor, Cook, Grand Dragon Robert Shelton and Grand Titan Hubert Page. Cook and Connor visited Atlanta on 11 May, to gather more intelligence on the Freedom Ride itinerary, and Shelton's klansmen held another meeting that night, to plan details of their "intervention." At that meeting, Page ordered his knights to stay away from the Greyhound bus depot when demonstrators arrived on 14 May. A team of sixty men hand-picked by Shelton would attack the riders, Page explained, during a fifteen-minute grace period granted by Connor. A message was conveyed from the police commissioner himself: "By God, if you are going to do this thing, do it right." Specifically, Connor instructed that the demonstrators should be beaten until they "looked like a bulldog got hold of them," then stripped of their clothes and chased from the depot—where police would charge them with indecent exposure. Klansmen were warned to leave their membership cards and unlicensed pistols at home. Any knights who overstayed their welcome and wound up in jail were guaranteed light sentences.

Gary Rowe was chosen as a squad leader, to coordinate the assaults. When informed of the Connor-Klan conspiracy, Rowe's FBI contact allegedly replied, "Jesus Christ, I can't believe this. This could never be allowed to happen. The American people would never stand for this." The G-man vowed to "get five thousand marshals or ten thousand troops in here, if necessary. We've got the 82nd Airborne, the 101st Airborne. We can pull more damn people in here than the Klan ever heard of. The Old Man [Director J. Edgar Hoover] will not allow this to go down." In fact, Hoover had known of Cook's ties to the Klan since 5 May, at the latest. On 12 May, he received a telex from the Birmingham field office, detailing the Klan's riot plan. One day later, Clement McGowan—chief of the FBI's civil rights section—ordered Birmingham to warn police chief Jamie Moore "that apparently several groups are interested in the arrival of the CORE party ... and there could be some violence." The warning should be couched in "general terms," McGowan said, with no specific mention of the KKK or any particular bus depot. No

Klansmen burned this "freedom ride" bus outside Anniston, Alabama, in May 1961 (Library of Congress).

information should be shared with Connor personally, since "we have to be careful to protect our informant and be alert to any possible 'trap.'" (Police in Anniston, sixty-six miles east of Birmingham, received a similar warning, devoid of details.) G-men apparently trusted Moore, a graduate of the FBI National Academy, to do his duty in spite of Connor, but their faith was misplaced. At 9:30 p.m. on 13 May, Moore called Agent Jenkins to say that he was leaving town, to visit family for Mother's Day. Moore left Tom Cook in charge, thereby effectively ceding control to the Klan.

CORE's team met only intermittent opposition in the first week of its odyssey. One rider was arrested at Charlotte, North Carolina, on 8 May; another was assaulted at Rock Hill, South Carolina, on 10 May; and two more were briefly jailed at Winnsboro, South Carolina, the same afternoon. By 14 May, when they left Atlanta bound for Birmingham, their numbers had swelled and the riders occupied two buses, one Greyhound and one Trailways. Atlanta's FBI office cabled Birmingham at 11:59 a.m. on 14 May, reporting that the first busload of riders should arrive by 3:30 p.m., with the second (Trailways) scheduled to reach Birmingham at 4:05. The Greyhound met a mob led by klansman Kenneth Adams at Anniston, bashing the bus with clubs and slashing at its tires with knives. The driver fled, pursued by a caravan of forty or fifty cars, but two of his tires went flat a few miles west of town. Surrounded, the riders huddled in the bus until one klansman pitched a firebomb through a window and set it ablaze. State Trooper Eli Cowling held the would-be lynchers at bay, firing shots over their heads until the mob dispersed. The riders were hospitalized for smoke inhalation, while their bus burned down to a blackened skeleton at roadside.

The Trailways bus reached Anniston an hour later, and found the Klan waiting. FBI agents and at least three local policemen watched the knights rush aboard, assaulting the riders and beating one—Walter Bergman—so severely that he suffered permanent brain damage. One smiling officer boarded the bus and told klansmen, "Don't worry about no lawsuits. I ain't seen a thing." The bus pulled out with eight knights still aboard, escorted by four police cars. Word flashed ahead to Birmingham, where Agent Jenkins telephoned Tom Cook and told him that the bus was on its way—this despite standing orders from Washington that G-men should furnish "information relating to racial matters ... only to reliable law enforcement officials and agencies." Cook wasted no time in alerting the Klan and National States Rights Party (whose contingent, led by Jesse Stoner and Ed Fields, had turned up uninvited for the party).

The Anniston ambush derailed Connor's initial plan in Birmingham. Despite the selection of a sixty-man strike team, eyewitnesses on 14 May describe 150 to 1,000 klansmen milling around the Greyhound depot by 3:00 p.m., across the street from City Hall. Tom Cook kept a phone line open for Gary Rowe at headquarters and made "a number of trips back and forth" to the Greyhound terminal, according to *Birmingham News* editor John Bloomer. After the Greyhound bus was burned at Anniston, Cook briefed Rowe on the incident and ordered klansmen to wait for the next load of riders. He signed off with "Give 'em hell," apparently still unaware that the remaining target was a Trailways bus. At 4:00 p.m., an unknown man—identified by

Rowe as a policeman—turned up at the Greyhound station, barking orders for the knights assembled there to rally at the Trailways depot. When the hijacked bus arrived at 4:15, klansmen were waiting for the demonstrators, wielding blackjacks, pipes, and leaded baseball bats. Gary Rowe waded in with the rest, beating riders and bystanders alike. His known victims included George Webb, a black man unconnected to the freedom riders, and a photographer from the Birmingham *Post-Herald*, whose camera Rowe smashed. Rowe was clubbing an unidentified black woman when Red Self arrived to warn him that the Klan's fifteen minutes were up. Retreating from the depot, Rowe and fellow knights attacked Clancy Lake, news director for a local radio station, and pummeled several blacks who were writing down the license numbers of Klan vehicles. In parting, Detective Self thanked Rowe and company for doing "a good job."

On Monday morning, Tom Cook telephoned Rowe and thanked him for doing "a goddamn good job down there. People [will] always love you for it." Unfortunately for Rowe, when he broke the *Post-Herald* photographer's camera he had not exposed its film. The paper ran a front-page picture of the riot, with a chunky klansman who resembled Gary Rowe in the thick of the action. Rowe's handler was furious, allegedly raging, "The Old Man's going to shit. He's going to climb the wall." When Rowe admitted that he was the subject in the photo, his contact replied, "Just think very carefully. Who else does that look like besides you?" Thus prodded, Rowe fingered a brother knight, Charles "Arnie" Cagle. "That's it," his handler said. "Cagle. To the day you die, if you're ninety-nine damn years old, I don't care who asks you—if the director comes down and looks you in the eyes and says, 'Goddamnit, Gary Thomas Rowe, Jr., I know that's you'—you're going to look him in the eye and say, 'No, sir. That's not me. That's Arnie Cagle.'" In a wire to FBI headquarters, Agent Jenkins told Hoover that Rowe "advised he was not personally involved in the fighting at the Trailways bus depot," and that Rowe had merely "obtained film from photographers' cameras peacefully and without incident." The bureau later gave Rowe fifty dollars for the doctor's tab and provided another $150 "for services rendered."

The action shifted northward to Montgomery on 20 May 1961. Once again, G-men warned authorities that freedom riders were on their way—and once again, police did nothing to prevent mayhem. At least 200 thugs were waiting when the bus arrived, reenacting the Birmingham riot while police commissioner L.B. Sullivan watched from his car, telling reporters, "We have no intention of standing guard for a bunch of troublemakers coming into our city." Ten minutes into the riot, police straggled onto the scene and watched from the sidelines. The mob, grown to at least a thousand by that time, turned from the freedom riders to assault black bystanders and journalists. Floyd Mann, the state's public safety director, flashed his pistol to protect two victims, but most were not so fortunate. When Mann asked a patrolman why Commissioner Sullivan had not summoned more police, the officer replied, "The men he would send out probably would join the mob." John Siegenthaler, a Justice Department attorney dispatched by Robert Kennedy, was clubbed unconscious in full view of FBI agents—who did nothing. He lay on the pavement while Sullivan told newsmen that "every white ambulance in town reported their vehicles had broken down." Finally, after an hour and fifteen minutes, police reinforcements and sheriff's deputies arrived to disperse the rioters with tear gas. The only persons arrested were a white couple, Fred and Anna Gach, jailed for "disorderly conduct" after shielding riot victims from their attackers.

After the Birmingham riot, FBI agents questioned various local klansmen. Without exception, the knights claimed their presence at the bus depot on Mother's Day was mere coincidence. Photos disproved that lie, but no federal charges were filed. Local police made a face-saving move on 16 May, bypassing Shelton's Alabama Knights to arrest three members of the U.S. Klans. A fourth knight—the proverbial "outside agitator" from Rome, Georgia—was charged on 26 May with beating a reporter. The defendants paid fines and received short jail terms for disorderly conduct, while more serious charges of assault with intent to murder were dismissed. Meanwhile, on 21 May, Assistant Attorney General William Orrick complained to Robert Kennedy about the FBI's negligence in Montgomery. Within an hour of that call, Montgomery's agent-in-charge promised Orrick "eager cooperation"—if he would stop criticizing the bureau. Early next morning, agents began arresting klansmen for the Anniston bus-burning, under a federal statute banning destruction of vehicles used in interstate commerce. A federal grand jury indicted nine knights on 1 September 1961. Two cases were soon dismissed, leaving seven defendants to face trial in October. On 3 November 1961, alleged ringleader Kenneth Adams was acquitted, while the judge declared a mistrial for his codefendants. Juror Lewis Parker was jailed for perjury on 28 November, for falsely denying Klan membership when he was picked for the panel. At their second trial, in January 1962, six defendants were convicted. Judge Hobart Grooms placed five on probation, subject to severance of all Klan ties, while defendant Robert Couch received a one-year prison term, concurrent with an outstanding burglary sentence. The convictions encouraged Governor Patterson to distance himself from the KKK. An FBI informant told headquarters that the governor advised one knight, "You need not think that because you all supported me you can take the law into your own hands. I'm going to start arresting you every time you get out of line and start causing trouble."

While the Anniston case wound its way through the courts, Justice attorney John Doar sought a federal injunction barring Alabama klansmen and police from conspiring against freedom riders. Doar's suit was filed before Judge Frank Johnson, a longtime Klan opponent who lived under guard from U.S. marshals. Tom Cook advised Robert Shelton to duck subpoenas for the hearing, scheduled to begin on 26 May 1961, but process servers traced the dragon to his lair. In court, Shelton drew a warning for evasive answers, then admitted knowing various Mother's Day conspirators, including Ken Adams, Hubert Page and Robert Thomas. Johnson ultimately banned three Ku Klux factions—the Alabama Knights, the Federated Knights and U.S. Klans—from interfering with the Freedom Rides. Also named in the injunction were Shelton, Grand Dragon Alvin Horn (of the U.S. Klans), Commissioner L.B. Sullivan and his police chief. Doar claimed the lawmen had "deliberately failed to take

measures to insure the safety of the students and to prevent unlawful acts and violence upon their persons."

Doar sought a similar injunction against Bull Connor and Chief Moore in Birmingham, but Judge Johnson dismissed them from the lawsuit on 30 May 1961. That decision was prompted in part by Agent Jenkins, who defended Connor on the witness stand, swearing that klansmen and police had not conspired to mob the Trailways bus on 14 May; he was not asked, and did not volunteer, Rowe's information that a plot was hatched against the *Greyhound* riders. Connor's case was strengthened by affidavits from two patrolmen, allegedly detailed to the Greyhound depot area at 3:00 p.m. on Mother's Day. The officers described a 4:15 radio alert reporting "a fight in progress" at the Trailways terminal, followed by announcements that two cars assigned to that district "were tied up." A time-stamped dispatch record indicated that other cars were sent to the Trailways depot "two minutes after the call was received." Outside the hearing room, Chief Moore told reporters, "There was no prearrangement [with the Klan] that I know of. Bull was certainly not in sympathy with those people, but he wouldn't shirk his duty." Neither Johnson nor the press were privy to comments from another Birmingham patrolman, who recalled his lieutenant's orders to remain at least six blocks distant from the Greyhound depot on Mother's Day. "If a call goes out to go to the bus station," he was told, "you don't hear it."

Fifteen years after the Mother's Day riot, Rowe appeared as a witness before the U.S. Senate's Church Committee, describing his work for the bureau. Those revelations prompted freedom riders Walter Bergman and James Peck to sue the FBI in 1983, charging that Hoover's agents knew about the ambush in advance and were responsible for failing to prevent it. The plaintiffs won their case in February 1984, with federal judge Richard Enslen finding that the freedom riders had faced a "statewide conspiracy and official involvement" in 1961. The court awarded Bergman $45,000 in damages, while Peck received $25,000.

1962—Oxford, Mississippi: On 25 June 1962, a federal court ordered the University of Mississippi—"Ole Miss," at Oxford—to admit James Meredith as its first black student. Governor Ross Barnett earned a contempt citation that same afternoon, followed by Lieutenant Governor Paul Johnson on 26 September, before the way was cleared for Meredith's admission on 30 September 1962. Outside agitators quickly seized upon the Oxford crisis, but they weren't the blacks and Reds depicted in segregationist propaganda. In Alabama, Imperial Wizard Robert Shelton huddled with officers of the UKA, declaring that Meredith's admission to Ole Miss might launch "another War Between the States." The UKA's leaders decided "that if they went to Mississippi to help defend Ole Miss, they would be armed and ready to fight." A "standby alert" flashed across the South, via telephone and CB radio, warning all UKA members to arm themselves and be ready to move on command from Tuscaloosa. Two crosses blazed on campus the night of 26 September, and Shelton's first "observers" reached Oxford the following day, joined by a team of nineteen Klansmen from northeastern Louisiana. In the meantime, another call to arms had

gone out nationwide, this one broadcast by a self-styled patriot in Texas.

Major General Edwin Walker had commanded U.S. troops assigned to protect the first black students at Little Rock's Central High School, in 1957. He performed that duty in a professional manner, but the experience seems to have unhinged his mind. Four years later, he resigned from the army after his superiors reprimanded him for indoctrinating his troops with far-right literature. In civilian life, Walker served as a paid orator for the John Birch Society, espousing doctrines so bizarre that even William Simmons of the Citizens' Councils branded him an extremist. Now, on 26 September 1962, Walker told a national radio audience, "It is time to make a move.... We have listened and we have been pushed around by the anti–Christ Supreme Court. It's time to rise. To make a stand beside Governor Ross Barnett at Jackson, Mississippi. He is showing the way. Now is the time to be heard. Ten thousand strong from every state in the nation. Rally to the cause of freedom. The battle cry of the Republic: Barnett, yes! Castro, no! Bring your flag, your tent and your skillet. It's now or never! I have been on the other side in such situations in a place called Little Rock, and I was on the wrong side. This time I will be in Jackson, Mississippi, on the right side."

Faulty geography aside, Walker's summons struck a responsive chord. Overnight, Barnett's office was flooded with telegrams and phone calls from militant racists, offering to "bring our guns and fight." FBI offices around the country logged tips on armed groups gathering as far away as southern California. L.P. Davis, head of the Gentilly, Louisiana Citizen's Council, cabled Walker: "You called for 10,000 volunteers nationwide for Ole Miss to fight against federal tyranny. Will pledge 10,000 from Louisiana alone, under your command." Louisiana Council boss William Rainach pledged another ten thousand to Governor Barnett. Fred Hockett, executive secretary of the Florida Citizens' Council, offered another 1,500 men. Sheriff Jim Clark of Selma, Alabama announced that he and Sheriff Hugh Champion were ready with "posses" of five hundred deputies each. Georgia Grand Dragon Calvin Craig declared that when his orders came, "a volunteer force of several thousand men would be on its way to Mississippi straight off." FBI informants reported six hundred knights already in Jackson, while a ham radio broadcast from Kansas City alerted "all Minutemen organizations, all ranger units, Illinois civilian control units, Washington militia" and allied groups to stand ready. The National States Rights Party wired Barnett from Alabama with a claim of "thousands" en route to Oxford. Milwaukee's field office warned Hoover that a wealthy racist was flying four P-51 fighter planes to Ole Miss, but they never arrived. Mississippi sheriff James Grimsley chartered buses for members of his Jackson County Citizens' Emergency Unit (JCCEU), embarking for Oxford on 27 September. Melvin Bruce, a sometime chauffeur for American Nazi Party leader George Rockwell, wired Barnett from Georgia on 30 September: "I volunteer my services, arms and munitions to you as a combat infantryman, and will serve under any officer you might designate. I would consider it an honor to serve under the patriot, General Walker." The same day, a caravan of "Citizens for the Preservation of Democracy" left Prichard, Alabama, trailed by journalists and an FBI surveillance team.

Edwin Walker landed in Jackson on 29 September, with a small band of Texas cronies. Before driving to Oxford, he held a press conference on the airport tarmac, telling reporters, "I am in Mississippi beside Governor Ross Barnett. I call for a national protest against the conspiracy from within. Rally to the cause of freedom.... There are thousands, possibly tens of thousands of people on their way to Mississippi from across the nation." James Meredith arrived at Ole Miss on 30 September, guarded by 300 U.S. marshals. At five o'clock that afternoon, Oxford's airport denied Robert Shelton permission to land, whereupon his UKA contingent circled briefly, then returned to Alabama. FBI resident agent Robin Cotton persuaded his superiors to send another dozen G-men, who fanned out to infiltrate the growing mob on campus. Rioting erupted after nightfall, with some 2,500 racists of all ages besieging Meredith's federal guards in the Lyceum, where they defended themselves with tear gas. Walker led one charge, followed by an estimated thousand rioters, while others rushed the Lyceum with a hijacked fire engine. Mississippi lawmen watched and did nothing, as gunfire erupted between snipers and the outnumbered marshals. Also on hand were two observers from Alabama, Al Lingo and Hunter Phillips, dispatched by gubernatorial candidate George Wallace to chart the progress of Mississippi's uprising for future reference.

At 10:00 p.m., Agent Cotton saw dozens of men armed with rifles and shotguns, leaping from pickup trucks on the campus outskirts. Soon they were blazing away at the Lyceum, in what author William Doyle calls "the beginnings of a Ku Klux Klan rebellion." Out-of-state knights by the dozens infested Ole Miss, mingling with students and apathetic police to burn cars, pummel bystanders, and bombard the Lyceum with everything from bricks to high-powered rifle fire. An old school bus bearing Louisiana license plates was parked outside the campus football stadium, loudspeakers blaring a fight song titled "Cajun Ku Klux Klan." Its lyrics ran: "You niggers listen now. I'm gonna tell you how to keep from being tortured when the Klan is on the prowl. Stay at home at night, lock your doors up tight. Don't go outside, or you will find them crosses burning bright." The racist guerrillas met no opposition from Mississippi officers, Attorney General Kennedy later complaining that "approximately 150 of the police were observed sitting in their automobiles within half a mile of the rioting and shooting."

The Ole Miss riot claimed two lives. One victim, Abbeville jukebox repairman Ray Gunter, had gone to Ole Miss with a friend "to see what's going on." A stray bullet struck him in the head as he stood watching rioters attack the Lyceum. Victim Paul "Flash" Guihard was a reporter for Agence France-Presse, assigned to cover the disorder. He arrived on campus at 8:40 p.m. and was found dying moments later, 165 yards northeast of the Lyceum. Unlike Gunter, Guihard was no accidental shooting victim. Forensic evidence revealed that he was shot in the back with a .38-caliber pistol from a distance of less than twelve inches. Investigators believe that Guihard's camera and goatee marked him for rioters or some "rogue" lawman as a "liberal" reporter, deserving of death. FBI technicians ultimately tested

450 weapons carried by federal officers during the riot, without identifying the guns that killed Guihard and Gunter. No tests were performed on the .38-caliber weapons carried by Mississippi officers at the scene.

The campus riot was quelled around 5:30 a.m. on 1 October 1962, then burst to life again at 9:00 a.m. in downtown Oxford. Some 13,500 troops—more than double the number of Oxford's year-round residents—crushed the second outbreak by noon. On campus, thirty U.S. marshals suffered gunshot wounds, while 136 more were otherwise injured; forty-eight soldiers also suffered various injuries. Within hours of the riot's end, Oxford was overrun by fifty FBI agents, two hundred other Justice personnel, twenty army intelligence agents and 31,000 regular troops—more than the total U.S. combat force in the Korean War. Ironically, black troops dispatched to Oxford were stripped of their rank, weapons and helmets to avoid offending local whites. The *New York Times* estimated that 375 civilians were injured, while another 300 were arrested by federal officers. (Mississippi lawmen made no arrests.) Those detained ranged in age from fourteen to fifty-seven, listing home addresses from California to Georgia, though the majority came from Mississippi, Alabama, Louisiana and Tennessee. Hundreds of weapons were seized in the riot, including a submachine gun and a souvenir Japanese pistol from World War II. On 1 October, troops raided the Sigma Nu fraternity house, confiscating twenty-five guns from frat brothers led by future U.S. senator Trent Lott. Of those arrested, only forty were registered college students; eight of those received mild disciplinary action from the student judicial council, but none were expelled. Most prisoners were freed by 3 October, after FBI interrogation.

Only four Ole Miss rioters, all from out of state, faced criminal charges. Edwin Walker stood accused of assaulting or opposing federal officers, preventing a federal officer from discharging his duty, inciting or engaging in an insurrection against the United States, and conspiracy to forcibly overthrow or oppose execution of U.S. laws. Briefly detained at the U.S. Medical Center in Springfield, Missouri, Walker posted $50,000 bond on 6 October 1962 and was released with a court order for psychiatric testing. A federal grand jury convened in January 1963 refused to indict Walker, and all charges were dropped. Melvin Bruce and three of Prichard's "Alabama volunteers" *were* indicted on federal charges, but one case was dropped and the other three defendants were acquitted after lawyer Jesse Stoner convinced jurors that the accused had been beaten by U.S. marshals. State authorities filed no charges.

Echoes from the battle of Ole Miss were heard for months to come. Leaders of the United Klans gathered at Bessemer, Alabama, on 2 October 1962, voting to "lay low for awhile and then try to get Meredith and hang him from a gate on the campus when the situation permitted." That same night, an FBI informant from Columbus, Georgia warned G-men of a Klan plot to bomb troops in Oxford with explosives charges dropped from small airplanes. Another group with designs on Meredith was Sheriff Grimsley's Jackson County Citizens' Emergency Unit, six hundred members strong, described in FBI memos as "being organized ... to secretly go to the University of Mississippi ... 'to get' or kidnap" Meredith. A separate Justice file confirmed that

the JCCEU's "main purpose, apparently, is to kill Meredith," though members also threatened and harassed moderate newspaper editor Ira Harkey in Pascagoula. Informants reported that Grimsley—a notorious drunkard known for corruption and sexual assaults on female prisoners—had conspired to murder Harkey, while his cronies bragged "that none had outdone them in brick throwing and vehicle burning" at Oxford. Nonetheless, the FBI's investigation of Grimsley was "suddenly dropped" in early 1963, "as if the government lost interest." On 23 December 1963, unidentified nightriders fired shotgun blasts into James Meredith's home at Kosciusko, Mississippi.

1964—St. Augustine, Florida: In early 1964, as St. Augustine prepared for its 1965 quadricentennial celebration, Dr. Martin Luther King's SCLC targeted the segregated city for a massive civil rights campaign. Arrayed against the demonstrators were the Ku Klux Klan and its local front group, the Ancient City Gun Club, many of whose members served as "special deputies" for Sheriff L.O. Davis. While Davis and his men brutalized protesters and prisoners, itinerant agitators Charles "Connie" Lynch and Jesse Stoner arrived in St. Augustine to stiffen Klan resistance. The result, during June 1964, was a series of riots wherein klansmen and members of Stoner's NSRP assaulted marchers, bystanders and journalists around the city's historic slave market and at local beaches during daylight "wade-in" demonstrations. The disorders made international headlines, prompting Dr. King to call St. Augustine "the most lawless community I have ever seen." Violence finally subsided in late June, after federal judge Bryan Simpson ordered Sheriff Davis to stop brutalizing prisoners and deputizing klansmen. An August injunction from Simpson banned Holsted Manucy and his Ancient City Gun Club from disrupting protests. Almost incredibly, no deaths resulted from the 1964 St. Augustine riots or their attendant shootings and arson attacks, though many demonstrators suffered injuries.

1966—Grenada, Mississippi: The UKA maintained a klavern in Grenada that stood ready to respond with violence when black civil rights demonstrations began in July 1966. Local police handled the early protests, clubbing and jailing protesters led by Dr. Martin Luther King's SCLC, but vigilantes joined the game on 10 July, firing shots at three white activists outside a black church. On the night of 9 August, a mob of 150–175 whites lobbed bricks, bottles, steel pipes and fireworks at 300 black marchers. Another mob, 500 strong, challenged police when the demonstrators marched again on 10 August. State police maintained order thereafter, until Grenada's schools opened with federal court orders demanding integration of all classes. On 12 September 1966, a mob of 200 to 400 whites armed with axe handles, chains and pipes barred 40 of 160 black students from entering John Rundle High School. Meanwhile, at Lizzie Horn Elementary School, black children entered classes peacefully that morning, but were mobbed and beaten with their parents in the afternoon, while Grenada police stood by and watched. Two boys suffered severe head injuries in that attack, while another's leg was fractured. The mob also beat three out-of-town reporters, including one who was blocked by a town constable from seeking refuge on school grounds. White rioting resumed

on 13 September, when mob victims included NAACP attorney Henry Aaronson (beaten while snickering police ignored his pleas for help). On 13 September, the DOJ filed suit against Grenada's mayor, police chief, city manager and Sheriff Suggs Ingram for "willful failure and refusal" to protect the children.

On 4 October 1966, a federal grand jury indicted five whites—including Justice of the Peace Richard Ayers—for conspiracy to intimidate black citizens and to willfully obstruct school integration.

10 POLICING VIGILANTES

While members of the KKK traditionally pledged to uphold the law (at least from 1867 through the 1970s), they frequently engaged in criminal behavior, ranging from threats and petty vandalism to arson, assault, mayhem and murder. This chapter examines the long and often frustrating campaign by American law enforcement to control the invisible empire and its satellite organizations. Subsections examine legislative efforts to control Ku Klux activity, some agencies involved in those efforts, and individuals who have (for good or ill) played roles in policing the KKK.

Legal Tools

Organizations such as the Ku Klux Klan cannot be banned by law under the U.S. Constitution. Freedom of speech, press, and peaceable assembly are guaranteed by the First Amendment, though many federal, state and local lawmakers have sought to punish unpopular speech (and even thought) throughout American history. Klansmen cross the line, however, when they seek to physically intimidate or harm their fellow citizens. Some of the laws passed to restrain them since the days of Reconstruction are described below.

Anti-mask Laws—Anonymity has long been one of the Ku Klux Klan's most effective weapons. With that in mind, since the early 1920s, various states and communities have passed anti-mask laws which typically forbid adults from wearing masks in public, particularly with intent to commit criminal acts or intimidate other persons. The Reconstruction-era Enforcement and Ku Klux Acts, passed by Congress in 1870–71, contained provisions against masked violence intended to deprive ex-slaves of their new civil rights, and while the U.S. Supreme Court subsequently gutted those federal statutes, state and local lawmakers used similar means to restrict the modern KKK. Michigan was an early leader in anti-mask legislation, with the Burns law passed in summer 1923, prohibiting assemblies of masked men. Enforcement of the statute was erratic, but when 5,000 Detroit klansmen rallied on 20 October 1923, none was masked. Wrightsville, Georgia, became the first southern community to ban masked demonstrations, in November 1948. Atlanta passed a similar ordinance on 2 May 1949, fixing punishment at thirty days in jail with a $200 fine. The Alabama state legislature responded to an outbreak of KKK violence with an anti-mask law in June 1949. In Arkansas, two black men were the first persons charged under a new anti-mask law, accused of donning Klan-type hoods to frighten black women out of dating white men. Georgia's assembly killed a statewide anti-mask law on 18 February 1950, but a new version passed eleven months later (also banning cross-burnings on private property without the owner's

Some klansmen still defy state laws banning masks in public (Florida State Archives).

304

consent). A South Carolina statute, enacted on 28 April 1951, imposed a one-year prison term and $500 fine for traveling masked or burning unauthorized crosses on private property. Florida followed suit with a new anti-mask law on 8 May 1951. Sheriff's deputies arrested fourteen knights for wearing masks at Conway, South Carolina's Can Branch Baptist Church, on 31 October 1951, but a pro–Klan deacon of the church retaliated with trespassing warrants against the lawmen. By 1967, twenty-two states and fifty-two southern communities had some form of anti-mask legislation on their statute books. (Louisiana's version exempts Mardi Gras participants, while others make allowances for Halloween.) In most areas, klansmen may avoid such laws by gathering on private property, but incidents persist. On 3 July 1966, participants in a National Knights rally at Lebanon, Ohio, stoned police who arrested two masked klansmen. Georgia's supreme court upheld the state's anti-mask law in 1990, denying the appeal of incarcerated klansman Shade Miller. Eight years later, a federal judge struck down the anti-mask law lately passed in Goshen, Indiana, on grounds that it "directly chilled speech" by denying klansmen the right to protest anonymously. No test of anti-mask laws had reached the U.S. Supreme Court at press time for this volume.

Civil Rights Act of 1957

This law included a provision punishing persons who used the telephone to threaten or intimidate others who attempt to exercise their legal rights (specifically where voting is concerned). While bomb threats and other forms of telephonic harassment are common forms of KKK activity, the FBI generally ignored its responsibilities under the 1957 statute, erroneously claiming that investigation of such crimes fell within the jurisdiction of local law enforcement agencies.

Civil Rights Act of 1960

Reluctantly signed by President Dwight Eisenhower, this statute made it a federal crime to transport explosives across state lines for purposes of terrorizing those who exercise their lawful rights (including but not limited to voting). Despite a southern bombing campaign that produced more than 200 explosions in the 1960s, the new law was rarely invoked by FBI agents under J. Edgar Hoover and no one was convicted on such charges during Hoover's tenure as FBI director.

Cross-burning Laws

The Reconstruction-era Klan burned no crosses, despite fictional portrayal of such rituals in the racist novels of Thomas Dixon (1902–05), but since 1915 the fiery cross has become an internationally recognized symbol of the KKK and its offensive racism. Large crosses are commonly burned at Klan rallies, while smaller ones traditionally have been burned at homes, schools, churches, and other targets owned by persons whom the Klan seeks to intimidate. In response to such activity, various states and local jurisdictions now have laws in place that penalize burning of crosses on private property without the owner's permission. Georgia was the first southern state to pass such a ban, in January 1951. South Carolina followed three months later, with a law imposing a one-year jail term and $500 fine for unauthorized cross-burnings on private property. Federal statutes also impose a minimum two-year prison term for acts of racial or religious intimidation, with an additional

Klansmen burned this cross to intimidate black residents of Waynesboro, Georgia, in 1961 (Georgia Department of Archives and History).

five-year minimum for using fire in the commission of a felony, so that cross-burners convicted in federal court may face a minimum of seven years in custody.

Still, cross-burnings continue throughout the U.S. to the present day, with 226 incidents recorded by the SPLC in 1994–98 alone. On 22 June 1992, the U.S. Supreme Court unanimously invalidated a cross-burning conviction from St. Paul, Minnesota, under a statute banning display of any symbol known to "arouse anger, alarm, or resentment in others on the basis of race, creed, religion, or gender." That law, in the court's view, imposed unreasonable limitations on symbolic speech under the First Amendment to the U.S. Constitution. Six months later, seven members of the Alabama Empire Knights were convicted in federal court of burning a cross at a black family's home in Marshall County, with intent to drive them from the area. The defendants in that case were sentenced to punishments ranging from four months' house arrest to 106 months in federal prison. In spring 1999, a federal jury in Chicago awarded $720,000 to a black couple whose white neighbor had burned a cross on their lawn three years earlier. Around the same time, Utah authorities charged defendant Michael Madley with four felony counts for burning a cross at the home of an interracial couple in Salt Lake City. If convicted, Madley faced a maximum of forty years in prison.

The year 1999 also produced a landmark case from Virginia, where state law made it a felony "for any person.., with the intent of intimidating any person or group..., to burn ... a cross on the property of another, a highway or other public place," and specified that "[a]ny such burning ... shall be prima facie evidence of an intent to intimidate a person or group." In June 1999, jurors convicted Keystone Knights Imperial Wizard Barry Black and two other klansmen of violating that law, and they were sentenced to prison. On appeal, Virginia's supreme court reversed those convictions and invalidated the state law on grounds that "[a] statute selectively addressed to the content of symbolic speech is not permitted under the First Amendment." Virginia's attorney general appealed that ruling to the U.S. Supreme Court, supported by briefs from nine other states—Alabama, Georgia, Kansas, Massachusetts, Missouri, Oklahoma, Utah and Washington—with similar laws on their books. On 7 April 2003, the Supreme Court issued a split decision, upholding Black's First Amendment claim but rejecting those of his codefendants. By a vote of six to three, the justices ruled that states may prohibit the burning of crosses with intent to intimidate. However, by a vote of seven to two, the court found that states may not define cross-burning as *prima facie* evidence of criminal intent. At press time for this volume, cross-burnings were banned by law in California, Connecticut, Delaware, the District of Columbia, Florida, Georgia, Idaho, Montana, North Carolina, South Carolina, South Dakota, Vermont, Virginia, and Washington.

Enforcement Act—Passed by Congress on 31 May 1870, this federal statute was designed to enforce provisions of the newly-ratified Fifteenth Amendment to the U.S. Constitution, guaranteeing former slaves the right to vote. Its key provisions lay in Sections 6 and 17. Section 6 read:

And be it further enacted, That if two or more persons shall band or conspire together, or go in disguise upon the public highway, or upon the premises of another, with intent to violate any provision of this act, or to injure, oppress, threaten, or intimidate any citizen with intent to prevent or hinder his free exercise and enjoyment of any right or privilege granted or secured to him by the Constitution or laws of the United States, or because of his having exercised the same, such persons shall be held guilty of felony, and, on conviction thereof, shall be fined or imprisoned, or both, at the discretion of the court—the fine not to exceed five thousand dollars, and the imprisonment not to exceed ten years—and shall, moreover, be thereafter ineligible to, and disabled from holding, any office or place of honor, profit, or trust created by the Constitution or laws of the United States.

Section 17 added:

And be it further enacted, That any person who, under color of any law, statute, ordinance, regulation, or custom, shall subject, or cause to be subjected, any inhabitant of any State or Territory to the deprivation of any right secured or protected by the last preceding section [giving all persons the same rights as white citizens] of this act, or to different punishment, pains, or penalties on account of such person being an alien, or by reason of his color or race, than is prescribed for the punishment of citizens, shall be deemed guilty of a misdemeanor, and, on conviction, shall be punished by fine not exceeding one thousand dollars, or imprisonment not exceeding one year, or both, in the discretion of the court.

The U.S. Supreme Court subsequently diminished those protections in a series of decisions rendered over seven decades. In *United States v. Reese* (1876), the court held that while the Fifteenth Amendment barred discrimination in voting, it did not confer a right to vote. *United States v. Cruikshank* (1876), springing from the Colfax massacre of 1873, dismissed the federal convictions of three Louisiana terrorists, permitting federal prosecution only of officials who conspired against free exercise of civil rights. Finally, in *Screws v. United States* (1948), the court decreed that policemen who brutalized or murdered prisoners could only be prosecuted under federal law if they possessed a specific intent to deprive their victims of federally protected rights (as opposed to acting out of simple racist sadism). The field was leveled once again in 1966, with a series of decisions reasserting the federal government's right and duty to prosecute terrorists (with or without badges) who deprive other citizens of their civil rights. By that time, the penalty for violations "under color of law" had been increased to ten years' imprisonment. Today, in cases where a victim dies, life prison terms may be applied.

Federal Bombing Statute—The federal response to bombing was erratic prior to 1972, when a new Federal Bombing Statute defined responsibility for such cases. Under this law, U.S. Postal Inspectors investigate mail-bombings and bombing attacks on post offices; the FBI handles bombings of federal property (excluding postal and Treasury Department facilities); and the ATF investigates all other domestic bombings unless the crimes are designated acts of terrorism—in which case they revert to FBI jurisdiction. During the past quarter-century, frequent conflicts have arisen over the FBI's narrow definition of "terrorism." In general, the Bureau has avoided most investigations of right-wing violence (except where G-men seek to claim credit for cases perfected by ATF or other agencies), and FBI headquarters has long avoided its statutory responsibility for investigation of crimes against women's clinics.

Gun Control Act of 1968—Passed by Congress in the wake of high-profile assassinations during 1963–68, this statute banned mail-order sale of firearms to anyone but federally licensed gun dealers. It also extended registration and transfer-tax provisions of the 1934 National Firearms Act to various "destructive devices," including explosives and certain military weapons (bazookas, flamethrowers, mortars, etc.). Consistent prosecution of klansmen and other racists on federal weapons charges began with passage of this statute and the simultaneous creation of the ATF.

Hate Crime Legislation—The federal Hate Crimes Statistics Act of 1990 defines these offenses (also called "bias crimes") as "crimes that manifest evidence of prejudice based on race, religion, sexual orientation or ethnicity, including where appropriate the crimes of murder, non-negligent manslaughter, forcible rape, aggravated assault, simple assault, intimidation, arson, and destruction, damage or vandalism of property." No federal hate crime legislation existed at press time for this work, but twenty-four states and the District of Columbia have comprehensive hate crimes statutes; twenty more have laws excluding sexual orientation as a factor; and seven states (Arkansas, Hawaii, Indiana, Kansas, New Mexico, South Carolina and Wyoming) have no legislation in place.

The Hate Crimes Statistics Act carries no enforcement provisions, merely requiring the FBI to collect and tabulate statistics voluntarily submitted by other law enforcement agencies around the U.S. How well has the statute worked in tracking hate crimes? A detailed study by the SPLC in 2003 revealed that while voluntary reports of such crimes increased from 2,215 to 12,122 between 1991 and 1999, the system remains "seriously flawed." Donald Green, a hate crimes expert at Yale University, went further, telling the SPLC that "the overall numbers are worthless." Among the many problems found with published FBI hate crime data, the following stand out:

* Hawaiian authorities refuse to participate on grounds that the federal definition of hate crimes is "very broad and subjective."
* Alabama, long a hotbed of KKK activity, reported "zero" hate crimes statewide for years on end, and has submitted no reports at all for "five or six years."
* In Kansas, only the Wichita Police Department reports hate crimes, and its clerks lag several years behind schedule. As of September 2001, they had not tabulated hate crimes for the years 1999–2000.
* In 1999, 83 percent of all reporting jurisdictions claimed "zero" hate crimes for the year. SPLC investigators found that officials in seven states arbitrarily reported "zero" hate crimes to the FBI on behalf of agencies that filed no reports for themselves.
* A report from the U.S. Justice Department, released in September 2000, found that nearly 6,000 law enforcement agencies had falsely reported "zero" hate crimes, when one or more offenses within their jurisdictions met the federal definition.

Ku Klux Act—Congress passed this statute—also known as the Third Enforcement Act, or simply the Force Act—on 20 April 1871, in response to rampant Ku Klux violence in Dixie. It stated:

> That if two or more persons within any State or Territory of the United States shall conspire together to overthrow, or to put down, or to destroy by force the government of the United States, or to levy war against the United States, or to oppose by force the authority of the government of the United States, or by force, intimidation, or threat to prevent, hinder, or delay the execution of any law of the United States, or by force to seize, take, or possess any property of the United States contrary to the authority thereof, or by force, intimidation, or threat to prevent any person from accepting or holding any office or trust or place of confidence under the United States, or from discharging the duties thereof, or by force, intimidation, or

> threat to induce any officer of the United States to leave any State, district, or place where his duties as such officer might lawfully be performed, or to injure him in his person or property on account of his lawful discharge of the duties of his office, or to injure his person while engaged in the lawful discharge of the duties of his office, or to injure his property so as to molest, interrupt, hinder, or impede him in the discharge of his official duty, or by force, intimidation, or threat to deter any party or witness in any court of the United States from attending such court, or from testifying in any matter pending in such court fully, freely, and truthfully, or to injure any such party or witness in his person or property on account of his having so attended or testified, or by force, intimidation, or threat to influence the verdict, presentment, or indictment, of any juror or grand juror in any court of the United States, or to injure such juror in his person or property on account of any verdict, presentment, or indictment lawfully assented to by him, or on account of his being or having been such juror, or shall conspire together, or go in disguise upon the public highway or upon the premises of another for the purpose, either directly or indirectly, of depriving any person or any class of persons of the equal protection of the laws, or of equal privileges or immunities under the laws, or for the purpose of preventing or hindering the constituted authorities of any State from giving or securing to all persons within such State the equal protection of the laws, or shall conspire together for the purpose of in any manner impeding, hindering, obstructing, or defeating the due course of justice in any State or Territory, with intent to deny to any citizen of the United States the due and equal protection of the laws, or to injure any person in his person or his property for lawfully enforcing the right of any person or class of persons to the equal protection of the laws, or by force, intimidation, or threat to prevent any citizen of the United States lawfully entitled to vote from giving his support or advocacy in a lawful manner towards or in favor of the election of any lawfully qualified person as an elector of President or Vice-President of the United States, or as a member of the Congress of the United States, or to injure any such citizen in his person or property on account of such support or advocacy, each and every person so offending shall be deemed guilty of a high crime, and, upon conviction thereof in any district or circuit court of the United States or district or supreme court of any Territory of the United States having jurisdiction of similar offences, shall be punished by a fine not less than five hundred nor more than five thousand dollars, or by imprisonment, with or without hard labor, as the court may determine, for a period of not less than six months nor more than six years, as the court may determine, or by both such fine and imprisonment as the court shall determine.

The law empowered President Ulysses Grant to suspend *habeas corpus* and declare martial law in areas where terrorists threatened the orderly operation of government, and while many parts of the South fit that description in 1870–72, Grant was cautious (some say negligent) in using his new power. He finally imposed military rule on nine of South Carolina's most violent counties, convicting sixty-five klansmen (out of 1,849 indicted) by late 1872. Ten years later, in the case of *United States v. Harris* (1882), the U.S. Supreme Court reversed the convictions of Tennessee lynchers and declared the criminal provisions of the Ku Klux Act unconstitutional, finding that federal authorities could not punish private conspiracies under the Fourteenth Amendment. Subsequent Supreme Court rulings in 1966 reversed that finding in turn, thus permitting federal prosecution of the klansmen who murdered Lemuel Penn, Viola Liuzzo, and three Mississippi civil rights workers.

National Firearms Act

National Firearms Act—Passed by Congress and signed by President Franklin Roosevelt in 1934, this law was aimed primarily at Depression-era bandits and gangsters. While it does not ban any weapons outright, it required federal registration of fully-automatic firearms (machine guns), silencers, and shotguns or rifles with barrels shortened below eighteen and sixteen inches respectively. In addition to registration, the law required payment of a $200 transfer tax each time a proscribed weapon changed hands. Although klansmen frequently stockpiled such weapons, they were rarely prosecuted during 1934–68, and cases abound wherein restricted weapons were first confiscated, then returned to Klan members by southern police.

Walker Law—On 22 May 1923, New York Governor Al Smith signed into law a statute introduced by state senator James Walker, which required that:

> Every existing membership corporation, and every existing unincorporated association having a membership of twenty or more persons, which corporation or association requires an oath as a prerequisite or condition of membership ... file with the secretary of state a sworn copy of its constitution, by-laws, rules, regulations, and oath of membership, together with a roster of its membership and a list of its officers for the current year.

The Walker Law also required such groups to file biannual reports "showing the names and addresses of such additional members as have been received." Furthermore, it stated that "[a]ny person who becomes a member of any such corporation or association, or remains a member thereof, or attends a meeting thereof, with knowledge that such corporation or association has failed to comply with any provision of this article, shall be guilty of a misdemeanor." Fraternities, benevolent societies and labor unions were specifically exempted.

Smith's signature on the law, coupled with his devout Catholicism, prompted klansmen to oppose his future presidential campaigns, while King Kleagle Emmett told a Long Island rally of 8,000 klansmen: "The Klan pledges itself never to reveal the names of its members. We will fight to the last breastwork to prevent public disclosure of our identities." On 31 May 1923, four Buffalo klansmen tried to incorporate their order under the name "Men's Fraternal Organization," but the ruse failed to work. State authorities subsequently prosecuted George Bryant of Buffalo for violating the Walker Law, and his case made its way to the U.S. Supreme Court in 1928. There, a majority of justices upheld the law as constitutional, ruling that:

> There are various privileges and immunities which under our dual system of government belong to citizens of the United States solely by reason of such citizenship. It is against their abridgement by state laws that the privilege and immunity clause in the Fourteenth Amendment is directed. But no such privilege or immunity is in question here. If to be and remain a member of a secret, oath-bound association within a state be a privilege arising out of citizenship at all, it is an incident of state rather than United States citizenship; and such protection as is thrown about it by the Constitution is in no wise affected by its possessor being a citizen of the United States. Thus there is no basis here for invoking the privilege and immunity clause.

Furthermore, the court recognized "the potentialities of evil in secret societies" and noted that "the danger of certain organizations has been judicially demonstrated." As to the KKK specifically, the justices decreed that it "was conducting a crusade against Catholics, Jews, and [N]egroes, and stimulating hurtful religious and race prejudices; that it was striving for political power, and assuming a sort of guardianship over the administration of local, state, and national affairs; and that at times it was taking into its own hands the punishment of what some of its members conceived to be crimes." With that in mind, the Walker Law was deemed to be a legitimate exercise of state police power.

Congressional Investigations

Congress has investigated the Klan repeatedly from Reconstruction through the latter 1970s, producing voluminous documentation of Ku Klux violence and financial corruption. None of those investigations produced viable legislation for controlling (much less eliminating) the Klan, but the published reports provide a wealth of information on the secret workings of the invisible empire.

1871—On 20 April 1871, the same day that Congress passed the federal Ku Klux Act, it also created a Joint Select Committee to Inquire into the Condition of Affairs in the Late Insurrectional States. Chaired by Pennsylvania Senator John Scott, the panel included seven Senators and fourteen Representatives drawn from both major parties, with Republicans in the majority. Public hearings in Washington, D.C., convened in May 1871 and continued through September. During autumn 1871, traveling subcommittees held hearings in Alabama, Florida, Georgia, Mississippi, North Carolina and Tennessee. The committee ignored Louisiana, Texas and Virginia (where the Klan had effectively disbanded by 1871), as well as Kentucky and Missouri (exempted as "loyal" Union States during the Civil War). Witnesses included military officers, public officials, victims of the KKK and known or suspected klansmen. Grand Wizard Nathan Forrest testified, denying membership in the Klan, but later told friends he had "lied like a gentleman" while speaking under oath. The committee's majority report, with thirteen volumes of supporting testimony, amply documented Ku Klux violence throughout the former Confederacy. The Democratic minority report, by contrast, virtually ignored white terrorism in Dixie while focusing on alleged corruption in various Reconstruction governments.

1921—Following a series of front-page exposés in the New York *World*, published in September 1921, the House Rules Committee convened preliminary hearings on the Ku Klux Klan in October of that year. Imperial Wizard William Simmons spent four days on the witness stand in Washington, D.C., capping his defense of the order with a dramatic fainting spell. While one committee member dismissed the swoon as a "cheap theatrical effect," the panel found no grounds for full investigation of the KKK, and the free publicity vastly increased Ku Klux recruiting. Before he was driven from office by Texas rival Hiram Evans, Simmons would declare, "Congress made us."

1942—Following a joint meeting of New Jersey klansmen with members of the German-American Bund, in August 1941, questions were raised concerning the KKK's loyalty to America. Imperial Wizard James Colescott testified before the Dies Committee (later HUAC) on 22 January 1942, informing the panel that only 10,000 dues-paying members remained in the invisible empire. The committee's chairman, Rep. Martin Dies of Texas, mildly chastised Colescott for opposing the Catholic Church (which Dies regarded as a bulwark against communism), and urged Colescott to lead his knights "back to the original objectives of the Klan." Still, the committee issued no wider condemnation of the KKK, and Rep. Joe Starnes of Alabama emerged from the hearings to proclaim that "the Klan was just as American as the Baptist or Methodist Church, as the Lions Club or the Rotary Club."

1965–66—By early 1965, Klan violence in the South had become an embarrassment to "respectable" segregationists, including most southern congressmen. On 30 March 1965, five days after Alabama klansmen murdered civil rights worker Viola Liuzzo, Rep. Edwin Willis of Louisiana announced that his House Committee on Un-American Activities would conduct a full inquiry on the KKK. HUAC's public hearings convened on 19 October 1965, grilling a total of 187 witnesses before the show ended on 24 February 1966. Most of those summoned were klansmen, and most refused to answer any substantive questions. The first round of hearings focused chiefly on Klan organization and alleged financial improprieties, while the latter phase revealed details of Ku Klux violence. Silent witnesses included Samuel Bowers, Byron De La Beckwith and Jesse Stoner, together with a host of others named as suspects in various crimes ranging from embezzlement to multiple murders. UKA Imperial Wizard Robert Shelton and three of his grand dragons were cited for contempt of Congress, over their refusal to produce Klan records on demand. Convicted by future Watergate judge John Sirica in September 1966, Shelton received a one-year prison sentence and was fined $1,000. Dragons James Jones (North Carolina) and Robert Scoggin (South Carolina) received identical terms and served nine months each, while Georgia's Calvin Craig escaped with a fine. HUAC climaxed its inquiry with legislative hearings in July 1966 and released its final report on the Klan in December 1967. Meanwhile, Chairman Willis drafted an "Organizational Conspiracies Act" that imposed life sentences on members of vaguely-defined "clandestine organizations" who conspired in acts of violence. The bill, introduced on 19 September 1967, was so poorly drafted and so broad in scope that vocal adversaries ranged from the Klan to black activist groups and the ACLU. It died in committee as the show wound to a close.

1975–76—Idaho senator Frank Church served as chairman of the U.S. Senate's Select Committee on Government Intelligence Agencies, better known as the Church Committee, ac-

tive during the term of the 94th Congress (1975–77). Although its mandate was investigation of various intelligence agencies—including the CIA, FBI, IRS and National Security Agency—the committee touched on Ku Klux Klan operations in its survey of the FBI's illegal COINTELPRO campaigns. Informant Gary Rowe appeared as a witness, speaking from behind a Klan-like mask to describe his involvement with the Bureau and the KKK in 1959–65. The committee's files contain extensive documentation of illicit FBI activities against the Klan and other hate groups during the 1960s and early 1970s.

1976–79—In January 1977, widespread public suspicion surrounding the murders of President John Kennedy (1963) and Dr. Martin Luther King, Jr. (1968), prompted creation of the House Select Committee on Assassinations, chaired by Ohio Rep. Louis Stokes. Over the next thirty months, the panel conducted 4,924 interviews, questioned 335 witnesses in public or executive hearings, and studied thousands of classified government documents. The Ku Klux Klan received particular attention in respect to Dr. King's death, since its members had frequently threatened his life. Accusations against specific klansmen were reviewed (including Sidney Barnes and William Morris of Alabama, Deavours Nix of Mississippi, and Jesse Stoner of Georgia). The committee also examined the relationship between attorney Arthur Hanes, Sr. (former mayor of Birmingham, later counsel for accused assassin James Early Ray), and Robert Shelton's UKA. Investigators noted "discrepancies between the testimony of Hanes and that of Shelton and [former acting imperial wizard Melvin] Sexton," but finally exonerated the Klan, NSRP and Minutemen from participation in King's murder. That finding failed to satisfy some private students of the King assassination and left certain questions unresolved at press time for this volume.

Agencies

Federal

Since the chaotic days of Reconstruction, various agencies of the U.S. government have tackled the daunting job of preventing and/or punishing Ku Klux crimes. This section examines their contributions and relative success, as documented from available sources.

ATF—The U.S. Treasury Department's Bureau of Alcohol, Tobacco and Firearms was created in 1968, evolving from such predecessor agencies as the Prohibition Bureau (1920–33), the Federal Alcohol Control Administration (1933–35), and the Alcohol Tax Unit (1940–68). Its mission included enforcement of various federal laws pertaining to manufacture and sale of alcoholic beverages or tobacco products, plus the 1934 National Firearms Act and the Gun Control Act of 1968. ATF responsibilities grew from there, with passage of the Federal Bombing Statute (1972) and Anti-Arson Act (1982). Responsibility for bombing cases was formally split between ATF, the FBI and U.S. Postal Inspectors, depending on the bomber's target and official designation of the crimes as acts of terrorism (at the FBI's discretion). On 24 January 2003, President George W. Bush transferred the ATF from Treasury to the Justice Department, formally renaming it the Bureau of Alcohol, Tobacco, Firearms and Explosives. Under provisions of the Homeland Security Act, ATF's tax and trade functions remained with Treasury, administered by a new Alcohol and Tobacco Tax and Trade Bureau.

ATF agents have long complained that the FBI manipulates definitions of terrorism to avoid responsibility for cases involving domestic far-right groups (including the Klan, neo–Nazis, and the "pro-life" bombers of American abortion clinics), while sometimes claiming credit for arrests and convictions secured by ATF personnel. In 1981 alone, ATF agents jailed four members of the Confederate Vigilante Knights of the KKK for plotting to bomb a Nashville, Tennessee, synagogue (sentences ranged from five to fifteen years); arrested Grand Wizard Richard Savina for conspiring to bomb the Baltimore home of an NAACP official (fifteen years); charged Adamic Knights Imperial Wizard Charles Sickles with weapons violations in Philadelphia (five years concurrent on each of eleven counts); disrupted a Klan plot to invade Dominica (with participants including KKKK leader Stephen Black and Canadian klansman Wolfang Droege); convicted six neo–Nazis of plotting to detonate bombs in Greensboro, North Carolina (sentences ranging up to fifteen years); jailed Death Knights of the KKK member Ralph Morgan for assaulting an ATF agent (eighteen months, with additional time on state arson charges); arrested IEKKKK activist William Riccio for possessing a sawed-off shotgun (ten years); and convicted New Jersey neo–Nazi Stanley LaBruna of shooting an ATF agent (thirty years). In 1984, ATF officers captured four Alabama klansmen responsible for torching SPLC headquarters in June 1983.

According to ATF historian James Moore, "The FBI liked these cases, liked them so much that, notwithstanding their minor assistance in no more than three investigations, they issued an official report taking full credit for almost all of them. The sad news is that 85 percent of all the cases the G-men claimed in that period were actually ATF's. The nice news is that the FBI might really deserve credit for 15 percent of the cases they claimed." When the ATF collaborated fully with the FBI, it made matters even worse. In 1992, ATF efforts to "turn" Aryan Nations associate Randall Weaver as an informant backfired tragically, producing the siege at Weaver's Idaho cabin, where an FBI sniper killed his unarmed wife. That incident, and the 1993 Branch Davidian siege near Waco, Texas—claiming the lives of four ATF agents and eighty-six cult members—sparked a decade of activity by the far-right "patriot militia" movement.

FBI—Active under various names since 1908, the Federal Bureau of Investigation is America's premier law enforcement agency, assigned to the enforcement of federal civil rights statutes and suppression of domestic terrorism. Media reports suggest that the FBI began investigating KKK activities in 1921, and while various published histories credit the Bureau with breaking Klan power nationwide, the fact remains that G-men arrested only one klansman prior to 1952. That case involved Imperial Kleagle Edward Clarke, who paid a fine in March 1924

for violating the Mann Act (transporting a woman across state lines for immoral purposes). Another twenty-eight years elapsed before the FBI made its first-ever arrests of Klan terrorists, jailing several Carolina klansmen who dragged their flogging victims across state lines in violation of the Lindbergh Law. Those prosecutions, during 1952–53, were rightly credited with breaking up Grand Dragon Thomas Hamilton's Association of Carolina Klans, but the FBI ignored simultaneous KKK violence in Alabama and Georgia, while its investigation of bombings and murders in Florida during 1949–51 produced no arrests. By the late 1950s, FBI headquarters had infiltrated various Klan factions with paid informants, but their efforts failed to produce more convictions. In March 1956, FBI Director J. Edgar Hoover told President Dwight Eisenhower that the KKK—then in the midst of its greatest recruiting drive since the early 1920s—was "pretty much defunct." Four years later, in July 1960, FBI agents arrested three Klan bombers in Little Rock, Arkansas, but charges were later dismissed when the Bureau refused to produce its informants as witnesses at trial. Ten months later, Alabama informant Gary Rowe informed G-men of police collusion with the KKK in Birmingham, plotting a riot against integrated "freedom riders," but the FBI did nothing to avert the violence—and, in fact, provided Klan-allied policemen with itineraries for the demonstrators. (Two decades later, a pair of victims from those riots won damage settlements from the FBI in federal court, for the Bureau's criminal negligence.) In 1963, after klansmen bombed Birmingham's Sixteenth Street Baptist Church, killing four black girls, G-men collected evidence identifying several of the bombers, then suppressed it until 1977. Two other klansmen avoided prosecution in that case until the twenty-first century.

In 1964, a rash of high-profile Klan murders and orders from President Lyndon Johnson forced Hoover to abandon his longstanding inaction on KKK cases. Typically, he then attacked the problem with illegal countermeasures, launching a "counter-intelligence program" (COINTELPRO) that included unlawful wiretaps and bugging, harassment via tax audits, anonymous mailings to klansmen or their relatives, plus employment of informants to seduce Klan wives and thus destroy their marriages. In Mississippi, G-men participated in a scheme to trap Klan bombers by hiring other klansmen (including one known murderer) to arrange the bombing of a Jewish businessman's home. The resultant ambush, which killed one terrorist and left another gravely wounded, embarrassed the Bureau when its full terms were exposed in 1970. Meanwhile, the FBI bankrolled at least two splinter Klans, supporting their activities financially in a bid to drain members from stronger factions. As late as 1980, the imperial wizard of America's largest and most violent Klan admitted serving as an FBI informant from the moment that he joined the KKK. Throughout the 1980s and 1990s, FBI agents generally avoided contact with the Klan, issuing definitions of "domestic terrorism" that excluded right-wing violence, thereby leaving prosecution of Klan terrorists to the rival ATF or local law enforcement agencies. Ironically, when Treasury agents or local police built cases against violent klansmen or neo–Nazis, FBI spokesmen often stepped in to claim credit for the results. Critics, inside the ATF and in the media, suggest that the FBI's long "secret war" against the KKK is more con game than conflict, a campaign of smoke and mirrors designed primarily to enhance the Bureau's reputation.

IRS—While FBI publicists commonly credit their bureau with "breaking up" the 1920s Klan, no such events transpired—and, in fact, the agency that had the greatest impact on the KKK before the 1950s was entirely divorced from the Justice Department. In April 1944, Atlanta IRS agent Marion Allen slapped Imperial Wizard James Colescott's Knights of the KKK with a lien for $685,355 in unpaid taxes from the order's glory days. That lien prompted Colescott to disband the national Klan (though he later denied doing so), and the Ku Klux movement has been splintered ever since. In August 1949, Agent Allen attracted more death threats with a new tax lien, this one demanding $9,332 from Dr. Samuel Green's AGK for taxes unpaid during 1946–48. Grand Dragon Samuel Roper paid that bill "under protest" on 12 September 1949, but Allen's office soon slapped the Klan with another lien, for an additional $8,383.

Secret Service—The U.S. Secret Service was created in July 1865, to suppress circulation of counterfeit currency. Two years later, its duties were expanded to include "detecting persons perpetrating frauds against the government." The agency's website reports that the extended mandate "resulted in investigations into the Ku Klux Klan, non-conforming distillers, smugglers, mail robbers, land frauds, and a number of other infractions against the federal laws." Authors Philip Melanson and Peter Stevens go further still, claiming that Secret Service agents "put an end to the Ku Klux Klan" in Reconstruction, but that assertion is completely unsupported and no available source offers any details of Secret Service activities against the KKK. Present-day investigation of klansmen or other extremists by the Secret Service might involve counterfeiting (as practiced in the 1980s by The Order and some factions of the Posse Comitatus) or threats against the President of the United States and other federal officials.

STATE AND LOCAL

Despite the Byzantine machinations at imperial headquarters, most Klans are grassroots organizations, acting on a state or local level. So it is that state, county and municipal law enforcement agencies historically have had more contact with the KKK—including frequent Klan infiltration of police ranks—than have various federal agencies. Any listing of police departments affected by Klan activities would run much longer than the present work, but this section provides a handful of examples from the twentieth century.

Alabama State Police—Klan membership was a virtual prerequisite for membership in the 1920s Alabama State Police. In December 1935, state legislators created a new Highway Patrol, whose officers divided their time between traffic enforcement and aiding county sheriffs who found themselves shorthanded, but the force received little attention outside Alabama until 1963, with the inauguration of Governor George Wallace. Elected with Klan support on a promise to preserve racial seg-

regation "forever," Wallace soon transformed the AHP into a notorious vehicle for crushing civil rights demonstrations. Under Col. Albert Lingo—a self-styled "good friend" of the Klan, known to friends as "hell on niggers"—Wallace renamed the AHP as Alabama State Troopers, ordering Confederate battle flags mounted on the front bumper of each patrol car. Lingo's troopers were notorious for their brutality against blacks and integrated demonstrators, frequently collaborating with hardline racist lawmen such as Birmingham's "Bull" Connor and Sheriff James Clark in Selma. State Attorney General Richmond Flowers and FBI files confirm that Lingo personally intervened on multiple occasions to subvert prosecution of Klan terrorists, including those responsible for bombing Birmingham's Sixteenth Street Baptist Church on 15 September 1963. Information flowed freely from Lingo's "antisubversive squad" to Klan leaders throughout Alabama, and troopers figured prominently in violence against peaceful demonstrators, as on Selma's "Bloody Sunday" in March 1965. During 1968's presidential campaign, a state trooper destroyed the film of a reporter who photographed Wallace shaking hands with Klan "wizard" Robert Shelton.

While Lingo left the force in 1966 to seek election as Jefferson County's sheriff, defeated by black votes, the state patrol remained a political tool (or weapon) for Governor Wallace. His 1970 gubernatorial campaign included TV ads attacking incumbent Albert Brewer's integration of the force. One ad depicted a white woman stopped for speeding on a lonely road at night, cringing as a black state trooper peers through her window.

Atlanta (Ga.) Police Department—Race has always been a law enforcement issue in Atlanta, which served as national headquarters of the Ku Klux Klan from 1915 to 1961. Many klansmen joined the city's all-white police force, some rising to command positions, and Atlanta's police union was essentially a KKK recruitment vehicle until its abolition in 1947. As late as 1949, detectives and patrolmen openly attended Klan meetings in Atlanta, often unmasked, and were sometimes featured as guest speakers. At one such gathering, in November 1948, Patrolman "Trigger" Nash was honored for killing his thirteenth black victim "in the line of duty." Nash told his brother klansmen that "he hoped he wouldn't have all the honor of killing the niggers in the South, and he hoped the people would do something about it themselves." Atlanta detective Sam Roper, formerly chief of the GBI under Governor Eugene Talmadge, served from 1949–52 as national leader of America's largest Klan faction, and reports persist that many Ku Klux crimes went unsolved through collaboration with racist police. Frame-ups were also fairly common, as when local resident Frank Bettis complained to police about a Klan parade in 1949. Soon afterwards, detectives and klansmen conspired to frame Bettis on a drunk-driving charge, but jurors acquitted him at trial. Subsequent integration of the force and election of a black mayor did not spare Atlanta from ongoing racial controversy in the 1970s and 1980s. A series of brutal murders terrorized Atlanta's black community from 1979 to 1982, prompting criticism of police who included adult ex-convicts on a published list of Atlanta's "missing and murdered children," while arbitrarily excluding thirty-odd minors who fit the established victim profile. Black suspect Wayne Williams was finally convicted of killing two adult males from the list, then was named without charges or trial as the slayer of twenty black children, but evidence in that case remains ephemeral and many black Atlantans regarded Williams as a scapegoat, charging that white racists committed the murders. That viewpoint was strengthened in 1985, with revelation that Klansmen had confessed at least one of the slayings on tape, in conversations recorded (and later withheld from the Williams defense team) by agents of the GBI.

Birmingham (Ala.) Police Department—Birmingham has long been Alabama's largest city and manufacturing center, ruled by "Big Mules" of the steel industry and politicians who served them. Police knew their place in that hierarchy, devoted in equal measure to suppressing organized labor and maintaining the hallowed southern tradition of white supremacy. Both goals were served, from 1915 through the 1960s, by collaboration with the Ku Klux Klan. The 1920s Klan boasted 14,000 members in Birmingham, including Police Chief Thomas Shirley. Historian William Snell asserts that under Shirley and his successors, most "if not all" Birmingham policemen were also members of the KKK. That symbiosis, masking Klan terrorism with virtual immunity, continued into the Great Depression and beyond World War II. In 1930, Alabama Klan leader John Murphy told Congress that his knights collaborated with Birmingham police and FBI agents to mount surveillance on suspected communists. Real or imagined CPUSA members were often arrested in Birmingham, then beaten by police or delivered to Klan whipping squads. On May Day 1933, Birmingham police, klansmen and White Legionnaires fought a pitched street battle with 3,000 hunger marchers. Future arrests were facilitated by the Downs Ordinance—named for police commissioner William Downs, an ex-sheriff and prominent klansman—which prescribed fines and jail time for any person possessing more than one copy of any "radical literature."

As bad as things already were in Birmingham, they worsened under public safety commissioner Eugene "Bull" Connor (1937–53, 1957–63). A bitter racist who once jailed a U.S. senator for walking through the "colored" entrance of a public building, Connor was so in synch with local vigilantes that he managed to predict the bombings of black homes and churches in advance. Unfortunately, his omniscience did not extend to catching the terrorists; in fact, his willful negligence earned Birmingham the nickname "Bombingham," while its central black district was dubbed "Dynamite Hill." (In one case, where a black witness identified the city's latest bomber as a uniformed policeman, furnishing the number of his patrol car, FBI agents stepped in to jail the witness on a federal perjury charge.) In May 1961, Connor authorized Klan riots against integrated "freedom riders," promising the racists fifteen minutes access to their victims without police interference. Two years later, he unleashed attack dogs and high-pressure hoses on demonstrators led by Dr. Martin Luther King, and thus helped ensure passage of 1964's Civil Rights Act. Harassment of civil rights workers and "liberals" did not end with Connor's removal from office in 1963.

Four years later, Birmingham police mounted surveillance on Vice President Hubert Humphrey, tracking his movements and eavesdropping on his telephone calls. Birmingham's primary civil rights organization, the Alabama Christian Movement for Human Rights, was still under full-time surveillance in 1969, with police employing wiretaps and informants to chart the progress of nonwhite "subversives."

Detroit (Mich.) Police Department—In October 1917, when Chief of Police James Couzens called Detroit "the best policed city in the United States," a local tabloid countered with reports that murders had increased by fifty-three percent under his regime, while robberies nearly tripled and auto thefts quadrupled. Nearly 300 policemen were hauled before Couzens on various charges in the last six months of 1917, eighty-nine of them for drinking on duty, but he only fired twenty-nine. Fifty-four holdups were recorded in the first six weeks of 1918, and Couzens virtually conceded defeat in mid–February, enlisting state troopers to patrol the streets at night. Statewide Prohibition, beginning in May 1918, inaugurated a fifteen-year reign of corruption surpassing anything Detroit had seen before. Police turned a blind eye while the number of saloons increased tenfold, with one observer christening Detroit "a city on a still." Detroit P.D. created its first "red squad"—the Special Investigation Bureau (SIB)—in 1930, primarily to help Henry Ford and other Motown industrialists combat the United Auto Workers union. Common tactics included mass arrests, raids on political meetings, random beatings and mounted charges into union picket lines. SIB officers also worked closely with members of the Black Legion, a spin-off faction of the KKK that practiced terrorism in the form of bombings, floggings and murder. After the Legion was exposed, with fifty-odd members shipped off to prison, Police Commissioner Heinrich Pickert was revealed as a secret member.

Racism was another pervasive problem for Detroit P.D., showcased during a deadly race riot in June 1943. The outbreak left thirty-four persons dead, twenty-five of them black, and police so obviously sided with white rioters that future U.S. Supreme Court Justice Thurgood Marshal issued a report comparing Detroit police to Adolf Hitler's Gestapo. A typical passage from Marshal's report described police handling of "looters":

> Throughout Monday the police, instead of placing men in front of stores to protect them from looting, contented themselves with driving up and down Hastings Street from time to time, stopping in front of the stores. The usual procedure was to jump out of the squad car with drawn revolvers and riot guns to shoot whoever might be in the store. The policemen would then tell the Negro bystanders to "run and not look back." On several occasions, persons running were shot in the back. In other instances, bystanders were clubbed by police. To the police, all Negroes on Hastings Street were "looters."

Little had changed in Detroit by July 1967, when another riot rocked the city's ghetto. Of forty-three persons killed in that riot, thirty-four were killed by police or by members of the National Guard. The late 1960s also witnessed a revival of the, assigned to conduct surveillance on black militants and anti-war protesters of the "New Left." The SIB's political bias was revealed in 1965, when its leaders released derogatory material on murdered civil rights worker Viola Liuzzo to Alabama sheriff James Clark and leaders of the KKK.

Georgia Bureau of Investigation—Law enforcement
in the Peach State was a strictly local affair until March 1937, when Governor Eurith Rivers and the state legislature established a Department of Public Safety. That agency, in turn, was divided into a uniformed Georgia State Patrol and a "plainclothes" unit originally called the Division of Criminal Identification, Detection, Prevention, and Investigation. Three years later, that long-winded handle was officially shortened to the Georgia Bureau of Investigation (GBI). Unfortunately, both Governor Rivers and successor Eugene Talmadge were machine politicians and active members of the Ku Klux Klan whose corruption and blatant racism tarnished the GBI's image. Georgia led the nation in unsolved lynchings, and Talmadge appointed Atlanta policeman Sam Roper (an active klansman) to lead the GBI during 1941–43. Some critics found the same mentality in play four decades later, when GBI agents taped conversations implicating several klansmen in Atlanta's ongoing murders of black children, then withheld that evidence from defense attorneys representing black suspect Wayne Williams in the same case.

Mississippi Highway Patrol—Founded in 1938, the
Mississippi Highway Patrol was tasked primarily with enforcement of traffic laws on state and U.S. highways. Patrolmen—commonly called state troopers—were also expected to assist local police departments with criminal cases and to cope with statewide emergencies at the governor's request. During 1954–70, Mississippi's chief "emergency" was the concerted suppression of black civil rights protests, and numerous complaints were filed against the Highway Patrol, alleging harassment or brutality against blacks and white civil rights workers. In July 1964, the FBI identified several highway patrolmen as members of the KKK, whereupon Governor Paul Johnson allegedly commanded them to quit the Klan or leave their jobs, but the patrol maintained its racist reputation through the remainder of the 1960s. In 1970, state troopers were involved with local police in a shooting that left two black students dead at Jackson State College, but none were disciplined for the illicit use of deadly force or their documented attempts to conceal evidence from federal agents. Today, state spokesmen assure us that "officers of the patrol exemplify the agency's motto of 'Courtesy, Service and Safety.'" Their goals are to enforce traffic laws "in a fair, impartial and courteous manner," while "enhanc[ing] the public esteem for law enforcement by precept and example of each member of the department."

Neshoba County (Miss.) Sheriff's Department—Neshoba County is located forty miles northwest of
Jackson, Mississippi. Its official history once boasted that Neshoba "enjoyed the largest annual per capita consumption of snuff and chewing tobacco of any county in the country." During the troubled 1960s, when Mississippi's black population struggled to achieve even the most basic civil rights, Neshoba was a die-hard island of resistance in a state already known for its devotion to the cause of white supremacy, and much of that re-

sistance emanated from the sheriff's office in the county seat, at Philadelphia.

For at least twelve years, between 1960 and 1972, the Neshoba sheriff's office was controlled by members of the Ku Klux Klan. Sheriff Ethel "Hop" Barnett was elected sheriff in 1959 and terrorized local blacks throughout his tenure, with help from deputies like Lawrence Rainey. Rainey killed one black man while a member of the Philadelphia Police Department, in October 1957, and later joined his chief in beating a black woman who criticized that unprovoked shooting. Rainey joined the sheriff's department in 1961, and killed a second black victim—prisoner Willie Nash—in May 1962. Evidence from that case reveals that Nash was handcuffed when Rainey, another deputy, and Sheriff Barnett shot him multiple times. In 1963, Rainey campaigned for sheriff on a promise to "handle the niggers and outsiders" expected to flood the state during Mississippi's 1964 "Freedom Summer." Voters elected him, and Rainey hired Cecil Price, a like-minded bigot, as his chief deputy. In 1964, federal prosecutors indicted Rainey and Price on charges for beating black mechanic Kirk Culbertson and fracturing his skull. Those charges were still pending when FBI agents identified Rainey and Price as prime suspects in the murders of three civil rights workers who vanished on 21 June 1964, after Price arrested them for speeding. Subsequent investigation revealed that Price—a member of the WKKKKM, as were Sheriffs Rainey and Barnett—had jailed the three activists, then released them after nightfall, only to stop them once more on the highway and deliver them to a Klan murder squad. Rainey, Price and Barnett were among twenty-one klansmen initially charged with conspiracy to violate the three victims' civil rights. Trial was delayed until 1967, at which time Price was convicted and sentenced to six years in prison. Rainey was acquitted, while the jury failed to reach a verdict on Barnett. Given the atmosphere in Mississippi at the time, it came as no surprise when Price and Barnett both campaigned for the sheriff's office in 1967, with criminal charges still pending against them. Price reminded voters of how he had worked to "maintain a buffer between our people and the many agitators who have invaded our county," adding: "You can be sure that I will be ready to serve you in the future." Still, voters chose Barnett for a second term, serving as sheriff until 1972. The federal charge against him was dismissed in January 1973.

Southern Conference on Bombing—The U.S.
Supreme Court's school desegregation orders of 1954–55 produced a wave of racist terrorism in the South unprecedented since the days of Reconstruction. Between January 1957 and May 1958, a series of forty-six bombings struck various southern targets, including schools, churches, synagogues and homes owned by African Americans. Most such crimes were traceable to factions of the KKK or other white-supremacist groups, but the rare cases of arrest usually led to acquittals by all-white juries.

The SCB was founded in response to those crimes, on 3 May 1958. Police officials from twenty-one southern cities gathered in Jacksonville, Florida, to compile dossiers on likely bombing suspects and offer rewards that finally totaled $55,700 for information leading to arrests. The FBI refused to participate, but a former G-man employed by the ADL, Milton Ellerin, compiled a list of prominent racists likely to plot terrorist bombings. (Conference participant Eugene "Bull" Connor—the Klan-allied public safety commissioner of Birmingham, Alabama, whose police had failed to solve thirty-odd bombings since 1949—was embarrassed to find his own name on the list.) Agents of the SCB reportedly infiltrated several racist groups, but no arrests resulted from their efforts. Indeed, while some participants were doubtless sincere in their wish to halt the bombings, the inclusion of Klan-friendly members like Connor and Jacksonville's Mayor Haydon Burns (who favored Klansmen with parade permits while jailing black demonstrators) prompted suggestions that the SCB may have been created as a publicity gesture, rather than a serious attempt to curb racist terrorism. The group passed from existence without fanfare, sometime in late 1958 or early 1959.

Tampa (Fla.) Police Department—From 1920 onward, Tampa police and klansmen closed ranks in brutal strike-breaking campaigns that blocked unionization of local citrus workers. By 1935, Chief R.G. Tittsworth and most of his policemen were recognized Klan members. That November, they collaborated in the murder of liberal activist Joseph Shoemaker and the near-fatal flogging of two other Socialists. Tittsworth and four others received prison terms in that case, but the verdicts were overturned on appeal, prompting Governor Cone to tell reporters, "I'm ashamed of Florida myself." Little changed in the aftermath of the Shoemaker case, where right-wing politics and union-busting was concerned. Klan terrorism continued into the early 1950s, and Tampa's police force fought racial integration through the 1960s, finally abandoning entrenched racism with obvious reluctance.

ROLL CALL

Over the past 140 years, countless American law enforcement officers, prosecutors and judges have joined, opposed, praised, denounced, investigated, defended, prosecuted or collaborated with the Ku Klux Klan. No definitive roster of those individuals exist, but this section presents some examples of persons whose relationships with the invisible empire are publicly recorded.

Aloia, Dennis—One of six Chicago policemen identified as Klan members in December 1967. Following a year-long internal investigation, Aloia was dismissed from the force.

Anders, Odell—Anders served as sheriff of Adams County, Mississippi, during 1964–68, when predecessor (and successor) William Ferrell, Sr., was barred by law from succeeding himself in office. On 20 August 1964, FBI agents provided Governor Paul Johnson with a list of fifteen Mississippi lawmen who were also klansmen. Anders made the list, with a notation that he was identified as a member of the WKKKKM "during February and April 1964." Questioned about that report three decades later, Anders told reporter Jerry Mitchell of the *Jackson Clarion-Ledger*, "I've never heard of it before." Anders admitted attend-

ing Klan meetings, but hedged on his reasons: "All the deputies and FBI went to these meetings. As far as me ever being a member, I was not involved in any way." Former Grand Dragon Edward McDaniel agreed that Anders was not a klansman, but allowed that "[h]e had a lot of friends in the Klan." Anders's tenure as sheriff coincided with the KKK's worst violence in Natchez and environs, including the murder of Ben Chester White and a rash of still-unsolved bombings (including blasts that maimed NAACP leader George Metcalfe and killed his successor, Wharlest Jackson). Ex-klansman Ernest Avants, a member of the wrecking crew that killed Ben White, once told police that the Klan had stockpiled "ammunition, hand grenades and a quantity of C-3 explosives ... [that] would be utilized only upon the instructions and command of the governor of the state of Mississippi or the sheriff of Adams County." Responding to that statement, Anders said, "That son of a bitch is crazy. I have no idea what he's talking about."

Baker, Wilson—As a captain on the Selma, Alabama police force in 1958, Baker ran against incumbent Jim Clark for the sheriff's post. Late in the campaign, Baker addressed a Klan rally outside of town, but the move backfired, gaining little white support and costing Baker the county's handful of black votes. In 1964, Mayor Joe Smitherman promoted the moderate Baker to chief of police, in an effort to minimize violence by Clark and his "special posse" of deputized klansmen. Baker restrained his police from attacking black protesters and jailed violent klansmen whenever possible (including the slayers of Rev. James Reeb), but he could not ensure convictions by the county's all-white juries.

Barnes, Sidney—While serving as police chief of Savannah, Georgia, Barnes appeared at a UKA rally on 20 July 1963. He accepted a Bible and a copy of the U.S. Constitution from Grand Dragon Calvin Craig, while 3,000 assembled klansmen chanted, "Barnes for mayor." Incumbent Malcolm MacLean had rejected a UKA lecture invitation and had banned Klan parades in the wake of recent violence. MacLean defeated Barnes on election day, winning a second term in office.

Barnett, Ethel Glenn ("Hop")—Barnett joined the WKKKKM while serving as sheriff of Neshoba County, Mississippi, during 1960–64. In May 1962, with Deputy Lawrence Rainey, he shot and killed Willie Nash, a black epileptic who was handcuffed and in custody. On 4 December 1964, Barnett was one of twenty-one klansmen arrested by FBI agents in connection with the murders of civil rights workers James Chaney, Andrew Goodman and Michael Schwerner. At trial, in October 1967, jurors failed to reach a verdict on the charges filed against Barnett. A month later, despite outstanding charges that might have sent him to prison, Neshoba County voters elected Barnett to another term as sheriff. Federal prosecutors dropped their case against him on 27 January 1973.

Beavers, James L.—While serving as Atlanta, Georgia's police chief in the early 1920s, Beavers defied the Peach State's political trend by opposing the KKK. Klansmen retaliated by branding him "the most incompetent chief of police Atlanta ever had." In 1922, Beavers opposed klansman Walter Sims in the Democratic mayoral primary, challenging all candidates to voice their opinions on the invisible empire. Beavers further promised that if elected, he would use every lawful means "to fight any improper influence the Klan may seek to exert in politics, or any hand it may seek to take in the affairs of this city." The effort backfired, as voters chose Sims to be mayor.

Behringer, John—A former New Jersey policeman, Behringer served as the Garden State's grand dragon during 1967–68.

Borland, Charles Barney—In 1921, while serving as chief of police in Norfolk, Virginia, Borland faced allegations of Klan membership. He denied ever joining the order, but his cover was blown by imperial headquarters on 10 June, when the latest issue of Imperial Kleagle Edward Clarke's *Weekly News Letter* carried a detailed description of Borland's initiation. Norfolk's exalted cyclops confirmed Borland's membership in the order, detailing his address to an audience of 300 klansmen whom Borland thanked for their pledge to help enforce the law in Norfolk.

Bridges, John—Witnesses identified Patrolman John Bridges as the Tampa, Florida, police officer who surrendered victims Eugene Poulnot, Samuel Rogers and Joseph Shoemaker to a KKK flogging party on 30 November 1935. All three were whipped with chains, then tarred and feathered, with fatal results in Shoemaker's case. Convicted at his first trial, in August 1936, Bridges received a four-year prison term for the assault on Poulnot, later reversed on appeal. At his trial for Shoemaker's murder, in October 1937, Judge Robert Dewell directed verdicts of acquittal. Tampa journalists described the whitewash as "a stench and a shame in the nostrils of the nation."

Brooks, Early L.—Brooks served as police chief of Fair Bluff, North Carolina, until 1947, when he was charged with shooting a fellow officer. Despite his acquittal at trial, public opinion forced his resignation and Brooks became a lightning-rod salesman, doubling as a part-time local constable. On the side, he also served as Fair Bluff's exalted cyclops for the Association of Carolina Klans. On 16 February 1952, FBI agents jailed Brooks on federal kidnapping charges, arising from the October 1951 flogging of victims Ben Grainger and Dorothy Martin. Eleven days later, local prosecutors charged him (with ten other klansmen) in the case of Esther Floyd, snatched from home and assaulted on 14 November 1951. On 8 May 1952, Brooks filed a plea of no contest for the December 1951 flogging of victim Woodrow Johnson, whereupon he received a two-year prison term. Five days later, conviction in the Grainger-Martin case earned him two concurrent five-year terms in federal prison.

Brown, C.A. ("Smitty")—As a sergeant with the Tampa (Fla.) Police Department, Brown led the raiding party that arrested members of the leftist Modern Democrats on 30 November 1935. Klan-allied policemen subsequently delivered three of the prisoners—Eugene Poulnot, Samuel Rogers and Joseph Shoemaker—to a Klan mob that flogged all three and left Shoemaker fatally injured. In May 1936, jurors convicted Brown of

assaulting Poulnot, and he received a four-year prison term (later reversed on appeal). Judge Robert Dewell directed verdicts of acquittal at his trial for Shoemaker's murder, in October 1937.

Bryan, J. Winder—In 1924, Klan leaders in Raleigh, North Carolina, demanded the dismissal of Police Chief A.E. Glenn and hand-picked J. Winder Bryan as his replacement. Raleigh's pliable mayor agreed to the switch.

Buchanan, Bob—As sheriff of McLennon County, Texas, Buchanan tried to stop an unauthorized Klan parade through Lorena in October 1921. Mayhem erupted, leaving Buchanan with a bullet in his leg, while one man was stabbed to death and several others injured. Local whites signed a complaint against Buchanan and a Klan-dominated grand jury rebuked him for "interfering with something that wasn't his business."

Burke, Joseph—While serving as the chief U.S. attorney in Los Angeles, California, Burke joined the KKK in 1921. His membership was exposed the following year, raising questions about his enforcement of various federal laws.

Butler, George—As a lieutenant with the Dallas (Texas) Police Department, Butler took charge of transferring alleged presidential assassin Lee Harvey Oswald from police headquarters to the county jail on 24 November 1963. Despite his best efforts, gangster Jack Ruby invaded the "secure" basement and shot Oswald to death before television cameras and numerous stupefied officers. After that shooting, Midlothian newsman Penn Jones recalled an incident from 1961, wherein Butler sought to have a Klan newsletter printed on Jones's press. According to Jones, "He told me that half of the Dallas police were members of the KKK."

Campbell, Clarence M.—In May 1921, a kleagle in Norfolk, Virginia, boasted publicly that "we have the chief of police, the commonwealth attorney, the postmaster, the police court judge, [and] members of the city council." Most of the officials thus identified denied Klan membership, including Chief of Police Clarence Campbell.

Candlish, William L.—In March 1924, as the price of KKK support during his mayoral campaign, Ben Stapleton named attorney and klansman William Candlish as chief of police for Denver, Colorado. Within a week of that appointment, critics circulated a recall petition against Stapleton, compelling him to face a second election (which he won) in August 1924. Chief Candlish, meanwhile, set about intimidating labor leaders and political opponents in Denver, using his authority to pack the August 1924 Denver Republican Assembly with Klan delegates. In April 1925, fed up with Candlish's malfeasance in office, Mayor Stapleton secretly deputized 125 members of the American Legion to raid gambling dens, speakeasies and brothels protected by Candlish and his handpicked vice squad of klansmen. As a result of the corruption thus exposed, Stapleton dismissed Candlish and twelve other Ku Klux policemen from the force.

Carlisle, C.W.—A Tampa, Florida, auxiliary police officer—fired for falsifying poll registry books, then hired by the city tax collector's office—joined the team of policemen who delivered victims Eugene Poulnot, Samuel Rogers and Joseph Shoemaker to a Klan flogging squad on 30 November 1935. At trial in May 1936, he was convicted of assaulting Poulnot and received a four-year prison sentence, later reversed on appeal. At his trial for Shoemaker's murder, in October 1937, Judge Robert Dewell directed verdicts of acquittal for all defendants.

Catterson, Robert F.—A former Union army officer, Catterson took charge of anti–Klan militia units in November 1868, after Governor Powell Clayton declared martial law in southwestern Arkansas. On 13 November, at Center Point, his troops defeated a force of 400 klansmen, thus effectively crushing the order's local resistance to Reconstruction. Catterson subsequently executed two Little River County klansmen for murder, then moved on in December 1868 to reinforce militia units in southeastern Arkansas. By early 1869, the Razorback Klan was effectively eradicated. Catterson subsequently served in the state legislature and as mayor of Little Rock (1871–73).

Chisolm, W.W.—As sheriff of Reconstruction-era Kemper County, Mississippi, Chisolm used federal troops to arrest Klan nightriders in early 1869. His efforts caused some local klansmen to flee the county, and Kemper was for several years the most peaceful of seven Klan-infested counties ranged along the Mississippi-Alabama border. The terrorists had long memories, however, and Sheriff Chisolm was assassinated several years later.

Clark, James G., Jr.—Born in 1924, Sheriff Jim Clark of Dallas County, Alabama, emerged in the mid–1960s as a symbol of racist defiance against black civil rights. His career was uneventful until early 1957, when Dr. Martin Luther King and other activists accused him of whitewashing an elderly black man's death outside Selma. Six years later, members of SNCC launched a black voter-registration drive in Selma, prompting Clark to recruit a civilian "posse" composed of Klan members and sympathizers. Armed with clubs, bullwhips and cattle prods, Clark's posse joined Al Lingo's state troopers to "operate in tandem as a mobile anti–civil rights force," ranging far beyond their legal jurisdiction. During 1964–65 Clark and his men surface on the racial battlefields of Gadsden, Hayneville, Marion, Notasulga and Tuscaloosa, assaulting and threatening civil rights workers. In February 1965, when he appeared with Lingo in Marion and watched police kill one unarmed demonstrator, Clark told reporters, "Things got a little too quiet for me over at Selma tonight, and it made me nervous." On 7 March 1965—memorialized as "Bloody Sunday"—Clark's posse and Lingo's troopers attacked a group of peaceful marchers in Selma, sending more than sixty to the hospital. That fiasco earned Clark a personal reprimand from Governor George Wallace, along with a federal court order to cease "any further use whatsoever of the Dallas County posse." Still, he found time to fraternize with the Klan, sharing derogatory information he received on murder victim Viola Liuzzo from the Detroit Police Department in April 1965, and visiting the jury room during deliberations on three klansmen who fatally beat Rev. James Reeb. Clark's comments to the jury were not recorded, but the panel voted to ac-

Sheriff Jim Clark (with club) threatens black protesters in Selma, Alabama, during 1965 (Library of Congress).

quit all three in record time. Newly enfranchised black voters rejected Clark's reelection bid in 1966, but he fought to the bitter end, suppressing some 1,600 "irregular" ballots cast for his opponent until court orders placed those votes on record. Clark then joined the John Birch Society as a traveling speaker who condemned civil rights as a "communist" plot, but his appeal faded with time and the society's dwindling membership. In 1978, Clark was indicted for smuggling three tons of marijuana into Alabama, valued at $4.3 million. He pled guilty and received a two-year federal prison sentence in December 1978. At the time of his plea, Clark also faced unrelated charges from New York, including three counts of fraud and one count of racketeering.

Cloe, W.B.—While serving as public safety commissioner of Birmingham, Alabama, in the 1920s, Cloe welcomed aid from the KKK in suppressing prostitution and other forms of "sexual immorality." As part of that campaign, in 1925, one hundred klansmen joined sheriff's deputies to raid a dance hall in Brookside, south of Birmingham, arresting four persons for liquor violations. Cloe subsequently told the press, "Klansmen are a good bunch of men or they wouldn't be knocked so much. Take that raid on the Brookside dance hall. I say, 'God bless them.' It may be your sons or daughters who are going to hell. They say the Ku Kluxers don't want the Jews to teach ... but if we want Christ and the Bible in our schools, then we must have Christ-like people to teach.... What we need here is more love of Jesus Christ."

Coleman, Thomas—In 1965, Tom Coleman was a well-connected engineer for Alabama's state highway department. The son of a former Lowndes County school superintendent, whose sister now held the same post, Coleman had a son—Thomas Jr.—employed as a state trooper and personal chauffeur to Col. Albert Lingo. He was also a close friend of Selma Sheriff James Clark, and a heavy drinker with a history of violence. (In August 1959, Coleman shot and killed black inmate Richard Jones at the Greenville prison camp, after guards unaccountably

asked him to help subdue their prisoner.) Coleman was a member of the Citizens' Council, and while he publicly denied membership in the KKK, SNCC activists described him as "a known klansman." On 10 August 1965, he confronted state Attorney General Richmond Flowers, threatening, "If you don't get off the Klan investigation, we'll get you off." Ten days later, he shot two white civil rights workers in Hayneville, killing Jonathan Daniels and wounding Rev. Richard Morrisroe. After the shooting, Coleman walked to the nearby courthouse. Sheriff Frank later told reporters he was out of town on 20 August. It was mere coincidence, he said, that Coleman answered the phone in his office when callers reported "a disturbance" at the shooting scene. From the sheriff's office, Coleman called Al Lingo and told him, "I just shot two preachers. You better get on down here." Lingo raced from Montgomery to Hayneville with a bondsman described by Richmond Flowers as "a known Kluxer," to secure Coleman's release on bail. Flowers described the shooting as "another Ku Klux Klan murder," telling reporters, "Everything points to another Klan killing, as the accused is strongly believed to be a Ku Klux Klan member."

FBI agents investigated the case to determine if Coleman had acted in his official capacity when he shot Daniels and Morrisroe. Lingo and Sheriff Ryals supported that contention in their early statements referring to Coleman as a deputy, and a card in Coleman's pocket identified him as a "special deputy" for Lowndes County. Ryals quickly changed his tune, however, after learning that official status might condemn his good friend to a federal prison cell. The card Coleman carried was nothing more than a common gun permit, Ryals now insisted, a privilege shared by numerous (white) citizens of Lowndes County. In fact, Ryals claimed, Coleman had never in his life performed any official duties for the sheriff's office. Testimony at Coleman's manslaughter trial, in September 1965, contradicted those statements. Deputy Joe Jackson testified under oath that Coleman had frequently aided the sheriff's department: on the day of the shooting, in fact, he was sent to retrieve riot gear from Montgomery "to maintain peace and order" in Hayneville. Coleman's attorney called the shooting self-defense, claiming that both victims were armed with weapons that subsequently disappeared, and Coleman's all-white jury acquitted him on 30 September 1965. A separate charge of assaulting Rev. Morrisroe was later dismissed without trial.

Colgrove, O.R.—The Republican sheriff of Jones County, North Carolina, Colgrove arrested several members of the Klan-allied CUG for terrorizing local blacks in early 1869. On 28 May 1869, terrorists ambushed Colgrove and a black companion on a rural highway, killing both men. In a bid to justify their crime, CUG leaders manufactured a spurious New York prison record for Colgrove, then held a barbecue to celebrate his death. State senator D.D. Colgrove asked Governor William Holden for troops to apprehend his brother's killers, telling Holden, "We cannot tell at night who will be living in the morning." Holden sent a militia detachment to Jones County, but the soldiers loitered in camp for six weeks, then departed without making a single arrest. D.D. Colgrove subsequently fled the district to avoid assassination.

Connor, Theophilus Eugene ("Bull")—Born at Selma, Alabama, on 11 July 1897, Connor dropped out of high school to work as a railroad telegrapher and radio sportscaster (where he earned his famous nickname for fabricating plays—i.e., "shooting the bull"—during broadcasts). Elected to the state legislature in 1934, three years later he became Birmingham's commissioner of public safety, commanding the city's police and fire departments. Connor held that post until 1953, declining to seek reelection that year in the wake of a 1951 sex scandal. Voters returned him to office in 1957, on a pledge to maintain strict segregation, and he held the job until Birmingham changed its form of municipal government in 1963. Connor's die-hard racism placed him in collaboration with the KKK, protecting nightriders responsible for forty-plus racist bombings between 1948 and 1963. Under Connor, the city was dubbed "Bombingham," while its largest black neighborhood earned the nickname "Dynamite Hill." On the rare occasions when he addressed the problem, Connor invariably blamed blacks for bombing their own homes and churches. An FBI memo filed on 7 December 1957, following the demolition of a black home, reported that "Connor did not intend to solve this bombing." Seven months later, FBI headquarters ordered the Birmingham

Birmingham police commissioner "Bull" Connor (in hat) collaborated with klansmen to terrorize black citizens (Library of Congress).

field office to "hold contacts with Connor to a minimum in view of his unsavory background." Connor reciprocated in October 1958, instructing his police to share no information with G-men on civil rights cases. That breakdown in communication hardly mattered, since FBI informants in the Klan kept agents fully advised on Connor's willful negligence. One such spy briefed Washington on Connor's May 1961 agreement to let klansmen assault integrated "freedom riders" without police interference. Rather than warn the demonstrators, FBI agents provided Birmingham police with an itinerary of the buses, thus facilitating brutal attacks in Birmingham and Anniston. After the riots in his city, Connor explained the absence of police by claiming that most of his men had stayed home for Mother's Day. Two years later, when a black witness identified one of Birmingham's phantom bombers as an on-duty patrolman, FBI agents charged the witness with perjury and DOJ prosecutors sent him to prison for a year. Stripped of his office by popular vote and court orders in summer 1963, Connor won election a year later to serve as president of Alabama's Public Service Commission. He held that post until 1972, when a series of strokes left him disabled and forced his retirement. A final stroke claimed his life on February 26, 1973.

Cook, Thomas H.—Cook served in the 1960s as a sergeant and lieutenant of the Birmingham Police Department, though declassified FBI reports claim that he "took most of his orders directly from [Commissioner of Public Safety Eugene] Connor and not from Chief [of Police Jamie] Moore." In that capacity Cook served as a liaison between Connor's office and the local KKK, leaking classified police and FBI documents to the Klan. On one occasion, Cook reportedly opened two drawers of his personal filing cabinet for klansman (and FBI informant) Gary Rowe, instructing Rowe to help himself to any available information "for the use of the Klan in general." Klansmen, in return, aided police by maintaining surveillance on civil rights workers, reporting the movements of "radical" blacks, and recording the license numbers of "suspicious" vehicles. In April 1961, Cook served as Connor's middleman with the KKK, arranging "spontaneous" riots against integrated "freedom riders" three weeks before the demonstrators reached Birmingham. FBI agents allegedly resented Cook's ongoing leaks to the Klan, but the flow of information continued unabated. Cook, in a bid to regain the Bureau's favor, tipped G-men to the fact that NSRP leader Edward Fields habitually carried a pistol, while boasting of his desire to kill a federal agent.

Copeland, J.D.—While serving as police commissioner of Austin, Texas, in early 1922, Copeland faced grand jury questions concerning his alleged membership in the KKK. On 16 March, Judge John Mullaly held Copeland in contempt for his refusal to answer, imposing a fifty-dollar fine and an indefinite jail term.

Crosby, Sam—Fellow officers identified Tampa, Florida, patrolman Sam Crosby as one of those who delivered victims Eugene Poulnot, Samuel Rogers and Joseph Shoemaker to a Klan flogging squad on 30 November 1935. Six months later, jurors convicted Crosby of assaulting Poulnot, but his four-year prison term was later quashed on appeal. At his trial for Shoemaker's murder, in October 1937, Judge Robert Dewell directed verdicts of acquittal for all defendants. The *Jacksonville Journal* described Dewell's handling of the case as "about all the disgrace Florida can stand for awhile."

Curry, Roland—Voters in Monroe County, Florida, elected klansman Roland Curry as their sheriff in 1921. That December, Key West klansmen under Exalted Cyclops Walter Decker targeted Canary Islander Manolo Cabeza for special attention, based on suspicion of bootlegging and Cabeza's selection of a mulatto prostitute as his mistress. After an initial beating that left him hospitalized, Cabeza went gunning for his assailants on Christmas Eve, killing Decker on the street and taking refuge in a downtown building. Sheriff Curry summoned U.S. Marines to smoke out Cabeza, then dismissed them from guard duty at the jail, permitting a party of fifteen knights to remove Cabeza from his cell and lynch him. While a grand jury exonerated Curry, citing Cabeza's "very bad reputation" and the "affront to society" he had committed by "living with a Negro woman," Curry finished his five-year term but did not escape retribution. Legend has it that Cabeza's mistress placed a voodoo curse on his killers, followed by the death of Sheriff Curry and at least three local klansmen in a series of freak accidents.

Daniels, Dan—In the 1970s, when Polk County, Florida, experienced a rash of cross-burning incidents, Sheriff Dan Daniels professed himself unable to find the culprits. A possible explanation for his failure was suggested when journalists learned that Daniels had recently hired two sergeants from the Lakeland Police Department, while fully aware (by their own admission) that both had "briefly" belonged to the KKK.

Davis, Lawrence O.—Although he was elected sheriff of St. Johns County, Florida, in 1949, most Americans heard of L.O. Davis for the first time in 1963, when four black NAACP members were beaten at a local Klan rally. Davis arrived in time to save their lives, then arrested the unconscious victims for assault. Four klansmen also went to jail, but their charges were soon dismissed, while the battered blacks faced trial and conviction for assaulting their would-be murderers. In early 1964, with an election pending, Davis visited St. Augustine's Lincolnville ghetto to announce his disdain for black votes. "I used the word 'nigger,'" he told reporters, "so they'd know I meant it." Davis further proved his bias by fraternizing with the KKK at every opportunity. He appeared at Klan rallies, allowed Klan meetings in his jail, and loaned patrol cars to visiting out-of-town klansmen. He also deputized 169 members of the Ancient City Gun Club, a Klan front group, as "special" deputies. In February 1964, a klansman sought on bombing charges in Jacksonville fled to St. Augustine, where FBI agents reported that Davis "was instrumental in helping the Klan hide" him. Civil rights activists filed a federal complaint against Davis in 1964, and Davis perjured himself in Judge Bryan Simpson's court, initially denying that he deputized any klansmen, then admitting that he had at least four Klan members on staff as full-time deputies. He also lied concerning weapons seized from civil rights protesters. After showing photographs of clubs and guns, claiming they had belonged to rowdy blacks, Davis confessed that they were seized from "anti-demonstrators"—and that all had been returned by him to their owners. Judge Simpson was outraged to find bootlegger Holsted Manucy's name on Davis's roster of "special" deputies, flaring, "That man is a convicted felon in this court!" Davis finally confessed that he had passed out badges to any white man who requested one. Still, it was Davis's treatment of prisoners that angered Simpson most. The sheriff's use of clubs and cattle prods was bad enough, but conditions in his jailhouse were Medieval—fifty-plus prisoners crammed into cells built for four; men and women packed together in outdoor, unshaded corrals, where shallow pits in the earth served as communal toilets. Judge Simpson ordered the abusive conduct discontinued, declaring: "More than cruel and unusual punishment is shown. Here is exposed, in its raw ugliness, studied and cynical brutality, deliberately contrived to break men physically and mentally." For all his glaring faults, Davis was beloved by most local white voters. The county sheriff's website still declares him "kindly," claiming that "with Sheriff Davis' leadership the community held together" under stress from outside agitators in the 1960s. Davis easily won reelection in 1964 and 1968, but Governor Claude Kirk removed him from office in 1970, citing allegations of corruption. Local jurors acquitted Davis of those charges, but his time was past. In 1972 he failed to recapture his office from Kirk appointee Dudley Garrett.

Deason, Mat—Deason served as sheriff of Wilkinson County, Georgia, during Reconstruction, when his wife was confined to an insane asylum. He subsequently took a black mistress, which in turn provoked attention from the local KKK. Deason responded to Klan threats by vowing to kill anyone who harmed his family. In August 1871, klansmen abducted Deason and his lover, beating and shooting the couple to death, then dumping their weighted corpses in a woodland creek.

Dixon, W. Lloyd—While serving as sheriff of Clayton County, Georgia (1961–64), Dixon was also an active member of two Klans—Klavern No. 297 of the U.S. Klans and Clayton County Klavern No. 52 of the UKA. He left office on 1 January 1965 but remained active in the UKA ten months later, when HUAC investigators exposed his Klan membership.

Dollar, William—Dollar became a target of KKK assassins while serving as a deputy sheriff in Reconstruction-era Monticello, Arkansas. In October 1868, nightriders invaded Dollar's home, seizing the deputy and a black visitor, one Fred Reeves. After linking their captives with a rope tied around both men's necks, the klansmen marched Dollar and Reeves 300 yards into the woods and shot both men to death. That done, the raiders bound Dollar and Reeves in a lover's embrace and left their corpses on display for curious passers-by.

Dunnaway, William—Declassified FBI reports from 1952 identify Dunnaway, then chief of police for Apopka, Florida, as an active member of the KKK. According to G-men, most of Dunnaway's officers were also klansmen.

Edwards, Charles—HUAC investigators identified Edwards as an officer of the UKA in January 1966. At the time, he

was employed as a policeman in Grimesland, North Carolina. According to HUAC, Edwards was responsible for organizing Klan attacks on black protesters in Plymouth, North Carolina, during August 1965.

Eidson, Herb—While serving as a deputy sheriff in Fulton County, Georgia, Eidson joined the AGK's violent Klavalier Klub and participated in numerous floggings during 1939–40. Assistant Attorney General Dan Duke convicted Eidson and seven other klansmen (including two more sheriff's deputies) in 1940, but Governor Eugene Talmadge released them all from prison a year later.

Elliott, J. Jefferson—J.J. Elliott joined the Ku Klux Klan in Georgia, while serving as an officer of the state highway patrol and personal bodyguard to Governor Eugene Talmadge (1941–42). Members of Elliott's family later described his Klan initiation as "just politics," claiming that he resigned from the order before he moved to Florida in 1949, as a special investigator for Governor Fuller Warren. His "special" cases included the 1949 Groveland rape investigation and allegations of brutality against Lake County Sheriff Willis McCall, as well as the 1951 Klan assassination of NAACP activist Harry Moore and his wife. Stetson Kennedy reported that Elliott once greeted him with secret Klan hand signs, and Elliott served as a pallbearer at the 1952 funeral of Dr. Clifford Adams, a klansman murdered by his black mistress shortly after his election to the state legislature.

Faris, John R.—A white resident of Reconstruction-era York County, South Carolina, Faris took charge of the state militia's anti–Klan campaign in October 1869. Local klansmen doubly resented the opposition, since most of Faris's soldiers were black. On 10 February 1871, fifty nightriders raided Faris's home, seizing a cache of rifles collected to army his militia detachment.

Fennell, Lewis—Florida native Lewis Fennell began his law enforcement career as sheriff of Alachua County (1892–95), but he proved such a "hardbitten" character that voters replaced him after one term in office. He moved on to the Gainesville Police Department, rising to the rank of chief in the early 1920s. In February 1924, three masked members of Alachua Klan No. 46 abducted Father John Conoley from St. Patrick's Church in Gainesville, castrated him, and left him near death on the steps of a church in Palatka. Conoley survived his wounds and fled the state without pressing charges, but he privately identified two of his assailants as Chief Fennell and Fennell's son-in-law, Mayor George Waldo.

Ferrell, William T., Sr.—A native of Natchez, Mississippi, born in 1923, Ferrell grew up as a childhood friend of future Grand Dragon Edward McDaniel and his two younger brothers. Ferrell joined the U.S. Army in 1942 and served in Europe during World War II. Returning to civilian life, he tried various jobs before finding his niche as sheriff of Adams County, elected for his first term in 1959. Three years later, he joined other Mississippi lawmen at Oxford, in a foiled attempt to stop black student James Meredith from enrolling at the University of Mississippi. Ferrell's role in the subsequent riot (which claimed two lives) remains unclear, but a photo snapped the day before shows him on campus, joking with other sheriffs while he brandishes a club. State law barred Ferrell from succeeding himself in 1963, and his office passed to Odell Anders (identified by FBI agents in 1964 as a klansman). Ferrell applied for a job with Mississippi's State Sovereignty Commission, but that covert segregationist group rejected him and Ferrell wound up serving as a Natchez policeman. In 1967, Ferrell's campaign for a second term as sheriff included a visit to a backwoods KKK rally, where FBI informants took notes on his speech. Declassified FBI files describe William Ferrell, Sr., as a member of Robert Shelton's UKA who was "said to handle propaganda and spread rumors." (Ferrell's relatives later denied the claim, noting that he was Catholic.) With restrictive legislation abolished, Ferrell held office in Adams County for the next twenty years, establishing a dynasty of sorts that passed to his son (William Jr.) in 1988. As sheriff, William Sr. kept a portrait of KKK Grand Wizard Nathan Bedford Forrest on his office wall. He also hired Bill and Jerry McDaniel (brothers of Grand Dragon Edward, but never identified as klansmen) to serve as his deputies. FBI agents opened an investigation of William Sr. in August 1976, pursuing allegations that he took bribes from local gamblers, pimps and prostitutes, but no charges were filed. Cancer claimed the former sheriff's life on 28 February 1999.

Garner, Thomas Heslip—While serving as sheriff of Orange County, Texas, Garner joined the local KKK. In 1922, he attended a rally in Beaumont where Judge W.H. Davidson was delivered by one of Garner's deputies. On that occasion, Garner told Davidson that "everybody wanted him in" and that "at the next meeting night he would be made a member," but Davidson allegedly refused.

Garrett, Floyd—Patrolman Floyd Garrett, of the Birmingham Police Department, was a nephew of Klan terrorist Robert Chambliss who plainly sympathized with the KKK. In 1961, when federal judge Frank Johnson investigated charges of police collusion in Birmingham's "freedom ride" riots, Garrett provided a sworn affidavit denying a conspiracy between Commissioner "Bull" Connor and the KKK. Two years later, according to journalist Diane McWhorter, Garrett provided a police escort for Chambliss and other klansmen when they bombed Birmingham's Gaston Motel on 11 May 1963. On the morning of 15 September 1963, shortly before a bomb demolished the Sixteenth Street Baptist Church, killing four young girls, Garrett visited his aunt (a sister of Chambliss) to tell her that a charge was planted at the church. A cousin heard him warn her, "Keep your damn mouth shut. If anybody asks, you don't know anything, understand?" After the blast, Garrett called on Chambliss and told him, "They will get your ass on this one. You have gone too far." Thanks to the Alabama State Police and FBI, however, Chambliss managed to evade justice for fourteen years.

Goodwin, Charles—In 1963, Goodwin was one of several sheriff's deputies assigned to infiltrate the UKA in Brunswick, North Carolina. Unlike his colleagues, Goodwin retained his Klan membership when the sheriff ordered him to resign, subsequently winning election as grand klaliff of the realm in January 1964. In that capacity, he collected dues from local klansmen and stored the money in the sheriff's safe. HUAC investigators exposed his double life in 1965.

Goodwin, John E.—Major John Goodwin commanded the Georgia Highway Patrol under Governor Eugene Talmadge (1941–43). On 10 October 1942, he was listed as an incorporating officer of Vigilantes, Inc., a white-supremacist group promoted by Talmadge and assumed by some observers to be Klan-connected. In December 1943, Goodwin and Talmadge attended a KKK rally in Porterdale, Georgia, accompanied by State Treasurer George Hamilton and Zack Cravey, Georgia's former Fish and Game Commissioner. On that occasion, Talmadge told the assembled klansmen, "Christian democracy and white supremacy are the greatest things which should emerge from [World War II]." When not engaged on official business for the Highway Patrol or the Vigilantes, Goodwin served as Talmadge's personal bodyguard.

Grimsley, James Ira—A Mississippi gulf coast native, born in 1912, Grimsley was a promising amateur boxer in his youth, before going to work in Pascagoula's shipyards. He pursued premed studies at Jackson's Millsaps College, but left school without graduating. Instead, Grimsley used his incomplete education to win election as Jackson County's coroner (1957–60), then as county sheriff (1961–65). The sheriff's job also incorporated tax collection, but a more lucrative field of income was graft from the operators of Pascagoula's illegal brothels, gambling clubs and moonshine stills. Harold Jones, one-time chief deputy who left Grimsley's force to join the U.S. Army, told FBI agents, "There was no bag man. Each guy paid off directly to the sheriff." Jones also described Grimsley's penchant for "cutting"—i.e., sexually assaulting—women other than his wife. According to Jones's sworn statement: "Worst part about the sheriff is that he'll try to cut every woman he gets alone. Women who come to visit their husbands in jail.... Wife of a guy we held on car theft charges. Every time she came in sheriff would cut her." A lifelong alcoholic who periodically vanished from Pascagoula to "dry out" in Alabama, Grimsley was also known for the intensity of his racism. In September 1962 he led three deputies and thirty-odd vigilantes to Oxford, where they joined in the riot against black student James Meredith's enrollment at the University of Mississippi. In the wake of that melee, Grimsley organized 600 bigots into a new Jackson County Citizens Emergency Unit, whose purpose was described by Ira Harkey, Jr., editor of the Pascagoula *Chronicle*.

> [T]hey outlined their program of civic improvement: to eradicate local "niggerlovers," to boycott all businesses that employed or sold goods to Negroes, to "attend to" persons placed on a list by an "action committee," to train a strongarm squad at weekly maneuvers ... and in the main and particular to put out of business the Pascagoula daily newspaper, the *Chronicle*, identified by them as "the leading niggerlover in the State."

In fact, FBI files document the JCCEU's plans "to do away with" Harkey and his newspaper. According to the same FBI files, the central purpose of Grimsley's goon squad was "to secretly go to the University of Mississippi … 'to get' or kidnap" Meredith. FBI investigation discouraged that plan, and the JCCEU rapidly lost members, while Sheriff Grimsley slid deeper into drunkenness. Jackson County voters rejected his reelection bid in 1964, and Grimsley lapsed into obscurity. He died in Pascagoula on 19 October 1987, on a street that bore his name, from the combined effects of liver disease and youthful exposure to asbestos.

Guy, George—While serving as chief of police in McComb, Mississippi, in 1964, Guy also acted as president of a notorious Klan front group, the APWR.

Harston, Dan—While serving as sheriff of Dallas County, Texas, Harston joined the KKK in 1921. Despite public exposure of his Klan membership, he easily won reelection to another term in 1922.

Hartline, William—In 1949, Hartline was a deputy sheriff in Dade County, Georgia, and an active member of the KKK. That spring, he joined in a campaign to drive black resident Mamie Clay from her home, so that local white buyers could claim it at a discount price. On 2 April 1949, Hartline joined Sheriff John Lynch in raiding Clay's home and arresting seven persons, whom they delivered to a Klan flogging squad. A federal grand jury indicted Hartline, Lynch, and ten other defendants for conspiracy to violate their victims' civil rights. At trial in November 1949, Hartline admitted constructing the cross klansmen burned at Clay's home on 2 April, but claimed that his presence during the raid was simply "a coincidence." Jurors acquitted two defendants in that trial, but failed to reach a verdict on Hartline, Lynch, and eight others. At their second trial, in March 1950, Hartline and Lynch were convicted, receiving the maximum penalty then provided under federal law (one year in prison and a $1,000 fine).

Haynes, A.J.—A captain of the Arkansas militia in 1868–69, Haynes faced charges of murder from prominent Democrats after his troops killed several klansmen in self-defense. Klan assassin Clarence Collier murdered Haynes on the main street of Marion, in July 1869.

Heath, Donald—A policeman assigned to the predominantly black Philmore District on Chicago's West Side, Heath was also a member of James Venable's National Knights in 1967. A year-long departmental investigation climaxed with a raid on Heath's home, where detectives seized various weapons (including a bazooka) and 200,000 rounds of ammunition. Prosecutors charged that the weapons had been stockpiled in a plot to kill Mayor Richard Daley and various other public officials. Heath was immediately relieved of duty, while two other klansmen resigned from the force.

Holland, Charles—While serving as a guard at New York's Wallkill Prison, Holland was exposed as a klansman in December 1974, after he addressed a Pennsylvania KKK rally. State investigators allowed Holland to keep his job after satisfying themselves that Klan membership did not affect his performance at the prison.

Huett, Joseph Thomas, Sr.—While serving as chief of police in Mt. Dora, Florida, Huett received a subpoena to testify before HUAC's investigation of the Ku Klux Klan. He first appeared willingly, without legal counsel, in February 1966, then balked at testifying when investigators named him as president of a Klan front group, the Mt. Dora Dunkers Club. Huett "couldn't remember" joining the Klan, though he recalled taking several "similar oaths" in recent months. Despite his self-description as a trained observer, Chief Huett also "couldn't rightly say" if he had ever attended Klan meetings in Florida or neighboring states. Pressed by the committee for a straight answer, Huett finally excused himself to consult an attorney, complaining, "I didn't know you were going to give me the third degree here." In fact, he was not recalled as a witness, but independent testimony demonstrated beyond reasonable doubt that the Dunkers Club was a front for the violent UFKKK.

Johnson, Frank Minis, Jr.—A native of Haleyville, Alabama, born 30 October 1918, Johnson graduated from the University of Alabama and its law school, then served with the U.S. Army in Europe during World War II. Back in civilian life, he entered private practice in Jasper (1946–53), then served as U.S. district attorney for the northern district of Alabama (1953–55). President Dwight Eisenhower appointed him to the U.S. district court for Alabama's middle district (Montgomery) in October 1955, and Johnson held that post until he was appointed to the Fifth Circuit Court of Appeals (1979–81). While serving in Montgomery, Judge Johnson antagonized the KKK with several landmark civil rights rulings. In 1956, he overturned Montgomery's longstanding ordinance segregating city buses. Subsequently, Johnson struck down biased "literacy tests" for voting applicants and ordered registration of qualified black voters; wrote the first statewide school integration decree; banned racial discrimination in libraries, transportation centers, and the state's agricultural extension service; and placed various state agencies under ongoing judicial review. In May 1961, after police collaborated with klansmen in attacks on integrated "freedom riders," Johnson issued sweeping injunctions forbidding further violence. Four years later, after state troopers and sheriff's deputies brutalized protesters in Selma, Johnson ruled that the right to demonstrate outweighed civic rules on obstruction of highways and sidewalks—a judgment that permitted Dr. Martin Luther King's epic march from Selma to Montgomery.

Not surprisingly, the KKK despised Judge Johnson, calling him the "most hated man in Alabama." Klan-allied Governor George Wallace agreed, denouncing Johnson as an "integrating, scalawagging, carpetbagging liar." Johnson received so many death threats that his family lived under constant federal protection from 1961 through 1975. Klansmen burned a cross in Johnson's yard, and later bombed his mother's home on 25 April 1967. In 1977, President James Carter asked Judge Johnson to become director of the scandalized FBI, but discovery of an aortal aneurysm forced him to decline that high-stress job. Instead, he accepted promotion to the Fifth Circuit Court of Appeals in June 1979, remaining in that post until his transfer to the Eleventh Circuit in October 1981. Johnson assumed senior status on that court in October 1991 and remained in federal service until his death on 23 July 1999. Before his death, Johnson received the American Bar Association's Thurgood Marshall Award for his work for civil rights (1993) and the Presidential Medal of Freedom (1995).

Journalist Bill Moyers opined that Judge Johnson's rulings "altered forever the face of the South." After his death, the U.S. Senate passed a resolution reading:

> Whereas in a time when men of lesser fortitude would have avoided direct confrontation of the highly unpopular issues of school desegregation and voting rights for African-Americans, Judge Johnson stood firm in upholding the Constitution and the law; ... Whereas in part because of Judge Johnson's upholding of the law, attitudes that were once intolerant and extreme have dissipated; ...
>
> Whereas the American people will always remember Judge Frank M. Johnson, Jr. for exemplifying unwavering moral courage in the advancement of the wholly American ideal that "all men are created equal" and deserve "equal protection of the laws" and for upholding the law; ...
>
> The Senate hereby honors the memory of Judge Frank M. Johnson, Jr. for his exemplary service to his country and for his outstanding example of moral courage.

Johnston, James Daniel—While serving as a police officer in Conway, South Carolina, Johnston joined the Association of Carolina Klans under Grand Dragon Thomas Hamilton. In July 1950, he won election as a magistrate, but Johnston did not survive to take office in March 1951. On the night of 26 August 1950, Johnston donned his hood and robe to join a raiding party that attacked a black nightclub outside Myrtle Beach. Owner Charlie Fitzgerald was seized and locked in the trunk of a car (later beaten, with both ears severed), before klansmen fired into the tavern, exchanging some 300 shots with patrons inside. When the smoke cleared, Officer Johnston lay dead, wearing his police uniform underneath his bloodied Klan robe. Grand Dragon Hamilton faced charges of conspiracy to incite mob violence in that case, but white jurors acquitted him.

Jones, Kenneth—Wyoming state authorities fired prison guard Kenneth Jones in February 1988, for donning a Klan hood and robe to terrorize black convicts in their cells.

Kennard, Adam—A black resident of Reconstruction-era Sumter County, Alabama, Kennard served simultaneously as a deputy sheriff and member of the Union League. Sometime in 1869 or 1870, he quit the League and joined the Democratic Party, while retaining his post with the sheriff's office. Thereafter, critics claimed that he collaborated with the KKK, illegally invading Mississippi several times in early 1871, to capture black fugitives from criminal charges or labor contracts. On at least one occasion, traveling with whites identified as Alabama klansmen, Kennard shot and wounded a black man while trying to arrest him. The raids provoked a violent response from Mississippi freedmen, who dragged Kennard from a Meridian rooming house and whipped him in February 1871. Kennard identified the leader of the flogging party as Daniel Price, a white Republican, and local police jailed Price pending trial. On the day of his preliminary hearing, Kennard appeared in Meridian with a dozen Alabama klansmen, calling for Price's

blood. The hearing was postponed to avert violence, but Kennard's posse beat and abducted three black men, carrying them back to Alabama on the next train. Kennard's border raids continued sporadically through late 1871, without further resistance.

Kirk, George W.—Tennessee native George Kirk commanded a Union army regiment in the Civil War, then served as a leader of Governor William Brownlow's anti–Klan militia in 1868. Two years later, North Carolina Governor William Holden recruited Kirk to lead his state's militia in a brief, abortive war against the Tarheel KKK.

Klinck, Earl—Hoosier klansmen Earl Klinck served as a personal aide and bodyguard to Grand Dragon David Stephenson in the early 1920s. In 1926, in return for Klan support in his bid to become mayor of Indianapolis, John Duval promised to make Klinck a detective with the Indianapolis Police Department. The ink was barely dry on that appointment, however, when Klinck was charged as an accomplice with Stephenson in the murder of Madge Oberholtzer. Jurors acquitted him, while convicting Stephenson, but the scandal effectively scuttled Klinck's law enforcement career.

Lawson, B.F.—In April 1923, while serving as chief of police in Fairmont, North Carolina, Lawson faced charges of leading a Klan flogging party that whipped two white women. According to the charges filed against Lawson and two other klansmen (Jules Brogden and John Hedgepeth), they snatched Mary Watson and Mrs. H.F. Purvis from Watson's home on the night of 14 April, carrying them to a local black church, where the women were stripped and forced to lie across logs while klansmen beat them with leather straps. The floggers accused both women of abusing Mrs. Purvis's husband while he was ill. Lawson and his codefendants denied all charges, and jurors subsequently acquitted all three.

Lewis, Hugh—While serving as sheriff of Suwannee County, Florida (1953–63), Lewis was also an active member of the KKK. He died in office, shortly before journalist William Bradford Huie exposed his Klan affiliation.

Lingo, Albert J.—Born 22 January 1910 in Clayton, Alabama, Lingo served briefly with the state highway patrol in the 1930s, then retired from law enforcement to operate a logging company. During his short stint in uniform, and afterward, he earned a reputation as a brutal racist who was "hell on niggers," prone to confrontation, with a violent temper that prompted him to take tranquilizers "by the handful" in later life. In the 1950s, he befriended a fellow resident of Barbour County, George Corley Wallace, and Wallace tapped Lingo as an aide to his 1962 gubernatorial campaign. In September of that year, Wallace sent Lingo to Oxford, Mississippi, where he observed police defiance of federal marshals at the state university and reported back to his employer on methods of stalling school integration. Upon inauguration, Wallace named Lingo to head the Alabama Department of Public Safety, where Lingo renamed the highway patrol Alabama State Troopers, affixing Confederate battle flags to the bumpers of each patrol car. The patrol was soon transformed into a mobile strike force for dis-

Al Lingo's state troopers attacked black protesters on Selma's "Bloody Sunday" in March 1965 (Library of Congress).

rupting civil rights demonstrations, armed with clubs, electric cattle prods, and guns which Lingo's troopers did not hesitate to use on unarmed blacks. Lingo did his best to honor Wallace's campaign promise of "segregation forever," once appearing on the dais at a Klan rally where the presiding officer introduced him as "a good friend of ours." In spring 1963, with two black students scheduled for court-ordered admission to the University of Alabama, Lingo ordered investigator Ben Allen to "find something on those two niggers" that would bar them from the school. (He failed.) Three months later, in Birmingham, Lingo met privately with leaders of the neo–Nazi NSRP, urging them to mount violent demonstrations outside local schools, thereby giving Wallace an excuse to close the schools before they were desegregated. Nor was Lingo's part in racial violence limited to an observer's role. After klansmen bombed Birmingham's Sixteenth Street Baptist Church in September 1963, killing four young girls, Lingo first blamed Black Muslims for the crime, then met with state Klan leaders in an effort to deflect blame from the KKK. As FBI agents built a case against the bombers, Lingo jailed three of them on misdemeanor dynamite-possession charges, thereby persuading FBI director J. Edgar Hoover to let the case die. In June 1964, after Mississippi Klansmen murdered three civil rights workers, Lingo falsified statements for Governor Wallace that the three victims had been seen alive in Alabama following their disappearance. In August 1965, after longtime friend and Klansman Tom Coleman shot two white ministers in Lowndes County, killing one, Lingo personally drove a Klan bondsman from Montgomery to post Coleman's bail, then took charge of the investigation and refused to share his information with FBI agents or state Attorney General Richmond Flowers. The night before his acquittal on manslaughter charges, Coleman attended Lingo's retirement party. Although he was leaving the state payroll, Lingo still craved a place in law enforcement. He ran for sheriff of Jefferson County (Birmingham) in 1966, but newly registered black voters ignored his belated attention, defeating him on election day. Lingo died in 1969.

Littlejohn, Frank N.—Near-legendary lawman Frank Littlejohn was born in 1885 and spent most of his life in the vicinity of Charlotte, North Carolina. He joined the local Klan in the early 1920s, though descriptions of his service to the order vary widely. Author Ben Haas reports that Littlejohn served as Charlotte's exalted cyclops and was close to Imperial Wizard Hiram Evans, while other accounts claim agents from some unspecified federal agency paid Littlejohn to infiltrate the KKK. If so, their money was wasted, since the effort produced no arrests. A decade later, in 1933, Littlejohn captured members of the Roger Touhy gang, a feat that prompted FBI Director J. Edgar Hoover to call Littlejohn "the finest detective in the United States." (G-men subsequently framed Touhy for a kidnapping that never occurred and sent him to prison for life.) Littlejohn joined the Charlotte Police Department in 1937 and rose through the ranks to become its chief in 1946. He supported segregation but refrained from harassing or brutalizing black protesters in the 1950s. In 1957, he personally scattered a Klan picket line outside a Charlotte theater, which was showing *Island in the Sun,* a film depicting an interracial love affair. Littlejohn retired in 1958, but his network of informants in the KKK produced the arrests and convictions of five klansmen who plotted to bomb a Charlotte school in 1959. Littlejohn died in 1965.

Logan, B.F.—During Reconstruction, Logan doubled as the sheriff of Cleveland County, North Carolina, and a leader of the local KKK. In spring 1871 he joined other Klan officers in a fruitless call for moderation, then fled the state in October 1871 to evade arrest on federal conspiracy charges.

Lollar, Coleman A. ("Brownie")—A member of the Federated KKK and "special" deputy sheriff in Jefferson County, Alabama, Lollar was identified in 1949 as a ringleader of nightriding terrorism around Birmingham. He lost his badge in June 1949, after standing guard at a KKK rally in Adamsville. Witnesses identified Lollar as a member of the flogging party that whipped four victims around the same time, and Lollar admitted Klan membership at his October 1949 trial, while denying any criminal activity. Jurors acquitted him on 29 October, to rousing applause from the spectator's gallery.

Lynch, John William—As sheriff of Dade County, Georgia, Lynch led several deputies to a rural black home on the night of 2 April 1949, allegedly responding to complaints of a loud party. They arrested seven persons, then delivered their prisoners to a waiting party of klansmen who whipped all seven. A federal grand jury convened to investigate the case on 3 August 1949, and Grand Dragon Samuel Green formally banished the Trenton klavern five days later, citing its involvement in the beating. The grand jury indicted twelve defendants, including Sheriff Lynch, three of his deputies, and six civilian klansmen. At least one klansman, James Berry, participated in the trial as an alternate juror, approved by Judge Frank Hooper. Defense witnesses included Grand Dragon Sam Roper (Green's successor), who denied the existence of a Dade County klavern, and Walter Arp, self-proclaimed exalted cyclops of Georgia's seventh province, who acknowledged the presence of a provisional klavern. Prosecutors countered with testimony from Katherine

Rogers, Green's former secretary, who identified Arp as Dade County's "cygraff" (presumably "kligrapp") and described an order for ten Klan robes placed with imperial headquarters by defendant Terrell Wheeler. On 28 November, victim Mamie Clay—owner of the home raided in April—described a campaign of police harassment following her refusal to sell her home on demand from local whites. Following rejection of the first offer, Sheriff Lynch had jailed her for running a brothel, but jurors acquitted Clay in that case. Clay and other victims testified that Lynch ignored their pleas for help on 2 April, joking with masked klansmen at the scene. Another witness recalled Lynch's comment on 3 April that "I don't think we'll be bothered by anything that happened last night." Lynch, meanwhile, insisted that the knights seized his prisoners at gunpoint while threatening his life. Deputy William Hartline admitted helping to build the cross klansmen burned at Clay's home on 2 April, but insisted that his presence at the raid was "a coincidence." Prosecutors rested on 1 December, after introducing a statement from Lynch in which he admitted working with the KKK to "get this thing cleared up" by driving Clay from her home. On 2 December, Judge Hooper directed verdicts of acquittal for defendants L.C. Spears and John Wilkins (city recorder for Trenton, Georgia) on grounds of insufficient evidence. Jurors deadlocked on charges against the remaining ten defendants, producing a mistrial on 17 December 1949. Prosecutors tried again in March 1950. Jurors acquitted eight of the remaining defendants on 17 March, while convicting Lynch and Hartline of conspiracy to violate their prisoners' civil rights. Both lawmen received the maximum one-year prison term and a $1,000 fine.

Mason, Simpson—A captain in the Arkansas state militia under Governor Powell Clayton, Simpson was ambushed and murdered by Fulton County klansmen on 19 September 1868. Authorities named several suspects, and local Klan leader N.H. Tracy fled the state to avoid prosecution. Four klansmen were arrested, and two of them—L.D. Bryant and Uriah Bush—confessed under conditions that local Democrats described as torture. While the informants were en route to Salem, Arkansas, for further questioning, masked riders seized both from their escorts and riddled them with bullets. Prosecutors soon freed the two remaining defendants for lack of evidence.

McCall, Herschel C.—A Michigan lawyer who moved south and served as a deputy sheriff, in Houston, Texas, McCall retired from law enforcement in 1921 to fill the post of Houston's grand titan. He argued that a bit of violence was good for Klan morale, a stance that later won his appointment as grand dragon of Texas. A friend of would-be wizard Hiram Evans, McCall participated in the palace coup that ousted Klan founder William Simmons from power in 1922. As his reward, McCall was transferred to Washington, D.C., where he served as the invisible empire's ambassador to the United States.

McCall, Willis Virgil—Ex–dairy farmer and federal fruit inspector Willis McCall was elected sheriff of Lake County, Florida, in 1944. Although financially supported by the county's leading gamblers, McCall promised a "good, clean, fearless and

Sheriff Willis McCall shot two of the Groveland rape defendants in November 1950 (Florida State Archives).

conscientious execution of my duties" if elected, and voters took him at his word. In 1945, acting under Florida's wartime "work or fight" statute, he jailed various blacks and "radicals" on trumped up charges, holding them in virtual slavery while he pocketed their fines. Strikers were "vagrants" in McCall's eyes, and he invaded their homes without warrants, beating those who "resisted arrest." His brutality toward union organizers was legendary, and he led a boycott against editor Mabel Reese of the *Mount Dora Topic,* who dared to publish exposés on McCall's lawless tactics. Still, it was Lake County's blacks who felt McCall's heavy hand most frequently. Identified in FBI reports as an active Klan member, McCall spared no efforts in harassing African Americans or those whom he suspected (often erroneously) as blacks trying to "pass for white." In 1949, McCall framed four black defendants on false charges of raping a local white woman. One suspect was killed by McCall's civilian posse, while two others received death sentences and the fourth (a minor already in jail for vagrancy when the alleged rape occurred) was imprisoned for life. Revelations of brutality and fabricated evidence led the U.S. Supreme Court to order a new trial for two of the defendants in 1951. While transporting them from prison to the county jail that November, McCall shot the two handcuffed prisoners, killing one and leaving the other gravely wounded. A local grand jury praised McCall for his action, while an elderly U.S. attorney (and friend of McCall's) subverted a federal investigation of presumed civil rights violations. McCall continued in that vein for the remainder of his career. He was suspected (though never charged) in the December 1951 bombing murder of NAACP leader Harry Moore. Twelve years later, McCall's Tavares office was the only public building in Florida which did not lower its flag to half-mast following President John Kennedy's assassination. McCall's explanation: he feared that lowering the flag would damage it, by causing it to flap against the courthouse wall. McCall threw Native American children out of Lake County's schools, lured interracial couples to the woods for beatings by his deputies, and maintained "Colored Only" signs in his waiting room long after they were banned by law. Governor Claude Kirk finally suspended McCall from office in April 1972, after McCall beat a black prisoner to death in his jail cell. McCall avoided conviction on second-degree murder charges, but voters were fed up at last, casting their ballots for a Detroit Yankee to defeat McCall's reelection bid that November. McCall died in April 1994, at age 84, at his home on a street that bore his name.

McLeod, J.R.—As sheriff of Hillsborough County, Florida, in the 1930s, J.R. McLeod opposed the local Ku Klux Klan. In 1935, he filed criminal charges against the klansmen and Tampa police officers responsible for the torture-slaying of victim Joseph Shoemaker, but a series of trials and appeals left the guilty parties unpunished.

McMullen, Robert—Deputy Robert McMullen lost his job with the Duval County (Fla.) Sheriff's Department in July 1988, after his dual life as a KKK kleagle was exposed. The courts upheld his dismissal on appeal.

Miller, Wallace—A police officer and member of the WKKKKM in Meridian, Mississippi, Miller testified as a prosecution witness in the October 1967 federal trial of klansmen charged with killing civil rights workers James Chaney, Andrew Goodman and Michael Schwerner. According to Miller's testimony, he was informed of the murder plot in advance and took no action to prevent it.

Miller, W.D.—In 1921, while serving as sheriff of Travis County, Texas, Miller admitted his Klan membership to a local grand jury. Charles Hamly campaigned against Miller in 1922, on an anti–Klan platform, but Miller retained his office.

Millis, Marion W.—While serving as sheriff of New Hanover County, North Carolina, Millis was subpoenaed to testify before HUAC in 1965. Millis admitted joining the UKA, along with six of his deputies, but insisted that he did so to gather intelligence on Klan activity in his county. Despite that assertion, congressional investigators demonstrated that Millis filed no surveillance reports on the KKK, although he stored Klan literature and dues in his office safe. HUAC described Millis as an "ideological member" of the Klan, but that report failed to sway local voters, who reelected him as sheriff in 1966.

Moore, Oneal—Sheriff Dorman Crowe of Washington Parish, Louisiana, risked his political future by hiring two black deputies—Oneal Moore and Creed Rogers—in June 1964. One year later, on the night of 3 June 1965, nightriders ambushed Moore and Rogers on a lonely rural road, riddling their patrol car with bullets. Moore died instantly, while Rogers survived with the loss of one eye. Police in nearby Tylertown, Mississippi, arrested suspect Ernest McElveen one hour later, riding with two pistols (one recently fired) in a pickup truck that matched descriptions of the murder vehicle. Investigators identified McElveen as a member of a Klan front group (United Conservatives), the Citizens' Council and the NSRP. HUAC identified a relative, D.D. McElveen, as a member of Bogalusa's Ku Klux "wrecking crew," and McElveen retained attorney Ossie Brown, who later defended the Original Knights against federal lawsuits stemming from violence in Washington Parish. Prosecutors filed murder charges against McElveen, but later dismissed them for "lack of evidence." Moore's slaying remains officially unsolved today.

Mosher, Marion B. ("Med")—On 22 April 1922, a raiding party of thirty-seven klansmen kidnapped two members of the Elduayen family from their home in Inglewood, California. They accused Fidel and Matias Elduayen of being bootleggers, and set off in search of a jail to receive the prisoners. Pursued by Inglewood's night marshal on a commandeered motorcycle, the knights opened fire and took fire in return. One of the marshal's bullets killed Marion Mosher, an Inglewood constable, while other shots wounded Mosher's son and a deputy sheriff. The Los Angeles County coroner ruled that Mosher died "while acting as a member of an illegal masked and armed mob, personally instigated and directed by members of the Ku Klux Klan." A grand jury subsequently indicted the surviving raiders, whose number included Grand Goblin William Coburn, King Kleagle Gus Price, and Kleagle Nathan Baker.

Murphy, Gordon—While serving as chief of police in Houston, Texas, during 1920, Murphy joined Mayor Oscar Holcomb as a member of Sam Houston Klan No. 1. He remained in the KKK long after Holcomb resigned, allowing klansmen to tap Catholic telephones, intercept messages at telegraph offices, and work as spies at the city post office.

Murray, Albert—The Democratic sheriff of Reconstruction-era Alamance County, North Carolina, Murray also served as chief of CUG Camp No. 4 and encouraged his deputies to join that Klan-allied group. It came as no surprise, therefore, when Murray failed to apprehend nocturnal terrorists in the Tarheel State's most violent county.

Nance, Silas—While serving as the city marshal of Jefferson, Texas, during Reconstruction, Nance was also active in the Knights of the Rising Sun. Witnesses identified him as a member of the lynch mob that murdered George Smith on 4 October 1868.

Nash, "Trigger"—An Atlanta policeman whose first name is lost to history, "Trigger" Nash earned his nickname for shooting numerous black men. His membership in the Klan was exposed by informant Stetson Kennedy after Nash attended a meeting of the AGK's Nathan Bedford Forrest Klavern No. 1 on 1 November 1948. Several Atlanta policemen addressed that gathering, and Nash drew a round of applause "for killing his thirteenth nigger in the line of duty." According to the minutes of that gathering: "Trigger Nash, also a policeman, got up and made a talk and said he hoped he wouldn't have all the honor of killing the niggers in the South, and he hoped the people would do something about it themselves." The Atlanta Police Department, controlled by klansmen in those days, took no disciplinary action against Nash.

Norris, John C.—As the Republican sheriff of Warren County, Georgia, during Reconstruction, Norris requested federal troops to suppress Klan activity in 1868. Gunmen ambushed Norris in December 1868, inflicting several bullet wounds, but he survived to identify his assailants as klansman James Cody and his two brothers. Though partially disabled by his wounds, Norris refused to leave office, but he took the advice of close friends and declined to prosecute his attackers. In spring 1869, while he was visiting Atlanta to request more troops, Warren County Democrats declared the sheriff's office vacant and appointed a klansmen to replace Norris. Armed with a special commission from the governor and federal commanders affirming his authority, Norris returned with troops to Warren County and deposed the interloper, but Klan threats drove him out of Warren County in autumn 1869. Norris returned once more, with a new federal commission as sheriff in January 1870, whereupon local Democrats tried a different tack to remove him. In February 1870, Norris foolishly accepted a $5,000 IOU in return for his promise to limit arrests of known klansmen, subsequently receiving $3,250 in cash before he was jailed on bribery charges. Removed from office and transported to Atlanta for trial, Norris later won dismissal of the charges, but klansmen had another warrant waiting, charging him with false arrest. This time, Norris remained in Atlanta, spared from further prosecution by a gubernatorial pardon.

Oaks, Louis D.—While serving as chief of the Los Angeles Police Department, in 1922, Oaks was identified as a member of the KKK. In response to that exposure, he claimed to have resigned from the Klan soon after his initiation.

Patrick, N.W. ("Pat")—While serving as the chief of police in Saraland, Alabama, Patrick was arrested with six fellow klansmen in September 1958, charged with burning a cross at the home of a Mobile minister and with illegally destroying political posters prior to Saraland's primary election on 6 May 1958. Mobile County Sheriff Ray Bridges made the arrests, describing the Saraland police station as a center of local KKK activity. According to Bridges, the arrests were also "definitely" linked to the August 1958 murder of Mayor Oscar Driver, but none of the prisoners were charged with that crime.

Peacock, Arthur—Florida klansman Arthur Peacock served as a Tampa policeman and as a deputy sheriff for Hillsborough County in the early 1930s, before abandoning law enforcement. On 20 March 1935, he joined the raiding party that abducted "playboy" victim Robert Cargell in St. Petersburg and castrated him. Cargell identified Peacock and filed charges against him, prompting his surrender on 11 April. Released without bond to his lawyer's custody, Peacock died under mysterious circumstances six days later. Authorities officially blamed his death on a stroke.

Peden, Alonzo—An active klansman in Reconstruction-era Giles County, Tennessee, Peden also served his father as a deputy sheriff. Witnesses identified him as a leader of harassment campaigns against Republicans and Union League members in Pulaski.

Peden, Bryant—While serving as sheriff of Giles County, Tennessee, during Reconstruction, Peden was recognized as a Klan sympathizer (if not a dues-paying member). He publicly declared that blacks were still slaves, despite the outcome of the Civil War, frequently boasted of whipping his servants, and offered ex-slave owners ten dollars per head for their human "property." Peden's son and deputy, Bryan, was known throughout Giles County as an active member of the KKK.

Pickert, Heinrich—While serving as police commissioner for Detroit, Michigan, in 1936, Pickert was scandalized by exposure of his membership in the Black Legion. He avoided prosecution when fifty-odd Legion members were packed off to prison for various crimes, and dodged dismissal from his job by "frantically promot[ing] all those police officers who could compromise him." Still, it only delayed the inevitable. Pickert was finally driven from office in 1939, after a local grand jury investigation disclosed widespread graft in the department. Indictments were filed against the mayor, Wayne County's prosecutor, Detroit's police superintendent and eight uniformed officers.

Plogger, William H.—One of five Chicago policemen identified as Klan members in December 1967, Plogger was fired in lieu of criminal prosecution for stockpiling illegal weapons and allegedly plotting to murder Mayor Richard Daley.

Pope, Henry H.—An ex-Union officer during the Civil War, Pope served as sheriff of St. Mary's Parish, Louisiana, during 1867–68. In October 1868, Klan terrorists murdered Pope and a local judge, Valentine Chase. Those crimes remain officially unsolved.

Price, Cecil Ray—As a deputy of Sheriff Lawrence Rainey in Neshoba County, Mississippi, and an active member of the WKKKKM, Price participated in the Klan's conspiracy to murder civil rights worker Michael Schwerner. On 21 June 1964, he arrested Schwerner, with companions James Chaney and Andrew Goodman, on a spurious traffic charge and held them until nightfall, while a Klan murder party assembled nearby. After releasing the trio from jail, Price then stopped them again on a rural highway and delivered the three to their killers. Federal prosecutors first indicted Price, with Rainey, for beating black prisoner Kirk Culbertson in custody, then charged both officers with conspiracy to violate the civil rights of Chaney, Goodman and Schwerner. Following his arrest on the latter charges, Price reported that he was an hour late for work because "I had to spend so much time shaking hands" with white townspeople. In 1967, prior to trial on the conspiracy charge, Price ran for sheriff of Neshoba County, reminding voters how he had worked to "maintain a buffer between our people and the many agitators who have invaded our county." He added: "You can be sure that I will be ready to serve you in the future." Voters rejected Price in favor of ex-sheriff (and fellow klansman) Ethel "Hop" Barnett, and federal jurors convicted Price in October 1967. He received a six-year prison term, delayed by appeals until 1970, and won parole from custody in 1974. In early 2001, Price agreed to cooperate with state authorities on a renewed investigation of the Neshoba County murders. Before he could provide significant information, however, Price died on 6 May 2001, from head injuries suffered when he fell from a lift in an equipment rental shop. No witnesses observed the accident.

Rainey, Lawrence A.—First hired as a policeman in Canton, Mississippi, Rainey transferred to the Philadelphia (Miss.)

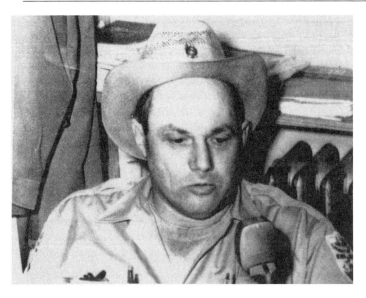

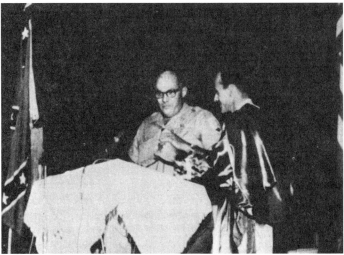

Top: **Sheriff Lawrence Rainey was among the klansmen charged with violating the rights of three civil rights workers murdered in June 1964.** *Above:* **Sheriff Rainey addresses a Mississippi Klan rally, sharing the stage with Grand Dragon Edward McDaniel. (both photographs: Library of Congress).**

Police Department two years later. There, in October 1957, he killed black resident Luther Jackson. When a female friend of Jackson's criticized the unprovoked shooting, she was beaten by Rainey and Philadelphia's police chief. Four years later, Rainey transferred to the Neshoba County Sheriff's Department, under Sheriff Ethel Barnett. In May 1962, with Barnett and another deputy, he shot and killed a handcuffed prisoner, Willie Nash, and escaped prosecution on a plea of self-defense. (Like Luther Jackson, Nash was black.) Elected as sheriff in 1963, Rainey campaigned on a promise to "handle the niggers and outsiders" expected during 1964's "Freedom Summer." Local blacks were so intimidated by Rainey that he once cleared a black county fair of 300 people by simply entering the room and standing silently until the crowd dispersed. In 1964, federal prosecutors charged Rainey and Deputy Cecil Price with beating black mechanic Kirk Culbertson, leaving him with a fractured skull. An active member of the WKKKKM, Rainey also faced charges of

conspiring to murder civil rights workers James Chaney, Andrew Goodman and Michael Schwerner in June 1964. Prior to his federal conspiracy trial, Rainey appeared as a guest speaker at UKA rallies across Mississippi, and he received an ovation from the state sheriff's association. Judge O.H. Barnett—a cousin of ex–Governor Ross Barnett, named in FBI files as a "Klan judge"—praised Rainey as "the bravest sheriff in America." Jurors acquitted Rainey in October 1967, and he left office two months later, finding work as a security guard (with a black supervisor).

Raley, John—As a klansman and town constable in Reconstruction-era Warrenton, Georgia, Raley participated in the March 1869 lynching of Dr. G.W. Darden, a local Republican activist. That spring, Raley was briefly named sheriff of Warren County in a Democratic bid to replace Sheriff John Norris, who was absent in Atlanta on official business. One of six klansmen subsequently arrested by Norris and federal troops in June 1869, charged with Darden's murder, Raley posted bail and escaped punishment when the charges were dismissed.

Robinson, J.T.—While serving as chief of police in Natchez, Mississippi, Robinson was arrested by the Adams County sheriff in December 1965, on a warrant filed by UKA Grand Dragon Edward McDaniel. The complaint accused Robinson with failure to enforce the state's anti-boycott law against black activists, but the charge was later dismissed.

Rogers, Calvin—A black constable in Marianna, Florida, during Reconstruction, Rogers was a repeated target of Ku Klux violence during 1869–70. Klansmen first tried to assassinate him at a picnic on 20 September 1869, but they missed their target, killing two bystanders instead. On 1 October 1869, unknown snipers fired on Klan leader James Coker at a local hotel. Again the marksmanship was faulty, leaving Coker unscathed while wounding companion James McClellan and killing McClellan's daughter. Klansmen blamed Rogers for the shooting, some claiming that they heard his voice give the order to fire, and a week-long pogrom ensued around Marianna, leaving several blacks dead. Rogers escaped that purge, but assassins finally killed him in spring 1870.

Roper, Samuel W.—An Atlanta policeman and member of the 1920s Klan, Roper led the Georgia Bureau of Investigation during the second term of Governor Eugene Talmadge (1941–43). In 1946, while serving as a detective with the Atlanta Police Department, Roper doubled as nighthawk for Grand Dragon Samuel Green and as exalted cyclops for Oakland City Post No. 297. When Green died from a heart attack in August 1949, Roper stepped into command of the AGK, which he publicly described as "an educational outfit." A public retreat from violence ultimately doomed the AGK, which apparently disbanded prior to the U.S. Supreme Court's 1954 "Black Monday" ruling on school integration.

Scarborough, W.W.—While serving as a deputy sheriff in Fulton County, Georgia, during 1939–40, Scarborough doubled as exalted cyclops of East Point Klan No. 61 and as an active member of the nightriding Klavalier Klub. His team committed at least fifty floggings, including the fatal beating of two young lovers on 2 March 1940 and the murder of barber Ike Gaston two weeks later. Jurors convicted Scarborough and seven other klansmen (including two more deputies) on various felony charges, but all were released from prison by Governor Eugene Talmadge in 1941.

Semet, Ernest—One of five Chicago police officers identified as klansmen in December 1967, Semet was forced from his job in lieu of prosecution on conspiracy and weapons charges.

Shirley, Thomas J.—While serving as chief of police for Birmingham, Alabama, in the early 1920s, Shirley joined the KKK and was named to serve on the order's imperial kloncilium. He valued Klan support so much, in fact, that he once urged the police chief of Nashville, Tennessee, to form his own klavern as an adjunct to local law enforcement. Dismissed by the city council in 1922, Shirley campaigned and won election as sheriff of Jefferson County. In that capacity, he praised klansmen who joined an off-duty deputy to raid three Chinese cafés in January 1926, performing "breath tests" and arresting six persons for supposed liquor violations. At headquarters, Chief Deputy Henry Hill (also a klansman) released the prisoners, tore up the warrants, and demanded the badge of the officer who joined the raid. Defendants in that case created a further rift in Klan ranks by hiring Ku Klux lawyer Hugo Black as their attorney, fielding him against Klan prosecutors George Frey and Hugh Locke. Controversy surrounding the raids cost Shirley his reelection bid in 1926, and he left office as sheriff in January 1927.

Stanton, Richard—A Chicago policeman, identified in December 1967 as a member of James Venable's National Knights, Stanton was permitted to resign in lieu of prosecution for stockpiling illegal weapons and allegedly plotting the murder of Mayor Richard Daley.

Star, S.D. ("Dave")—Star served for twenty-three years as sheriff of Orange County, Florida. Declassified FBI reports from 1952 identify him as an active member of the KKK.

Stirewalt, John—In 1966, voters in Rowan County, North Carolina, elected Stirewalt as their sheriff, despite his admission of membership in the UKA. Stirewalt publicly resigned from the Klan when he took office, but he subsequently named Grand Dragon James Jones as a "special deputy," after Jones warned Stirewalt of potential violence at a forthcoming UKA rally in Salisbury. Sheriff Stirewalt rescinded the appointment after media exposure sparked public outrage.

Switzer, F.W.—On 30 November 1935, Patrolman F.W. Switzer drove one of the cars that delivered prisoners Eugene Poulnot, Samuel Rogers and Joseph Shoemaker to a KKK flogging squad in Tampa, Florida. Shoemaker subsequently died from his injuries, and Switzer was one of those charged with his murder. Judge Robert Dewell created a national uproar by directing verdicts of acquittal in that case. Switzer was also a prime suspect (though never indicted) in the March 1935 castration of victim Robert Cargell, in St. Petersburg.

Tanner, Henry—While serving as the chief of police in Dallas, Texas, Tanner joined the KKK in 1921. He resigned from the order a year later, after his membership was exposed by the Dallas County Citizens League.

Tate, John K.—Longtime Tennessee klansman Jesse Stoner once recalled that "back in 1924 the Klan was extremely strong in Chattanooga and at that time elected city judge McCoy, Sheriff John Tate, and others." Stoner's memory was defective in at least one respect: Tate served as sheriff from 1932 through 1934.

Taylor, Woodford—While serving as a Virginia state prison guard, in January 1967, Taylor was one of five persons jailed for illegal cross-burning in Richmond. Spurred by two incidents on New Year's Day, the arrests spearheaded a crackdown on Klan activity by Governor Mills Goodwin.

Tittsworth, R.G.—As chief of police for Tampa, Florida, in the 1930s, Tittsworth welcomed klansmen into his department and used the KKK as an extralegal weapon against blacks, Hispanics, and labor organizers in the region's citrus industry. In 1935, his officers infiltrated a local leftist group, the Modern Democrats, and raided the organization's headquarters on 30 November, afterward delivering prisoners Eugene Poulnot, Samuel Rogers and Joseph Shoemaker to a Klan flogging party. Shoemaker died from his wounds, sparking an international scandal, but Tittsworth did everything within his power to stall the resultant investigation. He opposed suspension or arrest of any officers involved, even as a token show of fairness, and soon found himself indicted for conspiracy in the attack. Convicted at his first trial, in August 1936, Tittsworth received a four-year prison term for his complicity in the assault on Poulnot (later reversed on appeal). At his trial for Shoemaker's murder, in October 1937, Judge Robert Dewell directed verdicts of acquittal for all defendants.

Traeger, William I.—In May 1922, while serving as Sheriff of Los Angeles, California, Traeger was identified as a member of the KKK. He claimed that his affiliation with the order had been brief, terminated soon after his initiation.

Wallace, George—While serving as a deputy for Orange County, Texas, under Sheriff Thomas Garner, Wallace escorted Judge W.H. Davidson to a KKK rally in Beaumont. There, Garner and other klansmen tried unsuccessfully to recruit Judge Davidson for the order.

Ward, Harold—Wyoming authorities fired prison guard Harold Ward in February 1988, for donning KKK regalia to terrorize black inmates at the institution where he worked.

Webb, J.S.—While serving as sheriff of Reconstruction-era Rutherford County, Tennessee, Webb was dragged from his home by klansmen in April 1868 and threatened with lynching if he did not resign. He refused, and while klansmen later whipped his brother, they never again challenged Webb.

West, Thomas—West served as sheriff of Jackson County, Florida, after the Civil War, but he resigned in March 1871, following numerous threats from the Klan and a daylight assault in downtown Marianna.

Wiggins, Joe—In September 1924, while testifying in an embezzlement case in Raleigh, North Carolina, police detective Joe Wiggins was forced to admit his Klan membership on cross-examination.

Wiley, Frank A.—While an active member of the Reconstruction KKK, Wiley won election to serve as sheriff in Caswell County, North Carolina. In May 1870, he lured Republican state senator John Stephens into a courthouse trap where he was slain by klansmen. Afterward, Wiley claimed that Stephens was last seen alive in the company of "an unknown Negro." Arrested in July 1870, after Governor William Holden declared martial law, Wiley was never brought to trial.

Willis, Richard Andrew—A police officer in Philadelphia, Mississippi, Willis was among the klansmen jailed in February 1965, on federal charges of conspiring to kill civil rights workers James Chaney, Andrew Goodman and Michael Schwerner. Jurors acquitted him at trial, in October 1967.

Worley, Claude—During his 1926 campaign to become mayor of Indianapolis, Indiana, John Duval promised Grand Dragon David Stephenson that if elected, he would name Claude Worley as police chief. Duval kept his promise in January 1927.

Young, Alex—A Louisville, Kentucky, policeman who joined the 1980s KKK and later formed his own right-wing extremist group on the side, Young was slapped with various felony charges in 1986. At his trial in May, he described Klan infiltration of the Louisville Police Department as extensive.

PRIVATE EYES

Where law enforcement is unable or unwilling to move effectively against the Ku Klux Klan, private groups and individuals have sometimes filled the gap, opposing the order's criminal activities via public exposure, civil litigation, or armed force. The groups and individuals described below provide examples of such watchdog efforts from Reconstruction to the present day.

American Civil Liberties Union—The ACLU was founded in 1920, the same year in which the KKK began to spread nationwide from its Georgia stronghold. Based in New York City, the Union was pledged to defend the civil rights of any and all citizens—a broad mandate that quickly brought it into conflict with the Klan. From its early days, the ACLU has monitored and publicized Ku Klux activity designed to oppress or intimidate others. In 1923, ACLU attorneys opposed the efforts of Akron, Ohio's Klan-infested school board to dismiss Catholic teachers, and waged a national campaign against Klan-sponsored laws designed to ban parochial schools. After klansmen and police flogged several leftists in Tampa, Florida, killing one of their victims, ACLU member (and Secretary of the Interior) Harold Ickes addressed the Union's annual convention on the menace of "A Nation in Nightshirts." At the same time, however, ACLU attorneys often have been called upon to aid the Klan itself, where the order's First Amendment rights have been

unlawfully abridged. Union lawyers have supported the Klan's right to march and to express its hateful views in public. As ACLU founder Roger Baldwin explained, "We had some complaints about the denial of the Klan's right to parade in their nightgowns and pillowcases, and their rights to burn fiery crosses on private property. We decided that we had to defend their civil rights.... The Imperial Wizard responded by thanking us for our generous expressions of Americanism, and telling us that they would be glad to accept our services." Although generally friendly with the NAACP, the ACLU opposed that group's effort to ban Klan literature from the U.S. mails (1920), and protested bans on screenings of *The Birth of a Nation* in Detroit, Jersey City, Newark and Philadelphia. ACLU attorneys supported the Klan when its meetings or marches were banned by the mayors of Boston (1923) and Cudahy, Wisconsin (1924); when a Kansas judge barred demonstrations statewide (1925); and when New York's Walker Law required public registration for members of secret societies (1926). Only the latter incident produced a test case, and the U.S. Supreme Court upheld the Walker Law in 1928. Seven years later, the ACLU opposed New Jersey's statute banning any public statement "advocating hatred, abuse, violence, or hostility against any group or groups of persons by reason of race, color, religion, or manner of worship." Two years later, the Union successfully lobbied against passage of a similar law in New York.

In each case, the ACLU's defense of the KKK cost it black, Catholic and Jewish members. Controversy continued after World War II, as a new Red Scare produced "loyalty oaths" and lists of "subversive" organizations whose members were barred from public office. In 1947, Ernie Besig of the Northern California ACLU defended the right of policemen to join controversial groups, declaring, "It doesn't make any difference whether a Chief of Police is a member of the Ku Klux Klan or the Fellowship of Reconciliation. The test is how he performs his job." By contrast, six years later, ACLU board member Norman Thomas denied that klansmen or communists had any right to teach in public schools. In 1960, the Union supported ANP founder George Rockwell's right to hold public rallies, and six years later it defended Klan evangelist Connie Lynch against charges of inciting a Baltimore riot. In 1969, ACLU attorneys defended an Ohio klansman jailed under a 1919 criminal syndicalism statute for saying: "If our President, our Congress, our Supreme Court continues to suppress the white, Caucasian race, it's possible that there might have to be some revengeance [*sic*] taken." That case also found its way to the U.S. Supreme Court, where a majority decreed that the First Amendment protected even calls for violence (as long as no real violence was attempted). The 1970s brought a rash of controversial cases, as the ACLU defended U.S. Marines at Camp Pendleton against punitive action for starting a klavern on-base (1976); challenged a ban on Klan rallies at integrated schools by the school board of Harrison County, Mississippi (1977); and defended the right of Frank Collin's NSWPP to march through the Jewish enclave of Skokie, Illinois (1977). In the 1980s, the ACLU's Kansas City affiliate waged a long court fight in favor of the Klan's right to broadcast over public-access television. In the 1990s, ACLU attorneys also defended several klansmen in cross-burning cases, supporting their clients' right to engage in "symbolic speech."

Such choices have resulted in mass resignations and the splintering of certain Union chapters, but the ACLU's leaders remain steadfast in their commitment to defending anyone whose rights are jeopardized. In the 1920s, Roger Baldwin told reporters, "We make no distinctions whatever as to whose rights are involved. We will defend the Ku Klux Klan and the Communists, both of whom are opposed to free speech." Fifty years later, after the Skokie incident, ACLU president Norman Dorsen said his group was simply "keeping faith with our principles." Burt Neuborne, former legal director for the ACLU, was more pragmatic: "It's like taking out the garbage, but somebody's got to take the garbage out."

American Unity League—

The AUL was founded in Chicago, on 21 June 1922, by Joseph Keller, Grady Rutledge and Robert Shepherd. Their sole purpose was the eradication of the Ku Klux Klan, both in the Windy City and throughout America at large. While membership was open to all comers, and black Bishop Samuel Fallows of the Reformed Episcopal Church served as honorary chairman, the AUL's most influential proponents were three Catholic priests, Rev. E.A. Kelly, Rev. William McNamee, and Rev. J.F. Noll. Acting chairman (and later AUL president) Patrick O'Donnell was a successful criminal lawyer who traveled throughout the Midwest to speak against the KKK. O'Donnell estimated the AUL's membership at 27,000 by summer 1922 and 50,000 three months later. (The Klan, meanwhile, claimed some 200,000 knights in Chicago and environs.) The AUL's primary tactic lay in the exposure of closet klansmen, beginning with the first issue of *Tolerance* which identified 150 Chicago knights on 22 September 1922. The premier issue's print run of 2,700 sold out within hours, and 17,500 copies rolled off the presses a week later, expanding to a peak circulation of 150,000. Some membership lists were allegedly stolen, while the AUL purchased others—including a roster of 6,000 Chicago klansmen sold for $200 by Marvin Hinshaw, a former Midwestern king kleagle. AUL leaders considered their actions a public service, but critic and Klan historian John Mecklin opined that *Tolerance* matched "the most rabid Klan publications in its shrieking and hysterical condemnations of all things pertaining to the Klan."

Be that as it may, the tactic of "outing" Ku Kluxers was clearly successful. Augustus Olsen, named in the fifth issue of *Tolerance,* lost his job as president of Chicago's Washington Park National Bank after hundreds of Catholic and Jewish depositors closed their accounts in protest. Many lesser klansmen visited the AUL's headquarters to apologize for joining or to claim that they had been coerced into the order. When *Tolerance* named butcher Harry Junker as a klansman (over his denials), nocturnal bombers demolished his shop. Four days later, when a second bomb struck the former office quarters of the Klan newspaper *Dawn,* editor-klansman Edwin Parke accused *Tolerance*'s subscription editor of planting the charge. When the AUL began naming Hoosier klansmen in *Tolerance,* the Klan's own *Fiery Cross* retaliated by printing the name of Catholic businessmen in Indianapolis, branding the local Claypool Hotel as "the head-quarters of the Knights of Columbus, the Jewish B'nai B'rith and propagation headquarters for both." A federal judge subsequently impounded most of the 10,400 KKK membership lists printed in Indianapolis, and the AUL counted its local efforts as a failure.

The AUL's branch in New York failed in autumn 1922, after League leaders hired Klan double-agent Neufield Jones to run the satellite office. Jones pocketed some $30,000 from the AUL but never produced any lists of Klan members for publication. When headquarters recognized his duplicity, the AUL filed suit against the KKK for $500,000, but they failed to recover a penny. In Chicago, meanwhile, AUL leaders faced a series of defamation lawsuits filed by businessmen "exposed" in *Tolerance* who claimed that they were listed by mistake or out of spite. A doctor and a plumber sued for $25,000 apiece, followed by Catholic attorney J. William Brooks ($100,000) and chewing gum tycoon William Wrigley, Jr. ($50,000). Wrigley offered an additional $50,000 to any charitable group that could prove he was a klansman. His alleged signature on a Klan application printed in *Tolerance,* Wrigley maintained, was a "rank forgery and about as much like mine as the north pole like Vesuvius." Wrigley's claim prompted *Tolerance* editor and AUL secretary Grady Rutledge to secure an injunction against two staffers who, he claimed, inserted Wrigley's name in *Tolerance* over his own objections. Rutledge soon defected to the KKK, lending his talents to *Dawn* and revealing the names of various AUL informants. Thus betrayed, the AUL soon closed its doors.

Anti-Defamation League—

Sigmund Livingston of B'nai B'rith founded the ADL in October 1913, in response to anti–Semitic hysteria surrounding the Georgia murder trial of Leo Frank (whose lynchers, two years later, burned the first cross on American soil and subsequently joined the reborn KKK). According to its charter, "The immediate object of the League is to stop, by appeals to reason and conscience and, if necessary, by appeals to law, the defamation of the Jewish people. Its ultimate purpose is to secure justice and fair treatment to all citizens alike and to put an end forever to unjust and unfair discrimination against and ridicule of any sect or body of citizens." To that end, over the past nine decades, ADL investigators have maintained close watch on a variety of racist and anti–Semitic groups, including the Ku Klux Klan, the German-American Bund and other pro–Nazi groups of the 1930s, Father Charles Coughlin's Christian Front, the many vehicles of Gerald L.K. Smith, countless post-war neo–Nazi cliques, the Citizens' Councils, Posse Comitatus, the Nation of Islam, the "patriot militia" movement and modern neo–Confederate groups in the South. In the 1920s, ADL activists published the names of numerous klansmen, thus stripping away their mask of secrecy, and won a half-hearted apology from millionaire racist Henry Ford for his long-running attacks on Jews in the *Dearborn Independent.* (Despite that apology, Ford still fraternized with Nazis and employed many members of the Bund on his strike-breaking "security" force in Detroit.)

Klansmen and their neo-fascist allies typically attack the ADL as part of a "world Jewish conspiracy" that controls the news media, Congress, and American government in general (via "ZOG"). Some mainstream critics suggest that ADL spokesmen exaggerate (or even fabricate) incidents of anti–Semitism in their zeal to suppress any adverse commentary on Jews or the state of Israel. On 8 April 1993, after California congressman Pete McCloskey sued the ADL for invasion of privacy, police raided the League's offices in Los Angeles and San Francisco. They found files, consisting primarily of newspaper and magazine clippings, on some 12,000 individuals and 950 organizations (including the ACLU, the African National Congress, Greenpeace, Mills College, *Mother Jones* magazine, the National Lawyers Guild, and the United Auto Workers Union). Those revelations, in turn, prompted a lawsuit by the American-Arab Anti-Discrimination League, which the ADL settled out of court in 1998 (paying court costs for the plaintiffs and spending another $25,000 "to further Jewish-Muslim and Jewish-black relations").

While that case wound its way through the courts, in 1994, William and Dorothy Quigley sued the ADL over accusations of anti–Semitism arising from their feud with neighbors Mitchell and Candace Aronson in Evergreen, Colorado. Court documents indicate that ADL members secretly taped telephone conversations between the Quigleys, in which they discussed burning crosses on the Aronsons' lawn, placing fake oven doors outside their house (presumably in reference to the Holocaust), and dousing the Aronson children with gasoline. Upholding the Quigleys $10.5 million defamation claim in April 2001, U.S. District Judge Edward Nottingham ruled that "it is not unreasonable to infer that public charges of anti–Semitism leveled by the ADL will be taken seriously and assumed by many to be true without question. In that respect, the ADL is in a unique position of being able to cause substantial harm to individuals when it lends its backing to allegations of anti–Semitism." Nottingham opined that the ADL had not thoroughly investigated the Aronsons' case or weighed the consequences of its published findings. In March 2004, the U.S. Supreme Court refused to hear the ADL's appeal of that case (which represented its first legal defeat).

Anti-Klan Network *see* Center for Democratic Renewal

Berry, Isaac—With assistance from fellow Republicans, Berry organized an anti–Klan movement (including several disaffected ex-klansmen) in Reconstruction-era Blount County, Alabama. Armed bands visited the homes of known klansmen, warning them against future nightriding. The tactic proved effective, and terrorism in Blount County was substantially reduced.

Center for Democratic Renewal—The CDR began life in 1979 as the National Anti-Klan Network, founded by civil rights activists Anne Braden (whose husband was framed by Kentucky authorities in 1954, on a charge of bombing his own house) and Rev. C.T. Vivian. From humble beginnings, the Atlanta-based organization quickly grew into a coalition of sixty-odd human rights groups concerned with the resurgence of KKK and neo–Nazi violence in the late 1970s. Collaborating groups included the American Friends Service Committee, the

National Council of Churches, the Presbyterian Church of the USA, the Unitarian Universalist Church, the United Church of Christ and the United Methodist Church, in addition to various mosques, synagogues and independent political organizations. The NAKN changed its name in 1985, to become the CDR. It continues documenting racist violence to the present day and publishes its findings periodically. One such publication—*When Hate Groups Come to Town: A Manual of Effective Community Responses*—has been widely used throughout America to counter racist recruiting campaigns. In 1990, CDR's lobbyists successfully added mention of sexual orientation to the federal Hate Crimes Statistical Reporting Act. Over the next decade, as arson attacks on black churches multiplied in Dixie, CDR leaders founded the National Coalition of Burned Churches to press for a federal investigation. In 2000, the CDR's *Georgia State Climate Report* prompted legislators to enact the Peach State's first law defining and penalizing hate crimes. Most recently, the CDR's Southern Action Project has expanded to include a National Southern Coalition Against Racism and Bigotry, with eighty participating groups at press time for this volume.

Committee for Defense of Civil Rights in Tampa—New York leftists led by Norman Thomas formed this group in December 1935, after victim Joseph Shoemaker died from injuries inflicted by a Ku Klux flogging squad in Tampa, Florida. The group's intention was to publicize the case and thus "bring down upon the heads of government in the city of Tampa the full force of public indignation everywhere." That effort backfired in the trial of suspects charged with whipping Shoemaker and two companions, as defense attorneys branded Thomas a "nationally known communist propagandist," while maintaining of the CDCRT's "purpose was to destroy Americanism and American institutions by force of violence." When the defendants were acquitted, CDCRT spokesmen declared that "murder is safe in Florida if practiced by Klansmen with the support both of a political machine that would make Tammany Hall look like a Sunday school and of employing interests which have established American records in the exploitation of labor." A week after the verdict, Florida Governor Fred Cone met a six-member CDCRT delegation in New York City, telling them, "I'm ashamed of Florida myself." That said, Cone felt obliged to add a plug for vigilantism: "You go down there advocating the overthrow of the American government, you'll be run out of town on a rail. I think that a man ought to be hung on a tree if he advocates overthrow of government."

Dallas County Citizens League—The twentieth century's first formal anti–Klan group was founded in Dallas, Texas, on 4 April 1922. Its literature posed the question: "Who can teach Americanism, tried patriots or the Night Prowlers?"

Deacons for Defense and Justice—A black self-defense group, founded in Jonesboro, Louisiana, in summer 1964, the Deacons allegedly engaged in armed skirmishes with Klan nightriders around Bogalusa and elsewhere. On one occasion, members of the group took a black youth into protective custody after klansmen accused him of stealing a kiss from a

white girl. (The "victim" later recanted her story and charges were dropped.) FBI agents, ever alert to black assertiveness, sent reports on the "gun-carrying black vigilante group" to "appropriate ... authorities in the state of Louisiana." Claims of DDJ chapters in Alabama and Mississippi remained unconfirmed at press time for this work. HBO dramatized the group's activities in a made-for-cable movie, *Deacons for Defense*, in 2003.

Dees, Morris Seligman, Jr.—An Alabama native, born 16 December 1936, Dees graduated from the University of Alabama Law School in 1960 and practiced in Montgomery while operating a successful book publishing firm (Fuller & Dees Marketing Group). In 1969, after a self-described "night of soul searching at a snowed-in Cincinnati airport," Dees sold the company to Times Mirror (parent company of the *Los Angeles Times*) and launched a new career in civil rights litigation. In 1969, he filed suit to integrate Montgomery's all-white YMCA facility. Two years later, with Joe Levin, Dees founded the SPLC in Montgomery, using that nonprofit organization to strike crippling blows against several violent hate groups. His courtroom victories include a $7 million judgment against the UKA in Alabama (1987), $1 million against the IEKKKK (1988), $12.5 million against Tom Metzger's WAR (1990), $1 million against a Church of the Creator cultist (1994), $85,000 against National Alliance leader William Pierce (1995), and $6.5 million against the Aryan Nations. Those triumphs have made Dees the focus of hatred by denizens of the far-right fringe. Former klansman Louis Beam once challenged Dees to a duel, later posting Internet messages claiming that Dees had "earned two death sentences" for his anti-racist activities. Around the same time, North Carolina klansman Frazier Glenn Miller posted a "point" scale for would-be "Aryan warriors," with the highest number (888) reserved for anyone who murdered Dees. The SPLC leader's career was dramatized in a 1992 made-for-TV movie, *Line of Fire: The Morris Dees Story*.

Detroit Anti-Klan Coalition—This group organized to oppose Klan applications for a public demonstration during June 1980. Its members assaulted klansmen and neo–Nazis at a meeting of the Detroit city council on 26 June, resulting in ten arrests.

HateWatch—In summer 1995, Harvard Law School reference librarian David Goldman established a website titled *Guide to Hate Groups on the Internet*. In early 1996, he changed its name to *HateWatch* and expanded its coverage, providing both the URLs for various racist websites and critical commentary from a nonracist viewpoint. Goldman's operative motto came from Anglo-American essayist Logan Pearsall Smith: "How it infuriates a bigot, when he is forced to drag out his dark convictions." Goldman shut down his website on 16 January 2001, after running it single-handed for nearly five years.

Iron Ring—Founded in April 1921 by J. Finley Wilson, black publisher of the *Washington Eagle*, this group existed to fight the Klan, disseminate racial news, and monitor federal legislation in Congress. FBI agents compiled a dossier of rumors concerning the Iron Ring's "subversive" activity, but no details of any concrete action are available today.

John Brown Anti-Klan Committee—Based in Austin, Texas, this group exposed KKK paramilitary training exercises at Camp Puller (west of Houston) in November 1980. Adverse publicity surrounding Camp Puller produced lawsuits and a federal injunction barring maintenance of "private armies."

Kennedy, William Stetson—A native of Jacksonville, Florida, born in 1916, Kennedy traced his lineage to signers of the Declaration of Independence. His grandfather was a Confederate army veteran, and Kennedy's favorite uncle was a klansman in the 1920s. Kennedy's youthful fascination with the KKK turned to implacable hatred in 1923, after Jacksonville klansmen whipped and raped his family's black maid, to punish her for "insulting" a white streetcar driver who short-changed her on a fare. During the 1930s, Kennedy worked with the New Deal WPA's writer's project, then served as southeastern editorial director for the CIO's political action committee, observing at first hand the Klan's brutal war against organized labor in Dixie. During and after World War II, he helped the ADL and the Nonsectarian Anti-Nazi League, collecting inside information on the KKK and the neo–Nazi Columbians. As "John S. Perkins," Kennedy joined the AGK and furnished regular reports to his employers, as well as columnist Drew Pearson. He also published scathing articles under his own name while klansmen searched in vain for the elusive mole. (Grand Dragon Samuel Green offered a reward of $1,000 per pound for "the traitor's ass, FOB Atlanta.") When not embarrassing the Klan in print, Kennedy also leaked material to Georgia Assistant Attorney General Dan Duke, thereby aiding Duke's campaign to revoke the AGK's charter. Kennedy infiltrated Klavalier Klub flogging parties, warned some victims in advance, and soon began appearing in court as a prosecution witness. On the side, he furnished information to producers of the *Superman* radio program, launching the Man of Steel on a month-long crusade against the KKK. Kennedy subsequently hit the lecture circuit and published a book detailing his adventures with the Klan. In 1946, HUAC granted him a perfunctory interview, but the ap-

Longtime Klan opponent Stetson Kennedy (with "Frisk + Arrest" sign) protests a 1995 KKK parade in Ft. Lauderdale, Florida (Stetson Kennedy).

athetic congressional Red-hunters declined his evidence of Ku Klux terrorism. When Kennedy pressed for FBI action against the Klan, Director J. Edgar Hoover responded with a smear campaign, warning sponsors of a scheduled television interview that Kennedy was a "possible psychopathic case" who had participated in "various communist-inspired programs." Kennedy spent the years 1953–60 in Europe, then returned to Florida and settled in St. Augustine, launching a tutorial program for local blacks that paved the way for civil rights demonstrations in 1963–64. Continuing his work into the 1980s, Kennedy published articles alleging police complicity in the 1951 Harry Moore assassination, but his "evidence" against Lake County Sheriff Willis McCall failed to impress prosecutors.

Knights of the Blazing Ring—A Pennsylvania anti-Klan group, founded in 1923, the KBR existed simultaneously with the larger, better-known Knights of the Flaming Circle.

Knights of the Flaming Circle—Organized in Pennsylvania during 1923, the KFC soon expanded to plant chapters in New Jersey, New York and Ohio. While pledged to oppose the KKK, its members observed Klan-like rituals and burned large circles to counter the Klan's fiery crosses. In Steubenville, Ohio, members of the KFC beat attacked Klan meetings, dragging klansmen from their cars and beating them. The combination of arcane rites and violence ultimately doomed the KFC, described by the *New York Times* as "just about as ridiculous as the Klan itself." In December 1965, New Jersey resident Thomas A. Johnson announced plans to revive the group and thereby counter recent Klan recruiting efforts in Wanaque. His declaration prompted a rash of anonymous threats, and the new KFC failed to materialize, a victim of the same public apathy that ultimately doomed Wanaque's tiny klavern.

Knights of the Invisible Jungle of the Tiger's Eye—Founded in September 1922 by Klan opponents in Buffalo, New York, the KIJTE was a secret club "devoted to destroying the Knights of the Ku Klux Klan, Inc." in Buffalo. Operating from headquarters on Main Street, the group vowed to serve as "another link added to the chain that will soon drag the Klan from its hidden realm."

Knights of Liberty—Not to be confused with Tulsa, Oklahoma's Klan front group of the same name, New York's Knights of Liberty was an anti-Klan group organized by a penitent grand goblin.

Let Live League—Following the collapse of the American Unity League in late 1923, journalists Frank Poston and Thomas Shankle founded the LLL as Chicago's primary anti-Klan organization. No further details of its activities are presently available.

Loyal Legion of Lincoln—One of seven anti-Klan groups founded during 1923, the LLL planted scattered chapters across the Midwest. In place of the Klan's traditional fiery crosses, LLL members burned large wooden L's.

Minute Men of the West—Organized in 1923, this group of Klan opponents in San Francisco, California, mim-

icked the American Unity League by exposing klansmen to public scrutiny whenever possible.

Mossy-Backs—A Unionist, anti-Klan vigilante group, the Mossy-Backs were active in Fayette County, Alabama, during 1869–71. Members aided Sheriff F.N. Treadway in arresting Klan terrorists and waged sporadic guerrilla warfare against the numerically superior KKK when lack of evidence precluded indictments. Despite the group's best efforts, resistance to the Klan was crushed in 1871 and klansmen "redeemed" the district for white-supremacist "home rule."

National Vigilance Association—One of the nation's most effective anti-Klan groups of the 1920s, chartered in Washington, D.C., the NVA drew its membership from the upper ranks of education, politics and business. Together, they lobbied for passage of anti-mask laws in every state and for enactment of a federal statute banning mob violence. The latter goal was not achieved, but eight states—Arizona, Illinois, Iowa, Louisiana, Minnesota, New Mexico, North Dakota and Oklahoma—passed anti-mask laws during 1923–24.

Nonsectarian Anti-Nazi League—New Yorkers James Sheldon and Dr. S. William Kalb founded this group in the late 1930s, to expose and counteract the expansion of fascist groups in the United States. While their concern was initially triggered by the German-American Bund, which trained 4,000 young Americans to hate Jews and revere Adolf Hitler at New Jersey's Camp Nordland, many other groups came under scrutiny at the same time. Klansmen who fraternized with Nazis rated close investigation, along with allied groups as diverse as Father Charles Coughlin's Christian Front, William Pelley's Silver Shirt Legion, and Georgia Governor Eugene Talmadge's Vigilantes, Inc. The League used undercover agents such as Stetson Kennedy and Arthur Derounian (AKA John Roy Carlson) to infiltrate various hate groups and report on their activities. After World War II, Kennedy remained with the League for a time, penetrating the AGK, Atlanta's brown-shirted Columbians, and various Florida groups led by klansman Bill Hendrix. In 1948, the League petitioned Alabama Governor James Folsom to revoke the Klan's state charter, but Folsom rejected the plea after consultation with Ira Thompson, his chief counsel (and exalted cyclops of the 1920s Crenshaw County KKK). Still, publications by Derounian and Kennedy helped bring the Klan and its pro-fascist allies into disrepute limited their covert spread into mainstream society.

Order of Anti-Poke Noses—Anti-Klan residents of Searcy County, Arkansas, organized this group in 1923, declaring themselves "opposed to any organization that attends to everyone's business but its own." Spokesmen also voiced their support for elected officials who "do not need to be eternally prodded by the Ku Klux Klan."

Parker, Albert H.—The first of eleven private detectives hired by Arkansas Governor Powell Clayton to infiltrate the Reconstruction-era Klan, Parker entered White County in August 1868, posing as a cattle buyer. He sought to infiltrate the Klan's den in Searcy, thereby identifying the terrorists who murdered black state legislator Ban Humphries and attempted to

kill state senator Stephen Wheeler. Parker vanished without a trace two months later, and his fate remained unknown until March 1870, when klansman John McCauley confessed to participating in his murder. As McCauley explained, klansmen grew suspicious when Parker failed to purchase any cattle. Grand Titan Dandridge McRae and Grand Giant Jacob Frolich then ordered his death, and the hit team dumped Parker's body in an abandoned well. McRae and Frolich fled the county, but later returned for a farcical trial in 1871, wherein all defendants were acquitted despite eyewitness testimony from McCauley and another klansman who turned state's evidence.

Shepard, M.L.
—As a Republican leader in Reconstruction-era Jones County, North Carolina, Shepard organized several hundred blacks into an unofficial anti–Klan militia in spring 1869. His plea for regular troops fell on deaf ears in the state capital, but Shepard remained in Jones County after other GOP activists had fled for their lives. On 16 August 1869, klansmen murdered Shepard and two other men at his sawmill, in Trenton.

Southern Poverty Law Center
—Lawyers Morris Dees and Joe Levin founded the SPLC in 1971, operating from headquarters in Montgomery, Alabama. Chartered as a nonprofit organization, the group devotes itself to legal action on behalf of indigent clients, with a thriving sideline in education geared toward racial and religious tolerance. Former SNCC activist Julian Bond served as the SPLC's first president (1971–79). The group's noteworthy courtroom victories over violent hate groups include a federal injunction barring klansman Louis Beam from harassing Vietnamese fishermen in Texas (May 1981); a similar injunction against Alabama klansmen for their illegal training exercises at "Camp My Lai" (Nov. 1984); yet another injunction against paramilitary training exercises conducted by Frazier Miller's WPP in North Carolina (January 1985); a $7 million judgment against Robert Shelton's UKA for the lynching of Michael Donald in Mobile, Alabama (1987); a $1 million judgment against the IEKKKK for assaulting civil rights protesters in Forsythe County, Georgia (October 1988); a $12.5 judgment against Tom Metzger and WAR for the murder of an African student in Portland, Oregon (October 1990); a $1 million judgment against a Church of the Creator cultist for the slaying of a black Navy seaman in Florida (1994); an $85,000 judgment against neo–Nazi leader William Pierce for fraud related to the COC lawsuit (1995); a $37.8 million judgment against the Christian Knights for burning two South Carolina churches (1997); a $6.5 million judgment against the Aryan Nations, based on violent actions of security guards at the group's Idaho headquarters (2001); and a $1.35 million judgment against Ranch Rescue, a vigilante "border watch" group, for brutalizing Mexican-Americans (2005). In addition to legal action, the SPLC maintains ongoing surveillance on various hate groups, reporting their activities and tabulating hate crimes in its excellent quarterly *Intelligence Report.*

Such activities have prompted violent rhetoric and action by right-wing extremists. Members of Thomas Robb's KKKK torched the SPLC's Montgomery office on 28 July 1983 (and were arrested in December 1984). Louis Beam once challenged

Dees to a duel, and has posted Internet messages claiming that Dees "has earned two death sentences" for his anti–Klan litigation. Frazier Miller, likewise, offered an online "point" scale for prospective "Aryan warriors," with the highest possible score (888 points) reserved for whoever murdered Dees. On 9 November 1995, leaders of the Oklahoma Constitutional Militia were jailed for plotting to bomb various targets, including SPLC headquarters. (Defendant Willie Lampley received an eleven-year prison term in 1996.) Critics closer to the mainstream claim that the SPLC's lawsuits against racist organizations subject defendants to "guilt by association, rather than from direct involvement in violent hate crimes." And yet, every court case cited above involved criminal action—often including homicides—wherein jurors found specific hate groups and their leaders responsible for promoting and encouraging illegal conduct. (In Tom Metzger's case, for example, WAR leaders not only advocated random violence against blacks, but provided the very baseball bats used by Portland skinheads to kill victim Mulugeta Seraw.) Author Laird Wilcox, painting with a broad brush, asserts that the SPLC and three similar watchdog groups are guilty of "illegal spying, theft of police files, fund-raising irregularities, irresponsible and fraudulent claims, perjury, vicious and unprincipled name-calling, ritual defamation, libel, intolerance of criticism, harassment, stalking, and a callous disregard for the civil liberties of their opponents and critics." In 1994, the *Montgomery Advertiser* polled a handful of disgruntled ex-employees who accused Dees and other SPLC officers of financial chicanery and racial discrimination at headquarters. At press time for this work, none of those charges had been proved.

Aside from litigation and intelligence collection, the SPLC maintains a world-renowned civil rights memorial in Montgomery, unveiled in 1989, and at press time for this volume was preparing a new Civil Rights Memorial Center for public education. The group's award-winning "Teaching Tolerance" program, launched in 1991, provides innovative multimedia kits for teachers and students between kindergarten and high school, distributed free of charge to some 500,000 educators per year in the United States.

United Sons of America
—This anti–Klan group, founded in Buffalo, New York, during summer 1924, consisted primarily of business leaders and professionals pledged to oppose any "group of individuals who have plans for breaking down of this government, or the destruction of law and order." Like other groups of the period, it opposed KKK political initiatives and worked to identify members of the order.

USA Club
—The USA (*Unity, Service, and Americanism*) Club was organized in August 1924 to oppose the Klan in Anaheim, California. Its members paid a high-ranking klansman several hundred dollars for the order's state membership roster, then provided the list of names to Orange County District Attorney Alex Nelson, an outspoken critic of the Klan. Publication of the list resulted in defeat for several closet klansmen in that summer's primary election.

Whangs
—A short-lived anti–Klan group in Reconstruction-era Tennessee, the Whangs recruited freedmen to arm and or-

ganize against nightriders in spring 1868. Grand Dragon John Gordon publicly called on the group to disband, ordering his klansmen to disrupt its activities "at any cost." The Whangs apparently dissolved without seeing action against the KKK.

Wide Awakes—Another group of Tennessee blacks who armed against Klan terrorism in spring 1868, the Wide Awakes disbanded that July, after Grand Dragon John Gordon ordered his followers to disrupt black self-defense groups "at any cost." This group should not be confused with the white-supremacist Wide Awake Club, which collaborated with the KKK and KWC in Louisiana during 1868.

Williams, Robert F.—A black ex–Marine and leader of a militant NAACP chapter in Monroe, North Carolina, Williams chartered his group with the National Rifle Association in 1957, to obtain cheap guns and ammunition for defense against Ku Klux nightriders. Guards at his home exchanged shots with klansmen on 18 January 1958, and the violence resumed in August 1961, when a contingent of CORE's integrated "freedom riders" visited Monroe. On the night of 26 August, armed blacks barricaded their streets and repelled Klan raiders with rifle fire, briefly sheltering an innocent white couple who inadvertently drove into the battle zone. On 28 August, local authorities charged Williams and several other blacks with kidnapping. Williams fled the country and found refuge in Cuba. Upon returning for trial, several years later, he won acquittal on all charges.

11 Covering the Klan

Journalists

The individuals profiled below earned fame (or notoriety) for their public views on the KKK and/or violence committed by klansmen and their allies. The selection includes reporters and editors from Reconstruction to the present day.

Atkins, J.W.—As editor of the Gastonia (North Carolina) *Gazette,* Atkins ardently opposed the Ku Klux Klan during the 1930s. Nightriders burned a cross at his home in 1949, after he denounced efforts to revive the local klavern.

Beckerman, Milton—While serving as editor of Georgia's *Claxton Enterprise,* Beckerman stood in opposition to the Klan's revival after World War II. In August 1949, his editorials exposed a new "businessman's club" as a front for the KKK, prompting a series of telephone threats and one incident in which a klansman assaulted Beckerman with a hammer. In March 1950, the *Enterprise* called for a municipal anti-mask law and a ban on Klan meetings at Claxton's Masonic lodge. Klansmen retaliated with a horn-blowing motorcade that drove across Beckerman's lawn, then fled when he opened fire with a rifle. City council members passed the anti-mask ordinance, with support from local civic groups and churches, but Beckerman refused to take the credit. "We wrote the stories," he remarked, "and the people did the work."

Bellows, Jim—A reporter for the *Columbus* (Ga.) *Ledger,* Bellows was assigned—with colleague Carl Johnson and photographer Joe Talbott—to cover a KKK rally at Pine Mountain State Park on 13 March 1948. Following a speech by Grand Dragon Samuel Green, klansmen assaulted the three newsmen, injected them with drugs and forced them to drink liquor, then delivered them to police who jailed the trio overnight for public intoxication. Rally participants identified by Bellows included Fred New, editor of the white-supremacist *Georgia Tribune;* Rev. Evall "Parson Jack" Johnston, publisher of the *Georgia Tribune* and future grand dragon of the Original Southern Klans; and Hollis Cooper, an Alabama resident employed as the *Columbus Ledger's* circulation manager. Confronted with evidence of his role in framing three coworkers, Cooper resigned from the paper.

Blackburn, W. Jasper—A Republican congressman elected from Claiborne Parish, Louisiana, in 1868, Blackburn also served as editor of the "radical" Homer *Iliad.* In spring 1868, he traveled to New Orleans as a delegate to the state constitutional convention, but Klan death threats delayed his homecoming. Terrorists twice mobbed and demolished Blackburn's newspaper office, in July and November 1868.

Blumberg, Ralph—As the owner of radio station WBOX in Bogalusa, Louisiana, Blumberg became a target for Ku Klux harassment and threats. Klansmen first marked him in January 1965, as a member of the group that invited moderate Arkansas ex-congressman Brooks Hays to address a local church meeting. Anonymous threats canceled that event, and Klan pressure soon cost WBOX all but four of its regular seventy advertisers. Terrorists lobbed bricks through Blumberg's windows, sprinkled tacks in his driveway, and fired gunshots at the station's transmitter. The campaign drove WBOX from its rented quarters to a trailer, and finally out of existence. Persistent threats against his family prompted Blumberg to resettle his wife and children in St. Louis. In October 1965, Blumberg received the Paul White award for distinguished service in broadcasting, but it was too late to save WBOX. Announcing his plans to sell the station, Blumberg said, "When you become a target of the Ku Klux Klan, you soon learn that if there ever was a devil on the face of the earth, it lives, it breathes, it functions in the cloaked evil of the leaders of the Ku Klux Klan."

Burton, Pierce—As the Republican editor of the Demopolis (Ala.) *Southern Republic,* Burton made an easy target for the local KKK. In May 1871, while Burton was campaigning to become lieutenant governor, klansmen attacked and beat him on a public street in Eutaw, leaving him with permanent injuries. Burton subsequently fled the state for good, after receiving death threats from a Klan-allied group, the Knights of the Black Cross.

Carpenter, J.B.—While serving as clerk of the superior court in Reconstruction-era Rutherford County, North Carolina, Carpenter doubled as editor of the Rutherford *Star.* In that capacity, he spoke out frequently and strongly against the local KKK. In June 1871, he testified before a congressional panel investigating the Klan. Klansmen took advantage of his absence to destroy Carpenter's newspaper office.

Carter, William Hodding, III—A native of Hammond, Louisiana, born in 1907, Carter graduated from Maine's Bowdoin College in 1927, then returned to his home state and launched his first newspaper—the Hammond *Daily Courier*—in 1932. He subsequently moved to Greenville, Mississippi, where he edited the progressive *Delta Democrat-Times.* Carter won a Pulitzer Prize in 1946, for a series exposing ill treatment of Nisei soldiers returning from combat in World War II. After the U.S. Supreme Court delivered its "Black Monday" ruling on school integration, in 1954, Carter's editorials on racial and socioeconomic intolerance in Dixie earned him a reputation as "Spokesman of the New South." Those articles also made him a target of racist ire and threats, escalating in the 1960s when a violent new Klan organized in the Magnolia State. At one point, the harassment grew so ominous that Carter's son—later a White House aide to President James Carter (no relation)—reportedly confronted Greenville's exalted cyclops with a pistol, promising to kill him if any harm befell his father. Klansmen got the message, and Carter escaped injury while nightriders attacked journalist Hazel Brannon Smith and other Mississippi mavericks. Carter died of a heart attack in Greenville, on 4 April 1972.

Carter, W. Horace—As editor of the Tabor City (N.C.) *Tribune,* Carter waged a long, lonely, and hazardous campaign against Grand Dragon Thomas Hamilton's Association of Carolina Klans. Amid persistent death threats, klansmen twice snatched Carter's dogs, later releasing one and presumably killing the other. Carter's crusade climaxed in 1951–52 with the state and federal arrests of more than 100 klansmen (including Hamilton) on various criminal charges. In 1952, Carter received the Pulitzer Prize and the Sidney Hillman journalism award for his efforts.

Cole, Willard—Horace Carter was not alone in challenging Grand Dragon Tom Hamilton's Association of Carolina Klans in 1949–52. Willard Cole, editor of the Whiteville (N.C.) *News Reporter* won the Pulitzer Prize and the Sidney Hillman journalism award in 1952, for articles exposing Klan violence.

Dennett, Daniel—While serving as an officer of the KWC in Reconstruction-era St. Mary Parish, Louisiana, Dennett doubled as editor of the Franklin *Planter's Banner.* Predictably, the newspaper supported Democratic politicians and praised the actions of white-supremacist vigilantes.

Dorman, Michael—A reporter for *Newsday* during the June 1963 integration showdown at the University of Alabama, Dorman uncovered and published the story of Governor George Wallace's discharge from military service on grounds of mental instability. A short time later, two strangers began following Dorman around Tuscaloosa. U.S. marshals identified the men as UKA members, warning Dorman that his life might be in danger. UKA Imperial Wizard Robert Shelton subsequently tried to pick a fight with Dorman at the local Stafford Hotel, but bystanders separated the two men before either suffered any injury. Dorman subsequently published a memoir of the civil rights movement, *We Shall Overcome* (1964), and a book-length profile of the Klan's favorite governor, *The George Wallace Myth* (1976).

Gorman, John C.—Gorman served as editor of the Raleigh (N.C.) *Telegram* during Reconstruction. In 1868, he was also identified as the founder of a Klan-allied group, the White Brotherhood, yet Gorman publicly opposed nightriding by secret orders.

Grady, Henry W.—While serving as editor of the Rome (Ga.) *Commercial,* Grady was identified by a rival newsman as a participant in a January 1871 KKK demonstration. When a local grand jury began investigating racial terrorism one month later, the *Commercial* urged all members of secret societies "to remain perfectly quiet and orderly, for the present at any rate." The same editorial advised that klansmen should ride again only "if an inexorable necessity calls for action."

Gregory, C.E.—Atlanta *Journal* reporter C.E. Gregory earned the Klan's wrath by writing articles critical of Georgia Governor Herman Talmadge. He was also working on a book-length exposé of Georgia demagogues and race-baiters when klansmen bombed his house on 23 August 1947. Gregory escaped injury when the bomb, hurled toward an open window of his home, fell short and detonated on the porch outside. Gregory later served as director of the Georgia Historical Commission.

Hall, Grover Cleveland, Jr.—The son of crusading anti–Klan editor Grover Hall, Sr., Grover Jr. followed in his father's footsteps as a reporter for the *Montgomery* (Ala.) *Advertiser.* In 1949, when a new Klan reared its hooded head and launched fresh waves of terrorism in the Cotton State, Hall publicly condemned the KKK. A typical editorial read: "We thought we had outgrown such ... frightful deeds often inhuman in nature. Apparently we have not.... The Klan claims to be Christian. If it is, you may be sure that its main emphases are not the Christianity of Christ. It is anti–Jewish, and Christianity was founded by a Jew. It is anti-racial ... in open violation of Christ's tolerance.... It claims to be a true exponent of 'true Americanism.' but forgets that America is made up of heterogeneous national and racial groups, and ... constitutional and statutory laws.... It is anarchy in action. It thrives on ignorance, intolerance, prejudice and hate." Dismissing the KKK as a "misguided and ignoble movement," Hall concluded that "Alabama is bigger than ... the Klan."

Hall, Grover Cleveland, Sr.—A native of Henry County, Alabama, born in 1888, Hall was named for a Democratic president and devoted much of his life to supporting that party's conservative wing. As a journalist, however, his political commitment did not extend to supporting the Alabama Ku Klux Klan. After working on newspapers in Dothan, Enterprise, Pensacola and Selma, Hall was picked to serve as editor of the *Montgomery Advertiser* in 1926. He immediately launched a personal crusade against Klan terrorism in the Cotton State, penning a two-year series of hard-hitting editorials that earned him a Pulitzer Prize in 1928. Governor Benjamin Miller appointed Hall to serve as a probate judge during the Great Depression, while successor Frank Dixon named him to the state personnel board in 1939. Hall also served as a delegate to the Democratic National Convention in 1936.

Hanson, Victor—As Alabama's leading mogul of the press—publisher of the *Birmingham Ledger,* the *Birmingham News,* and the *Montgomery Advertiser*—Hanson welcomed the twentieth-century Klan as a response to "Negro uppitiness" after World War I. After 1925, however, he joined some of the states industrial "Big Mules" in condemning rampant Ku Klux violence, whereupon Grand Dragon James Esdale denounced Hanson and his associates as "leeches..., parasites..., [and] crooks."

Through his several editors, Hanson orchestrated a press campaign against the KKK, which reduced (but did not eliminate) the order's influence in Alabama politics and law enforcement.

Harkey, Ira B., Jr.

—Harkey settled in Mississippi in 1949, soon earning a dreaded "liberal" reputation as editor of the *Pascagoula Chronicle*. His challenges to white supremacy (including printed references to blacks as "Mr." and "Mrs.") angered local bigots, and nightriders burned a cross at his home on 1 September 1954. A sign planted beside the cross read: "We do not appreciate niggerlovers. We are watching you. KKK." A few days later, klansman Tommy Harper visited Harkey's office and warned him that blacks would not be the primary targets if Pascagoula schools were forced to integrate. "The one we'll get is the white man that's behind them," Harper said, "and we know who he is." Harkey survived that threat, moving on to criticize Governor Ross Barnett and the racists who rioted against James Meredith's admission to the University of Mississippi on 30 September 1962. One participant in that melee was local Sheriff Ira Grimsley, founder of the vigilante Jackson County Citizens Emergency Unit (initially organized as part of a scheme to kidnap and murder Meredith). On the night of the JCCEU's second meeting, 15 October 1962, a sniper fired into the *Chronicle* office. Days later, at another Unit meeting, Grimsley named Harkey's paper as "the state's leading niggerlover." Sheriff Grimsley and other whites harassed *Chronicle* delivery boys and threatened local stores with boycotts if they purchased ads in the paper. FBI agents launched an investigation after shotgun blasts shattered Harkey's windows, on 1 November 1962, and the JCCEU soon dissolved. Harkey left Mississippi in July 1963, as a new and more violent Klan organization spread throughout the state.

Harris, Julian

—As editor of the Columbus (Ga.) *Enquirer-Sun*, Harris was the only Georgia newsman to reprint the New York *World's* September 1921 exposés of Ku Klux violence and corruption. Four years later, he won a Pulitzer Prize for coverage of black community news and exposure of local KKK activity. In stinging editorials, Harris attacked klansmen as "grafters, blackmailers, spy-chiefs," and sometimes simply as "cluck-clucks." His newspaper named various public officials as klansmen, including Georgia's governor, attorney general, commissioner of agriculture, commissioner of fish and game, superintendent of public education, and chief justice of the state supreme court. Social critic H.L. Mencken described Harris's 1925 Pulitzer Prize selection as "the most intelligent award the committee has yet made."

Hartley, A.I.

—While serving as editor of the Warrenton (Ga.) *Clipper* in June 1869, Hartley was one of six Warren County klansmen jailed for the murder of state senator Joseph Atkins. Prosecutors subsequently released him without indictment.

Huie, William Bradford

—A native of Hartselle, Alabama, born on 13 November 1910, Huie graduated from the University of Alabama in 1930, then went to work for a Birmingham newspaper and published his first novel (*Mud on the Stars*) in 1942. Over the next forty-three years, Huie published seven more novels and fifteen nonfiction books, plus various articles for such national magazines as *Look, Time* and the *Saturday Evening Post*. In the 1950s, his articles focused on white opposition to the southern civil rights movement, including various exposés of violence by klansmen and affiliated racists. In 1955, after white jurors acquitted the lynchers of black teenager Emmett Till in Mississippi, Huie published their confession to the crime in *Look*. A year later, his book on a Florida murder case (*Ruby McCollum*) exposed Orange County lawmen as members of the KKK. In 1957, Huie covered the Alabama castration of Edward Aaron by members of Asa Carter's Original KKK of the Confederacy. Huie subsequently published articles on the Klan murders of Lemuel Penn in Georgia and the Mississippi slayings of COFO workers James Chaney, Andrew Goodman and Michael Schwerner (the latter published in book form as *Three Lives for Mississippi*, in 1965). Those publications prompted threats, cross-burnings at Huie's home, and occasional Klan motorcades that circled his home, while Huie and his wife stood guard with shotguns. The harassment escalated in 1967, after Huie published his penultimate novel, *The Klansman* (filmed by Hollywood in 1974).

Huie's strangest performance involved the April 1968 assassination of Dr. Martin Luther King, Jr. Soon after alleged triggerman James Earl Ray was captured in England, Huie struck a bargain with defense attorney Arthur Hanes, Sr., paying $40,000 for literary rights to Ray's story. As a prelude to his final book on the assassination, Huie wrote three articles for *Look* in November 1968 and April 1969. The first two installments described a plot by wealthy white-supremacists to murder King "for maximum bloody effect" during the 1968 election campaign, concluding: "Therefore, in this plot, Dr. King was the secondary, not the primary target. The primary target was the United States of America." The third article amazingly reversed Huie's previous claims, insisting that Ray had killed King on his own, in a quest for "criminal status." To explain that strange reversal, Huie wrote:

> [T]here are large conspiracies and little conspiracies. In large conspiracies, rich and/or powerful men are involved. Small conspiracies involve only little men.... I believe that one or two men other than James Earl Ray may have had foreknowledge of this murder, and that makes it a little conspiracy. But if there was a conspiracy, I now believe that James Earl Ray was probably its leader, not its tool or dupe.

That not-quite-lone-assassin view prevailed in Huie's book-length treatment of the case, *He Slew the Dreamer* (1970), and remains a point of controversy to the present day. Huie died at Guntersville, Alabama, in 1986.

Jenkins, Jay

—As a special reporter for the Raleigh (N.C.) *News & Observer*, Jenkins won a Sidney Hillman journalism award in 1952, for his articles exposing criminal activity by Grand Dragon Thomas Hamilton's Association of Carolina Klans.

Johnson, Carl

—On 13 March 1948, Johnson was one of three *Columbus* (Ga.) *Ledger* employees assaulted and drugged at a KKK rally in Pine Mountain State Park. Klan-allied police jailed the three victims (also including reporter Jim Bellows and photographer Joe Talbott) on charges of public intoxication, but the frame-up was soon exposed and all charges were dismissed.

Johnston, Rev. Evall G.—"Parson Jack" Johnston published the white-supremacist *Georgia Tribune* in the 1940s and early 1950s, while serving as a leader of the AGK in Columbus and later as head of his or Original Southern Klans. In 1952, *Tribune* editorials began to question the KKK's ability to enforce segregation, and Johnston sold the paper in January 1953, to pursue a full-time career as an evangelist of racism.

Loughery, R.W.—As the editor of two Texas newspapers, the Jefferson *Times* and the Marshall *Texas Republican,* Loughery supported the Reconstruction-era KKK and KRS, praising acts of violence against blacks and "radical" activists in the Lone Star State.

McCord, Frank O.—As editor of the Pulaski *Citizen,* McCord ran the only newspaper in Reconstruction-era Giles County, Tennessee. He was also one of the KKK's "immortal six" founders and served as the Klan's first grand cyclops. Historian Allen Trelease describes the *Citizen,* under McCord's leadership, as "the mouthpiece of the Klan leadership" in 1867–69. At various times, McCord published announcements of Klan demonstrations, made light of its activities with "humorous" articles, condoned vigilante action and finally condemned it. In late summer 1869, his paper carried calls for Klan disbandment that presumably issued directly from Grand Wizard Nathan Bedford Forrest.

McGill, Ralph Emerson—A Tennessee native, born in 1898, McGill attended Nashville's Vanderbilt University but was expelled during his senior year for criticizing school administrators in the campus newspaper. He soon found work as a reporter for the Nashville *Banner* and worked his way up to sports editor. Seeking more serious assignments, McGill traveled widely to cover the Cuban rebellion of 1933 and the Nazi seizure of Austria five years later. Those articles won him a job as editor (and later publisher) of the Atlanta *Constitution,* where his criticism of segregation and the Ku Klux Klan produced frequent death threats. In 1939, McGill published an invitation for ex–Imperial Wizard Hiram Evans to visit a new Roman Catholic church, constructed in place of the KKK's former imperial headquarters. (Evans obliged.) During the same period (1939–40), McGill's editorials spurred local authorities to investigate a rash of Klan floggings and murders. After World War II, McGill published exposés by Klan infiltrator Stetson Kennedy, prompting new threats and picket lines organized by Grand Dragon Samuel Green's AGK and Jesse Stoner's Christian Anti-Jewish Party. In the 1950s, McGill expanded his influence as a syndicated columnist, lambasting the "respectable" Citizens' Councils as "a scrubbed-up cousin of the Klan." McGill won a Pulitzer Prize for editorial writing in 1959, subsequently serving Presidents John Kennedy and Lyndon Johnson as ambassador to several African nations. McGill's book, *The South and the Southerner* (1963), included a critical chapter on the Ku Klux Klan. In 1964, he received a Presidential Medal of Freedom, while Atlanta's city fathers named Ralph McGill Boulevard in his honor. A heart attack claimed McGill's life on 3 February 1969.

Melton, Quimby, Jr.—In July 1960, editor Quimby Melton, Jr., penned an editorial in the Griffin (Ga.) *Daily News,* denouncing a recent cross-burning at the home of a local black family. As a result, police arrested two nightriders. Klansmen retaliated by burning a cross at Melton's house three nights later, on 25 July.

Mitchell, Jerry—A native of Texarkana, Texas, born in 1959, Mitchell moved to Mississippi in 1986 as a reporter for the Jackson *Clarion-Ledger.* Three years later, after viewing the Hollywood film *Mississippi Burning,* he undertook a crash course in self-education on the Magnolia State's troubled history of racial oppression and KKK violence. A tip directed Mitchell to the files of Mississippi's defunct State Sovereignty Commission, established in the 1950s to defend segregation by any available means. Mitchell's informant alleged that the commission had collected names of COFO volunteers during 1964's "Freedom Summer," including those of murder victims James Chaney, Andrew Goodman and Michael Schwerner. Although the files were sealed under court order, Mitchell procured documents proving that the commission had spied on Schwerner and furnished information to Neshoba County lawmen later charged with participating in Schwerner's slaying. In late 1989, Mitchell published a series of articles revealing those sinister links, and thus launched an unexpected career as Mississippi's preeminent Klan-fighting journalist.

Mitchell's subsequent exposés contributed to the 1994 conviction of klansman Byron De La Beckwith for the 1963 murder of NAACP leader Medgar Evers; prompted renewed investigation of black activist Vernon Dahmer's 1966 slaying (sending ex–Imperial Wizard Samuel Bowers to prison for life in 1998); revealed that state prosecutors suppressed a klansman's confession in the 1966 murder of Ben Chester White; spurred DOJ attorneys to reopen the 1964 murder of Klan victims Henry Dee and Charlie Moore on federal land; and destroyed the alibi of Birmingham church bomber Bobby Cherry. In the latter case, Cherry claimed he was at home, watching wrestling on TV, when fellow klansmen planted a fatal bomb at the Sixteenth Street Baptist Church, in September 1963. Mitchell's research proved that no wrestling was broadcast in Birmingham that night, and Cherry subsequently received a life sentence for murder of four young girls killed in the blast. Most recently, Mitchell published a sealed interview with Sam Bowers concerning the Neshoba County murders, resulting in 2005's conviction of ex-klansmen Edgar Killen on conspiracy charges.

Mitchell's one-man crusade has produced threats and insults from racists, while winning accolades from those concerned with justice. His reportage on Klan violence earned Mitchell the Heywood Broun Award, the Sidney Hillman Award for journalism and the Sigma Chi Award for Public Service. On 26 October 1998, he was one of four journalists honored by the ADL in Washington, D.C., for "their courage and conviction that the world must know of the brutality of hatred, injustice, and inhumanity." During that same year, the *Clarion-Ledger* published Mitchell's book-length work, *The Preacher and the Klansman,* detailing the complex relationship between ex-terrorist Thomas Albert Tarrants III and a black minister, Rev. John Perkins.

Moore, Charles—As editor of the Florence (S.C.) *Morning News,* Moore observed a local cross-burning on 13 August 1955. Several klansmen assaulted him when Moore questioned their reasons for lighting the cross, and a policeman stationed nearby refused to intervene because the incident occurred on private property. The cross-burning was South Carolina's first since the 1952 imprisonment of Grand Dragon Thomas Hamilton, coming eighteen months after Governor James Byrnes declared that the KKK "no longer exists" in the Palmetto State.

Moore, Jere—Editor Jere Moore of the Milledgeville (Ga.) *Union-Banner* published editorials criticizing the KKK in 1949. Klansmen retaliated by burning crosses at Moore's home and office.

New, Fred K.—An attorney in Columbus, Georgia, New was also a klansman and editor of the racist weekly *Georgia Tribune* after World War II. On 13 March 1948, he addressed an AGK rally at Pine Mountain, where three employees of the *Columbus Ledger* were assaulted, drugged, and delivered to local police on a charge of public intoxication. Three months later, New joined Alton Pate and Rev. Evall Johnston to organize the Original Southern Klans.

Pearson, Drew—An Illinois native, born 13 December 1897, Pearson moved to Pennsylvania with his family at age five. He attended Swarthmore College, where he edited the student newspaper, and afterward joined the *Baltimore Sun* as a reporter, in 1929. That paper's conservative editors frequently censored Pearson's articles supporting the New Deal, prompting his resignation to join the *Washington Post* in 1941. During World War II, Pearson doubled as a radio broadcaster, and in 1945 he hired reporter Jack Anderson to assist with production of his syndicated column, "Washington Merry-Go-Round." Pearson often criticized the KKK, prompting death threats in response to a scheduled speaking engagement at Stone Mountain, Georgia, on 16 June 1946. Pearson accepted the challenge, but Stone Mountain's owners forbade his appearance, whereupon he spoke instead from the steps of Georgia's state capitol, introduced by Governor Ellis Arnall. Pearson opposed Georgia gubernatorial candidate Eugene Talmadge in 1946, reporting that Talmadge had promised Atlanta Exalted Cyclops Samuel Roper a second term as chief of the GBI, with a collateral vow that "all race problems will be left up to the Klan" under Talmadge's administration. Five years later, Pearson was the object of a vulgar cartoon—depicting Pearson plunging into a toilet labeled "American Pot for Communists and Stooges"—which earned Florida klansman Bill Hendrix a $700 fine for criminal libel. During 1953–54, Pearson was one of the national journalists who challenged Senator Joseph McCarthy's witch hunts. In the 1960s, Pearson published a series of columns revealing anti–Semite Willis Carto's links to various Klan and neo–Nazi groups. Pearson died on 1 September 1969, leaving Jack Anderson to continue his column and tradition.

Philpott, Tom—In 1979, as a reporter for the *Army Times,* Philpott published findings of a Defense Department investigation that found Klan units active in every U.S. Army command worldwide. The same document reported that U.S. Air Force leaders were concerned about Ku Klux activity on bases in Germany.

Ryan, Abram J.—A Catholic priest from Knoxville, Tennessee, Ryan served as a chaplain with the Confederate army in the Civil War. Some sources also claim that he filled the same post for the Reconstruction-era KKK, although the Klan's prescripts mention no chaplain. In early 1868, Ryan left Tennessee and settled in Augusta, Georgia, where he edited and published the virulently anti–Yankee *Banner of the South.*

Saunders, William L.—An ex–Confederate army officer, Saunders served as editor of the Wilmington (N.C.) *Journal* during Reconstruction. The paper supported Democratic candidates for office and helped call the local KKK into action during March 1868. Several sources name Saunders as the Tarheel State's grand dragon during 1868–71.

Sawyer, B.F.—As editor of the Rome (Ga.) *Courier,* Sawyer was an ardent apologist for the Reconstruction-era KKK, but his public stance did not protect him from abuse. At midnight on 6 February 1871, several klansmen returning from a drunken raid stopped Sawyer on the street and forced him to dance at gunpoint.

Smith, Hazel Brannon—A resident of Lexington, Mississippi, Smith published two weekly newspapers during the troubled 1950s and 1960s, including the *Durant News,* the *Lexington Advertiser* and the *Northside Reporter* (in Jackson). In 1962–63, she also printed the tabloid *Mississippi Free Press,* brainchild of state NAACP leader Medgar Evers. Smith publicly opposed the racist Citizens' Council from its foundation in July 1954, and subsequently tackled the KKK when that order resurfaced in the Magnolia State. A typical offering from Smith's front-page editorial column, "Through Hazel Eyes," read:

> We cannot hold down more than 42 percent of our entire state population without staying down ourselves—and all intelligent people know it. This greatest of nations was not built by men who were afraid. The Magnolia State was not carved out of a wilderness by the fearful and timid. And we cannot live and truly progress in today's atmosphere of fear—an atmosphere engendered by the Citizens' Council and its professional agitators who apparently are now running our state and setting its policies, even to the point of intimidating the Legislature. If we lose our personal freedom, what does it matter what our masters call themselves? Gestapo rule in Mississippi? It is nearer than we think.

Threats and harassment followed. Smith's papers faced an advertising boycott, while her husband lost his job as a hospital administrator. Hate pamphlets warned Smith that "Her Communist holiday is about over." Citizens' Council members published a rival newspaper in Lexington, the *Holmes County Herald,* and lured Smith's foreman away to serve as its editor. Nightriders struck her home, burned a cross on Smith's lawn, and bombed the *Advertiser*'s office on 27 August 1964. Ten days later, a grand giant of the WKKKKM told FBI agents that Jackson klansmen has asked Imperial Wizard Samuel Bowers for permission to murder Smith. G-men warned Smith of the threat, and the plot was tabled indefinitely when Smith embarked on a vacation to New Jersey. The long war of attrition ultimately failed to silence Smith, but it cost her fifty percent of her normal advertising revenues, inflicting debts that forced Smith to mortgage her property and lay off two-thirds of her employees. In 1964, Smith won the first-ever Pulitzer Prize for a female editorial writer. Thirty years later, actress Jane Seymour portrayed Smith in a made-for-television movie, *A Passion for Justice: The Hazel Brannon Smith Story.*

Stallworth, Clarke—While writing for the *Birmingham Post,* in 1949, Stallworth investigated a cross-burning in nearby Sumiton, Alabama. Two men lured him into a local store with offers of information, then assaulted him, one hurling a hammer at Stallworth before he escaped. Police jailed klansmen Roscoe Fowler and Glen Godfrey for the attack.

Thompson, Jerry—In 1979, Nashville *Tennessean* reporter Jerry Thompson infiltrated David Duke's KKKK, posing as a military veteran in northern Alabama. He spent sixteen months inside the order and was present at several scenes of mob violence. Thompson's subsequent series of reports, also compiled into a book (*My Life in the Klan,* 1982), won him the prestigious National Headliner Award and a Pulitzer Prize nomination. Vice President Al Gore, a former colleague at the *Tennessean,* observed that Thompson "taught me about courage—living undercover so he could write in vivid detail about the hate mongering of the Ku Klux Klan." Thompson died in January 2000, at age fifty-nine, after a long battle with cancer.

Tolliver, Ken—As a reporter for the *Delta Democrat-Times* in Greenville, Mississippi, Tolliver published a May 1964 article that accused the APWR of using boycotts to keep "white" businesses segregated. A month after that piece appeared, Tolliver received an anonymous telephone call. The male caller informed him, "We have read your article on the Americans for the Preservation of the White Race, and we understand you plan to do a series. We want you to know that we know how to take care of you if you do." Within the hour, the same man called back, advising Tolliver, "We forgot to tell you that we've killed other people. You wouldn't be the first."

Trawick, Paul—Trawick, editor of the weekly *Jasper* (Ala.) *Union News,* was threatened by klansmen in 1949 for "meddling in Klan affairs." Although apparently disgruntled by his condemnation of recent Ku Klux violence, the knights did not follow up on their threat.

Turner, Josiah—A Reconstruction-era Klan apologist and Democratic editor of the Raleigh (N.C.) *Sentinel,* Turner actively suppressed reports of racist terrorism in the Tarheel State. When klansmen murdered blacks in his area, Turner printed editorials accusing Union League members of killing each other in a ploy to frame white Democrats. Meanwhile, in private conversations he praised the KKK as a political tool of the Democratic Party. State militia officers arrested Turner during Governor William Holden's 1870 anti–Klan campaign, but prosecutors failed to substantiate criminal charges against him.

Waterson, Henry—During the Civil War, Waterson served as an aide to Confederate cavalry general Nathan Bed-

ford Forrest, later grand wizard of the Reconstruction-era KKK. When Klan violence spread through Kentucky in 1868–69, Waterson's Louisville *Courier-Journal* first reported the crimes without editorial comment, then adopted the demonstrably false position that klansmen acted without racial or political motives, attacking white Democrats as often as blacks and Republicans. By late November 1870, Waterson was moved to condemn Klan terrorism and call for military force against the order, but he changed his mind two days later, condemning use of troops as part of a Republican conspiracy to dominate Kentucky politics.

West, J.W.—As editor of the Laurel (Miss.) *Leader-Call,* West took a courageous stand by criticizing Klan violence in the same town where Imperial Wizard Samuel Bowers made his home and headquarters of the WKKKKM. Klansmen bombed his office on 10 May 1964, prompting West to declare that henceforth, "Anything we write about Bowers will be strictly from the court record. We don't want to fool with him."

White, William Allen—A leading opponent of the 1920s Klan in Kansas, White used his position as editor of the Emporia *Gazette* to good effect. His editorials blasted the KKK as an "organization of cowards" led by "moral idiots," further proclaiming that the "picayunish cowardice of a man who would

Kansas journalist William Allen White was an outspoken opponent of the KKK (Library of Congress).

substitute clan rule and mob law for what our American fathers have died to establish and maintain should prove what a cheap screw outfit the Klan is." In 1923, White embarrassed the order by publishing a list of delegates to its statewide klorero, and a year later he launched an independent gubernatorial campaign against Klan candidate Ben Paulen. Although White polled less than half of Paulen's final vote tally on election day, he viewed the race primarily as a chance to "clear the atmosphere" with a campaign designed to "get out and spit in the face of the Klan." In his 1927 obituary of the Kansas realm, White wrote: "Dr. Hiram Evans, the Imperial Wizard of the kluxers, is bringing his imperial shirttail to Kansas this spring. He will see what was once a thriving and profitable hate factory and bigotorium now laughed into a busted community."

Wilkinson, Horace C.—A prominent lawyer and political fixer in Birmingham, Alabama, Wilkinson joined the 1920s Klan and used his influence to help Grand Dragon James Esdale promote the order statewide. Wilkinson also published the *Alabama Herald* in Jackson County, a racist tabloid that condemned even Birmingham's brutal police commissioner Eugene "Bull" Connor as a friend of blacks. Wilkinson initially supported legislation that would have imposed $25,000 fines on any newspaper that criticized Alabama's pro–Klan politicians, but he later promoted an anti-mask law and filed a $250,000 lawsuit against the KKK in Sylacauga, for its harassment of Catholics and Jews. (Wilkinson lost.) His waffling on the Klan issue was typical of Alabama politicians in the 1920s and 1930s.

Newspapers

Whenever possible, newspapers profiled below are listed alphabetically by the city or county in which they were published. States are indicated in parentheses where they are not explicit in the titles.

Abbeville **(Ala.)** *Herald*—Published in Henry County, Alabama, on the Georgia border, the *Herald* consistently supported the 1920s Klan.

Alabama *Baptist Leader*—Although described as a "progressive" in the 1920s, editor L.L. Gwaltney supported the Ku Klux Klan, ignored most of its nightriding violence, and later blamed rival newspapers for tarring Alabama's reputation with reports of the ongoing crime wave. On 11 January 1923, Gwaltney opined that Klan opponents should first ban the Catholic Knights of Columbus. In 1928, the *Baptist Leader* followed Ku Klux orthodoxy by opposing presidential candidate Al Smith both as a Catholic and as an enemy of Prohibition. In Gwaltney's view, the South's black population was itself sufficient reason to preserve the ban on alcoholic beverages. He wrote: "To give [them] free access to liquor—to place this passion inflamer in the hands of a child race not far removed from their savage haunts in the jungles of Africa, would be to court tragedy unspeakable."

Alabama Christian Advocate—This Protestant newspaper supported the 1920s Alabama Klan and attacked its crit-

ics. On 31 July 1927, for example, it complained that prosecutors of Klan floggers cast the whipping victims as "little saints—near Godworthy to be canonized. We don't know any of them, but from reports they were menaces to their several communities." During the contentious 1928 election campaigns, the *Advocate* parroted Ku Klux denunciations of Catholic presidential candidate Al Smith and defended Senator-klansman Thomas Heflin against denunciation from the state legislature and leaders of his own party.

Amarillo (Tex.) *News*—This Texas newspaper, while not always supportive of the 1920s Klan, nonetheless promoted some of the order's political initiatives.

Andalusia **(Ala.)** *Star*—An ardent supporter of the 1920s Ku Klux Klan in Alabama, the *Andalusia Star* blamed rival newspapers for soiling the state's reputation with their coverage of nightriding violence. When state attorney general Charles McCall (himself a klansman) sought to prosecute floggers, the *Star* condemned him as a publicity seeker and a dupe of the Catholic church.

Anniston **(Ala.)** *Star*—Historian Glenn Feldman calls *Anniston Star* editor Harry Ayers "a devout adversary" of the 1920s Klan in Alabama, although Ayers and his newspaper supported klansman Lycurgus Musgrove's unsuccessful campaign for the U.S. Senate in 1920, against incumbent Oscar Underwood. Anti-Catholicism was a major plank of Musgrove's platform, which drew no criticism from Ayers (himself a Baptist and American Legionnaire). Still, after World War II, the *Star* unquestionably condemned Ku Klux nightriding and compared the Cotton State's klansmen to Nazi storm troopers.

Athens (Ga.) *Banner-Herald*—*Banner-Herald* editor Andrew Irwin was an implacable enemy of the 1920s Klan, opposing the order both through his newspaper and as the two-term mayor of Athens, Georgia.

Atlanta (Ga.) *Constitution*—Atlanta's premier daily newspaper toed the Democratic line during Reconstruction, editorially chastising papers that condemned Klan violence in the Peach State. In 1871, while officially denying any sympathy for terrorists, the paper compared congressional investigations of southern violence to the Spanish Inquisition, insisting that Georgia produced no more civil disorders than any other state in the Union. Six decades later, with Ralph McGill as editor (and later publisher), the *Constitution* sang a different tune. Its editorials condemned Klan violence and encouraged prosecution of the knights responsible, subsequently branding the "respectable" 1950s Citizens' Council as a "scrubbed-up cousin of the Klan." Such editorials brought threats and pickets from the KKK and other racist groups, including Jesse Stoner's Christian Anti-Jewish Party, to the *Constitution*'s doorstep.

Atlanta (Ga.) *Daily New Era*—The *New Era* hardly qualified as a "radical" newspaper during Reconstruction, considering its February 1871 editorials that accused Republican Governor Rufus Bullock of coddling black murderers, but it earned condemnation from Democrats and Georgia klansmen nine months later, by reporting acts of Klan terrorism. Still, it joined Governor Bullock in opposing passage of the 1871 Ku Klux Act, insisting that law enforcement should be left to individual states. *New Era* editorials pleaded with white Georgians to end nightriding on their own, and thus forestall federal intervention, but the entreaties fell on deaf ears among klansmen.

Atlanta (Ga.) *Intelligencer*—Known during Reconstruction as a "Conservative" (i.e., Democratic) newspaper, the *Intelligencer* published Georgia's first announcement of the KKK's existence on 14 March 1868. Coincidentally or otherwise, Grand Wizard Nathan Bedford Forrest was in Atlanta that same week, ostensibly transacting railroad business.

Augusta (Ga.) *Banner of the South*—Father Abram Ryan, a former Catholic chaplain with the Confederate army (and alleged Klan chaplain during Reconstruction), moved from Knoxville, Tennessee, to Augusta in early 1868, where he founded this virulently anti–Yankee newspaper.

Augusta (Ga.) *Chronicle and Sentinel*—An outspoken Democratic organ during Reconstruction, the *Chronicle and Sentinel* never tired of attacking Governor Rufus Bullock or denying the existence of a Georgia KKK. In May 1869, the paper claimed that reports of Klan violence in the Peach State comprised a political fable concocted by "Booby Bullock and his pimps in Atlanta." In January 1870, with mayhem still ongoing, the *Chronicle and Sentinel* insisted that the KKK "does not now and never has existed in Georgia."

Batesville (Ark.) *North Arkansas Times*—This staunchly Democratic paper paved the way for Klan organizers in Arkansas with editorial attacks on the Loyal League and enthusiastic articles supporting KKK activity elsewhere. On 11 April 1868, it published Batesville's first incoherent Ku Klux notice, reporting that "perusal of the document makes one's blood run cold. We shut our eyes as we put in the type."

Birmingham (Ala.) *Age-Herald*—Editor Frederick Thompson's *Birmingham Age-Herald* hailed the KKK in June 1918 as an "awe inspiring" successor to the Reconstruction original. In January 1925, he accepted the Klan's invitation to send a reporter along on Ku Klux raids against local brothels. Thompson later experienced a change of heart, as Klan violence reached epidemic proportions, and assigned a reporter to infiltrate a local klavern. Subsequent *Age-Herald* reports alleged that Grand Dragon James Esdale had personally guaranteed immunity for floggers, whereupon Esdale filed a $300,000 libel suit. Thompson fired back by publishing a document wherein Esdale condemned Alabama's American Legion for choosing a Catholic leader. (Esdale blasted *Age-Herald* reporters for stealing the letter, but did not deny writing it.) The *Age-Herald* supported prosecution of Klan floggers, and while some convictions resulted, Thompson was clearly premature in declaring (on 30 July 1927) that Alabama was "free from the grip of sinister forces.... The day of the new independence is at hand." When the KKK unveiled its K-Trio rank in early 1928, the *Age-Herald* denounced it (2 February) as a "raffling scheme" and "stroke of despair" intended to fatten lean coffers. Such condemnation of the KKK, however, did not suggest any weakening of the paper's commitment to white supremacy or racial segregation.

Birmingham (Ala.) *Ledger*—Victor Hanson, who published the *Ledger* (as well as the *Birmingham News* and the *Montgomery Advertiser*) welcomed the 1920s Ku Klux Klan to Alabama and consistently supported its activities.

Birmingham (Ala.) *News*—As one of several newspapers run by Alabama publisher Victor Hanson, the *News* initially supported the 1920s KKK as a worthy successor to the Reconstruction-era original. On 15 May 1923, the paper ran a full-page advertisement purchased by the Klan, condemning use of public funds to support black schools. Escalating violence subsequently turned Hanson and his papers into critics of the KKK, and editors of the *News* praised themselves in 1927 as "men of moral perception and courage" for condemning terrorism. In fact, the paper's condemnation of flogging was sometimes equivocal. On 14 March 1925, after klansmen flogged Joseph Zimmerman, the *News* opined that "[s]ome of the [KKK's victims] undoubtedly deserved punishment," but then agreed that "the most flagrant guilt on the part of the victims does not justify" vigilantism. The editorial concluded: "Either we have a civilized community, or we haven't."

Birmingham (Ala.) *Post*—Editor E.T. Leech of the *Birmingham Post* ranked among the first local journalists to criticize the 1920s Klan for its vigilante activity against supposed bootleggers, questioning in January 1925 whether "all of this raiding is done by those who have never tasted a drink, never carried a gun and never broken a law." Two months later, Leech reminded Alabamians, "There never was a mob that didn't claim it was acting on behalf of the law while at the same time breaking it." The *Post* continued its campaign against Klan violence in 1948–49, when the Federated KKK resumed nightriding in post-war Alabama. In June 1949, two Sumiton klansmen assaulted *Post* reporter Clarke Stallworth, one lobbing a hammer at his head, then bought him dinner in a futile effort to suppress the incident.

Camden (Ark.) *Journal*—On 31 January 1869, this Arkansas newspaper dared to approve (at least in broad terms) of Governor Powell Clayton's militia campaign against the KKK. Its editorial read, in part: "If we look at affairs as they existed in those counties *before* being visited by Gen. [Robert] Catterson, and as they exist now, any man who loves order and deprecates indiscriminate murder, will be satisfied that the militia was a good institution in general. No one denies, or attempts to apologize for the wrongs committed by *individuals* belonging to the command. Many of them robbed innocent persons of their property, which was bad, and beyond the power of the officers to prevent; but we hope no good citizen will assert that the *stealing of property* was as great an evil as the shooting and hanging of men, for no other reason than their political opinions, as was common before Gen. Catterson went there. Those counties are now peaceable, quiet and law abiding." (Emphasis in the original.)

Centre (Ala.) *Coosa River News*—On 30 January 1928, after Alabama jurors convicted two Klan floggers (resulting in $100 fines but no jail time), the *Coosa River News* mocked the order's highly placed political supporters. "What has become," the editors asked, "of that flogging fan faronade that was so flamingly playcd up by the 'big papers' and their satcllites? Couldn't work juries, boys?"

Centreville (Ala.) Press—This Bibb County newspaper offered consistent support to the 1920s Ku Klux Klan.

Charleston (S.C.) Daily News—Editors of the *Daily News* welcomed the KKK to Charleston in March 1868, then turned against it two months later (7 May) with an editorial denouncing "thoughtless young men" who joined the KKK and thereby gave "our enemies at the North" a propaganda advantage. In the paper's view, "[N]o honorable and patriotic Southern man, who has the welfare of this people at heart, ought to sympathize with or countenance in any way this stupendous folly." The paper continued its attacks on terrorism throughout the chaotic election campaigns of 1868, but changed its tune two years later, when black votes carried another state election for the Republican party. At last, the *Daily News* opined, it was the duty of all white men to arm and organize themselves in defense of "decency, purity, and political freedom." That said, the editors waffled again in early 1871, supporting the state militia's campaign to suppress Klan terrorism in several counties. The paper's last flip-flop occurred in October 1871, after President Ulysses Grant declared martial law in parts of South Carolina and federal troops began jailing klansmen. In the face of those arrests, the *Daily News* somehow decided that the very acts of violence it had long decried were "either fabrications or gross perversions of the truth."

Charleston (S.C.) Daily Republican—Its masthead alone was enough to make the *Daily Republican* a target of Klan threats and vilification during Reconstruction, and the paper naturally opposed racist terrorism, calling for moderation even as it exposed cases of corruption within the state GOP. When white supremacists spoke of reclaiming state government, the *Daily Republican* answered (on 2 July 1870): "Such talk is as wickedly idle as for colored men to say that their race shall have complete control. It is not to be a matter of race at all. It is to be a matter of citizenship, in which colored and white are to have their rights and their due share of power; not because they are white, not because they are colored, but because they are American citizens. By-and-by we shall stop talking of the color of a man in relation to citizenship and power, and shall look at his wealth of mind and soul." Sadly, more than 135 years after that editorial was published, its goal has not been reached in the United States.

Charleston (S.C.) Mercury—In April 1868, this Democratic newspaper argued that secret societies such as the KKK were presently unnecessary in South Carolina. White voters could prevent their organization, the *Mercury* suggested, by defeating the state's new "radical" constitution at the polls. "But should they fail in their efforts, and negro [sic] governments be put over them," the paper warned, "we doubt not that every city, town, village and neighborhood in the South will have combinations of the white population, to protect themselves against negro [sic] rule."

Columbia (Tenn.) Herald—This Democratic paper collaborated with the Reconstruction-era Klan by publishing its notices and statements from local Ku Klux leadcrs. on 26 June 1868, for example, the *Herald* obligingly ran a pronouncement from the grand giant of Maury County, ordering local klansmen who had stepped outside the law to disband and destroy their regalia. The order, he said, was not created "to whip negroes [sic] ... radicals," or anyone else, "but to preserve law and order."

Columbia (S.C.) Phoenix—Like many other Democratic newspapers of the Reconstruction era, the *Phoenix* enjoyed an ambiguous relationship with the Ku Klux Klan. On 28 April 1868, for example, it published a story on klansmen who frightened Laurens County blacks with simple tricks, insisting that the KKK was no worse than the Union League. Two days later, the paper contradicted itself with a flat denial that the Klan existed anywhere in South Carolina, comparing its numerous threatening letters to comic Valentines or April Fools Day pranks. By autumn 1868, the *Phoenix* only mentioned the Klan's name in conjunction with violent crimes allegedly committed by freedmen or northern "carpetbaggers."

Columbia (S.C.) Record—This newspaper bucked the 1920s tide to criticized KKK activities in Dixie. In July 1927, its editors opined that rampant Klan activity in Alabama might pave the way for a fascist dictatorship nationwide.

Columbia (S.C.) Union—On 8 January 1871, the *Union* took an unusually strong stand against Klan violence in South Carolina, urging its readers to "shoot down, on sight, the first disguised man who is seen prowling about."

Columbus (Ga.) Daily Sun—The *Daily Sun* was yet another Democratic newspaper that praised the Reconstruction-era KKK and its activities, while simultaneously pretending to believe the Klan did not exist. On 24 March 1868, it reported the KKK's first meeting in Columbus, then (on 1 April) claimed that the Klan was a "wholly imaginary organization." The trigger for its change of tune was the Klan murder of prominent Republican George Ashburn on 30 March 1868. *Daily Sun* editorials blamed the slaying on members of Ashburn's own party, discounting any notion "that respectable white men should as a body plan murder."

Columbus (Ga.) Enquirer-Sun—Under editor Julian Harris, the *Enquirer-Sun* became a leading journalistic voice against the 1920s Ku Klux Klan in Georgia, where the order arguably held more power than in any other state. Satirizing the state's official motto—"It's great to be a Georgian"—Harris asked his readers, "Is it great to be a citizen of a state which is the proud parent of a cowardly hooded order founded and fostered by men who have been proved liars, drunkards, blackmailers, and murderers? Is it great to be a citizen of a state whose governor is a member of and subservient to that vicious masked gang, and whose officials are either members of or in sympathy with it? ... Is it great to be a citizen of such a state? Is it great to be a Georgian?"

Columbus (Miss.) Index—This Democratic newspaper made no secret of its admiration for the Reconstruction-era Ku

Klux Klan, going so far as to criticize klansmen when they failed to accomplish a murder. On 21 May 1871, after raiders bungled their attempt to lynch Republican Robert Fluornoy at Pontotoc, the *Index* lamented: "Fluornoy was not captured. For the Ku Klux this was a very badly managed affair, and there is something so at variance with the usual daring and success of the mysterious brotherhood, that we cannot receive the account without some grains of allowance. We are opposed to lawlessness, but we could have heard of the hanging of this ungodly wretch with a very great degree of fortitude, consoling ourselves with the conviction that 'his loss was Mississippi's gain.'"

Corvallis (Ore.) *Gazette Times*—The *Gazette Times* was one of several Oregon newspapers that opposed the powerful 1920s Ku Klux Klan.

Dadeville **(Ala.)** *Record*—On 7 January 1933, this newspaper in Tallapoosa County, Alabama, encouraged local klansmen to "quiet disturbances among our Negroes" and to deal forcefully with "outside interferences" by labor organizers.

Daily Austin **(Tex.)** *Republican*—Ranked by many Texas whites as a "radical" newspaper during Reconstruction, the *Daily Austin Republican* condemned violence by the KKK, KWC, and Knights of the Rising Sun. After KRS members lynched Republican George Smith at Jefferson, in October 1868, and Democratic newspapers posthumously accused Smith of urging blacks to practice arson against whites, the *Republican* replied on 21 October: "We have read your lying sheets for the last *eighteen* months, and this is the first time you have made any such charges." Klan historian Allen Trelease opines that the *Republican* "was surely justified in charging the Democratic editors of Texas with being accessories after the fact in Smith's murder."

Decatur (Ala.) *Republican*—In summer 1868, masked klansmen marched through the streets of Decatur, demanding that the *Republican*'s editor leave town within three days on pain of death.

Delta Democrat-Times **(Miss.)**—Published in Greenville by Hodding Carter III, the *Delta Democrat-Times* ranked among a handful of Mississippi newspapers that dared defy racist orthodoxy in the Magnolia State. Threats from the KKK and the Citizens' Council resulted, but Carter remained steadfast in opposition to white-supremacist dogma. Speaking of violent Greenwood in 1964, he told SNCC volunteer Sally Belfrage that the town "isn't run by the city government, but by a bunch of thugs." In spring 1963, klansman Byron De La Beckwith told his Greenwood employer that he planned to kill Carter "if I get my chance," but Beckwith subsequently murdered state NAACP leader Medgar Evers instead.

Demopolis (Ala.) *Southern Republican*—This Alabama newspaper was edited during Reconstruction by Pierce Burton, an outspoken Republican who ran for lieutenant governor in 1871. The paper naturally supported his candidacy and denounced Klan violence until Pierce was attacked and brutally beaten by klansmen in Eutaw. Death threats from the Knights of the Black Cross subsequently drove Burton from the state.

Des Moines (Ia.) *Register*—The 1920s KKK in Iowa met its most determined opposition from the Des Moines *Register*. While there was little or no local nightriding to report, the *Register* ran many front-page articles detailing Ku Klux crimes in other states, along with full reportage of scandals and power struggles surrounding imperial headquarters in Atlanta.

Dothan **(Ala.)** *Eagle*—Conservative editor Julian Hall opposed the 1920s Alabama Klan, albeit from curious motives at times. His attacks on Governor-klansman Bibb Graves, for example, focused chiefly on "liberal" state spending for public education, health and social reforms, derided by Hall as "Ku Klux-ism's latest gift to man in Alabama" and a "sickening story." Hall bitterly condemned the "wild debauchery of spending by a be–Kluxed Governor and a be–Kluxed Legislature," while praising Rep. Lister Hill for opposing a federal anti-lynching bill in Congress. When the *Dothan Eagle* attacked Senator-klansman Tom Heflin in 1928, it lampooned his ignorance rather than his ties to the KKK. On that occasion, Hall wrote: "And there you are—the senior Senator from our Great State talking like a half-civilized moron to a fellow Senator on the floor of our greatest lawmaking body! Oh, memories of [Sen. John Tyler] Morgan! Oh, shades of [Sen. Edmund] Pettus! Oh, features of [Sen. Oscar] Underwood! Oh, Heflin! Oh, Hell!" In August 1935, when state legislators passed a Klan-sponsored bill banning publication or possession of "radical" literature, Hall declared: "We advocate the overthrow of Alabama's government by violence. We urge the citizens to arm themselves with shillalahs, set out to Montgomery and whale hell out of the members of the Alabama legislature. After these ex-statesmen are thoroughly subdued, we advocate that the government of Alabama be changed from a so-called democracy to one of communism. Blood will be shed, of course, but capitalism and the curse of private profits must be destroyed."

Emporia (Kan.) *Gazette*—Under editor William Allen White, the *Gazette* served as the primary critic of the 1920s Klan in Kansas.

Esterhazy **(Saskatchewan)** *Observer*—A Canadian paper that favored the 1920s KKK, the *Observer* reported on a local cross-burning rally and found nothing to criticize, opining that the Klan simply stood for "a better control of immigration on such lines that the newcomers would not predominate and graft onto Canadian principles and ideals the objectionable features of the countries from which they come." Official criticism of the order, in the paper's view, "must be taken with a quantity of salt."

Eutaw (Ala.) *Whig & Observer*—This Democratic paper of the Reconstruction era praised the Ku Klux Klan and, in the words of historian Allen Trelease, "at least indirectly encouraged the [KKK's] terror in almost every issue." As a result, Greene County (near the Mississippi border) ranked among the Cotton State's most violent districts during 1868–71.

Evergreen **(Ala.)** *Courant*—This paper supported the Klan throughout the 1920s, even challenging Alabama press mogul Victor Hanson when his newspapers switched from supporting the KKK to criticizing its violence in 1926–27.

Fayette (Ala.) *Banner*—Published in Fayette County, Alabama, this newspaper openly supported Ku Klux violence during the 1920s. After klansmen kidnapped and whipped a white teenager, Jeff Calloway, for ridiculing a Blount County KKK meeting, the *Banner* dismissed Calloway (on 25 July) as a "drunken bully" whose "good whipping" was a favor to the community. The paper complained: "Just because of a 'poor little orphan,' ... full of booze and trying to bulldoze a whole community which was worshiping, ... Alabama is pictured as a state to be avoided."

Fayetteville (Tenn.) *Observer*—Another Democratic paper of the Reconstruction period, the *Observer* generally condoned Ku Klux violence. On 25 June 1868, for example, its editor applied his seal of approval to the lynching of a black rape suspect: "The community said amen to the act—it was just and right. We know not who did it, whether Ku Klux or the immediate neighbors, but we feel that they were only the instruments of Divine vengeance in carrying out His holy and immutable decrees."

Frankfort (Ky.) *Commonwealth*—During Reconstruction, the *Commonwealth* reported and opposed Klan violence throughout Kentucky. On 18 March 1871, ex–Governor John Stevenson made his first speech as a member of the U.S. Senate, claiming that the Bluegrass State had suffered only a dozen incidents of racial terrorism during his tenure as governor, the *Commonwealth* responded with a tabulation of eighty-one murders and seventy whippings or nonfatal shootings recorded during the same forty months.

Franklin (La.) *Planter's Banner*—As implied by its title, this Democratic newspaper of the Reconstruction era supported Louisiana's antebellum white aristocracy and promoted a return to "home rule" by white supremacists. That view is not surprising, since editor David Dennett was a high-ranking member of the local KWC.

Georgia Tribune—Klansmen Fred New and Rev. Evall "Parson Jack" Johnston produced this overtly racist newspaper after World War II. Johnston subsequently defected from the AGK to lead his own Original Southern Klans in June 1948, then resigned from the order with protests of poor health in February 1949. By 1952, *Georgia Tribune* editorials questioned the Klan's ability to preserve segregation in the South, and Johnston sold the paper in January 1953, to pursue his racist ministry full-time.

Goldsboro (N.C.) *Ku Klux Kaleidoscope*—This short-lived newspaper made no secret of its affiliation with the Klan, but it found no wide audience and survived for only a few months in 1868.

Grand Forks (N.D.) *Herald*—The 1920s Klan had few apparent enemies in North Dakota, but it still sought to organize statewide, opposed in that effort by the Grand Forks *Herald*. The *Herald* headlined stories of Klan crimes and scandals from other states, while lampooning critics of a state anti-mask law proposed in 1923. A particular target was Rev. F. Halsey Ambrose, a Grand Forks resident who lobbied hard against passage of the bill.

Greensboro (Ala.) *Beacon*—While a staunch supporter of Democratic causes and candidates throughout Reconstruction, the *Beacon* was also a voice of relative moderation in strife-torn Alabama. One of its editorials, published on 21 February 1871, acknowledged the role of Alabama's newspapers in fomenting terrorism: "So grossly personal and abusive have many of them been in their political discussions, that a portion of their readers have come to look upon it as not only no crime, but a patriotic duty, to do personal violence to those who render themselves obnoxious by their political opinions." It further called for educated white men to organize in opposition to nightriding terrorists, but that call to arms was generally ignored in the Cotton State.

Greensboro (N.C.) *Patriot*—The *Patriot* generally supported Democratic causes during Reconstruction and did its best to minimize Klan outrages, but it lodged a personal complaint against Grand Wizard Nathan Bedford Forrest on 10 February 1870, noting that he had recently persuaded "a large number of able-bodied blacks" to leave the district, lured away by higher wages paid to railroad laborers.

Greensboro (N.C.) *Register*—On 27 October 1869, the *Register* called for creation of a group "designed expressly to Kuklux the K.K.K.... Let this organization be one vast vigilance committee. Where ever an outrage is committed by the K.K.K., let them meet, follow the track, and avenge the blood that has been shed before it is yet cold in the earth. Let them have such a show of trial as they give their victims and *no more!* ... Let there be as many Ballard rifles in the hands of our men ... as there are K.K. masks and *let them be used* whenever the *masks are brought out!* Let us fight fire with fire, and shed blood! ... A dozen hangings will save a hundred murders! (Emphasis in the original.)

Hartsville (Tenn.) *Vidette*—While not apparently affiliated with the Klan, the editor of the *Vidette* mimicked a common Ku Klux notice in spring 1868, while trying to collect overdue bills. The "warning" read:

> Head Q'rs Everywhere!! Dark of the Moon!! Heavy Times!!! Halt and listen! Read and turn pale in the face!! Delinquent Subscribers hear your doom!!! Pay your Subscription!—The Vidette is looking for you! Death to Traitors!! Send the $3!?! Pay for your advertisements! Look out! Mule in the cellar! Dead man in the Loft!!—Guilty of Sedition if you don't send the Money!!!
>
> By Order of Two Cyclopses (Big Ones)

Hillsborough (N.C.) *Recorder*—During Reconstruction, the *Recorder* made sport of Ku Klux victims and occasionally blamed Klan crimes on freedmen. A typical mocking article, published on 15 September 1869, read: "An old negro [*sic*] came to town last week ... bringing something to eat to a son of his whom he said some disguised men had carried off ... for the purpose—as they said—of putting him in jail at this place. It seems that his son had threatened to ravish a white woman.... But the ole [*sic*] man didn't find his boy here. We reckon he was 'lost.'" Nine months later, after klansmen murdered Republican activist John Stephens, editors of the *Recorder* claimed (1

June 1870): "The evidence is becoming more palpable that the negroes [*sic*] killed him. It is known that most of the crimes committed in this State, have been done by disguised negroes [*sic*] and white Radical [i.e., Republican] Ku Klux or [Union] League men." In fact, the paper suggested, Governor William Holden may have triggered the murder by advising local freedmen to "kill off" Stephens politically.

Homer (La.) *Iliad*—As the only Republican newspaper in Reconstruction-era Claiborne Parish, Louisiana, the *Iliad* and its editor, W. Jasper Blackburn, suffered incessant threats from the KKK and KWC. White mobs destroyed the paper's office in July 1868, and again in November 1868, while death threats kept Blackburn from returning home after his election to Congress.

Hopkinsville (Ky.) *New Era*—During Reconstruction, editors of the *New Era* urged Governor John Stevenson to act decisively against Klan violence in Kentucky, a stance that prompted other Democratic newspapers to accuse the *New Era* of "treason to the party."

Houston (Tex.) *Daily Kuklux Vedette*—Another short-lived paper published by and for Reconstruction-era Texas klansmen, the *Daily Kuklux Vedette* existed only for a few weeks during 1868.

Houston (Tex.) *Telegraph*—This Democratic newspaper generally condoned Ku Klux violence against Texas blacks and Republicans during Reconstruction. A typical editorial, published on 14 July 1868, urged local whites to lynch two GOP leaders, Judge Charles Caldwell and Morgan Hamilton. "We say it solemnly," the *Telegraph* declared, "such men ought to die."

Indianapolis **(Ind.)** *Times*—In 1928, the *Times* won a Pulitzer Prize for meritorious public service, based upon its coverage of KKK activity in Indiana.

Jackson (Miss.) *Clarion*—Transplanted from Meridian to Jackson after the Civil War, the *Clarion* soon became Mississippi's leading Democratic newspaper. While cautiously denying any knowledge of the KKK, in April 1868 the *Clarion* urged all "young men of Mississippi" to organize "clubs" and vigilance committees for action during the June state elections. Thereafter, the paper maintained near-total silence on the Klan for two years, mentioning racial crimes only when they could be pinned on blacks. In April 1870, the paper ardently opposed Governor James Alcorn collection of a "secret service fund" to fight the Klan, denouncing the "slanderous assumption" that local sheriffs were remiss in prosecuting terrorists. Thirteen months later, the *Clarion* grudgingly changed its tune, supporting Alcorn's efforts to curb rampant violence in Mississippi's eastern counties. At the same time, however, the paper blamed such terrorist outbreaks on alleged abuses perpetrated by federal troops or militia units. It denied any knowledge of "Ku Klux combinations, but wrote: "If they really exist we count not recommend their disbandment so long as the Loyal League conspiracies whose operations they must have been designed to circumvent, are in full blast." (In fact, as noted by historian Allen Trelease, the Loyal League was virtually defunct by 1871.) A week later (28 March 1871), the *Clarion* compared Mississippi

klansmen to William Tell, for their brave resistance to tyranny. When Congress passed the Ku Klux Act that spring, the *Clarion* branded it "unconstitutional and hideously despotic." After 1888, the paper continued its racist tirades as the *Clarion-Ledger*.

Jackson (Miss.) *Clarion-Ledger*—Created in 1888 by a merger of the *Clarion* and the rival *State Ledger*, this newspaper maintained a stark racist tradition from its inception through the troubled 1960s. Cousins Robert and Thomas Hederman, both ardent segregationists, purchased the *Clarion-Ledger* in 1920 and merged it with the competing (but equally racist) *Daily News* in 1954. With a combined circulation of some 90,000, the Hedermans thus owned the only two daily papers available statewide in Mississippi, using that platform to promote unrelenting support for white supremacy. A *Clarion-Ledger* columnist once "joked" in print that scientists had discovered the cause of sickle cell anemia among blacks: licking food stamps. On 1 June 1963, columnist Charles Hills declared, "Times have changed to the extent that most folks down South consider it an honor to be termed a bigot, a reactionary, and a race-baiter. These are terms invented by the mentally depressed Yankee who thinks his skin ought to be black ... a situation in which he is unwanted either by the true white or the true Negro." Twelve days later, after a sniper killed state NAACP leader Medgar Evers, the *Clarion-Ledger* opined: "It is barely possible that desperately ruthless forces may have used him as a sacrificial offering, to rekindle the flames of unrest here and spur their drive for 'victory' everywhere." When klansman Byron De La Beckwith was arrested for the crime, the paper headlined: "Californian is Charged with Murder of Evers." (Beckwith was born in California, in 1920, but moved to Mississippi as an infant, with his parents.)

Throughout the remainder of the 1960s, the *Clarion-Ledger* maintained its intransigent support for white supremacy. Following Dr. Martin Luther King's triumphant march on Washington, D.C., the paper reported "Washington is Clean Again with Negro Trash Removed." Three months later, after Professor James Silver delivered a speech describing the Magnolia State as a "totalitarian society," the *Clarion-Ledger* complained that he had "abused the state of Mississippi, its people, officials and newspapers." (Silver subsequently lost his job at the University of Mississippi—and moved on to Notre Dame, where his salary more than doubled.) In the early 1970s, maverick Rea Hederman abandoned the paper's longstanding racist tradition, in favor of more balanced coverage. The Gannett corporation purchased both the *Clarion-Ledger* and the *Daily News* in 1982, formally merging them under the *Clarion-Ledger* masthead seven years later. The paper's dramatic reversal is epitomized by reporter Jerry Mitchell's investigative reporting on old Ku Klux crimes, resulting in new prosecutions during the 1990s and early 2000s.

Jackson County *Alabama Herald*—Under the ownership of klansman Horace Wilkinson, the *Alabama Herald* often served as a mouthpiece for the KKK, but diverged from the Klan line on various issues, including organized labor. Ironically, Wilkinson and his paper condemned Birmingham public safety commissioner Eugene "Bull" Connor as a friend of blacks, writing in 1937: "In due time, the NAACP ... will recognize [Connor's] distinguished service ... [on behalf of] negroes [*sic*], and if intelligence tests are not too high ... [will award him] the Senegambian Service medal and the Caucasian Double Cross."

Jackson County (Ala.) *Sentinel*—

On 16 April 1931, during the controversy surrounding arrest and trial of the black Scottsboro rape defendants, the *Sentinel* opined that a mass lynching of the prisoners was preferable to the "filthy insinuations ... [of] outsiders" who defended the accused. Klansmen debated the prospect, but international publicity forestalled mob violence in that case.

Jackson (Miss.) *Daily News*—

Editor Fred Sullens of the Jackson *Daily News* earned a reputation for intractable racism after World War II, with his bitter resistance toward any advance in black civil rights. On 23 June 1946, under a headline blaring "DON'T TRY IT!" Sullens warned all blacks within the reach of his voice: "Don't attempt to participate in the Democratic primaries anywhere in Mississippi on July 2nd. Staying away from the polls on that date will be the best way to prevent unhealthy and unhappy results." Seven months later, on 29 January 1947, another scare headline—"White Supremacy is in Peril"—preceded a warning to whites that "Negroes in large numbers are paying their poll taxes down at the courthouse." Sullens rhetorically asked his white readers whether "you want a white man's government, or will you take the risk of being governed by Negroes?" Before the U.S. Supreme Court's 1954 "Black Monday" ruling on school integration, Sullens sold the *Daily News* to the powerful Hederman family, owners of the Jackson *Clarion-Ledger* since 1920. With a combined circulation of some 90,000, both newspapers maintained Mississippi's strident racist tradition, frequently minimizing or denying incidents of racist violence against blacks. After klansmen murdered three civil rights workers in Neshoba County, on 21 June 1964, the *Daily News* quoted a Mississippi state trooper's opinion that their disappearance was a hoax arranged by communists. Family maverick Rea Hederman controlled both Jackson papers by the early 1970s, at last abandoning the long and unsavory race-baiting tradition in favor of more balanced reportage.

Jackson (Miss.) *Leader*—

Dr. William Compton assumed control of this Republican newspaper in 1871, marking a change from the earlier days of Reconstruction, when he edited a Democratic paper in Holly Springs, Mississippi, and doubled as grand giant of the Marshal County KKK. Soon after changing his allegiance and address, Compton was named superintendent of the state lunatic asylum, a job he carried out while simultaneously editing the *Leader*.

Jackson (Miss.) *Pilot*—

Standing in opposition to the strident *Clarion*, the *Pilot* served as Mississippi's leading Republican newspaper during Reconstruction. As such, the paper and its staff received constant threats from the KKK and other militant white supremacists.

Jacksonville *Florida Union*—

As the Sunshine State's leading Republican newspaper during Reconstruction, the *Florida Union* suffered incessant threats from klansmen and affiliated racists during 1869–71.

Jasper (Ala.) *Mountain Eagle*—

During 1949, this newspaper in Walker County, Alabama, condemned a resurgence of Ku Klux violence and compared local klansmen to Adolf Hitler's Nazis.

Jefferson (Tex.) *Jimplecute*—

This curiously-titled newspaper served during Reconstruction as the Democratic Party's voice in Jefferson, Texas. It implicitly supported political terrorism against blacks and Republicans, one printing (on 13 August 1868) a facsimile of a card signed by fifty-seven freedmen, promising that in the best interest of their loved ones they would "stick to their old-time friends, the white people of the South," by either voting Democratic or staying at home on election day.

Jefferson (Tex.) *Times*—

As the leading Democratic newspaper in Jefferson, Texas, edited by R.W. Loughery, the *Times* generally supported acts of violence committed by klansmen and other racist vigilantes. In October 1868, after local KRS members lynched Republican George Smith, the *Times* ignored eyewitness descriptions of the drunken mob, calling the lynchers "entirely sober and apparently well disciplined. After the accomplishment of their object they all retired as quietly and mysteriously as they came—none knowing who they were or from whence they came." In fact, according to the *Times*, the lynching "had become ... an unavoidable necessity. The sanctity of home, the peace and safety of society, the prosperity of the country, and the security of life itself demanded the removal of so base a villain." A month later, the paper opined: "Every community in the South will do well to relieve themselves [*sic*] of their surplus Geo. Smiths, and others of like ilk, as Jefferson rid herself of hers. This is not a healthy locality for such incendiaries, and no town in the South should be."

Jefferson (Tex.) *Ultra Ku Klux*—

Yet another tabloid published for Texas klansmen during Reconstruction, the *Ultra Ku Klux* enjoyed a short life during 1868.

Knoxville (Tenn.) *Whig*—

Published by outspoken Unionist William Brownlow, the *Whig* served as his public voice when Brownlow became governor of Tennessee in 1865. Klansmen despised the paper and its owner for statements like the following, published on 25 February 1867: "I have no concessions to make to traitors, or compromises to offer assassins and robbers; and if, in the seep of coming events, retributive justice shall overtake the lawless and violent, their own temerity will have called it forth. The outrages enumerated *must* and SHALL cease." (Emphasis in the original.) On 15 April 1868, Brownlow used his paper to announce the arrival of militia companies in Maury County, declaring that the troops would remain "until the disloyal, bushwhacking, jayhawking and murderous rebels learn lessons of moderation and acquire habits of decency."

Lashburn (Saskatchewan) *Comet*—

This Canadian newspaper opposed the 1920s KKK, commenting in June 1928 that residents of the province "certainly need no lessons ... from an organization with as unsavory a record and reputation as the Klan."

Lexington (Ky.) *Gazette*—

A Democratic paper of the Reconstruction era, the *Gazette* supported KKK activities even when the motive for Klan violence escaped its editors. A case in point involved the slaying of a black minister named Williams in September 1870. Reporting that crime, the *Gazette* declared: "We have not heard the reasons for the lawless act, but if Williams was not a bad character it is the first instance when the Ku Klux were mistaken." A subsequent editorial, published in March 1871, claimed that ninety percent of white Kentuckians supported the Klan (including many of those who publicly denounced its crimes).

Little Rock *Daily Arkansas Gazette*—As a mouthpiece for the Reconstruction-era Democratic Party, this paper predictably attacked every member and initiative of the GOP. On 8 February 1868, it described the recent state constitutional convention as "the most graceless and unconscionable gathering of abandoned, disreputable characters that has ever assembled in this state, outside of the penitentiary walls ... a foul gathering whose putridity stinks in the nostrils of all decency." A month later, on 18 March, the *Gazette* announced formation of the Razorback State's first KKK dens, explaining that the Klan effectively disrupted Union League activities "by taking advantage of the well-known superstitious fears of the negro [*sic*]." That said, the paper admitted:

> [W]e are inclined to regard this effect ... as only incident, and that the Klan is bent upon a much more earnest purpose than keeping the negro loyal leaguers close to home after night fall.... We take it ... that this organization proposes something towards the ultimate relief of the state, and when the proper time comes the members will be prepared for a concentrated movement in the right direction.

Although the *Gazette*'s editors professed to dislike secret societies, "[t]he radical party throughout the south [*sic*] is a sworn secret organization, and owing to this it has been able to manipulate the ignorant and superstitious negroes [*sic*] and vote them as one man." Democrats could only respond in kind, the paper opined: "It has always been and ever will be that where despotism bears cruel sway men will unite themselves for resistance to it and be prepared to avail themselves of opportunities that may offer to overthrow it. The state that is afflicted with the rule of its *canaille* must expect to be disturbed by conflicts." The KKK and similar groups would disappear, said the *Gazette,* once "a free and just government of the white race" had returned to Dixie.

Like other Democratic organs of the era, the *Gazette* tried to deny the KKK's existence even as it aided and abetted the secret order. An example of that schizophrenic mind-set surfaced on 15 May 1868, when the paper declared: "There is no evidence that the Klan has a member within the borders of our state." One day later, with no apparent consciousness of contradiction, the *Gazette* published a notice for a Klan meeting in Little Rock. Four months later, on 20 September 1868, the *Gazette* blamed recent Klan crimes against blacks on Republicans, alleging that GOP members donned masks and robes to brutalize freedmen in the hope of framing Democrats. ("They invited a carnival of blood that they might be sure of their spoils.") Conversely, in cases where white Democrats were indisputably guilty, the *Gazette* flatly denied any racial or political motive behind their

crimes. Predictably, the paper opposed Governor Powell Clayton's militia campaign against the KKK and welcomed subsequent disbandment of the troops as a victory for white rule.

Little Rock (Ark.) *Republican*—Launched as an antidote to the Reconstruction-era *Daily Arkansas Gazette,* the *Republican* condemned Ku Klux violence and supported Governor Powell Clayton's militia campaign against the KKK in 1868.

Livingston (Ala.) *Journal*—The Democratic (or "Conservative") *Journal* supported Reconstruction-era Klan activities in Alabama, commonly blaming black and Republican terrorist victims for their own misfortune. After klansmen raided the home of Republican Gerard Chotteau on 12 August 1869, killing one man and losing one of their own in the exchange of gunfire, the *Journal* blamed Chotteau for inciting the raid, by organizing the black Grant and Colfax Club during 1868's presidential election campaign. As described by the *Journal* (20 August):

> Gangs of from 25 to 75 negroes [*sic*] have night after night, for weeks in succession, been kept under arms in thickly populated neighborhoods. Armed gangs of the kind mentioned have held secret meetings in this town, and continued in session until mid-night. Parties of armed negroes have marched through the county ... in broad daylight, at the *order* of one man—their object being left for the public to conjecture. Threats have been made to reduce our town to ashes, if our citizens did not conduct themselves as the self-constituted commanders prescribed.

The same excuse was trotted out when klansmen murdered Rev. Richard Burke, one of the county's three black legislators, on 18 August 1869. Historian Allen Trelease describes the *Journal* as "part and parcel of the Ku Klux conspiracy until it achieved its political objective in November 1870," by reclaiming the state government for white Democratic rule.

Louisville (Ky.) *Courier-Journal*—The Bluegrass State's leading Democratic paper during Reconstruction was edited by Henry Watson, a former aide to Gen. Nathan Bedford Forrest in the Civil War. When Forrest's klansmen began terrorizing Kentucky in 1868, the *Courier-Journal* initially reported their crimes without comment, but evidence of Democratic collusion with the KKK later drove Watson to float the insupportable claim that Kentucky's nightriders victimized white Democrats as frequently as blacks or Republicans. The sheer volume of mayhem finally impressed Watson, prompting him to write (on 25 November 1870): "This thing of serving notices of exile upon Kentuckians at will, and hanging or hooting, at midnight and in their own door-yards, men who stand convicted of no crime, is a burning disgrace to the State, a positive injury to every interest cherished by her people." One day later, the *Courier-Journal* announced (and seemed to approve) plans for use of federal troops to suppress the KKK. On 28 November, however, Watson retreated to claim that Republicans wanted soldiers to help them dominate Kentucky's government. By 9 December 1870, the *Courier-Journal* insisted that the state could deal with any lawlessness unaided from outside. Still, Watson stopped short of blaming Ku Klux victims for their own misfortune, as some other

Democratic papers often did. On 24 March 1871, after state lawmakers emasculated proposed anti-Klan legislation, Watson wrote: "The idle gabble that the Ku Klux are all Radicals [i.e., Republicans] in disguise is even weaker than the silly platitude that there is no such thing as the Ku Klux at all. If the Ku Klux are radicals, the more reason to put them down. If there is no such order, there is outlawry which calls for extraordinary appliances. These appliances our Governor recommended. The press urged them. But the Legislature stood with a cigar in its mouth and a champagne glass in its hand, and would do nothing." The *Courier-Journal* continued reportage of Klan outrages until belated prosecutions finally dissolved the order in 1873.

Macon (Miss.) *Beacon*—Although a staunchly Democratic newspaper, based in one of Reconstruction-era Mississippi's most Klan-plagued counties, the *Beacon* denounced Ku Klux violence in spring 1868, with an editorial reading: "These midnight banditti are doing more to thwart the peace and prosperity of our country than a wise legislation of years can counteract. Our people should personally endeavor to remove these foul ulcers that now and then break out where bad blood exists, and apply remedies that will finally restore these diseased parts to healthy action.... It should be made disreputable to aid or countenance such outrages, and the very perpetrators will then pause and look back with horror on the deeds of darkness which they have blindly committed."

Marianna (Fla.) *Courier*—Located in the seat of Jackson County, where klansmen murdered at least 169 victims during Reconstruction, the Democratic *Courier* gleefully supported racist terrorism and lamented the loss of those few Republicans who escaped death during 1868–72.

Marshall *Texas Republican*—Despite its title, this newspaper was an outspoken Democratic Party organ during Reconstruction. Editor R.W. Loughery—who also ran the Jefferson *Times*—never hesitated to praise acts of violence committed by the KKK or KRS against blacks and Republicans. A typical editorial from 1868 decried the "terrible and revolting ordeal through which a refined, hospitable and intelligent people are passing, under radical rule."

McComb (Miss.) *Enterprise-Journal*—Editor Oliver Emmerich, of the *Enterprise-Journal*, displayed particular courage in speaking out against racist violence during Mississippi's 1964 "Freedom Summer." At the time, McComb was the epicenter of a Ku Klux bombing campaign, but the incessant terrorism failed to stop Emmerich and his paper from speaking out on behalf of law and order.

Memphis (Tenn.) *Appeal*—Following the Civil War, the *Appeal* was edited by ex–Confederate general Albert Pike, named by some historians as an author of the KKK's original prescript and/or Tennessee's grand dragon. While Pike's descendants deny any link to the Klan, the *Appeal* under his leadership was sympathetic to the KKK and lamented the arrest of twenty high-ranking klansmen in Memphis on 6 April 1868. As the Klan expanded, sparking debate over its origins, Pike's paper floated the false claim that its name was drawn from an ancient Jewish Text, *A True and Authentic History of the Great Rebellion of the Hebrews Against King Pharaoh, B.C.* When Governor Powell Clayton cracked down on Arkansas klansmen in 1868, the *Appeal* urged fugitives to seek refuge in Kentucky. The paper also falsely characterized Clayton's militia as predominantly black, when a majority of its members were white. On 30 December 1868, the *Appeal* declared: "The consequences of this act of the villain who calls himself governor of Arkansas, in arming these bands of negroes [*sic*] and sending them to murder and rob the peaceable inhabitants, are not only disastrous to the parties who suffer directly, but to the whole state. Just at the time when every hand is needed in the cotton fields this large force is drawn off and muskets thrust into their hands, that civil war, which is sure to follow, may rage throughout the state, to gratify "Governor" Clayton's hatred and fiendish thirst for blood."

Memphis (Tenn.) *Avalanche*—Another Democratic paper based in Memphis during Reconstruction, the *Avalanche* preferred to use humor when local authorities jailed twenty high-ranking klansmen on 6 April 1868. According to the paper's editorial of 8 April, lawmen had nabbed a band of innocents who "were simply members of baseball clubs and a serenading glee club." (The paper failed to mention that one incarcerated grand giant had lately been employed by the *Avalanche* as a reporter.) Like Albert Pike's *Appeal*, the *Avalanche* took great interest in Arkansas Governor Powell Clayton's anti–Klan campaigns of 1868. When klansmen boarded the steamboat *Hesper* on 15 October, destroying muskets earmarked for Clayton's militia, the *Avalanche* reported: "No one knows who these mysterious beings are that have exhibited so much antipathy to guns and blunderbuses. Some are of the opinion that they are mermaids riding upon the back of a dolphin; others believe that they are angels of mercy who believe in [General Ulysses] Grant's motto, 'Let us have peace,' and that they have destroyed them in order to prevent murder, and to give peace to the people of Arkansas. Still a larger portion of our people believed that these guns were sent to Memphis by Radicals [i.e., Republicans], to be destroyed by Radicals, in order to frighten the Northern people into the belief that another rebellion had bursted [*sic*] out in the South.... We know not, and care not, who it was that destroyed these weapons; but we do know that the party deserves the everlasting thanks of the people that they were intended to shoot and murder." Subsequently, on 17 January 1869, the *Avalanche* threatened a grassroots revolt if Tennessee Governor William Brownlow sought to emulate Clayton in suppressing the Klan with armed force.

Memphis (Tenn.) *Bulletin*—Although a staunchly Democratic (or "Conservative") paper throughout Reconstruction, the *Bulletin* opposed vigilantism in all forms and condemned the KKK as strongly as any Republican newspaper in Tennessee.

Memphis (Tenn.) *Commercial-Appeal*—In 1923, the *Commercial-Appeal* won a Pulitzer Prize for meritorious public service, based on its reportage of Ku Klux Klan activities in Tennessee.

Memphis (Tenn.) *Post*—As the leading Republican newspaper in Reconstruction-era Memphis, Tennessee, the *Post*

opposed the KKK and took delight in reporting the local arrest of twenty high-ranking klansmen on 6 April 1868. That exposure provided some of the earliest coverage on Klan ranks and rituals. In February 1869, the *Post* reported rumors of a general disbandment order (issued by Grand Wizard Nathan Bedford Forrest on 25 January), and a premature editorial of 20 March suggested that most Klan units in the Volunteer State had gone out of business.

Memphis (Tenn.) *Public Ledger*—Arguably the most racist Democratic newspaper published in Reconstruction-era Tennessee, the *Public Ledger* went beyond denial of the KKK's existence or general support for the order's aims and tactics to gushing praise of specific criminal acts. A case in point involved the July 1868 assassination of Arkansas militia captain A.J. Haynes in Marion, by klansman Clarence Collier. After Collier shot Haynes down in broad daylight, then fled to parts unknown, the *Public Ledger* trumpeted: "Gallant Clarence Collier! The blessings of an oppressed people go with you, and whenever the clouds lift you shall be known and honored throughout the lands [*sic*] as the William Tell of Crittenden County, Arkansas."

Mobile (Ala.) Press—On 29 September 1936, the *Mobile Press* publicly condemned the recent Klan flogging of CPUSA member Joseph Gelders, declaring that Alabama was "not going to have its good name blackened by would-be Fascists."

Montgomery (Ala.) Advertiser—One of three Alabama newspapers published by press mogul Victor Hanson, the *Advertiser* welcomed the Cotton State Klan in 1917–21, but changed its tune sharply after Grover Hall, Sr., became its editor in 1926. A relentless Klan opponent, Hall published daily reports and condemnations of Klan violence throughout Alabama, goading state officials to crack down on the hooded order. On 16 October 1927, he noted: "Whenever the state goes into action against floggers, Klansmen are indicted and convicted—because they are guilty." In 1928, Hall supported Catholic Al Smith's campaign for the White House and won a Pulitzer Prize for his many exposés of Ku Klux terrorism. The *Advertiser*'s opposition to the KKK continued through the 1930s, and resumed in 1949 with a series of stinging articles by Hall's son, Grover Jr.

Montgomery *Alabama Journal*—On 3 July 1949, this newspaper forthrightly addressed the latest wave of Ku Klux violence sweeping Alabama, noting that: "It's largely a matter of attitude ... of [the] men who have charge of law enforcement. That's the main thing needed today. Our state officials have been trifling with the subject for over a year. The whole present executive administration is studded with Klan leaders of yesterday. They have talked and at the same time secretly condoned. We were told a year ago that the law authorities knew all about a notorious Bessemer raid and would soon make arrests and round up the offenders. It was all bosh because cowardly police officials had no intention of offending [klansmen].... Alabama got into its present mess because we had no backbone in law enforcement ... from the governor on down.... [T]his new anti-masking law ... means absolutely nothing if the officials continue to sit and let matters take their own course. A mere law is futile in the hands of officials who are Klan-minded.... [E]ven laws would be useless so long as there was a great body of citizenship that was Klan-minded. Klan-mindedness include[s] many of those not–Klan members, those who d[o] not wear masks, but [are] secretly sympathetic to its covert and cowardly methods. Klan-mindedness [means] a man could still be a Klansman with all its evils and not wear a mask."

Montgomery *Alabama State Journal*—As Alabama's leading Republican newspaper during Reconstruction, the *Journal* opposed all Klan activity and did not hesitate to criticize Ku Klux leaders by name, where they could be identified. One such was Ryland Randolph, editor of the Tuscaloosa *Independent Monitor*, whose pathological street fighting made him a danger to everyone around him. In March 1870, a letter published in the *Journal* spurred Randolph to attack a friend of the author. The resultant gunfight resulted in amputation of Randolph's leg, while his intended target soon became secretary of Utah Territory. When Randolph subsequently picked a fight with Grand Wizard Nathan Forrest himself, the *Journal* was pleased to print Forrest's reply (13 October 1869): "His course as an editor has been constantly injurious, not to the Republicans, but to the Democratic party, and the true interests of the people of Alabama.... Unlike the editor of the *Monitor*, my object has been to bring peace to the country, and prosperity to the people; to soften down the prejudices of men of both parties; and in the development of the great material interests of the country, to smoothen the asperities engendered by the war, and efface alike the marks and memories of strife."

Montgomery (Ala.) Examiner—On 16 June 1949, racial moderate Charles Dobbins addressed Alabama's continuing KKK problem through this newspaper in the state's capital. "The Klan," he wrote, "is not a spontaneous expression. It is artfully contrived by leaders who want either money or political advantage."

Montgomery (Ala.) Journal—Unlike rival Victor Hanson, editor Frederick Thompson opposed the KKK's twentieth-century revival in Alabama and used his newspapers—including the *Montgomery Journal*, the Mobile *News-Item* and the Mobile *Register*—to opposed the order. His reporters infiltrated the Klan and published its innermost secrets, prompting a $300,000 lawsuit by Grand Dragon James Esdale.

Montgomery (Ala.) *State Sentinel*—A Republican newspaper in Reconstruction-era Alabama, the *State Sentinel* reported on 6 January 1868 that prominent "rebels" were collecting arms for use by all-white "Conservative clubs" during upcoming primary elections. The prophecy was realized one week later, when white terrorists repelled blacks from the polls at gunpoint. On 25 August 1868, klansman Ryland Randolph (also editor of the extremist Tuscaloosa *Independent Monitor*) complained that the *Sentinel* had published a letter from "an incendiary buck-nigger" in Tuscaloosa. The author of that letter, Randolph wrote, "is certainly a candidate before the Ku Klux for *grave* honors. Doubtless, his name will, if he keeps on scribbling, appear in the City Sexton's report, ere long."

Muncie (Ind.) *Post-Democrat*—No northern state was more thoroughly dominated by the 1920s Klan than Indiana, but some journalistic voices were still raised in opposition to the order. One such paper was the *Post-Democrat,* whose editor—George Dale—risked financial ruin to speak out forthrightly against Klan corruption and violence.

Nashville (Tenn.) *Gazette*—

A crude racist newspaper published during Reconstruction, the *Gazette* supported Ku Klux terrorism in Tennessee and elsewhere. On 16 April 1868, remarking on the KKK's activities in Alabama, the *Gazette* observed that "niggers are disappearing ... with a rapidity that gives color to the canibalistic [*sic*] threats of the shrouded Brethren. Run, nigger, run, or the Kuklux will catch you."

Nashville (Tenn.) *Press and Times*—

The Republican *Press and Times* was one of the first newspapers to report the organization of white-supremacist paramilitary groups in Reconstruction. On 12 July 1866, it noted that "in some portions of West Tennessee the rebels have formed a secret association, the object of which is to prevent the employment or patronage of Unionists in any capacity whatever, whether as day-laborers, clerks, book-keepers, teachers, physicians, lawyers or mechanics. In all cases rebels are to be employed, and the members of the association pledge themselves to starve out or drive out every Union man in that part of the country." Nearly three years later, on 12 March 1869, the *Press and Times* lamented "that of all the organized bands which have put Union men to violent deaths in Middle Tennessee within the last twelve months, not a single criminal has been punished or even arrested."

Nashville (Tenn.) *Republican Banner*—

Although nominally associated with the Republican Party, the *Banner* adopted a view of the Reconstruction-era Klan that mirrored the reportage of hard-line Democratic papers. After inadvertently naming many delegates to the Klan's April 1867 convention in Nashville, the *Banner* thereafter presumed that klansmen were such high-class individuals that they could not be guilty of criminal acts. On 13 December 1867, for instance, the paper responded to accounts of Ku Klux floggings in the rival *Press and Times* by claiming that Klan membership included "the most respectable young men of Giles and Maury Counties." On 8 February 1868, the paper went even further, publishing a Ku Klux threat of summary punishment for anyone who committed criminal acts while wearing Klan disguises.

New Orleans (La.) *Picayune*—

A typical Democratic newspaper in Reconstruction-era Louisiana (named for the Spanish coin that equaled its original price, 6¼ cents), the *Picayune* honored the "conservative" tradition of denying that the KKK or KWC existed, much less that members of those orders were responsible for any acts of terrorism. On 7 June 1868, the paper responded to the fears of harassed Republicans with quotations from scripture: "The wicked flee when no man pursueth" and "Guilty conscience is its own accuser."

New Orleans (La.) *Republican*—

The *Republican* was an early leader in exposure of Louisiana terrorist organizations during Reconstruction, including the KKK and KWC. In July and August 1868, it quoted two Catholic priests in New Orleans, who breached the seal of the confessional to describe alleged plans for an armed Democratic uprising against blacks and Republicans. (And in fact, more than 1,000 victims were slain in that year's election campaign.) On 19 November 1868, the *Republican* described nocturnal Klan parades through Alexandria, "enlivened by calls on the District and Parish Judge[s] and other parties obnoxious to them, storming their houses, and making night hideous by unearthly groans, yells, cat-calls, and whatever else their fancies suggest, to provoke some hostile demonstration which they can resent, of course in pure self-defense, by massacring the offending victim."

New Orleans (La.) *Times*—

During Reconstruction, the Democratic *Times* served as an unofficial organ for Louisiana's racial terrorists. On 1 May 1868, it printed the KWC's first public notice in New Orleans. Two weeks later, on 16 May, the paper denied the existence of a Louisiana Klan, except where rural jokers played tricks on freedmen "to keep them from stealing chickens and pigs in the night.... To this, and this alone, is due the existence of the frightful myth, the Ku Klux Klan." The KWC, meanwhile, continued to announce its meetings in the paper, while the *Times* warned Republicans (on 28 July 1868) that laws passed to mandate racial equality "have no binding force or moral sanction and will be disregarded and declared null and void as soon as the inalienable rights of the people are again recognized.... No privilege can be secured to the negro [*sic*] to which his white neighbors do not consent, and if he attempts to enforce privileges on the strength of carpetbag authority he will simply destroy his claims of future peace and heap up wrath against the day of wrath."

New Orleans (La.) *Times-Picayune*—

In 1914, the rival New Orleans *Times* and *Picayune* merged to become a single newspaper. Publisher S.I. Newhouse bought that paper and the competing *States-Item* in 1962, when the Bayou State was caught up in a fever of resistance to racial integration, marked by escalating Ku Klux violence. While hardly liberal, at least by northern standards, the *Times-Picayune* reported fairly and accurately on civil rights developments in neighboring Mississippi throughout the remainder of the decade.

New York *Daily Tribune*—

The *Tribune* began its Reconstruction-era coverage of the Ku Klux Klan with speculation in April 1868 that the order's name was derived from the sound of a gun being cocked. (That error later found its way into a Sherlock Holmes adventure penned by Sir Arthur Conan Doyle.) As Klan violence spread through the South, the paper sided with those who tried to suppress it. In March 1870, following the impeachment of North Carolina Governor William Holden, the *Tribune* noted that the state senate "virtually acknowledged the propriety of Gov. Holden's proclamation declaring Alamance and other counties in a state of insurrection, by acquitting him of charges of illegally and unnecessarily instituting martial law therein; while it condemns him for the employment of militia in suppressing the insurrection and restoring order. In other words, he was right in declaring the rebellion but wrong in suppressing it. For this decision there could be no respect, even if the trial had been otherwise fairly and decently conducted." One year later, on 17 March 1871, the *Tribune* called for federal action in an editorial titled "Mississippi is a Healthy State for Mayors":

> Mayor Crane of Jackson was shot by a murderer who goes unpunished. Mayor Sturgis of Meridian was expelled because he happened to be born in the North. And now Mayor Lacey of Aberdeen has been abducted by the Ku-Klux, probably because he was once an officer of the United States Army. Yet there are men in Congress who wish to spend a few months inquiring whether loyal men at the South really need protection.

New York *Herald*—During Reconstruction, the *Herald* was one of the few northern newspapers that engaged in fence-straddling where the KKK was concerned. Its first Klan article appeared in April 1868, quoting an unnamed "inside" source to date the order's birth from August 1866. Later, the *Herald* reported Klan atrocities but struck a "balance" by equating the KKK with the mostly-black (and nonviolent) Union League. In 1871, during congressional debates over passage of the Ku Klux Act, the *Herald* joined Democratic spokesmen in minimizing the extent of Klan terrorism throughout Dixie, noting that "similar" crimes occurred in the North and suggesting that many Klan victims were black criminals. Still, a *Herald* reporter in Rutherfordton, North Carolina, captured the spirit of local chaos in May 1871, when he wrote:

> There is probably no country in the world in which it is harder to obtain accurate and reliable information, whether as to actual occurrences or even as to the political sentiments of the people than in these Southern States. I am pretty sure that I could get more truth out of an interview by pantomimic signs with a Carib Indian or King Thakombau or the Gaekwar of Baroda than out of a Southern carpet-bagger or scallawag [*sic*] or a Southern conservative or a Southern out-and-out dyed-in-the-wool unterrified democrat. Ask these latter in turn about something which has come directly under their eyes or is clearly within the compass of their experience and you will get diametrically opposite testimony from them all. Each will flatly contradict the other two, and you will get to the end of your investigation with a very decided belief that as the Apostle Paul as said in Holy Scripture, "All men (excepting yourself) are liars."

New York *Journal-American*—Fired by a spirit of competition with the rival New York *World*, William Randolph Hearst's *Journal American* hired ex-klansman C. Anderson Wright to provide an inside view of the invisible empire. A former combat aviator from World War I, Wright described his efforts to organize a KKK air force, dubbed Knights of the Air, sabotaged by Imperial Kleagle Edward Clarke's personal greed. As with the *World*'s series of Ku Klux exposés, however, the *Journal-American*'s effort had the unexpected side effect of boosting KKK recruiting efforts.

New York *World*—The *World* took a skeptical view of Klan violence during Reconstruction, exemplified by coverage of congressional hearings in South Carolina, conducted in July 1871. According to the paper, visiting investigators "found everything in readiness for them when they came. The highways and byways had been scoured, and many a vagabond negro [*sic*], allured by the offer of $2 per day, exhibited himself marked with stripes which in many cases no doubt was done years ago at the pillory for crime. The evidence so far has not been important only as it discloses the miserable failure of the State Government." In fact, as noted by historian Allen Trelease, the evidence collected by Congress during 1871 documented a widespread conspiracy of terror and silence, abetted (where it was not actually initiated) by leading members of the Democratic Party.

The *World* adopted a very different stance toward the modern KKK, when it began to spread nationwide in 1920–21. In September 1921, the *World* produced a two-week series of articles hinging on revelations from ex–Kleagle Henry Peck Fry, detailing examples of Ku Klux financial chicanery and climaxing with a long, detailed list of Klan crimes during 1919–21. The series prompted hearings on the Klan in Congress, during October 1921, but it also had an unexpected beneficial effect on the invisible empire. Thousands of readers in the North learned of the KKK for the first time from the *World*'s exposé, and many of them subsequently joined the order—some using facsimile membership blanks from the paper itself to do so.

Oregon *Labor Times*—This union-oriented newspaper was one of several that steadfastly opposed the KKK's advance in 1920s Oregon.

Paris *Kentuckian*—A Democratic newspaper published during Reconstruction, the *Kentuckian* praised members of the original Klan for allegedly purging Jessamine County of immorality.

Pascagoula **(Miss.)** *Chronicle*—Editor Ira Harkey's *Pascagoula Chronicle* challenged the conventional "wisdom" of Mississippi racism during the 1950s and 1960s, thereby rating threats and cross-burnings. According to FBI reports, Sheriff Ira Grimsley and his Jackson County Citizens' Emergency Unit plotted Harkey's murder (along with that of black college student James Meredith), but Harkey left Mississippi in 1963 and thus escaped the mob's reach.

Pendleton (Ore.) *Tribune*—The *Tribune* proudly ranked among those Oregon newspapers that resisted Klan expansion in the early 1920s.

Petal **(Miss.)** *Paper*—P.D. East, owner and editor of the *Petal Paper*, earned a reputation for irascibility and opposition to doctrinaire racism during Mississippi's troubled 1950s and 1960s. That stance brought economic pressure from the Citizens' Councils and threats of violence from the Ku Klux Klan, but East proved too stubborn to recant in the face of pressure.

Pontotoc (Miss.) *Equal Rights*—Mississippi Unionist and Republican Robert Fluornoy edited this "radical" newspaper during Reconstruction, advocating equal rights for former slaves in all respects. Local klansmen attacked his home on the night of 12 May 1871, but Fluornoy and his friends repulsed the nightriders with gunfire, mortally wounding one klansman. The terrorists never returned, thereafter leaving Fluornoy to express himself in peace.

Portland (Ore.) *Telegram*—The *Telegram* was one of several newspapers that resisted advances by the powerful 1920s Klan in Oregon.

Prattville (Ala.) *Progress*—This newspaper was an early supporter of the 1920s Klan in Alabama. As late as 25 September 1925, after nightriding violence had engulfed much of the state, the *Progress* described KKK meetings as "beautiful and interesting," noteworthy for their "perfect order and good feeling."

Pulaski (Tenn.) *Citizen*

Historian Allen Trelease described the Pulaski *Citizen* as "the mouthpiece of the Klan leadership" in Reconstruction-era Tennessee. Its editor, Frank McCord, was one of the KKK's original six founders and served as the Klan's first grand cyclops. No journalist in Tennessee was better situated to report Klan news from the inside, or to communicate with klansmen in the field at large through articles and editorials. On 19 April 1867, soon after the Klan's great reorganizational meeting in Nashville, McCord reported a supposed visit to his Pulaski office by:

> the Grand Turk of the Kuklux Klan. We laid hold of the shooting stick and at once placed ourself in a position of defence [*sic*]. Our visitor appeared to be about nine feet high, with a most hideous face, and wrapped in an elegant robe of black silk, which he kept closely folded about his person. He wore gloves the color of blood, and carried a magic wand in his hand with which he awed us into submission to any demand he might make. In a deep coarse voice he inquired if we were the editor. In a weak timid voice we said yes. We tried to say no, but a wave of his wand compelled us to tell the truth. (A wicked printer in the office suggests that we ought to have a wand waving over us all the time.) Whereupon the mysterious stranger placed his hand under his robe and handed us the communication given below, and without uttering another word bowed himself out.

Despite McCord's tone, the appended announcement of local KKK activity warned: "This is no joke either. This is cold, hard earnest. Time will fully develop the objects of the 'Kuklux Klan.' Until such development takes place 'the public' will please be patient." A week later, the Klan used McCord's *Citizen* to announce a forthcoming "Rendezvous in the Forest." Two months later, McCord printed handbills announcing the Klan's first-anniversary parade, held in Pulaski on 5 June 1867.

Violence soon followed in Giles County and statewide, but McCord insisted that the KKK meant no one any harm. Those who called for militia companies to fight the Klan, he said, could only be "some transient, low down, hog stealing, black-hearted, white-livered, pusilanimous villian [*sic*]." While bestowing similar insults on the Union League and Freedmen's Bureau, the *Citizen* called for boycotts of Republican businessmen and social ostracism for all "scalawags." Still, mayhem escalated, prompting another editorial (on 14 February 1868) in which McCord denied any Ku Klux intent to "harm the poor African." Klansmen who wore their masks and robes outside the den, McCord decreed should face trial by the order itself. Still, McCord was not always opposed to violence. After a lynching on 29 June 1868, he wrote (3 July): "We need not be understood as encouraging mob violence when we express the opinion that the fate of this black would-be raper was merited. While we would not like to have his execution resting upon our shoulders, yet if those who ministered speedy justice to the scoundrel are satisfied, we

are, and shall not take the trouble to find out who they are. Let the black men of the community learn a lesson from this."

Shortly thereafter, the *Citizen* published an order from Giles County's grand giant, demanding that klansmen refrain from any "personal violence upon any citizen of this Province, regardless of color, without orders from these Head-quarters." McCord, in response, editorialized: "While we do not condemn all of the acts of the Kuklux Klan, yet there are many things done by them, or in their name and garb, which we do not hesitate to pronounce wrong, and which should be stopped by some means." No such pronouncements emerged during 1868's election campaign, wherein McCord ignored most incidents of terrorism, while minimizing those he deigned to report. McCord himself fled the county when Governor William Brownlow dispatched troops to quell local nightriding, but he soon returned to resume his post with the *Citizen*.

Grand Wizard Nathan Bedford Forrest himself ordered disbandment (of a sort) in January 1869, but Ku Klux violence continued in Tennessee and elsewhere, prompting McCord to write, on 3 September: "It is high time these masqueraders be unmasked and brought to justice. All good citizens deprecate and condemn such acts."

Raleigh (N.C.) *Daily Standard*

Owned by North Carolina Governor William Holden during Reconstruction, the *Standard* did its best to counter support for the Ku Klux Klan among Democratic newspapers in the Tarheel State. It deplored Klan violence, and on 5 October 1869 described an exodus of Ku Klux victims.

> Passing up Fayetteville street, Saturday night, our attention was drawn to a group of four or five women and children, gathered together under the light of a street lamp, quietly taking supper. They presented a discontented air, looked quite unhappy and equally dependant [*sic*]. We endeavored to find out something of their history and could only learn from one of them that they were going where there were no Ku Klux, in search of their male friends who had been compelled to come to Raleigh, to save their own lives.

On 30 October 1869, the *Standard* reported: "The guard house of this city is filled with destitute people from Orange County, who have been driven from their homes by Ku Klux. Some of these refugees are white and some are black. They represent the condition of affairs as fearful, and say they cannot stay at home unless something is done to check the murderous Ku Klux." Democratic editors, meanwhile, claimed that Holden's paper had "invented" the KKK as a political bogeyman, to win more Republican votes. On 23 May 1870, the *Standard* prescribed a drastic remedy for Klan violence: "We tell the people of North Carolina to ... load your guns and fire on these midnight assassins whenever they attack you. If they catch you at a disadvantage, take your gun down next day, if you are not too badly whipped, and fight it out then. A shot or two in every county in this State will break up these bands of outlaws and murderers."

Raleigh (N.C.) *News and Observer*

In 1923, editor Josephus Daniels of the *News & Observer* supported a proposed state law that would ban masked parades and criminal activity, while requiring secret societies to register lists of their members. State senators defeated the bill after long and acrimonious debate, passing instead a much weaker version favored by Klan lobbyists.

Raleigh (N.C.) *Sentinel*—As North Carolina's leading Democratic paper during Reconstruction, the *Sentinel* generally encouraged Klan activity. Its first mention of the order, on 30 April 1868, included what historian Allen Trelease terms "a thinly veiled call for more intensive Ku Klux organization." With that in mind, it was curious then, that editor Josiah Turner wrote (on 14 October 1869), "We do not pretend to know the object and purposes of the Ku Klux; indeed, we do not know that there is such an organization; we have always doubted the existence of a general organization of that kind for political or other purposes." Two years later, Turner tried to blame several Klan murders on the Union League, pretending to believe that freedmen often killed each other to elicit votes for the Republican Party. When that preposterous charade proved untenable, Turner and the *Sentinel* next switched to blaming Union League and Freedmen's Bureau members for the "necessary evil" of Klan violence. When Governor William Holden dispatched militia units to quell mayhem in Alamance County, the *Sentinel* lied doubly, denying any crime wave that required the "negro 'malish'"—when, in fact, the state militia was all white. When authorities jailed klansmen and the suspects started to confess their crimes, Turner opined that no man who violated the Klan's oath of secrecy could be trusted to tell the truth on any subject. Predictably, the *Sentinel* opposed passage of the Ku Klux Act in 1871, reverting to its earlier pretense that most of the crimes blamed on klansmen were committed by Republicans for political gain. Other Democratic papers followed the *Sentinel*'s lead in minimizing KKK activity statewide and blaming Ku Klux victims for their own misfortune. After President Ulysses Grant declared martial law in several Klan-infested South Carolina counties, Turner wrote: "Grant is a dictator, declares martial law when it suits his pleasure. Grant is master—the people his slaves.... Now, instead of civil law, we have kuklux acts, martial law, the despotism of bayonets."

Raleigh (N.C.) *Telegram*—During 1868, this Democratic newspaper was edited by a member of the Klan-allied White Brotherhood, John C. Gorman. Nonetheless, his editorials consistently opposed acts of terrorism committed by the KKK and other groups in North Carolina.

Rapides Parish (La.) *Tribune*—Mayor William McLean of Alexandria, Louisiana, launched this "radical" Republican newspaper in October 1868. Hours after the first printing press arrived from New Orleans, a mob of whites presumed to be klansmen raided the paper's office and destroyed the equipment. McLean ordered replacements, and klansmen returned to trash the place a second time on 15 November.

Richmond (Va.) *Dispatch*—The *Dispatch* greeted early Virginia klansmen with ridicule in 1868, exemplified by the following short article (which anticipated by nearly half a century Imperial Wizard William Simmons's fascination with the letter "K"):

The Ku-Klux klan are kalled upon to kastigate or kill any kullored kusses who may approve the konstitution being koncocted by the kontemptible karpet-baggers at the kapital. Each klan is kommanded by a karniverous kurnel, who kollects his komrade with kare and kaution kommensurate with the magnitude of the kause. Whenever konvened they must korrectly give four kountersigns. These are, kill the kullered kiss, klean out the karpet-baggers, krush the konvention, karry konservatism, konfusion to kongress, konfederate will konquer. Of course the klan kreates konsiderable konsternation among the kongoes and their kunning konductors, who kalkulate that their kareer may be kut short by katastrophes. Kowardly kirs, they kan't komplain.

Richmond (Va.) *Enquirer & Examiner*—Unlike the rival *Dispatch,* the *Enquirer & Examiner* welcomed the Klan's advent during Reconstruction with an editorial dated 26 March 1868:

It is now very evident that this "Ku-Klux-Klan" is not a meaningless Merry Andrew organization, but that under its cap and bells it hides a purpose as resolute, noble and heroic as that which Brutus concealed beneath the mask of well-dissembled [*sic*] idioticy [*sic*].

It is rapidly organizing wherever the insolent negro [*sic*], the malignant white traitor to his race and the infamous squatter are plotting to make the South utterly unfit for the residence of the decent white man. It promises, we hope, to bring into the field for the defence [*sic*] of our live, liberty and property hundreds of thousands of those heroic men who have been tried and indurated by the perils, dangers and sufferings of military service. It is, no doubt, an organization which is thoroughly loyal to the Federal constitution, but which will not permit the people of the South to become the victims of negro [*sic*] rule. It is purely defensive ,and for the protection of the white race, and has been rendered necessary by the organization of thousands of secret negro [*sic*] leagues, whose members have been stimulated to carry out the work of disfranchisement of the whites by the promise of pillage and wholesale confiscation.

If such is the purpose and real object of the new secret society, which is so rapidly increasing its numbers in Tennessee, Mississippi, Alabama, Georgia, North Carolina, and the other Southern States, it will arrest the progress of the secret negro [*sic*] conspiracy which has for its object the establishment of [*sic*] domination.

The *Enquirer & Examiner* called for organization of Klan dens to prevent "the Africanization of Virginia and the disfranchisement, outlawry and persecution of ever Virginian who was not a base traitor to his section during the late civil war." Loyal Virginians were duty-bound, said the paper, "to organize with such promptitude and stern resolution as to strike terror into the guilty souls of the secret negro [*sic*] societies and their delegates in the [state constitutional] 'Convention.'" While the paper's editors favored unmasked companies drilling in broad daylight, "if secret organizations, formed to sustain the constitution and restore peace and order, and suppress violence, wrong and outrage, shall be preferred by the people of Virginia to any other, the lawless adventurers and vile emissaries who have kindled the baleful fires of incendiarism[,] negro [*sic*] hate, and a war of races in eight hundred secret oath-bound negro [*sic*] leagues in this State, will have no right to complain." As if by prearrangement, over the next two days (27 and 28 March), the *Enquirer*

& Examiner announced the KKK's first appearances in Virginia, warning that Republicans would "soon find that 'this is a White Man's State.'" On 30 March, a "humorous" piece in the paper threatened Republican activist James Hunnicutt with a visit by klansmen. After the initial furor, however, the *Enquirer & Examiner* abandoned its public support for the KKK after April 1868.

Richmond (Ky.) *Register*—During September 1870, when violence by the Ku Klux Klan was at its worst in Madison County, Kentucky, the local Richmond *Register* blamed the crimes on Republicans, claiming that GOP members whipped and murdered each other to gain sympathy for their party.

Richmond (Va.) *Whig*—In April 1868, the *Whig* reported that the KKK was founded by a group of foreign merchants who smuggled opium into China. That report identified the founder of Virginia's Klan as one Humphrey Marshall, who allegedly launched the order's American branch during an innocent meeting at Brown's Hotel in Richmond, never guessing that the group would spin out of control to resist "radical" Reconstruction in Dixie. That same month, the paper claimed that Richmond alone boasted 4,000 klansmen, with 700 new recruits awaiting initiation.

Roanoke **(Ala.)** *Leader*—The editor of this newspaper, published in Randolph County, Alabama, denied any affiliation with the 1920s KKK, but still criticized the state's major dailies for allegedly "exaggerating" Ku Klux violence. As late as 22 August 1927, with hundreds of floggings and several murders recorded over the past three years, the *Leader* maintained: "The people of Alabama [are] not ... fools or lawless folk [that] ... have to be educated by incubator methods into the realization that mob law is pernicious, nor ... jerked up by the hair ... to be made to do their duty." The paltry number of convictions obtained against lawless klansmen during the same period proved that opinion invalid.

Rocanville **(Saskatchewan)** *Record*—A pro-Klan newspaper in the 1920s, the *Record* attacked Kleagle Pat Emmons for leaving the KKK and revealing its secrets. After Emmons won acquittal on charges of embezzling Klan funds, the paper editorialized: "Personally, we believe Emmons to be only a cheap grafter, apparently willing to sell out his friends to the highest bidder. At that he is very little lower than the gang who have obviously bought him."

Rome (Ga.) *Commercial*—In February 1871, after a party of klansmen stopped Rome *Courier* editor B.F. Sawyer on a public street and forced him to dance at gunpoint, Sawyer named rival *Commercial* editor Henry Grady as a member of the rowdy group. Grady denied it in print, joking that Sawyer "was excited, and besides he always shuts his eyes when he whistles." Denials notwithstanding, most locals regarded Grady as a klansman, if not the local den's cyclops. As Klan violence escalated, Grady adopted a cautious tone, warning that even "a half dozen murders" in Georgia could swing 100,000 votes to the GOP in 1872. As for the Klan itself, he asked "those of its friends who have any connection whatever with secret organizations *to remain perfectly*

quiet and orderly, for the present at any rate. Let there be no suspicion of disorder or lawlessness; let there be no parading of disguised men, no stopping of innocent men and forcing them to dance; this is all child's play and foolishness.... The exciting elections have all passed; the good cause has triumphed; the enemies of Georgia are beat to the dust.... Then let the harsh asperities that were necessary during the 'reign of terror' pass away like a dream." (Emphasis in the original.)

Grady was not calling for disbandment of the KKK, however. Instead, he wrote: "*Remember, brothers, that the strength and power of any secret organization rests in the attribute of mystery and hidden force, and in the fact that upon the thousand hills of our country a legion of brave hearts that are throbbing quietly can be called together by a tiny signal, and when the work is done, can melt away into shadowy nothing.*" (Emphasis in the original.) That time would only come, Grady asserted, "if an inexorable necessity calls for action," in which case the KKK would "act promptly, with decision, and do nothing more than is absolutely necessary."

Rome (Ga.) *Courier*—Reports differ on the role of editor B.F. Sawyer and his newspaper, the *Courier*, in dealing with the Reconstruction era KKK. Historian Allen Trelease calls Sawyer "an ardent Klan apologist," although Sawyer denounced the order by name for its violent acts, in January 1870. A year later, on 6 February 1871, a party of drunken klansmen stopped Sawyer on the street and compelled him to dance for them at gunpoint. Sawyer named Henry Grady—his former associate editor, later editor of the rival *Commercial*—as a member of that boozy band, writing: "We suspected all the while that we were exerting ourselves to please the ghostly crew, that we knew the form and recognized the snigger of the little fellow in the spotted shirt, who rode the little mule, and since no one but those engaged knew what transpired, we are now convinced that our suspicions were correct, and that the tail end of the Ku-Klux was no one else than our facetious young friend, Henry W. Grady." When violence escalated locally, Sawyer wrote: "Neither the interest of our people or the vindication of our peace and order requires their existence, and we unhesitatingly condemn their organization."

Rutherford County (N.C.) *Star*—The *Star*, edited by Rutherford County clerk J.B. Carpenter, courageously opposed the KKK from its first appearance during Reconstruction. On 11 June 1871, while Carpenter was testifying before Congress in Washington, D.C., a mob of klansmen demolished the newspaper's office and press. The pro-Klan Raleigh *Sentinel* blamed "radicals"—i.e., Republicans—for the attack.

Rutherfordton (N.C.) *Vindicator*—Republican activist Randolph Shotwell launched the *Vindicator* as a weekly in 1868, condemning Klan violence in Rutherford County, North Carolina, until bankruptcy forced him to sell the paper a few months later. It was purchased by a Democrat who generally ignored Klan violence until June 1871, when a mob of Kluxers demolished the rival *Star*'s office and presses.

St. Landry (La.) *Progress*—This bilingual newspaper was edited in 1868 by Emerson Bentley, a precocious eighteen-year-old who doubled as the only teacher at a local school for blacks. That role, and his support for the Republican Party, prompted three KWC members to visit the school on 28 September 1868, where they beat Bentley in front of his terrified students. Local blacks armed to retaliate for the assault, but Bentley calmed them and averted further bloodshed for the moment.

St. Martin Parish (La.) *Courier of the Teche*—A

Democratic newspaper during the Reconstruction era, the *Courier* publicly supported acts of violence by the Louisiana Klan and KWC. Its editor may well have gone beyond mere advocacy, since he later fled the state to avoid prosecution for the murder of a Republican state senator.

Salem (Ore.) *Capitol Journal*—Yet another anti–Klan

newspaper of the 1920s, the *Capitol Journal* resisted KKK political initiatives in Oregon despite the order's substantial membership and influence.

Salisbury (N.C.) *Old North State*—During Recon-

struction, the *Old North State* was one of only two North Carolina Democratic newspapers with editors bold enough to condemn the Ku Klux Klan. (The other was the Raleigh *Telegram*, ironically managed by a member of the Klan-allied White Brotherhood.) Threats of violence against its staff never materialized, and they failed to dissuade the paper from doing its civic duty.

Savannah (Ga.) *Republican*—Despite its name, this

Reconstruction-era newspaper was committed to support for Democratic candidates and causes. Nonetheless, it took a bold and lonely stand against the Georgia KKK in 1871, declaring on 6 January: "These secret bands of marauders and assassins are a disgrace to any civilized country, and it is hoped some plan may yet be devised of ridding the country of their presence."

Selma (Ala.) *Advocate*—Published in Dallas County, Al-

abama, this newspaper offered outspoken support to the 1920s KKK.

Shelby (N.C.) *Banner*—A pro-Klan newspaper in

Reconstruction-era North Carolina, the *Banner* complained bitterly when state authorities arrested Ku Klux terrorists in nearby Rutherford County. According to the *Banner*'s coverage of that event (23 August 1871), the raids victimized "helpless women and children, the aged and infirm, as well as the strong and athletic.... Honest citizens dare not speak their honest political sentiments. To be politically opposed to these petty tyrants is a passport to the black hole of the Rutherfordton jail, in which the best people of the county are ... crowded almost to suffocation, begging EVEN FOR WATER, like famished children. The young men of the country, who are as innocent of crime as a new born babe, are leaving for other parts, rather than summit [*sic*] to the oppression of these people." (Emphasis in the original.)

Shreveport (La.) *South-Western*—A Democratic

newspaper of the Reconstruction period, the *South-Western* warmly welcomed the formation of Louisiana's first Ku Klux dens in April 1868. A month later, as violence flourished, the paper closed its eyes to rampant acts of terrorism and denied any widespread paramilitary activity in the Bayou State. When crimes were acknowledged at all, as in the two-time mob destruction of the Homer *Iliad*'s office, *South-Western* editors blamed Republicans for staging the incidents in an attempt to frame Democrats. Nor was the paper's defense of violent klansmen restricted to Louisiana. When Georgia nightriders murdered Republican activist Rev. Joseph Adkins on 10 March 1869, the *South-Western* joined various Peach State tabloids in a campaign of posthumous character assassination, branding Adkins "a habitual inmate of negro [*sic*] brothels.... He was among the most degraded of the scalawags."

Spartanburg (S.C.) *Carolina Spartan*—A Democ-

ratic newspaper, generally supportive of the Reconstruction-era Klan, the *Carolina Spartan* accommodated Ku Klux terrorism by publishing notices from Republicans who received Klan death threats, announcing their conversion to the Democratic Party. It also published resolutions signed by local blacks, vowing to take no part in politics on either side. During 1871–72, the *Spartan* denied the existence of a Klan organization in Spartanburg County and angrily protested the federal arrests of Ku Klux murder suspects (including the principal of a boys' academy at Limestone Springs).

Spartanburg (S.C.) *Republican*—This Republican

newspaper tried to counter the rival *Carolina Spartan* by printing accurate reports of violent crimes committed by the Reconstruction-era Klan, but it made little headway. Democratic journalists accused the *Republican* of fabricating stories or parroting untrue reports contrived by GOP activists for political gain.

Stanford (Ky.) *Dispatch*—During Reconstruction, this

Democratic newspaper praised the KKK for its activities in Lincoln County, Kentucky.

Tabor City (N.C.) *Tribune*—This paper and its editor,

W. Horace Carter, won the Pulitzer Prize and the Sidney Hillman journalism award in 1952, for articles exposing Grand Dragon Thomas Hamilton's Association of Carolina Klans.

Taft (Calif.) *Midway Driller*—While the 1920s KKK

grew strong in Kern County, California, including the police chief of Taft among its members, the local *Midway Driller* raised a consistent voice in opposition to the invisible empire.

Tupelo (Miss.) *Daily Journal*—In the troubled 1950s

and 1960s, editor George McLean's *Tupelo Daily Journal* joined a handful of other Mississippi newspapers, bucking the dominant tide of racism supported by state government, the KKK, and the Citizens' Councils.

Tuscaloosa (Ala.) *Independent Monitor*—Ryland

Randolph settled in Tuscaloosa, Alabama, and purchased the *Independent Monitor* in 1867. His racist views were evident from the beginning, as the front page of his paper bore the motto: "White Man—Right or Wrong—Still the White Man!" On 4 December 1867, Randolph called for armed white resistance to the new state constitution, which he claimed would lead inexorably to racial intermarriage. The local Klan made its first appearance on 30 December, spiriting Randolph away into mock captivity, but he returned unscathed and henceforth served as the KKK's local mouthpiece. Historian Allen Trelease calls Randolph "the moving spirit behind the Klan" in Tuscaloosa County, and most accounts name him as the local den's cyclops. With Randolph at the helm, the *Independent Monitor* frequently published elaborate Ku Klux notices such as the following, printed on 1 April 1868:

Ku-Klux
Serpent's Den—Death's Retreat—
Hollow Tomb—Misery Cave of the
Great Ku-Klux Klan, No. 1,000

General Orders No. 1
Make ready! make ready! make ready!!!
The might Hobgoblins of the Confederate dead in
Hell-a-Bulloo assembled!

Revenge! Revenge!
Be secret, be cautious, be terrible!
By special grant, Hell freezes over for your passage.
Offended ghosts, put on your skates, and cross over to mother earth!

Work! Work!! Work!!!
Double, double, toil and trouble;
Fire burn and Cauldron bubble.
Ye white men who stick to black, soulless beasts! the time arrives for you to part. Z.Y.X.W.V.U., and so, from Omega to Alpha.

Cool it with a baboon's blood
Then the charm is firm and good.
Ye niggers who stick to low White—Begone, Begone, Begone!
The world turns around—the thirteenth hour approacheth.
S. one two and three—*beware!* White and yellow, J. and T——
P——and L——begone.—The handwriting on the wall warns you!

From the murderer's gibbet, throw
Into the flame. Come high or low.
By order of the Great BLUFUSTIN,
G.S.   K.K.K.
A true copy.
PETERLOO
P.S.   K.K.K.

Randolph was not all bluster, though. He soon became notorious for brawling in the street with critics and rival journalists, several times assaulting staffers of the Republican *Reconstructionist.* On one occasion, he claimed to have faced down 200 freedmen on his own, describing the event as follows: "I was determined to settle the matter of race supremacy right there and then.... I raised my gun as if to fire and, alone, started toward the crowd. The way that crowd of darkies scattered and scampered away was 'a caution,' as the saying is; indeed, so great was the 'skedaddle' that even I could not resist the temptation of laughing; and, to make the fun complete, I sighted my gun on the fleeing mob. Then there was not only running but actual 'hollering'; and in less than five minutes not a negro [*sic*] was to be seen on the streets." Charged with assault for the first time in April 1868, Randolph soon won acquittal and complained on 5 May that "Radical, nigger-worshipping vagabonds are protected by military authority, while the gentlemen of the land are persecuted by the same."

Ever the southern "gentleman," Randolph logged two more arrests by August 1868. On 1 September, the *Independent Monitor* published a cartoon depicting the lynching of Rev. A.S. Lakin, an Ohio native lately appointed as president of the state university in Tuscaloosa. The caption threatened Lakin with death if he did not flee the state by 4 March 1869. Lakin took the hint, and the university opened in April 1869 without him. Randolph's klansmen next pursued a campaign of death threats against the remaining faculty and thirty students which finally closed the school in 1871.

Randolph, meanwhile, had other issues on his mind. In October 1868, he offered his prescription for the proper handling of black voters: "Let the negro [*sic*] alone. If he attends barbecues let his province be to wait on the tables and brush off flies. He befits the speaker's stand about as well as a skunk would suit a sofa. Let him squall aloud for [Democratic national candidates] Seymour and Blair to his heart's content, for it is like a donkey braying for his food. Hallooing for the white man's candidate should be regarded as declaring in favor of white supremacy—nothing more or less; and all negroes [*sic*] who thus, with docility, fall into traces, should be rewarded with plenty of work, porridge and kind treatment." In truth, however, Randolph preferred slavery, as he explained on 23 February 1869.

[S]lavery was a God-send for the negro [*sic*] race. Negroes, as bondsmen, were happier, more sleek and greasy-looking, and better clothed, than they are now. We never hear the ringing horse-laughs, the picking on banjos, beating of tambourines, and knocking of feet against puncheon-floors, that formerly marked their *sans souci* existence. Instead thereof, they may be heard to grumble, in squads, collected in fence-corners; and may be seen with ashy faces, grum [*sic*] countenances, and squalid appearance generally.

On 22 June 1869, the *Independent Monitor* called for an end to Klan violence, with Randolph writing: "It is now time, we are free to announce, for murders and assassinations to cease." Various local klansmen were arrested over the next two months, and while Randolph grudgingly acknowledged on 14 September that criminals should be punished, he rebounded a week later with a sweeping dismissal of black testimony. "We contend," he wrote on 21 September, "that negro [*sic*] oaths are insufficient to establish a Southern white man's guilt. There exists a degree of cowardly, instinctive hatred, on the part of the tailless baboon race, for the whites, that can never be gotten rid of till the race itself shall be gotten rid of."

Advice aside, Randolph himself eschewed moderation. In March 1870, he lost a leg to wounds sustained in a public gunfight with a Republican enemy whom Randolph attacked on the street. By that time, even Grand Wizard Nathan Bedford Forrest was tired of his antics, telling the *Alabama State Journal* on 13 October 1869 that Randolph's "course as an editor has been constantly injurious, not to the Republicans, but to the Democratic party, and the true interests of the people of Alabama.... Unlike the editor of the *Monitor,* my object has been to bring peace to the country, and prosperity to the people; to soften down the prejudices of men of both parties; and in the development of the great material interests of the country, to smoothen the asperities engendered by the war, and efface alike the marks and memories of strife." Despite that verdict from his former leader, Randolph stayed his racist course and won election to a single term in the state legislature. He subsequently moved to Birmingham and died there on 7 May 1903, at age sixty-seven.

Tuscaloosa **(Ala.)** *News*—In 1949, this paper added its voice to the chorus of opposition to rampant Klan violence in Alabama. Its editors compared klansman to Adolf Hitler's Nazi storm troopers. Still, it stopped short of dealing the local KKK a mortal blow, refusing to publish a list of members that reporters had obtained after infiltrating Tuscaloosa's klavern.

Tuscaloosa (Ala.) *Reconstructionist*—This Republican newspaper struggled to survive in Tuscaloosa, Alabama, during Reconstruction. Klansmen threatened its staff constantly, and Ryland Randolph—editor of the rival *Independent Monitor*—periodically assaulted its editors on the streets.

Tuskegee (Ala.) *News*—The Democratic editors of this Reconstruction-era newspaper followed the familiar pattern of blaming some Ku Klux crimes on blacks or Republican "radicals," while ignoring most of the violence entirely.

Warrenton *Georgia Clipper*—A staunch Democratic paper in Reconstruction-era Warren County, Georgia, the *Clipper* generally supported KKK activity and waged a ceaseless campaign of vilification against Republican Sheriff John Norris. Historian Allen Trelease declared that the editor was "almost certainly" one of the Klan's local leaders. Wallace's successor in that post, A.I. Hartley, was subsequently named as a prime suspect in the December 1868 ambush-wounding of Sheriff Norris and the March 1869 lynching of Republican activist Dr. G.W. Darden.

Weldon (N.C.) *News*—Like other Democratic papers of the Reconstruction era, the *News* pretended to believe that no Klan existed in the Tarheel State. Reports of Ku Klux activity, its editors claimed, were fabricated for political effect by Governor William Holden's *Daily Standard.*

Whiteville (N.C.) *News Reporter*—This paper and its editor, Willard Cole, won the Pulitzer Prize and the Sidney Hillman journalism award in 1952, for articles exposing Grand Dragon Thomas Hamilton's Association of Carolina Klans.

Wichita Falls (Tex.) *Times*—Like the Amarillo *News,* this Texas newspaper endorsed some of the 1920s KKK's political initiatives without committing itself to wholehearted support of the order.

Wilmington (N.C.) *Journal*—A Democratic paper of the Reconstruction era, the *Journal* bore a measure of responsibility for calling the local Klan into existence in March 1868. Some historians claim that associate editor William Saunders was in fact the Tarheel State's grand dragon.

Wilson County (Tenn.) *Herald*—Based in Lebanon, Tennessee, during Reconstruction, this Democratic paper published a supposed disbandment order from unnamed KKK lead-

ers on 16 September 1869. It read: "Our mission on earth, to some extent is ended. Quiet and peace must be cast abroad in your land. Wherever possible, we have protected you from outrage and wrong. We will still lend a helping hand and the evil doers must remember that while we sleep we are not gone.... For the present, and we hope forever, we are done. When you see men, things or demons on your premises, claiming to be of me, shoot them down, for you may be certain that we are not there."

Yorkville (S.C.) *Enquirer*—As the only newspaper in Reconstruction-era York County, South Carolina, the Democratic *Enquirer* served as a de facto mouthpiece for the local Ku Klux Klan. On 30 March 1868, it printed the first announcement of a local Klan meeting, which read:

K.K.K. DEAD-MANS HOLLOW SOUTHERN DIV. Midnight, March 20. *General Order No.* 1. REMEMBER the hour appointed by our Most Excellent Grand Captain-General. The dismal hour draws nigh for the meeting of our mystic Circle. The Shrouded-Knight will come with pick and spade; the Grand Chaplain will come with the ritual of the dead. The grave yawneth, the lightnings flash athwart the heavens, the thunders roll, but the Past Grand Knight of the Sepulcher [*sic*] will recoil not. By order of the Great Grand Centaur SULEYMAN, G.G.S.

In 1870, the *Enquirer* denounced Klan nightriding in general terms, but considered the employment of a state militia (and especially one with black members) a much worse outrage. Throughout that year, the paper published party renunciations penned by black and white Republicans alike, intended to pacify klansmen who threatened their lives. On 9 February 1871, the *Enquirer* condemned Klan raiders and black barn-burners with equal vehemence, though it typically reserved most of its criticism for the Union League. On 9 March 1871, local Klan leaders used the paper as their vehicle for denouncing unauthorized threats in the KKK's name, but added that "the intelligent, honest white people (the tax-payers) of this county shall rule it! We can no longer put up with negro [*sic*] rule, black bayonets, and a miserably degraded and thievish set of lawmakers ... the scum of the earth, the scrapings of creation. We are pledged to stop it; we are determined to end it, even if we are 'forced, by force, to use force.'" Two months later, on 25 May, the *Enquirer's* editor joined with local Klan leaders to produce and publish a condemnation of future violent acts.

Still, such crimes remained widespread, and they produced some unfortunate effects. On 20 July 1871, the *Enquirer* complained that sixty black families were pulling up stakes for Liberia. As described in the paper: "The entire number is made up of the most industrious negroes [*sic*] in that section of the country, many of whom, since their emancipation, have shown themselves to be thrifty and energetic, and not a few of them had accumulated money." Days later, the *Enquirer* adopted a more familiar tone, mocking visiting members of the congressional "sub–Outrage committee" and denigrating the voluminous evidence of Klan terrorism statewide. Curiously, when federal arrests of klansmen began in York County and elsewhere, the *Enquirer* reported the round-ups with unusual self-restraint.

APPENDIX A:
A KU KLUX TIMELINE

Some events from the KKK's history can be dated precisely, while many others were deliberately obscured. The following timeline includes events specific to the Klan, as well as general events that had significant impact on the order's activities and evolution. Individual Klan rallies from the busy 1920s are not listed unless some particular importance was attached to the gathering, or it resulted in acts of violence. Likewise, individual minor assaults on civil rights workers in the 1960s are too numerous for inclusion here, unless specific evidence links them to the KKK, but serious acts of violence—including riots, shootings, arson and bombings—are recorded. Discrepancies in dating various incidents are common among published sources, and the dates cited below are those deemed most reliable after extensive research. No specific details are available for thousands of Klan assaults during Reconstruction and the period from 1915 through 1953, while media reports of violence during the civil rights era are much more detailed. That fact makes it appear that klansmen were more active during 1962–66 than during other periods when they actually claimed more victims, but since the Klan keeps no record of its crimes and press coverage was often lax in earlier times, we are left with the record as it stands, compiled from media reports and official investigations.

1864

12 April: Fort Pillow, TN—Gen. Nathan Bedford Forrest captures the Union stronghold, manned by 605 soldiers. An estimated 25–30 defenders die in combat before the post surrenders. Forrest then supervises the massacre of another 257 soldiers, mostly blacks, including some buried alive.

1865

14 April: Washington, DC—John Wilkes Booth assassinates President Abraham Lincoln. Andrew Johnson takes office as president on 15 April.

29 May: Washington, DC—President Johnson declares amnesty for all Confederates who accept the Thirteenth Amendment's ban on slavery.

22–25 November: Jackson, MS—State legislators enact the first Black Codes.

4 December: Washington, DC—Congress refuses to seat newly elected southern representatives and senators.

18 December: Ratification of the Thirteenth Amendment formally abolishes slavery.

1866

9 April: Washington, DC—Congress passes the first Civil Rights Act over President Johnson's veto.

30 April–2 May: Memphis, TN—White rioters kill at least 46 blacks and two "radical" whites, while destroying 90 black homes, 12 schools and 4 churches.

May/June: Pulaski, TN—The original Klan is founded by its "Immortal Six" creators.

13 June: Washington, DC—Congress sends the Fourteenth Amendment to the states for ratification.

July: Washington, DC—Congress extends the one-year life span of the Freedmen's Bureau.

24 July: Washington, DC—Congress readmits Tennessee to the Union.

30 July: New Orleans—A white pogrom led by police leaves 38 blacks dead and 146 injured.

November: South Carolina—Gen. Robert Scott reports that federal forces in the state are inadequate to suppress racist violence.

1867

12 February: Newnanville, FL—Self-declared klansmen murder a black man, Cooley Johnson.

2 March: Washington, DC—Congress passes the first Reconstruction Act.

29 March: Pulaski, TN—The Klan's first newspaper notice appears in the *Pulaski Citizen*, whose editor is one of the "Immortal Six" KKK founders.

April: Nashville, TN—Klansmen from various states gather to reorganize the KKK on paramilitary lines, approve a prescript, and elect Nathan Bedford Forrest grand wizard.

1 May: Gen. Phillip Sheridan begins registering black voters in Louisiana.

May: St. Mary Parish, LA—Militant whites organize the Knights of the White Camellia.

14 May: Mobile, AL—White rioters attack a black political meeting. One member of each race dies in the fighting.

5 June: Pulaski, TN—Klansmen stage their first anniversary parade.

1 August: Tennessee—Blacks vote for the first time in a southern state election, installing a Republican administration.

5 November: Montgomery, AL—Alabama's constitutional convention begins.

23 November: New Orleans—Louisiana's constitutional convention begins.

3 December: Richmond, VA—The Virginia constitutional convention begins.

9 December: Atlanta, GA—The Georgia constitutional convention begins.

30 December: Tuscaloosa, AL—Klansmen make their first public appearance in town.

1868

January: Pulaski, TN—Rioting erupts after a black man and a former slave quarrel over a black girl. Prominent klansmen join in the melee, which leaves at least one black dead and several wounded.

January: Marshall County, TN—Klansmen kidnap eight blacks and force them at gunpoint to renounce the GOP.

7 January: Constitutional conventions begin in Arkansas and Mississippi.

14 January: Constitutional conventions open in North and South Carolina.

20 January: Tallahassee, FL—Florida's constitutional convention begins.

February: Maury County, TN—Klansmen raid black homes, seizing at least 400 guns. Late in the month, after klansman John Bickell is murdered by a black robber, fellow knights take the suspect from jail and lynch him outside Columbia.

March: Tennessee—Klansmen issue statewide threats to prevent blacks from voting in county elections, afterward punishing those who ignore the warnings.

7 March: Davidson County, TN—Klansmen raid the home of black Union veteran Bob Anderson, five miles outside Nashville. Anderson kills one of the raiders. On 8 March, 50 whites "arrest" Anderson and several other blacks, ordering them to leave the county within 24 hours.

20 March: Eutaw, AL—Klansmen burn the Greene County courthouse.

21 March: Greensboro, AL: Townspeople foil a Klan attempt to burn the Hale County courthouse.

31 March: Columbus, GA—Klansmen murder Republican George Ashburn in his home.

31 March: Eutaw, AL—Klansmen murder the Republican county solicitor.

April: Danville, KY—Freedmen's Bureau agents report Klansmen terrorizing local blacks.

April: Murfreesboro, TN—Klansmen drag Sheriff J.S. Webb from his home and threaten to lynch him if he does not resign. Webb's brother is subsequently whipped.

May: Woodruff County, AR—Klansmen lynch a black man named Woodruff, jailed on vagrancy charges. Nightriders also raid a black couple's home whipping the husband and wife 200 lashes each.

May: Bienville Parish, LA—Amid general statewide terrorism, nightriders drag a black Republican from his home and behead him.

6 May: Claiborne Parish, LA—Gunmen ambush and murder William Meadows, a black delegate to the state constitutional convention.

June: Washington, DC—Congress reports that racial violence in the South has killed 373 blacks and 10 whites since Jan. 1866.

1 June: Austin, TX—The state's constitutional convention begins.

22 June: Washington, DC—Congress readmits Arkansas to the Union, followed on 25 June by Alabama, Florida, Georgia, Louisiana, North and South Carolina.

29 June: Pulaski, TN—100 klansmen remove a black rape suspect from jail, riddle him with bullets, and leave his body in the street.

July: Columbia, TN—50 klansmen drag a black man from his home, strangle him, and dump his corpse in the Duck River.

1 July: Texas—Federal authorities report 1,053 known murders since April 1865, one-third of them committed in 1867, and another one-third in the first half of 1868. White slayers are identified in 833; nearly half the victims are black, though whites hold a three-to-one majority in the state population.

4 July: Maury County, TN—Armed blacks ambush a nocturnal Klan procession, wounding at least three klansmen. By mid–July, at least three suspects are lynched, while others flee to Nashville for safety.

4 July: Cornersville, TN—Black leader William Burk dies in a shootout with klansmen at his home.

4 July: Jefferson, TX—300 armed whites seize the town to prevent a GOP rally. Mounted posses scour the surrounding countryside, hanging white Republicans, shooting blacks on sight or jailing them for "insurrection."

4 July: Shelbyville, TN—50 klansmen invade the town and whip two white victims. One, schoolteacher J.C. Dunlap, receives 200 lashes for teaching blacks.

8 July: Homer, LA—Whites destroy the presses of a GOP newspaper and flog a white Republican.

14 July: Woodruff County, AR—Klansmen launch a reign of terror that will claim 20 lives by 28 August, including eight persons murdered in one day.

21 July: Ratification of the Fourteenth Amendment confers citizenship upon former slaves.

1 August: Louisiana—Gov. Henry Warmouth calls for federal aid, reporting 150 political murders in six weeks. Democrats brand the report "a willful Radical fabrication."

1 August: Nashville, TN—Nathan Forrest, John Brown and 11 other former Confederate generals issue protests against Gov. Brownlow's efforts to raise a state militia.

August: Crittenden County, AR—Klansmen firing from ambush wound Republican state legislator and Freedmen's Bureau agent E.G. Barker.

August: Georgia—Klansmen launch a pre-election terror campaign lasting through October. At least 31 persons are murdered, 43 wounded by gunfire, 5 stabbed and 55 beaten, with 8 flogging victims receiving 300–500 lashes each.

15 August: Wayne County, TN—60 klansmen confront a group of black militiamen, ordering them to disband, then pursue the county sheriff to his jail in Waynesboro, where they besiege him with gunfire.

26 August: Mississippi County, AR—Klansmen assassinate state legislator A.M. Johnson. Six blacks are murdered in the county by 20 September.

29 August: Columbia County, AR—A state legislator reports 10 KKK murders of blacks in the county since 9 August.

September: Trinity County, TX—Masked whites murder several persons during a terror campaign against black would-be voters.

September: Lamar County, TX—Farmers arm and organize against Klan nightriders, but terrorism continues into November.

September: Searcy, AR—Private detective Albert Parker vanishes while investigating the local KKK. Klansmen admit knowledge of his murder in March 1870.

10 September: Northport, AL—Klansmen raid a black man's home, killing his wife while he hides in the chimney.

19 September: Bennett's Bayou, AR—Klansmen murder Capt. Simpson Mason while he registers black voters.

19 September: Camilla, GA—Whites shoot up a GOP rally, launching a pogrom that leaves 9 blacks dead and 30–40 wounded.

22 September: New Orleans—Rioting erupts after white Democrats fire on a GOP rally.

28 September: Opelousas, LA—Three members of the Seymour Knights beat Emerson Bentley, a white schoolteacher, in front of his black students. Elsewhere in the parish, terrorists murder 200–300 blacks.

Autumn: Columbia County, FL—White assassins fire on black GOP activist Prince Weaver at a black social gathering, killing his 13-year-old son and wounding three other victims.

October: Louisiana—A full-scale race war erupts in the month preceding the presidential election. Attacks by the KKK and KWC leave 1,723 persons dead or wounded by 8 November. In St. Landry Parish, more than 200 die in a two-day purge, with a pile of 25 half-buried bodies found in the woods. Authorities unearth another 162 corpses in Bossier Parish and report 297 political murders around New Orleans. Caddo Parish gunmen kill 42 victims, and locals count 25–30 black corpses drifting past Shreveport in the Red River. A mob in Alexandria demolishes the office of a GOP newspaper. In Franklinton, masked klansmen raid the homes of three black Republicans, seizing and destroying their GOP ballots.

October: Monticello, AR—Klansmen murder Deputy Sheriff William Dollar and a black companion, Frederick Reeves.

October: Live Oak, FL—Klansmen kidnap Doc Rountree, his wife and four children, whipping all six for the "crimes" of owning land and refusing to work for their prewar slave master.

October: Weakley County, TN—Klansmen invade the voting registrar's home, to prevent registration of blacks and Republicans, but the raiders quarrel and fight among themselves, finally fleeing with several self-inflicted gunshot wounds.

1 October: Cache Bottom, AR—Klansmen ambush white Republicans F.A. McClure and D.P. Upham, wounding both as they try to organize a militia company.

1 October: Abbeville, SC—Three klansmen assassinate B.F Randolph, a state senator and GOP chairman, at the railroad depot in broad daylight.

1 October: Sumter County, AL—Klansmen murder black Republican Ben Brown.

1 October: Jefferson, TX—Knights of the Rising Sun ambush "carpetbagger" George Smith at a black home. Smith wounds two attackers and is jailed for assault. KRS members return and kill Smith in jail on 4 October.

15 October: Crittenden County, AR—Klansmen on the tugboat *Netty Jones* capture the *Hesper*, destroying arms purchased for the Arkansas militia.

17 October: Franklin, LA—Members of the KKK and KWC assassinate Judge Valentine Chase and Sheriff Henry Pope.

22 October: Monroe County, AR—Klansmen murder congressman James Hinds, wounding future governor James Brooks in the same ambush.

23 October: Jefferson Parish, LA—KWC members provoke blacks into attacking them, then claim "self-defense" for a series of raids that leave 5 blacks dead, 9 wounded by gunfire, and 33 beaten or otherwise injured.

24 October: Rocky Comfort, AR—Klansmen murder Maj. Porter Andrews, U.S. revenue assessor, and Lt. Hiram Willis, of the Freedmen's Bureau. Other victims of the same ambush include one black man killed and two men wounded (one of them the county sheriff).

24 October: New Orleans—Whites fire on a GOP parade, leaving several blacks dead and wounded, then turn their wrath on white Republicans and the metropolitan police, killing 63 persons before order is restored.

25 October: Eutaw, AL—A pre-election pogrom leaves 4 blacks dead and 50 wounded, while 2 whites are slightly injured.

25 October: Algiers, LA—Authorities report 7 blacks murdered in recent days by members of the KWC and Wide Awakes.

29 October: Augusta, AR—Klansmen shoot up the town, killing George McElum and wounding Bill Cincinnati, narrowly missing the sheriff. Outside town, they raid and terrorize two black families at home.

29 October: Tangipahoa, LA—40 klansmen raid the home of black coroner John Kemp, murdering him and beating his wife. In other local raids, they wound two more blacks and rob a third.

31 October: Huntsville, AL—Parading klansmen clash with blacks and rioting erupts, leaving 2 dead and several wounded.

November: Gainesville, FL—Klansmen murder a black man named Stephens.

1 November: Tuscaloosa, AL—20 klansmen attack a pre-election GOP rally.

1 November: Monticello, AR—Klansmen stage multiple raids to frighten black voters, whipping two ministers.

1 November: Gordon, FL—Klansmen murder a black man, Moses Smith.

1 November: Warrenton, GA—Klan target Perry Jeffers resists nightriders, killing one klansman and wounding three more. Raiders try again on 5 November, killing one of Jeffers's sons and cremating his body on a bonfire built with the family's furniture. They also hang Jeffers's wife, but neighbors cut her down while still alive. Several days later, klansmen capture Jeffers and three of his sons on a train bound for Dearing, shooting all four in the woods and dumping their bodies down a well.

2 November: Franklinton, LA—Klansmen warn the board of election supervisors not to distribute Republican ballots during the next day's election.

2 November: Tennessee—Klan nightriders raid black and Republican homes in Franklin, Giles, Lincoln and Shelby counties on election eve.

3 November: South Carolina—Klansmen terrorize Republican voters in the northwestern part of the state. Only half of black registered voters cast ballots in Anderson and Lauren counties, while barely one-fifth vote in Abbeville County.

3 November: Pulaski, TN—Whites seize a Confederate veteran who voted Republican and subject him to mock auction as a "white nigger."

5 November: Greenville, FL—Klansmen board a train carrying arms for the militia from Jacksonville to Tallahassee, seizing and destroying the weapons.

9 November: Arkansas—Gov. Powell Clayton declares martial law in 10 counties, mobilizing a militia to oppose the KKK.

14 November: Sumter County, AL—A Klansman fires on the home of Republican Gerard Choutteau, narrowly missing his children. On 15 November they fire guns around the house all night to keep Choutteau's family awake.

14 November: Center Point, AR—Militiamen clash with 400 armed whites, leaving one man dead and five wounded before the racists scatter. The battle effectively ends local KKK activity.

15 November: Alexandria, LA—A white mob destroys the local GOP newspaper office.

30 November: Lewisburg, AR—Klansmen murder a black man, George Washington, at his home.

1 December: Lewisburg, AR—Klansmen torch the courthouse, destroying files required for prosecution of nightriders, but flames spread and level one-third of the town. Three arsonists are captured, one of them killed while "trying to escape."

December: Augusta, AR—Militia officers seize 15 white hostages and threaten to raze the town if a force of 200 racists proceeds with plans to attack the troops.

December: Warren County, GA—Klansmen ambush and wound Sheriff John Norris.

December: Overton County, TN—Armed blacks rout a Klan raiding party, capturing three horses and KKK regalia. Several nights later, 100 klansmen return and retrieve the horses. A black man defending his home kills one klansman, before he is shot and disemboweled. In a separate incident, klansmen allegedly hanged one of their own for killing "the wrong Negro" in another raid.

December: Chatham County, NC—Klansmen kidnap and torture a black theft suspect, Caswell Holt, in a fruitless effort to make him confess. They leave him alive, with a warning to vacate the county.

15 December: Lewisburg, AR—One week after a declaration of martial law, klansmen murder an elderly Republican merchant and burn his store.

18 December: Pulaski, TN—Masked whites remove a black prisoner from jail and lynch him.

1869

January: Palestine, TX—Nightriders terrorize blacks, shaving their heads and flogging them, shooting several persons and burning homes.

January: Shelbyville, TN—25–30 klansmen invade the town, seeking teacher J.C. Dunlap. Dunlap and friends fire on the raiders, killing one.

January: Georgetown, KY—Klansmen invade a black man's home, shooting him several times.

11 January: Columbia, TN—Klansmen abduct private detective Seymour Barmore, hired to infiltrate the KKK, from a local train, hanging him and riddling his body with bullets before dumping him in the Duck River.

24 January: Kinston, NC—CUG members remove five black prisoners from jail and execute them.

February: Hernando County, FL—Klansmen remove two black murder suspects from police custody and hang them.

20 February: Tennessee—Gov. W.C. Brownlow declares martial law in nine counties plagued by Klan violence.

26 February: Marianna, FL—Klansmen ambush state legislator W.J. Purman after a concert. A bullet passing through his body kills Purman's companion, county clerk John Finlayson.

March: Alamance County, NC—40 klansmen invade the county seat (Graham), firing into several black homes. Elsewhere, Joseph Harvey received 150 lashes, while klansmen club his infant child to death. In a third raid, a black woman armed with an axe wounds one klansman before the rest flee.

March: Jessamine County, KY—An intended Klan victim kills one of his would-be kidnappers and routs the rest.

March: Warrenton, GA—Dr. G.W. Darden kills Democratic newspaper editor Charles Wallace in a street confrontation. That night, black-robed klansmen drag Darden from jail and riddle him with bullets. Soon after the lynching, Klan raiders kill one black man, beat 11 others to the point of death, and gang-rape a teenage black girl.

13 March: Little Rock, AR—State legislators pass the first anti–Klan statute, banning both the KKK and KWC.

Spring: Columbia County, FL—Klansmen kidnap and murder black Republican Lishur Johnson. His body is never found.

April: Tuscaloosa County, AL—A black-white quarrel sparks raiding by the KKK, with one klansman killed in an exchange of gunfire. The next day, raiders burn every black home on one local plantation. Violence continues for another two days, with two more klansmen slain and several blacks wounded.

April: Garrard County, KY—Klansmen lynch a black jail inmate.

12 April: Raleigh, NC—State legislators enact an anti–Klan statute.

May: Sumter, AL—Klansmen kill two blacks and wound a third, then flee into neighboring Mississippi.

May: Jefferson County, GA—Klansmen murder Dr. Benjamin Ayer, a Republican state legislator.

10 May: Warren County, GA—Klansmen assassinate Republican state senator Joseph Adkins. Witnesses identify the gunman as Ellis Adams, who dies in a December 1869 shootout with authorities.

28 May: Jones County, NC—Klansmen ambush "carpetbag" Sheriff O.R. Colgrove, killing him and a black companion.

June: Lincoln County, KY—Klansmen raid a local Unionist's home, whipping his wife and burning the house.

June: Lawrence County, AL—Authorities jail eight klansmen after a lynching and several arson fires. A few days before their scheduled trial, masked men liberate the prisoners and execute those who confessed. Three are later recaptured, convicted, and sentenced to prison, but klansmen return to free them from the Athens prison on 14 July.

June: Tuscaloosa County, AL—Klansmen murder four persons during the month, with many more assaulted, beaten, and otherwise abused.

Summer: Lincoln County, NC—Klan arsonists burn the home of Rev. J.R. Peterson.

July: Harrodsburg, KY—Authorities report that in the past two years, klansmen have killed more than 25 persons and whipped or otherwise outraged at least 100, all within a 25-mile radius of town.

15 July: Marion, AR—A known klansman murders Capt. A.J. Haynes, a black militia officer, on a city street in broad daylight.

July: Jackson County, AL—Klan harassment of a British subject, James Weir, prompts official protests to Washington, DC.

31 July: Huntsville, AL—300 klansmen invade the town, hunting white Unionists and driving blacks at gunpoint from a religious service.

6 August: Tennessee—Klansmen terrorize blacks in Rutherford, Sumner and Wilson counties on election day, killing at least two and whipping, raping, or robbing numerous others. Scores of blacks abandon their farms to seek refuge in Nashville. A separate outbreak in Dyer and Weakley counties leaves one black prisoner lynched, one white man murdered, and three blacks whipped. The reign of terror permits white Democrats to recapture the state government.

August: Hillsborough, NC—100 masked klansmen remove two black arson suspects from jail, lynching one. A few nights later, Alamance County klansmen lynch two relatives of the victim, while a fourth black is hanged soon afterward, accused of trying to rape a white girl.

12 August: Livingston, AL—Nightriders storm Gerard Choutteau's home, killing security guard John Coblentz and losing one of their own in the gunfight. Other raiders wound black state legislator George Houston at his home, the same night.

16 August: Lenoir County, NC—Klansmen murder Republican leader M.L. Shepard and two other men at his sawmill.

September: Chapel Hill, NC—Parties of 50–100 klansmen repeatedly invade the town by night, beating blacks and driving white opponents from their homes, also whipping black inmates of the county poorhouse.

28 September: Robinson Spring, FL—Klansmen fire on a black picnic, killing Wyatt Young and 2-year-old Steward Livingston, slightly wounding Constable Calvin Rogers.

Autumn: Columbia County, FL—Klansmen mount a campaign against blacks and "radicals," murdering black Republicans Timothy Francis, James Green, Ike Ipswich and Thomas Jacobs in separate incidents. Authorities charge Ipswich's killer, but jurors acquit him in a trial packed with armed klansmen.

October: Live Oak, FL—Black Republican Doc Rountree survives his first attack by klansmen.

1 October: Marianna, FL—Snipers fire at local Klan leader James Coker, accidentally killing a companion, Maggie McClellan. Coker blames black constable Calvin Rogers and "carpetbag" state assemblyman M.I. Stearns. Armed whites threaten Stearns on 2 October and murder a black man, Oscar Granbury, in a separate incident.

4 October: Jackson County, FL—Klansmen raid a black home, killing Henry Reed, his wife and son, dumping their bodies in a lime pit.

5 October: Jackson County, FL—Klansmen wound Jerry Pridgeon, a black man, on a local plantation, then escort Jewish Republican Samuel Fleishman to the state line, with orders not to return.

6 October: Marianna, FL—Klansmen abduct a black man, Richard Pousser, from his home, but he escapes in transit to their would-be execution site.

8 October: Jackson County, FL—Klansmen kidnap Matt Nickles, his wife and son, killing all three and dropping their bodies into a lime sink.

11 October: Jackson County, FL—Klansmen ambush and kill returning exile Samuel Fleishman outside Marianna.

23 October: Jackson County, FL—Klansmen fire into the homes of two black Republicans, Alexander Bell and George Harvey.

24 October: Jackson County, FL—Klansmen raid the home of Adeline Failey, a black woman.

24 October: Marianna, FL—Lucy Griffin, a black woman, is assaulted on the street three times by whites, in separate attacks.

November: Alamance County, NC—A black man whipped by the Klan identifies two of his assailants as a deputy sheriff and a justice of the peace.

November: Lincoln County, NC—Authorities blame KKK raiders in four floggings.

26 November: Company Shops (now Burlington), NC—Klansmen visit Alonzo Corliss, a crippled white teacher in a school for blacks, whipping him and shaving half of his skull, then painting it black.

December: Marianna, FL—Klansmen wound Richard Pousser in a shooting at his home.

December: Pulaski, TN—50 masked klansmen invade the town to rescue a barrel of moonshine from revenue agents.

December: Alamance County, NC—Klansmen interrupt a party at a black home, whipping three men and fatally injuring a 4-month-old child. Subsequent raids included whipping of numerous other blacks.

December: Orange County, NC—Klansmen lynch two blacks accused of arson.

December: Obion County, TN—Klansmen raid the William Jones plantation, leaving one man killed and several wounded as Jones and his black field hands respond with gunfire. Authorities arrest Jones and several blacks, but the party is ambushed by klansmen en route to the county jail. Two blacks are killed and three wounded.

1870

January: Dallas, NC—Authorities blame black members of the Union League for fires that destroy nine barns owned by white Democrats in the space of one week.

January: Greene County, AL—Klansmen launch a reign of terror lasting through March, including at least seven murders and burning of seven black schools.

26 January: Washington, DC—Congress readmits Virginia to the Union.

February: Kentucky—Klansmen lynch two victims in Richmond and Winchester on successive nights.

10 February: York County, SC—Klansmen raid the home of militia captain John Farris, seizing rifles and ammunition.

12 February: Rutherford County, NC—Klansmen raid three Republican homes, abusing several women and flogging black GOP activist Almon Owens. Aaron Biggerstaff helps track the raiders to the home of his half-brother Samuel, where shots are exchanged.

Klansman William DePriest is subsequently killed by one of the night's targets, a white Republican named McGahey, whose wife he assaulted.

17 February: Washington, DC—Congress readmits Mississippi to the Union.

26 February: Graham, NC—Klansmen abduct and hang Wyatt Outlaw, a black town councilman and Union League leader.

7 March: Alamance County, NC—After klansmen murder William Puryear, a black witness to the Wyatt Outlaw lynching, Gov. William Holden declares a state of insurrection in the county.

18 March: Morgan County, AL—Klansmen assassinate Judge Charlton, a local GOP activist and founder of an anti–Klan action squad.

30 March: Ratification of the Fifteenth Amendment grants suffrage to blacks.

31 March: Eutaw, Alabama—30–40 klansmen drag county solicitor Alexander Boyd from his home and shoot him.

31 March: Union, AL—Klansmen murder a prominent black Republican, Jim Martin.

Spring: Jackson County, FL—Klan assassins finally locate and kill Constable Calvin Rogers.

1 April: Tuscaloosa, AL—A street duel between KKK leader Ryland Randolph and a rival leaves an innocent bystander dead, while Randolph's leg wound necessitates amputation.

8 April: Rutherford County, NC—Klansmen raid Aaron Biggerstaff's home, whipping Biggerstaff, his wife and daughter.

May: Franklin County, KY—Klansmen raid black homes around Frankfort, threatening the occupants with death if they vote in August's election.

11 May: Lincoln County, NC—Blacks report 16 attacks by klansmen since late March. Incidents include robbery, whippings and gang rape.

12 May: Cleveland County, NC—Klansmen ambush Aaron Biggerstaff, en route to testify concerning the raids of 12 February. The beating, his second, leaves Biggerstaff with a broken arm.

31 May: Washington, DC—Congress passes the first Enforcement Act to protect black voters in the South.

June: Live Oak, FL—Doc Rountree narrowly escapes a Klan ambush.

June: Tuskegee, AL—Klan threats drive James Alston, a leading black Republican, to leave the county.

July: Belmont, AL—200 armed blacks organize a militia troop and threaten to burn the town after several Klan raids, including disruption of a recent GOP meeting. Local whites import klansmen from Meridian, Mississippi, and launch a hunt for "insurrectionists." One black man kills a white in self-defense, then spends nearly a year in jail before he is finally lynched in September 1871.

8 July: Caswell County, NC—Gov. Holden declares a state of insurrection.

11 July: Cross Plains, AL—A fight between black and white youths ends in gunfire, with no injuries. On 12 July, three blacks and a white "carpetbag" teacher are jailed on assault charges. That night, klansmen abduct the four defendants and a black inmate held on unrelated charges. Leaving town, they abduct another black man from the street, eventually lynching all six men.

August: Versailles, KY—Klansmen invade the town by night and murder two black men.

1 August: Kentucky—White Democrats forcibly bar blacks from voting in several towns. Klansmen riot in Harrodsburg, afterward threatening to hang the U.S. commissioner and any other Republicans who file charges against the rioters.

4 August: North Carolina—Klan terrorism suppressed black votes on election day, permitting Democrats to recapture the state legislature.

18 August: Gainesville, AL—Klansmen assassinate black state legislator Richard Burke at his home.

September: Greene County, AL—Klansmen drag black Republican Guilford Coleman from his home, shoot him, and mutilate his corpse. Days later, the raiders murder a second black man.

Autumn: Chatham County, NC—Klansmen whip a black man, Henderson Judd, at his home.

Autumn: Moore County, NC—Klansmen burn a black school.

Autumn: Hale County, AL—Klansmen lynch a black man suspected of arson.

October: Madison County, FL—Klansmen ambush Sheriff David Montgomery, wounding his horse. Several days later, blacks fatally stab a klansman named Bryant in Montgomery's store. Federal authorities reject the governor's plea for troops to keep order in Madison County, and klansmen burn Sheriff Montgomery's store on 17 October.

October: Cookeville, TN—One night after a Klan parade, whites riot against blacks and Republicans, beating two Unionists and driving them from town.

October: Spartanburg, SC—Klansmen whip a Republican election manager and a black couple, forcing the latter to simulate sex before severing part of the man's ear. Several of the raiders are arrested, then released on bond and never prosecuted. Klansmen return to flog those responsible for the arrests, and in a later raid torture 69-year-old John Genobles into renouncing his GOP membership.

19–22 October: Clinton, SC—White terrorists drive a state constable from the polls and prevent blacks from voting on election day. Federal troops arrive in time to prevent a pogrom, but rioting erupts within hours of their departure on 20 October. Over the next two days, terrorists kill a dozen Republicans, most of them black. Victims include black state legislator Wade Perrin and a white probate judge.

25 October: Eutaw, AL—Whites fire on a GOP rally, killing 4 blacks and wounding 50.

November: Union County, NC—Klansmen murder a white justice of the peace whose home was used for GOP meetings. Soon afterward, raiders kill several blacks and whip dozens of victims, including a white probate judge. At least 200 blacks flee the county.

November: York County, SC—Klansmen launch a reign of terror continuing through September 1871. Best estimates reveal at least 11 murders, 600 serious beatings, plus numerous lesser assaults and abuses. Arsonists destroy five black schools and churches, including one burned and rebuilt on four separate occasions.

November: Spartanburg, SC—Masked klansmen demand the release of a white man jailed for killing a black, then depart empty-handed when the sheriff threatens to shoot anyone who enters the jail.

November: Noxubee County, MS—Klansmen whip and murder several black tenant farmers, also flogging three black women accused of sexual affairs with white men.

November: White County, GA—Klansmen murder a U.S. revenue agent.

November: Coosa County, AL—Klansmen begin a series of raids around Nixburg, continuing through summer 1871. Attacks include whippings, murders, and the burning of a black church.

7 November: Lake City, FL—Whites riot on election eve. The next morning, 100 armed men confine Republican state senator E.G. Johnson to his home under threat of death. GOP observers estimate that 250 blacks were barred from voting.

8 November: Florida—Armed whites bar blacks from the polls in Monticello and Quincy.

8 November: Tennessee—Klan terrorism ensures election of a Democratic slate.

15 November: Marianna, FL—Klansmen assault black constable Richard Pousser, stripping him as they brandish pistols.

20 November: Georgia—Klan terrorism carries the state elections for white Democrats.

December: Columbia County, FL—Klansmen assassinate black Republican Robert Jones, en route to a political meeting.

December: Kewaunee, MS—Klansmen murder Frank Diggs, a black mail agent on the railroad line between Selma, Alabama, and Meridian, Mississippi.

December: York County, SC—60 klansmen raid the home of Tom Roundtree, a black man, shooting him and cutting his throat.

14 December: Raleigh, NC—State legislators impeach Gov. Holden for his efforts to suppress Klan terrorism.

21 December: Chatham County, NC—Essic Harris, a black man, wounds two klansmen when they raid his home to confiscate guns. Authorities jail several klansmen in February 1871, then release them when all produce alibis.

26 December: Floyd County, GA—Klansmen raid the Waltemire plantation, whipping two black men and an elderly woman, gang-raping several black girls.

31 December: Union County, NC—Members of a black militia company kill Mat Stevens, a one-armed Confederate veteran and local bootlegger.

1871

January: Marion, AL—Officers foil an attempt to rescue several klansmen from the county jail.

January: Stamping Ground, KY—Klansmen raid several black homes, losing one of their own in an exchange of gunfire. They burn a black church in retaliation for the killing.

January: Chatham County, NC—Klansmen raid the Essic Harris home again, wounding Harris in the arm, while Harris wounds one of the raiders.

January: Frankfort, KY—Klansmen kidnap two blacks, rob them of a watch and $30, then force them to lie on ice until their clothes are stiff, with warnings to leave the county.

January: Big Poplar, NC—In three separate raids, klansmen burn a black church and whip two black men, Stokes and William Judd.

4 January: Union, NC—50 masked klansmen invade the county jail, removing five black prisoners suspected of murdering Mat Stevens on 31 December. The lynchers shoot all five captives, but two survive their wounds and are later rearrested.

7 January: Lexington, KY—Klansmen murder a black man outside town.

7 January: Shelbyville, KY—Klan raiders whip and shoot a local man, who survives his injuries.

12 January: Union, NC—500 robed klansmen return for the surviving killers of Mat Stevens. They remove 10 black prisoners from jail, hanging 2 and shooting 6 more outside town. Two escape from the mob but are later recaptured, convicted of murder, and legally executed.

14 January: Louisville, GA—Klansmen remove nine black prisoners from jail, hanging one accused arsonist, cropping the ears of seven charged with misdemeanors, and releasing one unharmed.

25 January: Yorkville, SC—Snipers fire into the headquarters of an anti–Klan militia, followed moments later by arson fires at three gin houses, a mill and a barn. Local whites accuse the militia of encouraging black incendiaries.

26 January: North Benson, KY—Klansmen assault W.H. Gibson, a black mail agent for the Louisville & Lexington Railroad. The line discontinues local mail service in February.

January–February: York County, SC—Freedmen retaliate for KKK violence by burning at least a dozen white-owned farm buildings. On 22 January, the Klan threatens to kill 10 prominent blacks and 2 white Republicans if the fires continue.

February: Shelby County, KY—Klansmen hang one of their own comrades, recently freed from jail after turning state's evidence against the KKK.

February: Colfax Township, NC—Klansmen burn a black school.

February: Rutherford County, NC—Klansmen flog Light Hall, a white Republican, and twice raid the home of Henry Houser, a black GOP member. They rob and whip Houser during the first raid, then beat members of his family the second time.

February: Kewaunee, MS—Klansmen threaten John Coleman, the white successor to murdered mail agent Frank Diggs.

February: Chattooga County, GA—Klansmen murder a black tenant on the Robert Foster plantation, harassing Foster and his sons when they try to prosecute the killers.

February: Cleveland County, NC—Klan gunmen wound Dick Beam, a black man.

February: Meridian, MS—Local klansmen whip Adam Kennard, a black deputy sheriff from Alabama, while he searches for fugitive klansmen.

6 February: Floyd County, GA—Klansmen wound one black man and whip at least two more in raids around Rome.

6 February: Rome, GA—Klansmen visit the home of Republican Thomas Drennon, who avoids flogging by denying sympathy with the party's "radical" wing.

8 February: Washington, DC—Congress passes a second Enforcement Act to protect black voters in Dixie.

10 February: York County, SC—50 klansmen raid the home of John Faris, seizing weapons collected for the state militia.

24 February: Frankfort, KY—75 klansmen liberate a white prisoner jailed for killing a black man.

25 February: Yorkville, SC—Klansmen tear up railroad tracks to delay the arrival of U.S. troops, then murder black arson suspect Anson Brown. The next morning, raiders ransack the office of Republican county treasurer E.M. Rose, then storm the home of black county commissioner Thomas Wright. Wright repulses them with gunfire, but the klansmen wound two more blacks in the ensuing week—one suspected of arson, the other accused of living with two white women.

28 February: Washington, DC—Congress passes a second Force Act to suppress southern terrorism and supplement safeguards for voters.

March: Rutherford County, NC—Klansmen whip the daughter of Ben Maize, a black man, for fighting with a white girl. Another victim, Thomas Wood, evades nightriders in the first raid on his home, but is caught and flogged a week later. After blacks complain of repeated attacks on their schools, federal authorities jail the county sheriff as a participant in Klan raids.

March: Jackson County, FL—The county sheriff resigns after numerous KKK threats and at least one assault.

March: Walton County, GA—Klansmen whip a black woman.

March: Locksville, NC—Klansmen flog a black woman, Frances Gilmore, then slash her with a knife and burn off her pubic hair.

March: Sandersville, GA—200 klansmen invade the town and lynch a black man accused of arson. One of the raiders is convicted and condemned in June, but fellow klansmen liberate him from jail in Milledgeville.

4 March: Meridian, MS—Whites disrupt a Republican rally by day, then torch the mayor's store at night. Police then arrest Republican activists William Dennis and Warren Tyler, with black state legislator Aaron Moore, for making "incendiary" speeches.

4 March: Chester County, SC—Militiamen repulse a Klan attack on the home of Capt. Jim Woods. A second, stronger attack is repelled the following night. By 6 March, KKK reinforcements from neighboring counties and North Carolina swell the local ranks, with a skirmish fought that evening. Near dawn on 7 March, klansmen rout the militia in a battle west of Chester.

6 March: Meridian, MS—Gunfire erupts during a court hearing for Republicans jailed on 4 March, killing the judge and two black bystanders. A pogrom ensues, leaving two white Republicans and three blacks dead. More blacks are killed and mutilated over the

next few days, as Klan reinforcements arrive from Eutaw, Alabama, and intermediate points. Six local whites are jailed on various charges, but a grand jury fails to indict them. The only defendant convicted is an Alabama resident charged with raping a black woman during the riot.

6 March: York County, SC—Klansmen hang former militia captain Jim Williams, then murder black militiaman Alex Leech and dump his body in a creek.

9 March: Monroe County, MS—Klansmen raid the home of George Ross, a white man, kidnapping and flogging Freedmen's Bureau representative Allen Huggins.

27 March: York County, SC—Federal troops arrive to maintain order.

April: Rutherford County, NC—Klansmen whip the same black man on two occasions, for "running after white women." They also flog a black woman, Adeline Beam, for bearing a "white" child. Other whipping victims include white Republican J.P. Gillespie and Henry Houser, previously flogged in February.

April: Clarendon County, SC—Klansmen assassinate a black county commissioner.

April: Newberry County, SC—Klansmen raid a black county commissioner's home, wounding him with gunfire, while one of their own is also injured.

April: Washington County, GA—Klansmen raid the home of a black man, Scipio Eager, flogging him and killing his brother.

3 April: Marianna, FL—Klansmen assassinate J.Q. Dickinson, the Republican county clerk.

14 April: Washington, DC: Congress passes the third Enforcement Act, defining the KKK conspiracy as an insurrection against the U.S. government, permitting the president to declare martial law and suspend habeas corpus in affected areas. President Grant signs the bill on 20 April.

29 April: Chatham County, NC—Klan nightriders murder one black man and whip five other victims, including a 60-year-old woman whom they also shoot in the leg.

May: Harrison County, GA—Klansmen murder a black man accused of consorting with white women. Three black women are whipped in a separate raid, with orders to stay home and mind their families. Raiders confiscate weapons from several black homes.

May: Baker County, FL—Klansmen whip two black men named Griffis and Smith at their homes.

May: Gwinnett County, GA—Klansmen whip and disarm several black tenants on a local plantation.

May: Rutherford County, NC—Klansmen storm the home of an interracial couple, Silas Weston and Polly Steadmen, killing Weston and his three oldest children before they burn the house. Steadman and her youngest child survive their wounds.

May: Attalla, AL—Klansmen from Etowah and St. Clair counties commandeer a train and ride it into town, whipping several blacks before they force the train crew to take them home.

May: Choctaw County, MS—A probate judge resigns after Klansmen threaten his life, shoot up his home, and wound him in a highway ambush.

May: Clay County, FL—Klansmen flog a black couple, Samuel Tutson and his wife, at home.

May: York County, SC—Klansmen raid the home of Elias Hill, an invalid black Republican, beating him with fists and a buggy whip. Leaders James Avery and Dr. Rufus Bratton issue fruitless calls for cessation of violence. Bratton flees to Canada after being indicted for murder.

12 May: Pontotoc County, MS—Klansmen searching for school superintendent Robert Fluornoy meet a posse of his friends, losing one raider in the exchange of gunfire.

21 May: White County, GA—Klansmen raid the home of Mary Brown, a black witness to the November 1870 murder of a federal revenue agent. They humiliate, whip, and torture Brown, her mother, and her daughter.

June: Bartow County, GA—Klansmen murder a black man. One of the killers is convicted and sentenced to life imprisonment in August.

June: Oxford, MS—Federal trials of Klan terrorists begin, ultimately convicting 243 of 930 klansmen indicted. Elsewhere, indictments charge 1,849 klansmen in North Carolina and 1,180 in South Carolina.

9 June: York County, SC—Maj. Lewis Merrill informs Washington of ongoing KKK terrorism.

July: Washington County, GA—Klansmen raid Scipio Eager's home again, chasing him through the woods with hounds, but he escapes.

July: White County, GA—White Unionists ambush klansmen on the highway, effectively ending local terrorism.

22 July: Yorkville, SC—A drunken racist assaults Republican congressman Alexander Wallace in a restaurant. Later the same night, a town constable and known klansman shoots a black man five times at close range.

August: Wilkinson County, GA—Klansmen murder Sheriff Mat Deason and his black mistress, weighting their corpses with iron bars and dumping them in a creek. Later in the month, klansmen castrate three blacks (one with fatal results) on suspicion of romancing white women. Republican Henry Lowther flees the county after death threats from the KKK.

7 August: Whites riot against blacks on election day, leaving two persons dead and several wounded. Later that night, klansmen invade the jail and lynch a black man charged with firing the riot's first shot. They also hang a second black, held on suspicion of rape.

September: Aspalaga, FL—Klansmen murder a black ferryman.

September: Belmont, Arkansas—Klansmen lynch Zeke High, a black man jailed for killing a white rioter in self-defense.

September: Gwinnett County, GA—Klansmen torch the county courthouse, destroying crucial evidence against 12 members held on various charges.

September: Morgan County, GA—Klansmen lynch Charles Clarke, a black man accused of rape.

14 September: Gainesville, FL—Klansmen murder a black man, Sandy Hocock.

19 September: York County, SC—A grand jury stacked with klansmen refuses to indict racial terrorists.

October: Walton County, GA—Klansmen return to whip the same black woman they flogged in March.

7 October: Alachua County, FL—Klansmen shoot and fatally wound Henry Washington, a black man.

8 October: Archer, FL—Klan gunmen wound a black man, Tom Williams.

8 October: Newnanville, FL—Klansmen murder black merchant W.M. Lucy.

12 October: Washington, DC—Attorney General Amos Akerman informs President Grant that federal officers have adequate evidence to charge Klan terrorists in South Carolina.

17 October: Washington, DC—President Grant suspends habeas corpus in nine South Carolina counties. 800 klansmen flee the state by year's end.

7 November: Marianna, FL—Klansmen assault black constable Richard Pousser on the street, as he escorts a white prisoner to jail.

24 November: Crittenden County, AR—Klansmen drag a black man, Alexander Farmer, from his home and shoot him. Farmer dies on 25 November, after local doctors refuse to treat him.

28 November: Columbia, SC—Federal trials of Klan terrorists begin.

19 December: Georgia—Terrorism carries state elections for the Democrats.

1872

19 February: Washington, DC—Congress completes its KKK investigation, issuing majority and minority reports with 13 volumes of supporting testimony.

March: South Carolina—U.S. troops begin arresting klansmen for terrorist activities. Of 500 charged, only 55 are finally convicted and sentenced.

June: York County, SC—Federal prosecutors extradite Dr. Rufus Bratton from Canada, but he escapes a second time, remaining in Ontario until 1877.

September: Wilkinson County, GA—After a period of inactivity, klansmen resume local raids, flogging several black Republicans.

1873

13 April: Colfax, Louisiana—White terrorists massacre 60+ unarmed blacks.

14 April: Washington, DC—The U.S. Supreme Court's decision in the *Slaughterhouse* cases begins dismantling federal enforcement of statutes supporting the Fourteenth and Fifteenth amendments.

1874

17 January: Austin, TX—Armed Democrats seize the state government, effectively ending Reconstruction.

27 April: Opelousas, LA—Democrats organize the White League to continue racist terrorism.

30 August: Coushatta, LA—Whites massacre 60+ Republicans, most of them black.

14 September: New Orleans—3,000 members of the White League stage a *coup d'etat* against the elected government, seizing city hall in a bloody clash that leaves 27 dead and 105 wounded. Federal troops crush the rebellion and restore order on 19 September.

3 November: Eufala, AL—White terrorists ambush black voters on election day, killing 2 and wounding 40. Two whites are killed and four wounded by blacks firing in self-defense. Democrats easily carry the election.

3 November: Mobile, AL—Whites fire on black voters en route to the polls, killing one and wounding four. Federal troops dismiss the incident as a "drunken brawl," leaving local police in charge while Democrats carry the election at gunpoint.

7 December: Vicksburg, MS—Democratic terrorists massacre 75 Republicans.

21 December: Washington, DC—President Grant issues a proclamation on Mississippi violence and prepares to dispatch federal troops.

1875

5 January: Vicksburg, MS—Federal troops arrive to suppress violence.

1 March: Washington, DC—Congress enacts a civil rights statute mandating equality in public accommodations.

4 July: Vicksburg, MS—White terrorists kill several blacks.

1 September: Yazoo City, MS—White Democrats attack Republicans, killing three blacks and one white.

4–6 September: Clinton, MS—White terrorists launch a racist pogrom, murdering 20–30 blacks.

8 September: Mississippi's governor requests federal aid to suppress terrorism, but Attorney General Edward Pierrepont refuses.

2 November: Mississippi—The Democratic "Shotgun Plan" suppresses Republican votes on election day and effectively ends Reconstruction.

1876

29 June: Horn Lakes, MS—Blacks complain to Congress that local whites have threatened to murder all Republican voters in future elections.

8 July: Hamburg, AR—White terrorists attack black Republicans, killing five.

6 September: Charleston, SC—Whites riot against blacks.

15–20 September: Ellenton, SC—White Democrats terrorize Republicans, killing 39 blacks and 2 whites.

16 October: Cainhoy, SC—Race riots kill five white Republicans and one black.

26 October: South Carolina—President Grant deploys federal troops.

7 November: Both parties claim victory in the presidential election, as violence and fraud obscure results in Florida, Louisiana and South Carolina.

1877

26 February: Washington, DC—A conference at the Wormley Hotel, including Georgia's former grand dragon, cedes the White House to loser Rutherford Hayes in return for cessation of southern Reconstruction, thus "redeeming" Dixie for white "home rule."

10 April: Columbia, SC—Federal troops withdraw and Democrats seize the state government.

20 April: New Orleans—U.S. troops withdraw, leaving white Democrats in control of the state.

1879

February: Southern blacks begin the mass "Exodus of 1879" from Dixie.

May: White terrorists led by ex–Gen. James Chalmers close the Mississippi River to black migrants at gunpoint.

1881

3 November: Danville, VA—White rioters kill four blacks.

24–31 December: Edgefield County, SC—5,000 blacks flee the county to escape terrorism and peonage.

1882

Tuskegee Institute reports 49 blacks lynched nationwide.

1883

Tuskegee Institute reports 53 blacks lynched nationwide.

1884

Tuskegee Institute reports 51 blacks lynched nationwide.

1885

Tuskegee Institute reports 74 blacks lynched nationwide.

1886

Tuskegee Institute reports 74 blacks lynched nationwide.

17 March: Carrollton, MS—White terrorists massacre 20 blacks.

1887

Tuskegee Institute reports 70 blacks lynched nationwide.

1888

Tuskegee Institute reports 69 blacks lynched nationwide.

1889

Tuskegee Institute reports 94 blacks lynched nationwide.

1890

Tuskegee Institute reports 85 blacks lynched nationwide.

12 August: Jackson, MS—A new state constitutional convention begins legal disenfranchisement of blacks.

1891

Tuskegee Institute reports 113 blacks lynched nationwide.

1892

Tuskegee Institute reports 161 blacks lynched nationwide.

1893

Tuskegee Institute reports 118 blacks lynched nationwide.

1894

Tuskegee Institute reports 134 blacks lynched nationwide.

1895

Tuskegee Institute reports 113 blacks lynched nationwide.

11–12 March: New Orleans—A white pogrom kills six blacks.

4 December: Columbia, SC—A new state constitutional convention disenfranchises blacks.

1896

Tuskegee Institute reports 78 blacks lynched nationwide.

January: Manatee County, FL—Following a fight between a black youth and the sheriff's son, the sheriff leads a lynch mob to seize the boy at home. The youth's father resists, killing the sheriff and two other whites as they storm his house. When their intended victims escape, a reinforced mob spends the night shooting into black homes and burning several, killing an uncertain number of blacks while many others flee the county.

18 May: Washington, DC—The U.S. Supreme Court's ruling in *Plessy v. Ferguson* approves racial segregation where "separate but equal" facilities are provided.

1897

Tuskegee Institute reports 123 blacks lynched nationwide.

1898

Tuskegee Institute reports 101 blacks lynched nationwide.

22 February: Lake City, SC—White terrorists lynch a black postmaster, then shoot his wife and three children, maiming all four for life.

21 April: The Spanish-American War begins.

12 May: New Orleans—A new state constitution strips blacks of their voting rights.

16 November: Wilmington, NC—White rioters kill eight blacks.

1899

Tuskegee Institute reports 85 blacks lynched nationwide.

1900

Tuskegee Institute reports 106 blacks lynched nationwide.

24–27 July: New Orleans—Whites stage a pogrom against blacks, killing an unspecified number. Two white policemen also die in the outbreak.

1901

Tuskegee Institute reports 105 blacks lynched nationwide.

19–20 August: Pierce City, MO—Whites lynch three black murder suspects, then run amok through the black community, burning at least five homes in a 15-hour pogrom. Peter Hampton, a 71-year-old black man, burns to death in his home, while indiscriminate gunfire from rioters kills a white child and wounds several other bystanders. The entire black population leaves town, except for a handful of railroad porters "known to be respectable."

11 November: Montgomery, AL—A new state constitution robs blacks of their voting rights.

1902

Tuskegee Institute reports 85 blacks lynched nationwide.

1903

Tuskegee Institute reports 84 blacks lynched nationwide.

26 April: Bloomington, IN—38 white men invade the home of Ira and Rebecca Stephens, whipping both white sisters and their black boarder, Joe Shively.

1904

Tuskegee Institute reports 76 blacks lynched nationwide.

1905

Tuskegee Institute reports 57 blacks lynched nationwide.

29–31 October: Salt Lake City, UT—Actors perform a stage play of *The Clansman.*

1906

Tuskegee Institute reports 62 blacks lynched nationwide.

22–25 September: Atlanta, GA—A white pogrom leaves 12 blacks dead, with at least 70 wounded. Police ignore the rioters, while forcibly disarming blacks.

22 October: Philadelphia, PA—3,000 blacks demonstrate and riot against a theatrical performance of *The Clansman.*

24–25 December: Meridian, MS—Blacks arm on Christmas Eve, after whites murder two black men. Federal troops are deployed, but white rioters still murder at least 12 more blacks on Christmas Day.

1907

Tuskegee Institute reports 58 blacks lynched nationwide.

27 October: St. Augustine County, TX—Texas Rangers arrive to quell a "race war," after three blacks are killed and numerous others flee the county.

1908

Tuskegee Institute reports 89 blacks lynched nationwide.

14–16 August: Springfield, IL—A white pogrom leaves at least 5 blacks dead and 75 injured, before federal troops restore order. The outbreak prompts blacks to create the NAACP.

1909

Tuskegee Institute reports 69 blacks lynched nationwide.

12 February: New York City—Blacks and white liberals found the NAACP, formally incorporated on 20 June 1911.

1910

Tuskegee Institute reports 67 blacks lynched nationwide.

1911

Tuskegee Institute reports 60 blacks lynched nationwide.

1912

Tuskegee Institute reports 61 blacks lynched nationwide.

10 September: Cumming, GA—The lynching of black murder suspect Robert Edwards erupts into a general pogrom, as white rioters drive 1,000 blacks from Forsyth County.

18 November: Wetumpka, AL—Two blacks fatally shoot a white man who tries to whip them after a buggy collision. A mob lynches one of the killers, but the other escapes, killing one of his pursuers in the process.

1913

Tuskegee Institute reports 51 blacks lynched nationwide.

12 March: Henderson, NC—Nightriders torch the home of a black man, Joe Perry, fatally shooting Perry and his son as they emerge. Perry's wife and a second child die in the flames.

11 April: Washington, DC—President Woodrow Wilson meets with cabinet members to discuss race relations in U.S. government departments, followed by wholesale segregation in federal agencies.

1914

Tuskegee Institute reports 51 blacks lynched nationwide.

15 April: Thomas Dixon sells D.W. Griffith screen rights to *The Clansman* for $2,500 and one-fourth of the film's profits.

14 July: Hollywood, CA—D.W. Griffith begins filming *The Birth of a Nation.*

1915

Tuskegee Institute reports 56 blacks lynched nationwide.

8 January: Los Angeles—*The Birth of a Nation* premieres.

3 February: Washington, DC—Thomas Dixon asks former college classmate Woodrow Wilson to view *The Birth of a Nation.*

18 February: Washington, DC—After watching *The Birth of a Nation* in a special White House screening, President Wilson endorses the film.

19 February: Washington, DC—Dixon secures another endorsement from former klansman Edward White, now chief justice of the U.S. Supreme Court.

20 February: New York City—Dixon and Griffith screen their film for the National Board of Censorship. The board approves it on 15 March.

1 March: New York City—D.W. Griffith offers an advance screening of his film, followed by the sold-out formal premiere on 3 March.

7 April: Boston, MA—Mayor James Curley orders special hearings on *The Birth of a Nation.* The debate results in editing of several inflammatory scenes.

17 April: Boston, MA—Blacks barred from viewing *The Birth of a Nation* sneak into the theater and pelt the screen with eggs. Mayor Curley closes the theater on 18 April, while Governor David Walsh calls for legislation banning racially inflammatory films on 19 April.

27 April: Marietta, GA—Mary Phagan is murdered at Leo Frank's pencil factory.

30 April: Washington, DC—President Wilson issues a disclaimer of his original endorsement for *The Birth of a Nation.*

12 August: Atlanta, GA—Tom Watson's *Jeffersonian* warns that Jews accused of rape or murder in Georgia are "going to get exactly the same thing that we give to Negro rapists."

16 August: Milledgeville, GA—The Knights of Mary Phagan remove Leo Frank from the state prison farm and hang him nearby.

2 September: Atlanta, GA—Tom Watson's *Jeffersonian* magazine calls for "another Ku Klux Klan" to "restore Home Rule."

15 September: Ogden, UT—The NAACP asks city commissioners to ban screenings of *The Birth of a Nation.*

16 October: Stone Mountain, GA—The Knights of Mary Phagan burn a cross atop the mountain.

26 October: Atlanta, GA—William Simmons and 34 others sign a charter application for the Knights of the KKK. State officials grant the charter on 14 December.

25 November: Stone Mountain, GA—William Simmons leads the Klan's first official cross-burning ceremony.

4 December: Atlanta, GA—Georgia authorities issue a preliminary charter for the KKK.

December: Blakely, GA—After a black man kills a white who tried to whip him, other whites launch a week-long pogrom, killing at least six blacks and burning a half-dozen lodge buildings used by local blacks for community meetings.

1916

Tuskegee Institute reports 56 blacks lynched nationwide.

1 January: Blakely, GA—Nightriders burn a rural black church as the local pogrom continues.

1 July: Atlanta, GA—Wizard Simmons incorporated the Klan under Georgia law.

1917

Tuskegee Institute reports 36 blacks lynched nationwide.

6 April: The U.S. enters World War I.

27–30 May: East St. Louis, IL—Whites riot over resentment of black competition for factory jobs, killing an uncertain number of victims.

1–3 July: East St. Louis, IL—Another pogrom erupts after blacks, armed in response to raids by white gunmen, accidentally fire on a carload of plainclothes policemen, killing one officer. Official casualty lists include 9 whites and 39 blacks dead in the riot, but some estimates claim 200 blacks killed. Four whites and 11 blacks are charged with murder, while three policemen plead guilty to rioting and pay $150 fines.

25–28 July: Chester, PA—At least five persons die in riots sparked by random white assaults on blacks.

November: Chicago—A bomb causes $1,000 damage to a home recently purchased by a black man, S.P. Motley.

4 November: St. Paul, MN—Bombs damage the parish house of a Catholic church.

9 November: Tulsa, OK—The Knights of Liberty whip, tar and feather 17 alleged IWW members.

24 November: Milwaukee, WI—A bomb removed from the basement of the Italian Evangelical Church explodes at police headquarters, killing 10 persons and wounding several more.

1918

Tuskegee Institute reports 60 blacks lynched nationwide.

June: Mobile, AL—Klansmen beat the union organizer of a shipyard strike. He subsequently disappears under circumstances suggesting murder.

25–28 July: Chester, PA—A race riot instigated by whites leaves three blacks and two whites dead.

26–29 July: Philadelphia, PA—Three blacks and one white die in another race riot.

11 November: Combatant nations declare an armistice ending the First World War.

1919

Tuskegee Institute reports 76 blacks lynched nationwide.

20 March: Salt Lake City, UT—State legislators pass a law requiring all non–English-speaking residents between ages 16 and 45 to attend "Americanization" classes.

10 May: Charleston, SC—White rioters kill two blacks.

28 May: Georgia—Authorities blame klansmen for the recent burning of five black churches. No charges are filed.

June: Chicago—A second bomb wrecks the home scheduled for purchase by SP. Motley, a black buyer.

13 July: Longview, TX—Whites riot against blacks, prompting a declaration of martial law and launching the "Red Summer" or 26 riots nationwide.

19–22 July: Washington, DC—White rioting, sparked by false rumors of black men assaulting white women, leaves at least 4 persons dead, with 70 injured and 100 arrested.

27 July–10 August: Chicago—Race riots erupt after whites stone a black youth to death for swimming at a segregated beach. Federal troops arrive on 30 July, but violence continues, with a final posted toll of 38 dead and 537 injured. At least 1,000 black families lose their homes to roving arson gangs.

28 August: Okmulgee, GA—Rumors of a "black uprising" spark a local reign of terror. Whites murder a black leader, Eli Cooper, in church and burn the building, moving on to torch several more churches and a black lodge hall.

30–31 August: Knoxville, TN—Rioting erupts after police foil the lynching of a black murder suspect. Six persons die in the outbreak, with at least 20 wounded and $50,000 in property damage. Federal troops deployed at the scene shoot up a black neighborhood, pursuing false rumors that blacks have killed two white men.

1 September: Georgia—Nightriders burn several black churches and schools in outlying areas.

22 September: Dooly County, GA—Three masked whites kidnap Ernest Glenwood, a black man accused of "inflaming local Negroes." Searchers pull his corpse from the Flint River on 2 October.

October: Atlanta, GA—Police arrest future KKK recruiters Edward Clarke and Elizabeth Tyler, half-naked, in a house of ill repute.

1–3 October: Elaine, AR—A white pogrom kills numerous blacks, with death tolls running as high as 200. Strangely, 79 blacks are charged with murder, 12 convicted at trial and sentenced to die. (Their convictions are overturned on appeal.)

10 October: Atlanta, GA—Klansmen stage their first public parade during a Confederate Reunion celebration. Afterward, John Boykin, solicitor-general of Atlanta's circuit court, pens a letter to William Simmons saying: "I want you and my brother Klansmen to know that I am with you in spirit."

28 October: Washington, DC—Congress passes the Volstead Act, enforcing prohibition under the Eighteenth Amendment.

29 October: Atlanta, GA—Police arrest future Klan publicists Edward Clarke and Elizabeth Tyler in their secret love nest. Both pay $100 fines on 31 October.

19 December: Washington, DC—An MID report condemns *The Messenger* for a "vicious" attack on the Klan, opining that the KKK merely seeks to block "encroachment of negroes in those neighborhoods populated by white people."

1920

Tuskegee Institute reports 53 blacks lynched nationwide.

7 June: Atlanta, GA—William Simmons signs a promotional contract with the Southern Publicity Assn., led by Edward Clarke and Elizabeth Tyler.

19 October: Trenton, SC—Klansmen whip, tar and feather chauffeur Peter McMahon before placing him on a northbound train.

19 October: Lake City, SC—Masked klansmen threaten black "loafers," warn white farmers to pay blacks less for picking cotton, and command Mayor W.H. Whitehead to enforce the town's vagrancy law more strictly.

30 October: Jacksonville, FL—500 klansmen parade downtown, warning blacks to "keep their place."

11 December: Washington, DC—An FBI report criticizes NAACP leader James Johnson for condemning the Klan.

20 December: Jacksonville, FL—Klansmen kidnap John Bischoff, tar and feather him, then dump him naked on a downtown street.

26 December: Daytona Beach, FL—Klansmen drag Arthur Hames from his home, fatally shooting his son Grandy when the boy resists. They drive Arthur into the woods and order him to leave town under pain of death. On the same night, raiders also whip Oscar Pellett and his brother.

1921

Tuskegee Institute reports 59 blacks lynched nationwide.

February: New Orleans—Police arrest Edward Clarke for violation of the Mann Act, after he transports a woman from Texas to Louisiana "for immoral purposes." Clarke announces his resignation from the Klan on 24 September, but later reconsiders and remains in his post as imperial kleagle.

4 February: Houston, TX—Klansmen whip, tar and feather attorney B.I. Hobbs for representing blacks.

13 March: Houston, TX—Klansmen castrate Dr. Lafayette Cockrell, a black dentist.

17 March: Houston, TX—Nightriders flog businessman A.V. Hopkins and warn him to leave town.

1 April: Dallas, TX—Klansmen whip a black man, Alex Johnson, and brand "KKK" on his forehead with acid "as a warning to other Negroes."

10 April: Webster, TX—KKK members whip stockman Gus Beck.

16 April: Washington, DC—FBI reports note the foundation of J. Finley Wilson's Iron Ring anti–Klan group.

18 April: Dallas, TX—Klansmen abduct Bill Harris, a black barber, and flog him in the woods outside town.

26 April: Houston, TX—Auto salesman J.W. McGee receives a Klan flogging with orders to leave the city.

1 May: Goose Creek, TX—Twelve klansmen whip, tar and feather victim Red Kemp.

6 May: Atlanta, GA—The KKK gives Wizard Simmons a car and a $40,000 home, called Klan Krest.

13 May: Vicksburg, MS—The town's exalted cyclops writes to the newspaper, airing the Klan's intention to "whip and rout" bootleggers, Catholics and Jews from Vicksburg.

18 May: Shreveport, LA—Klansmen tar and feather victim Jack Morgan.

20 May: Newport News, VA—A kleagle reports that the city's police chief, prosecutor, judge and other public officials are klansmen.

21 May: Dallas, TX—Streetlights go dark as 789 klansmen stage their first parade downtown.

25 May: Shreveport, LA—Police deliver alleged wife-beater Jack Morgan to a Klan tar-and-feather squad. He leaves town the next day.

31 May–1 June: Tulsa, OK—White rioters destroy the black community. Arsonists burn 1,115 homes, 31 restaurants, 24 grocery stores, 8 doctors' officers, 5 hotels, 4 drugstores and one school. Published estimates of the final death toll range from 27 to more than 250, with property damage approaching $2 million. A grand jury convened on 9 June recommends strict enforcement of segregation to prevent further outbreaks.

1 June: Chicago, IL—Kleagle C.W. Love arrives from Indianapolis.

9 June: Sea Breeze, FL—Klansmen drag Thomas Reynolds from his home, fatally beating and shooting him.

10 June: Springfield, IL—A federal grand jury clears Treasury agent Glenn Young for killing a man in Madison, during a warrantless liquor raid.

10 June: Brenham, TX—Klansmen tar and feather Dr. R.H. Lennet based on accusations of "disloyalty" during World War I.

10 June: Shreveport, LA—Klansmen drive several NAACP "propaganda spreaders" out of town.

11 June: Salt Lake City, UT—The *Deseret News* announces formation of a local klavern.

12 June: Portland, OR—Kleagle Bragg Calloway arrives from Texas.

16 June: Autreville, GA—Nightriders burn a black church, in retaliation for the unsolved murder of a white girl.

17 June: Bolton, TX—Klansmen flog John Bolton, a black man previously jailed on suspicion of "insulting a white woman." They leave him with a sign on his back reading "Whipped by the KKK."

18 June: Birmingham, AL—Klansmen whip C.S. Coley and Kate Alexander for befriending blacks.

18 June: Rockmart, GA—The town's mayor and city council members appear on-stage at a KKK rally.

20 June: Goose Creek, TX—Klansmen tar and feather two oilfield workers, B.L. Bloodworth and Olan Jones, on accusations of creating a "public nuisance."

20 June: West Columbia, TX—Klansmen tar and feather another male victim.

21 June: Dallas, TX—Klansmen whip Edwards Engers, a service station proprietor, and order him to leave town. He reports the attack to police, who arrest him on 3 July, filing charges of aggravated assault, burglary, threats to beat his wife, and threats to commit murder.

21 June: Houston, TX—Four klansmen flog victim Max Milansky.

21 June: Columbus, GA—Klansmen kidnap black victim Henry Allen and drive him into Alabama for a whipping. Alabama police arrest the floggers.

21 June: Wharton, TX—Nightriders whip, tar and feather victim Henry Schultz.

26 June: Yoakum, TX—Klansmen tar and feather a white female victim.

1 July: Fort Worth, TX—KKK members inflict twenty lashes on an accused wife-beater.

2 July: Denver, CO—Grand Goblin A.J. Pardon, Jr., reports enlistment of 175 klansmen, vowing 2,000 more in the next 90 days.

6 July: Muskogee, OK—Klansmen flog alleged burglar Billy Ware until he confesses his crimes.

6 July: Washington, DC—FBI agents report on a CPUSA pamphlet urging blacks to use "organized force" against klansmen and white rioters.

6 July: Union County, AR—75–100 klansmen whip Eddie Foreman for making a pass at a klansman's wife. The sheriff arrests five suspects, but a grand jury refuses to indict them on 19 July.

8 July: San Antonio, TX—Klansmen kidnap Hendry Adams, club him on the head, then dump him from their car upon discovering that he is "the wrong man."

8 July: Pensacola, FL—KKK members order Greek restaurateur Chris Lochas to leave the community.

9 July: Brenham, TX—City Marshal King refuses to discuss his recent kidnapping by klansmen, withdrawing a $300 reward for arrest of the raiders.

12 July: Enid, OK—Klansmen whip movie operator Walter Billings, afterward coating his body with crude oil and cotton.

14 July: Burkburnett, TX—Klansmen threaten to lynch D.E. Donnelly on accusations of molesting his two daughters. Police in Wichita Falls place Donnelly in protective custody.

14 July: Greenville, TX—Police remove black murder suspect Matt Gilsen from jail as a mob of 103 robed klansmen gather to lynch him.

16 July: Tenoha, TX—Klansmen tar and feather hotel maid Beulah Johnson. The following day, police charge her with bigamy.

16 July: Warrensburg, MO—Klansmen whip a 68-year-old farmer, Richard Johnson, and order him to leave the county.

16 July: Bay City, TX—Klansmen tar and feather bank cashier W.H. Hoopingarner, ordering him to leave town.

16 July: Deweyville, TX—Klansmen whip World War veteran R.F. Scott, then tar and feather him before dumping him in Beaumont.

16 July: Dickinson, TX—Nightriders whip G.C. Benson and order him to leave the area.

17 July: Rayville, LA—Race riots leave four blacks dead and one white man injured.

17 July: Nacogdoches, TX—Klansmen abduct and whip J.W. McKnight, a plumber and one-time deputy sheriff.

17 July: Dallas, TX—Klansmen kidnap black victim Alex Johnson and brand "KKK" on his forehead with acid. Those present later claim that future Imperial Wizard Hiram Evans led the raid.

17 July: Miami, FL—Klansmen whip, tar and feather Rev. Philip Irwin, a black bishop of the Episcopal Church.

18 July: Lufkin, TX—Klansmen tar and feather victim Ben Riley.

19 July: Lufkin, TX—Another raiding party tars and feathers Sherwood Vinson.

19 July: Chandler, TX—Klan members assault Harry Adams on the street, robbing him of $250.

19 July: Athens, TX—Nightriders kidnap Earl Peters, beat him unconscious, and dump him beside the highway.

19 July: Timson, TX—Klansmen flog victim J.W. McKnight for the second time.

21 July: Lufkin, TX—Klan raiders tar and feather chauffeur George Lee, then dump him in the downtown business district.

22 July: Goose Creek, TX—Klansmen tar and feather victim Will Stewart.

29 July: Austin, TX—KKK members whip black victim Jeff Smith for "loafing," then order him to leave town.

29 July: Matador, TX—A judge fines six klansmen $32 each for whipping victim Henry Adams. Adams killed the seventh member of the flogging party when they raided his home.

August: Mason City, IA—Klansmen snatch Socialist orator Ida Hazlett in the middle of a speech and drive her to the city limits, threatening violence if she returns.

1 August: Atlanta, GA—Wizard Simmons accepts a monthly income of $1,000, with $25,000 back pay for the lean years 1915–20.

2 August: Texarkana, TX—Klansmen whip black victim Warren Dickens and order him to leave town, based on accusations of his "familiarity" with white women.

6 August: Fort Worth, TX—Klansmen abduct Benny Pinto for the second time, holding police at bay with pistols. Driven to a field ten miles outside town, Pinto receives sixty lashes and a warning to leave town.

16–17 August: Augusta, GA—A white pogrom leaves five blacks dead, including one man dragged from a hospital bed and burned alive.

21 August: Indianapolis, IN—The KKK incorporates in Indiana.

4 September: Tennant, NJ—Farmer Wesley Smith reports that six klansmen snatched him from home and threatened him for allegedly mistreating his wife.

6 September: New York City—*The World* launches a series of exposé articles about the KKK, climaxing on 19 September with a list of 152 violent crimes committed by klansmen.

15 September: El Paso, TX—The city council passes an ordinance banning masked meetings and parades.

17 September: Chicago, IL—3,000 protesters hang a klansman in effigy at the Ragen Athletic Club. The city council passes an anti–Klan resolution on 19 September.

21 September: Washington, DC—The House of Representatives votes to investigate the Klan. On 24 September, Attorney General Harry Daugherty orders the FBI to "continue" its probe of the KKK.

24 September: Milwaukee, WI—The local archdiocese announces a Catholic investigation of the Klan.

26 September: New York City—The *New York World* launches a two-week series of exposés on Klan corruption and violence, ironically prompting a flood of membership applications.

30 September: Atlanta, GA—Wizard Simmons spends $2,000 on telegrams to congressmen and senators, encouraging an investigation.

1 October: Montreal, Québec—Newspaper reports announce the foundation of a local klavern.

1 October: Lorena, TX—Violence erupts when the sheriff tries to block a Klan parade. Eight persons suffer injuries, one dying from stab wounds on 5 October.

11–17 October: Washington, DC—The House Rules Committee holds hearings on the KKK, thereby sparking huge membership growth.

21 October: Texas—Klansmen kidnap two black youths from a rural prison farm and whip them.

21 October: Chicago, IL—Austin Klan No. 6 initiates 300 new recruits.

27 October: Enid, OK—Masked nightriders warn local blacks to leave town.

16 November: Baltimore, MD—Edward Clarke launches a KKK recruiting drive.

17 December: Wilson, OK—150 klansmen raid the home of alleged bootlegger Joe Carroll, killing him and losing two of their own in the battle. A grand jury indicts 11 raiders, the first facing trial in January 1923. The jury deadlocks on 3 February, but a second trial acquits defendant Jeff Smith on 28 February. Prosecutors then drop charges against Smith's 10 fellow klansmen.

21 December: El Paso, TX—10,000 citizens attend a debate between Catholic and Protestant clergymen, prompted by local KKK agitation.

22 December: Portland, OR—Rev. Reuben Sawyer praises the KKK before an audience of 6,000.

1922

Tuskegee Institute reports 51 blacks lynched nationwide.

7 January: Eugene, OR—Klansmen burn their first cross at Skinner's Butte.

26 January: Washington, DC—The Dyer anti-lynching bill passes the House of Representatives, but subsequently dies in the Senate as southern legislators mount a filibuster.

27 January: Harlingen, TX—Klansmen warn Mexican farm worker Manuel Duarte to leave town, but police tell him to ignore the threats. On 2 February, the knights return, assaulting Duarte and firing shots at him.

27 January: Denver, CO—Black janitor Ward Gosh receives a Klan threat for having "intimate relations with white women." The note warns him to leave town by 1 February.

28 January: El Paso, TX—The town's exalted cyclops and two other klansmen announce their candidacy for school board positions.

22 February: Salt Lake City, UT—A king kleagle reports initiation of nine klansmen.

22 February: Buffalo, NY—Klan spokesmen announce that klavern meetings have been held bi-weekly for the past eight months.

6 March: Salt Lake City, UT—The Klan runs its first newspaper advertisement.

7 March: Oklahoma City—Klansmen whip cab driver Edward Merriman for "immorality" and order him to leave town. He returns in April and identifies 18 of his attackers, but authorities refuse to prosecute and Merriman's employer vows to fire him if he presses charges.

10 March: Tulsa, OK—Klansmen whip a black victim, John Smitherman, then sever his ear and attempt to make him eat it.

10 March: Denver, CO—Grand jurors launch an investigation of the local KKK.

13 March: El Paso, TX—Armed citizens mass to prevent a rumored KKK parade, which fails to materialize.

16 March: Laredo, TX—Judge John Mullaly orders a grand jury investigation of the KKK.

20 March: Nashville, AR—Klansmen raid the home of Walter

Gibbs and Joel Harris, accused of dating black women. Gibbs dies in the exchange of gunfire, then klansmen beat Harris with a wooden plank.

4 April: Dallas, TX—5,000 residents meet to organize an anti-Klan organization, the Dallas County Citizens' League. Mayor Shawnie Aldredge endorses the League on 6 April, asking all city employees to quit the KKK.

10 April: Dallas, TX—Exalted Cyclops Hiram Evans departs to fill an imperial post in Atlanta.

14 April: Anaheim, CA—Voters elect four klansmen to the city council. On 21 April they choose klansman Elmer Metcalf as mayor.

14 April: Houston, TX—The county grand jury launches an investigation of the KKK.

19 April: Sandy, UT—Klansmen make their first public appearance in Utah, at the funeral of Deputy Sheriff Gordon Stewart.

22 April: Englewood, CA—Klan raiders kidnap alleged bootleggers Fidel and Matias Elduayen for delivery to jail. The town's night marshal intervenes, sparking a shootout that kills one klansman (an Inglewood constable), while leaving two others (his son and a deputy sheriff) wounded. A grand jury later indicts 37 klansmen, who face trial on 7 August. A judge sympathetic to the KKK directs their acquittal.

May: Tulsa, OK—Masked whites abduct black Deputy Sheriff John Smitherman, severing one of his ears.

8 May: Anaheim, CA—The city council hires 11 new policemen, 10 of them known klansmen.

17 May: Birmingham, AL—Nine klansmen kidnap and flog J.D. Dowling, Jefferson County's health inspector.

23 May: Buffalo, NY—The *Express* runs its first recruiting ad for the KKK.

28 May: Knoxville, TN—Klansmen initiate 800 new recruits at a rally outside town.

21 June: Chicago, IL—Klan opponents found the American Unity League.

24 June: New York City—The Democratic National Convention begins at Madison Square Garden. On 28 June, an epic fight ensues over a platform plank denouncing the KKK by name. After riotous demonstrations, delegates defeat the anti–Klan plank by one vote out of 1,083 cast. Ongoing bitterness over the Klan issue and Catholicism defeat front-running presidential hopefuls Oscar Underwood and Alfred Smith, ending with nomination of compromise candidate John Davis on 9 July.

July: New York City—Black "radicals" denounce Marcus Garvey for meeting with Edward Clarke.

10–12 July: Cleveland, OH—Delegates to the GOP National Convention carefully avoid the Klan issue and nominate incumbent "Silent Cal" Coolidge for president, thus ensuring an easy victory in November.

14 July: Denver, CO—Mayor Benjamin Stapleton addresses a KKK meeting, promising to "give the Klan the kind of administration it wants" if he is reelected.

17 July: Dallas, TX—Hiram Evans addresses 29,000 klansmen.

22 July: Texas—Klansman Earl Mayfield wins the Democratic primary for a U.S. Senate seat, qualifying for a runoff against ex–Gov. James Ferguson on 26 August. In El Paso, Klan candidates win 7 of 15 political races. Mayfield wins election to the Senate on 7 November.

26 July: Little Rock, AR—The local Klan publishes its list of candidates for Pulaski County's Democratic primary. All win election on 8 August.

22 August: Atlanta, GA—Wizard Evans announces that the KKK will support third-party presidential candidate Robert LaFollette.

22 August: Yazoo City, MS—Lynchers hang a black man, Parks Banks, outside town. Locals report that Banks ignored warnings to leave after verbal disputes with KKK members.

23 August: Texas—Miriam Ferguson wins a gubernatorial run-off election, campaigning on an anti-Klan platform. She prevails in the general election, on 4 November, after branding her opponent a klansman.

24 August: Mer Rouge, LA—Klansmen kidnap and whip five white men accused of earlier threatening Klan leaders. Two of the five, F. Watt Daniel and Thomas Richards, disappear.

26 August: Texas—Earl Mayfield wins the U.S. Senate runoff election.

5 September: New York City—A. Philip Randolph receives a severed hand with a note signed "KKK." He blames followers of Marcus Garvey for the mailing.

17 September: Chicago, IL—*Tolerance* publishes the names of 150 local klansmen. The newsletter will publish 4,000 names by 26 January 1923.

October: Salt Lake City, UT—The local klavern dissolves due to shortage of members.

2 October: Baton Rouge, LA—Gov. John Parker sends a letter to President Harding, seeking federal help for an investigation of the Louisiana Klan.

3 October: Boston, MA—A meeting of 1,000 klansmen sparks political and media attacks.

3–4 October: Noblesville, IN—D.C. Stephenson attends the 62nd annual meeting of the National Horse Thief Detective Assn., effectively co-opting the group as a Klan front.

4 October: Atlanta, GA—Edward Clarke announces his resignation from the Klan a second time, then reneges.

13 October: Atlanta, GA—One month after he addressed the Klan's second Imperial Klonvokation in Kansas City, Gov. Clifford Walker admits he is a klansman.

15 October: Birmingham, AL—7,000 klansmen cheer a mock funeral for Sen. Oscar Underwood, vowing to "retire him in 1926."

25 October: Buffalo, NY—Headlights of 297 cars illuminate a Klan rally, featuring a 40-foot fiery cross and initiation of 800 new members.

31 October: Chicago, IL—Officers of Washington Park National Bank remove klansman Augustus Olsen as president.

1 November: Herrin, IL—Ex-Prohibition agent Glenn Young arrives, hired by klansmen to lead a "clean-up" campaign.

5 November: Texas—Klansman Earle Mayfield wins election to the U.S. Senate.

7 November: Oregon—Walter Pierce wins election as governor with public Klan support. Voters also ban parochial and private schools.

8 November: Chicago, IL—The *Chicago Daily News* condemns Klan involvement in politics.

12 November: Horry County, NC—40–50 klansmen whip Mace Horn, who sometimes pays fines for convicted bootleggers, afterward cropping his ears.

17 November: Crassbrook, B.C.—Press reports herald the Klan's arrival in British Columbia.

21 November: La Grande, OR—Governor-elect and klansman Walter Pierce addresses a KKK rally.

27 November: Atlanta, GA—D.C. Stephenson and others persuade William Simmons to relinquish his post as imperial wizard, in favor of Hiram Evans.

28 November: Smackover, AR—200 klansmen raid a series of saloons, brothels and gambling dens, killing one man and whipping or tarring 12 others. Afterward, the sheriff praises klansmen for driving 2,000 "undesirables" from local oilfields.

4 December: Chicago, IL—Media reports expose an active klavern at an Austin fire station. Authorities force one kleagle to resign from the fire department on 13 December, suspending two more klansmen on 17 and 24 January 1923.

9 December: Horry County, NC—Klansmen threaten Daniel

Duncan for reporting local bootleggers to the authorities and for building a fence that blocked his neighbor's easement.

10 December: Buffalo, NY—75 policemen with riot guns guard a theater performance of the play *Ku Klux Klan.*

19 December: Moorehouse Parish, LA—Gov. John Parker declares martial law in response to Klan violence. On 22 December, dynamite blasts bring the corpses of murder victims F. Watt Daniel and Thomas Richards to the surface of Lake Lafourche.

20 December: Buffalo, NY—Vandals hurl a brick with a KKK note through the window of International Railway Co. motorman Edward Wild, warning him to quit his job.

1923

Tuskegee Institute reports 29 blacks lynched nationwide.

5 January: Moorehouse Parish, LA—Open hearings on KKK violence begin, continuing through 23 January. In April, authorities charge 18 klansmen with various crimes. On 21 November, four are convicted of carrying concealed weapons and fined $10 each. Local murders and other crimes remain unpunished.

10 January: Oklahoma City—John Walton is inaugurated as governor. Soon thereafter, he secretly joins the KKK as a "klansman at large."

11 January: Lillington, NC—Klansman Mark Moore receives an 11-month jail term for threatening critics of the KKK.

12 January: Circulation of the *Fiery Cross* tops 50,000 copies in the Midwest.

15 January: Washington, DC—The DOJ receives a letter signed by eight prominent blacks, seeking prosecution of Marcus Garvey and disbandment of his UNIA for collaborating with the Klan.

16 January: Springfield, IL—State legislators pass an anti-mask law.

20 January: Blanford, IN—White miners begin driving blacks from the area, after a white girl is molested. On 29 January, the miners kill three persons and fire on a sheriff investigating reports of the racist pogrom.

27 January: Horry County, NC—Masked klansmen fire 24 shotgun blasts at Daniel Duncan while he rides in a buggy. Police jail eight suspects, including a Baptist minister. Three confess and turn state's evidence, resulting in conviction of all eight defendants for rioting. Six receive 6-month jail terms, while the court levies fines of $50–$200.

28 January: New York City—The *New York Times* reports an ongoing DOJ investigation of the Louisiana Klan.

29 January: South Bend, IN—The AUL opens a new branch to oppose the KKK.

7 February: Chicago, IL—Mildred Erick reports that klansmen kidnapped her, carving crosses into her back, arms and legs to punish her for converting to Catholicism. She recants the story on 9 February, saying she lied to embarrass her klansman-father.

9 February: Baltimore, MD—Arsonists try to burn the local Klan headquarters.

23 February: El Paso, TX—500-plus cars join in a KKK motorcade through town.

26 February: Chicago, IL—The AUL holds an All-Nations Rally against the KKK.

1 March: Houston, TX—Federal prosecutors indict Edward Clarke for a February 1921 violation of the Mann Act. On 5 March, Wizard Evans banishes Clarke "for the good of the order." Clarke pleads guilty on 10 March 1924 and pays a $5,000 fine.

29 March: Portland, OR—Klansmen organize the Junior Citizens' Club for underage racists.

1 April: Pittsburgh, PA—Parishioners at Bellevue Methodist Episcopal church eject 16 klansmen, stripping them of their hoods and robes.

1 April: Indianapolis, IN—Thieves snatch a list of 12,208 klansmen, subsequently delivered to the AUL.

7 April: Chicago—A bomb wrecks the office of *Dawn,* a national KKK newsletter.

7 April: Atlanta, GA—William Simmons creates the order of Kamelia and installs himself as El Magus.

14 April: Lumberton, NC—Klansmen flog two white women, Mrs. H.F. Purvis and Mary Watson, in a black churchyard. On 25 April, prosecutors file criminal charges against three suspects, including Fairmont police chief B.M. Lawson.

15 April: Ogden, UT—Klansmen make their first public appearance at First Baptist Church. Rev. Lemuel Garrison endorses the Klan from his pulpit on 7 October.

25 April: Corpus Christi, TX—Police arrest the mayor and nine other city officials on charges of accepting kickbacks on a county road contract. The defendants accuse local klansmen of smearing the anti-Klan city administration.

27 April: Indianapolis, IN—The KKK retaliates for AUL release of klansmen's names by publishing names of Catholic businessmen, followed by a second list on 11 May.

May: Cheyenne, WY—The Wyoming realm receives its charter from Atlanta headquarters.

1 May: Atlanta, GA—Hiram Evans finally wins his legal battle with William Simmons for control of the KKK.

1 May: Bound Brook, NJ—100 protesters surround a church where Pentecostal fundamentalists are meeting to form a new klavern. Two persons are jailed for disorderly behavior.

2 May: New Brunswick, NJ—Klansmen brandish guns at hecklers during a KKK rally.

4 May: Columbus, OH—Klan opponents obtain an injunction banning a rally at Columbus Driving Park, east of town. The meeting proceeds on private property, with 1,500 new klansmen initiated.

5 May: Muskogee, OK—Dr. W.T. Tilley receives life membership in the KKK for recruiting Gov. Walton.

7 May: Atlanta, GA—White racists attack black railroad workers.

22 May: Albany, NY—Gov. Al Smith signs the Walker Law, requiring public registration of all oath-bound organizations with 20 or more members.

23 May: Grand Island, NY—Klansmen burn a large cross on this island in the Niagara River, with bonfires lining the shore.

4 June: Perth Amboy, NJ—A racially mixed group of hecklers disrupts a Klan meeting.

6 June: Plainfield, NJ—Opponents stone a Klan rally.

14 June: Bloomfield, NJ—Police narrowly avert a riot, after opponents pelt klansmen with eggs during a Flag Day parade.

19 June: Phoenix, AZ—Authorities charge two klansmen with whipping a black man.

24 June: Long Branch, NJ—A KKK opponent beats three klansmen during a street parade. Police jail the attacker.

July: Asheville, NC—At a convention of grand dragons, Wizard Evans announces plans to double Klan membership, for a projected total of 10 million.

2 July: Burleson County, TX—Klansmen raid Otto Lange's home, killing Lange, wounding his daughter, and pistol-whipping his elderly mother.

4 July: Kokomo, IN—The largest Klan rally in history draws 200,000 to witness installation of D.C. Stephenson as grand dragon.

12 July: Detroit, MI—5,000 klansmen gather to initiate 800 new members at a farm outside town.

13–15 July: Mooresville, IN—Indiana's Women of the KKK hold their first statewide gathering in the woods outside town.

14 July: Seattle, WA—50,000 klansmen and Royal Riders of the Red Robe rally for speeches and fireworks.

18 July: Indianapolis, IN—5,000 klansmen rally to test Mayor Samuel Shank's ban on cross-burning. Police arrest two demonstrators. Firefighters douse a second cross on 19 July.

21 July: Indianapolis, IN—D.C. Stephenson reports 117,969 klansmen initiated since 25 June 1922.

25 July: Buffalo, NY—3,000 klansmen and initiates rally outside town.

26 July: Okmulgee County, OK—Gov. Walton declares martial law and dispatches National Guardsmen after locals complain that their sheriff is "utterly indifferent" to Klan violence. At the same time, the state attorney general drops all charges against 27 Tulsa County klansmen linked to 12 floggings between 28 November 1921 and 25 July 1923.

2 August: San Francisco, CA—President Harding dies while returning from a visit to Alaska. Klansmen nationwide hold mourning ceremonies.

9 August: Tulsa, OK—Six klansmen kidnap and flog Jewish victim Nathan Hantaman. Gov. Walton meets him in Oklahoma City on 12 August and imposes martial law on Tulsa the following day. On 15 August, three companies of National Guardsmen relieve local police of their duties.

16 August: Steubenville, OH—Protesters mob 100 klansmen, producing numerous injuries and seven arrests.

19 August: Williamson County, IL—Every white protestant minister in the county urges parishioners to attend a Klan rally at Marion on 20 August. Some 2,000 persons answer the call, and klansmen initiate 300 new members.

20 August: Salt Lake City, UT—1,200 klansmen rally at the Orpheum Theatre.

25 August: Carnegie, PA—10,000 klansmen rally. Opponents attack a Klan parade, killing one klansman with gunfire.

29 August: Tulsa, OK—Klansmen kidnap another victim one block from the National Guard command post. Gov. Walton suspends habeas corpus for the entire county.

30 August: Perth Amboy, NJ—Rioters overrun police and firemen during an anti–Klan protest.

31 August: New Castle, DE—Gunfire wounds five persons at a KKK rally.

31 August: El Paso, TX—Klansmen tear down Mexican flags at Liberty Hall, during a celebration of Washington recognizing Mexico's Obregon regime.

9 September: Shreveport, LA—Klansmen from Arkansas, Louisiana and Texas gather for a tri-state konklave.

11 September: South Bend, IN—White threats prompt a partial evacuation of the black community.

11 September: Birmingham, AL—1,750 klansmen march to a mass initiation ceremony. New members include attorney Hugo Black.

12 September: Tulsa, OK—Chamber of Commerce leaders reject Gov. Walton's offer to lift martial law in return for selection of a new sheriff and police chief.

13 September: Oklahoma City—As a grand jury prepares to investigate Gov. Walton, he declares statewide martial law, proclaiming that the Klan has created a "state of virtual rebellion and insurrection." National Guardsmen prevent the grand jury from meeting on 16 September.

15 September: Aurora, IL—45,000 klansmen rally for a KKK Home Koming, including an air show.

21 September: Royal Oak, MI—2,000 klansmen rally.

22 September: Oklahoma City—Authorities charge Grand Dragon N. Clay Jewett with flogging Edward Merriman in March.

23 September: Ogden, UT—Klansmen burn two crosses during opening ceremonies at a Catholic parochial school.

26 September: Oklahoma City—Troops bar the state legislature from convening to impeach Gov. Walton. A special referendum on 2 October empowers legislators to meet without Walton's approval. The legislature impeaches Walton on 11 October, with his trial by the senate beginning on 1 November. On 18 November, Walton walks out on his continuing trial. Two days later, senators convict him on 11 of 22 charges, formally removing Walton from office.

29 September: Knoxville, TN—Knights flock to Klan Day at the East Tennessee Division of the State Fair.

11 October: Ogden, UT—Judge James Howell condemns the Klan at a KoC meeting.

11 October: Memphis, TN—Klansmen launch a "Bigger and Better Memphis" campaign, supporting W. Joe Wood for mayor.

18 October: Niagara County, NY—1,000 klansmen rally at Henry Pletcher's farm, east of Niagara Falls, to initiate 600 new recruits.

19 October: Ogden, UT—County Attorney David Wilson denounces the KKK at a WCTU meeting, at the First Baptist Church.

24 October: Kansas City, MO—Rioters stone a newly-opened KKK store.

24 October: Dallas, TX—75,000 klansmen attend Klan Day at the Texas State Fair. The KKK dedicates Hope Cottage for homeless children. Wizard Evans delivers a speech calling for revocation of black citizenship and declaring that assimilation of Catholics is "impossible."

24 October: Washington, DC—The U.S. Department of Labor reports that 500,000 blacks have fled the South over the past 12 months.

31 October: Memphis, TN—2,000 klansmen march downtown, protesting Election Commissioner John Brown's selection of precinct officials.

3 November: Eufala, OK—Klansmen kidnap a black man, Dallas Sewell, and hang him in a Klan leader's barn on charges of "passing for white and associating with white women."

7 November: Memphis, TN—The *Tri-State American* threatens banishment for any klansmen who bolt the KKK's political ticket on election day.

24 November: Chicago, IL—Grand Dragon Charles Palmer announces his plan to rid Illinois of "chronic revolutionists" who disrupt the Klan from within. He soon removes the exalted cyclopes of 10 Chicago klaverns.

22 December: Herrin, IL—Glenn Young and four other armed klansmen, deputized by U.S. Commissioner William Hart, raid a Catholic church in search of illegal liquor.

28 December: Herrin, IL—Sheriff George Galligan raids the home of klansman and state legislator Wallace Baudy, seizing illegal whiskey.

30 December: Marion, IL—Glenn Young's klansmen raid Paul Corder's café, beating Corder in the process. Corder files assault charges against the raiders. At trial, on 8 January 1924, Young and six other defendants enter the court armed with submachine guns, securing an immediate acquittal.

1924

Tuskegee Institute reports 16 blacks lynched nationwide.

5 January: Atlanta, GA—Wizard Evans announces banishment of William Simmons from the KKK.

7 January: Herrin, IL—Glenn Young's klansmen raid the home of Lewis Zosada, ordering him to eat a crucifix.

10 January: Herrin, IL—In a curious agreement brokered by state attorney general Carlos Black, the mayor fires all anti–Klan policemen and replaces them with klansmen, while Sheriff Galligan agrees to raid any liquor targets identified by informants. Black withdraws three militia companies from the troubled county on 15 January.

11 January: Washington, DC—A convention of grand dragons confirms the banishment William Simmons and Edward Clarke.

15 January: Oklahoma City—Gov. Martin Trapp signs the first U.S. anti-mask law, further requiring registration of all officers in secret societies.

20 January: Williamson County, IL—Glenn Young's klansmen stage 35 liquor raids on road houses, speakeasies and private homes.

21 January: Memphis, TN—A court order removes klansman N.T. Ingram as county coroner.

22 January: San Antonio, TX—Sheriff John Stevens disperses a parade of 150 klansmen, gathered to promote a Klan rodeo.

1 February: Johnston City, IL—Glenn Young assembles 1,200 deputized klansmen for a series of liquor raids, arresting 200+ suspects, robbing and pistol-whipping some.

8 February: Herrin, IL—Two Klan cops interrupt a meeting between anti–Klan sheriff's officers and members of the Shelton bootlegging gang. A 30-minute firefight rages, leaving one deputy dead, until militia troops return. Later the same night, anti–Klan gunmen kill klansman Caesar Cagle. On 9 February, police in Carbondale charge Sheriff Galligan and Herrin's mayor with Cagle's murder. The Klan stages a full-dress funeral for Cagle on 10 February. On 14 March, Herrin's grand jury indicts four suspects in Cagle's murder and 95 klansmen involved in the battle of 8 February. Glenn Young faces charges of robbery, assault with intent to kill, conspiracy, kidnapping and other felonies.

9 February: Atlanta, GA—Hiram Evans revokes the Memphis Klan's charter due to "unfavorable conditions existing in the local organization." A reconstituted klavern resumes operations on 26 April, under Exalted Cyclops W.A. Blankenship.

12 February: Atlanta, GA—Simmons accepts $14,000 to settle his claims against the Klan.

22 February: Oklahoma City—4,500 klansmen parade for the first time unmasked.

26 February: La Grande, OR—Dr. Ellis Wilson, a klansman, faces trial for performing an illegal abortion on his mistress. Jurors convict him on 3 March, resulting in a 3-year prison sentence.

12 March: Buffalo, NY—Klansmen raid roadhouses, saloons and hotels outside town.

13 March: Fort Worth, TX—Organizers of the Southwest Exposition and Fat Stock Show dedicate a day to the KKK.

16 March: Buffalo, NY—Klansmen raid the Auto Rest Inn, routing 150 patrons. On 17 March, Mayor Schwab receives a warning letter from the KKK.

17 March: Herrin, IL—A church rally collects more than $3 million to bail out klansmen indicted following the battle of 8 February.

21 March: Long Island, NY—Dynamite planted under several burning crosses injures participants in a Klan rally.

29 March: Buffalo, NY—Rev. Littleton Smith, a klansman, finds $10,000 worth of liquor at a "soft drink" shop.

1 April: La Grande, OR—Exalted Cyclops O.W. Jones resigns. The local klavern holds its last meeting on 15 April.

5 April: Lilly, PA—A riot between klansmen and anti–Klan demonstrators leaves 4 dead and at least 13 injured. On 1 July, 28 rioters receive 2-year jail terms.

7 April: Atlanta, GA—Wizard Evans banishes Indiana Grand Dragon D.C. Stephenson.

12 April: Buffalo, NY—Klansmen disrupt a speech by Mayor Schwab at Unity Masonic Temple.

3 May: Okawville Bottoms, IL—Bootleggers ambush klansman Glenn Young and his wife on the highway, wounding both. KKK members swarm local highways, killing gangster Jack Skelcher and wounding companion Charles Briggs.

6 May: Indianapolis, IN—Voters cast a record number of primary ballots, supporting gubernatorial hopeful Ed Jackson and other Klan candidates.

12 May: Indianapolis, IN—400 Klan officers elect D.C. Stephenson as grand dragon. On 13 May, Stephenson lays plans for a rift with Imperial Headquarters.

17 May: South Bend, IN—Notre Dame University students brawl with klansmen in the streets and besiege KKK headquarters. Rev. Jack Horton holds them at bay with a pistol.

18 May: Indianapolis, IN—Wizard Evans meets with new Grand Dragon Walter Bossert and others to reorganize the Indiana realm.

19 May: Conway, NC—Klansmen kidnap Jewish merchant Max Goldstein and order him to leave "white man's country."

30 May: Buffalo, NY—Klansmen rally near Clarence Center, with armed guards barring state troopers from the event.

2 June: Baton Rouge, LA—State legislators pass three anti–Klan laws, including a mask ban, prison terms for masked violence, and publication of membership in secret societies.

4 June: Atlanta, GA—A Klan tribunal sends D.C. Stephenson a list of charges lodged against him, with trial scheduled for 23 June. Stephenson ignores the summons.

10–12 June: Cleveland, OH—D.C. Stephenson attends the Republican National Convention.

16 June: Buffalo, NY—Mayor Schwab assigns Edward Obertean to infiltrate the local KKK.

17 June: Leeville, LA—A white pogrom kills one black and injures numerous others.

27 June: Cleveland, OH—D.C. Stephenson's yacht explodes and burns at its mooring in Bayview Park. John Bundy of Muncie, Indiana, confesses to starting the fire of 15 December, then recants his statement on 27 December, claiming he was coached by Stephenson's aides. No one is ever prosecuted.

30 June: Berkley, MI—Klansmen kidnap Rev. Oren Van Loon from his home. Searchers find him near Battle Creek, on 12 July, with "KKK" branded on his back.

2–4 July: Binghamton, NY—4,000 klansmen attend their second annual klorero. Opponents pelt one Klan sentry with bricks and fire a shotgun blast into the camp. 2,000 knights parade downtown on 4 July.

3 July: Buffalo, NY—Thieves steal Klan membership records and deliver the list of 5,574 names to Mayor Frank Schwab, who posts it for public viewing at police headquarters. Buffalo Klan leaders request help from imperial headquarters. Atlanta dispatches Thomas Austin to investigate. He arrives in Buffalo on 7 July and obtains a gun permit.

5 July: Binghamton, NY—Fighting erupts during a Klan meeting.

7 July: Staunton, VA—A masked victory parade celebrates the election of klansmen to 80 percent of city's public offices.

8 July: Darby, PA—Police administrators fire a patrolman for joining a Klan raid against an all-black Boy Scout camp.

26 July: Maryville, MD—The Klan warns Judge A.T. Brust that "something real" will happen if he investigates a recent tar-and-feathers incident.

29 July: Anaheim, CA—10,000 klansmen rally at a city park, then parade through town with a band and an airplane overhead, marching to a rally where 1,500 initiates take their oaths as knights.

29 July: Oklahoma City—The Klan endorses a member, Rep. E.B. Howard, for senator in the Democratic primary, opposing ex-governor Walton. On 2 August, the *Fiery Cross* endorses rival Charles Wrightman. Walton wins the primary on 4 August, but loses the general election in November.

30 July: Haverhill, MA—Gunfire wounds three persons during a riotous KKK rally. On 18 August, 13 defendants are sentenced to various jail terms.

31 July: East St. Louis, IL—On the day of his scheduled arraignment for attempted murder, Glenn Young leads 200 klansmen to the Labor Temple, near the courthouse, demanding that the judge come to him. A justice of the peace obliges and frees Young on bond pending trial.

1 August: Buffalo, NY—Mayor Schwab announces a tip to a cache of KKK documents. Police seize the papers, including names of

2,000 members. On 4 August, Schwab puts the names on public display. Embarrassed klansman Henry Lyon shoots his wife, two sons and himself on 7 August. On 13 August, vandals paint "KKK" on various Klan homes.

5 August: Blackstone, MA—Klansmen abduct and brand a newspaper reporter.

8 August: Fairmont, WV—Authorities charge seven klansmen with shooting Rev. Daniel Washington. Three defendants receive prison terms on 27 October.

11 August: Paxton, IL—Klansmen kidnap a Jew, Ralph Aaron, and brand him with the letters "KKK."

14 August: Logan, UT—City officials enact an anti-mask ordinance.

16 August: Burlington, VT—Police issue arrest warrants for klansman W.C. Moyers, charged with burning a Catholic church. Officers capture him on 20 August.

18 August: Memphis, TN—Gunfire erupts during a scuffle over KKK records. Authorities charge one klansman (a deputy sheriff from Birmingham, Alabama) with attempted murder of three local policemen. Officers jail three other knights for disorderly conduct.

19 August: Buffalo, NY—Mayor Schwab reports that a disgruntled klansman has sent him more membership names, spanning 70 towns in western New York. Police Chief Charles Zimmerman, uncle of a klansman, refuses to post the lists on 21 August. Schwab orders Zimmerman to comply on 28 August, while Catholic attorney and political candidate Charles Desmond files suit to obtain the lists. Private sources leak the names on 10 September, before a court order compels their publication on 15 September.

20 August: Helper, UT—Klansmen make their first appearance with a motorcade and a 15-foot fiery cross.

21 August: Little Rock, AR—Klan spokesmen charge the Democratic Central Committee with fraud against Klan candidates for office. Party leaders deny it on 26 August. A new roster of committee officers, selected on 9 September, includes 75 klansmen and 190 KKK opponents.

23 August: Sea Girt, NJ—Democratic vice presidential candidate John Davis publicly condemns the KKK.

29 August: Herrin, IL—Klansmen arrive as anti–Klan deputies seek to retrieve Jack Skelcher's car from a local garage. A pitched battle ensues, killing three klansmen, two Klan opponents, and two bystanders.

29 August: Buffalo, NY—Police jail klansman Albert Acker for illegally selling condoms. He pleads guilty in September and pays a $50 fine.

31 August: Tulsa, OK—State senator Wash Hudson leads the first in a series of Klansman's Klean-up Kommittee meetings, seeking replacement of Grand Dragon Jewett.

31 August: Buffalo, NY—Thomas Austin, Grand Kleagle George Bryant and klansman Carl Sturm ambush Edward Obertean. The resultant shootout kills Austin and Obertean, while leaving Sturm and Bryant wounded.

15 September: Mandy, UT—Greek immigrant Andrew Dallas marries a Mormon native, sparking a Klan parade and cross-burning in protest.

19 September: Ogden, UT—W. Earl Roche drives his car past klansmen blocking a city street. They fire shots at his car, but he escapes to file a complaint. Police take no action.

19 September: Buffalo, NY—Police charge Rev. Charles Penfold, a klansman, with "outraging public decency" by having sex with a woman in his car. Penfold initially identifies the woman as his wife, then admits lying under oath when he receives a 30-day sentence on the sex charge, on 26 September. Authorities indict him for perjury on 28 November 1924.

26 September: Atlanta, GA—Wizard Evans concedes that all future grand dragon selections will include approval by state members.

1 October: Buffalo, NY—George Bryant surrenders to police on

charges of violating the Walker Law. Court arguments challenge the statute on 1 October, but the judge upholds its constitutionality on 7 November. Bryant pleads guilty on 17 December 1928 and pays a $100 fine.

5 October: Loris, NC—Klansmen kidnap night marshal George Powers and warn him to stop liquor raids.

11 October: Oakland, MI—Fiery crosses and bomb explosions terrorize residents at a Catholic seminary.

17 October: Chicago, IL—After two months of Klan threats, arsonists burn the city's largest black church.

18 October: Worcester, MA—Rioting erupts during an anti–Klan demonstration.

20 October: Ogden, UT—City officials pass an anti-mask ordinance.

21 October: Detroit, MI—A tear-gas bomb scatters participants in an anti–Klan rally.

29 October: Niles, OH—A bomb wrecks the mayor's home, after he denies the KKK a parade permit.

1 November: Niles, OH—Rioting flares between klansmen and opponents at a tri-state rally, leaving at least 12 injured. Authorities indict 105 rioters on 5 December. Ten defendants plead guilty and pay fines on 25 March 1925.

2 November: Henryetta, OK—Angry miners attack a KKK parade.

4 November: Niles, OH—Police seize a cache of weapons at a KKK rally.

4 November: Indiana—Ed Jackson wins the gubernatorial election with KKK support.

4 November: Kansas—Ben Paulen wins election as governor with KKK support.

4 November: Seattle, WA—Voters reject a Klan initiative to ban parochial and private schools.

6 November: Ft. Worth, TX—Arsonists damage the local klavern.

19 November: Orange County, CA—Klansmen join police and members of the Anti-Saloon League in a series of liquor raids, jailing 52 persons.

17 December: Texas—Z.E. Martin resigns as grand dragon, replaced by Marvin Childers.

1925

Tuskegee Institute reports 17 blacks lynched nationwide.

January: Alabama—Klansmen launch a statewide campaign against brothels.

5 January: Oklahoma City—State legislators elect klansman Jess Harper speaker of the house.

19 January: Chicago—Bombers damage a synagogue recently sold to blacks.

24 January: Herrin, IL—Four persons die in a shootout between klansmen and anti–Klan Deputy Ora Thomas. The dead include Thomas and Klan leader Glenn Young. A coroner's jury convened on 1 February files no criminal charges.

1 February: Herrin, IL—The police chief fires one of his officers for joining the KKK.

2 February: Herrin, IL—A city policeman kills a man wearing a hat that bears the name of anti–Klan sheriff George Galligan. The victim proves to be an alcoholic thief who stole the hat.

3 February: Washington, DC—The U.S. Senate votes to seat klansman Earle Mayfield.

3 February: Anaheim, CA—The USA Club gathers enough petition signatures to force a recall election against Klan-supported officeholders.

11 February: Denver, CO—Klan opponents hold their first public rally.

21 February: Georgia—While returning from Florida, William Simmons suffers an auto accident and is hospitalized. His traveling companion dies in the crash.

23 February: Salt Lake City, UT—Several hundred klansmen stage a surprise parade downtown.

24 February: New Orleans—KKK members celebrate Mardi Gras as the only occasion when they can legally wear masks in Louisiana.

7 March: Austin, TX—Gov. Miriam Ferguson signs an anti-mask law.

15 March: Indiana—D.C. Stephenson rapes and tortures Madge Oberholtzer on a train traveling between Irvington and Chicago. Oberholtzer swallows poison on 16 March, but Stephenson withholds medical treatment for a crucial period. Oberholtzer gives a "dying declaration" to authorities on 28 March. Stephenson is charged with assault on 2 April. Oberholtzer dies on 14 April. Stephenson is arrested once more, this time for murder, on 20 April. Two of his aides are charged as accomplices. All three defendants plead not guilty on 15 May.

5–6 April: Salt Lake City, UT—Klansmen from Utah and Nevada stage their first interstate konklave.

28 April: Northbridge, MA—Hostile crowds besiege and menace a KKK rally.

1 May: Provo, UT—Kleagle Milfred Yant flees with the Klan treasury and other monies, in a stolen car. Police in Deland, Florida, arrest him on 13 October and return him for trial on 22 October. Yant pleads guilty to forgery on 26 October, receiving a prison term of 1–20 years on 28 October.

3 May: Berlin, MA—Klansmen brawl with opponents at a KKK rally.

3 May: Gardner, MA—Opponents stone a Klan parade, injuring its leader.

5 May: Denver, CO—Klan candidates win election to the school board.

19 May: Northbridge, MA—More rioting erupts at another Klan rally.

20 May: Denver, CO—Newspaper reports announce that Grand Dragon John Locke is under federal investigation for evading taxes during 1913–24.

11 June: Burlington, MA—Police arrest two persons after a KKK rally degenerates into violence.

19 June: Salt Lake City, UT—City officials enact an anti-mask law.

20 June: Clinton, MA—After another anti–Klan riot, police hold 38 persons over for grand jury action.

30 June: Denver, CO—Wizard Evans requests John Locke's resignation as Colorado grand dragon. Locke refuses on 1 July, before an audience of 20,000 klansmen. Two weeks later, after Evans demands the return of all Klan funds and property, Locke responds in July by founding the Minute Men of America.

3 July: Noblesville, IN—Unknown assailants fatally bludgeon 25-year-old Edith Dean, outside town. D.C. Stephenson, awaiting trial for murder in Noblesville, claims Dean visited him in jail on 2 July, informing him that klansmen asked her to falsely accuse him of rape with a statement similar to Madge Oberholtzer's dying declaration. Stephenson accuses the Klan of Dean's murder, but it remains officially unsolved.

9 July: Birmingham, AL—Hugo Black formally resigns from the KKK prior to launching his U.S. Senate campaign. On 2 September 1926, following his victory, Klan leaders welcome him back and present him with a gold "grand passport" indicating life membership.

12 July: Richfield, UT—LDS President Robert Young says any Mormon klansman "is not worthy of standing in the church."

23 July: Denver, CO—Mayor Stapleton dismisses klansman William Candlish as chief of police.

2 August: Westwood, MA—Police jail three klansmen for rioting after a KKK rally.

8 August: Washington, D.C.—40,000 klansmen and women's auxiliary members parade down Pennsylvania Avenue.

10 August: Framingham, MA—Klansmen ambush and wound five opponents after a KKK rally. A mob threatens the jail where 16 knights are held on assault charges.

12 August: Reading, MA—Rioting disrupts another KKK rally.

12 August: Denver, CO—A special election held to recall Klan mayor Ben Stapleton ends in victory for the KKK. Grand Dragon Locke serves as Stapleton's campaign manager.

22 August: Long Island City, NY—A mob stones klansmen whose car stalls while returning from a rally in Freeport.

8 September: Detroit, MI—Dr. Ossian Sweet, a black physician, moves his family into a previously all-white neighborhood. A Klan-led mob of 500 to 800 whites gathers outside the house that night but refrains from any violence. On 9 September, the mob returns and charges the house, hurling stones. Sweet's brother Henry fires a gunshot, killing rioter Leon Breiner. Police jail all 11 occupants of the house (exempting only a one-year-old infant). On 10 September, prosecutors announce that all 11 prisoners will be charged with first-degree murder. Trial convenes for Dr. Sweet on 30 October and ends with jurors deadlocked on 27 November. A second trial, for Henry Sweet, convenes on 19 April 1926. Jurors acquit him on 13 May, and prosecutors dismiss all charges against the other 10 defendants on 21 July 1927.

18 September: North Brookfield, MA—Police jail two persons after a KKK riot.

5 October: Salt Lake City, UT—Klansmen parade for the first time unmasked.

12 October: Noblesville, IN—Jury selection begins for the murder trial of D.C. Stephenson and two codefendants. Testimony begins on 29 October. Jurors convict Stephenson on 14 November, while acquitting defendants Earl Gentry and Earl Klinck. Stephenson receives a life prison term.

29 October: Anaheim, CA—Rev. Leon Myers, former exalted cyclops, resigns as pastor of the First Christian Church.

1 November: Buffalo, NY—E.D. Smith relinquishes his dual titles as grand kleagle of western New York and grand titan of Province No. 8.

3 November: Indianapolis, IN—Voters elect klansman John Duvall as mayor, while other KKK candidates sweep their races.

5 November: Colorado—Klan candidates sweep the state elections, while klansmen Rice Means and Lawrence Phipps win election to the U.S. Senate.

5 November: Little Rock, AR—Klan members deliver a no-confidence vote against Grand Dragon James Comer. Ladies' auxiliary members vote likewise on 11 November.

December: Salt Lake City, UT—Klansmen demand equal enforcement of the city's anti-mask law against Santa Claus impersonators.

1926

Tuskegee Institute reports 23 blacks lynched nationwide.

1 January: Washington, D.C.—Indianapolis mayor-elect John Duval, traveling at Klan expense, confers with Wizard Hiram Evans.

4 January: Birmingham, AL—Police and klansmen join in raids on several Chinese cafés, seeking liquor violations.

12 January: Albany, NY—The state court of appeals unanimously upholds the constitutionality of the Walker Law. A subsequent Klan appeal to the U.S. Supreme Court, filed on 10 October 1927, likewise proves fruitless.

30 January: Arkansas—Agnes Cloud sues Grand Dragon Comer and his wife for misappropriating Klan funds. A referee dismisses the case on 8 October, when Cloud fails to pay court costs.

10 March: Royston, GA—Klansmen raid Herman Bigby's home, killing him and a companion, Walton Adams.

12 March: Dallas, TX—Wizard Evans tells assembled klansmen that the KKK is "now completely out of politics."

13 April: Herrin, IL—42 klansmen and anti-Klan gangsters fight a pitched battle outside the Masonic Temple, killing three men on each side.

25 April: Carteret, NJ—One white man dies, and another is wounded, in a fight with six blacks. On 26 April, white rioters burn a black church and drive 100 black families out of town.

15 August: Wytheville, VA—A masked gang storms the jail and murders Raymond Bird, a black rape suspect.

2 September: Birmingham, AL—While attending the annual klorero, Gov. Bibb Graves receives a "grand passport" signifying his life membership in the KKK.

29 September: Indiana—D.C. Stephenson begins leaking information to reporters on his former political allies. He sits for a formal press interview on 25 October.

2 November: Marinette, WI—Jurors convict six men of inciting a riot at a June 1925 Klan rally.

1927

Tuskegee Institute reports 16 blacks lynched nationwide.

9 March: Mobile, AL—A white mob threatens attorney Clarence Darrow following his anti-lynching speech. Police escort him safely out of town.

8 April: Indianapolis, IN—Fred Butler, former secretary to D.C. Stephenson, testifies that Stephenson gave a car to Ed Jackson for use in Jackson's 1924 gubernatorial campaign.

15 May: Indianapolis, IN—Indictments charge Mayor John Duvall and city controller W.C. Buser with conspiracy, based on D.C. Stephenson's revelations.

30 May–1 June: Tampa, FL—Whites riot for three days, killing 4 persons and injuring 33, after National Guardsmen prevent the lynching of a black rape suspect.

31 May: Queens, NY—Klansmen battle police after they are ordered to withdraw from a Memorial Day parade.

July: Jefferson County, AL—Klansmen whip Arthur Hill, an elderly black man, and force him to sell his farm for $600 (10 percent of the fair market value).

July: Clay County, AL—Klansmen flog Greek-American victim Dan Mitchell for marrying a "pure American" woman.

July: Straight Mountain, AL—Klansmen whip a mentally retarded orphan who jeered at them. Seven defendants face trial in August, where five plead guilty on reduced charges and receive 6-month jail terms. Jurors convict Eugene Doss and another klansman, resulting in prison terms of 8–10 years.

13 July: Indiana—D.C. Stephenson produces 31 cancelled checks written to future Gov. Ed Jackson during 1924. A Marion County grand jury convenes on 19 July to investigate Klan-related political corruption. On 24 July, a reporter collects Stephenson's "black boxes" of evidence from a contact in Lick Skillet.

24 July: Grand Prairie, TX—Rioting erupts during a Klan march through town.

25 July: Crenshaw County, AL—Annie Simmons, an elderly black woman, dies from injuries inflicted by Klan floggers. White jurors later acquit the whipping squad's leader.

August: Clay County, AL—Klansmen try to whip Dan Mitchell a second time, but he drives them away with shotgun fire.

2 August: Black Hills, SD—Pres. Calvin Coolidge declines to run for reelection.

25 August: Virginia—C.W. Wilson defends his rural home against nightriders, killing one klansman.

3 September: Geneva, NY—Rioting disrupts another KKK parade.

4 September: Montgomery, AL—Grand Dragon James Esdale writes to Exalted Cyclops Ira Thompson in Luverne, asserting that he can make Gov. Graves terminate Attorney General Charles McCall's prosecution of Klan floggers.

7 September: Indianapolis, IN—New indictments charge 12 Republican officials, including Gov. Ed Jackson, with bribery and other crimes related to D.C. Stephenson and the Klan.

12 October: Indianapolis, IN—Jurors convict Mayor Duvall of conspiracy, related to the Stephenson scandals. He receives a 30-day jail term, pays a $1,000 fine, and is barred from public office for four years.

1928

Tuskegee Institute reports 10 blacks lynched nationwide.

7 February: Indianapolis, IN—Ex-governor Ed Jackson and two codefendants face trial on bribery charges. A two-year statute of limitations prevents their conviction.

23 May: Regina, Saskatchewan—1,500 klansmen assemble to burn an 80-foot cross.

June: Winnipeg, Manitoba—Klansmen hold their first public rally.

29 June: Houston, TX—The Democratic National Convention nominates Catholic Alfred Smith for president.

24 July: Denver, CO—200 klansmen burn a cross at the home of a woman convicted of child abuse.

20 September: Oklahoma City, OK—Al Smith publicly condemns the KKK.

29 October: Baltimore, MD—Al Smith attacks the Klan again.

1929

Tuskegee Institute reports seven blacks lynched nationwide.

17 March: Mayflower, MA—Hecklers pelt Sen. Tom Heflin with eggs and stones during a speech supporting the Klan.

18 March: Brockton, MA—Hecklers throw bottles at Sen. Heflin's car after another pro-Klan speech, injuring a policeman.

20 April: Missouri—Vigilantes invade a rural jail, removing black burglary suspect Fred Allen, and whip him before returning him to police custody.

14 July: Princess Anne, MD—Whites storm the black community, driving 300 blacks out of town.

23 August: Baltimore, MD—Racial street fighting leaves 20 persons injured.

1 November: Drumkeller, Alberta—Klansmen stage their first cross-burning.

28 November: Colorado—Investigation of a riot at the state prison reveals that white convicts have organized a KKK chapter behind bars.

1930

Tuskegee Institute reports 20 blacks lynched nationwide.

15 February: Spring Glen, UT—Kleagle Glen Jackson sells Klan property outside town to Slavic buyers.

28 February: Indiana—State authorities reject D.C. Stephenson's plea for clemency.

29 July: Ailey, GA—Masked raiders kidnap and beat S.S. Mincey, an elderly black Republican. Mincey dies from head injuries on 30 July.

29 July: Edmonton, Alberta—Klansmen burn a 50-foot cross at Riverside Flats.

September: Peekskill, NY—500 klansmen from four states stage a rally.

22 December: New York City—A revised print of *The Birth of a Nation* premieres on Broadway.

1931

Tuskegee Institute reports 12 blacks lynched nationwide.

25 March: Stevenson, AL—Police arrest nine blacks on charges of raping two white women aboard a train. Their first capital trial begins at Scottsboro on 6 April.

15 July: Camp Hill, AL—Sheriff Kyle Young leads a Klan posse to beat and disperse 80 SCU members. Victims regroup at the home of Tommy Gray, a black man, who drives the raiders off with gunfire. Sheriff Young and Dadeville's police chief lead a reinforced mob against the Gray home on 16 July, sparking a pitched battle. Ralph Gray, though shot in both legs, critically wounds Sheriff Young and repels the klansmen. They return after nightfall, killing Ralph Gray and burning the house, while police arrest 40 SCU members. Klansmen transport Gray's corpse to Dadeville, beating and shooting it for hours, then run amok throughout the district, killing an uncertain number of blacks and burning their homes.

1932

Tuskegee Institute reports six blacks lynched nationwide.
March: Dallas, TX—Klansmen kidnap and flog two CPUSA members who have spoken on behalf of blacks.
8 August: Edmonton, Alberta—Firefighters extinguish five burning crosses at the city racetrack.
7 November: Birmingham, AL—Klansmen rout black spectators gathered to protest the Scottsboro rape verdicts.
20 December: Talladega, AL—Police kill three blacks during an "uprising" by a local tenant farmer's union. A fourth victim dies from his wounds on 27 December.

1933

Tuskegee Institute reports 24 blacks lynched nationwide.
13 February: Blairmore, Alberta—Klansmen demonstrate against the Mine Workers Union.
1 May: Birmingham, AL—15 policemen resign over orders barring them from shooting unarmed CPUSA members.
16 November: Greenville, SC—Robed, masked raiders kidnap and murder a black man, George Green. Police supply no motive for the slaying.

1934

Tuskegee Institute reports 15 blacks lynched nationwide.
April: Lakeland, FL—Klansmen posing as police kidnap Frank Norman, a union organizer and ILD member. His body is never found.
May: Birmingham, AL—Klansmen join in the violence surrounding a strike by U.S. Steel miners.

1935

Tuskegee Institute reports 18 blacks lynched nationwide.
21 March: Poinsett County, AR—40 nightriders, including klansmen and police, raid the home of elderly STFU activist Rev. A.B. Brookins, riddling the house with bullets and killing his daughter.
21 March: Hernando, MS—Terrorists murder Rev. T.A. Allen, a black union organizer, dumping his chain-weighted body into the Coldwater River.
22 March: Marked Tree, AR—A mob besieges STFU organizers Clay East and Mary Hilliard, escorting them from town under threat of death if they return.
22 March: Poinsett County, AR—Raiders terrorize STFU president W.H. Stultz, attempting to bomb his home.
22 March: Mississippi County, AR—Nightriders invade the home of a black union member. His wife, Mary Green, dies of fright during the raid.
23 March: Marked Tree, AR—Nocturnal gunmen riddle the homes of several STFU members, including union attorney C.T. Carpenter. On 24 March, gunmen invade Carpenter's office, threatening to kill him if he does not sever his ties to the union.
25 March: Lawrence County, MS—White gunmen ambush and murder R.J. Tyrone, a prosperous black farmer, following arguments with a white neighbor.

27 March: Cross County, AR—STFU attorney John Allen escapes from a mob bent on lynching him. The mob ransacks homes in their search for Allen, beating numerous blacks, including a woman whose ear is severed by pistol-whipping.
30 March: Marked Tree, AR—Whites mob a group of blacks returning home from a rural church, indiscriminately beating men, women and children.
30 March: Hitchiecoon, AR—Arsonists destroy a black church lately used for union meetings.
2 April: Poinsett County, AR—Raiders storm the home of Rev. E.B. McKinney, STFU vice president, firing 250 machine-gun bullets into his house.
July: Selma, AL—The sheriff arrests five SCU organizers, then releases them to Klan floggers who whip them and burn their wounds. Two CPUSA investigators receive the same treatment after two hours in town, and klansmen subsequently torture a pair of ILD attorneys sent to defend the original prisoners.
30 November: Tampa, FL—Police raid a meeting of the Modern Democrats, arresting several members and delivering three to a Klan flogging squad. Victim Joseph Shoemaker dies from his injuries.

1936

Tuskegee Institute reports eight blacks lynched nationwide.
10 April: St. Petersburg, FL—Police charge klansmen with the 1935 kidnap-castration of Robert Cargell.
29 April: Lepanto, AR—Masked lynchers remove Willis Kees, a black rape suspect, from jail and fatally shoot him.
13 May: Detroit, MI—Police find Charles Poole murdered. On 23 May, prosecutors blame the Black Legion for his slaying and "scores" of others. Police jail 16 suspects and report that 7 have confessed to killing Poole because he allegedly beat his wife.
24 September: Birmingham, AL—Klansmen snatch CPUSA member Joseph Gelders from home and drive him to Chilton County for a near-fatal beating.

1937

Tuskegee Institute reports eight blacks lynched nationwide.
11 July: Atlanta, GA—Wizard Evans condemns the CIO as being "infested" with communists, vowing a Klan campaign against "alien labor agitation."
31 July: Atlanta, GA—Klansmen parade behind a fiery cross.
12 August: Washington, DC—FDR nominates Hugo Black to the U.S. Supreme Court. Reports of his KKK membership prompt Black to explain in a national radio address, on 1 October. Black takes his seat on the court on 4 October.

1938

Tuskegee Institute reports six blacks lynched nationwide.
August: Birmingham, AL—Klansmen flog several CIO members employed at the Scottsdale Mills.
20 November: Birmingham, AL—The SCHW holds its annual convention.
12 December: Washington, DC—The U.S. Supreme Court rules that states maintaining segregated schools must provide equal facilities for blacks. Missouri plaintiff Lloyd Gaines subsequently vanishes under mysterious circumstances.

1939

Tuskegee Institute reports two blacks lynched nationwide.
6 January: Atlanta, GA—Wizard Evans attends the consecration ceremony transforming his former imperial headquarters into the Roman Catholic Cathedral of Christ the King.
5 February: Atlanta, GA—40–50 klansmen in 10 cars snatch six persons from the streets, terrorizing them with threats.

1 May: Miami, FL—50 carloads of klansmen tour black neighborhoods, warning blacks not to vote in the next day's Democratic primary.

June: California—Grand Dragon Snelson urges klansmen to form "shooting clubs."

10 June: Atlanta, GA—James Colescott replaces Hiram Evans as imperial wizard.

7 August: Mattituck, NY—Klansmen burn a 10-foot cross with signs nearby, warning Jews to leave town.

3 October: Greenville, SC—The *News* carries Grand Klokard Fred Johnson's announcement of a new recruiting drive.

6 December: Aberdeen, WA—Klansmen and members of the Better Business Builders smash the windows of AFL and CIO offices.

1940

Tuskegee Institute reports four blacks lynched nationwide.

February: Rosedale, NJ—20 klansmen burn a 30-foot cross and distribute anti-Semitic pamphlets outside a synagogue. Police jail two for disorderly conduct.

2 March: Atlanta, GA—Klansmen beat a young couple to death in lover's lane. Investigators subsequently link the KKK to 50 floggings in the past two years.

13 March: Atlanta, GA—A coroner's jury convened to investigate the murder of Isaac Gaston, killed by the KKK for allegedly beating his wife, learns that three Fulton County sheriff's deputies are klansmen. On 29 March, authorities indict 10 klansmen for two kidnappings and 23 floggings. Police arrest the suspects on 30 March.

17 April: Atlanta, GA—Wizard Colescott formally bans hoods and limits cross-burnings to formal ceremonies.

18 August: Andover, NJ—Klansmen rally with the German-American Bund at Camp Nordland.

1941

Tuskegee Institute reports four blacks lynched nationwide.

May: Atlanta, GA—The Imperial Kloncilium seeks $1 million in donations for its "Americanization" fund, while denouncing the USO as dominated by Catholics and Jews.

30 May: Andover, NJ—New Jersey's attorney general closes Camp Nordland, declaring it "a Nazi agency."

August: California—Grand Dragon James Harvey condemns the USO and warns that klansmen must be ready "to take over the country" in times of crisis.

18 August: Miami, FL—Klansmen burn four crosses at the site of a proposed black housing project.

18 October: Washington, DC—California kleagle William Sahli testifies before the Dies Committee as a character witness for Frederick Van Meter, a member of the German-American Bund.

19 October: Detroit, MI—Klansmen convene a banquet to revive the local KKK.

7 December: Hawaii—Japanese aircraft attack Pearl Harbor. The U.S. enters World War II on 8 December.

1942

Tuskegee Institute reports six blacks lynched nationwide.

January: Atlanta, GA—Jurors convict Hiram Evans of conspiring with a state official to make $11,000 excess profit on a state printing contract. Klansman Wily Tucker, head salesman for the Williams Printing Co., faces charges in the same case.

12 January: Detroit, MI—Henry Ford writes to Wizard Colescott, disclaiming any taint of anti-Semitism.

22 January: Washington, DC—Colescott appears before the Dies Committee. Afterward, Alabama Rep. Joe Starnes described the KKK as "just as American as the Baptist or Methodist Church, as the Lions Club or the Rotary Club."

28 February: Detroit, MI—Robed klansmen join a mob of 1,200 armed whites gathered to repel black tenants from the Sojourner Truth housing project, leaving scores injured as rioting erupts. A federal grand jury indicts three mob leaders for conspiracy on 16 April. Some 2,000 police and National Guardsmen protect 14 black families when they finally move in, on 30 April.

21 March: Holt, AL—Klansmen burn crosses at the CIO hall and at a union leader's home, on the eve of an NLRB election at the Tennessee Coal, Iron & Railroad Co.

20 December: Orlando, FL—Kleagle Fred Bass tours the CIO Citrus Workers Union office, posing as "a boilermaker from New York."

1943

Tuskegee Institute reports two blacks lynched nationwide.

30 January: Orlando, FL—Klan leaders issue a radio "call for all klansmen." On 31 January, the *Sentinel-Star* runs an ad seeking 8,000 klansmen in three counties.

25 May: Mobile, AL—Whites riot over the promotion of 12 black shipyard workers.

16 June: Beaumont, TX—A white race riot leaves two victims dead.

20–21 June: Detroit, MI—A race riot instigated by whites leaves 25 blacks and 9 whites dead, with more than 700 persons injured and 600+ arrested. NAACP observer Thurgood Marshall describes city police as "the Gestapo" for their violence against blacks. On 22 October, white jurors convict two blacks of inciting the riot.

August: Beaufort, SC—The *Gazette* announces a Klan recruiting drive.

15 September: Apopka, FL—A Klan motorcade tours black neighborhoods on the eve of an NLRB election at a local citrus packing house. Klansmen jeer the CIO.

1944

Tuskegee Institute reports two blacks lynched nationwide.

15 January: Orlando, FL—100 klansmen parade at American Laundry, which employs CIO members, 15 days before commencement of a union contract.

17 February: Tallahassee, FL—Wizard Colescott announces a planned "unity meeting" with state attorney general Tom Watson to ban labor unions.

April: Atlanta, GA—The IRS files a lien against the KKK for $685,355 in back taxes and penalties from the 1920s.

3 April: Washington, DC—The U.S. Supreme Court bans white-only primary elections as unconstitutional.

23 April: Atlanta, GA—A special klonvokation disbands the Knights of the KKK, Inc., but Imperial Wizard James Colescott subsequently denies that the Klan has disbanded.

May: Lake County, FL—Willis McCall wins election to his first term as sheriff. FBI reports later identify him as a klansman.

21 May: Atlanta, GA—Samuel Green founds the AGK.

September: Tallahassee, FL—The KKK of Florida receives a state charter.

June: Washington, DC—A member of the GOP National Committee accuses Indiana committeeman Robert Lyons of being a former klansman. Lyons resigns from the committee two weeks later, without denying the charge.

23 October: Santa Clara, CA—Congressional candidate Hal Styles admits he was a klansman in the 1920s.

26 October: Peoria, IL—Vice presidential candidate Harry Truman denies former membership in the KKK. He later admits paying his klecktoken in the early 1920s, but insists that he was never initiated.

1945

Tuskegee Institute reports one black lynched nationwide.

April: Lake County, FL—Critics accuse Sheriff Willis McCall of beating six black men and holding them in peonage.

May: Atlanta, GA—William Simmons dies in obscurity.

August: DeKalb County, GA—Klansmen fatally stab Porter Turner, a black taxi driver, and dump his body on a doctor's lawn. The GBI reopens its investigation of the case on 7 June 1946.

2 September: Japan's formal surrender ends World War II.

October: Stone Mountain, GA—The AGK goes public with a ceremony falsely billed as "the first cross-burning since Pearl Harbor."

1946

Tuskegee Institute reports six blacks lynched nationwide.

7 February: Washington, DC—A filibuster by southern senators kills President Truman's Fair Employment Practices Committee.

13 February: Atlanta, GA—Klansmen flog a black navy veteran near the city airport.

26 February: Columbia, TN—Whites launch a pogrom against the black community, following an argument between a white store owner and two black customers. Vigilantes seize 300 guns in illegal searches of black homes, vandalizing the houses and various business establishments with "KKK" graffiti. The riot leaves 10 blacks injured and 70 in jail, where two blacks are shot dead during police "questioning" on 28 February. On 4 October, white jurors convict two blacks of attempted murder, while acquitting 23 others on all charges.

21 March: Flint, MI—Klansmen light several crosses after a black resident announces his candidacy for an elective city post.

22 March: Atlanta, GA—Attorney Morgan Belser files new incorporation papers for the Knights of the KKK, listing James Colescott as imperial wizard and paying fees for 1940–46.

5 April: Freeport, NY—Dorothy Langston, secretary of the New York Committee for Justice, receives a threatening letter signed by Great Kligrapp James Hanley.

21 May: Los Angeles, CA—Judge Alfred Paonessa revokes the Klan's California charter.

30 May: Atlanta, GA—Gov. Ellis Arnall moves to revoke the Klan's charter. The state officially files suit against the Klan on 20 June. On 21 June, FBI agents expose a "well-organized plot" by local klansmen to assassinate Gov. Arnall.

3 June: Washington, DC—The U.S. Supreme Court bans segregation aboard interstate buses.

9 June: Gordon, GA—Klansmen snatch black laborer Willie Dudley at gunpoint from his job at the P.M. Martin Clay Co. They order him to quit his union, beating Dudley with rubber hoses when he refuses.

16 June: Stone Mountain, GA—Klansmen threaten to kill journalist Drew Pearson if he appears for a scheduled speaking engagement. The mountain's owner refuses Pearson access, prompting him to speak instead from the steps of the state capital in Atlanta.

20 June: Frankfort, KY—State Attorney General Eldon Dummit files litigation to block the AGK from operating in Kentucky.

21 June: Birmingham, AL—William Morris founds the Federated KKK.

July: Albany, NY—Acting on a petition from the state attorney general, Judge Joseph Gavagan revokes the Klan's New York charter.

17 July: Atlanta, GA—Grand Dragon Samuel Green claims that the KKK delivered 100,000 votes to Gov. Eugene Talmadge in the recent Democratic primary.

22 July: Lexington, MS—Floggers fatally beat a black man, Leon McTatic, for allegedly stealing a saddle. Indictments charge six suspects with murder on 30 July, but jurors acquit them at trial.

26 July: Monroe, GA—A gang of 20 whites stops George Dorsey and Roger Malcolm on the road outside town, fatally shooting both black men and their wives.

31 July: Georgia—FBI agents report that klansmen have fired into homes as a warning to blacks against voting.

August: Soperton, GA—Following a campaign speech by Eugene Talmadge, white rioters raze a black church.

5 August: Miami, FL—Klansmen force a black CIO shop steward, Roosevelt Winfield, off the highway and threaten his life.

10 August: Athens, AL—White rioters injure 50–100 blacks.

17 August: Atlanta, GA—The Columbians, Inc. receive a Georgia state charter.

20 August: Magee, MS—White mobs attack black residents.

26 August: Crowley, LA—Police report mob violence against local blacks.

September: Birmingham, AL—The Federated KKK receives a state charter.

14 September: Los Angeles, CA—Black leaders launch a petition drive, seeking 1 million signatures for a drive to ban the KKK.

Autumn: Indianapolis—King Kleagle Harold Overton says kleagles are active in 60 of Indiana's 92 counties, processing 121,000 membership applications.

30 October: Atlanta, GA—The mayor orders investigation of recent incidents, including shootings, rock-throwing, and the 28 October beating of a black youth, Clifford Hines, by members of the neo–Nazi Columbians. On 31 October, a bomb wrecks the home recently purchased by black buyers in a formerly "white" neighborhood. Authorities jail four Columbians on 2 November, for inciting a riot. Jurors convict two defendants in February 1947.

1 November: Albany, NY—Democrats condemn Gov. Thomas Dewey for appointing klansman Horace Demarest to a post in state government.

14 November: Atlanta, GA—A tear-gas bomb drives the Columbians from their meeting hall.

December: Elba, AL—Klansmen kidnap and whip James Harden, a CIO organizer.

December: Madison, WI—State officials revoke the Klan's Wisconsin charter.

5 December: Washington, DC—President Truman creates an executive commission on civil rights.

1947

Tuskegee Institute reports one black lynched nationwide.

16 January: Lakeview, GA—Klansmen burn a cross at the home of high-school coach Walter Bowland. Bowland's wife kicks over the cross and berates the nightriders.

16 February: Atlanta, GA—Jurors convict Columbians member Homer Loomis of inciting a riot. A second jury convicts group leader Emory Burke on three misdemeanor charges, imposing a three-year sentence. On 27 March, conviction for usurping police earns Burke another 30-month sentence. The Columbians lose their state charter on 27 June and make the U.S. Attorney General's subversive list on 4 December.

9 April: CORE launches the first "freedom rides" to test desegregation aboard interstate buses.

3 May: Washington, DC—The U.S. Supreme Court bans restrictive covenants employed to segregate residential neighborhoods.

13 June: Atlanta, GA—The AGK voluntarily surrenders its state charter.

31 July: Birmingham, AL—A federal judge invalidates the city's segregated zoning law of 1926, in response to a lawsuit filed by black attorney Arthur Shores.

18 August: Birmingham, AL—Robert Chambliss bombs the home of Arthur Shores.

23 August: Atlanta, GA—Gov. M.E. Thompson announces a probe of recent floggings, including the attack on a CIO organizer and his wife at LaGrange. The same night, bombers strike the home of a reporter covering KKK political affiliations.

1948

Tuskegee Institute reports one black lynched nationwide.

20 February: Lakeview, GA—High school administrators fire coach Walter Bowland after a month-long campaign of KKK harassment.

2 March: Wrightsville, GA—300 robed klansmen march, announcing that "blood will flow in the streets of the South" if blacks seek equality. On 3 March, none of the town's 400 registered blacks cast ballots in the county primary.

9 March: Swainsboro, GA—Cardboard coffins labeled "KKK" appear on the porches of black homes overnight. On 10 March, less than one-third of the area's 1,500 registered black voters cast ballots in the primary election.

13 March: Columbus, GA—Klansmen seize three reporters covering a KKK rally, inject them with drugs, force them to drink whiskey, and photograph them in sexually compromising positions. Police arrest the three for public intoxication.

21 March: Mt. Vernon, GA—The NAACP charges that Klan threats kept 480 blacks from voting in the recent election.

April: Lake County, FL—Sheriff Willis McCall beats a black fruit picker for talking to CIO organizers. On the eve of state primary elections, a 250-car Klan motorcade tours Lake, Orange and Sumter Counties, burning a cross in Leesburg and warning blacks not to vote. McCall follows the procession in his patrol car but fails to intervene.

26 April: Birmingham, AL—Bull Connor warns leaders of the Sixteenth Street Baptist Church that klansmen may bomb it for hosting the SNYC.

9 May: Jackson, MS—Gov. Fielding Wright publicly warns blacks seeking equality to "make your home in some state other than Mississippi."

7 July: Birmingham, AL—Renegade "Dixiecrats" nominate Strom Thurmond as the States Rights Party's presidential candidate, with Fielding Wright for vice president. Numerous klansmen and professional anti–Semites use the convention as a recruiting forum.

14 July: Philadelphia, PA—Delegates from Alabama and Mississippi bolt from the Democratic National Convention in protest against the party's civil rights platform.

23 July: Stone Mountain, GA—10,000 persons attend a Klan rally.

23–25 July: Philadelphia, PA—The Progressive Party nominates Henry Wallace for president, with a public appeal for black votes.

26 July: Washington, DC—President Truman orders desegregation of the U.S. armed forces.

31 August: North Carolina—Whites hurling eggs and tomatoes disrupt speeches by presidential candidate Henry Wallace in Charlotte and Hickory.

8 September: Alston, GA—White gunmen execute a black man, Isiah Nixon, for voting. Jurors acquit one defendant on 5 November, accepting his plea of "self-defense."

27 September: Georgia—Progressive Party leaders seek federal protection, charging that their campaign workers have been kidnapped and threatened on two successive days.

November: Wrightsville, GA—City officials pass an anti-mask law.

1 November: Nashville, TN—Mayor Thomas Cummings says black neighborhoods have been "flooded" with threats against voting in tomorrow's election.

2 November: Montgomery, GA—Terrorists beat local NAACP leader D.V. Carter as he escorts black voters to the polls.

20 November: Lyons, GA—Robert Mallard, a black man, is ambushed and shot 18 times by klansmen wearing robes but no masks. GBI agents arrest Mallard's wife at his funeral, on 27 November, also jailing two other blacks and a white reporter as "material witnesses." Mrs. Mallard identifies five whites from the murder party, and police reluctantly arrest them on 4 December. A grand jury indicts them for murder on 10 December, but prosecutors later drop the case.

December: Milledgeville, GA—Police arrest three whites for firing into a black man's home, as part of a campaign to drive blacks from the area.

1949

Tuskegee Institute reports three blacks lynched nationwide.

18 February: Chattanooga, TN—Prosecutors charge a klansman with nine counts related to flogging and terrorist activities.

24 February: Columbus, GA—Klansmen kidnap three black high school students and drive them to the jail in Phenix City, Alabama, where they are questioned about ties to the NAACP. Afterward, the kidnappers beat them and shove them from a car, firing shots over their heads as they flee.

March: Dallas, TX—Bombers strike a black-owned home in a previously all-white neighborhood.

19 March: Birmingham, AL—Klansmen whip Jack Alexander and two other victims. State authorities charge A. Byrd Carradine, an officer of the Federated Klans, but jurors deadlock in his case on 12 December. Federal jurors convict Carradine and 17 other klansmen of civil rights violations on 6 October 1950.

26 March: Birmingham, AL—Klansmen bomb three black homes.

2 April: Hooker, GA—Sheriff John Lynch and Deputy William Hartline deliver seven blacks to a Klan flogging squad after reports of a "wild party." A federal grand jury convenes on 3 August, indicting Lynch, three deputies and eight klansmen. Samuel Green banishes the Trenton, Georgia, klavern on 8 August. Trial opens for 12 defendants on 22 November, ending with a directed acquittal of two defendants on 2 December and a mistrial for the rest on 17 December. A second federal jury convicts Lynch and Hartline on 9 March 1950, while acquitting eight other defendants. On 17 March, Lynch and Hartline receive one-year prison terms and $1,000 fines.

9 April: Chattanooga, TN—Police report that klansmen have whipped 16 victims in the past four months.

May: Birmingham, AL—Klansmen kidnap two white men without explanation, whipping one and forcing the other, a cripple, to watch.

2 May: Atlanta, GA—City officials pass an anti-mask ordinance.

21 May: Soperton, GA—Police jail two klansmen for assaulting the mayor. Moments later, two more flee town under police fire.

3 June: Dora, AL—Klansmen flog five victims, including two women, with prayers recited between whippings.

7 June: Birmingham, AL—A judge jails Grand Dragon William Morris for contempt of court, when he refuses to provide a list of Klan members. Briefly released in late July, Morris returns to jail on 2 August, after claiming the membership rolls have been stolen. The court releases him on 21 September, after he "recreates" the roster from memory.

11 June: Brookside, AL—Klansmen pack Steve Marshlar's diner, telling the Greek Orthodox proprietor, "We're tired of Catholics running this town."

11 June: Birmingham, AL—Klansmen whip Mrs. Hugh McDanal in her yard, beside a burning cross, on accusation of nude dancing, selling liquor to minors and running an "immoral house." Defendant Coleman Lollar faces trial on 26 October, winning acquittal on 29 October.

14 June: Birmingham, AL—Klansmen kidnap white navy veteran Billy Stoval and whip him for "immorality." Police call it the city's third flogging in a week.

28 June: Montgomery, AL—Gov. James Folsom signs an anti-mask law inspired by Klan violence.

1 July: Birmingham, AL—A grand jury convenes to investigate recent Klan terrorism. On 16 July, the panel indicts 16 klansmen (including Robert Chambliss) on 44 criminal counts.

2 July: Praco, AL—Authorities report at least a dozen Klan whippings in the past month.

16–19 July: Groveland, FL—Following reports that four black men have raped a white woman, locals and klansmen from Georgia run amok, burning homes and firing into others before the National Guard restores order. A civilian posse kills one of the suspects, Ernest Thomas, near Perry on 26 July. Jurors subsequently convict three others, based on fabricated evidence and confessions extracted through torture by Klan-allied Sheriff Willis McCall. A judge condemns two defendants on 8 September, while sentencing the youngest to life imprisonment. The U.S. Supreme Court orders a new trial for the two condemned defendants on 9 April 1951.

17 July: Iron City, GA—Mayor C.L. Drake repels eight carloads of klansmen from his home with gunfire, forcing the raiders to flee.

18 July: Birmingham, AL—Judge George Bailes, presiding over a grand jury investigation of Klan violence, admits being a klansman during 1920–25.

19 July: Goodwater, AL—Klansmen kidnap and flog white farmer S.G. Bailey and black Navy veteran S.J. Thomas.

19 July: Polk County, FL—Klansmen shoot up a black community, burning a cross at its school.

23 July: Chattanooga, TN—Bombers strike the first black home in a formerly all-white neighborhood.

24 July: Sandy Bottom, SC—Hooded men beat four blacks and fire shots at them, telling them, "This is your civil rights."

28 July: Birmingham, AL—Five klansmen demolish the new tower of WEDR, a black-owned radio station, causing $5,000 damage.

4 August: Ozark, AL—Police arrest four blacks under the new anti-mask law charging them with imitating klansmen to frighten black women from dating whites. One defendant receives a six-month jail term, another 60 days, while a third is remanded to juvenile authorities.

7 August: Iron City, GA—Mayor Drake and friends trade shots with a 16-car Klan caravan.

13 August: Birmingham, AL—Klansmen bomb two more black homes in a district zoned for white occupancy. Blacks fire on one of the fleeing cars.

18 August: Atlanta, GA—Samuel Green dies at home. Sam Roper replaces him as grand dragon of the AGK on 27 August.

23 August: Montgomery, AL—50 leaders of independent Klans from six states unite to form the Knights of the KKK of America, under Imperial Emperor Lycurgus Spinks.

24 August: Atlanta, GA—IRS agents impose a tax lien on the AGK for $9,332. Grand Dragon Sam Roper pays "under protest" on 12 September.

28 August: Peekskill, NY—White racists led by American Legionnaires beat and stone attendees at a scheduled concert by black singer Paul Robeson. Policemen join in the beatings. Southern Klan leaders claim the outbreak as proof of their strength in the North. Bigots stage a second riot against Robeson on 4 September.

28 August: Jacksonville, FL—Bill Hendrix announces his appointment as national adjutant of the Northern and Southern Knights.

24 September: Warrior, AL—Robert Chambliss strikes a reporter with a hammer at a KKK rally.

November: South Carolina—Thomas Hamilton founds the Association of Carolina Klans.

22 November: Atlanta, GA—Sam Roper and William Morris announce a "working agreement" between the AGK and Federated KKK, which soon falls apart.

18 December: Klan leaders Thomas Hamilton, Bill Hendrix and William Morris announce the merger of their independent factions to create the short-lived KKK of America.

1950

Tuskegee Institute reports one black lynched nationwide.

January: Alabama—Lycurgus Spinks expels J.B. Stoner from the Associated Klans of America for advocating mass-murder of Jews.

January: Nashville, TN—Builders drop plans for a new black housing project after a bomb blast and cross-burning.

18 February: Atlanta, GA—The state assembly defeats an anti-mask bill.

22 February: Pell City, AL—Klansmen try to kidnap Charlie Hurst, a white opponent of the KKK. Hurst dies in the exchange of gunfire, while his son is wounded. One of the raiders, Rev. Roy Heath, kills himself in Talladega on 26 February. Jurors convict Charles Carlisle of manslaughter on 28 June, resulting in a 5-year prison term. Defendant C.M. Hunter dies in a knife fight prior to trial, on 1 September. Prosecutors dismiss murder charges against Alabama's grand dragon, Rev. Alvin Horn, on 13 October 1952.

2 March: Eastman, GA—Klansmen kidnap and flog Jessie Goodman, a black farmhand accused of theft. A white farmer comes to his aid, trading shots with the kidnappers and forcing them to release Goodman.

17 March: Indianapolis, IN—Gov. Henry Schricker approves D.C. Stephenson's parole, on condition that Stephenson moves to Illinois and stays there. Stephenson agrees, then goes to Oklahoma instead.

25 March: Atlanta, GA—Sam Roper welcomes a rumored HUAC investigation of the Klan, but the probe does not occur.

25 March: Jackson, MS—Lycurgus Spinks announces relocation of his Klan headquarters from Montgomery, Alabama.

April: Birmingham, AL—Klan bombers strike a black minister's home, followed by the home of a black dentist nine days later.

May: Chattanooga, TN—For the second time in 10 months, klansmen bomb a black home in a "white" neighborhood.

1 July: Tulsa, OK—Birth of David Duke.

15 July: Birmingham, AL—Klansmen burn a cross and leave a threatening note at the home of CPUSA officer Sam Hall.

25 July: Soperton, GA—Will Robinson, a black man, becomes the latest victim in a series of Klan whippings that have prompted some residents to leave town. A white victim, Fred Mixon, moves to Savannah after recovering from wounds suffered in July.

12 August: Bishopville, SC—Leslie Boney, a YMCA swimming instructor, accidentally interrupts a KKK meeting. Klansmen drag him from his car, beating him as a suspected police spy. On 18 September, jurors convict Grand Dragon Tom Hamilton of conspiracy to incite mob violence.

26 August: Myrtle Beach, SC—Klansmen storm a black dance hall, trading 300 shots with defenders inside. They beat owner Charlie Fitzgerald and three others, shooting a fourth victim in the foot. The raiders then kidnap Fitzgerald for further whipping and cut off both his ears. At the club, authorities find policeman James Johnson dead, wearing his uniform beneath a Klan robe. On 31 August, police charge Grand Dragon Thomas Hamilton and 10 others as participants in the raid, releasing them on $5,000 bond. A grand jury refused to indict the suspects.

1 September: Pell City, AL—Unknown assailants at a carnival stab a Klan suspect in the Hurst murder case.

9 October: Charleston, SC—Klansmen stone the home of federal judge J. Waites Waring, who earlier struck down the state's "white primary."

9 November: Conway, SC—Klansmen raid a black family's rural home, beating Rufus Lee and his two sons, cutting off Lee's hair.

15 November: Robbinsdale, MN—Police arrest D.C. Stephenson for parole violation. On 23 November, the Minnesota Supreme Court orders him returned to Indiana.

December: Birmingham, AL—Klansmen bomb the home of a black woman who led a court fight against racial zoning laws. It marks the city's fifth racist bombing since spring 1949 and earns Birmingham the nickname "Bombingham."

5 December: Greenwood, SC—Klansmen whip Clayton Moore for "insulting a white woman. " Moore's son kills one of the floggers, while 13 others plead guilty to conspiracy charges on 12 February 1951. One defendant receives two years probation for aiding the prosecution, while the rest draw one-year jail terms.

1951

Tuskegee Institute reports one black lynched nationwide.

January: Atlanta, GA—State legislators pass a statewide anti-mask law and ban burning crosses on private property without the owner's consent.

17 January: Conway, SC—Klansmen whip two disabled war veterans, Sam and J.C. Gore.

18 January: Chadbourn, NC—Klansmen invade the home of a black woman, Evergreen Flowers, beating her with clubs and pistols, then shaving a cross in her hair with a razor.

22 January: Columbus County, VA—A black woman reports being whipped by nightriders.

March: Nashville, TN—Dynamite explodes in the yard of a home recently sold to blacks.

March: Atlanta, GA—Bombers strike a black home in a newly integrated neighborhood. Prosecutors indict AGK Grand Klaliff Charles Klein on 27 July 1952. Jurors deadlock in Klein's case on 25 January 1952.

31 March: Winter Garden, FL—Klansmen drag black victim Melvin Womack from his bed, beating and shooting him to death.

Spring: Jacksonville, FL—Klansman-attorney Edgar Waybright wins election as chairman of the Democratic Party in Duval County.

28 April: Columbia, SC—State legislators ban masks and unauthorized cross-burnings.

May: Birmingham, AL—Klansmen burn two black homes earlier damaged by bombs.

8 May: Tallahassee, FL—State legislators outlaw public wearing of masks and cross-burnings.

26 May: Norfolk, VA—Klansmen kidnap a black minister, Rev. Joseph Mann, telling him, "We want you to help us run some niggers out." They drive him to a black-owned home and force Mann inside before setting the house afire. Mann dies of burns on 29 May, after making a statement to police.

5 June: Miami, FL—Klansmen bomb an unfinished Jewish community center.

23 June: Columbia, SC—The state supreme court rules that racial segregation does not constitute discrimination. Judge E. Waites Waring dissents, subsequently becoming a target for KKK harassment.

July: Tabor City, NC—Klansmen snatch Bess, a dog belonging to anti-Klan journalist Horace Carter, and hold it captive for six months before it escapes and goes home.

July: Orlando, FL—Klansmen bomb a black apartment complex, the first of 12 bombings in six months.

14 July: Miami, FL—Klansmen defy the state's new law on cross-burnings by lighting four giant Ks around town. Police catch two men in the act. On 15 July, Bill Hendrix denies Klan involvement.

27 July: Tabor City, NC—Editor Horace Carter receives his first KKK threat, for an editorial condemning a 22 July Klan rally.

August: Miami, FL—Klansmen wound one person in a drive-by shooting at Carver Village, a black housing project.

11 August: Dallas, TX—Police report 13 black-owned homes bombed in the past 17 months.

25 August: Columbia, SC—Klansmen blackjack to spectators at a KKK rally, while police idly watch.

5 September: Swainsboro, GA—Klan floggers hospitalize black victim Otis Jordan.

22 September: Miami, FL—Klansmen bomb Carver Village.

30 September: Miami, FL—Nightriders vandalize a synagogue with anti-Semitic graffiti. On 1 October, congregants at a second synagogue find an unexploded bomb.

2 October: Dublin, GA—Klansmen beat Willie Brinson and his wife with a leather strap and axe handles, landing both in the hospital.

6 October: Fair Bluff, NC—Klansmen snatch Ben Grainger and Dorothy Martin, drive them into South Carolina, and whip both victims on charges of immorality and skipping church. On 18 February 1952, FBI agents and Sheriff Hugh Nance arrest 10 klansmen on federal kidnapping charges. Prosecutors charge an eleventh defendant on 12 May 1952. Trial begins on 13 May, in Wilmington. Jurors convict 10 defendants and acquit one. Six of those convicted receive prison terms, while three receive probation and one who turned state's evidence earns a suspended sentence. Seven defendants appeal their convictions in Richmond, Virginia, on 6 October 1952, claiming the floggings are justified as "church whippings." The court rejects their appeal.

8 October: Miami, FL—Klansmen toss a bomb at a Hebrew school, but the fuse extinguishes on impact.

11 October: Charbourn, NC—Klansmen flog black victim Dorsey Robinson.

20 October: Nichols, SC—Klansmen kidnap and flog George Smith. FBI agents arrest 19 suspects on 21 January 1953. Their federal kidnapping trial opens in Wilmington, North Carolina, on 18 May 1953. Jurors convict nine defendants. Their prison terms range from one to three years, with two sentences suspended.

30 October: Anderson, SC—Jurors convict Grand Dragon Tom Hamilton of criminal libel for his attacks on a journalist.

1 November: Allsbrook, NC—Sheriff's deputies arrest 14 klansmen at Cane Branch Baptist Church, for violating the state's anti-mask law. On 5 November, deacon A.L. Tyler files arrest warrants against the four deputies, for disrupting church services. Other congregants post their bail.

1 November: Miami, FL—Police find a stick of dynamite left by klansmen on the county courthouse steps.

2 November: Orlando, FL—Klansmen bomb a newly integrated ice cream stand.

6 November: Lake County, FL—Sheriff Willis McCall shoots two handcuffed prisoners, recently granted a new trial in the 1949 Groveland rape case. One victim dies, while the other survives. A grand jury rules the shooting "self-defense."

14 November: Chadbourn, NC—Klansmen kidnap Esther Floyd, a pregnant black woman, and cut off her hair for "going with white men." FBI agents arrest eight suspects on 25 February 1952, followed by four more arrests on 5 March.

30 November: Miami, FL—Klansmen bomb Carver Village again, causing $20,000 damage.

1 December: Whiteville, SC—Klansmen flog the first of six victims reported in less than two months.

2 December: Miami, FL—Bombs explode at Carver Village, a Jewish school, and a black home in a "white" neighborhood.

8 December: Whiteville, SC—Klansmen kidnap and flog Woodrow Johnson. A grand jury indicts 13 klansmen on 29 April

1952. Trial convenes on 9 May, and jurors convict 11 defendants of assault on 10 May, while acquitting two others. One klansman receives a 2-year prison term; 10 others have their 2-year terms suspended on payment of fines and court costs.

19 December: Columbus County, NC—KKK members whip tenant farmer Greer Wright.

23 December: Miami, FL—A defective fuse foils the bombing of a Catholic church.

25 December: Mims, FL—Klan bombers kill NAACP officer Harry Moore at his home. On 26 December, Gov. Fuller Warren assigns klansman Jefferson Elliott to investigate the bombing. Moore's wife dies from her injuries on 2 January 1952. Attorney General J. Howard McGrath orders an FBI investigation on 8 January. G-men question klansman Earl Brooklyn in Orlando, on 18 January, followed by a 20 January interview with suspect Tillman Belvin. On 29 January and 28 March, witnesses in Mims identify photos of Brooklyn as the man who stalked Moore prior to the bombing. G-men interview suspect Joseph Cox on 29 March 1952, prompting Cox to kill himself on 30 March. J. Edgar Hoover prepares a case summary for the DOJ on 28 April. The FBI's main informant refuses to testify on 1 May 1952. On 11 May 1952, two G-men urge Hoover to present Moore's case to a federal grand jury, but he refuses. Earl Brooklyn dies on 25 December 1952. Hoover marks the Moore case "inactive" on 1 July 1954 and formally closes it on 19 August 1955.

25 December: Nakina, NC—Three armed klansmen order white farmer Dan Ward to evict a black sharecropper from his land. Ward charges the knights with trespass and assault. At trial in January 1952, they receive five years probation and $1,000 fines.

29 December: Hallsboro, NC—Klansmen kidnap Grier Wright and flog him in Green Swamp.

30 December: Fort Payne, AL—Klansmen bomb the home of a woman who earlier stopped them from burning a cross in her yard.

1952

1 January: Hallsboro, NC—Klansmen drag L.W. Jernigan from his home and whip him.

12 January: Orlando, FL—Klansmen whip Arthur Holland and graze his scalp with a bullet "as a lesson to other Negroes."

13 January: Dallas, TX—A bomb explodes outside a black nightclub. Police call it the third "pointless" bombing in less than a month.

30 January: Cairo, IL—Bombers strike a black family's home. Police charge four whites with the crime on 2 February.

30 January: Whiteville, NC—Thomas Hamilton announces disbandment of the Fair Bluff klavern for "unklanish activities."

11 February: Gaffney, SC—Black candidate C.L.C. Glymph abandons his race for a city council seat after receiving Klan threats.

12 February: Tallahassee, FL—Police arrest Bill Hendrix for mailing obscene and libelous attacks against Gov. Warren, Drew Pearson and others. Jurors convict Hendrix of criminal libel on 20 February. He pays a $700 fine and receives a one-year suspended sentence.

27 February: Tabor City, NC—Klansmen steal and presumably kill a second dog owned by journalist Horace Carter.

6 March: South Carolina—FBI agents obtain a former Florida klansman's confession to five whippings since 1949.

7 March: Lumberton, NC—Police jail 16 klansmen on various misdemeanor charges.

10 March: Orlando, FL—FBI agents obtain a klansman's admission of lying about his KKK membership on a federal job application.

19 March: Orlando, FL—A klansman admits participation in three floggings, one performed with Harry Moore murder suspect Earl Brooklyn.

4 May: North Carolina—Two weekly newspapers receive Pulitzer Prizes for their anti-Klan reportage.

6 May: Lake County, FL—Willis McCall wins his third term as sheriff.

23 May: Whiteville, NC—Authorities charge Grand Dragon Tom Hamilton with conspiracy in the Evergreen Flowers whipping. He surrenders on 24 May and later pleads guilty, receiving a 4-year prison term on 30 July 1952. He surrenders to begin his prison time on 1 October. Authorities parole Hamilton on 23 February 1954.

20 June: Whiteville, NC—A grand jury indicts 25 klansmen in various flogging cases, followed by 18 more indictments on 22 June. Before summer's end, 63 klansmen draw terms ranging from 10 months to 6 years in the whipping of 10 victims. Ten klansmen enter prison on 1 September 1952, while 24 others pay fines totaling $15,850 and receive suspended sentences.

1 October: Louisville, KY—Federal prosecutors indict Emmett Carr for failure to divulge his KKK membership on a job application at Paducah's nuclear energy plant.

4 October: Washington, DC—Attorney General McGrath announces the creation of a federal grand jury to investigate Klan terrorism in Florida. The panel indicts three klansmen and a female KKK associate for perjury on 29 December.

30 December: Goretown, NC—Klansmen stage their first rally since Grand Dragon Hamilton's imprisonment.

1953

5 March: Miami, FL—A second federal grand jury convenes to investigate Klan violence in Florida. The panel issues its final report on 25 March, calling the "sadistic and brutal" KKK a "cancerous growth ... founded on the worst instincts of mankind." The panel indicts seven more klansmen for perjury on 3 June. Klan attorney Edgar Waybright moves to quash the indictments on 19 June, citing lack of federal jurisdiction. A federal judge dismisses one indictment on 30 December 1953, then drops the rest on 11 January 1954, denying the prosecution's motion for a rehearing on 25 June 1954. Federal authorities drop their appeal on 2 September 1954.

3 May: New York City—The NAACP and American Jewish Council report no lynchings in 1952, but they list at least 10 racist bombings of homes, public buildings and houses of worship during 1952.

5 May: Cleveland, OH—Explosives damage a black minister's home, while a second bomb planted next door fails to detonate. Two miles away, nightriders hurl a bottle containing a note signed "KKK" through the window of a third black-owned house.

August: Houston, TX—Bombs strike several black-owned homes.

3 August: Live Oak, FL—Ruby McCollum, a pregnant black woman, fatally shoots her white lover. The victim, Dr. Clifford Adams, is a klansman recently elected to the state senate. Klansmen in mufti patrol the streets to "keep things quiet," while McCollum is ruled insane and dispatched to a state asylum. The court refuses to acknowledge that Dr. Adams is the father of her child.

6–24 August: Norfolk County, VA—Police report three racist bombings within 18 days.

26 September: Mobile, AL—Klansman Elmo Barnard kills a 15-year-old black youth at his gunshop, during an alleged burglary.

October: River Junction, FL—C.L. Parker announces that his United Klan will accept black members into a segregated Negro Knights organization. None accept the offer.

1954

17 May: Washington, DC—The U.S. Supreme Court issues its *Brown v. Board of Education* ruling on school desegregation.

27 June: Louisville, KY—Bombers strike a black home in a previously all-white neighborhood. A cross was previously burned at the site, followed by stoning and drive-by shootings. Police frame and imprison a white man who purchased the home for black friends.

11 July: Indianola, MS—Whites organize the first Citizens' Council to oppose school integration "by all lawful means."

1 September: Pascagoula, MS—Klansmen burn a cross and leave a threatening note at the home of *Chronicle* editor Ira Harkey.

31 December: Media sources report 195 racist bombings and arson incidents during 1954.

1955

7 May: Belzoni, MS—White gunmen murder Rev. George Lee, a black NAACP activist. The sheriff blames "some jealous nigger."

31 May: Washington, DC—After a year with no visible progress, the Supreme Court orders school integration to proceed "with all deliberate speed."

21 June: Wadley, AL—An armed white mob disrupts an integrated meeting.

13 August: Brookhaven, MS—White gunmen murder Lamar Smith on the courthouse lawn, for urging blacks to register and vote.

13 August: Florence, SC—Klansmen assault Charles Moore, editor of the *Morning News,* as he observes a cross-burning.

September: Lake City, SC—A Klan motorcade circles the home of Rev. Joseph Delaine, a black litigant in a school-desegregation case, smashing windows with bricks and bottles. Previously, arsonists burned Delaine's home in Summerton.

18 September: Mobile, AL—100 klansmen in 18 cars burn a 10-foot cross at Dorothy Daponte's home, protesting her efforts to enroll her black maid's child in an all-white school. The knights burn a second cross, at the home of a Daponte friend, on 25 September.

October: Birmingham, AL—Asa Carter founds the North Alabama Citizens' Council.

6 October: Lake City, SC—Klansmen burn Rev. Delaine's church. On 10 October, Delaine trades shots with nightriders outside his home.

15 October: Loxley, AL—Parishioners welcome klansmen bearing cash at the Missionary Baptist Church.

22 October: Mayflower, TX—Acting in retaliation for construction of a new black school, white gunmen fire into a black café, killing 16-year-old John Reese and wounding two other victims.

24 October: Atlanta, GA—Eldon Edwards receives a state charter for the U.S. Klans.

1 December: Montgomery, AL—Police arrest black seamstress Rosa Parks for refusing to yield her bus seat to a white passenger, thus launching the city's historic bus boycott.

1956

30 January: Montgomery, AL—Klansmen bomb the home of Rev. Martin Luther King, Jr., black leader of a local bus boycott.

1 February: Montgomery, AL—Klansmen bomb the home of civil rights activist E.D. Nixon.

3–4 February: Tuscaloosa, AL—Klansmen and white students riot at the University of Alabama, protesting the admission of black coed Autherine Lucy. Those arrested include klansman Robert Chambliss. Another outbreak on 6 February prompts Lucy's expulsion. Chambliss and other jailed rioters subsequently file lawsuits against Lucy for "harassment."

18 February: Columbus, GA—A white gunman murders Dr. Thomas Brewer, local NAACP leader. Police deny that race was a motive.

9 March: Washington, D.C.—FBI Director J. Edgar Hoover tells President Eisenhower's cabinet that the KKK is "pretty much defunct."

25 March: Atlanta, GA—Klansmen bomb a black home in an integrated neighborhood.

23 April: Washington, DC—The U.S. Supreme Court agrees to review a lower court's ruling banning segregation in interstate bus travel.

28 May: Tallahassee, FL—Klansmen burn a cross at the home of a black coed earlier arrested for refusing to ride at the back of a city bus. Blacks begin a citywide bus boycott on 30 May.

June: Centreville, MS—Nine members of the black Taplin family die when arsonists burn their home, mistaking it for the house of a neighbor who kept a white mistress.

5 June: Montgomery, AL—A federal judge rules segregated seating on city buses unconstitutional. The U.S. Supreme Court upholds that decision on 13 December. Federal marshals serve the desegregation order in Montgomery on 20 December.

6 June: Memphis, TN—Klansmen burn a cross at the home of a black defendant in a bus desegregation case.

15 June: Kingstree, SC—Nightriders fire into a black religious meeting.

2 July: Atlanta, GA—Bombers strike a black home in a newly integrated neighborhood.

13 July: Camden, SC—Following proposals for an integrated work camp at the Methodist-run Mather School, klansmen burn a cross on campus and anonymous callers threaten to destroy the school.

23 July: Americus, GA—A bomb wrecks the roadside vegetable stand operated by members of Koinonia Farm, an integrated commune.

28 July: South Carolina—Klan rallies protest the *Brown* decision at Columbia and Hartsville.

1 August: Atlanta, GA—Eldon Edwards dies of a heart attack.

23 August: Charlottesville, VA—John Kasper disrupts a meeting of the Virginia Council on Human Relations, while klansmen burn a cross outside.

25 August: Montgomery, AL—Klansmen bomb the home of Rev. Bob Graetz, a civil rights activist.

25 August: Clinton, TN—John Kasper arrives in town to protest impending school integration. Police briefly jail him for disturbing the peace on 27 August. On 28 August, Kasper leads 100 whites in a demonstration at the town's high school. A second protest on 30 August draws 300 whites and lands Kasper in jail for eight days. Asa Carter leads the next protest rally, on 31 August, while racists march on the mayor's home and threaten to bomb it if Kasper is not released. Civilian volunteers use tear gas to rout the riotous mob, after gunmen fire on the home of the judge who ordered Kasper's arrest. Clinton's aldermen declare a state of emergency on 1 September and petition the governor for help. State police and National Guardsmen arrive with seven tanks on 3 September, to restore order. Kasper posts bond on 6 September, under a permanent injunction banning further agitation. On 25 September, prosecutors arraign him on charges of sedition and inciting a riot. Kasper's trial begins on 5 November. Jurors acquit him on 20 November. On 23 July 1957, a new jury convicts Kasper and six others of violating federal injunctions. Kasper enters prison in November 1957. At his parole, in August 1958, the reception committee includes Bill Hendrix, John Crommelin, and bomber George Bright.

28 August: Mansfield, TX—Whites post three black dummies bearing racist placards on Main Street and at a high school scheduled for integration. On 31 August a white mob gathers at the school. The mob returns on 5 September, barring black students from enrolling.

4 September: Oliver Springs, TN—Violence erupts over rumors of school integration. Two bombs explode in a black neighborhood, while a mob of 250 armed whites terrorizes black motorists. The mob wounds a deputy sheriff, and a black driver shoots one of the men attacking his car. National Guardsmen are dispatched from

Clinton, one of them stabbed by white thugs on arrival. Guardsmen disperse another mob on 5 September, as whites maul seven newsmen, destroying their equipment and threatening their lives.

5 September: Alvarado, TX—A white mob gathers on opening day of the local high school, drawn by rumors of integration. No blacks appear, but the mob hangs six effigies, while klansmen burn a cross in a black neighborhood.

5–6 September: Sturgis, KY—Mob violence flares at the prospect of school integration. National Guardsmen charge the crowd to clear a path for a black student leaving the school, while whites beat a plainclothes state policeman. Nightriders tour the black district on 8 September, warning against school desegregation.

6 September: Clinton, TN—Several whites, released on bond from riot charges, assault reporters waiting outside the courthouse.

6 September: Clay, KY—A white mob bars two black children from elementary school and threatens reporters nearby. The mob returns on 7 and 10 September, with protesters rocking one black motorist's car. Black parents abandon their desegregation plans on 10 September.

8 September: Mt. Gay, WV—125 whites bar teachers and pupils from a newly integrated grade school, shoving one black parent down a flight of stairs.

10 September: Texarkana, TX—300 whites bar two black students from entering a junior college.

18 September: Clarendon County, SC—NAACP organizer Bill Fleming reports that nightriders have twice fired on his house in recent days, while arsonists have burned his uncle's church.

27 September: Mobile, AL—Klansmen burn a "white" home briefly occupied by blacks, vacated after several shootings and rock-throwing incidents.

29 September: Atlanta, GA—3,000 klansmen gather outside town, for the largest rally since World War II.

October: Clinton, TN—125 carloads of klansmen parade through town, burning four crosses and chasing reporters away from a KKK rally.

6 October: Newton, GA—A white gunman murders a black woman, Mrs. M.A. Rigdon.

6 October: Warrior, AL—John Kasper addresses a KKK rally with Asa Carter and Kenneth Adams.

27 October: Wildwood, FL—Klansmen take Jesse Woods, a black man, from jail and whip him for "insulting a white woman" while intoxicated. Police charge seven suspects, but jurors acquit them on 12 December, after witnesses recant their testimony.

November: Summerville, GA—Klan threats close a high school's football field, where two black teams are scheduled to play.

24 November: Montgomery, AL—1,000 gather at a Klan rally outside town.

December: Kershaw, NC—Klansmen burn a black home.

December: Americus, GA—Drive-by shootings cause $300 damage to Koinonia Farm's roadside vegetable stand.

4 December: New Orleans—Whites beat Rev. Paul Turner, a white minister, as he escorts black children to a newly integrated school.

5 December: Montgomery, AL—Klansmen fire a shotgun blast into Martin Luther King's home.

19 December: Birmingham, AL—Klansmen fire shots at an integrated city bus.

20 December: Indianapolis, IN—Gov. George Craig grants D.C. Stephenson a discharge from his life prison term.

23 December: Montgomery, AL—Klansmen fire a shotgun blast into Martin Luther King's home.

25 December: Birmingham, AL—Robert Chambliss bombs the home of a black activist, Rev. Fred Shuttlesworth. The blast damages several nearby houses.

27–28 December: Montgomery, AL—Asa Carter announces plans for white "Minutemen" to patrol integrated buses. Klansmen fire on three buses, wounding a black woman on 28 December. Authorities resegregate bus seating to avert further violence, but racists still beat a black girl disembarking from another bus.

28 December: Camden, SC—Klansmen kidnap and flog the local high school's band director, Guy Hutchins, for "preaching integration." SLED agents arrest six suspects on 3 January 1957.

31 December: Birmingham, AL—Klansmen bomb a black home in a newly integrated neighborhood.

1957

January: Beaumont, TX—Segregationists bomb the city auditorium.

1 January: Montgomery, AL—Klansmen fire on a store owned by relatives of a bus boycott leader, and into the home of integrationist Rev. C.K. Steele, while burning a cross at Steele's church.

5 January: Clinton, TN—Police report a fourth bomb blast near an integrated high school.

9 January: Montgomery, AL—Klan bombs damage four black churches and the homes of two civil rights leaders.

10 January: Mobile, AL—Klansmen bomb a black home and attempt two other bombings, while burning crosses outside three more homes.

11 January: Chattanooga, TN—Two firebombs damage an interstate bus from which segregation signs have been removed.

15 January: Americus, GA—Klansmen bomb Koinonia Farm's roadside market, causing $5,000 damage.

23 January: Montgomery, AL—In a case of mistaken identity, klansmen kidnap black deliveryman Willie Edwards and force him at gunpoint to leap from a river bridge. He drowns, his body found on 26 January. Police list his death as accidental until 1976, when one of the klansmen confesses.

23 January: Birmingham, AL—Police briefly detain Imperial Wizard Asa Carter for shooting two of his klansmen in a personal dispute.

23 January: Chattanooga, TN—Klansmen detonate a bomb outside a home recently shown to black prospective buyers.

27 January: Montgomery, AL—Klansmen bomb a black home and fire into the home of a TV newscaster.

28 January: Montgomery, AL—Klan bombs damage a black home and a taxi stand owned by blacks. Martin Luther King finds an unexploded bomb at his home. Police arrest five klansmen for the bombings, two of them confessing on 10 February. At trial, jurors acquit both bombers, despite their confessions. Police free three others without trial, in a general amnesty extending to blacks charged with running an illegal boycott.

28 January: Birmingham, AL—Asa Carter and his brother scuffle with police during a Klan meeting.

February: Knoxville, TN—Klansmen bomb the city auditorium.

February: Charlottesville, NC—Klansmen bungle their attempted bombing of a black school.

13–14 February: New Orleans—Black delegates organize the SCLC, with Dr. Martin Luther King, Jr., as its leader.

14 February: Clinton, TN—A suitcase bomb explodes on the street in a black neighborhood, injuring two persons and shattering windows in 20 homes. The blast, audible for 20 miles, is Clinton's eighth racist bombing in recent months.

March: Mobile, AL—Klansmen bomb a black home in an integrated neighborhood.

March: Beaumont, TX—Racist bombers damage a truck, home and church owned by white "moderates."

16 March: Cleveland, TN—Speakers at a Klan rally denounce John Kasper as a "troublemaker" and race traitor who has dated black women.

22 March: Americus, GA—Nightriders fire shots at Koinonia Farm.

7 April: Wilmington, DE—Bombers strike a black home.

28 April: Bessemer, AL—Klansmen bomb a black church and the home of a black labor leader.

May: Chattanooga, TN—Klansmen bomb a black home in a newly integrated neighborhood.

11 May: Clinton, TN—Klansmen eject John Kasper from a KKK rally.

19 May: Americus, GA—Klan bombs damage three stores, two of which do business with Koinonia Farm.

July: Birmingham, AL—Klansmen bomb another black home on "Dynamite Hill."

23 July: Greenville, SC—Klansmen whip Claude Cruell, a black man, for baby-sitting his white neighbor's children. Jurors convict six floggers in January 1958, imposing prison sentences of one to six years.

August: Jersey, TN—Bombers strike a black home.

2 August: Wilmington, DE—Racists bomb another black home.

4 August: Nashville, TN—Police disrupt a Klan rally against school integration, featuring John Kasper.

8 August: Evergreen, AL—Klansmen whip four blacks, including Rev. Clifford Sheppard. Police call it the state's second flogging in one week.

9 August: Maplesville, AL—Klansmen flog six blacks.

28 August: Nashville, TN—John Kasper announces a campaign of harassment against black parents whose children enroll at integrated schools.

29 August: Washington, DC—Congress passes the 1957 Civil Rights Act.

2 September: Birmingham, AL—Klansmen kidnap and castrate a black man, Edward Aaron, as part of an initiation ceremony. Police jail six suspects on 7–8 September, with two confessing in custody. The first of four defendants charged receives a 20-year prison term on 7 November, with three others subsequently drawing identical terms. Gov. George Wallace releases all four in 1964–65, before completion of their statutory minimum terms.

4 September: Little Rock, AR—White mobs and National Guardsmen mobilized by Gov. Orval Faubus bar black students from Central High School. Klansmen burn a cross at the mayor's home on 6 September.

5 September: Prattville, AL—Klansmen fire shots at a black motorist, Rev. W.J. Bonner, who was active in the Montgomery bus boycott.

6 September: Levittown, PA—Klansmen burn a cross to intimidate black residents. Howard Bentcliffe pleads guilty to the offense on 26 February 1958.

9 September: Nashville, TN—A white mob stones black students and their parents outside Hattie Cotton School. Klansmen bomb the school on 10 September, with seven subsequently arrested.

9 September: Birmingham, AL—Klansmen beat Rev. Fred Shuttlesworth as he tries to enroll four black children in a white school.

10 September: Little Rock, AR—30 whites bar black students from Central High School.

23–25 September: Little Rock, AR—Riotous mobs protest enrollment of black students at Central High School. Pres. Dwight Eisenhower sends federal troops under Gen. Edwin Walker when Gov. Faubus refuses to intervene. The soldiers remain in place until 27 November, with federalized National Guardsmen left on duty until 8 May 1958.

October: Greensboro, NC—Klansmen bomb a black home.

October: Chattanooga, TN—Bombers strike two black homes.

25 October: Chattanooga, TN—Authorities grant a charter to the Dixie Klans, led by Harry and Jack Brown.

November: Charlotte, NC—Klansmen attempt to bomb a synagogue.

November: Chattanooga, TN—Klansmen bomb another black home.

November: Atlanta, GA—Eldon Edwards announces the purchase of land for construction of a new imperial palace.

1 November: Bessemer, AL—Klansmen bomb the home of a black integrationist.

20 November: Gaffney, SC—Klansmen bomb the home of a white woman who advocated racial moderation, then return to burn a cross in her yard on 23 November. Police arrest five bombing suspects on 7 December.

25 November: South Carolina—Delegates to a klonvocation of the Association of South Carolina Klans elect new officers for 1958.

December: Cowpens, SC—Racists bomb a black home.

December: Birmingham, AL—Klan bombs strike five black homes on "Dynamite Hill." A bombing on 7 December marks the city's seventh since terrorism resumed in 1956.

1958

January: Little Rock, AR—Klansmen bomb the home of an NAACP official.

1 January: Charlotte, NC—A Klan bomb damages the marquee of an integrated drive-in theater.

12 January: Lumberton, NC—Klansmen target Lumbee Indians with two fiery crosses.

18 January: Maxton, NC—Lumbee Indians raid a Klan rally held to protest mingling of whites and Indians in Robeson County. Klansmen flee on foot as Lumbees shoot up their cars, seizing regalia and loudspeakers. Authorities declare Grand Dragon James Cole a fugitive on 21 January. Jurors convict Cole and Grand Titan James Martin of inciting a riot on 14 March. Cole receives a sentence of 18–24 months, while Martin receives 6–12 months. An appellate court later reverses both verdicts. Following new convictions on 4 May 1959, Cole and Martin pay $250 fines.

19 January: Chattanooga, TN—A bomb causes $1,000 damage to a black school.

19 January: Tulsa, OK—Bombers damage a black home.

20 January: Little Rock, AR—Police defuse a bomb at a newly-integrated high school.

27 January: Chattanooga, TN—Klansmen bomb an integrated YWCA facility.

27 January: Columbus, GA—A bomb shatters windows of several black homes.

February: Chattanooga, TN—Klansmen bomb a newly-integrated school.

9 February: Gastonia, NC—Police find an unexploded bomb outside a synagogue.

15 February: Charlotte, NC—Police catch two klansmen, Imperial Wizard Lester Caldwell and Jack Ayscue, planting a bomb at a newly desegregated school. Officers arrest four other klansmen later in the evening. On 21 February, jurors convict five knights of illegal cross-burning, resulting in payment of fines. Their felony trial begins on 3 March, climaxed with conviction and imprisonment of three defendants on 20 March. Jurors acquit two other klansmen.

17 February: Atlanta, GA—Klansmen bomb a black home in a newly-integrated area.

20 February: Birmingham, AL—Klansmen bungle the bombing of a black church.

13 March: Tallahassee, FL—Gov. LeRoy Collins orders all Florida sheriffs to ban KKK and NAACP demonstrations "calculated to incite riot or disorder."

16 March: Miami, FL—Bombers strike a synagogue.

16 March: Nashville, TN—Racists bomb another synagogue.

17 March: Atlanta, GA—Klansmen bomb an unoccupied house, recently purchased by blacks in a "white" neighborhood.

27 April: Jacksonville, FL—Klansmen bomb a black school and a synagogue.

28 April: Birmingham, AL—Congregants find an unexploded bomb outside a synagogue.

3 May: Jacksonville, FL—Police from 29 southern cities convene to organize the Southern Conference on Bombing, pledged to solve 46 blasts recorded since 1 January 1957. Birmingham's Bull Connor is among the key participants, ensuring that the crimes remain unsolved.

8 May: Birmingham, AL—William Morris meets with Bull Connor to discuss means of entrapping J.B. Stoner in a bomb plot. On 14 June, Morris and Stoner discuss a proposed bombing of Fred Shuttlesworth's church with two undercover policemen. Stoner meets the detectives again on 21 June, accepting $100 as a "good faith" down-payment for the bombing contract. Two NSRP members bomb the church on 29 June, but police fail to arrest them, afterward suppressing evidence of the bungled "sting" for two decades.

17 May: Bessemer, AL—Klansmen bomb a black home.

24 May: Santiago, Chile—Police arrest several klansmen linked to the Aryan Knights of Texas.

29 May: Birmingham, AL—Vandals smear a black-owned radio station with KKK graffiti.

21 June: Beaumont, TX—Bombers strike the home of a white professor at an integrated college.

2 July: Columbus, GA—Klansmen bomb a black home.

7 July: Durham, NC—Bombers strike the home of a white minister in charge of the local Human Relations Committee.

17 July: Birmingham, AL—Blacks capture klansmen Ellis Lee and Crawford Neal at the scene of a bungled house bombing. In custody, the defendants name accomplice Herbert Wilcutt. All three receive 3-month jail terms on 4 May 1959.

5 August: Memphis, TN—Racists bomb a black church.

19 August: Oklahoma City, OK—The NAACP Youth Council launches sit-in demonstrations at whites-only lunch counters.

24–25 August: Deep Creek, NC—Arsonists raze two rural schools scheduled for racial integration.

27 September: Saraland, AL—State police charge seven whites, including the police chief, with burning crosses to intimidate blacks. Prosecutors claim the arrests are related to the 6 August slaying of Saraland's mayor, but they file no murder charges.

1 October: Wheelwright, KY—A white stone-throwing mob forces closure of a newly-integrated school.

5 October: Clinton, TN—Three dynamite blasts destroy an integrated school.

8 October: Greensboro, NC—A judge fines two klansmen for damaging property owned by an NAACP leader and another black victim.

12 October: Atlanta, GA—NSRP members bomb a synagogue. George Bright faces trial on 1 December, with jurors deadlocked on 10 December. A second jury acquits him in January 1959, while authorities drop all charges against his codefendants.

13 October: New York City—ADL spokesmen report 46 racist bombings or attempted bombings since 1 January.

14 October: Chicago, IL—Bombs destroy two black homes.

14 October: Peoria, IL—Bombers strike a synagogue.

25 October: Clinton, TN—Klansmen bomb an integrated school.

November: Arlington, VA—George Lincoln Rockwell founds the American Nazi Party.

10 November: Osage, WV—Dynamite damages an integrated school.

1959

23 February: Chattanooga, TN—White racists riot against sit-in demonstrators.

7 April: Wilmington, DE—Bombers strike a black home in a newly-integrated suburb.

25 April: Poplarville, MS—Lynchers, including a future county sheriff, remove black rape suspect Mack Parker from jail and drive him to Louisiana for summary execution. FBI agents identify the killers, but local authorities refuse to prosecute.

5 June: Little Rock, AR—A.C. Hightower charters the Arkansas realm of the U.S. Klans.

9 June: Little Rock, AR—One day after Arkansas Secretary of State C.G. Hall criticizes the KKK, arsonists set fire to his front porch. Rain douses the flames. Grand Dragon A.C. Hightower denies Klan involvement.

August: Atlanta, GA—J.B. Stoner writes to the NYPD, offering 5,000 klansmen to "clean up Harlem."

2 August: Wilmington, DE—Nightriders bomb a black home for the second time since April. On 8 August, police jail 13 whites on various related charges, while other white residents raise a defense fund for the accused.

10 August: Little Rock, AR—A.C. Hightower resigns as grand dragon, after quarreling with klansmen who advocate violent opposition to school integration.

12 August: Little Rock, AR—Authorities use fire hoses to disperse a racist mob outside the state capitol.

25 August: Little Rock, AR—Bombers strike a newly-integrated school. Police arrest two suspects.

27 August: Little Rock, AR—Two white women disrupt a school board meeting with tear-gas grenades.

7 September: Little Rock, AR—Bombs destroy the local school board office, damage the fire chief's car, and wreck property owned by the mayor. Police arrest five members of the Citizens' Council on 10–11 September. J.B. Sims pleads guilty on 18 September, receiving a 5-year prison term and a $500 fine. Jurors convict Jesse Perry on 28 October; he receives a 3-year sentence. Another jury convicts Council leader E.A. Lauderdale on 28 November, after testimony indicating that the bombings were planned at a KKK meeting. Lauderdale receives a 3-year sentence and $500 fine, but Gov. Faubus commutes the jail term to six months and refunds Lauderdale's fine. Gradon Beavers pleads guilty on 13 October 1960, receiving a 5-year sentence and $500 fine.

12 September: Montgomery, AL—Café owner James Peek, Jr., kills klansman William Horton, who allegedly threatened Peek's life for hiring black employees. Police charge Peek with first-degree murder, but jurors acquit him in May 1961.

October: Philadelphia, MS—Patrolman Lawrence Rainey fatally shoots a black man, Luther Jackson. Rainey and the town's police chief then beat a female friend of Jackson's for criticizing Rainey's action.

26 December: ADL investigators mark the start of a 9-week "swastika epidemic," logging 643 incidents of anti–Semitic vandalism in 42 states by February 1960.

1960

28 January: Kansas City, MO—Bombers strike a synagogue.

1 February: Greensboro, NC—Four black students from North Carolina A&T College stage a lunch counter sit-in. By 10 February the movement spreads to 15 cities in five southern states.

9 February: Little Rock, AR—Dynamite damages the home of a black student at Central High School.

21 February: Vienna, Austria—Police expose a neo–Nazi cell with links to the Aryan Knights of the KKK.

25 February: Montgomery, AL—Sit-in demonstrations begin. Klansmen armed with baseball bats assault blacks outside two variety stores on 27 February.

29 February: Jonesboro, GA—Klansmen elect H.H. Jones as imperial wizard of the Knights of the KKK.

7 March: Houston, TX—Four whites abduct Felton Turner, a black man, whipping him with chains, carving "KKK" on his abdomen, and leaving him bound upside-down in a tree.

15 March: Atlanta, GA—Sit-in demonstrations begin, soon countered by Klan pickets and random assaults on black protesters.

22 March: Petersburg, VA—Nightriders hurl a bottle containing a threat signed "KKK" through the window of a black minister active in the NAACP.

26 March: Klansmen coordinate nocturnal cross-burnings throughout the South.

27 March: Anniston, AL—A bomb explodes in a black family's yard. Later, police jail 13 whites for a series of cross-burnings.

12 April: Atlanta, GA—Bombers strike a black home in a newly-integrated area.

15 April: Chattahoochee, FL—Arsonists burn the home of a black rape-murder suspect.

15–17 April: Raleigh, NC—Activist students organize SNCC at Shaw University.

19 April: Nashville, TN—Bombs damage the homes of NAACP lawyer Z. Alexander Looby and a black city councilman.

19 April: Charleston, SC—A white mob attacks blacks picketing a department store.

24 April: Biloxi, MS—White rioters injure five blacks at a whites-only beach.

6 May: Washington, DC—President Eisenhower signs the 1960 Civil Rights Act, including federal penalties for racist bombings.

19 May: Ringgold, GA—A black housewife, Mrs. J. Green, dies when nightriders bomb her home.

23 June: Birmingham, AL—Gary Rowe joins the Alabama Knights as a paid FBI informant. He wins promotion to Night Hawk on 18 August.

1 July: Knoxville, TN—White mobs attack black protesters.

12 July: Little Rock, AR—FBI agents arrest three klansmen caught planting a bomb at Philander Smith College. Two hours later, a bomb damages a school warehouse and black homes nearby.

15 July: Chattanooga, TN—Klansmen burn the home of a black teacher. Nightriders also burned another house owned by the victim in 1956, and bombed his sister's restaurant in 1958.

13 August: Chattanooga, TN—Another bomb explodes in a newly-integrated neighborhood.

17 August: Chattanooga, TN—Two bombs damage the home of a white realtor who sold houses to blacks.

21 August: Chattanooga, TN—Klansmen bomb another black home.

26 August: Union, MS—Citizens' Council members beat a white minister helping to build a black seminary, afterward chasing several black workers and the town constable.

27 August: Jacksonville, FL—Klansmen riot against black sit-in demonstrators on "Axe-handle Saturday." Gunfire wounds two blacks, while police arrest 100 persons.

30 August: Buford, GA—Whites clash with black picketers, while five bombs damage stores and cars. Police blame out-of-town racists for the violence.

9 September: Chattanooga, TN—Klansmen burn a home in an integrated neighborhood.

2 October: Little Rock, AR—Bombers damage the car of a leading segregationist. Police deny a racial motive.

7 October: Whitesburg, GA—Klansmen flog a black couple.

27 October: Jackson, TN—White mobs assault black protesters.

8 November: Voters select John Kennedy as America's first Catholic president, despite Klan campaigning on nativist lines.

15 November: New Orleans—Rioting erupts during a Citizens' Council rally, with seven whites arrested at an integrated school.

18 November: Atlanta, GA—Klansmen bomb four homes in an integrated neighborhood.

23 November: Montgomery, AL—Police arrest five whites for threatening violence at a football game between two black teams.

On 24 November, officers find a KKK banner and a dummy bomb at the stadium.

29 November: Austin, TX—Bombers strike the building where members of the Texas University Religious Council have convened to plan integration of local restaurants.

29–30 November: New Orleans—White mobs demonstrate at an integrated Catholic school and the home of a priest who defied a white boycott.

3 December: St. Petersburg, FL—Police eject Klan leader Bill Hendrix from town, disrupting a planned racist demonstration.

5 December: New Orleans—White rioters stone cars carrying black children to an integrated school, while others damage the home of a liberal minister. On 7 December rioters stone the home of a white woman who defied their school boycott.

12 December: Atlanta, GA—Klansmen bomb a black elementary school, causing $5,000 damage. Police call it Atlanta's 18th racist bombing in four years.

1961

1 January: Greenville, MS—Gunmen on a motorcycle wound two blacks in a drive-by shooting.

5 January: Anniston, AL—Whites assault black protesters outside the courthouse where a white man faces trial for beating a black.

11 January: Athens, GA—600 whites riot at the University of Georgia, opposing enrollment of two black students. The nine rioters arrested include Grand Dragon Calvin Craig and seven other klansmen. School administrators suspend the black students on 12 January. On 15 January, campus security guards disarm an outsider who came seeking one of the new enrollees. On 19 January, authorities indict two students and nine adult Atlantans on riot-related charges.

18 February: Atlanta, GA—E.E. George resigns from the U.S. Klans.

21 February: Atlanta, GA—The UKA receives its state charter under Imperial Wizard Robert Davidson and Grand Dragon Calvin Craig.

1 April: Atlanta, GA—Robert Davidson formally resigns as imperial wizard of the U.S. Klans.

17 April: Bay of Pigs, Cuba—Cuban exiles trained in part by klansmen fail in their attempt to overthrow Fidel Castro.

4 May: Washington, DC—CORE's freedom riders begin their tour of Dixie.

9 May: Rock Hill, SC—Whites attack a busload of freedom riders.

11 May: Atlanta, GA—Birmingham policeman Tom Cook obtains a freedom ride itinerary and furnishes it to Alabama klansmen.

13 May: Talladega, AL—Klansmen whip three whites for allowing a black babysitter to discipline their children. Police arrest eight suspects on 23 May. One receives an 8-year prison term on 8 October.

14 May: Anniston, AL—Klansmen beat one busload of CORE freedom riders, then slash the tires of a second bus and burn it when it stops outside town. Federal prosecutors charge nine rioters with various offenses. Jurors deadlock at their first trial, while the judge at their second trial directs a verdict of acquittal on 3 November. Meanwhile, FBI agents identify one member of the first jury, L.M. Parker, as a klansman. On 28 November 1961, Parker receives a jail sentence for perjury (in falsely denying Klan membership when he was picked as a juror). Six rioters plead "no contest" to federal charges on 16 January 1962; one receives a jail term, while five others win probation by promising to sever all ties to the Klan.

14 May: Birmingham, AL—Klansmen and NSRP members beat CORE freedom riders, leaving one crippled for life. Police reluctantly arrest three rioters who overstay the deadline earlier imposed by Bull Connor for unrestrained mayhem.

20 May: Montgomery, AL—In a replay of Birmingham's riot, klansmen beat freedom riders while police make themselves scarce. That night, Attorney General Robert Kennedy sends U.S. marshals to protect a black church surrounded by whites, with congregants trapped inside. Federal judge Frank Johnson issues a temporary restraining order barring KKK interference with the freedom rides.

23 May: Washington, DC—New Jersey Rep. Charles Joelsen accuses UKA leaders of violating federal tax laws, by claiming that donations to the KKK are tax-deductible.

25 May: LaGrange, GA—Police jail five klansmen for trying to block passage of a CORE freedom bus at the state line. A judge fines the three on 29 May, for inciting a riot.

26 May: Rome, GA—Police arrest a local klansman for assaulting a reporter during the 14 May Birmingham riots.

2 June: Montgomery, AL—Judge Frank Johnson issues a preliminary injunction against KKK interference with the freedom rides.

16 June: Ocala, FL—Whites pummel two freedom riders at the bus depot. Police arrest the victims for assault.

16 June: Montgomery, AL—Gov. Patterson threatens to fire any state highway patrolmen who cooperate with FBI agents on hate crime investigations.

25 June: Jacksonville, FL—Leaders of the Florida KKK and the United KKK meet and merge to found the UFKKK.

8 July: Indian Springs, GA—Calvin Craig's UKA meets with Robert Shelton's Alabama Knights to finalize a merger.

22 July: Griffin, GA—Police arrest two klansmen for burning a cross in a black couple's yard.

21 August: Monroe, NC—Freedom riders arrive in town to lead civil rights demonstrations. Klan raids on the black community begin on 24 August, leaving one freedom rider wounded by gunfire and two others beaten on 25 August. NAACP members led by Robert F. Williams forcibly repel Klan motorcades on 26 August.

4 September: Atlanta, GA—Klan rally participants mob the police chief's car, after mistaking him for an FBI agent. Police jail Pennsylvania klansman Roy Frankhouser for assaulting an officer.

5 September: McComb, MS—A white mob beats a black man as he tries to register to vote.

25 September: Liberty, MS—State legislator E.H. Hurst fatally shoots black civil rights worker Herbert Lee in front of witnesses. A coroner deems the shooting self-defense.

16 November: Independence, MO—Police arrest D.C. Stephenson for molesting a 16-year-old girl. He pays a $300 fine and returns to Indiana, under a court order mandating his departure from Missouri.

29 November: McComb, MS—A white mob beats five freedom riders at a whites-only lunch counter. On 1 December, 700 whites menace the protesters, beating four out-of-town journalists. Rioters beat a carload of freedom riders on 2 December, and a segregationist assaults the editor of a "moderate" local newspaper on 3 December.

15 December: Birmingham, AL—Klansmen brawl with blacks at the Krystal Kitchen restaurant.

1962

16 January: Birmingham, AL—Klansmen bomb three black churches, damaging adjacent homes and a police car parked near the scene of one blast.

12 February: Macon, GA—Blacks launch a boycott of segregated city buses.

18 February: Shreveport, LA—Klansmen bomb a home under construction for NAACP leader C.O. Simpkins.

28 March: Birmingham, AL—Klansmen fire shots into the home of ACMHR treasurer Bill Shortridge.

11 April: Atlanta, GA—James Venable charters the Defensive Legion of Registered Americans.

24 April: Shreveport, LA—Klansmen bomb a black Masonic temple.

25 April: Talladega, AL—White rioters assault black protesters. Others hurl tear-gas grenades at the picket line from passing cars.

26 April: Bossier City, LA—Arsonists burn C.O. Simpkins's summer home.

May: Philadelphia, MS—Sheriff Ethel Barnett and Deputy Lawrence Rainey (both later identified as klansmen) beat a handcuffed black prisoner.

12–13 July: Savannah, GA—Whites riot against black protesters, climaxed by a rally of a racist group called Cavalcade of White Americans.

19 July: Birmingham, AL—UKA members plan to murder Rev. Fred Shuttlesworth during protests at a segregated café. Gary Rowe alerts the FBI, which in turn warns Shuttlesworth. He stays home, thus foiling the plot.

12 August: Albany, GA—City officials complain of incursions by "outsiders," Imperial Wizard Robert Shelton, Grand Dragon Calvin Craig, and members of the ANP.

17 August: Greenwood, MS—A mob of armed whites invades and vandalizes SNCC's office.

25 August: Monroe, NC—Klansmen wound one freedom rider in a drive-by shooting and beat two others on the street. On 26 August, racists armed with guns, knives and bottles mob a black picket line. Whites riot again on 27 August, injuring several blacks and shooting a policeman in the leg. That night, black residents trade gunfire with Klan raiders until dawn.

31 August: Lee County, GA—Klansmen fire into the homes of four blacks active in a voter registration drive.

1 September: Louisiana—Klansmen burn crosses at the state capital in Baton Rouge, at a black minister's home in Bastrop, at three black schools in Bosco and Hodge, and in 11 other north Louisiana towns.

5 September: Dawson, GA—Klansmen fire into a black home, wounding a civil rights worker. Police jail six suspects on 19 October.

5 September: Dallas, GA—Masked klansmen storm Kate Philpot's rural home, fleeing after Philpot's daughter fatally wounds Leroy Parks. On 19 October, jurors convict six surviving raiders of assault, riot, firing into an occupied dwelling, and violation of Georgia's anti-mask law.

7 September: New Orleans—Gunmen fire into an integrated Catholic school, while several others receive bomb threats.

9 September: Sasser, GA—Klansmen burn a black church.

9 September: Chickasawhatchee, GA—Klansmen burn a black church. FBI agents arrest a farmer who assaults them at the fire scene.

11 September: Ruleville, MS—Whites fire shotgun blasts into a black home, wounding two voter registration workers.

17 September: Dawson, GA—Nightriders burn another black church. Three defendants plead guilty to arson on 20 September.

19 September: Marksville, LA—Police jail two klansmen for assault and illegal cross-burning.

25 September: Macon, GA—Arson destroys the eighth black church burned by Georgia terrorists since 15 August.

28 September: Birmingham, AL—American Nazi Party member Roy James assaults Martin Luther King at an NAACP meeting.

30 September: Oxford, MS—Klansmen and white students riot to protest enrollment of black student James Meredith at the University of Mississippi. The outbreak leaves two white men dead, and some 375 injured, including 30 federal marshals wounded by sniper fire. Some 300 persons are arrested, mostly outside racists from Mississippi, Alabama, Louisiana and Tennessee. President Kennedy deploys 31,000 troops to restore order.

4 October: Greenville, MS—Klansmen burn a cross near the home of journalist Hodding Carter.

13 October: Birmingham, AL—Klansmen beat a spectator at a KKK rally, after he declares, "Mob violence is no answer to anything."

15 October: Pascagoula, MS—Snipers fire into the *Chronicle* office after editor Ira Harkey criticizes rioters at the University of Mississippi.

1 November: Pascagoula, MS—Nightriders fire shotgun blasts into Ira Harkey's home.

6 November: Alabama—George Wallace wins election as governor with Klan support.

14 December: Birmingham, AL—Klansmen bomb the New Bethel Baptist Church.

17 December: Birmingham, AL—Officials offer a $1,000 reward for information on recent bombings, increased to $3,000 on 18 December. By 11 April 1963, the unclaimed total reaches $87,125.

1963

11 January: Natchez, MS—Klansmen pursue two SNCC members, firing four shots into their car before they escape.

14 January: Montgomery, AL—Gov. Wallace delivers his "segregation forever" speech, adapted from KKK slogans by chief speech writer Asa Carter.

4 February: Mobile, AL—Klansmen burn a cross at the home of a white minister who urged desegregation of a local high school.

7 February: Bossier City, LA—Police arrest two klansmen for painting 30 "KKK" signs on walls and sidewalks.

20 February: Greenwood, MS—Arsonists destroy four buildings in the black business district, one day after SNCC received a truckload of food and clothes from Chicago. Police jail a SNCC member for calling it arson. He receives a 6-month jail term and a $500 fine for "inciting breach of the peace."

24 February: Greenville, MS—Klansmen machine-gun a carload of civil rights workers, wounding four.

28 February: Leflore County, MS—Drive-by gunmen wound James Travis, a black civil rights worker.

March: Greenwood, MS—Shotgun blasts damage the home of Moses Meredith, father of James.

2 March: Greenwood, MS—White gunmen fire shotgun blasts into a carload of blacks outside SNCC headquarters.

5 March: Birmingham, AL—Albert Boutwell leads Bull Connor in mayoral votes. He defeats Connor in a runoff election on 2 April.

6 March: Greenwood, MS—Drive-by gunmen wound four black voter registration workers outside a SNCC office.

8 March: Birmingham, AL—Edwin Walker addresses a "revival" meeting led by Billy James Hargis, before an audience packed with klansmen and NSRP members.

16 March: DeKalb County, GA—Police arrest UKA Grand Klokard John Brock and 37 others, including 10 children, during a wild party at the local klavern.

24 March: Birmingham, AL—Klansmen bomb a black home, injuring two occupants.

24 March: Greenwood, MS—Arsonists destroy a SNCC voter registration headquarters.

26 March: Greenwood, MS—Nightriders fire into a home linked to SNCC.

1–2 April: Macon, GA—White mobs attack black protesters at a segregated park, leaving one with stab wounds.

12 April: Clarksdale, MS—Racists firebomb the home of black civil rights activist Aaron Henry.

3 May: Birmingham, AL—Bull Connor deploys fire hoses and at-

tack dogs to disperse black demonstrators, arresting 450. The performance is repeated on 7 May, with 40 arrests.

4 May: Clarksdale, MS—The sheriff blames "lightning" for explosions that damage an NAACP member's store.

10 May: Birmingham, AL—City leaders and the SCLC reach an agreement on desegregation.

12 May: Birmingham, AL—Klansmen bomb Rev. A.D. King's home and the Gaston Motel, following a KKK rally. Black witness Roosevelt Tatum says a patrolman related to klansman Robert Chambliss planted the motel bomb. FBI agents charge Tatum with perjury on 28 June and he receives a 366-day prison term on 18 November.

12 May: Anniston, AL—Klansmen fire shots into a black church and two homes. Police arrest klansman Kenneth Adams on 20 May. Jurors convict him of assault in the residential shootings on 25 May, resulting in a 180-day jail term and $100 fine for each incident. On 8 April 1964, a separate jury acquits Adams of firing into the church.

17 May: Alexandria, LA—Klansmen burn a cross at the home of a black family related to a youth charged with raping a white woman.

27 May: Jackson, MS—Firebombers strike the carport of NAACP leader Medgar Evers.

2 June: Gainesville, FL—A white mob beats two persons and wounds one with gunfire during efforts to desegregate a theater.

6 June: Lexington, TN—500 armed whites rampage through a black neighborhood, where blacks resist with gunfire. One rioter dies, and a newsman is wounded. Police declare a state of emergency on 7 June, jailing 10 whites and 7 blacks on various charges.

7 June: Birmingham, AL—Bull Connor addresses a Citizens' Council rally, where a KKK meeting is announced for the same evening.

8 June: Clarksdale, MS—Nightriders shoot up the home of NAACP secretary Vera Page.

12 June: Jackson, MS—A sniper murders Medgar Evers at his home. Police charge Citizens' Council member and klansman Byron De La Beckwith, after finding his rifle at the scene. Beckwith faces trial on 27 January 1964, jurors deadlock on 7 February, followed by a second mistrial in April 1964.

13 June: Tuscaloosa, AL—Gov. Wallace briefly blocks black students from enrolling at the University of Alabama. Police arrest several carloads of UKA members, armed with a small arsenal including a bazooka, but a friendly judge releases them and orders return of all weapons.

14 June: Linden, AL—Klansmen burn a cross and throw rocks at the home of a minister who resigned his pulpit, rather than exclude blacks from his church.

17 June: Itta Bena, MS—Klansmen firebomb a black church.

18 June: Gillett, AR—Klansmen bomb a black church.

24 June: Canton, MS—Drive-by gunmen wound five blacks at a COFO voter registration rally.

26 June: Gulfport, MS—Bombers strike the home of a black doctor who doubles as local NAACP president.

30 June: Jackson, MS—Klansmen bomb a black home.

July: New York City—Police jail NSRP members for brawling with black picketers outside a restaurant, and for carrying illegal weapons in their car.

1 July: St. Augustine, FL—Klansmen trade shots with black guards at the home of a civil rights activist. Police jail three blacks.

7 July: Albany, GA—300 attend a UKA rally addressed by Grand Dragon Calvin Craig and city judge Clayton Jones.

11–12 July: Savannah, GA—White racists riot against black protesters. A mob spokesman declares that "the white people have shown remarkable restraint in not killing niggers wholesale."

13 July: Rosman, NC—White rioters rout campers from integrated Camp Summerland, stabbing one man and riddling a camp bus with gunfire, burning the gymnasium, then pouring gasoline into the lake and setting it afire.

20 July: Savannah, GA—Police Chief Sidney Barnes addresses a UKA rally, accepting the Klan's endorsement for mayor.

15 August: Birmingham, AL—Two tear gas bombs explode in a newly integrated store.

17 August: Spartanburg, SC—Connie Lynch shares the stage with Robert Shelton at a UKA rally.

21 August: Birmingham, AL—Klansmen bomb the home of black attorney Arthur Shores.

25 August: Birmingham, AL—The Cahaba River Group holds its first meeting.

26 August: Columbia, SC—Klansmen bomb the home of a black woman scheduled to enter the state university.

26 August: Buras, LA—Klansmen bomb an integrated Catholic school.

29 August: Folcroft, PA—White rioters bar a black couple from occupying their new home, and a firebomb damages the house. Police arrest seven whites for stoning cars on 30 August, finally restoring order on the 31st.

29 August: Montgomery, AL—A 75-car NSRP procession presents Governor Wallace with 30,000 signatures on petitions opposing school integration.

31 August: Jackson, MS—Klansmen bomb a black home.

1 September: Winnsboro, LA—Klansmen burn crosses at several schools.

3 September: Birmingham, AL—2,000 persons attend an NSRP rally.

4 September: Daisy City, AL—Robert Chambliss buys a case of dynamite, with caps and fuse.

4 September: Birmingham, AL—Klansmen bomb the home of Arthur Shores again, sparking a riot that leaves one person dead and 18 injured. Elsewhere, 125 NSRP members scuffle with police outside a newly integrated school. Eight are indicted for contempt of court on 23 September.

7 September: Birmingham, AL—Gov. Wallace addresses a UACG rally, with Robert Shelton, Edward Fields and Robert Chambliss in attendance.

8 September: Birmingham, AL—Klansmen bomb the home of black businessman A.G. Gaston.

10 September: Birmingham, AL—Police arrest 12 violent whites outside a high school. A concussion grenade explodes outside a black home.

12 September: Birmingham, AL—Three schools open with integrated classes. Two NSRP protest motorcades include 150 cars.

15 September: Anniston, AL—Whites mob and beat two black ministers at a white library.

15 September: Birmingham, AL—Klansmen bomb the Sixteenth Street Baptist Church, killing four girls and injuring a fifth. Black violence erupts in response, met by state troopers under Col. Al Lingo. During the riot, a policeman "accidentally" kills black youth Johnny Robinson, while 13-year-old Virgil Ware is murdered by two white teenagers linked to the NSRP.

16 September: Calhoun, FL—UFKKK members beat a 62-year-old white man for dating black women.

18 September: St. Augustine, FL—Klansmen beat four black NAACP members caught spying on a KKK rally. Sheriff L.O. Davis charges the victims and four of their attackers with assault. Jurors convict one of the blacks on 16 October, while another panel acquits one of the klansmen on 5 November. Prosecutors dismiss all charges against the other klansmen.

22 September: Birmingham, AL—Members of the Cahaba River Group hold a "kiss-of-death" meeting, vowing to murder anyone who reveals details of the 15 September church bombing.

25 September: Birmingham, AL—Klansmen detonate two shrapnel bombs in a black neighborhood.

26 September: Gardendale, AL—Charles Cagle guides FBI agents to a field outside town, where Robert Chambliss and John Hall allegedly concealed dynamite on 4 September. The agents find nothing.

29 September: Homestead, AL—Al Lingo meets with Arthur Hanes, Sr., Robert Shelton, and several UKA/UACG members before launching a series of raids to arrest bombing suspects. Those jailed include Charles Cagle, Robert Chambliss, John Hall, Ross Keith and Levi Yarbrough. On 1 October, Cagle leads Lingo to the same field near Gardendale that he visited with G-men on 26 September. This time, Lingo "finds" 130 sticks of dynamite. Police charge Cagle, Chambliss and Hall with illegal possession of dynamite. The city recorder finds them guilty on 9 October, imposing 180-day jail terms and $100 fines, then releases them on bond. Jurors acquit all three defendants on 16–18 June 1964.

29 September: Huntsville, AL—Klansman Hubert Page sits for an FBI polygraph test related to the 15 September church bombing.

1 October: Birmingham, AL—Thomas Blanton fails a polygraph test concerning his involvement in the 15 September church bombing. FBI agents search his home on 4 October and jail Blanton for assaulting a federal officer.

2 October: Birmingham, AL—Klansmen bomb a black butcher's shop.

6 October: Birmingham, AL—At a meeting of the Cahaba River Group, Robert Chambliss accuses Wizard Robert Shelton of conspiring with Gov. Wallace to link the klavern to the 15 September church bombing, thereby claiming outstanding rewards for the UKA.

9 October: Birmingham, AL—Bobby Cherry fails an FBI polygraph related to the 15 September bombing.

11 October: Birmingham, AL—Elizabeth Hood, a relative of Robert Chambliss, informs FBI agents of his admitted involvement in the 15 September bombing. G-men report the tip to J. Edgar Hoover on 12 October.

15 October: Whittier, CA—William Gale, founder of the California Rangers, meets with Connie Lynch and other KKK-NSRP members at the William Penn Hotel. Two of the 12 persons present are undercover policemen.

15 October: Selma, AL—Martin Luther King arrives to encourage SNCC's voter-registration volunteers.

19 October: Birmingham, AL—J.B. Stoner addresses an NSRP rally where Dr. King, Fred Shuttlesworth and Pres. John Kennedy are hanged in effigy. Witnesses note Robert Chambliss in the audience.

22 October: Detroit, MI—A witness to the 15 September Birmingham church bombing identifies Thomas Blanton's car from the scene. On 24 October she also picks Robert Chambliss from a photo lineup of suspects.

25 October: St. Augustine, FL—Gunfire kills a klansman as he rides with others, armed, through a black neighborhood.

26 October: College Park, GA—H.J. Jones deposes E.E. George as head of the U.S. Klans.

28 October: St. Augustine, FL—Klansmen fire into five black homes, throwing a hand grenade (which fails to explode) through the window of a sixth house.

29 October: Birmingham, AL—Klansman John Hall becomes an FBI informant. On 2 December he names the September church bombers as Thomas Blanton, Robert Chambliss and Troy Ingram.

31 October: Port Gibson, MS—Klansmen beat two civil rights workers. On 23 October 1964, police jail UKA member Myron Seale on charges of assault and battery with intent to kill. The officers also seize an arsenal of weapons from his home.

1 November: DeKalb County, GA—James Venable charters his National Knights of the KKK.

7 November: Lithonia, GA—E. E. George charters the Improved Order of U.S. Klans.

9 November: Quitman, GA—In conversation with a police informant, NSRP member Joseph Milteer predicts the place and manner of JFK's assassination. FBI agents question Milteer on 27 November, accepting his denials at face value. No mention of Milteer appears in the Warren Commission's report.

16 November: Tuscaloosa, AL—Two bombs explode on the state university campus, one near an integrated dormitory.

19 November: Tuscaloosa, AL—Another bomb explodes on campus, near the dorm housing a black coed. Police arrest five National Guardsmen on 22 December, and a grand jury formally indicts them on 8 January 1964.

20 November: Tuscaloosa, AL—FBI agents interview UKA Imperial Wizard Robert Shelton.

22 November: Dallas, TX—A sniper assassinates Pres. John Kennedy. Police arrest alleged communist Lee Harvey Oswald as a suspect. Transplanted Chicago gangster Jack Ruby murders Oswald on 24 November, during his transfer from Dallas Police Department headquarters to a more secure jail. Journalists later identify the officer in charge of the transfer, Lt. George Butler, as a klansman.

December: Mississippi—Douglas Byrd assumes office as temporary grand dragon for the Original Knights in Mississippi.

December: Wilkinson County, MS—Motorists find three blacks, two men and a woman, dead in a car 10 miles north of Woodville. Police and the press attribute their deaths to carbon monoxide poisoning, but a black mortician reports broken bones and gunshot wounds.

8 December: Dawson, GA—Klansmen fire 50 shots into a black civil rights worker's home, then hurl a bomb inside.

14 December: Mississippi—Dissident members of the Original Knights vote to defect and form the WKKKKM.

16 December: Washington, D.C.—The U.S. Supreme Court reverses a contempt citation against Edward Fields and another NSRP member for holding a banned rally at Fairfield, Alabama.

22 December: Hot Springs, AR—Arsonists burn the Roanoke Baptist Church after its pastor complains to the White House about local segregation.

1964

6 January: Birmingham, AL—Prosecutors refuse to charge a National Guardsman who confessed to detonating a bomb in a black neighborhood during October 1963. Residents did not report the blast, and no evidence remains.

18 January: Atlanta, GA—100 klansmen picket various newly-integrated downtown dining establishments.

18 January: Louisiana—Klansmen burn more than 150 crosses at black homes, churches and schools in five parishes.

19 January: Atlanta, GA—Klansmen pack a restaurant to keep out sit-in demonstrators and scuffle with protesters as they leave. Police arrest 78 persons.

23 January: Ratification of the 24th Amendment bans poll taxes in America.

25 January: Atlanta, GA—Klansmen brawl with black students during civil rights demonstrations.

31 January: Vicksburg, MS—Klansmen burn crosses at five locations in town.

31 January: Liberty, MS—Nightriders murder Louis Allen, a black witness to the 1961 slaying of Herbert Lee, at his home.

February: Atlanta, GA—James Venable creates the Committee of One Million Caucasians to March on Washington.

February: Charleston, MS—Klansmen trap two black youths in a white-owned grocery store, beating them with pistols and axe handles.

February: St. Augustine, FL—Klansmen burn the home of a black family whose child attends an integrated school. In a separate incident, racists beat a black man walking home from night school.

8 February: St. Augustine, FL—Klansmen fire four shotgun blasts into the home of NAACP leader R.N. Hayling, killing the family dog.

8–9 February: Birmingham, AL—The UKA holds its first known imperial klonvocation.

12 February: St. Augustine, FL—Klansmen burn a black family's car.

14 February: Natchez, MS—Klansmen kidnap and whip Alfred Whitley, a black employee at Armstrong Rubber Co.

15 February: Brookhaven, MS—Samuel Bowers leads 200 dissident klansmen out of the Original Knights to form the WKKKKM.

15 February: Natchez, MS—Klansmen lure black mortician Archie Curtis and an aide to a rural highway with false reports of a dying woman, then strip and beat them. Curtis moonlights as chairman of a black voter registration drive.

16 February: Jacksonville, FL—Klansmen bomb the home of a 6-year-old black boy who attends an integrated school. Police charge William Rosecrans with the crime on 3 March. Klan leader Holsted Manucy betrays Rosecrans to police on 4 March, mistaking him for the bomber of a local strikebound railroad. On 12 March, FBI agents arrest five more klansmen. Rosecrans pleads guilty on 13 March and receives a 7-year prison term on 17 April. The five other klansmen face trial on 30 June, with three acquitted a week later. Retrial of the other two begins on 16 November, with both acquitted on 25 November.

24 February: Princess Anne, MD—Two days after civil rights demonstrations at Maryland State College, bombers strike a black home.

28 February: Natchez, MS—Gunmen ambush and murder Clinton Walker, a black employee at International Paper. HUAC later lists Walker as the first known victim murdered by the White Knights of the KKK. Anne Moody suggests he was shot on suspicion of dating white women.

March: St. Augustine, FL—Racists smash windows in the home, car and office of John Kalivos, a restaurateur who served black customers during a sit-in.

March: Athens, GA—Police arrest klansman Joseph Sims for assaulting a black demonstrator outside a segregated restaurant.

1 March: Laurel, MS—Sam Bowers releases a White Knights "executive lecture" listing Klan security procedures.

2 March: Monticello, MS—Klansman Sterling Gillis robs a bank of $38,076. He confesses to FBI agents, following his September arrest on bombing charges, and later receives a 10-year prison term.

4 April: Neshoba County, MS—Klansmen burn 12 crosses.

5 April: Natchez, MS—White gunmen wound black farm worker Richard Butler. Police jail two suspects on 26 October, confiscating guns and blackjacks.

18 April: Notasulga, AL—Arsonists burn Macon County High School during a white student boycott against court-ordered integration.

18 April: Bogalusa, LA—Black-hooded klansmen kidnap, flog and pistol-whip a mill worker for failing to support his family.

18 April: Jackson, MS—Klansmen seize and beat newsman Bob Wagner near a KKK meeting.

24 April: Mississippi—Klansmen burn crosses in 64 of 82 counties.

24 April: Griffin, GA—Police arrest five UKA members and seize a small arsenal of weapons, after the klansmen burn a cross at a black-owned dry cleaning shop.

25 April: Jacksonville, FL—An explosion destroys the home of Grand Dragon Barton Griffin.

28 April: McComb, MS—Klansmen bomb the home of black NAACP member Curtis Bryant.

May: Ohio—James Venable charters a new realm of his National Knights.

May: McComb, MS—Nightriders smash windows of a COFO office twice in three days. In the second attack, a brick strikes a female occupant on the head.

2 May: Meadville, MS—Klansmen kidnap and murder black teenagers Henry Dee and Charles Moore, on suspicion of conspiring with Black Muslims. On 12 July, a fisherman finds their bodies in the Mississippi River, near Tallulah, Louisiana. On 6 November, police and FBI agents arrest klansmen Charles Edwards and James Seale, from Natchez. Despite an alleged confession from Seale, prosecutors never try the case.

2 May: Mississippi—Klansmen burn crosses in 64 counties.

3 May: Laurel, MS—Sam Bowers issues a list of "humorous" harassment techniques, including use of mad dogs and venomous snakes.

10 May: Laurel, MS—Klansmen bomb the office of a "moderate" newspaper.

28 May: St. Augustine, FL—White rioters, many of them klansmen, mob black demonstrators downtown.

29 May: St. Augustine, FL—Klansmen shoot up a beach cottage rented by SCLC staffers. In a separate incident, they also fire at one of Dr. King's aides on the highway. Racists assault newsman Gary Hanes twice within four hours, as he covers black protest marches.

June: Canton, MS—Klansmen stop a car driven by Rev. Edwin King, the white dean of mostly-black Tougaloo College. They debate killing King, but decide against it because they would also have to kill his wife and a Pakistani student riding in the car.

3 June: Jackson, MS—Two carloads of klansmen shoot up a COFO office.

7 June: Raleigh, MS—Sam Bowers convenes a secret WKKKKM meeting outside town, reading an "executive order" on approved techniques of violence.

8 June: McComb, MS—Three carloads of klansmen attack three blacks on the road outside town, beating them with guns and brass knuckles.

9 June: St. Augustine, FL—Klansmen attack black demonstrators, beating several.

10 June: St. Augustine, FL—Klansmen break through police lines to attack black marchers with bricks and sulphuric acid. Tear gas and police dogs finally disperse the rioters.

14 June: Oxford, OH—The COFO holds its final orientation meeting for Mississippi's "Freedom Summer" at Western College for Women.

16 June: Philadelphia, MS—Klansmen burn the Mt. Zion Methodist Church, after beating its congregants.

17 June: Jackson, MS—Hooded klansmen kidnap and beat a black man.

20 June: McComb, MS—Klan bombers strike a black barbershop, two black homes, and the homes of two whites who have publicly opposed Klan violence.

20 June: Athens, GA—Following a UKA rally at Covington, klansmen fire shotgun blasts into a black apartment house, wounding two tenants. On 30 June, two klansmen pay $105 fines.

21 June: Brandon, MS—Klansmen bomb the Sweet Rest Church of Christ Holiness.

21 June: Philadelphia, MS—Klansmen acting with police collusion kidnap and murder COFO workers James Chaney, Andrew Goodman and Michael Schwerner. Hunters find their burned-out car in Bogue Chitto Swamp on 22 June. Six FBI agents arrive to begin a federal investigation on 23 June. On 25 June, Allen Dulles recommends prompt White House action to "control and prose-

cute" Klan terrorists. Directed by informants, FBI agents recover their corpses from a klansman's property on 4 August, subsequently obtaining confessions from two members of the murder party. On 2 December, FBI agents meet with Governor Johnson to decide if state or federal authorities will prosecute the suspects. When Neshoba County's prosecutor refuses to answer by 3 December, the DOJ decides to proceed alone. G-men arrest 21 suspects on 4 December, but a U.S. commissioner dismisses all charges on 10 December. On 11 January 1965, DOJ attorneys present confessions from two klansmen to a federal grand jury, which indicts 18 of the suspects on 15 January. U.S. marshals arrest the 18 on 16 January. Federal judge Harold Cox dismisses the felony counts on 24 February, while ruling that 17 defendants must face trial on misdemeanor counts.

22 June: McComb, MS—Klansmen bomb the homes of two black civil rights workers. Seven sticks of dynamite fail to explode at a third home.

23 June: Jackson, MS—Klansmen fire into a black-owned café, wounding one customer, then shoot at a black minister's house.

23 June: Mossy Point, MS—Klansmen firebomb a Knights of Pythias hall used for black voter registration meetings.

24 June: Canton, MS—Klansmen fire into a civil rights worker's car.

25 June: Ruleville, MS—Klansmen firebomb a black church. Eight plastic bags of gasoline outside the church fail to ignite.

25 June: Longdale, MS—Klansmen firebomb another black church.

25 June: St. Augustine, FL—White mobs repeatedly assault black demonstrators throughout the day and evening. In one attack, police release five white prisoners on demand from the mob.

26 June: Clinton, MS—Klansmen burn a black church.

27 June: McComb, MS—Klansmen hurl a Molotov cocktail, bearing a note signed "KKK," against the front door of the *Enterprise Journal.*

28 June: Batesville, MS—Klansmen kidnap and beat a black man.

28 June: Cincinnati, OH—Klansmen burn a cross at an amusement park. Police arrest Clarence Brandenburg for criminal syndicalism on 17 August and jurors later convict him. On 9 June 1968, the U.S. Supreme Court reverses his conviction and declares the Ohio statute unconstitutional.

2 July: Washington, DC—LBJ signs the 1964 Civil Rights Act.

3 July: Soso, MS—Klansmen bomb a black café.

4 July: Washington, DC—James Venable's "mass" march on the capital attracts only a handful of racists, including George Rockwell's American Nazis.

4 July: Atlanta, GA—Whites attack four blacks, beating them with metal chairs at a political rally where Alabama Gov. George Wallace shares the stage with Lester Maddox and Georgia Grand Dragon Calvin Craig.

6 July: Jackson, MS—Klansmen set fire to a black church.

6 July: Moss Point, MS—Klansmen fire into a voter registration meeting, wounding a woman. Police arrest three blacks who pursue the gunmen.

7 July: Bovina, MS—Klansmen burn a black recreation center. Despite a smoldering torch left at the scene, the sheriff deems the fire "accidental."

7 July: McComb, MS—Three bombs rock a SNCC Freedom House, injuring two occupants.

10 July: Jackson, MS—J. Edgar Hoover inaugurates a new FBI field office.

10 July: Hattiesburg, MS—Whites armed with metal clubs beat three rabbis active in voter registration work, hospitalizing one victim. Two attackers plead guilty on 8 August, paying $500 in lieu of 90-day suspended jail terms.

10 July: Colbert, GA—Klansmen fire shots at black traveling salesman Clarence Ellington.

11 July: Shaw, MS—Whites offer a black man $400 to bomb a SNCC Freedom House. He declines and reports the offer.

11 July: Canton, MS—A firebomb explodes on the lawn of a SNCC Freedom House.

11 July: Browning, MS—Klansmen burn a black church.

11 July: Colbert, GA—UKA members ambush three black army reserve officers, killing Lt. Col. Lemuel Penn. FBI agents arrest four klansmen on 6 August. Two, Cecil Myers and Joseph Sims, face trial on 31 August, with the confession of a third defendant admitted as evidence. Jurors acquit both klansmen on 4 September, and the county sheriff joins in their victory celebration. A federal grand jury indicts Myers, Sims, and two other klansmen on 16 October, but a judge dismisses all counts on 29 December.

12 July: Kingston, MS—Klansmen burn two black churches.

12 July: Natchez, MS—Klansmen burn a black church and firebomb a black contractor's home. Police chief J.T. Robinson tells target Dorie Ladner, "The bomb was meant for you. I'm surprised you haven't been killed already."

13 July: Elm City, NC—Police arrest two klansmen for attempting to burn a black church. KKK leaders earlier warned the congregation against letting white students help paint the church.

14 July: Wesson, MS—Hooded klansmen abduct and beat a white gas station owner who hired black employees and refused to join the KKK.

16 July: Greenwood, MS—Klansmen kidnap black civil rights worker Silas McGhee, beating him with a board and pipe, shortly after he spoke to FBI agents about earlier assaults.

17 July: McComb, MS—Klansmen burn the Zion Hill Freewill Baptist Church and assault two bystanders.

18 July: Batesville, MS—The county sheriff holds two civil rights workers for 90 minutes without charges, then releases them to a white mob that beats them on the sidewalk.

18 July: McComb, MS—Klansmen burn the Sweet Home Missionary Baptist Church.

18 July: Laurel, MS—Nightriders smash a doctor's window with a rock, bearing a threatening note signed "KKK." Their apparent target, one floor higher, is the office of a dentist and NAACP member.

19 July: Madison County, MS—Klansmen burn the Christian Union Baptist Church.

22 July: McComb, MS—Klansmen burn a black church.

23 July: McComb, MS—Klansmen torch another black church.

24 July: St. Augustine, FL—Klansmen firebomb the newly-integrated Monson Motor Lodge. Later, five knights are jailed for burning a cross on private property.

24 July: Pinellas Park, FL—Bill Hendrix founds the American Underground.

25 July: Hattiesburg, MS—Klansmen firebomb the home of black MFDP activists.

26 July: McComb, MS—Klansmen twice try to bomb the home of black civil rights worker Charles Bryant, while the occupants defend themselves with gunfire.

26 July: Mileston, MS—Klansmen burn a SNCC worker's car outside a home housing civil rights workers.

26 July: Batesville, MS—Klansmen lob a tear-gas bomb into a home housing civil rights workers.

26 July: Greenwood, MS—200 whites mob Silas and Jake McGhee as they leave a movie theater. Both are cut by flying glass as the mob stones their car. Later, armed whites besiege the hospital where they seek treatment. The sheriff waits three hours to respond and disperse the mob.

27 July: Itta Bena, MS—Klansmen raid a voter registration office, smashing windows, ripping a door from its hinges, and tearing out porch supports.

30 July: Meridian, MS—Klansmen burn the Mount Moriah Baptist Church.

30 July: Gulfport, MS—Klansmen kidnap a black COFO volunteer and drive him to Biloxi, alternately threatening him and offering bribes for information on civil rights activities.

30 July: Batesville, MS—Klansmen fire three shots into the same house they tear-gassed four days earlier.

31 July: Brandon, MS—Klansmen burn the Pleasant Grove Baptist Church. Flames detonate a nearby propane tank.

2 August: Greenwood, MS—Klansmen fire four shots into the SNCC office.

2 August: Natchez, MS—Klansmen fire shots into the Archie Curtis Funeral Home.

2 August: Canton, MS—Klansmen fire on the SNCC Freedom House.

4 August: Natchez, MS—Klansmen burn a black church.

9 August: Mileston, MS—Klansmen detonate a bomb 40 yards from a black community center, leaving a crater six feet wide.

9 August: Aberdeen, MS—Civil rights workers find three tear-gas bombs on the lawn of the COFO Freedom House. Police dispose of them before FBI agents can lift fingerprints.

10 August: Gluckstadt, MS—Klansmen burn a church meeting hall used for civil rights meetings. Press reports call it the 17th attack on Mississippi churches since 16 June.

11 August: Brandon, MS—Klansmen burn a black church that doubles as a Freedom School.

11 August: Laurel, MS—Klansmen assault Eugene Keys, a black man, in a department store.

12 August: Hattiesburg, MS—Klansmen strafe a black home in a drive-by shooting.

13 August: Raleigh, NC—Klansmen burn a cross on the governor's lawn.

13 August: Cleveland, MS—A black man reports that police chief W.H. Griffin, of Shaw, offered him $300 to "get rid of" three voter registration workers.

14 August: McComb, MS—Klansmen bomb a black supermarket across the street from a COFO Freedom School.

14 August: Canton, MS—Klansmen fire shots at a COFO Freedom House.

14 August: Natchez, MS—Klan bombers demolish a nightclub and grocery across the street from a COFO Freedom School. The tavern is owned by an interracial couple.

15 August: Greenwood, MS—Gunmen wound Silas McGhee in his car, parked on a city street.

15 August: Jackson, MS—Klansmen club a white civil rights worker, wound a black man with gunfire, and burn six crosses throughout the city.

15 August: Louisiana and Mississippi—Klansmen burn scores of crosses, many lit simultaneously at 10 p.m.

15 August: Laurel, MS—Klansmen mob four civil rights workers at a lunch counter, beating them with fists and baseball bats.

17 August: Laurel, MS—Police arrest a klansman for assaulting a civil rights worker on the street.

18 August: Natchez, MS—A five-gallon gasoline bomb fails to explode beneath a black tavern. A Louisiana bar owned by the proprietor's brother was firebombed the previous weekend.

19 August: Collinsville, MS—Klansmen burn a black church.

20 August: Canton, MS—Blacks foil an arson attempt on the COFO Freedom House, causing klansmen to drop a firebomb and set their own pickup afire as they flee.

21 August: Itta Bena, MS—Klansmen burn a black church.

22 August: Jones County, MS—15 klansmen attack a picnic crowd of blacks and white civil rights workers outside Laurel, beating two persons with chains and firing shots at two others. One attacker is free on bail after an assault arrest on 17 August.

23 August: McComb, MS—Hooded klansmen abduct a white man who befriended blacks, holding him captive for three hours.

23 August: Tupelo, MS—Klansmen burn a voter registration office.

25 August: Madison, FL—Nightriders fire five shotgun blasts into a car owned by civil rights workers.

25 August: Cincinnati, OH—William Miller disbands his NAAWP, complaining that it has been "taken over by the Ku Klux Klan."

27 August: Jackson, MS—Klansmen bomb the office of a weekly newspaper whose editor won a Pulitzer Prize for her anti–Klan editorials.

29 August: Meridian, MS—The UKA charters its second Mississippi klavern.

30 August: Mt. Sterling, KY—Arsonists burn the DuBois School and a storage building owned by an NAACP leader.

31 August: Meridian, MS—Klansmen fire into a black home housing civil rights workers.

1 September: McComb, MS—UKA members hold a klavern drawing to determine who will bomb local targets. A second drawing is held on 15 September.

1 September: Holly Springs, MS—Klansmen firebomb a black Baptist college.

2 September: Washington, DC—J. Edgar Hoover orders an illegal COINTELPRO campaign against "white hate" groups.

2 September: McComb, MS—A klansman assaults a SNCC worker on a downtown street.

2–3 September: Enfield, NC—Klansmen burn several crosses on successive nights.

5–6 September: Birmingham, AL—The UKA stages another imperial klonvocation.

6 September: Atlanta, GA—Leaders of various independent Klans create the National Association of KKK and elect officers.

6 September: Canton, MS—Klansmen bomb a white-owned grocery in a black neighborhood.

7 September: Bogue Chitto, MS—Klansmen bomb a black-owned pool hall in a white neighborhood.

7 September: Auburn, MS—Klansmen bomb a black church.

7 September: Summit, MS—Predawn bombings damage a black-owned home, store and tool shed.

7 September: Magnolia, MS—Klansmen bomb the home of a black school principal.

7 September: Pickens, MS—Herbert Oarsby, a 14-year-old black boy, disappears while wearing a CORE T-shirt. Searchers pull his body from a nearby river on 9 September. Police list the death as accidental and deny Oarsby was active in civil rights work.

9 September: McComb, MS—Klansmen bomb the home of Rev. James Baker.

10 September: Jackson County, MS—Bombs cause minor damage to a black church.

13 September: Vidalia, MS—A bomb explodes in the yard of a white resident known to support LBJ.

14 September: Natchez, MS—Racists lob stink bombs at several stores owned by "moderates," including a supermarket owned by Mayor John Nosser.

17 September: Canton, MS—Klansmen burn two churches used for voter registration activity. Press reports place the state's tally of church attacks at 24 since 16 June.

18 September: Mississippi—Grand Dragon E.L. McDaniel clashes with Wizard Robert Shelton after a KKK rally.

19 September: Coy, MS—Klansmen burn another black church.

19 September: Kemper County, MS—Klansmen burn a rural black church.

20 September: McComb, MS—Klansmen bomb the Society Hill Baptist Church and the home of civil rights activist Aylene Quin.

21 September: Enfield, NC—Klansmen stage another cross-burning.

21 September: Biloxi, MS—A federal grand jury convenes to examine Klan crimes. A local grand jury in Philadelphia, Mississippi, orders all FBI agents having knowledge of recent race murders to appear on 28 September, but J. Edgar Hoover refuses.

23 September: McComb, MS—Klansmen bomb two more black homes, one owned by a former policeman.

23 September: Columbia, SC—Klansmen burn a cross outside the governor's mansion.

25 September: Natchez, MS—Klansmen bomb the home of Mayor John Nosser.

26 September: Farmville, NC—Klansmen search, harass and threaten a white minister at a KKK rally.

27 September: Jackson, MS—Klansmen bomb the carport of a black businessman's home.

30 September: Pike County, MS—FBI agents arrest three members of a Klan "wolf pack" linked to bombings around McComb. A fourth suspect confesses after his arrest on 2 October and identifies more bombers. Agents seize weapons and pipe bombs from the homes of Emery Allen and Sterling Gillis on 5 October. On 12–13 October, a grand jury indicts nine klansmen on charges including 16 bombings and several church arsons. All nine plead guilty or no contest on 23 October, whereupon a sympathetic judge releases them on probation, citing his belief that they were "unduly provoked" by civil rights activists.

4 October: Vicksburg, MS—Klansmen bomb a black church used for voter registration.

4 October: Meridian, MS—Nightriders fire into a black home housing civil rights workers.

11 October: Vicksburg, MS—WKKKKM officers plot a bombing of the local COFO office.

17 October: Clayton County, GA—The UKA conducts a "violence school" for local klansmen.

20 October: Anniston, AL—J.B. Stoner tells an NSRP rally that the "only good [blacks] are dead ones."

21 October: Marks, MS—Four whites force an MFDP activist off the highway, beat him unconscious, and urinate on his body. The victim suffers a concussion.

22 October: Indianola, MS—The one-plane Klan Air Force drops flares and explosives over an MFDP rally.

24 October: Tchula, MS—Nightriders fire four shots into the home of an MFDP activist.

28 October: Indianola, MS—Klansmen lob a tear-gas bomb into a black home housing civil rights workers, then try to burn the local SNCC Freedom School.

29 October: Ruleville, MS—Nightriders shoot out the windows of a black-owned store displaying Democratic Party posters.

31 October: Ripley, MS—Klansmen burn the Antioch Baptist Church, which doubles as a Freedom School.

3 November: Laurel, MS—A klansman assaults a civil rights worker.

15 November: Harrisville, MS—Sam Bowers convenes a WKKKKM meeting, ordering a moratorium on bombings and murders from 1 December 1964 until 1 March 1965.

17 November: Laurel, MS—Klansmen kidnap a black union official and whip him outside town.

23 November: Meridian, MS—Grand Dragon Julius Harper calls a WKKKKM meeting to collect legal defense funds.

29 November: Montgomery, AL—Klansmen bomb the carport of a black home in a newly-integrated neighborhood.

30 November: Laurel, MS—Klansmen attack a civil rights worker in a department store.

10 December: Ferriday, LA—Members of the Silver Dollar Group burn Frank Morris's shoe repair shop, forcing him at gunpoint to remain inside. Morris dies from burns on 14 December, after giving a statement to the FBI.

13 December: Montgomery, AL—Klansmen detonate explosives outside a black church. Police arrest three suspects, including one klansman indicted for bombings in 1957. All receive 6-month jail terms, but the judge releases them on probation after 10 days in custody.

19 December: Meridian, MS—A special meeting of the WKKKKM banishes policeman Wallace Miller.

1965

January: Louisiana—Leaders of the Original Knights incorporate the ACCA as a front group.

January: Charlotte, NC—Klansmen bomb a black civil rights worker's car.

January: Natchez, MS—Klansmen fire shots into the home of NAACP leader George Metcalfe, housing SNCC volunteers.

2 January: Selma, AL—Martin Luther King launches the SCLC's voter registration drive.

5 January: Bogalusa, LA—Klan threats force cancellation of a public address by former congressman Brooks Hays.

15 January: Selma, AL—NSRP member James Robinson assaults Martin Luther King at a downtown hotel.

15 January: Laurel, MS—Two klansmen assault a civil rights worker in a downtown parking lot.

17 January: Jonesboro, LA—Klansmen burn two rural black churches.

22 January: Brandon, MS—Klansmen torch another black church.

24 January: New Bern, NC—Two bombs explode outside a black church where an NAACP meeting is in progress. Another blast damages the mortuary owned by black civil rights activist Oscar Dove. FBI agents arrest UKA members on 29 January. They plead guilty and receive suspended sentences on 3 June.

26 January: Monroe, LA—Houston Morris incorporates the Original KKK of America.

29 January: Soso, MS—Klansmen fail in their attempt to burn a black home.

3 February: Bogalusa, LA—Three klansmen assault a civil rights worker.

9 February: Marion, AL—An FBI informant reports KKK plans to kill Martin Luther King during a visit on 15 February. King subsequently cancels the visit.

9 February: Laurel, MS—Klansmen fire into COFO headquarters.

18 February: Bessemer, AL—Striking klansmen, unwilling to work with blacks at the W.S. Dickey Clay Co., damage large pipe couplings at the plant and shoot up the car of a nonstriking worker. Gunfire damages a black worker's car on 19 February.

24 February: Mobile, AL—Nightriders fire on the mayor's home and the home of a black civil rights worker.

26 February: Marion, AL—Al Lingo's state troopers fatally wound Jimmie Lee Jackson, when he attempts to stop them from beating his mother.

28 February: Lowndes County, AL—Armed whites invade a church during services, warning the "moderate" minister to leave town under threat of death.

March: Laurel, MS—Klansmen burn a COFO Freedom House.

March: Vicksburg, MS—Two klansmen assault an elderly black man in a café, smashing eggs in his face and knocking him down. A few days later, they return and lob two firebombs through the windows, causing extensive damage.

2 March: Bessemer, AL—Klansmen stone a black employee leaving the W.S. Dickey Clay Co., then pursue his car and fire several shots before he escapes.

4 March: Ellisville, MS—Klansmen burn a black home.

5 March: Indianola, MS—Klansmen torch a Freedom School and library.

6 March: Bessemer, AL—Klansmen shoot up the car of a black employee leaving the W.S. Dickey Clay Co.

7 March: Selma, AL—On "Bloody Sunday," Al Lingo's state troopers and Sheriff Jim Clark's mounted posse attack civil rights marchers, sending 66 to the hospital. Hours later, NSRP members including James Robinson beat a black man on the highway outside town and assault an FBI agent who tries to intervene.

8 March: Bessemer, AL—Klansmen fire shotguns at another black employee outside the W.S. Dickey Clay Co.

9 March: Selma, AL—Klansmen attack three white ministers active in civil rights work, fatally beating Rev. James Reeb. Police arrest four suspects for assault on 10 March, upgrading the charge to murder when Reeb dies on 11 March. A grand jury indicts three of the men on 13 April. At trial, an all white jury acquits the three on 10 December, following an unexplained visit to the jury room by Sheriff Jim Clark.

10 March: Bessemer, AL—Klansmen attack a black employee from the W.S. Dickey Clay Co. on an errand for his boss, damaging a company vehicle before he escapes. In a separate incident, klansmen stone several trucks entering the factory grounds, smashing their windows.

15–16 March: Natchez, MS—A UKA klonvocation draws klansmen from Mississippi and seven other states.

21 March: Vicksburg, MS—Klansmen firebomb an integrated café.

21–22 March: Birmingham, AL—Residents find six unexploded time bombs in black neighborhoods.

21–25 March: Alabama—Civil rights protesters complete a march from Selma to Montgomery, protected by National Guardsmen.

25 March: Lowndes County, AL—UKA members ambush and murder Viola Liuzzo, a white civil rights worker, while she ferries marchers from Montgomery to Selma. FBI informant Gary Rowe is a member of the hit team and identifies the others. On 6 April, a federal grand jury indicts klansmen William Eaton, Eugene Thomas and Collie Wilkins. A local grand jury indicts the three for murder on 22 April. On 7 May, a jury deadlocks over Wilkins, resulting in a mistrial. Another jury, including known Citizens' Council members, acquits him of murder on 22 October. On 3 December, a federal jury in Montgomery convicts all three defendants on civil rights charges, resulting in 10-year prison terms. Eaton dies from a heart attack prior to his murder trial, on 10 March 1966. A white jury acquits Thomas of murder on 27 September 1966.

27 March: Tuscaloosa, AL—Robert Shelton describes the recent murders of Rev. James Reeb and Viola Liuzzo as part of a "trumped-up plot to destroy the right wing in America."

28 March: Meridian, MS—Klansmen firebomb two black churches.

29 March: Bogalusa, LA—Klansmen hurl a tear-gas grenade at a group of blacks.

30 March: Washington, DC—HUAC votes to investigate the KKK.

April: Birmingham, England—Visiting UKA Imperial Wizard Robert Shelton predicts a Klan resurgence in Britain.

1 April: Birmingham, AL—Klansmen bomb the home of a black accountant. Police defuse bombs at the homes of the mayor and a city council member.

2 April: Bessemer, AL—Klansmen fire a rifle shot into the W.S. Dickey Clay Co. as the strike against black workers continues.

5 April: Prosperity, SC—Robed, hooded men drag a black prisoner from his jail cell, threatening and slapping him. Prosecutors charge two policemen with second-degree lynching on 8 April.

7 April: Bogalusa, LA—Nightriders trade shots with civil rights workers at a black home, with 30 bullets striking the house and a parked car. In a separate incident, two armed klansmen threaten blacks at a civil rights meeting.

9 April: Bogalusa, LA—Klan-led white mobs attack civil rights workers, reporters, and an FBI agent.

10 April: Jonesboro, LA—Klansmen exchange shots with a black motorist.

11 April: Pittsburgh, PA—Unknown persons burn a cross in Point State Park, where vandals have twice smashed windows at a COFO Freedom Center during the previous week.

15 April: Bogalusa, LA—A black man, newly released from jail after a scuffle with whites, claims he was questioned in his cell by men wearing Klan hoods over police uniforms.

17 April: Hamburg, AR—Klansmen threaten a police officer and steal the car of a reporter who took "unauthorized" photos during a KKK rally.

18 April: St. Augustine, FL—White rioters pelt a black Easter parade with rocks and eggs. In a separate incident, whites also egg blacks entering a white church.

23 April: Ellisville, MS—Klansmen burn a black home.

25 April: Atlanta, GA—Police detour a march by 2,000 white racists after one detonates a smoke bomb.

1 May: Indianola, MS—Klan firebombs destroy two black homes, while damaging a third home, a store, and a COFO Freedom House.

9 May: Anniston, AL—A UKA parade features Viola Liuzzo's killers as guests of honor. Edward Fields joins the rally in a show of unity between the UKA and NSRP.

9 May: Bogalusa, LA—A white mob led by klansmen assaults black demonstrators at a city park with belts, clubs and other weapons.

11 May: New Orleans—Klansmen firebomb a Unitarian church.

12 May: New Orleans—Firebombs damage an ACLU member's car.

13 May: Oxford, AL—Klansmen bomb a black church.

13 May: Stockholm, Sweden—Police arrest Bjoern Lundahl, head of a neo–Nazi Klan organization linked to the Aryan Knights, for plotting to murder prominent local Jews.

15 May: Washington, DC—An FBI COINTELPRO memo targets Sam Bowers and other Klan leaders for special harassment.

16 May: Mt. Olive, MS—Klansmen burn a black-owned grocery.

16 May: Laurel, MS—Klansmen burn another black-owned grocery, a community recreation center, and a baseball park.

17 May: Atlanta, GA—Viola Liuzzo's murderers get the hero treatment in another UKA parade.

17 May: Laurel, MS—Klansmen set fire to a motel and gas station owned by outspoken KKK opponents.

24 May: Bogalusa, LA—A Klan-led mob of 300 tears down the gates of a city park to avert black demonstrations.

26 May: Crawfordsville, GA—Klansmen kidnap and beat a black civil rights worker, then deliver him to the sheriff.

June: Monroe, LA—Houston Morris and most of his klansmen defect to the UKA.

3 June: Washington Parish, LA—Nightriders ambush two black deputy sheriffs on patrol, killing O'Neal Moore and wounding Creed Rogers. Police arrest suspect Ernest McElveen—a klansman and NSRP member—in neighboring Mississippi and return him to face murder charges. On 5 June, gunmen fire into the home of a policeman assigned to the case. Prosecutors indict McElveen, but later drop all charges without trial.

7 June: Birmingham, England—Klansmen burn a cross at the home of an Indian immigrant.

13 June: Birmingham, England—16 Klan members hold their first public meeting.

13 June: London, England—Racists burn a cross at the home of a Pakistani merchant.

14 June: Vicksburg, MS—Klansmen firebomb the home of a Westinghouse officer who hired black secretaries for the local plant.

15 June: London, England—The British government bans Robert Shelton from further visits to England.

16 June: Laurel, MS—In separate incidents, klansmen shoot up a black nightclub and fire shots at the NAACP's state vice president.

July: Covington, LA—Members of the Original Knights plot a series of church-burnings.

1 July: Laurel, MS—Klansmen burn COFO headquarters and 13 homes occupies by civil rights activists.

1 July: Jones County, MS—Klansmen burn an integrated café.

1 July: Sharon, MS—Bombs destroy a barn owned by a white Klan opponent.

1 July: Mt. Olive, MS—Klansmen set the homes of three white "moderates" on fire.

3 July: Laurel, MS—Klansmen attempt to burn the home of another black activist.

8–11 July: Bogalusa, LA—Klan-led mobs repeatedly assault black demonstrators. Gunshots fired by the Deacons for Defense and Justice wounds one white rioter. J.B. Stoner exhorts 1,500 spectators at an NSRP rally on 8 July, then leads 2,000 on a 10 July protest march. Bystanders report klansmen distributing clubs to white youths along the route of a march on 11 July.

10 July: Meridian, MS—Sheriff Lawrence Rainey addresses a UKA recruiting rally, led by Robert Shelton and E.L. McDaniel.

15 July: Anniston, AL—Connie Lynch, J.B. Stoner and klansman Kenneth Adams address an NSRP rally. Afterward, nightriders shoot a black man, Willie Brewster, who dies on 18 July. Police charge three whites with murder, based on statements from a rally participant to whom they boasted of the shooting. A jury convicts Hubert Strange of second-degree murder on 2 December 1965, resulting in a 10-year prison term. Another jury acquits defendant Ira DeFries on 17 February 1966, and charges against Lewis Blevins are dismissed.

16 July: Bogalusa, LA—Klan-led mobs stage six attacks on black protesters while police idly watch, finally arresting two rioters during a seventh assault. On 17 July, whites spray black marchers with hoses, also pelting them with fruit and stones.

16 July: Greensboro, AL—A white mob armed with clubs, hammers and rubber hoses attacks 75 black protesters, sending 17 to the hospital.

18 July: Elmwood, AL—Klansmen burn a black church.

18 July: Greensboro, AL—Klansmen burn two black churches.

18 July: Jackson, MS—Addressing a KKK rally, Wizard Sam Bowers boasts that the Klan is responsible for more than 16 arson fires in Laurel, his hometown.

19 July: Laurel, MS—Klansmen burn the home of a white attorney hostile to the KKK.

19 July: Baton Rouge, LA—The DOJ files litigation against the Original Knights, ACCA and 38 individual klansmen, seeking injunctions against further violence in Bogalusa. Court hearings proceed in September, with injunctions issued on 1 and 22 December 1965.

27 July: Ferriday, LA—Klansmen firebomb two black homes.

27 July: New Orleans—Klansmen bomb a CORE office.

28 July: Americus, GA—White mobs stone black motorists. A white youth suffers fatal gunshots while attacking one car.

31 July: Columbia, MS—Klansmen riddle a civil rights office with bullets and set it afire.

31 July: Americus, GA—Klan-led mobs assault black demonstrators. Police report further attacks on 2 August.

31 July: Bear, DE—A UKA rally commemorates lost komrades Matt Murphy and Dan Burros.

1 August: Delaware—Robert Shelton installs Ralph Pryor, Jr., as the UKA's Delaware grand dragon.

3 August: Slidell, LA—Klansmen burn two black churches.

6 August: Washington, DC—LBJ signs the Voting Rights Act.

7 August: Jackson, AL—Gunmen fire into a restaurant where blacks seek service, wounding four persons.

8 August: West Point, MS—Klansmen fire shotguns into a home housing civil rights workers.

8 August: Valewood, MS Klansmen torch a Head Start office and burn several crosses nearby.

8 August: Sharon, MS—Klansmen fire into the home of a white "moderate" whose barn they bombed on 1 July. In a second raid, they shoot up and burn the home of a white anti–Klan minister.

9 August: Amherstburg, Ontario—Klansmen burn a cross downtown, defacing a nearby church with slogans reading: "Niggers beware" and "The Klan is coming."

12 August: Baton Rouge, LA—Klansmen bomb a hotel and motel housing civil rights workers.

14 August: Ft. Deposit, AL—A gang of whites armed with heavy walking sticks harass civil rights protesters, while klansmen burn a cross on the courthouse lawn and paint a large swastika on the town's water tower.

16 August: Meadville, MS—Police find ex-klansman Earl Hodges outside town, apparently beaten to death, but they rule his death "accidental." Informants claim he was murdered as a suspected FBI informant.

20 August: Hayneville, AL—Klansman and "special deputy" Tom Coleman shoots two white civil rights workers, killing Jonathan Daniels and critically wounding Rev. Richard Morrisroe. An all-white jury acquits Coleman of manslaughter charges on 30 September. Prosecutors later dismiss assault charges related to Morrisroe's shooting.

20 August: Greenwood, MS—Locals find Freddie Thomas, a black man, dead on the outskirts of town, apparently killed by a hit-and-run driver. Police decline to investigate.

21 August: Tuscaloosa, AL—UKA Imperial Klonsel Matt Murphy dies in an auto accident north of town.

23 August: Jackson, MS—Shotgun snipers wound Rev. D.A. Thompson, a white Unitarian minister active in civil rights.

23 August: Atlanta, GA—Dr. Andrew Stone, JBS leader from Emory, Georgia, addresses a UKA rally, afterward telling reporters he wants to "help the Klan all I can."

25 August: Baton Rouge, LA—Klansmen bomb a black nightclub.

26 August: Plymouth, NC—Klansmen beat 27 black protesters downtown, later clashing with hecklers at a KKK rally outside town.

27 August: Natchez, MS—A car bomb maims George Metcalfe, a black NAACP leader. FBI agents blame the Silver Dollar Group, but prosecutors file no charges.

30 August: Americus, GA—Six whites armed with bricks and stones attack black demonstrators at the courthouse.

31 August: Augusta, GA—Police charge three white youths with stealing grenades and other explosives from an army base, using them to terrorize blacks.

31 August: Plymouth, NC—Klansmen clash with black protesters outside police headquarters. Blacks wound one knight with gunfire and stab another.

2 September: Laurel, MS—Klansmen bomb a COFO truck.

5 September: Forrest, MS—Klansmen fire on the home of a black family whose child attends an integrated school, wounding one person.

7 September: Sandersville, MS—Klansmen burn a black home.

9 September: Greenwood, MS—Blacks request a DOJ investigation of the recent F.L. Thomas murder, claiming he was killed as a warning against black suffrage.

13 September: Atlanta, GA—Edwin Walker tells a JBS rally, "There will be a KKK in the USA longer than there will be an LBJ."

14 September: Sandersville, MS—Klansmen burn a black home.

16 September: Laurel, MS—Klansmen fire into the home of the state NAACP vice president. Police jail a suspect on 17 September.

26 September: Jones County, MS—Klansmen burn a rural black church.

30 September: Ovett, MS—Klansmen botch their attempt to burn a black home.

October: Jones County, MS—Authorities report 40+ cases of racist assault, arson and bombing in the county since May 1964.

October: Natchez, MS—Blacks organize a chapter of the Deacons for Defense and Justice, to guard civil rights protesters.

4 October: Crawfordsville, GA—Grand Dragon Calvin Craig assaults a black protester.

7 October: Crawfordsville, GA—Klansmen drag a white integrationist from his car and beat him during a black demonstration.

11 October: Laurel, MS—Klansmen shoot up and burn a black home first targeted in April.

12 October: Crawfordsville, GA—Klansmen assault an SCLC photographer.

16 October: Montgomery, AL—State attorney general Richmond Flowers issues a report linking the KKK to 40 of Birmingham's 45 racist bombings and 12 of 17 civil rights murders committed throughout the South since 1963.

17 October: Crawfordsville, GA—Armed klansmen force a black motorist off the road, assault him, and threaten his life.

17 October: Washington, DC—HUAC calls Robert Shelton as the first public witness in its probe of the KKK. Hearings continue through 24 February 1966. Legislative hearings in July 1966 fail to produce a viable anti–Klan statute.

18 October: Laurel, MS—Mayor Henry Bucklew denounces the WKKKKM on television.

22 October: Lincolnton, GA—30 whites attack black demonstrators. On 23 October, seven civil workers roll their car while fleeing nightriders in a high-speed chase.

22 October: Washington, D.C.—Klabee Joseph DuBois resigns from the UKA on the HUAC witness stand, disillusioned by other klansmen pleading the Fifth Amendment.

24 October: Melbourne, FL—Charles Riddlehoover leads UKA defectors to create the United Knights of the KKK.

24 October: Reading, PA—Grand Dragon Roy Frankhouser claims an attempt against his life.

26 October: Laurel, MS—Klansmen fire a shotgun blast into a black school.

29 October: Miami, FL—Police arrest Grand Dragon Charles Riddlehoover for speeding and reckless driving. Documents found in his car reveal a recent rift within the UKA, creating the United Knights.

30 October: Montgomery, AL—Two suspected klansmen assault Richmond Flowers at a football game.

31 October: Reading, PA—Dan Burros, New York grand dragon of the UKA, commits suicide after the *New York Times* reveals his Jewish lineage.

7 November: Wilmington, DE—Police arrest the state's top-ranking klansman for a shooting in Hartley, two weeks earlier.

8 November: Jones County, GA—Arsonists burn an abandoned home and a vacant black church.

8 November: Twiggs County, GA—Arsonists strike another black church. Police later charge a white Florida physician with setting both fires.

12 November: Lakeland, FL—Klansmen jam a 4-foot cross through a screen door at the home of Phyllis Johnson, daughter of a high-ranking knight who furnished information to HUAC.

18 November: Victoria, VA—Snipers fire at four civil rights workers, wounding one.

21 November: Ferriday, LA—Klansmen firebomb the home of a black civil rights activist.

22 November: Charlotte, NC—Klansmen bomb the homes of four blacks active in civil rights work.

29 November: Vicksburg, MS—A Klan car-bomb injures three

persons near a black grocery store, rumored to host civil rights meetings.

1 December: New Orleans—A federal court injunction bars the Original Knights from "acts of terror and intimidation" in Washington Parish.

5 December: Hamburg, AR—White gunmen shoot Lee Culbreath, a black newspaper delivery boy. Police charge two klansmen with his slaying. Jurors convict defendant Ed Vail of second-degree murder on 26 February 1966, resulting in a 21-year prison term. Prosecutors later dismiss charges against the second defendant.

10 December: Bogalusa, LA—Nightriders fire shots at the home of Robert Hicks, black leader of the Bogalusa Civic and Voters League.

11 December: Texas—UKA headquarters charters a Texas realm under Grand Dragon George Otto.

12 December: North Carolina—UKA Grand Klaliff Grady Mars commits suicide.

13 December: Laurel, MS—Sam Bowers orders the murder of NAACP officer Vernon Dahmer, in Hattiesburg.

24 December: Pulaski, TN—James Venable's National Knights erroneously celebrate the KKK's centennial.

1966

2 January: Newton, GA—Klansmen burn a black church. Anonymous callers threaten to kill the sheriff if he investigates.

3 January: Mississippi—Klansmen burn crosses in nine counties, firing shots at FBI agents in one instance. Police jail five knights for violation of state conspiracy statutes. G-men arrest brothers Allen and Bobby Byrd for the shooting on 4 January.

6 January: Alabama—William Brassel replaces Robert Creel as the UKA's grand dragon.

10 January: Hattiesburg, MS—Klansmen burn the home and store of black NAACP activist Vernon Dahmer, one night after Dahmer's announcement that he would collect poll taxes from black voters. Dahmer dies from his burns, while his wife and 10-year-old daughter are hospitalized. The DOJ issues complaints against 14 Klansmen on 27 March. FBI agents arrest 13 klansmen on 28 March, seizing weapons from the homes of Sam Bowers and Deavours Nix. Bowers surrenders on 31 March. A federal grand jury indicts 15 klansmen on 22 June, for violations of the 1965 Voting Rights Act. Agents arrest the 15th defendant on 23 June. The indictments are later dismissed, based on defense challenges to the grand jury's racial composition. A new panel indicts 12 of the original 15 on 27 February 1967. Defendant Billy Pitts pleads guilty to arson and murder on 8 March 1868, receiving a life sentence. On 13 March, authorities jail defense witness James Yount for perjury, based on his false denial of Klan membership. On 15 March 1968, jurors convict Cecil Sessum on state charges of first-degree murder, resulting in a life sentence. Federal prosecutors indict sixteen klansmen for conspiracy on 27 March. Billy Pitts receives a five-year federal sentence for conspiracy on 15 July. William Smith pleads guilty to murder and arson, receiving a life sentence on 19 July 1968. On 28 July, jurors deadlock over charges filed against Charles Wilson. Lawrence Byrd receives a 10-year sentence in state prison for arson, on 8 November 1968. Deadlocked juries result in mistrials for defendants Henry DeBoxtel (21 March 1968), Charles Wilson (28 July) and James Lyons (8 November). State authorities charge Bowers with murder on 18 November 1968. His first trial opens on 21 January 1969 and ends with a hung deadlocked jury on 25 January. Jurors subsequently deadlock on the Bowers case in two more trials. Authorities dismiss Bowers's charges in 1973.

12 January: Washington, DC—President Johnson asks Congress for laws to strengthen federal punishment of crimes related to civil rights.

24 January: Mississippi—Klansmen distribute leaflets advising white residents to refuse FBI interviews.

30 January: Atlanta, GA—The Southern Regional Council reports that Dixie racists killed 14 blacks and civil rights workers in 1965, with three blacks murdered so far in 1966.

2 February: Kosciusko, MS—Klansmen fire shotgun blasts into a home housing civil rights workers, wounding two persons.

3 February: Kosciusko, MS—Klansmen fire shots into a COFO Freedom House.

6 February: Zachary, LA—Klansmen bomb a black home.

9 February: Mississippi—A federal judge dismisses klansman Bernard Akin's libel suit against *Life* magazine, filed over coverage of his alleged involvement in the 1964 Neshoba County murders.

19 February: Birmingham, AL—Police discover a racist "bomb factory" in the woods outside town. One timing device is identical to those found on several unexploded bombs in April 1965.

24 February: Elba, AL—Two dynamite blasts damage a newly integrated high school.

11 March: Bogalusa, LA—Gunshots wound a black army captain in a public phone booth. Police later arrest two local whites for the shooting.

27 March: Maryland—Kleagle Xavier Edwards publicly resigns from the UKA, airing his fears that the Klan is "moving toward violence."

28 March: Washington, DC—The U.S. Supreme Court approves use of Reconstruction-era federal statutes to prosecute klansmen for the 1964 Lemuel Penn and Neshoba County, Mississippi, murders.

2 April: Baton Rouge, LA—Bombs explode at two swimming pools scheduled for desegregation.

4 April: Titusville, FL—Robert Shelton banishes UKA Imperial Kludd George Dorsett for exposing Klan secrets to HUAC. Release of FBI documents in January 1976 exposes Dorsett as an informant.

9 April: Ernul, NC—Klansmen bomb a black church.

10 May: Cincinnati, OH—Jurors convict NSRP member Jerrold Black under Ohio's syndicalism law, for illegally distributing hate literature. A federal court overturns his conviction on 13 June and rules the law unconstitutional.

June: New Jersey—Ralph Rotella resigns as UKA grand dragon.

6 June: Hernando, MS—Memphis resident Aubrey Norvell wounds James Meredith with three shotgun blasts on the third day of Meredith's one-man "March Against Fear." In 2003, David Chalmers identified Norvell as a klansman.

10 June: Natchez, MS—Klansmen kidnap and murder Ben White, an elderly black man, in hopes that his murder may lure Martin Luther King to the city. A jury acquits two defendants of murder on 9 December 1967. White's family files a wrongful-death lawsuit against the killers and the White Knights of the KKK, winning a damage judgment of $1,021,500 on 13 November 1968.

17 June: Greenwood, MS—Reporters covering a civil rights rally escape injury after klansmen place two venomous snakes in their car. Byron De La Beckwith circulates through the crowd, seeking Charles Evers, brother of the NAACP leader Beckwith murdered in 1963.

21 June: Philadelphia, MS—White mobs stone civil rights marchers, while police stand by watching. After nightfall, klansmen fire on four homes in the black community. Security guards wound a white gunman as he fires on the local MFDP office.

21 June: Louisiana—Police arrest six klansmen for a series of firebombings that struck two churches, a furniture store and several homes between 1 March 1965 and 11 May 1965.

22 June: Canton, MS—Blacks wound a klansman following a firebomb attack on a local civil rights headquarters.

24 June: Philadelphia, MS—Whites pelt Martin Luther King and other demonstrators with eggs and bottles.

24 June: Carthage, MS—Klansmen burn a Catholic church.

28 June: Jonesboro, TN—Former Indiana grand dragon D.C. Stephenson dies.

28 June: Cordele, GA—25–30 armed whites gather at a black-owned gas station, firing shots after a black youth throws a bottle at their cars. Blacks return fire in a shootout lasting 90 minutes.

Summer: Crenshaw County, AL—The DOJ seeks an injunction to ban UKA interference with school desegregation.

1 July: Milwaukee, WI—Klansmen bomb a linoleum store owned by the former president of the Wisconsin Civil Rights Conference.

3 July: Lebanon, OH—Klansmen stone police after the officers arrest two knights for violating the state's anti-mask law.

4 July: Norborne, MO—Minutemen leader Robert DePugh creates the Patriotic Party.

10 July: Grenada, MS—Police jail two whites for firing sub-machine-gun bursts at an FBI agent and two blacks outside a black church.

17 July: Cordele, GA—Police jail seven klansmen for illegal possession of riot equipment at a KKK rally.

18 July: Jacksonville, FL—Rioting erupts after whites attack civil rights marchers. Police arrest Warren Folks for trying to serve a "Klan warrant" on NAACP officials.

20 July: Jacksonville, FL—Bombers strike a black-owned store.

28 July: Baltimore, MD—Following an NSRP rally addressed by Connie Lynch, white gangs invade a black neighborhood. Police jail Lynch and two others for inciting the riot, while an August court order bars all three from Baltimore. Jurors convict the defendants on 21 November, resulting in two-year prison terms.

30 July: Bogalusa, LA—White gunmen murder Clarence Triggs, a black man.

31 July: Raleigh, NC—Klansmen brawl with blacks at a KKK rally.

9 August: Grenada, MS—175 whites hurl bricks, stones, bottles, steel pipes and firecrackers at black protest marchers. Police stand by, laughing, as a riot erupts.

9 August: Milwaukee, WI—Klansmen bomb an NAACP office. On 26 September, police arrest Illinois Grand Dragon Turner Cheney and two others for this crime and another bombing on 1 July. On 1 May 1967, prosecutors charge Cheney with soliciting the murder of codefendant Robert Schmidt, to prevent Schmidt from turning state's evidence.

11 August: Carthage, MS—Klansmen bomb the home of a black activist.

12 August: Chicago, IL—White mobs, including a robed klansman and uniformed ANP members, stone civil rights marchers in Marquette Park.

14 August: Chicago, IL—White rioting continues in Marquette Park, while other mobs repeatedly assault black demonstrators in Bogan and Gage Parks, injuring several blacks and two policemen.

21 August: Chicago, IL—White rioters stone another civil rights march.

23 August: South Deering, IL—Whites stone civil rights marchers in this Chicago suburb.

12 September: Grenada, MS—150 black students enter local schools unchallenged, but face mob assaults by 75 whites as they leave at noon. The sheriff, police, and FBI agents watch from the sidelines, while 30 students suffer beatings, one including a broken leg. (The victim's father loses his job the same day.) Governor Johnson sends state troopers that night, but riotous assaults by 200–400 whites resume on 13 September. Police take no action as rioters beat blacks and reporters with axe handles, chains and steel pipes. That evening, racists armed with slingshots fire lead sinkers at a black protest march. On 16 September, a judge finally orders police to protect the children. FBI agents arrest 13 rioters, including a local justice of the peace, on 17 September. White jurors acquit the defendants on 16 June 1967.

24 September: Cleveland, OH—Arsonists burn the home of a black minister, Rev. John Compton.

5 October: Richmond, VA—Klansmen bomb a black church.

6 October: Philadelphia, PA—Police jail Grand Dragon Roy Frankhouser and two other klansmen for disorderly conduct during an NAACP demonstration at Girard College.

8 October: Waukesha, WI—Unknown snipers fire a shotgun blast into the home of Grand Dragon David Harris.

8 November: Authorities report outbreaks of election-related violence against blacks in Lowndes County, Alabama, and Amite County, Mississippi.

19 November: Natchez, MS—Klansmen firebomb a jewelry store and damage the home of an Adams County supervisor with a hand grenade.

7 December: Richmond, VA—Governor Mills Goodwin offers a $1,000 reward for the arrests of those responsible for 18 recent cross-burnings. Klansmen light another cross one hour after Goodwin announces his reward and burn one outside the governor's mansion on 10 December.

1967

1 January: Richmond, VA—Police jail five whites, including one woman and a state prison employee, for illegal cross-burning.

1 January: Indiana—William Chaney becomes James Venable's grand dragon, serving until 31 May 1976.

10 January: New Orleans—Anti-Semitic vandals strike two Jewish cemeteries, desecrating 100+ graves.

21 January: Collins, MS—Klansmen burn a black church.

23 January: Grenada, MS—Klansmen burn a black church used for civil rights activity. Police list the fire as "accidental."

28 January: Atlanta, GA—Black parishioners at the James Avenue Church of Christ find a pile of kerosene-soaked rags burning in the office of Rev. George Briley. Shortly after midnight on 29 January, Briley's wife Lillian answers the doorbell at her home and dies from a point-blank shotgun blast. Both Klan-type crimes remain unsolved.

February: Mississippi—KKK assassin Byron De La Beckwith announces his candidacy for lieutenant governor, billing himself as a "straight-shooter."

11 February: Meridian, MS—Klansmen fire on the home of Rev. Delmar Dennis, a former White Knight who turned FBI informant. Dennis returns fire and the raiders flee.

23 February: New Orleans—Klansmen Jack Helm and Jules Kimble visit the apartment of JFK assassination suspect David Ferrie, one day after Ferrie's death from a "stroke."

27 February: Natchez, MS—A car bomb planted by the Silver Dollar Group kills Wharlest Jackson, George Metcalfe's replacement as head of the local NAACP.

4 March: Grenada, MS—Klansmen burn a black church.

4 March: Pascagoula, MS—Klansmen kidnap ex-convict Jack Watkins and threaten his life in an effort to elicit false testimony against FBI agents in the Dahmer murder case. On 9 March, police charge klansman Billy Roy Pitts and WKKKKM lawyer Travis Buckley with kidnapping and obstruction of justice. State authorities indict and convict both defendants, while Buckley is temporarily disbarred from practicing law.

8 March: Prattville, AL—White rioters against integration damage four school buses.

12 March: Hayneville, AL—Klansmen burn a black church.

13 March: Ft. Deposit, AL—Klansmen burn another black church.

13 March: Hayneville, AL—Klansmen burn an Episcopal church used as a Head Start center.

13 March: Liberty, MS—Klansmen bomb a Head Start office.

28 March: Mobile, AL—Klansman Thomas Tarrants robs a supermarket.

25 April: Birmingham, AL—Bombs damage the home of Judge Frank Johnson's mother.

10 May: Jackson, MS—Thomas Tarrants robs a grocery store.

14 May: Cleveland, OH—Bombers strike a black home in a newly-integrated suburb.

27 May: Meridian, MS—Thomas Tarrants bombs the Temple Beth Israel.

23 June: Newark, NJ—Klan leader John Behringer tells reporters that he initiated Anthony Imperiale, leader of the vigilante North Ward Citizens Committee, into the KKK on 19 April.

28 June: Mobile, AL—Klansmen bomb a black civil rights worker's home.

30 June: Wadesboro, NC—Klansmen bomb three homes, a business office and a lodge owned by school board members who support integration.

18 July: North Carolina—FBI agents arrest 12 whites, including 7 identified klansmen, for acts of racist terrorism spanning the past 21 months in Anson, Cabarrus and Rowan Counties. In a separate incident at Greensboro, police jail two klansmen for illegal cross-burning.

19 July: Baton Rouge, LA—Bombs destroy one car, damage another, and shatter windows at the home of a Victor Bussie, an AFL-CIO leader who publicly condemned the KKK.

11 August: Indianapolis, IN—A court order cancels Bill Chaney's scheduled KKK rally.

15 August: Satsuma, LA—15 whites attack black protesters.

16 August: Holden, LA—75 whites assault black marchers.

19 August: Shelby, NC—A bomb strikes the chemical company owned by Grand Dragon Woodrow Lynch.

24 August: Philadelphia, MS—Klansmen fire shotguns at two busloads of black students, wounding two children with flying glass. As a result, black parents launch a school boycott.

28 August: Milwaukee, WI—White mobs stone NAACP protesters, while shouting, "We want slaves!" and "Get yourself a nigger!" More rioters attack black marchers on 29 August, while arsonists burn a Freedom House and snipers harass firefighters summoned to fight the blaze.

18 September: Jackson, MS—Klan members Thomas Tarrants and Kathy Ainsworth bomb the Temple Beth Israel. Three other klansmen are jailed the same night, for threatening FBI agents and ramming their car. J. Edgar Hoover orders further investigation on 28 September.

29 August: Arlington, VA—Ex-ANP member John Patler assassinates party leader George Lincoln Rockwell.

Autumn: Louisiana—David Duke joins the KKKK.

6 October: Jackson, MS—Klansmen bomb the home of a white dean at Tougaloo College.

6 October: Carthage, MS—Klansmen fire into the home of a black NAACP activist.

8 October: Bastrop, LA—An explosive booby-trap at a rural KKK hangout injures two trespassing hunters.

9 October: Meridian, MS—Eighteen WKKKKM members face trial on federal charges in the slaying of victims James Chaney, Andrew Goodman and Michael Schwerner. On 20 October jurors convict seven defendants, acquit eight, and deadlock on three. Judge Harold Cox sentences the convicted defendants to prison on 29 December. An appellate court upholds the verdicts on 17 July 1969. The U.S. Supreme Court declines to review the case on 27 February 1970.

15 November: Laurel, MS—Klansmen bomb the parsonage of St. Paul's Church, whose pastor doubles as a local NAACP leader.

19 November: Jackson, MS—Thomas Tarrants and Kathy Ainsworth bomb the home of white civil rights activist Robert Kochtitzky.

21 November: Jackson, MS—Klansmen bomb the home of Rabbi Perry Nussbaum. Some media reports cite it as the home's second bombing. Jewish community leaders meet to discuss countermeasures on 22 November, expanding their discussions to include the FBI and Mayor Allen Thompson on 23 November.

20 December: Collins, MS—Police stop Thomas Tarrants for reckless driving, briefly detaining him and passenger Sam Bowers after seeing a submachine gun in the car.

21 December: Heidelberg, MS—Unknown kidnappers snatch former WKKKKM Grand Titan Donald Hinshaw, then release him outside town.

25 December: Louisburg, NC—Klansmen fire on the home of a black civil rights activist.

1968

February: Hattiesburg, MS—Klansmen fire on the home of NAACP activist Kaley Duckworth.

20 February: Meridian, MS—Klansmen burn a store owned by turncoat former klansman Wallace Miller. The attack inaugurates a local reign of terror, including arson fires at two black churches used as Head Start centers and the home of a black Head Start bus driver.

3 March: Jackson, MS—Guards at the home of Charles Evers exchange shots with nightriders. Police arrest one white youth the next day.

7 March: Jackson, MS—Klansmen bomb the Blackwell Real Estate office for accepting black customers. A grand jury indicts Sam Bowers and nine others on 10 April. Jurors deadlock in the case of James Harper, caught with 115 sticks of dynamite, on 31 July. Another panel acquits Joe Daniel Hawkins, Jr., on 7 August.

23 March: Mobile, AL—Thomas Tarrants escapes an FBI trap at his home and flees to North Carolina.

4 April: Memphis, TN—A sniper's bullet kills Dr. Martin Luther King, Jr., at the Lorraine Motel. Over the next week, rioting erupts in 125 cities nationwide, leaving 46 persons dead, 2,600 injured, and 21,270 arrested, with $45 million in property damage reported. British police capture suspect James Earl Ray in London, on 8 June. He initially retains frequent Klan attorney Arthur Hanes, Sr., then switches to lawyer Percy Foreman before pleading guilty on 10 March 1969. Sentenced to 99 years in prison, Ray maintains that King was killed as the result of a conspiracy. In April 1969 he retained klansman J.B. Stoner as his new lawyer.

4 April: Meridian, MS—FBI agents spy on an NSRP meeting led by J.B. Stoner, thus "eliminating" him as a suspect in the King assassination.

11 April: Washington, DC—LBJ signs the 1968 Civil Rights Act.

28 April: Atlanta, GA—Grand Dragon Calvin Craig resigns from the UKA, declaring that all races should cooperate "in a united America."

2 May: Sandhill, MS—Klansmen strafe the home of Head Start worker Flossie Lindsey with machine-gun fire.

15 May: Hattiesburg, MS—A car-bomb injures civil rights activist Kaley Duckworth.

28 May: Meridian, MS—Albert Tarrants and Joe Daniel Hawkins, Jr., bomb the Temple Beth Israel.

2 June: New Orleans—The mayor and police chief of Meridian, Mississippi, meet with ADL leaders to discuss cash payments for Klan bombing informants.

8 June: Meridian, MS—Brothers Alton and Raymond Roberts agree to betray fellow klansmen for cash. ADL sources deliver $25,000 to local leaders on 11 June, with $1,000 paid to the Roberts brothers and $1,000 to a middleman. On 12 June, the brothers meet with FBI agents but refuse to testify in court. The brothers meet with Joe Daniel Hawkins, Jr., on 13 and 17 June, to plot a bombing at Meyer Davidson's home. Raymond Roberts receives $850 from the FBI on 18 June, followed by another meeting with Hawkins on

19 June. Hawkins meets Thomas Tarrants on 24 June. Fear of FBI surveillance on Hawkins scuttles the plan for a bombing on 27 June.

29 June: Meridian, MS—Police ambush Klan terrorists Thomas Tarrants and Kathy Ainsworth at Meyer Davidson's home, killing Ainsworth and critically wounding Tarrants in running gun battle. Gunfire also wounds a policeman and an innocent bystander during the chase. Tarrants receives a 30-year prison term on 27 November.

5 August: Charlotte, NC—Bombers strike the home of a known klansman.

14 August: Louisville, KY—Nightriders bomb the church of Rev. A.D. King.

19 August: Shelby, NC—A bomb explodes at a chemical plant owned by a KKK member.

26 August: New York City—Police arrest KKK-NSRP members Paul Dommer and William Hoff for supplying explosives to an undercover officer, in an alleged plot to bomb the home of a local draft resistance leader. Dommer pleads guilty to third-degree conspiracy in February 1969.

1 September: Berea, KY—Following a speech by Connie Lynch, shooting erupts at an NSRP rally, killing two persons.

4 September: Lexington, KY—A bomb wrecks the home of Dr. Z.A. Palmer, a member of the Kentucky Human Rights Commission, injuring Palmer and members of his family.

26 September: Salisbury, NC—Rowan County Sheriff John Stirewalt recruits Grand Dragon James Jones as a "special deputy."

24 December: Monroe, LA—Gunmen fire into the home of a black OEO administrator, narrowly missing his wife. Police arrest a klansman for the crime, then release him on 29 February 1969, due to a legal technicality.

1969

5 January: New York City—The mayor reports arson attacks on 32 religious institutions, including 14 synagogues, during 1968.

15 January: Cairo, IL—Snipers drive police and firefighters from a burning warehouse. Authorities report three more firebombings on 16 January, in an area patrolled by volunteer members of the vigilante White Hats. On 19 January, state troopers officially relieve the White Hats of all patrol duties.

14 February: Texarkana, AR—Robert Shelton enters federal prison, to serve a one-year sentence for contempt of Congress.

27 June: Cairo, IL—White and black mobs stone each other during a "mother's march" on police headquarters, demanding "equal rights for whites." A warehouse arson fire forces evacuation of 3,000 residents from the immediate area.

4 July: Swan Quarter, NC—A shootout following a UKA rally leaves one woman wounded. Police charge Grand Dragon Joseph Bryant and 16 other klansmen with inciting a riot. All are convicted at trial, paying $1,000 fines in lieu of suspended jail terms.

23 July: Parchman, MS—Thomas Tarrants and two other inmates escape from Mississippi's state prison. Joe Daniel Hawkins, Jr., and another klansman meet them with guns and a getaway car. Authorities recapture Tarrants the same night, adding eight years to his 30-year sentence for the escape.

27 August: Forrest City, AR—Would-be lynchers storm the jail attempting to reach a black prisoner. State police and National Guardsmen disperse the mob.

9 September: Fayette, MS—Police arrest three klansmen with a carload of weapons, outside a store owned by newly-elected mayor Charles Evers.

16 September: North Carolina—Joseph Bryant leads dissident klansmen into the new North Carolina Knights, secretly funded by the FBI. Defecting UKA members rally and nail their membership cards to a cross before burning it.

11 November: Baton Rouge, LA—*The Reveille* runs its first article on David Duke's collaboration with the NSLF at LSU.

21 November: Ashville, AL—2,200 whites rally to protest the sale of a nearby farm to Black Muslims. Several nights later, snipers kill six cows at the farm. On 16 March 1970, NOI spokesmen announce plans to sell the farm.

26 November: Sandersville, GA—Nightriders fire on the home of a black civil rights leader.

8 December: Pell City, AL—Arsonists damage the auto dealership of a white man who sold land to Black Muslims.

1970

January: Clay County, MS—A segregationist bomb damages the county courthouse.

3 March: Lamar, SC—White rioters armed with axe handles attack school buses carrying black students to a newly-integrated school. Jurors convict three of the mob on 17 February 1971.

15 March: Ashville, AL—The sheriff announces that 63 cows on a farm owned by the NOI have been poisoned with cyanide since October 1969. He names unspecified klansmen as the prime suspects.

3 April: Imperial Wizard Sam Bowers begins his prison sentence for the murders of three civil rights workers in Neshoba County, Mississippi. Authorities parole him in 1976.

May: Houston, TX—Klansmen bomb Pacifica radio station KPFT.

14 May: Jackson, MS—City and state police fire on unarmed black students at Jackson State College, killing two. Despite an FBI investigation proving that officers fired without provocation and later destroyed evidence, white jurors acquit all concerned.

3 June: Frankfurt, West Germany—A U.S. Army report denies rumors of KKK activity among soldiers stationed in the city.

27–28 June: Salisbury, NC—Dissent splits a UKA convention between followers of Robert Shelton and Grand Dragon J.R. Jones.

5 July: Longview, TX—Two dozen bombs explode, damaging 36 school buses scheduled for use in court-ordered integration.

20 July: Brooklyn, NY—Bombers damage the Crown Heights Jewish Community Council building.

August: A Gallup poll reveals that 76 percent of all Americans surveyed disapprove of the KKK.

28 August: Rocky Mount, NC—Bombers strike a school scheduled for desegregation.

23 July: New Orleans—David Duke pickets attorney William Kinstler at Tulane University, in full Nazi uniform.

6 September: Washington, DC—David Duke addresses a NSWPP rally led by Matt Koehl.

19 September: Sumter, SC—Police charge Grand Dragon Robert Scoggin and nine klansmen as accessories to murder, after KKK security guards kill W.L. Odom at a Klan rally. Additional charges include conspiracy to commit robbery.

Autumn: Baton Rouge, LA—David Duke joins the White Student Alliance at LSU.

6 October: Houston, TX—Klan bombers strike radio station KPFT for the second time.

8 November: Cairo, IL—White snipers wound three blacks, including soldier Wiley Anderson, while firing into a black housing project. Elsewhere, arsonists burn a lumberyard owned by the founder of the racist White Hats.

24 November: Savannah, GA—Jurors acquit Jerry Ray of aggravated assault in the wounding of ANP member and future klansman Don Black, shot during an alleged burglary attempt at NSRP headquarters.

5 December: Cairo, IL—Police resume deputizing of White Hat vigilantes after black snipers wound a white deputy sheriff. Authorities jail 12 blacks for that shooting, later releasing eight.

1971

20 January: Houston, TX—Police acting on an FBI tip arrest klansman Jimmy Hutto for conspiracy to terrorize Pacifica radio stations in Texas and California.

4 February: Chapel Hill, NC—Arsonists cause $50,000 damage to the office of J.L. Chambers, a black lawyer active in civil rights litigation.

5 February: Wilmington, NC—Violence erupts after bomb threats to a black church. Armed youths fortify the church and trade shots with white gunmen. Sniper fire kills one white man and police slay a black youth before National Guardsmen restore order on 8 February.

March: Toronto, Ontario—David Duke visits the city to recruit Canadian klansmen.

6–7 March: Texarkana, TX—Arsonists burn four black churches.

9 March: Baton Rouge, LA—A letter from George Tully, Jr., accuses *The Reveille* of letting David Duke use the paper as a neo-Nazi propaganda vehicle. The paper never mentions him again.

12 March: Houston, TX—Klansmen bomb an SWP office.

April: Hightstown, NY—UKA members clash with JDL militants.

2 April: Ypsilanti, MI—Armed UKA members abduct Dr. R.W. Brownlee, principal of Willow Run High School, to tar-and-feather him for promoting racial harmony on campus. Federal prosecutors indict Grand Dragon Robert Miles and four others on 22 June 1972.

20 April: Washington, DC—The U.S. Supreme Court approves busing to achieve school integration.

5 May: Baton Rouge, LA—David Duke and the White Youth Alliance picket an anti-war rally at LSU.

26 May: Drew, MS—Drive-by gunmen murder black teenager Jo Etta Collier following her high school graduation ceremony. Police charge three white suspects, and jurors convict the triggerman of manslaughter on 30 October, resulting in a 20-year prison term. Prosecutors drop all charges against the other defendants on 5 March 1972.

11 June: Houston, TX—Prosecutors charge Louis Beam, Jimmy Hutto and two other klansmen with bombing Pacifica radio station KPFT, the local SWP office, a "hippie" restaurant, an architect's office and a motorcycle dealership. None of the charges finally produce convictions.

30 August: Pontiac, MI—Bombs destroy 10 school buses scheduled for use in desegregation. FBI agents arrest seven UKA members, including Grand Dragon Robert Miles, on 9 September. Jurors later convict Miles and Dennis Ramsey of conspiracy, but prosecutors dismiss all charges against the other five defendants on 22 October 1974, after a key witness suffers brain damage from a prison beating.

September: Wilmington, NC—Racists pour sand into the fuel tanks of 19 school buses scheduled for use in desegregation.

7 September: Pontiac, MI—Police jail five UKA members for creating a disturbance at the school bus depot.

10 September: Jacksonville, FL—Police defuse a bomb with 10 sticks of dynamite, found under a school bus.

9 October: Arkansas—Reports from Forrest City, Madison and Marianna suggest that recent rapid growth of the KKK has been accompanied by violence. In the preceding year, arsonists destroyed several buildings and racially-motivated shootings wounded at least 10 victims.

November: Rochester, NY—Bombers damage a black church.

1972

January: New Orleans—David Duke creates the National Party with Klan backing, to recruit young people. Police subsequently charge Duke and two other party members (including his future wife Chloe) with illegally collecting campaign donations for the AIP.

19 January: New Orleans—Blacks armed with bricks injure Imperial Wizard H.R. Thompson during a parade celebrating the birthday of Confederate Gen. Robert E. Lee.

21 January: New Orleans—David Duke organizes a march protesting the rape of a white woman by a black assailant on Christmas Eve. Police jail Duke and two others for lighting a homemade torch, but they drop all charges after Jim Lindsay intervenes. The march proceeds after nightfall with 300 participants.

19 February: Detroit, MI—Leaders of Canada's Western Guard meet with Michigan klansmen.

1 May: Toronto, Ontario—The Toronto *Sun* announces renewed KKK activity in the city.

11 September: Tuscaloosa, AL—As a hedge against informers, Robert Shelton orders all UKA members to take polygraph tests.

14 November: Baton Rouge, LA—David Duke pickets activist Jerry Rubin in full Nazi uniform.

1973

12 January: Rochester, NY—Arsonists destroy a black church, closed since it was bombed by nightriders in November 1971.

May: Wilmington, NC—Police jail Leroy Gibson, leader of the Rights of White People, for bombing a bookstore.

September: Trenton, NJ—Police jail Grand Dragon Frank Drager for buying a pistol without a permit. He receives a six-month jail term on 6 November 1976.

26 September: Jackson, MS—FBI agents watch as Byron De La Beckwith receives a time bomb from klansman L.E. Matthews in a restaurant. On 27 September, New Orleans police arrest Beckwith with the bomb and five guns in his car, allegedly bound for a raid on an ADL leader's home. On 9 October, federal prosecutors charge Beckwith with illegally transporting explosives across state lines. The Louisiana Klan begins fund-raising for Beckwith's defense on 10 October. Jurors acquit him of all charges on 16 January 1974.

26 November: Gadsden, AL—Klansmen murder a black minister, Rev. Edward Pace, at his home. Police arrest three UKA members. Jurors convict defendant Bruce Botsford on 6 March 1974, resulting in a 30-year prison term. A second panel deadlocks on defendant Aubrey Arledge in April.

1974

3 January: Asbury Park, NJ—An appeals court upholds the conviction of a klansman jailed for burning a cross at a black home.

7 January: New York City—David Duke appears on NBC's *Tomorrow* show, hosted by Tom Snyder.

1 March: Philadelphia, PA—A grand jury indicts Grand Dragon Roy Frankhouser and two others for trafficking in stolen explosives.

1 March: Ann Arbor, MI—Klansmen Elmer Tackett, dying of leukemia, confesses to the 1971 bombing of school buses at Pontiac. Authorities ignore his claim that the knights convicted in that case are innocent.

17 May: Baton Rouge, LA—David Duke graduates with a B.A. from LSU after six years of study.

27 July: Kokomo, IN—Police report shooting incidents during a Klan recruiting drive.

17 August: Kokomo, IN—Authorities report more Klan-related shootings.

19 September: Boston, MA—David Duke and two other klansmen lead an anti-busing rally attended by 2,000 racists. Police cancel a planned KKK parade on 20 September, ordering Duke and his comrades out of town. Despite Duke's absence, anti-busing riots erupt at several points on 20 September, with mobs stoning school buses and battling police. Violence continues through 22 September, when armed whites invade a black housing project and terrorize its occupants. National Guard troops mobilize to suppress new outbreaks on 15 October.

23 December: Pine Bush, NY—Janice Schoonmaker, wife of New York's grand dragon, refuses calls to resign from her school board position.

1975

January: Pensacola, FL—Simmering racial animosity sparked by KKK recruiting erupts into violence, with shots fired into the state attorney's home and a brick hurled through the window of a black leader's residence. Police arrest 50 persons during the month.

4 April: Walker, LA—David Duke leads a rally attended by 2,700 persons. Female jockey Mary Bacon reveals her Klan membership, thus effectively ending her career.

May: Kankakee, IL—UKA Imperial Representative Wilburn Foreman meets with leaders of the Devil's Advocates motorcycle gang. Imperial Wizard Robert Shelton fires Foreman soon afterward.

12 June: Metairie, LA—Jim Lindsay's still-unsolved murder leaves David Duke in charge of the Klan. Duke incorporates his Knights of the KKK in August.

2 July: Boston, MA—100 whites, some armed with baseball bats, attack six black bible salesmen at Carson Beach. Police jail two rioters for assault with deadly weapons.

27 July: Tuscumbia, AL—Stephen Black joins the KKK, becoming David Duke's Alabama grand dragon.

29 July: Boston, MA—Racial clashes injure two more persons.

10 August: Boston, MA—Rock fights erupt after whites stone blacks at a public beach. Police jail 17 suspects after black youths attack white motorists on 12 August. Race riots on 13 August leave 17 injured, including 6 policemen, while officers arrest two brawlers. By 14 August, police have jailed 83 persons, reporting 36 injured. Racial fighting injures two more persons on 15 August.

16 August: Greenville, AL—A car bomb injures Judge Arthur Hamble, who signed murder indictments against Viola Liuzzo's killers in 1965.

26 August: Boston, MA—Police jail 10 persons after a series of racial brawls, including one charged with assaulting an officer.

30 August: Stone Mountain, GA—Assembled klansmen assault five men, including two blacks and one Asian, expelling them from the convention.

5 September: Louisville, KY—Whites riot against school busing for desegregation, overrunning police lines at Valley High School, burning one school bus and damaging 30 more, then vandalizing nearby shops. National Guardsmen restore order on 6 September, while police arrest Grand Dragon Phillip Chopper and 74 others during an unauthorized protest march.

October: Louisville, KY—Police extradite Phillip Chopper to Louisiana for trial on charges of writing bad checks.

13 October: The grand dragons of Maryland, Ohio, Pennsylvania, South Carolina and West Virginia defect from James Venable's National Knights to found the Invisible Empire, Knights of the KKK.

1 November: Baton Rouge, LA—David Duke loses his race for the state senate to opponent Ken Osterberger, polling 11,079 votes (33.2 percent of the total).

1976

15 January: Albany, NY—New York's supreme court rules that the KKK is not an "oath-bound" organization covered by terms of the Walker Law.

21 February: Montgomery, AL—Police arrest klansmen Henry Alexander, Sonny Livingston and James York for the 1957 murder of Willie Edwards. Grand jurors indict all three on 5 March, but prosecutors dismiss the charges for "lack of evidence" on 14 April.

March: St. Louis, MO—Rev. James Betts offers 40 klansmen to help police patrol the city. Department leaders decline.

29 May: Pulaski, TN—The UKA stages a Klan "bicentennial" demonstration.

3 July: Lebanon, OH—Police arrest two Klan members at a rally led by James Venable, for violation of anti-mask laws. Angry klansmen stone the officers.

3 July: Shepherdsville, KY—UKA Grand Dragon Sherman Adams leads 260 klansmen on an unauthorized parade. Police fail to intervene.

7 July: Birmingham, AL—Police jail eight whites, including at least one klansman, on weapons charges after shooting incidents in a racially troubled neighborhood.

15 August: Okolona, KY—Three hooded horsemen lead several hundred klansmen through this Louisville suburb torn by dissent over busing to achieve school integration.

September: New Orleans—The KKKK participates in a 5-day World Nationalist Congress, with 1,000 persons attending. Police arrest James Warner for disorderly conduct.

6 September: Atlanta, GA—Former klansman Joseph Paul Franklin follows an interracial couple for 10 miles before stopping them and spraying both with mace. Police arrest him for assault.

9 October: Denver, CO—District Attorney Dale Tooley tells Grand Dragon Jerry Dutton to leave town. The ACLU supports Dutton's protest.

5 November: New Jersey—The state's grand dragon draws a six-month jail term for carrying an unlicensed gun.

13 November: Camp Pendleton, CA—Black marines raid a barracks occupied by members of an on-base klavern. Military police seize a list of 16 klansmen on 14 November. Klavern leader Daniel Bailey faces arrest for refusing transfer orders on 4 December.

6 December: Camp Pendleton, CA—Anti-Klan picketers assault David Duke during a public demonstration. The ensuing brawl leaves six whites hospitalized, while police charge 14 blacks with assault and conspiracy.

13 December: Jackson, MS—Gov. Cliff Finch approves the release of Thomas Tarrants from state prison, to attend Ole Miss.

1977

4 February: Plains, GA—An anti-Klan motorist drives his car into the crowd at a KKK rally.

14 February: New Rochelle, NY—NSRP member Frank Cowan, recently suspended from his job after altercations with a Jewish supervisor, returns to work with a small arsenal, killing five persons and wounding five others before he commits suicide.

March: Louisville, KY—Authorities indict Grand Dragon Sherman Adams and 10 other klansmen for staging a private drug raid, ransacking and vandalizing the suspect's home.

2 March: Baltimore, MD—Police arrest klansman William Aitcheson with bomb components at the University of Maryland, charging him with a series of threats and cross-burnings. Aitcheson pleads guilty to threatening Martin Luther King's widow and begins serving a 90-day federal jail term on 7 September. In state court, he pleads guilty on two cross-burnings and charges of manufacturing explosives without a license. He receives a 2-year sentence with all but 30 days suspended, to be served concurrently with his federal term.

April: Los Angeles, CA—Police jail three klansmen on charges of plotting to kill local JDL leaders. Jurors convict all three in December 1978.

15–17 April: Elwood, IN—A weekend outbreak of Klan activity includes cross-burnings, garbage strewn on lawns, and a shotgun blast fired into the mayor's home.

29 April: Birmingham, AL—Former klansman Uriel Miles and his wife Laura file a $250,000 lawsuit against the FBI for circulating letters that falsely accused Laura of adultery in 1966.

5 June: A secret "unity conference" installs William Chaney as head of a new Confederation of Independent Orders.

11 July: Birmingham, AL—Robert Shelton sues the FBI to halt destruction of COINTELPRO records from the 1960s.

29 July: Chattanooga, TN—Joseph Franklin bombs a synagogue. Prosecutors indict Franklin on 8 March 1984, and jurors convict him on 12 July 1984.

7 August: Madison, WI—Joseph Franklin fatally shoots an interracial couple, Alphonse Manning and Toni Schwenn. Jurors convict Franklin on 14 February 1986. He receives a life prison term.

12 August: Birmingham, AL—A grand jury begins reviewing evidence in the 15 September 1963 bombing of the Sixteenth Street Baptist Church. On 24 September, the panel indicts Robert Chambliss of four murder counts. He faces trial on 14 November, on a single charge of murdering victim Denise McNair. On 17 November (McNair's birthday), jurors convict Chambliss. He receives a life sentence and later dies in custody on 19 October 1985.

12 August: Yukon, PA—Following an arson attack on a home he planned to buy, American Knights member Ed Foster allegedly threatens to kill the suspects and burn their home.

5 September: Columbus, OH—Klansmen battle hecklers at an anti-busing rally.

24 September: Mobile, AL—Brawling erupts between klansmen and hecklers at a KKK rally.

29 September: Marietta, GA—J.B. Stoner surrenders to face trial on charges of bombing Fred Shuttlesworth's Birmingham church in 1958.

8 October: St. Louis, MO—Sniper Joseph Franklin murders Gerald Gordon as he leaves a bar mitzvah in suburban Richmond Heights. Franklin receives a life sentence for the murder on 30 January 1997.

18 November: Wilkes County, GA—Nightriders burn four black churches. A white defendant pleads guilty on 28 April 1978, receiving a 6-year prison term.

26 December: Mims, FL—400-plus demonstrators join in a "Harry Moore pilgrimage," sparking new interest in Moore's 1951 assassination.

28 December: Detroit, MI—Relatives of Viola Liuzzo file a $2 million lawsuit against the FBI. A federal judge later dismisses their case.

1978

16 January: Brevard County, FL—Ex-klansman Edward Spivey claims knowledge of the 1951 Harry Moore murder, claiming the bomber committed suicide. Spivey refuses to testify before a grand jury.

March: England—David Duke plays a highly-publicized game of hide-and-seek with British authorities, meeting with native racists and journalists before he is finally caught and expelled from the country.

1 March: Fort Pierce, FL—Raymond Henry, Jr., claims a role in the Harry Moore bombing, allegedly funded by Sheriff Willis McCall. Despite inconsistent details, Stetson Kennedy publishes the story in the May 1982 *Crisis.*

April: Cohoctah, MI—Robert Miles hosts a series of meetings attended by representatives of the KKKK, NSWPP, National Alliance, Aryan Nations and Euro-American Alliance.

27 April: Lakeside, CA—Terry Martin murders fellow klansman Everett Henson, for informing on Martin's illegal drug business. Martin receives a life prison term on 15 June 1979.

May: Montgomery, AL—Federal agents charge ex-sheriff James Clark with smuggling marijuana. Clark pleads guilty and receives a 2-year prison term in December.

8 July: Birmingham, AL—State prosecutors name Gary Rowe as a possible *agent provocateur* within the KKK, announcing that Rowe failed a 1963 polygraph test concerning his involvement in local bombings, and that he confessed to murdering a black man in

1963, claiming his FBI handlers suppressed evidence in that case. The DOJ announces its own investigation of Rowe, which finds no grounds for federal prosecution.

August: Okolona, MS—Klansmen shoot out the windshield of a car owned by Dr. Howard Gunn, head of the Unity League.

2 October: Cullman, AL—Black defendant Tommy Lee Hines faces trial on charges of raping a white woman. Klansmen block 26 SCLC protesters from entering the town, after which state police arrest the marchers for parading without a permit. Prosecutors later drop those charges.

30 November: Birmingham, AL—Klansmen fire shots into the homes of NAACP members Willie Williams and Charles Woods.

15 December: Cullman, AL—White men kidnap and beat a black minister, Rev. Manuel Whitfield. Klan spokesmen subsequently claim responsibility for the attack.

1979

February: Atlanta, GA—Georgia's governor approves extradition of Gary Rowe to face Alabama murder charges in Viola Liuzzo's slaying. Lowndes County prosecutors drop the case in autumn.

1 April: Vancouver, B.C.—Police arrest David Duke after a radio interview, expelling him from Canada for violation of immigration laws.

4 April: Birmingham, AL—A federal grand jury indicts 21 klansmen on charges of firing shots into the homes of NAACP members and interracial couples. The defendants include both UKA and KKKK members. The panel also charges nine klansmen with impersonating FBI agents in a failed effort to "arrest" a civil rights activist. At trial, a judge dismisses charges against four of 17 defendants on 8 June.

27 April: Lakeside, CA—A klansmen kills fellow knight Everett Henson, in what police describe as a drug-related murder. The slayer receives a life prison term on 15 June 1979.

9 June: Riverton, UT—The Klan makes its public debut with a cross-burning at City Park.

9 June: Decatur, AL—1,200 SCLC members parade past 150 klansmen, while 500 police keep the two groups apart.

9 June: Little Rock, AR—Police arrest Grand Dragon Randy Howard and four others, after violence erupts between klansmen and hecklers at a KKK rally.

18 June: Hamburg, AR—Robert Shelton claims that the FBI financed several Klan factions between 1964 and 1971. FBI documents later prove the charge.

July: Lochearn, MD—Police jail three klansmen for plotting to bomb a synagogue and a black congressman's home. Jurors later convict all three defendants.

10 July: Birmingham, AL—Ex-klansman Gary Rowe confesses that he killed a black man during a 1963 race riot, then concealed the crime on orders from FBI agents who paid him to infiltrate the KKK.

October: Riverton, UT—Klansmen hang an effigy peppered with shotgun pellets above a cemetery gate, with dead ducks scattered at its feet and a sign warning "niggers" to leave town. They soon return to hang a second effigy at the same site, with a sign reading: "KKK Kills Niggers."

15 October: Boston, MA—Anti-Klan picketers assault two knights at a Klan-sponsored anti-busing rally.

30 October: Camp Pendleton, CA—A white marine identified as a klansman dies from gunshot wounds inflicted by a Hispanic marine. Investigators call the shooting "accidental."

10 November: Riverton, UT—Klansmen hang a third effigy at the local cemetery entrance, adding KKK graffiti and shooting out a nearby streetlight.

24 November: Vineland, NJ—Police arrest 22 klansmen and

neo–Nazis on weapons charges prior to a public rally. The officers confiscate 20 weapons, including guns, knives and clubs.

26 November: Algiers, LA—Police jail a klansman for firing shots at officers sent to investigate complaints of unusual noise at a KKK rally.

1979

4 April: Birmingham, AL—Federal prosecutors indict 21 klansmen, including a policeman, for firing shots into the homes of NAACP members and interracial couples in Childersburg and Sylacauga. On 4 June, police find prosecution witness Lloyd Bailey dead near the federal courthouse, charging a klansman with his murder on 5 June. Jurors convict 12 of the original defendants on 14 June.

29 April: Decatur, AL—A robed klansmen suffers gunshot wounds while "patrolling" a black neighborhood. Snipers fire into a white home on 3 May, while a black home suffers gunfire damage on 5 May. On 28 May, police charge a black suspect with wounding the klansman. Racial tensions stem from the arrest of a retarded black man, charged with raping three white women, with Klan leaders using the case as a recruiting tool.

26 May: Decatur, AL—Klansmen clash with blacks during a public demonstration. Gunfire erupts, wounding two klansmen and a black woman. On 29 May, police charge three klansmen with assaulting officers during the riot. Federal prosecutors indict nine klansmen for civil rights violations on 17 May 1984.

30 June: Vineland, NJ—Prosecutors charge two klansmen with raping a female JDL member, caught spying on one of their meetings. Jurors acquit both defendants on 1 March 1980.

6 July: Birmingham, AL—Police arrest several whites, including Klan members, for bullying blacks on the street.

19 July: Birmingham, AL—Officers jail two white gunmen for firing into black homes.

22 July: Doraville, GA—Sniper Joseph Franklin kills black victim Harold McIver at a restaurant.

11 August: Selma, AL—Police seize weapons and arrest 11 klansmen during a KKK demonstration.

19 August: Castro Valley, CA—A clash between klansmen and hecklers leaves one person hospitalized with head injuries.

21 October: Oklahoma City—Joseph Franklin murders an interracial couple, Jessie Taylor and Marion Bresette, in a parking lot. Prosecutors later charge him with the killings, then dismiss the indictments in January 1983.

31 October: Greensboro, NC—Informant Edward Dawson warns police of KKK plans to attack an anti–Klan parade on 3 November. Dawson repeats his warning on the day of the march.

3 November: Greensboro, NC—Klansmen and neo–Nazis fire on a "Death to the Klan" parade, killing four members of the Revolutionary Communist Party and wounding eight others. A fifth victim dies on 5 November. Authorities charge 13 defendants with murder on 13 December, followed by formal indictments of 14 suspects on 17 January 1980. Authorities later dismiss charges against eight defendants. Jurors acquit the remaining six on 17 November 1980.

24 November: Vineland, NJ—Police arrest 22 klansmen and neo–Nazis on weapons charges prior to a scheduled public demonstration.

29 November: Metairie, LA—David Duke receives a 6-month jail term (suspended) and one year's probation following conviction for inciting a riot in 1976.

1980

SPLC investigators report nine cross-burnings nationwide.

January: Muscle Shoals, AL—Two klansmen plead guilty to assaulting black ministers in a local restaurant.

8 January: Indianapolis, IN—Sniper Joseph Franklin murders Larry Reese, a black man, at a fast-food restaurant.

14 January: Indianapolis, IN—Joseph Franklin kills another black victim, shooting Lee Watkins outside a supermarket.

February: Barnegat Township, NJ—Klansmen fire shots into the home of a black couple, Joseph and Shirley Sanders. Police arrest three suspects, seizing an arsenal at the home of one KKK member. On 11 April 1981, two defendants receive 6-month jail terms. On 29 October 1981, police jail a local physician (and the father of one Klan defendant) for plotting to murder another of his sons, who testified for the prosecution at trial.

March: Hayden, AL—Prosecutors indict a klansman for raiding an interracial couple's home and injuring a black man.

3 March: Orlando, FL—20 armed men disrupt a KKK rally, firing shots at klansmen as they flee. Police arrive to find two klansmen handcuffed and badly beaten, arresting one of the raiders.

15 March: Oceanside, CA—150 hecklers brawl with 30 klansmen at a KKK rally.

April: Jersey City, NJ—Bombs explode at the local office of Jesse Jackson's Operation PUSH.

1 April: North Carolina—The state's grand dragon and another klansman draw prison terms for illegal cross-burning.

8 April: Wrightsville, GA—200 white rioters attack black demonstrators, setting fire to several buildings in a black neighborhood and trading shots with black residents. On 1 February 1983, federal jurors reject a $21.3 million lawsuit filed by blacks against the local sheriff and 10 klansmen accused of leading the mob.

19 April: Wrightsville, GA—Two klansmen fire on black residents, wounding a 9-year-old child.

19 April: Chattanooga, TN—Three klansmen fire into a crowd of blacks, wounding five women. Police arrest the gunmen, but jurors acquit one defendant on 22 July, while convicting the other two on reduced charges. That verdict sparks three nights of black rioting. On 27 February 1982, federal jurors award the five shooting victims $5.35 million in damages.

20 April: North Carolina—Klansmen join NSPA members for a "Hitlerfest," celebrating Adolf Hitler's birthday.

29 April: Las Vegas, NV—Vandals deface the home of black comedian Redd Foxx with KKK graffiti.

May: New Britain, CT—Police blame klansmen for acts of racist vandalism around town.

2 May: Greensboro, NC—Prosecutors file riot charges against eight participants in the deadly anti–Klan rally of 3 November 1979. Fighting erupts in court as the trial begins on 16 June. Police arrest three anti–Klan protesters in that incident. On 4 August, police arrest the widows of two Klan murder victims for disrupting the trial.

3 May: Tomah, WI—Racist serial killer Joseph Franklin kills Rebeccah Bergstrom and dumps her corpse outside town.

29 May: Ft. Wayne, IN—Sniper fire wounds Vernon Jordan, black leader of the National Urban League, as he sits in a car with a white woman, outside a motel. Police later accuse Joseph Franklin of the crime, then dismiss the charges.

8 June: Cincinnati, OH—Sniper Joseph Franklin kills two blacks, Dante Brown and Darrell Land, as they walk across a railroad trestle. Jurors convict Franklin on 21 October 1998, resulting in a double life sentence.

10 June: San Francisco, CA—Anti-Klan demonstrators mob and vandalize a theater screening *The Birth of a Nation,* forcing the theater to close.

15 June: Johnstown, PA—Joseph Franklin murders an interracial couple, Arthur Smothers and Kathleen Mikula, who are engaged to be married.

July: Forsyth County, GA—White gunmen fire shots at a black fireman during a picnic.

July: Muncie, IN—Bombers strike at a black home. Police charge klansman Clifford Redwine, his son Sam, and associate Chester Strong. Jurors later convict all three, resulting in 6-year jail terms.

4 July: Wrightsville, GA—Police announce the murder of Mike Salter, an elderly civil rights activist. Unofficial reports claim the letters "KKK" were scrawled on Salter's body.

24 July: Metairie, LA—David Duke resigns as leader of the KKKK to found a new NAAWP.

August: Detroit, MI—Klansmen fire shotguns at a black man in a drive-by shooting. On learning that he is unharmed, they return and fire into his home. In November, three defendants plead guilty to firing on the victim because he entered a "white" tavern. A fourth klansman also pleads guilty to harassing a black family in nearby Romulus, trying to drive them from their home. After protracted delays, the four receive prison terms on 12 December 1981.

August: Lansing, MI—KKK/NSRP member Gerald Carlson wins the GOP congressional primary with 3,759 votes. He loses the general election in November, but still polls 53,570 votes.

20 August: Salt Lake City, UT—Sniper Joseph Franklin murders two black joggers, Ted Fields and David Martin. He receives a life sentence for the slayings on 23 September 1981.

1 September: Centralia, IL—Police hold Grand Dragon James McKinney for questioning in burglaries spanning seven counties. A search of his home reveals stolen guns, explosives, furniture and stereo equipment. Jurors later convict him of burglary and theft, resulting in two concurrent 3-year prison terms. Accomplice-klansman Robert Hansen receives two years' probation and pays a $4,000 fine.

16 September: San Diego, CA—A man armed with a pistol attempts to kill klansman and political candidate Tom Metzger at one of Metzger's campaign rallies.

20 September: Orlando, FL—Jurors acquit two Klan leaders on charges of beating dissident members.

28 September: Toronto, Ontario—The Canadian Klan announces its merger with the Nationalist Party of Canada to "promote cooperation in the white nationalist ranks."

October: Manchester, CT—A firebomb damages a black home in a newly-integrated neighborhood.

22 October: Powderly, AL—Police defuse a bomb planted at a black church.

November: Pensacola, FL—White men armed with iron pipes and sharpened steel clubs assault three black men. Police identify the attack's leader as a klansman.

November: Toronto, Ontario—Klansman Armand Siksna receives 867 votes for mayor.

November: Jackson, MS—Two white youths, one of them a klansman's son, tear-gas black students on a school bus.

November: Norfolk, VA—Jurors convict a white man of burning a cross at the home of an interracial couple.

19 November: Maiden, NC—One of the Greensboro KKK murder defendants trades shots with an unknown gunman at his home.

December: Tuscaloosa, AL—Unknown killers fatally beat a black 12-year-old, James Herrod, Jr., at a housing project where racial tension prevails. Gunmen fire at search parties seeking Herrod, and nightriders burn a cross at the complex shortly before his corpse is found, in March 1981.

December: San Pablo, CA—Arsonists burn a black woman's home. Police also report white assaults on a Hispanic victim and the wife of a candidate running for office against klansman Tom Metzger. Informants claim that local klansmen boast of decapitating an unidentified Mexican.

31 December: New Orleans—David Duke meets with Michael Purdue to secure a charter boat for the planned KKK invasion of Dominica.

1981

SPLC investigators report twelve cross-burnings nationwide.

January: Contra Costa County, CA—Vandals mark an interracial couple's home with Klan graffiti and hurl a sledgehammer through one window.

1 January: Smithburg, WV—Rev. Michael Curry goes into hiding, after a 6-month reign of terror sparked by his refusal to permit Klan meetings in his church.

3 January: Delta, B.C.—A firebomb damages the home of an East Indian family. Spokesmen for the British Columbian Organization to Fight Racism accuse the KKK.

18 January: Salt Lake City, UT—Racist vandals strike local NAACP and SWP offices. Both groups blame the Klan.

February: Tuscaloosa, AL—Nightriders fire into a black home.

February: Denver, CO—Police charge a Klan leader with harassing and threatening a black family.

25 February: Salt Lake City, UT—A bomb scare disrupts Joseph Franklin's murder trial.

2 March: Greensboro, NC—ATF agents arrest six neo-Nazis for conspiring to bomb the city if various KKK-Nazi defendants were convicted of murder at their trial in 1980. Targets include a shopping mall, a chemical fertilizer plant, an oil storage facility, and various downtown shops. Jurors convict all six defendants on 18 September 1981. Three receive 5-year prison terms, while the others receive suspended sentences or probation.

21 March: Mobile, AL—Klansmen lynch black teenager Michael Donald across the street from the home of a UKA grand titan. Three years pass before FBI agents and local police charge klansmen Henry Gays and James Knowles with Donald's murder, on 16 June 1983. Jurors convict Hays in February 1984, resulting in a death sentence. Knowles cooperates with the prosecution and receives a life prison term. In August 1987, a grand jury indicts UKA Grand Titan Bennie Hays (Henry's father) and Exalted Cyclops Benjamin Cox as accomplices. They win a mistrial based on Bennie's failing health in February 1988, but jurors convict Cox at a second trial, in May 1989, and he receives a life sentence. Donald's mother and the SPLC sue Robert Shelton's Klan for wrongful death and win a $7 million damage award in February 1987, forcing Shelton to surrender his imperial headquarters. Henry Hays dies by lethal injection on 7 June 1997.

Spring: Jefferson County, KY—A white teenager affiliated with the KYC assaults a black classmate.

April: Merced, CA—Jurors convict a klansman of brandishing a gun to threaten students on a school bus.

1 April: Sacramento, CA—Klansmen and hecklers clash at a KKK rally. Police jail one brawler.

4 April: Vancouver, B.C.—750 persons join in a "Ban-the-Klan" march.

11 April: San Jose, CA—Police jail 23 persons for stoning Klan demonstrators.

27 April: Lake Pontchartrain, LA—Federal agents arrest klansmen assembled to prepare their invasion of Dominica. A federal grand jury indicts 10 conspirators on 7 May. Jurors convict Stephen Black and Joe Daniel Hawkins on 20 June, resulting in three-year prison terms. The same panel acquits defendant Michael Norris based on his belief that he was working for the CIA. Attorney J.W. Kirkpatrick, a financial backer of the plot, commits suicide at Earle, Arkansas, on 20 June, after the verdicts are announced. Defendants Christopher Anderson, Wolfgang Droege and Michael Purdue receive three-year sentences on 2 July, while Larry Jacklin receives a sentence of indeterminate confinement in a juvenile prison.

14 May: Houston, TX—In a lawsuit filed by the SPLC, a federal judge orders Louis Beam's klansmen and white fishermen to cease harassment of Vietnamese refugees on the Gulf Coast. The order specifically bans "armed boat patrols," wherein robed klansmen brandish weapons to frighten Vietnamese fishermen.

21 May: ATF agents raid Adamic Knights klaverns in Delaware, Maryland and New Jersey, arresting 10 klansmen for conspiracy to bomb a Baltimore NAACP office.

27–28 May: Nashville, TN—FBI agents arrest six klansmen for conspiring to bomb a TV tower, a synagogue, and several Jewish-owned businesses. Their trial convenes on 7 November.

July: Rodeo, CA—The sheriff blames klansmen for recent shootings at a black housing project.

July: Massachusetts—Police defuse a pipe bomb at an NAACP office.

July: Suffolk County, NY—Whites firebomb a black home and burn a cross nearby.

11 July: Meriden, CT—Hecklers mob a Klan rally, leaving two persons injured and four in custody.

27 July: Willacoochee, GA—FBI agents launch an investigation of cross-burnings, threats, and shootings directed at interracial couples in Atkinson County.

29 August: Baltimore, MD—Federal jurors convict a Klan leader of attempting to firebomb an NAACP office. He receives a 15-year prison term on 26 September.

22 November: Meriden, CT—Brawling at a KKK rally injures 19 policemen and 6 other persons.

December: Talladega, AL—Police charge a klansman with stabbing three blacks.

December: Jackson, MS—Klansmen fire 32 shots into the office of an anti–Klan newspaper, *The Advocate.*

16 December: Yuma, AZ—Police hold a klansman from San Bernardino, California, pending extradition for trial on charges of arson, assault with a deadly weapon, and making terrorist threats.

1982

SPLC investigators report eight cross-burnings nationwide.

January: Iredell County, NC—A black rape suspect rejects attempts by 15 klansmen to bail him out of jail.

January: Jackson, MS—Klansmen fire 84 shots into *The Advocate*'s office. Police arrest two suspects, with a third surrendering on 22 January.

3 January: Raleigh, NC—Robed klansmen protest the recent conviction of their regional leader in a firebombing case.

5 January: New York City—The ADL reports that nationwide anti–Semitic incidents more than doubled in 1981, for the third consecutive year.

February: Atlanta, GA—Police find Frederick York, a black man, hanging from a tree downtown. They initially call his death suicide, then reverse that finding.

February: Springfield, MO—Racist serial killer Joseph Franklin suffers 15 stab wounds in prison. He survives the attack and refuses to name his assailant.

February: North Carolina—Nightriders fire into black homes in Alexander and Iredell Counties. In July 1985, a member of the WKL pleads guilty on multiple counts and turns state's evidence against his comrades at a trial resulting in several convictions.

February: Cleveland, OH—Frank Spisak, a transvestite neo-Nazi, launches a series of "search and destroy" missions, killing three blacks and one suspected Jew before his September arrest. Prior to Spisak's August 1983 conviction and death sentence, the leader of a neo–Nazi splinter group claims Spisak was "acting under orders from the party" to "kill niggers until the last one is dead."

11 February: Toronto, Ontario—Canadian authorities arrest klansmen James McQuirter and Charles Yanover for their role in the abortive Dominica invasion. McQuirter pleads guilty on 24 September. Yanover pleads guilty on 10 June 1983.

March: Baltimore County, MD—Two knife-wielding klansmen assault blacks on the street. One black family flees the area after repeated acts of racist vandalism.

16 April: Texas—The SPLC sues Louis Beam and his klansmen over harassment of Vietnamese fishermen. Judge Gabrielle McDonald issues a preliminary injunction against KKK intimidation on 14 May, followed by a permanent injunction on 3 June.

24 April: Hannibal, MO—Black protesters disrupt a KKK rally.

May: Cobb County, GA—Armed klansmen assault blacks and American Indians in a national park. In 1983, one defendant pleads guilty, while federal jurors convict two others.

May: Gloucester, RI—Members of a white racist group, the Guardian Knights of Justice, fire shots into a local resident's home and attempt to bomb the house.

May: Seattle, WA—A gang of whites, including at least two klansmen, assault black victim Wendell Dixon.

6 May: Denham Springs, LA—NAACP spokesmen ask Louisiana's governor to investigate the "nightrider, KKK-type" murder of a black man.

June: North Carolina—White gunmen fire on an interracial couple, killing Curtis Anderson and wounding his girlfriend.

June: Louisville, KY—White men claiming to be KKK members attack two women (a Puerto Rican and a white with dark-skinned children), leaving both victims hospitalized.

June: Meridian, MS—Black teenager Beverly Parnell disappears from home. In July, police find her murdered in a warehouse, with KKK graffiti painted on the floor beside her corpse.

July: Knoxville, TN—Police blame klansmen for the burning of a black family's home.

July: Alexander County, NC—Nightriders fire on a black home.

28 July: Toronto, Ontario—James McQuirter solicits an undercover policeman to murder the husband of klanswoman Jean MacGarry. On 8 February 1983, McQuirter and MacGarry confess the plot and plead guilty to fraud.

August: Lansing, MI—KKK/NSRP member Gerald Carlson gets 7,486 votes in his third congressional race.

September: Edinburgh, IN—Arsonists damage the home and car of Frank McGrone, a black Job Corps supervisor. Later in the month, white men kidnap McGrone, branding "KKK" on his back and a single "K" on his forehead.

4–6 September: Stone Mountain, GA—Leaders of seven independent Klans gather for a "unity conference." Despite his resignation from the KKK, David Duke also attends.

14 October: Boston, MA—During the live broadcast of a KKK TV program, hecklers pelt the host with eggs and fighting breaks out in the audience.

November: Amelia County, VA—Police charge Klan leader William Church with raping a 7-year-old girl.

November: North Carolina—The WKL launches a 2-month reign of terror against black families, including firing guns into homes.

23 November: Waco, GA—Klansmen whip a white woman, Peggy French, for socializing with black friends. On 18 December 1984, three defendants receive 40-year prison terms for that crime and for flogging a black man who married a white woman.

December: Colorado Springs, CO—Jurors convict a klansman of robbery.

December: Salem, OR—Fire guts the home of an interracial couple. Graffiti painted on a nearby fence reads: "KKK Merry Christmas Niggers."

December: Oakdale, LA—A local Klan leader launches a 2-month terror campaign against an interracial couple. He receives a 3-year prison term on 3 April 1984.

December: DeKalb County, GA—A klansman fires rifle shots at blacks in a restaurant, wounding one man.

December: Montgomery County, MD—The state Human Rights Commission reports 185 incidents of racist vandalism and harassment during 1982.

1983

SPLC investigators report thirteen cross-burnings nationwide.

January: Metairie, LA—Bill Wilkinson and the IEKKKK file for bankruptcy.

February: Tallapoosa, GA—Six masked klansmen invade an interracial couple's home, beating black victim Warren Coakley. Federal jurors later convict four defendants on civil rights charges.

February: Sturgis, IN—Police jail a klansman for armed harassment of a female city resident.

19 February: Austin, TX—Police and anti–Klan hecklers clash at a KKK rally, leaving at least 10 persons injured.

April: Toronto, Ontario—Jurors convict klansman Charles Yanover of plotting an insurance-related bombing from prison, in April 1980.

2 April: Houston, TX—Police jail six persons after an egg-hurling melee erupts at a KKK rally.

22 May: Farmington, CT—A mob attack on Klan members leaves three policemen injured and three persons in jail.

June: Buford, GA—White men attempt to kidnap the mulatto child of a women recently threatened by racists.

25 June: New Britain, CT—Police arrest four persons during an outbreak of anti–Klan violence.

July: Muscogee County, GA—Nightriders bomb three black churches and a black woman's home.

28 July: Montgomery, AL—Klansmen torch SPLC headquarters, seeking to destroy legal records in pending lawsuits. Klansman Tommy Downs subsequently receives a federal prison term.

August: Carroll County, GA—Three armed white men kidnap two blacks after a Klan rally. Police also report racist vandalism at two black homes.

August: Bloomington, IN—CSA members burn a Jewish community center.

11 August: West Hartford, CT—Arsonists destroy a synagogue.

16 September: Asheville, NC—Jurors convict six neo–Nazis of conspiracy to firebomb various Greensboro targets in 1979, in a show of support for klansmen and fascists facing trial on murder charges.

18 September: New York City—A sniper firing at Jewish high school students kills bystander Lucille Rivera. Police report the same weapon used in four other shootings since 22 June.

October: Sacramento, CA—Fumes from toxic chemicals scattered by vandals in a black residence hospitalize four tenants and two firefighters. Police find KKK graffiti at the scene.

October: Cedartown, GA—Police catch three white men trying to booby trap the residence of Casiano Zamudio's widow. Zamudio was an outspoken critic of the Klan and neo–Nazi groups.

October: Cobb County, GA—Terrorists protesting desegregation of a "white" neighborhood fire into a black family's home and car, slash the car's tires, poison the family dog, and detonate fireworks in the yard.

November: Pittsboro, NC—Gunfire erupts at a KKK meeting, killing Klan leader David Wallace. The shooter, also a klansman, receives an 18-year prison term on 14 July 1984.

November: Goulds, FL—Callers claiming to be klansmen threaten to bomb a grocery patronized by blacks. Later, whites assault several patrons at the store.

November: Arkansas—Six CSA members bomb a natural gas pipeline along the Red River.

2 November: Washington, DC—Pres. Ronald Reagan signs an act making Martin Luther King's birthday a federal holiday.

20 December: Seattle, WA—Robert Mathews stages The Order's first bank robbery, stealing $25,900.

1984

SPLC investigators report six cross-burnings nationwide.

January: Grand Prairie, TX—Robed klansmen harass worshippers at a Buddhist temple.

January: Dallas, TX—A bomb kills Ward Keeton, a police informant against the KKK and ANP. Authorities later charge two klansmen with the slaying.

30 January: Spokane, WA—The Order robs a bank of $3,600.

February: Orange County, CA—Bombers strike a black home.

7 February: Michigan—A federal court orders the FBI to pay Walter Berg $45,000 for injuries suffered by Klan attacks on the 1961 freedom rides.

18 March: Seattle, WA—The Order loots $43,000 from an armored car.

Spring: Chicago, IL—Bombers strike a black family's home, painting a swastika on an outbuilding. Later, racist vandals deface and set fire to a second black home.

Spring: Baltimore County, MD—Armed klansmen assault two black men.

April: Cedartown, GA—Klansmen attack Tim Carey, a black youth, spraying him with mace and beating him with brass knuckles when he rides his bicycle past a KKK rally. Police charge one defendant with assault on 8 May 1985.

April: Guilford County, GA—Nightriders fire into an elderly black man's home, burning a cross topped with a severed dog's head in his yard.

April: Muscogee County, GA—Terrorists bomb a black church.

April: Boise, ID—A member of The Order bombs a synagogue.

April: Henderson County, NC—Bombers strike a black church.

April: Baltimore, MD—Klansmen armed with knives attack two black men in a bar. Police charge two suspects with attempted murder.

22 April: Seattle, WA—Members of The Order bomb an adult theater. A bomb threat to the same theater on 23 April distracts police while the terrorists rob an armored car of $500,000.

June: Danbury, CT—Street fighting erupts after whites attending a Klan rally taunt black pedestrians.

June: Indianapolis, IN—One day after leaving a written threat signed "KKK," arsonists burn a black woman's new home.

18 June: Denver, CO—Members of The Order, including klansman David Lane, murder Jewish radio host Alan Berg at his home. Jurors convict Lane and Bruce Pierce on 17 November 1987, resulting in 150-year prison terms for both.

July: Lancaster, SC—Arsonists burn three black churches. Police catch two white men attempting to torch a fourth church.

July: Enterprise, AL—A klansman assaults two boys in a parking lot. Upon conviction, he receives a one-year jail term.

19 July: Ukiah, CA—Members of The Order rob a Brinks truck, fleeing with $3.6 million while dropping a pistol at the crime scene.

August: Hickory Hills, IL—Rev. Enell Hall, a black minister, finds an unexploded firebomb at his home. Prosecutors indict Chicago klansman Willis Pernic on 20 June 1985, but he evades arrest.

August: Daytona Beach, FL—KKK graffiti and bomb threats target a newspaper that published anti–Klan editorials.

10 August: Georgia—FBI agents arrest five klansmen for invading the homes of interracial couples and assaulting the residents. The raids bring total Georgia Klan arrests to 29 since October 1982.

31 August: Louisiana—Bill Wilkinson resigns as imperial wizard of the IEKKKK, replaced by James Blair of Alabama.

September: Jackson, MS—A hooded white man terrorizes black children in a series of incidents.

September: Carroll County, GA—Arsonists burn the home of an interracial couple.

September: West Point, GA—Klansman James Harry pleads guilty to displaying a weapon during a KKK demonstration. He pays a $105 fine.

Autumn: Louisville, KY—Nightriders burn a black home.

October: Doraville, GA—Racists torch a black family's car and burn a cross on their property.

October: Hobart, IN—Racists burn a cross at a black couple's home. Jurors convict two whites of the crime on 19 April 1988.

18 October: Sandpoint, ID—A member of The Order flees his home after a shootout with FBI agents. G-men recover the gun used to kill Alan Berg in June.

23 October: Cairo, NE—Posse Comitatus member Arthur Kirk mistakes police officers for agents of the Israeli Mossad and dies in the ensuing gunfight.

November: Frederica, DE—Arsonists damage a store being converted to a Puerto Rican church. Days later, vandals spray the building with KKK graffiti and racist threats.

9 November: Atlanta, GA—Federal jurors convict three klansmen in a series of 1982 floggings throughout western Georgia. They also convict a fourth klansman of perjury in the same case.

20 November: Baltimore, MD—Five klansmen receive jail terms for illegal cross-burnings. Grand Titan Benjamin Burton draws a one-year term, while the rest get 60 days each.

24 November: Portland, OR—Robert Mathews escapes from an FBI trap, while agents wound and capture Gary Yarborough. On 25 November, The Order declares war on "ZOG."

December: Rutherford County, NC—Klansmen jailed for shooting a black man defend their actions with claims that they targeted drug dealers.

December: Murfreesboro, TN—Klansmen fire at a suspected drug house. One suspect pleads guilty on 9 April 1985.

7 December: Whidbey Island, WA—Robert Mathews dies in a shootout with FBI agents. G-men capture several other members of The Order.

1985

SPLC investigators report seven cross-burnings nationwide.

January: Cobb County, GA—Arsonists firebomb a black home in a newly-integrated neighborhood.

January: Tallapoosa, GA—White gunmen fire shots into a black woman's car.

15 January: Scottsboro, AL—Bomb threats from self-proclaimed klansmen evacuate the courthouse, city jail and a radio station on Martin Luther King Day.

16 January: New York—The ADL reports 715 acts of anti-Semitic violence in 1984, a 6.7-percent increase after two years of declining mayhem.

February: Ulster County, NY—Six white prisoners dressed in Klan-style robes assault a black jail inmate.

February: Weslaco, TX—Mayor Hector Farias blames white racist groups for a bomb blast at his home.

February: Iredell County, NC—Nightriders fire into a black home, wounding three residents.

February: New Orleans, LA—Canadian klansman Walter Droege pleads guilty to federal drug, weapons and immigration charges, receiving a 13-year sentence.

March: Long County, GA—Klansmen launch a recruiting drive, after racial brawls at a local high school.

March: Louisville, KY—Purported klansmen phone bomb threats to a motel, the Braden Memorial Center, and the Kentucky Alliance Against Racist and Political Repression.

18 March: Metairie, LA—David Duke grants an interview to Evelyn Rich, including denials that the Holocaust occurred.

April: Long County, GA—Arsonists burn a black home.

April: Northbrook, IL—A pipe bomb explodes at a synagogue.

9 April: St. Petersburg, FL—Police jail five klansmen for plotting to bomb property owned by blacks and Jews.

15 April: Ridgedale, MO—A fugitive member of The Order kills state trooper Jimmie Linegar and wounds his partner.

25 April: Evansville, IN—Police jail two Klan/Nazi activists for firing a rifle into a teenager's car.

May: Houston, TX—Police charge local klansmen with setting fire to several black homes.

May: Clayton County, GA—Klansmen beat a black woman in broad daylight, on a public street.

July: Belle Glade, FL—Police charge three members of the WPP with multiple crimes against blacks, including three assaults, several shootings, slashing of car tires, and rock-throwing incidents.

10 July: Montgomery, AL—A klansmen convicted of illegal cross-burning receives a 9-month jail term.

11 July: Dunlap, TN—Klansman Rocky Coker, jailed for illegal possession of explosives in 1980, receives a death sentence for murdering a black businessman.

August: Clark, NH—The town's first black residents suffer arson threats, racist vandalism, and a cross-burning.

August: Hayden Lake, ID—Authorities charge an Aryan Nations security guard with paying $1,800 to arrange the decapitation of a suspected police informant. On 7 January 1986, federal jurors convict the defendant of plotting a contract murder and tampering with witnesses. He receives a 12-year prison term on 21 March 1986.

September: Villa Rica, GA—A klansman assaults a black youth on the street.

September: Iredell County, NC—Nightriders fire on the home of a black policeman.

October: California—Police jail Lisa Bonilla for killing an elderly Hispanic man. At trial, she reads aloud from the Bible and chants KKK slogans in court.

October: Atlanta, GA—Vandals deface and firebomb a black home.

October: Dallas, GA—Four hooded white men kidnap and threaten a black woman.

31 October: Robeson County, NC—A "white man wearing white" kidnaps, rapes and murders black victim Joyce Sinclair, dumping her corpse near the site of a recent Klan rally.

November: Concord, CA—Residents find Timothy Lee, a gay black man, hanged near the site where robed klansmen assaulted two other blacks. Civil rights activists reject the official verdict of suicide.

November: Forest Hills, PA—Bombers strike a black home.

November: Wren, MS—Arsonists burn a black home in a newly-integrated neighborhood.

November: Dover, DE—Firebombs damage an NAACP office.

28 November: DeKalb County, GA—Nightriders hurl four firebombs into a home purchased for blacks in a "white" neighborhood. Rain-dampened fuses foil the arson attack.

18 December: Statesville, NC—Four whites, including two Klan officers, plead guilty to federal civil rights violations stemming from cross-burnings at the homes of interracial couples.

1986

SPLC investigators report 18 cross-burnings nationwide.

January: Chicago, IL—Klansmen and neo-Nazis disrupt an interracial meeting.

February: Springfield, IL—Bombs strike a housing project where several black tenants reside.

February: Cobb County, GA—Klansmen and NSRP members assault a black CDC staffer.

March: Hayden Lake, ID—Bombers strike a Jewish-owned business.

April: Leavenworth, KS—Vandals smash a window of a black home, while burning a cross in the yard.

June: Mt. Airy, NC—Klansmen pummel a heckler at a KKK rally.

June: Baltimore, MD—Bombers strike a black-owned store.

June: Rock Springs, WY—Three masked whites shout racial epithets at a black traveler and fire shots at his car.

June: Zion, IL—Klansmen brawl with blacks in a state park.

June: Nash County, NC—A WKL member disrupts an NAACP parade, brandishing a gun at marchers.

July: Charlotte, NC—Police blame klansmen for vandalism at a black woman's home.

July: Scott County, IA—Vandals deface a church with a predominantly black congregation, then return two weeks later and set it afire.

July: Zion, IL—A white gunman shouting, "Klan! Klan! Klan!" fatally wounds Fahim Ahmad, a black teenager.

2 July: Washington, DC—The U.S. Supreme Court upholds affirmative action by a vote of six to three.

August: Federal Way, WA—Bomb threats from a self-proclaimed Aryan Nations member close the same bank twice in one week.

August: Chicago, IL—Hundreds of whites disrupt a small anti–Klan demonstration in Marquette Park.

September: Cumberland County, NC—Police charge WPP members with plotting robberies to purchase weapons for racist attacks.

September: Connecticut—James Farrands replaces James Blair as imperial wizard of the IEKKKK.

15 September: Coeur d'Alene, ID—Bombers strike the home of Rev. William Wassmuth, an outspoken critic of the Aryan Nations.

29 September: Coeur d'Alene, ID—Aryan Nation bombs damage three downtown businesses.

1987

SPLC investigators report 21 cross-burnings nationwide.

17 January: Cumming, GA—400 klansmen and sympathizers attack a brotherhood parade, injuring four marchers. Police arrest eight whites.

23 January: Cumming, GA—5,000 whites follow David Duke in a march on the county courthouse. Police arrest Duke, Don Black and 62 others for blocking the street. Duke posts $2,000 bond, with a promise to appear in court on 23 February.

24 January: Cumming, GA—Klan-led whites menace a new March Against Fear, but police prevent violence, arresting David Duke and 54 other white hecklers. On 10 February, prosecutors indict seven whites for racial incidents spanning the past month.

February: Howard Beach, NY—David Duke arrives to exploit recent incidents of racial violence.

22 February: Cumming, GA—125 persons attend a rally outside town, led by David Duke.

30 April: Ozark, MO—Police arrest Glenn Miller and three others. In September, Miller pleads guilty to stockpiling weapons and mailing threatening letters. He receives a six-month jail term, with three years' probation.

8 June: Marietta, GA—White supremacist leaders gather to launch David Duke's 1988 presidential campaign. Duke formally announces his candidacy on 9 June.

22 June: Cumming, GA—David Duke pleads no contest to misdemeanor charges filed in January, pays a $55 fine, and promises to stay out of Forsyth County for one year. The judge suspends his one-year jail term.

14 July: Washington, DC—FBI leaders place Louis Beam on the "Ten Most Wanted" list.

30 October: Louisiana—David Duke files suit to win inclusion in a Democratic presidential debate, scheduled for 2 November at Tulane University. He also seeks $1 million in damages for an alleged conspiracy to exclude him. A federal judge dismisses the lawsuit on 2 November.

6 November: Guadalajara, Mexico—Police arrest Louis Beam and his wife after a shootout that leaves one officer wounded.

December: Boston, MA—Jurors convict Roy Frankhouser of conspiring to obstruct investigations of alleged credit card fraud connected to the Lyndon LaRouche presidential campaign.

15 December: Raleigh, NC—State authorities report 45 attacks on racial and religious minorities statewide in 1987, an increase from 31 incidents in 1985 and 37 in 1986.

1988

SPLC investigators report 31 cross-burnings nationwide.

24 January: Durham, NH—Democrats exclude David Duke from another presidential debate. He distributes leaflets outside and sits for an MTV interview.

26 January: Lincoln City, IN—Racists burn a cross to intimidate black members of a local basketball team. Three whites plead guilty on 28 June.

28 January: New York City—The ADL reports a 17-percent increase in anti–Semitic incidents during 1987, with 207 violent acts reported in New York alone.

February: Pennsylvania—Grand Dragon Roger Kelly receives six months' probation for illegal cross-burning.

8 March: Louisiana—David Duke receives 23,390 votes (3.8 percent of the total) in the state's Democratic primary.

13 March: Cincinnati, OH—The Populist Party delegates choose David Duke as their presidential candidate, with Bo Gritz for vice president.

7 April: Fort Smith, AR—White jurors acquit white supremacist leaders on sedition charges related to their affiliation with The Order.

23 April: Bloomington, IN—Vandals torch a black student's dormitory room at Indiana University, scrawling "KKK" and "Nigger" on the door.

4 August: Oxford, MS—Police blame arson for the fire that destroys a building scheduled to house the University of Mississippi's first black fraternity.

8 November: David Duke polls 48,267 presidential votes nationwide (.05 percent of the total votes cast).

22 November: Metairie, LA—David Duke moves his home address to a new district, seeking reelection to the state legislature.

1989

SPLC investigators report 29 cross-burnings nationwide.

15 January: Longmont, CO—Police catch five white supremacists with 300 pounds of plastic explosives, several guns, and a large cache of ammunition. One prisoner tells detectives the group planned to bomb local police stations.

18 February: Metairie, LA—David Duke wins election to the state legislature.

May: Poplarville, MS—Angry klansmen depose Jordan Gollub as head of the Mississippi Christian Knights after learning that he is a Jew from Pennsylvania.

July: Montgomery, AL—Jurors in a civil lawsuit filed by the SPLC order each of 10 klansmen involved in the Decatur riots of 1979 to pay their black victims $11,500.

22 August: Atlanta, GA—White supremacists issue a declaration of war against the Eleventh Circuit of the U.S. federal courts, threatening poison gas attacks at unspecified locations. On the same day, a tear-gas parcel bomb detonates at the Atlanta NAACP office, injuring eight persons.

16 December: Birmingham, AL—A mail bomb kills federal judge Robert Vance, known for opposition to the Klan and rulings favorable to black civil rights groups.

18 December: Atlanta, GA—Police evacuate a federal courthouse and defuse a mail bomb identical to the one that killed Judge Vance two days earlier.

19 December: Jacksonville, FL—Police defuse a mail bomb at the NAACP office. FBI spokesmen link the recent incidents to August's declaration of war by white racists.

24 December: New Orleans—David Duke announces his candidacy for the 1990 U.S. Senate race.

1990

SPLC investigators report 54 cross-burnings nationwide.

8 March: Beaumont, TX—Police jail two white youths for kidnapping an Arab man and carving "KKK" into his flesh.

21 March: Jackson County, OH: Elderly klansman William Donta, Jr., shoots and kills black neighbor Rick Ratliff in an argument over a chainsaw. Police charge Donta with murder.

April: Bartow, FL—Police charge Klan leader Donald Spivey with sexual battery of a 16-year-old girl. Jurors convict him on 6 December 1991, resulting in a 30-year prison sentence on 18 December.

1 April: Smithville, TX—Police arrest a klansman for threatening a black family.

28 April: Washington, D.C.—President George H.W. Bush signs the federal Hate Crimes Statistics Act, mandating FBI data collection from the 50 states. Many state and local agencies refuse to participate.

1 May: Forrest, MS—The father of a local kludd fires shots at a black motorist.

9 May: Hamilton, OH—Tarvie Collins, son of a local Klan leader, fatally shoots black teenager Roy Printup, Jr. On the same day, Collins also beats a second black teenager with a baseball bat. Upon conviction of murder, Collins receives a prison term of 15 years to life. In November 1991, Printup's family wins a $1 million wrongful-death lawsuit against Collins.

21 May: Andrews, NC—Police jail a klansman after a street fight with another man.

June: Nashville, TN—White Knights Grand Dragon Leonard Armstrong fires shots into a synagogue. He pleads guilty on 10 April 1992.

July: Picayune, MS—Men wearing Klan hoods threaten a black inmate in jail.

16 July: Riverdale, GA—Nightriders firebomb an NAACP office. Four more firebombs hit the same building on 24 July, while a black family's home is bombed the same week.

18 August: Guntersville, AL—A man dressed in Klan regalia assaults another white man in a dispute over drugs.

15 October: Louisiana—David Duke loses his U.S. Senate race but surprises opponents by polling 605,681 votes—60 percent of the white vote and almost 40 percent of all ballots cast.

22 October: Portland, OR—Jurors order Tom Metzger, son John, WAR, and two local skinheads to pay $12.5 million for the wrongful death of an Ethiopian victim murdered in 1998.

November: Gloucester City, NJ—IEKKKK Grand Dragon Joseph Doak conspired with other klansmen to murder Klan defectors Joseph Bednarsky and Andy Jones. Police arrest Doak, his wife, and Grand Nighthawk Harold Patterson, Jr., on 17 December. All three defendants plead guilty in July 1992. Doak receives a three-year prison term on 28 August 1992, while his wife receives a sentence of one year's probation and 100 hours of community service.

30 November: Talladega, AL—Former klansman Charles Randall

Stewart murders his ex-wife, Betty Sue Lang. Jurors subsequently convict him and recommend execution.

14 December: Jackson, MS—A grand jury indicts Byron De La Beckwith once more, for the 1963 murder of Medgar Evers. Jurors convict Beckwith on 5 February 1994, resulting in a life prison term. The state supreme court upholds that verdict on 22 December 1997. Beckwith dies in prison on 21 January 2001.

1991

SPLC investigators report 94 cross-burnings nationwide.

23 January: Fort Bragg, NC—Federal prosecutors indict two active-duty soldiers and a postal employee for stealing military weapons and explosives in 1987, telling one bystander, "This is for the KKK." Agents recovered most of the weapons in October 1990, from a storage locker in Fayetteville, North Carolina.

4 February: New Orleans—David Duke announces his candidacy for president in 1992.

March: Albertville, AL—Members of the Alabama Empire Knights burn a cross at a black family's home. Federal prosecutors indict seven klansmen on various charges in June 1992. Three defendants plead guilty on reduced charges, while the rest are convicted at trial. All are sentenced as follows on 5 November 1992: Grand Dragon Stevie Stone, 106 months in prison; Grand Klabee Christopher Daniel, 90 months; Dennis Stewart, 90 months; Clarence Whitlock, Jr., 30 months; Thomas Murphree, 24 months; J.P. Warren, 18 months; and Marion Gibson, four months home detention and four months community service.

1 May: Gainesville, GA—Violence erupts after klansman John Land appears in KKK regalia outside a Hispanic housing complex. On 11 December, jurors convict Land of inciting a riot. He receives a sentence of one year's probation and 100 hours of community service.

7 May: Shreveport, LA—Members of the IEKKKK burn several crosses throughout the city. FBI agents arrest Grand Dragon Wayne Pierce and thirteen other Klan members on various federal charges stemming from the demonstrations. On 30 January 1992, defendant Ernest Palmer receives an 18-month sentence for conspiracy to intimidate blacks. Other defendants sentenced in January 1991 include Marissa Bamburg (three months' probation); Marlon Bamburg (one year); Herbert Hayes (one year of house arrest); Howard Hunter (one year); David Lively (one year); Fred Massey, Jr. (one year); Edward McGee (one year and a $2,000 fine); Gary Moore (one year of house arrest); Bobbie Pratt (three months' probation); and Norman Temple (five months in jail and five months house arrest). Pierce receives a six-year prison term on 21 February 1992, while the former Grand Klaliff gets 27 months.

19 August: Charlottesville, VA—Police jail former IEKKKK Grand Dragon Dennis Snellings for assaulting a black student.

23 August: Houston, TX—A white man with KKK tattoos attempts to rape a black woman.

24 August: Lancaster, PA—Police jail IEKKKK Imperial Wizard James Farrands for disorderly conduct, after he refuses to let them frisk him for weapons. Jurors acquit him on 8 January 1992.

26 August: Tallahassee, FL—Stetson Kennedy sends Gov. Lawton Chiles a taped interview with Dottie Harrington, naming her husband Frank as Harry Moore's killer. Chiles orders an FDLE investigation on 30 August. Agents interview Dottie on 1 October, then locate Frank in Hollywood, Florida, on 29 October. He denies any part in the crime or link to the KKK and passes a polygraph test. Dottie recants her story on 13 November.

29 August: Muskogee, OK—Police capture self-styled Phineas Priest Walter Thody after he robs the same thrift store for the second time in six weeks, fleeing with $52,000.

5 October: Tylertown, MS—Two "drinking buddies" fatally beat klansman Jeffrey Smith, stealing $700 in Klan funds from his body.

Defendants Olin McKenzie and Luther Roden, Jr., receive life prison terms for murder on 8 November.

6 October: Louisiana—David Duke polls 607,391 votes (31.7 percent of all ballots cast) in his race for governor, running second in a field of 12 contenders. In his 16 November runoff against opponent Edwin Edwards, Duke receives 671,009 votes (39 percent of all votes cast and 55 percent of the white vote).

22 October: Salisbury, NC—Rev. Virginia Herring sues the Confederate Knights for calling her a "whore" on the group's White Power Message Line.

December: Bowling Green, KY—Arsonists burn a church whose pastor criticized the KKK. On 8 June 1992, police arrest Kentucky Knights Grand Dragon Ernest Pierce and three other klansmen for the crime. Pierce subsequently receives a sentence of four years and four months for ordering the attack. On 30 August 1994, Brian Tackett receives a 12-year sentence without parole for setting the fire. On 20 October 1994, jurors convict klansman Chris Conner of threatening to kill an ATF agent assigned to the arson investigation and threatening to shoot up a local employment office.

5 December: Vero Beach, FL—FBI agents locate Raymond Henry, Jr., and take a new statement on his alleged involvement in Harry Moore's slaying.

1992

SPLC investigators report 96 cross-burnings nationwide.

7 January: Dubuque, IA—Police arrest klansman Arnold Hood for illegally burning two crosses on 7 December 1991.

10 January: Lanett, AL—A review board upholds the dismissal of two policemen who taunted a black prisoner with racial epithets and made him wear a Klan hood.

13 January: Lake City, FL—FBI agents interview ex-sheriff Willis McCall concerning his alleged involvement in Harry Moore's murder. McCall denies complicity but refuses a polygraph test.

19 January: Denver, CO—Two sheriff's deputies don Klan regalia to frighten black jail inmates.

21 January: Cleveland, OH—Nightriders firebomb a black couple's apartment, hours after vandalizing the building with KKK and SWP (Supreme White Power) graffiti. Police arrest three teenagers.

29 January: Clifton, MD—Police jail self-described klansman David Black for an illegal cross-burning the previous night.

30–31 January: South Carolina—David Duke campaigns in the state's presidential primary. He receives seven percent of the votes cast on 7 March.

February: Ex-klansman and self-styled seditionist Louis Beam calls for "leaderless resistance" to destroy the U.S. government.

23 February: Blairstown, PA—Police cite Kleagle Brent Tieber for obstructing a highway during a Mountaineer Knights demonstration. Jurors convict him on 15 April.

1 March: Grovetown, GA—Police charge former klansman and fire chief Scott Lowe with a 1987 cross-burning at the home of a man who vandalized Lowe's church.

10 March: David Duke appears on presidential ballots in seven states on "Super Tuesday," winning none of the primary elections.

13 March: Atlanta, GA—Jurors convict klansman Dave Holland on three counts of perjury related to his testimony in a civil case stemming from Klan riots in Forsyth County. On 3 June he receives a sentence of two years' probation (including six months' home detention), 250 hours of community service, and $211.50 in financial restitution to the court.

31 March: Arkansas—KKKK National Director Thom Robb files as a Republican to run for a seat in the state legislature.

1 April: Tallahassee, FL—The FDLE closes its investigation of Harry Moore's murder.

8 April: Corbin, KY—U.S. Knights Imperial Wizard Pete Collins opens a new realm office and appoints state officers.

14 April: Montreal, Quebec—Canadian KKK members Jean-Pierre Bergeron, Stephane Pigeon and Eric Vachon plead guilty to illegally importing 1,250 copies of *The Klansman* in November 1991. The court orders each to pay a $500 fine.

23 April: Millville, NJ—Police charge Confederate Knights Grand Dragon Joseph Bednarsky and klansman Anthony Trask with harassing and threatening Hispanic neighbors. Bednarsky pleads guilty on 9 September.

19 May: Conyers, GA—Federal agents jail Grand Dragon Greg Walker for selling illegal drugs and weapons to undercover officers.

21 May: Hartford, CT—William Hoff's black employers fire him after they discover he is New York's grand dragon for the IEKKKK.

3 June: Dubuque, IA—Three black women punch and kick a 16-year-old female Klan member.

6 June: London, KY—U.S. Knights clash with blacks at an outdoor concert.

10 June: Meriden, CT—Jurors convict Carl Tillbrook, Jr., of criminal trespass and harassment, for mailing and distributing threatening KKK messages during 1991.

23 June: Birmingham, AL—Prosecutors charge Klan leader Roger Handley with sodomy charges involving a teenage boy. Sheriff's deputies raid Handley's home on 25 June, recovering a copier stolen from a local church. On 7 August, officers arrest Handley on a second sodomy charge, involving a different boy.

23 June: Janesville, WI—Police arrest National Knights Imperial Wizard Ken Peterson for disorderly conduct after a quarrel related to sale of a car. On 26 August Peterson announces plans to disband his Klan and leave town. In October, Peterson donates all his KKK materials to a social justice organization and vanishes "underground."

July: Tulsa, OK—Former White Knights Grand Dragon and WAR organizer Dennis Mahon announces his candidacy for mayor.

7 July: Louisville, KY—Police arrest Marx Walker and his wife Belinda after a raid on drug charges. Other items seized at their home include a cache of weapons and photos of people in Klan regalia.

8 August: St. Clair County, AL—During a routine driver's license check near an Aryan Youth concert, police arrest four white supremacists. Officers charge Confederate Knights Imperial Wizard Terry Boyce, New National Socialist leader Hank Schmidt and skinhead Mack Frizzell with carrying concealed pistols. Another skinhead, Terry Sergent II, is held on a California fugitive warrant.

18 August: Erie, PA—Ella Mae Buren receives a 17-year prison sentence for assaulting black youths near her Franklin Township home in April 1991. Shortly before that incident, she invited klansmen to rally on her property.

27 August: Birmingham, AL—Authorities jail eight white supremacists, including longtime klansman and Aryan National Front leader Bill Riccio, on state and federal charges involving stolen military weapons and explosives.

17 September: Winter Haven, FL—Police arrest a 16-year-old boy for wearing KKK regalia in public and carrying brass knuckles. Charges include carrying a concealed weapon and wearing a mask to intimidate.

October: Georgia—Following his ouster from the Nationalist Movement for drunk and disorderly behavior, Jerry Lord founds the Rebel Knights of the KKK.

1 October: Vista, CA—A Latino man reports that his home was set afire by a disgruntled ex-employee with ties to the Klan.

5 October: Vidor, TX—Klansmen throw racist literature at a black woman and warn her to leave town.

7 October: Ocean City, MD—Herbert Cox receives two concurrent three-year prison terms for assaulting police officers at a KKK rally.

15 October: Stuart, FL—Police jail IEKKKK officer Jack Bullock and Belgian racist Steve Cirock for aggravated assault, after they chased and fired shots at a black man.

23 October: Estes Park, CO—White supremacists and far right "patriots" gather for an anti-government "Rocky Mountain Rendezvous" that spawns the 1990s militia movement. Featured speakers include Louis Beam and Christian Identity spokesman Pete Peters.

1993

10 March: Pensacola, FL—Michael Griffin, an associate of ex-klansman and "pro-life" crusader John Burt, kills Dr. David Gunn in the first U.S. assassination of an abortion provider.

20 May: Forsyth County, GA—The verdict in a federal lawsuit filed by the SPLC over Klan attacks on black demonstrators during 1987 forces the IEKKKK to disband, destroy its membership lists, and surrender all assets to pay a $37,500 judgment to the plaintiffs.

1994

21 January: Wallingford, CT—Police jail four members of the Unified KKK on weapons charges. The raids follow a sting operation in which UKKK leader William Dodge purchased a pipe bomb from undercover officers. Defendant George Steele pleads guilty on 5 April but later commits suicide prior to sentencing. Ex-convict Stephen Gray pleads guilty on 3 May; on 8 September he receives a six-month sentence at a halfway house. Dodge pleads guilty to possessing a pipe bomb on 26 May; he receives a 63-month prison term on 28 July. On 10 June, jurors convict defendant Edmund Borkoski of conspiring to purchase a firearms silencer that he threatened to use on his sister's black boyfriend; he receives a 54-month sentence. On 9 September, defendant Scott Palmer receives a 63-month sentence.

24 March: South Bend, IN—Federal jurors convict klansman Robert Rogers on weapons charges and one count of conspiracy to harass a black couple in 1992. Five other knights previously pled guilty in the same case. Rogers receives a 22-year prison term on 2 June, while codefendant Douglas Martin receives nine years for his role in the attack.

April: Arkansas—Ed Novak defects from Thomas Robb's KKKK to lead a more militant faction aligned with neo–Nazi groups. Another rift in August further weakens Robb's Klan.

16 April: Hollywood, FL—Police jail five persons during a Populist Party march in support of the Confederate battle flag. One of those arrested, klansman Hank Pritchard, faces charges of threatening to kill policemen.

16 September: Vidor, TX—Klan members Judith Foux and her two sons, David and Steven, plead guilty to various charges stemming from their harassment of black tenants at a newly-integrated housing project.

2 October: Huntingdon, PA—Authorities jail klansman Romie Young for conspiring to bomb a nearby dam.

14 October: Elkton, MD—Pennsylvania klansman Michael Birkl invades a doctor's office and holds the receptionist hostage in a bid to "get his message out." He surrenders after a 6½-hour standoff with police.

24 October: Hull, GA—Police charge four KKK members with murdering klansman William Eddie Tucker. The defendants include Terry Allen, Mary Doster, Christopher Hattrup and William Mize. Hattrup faces additional charges of giving false information and tampering with evidence.

21 November: Reading, PA—FBI agents charge Roy Frankhouser with conspiracy to obstruct an investigation of the New Dawn Hammerskins gang in Massachusetts. He allegedly induced witnesses in that case to conceal or destroy evidence. Jurors convict him on three counts, on 16 February 1995.

1995

5 January: Denver, CO—Police jail eleven past and present klansmen for acts of racist vandalism committed in April 1994, seizing a "small arsenal" of weapons. Charges later expand to include twenty-one members of the KKK, the White Order, the Nationalist Movement, the Colorado Skinheads, and the Confederate Hammerskins.

13 January: Bells, TN—Arsonists burn the black Johnson Grove Baptist Church.

13 January: Denmark, TN—Nightriders burn the black Macedonia Baptist Church.

31 January: Hardeman County, TN—Arsonists burn another black church, Mt. Calvary Baptist.

19 April: Oklahoma City, OK—Former klansman Timothy McVeigh bombs the Alfred P. Murrah Federal Building, killing 168 persons. McVeigh is executed for his crime in June 2001, while accomplice Terry Nichols receives life sentences in both state and federal prison. A third accomplice, known only as "John Doe No. 2," remains at large today.

June: Berkeley County, SC—Two members of the Christian Knights, Gary Cox and Timothy Welch, beat and stab a mentally retarded black man. Both receive 20-year prison terms on 2 April 1997. At the time of sentencing, both are already imprisoned on arson charges.

20 June: Greeleyville, SC—Klansmen burn the Mt. Zion AME Church.

21 June: Bloomville, SC—Klan arsonists destroy the 100-year-old Macedonia Baptist Church. Gary Cox and Timothy Welch, both members of the Christian Knights, plead guilty to this and the Greeleyville arson on 14 August 1996, naming accomplices. On 16 August 1996, authorities charge klansmen Arthur Haley and Hubert Rowell with conspiracy in the church fires, plus arson attacks on a migrant labor camp, a Clarendon County service center, and a black man's car. On 20 February 1997, Cox receives a 19½-year prison term, while Welch gets 18 years. In August 1997, Haley receives a 21½-year sentence, while Rowell gets 15 years in federal prison. On 14 July 1998, Cox and Welch win a reduction of their sentences to 14 and 12 years, respectively, as a reward for their cooperation with the prosecution. On 24 July 1998, jurors in a civil lawsuit levy damages of $37.8 million against the Christian Knights, Grand Dragon Horace King, and the four convicted klansmen.

August: Auburn, IN—Police jail Klan member Edna Berry for harassing her neighbors and brandishing a firearm. On 13 February 1997, she receives a sentence of one year's probation and 30 hours of community service.

9 October: Hyder, AZ—Saboteurs derail an Amtrak passenger train, killing one passenger and injuring dozens. Investigators find an antigovernment note at the scene, signed by the "Sons of Gestapo." The case remains unsolved.

9 November: Oklahoma—Federal agents arrest Oklahoma Constitutional Militia leader Willie Lampley, his wife, and two other suspects on charges of plotting to bomb abortion clinics, gay bars, welfare offices, and the SPLC's headquarters in Montgomery, Alabama. Jurors subsequently convict all four defendants.

22 December: Boligee, AL—Arsonists burn the black Mt. Zion Baptist Church.

30 December: Gibson County, TN—Fire destroys the black Salem Baptist Church.

1996

8 January: Knoxville, TN—Arsonists burn black Inner City Church.

11 January: Green County, AL—Nightriders burn two black churches, Little Mt. Zion Baptist and Mt. Zoar Baptist.

18 January: Ohio—FBI agents capture Peter Langan, commander of the Aryan Republican Army, after a fierce shootout. Langan subsequently receives a life sentence plus 55 years for his role in 22 Midwestern bank robberies committed during 1994–96. Four other ARA members receive varying prison terms, while a fifth commits suicide.

19 January: Wolfe City, TX—Arsonists level the Mt. Zion Missionary Baptist Church.

26 January: Orrum, NC—Fire destroys the Ohova AME Church.

1 February: Baton Rouge, LA—Arson fires raze four black churches in one night.

21 February: Richmond, VA—Arsonists burn the black Glorious Church of God.

5 March: Haley, MS—Fire destroys the St. Paul AME Church.

10 March: West Point, MS—Nightriders set fire to the Falling Meadows Baptist Church.

20 March: Ruleville, MS—Arsonists burn the black New Mt. Zion Baptist Church.

27 March: Millen, GA—Terrorists burn the Gays Hill Baptist Church, whose congregation is black.

31 March: Orangeburg, SC—Fire levels the Butler Chapel AME Church.

11 April: Paincourtville, LA—Arsonists destroy the all-black St. Charles Baptist Church.

13 April: Barnwell, SC—Fire destroys the black Rosemary Baptist Church.

26 April: Effingham, SC—Arsonists burn another black church, Effingham Baptist.

14 May: Tigrett, TN—Fire razes the all-black Mt. Pleasant Baptist Church.

23 May: Cerro Gordo, NC—Terrorists burn the Mt. Tabor Baptist Church.

24 May: Lumberton, NC—Arsonists level the Pleasant Hill Baptist Church.

June: Millville, NJ—Klan leader Joseph Bednarsky, Jr., shoots a black woman with a slingshot. He receives a one-year jail sentence on 3 June 1998.

3 June: Greensboro, AL—Arsonists burn the Rising Star Baptist Church.

6 June: Charlotte, NC—Nightriders torch the all-black Matthews-Murkland Presbyterian Church.

9 June: Greenville, TX—Fire destroys another black church, the New Light House of Prayer.

10 June: Greenville, TX—Arsonists strike again, burning the Church of the Living God.

October: Fort Worth, TX—Klansman Eric Brandon Lane sexually assaults two teenage runaways. He receives a 10-year prison term on 15 May 1998.

October: Columbia, SC—Klansmen shoot three black teenagers outside a nightclub, following a KKK rally. On 13 July 1998, Joshua England pleads guilty on four felony counts; he receives a 26-year federal prison term on 29 September 1998. Klansman Clayton Spires, Jr., receives an identical federal sentence on 3 March 1999. On 24 June 1999, England and Spires receive 25-year state prison terms for the same incident, concurrent with their federal penalties.

8 October: Spokane, WA—Authorities charge three self-styled Phineas Priests in connection with two bank robberies, detonation of banks at both bombs, and a conspiracy to bomb other targets (including a Planned Parenthood office). Defendants Charles Barbee, Ray Berry and Jay Merrell subsequently receive life prison terms, while Brian Rattigan gets 55 years. Police assume that $108,000 still missing from the holdups has been given to various radical white supremacists.

1997

SPLC investigators report 11 cross-burnings nationwide.

9 January: Oskaloosa, KS—Two former klansmen receive their sentences for a homicide committed in 1993. One-time Klan leader Michael Bittle gets 11 years in prison for conspiracy to commit murder and aggravated robbery, while Michael Wilkins receives a 29-year minimum sentence as the actual slayer.

22 January: Martinton, IL—Authorities raid the home of ex–Marine and klansman Ricky Salyers, seizing 35,000 rounds of heavy ammunition plus grenades, smoke bombs, and other military gear. Upon conviction, Salyers serves three years in prison and is paroled in 2000.

22 April: Fort Worth, TX—FBI agents acting on a tip from Klan leader Robert Spence jail three klansmen for plotting to bomb a natural gas refinery; they also subsequently arrest a fourth suspect. On 7 October 1997, defendants Shawn Adams, his wife Catherine, and Edward Taylor, Jr., plead guilty to conspiracy and possessing a destructive device. Defendant Carl Waskom pleads guilty, receiving a sentence of nine years and two months on 23 January 1998. Shawn Adams receives a 14-year sentence on 23 January 1998, while Edward Taylor receives 21 years and 10 months. Catherine Adams receives a 15-year sentence on 29 January 1998. Spence enters the federal witness protection program.

26 April: McKinney, TX—Seeking "to make a point," klansman and Aryan Nations member Donald Ray Anderson invades the Baruch Ha Shem synagogue, firing shots into the ceiling during worship services. On 5 May 1998, Anderson receives a 12-year federal prison sentence.

30 June: Little River, AL—Fire destroys the all-black St. Joe Baptist Church. FBI agents arrest five white teenagers on 5 July, charging two with additional counts for vandalizing the Tate Chapel AME Church. Bureau spokesmen report that the teens attended a White Knights rally in Tenesaw on 28 June, ten miles from the site of the fire.

25 August: Cincinnati, OH—Police jail Tony Gamble, imperial wizard of the Tristate Knight Riders of the KKK, on rape and sodomy charges related to sexual abuse of a thirteen-year-old girl spanning the past eighteen months.

27 August: Independence, KY—Imperial Wizard Tony Gamble, of the Tristate Knight Riders, pleads not guilty to rape and sodomy charges. Prosecutors claim that he sexually abused two adolescent girls over a three-year period. Upon conviction, he receives a 55-year prison sentence in March 1998.

3 September: Covington, LA—David Duke wins election to serve as chairman of St. Tammany Parish Republican Executive Committee, which sets GOP policy for the county.

1998

SPLC investigators report 48 cross-burnings nationwide.

9 January: Starkville, MS—Police administrators place Patrolman David Lindley on six months' probation for wearing a Klan robe while on duty.

17 January: Jackson, MS—The *Clarion-Ledger* reveals that klansmen Billy Pitts never served a day of his 1968 life sentence for killing Vernon Dahmer. Authorities issue an arrest warrant, whereupon Pitts surrenders and becomes a key witness in the prosecution of ex–Imperial Wizard Sam Bowers.

24 February: East St. Louis, IL—Federal agents charge three members of the New Order—group leader Dennis McGiffen, Wallace Weicherding and Paul Bock—with multiple weapons and explosives charges involving an alleged conspiracy to bomb public buildings across the U.S., poison water supplies, rob banks and assassinate various individuals. McGiffen and Weicherding are both former klansmen who left the KKK in search of a more radical movement. Agents arrest Glenn Lowtharp on 6 March, charging him with illegal manufacture of automatic weapons. Daniel Rick, jailed on 16 March, faces multiple charges involving illegal weapons. McGiffen strikes a plea bargain with prosecutors on 27 April. Bock and Lowtharp follow suit on 14 May. A sixth defendant, Karl Schave, pleads guilty to possession of a homemade bomb on 15 May. Weicherding faces new charges on 27 May, for compiling a list of assassination targets. Daniel Rick pleads guilty to three charges on 29 May. McGiffen receives a seven-year prison sentence on 11 September.

26 February: Goldvein, VA—Three whites shouting Ku Klux slogans fire shots at a black family dining at a fast-food restaurant. Police charge Ashley Kiser, Alicia Martini and an unnamed teenager with multiple felony counts including conspiracy to commit murder.

12 March: Jackson, MS—The *Clarion-Ledger* publishes FBI documents that reveal jury-tampering in the 1968 murder trial of Sam Bowers.

28 April: Milford, CT—Stanley Hicks receives a five-year prison term for writing "KKK" in his own blood on a gay couple's home.

15 May: Texas—Klansman and Aryan Nations member Donald Ray Anderson receives a 12-year federal prison term for his shooting spree at a synagogue.

15 May: Tarrant County, TX—Eric Brandon Lane, former imperial wizard of the True Knights of the KKK, receives a 10-year prison term for sexually assaulting two teenagers during a Klan initiation ceremony.

28 May: Mississippi—State authorities arrest three former WKKKKM members in connection to the 1966 slaying of Vernon Dahmer. Imperial Wizard Sam Bowers faces murder charges; Deavours Nix is accused of arson; Charles Noble faces trial for arson and murder. Nix avoids jail by pleading critical illness, but police re-arrest him on 10 June, after witnesses report him playing golf. Forrest County jurors convict Bowers of murder on 21 August, resulting in a mandatory life prison term. Nix dies of lung cancer on 19 September, while still awaiting trial. Jurors deadlock in Noble's trial on 15 June 1999. A judge dismisses Noble's charges on 16 January 2002.

6 June: Jasper, TX—Three ex-convicts with ties to the Klan and the Aryan Brotherhood drag black victim James Byrd, Jr., behind their pickup truck until he is decapitated. Police arrest Shawn Berry, Lawrence Brewer and John William King for the crime. Jurors convict King of murder on 23 February 1999, resulting in a death sentence on 22 July 1999. A second jury convicts Brewer on 20 September 1999, recommending execution. Jurors in a third trial convict Shawn Berry of murder on 18 November 1999, mandating a term of life imprisonment without parole.

4 July: Jackson, MS—The *Clarion Ledger* destroys Alabama klansman Bobby Cherry's alibi for the fatal 1963 bombing of Birmingham's Sixteenth Street Baptist Church. Cherry claimed that he was watching wrestling on TV when the bomb was planted, but investigative journalists discover that no such program was broadcast on the night in question.

10 July: California—Police jail klansman John Varela on felony assault charges after he attacks a witness at a preliminary hearing for a pending hate-crime case.

25 July: Boswell, PA—Armed members of the Keystone Knights surround State Trooper George Emigh and threaten his life after they spot him in a tree, spying on their "White Pride Day" festivities. Police charge four klansmen—Michael Abraham, Ronald Bedics, Adam Moyer and Donald Penrod—with assault, reckless endangerment and making terroristic threats. Jurors convict Abraham, Bedics and Penrod on 27 May 1999, while acquitting Moyer. Bedics receives a prison term of 14 to 30 months on 11 June 1999.

27 July: North Carolina—Klan members Donald Druck, Allison Johnson, Robert Johnson and Tony Vance plead no contest on charges of assaulting victim Calvin Cothern with a deadly weapon. They receive jail terms ranging from three to six months. On 9 July 1999, Abraham receives a sentence of 9 to 23 months in jail, while Penrod gets a term of 6 to 23 months.

8 August: Lexington, NC—Police arrest klansman Jimmy Ray Shelton for carrying a concealed weapon at a KKK rally.

14 August: Huntington, CA—Klansman Erik Anderson receives a prison term of 30 years to life for stabbing a Native American man in 1996.

22 August: Hillsville, PA—Police jail Keystone Knights Imperial Wizard Barry Black for unauthorized cross-burning at a Klan rally.

2 October: Greensboro, NC—Former klansman E.H. Hennis, a retired demolitions engineer, brings a fake bomb to a county commission meeting, threatening commissioners with injury or death by car-bombing. Police jail Hennis for making threats and staging a bomb hoax.

5 October: Greenville, NC—A group of hooded men armed with clubs beat a black minister, carve a Nazi symbol into his chest, and urinate on him.

2 November: Virginia—Police jail visiting North Carolina Grand Dragon J.J. Jones for check fraud.

13 November: Denver, CO—Skinhead-klansman and Aryan Nations associate Matthaeus Jaehnig murders policeman Bruce Vander Jagt following a burglary, then commits suicide.

December: Moscow, ID—Nightriders bomb an anti-Nazi protester's home and burn a cross on the lawn.

27 December: Mississippi—Relatives of 1964 murder victims James Chaney, Andrew Goodman and Michael Schwerner call for a renewed investigation of the case, based on published statements from Sam Bowers that he didn't mind serving time while a fellow klansman got away with murder. State Attorney General Mike Moore officially reopens the case on 25 February 1999. Moore's office received 40,000 documents on the case from FBI files in December 1999.

1999

SPLC investigators report 11 cross-burnings nationwide.

2 February: McGrady, NC—Police jail James M. Anderson for allegedly beating a fellow klansman with a tire iron, when the victim tried to quit the KKK. Four other defendants receive suspended sentences in the same case.

4 February: Fort Payne, AL—Jurors convict klansman Gregory Garrett of sexually assaulting a child in 1997. He receives a 15-year sentence for rape and 10 years for sexual abuse.

4 March: Sylacauga, AL—Police charge "wannabe" klansman and skinhead Steven Mullins and accomplice Charles Butler with murdering gay victim Billy Jack Gaither and burning his corpse.

29 March: Austin, TX—North Carolina klansmen Eddie Bradley and Jimmy Ray Shelton exchange gunfire with police during a high-speed chase outside town. Documents found in the car identify Shelton as imperial wizard of the Confederate Ghost Knights. On 13 April, a grand jury indicts both defendants on charges of attempted capital murder. Jurors in Bastrop convict Shelton on 17 September, resulting in a 99-year prison term.

20 May: Baton Rouge, LA—Police charge klansman Greg Davis with aggravated rape, oral sexual battery and crimes against nature for his 1997 sexual assault on a black man.

12 June: Fort Payne, AL—Police jail five klansmen on firearms charges following a rally at the De Kalb County courthouse.

12 July: Cumberland County, OR—Klansman Rocky Libby, charged with ramming a black deputy sheriff's patrol car, pleads guilty to attempted murder and assault. He receives a three-year prison sentence.

3 August: Cleveland, OH—ACLU spokesmen support Mayor

Michael White's decision to don their regalia in the city's police garage, prior to a demonstration scheduled for 21 August. Mayor White explains his decision as "a public safety issue."

6 October: Pemiscot County, MO—State authorities ask FBI agents to aid in their search for Arkansas Kleagle Gregory Reid, sought for injuring a black girl in a hit-and-run collision. Witnesses claim that Reid deliberately swerved his car to hit the child.

12 October: Charleston, SC—The city council issues a resolution branding the KKK a terrorist group.

November: Mississippi—FBI agents reopen their investigation of Ben White's 1966 murder after journalists "remind" them that White was killed on federal property.

November: Auburn, IN—American Knights Imperial Wizard Jeff Berry briefly holds two TV reporters captive in his home, after an interview goes sour. On 10 November 2000, police charge Berry with multiple felony counts including conspiracy, theft and criminal mischief. Berry receives a seven-year prison sentence on 3 December 2001.

4 November: Rutherford County, NC—Police raid the home of Robert Guffey and his son Anthony, seizing homemade bombs, drugs, stolen property, and a cache of KKK literature.

December: Louisiana—David Duke publishes *My Awakening,* an unabashedly racist autobiography praised in its foreword by Florida State University Prof. Glayde Whitney as an "academically excellent work" with the potential to "change the course of history."

16 December: Pennsylvania—Police charge Klan leader C. Edward Foster with arson and insurance fraud, related to the burning of his ex-wife's home while Foster was out of state on Klan business.

18 December: Montgomery, AL—The SPLC releases a report exposing the "mainstream" CCC's many ties to extremist groups including the KKK, neo–Nazi factions and the original Citizens' Council.

2000

SPLC investigators report 21 cross-burnings nationwide.

13 January: Jackson, MS—FBI agents renew investigation of the 1964 Charlie Dee-Henry Moore slayings, after the *Clarion Ledger* reveals that the victims may have been killed on federal land. The same article proves that G-men lied about destroying their files on the case.

7 May: Jackson, MS—The *Clarion Ledger* reveals that a lone holdout juror violated her oath in the 1967 mistrial of klansman Edgar Killen, charged with conspiracy to murder victims Chaney, Goodman and Schwerner. The woman told other jurors that she "could never convict a preacher."

14 May: Jackson, MS—Bob Stringer, a former employee of Samuel Bowers, tells the *Clarion Ledger* that he heard Bowers order Edgar Killen to "eliminate" Michael Schwerner in 1964. Killen denies the report.

17 May: Birmingham, AL—Police arrest Thomas Blanton and Bobby Cherry on murder charges related to the church bombing of 15 September 1963. Jurors convict Blanton on 1 May 2001, resulting in a life prison term. A separate jury convicts Cherry of murder on 22 May 2002, whereupon he receives a life sentence.

7 June: Bogue Chitto, MS—Federal authorities belatedly charge ex-klansman Ernest Avants in the June 1966 murder of Ben White on U.S. government property. His trial begins on 24 February 2003 and jurors convict Avants on 1 March 2003, resulting in a life sentence. He dies in prison on 16 June 2004.

8 June: St. Louis, MO—Police charge former KKKK leader Michael Cuffley with burglary and theft.

12 August: Hazard, KY—Following a rally by his American Knights, Imperial Wizard Jeff Berry argues with black resident James Beatty in a parking lot, then pursues Beatty's car for two miles and rams it with his van. Police jail Berry on felony charges

of wanton endangerment, criminal mischief and terrorist threats, holding him in lieu of $10,000 cash bond.

30 August: Kokomo, IN—James Colvin receives a 22-year prison sentence for a 1996 cross-burning incident.

16 December: Skokie, IL—Grand Dragon Michael McQueeney leads 20 klansmen in a demonstration at the local courthouse, while 200 police hold 400 angry protesters at bay. Violence erupts after the klansmen leave, with rioters smashing squad car windows and slashing tires. Police jail 20 persons, including one Wisconsin resident caught with a concealed firearm.

2001

SPLC investigators report 20 cross-burnings nationwide.

23 March: Flint, MI—Nightriders firebomb a black family's barn and leave a wooden cross on their back porch.

6 May: Mississippi—Ex-deputy and klansman Cecil Price, assisting state authorities with their investigation of the 1964 Chaney-Goodman-Schwerner slayings, dies from injuries suffered in a fall.

7 May: South Bend, IN—Police charge National Knights officer Railton Loy with telephone harassment, after he leaves a menacing message on a reporter's voice mail. On 31 October, Loy receives a sentence of six months' probation.

19 July: Jackson, MS—Retired investigator George Metz tells the *Clarion Ledger* that klansman Edgar Killen once admitted cleaning up the Chaney-Goodman-Schwerner murder scene on 22 June 1964.

2002

SPLC investigators report five cross-burnings nationwide.

March: Dawson Springs, KY—Without explanation, the Imperial Klans of America expels former Imperial Wizard and Illinois Grand Dragon Dale Fox.

19 July: Johnston County, NC—Federal and local authorities arrest Nation's Knights Grand Dragon Charles Barefoot, Jr., on multiple felony counts. State officers charge Barefoot with plotting to bomb the county jail and sheriff's office, while federal agents add a charge of illegally possessing firearms while subject to a domestic protection order. A search of Barefoot's home reveals numerous guns (including two illegal automatic weapons), two homemade bombs, and bomb-making components. On 23 June 2003, Barefoot receives a 27-month federal prison term for weapons violations.

4 August: Durant, OK—After a series of threatening calls from self-described Klan members, arsonists set fire to a church with a racially mixed congregation.

16 November: Lafayette, LA—Federal authorities charge Klan members Christopher Aaron, Robert Dartex, David Fusilier and Samuel Trahan with multiple felonies after they burn a cross in a black family's yard. Charges include conspiracy, interfering with their victims' housing rights, and using fire to commit a felony.

2003

SPLC investigators report four cross-burnings nationwide.

2 January: Sampson County, NC—Police unearth a man's decomposed corpse in a rural field. On 10 January, investigators seize a bloodstained van at the home of Sharon Barefoot, estranged wife of Klan leader Charles Barefoot, Jr. Others charged over the next two weeks include Barefoot himself, Grand Dragon Michael Brewer, and two other klansmen, Mark Denning and Marvin Gautier. Police spokesmen link the murder to an alleged July 2002 bombing plot against the Sampson County Sheriff's Department, in which Charles Barefoot already faces conspiracy charges.

8 January: Chicago, IL—Authorities charge WCOC leader Matt Hale with soliciting the murder of federal judge Joan Lefkow. Jurors subsequently convict Hale, resulting in a 40-year prison sentence.

25 January: Montgomery, AL—65 white supremacists representing two Klan factions, the CCC, Aryan Nations, White Revolution and World Church of the Creator stage a demonstration outside SPLC headquarters.

13 February: Amwell, PA—Officers of Pennsylvania's Joint Anti-Terrorism Task Force arrest White Knights Imperial Wizard David Hull on multiple weapons and explosives charges. Jurors convict him of firearms violations on 28 Mary 2004, but acquit Hull of possessing pipe bombs. Hull receives a 12-year prison term on 28 February 2005

28 May: Decatur, AL—Lee Wayne Bray receives a six-year federal prison term for burning a cross at the home of a white woman who has black friends.

12 August: Valley Forge, PA—Ex-klansman Joseph Holleran, Jr., receives a 27-month prison term for vandalizing a black patriots' memorial and a suburban synagogue.

22 November: Johnson City, TN—Police jail Gregory Freeman on charges of aggravated assault and reckless endangerment after he fires a gun at a KKK rally.

2004

SPLC investigators report nine cross-burnings nationwide.

9 February: Washington, D.C.—Charles Lambert receives a 27-month federal prison sentence for burning a cross at the home of an interracial couple in July 2001.

7 May: Trenton, GA—White defendants Steven Garland, Terrel Garner, Stacy Jones, Jeremy Sims, Eric Sullivan and Billy Wells plead guilty to a hate crime charge of conspiring to deprive civil rights by burning a cross at the home of a woman whose daughter has a biracial boyfriend.

1 October: Sacramento, CA—Christopher Easely receives a 41-month federal prison term for a January cross-burning at a black family's home.

28 December: Townsville, North Queensland, Australia—Klansmen raid an Aboriginal shanty town and harass its occupants.

2005

SPLC investigators report five cross-burnings nationwide.

9 March: Balton Spa, NY—Michael Robinson receives a six-month jail term for writing KKK graffiti on the auto of a neighbor involved in an interracial romance.

16 March: Carlsbad Springs, Ontario—Arsonists burn the home of Ian Macdonald, former advisor to the Canadian Klan and various neo–Nazi groups in the 1980s.

19 May: Greenville, SC—ATF agents arrest klansman Daniel Schertz for selling five pipe bombs to undercover officers, as part of an alleged conspiracy to kill Haitian and Hispanic immigrants. Schertz pleads guilty to six federal counts on 4 August. He receives the maximum 14-year prison term on 4 November 2005.

3 June: Montgomery, AL—George Wallace, Jr., Alabama's public service commissioner, addresses the CCC's annual convention, including delegates linked to the KKK. On 2 June, "former" klansmen lead 50 CCC members in a protest demonstration outside SPLC headquarters.

APPENDIX B:
SELECTED KLAN DOCUMENTS

I. KKK Prescript of 1867

PRESCRIPT

OF THE

❀   ❀

·—·—·—·

What may this mean,
That thou, dead corse, again, in complete steel,
Revisit'st thus the glimpses of the moon,
Making night hideous; and we fools of nature,
So horridly to shake our disposition,
With thoughts beyond the reaches of our souls?

·—·—·—·

An' now auld Cloots, I ken ye're thinkin',
A certain *Ghoul* is rantin', drinkin',
Some luckless night will send him linkin',
                    To your black pit;
But, faith! he'll turn a corner jinkin',
                    An' cheat you yet.

CREED

We, the * * , reverently acknowledge the Majesty and Supremacy of the Divine Being, and recognize the Goodness and Providence of the Same.

PREAMBLE

We recognize our relations to the United States Government, and acknowledge the supremacy of its laws.

APPELLATION

ARTICLE I. This organization shall be styled and denominated the * *

TITLES

Art. II. The officers of this * shall consist of a Grand Wizard of the Empire and his ten Genii; a Grand Dragon of the Realm and his eight Hydras; a Grand Titan of the Dominion and his six Furies; a Grand Giant of the Province and his four Goblins; a Grand Cyclops of the Den and his two Night Hawks; a Grand Magi, a Grand Monk, a Grand Exchequer, a Grand Turk, a Grand Scribe, A Grand Sentinel, and a Grand Ensign.

Sec. 2. The body politic of this * shall be designated and known as 'Ghouls,'

DIVISIONS

Art III. This * shall be divided into five departments, all combined, constituting the Grand * of the Empire. The second department to be called the Grand * of the Realm. The third, the Grand * of the Dominion. The fourth, the Grand * of the Province. The fifth, the * of the Den.

DUTIES OF OFFICERS

GRAND WIZARD

Art. IV. Sec. 1. It shall be the duty of the Grand Wizard, who is the Supreme Officer of the Empire, to communicate with and receive reports from the Grand Dragons of Realms, as to the condition, strength, efficiency and progress of the *s within their respective Realm. And he shall communicate from time to time, to all subordinate *s, through the Grand Dragons, the condition, strength, efficiency, and progress of the *s throughout his vast Empire; and such other information as he may deem expedient to impart. And it shall further be his duty to keep by his G Scribe a list of the names (without any caption or explanation whatever) of the Grand Dragons of the different Realms of his Empire, and shall number such Realms with the Arabic numerals, 1, 2, 3, &c., *ad finem*. And he shall instruct his Grand Exchequer as to the appropriation and disbursement which he shall make of the revenue of the * that comes to his hands. He shall have the sole power to issue copies of this Prescript, through his Subalterns and Deputies, for the organization and establishment of subordinate *s. And he shall have the further power to appoint his Genii; also, a Grand Scribe and a Grand Exchequer for his Department, and to appoint and ordain Special Deputy Grand Wizards to assist him in the more rapid and effectual dissemination and establishment of the * throughout his Empire. He is further empowered to appoint and instruct Deputies, to organize and control Realms, Dominions, Provinces, and Dens, until the same shall elect a Grand Dragon, a Grand Titan, a Grand Giant, and a Grand Cyclops, in the manner hereinafter provided. And when a question of paramount importance to the interest or prosperity of the * arises, not provided for in this Prescript, he shall have power to determine such question, and his decision shall be final, until the same shall be provided for by amendment as hereinafter provided.

GRAND DRAGON

Sec. 2. It shall be the duty of the Grand Dragon who is the Chief Officer of the Realm, to report to the Grand Wizard when required by that officer, the condition, strength, efficiency, and progress of the * within his Realm, and to transmit through the Grand Titan to the subordinate *s of his Realm, all information or intelligence conveyed to him by the Grand Wizard for that purpose, and all such other information or instruction as he may think will promote the interests of the *. He shall keep by his G. Scribe a list of the names (without any caption) of the Grand Titans of the different Dominions of his Realm, and shall report the same to the Grand Wizard when required; and shall number the Dominions of his Realm with the Arabic numerals, 1, 2, 3, &c., *ad finem*. He shall instruct his Grand Exchequer as to the appropriation and disbursement of the revenue of the * that comes to his hands. He shall have the power to appoint his Hydras; also, a Grand Scribe and a Grand Exchequer for his Department, and to appoint and ordain Special Deputy Grand Dragons to assist him in the more rapid and effectual dissemination and establishment of the * throughout his Realm. He is further empowered to appoint and instruct Deputies to organize and control Dominions, Provinces and Dens, until the same shall elect a Grand Titan, a Grand Giant, and Grand Cyclops, in the manner hereinafter provided.

GRAND TITAN

Sec. 3. It shall be the duty of the Grand Titan who is the Chief Officer of the Dominion, to report to the Grand Dragon when required by that officer, the condition, strength, efficiency, and progress of the * within his Dominion, and to transmit, through the Grand Giants to the subordinate *s of his Dominion, all information or intelligence conveyed to him by the Grand Dragon for that purpose, and all such other information or instruction as he may think will enhance the interests of the *. He shall keep, by his G. Scribe, a list of the names (without caption) of the Grand Giants of the different Provinces of his Dominion, and shall report the same to the Grand Dragon when required; and he shall number the Provinces of his Dominion with the Arabic numerals, 1, 2, 3, &c., *ad finem*. And he shall instruct and direct his Grand Exchequer as to the appropriation and disbursement of the revenue of the * that comes to his hands. He shall have power to appoint his Furies; also to appoint a Grand Scribe and a Grand Exchequer for his department, and appoint and ordain Special Deputy Grand Titans to assist him in the more rapid and effectual dissemination and establishment of the * throughout his Dominion. He shall have further power to appoint and instruct Deputies to organize and control Provinces and Dens, until the same shall elect a Grand Giant and a Grand Cyclops, in the manner hereinafter provided.

GRAND GIANT

Sec. 4. It shall be the duty of the Grand Giant, who is the Chief Officer of the Province, to supervise and administer general and special instruction in the formation and establishment of *s within his Province, and to report to the Grand Titan, when required by that officer, the condition, strength, progress and efficiency of the * throughout his Province, and to transmit, through the Grand Cyclops, to the subordinate *s of his Province, all information or intelligence conveyed to him by the Grand Titan for that purpose, and such other information and instruction as he may think will advance the interests of the *. He shall keep by his G Scribe a list of the names (without caption) of the Grand Cyclops of the various Dens of his Province, and shall report the same to the Grand Titan when required; and shall number the Dens of his Province with the Arabic numerals, 1, 2, 3, &c., *ad finem*. And shall determine and limit the number of Dens to be organized in his Province. And he shall instruct and direct his Grand Exchequer as to what appropriation and disbursement he shall make of the revenue of the * that comes to his hands. He shall have power to appoint his Goblins; also, a Grand Scribe and a Grand Exchequer for his department, and to appoint and ordain Special Deputy Grand Giants to assist him in the more rapid and effectual dissemination and establishment of the * throughout his Province. He shall have the further power to appoint and instruct Deputies to organize and control Dens, until the same shall elect a Grand Cyclops in the manner hereinafter provided. And in all cases, he shall preside at and conduct the Grand Council of Yahoos.

GRAND CYCLOPS

Sec. 5. It shall be the duty of the Grand Cyclops to take charge of the * of his Den after his election, under the direction and with the assistance (when practicable) of the Grand Giant, and in accordance with, and in conformity to the provisions of this Prescript, a copy of which shall in all cases be obtained before the formation of a * begins. It shall further be his duty to appoint all regular meetings of his * and to preside at the same — to appoint irregular meetings when he deems it expedient, to preserve order in his Den, and to impose fines for irregularities or disobedience of orders, and to receive and initiate candidates for admission into the * after the same shall have been pronounced competent and worthy to become members by the Investigating Committee. He shall make a quarterly report to the Grand Giant, of the condition, strength and efficiency of the * of his Den, and shall convey to the Ghouls of his Den, all information or intelligence conveyed to him by the Grand Giant for that purpose, and all such other information or instruction as he may think will conduce to the interests and welfare of the *.

He shall preside at and conduct the Grand Council of Centaurs. He shall have power to appoint his Night Hawks, his Grand Scribe, his Grand Turk, his Grand Sentinel, and his Grand Ensign. And he shall instruct and direct the Grand Exchequer of his Den, as to what appropriation and disbursement he shall make of the revenue of the * that comes to his hands. And for any small offense he may punish any member by fine, and may reprimand him for the same: And he may admonish and reprimand the * of his Den for any imprudence, irregularity or transgression, when he is convinced or advised that the interests, welfare and safety of the * demand it.

GRAND MAGI

Sec. 6. It shall be the duty of the Grand Magi, who is the Second Officer, in authority, of the Den, to assist the Grand Cyclops and to obey all the proper orders of that officer. To preside at all meetings in the Den in the absence of the Grand Cyclops; and to exercise during his absence all the powers and authority conferred upon that officer.

GRAND MONK

Sec. 7. It shall be the duty of the Grand Monk, who is the third officer, in authority, of the Den, to assist and obey all the proper orders of the Grand Cyclops and the Grand Magi. And in the absence of both of these officers, he shall preside at and conduct the meetings in the Den, and shall exercise all the powers and authority conferred upon the Grand Cyclops.

GRAND EXCHEQUER

Sec. 8. It shall be the duty of the Grand Exchequers of the different Departments of the * to keep a correct account of all the revenue of the * that shall come to their hands, and shall make no appropriation or disbursement of the same except under the orders and direction of the chief officer of their respective departments. And it shall further be the duty of the Grand Exchequer of Dens to collect the initiation fees, and all fines imposed by the Grand Cyclops.

GRAND TURK

Sec. 9. It shall be the duty of the Grand Turk, who is the Executive Officer of the Grand Cyclops, to notify the ghouls of the Den of all informal or irregular meetings appointed by the Grand Cyclops, and to obey and execute all the lawful orders of that officer in the control and government of his Den. It shall further be his duty to receive and question at the Out-Posts, all candidates for admission into the *, and shall *there* administer the preliminary obligation required, and then to conduct such candidate or candidates to the Grand Cyclops at his Den, and to assist him in the initiation of the same. And it shall further be his duty to act as the Executive officer of the Grand Council of Centaurs.

GRAND SCRIBE

Sec. 10. It shall be the duty of the Grand Scribes of the different departments to conduct the correspondence and write the orders of the chiefs of their departments, when required. And it shall further be the duty of the Grand Scribes of the Den to keep a list of the names (without caption) of the ghouls of the Den — to call the Roll at all regular meetings and to make the quarterly report under the direction of the Grand Cyclops.

GRAND SENTINEL

Sec. 11. It shall be the duty of the Grand Sentinel to detail, take charge of, post and instruct the Grand Guard under the direction and orders of the Grand Cyclops, and to relieve and dismiss the same when directed by that officer.

GRAND ENSIGN

Sec. 12. It shall be the duty of the Grand Ensign to take charge of the Grand Banner of the *, to preserve it sacredly, and protect it carefully, and to bear it on all occasions of parade or ceremony, and on such other occasions as the Grand Cyclops may direct it to be flung to the night breeze.

ELECTION OF OFFICERS

ART. V. Sec. 1. The Grand Cyclops, the Grand Magi, the Grand Monk, and the Grand Exchequer of Dens, shall be elected semi-annually by the ghouls of Dens. And the first election for these officers may take place as soon as seven ghouls have been initiated for that purpose.

Sec. 2. The Grand Wizard of the Empire, the Grand Dragons of Realms, the Grand Titans of Dominions, and the Grand Giants of Provinces, shall be elected biennially, and in the following manner, to wit: The Grand Wizard by a majority vote of the Grand Dragons of his Empire, the Grand Dragons by a like vote of the Grand Titans of his Realm; the Grand Titans by a like vote of the Grand Giants of his Dominion, and the Grand Giant by a like vote of the Grand Cyclops of his Province.

The first election for Grand Dragon may take place as soon as three Dominions have been organized in a Realm, but all subsequent elections shall be by a majority vote of the Grand Titans throughout the Realm, and biennially as aforesaid.

The first election for Grand Titan may take place as soon as three Provinces have been organized in a Dominion, but all subsequent elections shall be by a majority vote of all the Grand Giants throughout the Dominion and biennially as aforesaid.

The first election for Grand Giant may take place as soon as three Dens have been organized in a Province, but all subsequent elections shall be by a majority vote of all the Grand Cyclops throughout the Province, and biennially as aforesaid.

The Grand Wizard of the Empire is hereby created, to serve three years from the First Monday in May, 1867, after the expiration of which time, biennial elections shall be held for that office as aforesaid. And the incumbent Grand Wizard shall notify the Grand Dragons, at least six months before said election, at what time and place the same will be held.

JUDICIARY

ART. VI. Sec. 1. The Tribunal of Justice of this * shall consist of a Grand Council of Yahoos, and a Grand Council of Centaurs.

Sec. 2. The Grand Council of Yahoos, shall be the Tribunal for the trial of all elected officers, and shall be composed of officers of equal rank with the accused, and shall be appointed and presided over by an officer of the next rank above, and sworn by him to administer even handed justice. The Tribunal for the trial of the Grand Wizard, shall be composed of all the Grand Dragons of the Empire, and shall be presided over and sworn by the senior Grand Dragon. They shall have power to summon the accused, and witnesses for and against him, and if found guilty they shall prescribe the penalty and execute the same. And they shall have power to appoint an Executive officer to attend said Council while in session.

Sec. 3. The grand Council of Centaurs shall be the Tribunal for the trial of ghouls and non-elective officers, and shall be composed of six judges appointed by the grand Cyclops from the ghouls of his Den, presided over and sworn by him to give the accused a fair and impartial trial. They shall have power to summon the accused, and witnesses for and against him, and if found guilty they shall prescribe the penalty and execute the same. Said Judges shall be selected by the Grand Cyclops with reference to their intelligence, integrity and fair mindedness, and shall render their verdict without prejudice or partiality.

REVENUE

ART. VII. Sec. 1. The revenue of this * shall be derived as follows: For every copy of this Prescript issued to the *s of Dens, Ten Dollars will be required. Two dollars of which shall go into the hands of the Grand Exchequer of the Grand Giant; two into the hands of the Grand Exchequer of the Grand Titan; two into the hands of the Grand Exchequer of the Grand Dragon, and the remaining four into the hands of the Grand Exchequer of the Grand Wizard.

Sec. 2. A further source of revenue to the Empire shall be ten per cent of all the revenue of the Realms, and a tax upon Realms, when the Grand Wizard shall deem it necessary and indispensable to levy the same.

Sec. 3. A further source of revenue to Realms shall be ten per cent of all the revenue of Dominions, and a tax upon Dominions when the Grand Dragon shall deem such tax necessary and indispensable.

Sec. 4. A further source of revenue to Dominions shall be ten per cent of all the revenue of Provinces, and a tax upon Provinces when the Grand Titan shall deem such tax necessary and indispensable.

Sec. 5. A further source of revenue to Provinces shall be ten per cent, on all the revenue of Dens, and a tax upon the Dens, when the Grand Giant shall deem such tax necessary and indispensable.

Sec. 6. The source of revenue to Dens, shall be the initiation fees, fines, and a *per capita* tax, whenever the Grand Cyclops shall deem such tax indispensable to the interests and purposes of the * .

Sec. 7. All of the revenue obtained in the manner herein aforesaid, shall be for the exclusive benefit of the *. And shall be appropriated to the dissemination of the same, and to the creation of a fund to meet any disbursement that it may become necessary to make to accomplish the objects of the *, and to secure the protection of the same.

OBLIGATION

ART. VIII. No one shall become a member of this *, unless he shall take the following oath or obligation:

'I, ——— of my own free will and accord, and in the presence of Almighty God, do solemnly swear or affirm that I will never reveal to any one, not a member of the * * by any intimation, sign, symbol, word or act, or in any other manner whatever, any of the secrets, signs, grips, pass-words, mysteries or purposes of the * *, or that I am a member of the same or that I know any one who *is* a member, and that I will abide by the Prescript and Edicts of the * *. So help me God.'

Sec. 2. The preliminary obligation to be administered before the candidate for admission is taken to the Grand Cyclops for examination, shall be as follows:

'I do solemnly swear or affirm that I will never reveal anything that I may this day (or night) learn concerning the * *. So help me God.'

ADMISSION

ART. IX. Sec. 1. No one shall be presented for admission into this *, until he shall have been recommended by some friend or intimate, who *is* a member, to the Investigating Committee, which shall be composed of the Grand Cyclops, the Grand Magi and the Grand Monk, and who shall investigate his antecedents and his past and present standing and connections, and if after such investigation, they pronounce him competent and worthy to become a member, he may be admitted upon taking the obligation required and passing through the ceremonies of initiation. *Provided*, That no one shall be admitted into this * who shall have not attained the age of eighteen years.

Sec. 2. No one shall become a member of a distant * when there is a * established and in operation in his own immediate vicinity. Nor shall any one become a member of any * after he shall have been rejected by any other *.

ENSIGN

ART. X. The Grand Banner of this * shall be in the form of an isosceles triangle, five feet long and three wide at the staff. The material shall be Yellow, with a Red scalloped border, about three inches in width. There shall be painted upon it, in black, a Draco-volans, or Flying Dragon, with the following motto inscribed above the Dragon, 'QUOD SEMPER, QUOD UBIQUE, QUOD AB OMNIBUS.'

AMENDMENTS

ART. XI. This Prescript or any part or Edicts thereof, shall never be changed except by a two-thirds vote of the Grand Dragons of the Realms, in Convention assembled, and at which Convention the Grand Wizard shall preside and be entitled to a vote. And upon the application of a majority of the Grand Dragons, for that purpose, the Grand Wizard shall appoint the time and place for said Convention; which, when assembled, shall proceed to make such modifications and amendment as it may think will advance the interest, enlarge the utility, and more thoroughly effectuate the purposes of the *.

INTERDICTION

ART. XII. The origin, designs, mysteries and ritual of this * shall never be written, but the same shall be communicated orally.

REGISTER

I.	1st—Dismal.	7th—Dreadful.
	2nd—Dark.	8th—Terrible.
	3rd—Furious.	9th—Horrible.
	4th—Portentous.	10—Melancholy.
	5th—Wonderful.	11—Mournful.
	6th—Alarming.	12th—Dying.
II.	I—White.	IV—Black.
	II—Green.	V—Yellow.
	III—Blue.	VI—Crimson.

VII—Purple.

III.	1—Fearful.	7—Doleful.
	2—Startling.	8—Sorrowful.
	3—Awful.	9—Hideous.
	4—Woeful.	10—Frightful.
	5—Horrid.	11—Appalling.
	6—Bloody.	12—Last.

EDICTS

I. The Initiation Fee of this * shall be one dollar, to be paid when the candidate is initiated and received into the *.

II. No member shall be allowed to take any intoxicating spirits to any meeting of the * Nor shall any member be allowed to attend a meeting when intoxicated; and for every appearance at a meeting in such a condition, he shall be fined the sum of not less than one nor more than five dollars, to go into the revenue of the *.

III. Any member may be expelled from the * by a majority vote of the officers and ghouls of the Den to which he belongs, and if after such expulsion such member shall assume any of the duties, regalia or insignia of the * or in any way claim to be a member of the same, he shall be severely punished. His obligation of secrecy shall be as binding upon him after expulsion as before, and for any revelation made by him thereafter, he shall be held accountable in the same manner as if he were then a member.

IV. Every Grand Cyclops shall read or cause to be read, this Prescript and these Edicts to the * of his Den, at least once in every three months — And shall read them to each new member when he is initiated, or present the same to him for personal perusal.

V. Each Den may provide itself with the Grand Banner of the *

VI. The *s of Dens may make such additional Edicts for their control and government as they shall deem requisite and necessary. *Provided*, No Edict shall be made to conflict with any of the provisions or Edicts of this Prescript.

VII. The strictest and most rigid secrecy, concerning any and everything that relates to the * shall at all times be maintained.

VIII. Any member who shall reveal or betray the secrets or purposes of this * shall suffer the extreme penalty of the Law.

Hush, thou art not to utter what I am. Bethink thee; it was our covenant. I said that I would see thee once again.

L'ENVOI

To the lovers of Law and Order, Peace and Justice, we send greeting; and to the shades of the venerated Dead, we affectionately dedicate the * *

II. KKK Prescript of 1868

REVISED AND AMENDED

PRESCRIPT

OF THE

ORDER

OF THE

*

*   *

Damnant quod non intelligunt.

APPELLATION

T<small>HIS</small> Organization shall be styled and denominated, the Order of the * * *.

CREED

We, the Order of the * * *, reverentially acknowledge the majesty and supremacy of the Divine Being, and recognize the goodness and providence of the same.   And we recognize our relation to the United States Government, the supremacy of the Constitution, the Constitutional Laws thereof, and the Union of States thereunder.

CHARACTER AND OBJECT OF THE ORDER

This is an institution of Chivalry, Humanity, Mercy, and Patriotism; embodying in its genius and its principles all that is chivalric in conduct, noble in sentiment, generous in manhood, and patriotic in purpose; its peculiar objects being,

First: To protect the weak, the innocent, and the defenceless, from the indignities, wrongs, and outrages of the lawless, the violent, and the brutal; to relieve the injured and oppressed; to succor the suffering and unfortunate, and especially the widows and orphans of Confederate soldiers.

Second: To protect and defend the Constitution of the United States, and all laws passed in conformity thereto, and to protect the States and the people thereof from all invasion from any source whatever.

Third: To aid and assist in the execution of all constitutional laws, and to protect the people from unlawful seizure, and from trial except by their peers in conformity to the laws of the land,

ARTICLE I
TITLES

S<small>ECTION</small> 1. The officers of this Order shall consist of a Grand Wizard of the Empire, and his ten Genii; a Grand Dragon of the Realm, and his eight Hydras; a Grand Titan of the Dominion, and his six Furies; a Grand Giant of the Province, and his four Goblins; a Grand Cyclops of the Den, and his two Night-hawks; a Grand Magi, a Grand Monk, a Grand Scribe, a Grand Exchequer, a Grand Turk, and a Grand Sentinel.

S<small>EC</small>. 2. The body politic of this Order shall be known and designated as 'Ghouls.'

ARTICLE II
TERRITORY AND ITS DIVISIONS

S<small>ECTION</small> 1. The territory embraced within the jurisdiction of this Order shall be coterminous with the States of Maryland, Virginia, North Carolina, South Carolina, Georgia, Florida, Alabama, Mississippi, Louisiana, Texas, Arkansas, Missouri, Kentucky, and Tennessee; all combined constituting the Empire.

S<small>EC</small>. 2. The Empire shall be divided into four departments, the first to be styled the Realm, and coterminous with the boundaries of the several States; the second to be styled the Dominion, and to be coterminous with such counties as the Grand Dragons of the several Realms may assign to the charge of the Grand Titan. The third to be styled the Province, and to be coterminous with the several counties; *provided*, the Grand Titan may, when he deems it necessary, assign two Grand Giants to one Province, prescribing, at the same time, the jurisdiction of each. The fourth department to be styled the Den, and shall embrace such part of a Province as the Grand Giant shall assign to the charge of a Grand Cyclops.

ARTICLE III
POWERS AND DUTIES OF OFFICERS
GRAND WIZARD

S<small>ECTION</small> 1. The Grand Wizard, who is the supreme officer of the Empire, shall have power, and he shall be required to, appoint Grand Dragons for the different Realms of the Empire; and he shall have power to appoint his Genii, also a Grand Scribe, and a Grand Exchequer for his Department, and he shall have the sole power to issue copies of this Prescript, through his subalterns, for the organization and dissemination of the Order; and when a question of paramount importance to the interests or prosperity of the Order arises, not provided for in this Prescript, he shall have power to determine such question, and his decision shall be final until the paramount importance to the interests or prosperity of the Order arises, not provided for in this Prescript, he shall have power to determine such question, and his decision shall be final until the same shall be provided for by amendment as hereinafter provided. It shall be his duty to communicate with, and receive reports from, the Grand Dragons of Realms, as to the condition, strength, efficiency, and progress of the Order within their respective Realms. And it shall further be his duty to keep, by his Grand Scribe, a list of the names (without any caption or explanation whatever) of the Grand Dragons of the different Realms of the Empire, and shall number such Realms with the Arabic numerals 1, 2, 3, etc., *ad finem*; and he shall direct and instruct his Grand Exchequer as to the appropriation and disbursement he shall make of the revenue of the Order that comes to his hands.

GRAND DRAGON

SEC. 2. The Grand Dragon, who is the chief officer of the Realm, shall have power, and he shall be required, to appoint and instruct a Grand Titan for each Dominion of his Realm, (such Dominion not to exceed three in number for any Congressional District) said appointments being subject to the approval of the Grand Wizard of the Empire. He shall have power to appoint his Hydras; also, a Grand Scribe and a Grand Exchequer for his Department.

It shall be his duty to report to the Grand Wizard, when required by that officer, the condition, strength, efficiency, and progress of the Order within his Realm, and to transmit, through the Grand Titan, or other authorized sources, to the Order, all information, intelligence, or instruction conveyed to him by the Grand Wizard for that purpose, and all such other information or instruction as he may think will promote the interest and utility of the Order. He shall keep by his Grand Scribe, a list of the names (without caption) of the Grand Titans of the different Dominions of his Realm, and shall report the same to the Grand Wizard when required, and shall number the Dominion of his Realm with the Arabic numerals 1, 2, 3, etc., *ad finem*. And he shall direct and instruct his Grand Exchequer as to the appropriation and disbursement he shall make of the revenue of the Order that comes to his hands.

GRAND TITAN

SEC. 3. The Grand Titan, who is the chief officer of the Dominion, shall have power, and he shall be required, to appoint and instruct a Grand Giant for each Province of his Dominion, such appointments, however, being subject to the approval of the Grand Dragon of the Realm. He shall have the power to appoint his Furies; also, a Grand Scribe and a Grand Exchequer for his Department. It shall be his duty to report to the Grand Dragon when required by that officer, the condition, strength, efficiency, and progress of the Order within his Dominion, and to transmit through the Grand Giant, or other authorized channels, to the Order, all information, intelligence, instruction or directions conveyed to him by the Grand Dragon for that purpose, and all such other information or instruction as he may think will enhance the interest or efficiency of the Order.

He shall keep, by his Grand Scribe, a list of the names (without caption or explanation) of the Grand Giants of the different Provinces of his Dominion, and shall report the same to the Grand Dragon when required; and shall number the Provinces of his Dominion with the Arabic numerals 1, 2, 3, etc., *ad finem*. And he shall direct and instruct his Grand Exchequer as to the appropriation and disbursement he shall make of the revenue of the Order that comes to his hands.

GRAND GIANT

SEC. 4. The Grand Giant, who is the chief officer of the Province, shall have power, and he is required, to appoint and instruct a Grand Cyclops for each Den of his Province, such appointments, however, being subject to the approval of the Grand Titan of the Dominion. And he shall have the further power to appoint his Goblins; also, a Grand Scribe and a Grand Exchequer for his Department.

It shall be his duty to supervise and administer general and special instructions in the organization and establishment of the Order within his Province, and to report to the Grand Titan, when required by that officer, the condition, strength, efficiency, and progress of the Order within his Province, and to transmit through the Grand Cyclops, or other legitimate sources, to the Order, all information, intelligence, instruction, or directions conveyed to him by the Grand Titan or other higher authority for that purpose, and all such other information or instruction as he may think would advance the purposes or prosperity of the Order. He shall keep, by his Grand Scribe, a list of the names (without caption or explanation) of the Grand Cyclops of the various Dens of his Province, and shall report the same to the Grand Titan when required; and shall number the Dens of his Province with the Arabic numerals 1, 2, 3, etc., *ad finem*. He shall determine and limit the number of Dens to be organized and established in his Province; and he shall direct and instruct his Grand Exchequer as to the appropriation and disbursement he shall make of the revenue of the Order that comes to his hands.

GRAND CYCLOPS

SEC. 5. The Grand Cyclops, who is the chief officer of the Den, shall have power to appoint his Night-hawks, his Grand Scribe, his Grand Turk, his Grand Exchequer, and his Grand Sentinel. And for small offenses he may punish any member by fine, and may reprimand him for the same. And he is further empowered to admonish and reprimand his Den, or any of the members thereof, for any imprudence, irregularity, or transgression, whenever he may think that the interests, welfare, reputation or safety of the Order demand it. It shall be his duty to take charge of his Den under the instruction and with the assistance (when practicable) of the Grand Giant, and in accordance with and in conformity to the provisions of this Prescript — a copy of which shall in all cases be obtained before the formation of a Den begins. It shall further be his duty to appoint all regular meetings of his Den, and to preside at the same; to appoint irregular meetings when he deems it expedient; to preserve order and enforce discipline in his Den; to impose fines for irregularities or disobedience of orders; and to receive and initiate candidates for admission into the Order, after the same shall have been pronounced competent and worthy to become members, by the Investigating Committee herein after provided for. And it shall further be his duty to make a quarterly report to the Grand Giant of the condition, strength, efficiency, and progress of his Den, and shall communicate to the Officers and Ghouls of his Den, all information, intelligence, instruction, or direction, conveyed to him by the Grand Giant or other higher authority for that purpose; and shall from time to time administer all such other counsel, instruction or direction, as in his sound discretion, will conduce to the interests, and more effectually accomplish, the *real* objects and designs of the Order.

GRAND MAGI

SEC. 6. It shall be the duty of the Grand Magi, who is the second officer in authority of the Den, to assist the Grand Cyclops, and to obey all the orders of that officer; to preside at all meetings in the Den, in the absence of the Grand Cyclops; and to discharge during his absence all the duties and exercise all the powers and authority of that officer.

GRAND MONK

SEC. 7. It shall be the duty of the Grand Monk, who is the third officer in authority of the Den, to assist and obey all the orders of the Grand Cyclops and the Grand Magi; and, in the absence of both of these officers, he shall preside at and conduct the meetings in the Den, and shall discharge all the duties, and exercise all the powers and authority of the Grand Cyclops.

GRAND EXCHEQUER

SEC. 8. It shall be the duty of the Grand Exchequers of the different Departments to keep a correct account of all the revenue of the Order that comes to their hands, and of all paid out by them; and shall make no appropriation or disbursement of the same except under the orders and direction of the chief officer of their respective Departments. And it shall further be the duty of the Exchequers of Dens to collect the initiation fees, and all fines imposed by the Grand Cyclops, or the officer discharging his functions.

GRAND TURK

SEC. 9. It shall be the duty of the Grand Turk, who is the executive officer of the Grand Cyclops, to notify the Officers and Ghouls of the Den, of all informal or irregular meetings appointed by the Grand Cyclops, and to obey and execute all the orders of that officer in the control and government of his Den. It shall further be his duty to receive and question at the outposts, all candidates for admission into the Order, and shall *there* administer the preliminary obligation required, and then to conduct such candidate or candidates to the Grand Cyclops, and to assist him in the initiation of the same.

GRAND SCRIBE

SEC. 10. It shall be the duty of the Grand Scribes of the different Departments to conduct the correspondence and write the orders of the Chiefs of their Departments, when required. And it shall further be the duty of the Grand Scribes of Dens, to keep a list of the names (without any caption or explanation whatever) of the Officers and Ghouls of the Den, to call the roll at all meetings, and to make the quarterly reports under the direction and instruction of the Grand Cyclops.

GRAND SENTINEL

SEC. 11. It shall be the duty of the Grand Sentinel to take charge of post, and instruct the Grand Guard, under the direction and orders of the Grand Cyclops, and to relieve and dismiss the same when directed by that officer.

THE STAFF

SEC. 12. The Genii shall constitute the staff of the Grand Wizard; the Hydras, that of the Grand Dragon; the Furies, that of the Grand Titan; the Goblins, that of the Grand Giant; and the Night-hawks, that of the Grand Cyclops.

REMOVAL

SEC. 13. For any just, reasonable and substantial cause, any appointee may be removed by the authority that appointed him, and his place supplied by another appointment.

ARTICLE IV

ELECTION OF OFFICERS

SECTION 1. The Grand Wizard shall be elected biennially by the Grand Dragons of Realms. The first election for this office to take place on the 1st Monday in May, 1870, (a Grand Wizard having been created, by the original Prescript, to serve three years from the 1st Monday in May, 1867); all subsequent elections to take place every two years thereafter. And the incumbent Grand Wizard shall notify the Grand Dragons of the different Realms, at least six months before said election, at what time and place the same will be held; a majority vote of all the Grand Dragons *present* being necessary and sufficient to elect a Grand Wizard. Such election shall be by ballot, and shall be held by three Commissioners appointed by the Grand Wizard for that purpose; and in the event of a tie, the Grand Wizard shall have the casting-vote.

SEC. 2. The Grand Magi and the Grand Monk of Dens shall be elected annually by the Ghouls of Dens; and the first election for these officers may take place as soon as ten Ghouls have been initiated for the formation of a Den. All subsequent elections to take place every year thereafter.

SEC. 3. In the event of a vacancy in the office of Grand Wizard, by death, resignation, removal, or otherwise, the senior Grand Dragon of the Empire shall immediately assume and enter upon the discharge of the duties of the Grand Wizard, and shall exercise the powers and perform the duties of said office until the same shall be filled by election; and the said senior Grand Dragon, as soon as practicable after the happening of such vacancy, shall call a convention of the Grand Dragons of Realms, to be held at such time and place as in his discretion he may deem most convenient and proper. *Provided*, however, that the time for assembling such Convention for the election of a Grand Wizard shall in no case exceed six months from the time such vacancy occurred; and in the event of a vacancy in any other office, the same shall immediately be filled in the manner herein before mentioned.

SEC. 4. The Officers heretofore elected or appointed may retain their offices during the time for which they have been so elected or appointed, at the expiration of which time said offices shall be filled as herein-before provided.

ARTICLE V

JUDICIARY

SECTION 1. The Tribunal of Justice of this Order shall consist of a Court at the Head-quarters of the Empire, the Realm, the Dominion, the Province, and the Den, to be appointed by the Chiefs of these several Departments.

SEC. 2. The Court at the Head-quarters of the Empire shall consist of three Judges for the trial of Grand Dragons, and the Officers and attachés belonging to the Head-quarters of the Empire.

SEC. 3. The Court at the Head-quarters of the Realm shall consist of three Judges for the trial of Grand Titans, and the Officers and attachés belonging to the Head-quarters of the Realm.

SEC. 4. The Court at the Head-quarters of the Dominion shall consist of three Judges for the trial of Grand Giants, and the Officers and attachés belonging to the Head-quarters of the Dominion.

SEC. 5. The Court at the Head-quarters of the Province shall consist of five Judges for the trial of Grand Cyclops, the Grand Magis, Grand Monks, and the Grand Exchequers of Dens, and the Officers and attachés belonging to the Head-quarters of the Province.

SEC. 6. The Court at the Head-quarters of the Den shall consist of seven Judges appointed from the Den for the trial of Ghouls and the officers belonging to the Head-quarters of the Den.

SEC. 7. The Tribunal for the trial of the Grand Wizard shall be composed of at least seven Grand Dragons, to be convened by the senior Grand Dragon upon charges being preferred against the Grand Wizard; which Tribunal shall be organized and presided over by the senior Grand Dragon *present;* and if they find the accused guilty, they shall prescribe the penalty, and the senior Grand Dragon of the Empire shall cause the same to be executed.

SEC. 8. The aforesaid Courts shall summon the accused and witnesses for and against him, and if found guilty, they shall prescribe the penalty, and the Officers convening the Court shall cause the same to be executed. *Provided* the accused shall always have the right of appeal to the next Court above, whose decision shall be final.

SEC. 9. The Judges constituting the aforesaid Courts shall be selected with reference to their intelligence, integrity, and fair-mindedness, and shall render their verdict without prejudice, favor, partiality, or affection, and shall be so sworn, upon the organization of the Court; and shall further be sworn to administer even-handed justice.

SEC. 10. The several Courts herein provided for shall be governed in their deliberations, proceedings, and judgments by the rules and regulations governing the proceedings of regular Courts-martial.

ARTICLE VI

REVENUE

SECTION 1. The revenue of this Order shall be derived as follows: For every copy of this Prescript issued to Dens, $10 will be required;

$2 of which shall go into the hands of the Grand Exchequer of the Grand Giant, $2 into the hands of the Grand Exchequer of the Grand Titan, $2 into the hands of the Grand Exchequer of the Grand Dragon, and the remaining $4 into the hands of the Grand Exchequer of the Grand Wizard.

SEC. 2. A further source of revenue to the Empire shall be ten per cent of all the revenue of the Realms, and a tax upon Realms when the Grand Wizard shall deem it necessary and indispensable to levy the same.

SEC. 3. A further source of revenue to Realms shall be ten per cent of all the revenue of Dominions, and a tax upon Dominions when the Grand Dragon shall deem it necessary and indispensable to levy the same.

SEC. 4. A further source of revenue to Dominions shall be ten per cent of all the revenue of Provinces, and a tax upon Provinces when the Grand Giant shall deem such tax necessary and indispensable.

SEC. 5. A further source of revenue to Provinces shall be ten per cent of all the revenue of Dens, and a tax upon Dens when the Grand Giant shall deem such tax necessary and indispensable.

SEC. 6. The source of revenue to Dens shall be the initiation fees, fines, and a *per capita* tax, whenever the Grand Cyclops shall deem such tax necessary and indispensable to the interests and objects of the Order.

SEC. 7. All the revenue obtained in the manner aforesaid, shall be for the *exclusive* benefit of the Order, and shall be appropriated to the dissemination of the same and to the creation of a fund to meet any disbursement that it may become necessary to make to accomplish the objects of the Order and to secure the protection of the same.

ARTICLE VII

ELIGIBILITY FOR MEMBERSHIP

SECTION 1. No one shall be presented for admission into the Order until he shall have first been recommended by some friend or intimate who *is* a member, to the Investigating Committee, (which shall be composed of the Grand Cyclops, the Grand Magi, and the Grand Monk,) and who shall have investigated his antecedents and his past and present standing and connections; and after such investigation, shall have pronounced him competent and worthy to become a member. *Provided*, no one shall be presented for admission into, or become a member of, this Order who shall not have attained the age of eighteen years.

SEC. 2. No one shall become a member of this Order unless he shall *voluntarily* take the following oaths or obligations, and shall *satisfactorily* answer the following interrogatories, while kneeling, with his right hand raised to heaven, and his left hand resting on the Bible:

PRELIMINARY OBLIGATION

'I ——— solemnly swear or affirm that I will never reveal any thing that I may this day (or night) learn concerning the Order of the * * *, and that I will true answer make to such interrogatories as may be put to me touching my competency for admission into the same. So help me God.'

INTERROGATORIES TO BE ASKED:

1st. Have you ever been rejected, upon application for membership in the * * *, or have you ever been expelled from the same?

2d. Are you now, or have you ever been, a member of the Radical Republican party, or either of the organizations known as the 'Loyal League' and the 'Grand Army of the Republic?'

3d. Are you opposed to the principles and policy of the Radical party, and to the Loyal League, and the Grand Army of the Republic, so far as you are informed of the character and purposes of those organizations?

4th. Did you belong to the Federal army during the late war, and fight against the South during the existence of the same?

5th. Are you opposed to negro equality, both social and political?

6th. Are you in favor of a white man's government in this country?

7th. Are you in favor of Constitutional liberty, and a Government of equitable laws instead of a Government of violence and oppression?

8th. Are you in favor of maintaining the Constitutional rights of the South?

9th. Are you in favor of the re-enfranchisement and emancipation of the white men of the South, and the restitution of the Southern people to all their rights, alike proprietary, civil, and political?

10th. Do you believe in the inalienable right of self-preservation of the people against the exercise of arbitrary and unlicensed power?

If the foregoing interrogatories are satisfactorily answered, and the candidate desires to go further (after something of the character and nature of the Order has thus been indicated to him) and to be admitted to the benefits, mysteries, secrets and purposes of the Order, he shall then be required to take the following final oath or obligation. But if said interrogatories are not satisfactorily answered, or the candidate declines to proceed further, he shall be discharged, after being solemnly admonished by the initiating officer of the deep secresy to which the oath already taken has bound him, and that the extreme penalty of the law will follow a violation of the same.

FINAL OBLIGATION

'I ——— of my own free will and accord, and in the presence of Almighty God, do solemnly swear or affirm, that I will never reveal to any one not a member of the Order of the * * *, by any intimation, sign, symbol, word or act, or in any other manner whatever, any of the secrets, signs, grips, pass-words, or mysteries of the Order of the * * *, or that I am a member of the same, or that I know any one who *is* a member; and that I will abide by the Prescript and Edicts of the Order of the * * *. So help me God.'

The initiating officer will then proceed to explain to the new members the character and objects of the Order, and introduce him to the mysteries and secrets of the same; and shall read to him this Prescript and the Edicts thereof, or present the same to him for personal perusal.

ARTICLE VIII

AMENDMENTS

This Prescript or any part or Edicts thereof shall never be changed, except by a two-thirds vote of the Grand Dragons of the Realms, in convention assembled, and at which convention the Grand Wizard shall preside and be entitled to a vote. And upon the application of a majority of the Grand Dragons for that purpose, the Grand Wizard shall call and appoint the time and place for said convention; which, when assembled, shall proceed to make such modifications and amendments as it may think will promote the interest, enlarge the utility, and more thoroughly effectuate the purposes of the Order.

ARTICLE IX

INTERDICTION

The origin, mysteries, and Ritual of this Order shall never be written, but the same shall be communicated orally.

ARTICLE X

EDICTS

1. No one shall become a member of a distant Den, when there is a Den established and in operation in his own immediate vicinity; nor shall any one become a member of any Den, or of this Order in any way, after he shall have been once rejected, upon application for membership.

2. No Den, or officer, or member, or members thereof, shall operate beyond their prescribed limits, unless invited or ordered by the proper authority so to do.

3. No member shall be allowed to take any intoxicating spirits to any meeting of the Den; nor shall any member be allowed to attend a meeting while intoxicated; and for every appearance at a

meeting in such condition, he shall be fined the sum of not less than one nor more than five dollars, to go into the revenue of the Order.

4. Any member may be expelled from the Order by a majority vote of the Officers and Ghouls of the Den to which he belongs; and if after such expulsion, such member shall assume any of the duties, regalia, or insignia of the Order, or in any way claim to be a member of the same, he shall be severely punished. His obligation of secrecy shall be as binding upon him after expulsion as before, and for any revelation made by him thereafter, he shall be held accountable in the same manner as if he were then a member.

5. Upon the expulsion of any member from the Order, the Grand Cyclops, or the officer acting in his stead, shall immediately report the same to the Grand Giant of the Province, who shall cause the fact to be made known and read in each Den of his Province, and shall transmit the same, through the proper channels, to the Grand Dragon of the Realm, who shall cause it to be published to every Den in his Realm, and shall notify the Grand Dragons of contiguous Realms of the same.

6. Every Grand Cyclops shall read, or cause to be read, this Prescript and these Edicts to his Den, at least once in every month; and shall read them to each new member when he is initiated, or present the same to him for personal perusal.

7. The initiation fee of this Order shall be one dollar, to be paid when the candidate is initiated and received into the Order.

8. Dens may make such additional Edicts for their control and government as they may deem requisite and necessary. *Provided,* no Edict shall be made to conflict with any of the provisions or Edicts of this Prescript.

9. The most profound and rigid secrecy concerning any and everything that relates to the Order, shall at all times be maintained.

10. Any member who shall reveal or betray the secrets of this Order, shall suffer the extreme penalty of the law.

ADMONITION

Hush! thou art not to utter what I am; bethink thee! it was our covenant!

REGISTER

I

1. Dismal,	7. Painful,
2. Mystic,	8. Portentous,
3. Stormy,	9. Fading,
4. Peculiar,	10. Melancholy,
5. Blooming,	11. Glorious,
6. Brilliant,	12. Gloomy.

II

I. White, II. Green, III. Yellow, IV. Amber, V. Purple, VI. Crimson, VII. Emerald.

III

1. Fearful,	7. Hideous,
2. Startling,	8. Frightful,
3. Wonderful,	9. Awful,
4. Alarming,	10. Horrible,
5. Mournful,	11. Dreadful,
6. Appalling,	12. Last.

IV

Cumberland.

L'ENVOI

To the lovers of law and order, peace and justice, we send greeting; and to the shades of the venerated dead we affectionately dedicate the Order of the * * *.

Resurgamus

III. The Kloran

KLOKARD. Your excellency, the sacred altar of the klan is prepared; the fiery cross illumines the klavern.
E.C. Faithful Klokard, why the fiery cross?
KLOKARD. Sir, it is the emblem of that sincere, unselfish devotedness of all klansmen to the sacred purpose and principles we have espoused.
E.C. My terrors and klansmen, what means the fiery cross?
ALL. We serve and sacrifice for the right.
E.C. Klansmen all: You will gather for our opening devotions.

· · · · · · ·

(The stanzas are sung to the tune From Greenland's Icy Mountains and the chorus, Home, Sweet Home.)

I.

We meet with cordial greetings
  In this our sacred cave
To pledge anew our compact
  With hearts sincere and brave;
A band of faithful klansmen,
  Knights of the K.K.K.,
We all will stand together
  Forever and for aye.

CHORUS.

Home, home, country and home,
  Klansmen we'll live and die
For our country and home.

II.

Here honor, love, and justice
  Must actuate us all;
Before our sturdy phalanx
  All hate and strife shall fall.
In unison we'll labor
  Wherever we may roam
To shield a klansman's welfare,
  His country, name, and home.

After singing, the Kludd at the sacred altar leads in the following prayer: (All must stand steady with heads reverently bowed.)

Our Father and our God, we, as klansmen, acknowledge our dependence upon Thee and Thy lovingkindness toward us; may our gratitude be full and constant and inspire us to walk in Thy ways.

Give us to know that each klansman by the process of thought and conduct determines his own destiny, good or bad: May he forsake the bad and choose and strive for the good, remembering always that the living Christ is a klansman's criterion of character.

Keep us in the blissful bonds of fraternal union, of clannish fidelity one toward another and of a devoted loyalty to this, our great institution. Give us to know that the crowning glory of a klansman is to serve. Harmonize our souls with the sacred principles and purposes of our noble order that we may keep our sacred oath inviolate, as Thou art our witness.

Bless those absent from our gathering at this time; Thy peace be in their hearts and homes.

God save our Nation! And help us to be a Nation worthy of existence on the earth. Keep ablaze in each klansman's heart the sacred fire of a devoted patriotism to our country and its Government.

We invoke Thy blessing upon our emperor, the imperial wizard, and his official family in the administrations of the affairs pertaining to the government of the invisible empire. Grant him wisdom and grace; and may each klansman's heart and soul be inclined toward him in loving loyalty and unwavering devotion.

Oh, God! For Thy glory and our good we humbly ask these things in the name of Him who taught us to serve and sacrifice for the right. Amen! (All say "Amen!")

CLOSING CEREMONY, KNIGHTS OF THE KU-KLUX KLAN.

The order of business having been finished, the E.C. will arise, give one rap with his gavel and say:

"My terrors and klansmen, the sacred purpose of the gathering of the klan at this time has been fulfilled; the deliberations of this klonklave have ended."

E.C. Faithful Klaliff: What is the fourfold duty of a klansman?

The klaliff will arise and say:

"To worship God; be patriotic toward our country; be devoted and loyal to our klan and emperor, and to practice clannishness toward his fellow klansfen." (And remains standing.)

E.C. Faithful Kludd: "How speaketh the oracles of our God?"

The kludd will arise and say:

"Thou shalt worship the Lord thy God. Render unto the state the things which are the state's. Love the brotherhood: honor the king. Bear ye one another's burdens, and so fulfill the law of Christ." (And remains standing.)

E.C. Faithful Klokard: "What does a klansman value more than life?"

The klokard will arise and say:

"Honor to a klansman is more than life." (And remains standing.)

[Tune, America.]

God of Eternity
Guard, guide our great country,
Our homes and store.
Keep our great state to Thee,
Its people right and free.
In us Thy glory be,
Forevermore.

After the singing all look toward the mounted flag and will gtnh and then stand with bowed heads; the kludd standing at the sacred altar will pronounce the following benediction:

THE BENEDICTION.

May the blessings of our God wait upon thee and the sun of glory shine around thy head; may the gates of plenty, honor, and happiness be always open to thee and thine, so far as they will not rob thee of eternal joys.

May no strife disturb thy days, nor sorrow distress thy nights, and when death shall summons thy departure may the Saviour's blood have washed thee from all impurities, perfected thy initiation, and thus prepared, enter thou into the empire invisible and repose thy soul in perpetual peace.

Amen! (All say, "Amen.")

QUALIFYING INTERROGATORIES.

The klokard will first ask each candidate his name and then speak to the candidates in the outer den as follows:

SIRS: The Knights of the Ku-Klux Klan, as a great and essentially a patriotic, fraternal, benevolent order, does not discriminate against a man on account of his religious or political creed, when same does not conflict with or antagonize the sacred rights and privileges guaranteed by our civil government and Christian ideals and institutions.

Therefore, to avoid any misunderstanding and as evidence that we do not seek to impose unjustly the requirements of this order upon anyone who can not, on account of his religious or political scruples, voluntarily meet our requirements and faithfully practice our principles, and as proof that we respect all honest men in their sacred convictions, whether same are agreeable with our requirements or not, we require as an absolute necessity on the part of each of you an affirmative answer to each of the following questions:

Each of the following questions must be answered by (each of) you with an emphatic "Yes."

First. Is the motive prompting your ambition to be a klansman serious and unselfish?

Second. Are you a native-born white, Gentile American citizen?

Third. Are you absolutely opposed to and free of any allegiance of any nature to any cause, Government, people, sect, or ruler that is foreign to the United States of America?

Fourth. Do you believe in the tenets of the Christian religion?

Fifth. Do you esteem the United States of America and its institutions above any other Government, civil, political, or ecclesiastical, in the whole world?

Sixth. Will you, without mental reservation, take a solemn oath to defend, preserve, and enforce same?

Seventh. Do you believe in clannishness and will you faithfully practice same towards klansmen?

Eighth. Do you believe in and will you faithfully strive for the eternal maintenance of white supremacy?

Ninth. Will you faithfully obey our constitution and laws, and conform willingly to all our usages, requirements, and regulations?

Tenth. Can you be always depended on?

KLADD. The distinguishing marks of a klansman are not found in the fiber of his garments or his social or financial standing, but are spiritual: namely, a chivalric head, a compassionate heart, a prudent tongue, and a courageous will. All devoted to our country, our klan, our homes, and each other: these are the distinguishing marks of a klansman, oh faithful klexter! And these men claim the marks.

KLEXTER. What if one of your party should prove himself a traitor?

KLADD. He would be immediately banished in disgrace from the invisible empire without fear or favor, conscience would tenaciously torment him, remorse would repeatedly revile him, and direful things would befall him.

KLEXTER. Do they (or does he) know all this?

KLADD. All this he (or they) now know. He (or they) has (or have) heard, and they must heed.

KLEXTER. Faithful kladd, you speak the truth.

KLADD. Faithful klexter, a klansman speaketh the truth in and from his heart. A lying scoundrel may wrap his disgraceful frame within the sacred folds of a klansman's robe and deceive the very elect, but only a klansman possesses a klansman's heart and a klansman's soul.

KLOKARD:

God give us men! The invisible empire demands strong
  Minds, great hearts, true faith, and ready hands.
Men whom the lust of office does not kill;
  Men whom the spoils of office can not buy;
Men who possess opinions and a will:
  Men who have honor; men who will not lie;
  Men who can stand before a demogogue
And damn his treacherous flatteries without winking!
Tall men, sun-crowned, who live above the fog
  In public duty and in private thinking;
For while the rabble, with their thumb-worn creeds,
Their large professions and their little deeds,
Mingle in selfish strife, Lo! freedom weeps,
Wrong rules the land, and waiting justice sleeps.
God give us men!
Men who serve not for selfish booty,
But real men, courageous, who flinch not at duty;
Men of dependable character; men of sterling worth;
Then wrongs will be redressed, and right will rule the earth;
God give us men!

After a pause, the klarogo faces the candidates and says:

"SIRS: Will you (or each of you) by your daily life as klansmen earnestly endeavor to be an answer to this prayer?"

The exalted cyclops will arise and address the candidates as follows:

"Sirs, is the motive prompting your presence here serious and unselfish?

"It is indeed refreshing to meet face to face with men (or a man) like you, who, actuated by manly motives, aspire to all things noble for yourselves and humanity.

"The luster of the holy light of chivalry has lost its former glory and is sadly dimmed by the choking dust of selfish, sordid gain. Pass on:"

The exalted cyclops will resume his seat, and the kladd will face his party toward the nighthawk and advance behind the nighthawk until he hears the signal of allw from the klokard. On hearing the signal from the klokard, the nighthawk stops and stands steady; the kladd will also stop his party immediately in front of the klokard's station and face them to the klokard's station and answer the signal by the same. On receiving the answer, the klokard will arise and address the party as follows:

"Real fraternity, by shameful neglect, has been starved until so weak her voice is lost in the courts of her own castle, and she passes unnoticed by her sworn subjects as she moves along the crowded streets and through the din of the market place. Man's valuation of man is by the standard of wealth and not worth: selfishness is the festive queen among humankind, and multitudes forget honor, justice, love, and God and every religious conviction to do homage to her; and yet, with the cruel heart of Jezebel, she slaughters the souls of thousands of her devotees daily. Pass on!"

The kludd will resume his seat, and the kladd will face his party as before and advance behind the nighthawk until he hears the signal of allw from the exalted cyclops. On hearing the signal of the exalted cyclops, the nighthawk stops and goes to and takes position at the sacred altar; the kladd will also stop his party immediately in front of the exalted cyclops's station, facing them to the exalted cyclops, and then answer the signal with the same. On receiving the answer, the exalted cyclops will arise and address the party as follows:

"Sirs, we congratulate you on your manly decision to forsake the world of selfishness and fraternal alienation and emigrate to the delectable bounds of the invisible empire and become loyal citizens of the same. The prime purpose of this great order is to develop character, practice clannishness, to protect the home and the chastity of womanhood, and to exemplify a pure patriotism toward our glorious country.

"You as citizens of the invisible empire must be actively patriotic, toward our country and constantly clannish toward klansmen socially, physically, morally, and vocationally; will you assume this obligation of citizenship?

"You must unflinchingly conform to our requirements, regulations, and usages in every detail and prove yourselves worthy to have and to hold the honors we bestow; do you freely and faithfully assume to do this?

"Sirs, if you have any doubt as to your ability to qualify, either in body or character, as citizens of the invisible empire, you now have an opportunity to retire from this place with the good will of the klan to attend you; for I warn you now if you falter or fail at this time or in the future as a klansman, in klonklave or in life, you will be banished from citizenship in the invisible empire without fear or favor.

"This is a serious undertaking; we are not here to make sport of you nor indulge in the silly frivolity of circus clowns. Be you well assured that 'he that putteth his hands to the plow and looketh back is not fit for the kingdom of heaven' or worthy of the high honor of citizenship in the invisible empire, or the fervent fellowship of klansmen. Don't deceive yourselves; you can not deceive us, and we will not be mocked. Do you wish to retire?"

E. C. Faithful kladd, you will direct the way for these worthy aliens to the sacred altar of the empire of chivalry, honor, industry, and love, in order that they may make further progress toward attaining citizenship in the invisible empire, Knights of the Ku-Klux Klan.

DEDICATION.

The E. C. addresses the candidates as follows:

"Sirs, have (each of) you assumed without mental reservation your oath of allegiance to the invisible empire? Mortal man can not assume a more binding oath; character and courage alone will enable you to keep it. Always remember that to keep this oath means to you honor, happiness, and life; but to violate it means disgrace, dishonor, and death. May honor, happiness, and life be yours."

(Then he folds up the vessel from the sacred altar, containing the dedication fluid, and addresses the candidates as follows:)

"With this transparent, life-giving, powerful, God-given fluid, more precious and far more significant than all the sacred oils of the ancients, I set you (or each of you) apart from the men of your daily association to the great and honorable task you have voluntarily allotted yourselves as citizens of the invisible empire, Knights of the Ku-Klux Klan.

"As a klansman may your character be as transparent, your life purpose as powerful, your motive in all things as magnanimous and as pure, and your clannishness as real and as faithful as the manifold drops herein, and you a vital being as useful to humanity as is pure water to mankind.

"You will kneel upon your right knee."

Just here the following stanza must be sung in a low, soft, but distinct tone, preferably by a quartet:

[Tune, Just As I Am Without One Plea.]

To Thee, oh God! I call to Thee—
True to my oath, oh, help me be!
I've pledged my love, my blood, my all;
Oh, give me grace that I not fall.

E.C. Sirs, 'Neath the uplifted fiery cross which by its holy light looks down upon you to bless with its sacred traditions of the past I dedicate you in body, in mind, in spirit, and in life to the holy service of our country, our klan, our homes, each other, and humanity.

DEDICATORY PRAYER.

God of all, author of all good, Thou who didst create man and so proposed that man should fill a distinct place and perform a specific work in the economy of Thy good government. Thou has revealed Thyself and Thy purpose to man, and by this revelation we have learned our place and our work. Therefore we

have solemnly dedicated ourselves as klansmen to that sublime work harmonic with Thy will and purpose in our creation.

Now, oh, God, we, through Thy goodness, have here dedicated with Thine own divinely distilled fluid these manly men at the altar kneeling, who have been moved by worthy motives and impelled by noble impulses to turn from selfishness and fraternal alienation and to espouse with body, mind, spirit, and life the holy service of our country, our klan, our home, and each other. We beseech Thee to dedicate them with the fulness of Thy spirit, keep him (or each of them) true to his (or their) sacred, solemn oath to our noble cause, to the glory of Thy great name. Amen. (All say "amen.")

THE KLONVERSATION.

After the instructions have been given the klokard will say:

"The kladd will now conduct you to the exalted cyclops, where you will receive from him the CS and PW, the sacred symbol and imperial instructions, to which give earnest heed."

The kladd conducts the party to the station of the E.C. and says:

"Your excellency, these klansmen (or this klansman), having been instructed in the way of the klavern, now awaits to receive from you the CS and PW, the sacred symbol of the klan and imperial instructions."

E.C. will arise and say:

"My fellow klansman (or klansmen) the insignia or mark of a klansman is honor. All secrets and secret information of the invisible empire is committed to you on your honor. A klansman values honor more than life itself. Be true to honor, then to all the world you will be true. Always remember that an honorable secret committed is a thing sacred.

"I am about to commit to you three vital secrets of the invisible empire—the CS and PW and the sacred symbol, the mioak. Do you swear to forever hold them in sacred, secret reverence, even unto death?

"The CS and PW enables you to meet with and enjoy the fellowship of klansmen in klonklave assembled.

"For the present and until changed the CS is ——— and the PW is ———.

"The mioak, the sacred symbol of the klan is that (he explains what it is) by which klansmen recognize each other without word, sound, or sign.

"I now present you with the material insignia of a klansmen, the sacred symbol of the plan, by name the mioak. Be faithful in its wearing. It must be morn on your person where it may be readily seen. Tell no person in the whole world what it is, its meaning and significance, even by hint or insinuation, as it is a positive secret of the plan. Don't fail to recognize it by whomsoever it is worthily worn; always appreciate its sacred significance and be true to same. As a test of your honor I invest you with this symbol and commit to you its sacred secret."

He pins on the breast of the new klansman the insignia and explains its symbolic meaning.

"You will now receive imperial instructions. Carefully preserve and seriously study this document and give earnest heed to same, for on the practice of its teachings in your daily life depends your future advancement."

"You (or each of you) now are instructed klansmen, possessing all the rights, privileges, and protection as such will take your place with klansmen in the sacred fellowship of the invisible empire."

The E.C. will then give two raps with his gavel, take his seat and proceed with the other business.

THE IMPERIAL PROCLAMATION.

To all nations, people, tribes, and tongues, and to the lovers of law and order, peace and justice, of the whole earth, greeting:

I, and the citizens of the invisible empire through me, proclaim to you as follows:

We, the members of this order, desiring to promote real patriotism toward our civil Government; honorable peace among men and nations; protection for and happiness in the homes of our people; love, real brotherhood, mirth, and manhood among ourselves, and liberty, justice, and fraternity among all mankind; and believing we can best accomplish these noble purposes through the channel of a high-class mystic, social, patriotic, benevolent association, having a perfected lodge system with an exalted, ritualistic form of work and an effective form of government, not for selfish profit but for the mutual betterment, benefit, and protection of all our oath-bound associates, their welfare, physically, socially, morally, and vocationally, and their loved ones, do proclaim to the whole world that we are dedicated to the sublime and pleasant duty of providing generous aid, tender sympathy, and fraternal assistance in the effulgence of the light of life and amid the sable shadows of death, amid fortune and misfortune, and to the exalted privilege of demonstrating the practical utility of the great, yet most-neglected, doctrine of the fatherhood of God and the brotherhood of man as a vital force in the lives and affairs of men.

In this we invite all men who can qualify to become citizens of the invisible empire to approach the portal of our beneficent domain and join us in our noble work of extending its boundaries; in disseminating the gospel of "klankraft," thereby encouraging, conserving, protecting, and making vital the fraternal human relationship in the practice of a wholesome clanishness; to share with us the glory of performing the secred duty of protecting womanhood; to maintain forever white supremacy in all things; to commemorate the holy and chivalric achievements of our fathers; to safeguard the sacred rights, exalted privileges, and distinctive institutions of our civil Government; to bless mankind, and to keep eternally ablaze the secred fire of a fervent devotion to a pure Americanism.

The invisible empire is founded on sterling character and immutable principles based upon a most sacred sentiment and cemented by noble purposes; it is promoted by a sincere, unselfish devotion of the souls of manly men, and is managed and governed by the consecrated intelligence of thoughtful brains. It is the soul of chivalry and virtue's impenetrable shield—the devout impulse of an unconquered race.

Done in the aulic of his majesty, the imperial wizard and emperor of the invisible empire, Knights of the Ku-Klux Klan, in the imperial palace, in the imperial city of Atlanta, Commonwealth of Georgia, United States of America, this the 4th day of July, A.D. 1916 Anno Klan L.

Signed by his majesty,

[SEAL.]

WILLIAM JOSEPH SIMMONS
Imperial Wizard.

°   °   °   °   °   °   °

A SACRED DUTY—A PRECIOUS PRIVILEGE.

A true American can not give a higher and more sincere expression of appreciation of and gratitude for what was accomplished by our fathers in the defense of home and the sacred rights of our people than by becoming a "citizen of the invisible empire, Knights of the Ku-Klux Klan." He can not align himself with any institution that will mean so much for himself, his home, and his country as this great order.

It stands for America first—first in thought, first in affections, and first in the galaxy of nations. The Stars and Stripes forever above all other and every kind of government in the whole world.

Benevolence—in thought, word, and deed based upon justice and practically applied to all. To right the wrong; to succor the weak and unfortunate; to help the worthy and to relieve the distressed.

Clannishness—real fraternity practically applied—standing by and sticking to each other in all things honorable. Encouraging, protecting, cultivating, and exemplifying the real "fraternal human relationship" to shield and enhance each other's happiness and welfare. A devoted, unfailing loyalty to the principles, mission, and purposes of the order in promoting the highest and best interest of the community, State and Nation.

What it is: It is a standard fraternal order enforcing fraternal conduct, and not merely a "social association." It is a duly incorporated, legally recognized institution, honest in purpose, noble in sentiment and practical in results that commands the hearty respect of all respectable people throughout the Nation. It is not encouraging nor condoning any propaganda of religious intolerance nor racial prejudice. It is an association of real men who believe in being something, in doing things worth while, and who are in all things 100 per cent pure American. Yet it is vastly more than merely a social fraternal order.

Its initial purpose: An enduring monument to the valor and patriotic achievements of the Ku-Klux Klan. That this monument be not embodied in cold, emotionless stone, but in living, pulsating human hearts and active human brains, and find a useful expression in the nobility of the character of real manly men; this is the only memorial that will adequately befit the memory of the valiant Ku-Klux Klan.

Its lineage: The most sublime lineage in history, commemorating and perpetuating, as it does the most dauntless organization known to man.

Its secret: Sacred guardianship to the most sacred cause.

Its courage: The soul of chivalry and virtue's impenetrable shield. The impulse of an unconquered race.

Its teachings: To inculcate the sacred principles and noble ideals of the world's greatest order of chivalry; and direct the way of the initiate through the veil of mystic philosophy into the empire invisible.

Its character: The noblest concepts of manhood idealized in thought and materialized in practice in all the relationships of life—mystery and action mastery and achievement.

Its ritualism is vastly different from anything in the whole universe of fraternal ritualism. It is altogether original, weird, mystical, and of a high class, leading up through four degrees. Dignity and decency are its marked features. It unfolds a spiritual philosophy that has to do with the very fundamentals of life and living, here and hereafter. He who explores the dismal depths of the mystic cave and from thence attains the lofty heights of superior knighthood may sit among the gods in the empire invisible.

Its patriotism: An uncompromising standard of pure Americanism untrammeled by alien influences and free from the entanglements of foreign alliances. Proclaiming the brotherhood of nations but wedding none, thereby unyielding in the dignity of our own independence and forever faultless in our freedom.

Its mission: Duty—without fault, without fail, without fear, and without reproach.

Its society: The practical fraternal fellowship of men whose standard is worth not wealth; character, not cash, courageous manhood based upon honor untarnished by the touch of hypocrisy or the veneering of society's selfish social valuations.

Its place: In the heart of every "true American," alongside of every other fraternal order, and in its original casting, unique mannerism, sacred sentiment, noble purpose, and peculiar mysticism it is separate and apart from any and all and peerless in its distinctive peculiarities.

Its fraternity: Not merely reciting in ceremony pretty, time-worn platitudes on brotherly love, but to enforce a fraternal practice of clanishness, thereby making devotion to its standard worth while. "The glory of a klansman is to serve."

Its origin: This great institution, as a patriotic, ritualistic fraternal order, is no hastily "jumped-up" affair. It has been in the making for the past 20 years. It is a product of deliberate thought. The one man (William Joseph Simmons) who is responsible for it conceived the idea 20 years ago. For 14 years he thought, studied, and worked to prepare himself for its launching. He had dedicated his life to this noble cause. He kept his own counsel during these years and in the silent recesses of his soul he thought out the great plan. During the early days of October, 1915, he mentioned his ambition to some friends, among whom were three men who were bona fide members of the original klan when it disbanded. They most heartily cooperated with him. Having met with such encouragement, he invited several of his friends to a meeting on the night of October 26, 1915, at which time he unfolded his plans, and as a result all present, 34 in number, signed a petition for a charter. The petition was accepted and on Thanksgiving night, 1915, when were seen emerging from the shadows and gathering around the spring at the base of Stone Mountain (the world's greatest rock, near Atlanta, Ga.) and from thence repaired to the mountain top and there, under a blazing fiery cross, they took the oath of allegiance to the invisible empire, Knights of the Ku-Klux Klan. The charter was issued by the State of Georgia, December 4, 1915, and signed by Hon. Philip Cook, secretary of state. In the development of the order a petition was made to the superior court, Fulton County Ga., for a special charter, and said charter was issued July 1, 1916. The imperial wizard issued his imperial proclamation July 4, 1916.

And thus on the mountain top that night at the midnight hour while men braved the surging blasts of wild wintry mountain winds and endured a temperature far below freezing, bathed in the sacred glow of the fiery cross, the invisible empire was called from its slumber of half a century to take up a new task and fulfill a new mission for humanity's good and to call back to mortal habitation the good angel of practical fraternity among men.

PREREQUISITES TO CITIZENSHIP IN THE INVISIBLE EMPIRE.

This order is founded upon dependable character. It is not an ultra-exclusive institution, but its membership is composed of "picked" men.

No man is wanted in this order who hasn't manhood enough to assume a real oath with serious purpose to keep the same inviolate.

No man is wanted in this order who will not or can not swear an unqualified allegiance to the Government of the United States of America, its flag, and its Constitution.

No man is wanted in this order who does not esteem the Government of the United States of America above any other government, civil, political, or ecclesiastical, in the whole world.

No man is wanted in this order who can not practice real fraternity toward each and every one of his oath-bound associates.

Only native born American citizens who believe in the tenets of the Christian religion and owe no allegiance of any degree or nature to any foreign Government, nation, political institution, sect, people, or person, are eligible.

DEGREE FEES.

Membership in this order can not be bought; it is given as a reward for service unselfishly rendered. If you really believe in the order, and will practice its principles, and conform to its regulations and usages and contribute the sum of $10 toward its propagation and can otherwise qualify then membership is awarded you upon this service rendered and pledged of future fidelity to the institution. This is not a selfish, mercenary, commercialized proposition, but the direct opposite.

THE KU-KLUX KREED.

We, the order of the Knights of the Ku-Klux Klan, reverentially acknowledge the majesty and supremacy of the Divine Being, and recognize the goodness and providence of the same.

We recognize our relation to the Government of the United States of America, the supremacy of its Constitution, the Union of States thereunder, and the constitutional laws thereof, and we shall be ever devoted to the sublime principles of a pure Americanism and valiant in the defense of its ideals and institutions.

We avow the distinction between the races of mankind as same has been decreed by the Creator, and we shall ever be true to the faithful maintenance of

White Supremacy and will strenously oppose any compromise thereof in any and all things.

We appreciate the intrinsic value of a real practical fraternal relationship among men of kindred thought, purpose, and ideals and the infinite benefits accruable therefrom, and we shall faithfully devote ourselves to the practice of an honorable clannishness that the life and living of each may be a constant blessing to others.

"Non silba sed anthar."—Original creed revised.

OBJECTS AND PURPOSE.

ARTICLE II.

SECTION 1. The objects of this order shall be to unite only white male persons, native-born gentile citizens of the United States of America, who owe no allegiance of any nature or degree to any foreign Government, nation, institution, sect, ruler, person, or people; whose morals are good; whose reputations and vocations are respectable; whose habits are exemplary; who are of sound minds and at or above the age of 18 years, under a common oath into a common brotherhood of strict regulations for the purpose of cultivating and promoting real patriotism toward our civil Government; to practice an honorable clanishness toward each other; to exemplify a practical benevolence; to shield the sanctity of the home and the chastity of womanhood; to forever maintain white supremacy; to teach and faithfully inculcate a high spiritual philosophy through an exalted ritualism, and by a practical devotedness to conserve, protect, and maintain the distinctive institutions, rights, privileges, principles, traditions, and ideals of a pure Americanism.

SEC. 3. This order is an institution of chivalry, humanity, justice, and patriotism; embodying in its genius and principles all that is chivalric in conduct, noble in sentiment, generous in manhood, and patriotic in purpose; its peculiar objects being: First, to protect the weak, the innocent, and the defenseless from the indignities, wrongs, and outrages of the lawless, the violent, and the brutal; to relieve the injured and the oppressed; to succor the suffering and unfortunate, especially widows and orphans. Second, to protect and defend the Constitution of the United States of America and all laws passed in conformity thereto, and to protect the States and the people thereof from all invasion of their rights thereunder from any source whatsoever. Third, to aid and assist in the execution of all constitutional laws, and to preserve the honor and dignity of the State by opposing tyranny in any and every form or degree attempted from any and every source whatsoever by a fearless and faithful administration of justice, and to promptly and properly meet every behest of duty without fear and without reproach.

TERRITORIAL JURISDICTIONS, ASSEMBLIES, ETC.

ARTICLE III.

SEC. 1. *The invisible empire.*—The phrase "invisible empire" in a material sense denotes the universal geographical jurisdiction of this order and it shall embrace the whole world. The convention of the invisible empire shall be known as the imperial klonvokation. The phrase "invisible empire" in a spiritual sense denotes or applies to all the secrets and secret knowledge and information, secret work and working and things of this order, and to all that has been, to all that now is, and to all that is to be, the past, the present, and the future, yesterday, to-day, and forever; the dead of yesterday, the living of to-day, and the contemplated of to-morrow of the life that now is and of that which is to come.

MEMBERSHIP.

ARTICLE IV.

SECTION 1. The qualification for membership in this order shall be as follows: An applicant must be white male gentile person, a native-born citizen of the United States of America, who owes no allegiance of any nature or degree whatsoever to any foreign Government, nation, institution, sect, ruler, prince, potentate, people, or person; he must be at or above the age of 18 years, of sound mind, good character, of commendable reputation, and respectable vocation, a believer in the tenets of the Christian religion, and whose allegiance, loyalty, and devotion to the Government of the United States of America in all things is unquestionable.

KLANS.

ARTICLE XVII.

SEC. 25. A klan, or a member of this order, must not use the official costume or any part of same of the order on any occasion, or for any purpose other than in ceremony of this order, or in an official klavalkade (parade) under penalty of forfeiture of charter of the klan or expulsion from this order of the member.

SEC. 26. No klan and no member of this order shall use the name of this order or any part thereof for any purpose that contravenes in any manner the laws of the land, or in any manner that will in any way reflect, or probably reflect, upon the reputation and good name of this order, or compromise or injure this order or any member of this order in any way.

OFFENSES AND PENALTIES.

ARTICLE XIX.

SECTION 1. Offenses against this order deserving penalties shall be: Treason against the United States of America: violating the oath of allegiance or any supplementary oaths or obligations thereto of this order; criminal act or acts proven; disregard of public decency; disrespect for virtuous womanhood; betraying or violating a sacred trust of a klansman; a purposely violation of this constitution and the laws of this order, or the by-laws of a klan of this order; excessive drunkenness in public places, drunkenness or drinking intoxicating liquors during a klonklave or on the premises thereof, or entering a klonklave in an intoxicated condition; the frequent use of profane language or vulgarity during a klonklave, or in an assembly of klansmen just prior thereto; conspiring against the interest and prosperity of this order or any klansman in any way, or being a party thereto, or being a party to any move, conspiracy, or organization whose existence or purpose is antagonistic or injurious to or is an imitation or counterfeit of this order, or whose name, style, or title is a colarable imitation of the name of this order; swearing allegiance to or otherwise becoming a citizen or subject of any nation, government, or institution of any nature or classification, or any ruler, potentate, prince, or person, or any cause whatsoever that is foreign to or is inimical to the Government of the United States of America and its established institution, or aiding or abetting such a government, nation, institution, ruler, potentate, prince, or person against the interest, well being, or dignity of the United States of America or the distinctive institutions of its Government.

THE PRACTICE OF KLANISHNESS.

(1) *Patriotic klanishness.*—An unswerving allegiance to the principles of a pure Americanism as represented by the flag of our great Nation, namely, liberty, justice, and truth. Real, true Americanism unadulterated; a dogged devotedness to our country, its government, its ideals, and its institutions. To keep our Government forever free from the alien touch of foreign alliances and influences that liberty's effulgent torch be not dimmed. By your vote as a citizen select only men of pure patriotic impulses to serve in positions of public trust. Vote not politics but patriotism. Exercise your rights and prerogatives as a civil citizen for the best interest of your state and community and for the general public weal; the making of just and equitable laws and the righteous enforcement of same; bitterly oppose tyranny in any and every form and degree, and displace the corrupt politicians with dependable patriotic statesmen: "He who saves his country saves all things and all things saved bless him; but he who lets his country die lets all things die and all things dying curse him."

THE KU-KLUX KLAN YESTERDAY, TODAY, AND FOREVER.

The purpose of the modern Ku-Klux Klan is to inculcate the sacred principles and noble ideals of chivalry, the development of character, the protection of the home and the chastity of womanhood, the exemplification of a pure and practical patriotism toward our glorious country, the preservation of American ideals and institutions and the maintenance of white supremacy.

While membership in the Ku-Klux Klan is open only to white American citizens, the organization wages war on no individual or organization, regardless of race, color, or creed. It takes no part as an organization in any political or religious controversy, and it concedes the right of every man to think, vote, and worship God as he pleases.

Among the principles for which this organization stands, in addition to those already enumerated, are: Suppression of graft by public officeholders; preventing the causes of mob violence and lynchings; preventing unwarranted strikes by foreign agitators; sensible and patriotic immigration laws; sovereignty of State rights under the Constitution; separation of church and state; and freedom of speech and press, a freedom of such that does not strike at or imperil our Government or the cherished institutions of our people.

If there be any white American citizen who owes allegiance to no flag but the Star Spangled Banner and who can not subscribe to and support these principles let him forever hold his peace, for he is basely unworthy of the great flag and its Government that guarantees to him life, liberty, and the pursuit of happiness. That person who actively opposes these great principles is a dangerous ingredient in the body politic of our country and an enemy to the weal of our National Commonwealth.

*   *   *   *   *   *   *

The Anglo-Saxon race, the only race that has ever proved its ability and supremacy and demonstrated its determination to progress under any and all conditions and handicaps, owes its high place in the world to-day to the fact that this spirit has been kept alive from the foundation of the world and has never lagged in any land or clime.

And if the Anglo-Saxon race is to maintain its prestige, if it is to continue as the leader in the affairs of the world and to fulfill its sacred mission it must maintain and jealously guard its purity, its power, and its dignity; and while it should aid and encourage to the limit of its ability all men of whatever race or creed, it must forever maintain its own peculiar identity as the Anglo-Saxon race and preserve the integrity of its civilization, for the shores of time hold the shipwreck of all the mongrel civilization of the past which is evidence that in keeping with the laws of creative justice nature has decreed that mixed civilizations, together with governments of mixed races, are doomed to destruction and oblivion.

From the past the voice of the great Lincoln must be heard:

"There are physical differences between the races which would forever forbid them living together on terms of political and social equality."

The imperative call of higher justice to the real patriots of our Nation is:

"In the name of our valiant and venerated dead and in due respect to their stainless memory and in the interest of peace and security of all peoples now living and for the sake of all those yet to be, keep Anglo-Saxon American civilization, institutions, politics, and society pure, since we have received this sacred heritage, transmit it with clean hands and pure hearts to generations yet unborn, thereby keeping faith with the mind, soul, and purpose of our valiant sires and transmit our name into the future without dishonor and without disgrace.

"Let the solemn behest of higher duty be promptly and properly met in all the relationships of life and living without fault, without fail, without fear, and without reproach, now and forevermore."

The Ku Klux may be antagonized and forced to fight many battles, but perish? Never! To destroy it is an impossibility, for it belongs in essence to the realms spiritual. It is unshaken by unjust criticisms, no power can thwart it in its onward conquest of right; it courts not the plaudits of the populace, nor is it swerved from its course by the libel of its foes. Attuned with Deity, functioning only for all humanity's good, misjudged by ignorance, misunderstood by many, slandered by prejudice, sweeping on under the divine leadership of Deity, it never falters and will never fall.

The spirit of the Ku-Klux Klan still lives, and should live, a priceless heritage to be sacredly treasured by all those who love our country, regardless of section, and are proud of its sacred traditions. That this spirit may live always to warm the hearts of manly men, unify them by the force of a holy clannishness, to assuage the billowing tide of a fraternal alienation that surges in human breasts, and inspire them to achieve the highest and noblest in the defense of our country, our homes, humanity, and each other is the paramount ideal of the Knights of the Ku-Klux Klan.

IV. Constitution and Laws of the UKA

Constitution And Laws

Of The

United Klans Of America, Inc.

Knights Of The Ku Klux Klan

As amended, ratified and approved by the Imperial Kloncilium at Birmingham, Alabama, September, 1964.

Imperial Palace — Invisible Empire
United Klans of America, Inc.
Knights of the Ku Klux Klan
Tuscaloosa, Alabama

IMPERIAL PROCLAMATION

To: All Klanmen Klansmen And To All True Americans,

Greetings:

By viture of authority vested in me, I, and members of the Imperial Kloncilium of September, 1964, held in Birmingham, Alabama Proclaim to you:

We have adopted this Constitution and I hereby proclaim it to be the Supreme and Fundamental Law of our Order, to which we all own and give complete and loyal obedience, and which is immutable except as it, itself, provides.

Done in the Aulic of his Majesty, the Imperial Wizard of the United Klans of America, Inc., Knights of the Ku Klux Klan, this 1st day of January, Anno Domini Nineteen Hundred and Sixty-Five, Anno Klan. Signed by His Majesty.

DECLARATION

WE, THE UNITED KLANS OF AMERICA, INC., KNIGHTS OF THE KU KLUX KLAN SOLEMNLY DECLARE TO ALL MANKIND: that the principle and spirit of Klankraft will at all time be dedicated in thought, spirit and affection to our Founding Fathers of the Original Ku Klux Klan organization in the year 1866, and active during the period of Reconstruction History; and to their predecessors in the years (1915 & 16).

WE DO FURTHER DECLARE TO THE WORLD: 'that our original Prescript used as the governing law of the Ku Klux Klan, during the period of its former activities, and all official titles, mannerisms, usages and things therein prescribed, have not been abandoned by us; but is Held in Esteem as dedication, all of these, together with designs of paraphernalia, regalia, flags, banners, emblems, symbols, or other insignia and things prescribed or previously used by or under the authority of the Ku Klux Klan, are the property of the Ku Klux Klan under and by virtue of its name of Knights of the Ku Klux Klan, and are held sacred by us as a precious heritage, which we shall jealously preserve, forever maintain and valiantly protect from profanation.

THE IMPERIAL PROCLAMATION

To the lovers of law, order, peace and justice of all nations, people, tribes and tongues of the whole earth, Greetings:

I, and the citizens of the Invisible Empire, through me, make dedication to you:

We, the members of this order, desiring to promote patriotism toward our civil government; honorable peace among men and nations; protection for and happiness in the homes of our people; manhood, brotherhood, and love among ourselves, and liberty, justice and fraternity among all mankind; believing we can best accomplish these noble purposes through a mystic, social, patriotic, benevolent association, having a perfected lodge system, with an exalted ritualistic form of work and an effective form of government, not for selfish profit, but for the mutual betterment, benefit and protection of our oath-bound associates, and their loved ones; do physically, socially, morally and vocationally;

PROCLAIM TO THE WORLD

That we are dedicated to the sublime duty of providing generous aid, tender sympathy and fraternal assistance and fortune and misfortune,

in the effulgent light of life and amid the sable shadows of death, and to the exalted privilege of demonstrating the practical utility of the great (yet most neglected,) doctrine of the Fatherhood, of God and the brotherhood of man as a vital force in the lives and affairs of men.

We invite all men who can qualify, to become citizens of the Invisible Empire, to approach the portal of our beneficent fomain, join us in our noble work of extending its boundaries, and in disseminating the gospel of "Klankraft", thereby encouraging, conserving, protecting and making vital the fraternal relationship in the practice of an honorable clannishness; to share with us the glory of performing the sacred duty of protecting womanhood; to maintain forever the God-given supremacy of the White race; to commemorate the holy and chivalric achievements of our fathers; to safeguard the sacred rights, privileges and institutions of our civil government; to bless mankind and to keep eternally ablaze the sacred fire of a fervent devotion to a pure Americanism.

The Invisible Empire is founded on sterling character, and immutable principles based upon sacred sentiment and cemented by noble purposes. It is promoted by a sincere, unselfish by their consecrated intelligence. It is the soul devotion of the souls of men, and is governed by chivalry, virtue's impenetrable shield and the devout impulse of an unconquered race.

UNITED KLAN KREED

We, the order of the United Klan of America, Inc., Knights of the Ku Klux Klan, reverentially acknowledge the majesty and supremacy of Almighty God and recognize His goodness and providence through Jesus Christ our Lord.

Recognizing our relation to the government of the United States of America, the supremacy of its Constitution, the union of states thereunder, and the Constitutional laws thereof, we shall ever be devoted to the sublime principles of a pure Americanism, and valiant in the defense of its ideals and institutions.

We avow the distinction between the races of mankind as decreed by the Creator, and we shall ever be true to the maintenance of White supremacy and strenously oppose any compromise thereof.

We appreicate the value of practical, fraternal relationship among men of kindred thought, purpose and ideals, and the infinite benefits accuring therefrom; we shall faithfully devote ourselves to the practice of an honorable clannishness that the life each may be a constant blessing to others.

"NON SILBA SED ANTHAR"

PREAMBLE

We, the members of this order, citizens and probationers of the United Klans of America, Inc., Knights of the Ku Klux Klan in order of insure unity of organization; to guarantee an effective form of government; to perpetuate our great institution through patriotic and fraternal achievements, to preserve forever its holy principles; to continue and make vital its spiritual purposes; to achieve its laudable objects; to attain its lofty ideals; to consummate its mission and to promote effectively all things set forth in the National Klonvokation herein; do declare this Constitution of the United Klans of America, Inc., Knights of the Ku Klux Klan, in lieu of the original Prescript of the Ku Klux Klan, as the supreme law of this society, and pledge our voice, our loyalty, our manhood and our sacred honor to enforce the same. In our endeavor toward the faithful fulfillment of this, our honorable mission, we solemnly invoke the guidance and blessing of Almighty God in behalf of our country, our homes, our race and each other, now, and unto generations yet unborn.

APPELLATION AND GOVERNMENT

Article I

Section 1. To the name of this society, Ku Klux Klan has been prefixed the words "Knights of the," and forever hereafter it shall be known as the United Klans of America, Inc., "Knights of the Ku Klux Klan." The United Klans of America, Inc., is and shall continue to be a patriotic, military, benevolent, ritualistic, social or Faternal order or society.

Section 2. The government of this order shall ever be military in character, especially in its executive management and control; and no legislative enactment of Constitutional amendment hereafter shall encroach upon, effect or change this fundamental principle of the Invisible Empire.

Section 3. The government of this Order shall be vested primarily in the Imperial Wizard, with official Board, who shall be supreme within the restrictions of this constitution, and as otherwise provided, and whose decisions, decrees, edicts, mandates, rulings and instructions shall be of full authority and unquestionably recognized and respected by each and every citizen of the Invisible Empire.

OBJECTS AND PURPOSES

Article II

Section 1. The objects of this Order shall be to unite white male persons, native-born Gentile citizens of the United States of America, who owe no allegiance of any nature or decree to any foreign government; nation, institution, sect, ruler, person or people; whose morals are good; whose reputations and vocations are respectable; whose habits are exemplary; who are of sound minds and twenty-one years or more of age, under a common oath into a brotherhood of strict regulations; to cultivate and promote patriotism toward our civil government.

Section 2. This Order is an institution of chivalry, humanity, justice and patriotism; embodying in its genius and principles all that is chivalric in conduct, noble in sentiment, generous in manhood and patriotic in purpose. Its peculiar objects are: First, to protect the weak, the innocent, and the defenseless from the indignities, wrongs and outrages of the lawless, the violent and the brutal; to relieve the injured and the oppressed; to succor the suffering and unfortunate, especially widows and orphans. Second, to protect and defend the Constitution of the United States of America, and all laws passed in conformity thereto, and to protect the states and the people thereof from all invasion of their rights from any source whatsoever.

TERRITORIAL JURISDICTIONS AND ASSEMBLIES

Article III

Section 1. THE INVISIBLE EMPIRE. The phrase "Invisible Empire" in a material sense denotets the universal geographical jurisdiction of this Order and it shall embrace the whole world. The convention of the Invisible Empire shall be known as the Imperial Klonvokation.

The phrase "Invisible Empire" in a spiritual sense applies to all the secrets and secret knowledge and information, secret work and working and things of this Order, and to all that has been, to all that now is and to all that is to be, the past, the present and the future, yesterday, today and forever; the dead of yesterday, the living of today and the contemplated of tomorrow, of the life that now is and of that which is to come.

Section 2. In a material sense, the territorial division of the Invisible Empire into a subordinate jurisdiction shall be known as a "Realm," and same shall embrace a part of a state or states or a territorial possession of the United States of America.

Section 3. A territorial division of a Realm shall be known as a "Province" and shall embrace a Congressional District of a state. Provinces shall be designated by number. The convention of a Province shall be known as the "Klonverse."

Section 4. A "Klan" is the unit of this Order; it is the local or subordinate body, lodge, or organization, and its territorial jurisdiction shall be known as the "Klanton," which shall extend in all directions to a distance midway between the location of the Klan and the nearest Klan thereto, except as otherwise designated by the Imperial Wizard or Grand Dragon and with the approval of their respective Boards. The boundaries of a Klanton shall be fixed, so far as is possible, on the delivery of the Klan charter. A convention or an assembly of a Klan in secret session shall be known as the "Klonklave."

Section 5. All things and matters which do not exist within this Order or are not authorized by or do not come under its jurisdiction shall be designated as the "Alien World." All persons who are not members of this Order shall be designated as "Aliens."

MEMBERSHIP

Article IV

Section 1. The qualifications for membership in this Order shall be: An applicant must be a White male Gentile person, a native-born citizen of the United States of America, who owes no allegiance of any nature of degree whatsoever to any foreign government; nation, institution, sect, ruler, prince, potentate, people or person; he must have attained the age of twenty-one years, be of sound mind, good character, of commendable reputation and respectable vocations, a believer in the tenats of the Christian religion, and one whose allegiance, loyalty and devotion to the government of the United States of America in all things in unquestionable.

Section 2. Application for membership in this Order must be on a regular charter petition by charter applicants of a Klan, and on a regular application blank after a Klan has been chartered. The applicant must state whether he ever has applied for membership in this Order, and such application made to a chartered Klan must be endorsed by at least two Klansmen, or by a Kleagle.

Section 3. The "Klectokon" (initiation fee) is given by an applicant and accepted by this Order as a donation to its propagation and general fund and not in the sense of purchasing membership in this Order by the applicant, and this donation must accompany each application for citizenship. The Klectokon is a sum of money of not less than Ten ($10.00) Dollars, nor more than Twenty-five ($25.00) Dollars.

Section 4. An applicant's qualifications must be known before he is accepted for membership of this Order. Great care must be exercised on the part of a Kleagle or a Klan in ascertaining an applicant's qualifications under Section I, of this Article.

THE IMPERIAL KLONVOCATION

Article V

Section 1. The Imperial Klonvokation shall be the sole legislative body of this Order, therefore, it shall have original jurisdiction in all matters pertaining to creating and amending this Constitution and Laws, the regulation, government and general Welfare of this Order. It shall have power to enact laws for the regulation of its own procedure, for the government of the Invisible Empire, Realms, Provinces and Klans, and for the general control and management of the business of this Order, and to provide penalities for the violation thereof. It shall have power to prescribe the rights, privileges, duties and responsibilities of the Realms, Provinces, and Klans, and all officers and members of this Order, and finally to determine the same. The Imperial Klonvokation shall meet biennially in the month, date and place to be fixed by the Imperial Wizard with approval of Imperial Board.

Section 2. The Imperial Klonvokation shall be composed of all Imperial Officers, Grand Dragons, Titans, Kleagles, and Realm or Province Officers, each Organized and Chartered Unit shall be represented by 3 voting delegates, when their unit membership is 50 or less. Units may increase voting delegates by one for each additional 50 men. In order for any Officer to vote, he must be an elected or appointed delegate in good standing from a Chartered Unit.

Section 3. The State or Realm Klonvokation shall be composed of all State Officers and Realm Officers, and each Organized and Chartered Unit shall be represented by 3 voting delegates, when when their unit membership is 50 or less. Units may increase voter delegates by one for each additional 50 men. In order for any Officer to vote, he must be an elected or appointed delegate in good standing from a Chartered Unit.

THE IMPERIAL KLONCILIUM

Article VI

Section 1. The Imperial Kloncilium shall be the supreme advisory board of this Order and shall be composed of all the Imperial officers named in Article VII.

Section 2. The Imperial Kloncilium shall be the Supreme Tribunal of justice of this Order and shall have full appellate jurisdiction to hear and finally determine all appeals of whatsoever nature presented to it affecting the relationship and constitutional rights and privileges of Realms, Provinces, Klans and members of this Order.

Section 3. It shall have full power and authority, acting in the presence of the Imperial Wizard of his authorized representative, to act in the interium between sessions of the Imperial Klonvokations.

Section 4. It shall meet in regular session at a time to be determined by the Imperial Wizard and Imperial Board.

Section 5. Nine members of the Imperial Kloncilium shall constitute a quorum.

Section 6. Decisions of the Imperial Kloncilium on all matters of a judiciary nature coming before it for adjudication shall be final when same are ratified by the Imperial Wizard.

Section 7. Between the meetings of the Imperial Kloncilium, whenever, in the judgment of the Imperial Wizard, it shall become necessary for it to consider any matter or thing whatsoever, he may submit the matter to the members of the Imperial Kloncilium in writing by mail or otherwise, and their votes thereon shall be case in writing by mail or otherwise within a time limit to be fixed by the Imperial Wizard.

Section 8. The Imperial Kligrapp shall be the secretary and recording officer of the Imperial Kloncilium.

IMPERIAL OFFICERS

Article VII

Section 1. Hereafter the Imperial officers of this order shall be sixteen in number, and their official titles shall be as follows:

The Imperial Wizard (Supreme Chief Executive),
Imperial Klaliff (Supreme Vice-Pres.),
Imperial Klokard (Supreme Lecturer),
Imperial Kludd (Supreme Chaplain),
Imperial Kligrapp (Supreme Secretary),
Imperial Klabee (Supreme Treasurer),
Imperial Kladd (Supreme Conductor),
Imperial Klarogo (Supreme Inner-Guard),
Imperial Klexter (Supreme Outer-Guard),
Imperial Klonsel (Supreme Attorney),
Imperial Night-Hawk (Supreme Courier),
and five Imperial Klokann (consisting a Board of Auditors and Supreme advisors).

These shall be known as the Imperial Wizard and his fifteen GENI.

Section 2. The term of office is as follows: Imperial Klaliff — 2 years, Imperial Klokard — 1 year, Imperial Kludd — 1 year, Imperial Kligrapp — 2 years, Imperial Klabee — 2 years, Imperial Kladd — 1 year, Imperial Klarogo — 1 year, Imperial Klexter — 1 year, Imperial Klonsel — 2 years, Imperial Night-Hawk — 2 years.

IMPERIAL WIZARD

Article VIII

Section 1. Upon the death or removal of the Imperial Wizard from office, the Imperial Klaliff shall immediately succeed to that office and shall govern until a successor to the Imperial Wizard is installed. In the event the Imperial Wizard is removed from office, a successor shall be named at the earliest possible date thereafter, consistent with careful judgment in the selection.

Section 2. The Imperial Wizard shall be an elected Officer and his term of office shall be three years.

DUTIES, PREROGATIVES AND POWERS OF THE IMPERIAL WIZARD

Article IX

Section 1. Being the Supreme Chief Executive of this Order, the Imperial Wizard shall have and hold supreme authority and power within this Constitution in all administrative matters, and to act in any and all matters not prescribed in this Constitution, when in his judgment the best interest of this Order warrants. He may delegate such authority to his subordinate executives or administrative officers as he may deem necessary.

Section 2. He shall specify the duties of all officers regardless of rank or station, of whatever department, bureau, or division, other than those duties enumerated in this Constitution, and shall require such duties to be properly performed on penalty of removal from office.

Section 3. He shall issue charters for Klans, specify conditions on which charters shall be issued, and shall have the power to open and close charters of Klans at his discretion or upon request of a Klan. He shall have full authority and power to suspend or revoke charters of Klans, for cause.

Section 4. He shall promulgate all counter-signs and passwords, and any and all other secret signs and work of this Order.

Section 5. He shall have supreme supervision over all departments of this Order.

Section 6. He shall have full authority to issue decrees, edicts, mandates, rulings and instructions covering any matter not specifically set forth in this Constitution, or emphasizing any matter of this Constitution, and all such decrees, edicts, mandates, ruling and instructions must be respected and obeyed promptly and faithfully by all members of this Order on penalty of Suspension, upon approval of the Imperial Board.

Section 7. All paraphernalia, regalia, uniforms, costumes, emblems, insignia, flags, banners, jewelry for individual wear, jewels for official use, clerical forms, books, pamphlets, literature, advertising matter, stationery, etc., etc., may be manufactured upon the Recommendation of the Imperial Board and no other design, emblem, insignia or form or thing, article or articles shall be recognized, countenanced or used by this Order or any member of same. All designs, emblems or other insignia officially adopted by the Imperial Board whether created by them or not, shall be recognized as official and duly respected by all members of this Order.

Section 8. They shall request of the Imperial Klonvokation such legislation as they deem wise for the best interest of this Order in its government, regulation and promulgation.

Section 9. He shall have full power and authority to suspend from office at any time any officer of this Order, or any rank or station or capacity, or any employee whomsoever, on the ground of incompetency, disloyalty, neglect of duty, or for unbecoming conduct.

Section 10. He shall have and hold full and original authority and power, office and title of "Supreme Kleagle."

Section 11. He shall issue and sign all commissions or other credentials of this Order in promulgating same, and affix the Imperial Seal thereto; and he shall contract, in the name of this Order, with other members for its extension, financing, management, operation and business interests.

Section 12. Whenever a question of paramount importance to the interest, well-being or prosperity of this Order arises, not provided for in this Constitution, he shall have full power and authority to determine such question, and his decision, which he shall report to the Imperial Board, if requested, shall be final.

DUTIES OF IMPERIAL OFFICERS

Article X

Section 1. IMPERIAL KLALIFF: Is the second highest officer of this Order; He shall be the president of the Imperial Klonvokation, and perform such other duties as may be required of him by the Imperial Board.

Section 2. IMPERIAL KLOKARD: The duties of the Imperial Klokard shall be to disseminate Klankraft, and perform such duties as may be required by the Imperial Wizard on approval of the Imperial Board.

Section 3. Imperial KLUDD: Is the chaplain of the Imperial Klonvokation and shall perform such other duties as may be required by the Imperial Wizard on approval of the Imperial Board.

Section 4. IMPERIAL KLIGRAPP: Is the Supreme Secretary and recording officer of this Order. He shall be the secretary of the Imperial Klonvokation and shall act as secretary of the Imperial Kloncilium and shall have general supervision of all the clerical work and workings. He shall keep an accurate account of the receipts and disbursements. He shall sign all papers, vouchers and other documents requiring his signature of attestation. He shall prepare and submit a report of the workings of his office to each session of the Imperial Klonvokation. He shall furnish the Imperial Kloncilium, when requested, with such information as they desire with reference to his office. In the event additional clerical help is needed in the Imperial office it may be secured upon recommendation of the Imperial Wizard and approval of Imperial Board.

Section 5. IMPERIAL KLABEE: Is the Supreme Treasurer of this Order and is, therefore, the custodian of its funds, and he shall countersign all checks with the Imperial Wizard, and he shall make a full and complete report of his office to the regular Klonvokation each and every year.

Section 6. IMPERIAL KLADD: Shall perform such duties as may be required of him by the Imperial Wizard on approval of Imperial Board.

Section 7. IMPERIAL KLAROGO: Is inner guard at all Imperial Kloncilium and Imperial Klonvokation, and shall perform such other duties as may be required by the Imperial Wizard on approval of Imperial Board.

Section 8. IMPERIAL KLEXTER: Is outer guard at all meetings of the Imperial Kloncilium and Imperial Klonvokation, and shall perform such other duties as may be required by the Imperial Wizard on approval of Imperial Board.

Section 9. Imperial Klonsel: Is Supreme Attorney or legal advisor of this Order and shall perform such other duties as may be required by the Imperial Wizard on approval of Imperial Board.

Section 10. IMPERIAL NIGHT-HAWK: Is the Supreme Board of Auditors and Special advisors. It shall be the responsibility of the Imperial Board to select not more than 5 and not less than 3 responsible persons to serve in the capacity of auditors and advisors of the Imperial office for purpose of auditing the records and generally serving in the capacity as advisors. It shall recommend to the Imperial Wizard such plans and methods as it deems wise for the welfare of this Order, and it shall perform such other duties as may be required of it, and each member thereof, individually, shall perform such other duties as may be required of him by the Imperial Wizard on approval of Imperial Board.

KLEAGLES AND GIANTS

Article XII

Section 1. A Kleagle is an organizer or field worker of this Order. On the approval of the Imperial Board and where by an established Realm exist the Grand Dragon and his staff will have the authority to appoint Kleagles for his respective Realm and he shall work by and under their instructions.

Section 2. The Imperial Wizard, being by virtue of his office the Supreme Kleagle shall have full power and authority to commission and appoint members of this Order as Kleagles, and he shall have full power to remove from office any Kleagle of any rank, grade or station on due cause.

Section 3. Any Kleagle of any rank is entitled to receive $3.00 Commission on new applicants not to exceed charter strength of 25 members. He is also entitled to the sum of $2.00 Commission on any re-instatement in acquiring charter strength of 25 men. This commission to be used at his discretion to bear expenses in securing charters.

Section 4. Kleagles of whatever rank, grade or station must thoroughly familiarize themselves with the Kloran, laws, principles, objects, history, usages and mannerisms of this Order, and must be able to demonstrate same in an intelligent and proficient manner.

Section 5. The title of Giant may apply by gradation to all officers who have served one or more terms as the chief executive officer of the Invisible Empire and of subordinate jurisdictions thereof. A Klan Giant is one who has served as Exalted Cyclops; a Great Giant is one who has served as Great Titan; A Grand Giant is one who has served as Grand Dragon; an Imperial Giant is one who has served as Imperial Wizard. The title is not conferred on an officer until his successor has been duly installed. The title Giant shall in all cases be conferred upon the recommendation of the next officer above in rank. This honorary title shall be conferred in recognition of regular and faithful services performed as prescribed by the Constitution and Laws of this Order. The Grand Dragon of a Realm shall, whenever possible, use such Giants for special service.

PARAPHERNALIA, REGALIA, EMBLEMS, ENSIGNS, INSIGNIA, ETC.

Article XIII

Section 1. Members robes shall be classified as their personal property. In the event that such member is suspended, banished, or voluntarily quits the organization the unit may, if agreeable with member, re-purchase robe at an agreed price. All paraphernalia, clerical records, standard bearers, flags, and other materials referred to as properties of this order shall be surrendered upon request by proper authority upon the member disassociating from this Order.

Section 2. All designs, ensigns, flags, standards, banners, emblems, insignia, seals, paraphernalia, regalia, uniforms, costumes, etc., and all clerical forms or matters to be printed, shall be adapted by or designed by or under the directions of the Imperial Board.

Section 3. All articles, designs and things referred to or implied in Sections 1 and 2, above, and Article X, Section 7, of this Constitution, and all property, real and personal, shall ever be and remain the property of this Order and such supplies can only be procured from the Imperial Wizard by the required requisition therefor, and this also shall apply to all supplies used by any subordinate jurisdiction, and any and all jewelry or other articles used by a member upon the approval of the Imperial Board.

Section 4. Any article or things, regardless of form, or of that material it shall be made, or for what purpose it shall be made, or to what use it shall be subjected, if it bears an emblem or an insignia of this Order, shall belong to and is the property of this Order; and such articles or things cannot legally bear an emblem, insignia, or design of this Order without written authority of the Imperial Wizard. If a member has in his possession any article or property of this Order, and voluntarily discontinues his membership, or is banished from membership, or in any other manner his connection with this Order is served, such article or articles, thing or things, must be immediately returned or surrendered by him to an Exalted Cyclops, Great Titan, Grand Dragon, or to the Imperial Wizard, and he shall be given a receipt for same.

Section 5. It shall be unlawful for any person or persons, company, firm or corporation, to manufacture or cause to be manufactured, catalog or cause to be cataloged, advertise or cause to be advertised, sell or offer for sale, or cause same to be done, any article or design whatsoever of this Order, or anything used by or properly belonging to this Order, unless such person or persons, company, firm, or corporation, be duly licensed by the Imperial Board to manufacture, advertise, or sell such article, designs or things, and even then, only by a strict adherence to the conditions, restrictions and directions specified in said license.

Section 6. It shall be unlawful for any member of this Order to purchase, cause to be purchased, or otherwise come into possession of any article or property of this Order from any person, company, firm or corporation, without authority to do so from the Imperial Wizard; he can procure such article from the Imperial Wizard only by making requisition therefor, and remitting the amount of money required. It shall be unlawful for any subordinate jurisdiction to procure any article or property of this Order, or any supplies, etc., used by it from any other source than the Imperial Wizard, or by his authority.

Section 7. If an unauthorized person shall have in his possession any article, or property of this Order, and this fact shall become known to a member, it shall be the sworn duty of such member to regain for this Order the actual possession of such article without delay; his failure to do so will jeopardize his membership.

COSTUMES, SEALS, ENSIGNS, SYMBOLS, ETC.

Article XIV

Section 1. KLAN PARAPHERNALIA: Shall consist of altar furnishings as per Kloran, and such account books, forms, and other things as are necessary.

Section 2. COSTUMES: The official costume of this Order shall be a white robe of lightweight cotton cloth, made with cape of same material, and of proper length, with white girdle around waist, and insignia of this Order worn on the left breast. The cowl or helmet shall be made of this same material as the robe, and with whatever material necessary to give it the proper stiffness, and so made that it will be collapsible, and when worn shall be of a cone shape. There shall be one red tassel attached to the peak of same. There shall be an apron of the same material in both front and rear, so as to completely conceal the identity of the wearer. The front apron shall have two holes of the proper size and location to facilitate the vision of the wearer. This shall be known as the Klansman's robe or costume. Costumes to be worn by active officers, of whatever rank or station, shall be of such design, and made of such material, and with the use of such colors, as may be prescribed by the recommendation of the Imperial Board.

Section 3. EMBLEMS, AND SYMBOLS: Shall be such as may be designated or authorized by the Imperial Board.

Section 4. ENSIGNS, FLAGS AND STANDARDS: The official ensigns, flags, and standards of this Order, together with all official banners, shall be of such shape, size and design as may be authorized by the Imperial Board.

Section 5. THE GRAND ENSIGN: The "Grand Ensign," or banner of this Order shall be in the form of an isosceles triangle, five feet long and three feet wide at the staff. The material shall be yellow, with a red scalloped border about three inches in width. There shall be painted upon it in black, a Dracovolans, or flying dragon, with the following motto inscribed on it: "Quod Semper, Quod ubique, quod ab ominibus." The tongue shall be painted in red with an arrow head end. The tail shall also end with an arrow head.

Section 6. SEAL: There shall be a Seal of this Order, which shall be known as the Great Imperial Seal. It shall bear the words: United Klans of America, Inc., Knights of the Ku Klux Klan," and shall be of such design as the Imperial Wizard shall direct. Each chartered Klan of this Order shall have a seal bearing the name, number and Realm of the Klan, together with the name of this Order: United Klans of America, Inc.", and shall be of such design as directed by the Imperial Board. This seal must be procured by the Klan immediately after it shall have been chartered. Seals to be used by the various subordinate jurisdictions shall bear the name: "United Klans of America, Inc., Knights of the Ku Klux Klan," and be of such design as the Imperial Board may direct.

Section 7. KLIKON AND SYMBOLS: The Klikon is the sacred picture of this Order, and as such must be rigidly safeguarded by whatever Klan or Klansman to whom it may be intrusted. The various symbols of this Order, used in its several Kloranic orders, shall be such as are designed and authorized by the Imperial Board.

REVENUES AND PROPERTY TITLES

Article XV

Section 1. The revenues of this Order shall consist of: First, a per capita tax, which shall be known as the Imperial Tax, which shall be a sum of fifty cents ($.50) per month. Second, all profits realized from the placing of paraphernalia, regalia, supplies, jewelry, uniforms, costumes, stationery, and any and all other articles used in the work of this Order or by any member. Third, all interest accuring on investments made by this Order.

Section 2. The Imperial Tax shall begin with the month immediately succeeding the month in which a Klan is chartered, and is due and payable on the first day of each calendar month thereafter; the Kligrapp of each Klan shall remit the same with his regular monthly report — his failure to do so will subject the charter of that Klan to suspension or cancellation. The Imperial Tax is hereby levied upon each and every Klan now chartered and which may be hereafter chartered, and the Imperial Authorities have full authority and power to collect same.

Section 3. The revenues of a Realm shall consist of: First, such portion of the Imperial revenue received from that Realm as may be fixed by proclamation of the National Klonvokation. Second, a per capita tax, to be known as a Realm Tax, in such amount as the Klorero may determine, in no case to be less than 25¢ cents per month.

REALMS

Article XVI

Section 1. A Realm may be organized within a state or states of the United States, or other territorial sub-division.

Section 2. A Realm is organized on the declaration of the Imperial Wizard, and with such declaration he shall appoint and name all officers thereof and shall furnish laws and regulations for the government of that Realm, and such appointment of officers and such laws if not in conflict with the Constitution, shall be effective until the convention of the initial Klorero of that Realm after its organization; at which time the Klorero will proceed to elect all of its elective officers, and adopt laws for the government of that Realm, but such laws adopted and such elections held shall not be inconsistent with this Constitution and the laws of this Order. Such laws and amendments of laws adopted at this time or at any future Klorero must be ratified by the Grand Dragon or the Imperial Wizard before the same become effective as law.

Section 3. The Klorero of a Realm shall be composed of all Grand Officers within that Realm, and Kleagles, Titans and their Furies from each Province in said Realm. Grand Officers, Great Titans and Great Officers shall be entitled to one vote each. Each unit by virtue of their Charter and up to 50 men have 3 delegate votes and for each 50, 1 additional delegate vote.

Section 4. The Klorero shall possess no power to interfere with the Imperial Boards plan and purposes in the promulgation of this Order within its respective bounds.

Section 5. The Klorero shall provide its own revenue to meet the expenses of its convention and clerical obligations.

Section 6. The officers of A Realm shall be a Grand Dragon, who shall be President of the Klorero; he shall be elected by the Realm for a term of three years, and shall govern his Realm in a manner not inconsistent with this Constitution, or the instructions and directions of his Imperial Klaliff; Grand Klaliff, second highest officer of a Realm, who shall be vice-president of the Klorero; Grand Klokard, lecturer; Grand Kludd, chaplain; Grand Kligrapp, secretary; Grand Klabee, treasurer; Grand Kladd, conductor; Grand Klarogo, inner guard; Grand Klexter, outer guard; and a Grand Night-Hawk. These shall be known as the Grand Dragon and his nine Hydras. They are to be elected by proper delegation of their respective Realm.

Section 7. It will be the responsibility of the Grand Dragon to call a meeting with the Great Titans of each Realm, at his discretion, to disperse of Klan business within the Realm. This meeting manditory at least once each year.

PROVINCES

Article XVII

Section 1. A Province will consist of a respective Congressional District of the said Realm.

Section 2. At the initial convention of a Klonverse of a Province, the elective officers of that Province shall be elected, but such election must be ratified by the Grand Dragon of that Realm, and such officers elected and ratified shall be installed by the Grand Dragon or by his duly appointed deputy, and they shall govern the Province under the direction and instructions of the Grand Dragon.

Section 3. The officers of a Province shall hereafter be: A Great Titan, the highest officer of a Province, and president of the Klonverse; three great Klaliffs, who shall compose an Advisory Board; a Great Kligrapp, secretary; a Great Klabee, treasurer; a Great Kludd, Chaplain; and a Great Night-Hawk. These officers shall be known as the Great Titan and his seven Furies, and their terms of office shall be from the date of their installation until the next convention of the Klonverse, or until their successors shall have been elected and installed.

Section 4. The Great Titan and all officers of a Province shall be elected by the Klonverse of that Province.

Section 5. The function of the Klonverse is social and fraternal, for the purpose of promoting good fellowship within the bounds of that Province, and stimulating and developing interest in this Order, and its mission and work.

Section 6. The Klonverse shall meet at the discretion of that Titan of that Province. Meeting to be held at least once monthly.

KLANS

Article XVIII

Section 1. In states having no Realm organization the King Kleagle shall be the judge of the location to institute a new Klan.

Section 2. The Grand Dragon in Realm organizations, or the Imperial Board in states without Realm organization, shall, upon being authorized by the Imperial Wizard, upon re-

commendation of the Imperial Board have power to order the disbandment of any provisional Klan for the same cause that the charter of a chartered Klan may be revoked; and such order of disbandment shall have the same effect as a revocation of the charter of a chartered Klan.

Section 3-a. Upon the organization of a Klan, a vote shall be had on the petitioners, and if there be three negative votes cast on the ballot as a whole, then an individual ballot shall be had by balloting on the petitioners one at a time, three negative ballots rejecting. After a Klan has been organized and prior to the issuance and closing of its charter, charter applicants must be submitted to the Klan in Klonklave assembled; if any Klansman present knows any just reason that disqualifies an applicant for membership, he must rise to his feet and challenge that applicant and state his reasons for so doing; this done, the Provisional Exalted Cyclops, or the Kleagle in charge acting as such, shall refer the application to the Klokann and the Klokann shall investigate the application on the basis of the grounds of objection, and they shall report on such applicant at the next subsequent Klonklave, if possible, or at which Klonklave final action shall be taken. An applicant who has been finally rejected cannot apply again until after the expiration of twelve months from date of rejection. If after a careful investigation the Klokann finds that the objector was in error, they shall report accordingly and recommend the passage of the applicant, and the Klan shall take definite and final action on the report of the Klokann.

Section 3-b. Applications for membership in chartered Klans shall be read three times in Klonklave assembled, and opportunity given each member present to make objections. All objections may be made in writing, signed by the objector and delivered to the Klokann, whose duty it shall be to investigate the objections and make their findings and report the same to the Klan body for its adoption or rejection. All petitions must be made in writing on Form K-115.

Section 3-c. An applicant who has been finally rejected cannot apply again until after the expiration of twelve months from date of rejection and shall be within the jurisdiction of that Klan for a period of three years. Provided, however, upon request of the Klokann of that Klan through regular channels the Grand Dragon and Staff or organized Realms or the Imperial Wizard and Staff in unorganized states, a special dispensation may be granted ordering another ballot taken immediately.

Section 4. A Klansman who presents the name of an applicant for membership in this Order must know the applicant personally and be familiar with his qualifications according to this Constitution and Laws. All members of a Klan must faithfully guard the portal of the Invisible Empire so that no person not qualified to enter therein shall be admitted.

Section 5. In the event a petitioner or an applicant is denied membership in this order, the sum of his Klectokon shall be immediately returned to him.

Section 6. All actions of a Klan in rejecting an applicant for membership, as to the votes cast, and by whom objections were made, are a positive secret of this Order; members who have knowledge of same and divulge or intimate in the slightest degree or cause such knowledge to be in any way communicated to any person not a member, shall be at once banished from the Invisible Empire for the violation of his oath.

Section 7. When the required number of charter petitioners have been obtained in a community where a Klan is to be located, a regular petition for the issuance of charter shall be forwarded to the Imperial Wizard through regular channels. Such petition must give the name selected for that Klan, time of the meeting of regular Klonklave and must be signed by the Kleagle in charge of the officers, giving the address of that Klan.

Section 8. The Klan charter shall contain the following text.

IMPERIAL PALACE, INVISIBLE EMPIRE,
UNITED KLANS OF AMERICA, INC.
KNIGHTS OF THE KU KLUX KLAN

To All Who Read and Respect These Lines, Greetings:

WHEREAS, The Imperial Wizard has received a petition from the following named Klan of the Invisible Empire,

Praying for themselves and others and their successors to be instituted a Klan of the Order under the name and number of _____ Klan No. _____ Realm of _____ and same to be located at _____ in the County of _____, State of _____, United States of America, and they having given assurance of their fidelity to this order and their competency to render the service required, and their willingness to take upon themselves and their successors the duties and responsibilities thereof, and their serious determined purpose, to rightly use and not abuse the powers, privileges and prerogatives

to render the service required, and their willingness to take upon themselves and their successors the duties and responsibilities thereof, and their serious determined purpose, to rightly use and not abuse the powers, privileges and prerogatives conferred on them as such, and be faithful and true in all things committed to them;

NOW KNOW YE, that I, the Imperial Wizard of the Knights of the Ku Klux Klan, on this the _____ day of the _____ Month of the Year of Our Lord Nineteen Hundred and _____, and on the _____ day of the _____ week of the _____ Month of the Year of the Klan _____ and in the _____ Cycle of the Seventh Reign of the Reincarnation, under the authority possessed by me, do issue this Charter to the aforesaid petitioners, their associates and successors, under the name and number aforesaid from the day and date hereon, and same is effective from the date of its acceptance by said Klan as certified below.

The said Klan is hereby authorized and empowered to do and perform all such acts and things as are prescribed by the Kloran, Laws, Imperial decrees, edicts, mandates and usages of the Order, and to enjoy all the rights, privileges and prerogatives authorized by the Constitution thereof; and all Klansmen are strictly enjoined to valiantly preserve and persistently practice the principles of pure patriotism, honor, Klannishness and White supremacy, ever keeping in mind and heart the sacred sentiment, peculiar purpose, manly mission, and lofty ideals and objects of this Order, a devoted loyalty to their Emperor and their Imperial Wizard, a steadfast obedience to the Constitution of this Order, a faithful keeping of their Oath of Allegiance, and a constant unwavering fidelity to every interest of the Invisible Empire, to the end that progress, power, purpose and influence of Klankraft be property promoted, the knowledge of the faithful self-sacrificing service and noble achievements of our fathers be not lost to posterity, and all those things for which this, our beloved Order, is founded to do and to perform and to protect and to preserve and to pereptuate, be diligently done and scrupulously maintained and that they be blameless in preserving the grace, dignity and intent of this Charter forever.

I solemnly charge you to hold fast to the dauntless faith of our fathers and to keep their spotless memory secure and unstained, and true to the traditions of our valiant sires, meet every behest of duty, in all the relationships of life and living, promptly and properly, without fault without fail, without fear and without reproach.

The Imperial Wizard has and holds the full

The Imperial Wizard has and holds the full and unchallengeable authority, right and power to cancel, to suspend or revoke this Charter, and to annul all the rights, powers, preorgatives and immunities conferred hereby, for the neglect or refusal on the part of the said Klan to conform to and comply with the Kloran, Constitution and Laws of this Order, and the Imperial decrees, edicts, mandates, rulings and instructions thereof, or its failure to respect the usages of this Order as proclaimed by and maintained under the Imperial Authority of same.

In testimony whereof, I, the Imperial Wizard of the Knights of the Ku Klux Klan, have caused to be affixed hereon the Great Imperial Seal of the Invisible Empire, and do hereunto set my hand and impress my official seal, and same is duly attested — "Non Silba Sed Anthar."

Done in the Executive Chambers of His Lordship.

BY HIS LORDSHIP,

_____
Imperial Wizard, of the Invisible Empire, Knights of the Ku Klux Klan (United Klans of America, Inc.)

ATTEST:

_____
Imperial Kligrapp

CERTIFICATE OF ACCEPTANCE:

This certifies that above Charter was read to and duly adopted by above named Klan, in session assembled, with all stipulations and conditions herein stated or implied, on the _____ day of _____ A. D. 19 _____, AK _____ Signed _____
Exalted Cyclops of Above Named Klan in behalf of all present and future members thereof.
(Witness)

_____
Grand Dragon of Realm

Section 9. Upon the receipt of the charter, Kleagle or other officer in charge, shall notify, of cause to be notified, the members, of that Klan to assemble at the earliest convenient time in Klonklave, at which Klonklave the charter shall be read and accepted by the Klan and a record made in the minutes of the Klan. The charter of the Klan is then closed and the Klan will proceed to elect its elective officers, exercising care to select officers who are competent and fitted for the respective offices. This done, the Klan proceeds at once to supply itself with a seal and with adequate and suitably bylaws for its government and the regulation of its affairs and for the rigid protection and interests of this Order within its Klanton.

Section 10. By-Laws of the Klan shall not conflict with or be inconsistent with the Constitution and Laws of this Order, and after same have been prepared by the Klan, they must be immediately sent to the Imperial Wizard or Grand Dragon to be approved and ratified by him, corrected and amended by him, if necessary and upon his ratification such By-Laws become effective as law for the regulation of that Klan.

Section 11. The charter of a Klan may be reopened by the Grand Dragon of a Realm or by the Imperial Wizard upon a request by the Klan, signed by its Exalted Cyclops and Kligrapp. When a charter is reopened, the Grand Dragon or the Imperial Wizard will provide a Kleagle for this Klan for work under their direction.

Section 12. The elective officers of a Klan shall hereafter be as follows: the Exalted Cyclops, president; Klaliff, vice-president; Klokard, lecturer; Kludd, chaplain; Kligrapp, secretary; Klabee, treasurer; Kladd, conductor; Klarogo, inner guard; Klexter, outer guard; Night-Hawk, in charge of candidates; and three Klokann, board of investigators, auditors, and advisors, each of whom shall bear the title of "Klokann." These shall be known as the Exalted Cyclops and his twelve Terrors.

Section 13. The term of office for officers of a Klan shall be for twelve months or until their successors have been elected and installed.

Section 14. An officer of a Klan elected and who is absent on the night of installation shall be installed at the next Klonklave, and if he should be absent from this Klonklave, he shall be notified to be present at the next Klonklave for installation; then, if he fails to present himself, and has no providential excuse, his office shall be declared vacant by the Exalted Cyclops and the Klan shall proceed to elect at that Klonclave a member to fill that vacancy, and such member elected shall be installed at that Klonklave.

Section 15. Officers-elect shall not in any case be installed unless their Klan dues are paid up to and including the calendar quarter of installation and their respective offices shall become vacated, if, at any time, their Klan dues become in arrears, and no Klan installation of officers shall be recognized within the Invisible Empire as being official unless that Klan be in good standing with the Imperial Palace, Realm and Province offices.

Section 16. When a Klan becomes in arrears in payment of its Imperial, Realm of Provincial tax for a period of one hundred days, its several offices are automatically vacated, its members denied visiting privileges in other Klans, and its acts subsequent thereto are invalid unless the time is extended by the Grand Dragon in organized Realms, or the Imperial Wizard in unorganized Realms, either of whom shall have the authority to order a complete audit of this Klan's affairs at the expense of the local Klan. Such Klan shall not be entitled to representation in any Klonverse, Klorero or Imperial Klonvokation. It shall be the duty of all Grand Dragons of Realms and Great Titans of Provinces to file with the Imperial Kligrapp, at least ten days preceding the Klonvokation, a list of all Klans in their respective territories which have paid their Realm or Province Tax, and the numberical strength of the individual Klans.

Section 17. Immediately upon the election of officers, the Kligrapp shall transmit the names of the Exalted Cyclops and Kligrapp to the Great Titan of the Province. The Great Titan shall immediately forward a copy of the list to the Grand Dragon of that Realm, who shall in turn file a copy in his office and transmit a copy immediately to the Imperial Wizard. No office-elect shall be inducted into office unless he be worthy and well qualified to fulfill the duties of that office and his election duly ratified by the Great Titan or Grand Dragon.

Section 18. Klan dues shall be paid in advance. A new member shall begin paying dues the month immediately succeeding the month in which he was naturalized. A member failing to pay his dues for three successive months shall be automatically suspended from the Klan, and his name dropped from the roll and he shall be so reported in the next monthly report. Up on the payment of his arrears he shall be automatically reinstated and shall be so reported by the Kligrapp in the next monthly report.

Section 19. Each and every member naturalized in this Order must supply himself with a robe and helmet by sending, through his Kligrapp, his measurement to agreed party to supply robe.

Section 20. A Klan under any and all circumstances shall accord full respect to its charter, and thereby strictly observe the Constitution and Laws, mannerisms, usages and Kloranic (ritualistic) regulations and requirements of this Order as same are promulgated by the Imperial Wizard; and shall give due respect and obedience to all Imperial, Realm and Provincial decrees,

edicts, mandates, rulings and instructions issued by the said officers; and failure on the part of a Klan to do so shall be cause for revocation of its charter and the suspension of its entire membership from this Order.

Section 21. A Klan shall meet in Klonklave at least once every week, when possible, and gather promptly at the hour agreed upon. Six members of a Klan shall constitute a quorum for the transaction of any business at any regular Klonklave.

Section 22. Special Klonklaves may be held at any time whenever same are deemed necessary by the Exalted Cyclops or when he is requested to do sy by twenty-five per cent of the membership in good standing and ten per cent in cases where the membership in good standing is greater than one thousand; provided, however, in no event under the provisions of this section shall the number require be less than one hundred in Klans having a membership in good standing greater than four hundred. If this meeting is called upon petition in accordance with the provisions of this section, forty per cent of the membership in good standing at the time of such call shall constitute a quorum.

Section 23. In the event the charter of a Klan has been revoked or cancelled for any cause, whatsoever, and in the event of disbandment of a Klan, whether it be a Chartered or Provisional Klan, all books, papers, manuscripts, Klorans, records, seal, Klan paraphernalia, and any and all other things used by the Klan, and all articles or things appertaining to this Order as may have been used by or are in the possession of any individual member thereof shall be properly surrendered to proper authority.

Section 24. A Klan, or member of this Order shall not use the official costume or any part of same on any occasion outside the Klavern without permission of the Grand Dragon in organized Realms, or the Imperial Wizard in unorganized states under penalty of forfeiture of their charter or banishment from this Order.

Section 25. No Klan or member shall use the name of this Order or any part thereof for any purpose that contravenes in any manner the laws of the land, that will reflect or probably reflect upon the reputation and good name, or compromise, or injure this Order, or any member thereof, in any way.

DUTIES OF KLAN OFFICERS

Article XIX

Section 1. EXALTED CYCLOPS: The Exalted Cyclops in the supreme officer of a Klan and its official head. He shall preside over the Klonklaves and govern same with dignity, devotion and impartiality. He shall be faithful in the prompt and efficient discharge of every duty prescribed or implied, incumbent upon him and fearless without respect to individual persons in the administration of the affairs of his office in promoting the welfare of this Order within the bounds of his Klanton, and he shall set a laudable example to all Klansmen of patriotism, Klanishness, benevolence, love, justice, every respect. He shall require a faithful honor and devoted loyalty to this Order in observance on the part of all Klansmen within his Klanton of the Constitutions, laws, usages, etc., of this Order, and all Imperial, Realm or Province decrees, edicts, mandates, rulings and instructions, and seek to make vital and effective the principles, objects and purposes of this Order. He shall call the Klonklave to order promptly on the hour designated, if there be a quorum present, and see that his Terrors fill their respective offices in an acceptable manner. He shall diligently safeguard the sanctity and dignity of the Charter of his Klan and suffer no encroachment thereon, nor any departure therefrom. He shall require the ritualistic work of the Kloran to be exemplified with the highest degree of perfection possible, and he shall do such other things as may be required of him by the Laws of this Order, the Kloran, the By-Laws of his Klan, and faithfully execute all orders and special instructions of the Great Titan, Grand Dragon or the Imperial Wizard.

Section 2. KLALIFF: The Klaliff is the vice-president of his Klan, and he shall preside over the Klonklave in the absence of the Exalted Cyclops. He shall preserve order during the deliberations of a Klonklave, and otherwise assist the Exalted Cyclops in Klonklave assembled and perform such other duties as may be required of him by the Exalted Cyclops, the Kloran and By-Laws of his Klan.

Section 3. KLOKARD: The Klokard is the lecturer or instructor and the Klan censor or critic. He shall administer the oaths, deliver the Kloranic lectures, instruct in secret work, do those things commonly required of a critic, and perform such other duties as may be required of him by the Exalted Cyclops, the Kloran and the By-Laws of his Klan. He shall be responsible for the proper performances of all ritualistic work within his Klan, and shall disseminate Klankraft throughout his Klanton.

Section 4. KLUDD: The Kludd is the chaplain of the Klan. He shall perform the duties peculiar to his sacred office, and such other duties as may be required of him by the Exalted Cyclops, the Kloran and the By-Laws of his Klan. He shall be responsible for such musical program as may be presented; and for the general spiritual welfare of his Klan.

Section 5. KLIGRAPP: The Kligrapp is the secretary and recording officer of the Klan. He shall keep an accurate and complete record of all the proceedings of his Klan assembled, and a correct and systematic record of its membership, and of the date each member was naturalized, etc., as required by the record book for that purpose. He shall make a report through the proper channles to the proper officers not later than the 10th of the month for the calendar month last past on the regular blanks therefor; and with his reports he shall remit to said officer or officers, all monies belonging to this Order, such as Imperial Tax, Realm or Provincial Tax, Klectokons monies due for supplies and any and all other monies due and payable to said officers. He shall witness all requisitions made for any article or paraphernalia, regalia, jewelry, or other property of this Order, to be used by the Klan or a member thereof, and see that the required sum of money is sent therewith. He shall notify all members who are in arrears three months, and shall notify the Imperial office of the arrears of a member for three months. He shall be the custodian of the seal of the Klan and shall impress it on all papers and documents requiring same and perform such other duties as may be required of him by the Exalted Cyclops, the Kloran and the By-Laws of his Klan.

Section 6. KLABEE: The Klabee is the treasurer of the Klan. He shall be the custodian of its funds, and shall receive from the Kligrapp all monies due to be turned over to him, giving his receipt for same, and keeping same apart from his personal funds and secure for the sole use of the Klan. He shall keep an accurate account of all monies received by him, and pay same out only on order of the Klan, signed by the Exalted Cyclops and the Kligrapp, except the monies due by the Klan to the Imperial, Realm and Province offices, which monies do not require action of the Klan, and make a faithful record of such disbursements. He shall make a complete and itemized report of his office to the Klan when same is requested by the Exalted Cyclops or the Klan, and shall perform such other duties as may be required of him by the Exalted Cyclops and the By-Laws of the Klan.

Section 7. KLADD: The Kladd is the conductor of the Klan and the custodian of its paraphernalia and other properties. He shall conduct candidates for naturalization, collect the countersign and password at the opening of a Klonklave, and perform such other duties as may be required of him by the Exalted Cyclops, the Kloran and the By-Laws of his Klan.

Section 8. KLAROGO: The Klarogo is the inner guard of the Klan. He shall keep a diligent watch at the inner door and permit only those to enter the Klavern who are qualified to have the permission of the Exalted Cyclops. If he should be in doubt as to the qualifications of the one seeking admission, he must satisfy himself from the Klaliff or Kligrapp. He shall perform such other duties as may be required of him by the Exalted Cyclops, the Kloran and the By-Laws of his Klan.

Section 9. KLEXTER: The Klexter is the outer guard of a Klan. He shall keep a diligent faithful watch at the outer door, and allow no one to pass him from the outside except those who are qualified and have permission of the Exalted Cyclops. He shall observe from time to time the outside premises of the Klavern to see that no eavesdroppers or other persons are around, who are liable to obtain information or knowledge concerning the acts or procedure of the Klonklave. He shall in no case leave his post of duty unless summoned therefrom by the Exalted Cyclops, and even then, a substitute must be placed in his stead to watch until his return. He shall perform such other duties as may be required of him by the Exalted Cyclops, the Kloran and the By-Laws of his Klan.

Section 10. NIGHT-HAWK: The Night-Hawk is the special courier of the Exalted Cyclops. He shall have charge of and shall entertain the candidate or candidates in the outer den of the Klavern until he is signalled to enter the Klavern at the beginning of the ceremony of naturalization. He shall carry the Fiery Cross in the ceremony and on all public exhibitions where same is used, and shall perform such other duties as may be required of him by the Exalted Cyclops and the By-Laws of his Klan.

Section 11. KLOKLANN: The Klokann is the board of auditors, advisors and trustees, and the investigating committee of the Klan. It shall be composed of three members, each of whom shall bear the title of "Klokan." It shall be their duty to audit the books and records of the Kligrapp and the Klabee in the month of June each year, and

oftener if so required by the Klan in writing. They shall see that all paraphernalia, regalia and other property of the Klan and of this Order is properly kept, and shall perform such other duties as may be required of them by the Exalted Cyclops and By-Laws of their Klan. The Klokann may select such assistants as in their judgment seems necessary.

Section 12. An officer of a Klan who allows himself to get in arrears for three months, or who absents himself from three consecutive Klonklaves without a providential excuse, or who fails to master his part of the Kloranic work within sixty days after he is placed in office, shall forefit all right, prerogatives and honors of his office; the Exalted Cyclops must declare his office vacant and will at once appoint a successor thereto. If the Exalted Cyclops shall be guilty of negligence as above, the Klan in Klonklave shall demand his resignation and whether tendered by him or not, they shall proceed to elect his successor at the following Klonklave if he is not present to apologize to the Klan and take up his duties of office.

Section 13. The Grand Dragon or the Great Titan shall have the power to remove any officer of a local Klan for cause, but must immediately report said removal to the Tribunal of the Realm whose duty it shall be to immediately pass on the correctness of his act. If he is sustained the Klan shall proceed to elect a successor to the officers removed; if he is not sustained, the officer removed resumes the duties of his office. This applies in Realms that have perfected Realm organizations. In all other jurisdictions this power is vested in the Imperial Wizard, who shall report same to the Imperial Kloncilium for review in the same manner as above set forth.

OFFENSES AND PENALTIES

Article XX

Section 1. Offenses against this Order shall be divided into two classes — major offenses and minor offenses.

Section 2. Major offenses shall consist of: (1) treason against the United States of America; (2) violating the Oath of Allegiance to this Order or any supplementary oath or obligation thereof; (3) disrespect of virtuous womanhood; (4) violation of the Constitution or the laws of this Order; conspiring against the interest and prosperity of this Order or any Klansman in any way or being a party thereto, or being a party to any move, conspiracy or organization whose existence is antagonistic or injurious to or is an imitation of this Order; whose name, style or title is a colorable imitation of this Order; swearing allegiance to or otherwise becoming a citizen or subject of any nation, government or institution of any nature or classification whatsoever, or any ruler or potentate, prince or person of any court whatever that is foreign to or is inimical to the government of the United States of America and its established institution, or aiding or abetting such a government, nation, institution, ruler, potentate, prince or person, against the interest, wellbeing or dignity of the United States of America or the distinctive institutions of its government; violating the By-Laws of a Klan of this Order; excessive or habitual drunkeness; drunkeness or the drinking of intoxicating liquor during a Klonklave or on the premises thereof, or entering a Klonklave in an intoxicated condition; the habitual use of profane language or vulgarity during a Klonklave or during an assembly of Klansmen just prior thereto; (5) being responsible for the polluting of Causasian blood through miscegenation, or the commission of any act unworthy of a Klansman; (6) the repeated commission of a minor offense shall in itself constitute a major offense.

Section 3. Minor Offenses. Minor offenses shall consist of drunkeness, drinking intoxicating liquor during a Klonklave or on the premises thereof, entering a Klonklave in an intoxicated condition, use of profane language or vulgarity during a Klonklave or in an assembly of Klansmen just prior thereto, or committing any other act which might operate against the best interest of the Klan or Klansmen, refusal or failure to obey the mandates, rules, edicts and orders of the Exalted Cyclops or the Klan, or the failure or refusal on the part of any Klansman, upon demand by the Exalted Cyclops, to respond to any summons issued by him, unless he has a providential excuse; or failure or refusal to surrender his credentials when called for by the Exalted Cyclops.

Section 4. PENALTIES: All offenses enumerated above under the head of major offenses, shall be tried and penalties assessed by the Tribunal hereinafter provided for. All offenses enumerated as minor offenses shall be heard and determined and penalties assessed by the Exalted Cyclops of the Klan. Penalties shall be of four classes, as follows: (1) reprimand; (2) suspension; (3) banishment; (4) extreme penalty — banishment forever, and there shall be added thereto complete ostracism in any and all things by each and every member of this Order.

Section 5. A member who fails to respect the penalty imposed on another member shall receive the same penalty as if he himself were guilty of that offense.

Section 6. All charges against a Klansman, involving a major offense under the Constitution and Laws of the United States of America, Inc., Knights of the Ku Klux Klan shall be in writing, specifying the acts complained of, which shall be submitted to the Klokann of the Klan, of which the accused is a member, or in whose jurisdiction the offense was committed.

Section 7. Upon the filing of such charges the Klokann shall consider and investigate the same and take action thereon within thirty days from the time such charges are filed. The Klokann shall determine the sufficency of the charges presented and the advisability of a trial as herein provided, and their action on such charges shall be final.

If the judgment of the Klokann is not unanimous, then the decision of a majority of the Klokann, when approved by the Exalted Cyclops, shall be final.

Section 8. Upon the filing of such charges the Klokann shall have the right in its discretion, through the Exalted Cyclops, to suspend the accused during the period of investigation of such charges or until his acquittal (if trial is ordered).

If, in the opinion of the Klokann, the charges presented constitute a minor offense, as herein defined, the same shall be referred to the Exalted Cyclops for such action as he shall deem proper.

Section 9. If the Klokann shall order a trial of the accused, the charges and specifications shall be published in regular Klonklave by the Klaliff.

Section 10. The Exalted Cyclops shall in such event set the date of the trial which shall be not more than thirty days after report of the Klokann, and shall serve the accused with a copy of the indictment or charges not less than ten days before the date of the trail.

Section 11-a. The accused shall be tried before a Tribunal selected as follows: The Exalted Cyclops, Klaliff, Klokard and Kludd shall each select from the membership in good standing six Klansmen, whose names shall be placed in some suitable receptacle and from this receptacle the Kludd, wearing hoodwink, shall withdraw eight names, and the remaining sixteen Klansmen shall constitute the Tribunal whose attendance at the trial is compulsory. In the event any one or more of the Sixteen Klansmen thus selected shall fail to appear, that number which do appear may select from the Klay body sufficient Klansmen to fill their places.

Section 11-b. In event of charges being presented against the Exalted Cyclops of a Klan, he shall immediately vacate his office and he shall remain out of office until the case against him is finally adjudicated. In such event the Klaliff shall immediately assume the office, duties and responsibilities of the Exalted Cyclops and shall appoint a Klaliff. The Klaliff in all respects shall be Exalted Cyclops in fact and the one appointed by him to the office of Klaliff shall be Klaliff in fact until the case against the Exalted Cyclops is finally adjudicated. In event the Exalted Cyclops so accused shall have been found guilty and duly penalized, the acting Exalted Cyclops and Klaliff shall remain in their respective offices until the end of the term, or until he shall have been reinstated. In the event charges are preferred against a Terror of a Klan he shall vacate his office immediately and shall remain out of office until the case against him has been finally adjudicated. Immediately upon his vacating office, the Exalted Cyclops shall appoint a substitute thereto and this substitute shall act in this office until the case against the Terror in question has been finally adjudicated. In the event the Terror in question is convicted and penalized, the substitute in his former office shall become the Terror in fact of that office unless or until the said Terror shall have been reinstated. In the event the Exalted Cyclops or any Terror of the Klan is accused and tried and acquitted, such Exalted Cyclops or Terror shall immediately resume his former office and proceed with the affairs of his office as before.

Section 12. Such Tribunal shall select one of their number as Triton, who shall preside, and one as Scribe, and the duty of the Scribe shall be to make a record of the proceedings, write the testimony of witnesses, or cause same to be done by a competent Klansman stenographer. Said Tribunal shall have authority and power to issue summons directed to any Klansman, commanding him to appear and give testimony for or against the accused, and hear the charges and evidence and to render judgment in conformity with the laws of this Order and the evidence adduced.

Section 13. The Tribunal and the accused may take testimony touching the issues involved, except where Klan secrets and secret information of the Klan are involved, by interrogatories and cross interrogatories, first giving either party timely notice thereof, and such evidence when so taken may be received as evidence in the case and may be used by either party.

Section 14. On the date set for trial the accused shall be required to be present in person or by counsel (who shall be a Klansman in good standing,) Providence alone preventing; and in the event of his failure or refusal to be present or represented by counsel the said Tribunal shall select a member in good standing in that Klan as counsel for the defense and render its decision in accordance with the laws of this Order and the evidence adducted at such trial; and said Tribunal in rendering its decision shall find whether or not service of the charges has been made upon the accused and notice of the time and place of hearing has been given to the defendant. Service of the time and place of the trial of the accused shall be made upon him in person or by registered letter, and a return card from the postoffice showing delivery thereof to such Klansman, coupled with an affidavit from the Night-Hawk of such Klan to the effect that a copy of the charges or indictment and a notice to the accused Klansman, specifying the time and place of trial, was placed in a letter in an envelope with proper postage and directed to such Klansman at his last known address, shall constitute service and notice on such Klansman.

Section 15. No evidence shall be offered at such trial except such as may be pertinent to the charges presented.

Section 16. At a trial held under this article on the following may be present: (a) the Tribunal in full regalia of the Order; (b) the prosecutor appointed by the Klokann; (c) the defendant and his representative or representatives; (d) witnesses who are Klansmen; (e) the Great Titan or his representatives; (f) the Grand Dragon or his representatives; (g) the Imperial Wizard of his representatives; (h) a stenographer reporting the case, who must be a Klansman.

Section 17. At the conclusion of the evidence, the prosecutor and counsel for the accused shall have the right to argue the case to the Tribunal and the accused shall have the right to be heard in his own behalf, and at the conclusion of the arguments all persons except the Tribunal immediately shall retire.

Section 18. After fully considering the charges and evidence thereon, such Tribunal shall determine the guilt or innocence of the accused by written ballot. Twelve or more votes shall be necessary to convict or acquit.

Section 19. If the accused shall be found guilty, the Tribunal shall assess the penalty to be imposed and the Exalted Cyclops shall enforce the same, and such judgment shall be published by the Klaliff at the next regular Klonklave.

Section 20. If the accused shall be acquitted, the Exalted Cyclops shall be notified thereof and such acquittal shall be published by the Klaliff at the next regular Klonklave.

Section 21. If the Tribunal is unable to reach a decision as herein provided, then such Tribunal shall be discharged, another Tribunal composed altogether of different members from the former Tribunal shall be created as herein provided, who shall proceed to try the case as herein set forth.

Section 22. Should the accused be acquitted, a majority of the Klokann shall have the right to appeal from the judgment of the Tribunal and such majority of the Klokann shall also have the right to suspend the accused through the Exalted Cyclops until such appeal shall have been finally determined.

Section 23. Should the accused be convicted he shall have the right to appeal from the judgment of the Tribunal; but he shall remain suspending until such appeal shall have been finally determined.

Section 24. Notice of appeal shall be in writing signed by the party or parties appealing and filed with the Kligrapp of the Klan in which the accused was tried, not more than 15 days from the date and judgment of the Tribunal was published in regular Klonklave.

Section 25. Upon the filing of such appeal, the Kligrapp, Titan and Scribe of the Tribunal shall, within 30 days, make up a complete transcript of the proceedings had upon the trial, which shall be duly certified to by the Kligrapp and forwarded by him immediately to the Grand Dragon of that Realm; provided, however, that any member shall be found guilty by a Tribunal in a Realm other than that in which he holds membership, shall have the right, at his option, to take his appeal to the Imperial Kloncilium, instead of to the Grand Tribunal of the Realm where the trial is held.

Section 26. In states where Realm organizations has not been instituted, the appeal shall be taken to the Imperial Kloncilium and a transcript of appeal filed with the Imperial Kligrapp in like manner as is provided in appeals to the Grand Tribunal of a Realm.

Section 27. In organized Realm, the Grand Dragon shall annually select a Grand Tribunal composed of 12 Hydras or Giants, provided that for the first two years after a Realm is instituted

the Tribunal may be composed of Hydras, Furies, Exalted Cyclops and Klaliffs.

Section 28. The Grand Tribunal shall meet at the annual meeting of the Klorero and at such other times as the Grand Dragon thereof may direct.

Section 29. The Grand Dragon shall designate one of said Grand Tribunal as Triton and he shall select his Scribe therefor from the membership of the Grand Tribunal. The decision of nine or more members of said Grand Tribunal shall render judgment.

Section 30. Until Realm organization is instituted all appeals from judgments of the Tribunal of the individual Klans in such states shall be reviewed by the Imperial Kloncilium whose judgments thereon shall be final.

Section 31. The procedure shall in all cases refer and apply to major offenses against the Order and shall in no sense alter or affect Sections 3 and 4 of Article XX of the Constitution and Laws.

Section 32. All judgments of the Tribunal shall be reported promptly by the Kligrapp of the Klan within five days to the Grand Dragon; or where a Realm organization has not been perfected, to the Imperial Kligrapp.

Section 33. Where banishment has been imposed, the Grand Dragon or the Imperial Kligrapp, as the case may be, shall so notify all Klans within the Realm where the case originated. Where the extreme penalty has been imposed, the Imperial Wizard shall decree, proclaim and publish same or cause the same to be done to all Klans throughout the Invisible Empire.

Section 34. In the event the preceding sections of this Constitution fail to provide for punishment of any Klansman for any of the offenses herein referred to, or for any other offenses that is inimical to the best interest of this Order, the Imperial Wizard is hereby vested with authority and power to prefer charges against such Klansman in accordance with the provisions of this article, or at his discretion to issue banishment order against such Klansman, who shall have the right of appeal to the Imperial Kloncilium for a period of 90 days after date of banishment. The Imperial Kligrapp shall publish the decree of banishment to Klans in the realm in which such person holds membership, or throughout the bounds of the Invisible Empire in accordance with the decree.

KU KLUX KALENDAR
KU KLUX KULLORS, ETC.

Article XXI

Section 1. Hereafter the calendar of this Order, by which days, weeks, months and years shall be designated in all official documents, is as follows:

Days —	Weeks —	Months —
7. Desperate	5. Weird	12. Appalling
6. Dreadful	4. Wonderful	11. Frightful
5. Desolate	3. Wailing	10. Sorrowful
4. Doleful	2. Weeping	9. Mournful
3. Dismal	1. Woeful	8. Horrible
2. Deadly		7. Terrible
1. Dark		6. Alarming
		5. Furious
		4. Fearful
		3. Hideous
		2. Gloomy
		1. Bloody

YEAR OF THE KLAN: The year of the Klan (Anno Klan) begins with the month of December each year.

REIGN: The reign of Incarnation includes all time up to the American Revolutionary War. The first reign of our Re-incarnation dates from the beginning of the Revolutionary War and the establishment of our government to the organization of the Ku Klux Klan of the Reconstruction, in the year A. D. 1866. The second reign of our Re-incarnation dates from the year A. D. 1866 to the year A. D. 1872. The third reign of our Re-incarnation dates from the year A. D. 1915 on to the present and future.

Section 2. The Kardinal Kullors of this Order hereafter shall be white, crimson, gold and black. The secondary Kullors shall be gray, green and blue. The official Kullors of the Emperor shall be such as he may designate; those of the Imperial Wizard, Royal purple. The significance and the mystery of these Kullors in the Invisible Empire shall be revealed Kloranically.

Section 3. There shall be four Kloranic orders of this Order, namely: the order of citizenship of K-UNO (probationary); Knights Kamellia or K-DUO (primary order of knighthood); Knights of the Great Forest or K-TRIO (the order of American chivalry); and Knights of the Mid-night Mystery or K-QUAD (superior order of knighthood and spiritual philosophies.)

Section 4. These several orders of Klannish achievement and Kloranic advancement shall be communicated, and their Kloranic regulations, requirements and governments shall be established and promulgated by and in the discretion of the Emperor of this Order in the unfoldment of its philosophies and in the revelation of its spiritual mysteries.

ANNIVERSARY

Article XXII

Section 1. The Order was first organized and operated under the appellation of the Ku Klux Klan, or Invisible Empire, in the town of Pulaski, Tennessee, in the month of May, in the year Eighteen Hundred and Sixty-Six (1866), by six young men as a "social club." In the year Eighteen Hundred and Sixty-Seven (1867), it was reorganized into a "regulative and protective organization" and as such it actively existed as a cohesive organization until about the year Eighteen Hundred and Seventy-Two (1872), at which time it voluntarily disbanded in pursuance of an order issued by its Grand Wizard General Sathan Bedford Forrest. In the month of October, in the year Nineteen Hundred and Fifteen (1915) it was resurrected, reconstructed and remodeled into its present incorporated from and character as a "historical, social, patriotic, military, benevolent, ritualistic, fraternal order or society, under its present appellation by William Joseph Simmons, of Atlanta, Georgia, and thirty-three associates, three of whom were bona fide members in good standing of this Order when it disbanded as a regulative and protective organization, as above stated.

Section 2. The anniversary date of this Order hereafter shall be the Sixth (6th) day of the month of May each year.

Article XXIII

Section 1. This Constitution may be amended by the Imperial Klonvokation, at any regular session thereof, provided that such proposed amendment be indorsed by the Klorero of three or more Realms, or such amendments shall become a part of this Constitution when same has (or have) been passed by a two-thirds vote of the Klonvokation and also ratified by the Imperial Wizard, provided further that no amendment shall affect in any way the fundamental principles, objects, purposes and ideals of this Order, or the military character of its government.

Section 2. All laws and parts of laws in conflict hereiwth are hereby repealed and this Constitution shall go into effect immediately.

INSTALLATION CEREMONIES

of the

UNITED KLANS OF AMERICA, INC.

KNIGHTS OF THE KU KLUX KLAN

PREPARATION

All officers elected will form in line in front of the Sacred Altar facing the station of the Exalted Cyclops in order as named, left to right: Exalted Cyclops, Klaliff, Klokard, Kludd, Kligrapp, Klabee, Kladd, Klarogo, Klexter, Klokann, Night-Hawk.

Installation officers will consist of a Master of Ceremonies and a Marshal of Ceremonies.

The duties of the Master of Ceremonies will be to perform the installation ceremony and shall stand in front of the Sacred Altar between it and the station of the Exalted Cyclops.

The duties of the Marshal of Ceremonies will be to assist the Master of Ceremonies as he may direct, and shall stand at the right of the Exalted Cyclops in line, facing Master of Ceremonies when not filling order of the Master of Ceremonies.

PRECEDURE

(When All is in readiness)

Master of Ceremonies: "Marshal of Ceremonies publish the names of the newly elected officers to the Klansmen now in Klonklave Assembly."

After concluding this the Marshal of Ceremonies shall ask all to attend prayer, which will be given by the Marshal of Ceremonies or one substituted in his stead.

Prayer to be as follows:

Almighty God, we beseech Thee to grant these manly men who have been elected to fill the offices of this Klan, wisdom and grace and may their every effort be for the betterment of Thy great name and for the best interest of this our great Order, help them to despatch with dignity, devotion and impartiality every duty incumbent upon them.

Grant them power that they may set an example to all Klansmen and be able to teach their fellow Klansmen that which is right according to Thine Own divine wishes.

Oh, God, we ask these things for our good and to the glory of Thy great name, Amen.

Master of Ceremonies: "Marshal of Ceremonies, present the Exalted Cyclops."

The Marshal of Ceremonies takes the Exalted Cyclops by the right arm and left faces, marching to the center and in front of the Sacred Altar, turns, facing the Master of Ceremonies.

Master of Ceremonies: "Klansman (pronounces name of Exalted Cyclops) you have been elected to that highest and most supreme office of this Klan. Your duties are many in number and before you can be installed and declared Exalted Cyclops of (name of Klan) (number), Realm of (state) it is necessary that you answer each of the following questions with an emphatic 'yes.'"

"Will you preside over the Klonklaves and govern same with dignity, devotion and impartiality?

"Will you be faithful in the prompt and efficient discharge of every duty prescribed or implied incumbent upon you?

"Will you, with respect to individual persons, fearlessly administer the duties of this office in promoting the welfare of the Order in this Klanton?

"Will you set a laudable example to all Klansmen of patriotism, Klannishness, benevolence, love and justice?

"Will you require a faithful honor and a devoted loyalty to this Order in observance on the part of all Klansmen within this Klanton the Constitution, Laws, usages, etc., of this Order, and all Imperial, Realm or Province Decrees, Edicts, Mandates, Rulings and Instructions and seek to make vital and effective the principles, objects and purposes of this Order?

"Will you call the Klonklave to Order promptly on the hour designated if there be a Quorum present, and see that your terrors fill their respective offices in an acceptable manner?

"Will you diligently safeguard the safety and dignity of the Charter of this Klan and suffer no encroachment thereon, nor any departure therefrom?

"Will you require the Ritualistic work of the Kloran to be exemplified with the highest degree of perfection possible?

"Will you do such other things as may be required of you by the Laws of this Order, the Kloran, the By-Laws of this Klan?

"Will you faithfully execute all orders and special instructions of the Great Titan, Grand Dragon, Imperial Representative or the Imperial Wizard?

"Klansman (pronounces name of Exalted Cyclops) since you have before God and these mysterious men answered the questions with an emphatic 'yes' I now officially proclaim you duly installed Exalted Cyclops of (name of Klan) (number) Realm of (state) and sincerely hope that you will forever perform your duties with despatch and dignity and for the best interest of this Order."

Master of Ceremonies: "Marshal of Ceremonies, you will escort the Exalted Cyclops to his station."

The Marshal of Ceremonies will take Exalted Cyclops by right arm, left face and march to the station of the Exalted Cyclops (turning to the right at corners). The Exalted Cyclops will remain standing, the Marshal of Ceremonies returning to his proper place at the line of officers. The Master of Ceremonies to take position at the left of the Exalted Cyclops and give two raps with the gavel which calls all Klansmen to their feet. Then the Master of Ceremonies says:

Master of Ceremonies: "Klansmen, greet your Excellancy."

All Klansmen to give the sign of greeting and the Exalted Cyclops will return the sign and the Master of Ceremonies will seat the Klansmen with one rap of the gavel. Then the Master of Ceremonies addresses the Exalted Cyclops.

Master of Ceremonies: "It is with pleasure that I present you with this implement of your office."

And then the Master of Ceremonies hands the Exalted Cyclops the gavel and returns to his place in front of the Sacred Altar.

Master of Ceremonies: "Marshal of Ceremonies, you will present the Klaliff."

The Marshal of Ceremonies takes the Klaliff by the right arm, left faces, marching to the Sacred Altar and right faces, facing the Master of Ceremonies.

Master of Ceremonies: "Klansman (pronounces the name of the Klaliff) you have been elected to a very important office of this Klan. You are Vice-President of this Klan and shall

preside over the Klonklaves in the absence of the Exalted Cyclops and when so acting as Exalted Cyclops you shall preserve order during the deliberations of a Klonklave and otherwise assist the Exalted Cyclops in the Klonklave assembled and perform such other duties as may be required of you by the Exalted Cyclops, the Kloran and By-Laws of this Klan.

"Will you perform these duties with despatch and dignity and ever strive for the betterment of this Klan and its affairs?

(Answer should be yes).

Master of Ceremonies: "Marshal of Ceremonies, will you escort the Klaliff to his station.

Marching as before, turning to the right at corners, then after seating the Klaliff, he will return to his place in line.

Master of Ceremonies: "Marshal of Ceremonies, you will present the Klokard."

The Marshal of Ceremonies takes the Klokard by the right, left faces, marching to the Sacred Altar and right faces; facing the Master of Ceremonies.

Master of Ceremonies: "Klansman (pronounces the name of the Klokard) you have been elected to a very important office of this Klan. You have been elected to that of Lecturer or Instructor and the Klan Censor or Critic. You shall administer the Oaths, deliver the Kloranic Lectures, instruct in secret work, do those things commonly required of a Critic, and perform such other duties as may be required of you by the Exalted Cyclops, the Kloran and the By-Laws of this Klan. You shall be responsible for the proper performance of all Ritualistic Work within this Klan, and shall disseminate Klankraft throughout your Klanton. Will you faithfully perform these duties?

(Answer should be yes).

Marshal of Ceremonies will then escort the Klokard to his station and return to his place in line.

Master of Ceremonies: "Marshal of Ceremonies, you will present the Kludd."

The Marshal of Ceremonies makes same movement to Altar as previously done.

Master of Ceremonies: "Klansman (pronounces the name of the Kludd) you have been elected to the office of Chaplain of this Klan. You shall perform the duties peculiar to your sacred office and such other duties as may be required of you by the Exalted Cyclops, the Kloran and the By-Laws of this Klan. You shall be responsible for such musical programs as may be presented, and for the general spiritual welfare of this Klan. Will you conform to the requirements of your office?

(Answer should be yes).

Marshall of Ceremonies will then take the Kludd to his station, returning to his place in line, going through the same movements.

Master of Ceremonies: "Marshal of Ceremonies, you will present the Kligrapp.

The Marshal of Ceremonies presents the Kligrapp.

Master of Ceremonies: "Klansman (pronounces the name of the Kligrapp) you have been elected as the Secretary and Recording officer of this Klan. You shall keep an accurate and complete record of all the proceedings of this Klan assembled, and a correct and systematic record of its membership, and of the date each member was naturalized, etc., as required by the record book for that purpose. You shall make a report through the proper channels to the proper officers not later than the tenth of the month for the calendar quarter last past on the regular blanks therefor and with your report you shall remit to said officer or officers all monies belonging to this order, such as Imperial tax, Realm or Provincial tax, Klectokans, monies due for supplies and any and all other monies due and payable to said officers. You shall witness all requisitions made for any article or paraphernalia, regalia, jewelry, or other property of this order to be used by this Klan, or a member thereof, and see that the required sum of money is sent therewith. You will notify all members who are in arrears three months and shall notify the Imperial office of the arrears of a member for three months. You will be the custodian of the Seal of this Klan and shall impress it on all papers and documents, requiring same, and perform such other duties as may be required of you by the Exalted Cyclops, the Kloran and the By-Laws of this Klan. Will you faithfully perform the duties pertaining to your office?

(Answer should be yes).

The Marshal of Ceremonies will escort the Kligrapp to his station and take his place in line.

Master of Ceremonies: "Marshal of Ceremonies, you will present the Klabee."

The Marshal of Ceremonies presents the Klabee.

Master of Ceremonies: "Klansman (pronounces the name of the Klabee) you have been elected as the Treasurer of this Klan. You will be the custodian of its funds, and shall receive from the Kligrapp all monies due to be turned over to you, giving your receipt for same, and keep same apart from your personal funds and secure for the sole use of this Klan. You will keep an accurate account of all monies received by you and pay same out only on order of this Klan signed by the Exalted Cyclops and the Kligrapp, except the monies due by this Klan to the Imperial, Realm or Province officers, which monies do not require action of this Klan and make a faithful record of such disbursements. You will make a complete and itemized report of your office to this Klan when same is requested by the Exalted Cyclops or this Klan and you will perform such other duties as may be required of you by the Exalted Cyclops and the By-Laws of this Klan. Will you truthfully and faithfully perform the duties of your office?

(Answer should be yes).

The Marshal of Ceremonies will escort the Klabee to his station and take is place in line.

Master of Ceremonies: "Marshal of Ceremonies, you will present the Kladd."

The Marshal of Ceremonies presents the Kladd.

Master of Ceremonies: "Klansman (pronounces the name of the Kladd) you have been elected Conductor of this Klan and the Custodian of its paraphernalia and other properties. You will conduct candidates for naturalization, collect the Countersign and Password at the opening of a Klonklave, and perform such other duties as may be required of you by the Exalted Cyclops, the Kloran and the By-Laws of this Klan. Will you willingly and faithfully perform the duties of your office?"

(Answer should be yes).

The Marshal of Ceremonies will escort the Kladd to his station and take his place in line.

Master of Ceremonies: "Marshal of Ceremonies, you will present the Klarogo."

The Marshal of Ceremonies presents the Klarogo.

Master of Ceremonies: "Klansman (pronounces the name of the Klarogo) you have been elected Inner Guard of this Klan. You will keep a diligent watch at the Inner Door and permit only those to enter the Klavern who are qualified or have permission of the Exalted Cyclops. If you should be in doubt as to the qualifications of the one seeking admission, you must satisfy yourself from the Klaliff or Kligrapp. You will perform such other duties as may be required of you by the Exalted Cyclops, the Kloran and the By-Laws of this Klan. Will you faithfully perform the duties of your office?"

(Answer should be yes).

The Marshal of Ceremonies will then escort the Klarogo to his station and take his place in line.

Master of Ceremonies: "Marshal of Ceremonies, you will present the Klexter."

The Marshal of Ceremonies presents the Klexter.

Master of Ceremonies: "Klansman (pronounces the name of the Klexter) you have been elected Outer Guard of this Klan. You will keep a diligent and faithful watch at the Outer Door and allow no one to pass you from this outside except those who are qualified and have permission of the Exalted Cyclops. You will observe from time to time the outside premises of the Klavern to see that no eaves droppers or other persons are around, who are liable to obtain information or knowledge concerning the acts or procedure of the Klonklave. You will in no case leave your post of duty unless summoned therefrom by the Exalted Cyclops and even then a substitute must be placed in your stead to watch until your return. You will perform such other duties as may be required of you by the Exalted Cyclops, the Kloran and the By-Laws of this Klan. Will you faithfully perform the duties of your office?

(Answer should be yes).

The Marshal of Ceremonies will escort the Klexter to his station and take his place in line.

Master of Ceremonies: "Marshal of Ceremonies, you will present the Klokann."

The Marshal of Ceremonies presents the three members of the Klokann.

Master of Ceremonies: "Klansmen (pronounces the names of the Klokann) you have each been elected as members of the Board of Investigators of this Klan. It will be your duty to audit the books and records of the Kligrapp and the Klabee in the month of June each year and oftener if so required by the Klan in writing. You shall see that all paraphernalia, regalia and other property of this Klan and of this order is properly kept, and shall perform such other duties as may be required of you by the Exalted Cyclops and the

By-Laws of this Klan. You may select such assistants as in your judgment seems necessary. Will each of you faithfully perform the duties of your office?

(Answer should be yes).

The Marshal of Ceremonies will escort the Klokann to their station and take his place in line.

Master of Ceremonies: "Marshal of Ceremonies, you will present the Night-Hawk."

The Marshal of Ceremonies presents the Night-Hawk.

Master of Ceremonies: "Klansman (pronounces name of the Night-Hawk) you have been elected as the Special Courier of the Exalted Cyclops, you will have charge of and will entertain the candidate or candidates in the Outer Den of the Klavern until you are signaled to enter the Klavern at the beginning of the Ceremony of Naturalization. You will carry the Firey Cross in the Ceremony and on all public exhibitions where same is used, and will perform such other duties as may be required of you by the Exalted Cyclops, the Kloran and the By-Laws of this Klan. Will you faithfully perform the duties of your office?

(Answer should be yes).

The Marshal of Ceremonies will escort the Night-Hawk to his station and take a position in front of the Sacred Altar between the Sacred Altar and the station of the Klaliff facing the Master of Ceremonies.

Marshal of Ceremonies: "Master of Ceremonies, I duly declare all the newly elected officers installed and at their proper stations."

Master of Ceremonies: "Your Excellency, the Marshal of Ceremonies declares all officers duly installed and in their proper stations. I therefore place in your care and charge the affairs of this Klan to be handled in a conservative and reverential manner throughout the term of your office."

The Master of Ceremonies and the Marshal of Ceremonies take seats with the Klansmen. The Exalted Cyclops handles the meeting therefrom.

NOTES

Manner of handling meeting for Installation Ceremonies at Klans having a Charter:

Open meeting in form and first matter in General Business perform the Installation Ceremonies.

Each retiring officer will remain at his station until relieved by the newly elected and installed officer.

In case of re-election of an officer a substitute will fill this particular station during Installation Ceremonies until he is relieved by the newly elected and installed officer.

Manner of handling meeting for Installation Ceremonies of Klans receiving their Charter at the same meeting:

Master of Ceremonies will have charge of meeting and will call meeting to order and proceed to deliver charter. After this has been done, next comes the Installation of Officers.

No stations are occupied until so filled by newly elected and installed officers.

V. Seven Symbols of the Klan

The Seven Symbols of The Klan

Imperial Instructions
Document No. II
Series A.D. 1960, A.K. LXXXXIV

Being Official Instructions in K-uno in the border Realm of Karacter from the one who traversed the Realm of the Unknown, wrested the solemn Secret from the grasp of Night and became the Imperial Master of the great lost Mystery. Words of timely Wisdom from the soul of the great Imperial Wizard, who out of Mystic Darkness brings Light.

Imperial Instructions
Documeiit No. II
Series A.D. 1960, A.K. LXXXXIV

To Each and Every Citizen of the Invisible Empire, Knights of the Ku Klux Klan, My Cordial Greetings:
To You I speak, Oh, Noble Klansman!

The language of symbolism is the most beautiful, the most expressive and the most impressive of any language known to mankind. Who can read the story of Noah's Ark without thinking of the church; or the story of the scape goat, the brazen serpent or the feast of the Passover without thinking of the Christ who takes away all our iniquities and delivers us from the bondage of sin?

In the sublime ceremonies of Klankraft, I take it that we use seven significant symbols, each of which conveys and inculcates a very beautiful lesson, and emphasizes a great Klan principle, when the language of symbols is properly understood. They are, in the order of their importance; The Bible, the Cross, the Flag, the Sword, the Water, the Robe and the Hood.

Not many Klansmen have ever thought of these commonplace things as having any special significance, or as being especially expressive of fundamental Klan principles. Whether the founder of the Klan had this idea in mind or not, we do not know; but we do know that the symbolical meaning of these things makes a wonderful impression of Klansmen, and gives a most surprising emphasis to the sacred, and sublime principles of Klankraft.

Everywhere we have lectured on this great subject and explained the meaning of these symbols, men have listened with an intense wonderment, saying afterwards: "We have never heard it-like that before. That is wonderful, beautiful and strangely gripping. I want a copy of the explanation."

As we have no copyright on it, and seek to contribute our small bit to the success of our great Order, we are giving you the benefit of our ideals, with the sincere and unselfish hope that it will help every Klansman who reads it to be a better Klansman, and have a higher, nobler and holier regard for, and opinion of the EMPIRE of CHIVALRY, HONOR, INDUSTRY, PATRIOTISM and LOVE.

THE BIBLE

THIS BOOK DIVINE signifies that there is a GOD. No sane man of reasonable intelligence can look upon this sacred volume without thinking of GOD as its author, righteousness as its aim, and eternal life as its end. It is a constant reminder that GOD is OUR FATHER, LIFE is our opportunity, and HEAVEN is our HOME. It reveals the way of life, and the cause of death. It is a LAMP unto our feet, a light unto our pathway, and the only sure guide to right living. It is the book of books and reveals the only TRUE GOD.

In a Klavern you will always find this wonderful book opened at the twlefth chapter of Romans. This is the most practical and the most complete chapter in the whole Bible on CHRISTIAN living. It is a constant reminder of the tenets of the CHRISTIAN RELIGION, and is a KLANSMAN'S LAW OF LIFE. Every Klansman should read it the first thing every morning and endeavor to live by it during the day. "I BESEECH YOU THEREFORE BRETHREN BY THE MERCIES OF GOD", that you follow its teachings.

THE CROSS

Out of the wonderful story of the sacred pages of this old BOOK DIVINE comes the sad, sweet story of CALVARY'S rugged but HOLY CROSS. This old cross is a SYMBOL of SACRIFICE and SERVICE, and a sign of the CHRISTIAN RELIGION. Sanctified and made holy nearly nineteen centuries ago by the suffering and blood of fifty million martyrs who died in the most holy faith, it stands in every Klavern of the U.S. Klans, Knights of the Ku Klux Klan as a constant reminder that CHRIST is our criterion of character, and His teachings our rule of life-blood-bought, holy sanctified and sublime.

It was once a sign of ignominy, disgrace and shame, but being bathed in the blood of the lowly Nazarene, it has been transformed into a symbol of FAITH, HOPE and LOVE. It inspired the Crusaders of the Middle Ages in their perilous efforts to rescue the Holy Land from the heathern Turks; and is today being used to rally the forces of Christianity against the ever increasing hordes of anti-Christ and the principles of pure Americanism.

We have added the fire to signify that "CHRIST IS THE LIGHT OF THE WORLD". As light drives away the darkness and gloom, so a knowledge of the truth dispels ignorance and superstition. As fire purifies gold, silver and precious stones, but destroys the dross, wood, hay and stubble; so by the fire of Calvary's cross we mean to purify and cleanse our virtues by burning out our vices with the fire of HIS SWORD. Who can look upon this sublime symbol, or sit in its sacred, holy light without being inspired with a holy desire and determination to be a better man? "BY THIS SIGN WE CONQUER."

THE FLAG

This old flag, purchased by the blood and suffering of AMERICAN HEROES, represents the price paid for American liberties. It is the symbol of the Constitution of the UNITED STATES of AMERICA, free speech, free press, free schools, freedom of worship, and all CONSTITUTIONAL LAWS, BOTH STATE AND NATIONAL.;

Its RED is the BLOOD of American heroes that stained a hundred battlefields. Its WHITE symbolizes the PURITY of AMERICAN WOMANHOOD and the sanctity of AMERICAN HOMES. Its BLUE is but a patch of America's unclouded sky, snatched from the diamond-studded canopy that bends over our native land. Its STARS represent an aggregation of UNDEFEATED STATES bound together in an inseparable union.

"Its red is the red of the sunset's evening glow,
Its white is the white of the winter's driven snow;
Its blue is the blue of the ocean, sea and sky,
Its stars, the states of a union THAT MUST NOT DIE."

It has never been trailed in the dust, trampled in the mud or defeated in battle. It has never led a retreat or been hauled down at the command of any enemy. It is the greatest and most glorious flag that every floated in a breeze or waved over land or sea. It was purchased by the sacrifice and blood and we have most SACREDLY VOWED that we will uphold and defend it with our sacred honor, our property, our blood and our lives. May we ever be true to our VOW. Under its fluttering folds, as it floats in the gentile breeze in every Klavern, the U.S. Klans, Knights of the Ku Klux Klan will forever defend the principles of a pure Americanism, and thus perpetuate the sacred memory of our venerable and heroic dead.

Who can stand under these Stars and Stripes, remembering the sacred traditions that entwine about its holy past, without feeling that sublime patriotism that inspired our noble sires to die for OUR OWN, OUR NATIVE LAND?

THE SWORD

This unsheathed sword of steel is a symbol of law enforcement. It represents the military, or enforcement powers of our government from the president down to the constable. Its presence on our sacred altar signifies that we, as an organization, are solidly behind every enforcement officer in the land, to help, aid, and assist in the PROPER PERFORMANCE of their LEGAL duties. We stand unconditionally and unqualifiedly for the just and impartial enforcement of the law, and for the defense and protection of all rights and privileges of all citizens alike.

This SWORD also signifies that we are set for the defense of our Flag and all that it symbolizes against the attack and invasion of every foreign power, government, sect, ruler or people in the whole world. We believe in AMERICA FOR AMERICANS, and are sworn to defend it by all justifiable means and methods, from any encroachment whatever. This SWORD is a constant reminder of our obligation to defend our country and enforce its laws, through DULY CONSTITUTED authorities and justifiable means and methods. May we wield it wisely and well in defense of our COUNTRY, OUR HOMES, OUR FLAG, OUR LIBERTIES AND HUMANITY.

THE WATER

"This God-given, powerful, Life-giving fluid, more precious and far more significant than all the sacred oils of the ancients" is a symbol of the purity of life and the unity of purpose. With this divinely distilled fluid we have been dedicated and set apart, in body, in mind, in spirit and in life, to the sacred, sublime and holy principles of Klankraft. In this dedicatory service we are solemnly admonished to keep our character as transparent and as clear and clean as the liquid in this glass. A drop of ink of blood in this crystal fluid will have the same effect as sin in our lives. May we keep our record clear and transparent free from the sinstains of evil and wrong doing.

As water is useful to human life, so may we as Klansmen, be useful to humanity. As drops of water mingle and intermingle, thus becoming one solid mass, may we, as Klansmen become so united, each with the other, that we will become one solid mass, or one body in Klankraft. Thus we see the water is a beautiful symbol of unity, usefulness and purity. Who can fail to learn from these drops of water, the lesson of real Klanishness, and of brotherhood in a common service to mankind?

THE ROBE

"THE distinguishing marks of a Klansman are not found in the fiber of his garment, or in his social, political or financial standing; but they are spiritual, viz: a chivalric head, a compassionate heart, a prudent tongue and a courageous will; all devoted and consecrated to our country, our homes, our Klan and each other.

We use the robe to signify that we do not judge men by the clothes they wear, and to conceal the difference in our clothing as well as our personality. There are no rich or poor, high or low, in Klankraft. As we look upon a body of Klansmen robed in white we are forcibly reminded that they are on a common level. By this means we also help to conceal our identity, which is an essential principle of Klankraft.

This white robe is also a symbol of the robe of righteousness to be worn by the saints in the land of YET-TO-COME. The age apostle, a prisoner on the Island of Patmos, peeped into the portals of the Great Beyond, and caught a glimpse of that saints, robed in white, "Which was the righteousness of Christ." Taking Christ as our criterion of character, and endeavoring to follow His teachings, Klansmen wear this white robe to signify that they desire to put on that white robe which is the righteousness of Christ, in that Empire Invisible, that lies out beyond the vale of death where there will be no more parting and no more tears.

"A lying scoundrel may wrap his disgraceful frame in the sacred folds of a Klansman's robe and deceive the very elect, but ONLY A KLANSMAN POSSESES A KLANSMAN'S HEART and a KLANSMAN'S SOUL." Therefore, as we seek to cover here our filthy rage and imperfect lives with the robe of a Klansman, may we through the grace of God and by following HIS CHRIST, be able to hide the scars and stains of sin with the righteousness of CHRIST when we stand before HIS GREAT WHITE THRONE.

THE HOOD

That hated hood, the terror of every evil force in the land, how they cry, "take off the hood." But they don't know what they say. They do not understand why we wear it or what it means. "If they only knew!"

In the first place it helps to conceal our membership. The secret of our power lies in the secrecy of our membership. We are a great secret organization to aid the officers of the law and we can do our best work when we are not known to the public. By this means we see and hear everything. We know the evil forces but they do not know us. By our secret membership we gather thousands into the meshes of the law that would otherwise escape.

It is also a symbol of UNSELFISHNESS. With the hood we hide our individuality and sink ourselves into the sea of Klankraft. Not as individuals but as Klansmen, "WE SACRIFICE TO SERVE." Our motto is, "NON SILBA SED ANTHAR--not for self but for others." Therefore, we hide self behind the hood that we may be unselfish in our service.

Who can look upon a multitude of white robed Klansmen without thinking of the equality and unselfishness of that throng of white robed saints in the GLORY LAND? May the God of Heaven, Who looks not upon the outward appearance but upon the heart, find every Klansman worthy of the robe and hood he wears. Then when we "DO THE THINGS WE TEACH" and "LIVE THE LIVES WE PREACH," the title of Klansman will be the most honorable title among men.

Thus with our symbols we seek to emphasize and impress the sacred, sublime and holy principles of Klankraft. WITH GOD AS OUR FATHER, CHRIST AS OUR CRITERION, THE BIBLE AS OUR GUIDE, THE CROSS AS OUR INSPIRATION, AND THE FLAG AS OUR PROTECTION, WE MEAN TO MARCH ON TO A TRIUMPHANT VICTORY FOR THE PRINCIPLES OF RIGHT IN THE U.S. KLANS, KNIGHTS OF THE KU KLUX KLAN.

**UNITED KLANS OF AMERICA
KNIGHTS OF THE KU KLUX KLAN
REALM OF ALABAMA**

**SUITE 401, ALSTON BUILDING
TUSCALOOSA, ALABAMA**

VI. Constitution of the Original Knights of the Realm of Louisiana

Since 1866

PROCLAMATION

TO ALL WHO SHALL SEE THESE PRESENTS, GREETING:

KNOW YE that in order to insure an effective organization within the Realm of Louisiana, to assist in the accomplishment of our worthy objects and purposes, to perpetuate our great fraternity, to preserve forever its principles, and to consumate its mission, I, the Grand Dragon of the Realm of Louisiana, Original Ku Klux Klan, do hereby proclaim this Konstitution, embodying all of·the original precepts, to be the Supreme Law of the Realm, and do invoke the blessing and guidance of Almighty God in behalf of our united effort to save our country, our homes and our race from the works of the Devil and the designs of the enemies of liberty;

KNOW YE FURTHER that·for a period of ten days from the date of this proclamation each Klavern, through its Exalted Cyclops, shall have the right to submit in writing to the Grand Kligrapp, specific amendments to this Konstitution, which amendments shall be considered by the Kabinet for proposal under Article IX of this· Konstitution.

KONSTITUTION

of the

ORIGINAL KU KLUX KLAN

REALM OF LOUISIANA

PREAMBLE

We, the members of the Original Ku Klux Klan, Realm of Louisiana, reaffirming the principles for which our forefathers mutually pledged and freely sacrificed their lives, their fortunes and their sacred honor two centuries ago; reaffirming the principles and honoring the accomplishments of our courageous fathers who established the invisible empire a century ago; and met in our own time by a renewed assault of the skilled and godless enemies of liberty; do ordain and establish this Konstitution, that we may best preserve, protect and transmit to our posterity the priceless heritage so painfully delivered to us. Let all mankind know that as freeborn Christian men and as worthy sons of our Fathers, we will do no less.

ARTICLE I

The objects and purposes of this organization shall be:

To foster and promote the tenets of Christianity;

To preserve, protect and defend the Constitution of the United States against all enemies whomsoever, both Foreign and Domestic;

To teach and practice pure Patriotic Americanism;

To maintain forever Segregation of the races and the Divinely directed and historically proven supremacy of the White Race;

To preserve public peace and good order; to maintain Justice under the Law and to protect the weak, the innocent and the defenseless from the indignities, wrongs and outrages of the lawless, and from all impositions and oppressions whatsoever;

To relieve the injured and the oppressed; to succor the suffering and, especially to aid and support those, and the widows and orphans of those, who may suffer and fall in our cause; and

To promote true responsible manhood, loyal fraternity or brotherhood, and generous mutual cooperation and assistance among ourselves; to further happiness among our people by constantly practicing and teaching our children to practice all of these objects and purposes.

ARTICLE II

Membership in this Organization shall be by invitation only, and shall be limited to Mature, Native-born, White, Gentile Men, of the age of eighteen years and upwards, who profess and practice the Christian Faith but who are not members of the Roman Catholic church

No Alien shall be invited nor shall he be admitted to membership until he shall have been vouched for in klavern as fully qualified, unquestionable loyal to the objects and purposes of this organization, and dependable to death, by at least two members in good standing who have known him personally for at least three years and intimately for at least two years. Each such Alien so vouched for shall be voted upon in klavern on two separate occasions, and upon each such occasion one negative vote shall require careful investigation and report before proceding further and two negative votes shall require rejection.

Upon approval as aforesaid, or where for the manifest good of the organization the Grand Dragon has expressly authorized approval in another manner, and upon solemnly swearing the oaths of obedience, secrecy, fidelity and klanishness, before an officer of this organization authorized to administer the same, qualified aliens shall become full members of, assume all of the obligations of, and be entitled to all of the rights and privileges of this organization.

Any member who, after fair notice and opportunity to be heard, shall be found to lack the qualifications, the loyalty or the dependability required for membership, or who shall be so found to be guilty of acts or omissions violative of his oaths or otherwise detrimental to the organization or its objects and purposes, shall be forthwith expelled or banished. The Grand Dragon shall, by edict, prescribe the form of notice, the form and manner of hearing, and the offenses for which banishment may be decreed. Banished persons shall be forever ostracized by all members of this organization.

No member shall ever be required to perform any act or accept any obligation contrary to the dictates of his conscience, in violation of his Religious convictions or against which he has real moral scruples, provided only that he timely make his objection known. Any member in good standing and against whom no charges which might result in his expulsion or banishment are pending, may resign his membership under honorable conditions upon solemnly swearing the discharge oath before an officer of the organization authorized to administer the same and, where physically possible, in the presence of one or more members of his klavern.

ARTICLE III

This organization is and shall remain absolutely sovereign in the Realm of Louisiana, recognizing the authority of no other so-called Ku Klux Klan organization in the Realm. For the furtherance of our objects and purposes and the protection of our members, no such person or persons not members of and subject to the discipline of this organization will be permitted to act in the name of the Ku Klux Klan within the Realm. Such persons are not Klansmen and, under penalty of banishment, may not be dealt with as Klansmen within the Realm by members of this organization.

The Grand Dragon, with the advice and consent of the Kabinet, may recognize, exchange envoys with, enter into treaties and agreements with, and otherwise mutually cooperate with any and all Ku Klux Klan organizations exercising actual effective jurisdiction over all or a substantial part of another Realm, having substantially the same objects and purposes as this organization, and governed by substantially the same oaths and discipline as this organization.

ARTICLE IV

The Government of this Realm shall consist of the Grand Dragon and his Kabinet of nine Hydras. The Grand Dragon shall be the Chief Executive Officer of this organization, his orders, edicts and proclamations issued in conformity with this Konstitution shall be law in the Realm, and he shall, by and with the advice and consent of his Kabinet, commission all Realm and Province Officers, and charter all organized Klaverns. He shall have the power to suspend any such officer so commissioned and to suspend the charter of any organized Klavern when, in his judgment alone, the best interests of the organization require such suspension. The power of impeachment of all Realm and Province officers, as well as the power to revoke charters, shall be vested exclusively in the Kabinet, by a vote of two-thirds of the members thereof. No impeachment or revocation shall be had except after fair notice and opportunity to be heard, the form and manner of which shall be provided by the Kabinet by decree; nor shall any impeachment or revocation be considered except upon detailed charges lodged in the Kabinet and showing on their face that if such charges are true such impeachment or revocation is manifestly necessary for the good of the organization.

The Grand Titan shall be the principal Assistant to the Grand Dragon, shall perform such duties as the Grand Dragon may direct, and in the event of the death, resignation, or other inability of the Grand Dragon to discharge the duties of his office, shall succeed to or perform the duties of that office. The method of further succession to the office of Grand Dragon shall be prescribed by the Grand Dragon by edit from time to time.

The Grand Klokard, the Grand Kludd, the Grand Klokan, the Grand Kleagle, the Grand Kligrapp, the Klabee, and two additional Hydras whose titles and duties shall be prescribed by the Grand Dragon, shall together with the Grand Titan, constitute the Kabinet. The duties and authority of each of the said Hydras shall be specified by the Grand Dragon and they shall perform their duties under his supervision and control.

The Realm Klorero shall consist of the Grand Dragon, his Kabinet, all Great Titans, and the Exalted Cyclops or his Representative of all chartered Klaverns. The Klorero shall meet from time to time at the call of the Grand Dragon to receive information and instructions and to report on progress of the activities of the organization. It shall act in an advisory capacity only, having authority to make recommendations and to maintain order during its meetings, but no more.

ARTICLE V

The Realm shall be divided into eight Provinces, each coextensive with and bearing the same number as the Congressional Districts of the State of Louisiana. Subject to the provisions of this Konstitution and the supremacy of the Realm in all things, the Government of a Province shall consist of a Great Titan and his Kommittee of twelve Furies. The Great Titan shall be the Principal Executive Officer of the Province, responsible in all things to the Grand Dragon. His Kommittee shall be advisory only, but shall be consulted to the greatest extent possible concerning activities within the Province.

The Province Klonverse shall consist of the Great Titan, his Kommittee, and the Exalted Cycles, Klaliffs and Klokans of all Klaverns within the Province. The Klonverse shall meet from time to time at the call of the Great Titan to receive information and instructions and to report on the progress of activities of the organization. It shall act in an advisory capacity only, having authority to make recommendations and to maintain order during its meetings, but no more.

There shall be commissioned in each Province a Great Klaliff, who shall be the principal assistant to the Great Titan, shall perform such duties as the Great Titan may direct, and in the event of the inability of the Great Titan to discharge the duties of his office for any reason, shall succeed to or perform the duties of that office until the pleasure of the Grand Dragon be known.

The Great Klaliff, together with the Great Klokard, the Great Kludd, the Great Klokan, the Great Kleagle, the Great Kligrapp, the Great Klabee, and five additional Furies whose titles and duties shall be prescribed by the Great Dragon, constitute the Kommittee. The duties of each of the said Furies shall be the same as those specified by the Grand Dragon for Hydras bearing the same title, except that their jurisdiction shall be limited to their Province and they shall operate under the general direction of the corresponding Hydra and the specific supervision and control of the Great Titan.

Each Great Titan shall have full authority to divide his Province into Districts and to alter the Boundaries of such Districts when circumstances indicate. He shall recommend to the Grand Dragon persons to be commissioned as Deputy Titans, and shall assign a Deputy Titan to each such District so created. The duties of each Deputy Titan shall be as prescribed by the Great Titan and shall be performed under his supervision and control, but not outside of the District to which he is assigned.

ARTICLE VI

The Klavern shall be the local unit of this organization, a subordinate body operating solely under the authority of the Realm. It shall have jurisdiction over the territory known as its Klanton and specifically described in its charter. It may also be granted temporary jurisdiction over additional territory adjacent to its Klanton pending the chartering of one or more additional Klaverns in such territory. All officers and members of this organization shall at all times recognize and respect the primary concern of a chartered Kiavern over any activities within its own Klanton.

A Klavern shall be eligible for charter when it has attained a membership of 25 or more Klansmen and has demonstrated its capacity to conduct its affairs in conformity to the high standards expected of all units of this order.

Except under special circumstances, and then only with the express permission of the Grand Dragon, no Klavern shall consist of more than 100 members. In such circumstances every reasonable effort will be made to divide the Klanton and charter another strong unit in the vicinity of the oversize Klavern.

Officers of the Klavern shall be the Exalted Cyclops and his 12 Terrors, who shall be elected annually by the members in good standing. A majority shall be required to elect. Officers so elected shall serve for a term of one year or until their successors have been elected and qualified. Where it is for the manifest good of the order to do so, the Grand Dragon shall have the power and authority to suspend Klavern officers, but the power of removal shall be vested in the Klavern by majority vote and in such manner as the Grand Dragon shall prescribe by edict.

The Klavern Executive Board shall consist of the Klaliff, the Klokard, the Kludd, the Kligrapp, the Klabee, the Kladd and the Klokan, together with the Exalted Cyclops, and shall meet at least weekly to organize and plan the program and activities of the Klavern.

The duties of all Klavern officers and of all Klavern committees shall be specified by edict of the Grand Dragon from time to time.

ARTICLE VII

The Grand Dragon, with the advice and consent of the Kabinet, may by edict levy a tax for the operating expenses of the Realm, but any taxes so levied will be uniform throughout the Realm.

Klavern dues shall be fixed by each chartered unit, but shall never exceed the sum of $5.00 per member per month. Dues for unchartered units shall be fixed at the sum of $2.00 per member per month, subject to increase or decrease by the Klavern when chartered.

ARTICLE VIII

The uniform or regalia of this order shall consist of the Robe, cape and helmet traditional with the Invisible Empire. The design, style, material and color of the regalia shall be specified by edict by the Grand Dragon.

Under no circumstances will regalia be worn or displayed in public without the express consent of the Grand Dragon, nor shall the traditional firery cross be exhibited or displayed in public without the express consent of the Grand Dragon.

ARTICLE IX

The Kabinet, whenever two-thirds of the members shall deem it necessary, shall propose amendments to this Konstitution, or, on the application of the Exalted Cyclops of two-thirds of the chartered Klaverns shall call a Konvention for proposing amendments, which, in either case, shall be valid to all intents and purposes as part of this Konstitution when ratified by the Exalted Cyclops of three-fourths of the chartered Klaverns, or by an affirmative vote in three-fourths of the chartered Klaverns, as one or the other mode of ratification may be proposed by the Kabinet.

P R O C L A M A T I O N

WHEREAS:
There is a definite need for a better organized meeting within the KLAVERNS;
WHEREAS:
All new members shall be made aware of the importance of organization and secrecy;
AND WHEREAS:
The duties of the officers are many and varied and there

exists a need for a general guide for conducting KLAVERN meetings.

BE IT THEREFORE RESOLVED AND PROCLAIMED THAT THE FOLLOWING WILL BE STRICTLY ADHERED TO:

E.C. is elected by majority vote of his KLAVERN and shall have complete responsibility for all actions of his KLAVERN and shall answer to the GRAND DRAGON for same.

ALL REALM work is carried on by a chain of command. No PROVINCE or REALM OFFICER shall be by passed by the EXALTED CYCLOP when securing assistance or information, unless this officer should fail to function, then it shall be carried to the next in line and the failure of the other officer reported.

There are THREE divisions in the ORGANIZATION. Each has its respective DUTIES. Do not request one officer to do the work of another.
KLEAGLES . . . . Organizational Work
TITANS . . . . .Executive Work
KLOKANS . . . . Investigative Work
Their DUTIES are as follows:

DEPUTY TITANS

They shall work under the supervision and instructions of the PROVINCE TITAN, in the AREA assigned to him and in that area ONLY.

DUTIES: Promote any program outlined by the GRAND DRAGON and handed down to him by the PROVINCE TITAN.

VISIT KLAN UNITS and give assistance, when requested by EXALTED CYCLOPS.

He shall carry messages from the PROVINCE TITAN to the EXALTED CYCLOPS and shall be responsible for the distribution of literature given him by the PROVINCE TITAN.

He shall make weekly reports in writing to the PROVINCE TITAN.

He shall act as a personal AMBASSADOR for the PROVINCE TITAN, but he does not have any authority to make decisions or rulings pertaining to the work of the KLAN UNITS.

He shall NEVER INTERFERE with the actions of the KLOKANS OR KLEAGLES.

GREAT TITAN

He shall work under the supervision and instructions of the GRAND TITAN, in the PROVINCE assigned to him in that PROVINCE only, unless requested otherwise by the GRAND TITAN.

DUTIES: He shall secure COMMISSIONS for as many DEPUTY TITANS as he needs to insure proper supervision over his PROVINCE.

He shall supervise and coordinate their work in order to promote any program outlined by the GRAND DRAGON and handed down to him by the GRAND TITAN.

He shall hold a PROVINCE MEETING once each month and shall preside over said meeting. He shall appoint a DEPUTY TITAN to act as secretary, and take an accurate record of the meeting.

He shall visit KLAN UNITS, give them assistance, and keep them informed as to the progress of the INVISIBLE EMPIRE.

He shall be present at the chartering of all KLAN UNITS in his PROVINCE, or have his deputy act for him, present them with their material, and instruct them in the operation of a KLAN UNIT.

He shall make weekly reports in writing to both the GRAND DRAGON and the GRAND TITAN.

He shall be fully responsible for all the actions of the DEPUTY TITANS and has the authority to replace any DEPUTY TITAN if he fails to discharge his DUTIES.

GRAND TITAN

He shall work under the supervision and instruction of the GRAND DRAGON. His jurisdiction shall extend over the entire REALM.

DUTIES: He shall select and secure COMMISSIONS for one PROVINCE TITAN in each PROVINCE.

He shall supervise and coordinate the work of the PROVINCE TITANS in order to carry out any program outlined by the GRAND DRAGON.

He shall be directly responsible to the GRAND DRAGON for all of the actions of the PROVINCE TITANS and has the authority to replace any PROVINCE TITAN who fails to perform his duties.

DEPUTY KLOKAN

He shall work under the supervision and instructions of the PROVINCE KLOKAN, in the area assigned to him and in that area only.

DUTIES: He shall visit KLAN UNITS, giving assistance when requested by UNIT KLOKANS and check out SECURITY of UNIT.

He shall act as personal AMBASSADOR for the PROVINCE KLOKAN but does not have the AUTHORITY to make decisions or take action on any JOB, until he has requested and received permission from the PROVINCE KLOKAN.

He shall attend PROVINCE KLOKAN MEETINGS and assist PROVINCE KLOKAN when needed.

He shall make weekly reports in writing to the PROVINCE KLOKAN.

He shall NEVER INTERFERE with the work of the EXALTED CYLCOPS, TITANS OR KLEAGLES.

GREAT KLOKAN

He shall work under the supervision and instruction of the GRAND KLOKAN, and in the PROVINCE ASSIGNED to him, and that PROVINCE ONLY, unless requested, otherwise, by the GRAND KLOKAN.

DUTIES: He shall secure commissions for as many DEPUTY KLOKANS as he needs, to insure PROPER SUPERVISION over his PROVINCE.

He shall supervise and coordinate their work in a manner to insure proper investigative PROCEDURE OF ALL ACTION in his PROVINCE.

He shall hold PROVINCE MEETINGS once each month, and shall preside over said meeting.

He shall visit KLAN UNITS and see that they maintain proper security.

He shall be present at the chartering of all New Klan Units, in his PROVINCE, and instruct them in the proper procedure for handling all investigative work, and the necessity of maintaining good security at all times.

He shall make weekly reports in writing to both the GRAND KLOKAN AND THE GRAND DRAGON.

He shall be FULLY responsible for all the actions of the DEPUTY KLOKANS and has the authority to replace any DEPUTY KLOKAN if he fails to properly discharge his duties.

He shall never interfere with the action of TITANS OR KLEAGLES.

GRAND KLOKAN

He shall work under the supervision and instructions of the GRAND DRAGON. His jurisdiction shall extend over the entire REALM.

DUTIES: He shall select and secure COMMISSIONS for one PROVINCE KLOKAN for each PROVINCE.

He shall supervise and coordinate the work of the PROVINCE KLOKAN in order to carry out the investigative work properly.

He shall visit PROVINCE meetings and KLAN UNITS, giving instructions and assistance when needed.

He shall be present or visit as soon as possible, each newly Chartered KLAN UNIT.

He shall make weekly reports in writing to the GRAND DRAGON

He shall be directly responsible to the GRAND DRAGON for the actions of the PROVINCE KLOKANS, and has the authority to replace any PROVINCE KLOKAN who fails to properly perform his DUTIES.

He shall never interfere with the actions of the TITANS OR KLEAGLES.

KLEAGLES

He shall work under the supervision and authority of the GRAND KLEAGLE and in the area assigned to him and in that area only.

DUTIES: He shall be fully informed in the proper method of starting, building and chartering new KLAN UNITS.

He shall be careful to maintain security and not divulge KLAN SECRETS to Aliens.

He shall keep as compensation for his efforts, $5.00 of the KELECKTOKEN he receives from each application.

He shall send the remaining $5.00 of the KELECKTOKEN to the GRAND KLIGRAPP, along with a weekly report.

He shall make WEEKLY REPORTS in WRITING to both the GRAND KLIGRAPP and the GRAND KLEAGLE.

He shall be fully responsible for the action of all units until they are chartered.

He shall be PRESENT and PRESENT the charter to all newly chartered units in his area, then INTRODUCE and turn UNIT over to the PROVINCE TITAN.

He shall never interfere with the actions of the TITANS or KLOKANS.

GRAND KLEAGLE

He shall work under the supervision and by authority of the GRAND DRAGON. His jurisdiction shall extend over the entire REALM.

DUTIES: He shall SELECT, INSTRUCT and SECURE COMMISSIONS for as many KLEAGLES as he needs for the proper performance of his duties.

He shall supervise and coordinate the work of all the KEAGLES in the REALM.

He shall keep as compensation for his efforts, $9.00 of the KELECKTOKEN he receives from each application, and $1.00 from each KELECKTOKEN secured by each KLEAGLE.

He shall send the remaining $1.00 of each KELECKTOKEN to the GRAND KLIGRAPP, along with a report weekly, in writing.

He shall be fully responsible for the actions of all KLEAGLES, and has the authority to replace any KLEAGLE who fails to properly perform his duties.

He shall be present at the CHARTERING of all UNITS that he builds. He shall present them with their CHARTER, introduce the PROVINCE TITAN and turn the UNIT over to him.

He shall never interfere with the work of the TITANS or KLOKANS.

DUTIES OF KLAVERN OFFICERS

I. EXALTED CYCLOPS: The duty of the E.C. is to govern the meeting of the Klavern.
   (a) See that the meeting is opened at the exact time specified.
   (b) See that the business is conducted in an orderly manner.
   (c) He shall complete the order of business at every regular meeting.
   (d) He shall appoint all committee chairmen
   (e) He shall attend all Province meetings and give a progress report of his Klavern.
   (f) He shall take charge of and advise on all matters concerning his Klavern not mentioned above.
   (g) He is in complete charge of his unit.
   (h) He shall attend each meeting if at all possible.
   (i) He shall attend every Province meeting of his respective Province if at all possible.
   (j) He shall maintain order at all times during meeting.
   (k) He shall serve a one year term of office unless voted out of office by a majority of the membership.
   (l) He is responsible for the conduct of each Klansman in his Unit.
   (m) He should study naturalization ceremony and be able to give same from memory.
   (n) He will serve as chairman of the Klavern Executive Board.

II. KLALIFF:
   (a) The Klaliff shall serve in the absence of the E.C.

(b) He shall assist the E.C. in all Klavern business at the E.C.'s request.

(c) Shall assist and direct committees and see that all members serve on at least one committee.

III. KLOKORD:
(a) He shall study and master the KLORAN, the KONSTITUTION and all other laws and rulings of the Invisible Empire and be prepared to advise Klavern on same at any and all times.

(b) He shall be prepared to lecture at each meeting of Klavern.

(c) He shall instruct new members in The Way of the Klavern.

IV. KLUDD:
(a) He is the Klavern Chaplain and shall be prepared to give religious inspiration to the Klavern.

(b) He shall open and close each meeting of Klavern with prayer.

(c) He should study and be prepared to explain the 12th chapter of ROMANS at any time, as this is the religious foundation of the Invisible Empire.

V. KLIGRAPP:
(a) He is the secretary of the Klavern and keeps a record of the Klavern business. Takes the minutes of the meeting and sends reports of same to State Secretary.

VI. KLABEE:
(a) He is the treasurer of the Klavern and keeps a record of all Klavern finances and should be prepared to report same on request.

(b) He makes all bank deposits and signs all checks.

VII. KLADD:
(a) He is the conductor and accertains with care if all present at meeting are members of the INVISIBLE EMPIRE.

(b) He introduces all visitors to the Klavern members.

VIII. KLOROGO:
(a) He is the inner guard and permits no one to enter or leave Klavern during opening or closing ceremonies.

(b) Let no one enter except those duly qualified.

(c) He sees that each member gives station officer the S.O.S. upon entering or leaving Klavern in Klonklave assembled.

IX. KLEXTER:
(a) He is the outer guard and takes the password and ascerts that all persons entering the Klavern are members of the INVISIBLE EMPIRE and informs Klorogo of same.

KLOKAN:
(a) He is the Klavern Investigator and it shall be his duty to investigate all questionable matters pertaining to the Klavern.

(b) He shall appoint as many members as he deems necessary to assist him in his work.

(c) He shall report to the E.C. all findings resulting from his investigations.

(d) He shall attend all Province meetings for the purpose of receiving instructions and give reports.

XI. KNIGHT HAWK:
(a) He is the keeper of the Klavern and is responsible for aliens brought to the Klavern.

(b) It shall be his duty to see that the aliens are not exposed to the membership until naturalization ceremony beings.

XII. CAPTAIN OF THE GUARD:
(a) He is in charge of the Klavern security.

(b) He appoints members for guard duty.

XIII. SARGENT OF THE GUARD:
(a) He assists the Captain of the Guard.

(b) He serves in the absence of the Captain of the Guard.

Each Officer shall have an assistant capable of assuming his duties, who will be appointed by himself with E.C.'s approval.

In the event that any officer cannot be present at a meeting, it shall be his duty to see that his assistant is present to serve in his place.

NOTATION: Each officer shall attend all meetings, learn a n d practice Kloran Proceedures. Each Unit shall hold regular meetings at least once EACH WEEK.

DUTIES OF COMMITTEES

POLITICAL ACTION COMMITTEE
(a) The duty of the political action committee is to study all political activities in the jurisdiction of the Klavern.

(b) Keep the E.C. and the members of the Klavern informed on all matters of political interest. This includes State, National and International.

(c) Be well enough informed to recommend what political candidate: or issues to support or oppose and give recommendations to Klavern on such.

(d) Keep a record of all political activities within the jurisdiction of the Klavern, and be prepared to present it or any part of it to the Klavern upon request of E.C.

(e) Stay out of other Klavern Klanton unless otherwise agreed by same.

(f) From time to time the members of this committee will be requested to effectively contact their State Representatives and State Senator, as well as their Democratic State Central Committeemen for one or more of the following purposes:
(1) To determine their position on a specific matter then before them.
(2) To obtain their support and cooperation in either passing, amending or defeating that measure, or
(3) To learn and report the person or persons most able to influence them on such matters.

THE MEMBERS OF THIS COMMITTEE WILL BE CONTACTED, FREQUENTLY ON VERY SHORT NOTICE, FROM TIME TO TIME TO ASSIST IN LINING UP THEIR REPRESENTATIVES, SENATORS AND COMMITTEEMEN IN SUPPORT OF OUR POSITION.

EDUCATION COMMITTEE
(a) The Education Committee is responsible for the educating of the public in all matters of interest within the jurisdiction of the Klavern.

(b) Collect and distribute any literature that they can obtain that will further the cause of our organization.

(c) Write letters to the public on political or other issues of interest within the jurisdiction of the Klavern.

(d) Check books in the libraries of Schools, Churches, etc, a n d check any books or literature that is exposed to the public to assure that it does not contain communist influence material, (or integration material)..

(e) Write letters of protest to individuals or organizations t h a t publicly advocate integration, or communism.

(f) Write letters of appreciation to those who are working to further Americanism, Segregation, and etc.

MEMBERSHIP COMMITTEE:
(a) The membership committee keeps all records of the members, (Not excluding the sect.) prospective members, and rejected and/or suspended members.

(b) See that all material and literature in the possession of an expelled or suspended member is returned to the unit.

(c) Incourage regular attendance of members.

(d) Report on all members unable to attend regularly.

(e) Attempt to notify all members of special events, called meetings, summons, etc.

BENEVOLENCE COMMITTEE:
(a) The Benevolence Committee is in charge of all charity activity within the unit.

(b) Reports on all sick members, send flowers or cards to them and asks for any assistance that the unit might provide for same.

(c) Reports on and asks for assistance for persons other than members where the unit can be of assistance.

BUILDING COMMITTEE:

(a) The building committee is in charge of the construction and maintenance of the Klavern.

(b) Asks for or appoints members to work on the building or the grounds of same.

(c) Sees that the building is kept clean, the grass is cut, all necessary repairs are made, and recommends changes or additions to the building.

PUBLIC RELATIONS COMMITTEE:

(a) The Public Relations Committee is responsible for the relations between the organization and the non-member public.

(b) Their duties are advisory only.

(c) Inspect all out going literature and determine if it will create a good image.

(d) Advise on all activities of the unit that concern the public to assure prestige and a good public image for the organization.

KLOKAN COMMITTEE:

(a) This committee is appointed by the Klokan of the Klavern and is under the direct supervision of the Klokan.

(b) Takes no action other than that specifically ordered by the Klokan.

THE WAY OF THE KLAVERN

The following should be given to each new member immediately after the naturalization ceremony.

The newly made member be conducted to the Klocards' station by the Kladd. The Klocard will then instruct the new members as follows:

1. Destroy application
2. Instruct the member in the use of the gavel.
3. The National Password.
4. The Klavern Password.
5. The Signs of Recognition.
   (a) Lapel Sign
   (b) Foot Sign.
   (c) Hand Sign
   (d) Grip
   (e) Words of Recognition
6. Word of Caution.
7. Word of Distress
8. Instruct the members in the necessity of security.
9. Instruct the members as to the best way to approach prospective members.
10. Explain to the member the regulation concerning profanity and intoxication.
11. Impress upon the member the necessity of regular attendance.

Titans and Investigators should be given the same courtesy as your Grand Dragon or any other staff officer.

You will receive out of this office new rules and rule changes from time to time. Please study these and if the majority of your unit objects to any one or part of one, notify us immediately.

1. No action may be taken by any Kloklan committee without the consent and approval of E.C. in locality.
2. No new unit may be installed in any Klavern territory without said Klaverns approval.

3. Uniforms (robes) will all be made by the same standards by Klansmen in Realm. We shall have at least two manufacturers. One for South La. and one for North La. Since there is considerable profit envolved in this project, the following has been suggested: Determine amount of profit and pay makers accordingly out of realm treasury. Orders to be placed with secretary who will collect $10.00 for each. Profit will thereby go to Realm to be used for Klan expenses.

4. The Realm Secretary will keep records that may be audited at any time. He will furnish each Prov. Giant a financial statement each month to be examined by any E.C. at the monthly province meeting.

5. Before any payments are made out of realm funds, the secretary will have a voucher from the Grand Dragon authorizing same. All checks will be signed by the treasurer and secretary.

All Kleagles or anyone interested in organizing any new units should contact H. P. Morris, Zackary, La., Phone 654-4459 immediately.

6. Any candidate for public office that the Klan backs will be supported by all Klansmen. If there are any Klansmen that will not, then they will either resign or be expelled. The candidates shall be voted on by all concerned after they have been investigated and there must be 2/3 majority or no action will be taken.

7. Any Klansman who is known to violate our rules, especially those that give information to any aliens, shall be expelled immediately, then is to be watched and visited by the Wrecking Crew if necessa

8. All Klansmen should attend all meetings except when providentially hindered. Dues must be paid and those 30 days delinquent on dues will be dropped from the rolls.

9. All units will have and use the following:
   1. Holy Bible
   2. 2' x 3' U.S. Flag
   3. 2' x 3' Confederate Flag
   4. 2' x 3' Cross (should be able to light it by electrical means)
   5. (2) Sabres or swords
   6. 1 glass or tumbler

10. The organization shall have a Realm Naturalization Team who will demonstrate method of opening and closing and naturalization ceremony.

11. Each unit will set up at least one team of six men to be used for wrecking crew. These men should be appointed by the Klokan in secrecy.

12. All Klaverns will have at least five armed guards with flashlights posted during regular meetings.
    (a) No one will be allowed to carry a gun inside the Klavern during regular meetings except the Night Hawk.
    (b) No one will carry a gun inside during a state or province meeting except those appointed by the Chief KBI or Province KBI.

13. Any Klansman that leaves the organization for any reason shall be voted on as any alien when applying for readmittance.

14. A Klansman may be expelled from this organization after being given a hearing by a 2/3 majority vote of the membership. All members shall be contacted and urged to attend when a vote of this kind is taken.

15. All Klansmen shall bring their robes to the meeting. Any without a robe shall not sit in during degree ceremony.

16. All Klansmen shall practice klanishness, not only at meetings but in all phases of life.

17. No member will discuss Klan business with members who have missed meetings. Klansmen who are interested will attend. If providentially hindered, they may be informed of proceedings by E.C. only.

18. Security - Responsibility of Klavern security to rest upon Captain of Guard, and Sargeant of Guard in his absence. All other Security measures will be under the Klokan's supervision.

KLAVERN EXECUTIVE BOARD

The Klavern Executive Board shall consist of the eight highest ranking officers of the Klavern. They are as follows:

1. Exalted Cyclops
2. Klaliff
3. Klokard
4. Kludd
5. Kligrapp
6. Klabee
7. Kladd
8. Klokan

They shall meet at least once each week to map program and discuss plans for each weekly Klavern meeting.

VII. Constitution of the WKKKKM

THE CONSTITUTION

of the White Knights of the KU KLUX KLAN of the Sovereign Realm of Mississippi

(PREAMBLE)

We, the White Knights of the KU KLUX KLAN of Mississippi, FIRST recognizing Almighty God as our Creator, our Savior, and our Inspiration, in order to form a more Christian and Effective Klan, Provide a vehicle for the preservation of the Constitution of the United States of America according to its original Spirit, to Establish Justice, Insure Domestic Tranquility, Provide for the Common Defense, Promote the Welfare of Christians and the Christian Civilization, to Secure the Blessings of Liberty to ourselves and our posterity, to Promote the Purity and Integrity of the Separate Races of Mankind, Do Ordain and Establish this Constitution for the Government of the White Knights of the KU KLUX KLAN of the Sovereign Realm of Mississippi.

Article I
(Legislative Branch)

Section 1. All legislative powers herein granted shall be vested in two houses, not sitting concurrently, which shall be known as the Klongress. The upper house shall be known as the KLONVOCATION, and the lower house shall be known as the KLANBURGESSES. The KLAN-BURGESSES shall have the exclusive power to call the KLONVOCATION into session by means of passing a Convening Act.

Section 2. The members of the KLONVOCATION, who shall be known as Senators, shall be chosen as follows: All Klansmen within each of the several counties of the Realm, shall convene at a time and place within their respective counties, which shall previously have been determined and advertised, and then and there, by popular election among all individual Klansmen in good standing from within the respective counties, elect Senators to represent the counties in the Klonvocation. Each county may elect one and one only Senator, but the Senators shall have the power to designate a proxy to stand in their stead.

Section 3. The KLANBURGESSES shall consist of all Klansmen in good standing, who shall have voice and vote, unless a great disorder or a grossly unbalanced representation should occur, WHEREUPON either the Speaker, or any Klansman in good standing, may call for a UNIFORM REPRESENTATION RULE. Upon such call the floor shall

be reduced to one delegate. Only Khartered Klaverns and UnKhartered Klaverns with a minimum membership of twenty-five (25) Klansmen in good standing shall be entitled to vote in the Klanburgesses under the UNIFORM REPRESENTATION RULE.

Section 4. The proceedings of the KLONVOCATION shall be conducted according to strict interpretation of Parliamentary Rules at all times. The proceedings of the KLANBURGESSES shall be conducted under a loose Parliamentary procedure and the KLANBURGESSES shall forever remain popular in character.

Section 5. The powers of the KLANBURGESSES shall be as follows:

A. To hear reports and questions.
B. To make recommendations to all Grand and Province Officers.
C. Exclusively, to elect temporary Grand and Province Officers.
D. Exclusively, to call for evidence and Impeach, on a 3/4 vote, any Grand or Province Officer.
E. To debate any issue of business of concern to the Klan, and to hear any member Klansman in good standing who may wish to speak.
F. To authorize commercial operations.
G. Exclusively, to determine a set of rules and an order of business for the KLANBURGESSES.
H. Order investigations upon probable cause.
I. To authorize disbursements, the aggregate of which shall not exceed the sum of five hundred dollars ($500.00) per session.
J. The KLANBURGESSES shall have the power to constitute itself as a tribunal to investigate, try and punish disciplinary cases within the Klan, and may fine Klavern Officers a maximum of $25.00, Province or District Officers a maximum of $50.00, and/or Grand Officers a maximum of $100.00 for malfeasance or misconduct. The Exaulted Cyclops of each Klavern shall be held responsible to the Klan for the conduct of each member of his Klavern.
K. The KLANBURGESSES shall have the power to vote fines upon any klansman, not to exceed Five Dollars ($5.00) for misconduct at the KLANBURGESSES.
L. Exclusively, to call the KLONVOCATION into session, by means of passing a CONVENING ACT for the following purposes:

  1. To try impeachments with a 2/3 vote required for conviction.
  2. Amend the Constitution on specific points, but NOT Article VI, Section 1.
  3. Enact Specific Laws.

4. Fix or change emoluments for officers.
5. Authorize disbursements in excess of five hundred dollars ($500.00).
6. Fix or change uniform dues, rates and allowances, but all shall be uniform throughout the Klan, at the KLAN-LEVEL.
7. Establish a Klan Headquarters.
8. Elect all Grand Officers.
9. Confirm all executive appointees and Klan of Province fines, with a 2/3 vote required; but the Klonvocation shall not be convened solely for confirmation purposes.
10. The Klonvocation shall have the power to appoint from within their own membership any special or standing committee which they may deem necessary without specific authorization, Section 9 of this article notwithstanding.

Section 6. The KLANBERGESSES shall appoint the time, place and manner for the election of province officers which shall be held in the proper province. Each Klavern shall have but one vote in the Province Elections, but no Province elections shall be held in any Province which may have less than five (5) Khartered Klaverns within that Province. To meet any such deficiency, the Klanburgesses shall elect temporary officers for such provinces, but elections for full-term, permanent Province Officers shall be held in the Respective Provinces as soon as practicable after the Fifth Klavern is Khartered within the Province, after the Second Tuesday in January, 1965.

Section 7. The KLANBURGESSES shall meet not less than once each ninety (90) days. The meeting place shall alternate equitably among the Provinces, and no two consecutive sessions shall be held within the same Province. The time and place of the first session shall be set by the Imperial Wizard, and all subsequent sessions shall be set by the immediately preceeding session of the KLANBURGESSES. The Imperial Wizard shall notify the Exalted Cyclops of all Klaverns as to the time and place of all future sessions of the Klanburgesses. The Imperial Wizard shall have the power to call a Special Session of the Klanburgesses.

Section 8. The KLANBURGESSES shall be called to order at the appointed time and place by the highest ranking officer present, who shall immediately appoint a member to open the proceedings with Prayer. All Grand and Province Officers shall be required to attend all sessions of the KLAN-BURGESSES, Providence alone preventing. The adjournment of all sessions of the KLAN-BURGESSES shall be automatic six (6) hours after the call to order, but may be adjourned prior to that time by majority vote.

Section 9. The CONVENING ACT by which the KLANBURGESSES shall call the KLONVOCATION into session shall specifically state, define and outline the matter(s) to be legislated or rejected, and thereby restrict and limit the particular legislative area to which the particular session of the KLONVOCA-TION shall be confined, except as noted in Section 5, SS-L, Item 10 of this Article.

Section 10. The KLONVOCATION shall be called to order at the time and place specified in the CONVENING ACT by the Grand Giant, and the First Order of business shall be a Prayer, followed by the election of a Presiding Officer, if none shall have been elected. A period of time shall then be given over to opening declaratory remarks by the Senators, or their Proxies, and any Grand Officer upon Majority Invitation, not debatable. This period of opening remarks shall be followed by a recess, and then the specified order of business shall be considered, with only necessary and proper recesses, until such business shall be properly legislated or rejected, and a 2/3 majority of the Senators shall vote to adjourn.

Section 11. No one save the Senators or their Proxies shall be permitted upon the floor of the KLONVOCATION, and none but they shall speak, except those who may receive an invitation by majority vote.

Section 12. This Constitution and all Laws enacted pursuant to it, SHALL BE THE SUPREME LAW OF THE WHITE KNIGHTS OF THE KU KLUX KLAN OF THE SOVEREIGN REALM OF MISSISSIPPI, AND BINDING THEREOF UPON ALL MEMBERS, REGARDLESS OF RANK. The election and confirmation or removal of officers shall not require ratification. Printed copies of this Constitution shall be made available to the Klansmen at a nominal fee.

Section 13. All Grand and Province Officers shall be required to attend the KLONVOCATION and shall be provided with stations behind the chair from whence they may be invited to speak upon majority invitation. The chair shall recognize none other than a duly elected Senator or his Proxy, and none shall vote in the Klonvocation save a proper Senator or his Proxy.

Section 14. The Klonvocation is prohibited from voting its members any emoluments.

Section 15. No money shall be drawn from the Treasury but in the consequence of appropriations made by law. A regular statement of all the receipts, expenditures and balances on hand shall be furnished to the Klongress, all Grand Officers and the Klavern Kligraphs by the Chief Klabursar.

Section 16. The President of the Klonvocation shall be a Senator, and shall be elected for a term of two (2) years, and shall vote only to break a tie.

Section 17. Both Houses of the KLONGRESS shall have the power to determine the rules of order for their respective houses, except as herein noted.

Article II
(Executive Powers)

Section 1. The Executive Department of the Klan shall consist of the following elected Grand Officers: 1. The Imperial Wizard, 2. The Grand Dragon, 3. The Grand Giant, 4. The Grand Chaplain, 5. The Grand Director of the Klan Bureau of Investigation. These officers shall all be limited to a maximum of three (3) consecutive terms of four (4) years each, which is a maximum total of twelve (12) years service. This shall not include a fractional part of a year or term which may have been arranged to adjust to a rotational convenience of staggered terms. No officer shall have the power to appoint or commission an officer or Klansman to a term extending past the then current term of the appointing officer.

Section 2. The Realm of Mississippi shall be divided into five (5) Districts, which shall correspond to, and adjust to, any changes in the United States Congressional Districts of the State of Mississippi, as geographical boundaries based on population.

Section 3. Commencing in 1964, and so remaining until changed by a Congressional Re-districting the Districts of the Klan shall be as follows:

A. The counties of Alcorn, Tishomingo, Prentiss, Lee, Itawamba, Monroe, Pontotoc, Calhoun, Chickasaw, Webster, Clay, Lowndes, Attala, Choctaw, Winston, Oktibbeha, and Noxubee taken together shall constitute Klan District # 1.
B. The Counties of DeSoto, Marshall, Tippah, Benton, Union, Lafayette, Tate, Panola, Tunica, Coahoma, Quitman, Bolivar, Tallahatchie, Yalobusha, Grenada, Montgomery, Carroll, LeFlore, Sunflower, Holmes, Washington, Humphreys, Sharkey, and Issauena taken together shall constitute Klan District # 2.
C. The counties of Yazoo, Warren, Hinds, Claiborne, Copiah, Lincoln, Jefferson, Amite, Franklin, Adams, Wilkinson, Pike and Walthall taken together shall constitute Klan District # 3.
D. The counties of Madison, Leake, Neshoba, Kemper, Rankin, Scott, Clarke, Lauderdale, Newton, Jasper, Smith and Simpson shall constitute Klan District # 4.
E. The counties of Lawrence, Jeff Davis, Covington, Jones, Wayne, Marion, Lamar, Forrest, Perry, Greene, George, Stone, Pearl River, Hancock, Harrison and Jackson shall constitute Klan District # 5.

Section 4. Each of the Klan Districts shall elect, by vote of all the Klaverns within the respective Klan Districts one Financial Officer who shall be known as a Klabursar, and also one Judicial Officer who shall be known as a Klan Justice, and each Klavern in the respective Districts shall have one vote in their District Elections.

Section 5. The Realm of Mississippi shall also be divided into geographical divisions without regard to population, which shall be known as Provinces:

A. The counties of Hinds, Copiah, Lincoln, Franklin, Amite, Pike and Walthall taken together shall be known as Province # 1.
B. The counties of Bolivar, Washington, Sharkey, Isaquena, Humphreys, Sunflower, LeFlore, Holmes, Tallahatchie, Yalobousha, Grenada, Carroll and Montgomery, taken together shall be known as Province # 2.
C. The counties of Coahoma, Tunica, Quitman,

Panola, Tate, DeSoto, Marshall, Lafayette, Benton, Tippah, and Union taken together shall be known as Province # 3.
D. The counties of Alcorn, Tishomingo, Prentiss, Itawamba, Lee, Pontotoc, Calhoun, Chickasaw and Monroe, taken together shall be known as Province # 4.
E. The counties of Clay, Webster, Lowndes, Oktibbeha, Choctaw, Attala, Winston, and Noxubee taken together shall be known as Province # 5.
F. The counties of Madison, Leake, Neshoba, Kemper, Rankin, Scott, Clarke, Lauderdale, Simpson, Smith, Jasper and Newton taken together shall be known as Province # 6.
G. The counties of Lawrence, Jeff Davis, Covington, Jones, Wayne, Marion, Forrest, Perry, and Greene shall be known as Province # 7, together with Lamar.
H. The counties of Pearl River, Stone, George, Hancock, Harrison and Jackson taken together shall be known as Province # 8.
I. The counties of Yazoo, Warren, Claiborne, Jefferson, Adams, Wilkinson taken together shall be known as Province # 9.

Section 6. Each of the Provinces shall elect by Klavern vote, one Province Giant and also one Province Klan Bureau Investigator, and each Klavern in the respective Provinces shall have one vote in their Province Elections.

Section 7. No Officer or Klansman shall make any treaty, or enter into any negotiation with any other person or organization, domestic or foreign, without the advice and consent of the Klonvocation, but this shall not be construed so as to limit the power of the Imperial Wizard to render temporary material assistance to other organizations. Article VI, Section 1 is absolutely paramount to this entire constitution, and essential to it, and shall not be abrogated or modified by any means. No treaty shall be valid until approved by a 2/3 vote of the Klonvocation.

Section 8. The Imperial Wizard shall direct the Political, Educational, and other activities of the Klan, and shall have the necessary powers to initiate action and issue orders to accomplish the purposes of the Klan, except as restricted by this constitution. The Imperial Wizard shall enjoy the right of secrecy, and his own, private council for his private deliberations; however, he or they may be held accountable for all past actions in connection with his office of the Klan, and they and he shall be subject to censure, fine and impeachment, for misconduct or any act of malfeasance, and his Purse power shall always remain in the hands of the Klongress.

Section 9. The Imperial Wizard shall appoint the Klan Kleagle, and all other Kleagles and all private, executive investigators, and shall make all other appointments which may become necessary to accomplish the purposes of the Klan. All Executive appointees and commissions shall be subject to confirmation of the Klonvocation, except the private, executive investigators, who shall be private to the Imperial Wizard. All of the Executive appointees and commissions may act and serve until confirmed by the Klonvocation, but may later be rejected, and thus removed, by the Klonvocation.

Section 10. The Imperial Wizard shall be required to notify the Exalted Cyclops of all the Several Klaverns of the Realm, regarding the time and place of the Future Sessions of the Klonvocation and Klanburgesses, INSTANTER, it becomes known to him, and process will admit.

Section 11. In the event of the death or incapacity of the Imperial Wizard, the Grand Dragon shall immediately assume the position of Imperial Wizard, and shall call an immediate session of the Klanburgesses to elect a new and temporary Grand Dragon. If the first Grand Dragon should die or become incapacitated before such election can be held, the then third-ranking Grand Officer shall assume the position of Imperial Wizard, and the election shall fill the two vacancies, and so on. The Rank of the Grand Officers, and their order of succession to the position of Imperial Wizard shall be as follows:

1. The Imperial Wizard
2. The Grand Dragon
3. The Grand Giant
4. The Grand Chaplain
5. The Grand Director of the Klan Bureau of Investigation
6. The Speaker of the Klanburgesses
7. The President of the Klonvocation

Section 12. The Klonvocation shall be the sole judge of the capacity of the Imperial Wizard or any other Grand Officer by a 2/3 vote.

Section 13. Upon demand of the Imperial Wizard or the Chief Klanbursar any Klavern must furnish information concerning its total membership and active strength, but no Klavern shall be required at any time to divulge the names of its regular Klansmen, nor their individual numbers, but the Officers of the Klavern are excepted and must reveal their identy to the other Officers of the Klan, if necessary.

Section 14. The Imperial Wizard may investigate without interference to see that the Law of the Klan is being observed.

Section 15. The Grand Dragon shall understudy the duties of the Imperial Wizard in order to quality himself for the position of Imperial Wizard, and shall receive compensation according to law.

Section 16. The Grand Giant shall conduct all Province and District elections with the assistance of the Province Giants and the Province Klan Bureau Investigators. The proper Province Giant shall forward the election returns of their respective Province elections to the Grand Giant, who shall certify same. The proper Klavern Kligraphs shall forward the election returns of their respective Klavern elections to their proper Province Giants, who shall forward them in to the Grand Giant for certification. The Klavern Kligraph of the oldest Khartered Klavern in each respective county shall forward the election results for the post of county Senator to the proper Province Giant, who shall forward them in to the Grand Giant for certification. The Grand Giant shall, in a rotational manner, select a

proper Province Giant and a proper Province Klan Bureau Investigator to conduct the District elections, and the selected Province Giant shall forward the bonafide District Election results to the Grand Giant. The Grand Giant shall present all certified results to the Klonvocation at its first session following the election.

Section 17. The Province Giants and the Province Klan Bureau of Investigators shall, upon a Klavern authorization conduct the purposes of the Klan in their respective Provinces which are not of a Great Magnitude or Complex in nature. All projects which arise in a Klavern or in the Klan, which are of a Great Magnitude or Complex in Nature shall be forwarded through the Chain of Command to the Imperial Wizard, who shall seek the advice and counsel of all Grand Officers.

Section 18. The Grand Chaplain shall serve in the capacity of Christian advisor on all questions of morals and idealistic Klavern conduct.

A. In cases of extreme penalties the advise of the Grand Chaplain shall be sought and considered.
B. The Grand Chaplain shall appoint a Province Chaplain for and from each of the respective Provinces. A 2/3 vote by the KLONVOCATION shall be required to confirm each of these appointments.
C. The Spiritual Conduct of all Klan Functions shall be under the direct supervision of the Grand Chaplain.

Section 19. The Grand Director of the Klan Bureau of Investigation shall coordinate the Investigative effort of the Klan in such a manner as to insure maximum balance and efficiency between the Executive Investigators down, and the Elected Investigators up and down.

Section 20. All officers of the Klan, elective or appointive, at all levels shall be Klansmen in good standing, of sound mind, good moral standing, and meet the following particular requirements for the Individual Offices:

A. The Imperial Wizard shall have attained his thirty-fifth birthday anniversary prior to taking office.
B. The Grand Dragon shall meet the same age requirement as the Imperial Wizard.
C. The Grand Giant shall be at least twenty-five years of age prior to taking office.
D. The Grand Chaplain shall be at least twenty-five years of age prior to taking office and shall be an Ordained Minister of the Christian Faith, and of a Christian Protestant Church.
E. The Grand Director of the Klan Bureau of Investigation shall be thirty-five years of age prior to taking office.
F. The Klan Kleagle shall be at least twenty-five years of age prior to taking office.
G. Each Klan Justice shall be at least forty years of age prior to taking office.
H. Each Klanbursar shall be at least thirty-five years of age prior to taking office.

I. Each County Senator and his Proxy shall be at least twenty-one years of age prior to taking office.

Section 21. The Imperial Wizard shall have the power to veto any legislative act within ten (10) days of the passage date, but shall explain in detail his reasons for all vetos.

Section 22. The Klongress shall have the power to override the veto of the Imperial Wizard by a 2/3 vote of both houses.

Section 23. The confirmation or rejection of any Executive Appointee of Commissions shall not be construed as legislative acts, and are therefore not subject to the Executive veto power granted in Section 21 of this article.

Section 24. The administration of the Klan shall consist of three levels of command, which shall be known as the Klan Chain of Command. All problems and administration shall proceed through this Klan Chain of Command in orderly fashion, up and down. The three levels are:

A. Klan-Level (All Grand Officers and other Klan-Level Appointed Officers)
B. Province-Level (All Elected and Appointed Province Officers)
C. Klavern-Level (All Elected and Appointed Klavern Officers)

Section 25. The Province Officers shall be the connecting link between the Klavern and the Klan-Level Officers.

A. The Province Giants are Second in Command to the Grand Giant.
B. The Klavern Kligraphs are Second in Command to the Province Giants.
C. The Province Bureau of Investigators are second in command to the Grand Director of the Klan Bureau of Investigation, but not under his Exclusive Control.
D. The Klavern Investigators are second in command to their respective Province Bureau Investigators, but not under their exclusive control.
E. The Klavern Exalted Cyclops shall use the Province Officer most convenient to him for transmission of administrative problems through the Chain of Command.

Article III
(Judicial Department)

Section 1. The Judicial Department of the Klan shall consist of five (5) elected Klanjustices, one each elected from their respective Districts in accordance with Article II Sections 3 & 4. They shall select one of their number to serve as Chief Klanjustice who shall, with 5-0 consent, select their meeting places.

Section 2. To serve as a Klan Justice, a Klansman shall not be required to be a licensed lawyer, and due notice shall be taken at all elections of possible conflict between the Bar and Klan loyalty of candidates.

Section 3. The Klanjustices shall be required to return a ruling on any proper legal question that may arise concerning the Klan within ten (10) days after such a ruling is requested by the Klangurgesses or the Imperial Wizard. Only 5-0, 4-0 and 4-1 rulings shall be valid, and the dissenting opinions shall be written and presented to the future sessions of the Klanburgesses.

Section 4. All of the Klanjustices shall be required to attend the Klonvocation, Providence alone preventing, and render legal assistance upon request of the Klonvocation. The Chief Klanjustice, may, with 5-0 consent of the other Klanjustices, submit legislative recommendations.

Section 5. The Klanjustices shall be subject to censure, fine, impeachment and removal by the Klongress for misconduct or malfeasance. The Klanjustices shall be entitled to travel and per diem allowances to be fixed by law.

Section 6. The Klonvocation shall confirm the election of all Klanjustices by a 2/3 vote.

Section 7. The Judicial Department shall have no Executive Powers save those minimum ones necessary to conduct their own private affairs, and no legislative powers whatsoever.

Section 8. The terms of office of the Klanjustices shall be for six (6) years, EXCEPT the initial terms of office, shall, in each individual case, correspond to a number of whole years which is equal to the numerical number of the U. S. Congressional district from which the respective Klanjustices shall have been elected. After this initial term, which will provide a staggered system of terms, the individual Klanjustices shall be elected for terms of six (6) years.

Article IV
(Financial Department)

Section 1. All financial transactions and disbursements of the Klan shall be administered by a Board of Klabursars, each of whom shall have been elected in accordance with Article II, Sections 3 and 4, from the respective Districts of the Realm. The Chief Klabursar shall make all disbursements, with the knowledge of all the other Klabursars. No disbursements shall be made, except those which have been authorized by proper legislative Acts of the KLANBURGESSES and/or the KLONVOCATION. The Chief Klabursar shall submit copies of the financial statement to each session of the Houses of the Klongress. At least one Klabursar shall attend each session of the KLANBURGESSES, and all Klabursars shall attend each session of the KLONVOCATION, Providence alone preventing.

Section 2. The Board of Klabursars shall meet once each month at a time and place specified by the Chief Klabursar, and shall then and there conduct all of the regular monthly transactions of the Klan. The Klabursars shall be required to admit to their meeting any Grand Officer or any Province Officer on their own authority, and any Klansman upon presentation of written authority from his Klavern.

Section 3. The Board of Klabursars shall not make any disbursements without specific authorization from the Klongress, and then only at their scheduled meeting.

Section 4. The Chief Klabursar shall be the Treasurer of the Klan, and he shall be elected from among and by the duly elected Klabursars. The Chief Klabursar may assign custody of separate portions of the Treasure among the Klabursars for safekeeping, however, there shall be but one, common Klan Treasure in theory, which may be divided into separate portions for safety, in practice.

Section 5. The District Elections of all Klabursars shall be confirmed by a 2/3 vote of the Klonvocation.

Section 6. The Klabursars shall be entitled to travel, per diem and other allowances to be fixed by Law.

Section 7. The Klabursars shall be subject to censure, fine and impeachment and removal by the Klongress, and if convicted of financial dishonesty, misconduct or malfeasance, shall be required to restore any short funds to the Treasury.

Section 8. All initiation fees, fines and other monies due the Klan shall be placed in the hands of the proper District Klabursar to be held and used for the expenses of the Klan as provided in this Constitution, and by Appropriation Acts of the Klongress enacted pursuant to it.

Section 9. The Klongress shall, when sufficient funds become available, appropriate and set aside by proper legislative acts, certain specific funds for particular use as follows:

    A. Legal Defense
    B. Benevolent Assistance
    C. Incentive of the Klansmen

The Imperial Wizard shall have complete control of the Legal Defense Fund, but shall be held accountable, and shall answer to the Klongress for any money used from the Legal Defense Fund.

The Klonvocation shall select a committee of eleven (11) of its members who shall make legislative recommendations relative to the use of all monies appropriated into the Benevolent Fund. A 2/3 vote of the Klonvocation shall be required to authorize the disbursement of any Benevolent Funds.

The Klonvocation shall select a committee of eleven (11) of its members, who are not members of the Benevolent Fund Committee, who shall make legislative recommendations relative to the use of all monies appropriated into the Incentive Fund. A 2/3 vote of the Klonvocation shall be required to authorize the disbursement of any Incentive Funds.

If any apportionment of Specific Funds which are outlined and described in this Section

shall become excessive or inconvenient to the best interests of the Klan, the Klongress may, by a majority vote, transfer sums of money from one fund to another as may be deemed necessary and practical by the legislators.

Section 10. A uniform receipt system shall be used by all Klabees, Kleagles, Organizers, Executive Appointees, Executive Officers, Klabursars, and all other Officers and Klansmen who may be engaged in the handling of funds, in order that the financial efficiency and integrity of the Klan shall be maintained at the highest practical level.

Section 11. Every person who is accepted for membership in the White Knights of the KU KLUX KLAN shall be required to pay a Klectoken Fee of Ten Dollars ($10.00) prior to receiving the Initiation Oath, and the Kleagle in charge of the Induction Ceremony shall be required to collect this Clectoken in full as a necessary part of the Application for Citizenship in the Invisible Empire.

Section 12. Kleagles who perform ceremonies of Initiation in Klaverns other than their own home Klavern shall be entitled to deduct Four Dollars ($4.00) of the Klectoken fee as their own personal fee, and shall remit the remaining Six Dollars ($6.00) to the proper District Klabursar not later than the fifteenth day following the Initiation Ceremony. No Kleagle who conducts Initiation Ceremonies in his own home Klavern shall be entitled to deduct any portion of such home klavern klectoken fees for his own personal benefit.

Section 13. Grand Officers and Klansmen who are authorized to travel on Official Klan business shall be paid ten cents (10¢) per mile and One Dollar and twenty-five cents ($1.25) per meal, with a maximum of two meals per diem allowed, and local activities shall be locally financed. Any officer or member who is authorized to receive travel and meal allowances shall not be permitted to receive any Kleagle fee if he should perform an Initiation Ceremony, but all such officers or members shall be required to turn in the entire Ten Dollar Klectoken fee to the proper District Klabursar without deductions.

Section 14. All Klansmen of the Realm shall pay regular dues to their Klavern Klabee which shall not be less than Three Dollars ($3.00), nor more than Four and one-half Dollars ($4.50) per Calendar Quarter. All Klavern Klabees shall remit to their proper District Klabursar the Klavern Realm Dues within fifteen days after the start of each Calendar Quarter. The Klavern Realm Dues shall be uniform throughout the Realm and shall consist of a sum of money computed at the uniform rate of One Dollar and ninety-five cents ($1.95) per member, per quarter. The Klavern Klabees shall remit One Dollar and ninety-five cents for each member carried upon the Klavern Roll each quarter.

Section 15. The Klanburgesses shall appropriate five cents (5¢) per Klansman per month for the exclusive use in the Province from which the Klansmen's Realm Dues were collected.

Section 16. Upon reaching an enrolled strength of Forty Klansmen a Klavern shall be considered as having a probationary Khartered Status, and shall then be entitled to elect their full slate of Regular Klavern Officers including the Klokard, who shall serve as the Klavern Kleagle. The Klavern Klabee shall be entitled to withhold Five Dollars ($5.00) of the Klectoken fee of Ten Dollars ($10.00) of the Forty-first (41st.) and all subsequent initiates for the Klavern Treasury, but shall remit the remaining Five Dollars ($5.00) of each Klectoken fee to the proper District Klabursar not later than the fifteenth day following the Initiation Ceremony. No Kleagle who conducts Initiation ceremonies in his own home Klavern shall be entitled to deduct any portion of such home Klavern Klectoken fees for his own personal benefit.

Section 17. Upon reaching an enrolled strength of Forty Klansmen each Klavern shall be required to remit the current quarterly dues for each of its enrolled members to the proper District Klabursar within fifteen days, PROVIDED, that less than Forty-five days of the current calendar quarter shall not have elapsed prior to the Initiation of the Fortieth member. If the calendar quarter shall be more than forty-five days elapsed at the time of the Initiation of the Fortieth Klavern member, dues shall not be paid until the next calendar quarter.

Article V
(Recruiting)

Section 1. All Kleagles and Organizers shall be selected on the basis of their depth of Christian Dedication, Ability to Organize and Instruct, their Domestic Situation, and their Moral Integrity.

Section 2. The Klan Kleagle and his selected Kleagles shall be primarily responsible to the Klan for the further expansion and organization of the Klan.

Section 3. All Kleagles must possess the clerical ability to perform the work which the office requires.

Section 4. All Kleagles shall, as a part of each Initiation Ceremony, prepare a receipt in quadruplicate form, and shall number same, and shall obtain thereon the number of the Klavern Kligraph, or the temporary officer in charge of the Klavern, if UnKhartered. The Kleagle shall then leave one copy with the Kligraph or temporary officer. The Kleagle shall then, within fifteen days, present the remaining three copies of the quadruplicate receipt form to the proper District Klabursar thereon, and leave one copy with the Klabursar. The Kleagle shall then forward both remaining copies of the receipt to the Grand Giant who shall number both copies, retain one and return the other to the Kleagle. The four copies shall be retained by their respective holders and surrendered upon call of a bona-fide Klan Auditor. The Klabees of Khartered Klaverns shall perform the clerical duties outlined in this section.

Section 5. All Kleagles may be compensated by law.

Section 6. No Kleagle, Officer or Klansman in any capacity shall ever attempt to recruit an alien for membership into the Klan who is a negro, jew or papist, not shall any alien who is cohabiting with or married to, by common law or pagan ways, a negro, jew or papist ever be allowed membership in the Klan.

Section 7. No person who professes atheism, or who refuses to acknowledge Almighty God as his Creator, Savior and Inspiration shall ever be allowed membership in the Klan.

Section 8. No person who espouses any allegiance in any form to any government or governmental system, social, ecclesiastical or political, which is in any way incompatible with the Lawful, Constitutional, Governmental System of the United States of America shall ever **be allowed membership in the Klan. No person who advocates the overthrow or erosion of the Lawful, Constitutional Government of the United States of America shall ever be allowed membership in the Klan. No person shall ever be recruited who is not a White, Gentile, American-born Citizen.**

Section 9. Kleagles shall scout into new areas and contact prospective Christian militant aliens for membership in a careful and Judicious manner using maximum possible secrecy, after being commissioned for this work by the Imperial Wizard.

Section 10. The membership of the Klan shall be composed of Christian men who meet the requirements heretofore stated and who are Twenty-One Years of Age, or older, sound of mind, sober in habits, of good moral character and not guilty of rape, murder, or treason.

Section 11. After the Initial men have begun a new Klavern, or a Klavern has been established, the Exalted Cyclops or temporaty officer in Charge shall call for names of men to be submitted as prospective candidates for membership. All members of the particular Klavern who are Klansmen in good standing shall be allowed to submit names of persons whom they have known for at least <u>five</u> years personally, and for <u>two</u> years intimately, at least. A submitted <u>name</u> must be accompanied by the vouch of an additional Klavern member in good standing. All submitted names shall be immediately recorded on the Prospective Candidate Roll within the Klavern.

The Exalted Cyclops or Temporary Officer in Charge of the Klavern shall require that all names of Prospective Candidates shall be called and read aloud at two consecutive meetings of the Klavern without a dissenting vote being cast against any particular prospective candidate, before the sponsor of that particular candidate shall be granted permission to approach that particular candidate for membership. If no dissent is heard on a particular candidate for two consecutive Klavern Readings of his name , the sponsor shall have permission to contact the candidate for membership.

If a submitted name receives one objection at either of the two required readings, and his sponsor insists, a previously selected standing committee from within the Klavern shall interview the objector in private, investigate his objections with care, and report their findings back to the Klavern at a later date. After the report of the committee a new vote shall be taken and if but one dissenting vote is cast, it shall be overruled and the prospective candidate shall be approved for his sponsor to contact for membership.

If the name of any Prospective Candidate shall receive two or more objections at any call, reading or vote, that name shall be dropped from consideration for a period of one year, and the Officer in charge of the Prospective Candidate roll shall enter all such pertinent information on the Roll immediately.

The Kligraphs of all of the respective Klaverns within the respective Counties shall maintain a current list for circulation among themselves which contains all names that have been rejected for membership in order to assist each other in the exclusion of undesirables.

No Klansman shall approach any alien or other person to enlist him or recruit him into the Klan until the conditions specified in this article have been fulfilled regarding each individual Prospective Candidate, except that Kleagles who are Holders of Commissions and are duly authorized by the Imperial Wizard may start new Klaverns on their own authority by contacting Christian, militant aliens whom they may judge to be good prospective Klansmen. Once a Klavern meeting has been established, however, no Kleagle shall bring any person to that meeting as a recruit unless he shall have been approved in the regular specified Klavern manner herein stated.

Section 12. No Klansman shall be allowed to transfer from one Klavern to another without proper reason and approval by his home Klavern. A Klansman who desires to transfer into another Klavern must be approved by that Klavern in exactly the same manner as any other Prospective Candidate who is alien to that Klavern.

Section 13. The Exalted Cyclops or Temporary Officer in Charge of a Klavern may call for a secret ballot on any vote of recruiting or any other issue on his own authority.

Section 14. The Imperial Wizard shall have the power to Commission Kleagles for the specific purpose of Recruiting certain persons such as professional men into the Klan as Secret Members.

The identity of a secret member shall never be revealed to the Klan at large, nor shall any information concerning the Klan at large ever be revealed to a secret member, save that bare minimum necessary to enable him to perform a particular task efficiently.

A secret member shall be attached to a regular Klavern Roll, and shall be carried on that roll as a number, together with his contact number or numbers, and secret members shall be required to pay regular dues through their contact number or numbers.

Article VI
(Bill of Rights)

Section 1. No Klansman shall at any time be required to perform any act or accept any duty that may conflict with his conscience, religious convictions or moral scruples, but a Klansman in good standing may resign and be sworn out of the Klan at any time.

Section 2. The Imperial Wizard may rescind and remove the Kharta of a Klavern for Cause, but a Klavern shall enjoy the right of appeal to the Klongress for review, and a 2/3 vote of the Klongress shall be required to sustain the removal.

Section 3. All Klansmen shall enjoy the right to pay the exact and same dues to the Klan at the Realm level.

Section 4. All Klansmen shall enjoy the right to freedom from the exposure of their identity and the right to privacy. No alien shall ever be brought to, nor suffered to remain at any Klan Meeting, save duly approved recruits to Initiation Ceremonies. No open, public meeting of the Klan shall be held without the Direction of the Imperial Wizard and approval of the Klanburgesses for the specific occasion.

Section 5. Any member expelled by a Klavern shall have the right of appeal at the next session of the Klanburgesses, and may continue without a voice or vote until such time as his appeal may be heard, with a 2/3 vote of the Klanburgesses required for reinstatement.

Section 6. A secret member as described in Article V, Section 14 of this Constitution shall enjoy the right to privacy and freedom from exposure to all save his Contact Klansman.

Section 7. The internal affairs of a Klavern shall not be interfered in by outside Klansmen or any officers, except by invitation of the Exalted Cyclops or by petition of fifteen (15) aggrieved Klansmen in good standing within the Klavern, sworn and presented to the Imperial Wizard, but all Klavern shall conform to the Laws of the Klan.

Section 8. No Klansman shall visit a Klavern of which he is not a member, save by invitation of a Klansman in good standing from within the Klavern, and unanimous approval of the meeting prior to entry.

Section 9. Every Klansman shall enjoy the right to be heard at the Klanburgesses and may commission another member to speak for him. Every Klansman shall have the right of appeal to the Klanburgesses for the confirmation of fines, penalties and punishments short of expulsion by majority vote of the Klanburgesses. No penalty imposed upon a Klansman by his Klavern shall be effected, if appealed, until the Klanburgesses confirms such penalty. Any such appeal must be filed within one hundred twenty (120) days from the sentence.

Section 10. No Klansman shall be fined or otherwise punished more than once for the same offensive act by any of the several jurisdictions of the Klan.

Section 11. All Klansmen and Officers shall have the right to appeal the need of special funds, emolument increases, or the establishment of New emoluments, or the defrayal of past expenses, or any other appropriations which they may feel are necessary in connection with the work of the Klan.

Article VII
(Investigative Department)

Section 1. The Investigative Department of the Klan shall consist of the Grand Director of the Klan Bureau of Investigation, two Klan-level branches of Investigators, and the Klavern Investigators. The two, separate Klan-level branches shall be: (1) The Province Klan Bureau Investigators, duly elected from their respective Provinces, and such Special Legislative Investigators as may be appointed by the Klongress at their discretion, who shall report to their Klongress; and (2) The Executive Investigators who shall be appointed by and report to the Imperial Wizard.

Section 2. The Klavern Investigators shall be elected by their respective Klaverns, which election shall be private to the Klavern.

Section 3. The Investigative Department may petition the Klongress for funds with which to conduct investigations without disclosure of the specific business for which the funds are to be used, but they may be held accountable for wasted and misused funds at a later date.

Section 4. All Investigators may be held accountable for any false accusations or mistakes in the conduct of their office by the Imperial Wizard or the Klongress within the proper limits of security.

Article VIII
(Klavern Regulations)

Section 1. All klan meetings shall be conducted in a Christian manner calculated to stimulate the Spiritual Awareness and Reverence for Almighty God in all Klansmen. No cursing, intoxicated persons, nor those partaking of any form of intoxicating beverages shall be allowed in or suffered to remain at any Klan meeting or in its vicinity. Punishments shall be assessed against members for the violation of Christian Reverence during the meetings.

Section 2. A Klavern may hold secret ballots on the vote of any issue, and may require a vote on any issue to determine the will of the Klavern. The Exalted Cyclops of the Klavern or Temporary Officer in Charge of the Klavern may call for a secret ballot on any issue without any other authority or authorization.

Section 3. A loose parliamentary proceedure shall govern the business sessions of the Klavern. Kleagles who are building Klaverns to Kharter strength and all Officers of Khartered Klaverns shall be responsible for maintaining Reverence and Dignity at Klavern Meetings and shall require that all Klavern Meetings at which they are present shall be conducted in a militant and orderly manner. The

Exalted Cyclops of Khartered Klaverns, or his assignee shall be the Chairman at all Khartered Klavern meetings.

Section 4. The Exalted Cyclops shall be allowed to appoint any or all special or standing committees which he may deem necessary to insure the proper functioning of his Klavern.

Section 5. Should any Klansman commit an Act of Violation of the Klan Law, or of his lawful Klavern Regulations, or should there be presumptive indication that he is the probable cause of any such violation, he shall be tried by his Klavern and all penalties shall be final unless under appeal as provided in Article VI, Sections 5 and 9.

Section 6. The Klavern Officers and their order of rank shall be as follows:

1. The Exalted Cyclops – The President
2. The Klaliff – – The Vice-President
3. The Klokard – – – – – The Lecturer
4. The Kligraph – – – – The Secretary
5. The Klabee – – – – – The Treasurer
6. The Kludd– – – – – – The Chaplain
7. The Kladd – – – – – – The Conductor
8. The Klarogo – – – – – The Inner Guard
9. The Klexter – – – – – The Outer Guard
10. The Klokan – – – The Klavern Investigator
11. The Night Hawk – The Assistant to the Klokard and Kladd
12. The Klepeer– – – The Klavern Representative to the Klanburgess

Section 7. All approved recruits who shall be sworn into the Klan in a Khartered Klavern shall be given the Oath of Allegiance, Dedicated, Given all Lectures, pay the Initiation Fee and be given all signs, words, ways and grips in a place which is separate and apart from the Inner Klavern. The Last order of business prior to the Closing Ceremony shall be the introduction of the new Klansmen into the Inner Klavern. The Kleagle and Klokard shall be held responsible for the proper conduct of the Initiation Ceremony and shall be assisted by the Kladd and the Nighthawk.

Article IX
(Elections)

Section 1. The first terms of regular office shall run from noon of the second Tuesday in January, 1965 through as many years later as the respective terms of office shall have been designated to run by law; and subsequent elections shall be held in the year preceeding the expiration of those terms as herein specified. No elections shall be held for any office, the term of which shall be not definitely specified, after noon of the second Tuesday in January, 1965. No Klansman shall hold any office in the Klan Government for an unspecified term after that time.

Section 2. The election of Officers for the several Klaverns throughout the Realm shall be held during the first fifteen (15) days of September in the calendar years which immediately preceed the years in which the terms of office shall expire. The terms of the Klavern Officers shall be for not less than one (1) year, nor for more than four (4) years. The Klavern Kligraphs shall certify the Klavern election results in their respective Klaverns and shall send same to their respective Province Giants for certification and forwarding to the Grand Giant prior to the last day of September in the years in which elections are held.

Section 3. The elections of the Senators shall be held in their respective counties during the last ten (10) days of September in an election year. The Exalted Cyclops of the oldest Khartered Klavern in each of the several counties of the Realm shall summons all of the Klansmen within their respective counties into a common meeting, and there shall be elected by popular vote of all the Klansmen present, a County Senator who shall meet the lawful requirements herein specified. The Kligraph of the oldest Khartered Klavern within each of the respective counties shall certify the election results for the office of Senator and shall send same to the Grand Giant for certification and recording prior to the fifteenth day of October in an election year. The terms of the Senators shall be for six years; but immediately after they shall be assembled in consequence of the first election, they shall be divided as equally as may be into three classes, by lot. The seats of the senators of the first class shall be vacated at the expiration of the second year, of the second class at the expiration of the fourth year, and of the third class at the expiration of the sixth year, so that one-third may be chosen every second year thereafter for the full six-year term; and if vacancies happen by resignation or otherwise, the Exalted Cyclops of the oldest Khartered Klavern in the affected county shall appoint a Senator to fill the unexpired term.

Section 4. The Province and District elections shall be conducted and certified in accordance with Article II, Section 16 of this Constitution. The vote in all Province and District elections shall be by Klaverns, and each Klavern shall have one vote. The Province elections shall be held during the first fifteen days of October of an election year. The District elections shall be held during the last ten days of October in an election year. Multiple primaries shall be held in all Province and District elections, until one candidate shall have received fifty-one (51) per cent of all votes cast and be thereby elected.

Section 5. All candidates for Grand Office shall qualify between the first day of August and the tenth day f September in an election year by a registered letter containing their application and affidavit to the Grand Giant; and such registered letter postmarked prior to the deadline shall constitute due notice of candidacy. The Grand Giant shall circulate a list containing the names of all qualified candidates for Grand Office among all of the several Klaverns of the Realm prior to the First day of November in an election year. In addition, the Grand Giant shall circulate among the Klaverns any pertinent information concerning the various candidates for Grand Office, which may be authorized by the Individual Candidates.

Section 6. The Imperial Wizard shall call a session of the Klanburgesses at a conveni-

ent time in an election year, and inform them of the pending elections for Grand Office. The Klanburgesses shall then order the Klonvocation to assemble and elect the Grand Officers during the last fifteen days of November in that same year.

Section 7. The Klonvocation shall elect the Grand Officers and multiple primaries shall be held in each election for each Grand Office until one candidate shall receive sixty (60) per cent of the votes cast, and be thereby elected.

Section 8. No person shall serve in more than one elective or appointive office at either the Klavern, Province, District or the Klan Lever - Kleagles excepted.

Section 9. The White Knights of the Ku Klux Klan of the Sovereign Realm of Mississippi shall function under temporary and provisional Province, District and Grand Officers until noon of the second Tuesday in January, 1965, at which time the Duly Elected Regular Officers will assume the offices to which they have been elected.

Article X
(Robes)

Section 1. The cost of a robe shall be ten dollars ($10.00), and shall be paid for by the individual Klansman upon receipt of same.

Section 2. The manufacture and distribution of all robes shall be by contracts between qualified Klansmen and the Imperial Wizard, endorsed by a majority of the Grand Officers. All robe contractors shall agree to pay the Klan One Dollar ($1.00) into the hands of the proper Klabursar for each robe delivered within fifteen days of each delivery. Each robe shall be serially numbered with indelible ink by the robe contractor.

Section 3. The robe shall never be worn except for officially authorized purposes. The Grand Officers shall determine the style of the officers robes, but all robes shall be basically White.

Section 4. Any Klansman leaving the Klan under honorable conditions may be entitled to retain his robe, but all Klansmen leaving the Klan under dishonorable conditions shall be compelled to surrender his robe. Any Klansman leaving the Klan under honorable conditions and surrendering his robe may be entitled to a robe refund, but any Klansman leaving the Klan under dishonorable conditions shall not be entitled to a robe refund.

Article XI
(Proceedure for amending)

Section 1. No portion of this Constitution shall ever be altered, construed or amended in any way that would cause it to become in conflict with the Lawful Constitution of the United States of America.

Section 2. Article VI, section 1 is absolutely paramount and seential to this entire Constitution and shall not be abrogated or amended in any manner at any time.

Section 3. This Constitution may be otherwise lawfully amended by the introduction of a bill which shall be specifically labeled as a Constitutional Amendment in the Klanburgesses; if the amendment shall receive a 3/4 vote in the Klonburgesses, then the Klonvocation shall be called into session for the specified purpose of considering the amendment; if the amendment shall receive a 3/4 vote in the Klonvocation, it shall be sent to the Imperial Wizard for approval or rejection; if the Imperial Wizard shall approve the amendment, it shall then be sent to the Klanjustices where a 5-0 or 4-1 vote shall be required for approval; if the Klanjustices do then approve the amendment it shall become a legal part of this Constitution, but if the amendment should fail at any of these stated requirements of passage it shall fail, proceed no further and become void.

Article XII
(Klan Prayers and Oaths)

Section 1. The prayers and oaths included in this section of this Constitution are to be used as herein prescribed and shall not be modified, misconstrued or altered or used for any other purpose than as herein stated.

Section 2. The Invocation Prayer shall open all Klan Functions unless there be Klansmen present who shall offer suitable prayers. The Invocation Prayer of the Klan:

"OH GOD, OUR HEAVENLY GUIDE, AS FINITE CREATURES OF TIME AND AS DEPENDENT CREATURES OF THINE, WE ACKNOWLEDGE THEE AS OUR SOVEREIGN LORD. PERMIT FREEDON AND THE JOYS THEREOF TO FOREVER REIGN THROUGHOUT OUR LAND. MAY WE AS KLANSMEN FOREVER HAVE THE COURAGE OF OUR CONVICTIONS AND THAT WE MAY ALWAYS STAND FOR THEE AND OUR GREAT NATION. MAY THE SWEET CUP OF BROTHERLY FRATERNITY EVER BE OURS TO ENJOY AND BUILD WITHIN US THAT KINDRED SPIRIT WHICH WILL KEEP US UNIFIED AND STRONG. ENGENDER WITHIN US THAT WISDOM KINDRED TO HONORABLE DECISIONS AND GODLY WORK. BY THE POWER OF THY INFINITE SPIRIT AND THE ENERGIZING VIRTUE THEREIN, EVER KEEP BEFORE US OUR OATHS OF SECRECY AND OUR PLEDGE OF RIGHTEOUSNESS. BLESS US NOW IN THIS ASSEMBLY THAT WE MAY HONOR THEE IN ALL THINGS, WE PRAY IN THE NAME OF CHRIST OUR BLESSED SAVIOR. AMEN."

Section 3. The Benediction Prayer shall be used to close all Klan Meetings as follows:

"OUR HEAVENLY FATHER, WE INVOKE THY DIVINE BENEDICTION UPON US. KEEP US UNFETTERED FROM THE WORLD THAT WE MIGHT FIGHT THE GOOD FIGHT AND RUN A TRUE COURSE AND BE WORTHY TO CLAIM THE PRIZE. MAY WE AS BRETHREN AND KLANSMEN BE STEADFAST AND UNREMOVABLE, ALWAYS ABOUNDING IN THE WORK OF OUR LORD KNOWING THAT OUR LABOR IS NOT IN VAIN. THROUGH JESUS CHRIST WE PRAY. AMEN."

Section 4. The Dedication Prayer shall be used at the close of the Initiation Ceremony, as follows:

"OUR HEAVENLY FATHER WE BESEECH THEE THAT AN OVERWHELMINGLY SENSE OF DEDICATION WILL EMBRACE THESE MEN KNEELING BEFORE THEE. LOOK WITH FAVOR UPON THAT TO WHICH THEY ASPIRE AND BLESS THEM IN THAT WHICH THEY HOPE TO OVERCOME. DEDICATE THEM THEREFORE TO THE FIGHT FOR RIGHT, FREEDON AND A KLANSMAN LIKE SPIRIT. ALLOW THE NOBLE ATTITUDES OF HONOR, TRUTH, AND BROTHERLY AFFILIATION TO EVER PERMEATE THEIR LIVES, THEIR HONOR, THEIR HOMES AND IDEALS. THROUGH CHRIST OUR LORD WE PRAY. AMEN."

Section 5. All Klan functions, regardless of time, place and manner, shall begin with prayer, and end with prayer to Almighty God.

Section 6. All persons being admitted to membership in the Klan shall be bound by the following oath which shall be administered by the Kleagle in charge of the Initiation Ceremony:

"I, _____ consciously, willingly and soberly _____ standing in the presence of Almighty God and these mysterious Klansmen _____ do hereby pledge, swear, and dedicate my mind, my heart, and my body _____ to the Holy Cause of preserving Christian Civilization, _____The diginity and integrity of the Holy Writ _____ And the constitution of The United States of America as originally written _____ as the greatest safeguards of Justice and True Liberty ever written ___ I swear that I will preserve, protect and defend _____ The Constitution of _____ The White Knights of The Ku Klux Klan of Mississippi ___ and obey the laws enacted thereunder ___ and the lawful orders of the officers of the Klan.

I swear that I will ___ wholeheartedly embrace ___ the Spirit of Christian militancy ___ which is the basic philosophy of this order ___ and I swear that I will pray for daily guidance ___ to help me determine my proper balance ___ between the humble ___ and the militant ___ approach to my problems ___ in order that my arms ___ shall always remain ___ as instruments of justice ___ in the hands of Almighty God ___ and not become tools of my own vengance ___ I swear that I will constantly ___ and continuously prepare myself ___ Physically, Morally, Mentally and Spiritually ___ in order that I may become ___ an increasingly useful instrument ___ in the hands of Almighty God ___ and that His will be done through me ___ as part of His Divine Purpose.

I swear that I will remain ___ constantly alert ___ to the satanic force of evil ___ which is and shall remain ___ my enemy and I swear that I will ___ oppose and expose this force ___ at every opportunity ___ in klonclave ___ and in life.

I swear that I will offer ___ the utmost of
both my physical courage ___ and my moral
courage ___ which may require the sacrifice
both of bodily comfort ___ in combat with
the enemy ___ and also the sacrifice ___ of
my ego in daily life ___ I hereby dedicate
my Being ___ not only to combat satan ___
but God willing ___ to the triumph ___ over
his malignant forces ___ and agents here on
earth ___ Not only will I die ___ in order to
preserve ___ Christian Civilization ___ but
I will live and labor mightily ___ for the
Spirit of Christ ___ in all men.

I swear that I will cleave ___ to my brethern
___ in this order ___ and their families ___
above all others ___ and will defend and protect them against all of our enemies ___ both
foreign and domestic.

I swear that I will never be ___ the cause of
a breach of secrecy ___ or any other act ___
which may be detrimental ___ to the integrity
of ___ the White Knights of the Ku Klux Klan
of Mississippi.

All of these things I do swear to do ___ and
I will daily beseech Almighty God, my Creator
and Saviour ___ that I may be granted ___ the
strength ___ the ability ___ and the grace ___
that I may be eminently successful in my performance ___ of this sacred obligation.

I do hereby bind myself to this oath ___ unto
my grave ___ so help me ___ Almighty God."

Section 7. The discharge oath shall be used
upon the discharge of any Klansman from this
order, provided he be discharged in accordance with instructions in this constitution.
The Discharge Oath of the Klan:

"I, _____ Hereby surrender all property not held by me that belongs to the Klan
___ give up my citizenship and all rights ___
in the Klan ___ and hereby swear ___ before
Almighty God ___ and in the presence of men
___ that I will never betray ___ nor divulge
___ at any time ___ any information that I
have ___ concerning the Klan ___ and shall
always ___ remain absolutely neutral ___
forevermore ___ so help me God."

ALL AMENDMENTS BELOW PASSED APRIL 19, 1964

Amendment 1

Section 1. No Officer nor member shall be
permitted to compose, print or distribute
any literature which contains the classic
name of KU KLUX KLAN; nor write this name
in public, nor in any way use or expose
this name where alien eyes or ears can see

or hear it without the knowledge and consent of the Imperial Wizard.

Section 2. The Twenty Reasons recruiting
aid shall be exempt from the above rule,
but great care shall still be used in its
distribution to avoid alien familiarity
with the classic name.

Section 3. The Klanburgesses shall have
the power to invoke disciplinary measures
for violations of this article.

Section 4. A person who is a prospective
recruit who has been approved by the Klavern shall not be considered an alien in
construing this article.

Amendment 2

Section 1. No disciplinary cross shall
be burned on private property without
prior approval and investigation by the
Province Investigators and Province Titan.

Section 2. No Province Titan shall authorize a disciplinary cross burning without a complete and prior plan of follow-
up information in hand.

Section 3. This amendment shall take
effect thirty (30) days after passage.

Amendment 3

Section 1. All Grand, Province and District, Shire and other officers and members who become detached from their home
Klaverns as a result of service to the
higher levels of the Klan shall be permitted to form themselves into an Imperial Klavern, and shall pay regular dues
to the Klan.

Section 2. The Imperial Klavern shall
not have a regular vote in the Klanburgesses under the uniform representation
rule, nor shall its members vote in any
Province or district election.

Section 3. All members of the Imperial
Klavern shall have the privilege of membership in the Imperial Klavern for so
long as their dues are paid and their
conduct is honorable. They may transfer
out of the Imperial Klavern voluntarily,
but may not be retired without their individual consent.

Section 4. The Imperial Klavern shall
pay their own Klavern expenses of operation as do all Klaverns.

BIBLIOGRAPHY

Abbey, Sue. "The Ku Klux Klan in Arizona, 1921–1925." *Journal of Arizona History* 14 (Spring 1973): 10–30.

Abrams, Charles. "Invasion and counterattack." *Violence in America.* Edited by Thomas Rose. New York: Vintage, 1970.

"Activities of the Ku Klux Klan in Saskatchewan." *Queen's Quarterly* 35 (Autumn 1928): 1592–609.

"AFSC deplores KKK." *Christian Century* 98 (14 Oct. 1981): 1016–1017.

"Again, the Klan." *Time* 47 (20 May 1946): 20.

Aho, James. *The Politics of Righteousness: Idaho Christian Patriotism.* Seattle: University of Washington Press, 1990.

Aikman, Duncan. "Prairie fire." *American Mercury* 6 (Oct. 1925): 209–214.

_____. "Savonarola in Los Angeles." *American Mercury* 21 (Dec. 1930): 423–430.

"Ain't nothing you can do but join the Klan." *Esquire* 92 (March 1980): 27–37.

"Alabama aroused." *Outlook* 147 (2 Nov. 1927): 261.

Alabama General Assembly, Joint Committee on Outrages. *Report of Joint Committee on Outrages.* Montgomery: J.G. Stokes & Co., 1868.

"Alabama's floggers." *Literary Digest* 95 (29 Oct. 1927): 11–12.

Alexander, Charles. *Crusade for Conformity: The Ku Klux Klan in Texas, 1920–1930.* Houston: Texas Gulf Coast Historical Assn., 1962.

_____. "Defeat, decline, disintegration: The Ku Klux Klan in Arkansas, 1924 and after." *Arkansas Historical Quarterly* 22 (Winter 1963): 310–331.

_____. "Kleagles and cash: The Ku Klux Klan as a business organization, 1915–1930." *Business History Review* 39 (Autumn 1965): 348–367.

_____. *The Ku Klux Klan in the Southwest.* Lexington, KY: University of Kentucky Press, 1965.

_____. "Secrecy bids for power: The Ku Klux Klan in Texas politics in the 1920s." *Mid-America* 46 (Jan. 1964): 3–28.

_____. "White robed reformers: The Ku Klux Klan comes to Arkansas, 1921–1922." *Arkansas Historical Quarterly* 22 (Spring 1962): 8–23.

_____. "White robes in politics: The Ku Klux Klan in Arkansas, 1922–1926." *Arkansas Historical Quarterly* 22 (Fall 1963): 195–214.

Alexander, T.B. "Ku Kluxism in Tennessee, 1865–1869: A technique for the overthrow of radical Reconstruction." *Tennessee Historical Quarterly* 8 (Sept. 1949): 195–219.

Allen, Devere. "Substitutes for brotherhood." *World Tomorrow* 7 (March 1924): 74–76.

Allen, Frederick. "KKK." *Literary Digest* 124 (9 Oct. 1937): 15–17.

Allen, Lee. "The Democratic presidential primary election of 1924 in Texas." *Southwestern Historical Quarterly* 61 (April 1958): 474–493.

_____. "The McAdoo campaign for the presidential nomination in 1924." *Journal of Southern History* 29 (May 1963): 211–228.

Allen, Ward. "A note on the origin of the Ku Klux Klan." *Tennessee Historical Quarterly* 23 (June 1964): 182.

"Alma mater, KKK." *New Republic* 36 (5 Sept. 1923): 35–36.

"The American Legion—Our national Ku Klux Klan." *Messenger* 8 (April 1926): 124–125.

Ames, Jessie. *The Changing Character of Lynching.* Atlanta: Commission on Interracial Cooperation, 1942.

"And these are the children of God." *Collier's* 124 (6 Aug. 1949): 74.

Angleton, Paul. *Bloody Williamson: A Chapter in American Lawlessness.* New York: Alfred A. Knopf, 1952.

Anti-Defamation League. "Neo-Nazi skinheads: A 1990 status report." *Terrorism* (1990): 243–275.

"Anti-Klan group wrecks Frisco theater showing 1915 *Birth of a Nation.*" *Variety* 299 (18 June 1980): 1.

Armbrister, Trevor. "Portrait of an extremist." *Saturday Evening Post* 237 (22–29 Aug. 1964): 80–83.

Arnall, Ellis. "My battle against the Klan." *Coronet* 20 (Oct. 1946): 3–8.

"Arnall moves to dissolve Klan." *Christian Century* 63 (3 July 1946): 829.

"Attorney General Daugherty and the Ku Klux." *Messenger* 4 (Oct. 1922): 498.

"Backfire: South Carolina's Myrtle Beach." *Time* 56 (11 Sept. 1950): 26–27.

"Bad medicine for the Klan." *Life* 44 (27 Jan. 1958): 26–28.

Bagnall, Robert. "The spirit of the Ku Klux Klan." *Opportunity* 1 (Sept. 1923): 265–267.

_____. "The three false faces of civilization." *Messenger* 5 (Aug. 1923): 789–791.

Bain, Donald. *War in Illinois.* Englewood Cliffs, NJ: Prentice-Hall, 1978.

Baldwin, Neil. *Henry Ford and the Jews: The Mass Production of Hate.* New York: Public Affairs, 2001.

Baldwin, Roger. "Haters among us." *Saturday Review of Literature* 48 (19 June 1965): 36.

"Baltimore bookman fights against KKK terrorism." *Publisher's Weekly* 191 (27 March 1967): 35–36.

"Ban the Klan." *Jet* 59 (2 Oct. 1980): 5.

Barkun, Michael. "Militias, Christian Identity and the radical right." *Christian Century* 112 (2–9 Aug. 1995): 738–740.

_____. *Religion and the Racist Right: The Origins of the Christian Identity Movement.* Revised edition. Chapel Hill, NC: University of North Carolina Press, 1997.

Barrett, Stanley. *Is God a Racist?: The Right Wing in Canada.* Toronto: Toronto University Press, 1987.

Barron, John. "The FBI's secret war against the Ku Klux Klan." *Reader's Digest* 88 (Jan. 1966): 87–92.

Bartley, Numan. *The Rise of Massive Resistance: Race and Politics in the South During the 1950s.* Baton Rouge: Louisiana University Press, 1969.

Bass, Jack. *Taming the Storm: The Life and Times of Judge Frank M. Johnson, Jr., and the South's Fight Over Civil Rights.* New York: Doubleday, 1993.

Bates, Daisy. *The Long Shadow of Little Rock.* New York: David McKay, 1962.

Beal, Francis. "Let's unite to stamp out the Klan." *Black Scholar* 11 (March/April 1980): 2–9.

Beals, Carleton. *Brass-Knuckle Crusade: The Great Know-Nothing Conspiracy, 1820–1860.* New York: Hastings House, 1960.

Beard, James. *KKK Sketches, Humorous and Didactic, Treating the More Important Events of the Ku Klux Movement in the South.* Philadelphia: Claxton, Remsen & Haffelfinger, 1877.

Beazell, W.P. "The rise of the Ku Klux Klan." *World Tomorrow* 7 (March 1924): 414–418.

Beckett, R.C. "Some effects of military reconstruction in Monroe County, Mississippi." *Publications of the Mississippi Historical Society* 8 (1904): 177–186.

Belfrage, Sally. *Freedom Summer.* New York: Viking, 1965.

Belknap, Michael. *Federal Law and Southern Order: Racial Violence and Constitutional Conflict in the Post-Brown South.* Athens, GA: University of Georgia Press, 1987.

Bell, Edward. "Israel Zangwill on the Ku Klux Klan." *Landmark* 6 (June 1924): 30–32.

Bell, Leland. *Hitler's Shadow.* New York: Kennikat, 1973.

Bellant, Russ. *Old Nazis, the New Right and the Republican Party.* Boston: South End Press, 1991.

Bendersky, Joseph. *The "Jewish Threat": Anti-*

Semitic Policies of the U.S. Army. New York: Basic Books, 2000.

Bennett, Carl. "Methodists not alone in Georgia." *Christian Century* 66 (26 Jan. 1949): 114–115.

_____. "Ministers denounce Georgia Klan; Reply." *Christian Century* 66 (26 Jan. 1949): 114.

Bennett, David. *The Party of Fear: From Nativist Movements to the New Right in American History.* Chapel Hill, NC: University of North Carolina Press, 1988.

Bentley, Max. "The Ku Klux Klan in Indiana." *McClure's Magazine* 56 (May 1925): 23–25.

_____. "Let's brush them aside." *Collier's* 74 (22 Nov. Nov. 1924): 21.

_____. "A Texan challenges the Klan." *Collier's* 72 (3 Nov. 1923): 12, 22.

Berman, Daniel. "Hugo L. Black: The early years." *Catholic University of America Law Review* 8 (May 1959): 103–116.

Bermanzohn, Paul, and Sally Bermanzohn. *The True Story of the Greensboro Massacre.* New York: Cesar Cauce, 1982.

Besal, Dorothy. "Reasonable racism." *Community* 23 (May 1965): 3.

Betten, Neil. "Nativism and the Klan in town and city: Valparaiso and Gary, Indiana." *Studies in History and Society.* 4 (Spring 1973): 3–16.

"Bill outlawing violence." *Criminal Justice Issues* 6 (June 1981): 10.

"Bill to outlaw KKK paramilitary training by Ala. Rep." *Jet* 59 (23 Oct. 1980): 5.

Billington, Roy. *The Protestant Crusade, 1800–1900, a Study of the Origins of American Nativism.* New York: Macmillan, 1928.

"Black: A Klan member on the Supreme Court? New evidence comes to light." *Newsweek* 10 (20 Sept. 1937): 9–12.

"Black ballots." *Time* 33 (15 May 1939): 19.

Black, Earl. *Southern Governors and Civil Rights: Racial Segregation as a Campaign Issue in the Second Reconstruction.* Cambridge, MA: Harvard University Press, 1976.

"Black lawyer challenges right of KKK to exist." *Jet* 58 (21 Aug. 1980): 4.

"Black lawyers in Calif. urge outlawing KKK." *Jet* 59 (13 Nov. 1980): 8.

"Black leader calls for Nazis, Klansmen retrial." *Jet* 59 (4 Dec. 1980): 15.

"Black marines battle Ku Klux Klan at Camp Pendleton." *Black Scholar* 8 (April 1977): 46–49.

"Black ministers help calm Chattanooga, Tenn." *Jet* 58 (14 Aug. 1980): 6.

"Black police group asks for FBI probe on Klan." *Jet* 56 (12 July 1979): 7.

"Black protester slain while protecting children at N.C. anti–Klan rally." *Jet* 57 (2 Nov. 1979): 6–7.

"Black shirts and lynching." *World Tomorrow* 13 (Nov. 1930): 437–438.

"Black students in Atlanta attempt debate with KKK." *Jet* 60 (26 March 1981): 26.

"Black veterans plan training to fight KKK." *Jet* 54 (13 Nov. 1980): 5.

Blake, Aldrich. "Oklahoma's Klan-fighting governor." *Nation* 117 (3 Oct. 1923): 353.

Blankenship, Gary. "The *Commercial Appeal*'s attack on the Ku Klux Klan, 1921–1925." *West Tennessee Historical Society Papers* 31 (1977): 44–58.

Blee, Kathleen. *Inside Organized Racism: Women in the Hate Movement.* Berkeley: University of California Press, 2002.

_____. *Women of the Klan: Racism and Gender in the 1920s.* Berkeley: University of California Press, 1991.

Bliss, David. "Antiwar movement attacks links of Houston police to Ku Klux Klan." *Militant* 34 (27 Nov. 1970): 3.

Bliven, Bruce. "From the Oklahoma front." *New Republic* 36 (17 Oct. 1923): 202–205.

Bohn, Frank. "The Ku Klux Klan interpreted." *American Journal of Sociology* 30 (Jan. 1925): 385–407.

Bonventre, Peter. "KKK tries to rise again." *Newsweek* 93 (18 June 1979): 31.

Booth, Edgar. *The Mad Mullah of America.* Columbus, OH: Boyd Ellison, 1927.

Boskin, Joseph. *Urban Racial Violence in the Twentieth Century.* Beverly Hills, CA: Glencoe, 1976.

"The 'Boy Scout' boot camp." *Newsweek* 96 (15 Dec. 1980): 32.

Boyd, T. "Defying the Klan: Julian Harris and the *Enquirer-Sun*." *Forum* 76 (July 1926): 48–56.

Braden, Anne. "A Klan revival." *The Review* 1 (Jan. 1981): 14–16.

_____. "Lessons from a history of struggle." *Southern Exposure* 8 (Summer 1980): 56–61.

Braden, George. "The Ku Klux Klan: An apology." *Southern Bivouac* 4 (Sept. 1885): 103–109.

Bradley, P. "Psycho-analyzing the Ku Klux Klan." *American Review* 2 (Nov./Dec. 1924): 683–686.

Branch, Taylor. *Parting the Waters: America in the King Years, 1954–1963.* New York: Simon & Schuster, 1988.

_____. *Pillar of Fire: America in the King Years, 1963–65.* New York: Simon & Schuster, 1998.

Braxton, Lee. "They spoke out for decency." *Rotarian* 83 (Sept. 1953): 29, 55–56.

Bridges, Tyler. *The Rise of David Duke.* Jackson: University Press of Mississippi, 1994.

Brier, Royce. "Nightshirt knights." *Forum* 106 (July 1946): 54–55.

Brinkley, Alan. *Voices of Protest: Huey Long, Father Coughlin, and the Great Depression.* New York: Knopf, 1982.

"Broken monopoly." *Time* 55 (20 March 1950): 20.

Brooks, Fred. "Criminal violence escalates against minorities." *Criminal Justice Issues* 6 (June 1981): 1–2.

Broun, Haywood. "Up pops the wizard." *New Republic* 99 (21 June 1939): 186–187.

Brown, Bertram. *Southern Honor: Ethics & Behavior in the Old South.* Oxford: Oxford University Press, 1982.

Brown, William. "The Ku Klux movement." *Atlantic Monthly* 87 (May 1901): 634–644.

Brownell, Blaine. "Birmingham, Alabama: New South city in the 1920s." *Journal of Southern History* 28 (Feb. 1972): 21–48.

Bryant, Benjamin. *Experience of a Northern Man Among the Ku Klux: or, the Condition of the South.* Hartford, CT: The Author, 1872.

Buckner, George Jr. "Probe a rebirth of Hoosier Klan." *Christian Century* 63 (27 Nov. 1946): 1446.

Budenz, Louis. "There's mud on Indiana's white robes." *Nation* 125 (27 July 1927): 81–82.

Bullard, Sarah (ed.). *The Ku Klux Klan: A History of Racism and Violence.* 4th edition. Montgomery, AL: SPLC, 1991.

Burbank, Garin. "Agrarian radicals and their opponents: Political conflict in southern Oklahoma, 1910–1924." *Journal of American History* 58 (June 1971): 5–23.

Burner, David. "The Democratic Party in the election of 1924." *Mid-America* 46 (April 1964): 92–113.

"'Burning Cross' is daring expose of the Ku Klux Klan." *Pulse* 5 (Nov. 1947): 114–15.

Burton, Annie. *The Ku Klux Klan.* Los Angeles: W.T. Potter, 1916.

Busch, Francis. *Guilty or Not Guilty?* Indianapolis: Bobbs-Merrill, 1952.

Bushart, Howard, John Craig, and Myra Barnes. *Soldiers of God: White Supremacists and Their Holy War for America.* New York: Pinnacle, 1998.

Butler, Benjamin. *Ku Klux Outrages in the South.* Washington, DC: M'Gill & Witherow, 1871.

Butler, Robert. *So They Framed Stephenson.* Huntington, IN: The Author, 1940.

"Button down bed sheets." *Newsweek* 62 (26 Aug. 1963): 32–33.

Byrne, Kevin, and Oliver Houghton. "Texas Klan rally: Cow pasture politics." *Space City* 3 (31 Aug. 1971): 15.

Cagin, Seth, and Philip Dray. *We Are Not Afraid: The Story of Goodman, Schwerner and Chaney and the Civil Rights Campaign for Mississippi.* New York: Macmillan, 1988.

Calbreath, Dean. "Kovering the Klan." *Columbia Journalism Review* 19 (March/April 1981): 42–45.

Calderwood, William. "The decline of the Progressive Party in Saskatchewan, 1925–1930." *Saskatchewan History* 21 (Autumn 1968): 81–99.

_____. "Religious reactions to the Ku Klux Klan in Saskatchewan." *Saskatchewan History* 26 (Autumn 1973): 103–114.

"Calif. senate OKs bill to reduce KKK violence." *Jet* 60 (6 Aug. 1981): 8.

"California Klansman runs for Congress." *National Catholic Reporter* 16 (4 July 1980): 6–7.

Callaway, E.E. "Notes on a kleagle." *American Mercury* 43 (Feb. 1938): 248–249.

Campbell, Sam. *The Jewish Problem in the United States.* Atlanta: Ku Klux Klan, 1923.

Campbell, Will. "Clean up the botulism." *Southern Exposure* 8 (Summer 1980): 99.

"Can the Ku Klux Klan survive in Oklahoma?" *Harlow's Weekly* 23 (6 Sept. 1924): 6–7.

"Canada's 'keep out' to Klanism." *Literary Digest* 76 (3 Feb. 1923): 20–21.

Carlson, John. *The Plotters.* New York: E.P. Dutton, 1946.

_____. *Undercover: My Four Years in the Nazi Underworld of America.* New York: E.P. Dutton, 1943.

Carlton, Luther. *Assassination of J.W. Stephens.* Durham, NC: Duke University, 1898.

"Carter and the KKK." *New Republic* 136 (4 Feb. 1957): 6.

Carter, Dan. *The Politics of Rage: George Wallace, the Origins of the New Conservatism, and the Transformation of American Politics.* 2d edition. Baton Rouge: Louisiana State University Press, 2000.

Carter, Elmer. "The Ku Klux Klan marches again." *Opportunity* 17 (June 1939): 163.

Carter, Everett. "Cultural history written with lightning: The significance of *The Birth of a Nation*." *American Quarterly* 12 (Fall 1960): 347–357.

Carter, Hodding. *The Angry Scar: The Story of Reconstruction*. Garden City, NY: Doubleday, 1959.

Carter, L. Edward. "Rise and fall of the Invisible Empire: Knights of the Ku Klux Klan." *Great Plains Journal* 16 (1977): 82–106.

Carter, Ulish. "Ku Klux Klan is not the real problem." *Florida Courier* (8 Nov. 1980): 1, 3.

"Carter urges Klan probe after talks with blacks." *Jet* 57 (22 Nov. 1979): 8.

Carter, W. Horace. *Virus of Fear*. Tabor City, NC: The Author, 1991.

"Casting out the Klan." *Independent* 113 (13 Sept. 1924): 141.

Catchpole, Terry. "Operation Contempt: HUAC vs. KKK." *National Review* 18 (22 Feb. 1966): 152.

Catholic, Jews, Ku Klux Klan: What They Believe, Where They Conflict. Chicago: Nutshell Publishing, 1924.

"Caucasian crusade." *Outlook* 155 (6 Aug. 1930): 539.

Caughey, John (ed). *Their Majesties the Mob*. Chicago: University of Chicago Press, 1974.

Center for Democratic Renewal. *They Don't All Wear Sheets: A Chronology of Racist and Far Right Violence, 1980–1986*. Atlanta: CDC, 1987.

_____. *When Hate Groups Come to Town: A Handbook of Model Community Responses*. Montgomery, AL: Black Belt Press, 1992.

_____. *Procreating White Supremacy: Women and the Far Right*. Atlanta: CDC, 1996.

Chalk, David. "Klanswomen: In the new South the Ku Klux Klan is very much a family affair." *New Dawn* 1 (Sept. 1976): 37–41.

Chalmers, David. *Backfire: How the Ku Klux Klan Helped the Civil Rights Movement*. Lanham, MD: Rowman & Littlefield, 2003.

_____. *Hooded Americanism: The First Century of the Ku Klux Klan, 1865–1965*. Garden City, NY: Doubleday, 1965.

_____. *Hooded Americanism: The History of the Ku Klux Klan*. 2nd edition. New York: New Viewpoints, 1981.

_____. "The Ku Klux Klan in politics in the 1920s." *Mississippi Quarterly* 18 (Fall 1965): 234–247.

_____. "The Ku Klux Klan in the Sunshine State: The 1920s." *Florida Historical Quarterly* 43 (1964): 209–215.

_____. "The rise and fall of the Invisible Empire of the Ku Klux Klan." *Contemporary Review* 237 (Aug. 1980): 57–64.

"Changing values." *Forbes* 120 (15 Sept. 1977): 241–248.

Chidley, Joe. "Spreading hate on the Internet." *Maclean's* 108 (8 May 1995): 37.

Chomel, M. "The Klan issue in Indiana." *America* 32 (25 Oct. 1924): 31–32.

"Church urges members to struggle against KKK." *Jet* 60 (2 April 1981): 36.

"Churches vow KKK offensive." *National Catholic Reporter* 16 (28 Dec. 1979): 1.

"Clash in the Klan." *Literary Digest* 77 (21 April 1923): 13.

Clason, George. *Catholic, Jew, Ku Klux Klan*. Chicago: Nutshell, 1924.

Clayton, Powell. *The Aftermath of the Civil War in Arkansas*. New York: Neale Publishing, 1915.

Cline, Leonard. "In darkest Louisiana." *Nation* 116 (14 March 1923): 292–293.

Coates, James. *Armed and Dangerous: The Rise of the Survivalist Right*. New York: Noonday Press, 1987.

Cobbs, Elizabeth, and Petric Smith. *Long Time Coming: An Insider's Story of the Birmingham Church Bombing That Rocked the World*. Birmingham: Crane Hill Publishers, 1994.

Cole, Nancy. "How FBI aided Klan terrorists." *Militant* 39 (12 Dec. 1975): 3.

_____. "Informer reveals FBI's role in Ku Klux Klan attacks." *Intercontinental Press* 13 (15 Dec. 1975): 758–759.

Coleman, Louis. "The Klan revives." *Nation* 139 (4 July 1934): 20.

Collins, Frederick. "Way down east with the Ku Klux Klan." *Collier's* 72 (15 Dec. 1923): 12, 29.

"Colonel Simmons and $146,500 from KKK to KFS." *Literary Digest* 80 (8 March 1924): 36, 38, 40.

Commager, Henry. "Does the Klan ride to its death?" *Scholastic* 49 (7 Oct. 1946): 7–8.

Committee for the Defense of Civil Rights in Tampa. *Terror in Tampa: The Ku Klux Klan in Florida*. New York: Workers Defense League, 1937.

"Confirmation from a strange source." *American Federationist* 29 (Dec. 1922): 905–906.

Connor, R.D.W. "Ku Klux Klan and its operations in North Carolina." *North Carolina University Magazine* 30 (April 1900): 224–234.

Conroy, Thomas. "The Ku Klux Klan and the American clergy." *Ecclesiastical Review* 70 (Jan. 1924): 47–59.

"Constitution week in Oklahoma." *Literary Digest* 79 (13 Oct. 1923): 12–13.

Cook, Ezra. *Ku Klux Secrets Exposed*. Chicago: Cook, 1922.

Cook, Fred. *The Ku Klux Klan: America's Recurring Nightmare*. New York: Julian Messner, 1980.

Cook, James. *The Segregationists*. New York: Appleton-Century-Crofts, 1962.

Cook, Walter. *Secret Political Societies in the South During the Period of Reconstruction*. Cleveland: Press of the Evangelican Publishing House, 1914.

Corcoran, James. *Bitter Harvest: The Birth of Paramilitary Terrorism in the Heartland*. New York: Viking, 1990.

Coughlan, Robert. "Klonklave in Kokomo." *The Aspirin Age*. Edited by Isabel Leighton. New York: Simon & Schuster, 1949.

Coy, Harold. "The Klan hates them all." *Equality* 2 (April 1940): 9–14.

"Crackdown on the Klan." *Time* 59 (25 Feb. 1952): 28.

Craven, Charles. "Robeson County Indian uprising against the KKK." *South Atlantic Quarterly* 57 (Fall 1958): 433–442.

Crew, Danny. *Ku Klux Klan Sheet Music: An Illustrated Catalogue of Published Music, 1867–2000*. Jefferson, NC: McFarland, 2003.

Crews, Harry. "The buttondown terror of David Duke." *Playboy* 27 (Feb. 1980): 102–108.

Cripps, Thomas. "The reaction of the Negro to the motion picture 'Birth of a Nation.'" *Historian* 25 (May 1963): 344–362.

Crockett, Phyllis. "Ku Klux Klan." *Dollars & Sense* 6 (June/ July 1980): 94, 96–99.

Cronon, Edmund. *Black Moses: The Story of Marcus Garvey and the Universal Negro Improvement Association*. Madison, WI: University of Wisconsin Press, 1955.

"Crosses of fire." *Newsweek* 27 (8 April 1946): 21–22.

Crowell, C.T. "Collapse of constitutional government." *Independent* 109 (22 Dec. 1922): 333–334; 110 (6 Jan. 1923): 8–9.

Crowell, Evelyn. "My father and the Klan." *New Republic* 114 (1 July 1946): 930–931.

Crowther, Bosley. "The birth of 'The Birth of a Nation.'" *New York Times Magazine* 116 (7 Feb. 1965): 85.

Crozier, Ethelred. *White Caps and Blue Bills: The White Caps of Sevier County, a Story of Women & Kluxers in the Great Smoky Mountains*. Knoxville: Sevier Publishing and Distributing, 1937.

"Curriculum on KKK now available." *International Books for Children* 12 (1981): 32–33.

Curry, LeRoy. *The Ku Klux Klan Under the Searchlight*. Kansas City: Western Baptist, 1924.

Dabney, Dick. "Mean talk, mean times." *Nation* 153 (8 Nov. 1941): 456–457.

Dalrymple, A.V. *Liberty Dethroned*. Philadelphia: Times Publishing, 1923.

Damer, Eyre, *When the Ku Klux Rode*. New York: Neale Publishing, 1912.

Daniel, Mike. "The arrest and trial of Ryland Randolph: April–May, 1868." *Alabama Historical Quarterly* 40 (1978): 127–143.

Daniel, Pete. *In the Shadow of Slavery: Peonage in the South, 1901–1969*. London: Oxford University Press, 1973.

"Dark days in weird week." *Time* 86 (29 Oct. 1965): 29–30.

Davis, Daryl. *Klan-Destine Relationships: A Black Man's Odyssey in the Ku Klux Klan*. Far Hills, NJ: New Horizon Press, 1997.

Davis, Jack. *Race Against Time: Culture and Separation in Natchez Since 1930*. Baton Rouge: Louisiana State University Press, 2001.

Davis, James. "Colorado under the Klan." *Colorado Magazine* 42 (Spring 1965): 93–108.

Davis, Lenwood, and Janet Sims-Wood. *The Ku Klux Klan: A Bibliography*. Westport, CT: Greenwood Press, 1984.

Davis, Susan. *Authentic History, Ku Klux Klan, 1865–1877*. New York: American Library Service, 1924.

Deaton, Ron. "Klan revival: Work of D. Duke." *Progressive* 39 (June 1975): 29.

Dees, Morris. *A Season for Justice: The Life and Times of Civil Rights Lawyer Morris Dees*. New York: Charles Scribner's Sons, 1991.

Dees, Morris, and James Corcoran. *Gathering Storm: America's Militia Threat*. New York: HarperPerennial, 1996.

Dees, Morris, and Steve Fiffer. *Hate on Trial: The Case Against America's Most Dangerous Neo-Nazi*. New York: Villard Books, 1993.

"A defense of the Ku Klux Klan." *Literary Digest* 76 (20 Jan. 1923): 18–19.

Degler, Carl. "A century of the Klan: A review article." *Journal of Southern History* 31 (Nov. 1965): 435–443.

Del Boca, Angelo, and Mario Giovana. *Fascism Today: A World Survey.* New York: Pantheon, 1969.

Delaughter, Bobby. *Never Too Late: A Prosecutor's Story of Justice in the Medgar Evers Case.* New York: Scribner, 2001.

"Democracy or Invisible Empire?" *Current Opinion* 75 (Nov. 1923): 521–523.

Dent, Sanders. *The Origin and Development of the Ku Klux Klan.* Durham, NC: Duke University, 1897.

De Silver, Albert. "The Ku Klux Klan: 'Soul of chivalry.'" *Nation* 113 (14 Sept. 1921): 285–286.

Desmond, Humphrey. *The A.P.A. Movement: A Sketch.* Washington, DC: New Century Press, 1912.

Desmond, Shaw. "KKK: The strongest secret society on Earth." *Wide World Magazine* 47 (Sept. 1921): 335–365.

Dever, Lem. *Confessions of an Imperial Klansman.* Portland, OR: The Author, 1924.

Devine, Edward. "The Klan in Texas." *Survey* 48 (1 April 1922): 10–11; (13 May 1922): 251–253.

_____. "More about the Klan." *Survey* 48 (8 April 1922): 42–43.

Dinnerstein, Leonard. *Anti-Semitism in America.* New York: Oxford University Press, 1994.

_____. *Uneasy at Home.* New York: Columbia University Press, 1987.

"Disrobing the Klan." *New Republic* 126 (256 May 1952): 6.

Dittmer, John. *Local People: The Struggle for Civil Rights in Mississippi.* Urbana, IL: University of Illinois Press, 1995.

"Divisible Invisible Empire." *Newsweek* 32 (19 July 1948): 20.

Dixon, Edward. *The Terrible Mysteries of the Ku Klux Klan.* New York: The Author, 1868.

Dobratz, Betty, and Stephanie Shanks-Meile. *"White Power, White Pride!": The White Separatist Movement in the United States.* New York: Twayne, 1997.

Doherty, Herbert Jr. "Florida and the presidential election of 1928." *Florida Historical Quarterly* 26 (Oct. 1947): 174–186.

Dorman, Michael. *We Shall Overcome.* New York: Delacorte Press, 1964.

Douglas, Lloyd. "The patriotism of hatred." *Christian Century* 40 (Oct. 25 1923): 1371–1374.

Douglas, W.A.S. "Ku Klux." *American Mercury* 13 (March 1928): 272–279.

Doyle, William. *An American Insurrection: James Meredith and the Battle of Oxford, Mississippi, 1962.* New York: Anchor Books, 1962.

Dray, Phillip. *At the Hands of Persons Unknown: The Lynching of Black America.* New York: Modern Library, 2002.

"Drive to expose Klan." *U.S. News & World Report* 58 (12 April 1965): 69.

Du Bois, W.E.B. *Black Reconstruction.* New York: Russell & Russell, 1935.

_____. "Fighting race calumny." *Crisis* 10 (May 1915): 40.

_____. "The shape of fear." *North American Review* 223 (June-Aug. 1926): 291–303.

_____. "The slanderous film." *Crisis* 10 (Dec. 1915): 76–77.

Duffus, Robert. "Ancestry and end of the Ku Klux Klan." *World's Work* 46 (Sept. 1923): 291–303.

_____. "Counter-mining the Ku Klux Klan." *World's Work* 46 (July 1923): 275 284.

_____. "The Ku Klux Klan in the Middle West." *World's Work* 46 (Aug. 1923): 367–373.

_____. "Salesmen of hate." *World's Work* 42 (Oct. 1923): 461–469.

Duke, David. *My Awakening: A Path to Racial Understanding.* Mandeville, LA: Free Speech Press, 1998.

Dunbar, Anthony. "Conspiracy on conspiracy." *Katallagete* 3 (Winter 1971): 33–38.

Dunning, Frederick. "Ku Klux Klan fulfills the scripture." *Christian Century* 41 (28 Sept. 1924): 1205–1207.

Dyer, Joel. *Harvest of Rage: Why Oklahoma City is Only the Beginning.* Boulder, CO: Westview Press, 1997.

Dykeman, Wilma, and James Stokely. "The Klan tries a comeback in the wake of desegregation." *Commentary* 29 (Jan. 1960): 45–51.

Eagles, Charles. *Outside Agitator: Jon Daniels and the Civil Rights Movement in Alabama.* Chapel Hill, NC: University of North Carolina Press, 1993.

Early, Tracy. "Klan Kludd: To be or not to be." *Christian Century* 84 (22 Feb. 1967): 236–237.

Eastland, Terry. "The Communists and the Klan." *Commentary* 69 (May 1980): 65–67.

Edmonson, Ben. "Pat Harrison and Mississippi in the presidential elections of 1924 and 1928." *Journal of Mississippi History* 33 (Nov. 1971): 333–350.

"Educators publish guide to fight racism, Klan." *Jet* 60 (30 July 1981): 23.

"1871: Visitor from hell; Excerpts from congressional hearings on the KKK." *Southern Exposure* 8 (Summer 1980): 62–63.

"Election eve in Georgia." *New Republic* 119 (6 Sept. 1948): 10.

Elshtain, J.B. "Revolutionary Pulaski." *Commonweal* 117 (6 April 1990): 206–207.

"End of hearings on the Klan." *America* 114 (12 March 1966): 343.

The Englewood Raiders: A Story of the Celebrated Ku Klux Case at Los Angeles and Speeches to the Jury. Los Angeles: L.L. Bryson, 1923.

"Episcopalians assail Ku Klux." *Messenger* 4 (Oct. 1922): 497–498.

Epstein, Benjamin, and Arnold Forster. *The Radical Right: A Report on the John Birch Society and Its Allies.* New York: Vintage, 1967.

_____. *Report on the John Birch Society 1966.* New York: Random House, 1966.

Eskew, Glen. *But for Birmingham.* Chapel Hill, NC: University of North Carolina Press, 1997.

Evans, Hiram. *The Attitude of the Ku Klux Klan Toward the Jew.* Atlanta: Ku Klux Klan, 1923.

_____. "Ballots behind the Ku Klux Klan." *World's Work* 55 (Jan. 1928): 243–252.

_____. "The Catholic question as viewed by the Ku Klux Klan." *Current History* 26 (July 1927): 563–568.

_____. "The Klan: Defender of Americanism." *Forum* 74 (Dec. 1925): 801–814.

_____. "The Klan's fight for Americanism." *North American* 223 (March 1926): 33–63.

_____. *The Rising Storm: An Analysis of the Growing Conflict over the Political Dilemma of Roman Catholics in America.* Atlanta: Buckhead Publishing, 1930.

Evans, Margaret. "Like a thief." *New Republic* 28 (31 Aug. 1921): 16–17.

"Even the Klan has rights." *Nation* 115 (13 Dec. 1922): 654.

Ezekiel, Raphael. *The Racist Mind: Portraits of American Neo-Nazis and Klansmen.* New York: Penguin, 1995.

Ewing, Cortez. "The Reconstruction impeachments." *North Carolina Historical Review* 15 (July 1938): 204–230.

Fairclough, Adam. *Race and Democracy: The Civil Rights Struggle in Louisiana, 1915–1972.* Athens, GA: University of Georgia Press, 1995.

Fanning, Jerry, and Andy Bustin. "KKK grand dragon indicted in Houston." *Militant* 35 (17 Sept. 1971): 24.

Feidelson, Charles. "Alabama's super government." *Nation* 125 (28 Sept. 1927): 311–312.

Feldman, Glenn. *Politics, Society, and the Klan in Alabama, 1915–1949.* Tuscaloosa: University of Alabama Press, 1999.

"Fight for freedom of the press." *Literary Digest* 90 (14 Aug. 1926): 9–10.

Finch, Phillip. *God, Guts, and Guns.* New York: Seaview/ Putnam, 1983.

Fisher, William. *The Invisible Empire: A Bibliography of the Ku Klux Klan.* Metuchen, NJ: Scarecrow Press, 1980.

Fleming, Walter. "A Ku Klux document." *Mississippi Valley Historical Review* 1 (March 1915): 575–578.

_____. "The Ku Klux testimony relating to Alabama." *Gulf State Historical Magazine* 2 (Nov. 1903): 155–160.

_____. "Prescript of the Ku Klux Klan." *Publications of the Southern History Association* 7 (Sept. 1903): 327–348.

"A flogging for the Klan." *Time* 60 (11 Aug. 1952): 21.

"Florida is being lobbied for anti–Klan legislation." *SCLC Magazine* 10 (March/April 1981): 51.

"Florida panels approve unmasking Klan bill." *Jet* 60 (21 May 1981): 19.

Flowers, Richmond. *Preliminary Results of Investigation: United Klans of America, Incorporated, Knights of the Ku Klux Klan and Other Klan Organizations.* Montgomery, AL: Attorney General's Office, 1965.

Floyd, Nicholas. *Thorns in the Flesh. A Voice of Vindication from the South in Answer to "A Fool's Errand" and Other Slanders.* Philadelphia: Hubbard Brothers, 1884.

Flynn, Kevin, and Gary Gerhardt. *The Silent Brotherhood: Inside America's Racist Underground.* New York: Free Press, 1989.

Flynn, Laurie, and Paul Greenglass. "The Klan's latest method of propagating its gospel—TV." *Listener* 105 (16 April 1981): 497.

Foley, Albert. "KKK in Mobile, Ala." *America* 96 (8 Dec. 1956): 298–299.

Footlick, Jerrold, and Anthony Marro. "G-men and Klansmen." *Newsweek* 86 (25 Aug. 1975): 74–75.

"For and against the Ku Klux Klan." *Literary Digest* 70 (28 Sept. 1921): 34, 36, 38, 40.

Forster, Arnold. *A Measure of Freedom.* Garden City, NY: Doubleday, 1950.

Forster, Arnold, and Benjamin Epstein. *Danger*

on the Right: The Attitudes, Personnel and Influence of the Radical Right and Extreme Conservatives. New York: Random House, 1964.

_____. *The New Anti-Semitism.* New York: McGraw-Hill, 1974.

_____. *Report on the Ku Klux Klan.* New York: ADL, 1966.

_____. *The Troublemakers.* Garden City, NY: Doubleday, 1952.

"The four Klansmen." *Newsweek* 64 (17 Aug. 1964): 29–30.

Frady, Marshall. *Wallace.* New York: Random House, 1996.

Frank, Glenn. "Christianity and racialism." *Century* 109 (Dec. 1924): 279.

Franklin, John. "'The Birth of a Nation'—Propaganda as history." *Massachusetts Review* 30 (1979): 433.

_____. *Reconstruction: After the Civil War.* Chicago: University of Chicago Press, 1961.

Frederickson, Kari. *The Ku Klux Klan of the 1920s.* Armonk, NY: M.E. Sharpe, 2002.

"From the kreed of klanishness." *World Tomorrow* 7 (March 1924): 76–77.

Frost, Stanley. "Behind the white hoods: The regeneration of Oklahoma." *Outlook* 135 (21 Nov. 1923): 492–494.

_____. *The Challenge of the Klan.* Indianapolis: Bobbs-Merrill, 1924.

_____. "The Klan, the king, and a revolution: Regeneration in Oklahoma." *Outlook* 135 (28 Nov. 1923): 530–531.

_____. "Klan restates its case." *Outlook* 138 (15 Oct. 1924): 244–245.

_____. "The Klan shows its hand in Indiana." *Outlook* 137 (4 June 1924): 187–190.

_____. "Klan's 1/2 of 1 percent victory." *Outlook* 137 (9 July 1924): 384–387.

_____. "Masked politics of the Klan." *World's Work* 55 (Feb. 1928): 399, 407.

_____. "Night-riding reformers: The regeneration of Oklahoma." *Outlook* 135 (14 Nov. 1923): 438–440.

_____. "The Oklahoma regicides act." *Outlook* 135 (7 Nov. 1923): 395–396.

_____. "When the Klan rules." *Outlook* 135 (19 Dec. 1923): 674–676, 716–718; 136 (27 Feb. 1924): 20–24, 64–66, 100–103, 144–147, 183–186, 217–219, 261–264, 308–311, 350–353.

Fry, Gladys-Marie. *Night Riders in Black Folk History.* Knoxville: University of Tennessee Press, 1975.

Fry, Henry. *The Modern Ku Klux Klan.* Boston: Small, Maynard & Co., 1922.

Fuller, Edgar. *Maelstrom; The Visible of the Invisible Empire: A True History of the Ku Klux Klan.* Denver: Maelstrom Publishing, 1925.

Furness, Jim. *Tennessee's Klan Kleagle Only 22, but Has He Murder Plan?* Atlanta: Southern Regional Council, 1946.

Gallagher, Eugene. "God and country: Revolution as religious imperative on the radical right." *Terrorism and Political Violence* 9 (Autumn 1997): 63–79.

Gallman, Vanessa. "The continuing saga of the KKK." *Southern Changes* 2 (Sept. 1979): 18–21.

_____. "1979–1980: Klan confrontations." *Southern Exposure* 8 (Summer 1980): 76–78.

"Gambling on HUAC." *Commonweal* 82 (16 April 1965): 101.

Gannon, William. *The G.A.R. vs. the Ku Klux.* Boston: W.F. Brown, 1872.

Gardner, Virginia. "Fellow-travelers of the Klan." *New Masses* 54 (25 June 1946): 20–21.

_____. "Klansmen crusade for Dewey." *New Masses* 53 (31 Oct. 1944): 3–8, 16.

Garner, James. *Reconstruction in Mississippi.* New York: Macmillan, 1901.

Garrow, David. *Bearing the Cross: Martin Luther King, Jr., and the Southern Christian Leadership Conference.* New York: Morrow, 1986.

_____. *Protest at Selma: Martin Luther King, Jr., and the Voting Rights Act of 1965.* New Haven, CT: Yale University Press, 1978.

Garson, Robert. "Political fundamentalism and popular democracy in the 1920s." *South Atlantic Quarterly* 76 (Spring 1977): 219–233.

Gatewood, William Jr. "Politics and piety in North Carolina: The fundamentalist crusade at high tide, 1925–1927." *North Carolina Historical Review* 42 (July 1965): 275–290.

Gerlach, Larry. *Blazing Crosses in Zion: The Ku Klux Klan in Utah.* Logan, UT: Utah State University Press, 1982.

Gibbs, C.R. "How the Ku Klux Klan changes with the times." *Sepia* 29 (June 1980): 24–25.

Gibson, James. *Warrior Dreams: Paramilitary Culture and Manhood in Post-Vietnam America.* New York: Hill & Wang, 1994.

Gillette, Paul, and Eugene Tillinger. *Inside Ku Klux Klan.* New York: Pyramid Books, 1965.

Ginzburg, Ralph. *100 Years of Lynchings.* New York: Lancer, 1962.

"'God don't like ugly': The Klan rises in the new South." *Encore* 8 (15 Oct. 1979): 12–16.

Gohdges, Clarence. "The Ku Klux Klan and the classics." *Georgia Review* 7 (Spring 1953): 18–24.

Gohman, Mary. *Political Nativism in Tennessee to 1860.* Washington, DC: Catholic University of America, 1938.

Goldenweiser, Alexander. "Prehistoric KKK." *World Tomorrow* 7 (March 1924): 81–82.

Goldberg, Robert. "Beneath the hood and robe: A socioeconomic analysis of Ku Klux Klan membership in Denver, Colorado, 1921–1925." *Western Historical Quarterly* 11 (April 1980): 181–198.

_____. *Enemies Within: The Culture of Conspiracy in Modern America.* New Haven, CT: Yale University Press, 2001.

_____. *Hooded Empire: The Ku Klux Klan in Colorado.* Urbana, IL: University of Chicago Press, 1981.

_____. "The Ku Klux Klan in Madison, 1922–1927." *Wisconsin Magazine of History* 58 (Autumn 1974): 31, 44.

Goldenweiser, Alexander. "Prehistoric KKK." *World Tomorrow* 7 (March 1924): 81–82.

Goodman, Walter. *The Committee: The Extraordinary Career of the House Committee on Un-American Activities.* New York: Farrar, Straus and Giroux, 1968.

Goodwyn, Larry. "Anarchy in St. Augustine." *Harper's Magazine* 230 (Jan. 1965): 74–81.

Goodwyn, Lawrence. *The Populist Movement: A Short History of the Agrarian Revolt in America.* Oxford: Oxford University Press, 1978.

"GOP senator speaks out against ignoring the Klan." *Jet* 60 (23 July 1981): 7.

Gordon, John. *Unmasked.* Brooklyn, NY: The Author, 1924.

"Grand drag: Investigation by House Committee on Un-American Activities." *Reporter* 33 (18 Nov. 1965): 10, 12, 14.

"The Grand Dragon runs for Congress." *Present Tense* 8 (Summer 1981): 25–30.

Grant, George. "Garveyism and the Ku Klux Klan." *Messenger* 5 (Oct. 1923): 835–836, 842.

Great Ku Klux Trials: Official Report of the Proceedings Before the U.S. Circuit Court, November Term, 1871. Columbia, SC: The Columbia Union, 1872.

Green, John. *Recollections of the Inhabitants, Localities, Superstitions and Ku Klux Outrages of the Carolinas, by a "Carpet-Bagger" Who Was Born and Lived There.* Cleveland: The Author, 1880.

Greene, Ward. "Notes for a history of the Klan." *American Mercury* 5 (June 1925): 240–243.

Gregory, Dick. "And I ain't just whistlin' Dixie." *Ebony* 26 (Aug. 1971): 149–150.

Greuning, Martha. *Reconstruction and the Ku Klux Klan in North Carolina.* NY: NAACP, n.d.

Griffith, Charles, and Donald Stewart. "Has a court of equity power to enjoin parading by the Ku Klux Klan in mask?" *Central Law Journal* 96 (20 Nov. 1923): 384–393.

Grimshaw, Allen. *Racial Violence in the United States.* Chicago: Aldine, 1970.

Grizzard, Vernon. "Fraternity and brotherhood; Police and the Klan." *Kudzu* 3 (Sept. 1970): 8–9.

Grossup, Beau. *The Newest Explosions of Terrorism.* Far Hills, NJ: New Horizons Press, 1997.

"Gun play and sudden death in Herrin." *Literary Digest* 86 (21 Feb. 1925): 34, 36, 38, 40.

"Gunfire in Greensboro." *America* 141 (17 Nov. 1979): 292–310.

Haas, Ben. *KKK.* San Diego: Regency Books, 1963.

Hadden, Sally. *Slave Patrols: Law and Violence in Virginia and the Carolinas.* Cambridge, MA: Harvard University Press, 2001.

Hall, Grover. "We southerners." *Scribner's Magazine* 83 (Jan. 1928): 82–88.

"Halt Klan probe!" *Messenger* 3 (Nov. 1921): 273.

Hamilton, Virginia. *Hugo Black: The Alabama Years.* Baton Rouge: Louisiana University Press, 1972.

Harkey, Ira. *The Smell of Burning Crosses: An Autobiography of a Mississippi Newspaperman.* Jacksonville, IL: Harris-Wolfe & Co., 1967.

Harlow, Victor. "The achievement of the Klan." *Harlow's Weekly* 23 (19 June 1924): 1.

_____. "A new place in the Klan." *Harlow's Weekly* 23 (6 Dec. 1924): 1.

Harris, Abraham. "The Klan on trial." *New Republic* 35 (13 June 1923): 67–69.

Harris, Ronald, and D. Michael Cheers. "Ku Klux Klan: Robed racists are active from coast to coast." *Ebony* 34 (Oct. 1979): 164–165.

Harrison, Morton. "Gentlemen from Indiana." *Atlantic Monthly* 141 (May 1928): 676–686.

Harsch, Ernie. "Klansmen arrested in Michigan bombing." *Militant* 35 (24 Sept. 1971): 14.

Hartt, Rollin. "The new Negro." *Independent* 105 (15 Jan. 1921): 59–60.

Haskell, H.J. "Martial law in Oklahoma." *Outlook* 135 (26 Sept. 1923): 133.

Haynes, George, and Horace Wolff. "How shall we meet the Klan?" *World Tomorrow* 7 (March 1924): 85–86.

"Heap bad Kluxers armed with gun. Indian angry, paleface run." *Ebony* 13 (April 1958): 25–26, 28.

Hendrickson, Paul. *Sons of Mississippi: A Story of Race and Its Legacy.* New York: Alfred A. Knopf, 2003.

Herring, Hubert. "Ku Klux to the rescue." *New Republic* 34 (23 May 1923): 341–342.

Herring, Mary. "The why of the Ku Klux." *New Republic* 33 (7 Feb. 1923): 289.

Herzog, Frederick. "Was justice done in Greensboro?" *Christian Century* 97 (17 Dec. 1980): 1236–1237.

Higham, Charles. *American Swastika.* Garden City, NY: Doubleday, 1985.

Higham, John. *Strangers in Our Land: Patterns of American Nativism, 1860–1925.* New Brunswick, NJ: Rutgers University Press, 1955.

Hirsch, James. *Riot and Remembrance: The Tulsa Race War and Its Legacy.* Boston: Houghton Mifflin, 2002.

"The history of the Ku Klux Klan: Rule by terror." *American History Illustrated* 14 (Jan. 1980): 8–15.

Hockenos, Paul. *Free to Hate: The Rise of the Right in Post-Communist Eastern Europe.* New York: Routledge, 1993.

Hodes, Martha. *White Woman, Black Man: Illicit Sex in the 19th-Century South.* New Haven, CT: Yale University Press, 1997.

Hodsden, Harry. *Stephenson Was Framed in a Political Conspiracy.* La Porte, IN: La Porte Press, 1936.

Hoffman, Edwin. "The genesis of the modern movement for equal rights in South Carolina, 1930–1939." *Journal of Negro History* 44 (Oct. 1959): 346–369.

Hofstadter, Richard, and Michael Wallace (eds.). *American Violence: A Documentary History.* New York: Vintage, 1970.

"Hold everything." *Time* 54 (25 July 1949): 12.

Holsinger, M. Paul. "Oregon school controversy, 1922–25." *Pacific Historical Review* 37 (Aug. 1968): 327–341.

"Hooded horsemen gallop out of the past in a sudden revival of the KKK." *Life* 58 (23 April 1965): 28–35.

"The hooded knights revive rule by terror in the Twenties." *American History Illustrated* 14 (Feb. 1980): 28–36.

"Hoods banned in W. Va. city to restrain KKK." *Jet* 59 25 Sept. 1980): 5.

"Hoods down in Claxton." *Newsweek* 35 (17 April 1950): 67.

"Hoods off the Klan." *Economist* 217 (23 Oct. 1965): 386–387.

"Hoover hid KKK's role in Alabama church bombing." *Jet* 57 (13 March 1980): 7.

Horn, Stanley. *Invisible Empire: The Story of the Ku Klux Klan, 1866–1871.* Boston: Houghton Mifflin, 1939.

Horowitz, David (ed.). *Inside the Klavern: The Secret History of the Ku Klux Klan in the 1920s.* Carbondale, IL: Southern Illinois University Press, 1999.

Horrible Disclosures: A Full and Authentic Expose of the Ku Klux Klan, from Original Documents of the Order, and Other Official Sources. Cincinnati: Padrick & Co., 1868.

Hoskins, Kelly. *Vigilantes of Christendom: The Story of the Phineas Priesthood.* Lynchburg, VA: Virginia Publishing Co., 1990.

"Houston Socialist candidate debates Klan leader." *Militant* 35 (18 June 1971): 12–14.

"How 'Al' Smith fared in Mississippi." *Nation* 125 (14 Sept. 1927): 244–245.

Howe, Elizabeth. "A Ku Klux uniform." *Buffalo Historical Society Publications* 25 (1921): 9–41.

"HUAC versus the Klan." *Reporter* 32 (22 April 1965): 9–10.

Huff, Theodore. *A Short Analysis of D.W. Griffith's The Birth of a Nation.* New York: Museum of Modern Art, Film Library, 1961.

Hughes, Llewellyn. *In Defense of the Klan.* New York: The Author, 1924.

Huie, William. "Murder: The Klan on trial." *Saturday Evening Post* 238 (19 June 1965): 86–89.

_____. *Three Lives for Mississippi.* New York: WCC Books, 1965.

Hull, Robert. "The Klan aftermath in Indiana." *America* 38 (15 Oct. 1927): 8.

"If ever a devil..." *Time* 86 (5 Nov. 1965): 109–110.

Illinois General Assembly, Legislative Investigating Commission. *Ku Klux Klan: A Report to the Illinois General Assembly.* Chicago: The Commission, 1976.

"The imperial emperor of the KKK meets the press." *American Mercury* 69 (Nov. 1949): 529–538.

"Imperial lawlessness." *Outlook* 129 (14 Sept. 1921): 46.

"Imperial wizard and his Klan." *Literary Digest* 68 (5 Feb. 1921): 40–46.

"Indians back at peace and the Klan at bay." *Life* 44 (3 Feb. 1958): 36.

"Indians rout the Klan." *Commonweal* 67 (31 Jan. 1958): 446.

Ingalls, Robert. *Hoods.* New York: Putnam, 1979.

_____. "1935: The murder of Joseph Shoemaker." *Southern Exposure* 8 (Summer 1980): 64–68.

"Initiating a Negro into the Ku Klux Klan." *Messenger* 5 (Jan. 1923): 562–563.

"Interesting facts about the Ku Klux Klan." *Messenger* 3 (March 1921): 194–195.

"Intolerance in Oregon." *Survey* 49 (15 Oct. 1922): 76–77.

"Investigating the Ku Klux Klan." *Crisis* 72 (May 1965): 279–280.

"Invisible Empire in the spotlight." *Current Opinion* 71 (Nov. 1921): 561–564.

"Invisible government." *Outlook* 132 (13 Dec. 1922): 643.

Irwin, Theodore. "The Klan kicks up again." *American Mercury* 50 (Aug. 1940): 470–476.

"Is the Ku Klux Klan returning?" *Messenger* 4 (Feb. 1922): 356–357.

"Is the Ku Klux Klan un-American?" *Forum* 75 (Feb. 1926): 305–308.

"It sure was pretty." *Time* 54 (7 Nov. 1949): 24.

"Jack, the Klan-fighter in Oklahoma." *Literary Digest* 79 (20 Oct. 1923): 38, 40, 42, 44.

Jackson, Charles. "William J. Simmons: A career in Ku Kluxism." *Georgia Historical Quarterly* 50 (Dec. 1966): 351–365.

Jackson, Kenneth. *The Ku Klux Klan in the City, 1915–1930.* New York: Oxford University Press, 1967.

Jarvis, Mary. "The conditions that led to the Ku Klux Klan." *North Carolina Booklet* 1 (10 April 1902): 3–24.

_____. "The Ku Klux Klans." *North Carolina Booklet* 2 (10 May 1902): 3–26.

Jaworski, Leon. "Knights of the Invisible Empire." *Crisis* 88 (July 1981): 274–276.

Jeansonne, Glen. *Gerald L.K. Smith: Minister of Hate.* New Haven, CT: Yale University Press, 1988.

Jenkins, Philip. "Home-grown terror." *American Heritage* 46 (Sept. 1955): 38–46.

_____. *Hoods and Shirts: The Extreme Right in Pennsylvania, 1925–1950.* Chapel Hill, NC: University of North Carolina Press, 1997.

Jenkins, Ray. "Again, the Klan: Old sheets, new victims." *Reporter* 6 (4 March 1952): 29–31.

Jenkins, William. "The Ku Klux Klan in Youngstown, Ohio: Moral reform in the Twenties." *Historian* (Nov. 1978): 76–93.

_____. *Steel Valley Klan: The Ku Klux Klan in Ohio's Mahoning Valley.* Kent, OH: Kent State University Press, 1990.

Jenness, Linda. "Not in the name of feminism." *Militant* 39 (27 June 1975): 11.

"'Jesus no!'" *Newsweek* 64 (21 Dec. 1964): 21–22.

Johnsen, Julia. *Ku Klux Klan.* New York: H.W. Wilson, 1923.

Johnson, George. *Architects of Fear: Conspiracy Theories and Paranoia in American Politics.* Los Angeles: Jeremy P. Thacher, 1983.

Johnson, Gerald. "The Ku-Kluxer." *American Mercury* 1 (Feb. 1924): 207–211.

Johnson, Guy. "The race philosophy of the Ku Klux Klan." *Opportunity* 1 (Sept. 1923): 268–270.

_____. "A sociological interpretation of the new Ku Klux movement." *Social Forces* 1 (March 1923): 440–444.

Johnson, Tom. "Dixie Jew." *New Masses* 12 (24 July 1934): 21–22.

"Joke that became a terror." *Illustrated World* 33 (March 1920): 110.

Jones, Lila. "The Ku Klux Klan in eastern Kansas during the 1920s." *Emporia State Research Studies* 23 (Winter 1975): 5–41.

Jones, Paul. "The Ku Klux goes calling." *New Republic* 85 (8 Jan. 1936): 251.

_____. "What brotherhood demands." *World Tomorrow* 7 (March 1924): 82–8/3.

Jones, Winfield. *Knights of the Ku Klux Klan.* New York: Tocsin Publishers, 1941.

_____. *The Story of the Ku Klux Klan.* Washington, DC: American Newspaper Syndicate, 1921.

Joshi, S.T. (ed.). *Documents of American Prejudice: An Anthology of Writings on Race from Thomas Jefferson to David Duke.* New York: Basic Books, 1999.

"Judge refuses to dismiss federal tort claim." *Criminal Justice Issues* 6 (June 1981): 8–9.

"Judicial spanking for the Klan." *Literary Digest* 97 (28 April 1928): 8–9.

"'Justice' by violence." *World Tomorrow* 7 (March 1924): 78–79.

Kaplan, Jeffrey. *Encyclopedia of White Power.* Walnut Creek, CA: AltaMira Press, 2000.

_____. "Leaderless resistance." *Terrorism and Political Violence* 9 (Autumn 1997): 80–95.

"Kashing in." *Newsweek* 66 (1 Nov. 1965): 34–35.

Katagiri, Yasuhiro. *The Mississippi State Sovereignty Commission: Civil Rights and States' Rights.* Jackson: University Press of Mississippi, 2001.

Keith, Adam. "KKK ... Klose Kall in Kolorado." *Denver* 1 (Aug. 1965): 24–27.

Kennedy, Stetson. *I Rode with the Ku Klux Klan.* London: Arco Publishers, 1954.

_____. *Jim Crow Guide: The Way It Was.* Boca Raton: Florida Atlantic University Press, 1990.

_____. "KKK vs. labor: A sampler." *Southern Exposure* 8 (Summer 1980): 61.

_____. *The Klan Unmasked.* Boca Raton: Florida Atlantic University Press, 1990.

_____. "The Ku Klux Klan." *New Republic* 114 (1 July 1946): 928–930.

_____. "The Ku Klux Klan in America." *New Republic* 114 (1 July 1946): 928–930.

_____. "Murder without indictment." *Nation* 173 (24 Nov. 1951): 444–446.

_____. *Southern Exposure.* Garden City, NY: Doubleday, 1946.

_____. "Who cares who killed Harry T. Moore?" *Crisis* 89 (May 1982): 18–21.

Kent, Frank. "Ku Klux Klan in America." *Spectator* 130 (17 Feb. 1923): 279–280.

Kent, Grady. *Flogged by the Ku Klux Klan.* Cleveland, TN: White Wing, 1942.

Keresey, John. "How shall we meet the Klan?" *World Tomorrow* 7 (March 1924): 86.

Key, Valdimer. *Southern Politics in State and Nation.* New York: Random House, 1949.

"Kidnapped by the Klan." *Newsweek* 29 (26 May 1952): 30.

"Killed by Kluxers." *Newsweek* 35 (13 March 1950): 22.

King, Martin Luther Jr. *Stride Toward Freedom.* New York: Ballentine, 1958.

"KKK." *Indiana State Journal.* 74th session. (1925): 132, 792.

"KKK." *Messenger* 5 (Feb. 1923): 594.

"The KKK." *New Republic* 28 (21 Sept. 1921): 88–89.

"KKK." *Opportunity* 2 (June 1924): 191.

"The KKK candidate for Congress." *Newsweek* 95 (16 June 1980): 11.

"KKK chief tells group to stop run-ins with police." *Jet* 60 (9 July 1981):6.

"KKK crusades in Selma, as blacks shout insults." *Jet* 56 (3 May 1979): 5.

"KKK feeding off hard times, says NAACP head." *Jet* 56 (13 Sept. 1979): 7.

"KKK: Festering sore in Chicago." *Sepia* 17 (June 1963): 60–65.

"The KKK goes military." *Newsweek* 96 (6 Oct. 1980): 52.

"KKK grows in W. Va. as job problems worsen." *Jet* 57 (6 March 1980): 5.

"KKK in Oregon." *Nation* 113 (1921): 233–234.

"KKK in Oregon." *Nation* 116 (1922): 6, 325.

"KKK in Oregon." *Survey* 49 (1922): 76–77.

"KKK in Pennsylvania." *Literary Digest* 68 (5 Feb. 1921): 42, 45, 46.

"KKK in Pennsylvania." *Nation* 113 (1922): 285–286.

"KKK looks to Pitt steel mills for new membership." *Jet* 57 (28 Feb. 1980): 7.

"KKK offers jobs to all in sheet-sewing drive." *Jet* 58 (19 June 1980): 5.

"KKK philosophy." *Opportunity* 2 (Jan. 1924): 30.

"KKK plot to bomb NAACP chapter foiled." *Jet* 60 (11 June 1981): 8.

"KKK resurgence." *Crisis* 88 (June 1981): 252.

"KKK wants to parade in Detroit." *Jet* 58 (26 June 1980): 53.

"KKK wizard was FBI informant, paper says." *Jet* 61 (24 Sept. 1981): 10.

"Klan and the bottle." *Nation* 117 (21 Nov. 1923): 570–572.

"The Klan and the candidates." *Literary Digest* 82 (6 Sept. 1924): 10–11.

"The Klan and the Democrats." *Literary Digest* 81 (14 June 1924): 12–13.

"The Klan as a national problem." *Literary Digest* 75 (2 Dec. 1922): 12–13.

"Klan as an issue." *Outlook* 138 (3 Sept. 1924): 5–6.

"Klan as the victim of mob violence." *Literary Digest* 78 (8 Sept. 1923): 12–13.

"Klan at bay." *Current Opinion* 77 (Oct. 1924): 419–422.

"The Klan 'backs' a college." *Literary Digest* 78 (15 Sept. 1923): 43–46.

"Klan celebrated Mother's Day." *Christian Century* 42 (21 May 1925): 677–681.

"Klan credited in theft of Kunta Kinte memorial." *Jet* 61 (15 Oct. 1981): 7.

"The Klan defies a state." *Literary Digest* 77 (9 June 1923): 12–13.

"Klan dissolves but subject to revival." *Pulse* 2 (July 1944): 14.

"The Klan enters the campaign." *Literary Digest* 82 (12 July 1924): 9–10.

"Klan fight causes statewide martial law." *Harlow's Weekly* 22 (22 Sept. 1923): 8–9.

"Klan for Negroes?" *Newsweek* 42 (26 Oct. 1953): 7.

"Klan goes in for face-lifting." *Literary Digest* 96 (10 March 1928): 15–16.

"The Klan in Oklahoma attempts to come back." *Harlow's Weekly* 30 (24 Sept. 1931): 4–7.

"The Klan in defeat and retreat." *Independent* 113 (30 Aug. 1924): 114–115.

"Klan in Florida." *New Republic* 91 (9 June 1937): 118.

"The Klan in Oklahoma attempts to come back." *Harlow's Weekly* 30 (24 Sept. 1931): 4–7.

"Klan in politics: Force or farce?" *U.S. News & World Report* 89 (15 Sept. 1980): 13.

"The Klan in retreat and defeat." *Independent* 113 (30 Aug. 1924): 114–115.

"The Klan in Texas and Maine." *Messenger* 6 (Oct. 1924): 312.

"Klan is dead; Long live the—?" *Christian Century* 45 (8 March 1928): 306–307.

"Klan is guilty." *Newsweek* 39 (26 May 1952): 31.

"Klan is in trouble." *Life* 32 (31 March 1952): 44–46.

"Klan is major topic for Black History Month." *Jet* 59 (26 Feb. 1981): 30.

"Klan is outlawed in Kentucky." *Christian Century* 63 (25 Sept. 1946): 114–116.

"The Klan issue." *Nation* 231 (15 Sept. 1980): 110.

"Klan kash & karry: 'No comment.'" *Southern Exposure* 8 (Summer 1980): 54–55.

"Klan knights put out of church." *Literary Digest* 77 (5 May 1923): 37–38.

"Klan kurbed in South Carolina." *Newsweek* 35 (29 Jan. 1940): 15.

"Klan leader fined for inciting riot in La." *Jet* 57 (3 Jan. 1980): 8.

"Klan leader, followers arrested in Tennessee,

more face charges in Texas." *Jet* 60 (21 May 1981): 8.

"Klan leaders ordered to reveal their identities." *Jet* 62 (8 March 1982): 5.

"Klan members sued for personal injuries." *Southern Exposure* 10 (Jan./Feb. 1982): 6.

"Klan on the pan." *Senior Scholastic* 86 (15 April 1965): 27.

"Klan ordered to pay five black women hurt in shooting spree $535,000." *Jet* 62 (22 March 1982): 28.

"The Klan parade." *Opportunity* 3 (Sept. 1925): 279–280.

"Klan rears its head again." *Literary Digest* 118 (21 July 1934): 19.

"Klan recruitment efforts increase." *Interracial Books for Children* 12 (1981): 32.

"Klan resurgence a big threat: union official." *Jet* 59 (19 Feb. 1981): 29.

"Klan revives." *Commonweal* 65 (12 Oct. 1956): 38.

"Klan rule." *Crisis* 35 (Jan. 1928): 12–13.

"Klan, SCLC promise summer will be 'hot' and long in the South." *Jet* 56 (28 June 1979): 5.

"A Klan senator from Indiana." *Literary Digest* 87 (14 Nov. 1925): 16–17.

"Klan sets up branches on Air Force bases." *Jet* 60 (9 July 1981): 38.

"The Klan sheds its hood." *New Republic* 45 (10 Feb 1926): 310–311.

"A Klan shock in Indiana." *Literary Digest* 81 (24 May 1924): 14.

"Klan terrorism will escalate by spring." *Jet* 60 (26 March 1981): 38.

"Klan victories and defeats." *Literary Digest* 83 (22 Nov. 1924): 16.

"Klan victories in Oregon and Texas." *Literary Digest* 75 (25 Nov. 1922): 12–13.

"Klan violence becomes nat'l. problem: Vivian." *Jet* 58 (24 April 1980): 6.

"The Klan walks in Washington." *Literary Digest* 86 (22 Aug. 1925): 7–8.

"Klan writes a violent new chapter." *U.S. News & World Report* 87 (19 Nov. 1979): 59.

"The Klan—ye shall have always." *Pulse* 5 (Nov. 1947): 8.

"The Klandidate." *Nation* 231 (5 July 1980): 4–5.

"Klans and councils." *New Republic* 137 (23 Sept. 1957): 6.

"The Klan's archnemesis speaks: 'Kind treatments whip a devil.'" *Encore* 8 (15 Oct. 1979): 4–15.

"Klan's challenge and the reply." *Literary Digest* 79 (17 Nov. 1923): 32–33.

"Klan's new krisis." *Christianity Today* 10 (19 Nov. 1965): 42–43.

"The Klan's political role." *Literary Digest* 79 (24 Nov. 1923): 13–14.

"Klansman admits theft." *Messenger* 6 (Dec. 1924): 373.

"Klansman Black?" *Commonweal* 26 (24 Sept. 1937): 1, 3.

"Klansman wins Calif. congressional primary." *Jet* 58 (26 June 1980): 5.

"The Klansmen." *Newsweek* 84 (16 Dec. 1974): 16–16A.

"Klansmen kluxed by the Klux: Just kluxin' around." *Messenger* 5 (Dec. 1923): 920.

"Klansmen must surrender jobs." *Messenger* 4 (April 1922): 387–388.

Kleber, Louis. "The Ku Klux Klan." *History Today* 21 (Aug. 1971): 567–574.

"Klobbered in Karolina." *Newsweek* 40 (11 Aug. 1952): 24.

Kluger, Richard. *Simple Justice: The History of Brown v. Board of Education and Black America's Struggle for Equality.* New York: Alfred A. Knopf, 1976.

"Kluxers on the prowl." *Newsweek* 34 (11 July 1949): 21–22.

Knebel, Fletcher, and Clark Mollenhoff. "Eight Klans bring new terror to the South." *Look* 21 (30 April 1957): 59–60.

"Konstitutional rites." *Newsweek* 66 (8 Nov. 1965): 34.

"The Koo Koo Klan again." *Messenger* 4 Sept. 1922): 489–490.

Kornweibel, Theodore Jr. *Seeing Red: Federal Campaigns Against Black Militancy, 1919–1925.* Bloomington, IN: Indiana University Press, 1998.

Kroll, Eric. "A documentary photographer takes a ride with the Ku Klux Klan." *American Photographer* 4 (April 1980): 28–30.

"Ku Klux and crime." *New Republic* 33 (17 Jan. 1923): 189–190.

"The Ku Klux are riding again." *Crisis* 17 (March 1919): 229–231.

"Ku Klux condemned by the religions press." *Literary Digest* 71 (1 Oct. 1921): 30–31.

"The Ku Klux in politics." *Literary Digest* 73 (10 June 1922): 15.

"Ku Klux Kanada." *MacLeans* 90 (4 April 1977): 70–71.

"Ku Klux Klan." *American Federationist* 30 (Nov. 1923): 919.

"Ku Klux Klan." *Catholic World* 116 (Jan. 1923): 433–434.

"Ku Klux Klan." *Century* 28 (Aug. 1884): 948–950.

"The Ku Klux Klan." *Messenger* 5 (Jan. 1923): 564.

"The Ku Klux Klan." *Messenger* 8 (Nov. 1926): 345.

"Ku Klux Klan." *Nation* 162 (8 June 1946): 678.

"Ku Klux Klan activities in Saskatchewan." *Queen's Quarterly* 35 (Autumn 1928): 592–602.

"The Ku Klux Klan again." *New Republic* 114 (10 June 1946): 822.

"Ku Klux Klan again." *Outlook* 129 (21 Sept. 1921): 79.

"The Ku Klux Klan and the election." *Christian Century* 41 (20 Nov. 1924): 1496–1497.

"The Ku Klux Klan and the next election." *World's Work* 46 (Oct. 1923): 573–575.

"Ku Klux Klan; Attempts to establish Ku Klux Klan in Canada." *Canadian Forum* 10 (April 1930): 233.

"Ku Klux Klan: Bigotry in the guise of politics." *Nation* 173 (4 Aug. 1951): 82.

"The Ku Klux Klan—how to fight it." *Messenger* 3 (Nov. 1921): 276–277.

"Ku Klux Klan in Germany." *Living Age* 327 (17 Oct. 1925): 128.

"Ku Klux Klan in Oklahoma." *Current Opinion* 75 (Nov. 1923): 523–524.

"Ku Klux Klan in politics." *Literary Digest* 73 (10 June 1922): 15.

"The Ku Klux Klan is riding again." *Crisis* 17 (March 1919): 229–231.

"Ku Klux Klan leaders well fitted to correct morals of communities." *Messenger* 3 (Oct. 1921): 261–262.

"Ku Klux Klan on the downgrade." *Christian Century* 40 (13 Sept. 1923): 1158–1160.

"Ku Klux Klan on the way back." *U.S. News & World Report* 57 (19 Oct. 1964): 51–52.

"Ku Klux Klan seizing the government." *Messenger* 4 (Dec. 1922): 537–538.

"Ku Klux Klan; symposium." *North American* 223 (March 1926): 33–63; 223 (June 1926): 268–309.

"Ku Klux Klan tokens." *Antiques Journal* 36 (Oct. 1981): 48.

"Ku Klux Klan: The violent history of a hooded society." *Senior Scholastic* 87 (2 Dec. 1965): 5–8.

"The Ku Klux Klan tries a comeback." *Life* 20 (27 May 1946): 42–44.

"Ku Klux Klan tries for a comeback." *U.S. News & World Report* 78 (23 June 1975): 32–34.

"The Ku Klux Klan unmasked." *Time* 11 (5 March 1928): 10–11.

The Ku Klux Klans. Raleigh, NC: Capital Printing, 1902.

"Ku Klux Klan's white knights." *Newsweek* 64 (21 Dec. 1964): 22–24.

"Ku Klux kourts." *Messenger* 6 (Dec. 1929): 373.

"The Ku Klux trial." *American Missionary Magazine* 16 (Feb. 1872): 39–40.

"The Ku Klux victory in Texas." *Literary Digest* 74 (5 Aug. 1922): 14–15.

"Ku Klux violence in Haywood County, Tennessee." *American Missionary Magazine* 13 (Feb. 1869): 40–42.

"Ku Klux violence to teachers in the South." *American Missionary Magazine* 18 (Sept. 1874): 208–209.

Langer, Elinor. "The American neo–Nazi movement today." *Nation* 251 (16–23 July 1992): 82–108.

Laqueur, Walter. *Black Hundred: The Rise of the Extreme Right in Russia.* New York: HarperPerennial, 1993.

"Law for others, not for the Ku Klux Klan?" *Outlook* 134 (9 June 1924): 79–80.

Lay, Shawn. *Hooded Knights on the Niagara: The Ku Klux Klan in Buffalo, New York.* New York: New York University Press, 1995.

_____ (ed.). *The Invisible Empire in the West: Toward a New Historical Appraisal of the Ku Klux Klan of the 1920s.* Urbana, IL: University of Illinois Press, 1992.

_____. *War, Revolution, and the Ku Klux Klan: A Study of Intolerance in a Border City.* El Paso: Texas Western Press, 1985.

Lee, Kendrick. "Ku Klux Klan." *Editorial Research Report* 2 (10 July 1946): 449–464.

Lee, Martin. *The Beast Reawakens: Fascism's Resurgence from Hitler's Spymasters to Today's Neo-Nazi Groups and Right-Wing Extremists.* Boston: Little, Brown, 1997.

Leland, John. *A Voice from South Carolina: Twelve Chapters Before Hampton, Two Chapters After Hampton, with a Journal of a Reputed Ku Klux, and an Appendix.* Charleston, SC: Walker, Evans & Cogswell, 1879.

Lester, John, and D.L. Wilson. *The Ku Klux Klan: Its Origin, Growth and Disbandment.* Nashville, TN: Wheeler, Osborn & Duckworth, 1884.

Leuchtenberg, William. "A klansman joins the court: The appointment of Hugo L. Black." *University of Chicago Law Review* 41 (1973): 121.

Levitas, Daniel. *The Terrorist Next Door: The Militia Movement and the Radical Right.* New York: Thomas Dunne, 2002.

Lewis, Anthony. *Portrait of a Decade.* New York: Bantam, 1965.

"A license to murder." *Ebony* 21 (Dec. 1965): 148–149.

Likens, William. *Patriotism Capitalized, or Religion Turned Into Gold.* Uniontown, PA: Watchman Publishing, 1925.

_____. *The Trail of the Serpent.* Uniontown, PA: Watchman Publishing, 1928.

Lincoln, C. Eric. *The Black Muslims in America.* Boston: Beacon, 1961.

Linder, John. "Minn. students picket speech by Klansman." *Militant* 38 (25 Oct. 1974): 23.

Lindsey, Ben. "The beast in new form." *New Republic* 41 (24 Dec. 1924): 121.

_____. "My fight with the Ku Klux Klan." *Survey Graphic* 54 (1 June 1925): 271–274.

Lipset, Seymour. "An anatomy of the Klan." *Commentary* 40 (Oct. 1965): 74–83.

Lipset, Seymour, and Earl Raab. *The Politics of Unreason: Right-Wing Extremism in America, 1790–1970.* New York: Harper & Row, 1970.

Lipstadt, Deborah. *Denying the Holocaust: The Growing Assault on Truth and Memory.* New York: Free Press, 1993.

"A litany of 'not guilty.'" *Time* 116 (1 Dec. 1980): 25–26.

Loftis, Randy. "Has the KKK duped the press?" *Civil Rights Quarterly Perspectives* 12 (Fall 1980-Winter 1981): 14–15.

Loggins, Kirk, and Susan Thomas. "The menace returns." *Southern Exposure* 8 (Summer 1980): 50–54.

"London's view of the Klan row." *Literary Digest* 77 (19 May 1923): 20.

"'Long, hot summer' flaring in the South?" *U.S. News & World Report* 86 (25 June 1979): 12.

"A long white summer for KKK kids." *Life* 2 (Aug. 1979): 108–109.

Loucks, Emerson. *The Ku Klux Klan in Pennsylvania: A Study in Nativism.* New York: Telegraph Press, 1936.

Lowe, David. *KKK: The Invisible Empire.* New York: W.W. Norton, 1967.

Lumpkin, Benjamin, and Thomas Malone. *Full Report of the Great Ku Klux Trial in the United States Circuit Court at Oxford, Miss.* Memphis: W.J. Mansford, 1871.

Lutholtz, M. William. *Grand Dragon: D.C. Stephenson and the Ku Klux Klan in Indiana.* West Lafayette, IN: Purdue University Press, 1991.

Lytle, Andrew. *Bedford Forrest and His Critter Company.* New York: McDowell, Obolensky, 1960.

"Ma Ferguson and the KKK." *New Statesman* 23 (4 Oct. 1924): 728–729.

MacKaye, Milton. "'The Birth of a Nation.'" *Scribner's Magazine* 102 (Nov. 1937): 44.

MacLean, Nancy. *Behind the Mask of Chivalry: The Making of the Second Ku Klux Klan.* New York: Oxford University Press, 1994.

Madigan, Tim. *The Burning: Massacre, Destruction, and the Tulsa Race Riot of 1921.* New York: Thomas Dunne, 2001.

Mahoney, William. *Some Ideals of the Ku Klux Klan.* Atlanta: Ku Klux Klan, n.d.

"Make cross-burning a felony: Baltimore group." *Jet* 58 (20 March 1980): 7.

"Malice toward some." *Newsweek* 67 (11 April 1966): 39–40.

March, William. "Greensboro rallies blast Klan,

recall civil rights anniversary." *National Catholic Reporter* 16 (15 Feb. 1980): 4–5.

"Mark of the beast: Special section on the Ku Klux Klan." *Southern Exposure* 8 (Summer 1980): 49–100.

Markmann, Charles. *The Noblest Cry: A History of the American Civil Liberties Union.* New York: St. Martin's Press, 1965.

Marriner, Gerald. "Klan politics in Colorado." *Journal of the West* 15 (Jan. 1976): 76–101.

Mars, Florence. *Witness in Philadelphia: A Mississippi WASP's Account of the 1964 Civil Rights Murders.* Baton Rouge: Louisiana State University Press, 1977.

Marsh, Charles. *Gods Long Summer: Stories of Faith and Civil Rights.* Princeton, NJ: Princeton University Press, 1997.

"Martial law in Oklahoma." *Outlook* 135 (26 Sept. 1923): 133–134.

Martin, Harold. "The truth about the Klan today." *Saturday Evening Post* 222 (22 Oct. 1949): 17–18, 122–126.

Martin, John. "Beauty and the beast: The downfall of D.C. Stephenson, Grand Dragon of the Indiana KKK." *Harper's* 189 (Sept. 1944): 319–329.

_____. *The Deep South Says "Never."* New York: Ballantine, 1957.

Martinez, Thomas, and John Guinther. *Brotherhood of Murder.* New York: McGraw-Hill, 1988.

Marx, Andrew, and Tom Tuthill. "1978: Mississippi organizes." *Southern Exposure* 8 (Summer 1980): 73–76.

"Masked floggers of Tulsa." *Literary Digest* 78 (22 Sept. 1923): 17–18.

Massengill, Reed. *Portrait of a Racist: The Real Life of Byron De La Beckwith.* New York: St. Martin's Griffin, 1996.

Mast, Blaine. *KKK, Friend or Foe: Which?* Pittsburgh: Herbick & Held, 1924.

May, Gary. *The Informant: The FBI, the Ku Klux Klan and the Murder of Viola Liuzzo.* New Haven, CT: Yale University Press, 2005.

Mazzulla, Fred, and Jo Mazzulla. "A Klan album." *Colorado Magazine* 42 (Spring 1965): 109–113.

McBee, William. *The Oklahoma Revolution.* Oklahoma City: Modern Publishers, 1956.

McClean, Phillip. "Klan reborn on Stone Mountain." *Christian Century* 63 (5 June 1946): 726.

_____. "Southern liberals oppose the Klan." *Christian Century* 63 (5 June 1946): 726.

McConville, Edward. "Portrait of a Klansman: The prophetic voice of C.P. Ellis." *Nation* 217 (15 Oct. 1973): 361–366.

McCord, William. *Mississippi: The Long, Hot Summer.* New York: W.W. Norton, 1965.

McCorvey, Thomas. "The Invisible Empire." *Alabama Historical Sketches.* Edited by George Johnson. Charlottesville, VA: University of Virginia Press, 1960.

McDonald, Marci. "The enemy within: The far right's racist war against society is opening new fronts across Canada." *Maclean's* 108 (8 May 1995): 34–40.

McGill, Ralph. *The South and the Southerner.* Boston: Little, Brown and Co., 1963.

McIlhany, William. *Klandestine: The Untold Story of Delmar Dennis and His Role in the FBI's War Against the Ku Klux Klan.* New York: Arlington House, 1975.

McIver, Stuart. "The murder of a scalawag." *American History Illustrated* 8 (April 1973): 12–18.

McLennan, Paul, Trisha McLennan, and David Chalmers. *Solidarity or Division: The True Story of the Ku Klux Klan vs. Organized Labor.* Atlanta: Center for Democratic Renewal, 1985.

McMillen, Neil. *The Citizens' Council: Organized Resistance to the Second Reconstruction, 1954–64.* Urbana, IL: University of Illinois Press, 1971.

McNeilly, J.S. "Enforcement Act of 1871 and Ku Klux Klan in Mississippi." *Mississippi Historical Society Publications* 9 (Nov. 1906): 107–171.

_____. "Reconstruction and the Ku Klux." *Confederate Veteran* 30 (March 1922) 96–97.

McWhiney, H. Grady, and Francis Simkins. "Ghostly legend of the Ku Klux Klan." *Negro Historical Bulletin* 14 (Feb. 1951): 109–112.

McWhorter, Diane. *Carry Me Home: Birmingham, Alabama: The Climactic Battle of the Civil Rights Revolution.* New York: Simon & Schuster, 2001.

McWilliams, Carey. "The Klan: Post war model." *Nation* 163 (14 Dec. 1946): 691–692.

_____. *Prejudice—Japanese Americans: Symbol of Racial Intolerance.* Boston: Little, Brown, 1944.

"Measure to keep KKK off school grounds passed." *Jet* 59 (20 Nov. 1980): 22.

Mecklin, John. *The Ku Klux Klan: A Study of the American Mind.* New York: Harcourt, Brace and Co., 1924.

_____. "Ku Klux Klan and the democratic tradition." *American Review* 2 (May 1924): 241–251.

_____. *The Ku Klux Klan in Pennsylvania.* New York: Telegraph Press, 1936.

Melching, Richard. "The activities of the Ku Klux Klan in Anaheim, California, 1923–1925." *Southern California Quarterly* 56 (Summer 1974): 175–196.

Mellett, Lowell. "Klan and church in Indiana." *Atlantic Monthly* 132 (Nov. 1923): 586–592.

Meltzer, Milton. *The Truth About the Ku Klux Klan.* New York: Franklin Watts, 1982.

"Membership in the American fascisti: disclaimed." *Messenger* 4 (1 Nov. 1922): 518–519.

Mendelsohn, Jack. *The Martyrs: Sixteen Who Gave Their Lives for Racial Justice.* New York: Harper & Row, 1966.

Meriweather, Elizabeth. *The Ku Klux Klan, or the Carpet-Bagger in New Orleans.* Memphis: Southern Baptist Publication Society, 1877.

Merkl, Peter, and Leonard Weinberg (eds.). *Encounters with the Contemporary Radical Right.* Boulder, CO: University of Colorado Press, 1993.

Merritt, Dixon. "Klan and anti-Klan in Indiana." *Outlook* 144 (8 Dec. 1926): 465–469.

_____. "Klan on parade." *Outlook* 140 (19 Aug. 1925): 553–554.

"Mer Rouge murders unpunished." *Literary Digest* 76 (31 March 1923): 10–11.

Merz, Charles. "The new Ku Klux Klan." *Independent* 118 (12 Feb. 1927): 179–180, 196.

Middlebrooks, A.E. "Alabama votes to unmask the Klan." *Christian Century* 66 (20 July 1949): 871.

Miller, Robert. "Note on the relationship between the Protestant churches and the revived Ku Klux Klan." *Journal of Southern History* 22 (Aug. 1956): 355–368.

_____. "The social attitudes of the American Methodists, 1919–1920." *Religion in Life* 28 (Spring 1958): 185–198.

Miller, Stuart. *The Unwelcome Immigrant.* Berkeley: University of California Press, 1969.

"Ministers denounce Georgia Klan." *Christian Century* 66 (5 Jan. 1949): 6.

"Ministers suspect racism after five churches burned." *Jet* 58 (29 May 1980): 8–9.

"Miss KKK." *Newsweek* 32 (20 Dec. 1948): 22.

"Mr. White challenges the Klan." *Outlook* 138 (1 Oct. 1923): 154.

Mitchell, Enoch. "The role of George Washington Gordon in the Ku Klux Klan." *West Tennessee Historical Society Papers* (1947): 73–80.

Mitchell, J. Paul. *Race Riots in Black and White.* Englewood Cliffs, NJ: Prentice-Hall, 1970.

Mitchell, Louis. "Klan today." *Crisis* 85 (Feb. 1978): 48–53, 56.

Mitchell, Robert. *The Nation's Peril. Twelve Years' Experience in the South. Then and Now. The Ku Klux Klan, a Complete Exposition of the Order; Its Purpose, Plans, Operations, Social and Political Significance; the Nation's Salvation.* New York: Friends of the Compiler, 1872.

"Mob violence and the Ku Klux Klan." *Messenger* 3 (Sept. 1921): 244–246.

Mockler, William. "Source of Ku Klux." *Names* 3 (March 1955): 14–18.

Moffat, John. *The Ku Klux Klan.* New York: Russell & Russell, 1963.

Monk, A.D. "Knights of the nightshirt organized in Canada." *Canadian Magazine* 66 (Oct. 1926): 31.

Montveal, Marion. *The Klan Inside Out.* Chicago: The Author, 1924.

Moore, Edmund. *A Catholic Runs for President.* New York: Ronald Press, 1956.

Moore, John. "Communists and fascists in a southern city: Atlanta, 1930." *South Atlantic Quarterly* 67 (Summer 1968): 437–454.

Moore, Leonard. *Citizen Klansmen: The Ku Klux Klan in Indiana, 1921–1928.* Chapel Hill, NC: University of North Carolina Press, 1997.

Moore, Samuel. "Consequences of the Klan." *Independent* 113 (20 Dec. 1924): 534–536.

_____. "How the kleagles collected the cash." *Independent* 113 (13 Dec. 1924): 517–519.

_____. "A Klan kingdom collapses." *Independent* 113 (6 Dec. 1924): 473–475.

"Moral lashes for Alabama floggers." *Literary Digest* 95 (17 Dec. 1927): 32.

Moseley, Clement. "Latent Klanism in Georgia, 1890–1915." *Georgia Historical Quarterly* 56 (Fall 1972): 365–386.

_____. "The political influence of the Ku Klux Klan in Georgia, 1915–1925." *Georgia Historical Quarterly* 57 (Summer 1973): 235–255.

Mugleston, William. "Julian Harris, the Georgia press, and the Ku Klux Klan." *Georgia Historical Quarterly* 59 (Fall 1975): 284–295.

"Murders of Mer Rouge." *Literary Digest* 76 (13 Jan. 1923): 10–12.

Murphy, Robert. "The south fights bombing." *Look* 23 (6 Jan. 1959): 13–17.

Murray, Robert. *Red Scare: A Study in National Hysteria.* Minneapolis: University of Minnesota Press, 1955.

Muse, Benjamin. *Ten Years of Prelude: The Story of Integration Since the Supreme Court's 1954 Decision.* New York: Viking Press, 1964.

"Mutine in the Invisible Empire." *Independent* 116 (16 Jan. 1959): 58–59.

Myers, Gustavus. *History of Bigotry in the United States.* New York: Random House, 1943.

Myers, William. "Know Nothing and Ku Klux Klan." *North American Review* 219 (Jan. 1924): 1, 7.

_____. "The Ku Klux Klan of today." *North American Review* 223 (June-Aug. 1926): 304–309.

NAACP. *M is for Mississippi and Murder.* New York: NAACP, 1956.

_____. *Thirty Years of Lynching in the United States.* New York: NAACP, 1919.

"The nation and the Klan." *Messenger* 6 (March 1924): 69–70.

"National affairs: Ku Klux Klan." *Time* 4 (18 Aug. 1924): 3–4.

"A national plot to kill blacks." *U.S. News & World Report* 87 (3 Nov. 1980): 7.

"Natives are restless." *Time* 71 (27 Jan. 1958): 20.

"NBA immediate past president drafts legislation to ban KKK violence." *National Bar Bulletin* 13 (Feb. 1981): 1.

"Negroes: Darrow vs. Klan." *Time* 9 (21 March 1927): 12.

"Negroes defeat Klan candidates in Chattanooga." *Messenger* 5 (June 1923): 733–734.

Neier, Aryeh. "Mississippi relives its '60s." *Nation* 227 (23 Sept. 1978): 265–267.

Nelson, Jack. *Terror in the Night: The Klan's Campaign Against the Jews.* Jackson: University Press of Mississippi, 1993.

Nelson, Llewellyn. "The KKK for boredom." *New Republic* 41 (14 Jan. 1925): 196–198.

Neuringer, Sheldon. "Governor Walton's war on the Ku Klux Klan: An episode in Oklahoma history, 1923 to 1924." *Chronicles of Oklahoma* 45 (Summer 1967): 153–179.

"The new crusaders." *Opportunity* 2 (Aug. 1924): 227–228.

"New furor over an old informant." *Time* 112 (24 July 1978): 17.

"'New' KKK drawing students: Schools must combat influence." *Vibration* 68 (July–Sept. 1981): 8.

"New Ku Klux Klan activity." *Scholastic Magazine* 36 (13 May 1940): 2.

"New York's anti–Klan outburst." *Literary Digest* 75 (23 Dec. 1922): 31–32.

"Newly resurgent Ku Klux Klan exploits racial tensions in American schools." *NEA Reporter* 20 (June 1981): 8–9.

Newton, Michael. *The FBI and the KKK: A Critical History.* Jefferson, NC: McFarland, 2006.

_____. *The Invisible Empire: The Ku Klux Klan in Florida.* Gainesville: University Press of Florida, 2001.

"Next step: Button-down robes." *Time* 83 (1 May 1964): 23–24.

Nicholson, Meredith. "Hoosier letters and the Ku Klux." *Bookman* 67 (March 1928): 7.

"The nightriders in Missouri." *Missouri Historical Review* 37 (Oct. 1942–July 1943): 441–450.

"Night riding in Alabama." *Commonweal* 50 (8 July 1949): 309.

"1940: 'The police just laughed.'" *Southern Exposure* 8 (Summer 1980): 69.

"No place for fanatics." *Collier's* 100 (23 Oct. 1937): 74-75.

"No room for KKK, racist pranks at Purdue." *Jet* 59 (9 Oct. 1980): 30.

"Nobody turn me 'round." *Time* 86 (15 Oct. 1965): 31–32.

"North Carolina Indian raid." *Newsweek* 51 (27 Jan. 1958): 27.

Nossiter, Adam. *Of Long Memory: Mississippi and the Murder of Medgar Evers.* Reading, MA: Addison-Wesley, 1994.

Nunnelley, William. *Bull Connor.* Tuscaloosa: University of Alabama Press, 1991.

"Officials probe charges of Klansmen among Pa. police." *Jet* 59 (13 Nov. 1980): 54.

"Okla. youth buried, KKK recruiting mission fails." *Jet* 57 (21 Feb. 1980): 7.

"Oklahoma kingless, not Klanless." *Literary Digest* 79 (8 Dec. 1923): 9–11.

"Oklahoma's Klan war from over the border." *Harlow's Weekly* 22 (22 Sept. 1924): 4–5.

"Oklahoma's uncivil civil war." *Literary Digest* 78 (29 Sept. 1923): 10–11.

"Old South." *Newsweek* 94 (12 Nov. 1979): 50.

Olsen, Otto. *Carpetbagger's Crusade: The Life of Albion Winegar Tourgee.* Baltimore: Johns Hopkins Press, 1965.

_____. "The Ku Klux Klan: A study of Reconstruction politics and propaganda." *North Carolina Historical Review* 39 (July 1962): 340–362.

O'Mahony, Joseph. "The Ku Klux Klan in Indiana." *America* 30 (15 Dec. 1923): 202.

O'Reilly, Kenneth. *"Racial Matters": The FBI's Secret File on Black America.* New York: Free Press, 1989.

"Oscar Underwood's great service." *World's Work* 48 (July 1924): 242–243.

Ottley, Roy. "I met the Grand Dragon." *Nation* 169 (2 July 1949): 10–11.

"Our own secret fascisti." *Nation* 115 (15 Nov. 1922): 514–515.

"Out of the cave." *Time* 47 (3 June 1946): 25.

Overstreet, Harry, and Bonaro Overstreet. *The FBI in Our Open Society.* New York: W.W. Norton, 1969.

_____. *The Strange Tactics of Extremism.* New York: W.W. Norton, 1964.

Owens, John. "Does the Senate fear the Ku Klux Klan?" *New Republic* 37 (26 Dec. 1923): 113–114.

Papikolas, Helen. "The Greeks of Carbon County." *Utah Historical Quarterly* 22 (April 1954): 163.

_____. "Tragedy and hate." *Utah Historical Quarterly* 38 (Spring 1970): 176–181.

Parker, Thomas. *Violence in the United States.* New York: Facts on File, 1974.

Pattangall, William. "Is the Ku Klux Klan un–American?" *Forum* 74 (Sept. 1925): 321–332.

Patterson, Barbara. "Defiance and dynamite." *New South* 18 (May 1963): 8–11.

Patton, R.A. "Ku Klux Klan reign of terror." *Current History* 28 (April 1928): 51–55.

Paul, Justus, "The Ku Klux Klan in the 1926 Nebraska election." *North Dakota Quarterly* 39 (Autumn 1971): 64–70.

Payne, George. "Does the Ku Klux Klan need the Jew?" *Forum* 74 (Dec. 1925): 915–917.

Peek, Ralph. "Lawlessness in Florida: 1868–1871." *Florida Historical Quarterly* 40 (Oct. 1961): 164–185.

Percy, Leroy. "The modern Ku Klux Klan." *Atlantic Monthly* 130 (July 1922): 122–128.

Percy, William. *Lanterns on the Levee: Recollections of a Planter's Son.* New York: Alfred A. Knopf, 1941.

Perlmutter, Nathan. "Bombing in Miami, Anti-Semitism and the segregationists." *Commentary* 25 (June 1958): 498–503.

Phillips, John. *The Sign of the Cross: The Prosecutor's True Story of a Landmark Trial Against the Klan.* Louisville, KY: Westminster John Knox Press, 2000.

Phillips, Paul. "White reaction to the Freedmen's Bureau in Tennessee." *Tennessee Historical Quarterly* 25 (Spring 1966): 50–62.

Pierce, Neal. *The Deep South States of America.* New York: W.W. Norton, 1972.

Pike, D.W. *Secret Societies: Their Origin, History & Ultimate Fate.* London: Oxford University Press, 1939.

"Pink ballots for the Ku Klux Klan." *Outlook* 137 (25 June 1924): 306–309.

"Platforms of the people and the mind of the Ku Klux Klan." *Outlook* 137 (25 June 1924): 307–309.

"Playing with fire." *Time* 53 (3 Jan. 1949): 42.

Posner, Gerald. "A murder in Alabama." *Talk* (Aug. 2000): 96–101, 126–127.

Post, Louis. "A 'carpetbagger' in South Carolina." *Journal of Negro History* 10 (Jan. 1925): 10–79.

Powell, John. "The Klan un-klandestine." *Nation* 173 (29 Sept. 1951): 255.

"Powerful aid for the Klan." *Crisis* 46 (Aug. 1939): 241–242.

Preece, Harold. "The Klan declares war." *New Masses* 57 (16 Oct. 1945): 3–7.

_____. "Klan 'Murder, Inc.' in Dixie." *Crisis* 53 (Oct. 1946): 299–301.

_____. "The Klan's 'revolution of the right.'" *Crisis* 53 (July 1946): 202–203, 219–220.

"The press are unwitting ally to the Klan." *American Federationist* 88 (Aug. 1981): 22–23.

"Protectors of womanhood." *Time* 51 (16 Feb. 1948): 26.

"Protestants disowning the Ku Klux." *Literary Digest* 75 (25 Nov. 1922): 33–34.

"Quaint customs and methods of the Ku Klux Klan." *Literary Digest* 74 (5 Aug. 1922): 44–52.

Quarles, Chester. *The Ku Klux Klan and Related American Racialist and Antisemitic Organizations: A History and Analysis.* Jefferson, NC: McFarland, 1999.

"Race problem in Texas." *The Freeman* 5 (30 Aug. 1922): 578–5791 (20 Sept. 1922): 42–43.

Racine, Philip. "The Ku Klux Klan, anti-Catholicism, and Atlanta's board of education." *Georgia Historical Quarterly* 57 (Spring 1973): 63–75.

Rambow, Charles. "The Ku Klux Klan in the 1920s: A concentration on the Black Hills." *South Dakota History* 4 (Winter 1973): 63–81.

"Rampages of Ku Klux Klan on Pacific coast." *Messenger* 4 (June 1922): 419–420.

Randel, William. *The Ku Klux Klan: A Century of Infamy.* Philadelphia: Chilton Books, 1965.

Randolph, A. Philip. "The election in retrospect." *Messenger* 6 (Dec. 1924): 369–371, 390.

Raper, Arthur. *The Tragedy of Lynching.* Chapel Hill, NC: University of North Carolina Press, 1938.

"The reformation of Herrin." *Literary Digest* 86 (1 Aug. 1925): 28–29.

Reich, Frances. "The Klan rides Hitler." *Jewish Survey* 2 (June 1942): 4–6.

"The reign of the tar bucket." *Literary Digest* 70 (27 Aug. 1921): 12–13.

Reinholz, Mary. "A visit to a KKK koffee klatch in upstate New York." *New Dawn* 1 (Sept. 1976): 36.

"Report Klan growth up 50% over last four years." *Jet* 57 (3 Jan. 1980): 14.

"Resolution on KKK at Synod 12." *Criminal Justice Issues* 6 (June 1981): 11.

"The return of the KKK." *Present Tense* 6 (Summer 1979): 14–15.

"Revised and amended prescript of the order of the..." *American Historical Society Quarterly* 5 (Jan. 1900): 3–26.

Reynolds, John. *Reconstruction in South Carolina, 1865–1877.* Columbia, SC: State Co., 1905.

Ribuffo, Leo. *The Old Christian Right: The Protestant Far Right from the Depression to the Cold War.* Philadelphia: Temple University Press, 1988.

Riccio, Bill, and Bill Wilkinson. "The Klan speaks." *Southern Exposure* 8 (Summer 1980): 88–90.

Rice, Arnold. *The Ku Klux Klan in American Politics.* Washington, DC: Public Affairs Press, 1962.

Richards, Leonard. "*Gentlemen of Property and Standing*": *Anti-Abolition Mobs in Jacksonian America.* London: Oxford University Press, 1970.

Ridgeway, James. *Blood in the Face: The Ku Klux Klan, Aryan Nations, Nazi Skinheads, and the Rise of a New White Culture.* New York: Thunder's Mouth Press, 1990.

Riley, Clayton. "Macho imagery versus human rights." *Crisis* 88 (March 1981): 64–69.

Riley, Rochelle. "Board seeks to ban Klan." *National Bar Bulletin* 12 (April-June 1980): 2.

Ring, Harry. "Houston election campaign puts Socialists on the map." *Militant* 35 (24 Dec. 1971): 12–13.

"The riot at Niles." *Outlook* 138 (12 Nov. 1924): 396.

"The rise and fall of the KKK." *New Republic* 53 (30 Nov. 1927): 33–34.

"Rise and fall of the Ku Klux Klan." *Outlook* 138 (15 Oct. 1924): 237–238.

"The rise of the Klan." *Crisis* 88 (March 1981): 62–69.

"Robert Guillaume hopes to film movie on Klan." *Jet* 61 24 Sept. 1981): 58.

Roberts, Waldo. "The Ku-Kluxing of Oregon." *Outlook* 133 (14 March 1923): 490–491.

Robinson, Steve, and Jed Horne. "A virulent Ku Klux Klan returns." *Life* 4 (June 1981): 32–40.

Rogers, John. *The Murders of Mer Rouge.* St. Louis: Security Publishing Co., 1923.

Rogers, William. "Boyd incident: Black Belt violence during Reconstruction." *Civil War History* 21 (Dec. 1975): 302–329.

Romine, William. *A Story of the Original Ku Klux Klan.* Pulaski, TN: The Pulaski Citizen, 1924.

Rork, C.M. "A defense of the Klan." *New Republic* 37 (5 Dec. 1923): 44–45.

Rose, Douglas (ed.). *The Emergence of David Duke and the Politics of Race.* Chapel Hill, NC: University of North Carolina Press, 1992.

Rose, Laura. *The Ku Klux Klan or Invisible Empire.* New Orleans: Graham, 1914.

Rose, Thomas (ed.). *Violence in America.* New York: Vintage, 1970.

Rosenthal, A.M., and Arthur Gelb. *One More Victim.* New York: New American Library, 1967.

Rovere, Richard. "The Klan rides again." *Nation* 150 (6 April 1940): 445–446.

Roy, Ralph. *Apostles of Discord: A Study of Organized Bigotry and Disruption on the Fringes of Protestantism.* Boston: Beacon Press, 1953.

Ruark, H.G. "Fear Klan revival in the Carolinas." *Christian Century* 75 (26 Feb. 1958): 257.

Rubin, Jay. *The Ku Klux Klan in Binghamton, New York, 1923–1928.* Binghamton: Broome County Historical Society, 1973.

Ruiz, Jim. *The Black Hood of the Ku Klux Klan.* Lanham, MD: Austin & Winfield, 1997.

"Same old HUAC." *Nation* 201 (1 Nov. 1965): 290–291.

"San Diego bishop urges defeat of Klansman." *National Catholic Reporter* 16 (17 Oct. 1980): 3–4.

"San Jose protesters thwart KKK rally." *Jet* 60 (7 May 1981): 5.

Sawyer, Reuben. *The Truth About the Invisible Empire, Knights of the Ku Klux Klan.* Portland, OR: Northwest Domain, 1922.

Schaefer, Richard. "Ku Klux Klan: Continuity and change." *Phylon* 32 (Summer 1971): 143–157.

Schardt, Arlie. "A Mississippi mayor fights the Klan." *Reporter* 34 (27 Jan. 1966): 39–40.

Schonbach, Morris. *Native American Fascism During the 1930s and 1940s.* New York: Garland, 1985.

"School accepts KKK book for students, limits use." *Jet* 58 (31 July 1980): 54.

Schwartz, Alan. *Danger—Extremism: The Major Vehicles and Voices on America's Far-Right Fringe.* New York: ADL, 1996.

Scott, Martin. "Catholics and the Ku Klux Klan." *North American Review* 223 (June 1926): 268–281.

Sendor, Elizabeth. "When terror rode at night." *Senior Scholastic* 111 (8 Feb. 1979): 17–19.

Shankman, Arnold. "Julian Harris and the Ku Klux Klan." *Mississippi Quarterly* 28 (Spring 1975): 147–169.

_____. "Julian Harris and the Negro." *Phylon* 35 (1974): 442–456.

Shapiro, Herman. "The Ku Klux Klan during Reconstruction: The South Carolina episode." *Journal of Negro History* 49 (Jan. 1964): 35–55.

Shay, Frank. *Judge Lynch: His First Hundred Years.* New York: Washburn, 1938.

"Shed a tear for the Klan." *Nation* 119 (9 Oct. 1924): 351–352.

"Sheet, surgar sack and cross." *Time* 51 (15 March 1948): 29.

"The 'sheeted jerks' of the Ku Klux Klan." *Nation* 169 (2 July 1949): 2–4.

Shepherd, William. "How I put over the Klan." *Collier's* 82 (14 July 1928): 5–7, 32, 34–35.

_____. "Indiana's mystery man." *Collier's* 79 (8 Jan. 1927): 8–9, 47–49.

_____. "Ku Klux koin." *Collier's* 82 (21 July 1928): 8–9, 38–39.

_____. "The whip hand in Alabama." *Collier's* 81 (7 Jan. 1928): 44–45.

_____. "The whip wins." *Collier's* 81 (14 Jan. 1928): 10–11, 30, 32.

Sherrill, Robert. "Expose of tedium, terror and fiscal tricks at HUAC." *New South* 21 (Winter 1966): 57–63.

_____. *Gothic Politics in the Deep South.* New York: Grossman, 1968.

Shipp, Bill. *Murder at Broad River Bridge: The Slaying of Lemuel Penn by Members of the Ku Klux Klan.* Atlanta: Peachtree Publishers, 1982.

"Shooting at the Klan but wounding the Negro." *Christian Century* 82 (22 Sept. 1965): 1149.

"Shots in the shadows." *Newsweek* 49 (4 Feb. 1957): 26.

"The sign on the cross." *America* 173 (15–22 July 1995): 3.

Sikora, Frank. *Until Justice Rolls Down: The Birmingham Church Bombing Case.* Tuscaloosa: University of Alabama Press, 1991.

Silverman, Joseph. "The Ku Klux Klan a paradox." *North American Review* 223 (June-Aug. 1926): 282–291.

Simkins, Francis. "The Ku Klux Klan in South Carolina, 1868–1871." *Journal of Negro History* 12 (Oct. 1927): 606–647.

Simmons, William. *America's Menace or the Enemy Within.* Atlanta: Patriotic Books, 1926.

_____. *The Klan Unmasked.* Atlanta: W.F. Thompson, 1923.

Sims, Patsy. *The Klan.* New York: Stein & Day, 1978.

Singer, Sty. "Armed Klansmen threaten socialites." *Militant* 39 (7 March 1975): 28.

Singular, Stephen. *Talked to Death.* New York: Berkley, 1987.

The Skinhead International: A Worldwide Survey of Neo-Nazi Skinheads. New York: ADL, 1995.

Skinner, R. Dana. "Is the Ku Klux Klan Katholik?" *Independent* 111 (24 Nov. 1923): 242–243.

Skolnick, Jerome. *The Politics of Protest.* New York: Simon & Schuster, 1969.

Sletterdahl, Peter. *The Nightshirt in Politics.* Minneapolis: Ajax Publishing, 1926.

Sloan, Charles Jr. "Kansas battles the Invisible Empire: The legal ouster of the KKK from Kansas, 1922–1927." *Kansas Historical Quarterly* 57 (Autumn 1974): 393–409.

Sloan, John. "The Ku Klux Klan and the Alabama election of 1872." *Alabama Review* 17 (April 1965): 113–124.

Smiley, Wendell. *The North Carolina Press Views the Ku Klux Klan from 1964 through 1966.* Greenville, NC: The Author, 1968.

Smith, Baxter. "The Klan rides at Naponoch."

Militant 39 (24 Jan. 1975): 11; (4 April 1975): 24.

_____. "The resurgence of the KKK." *Black Scholar* 12 (Jan.-Feb. 1981): 225–30.

Smith, Brent. *Terrorism in America: Pipe Bombs and Pipe Dreams.* Albany: State University of New York Press, 1994.

Smith, Norman. "The Ku Klux Klan in Rhode Island." *Rhode Island History* 37 (1978): 35–45.

Smith, Philip. "Same problems, new faces." *Dollars and Sense* 6 (Feb./March 1981): 45, 49.

Smith, Robert. "Klan spooks in Congress." *Independent* 116 (19 June 1926): 718–719.

Smith, Vern. "Unsolved murders." *Emerge* 7 (April 1996): 30–37.

"Snake-pit." *Newsweek* 67 (24 Jan. 1966): 29–30.

Snell, William. "Fiery crosses in the Roaring Twenties: Activities of the revised Klan in Alabama, 1915–1930." *Alabama Review* 23 (Oct. 1970): 256–276.

"Solemn but undignified penguins." *Nation* 116 (3 Jan. 1923): 6–7.

Sonnichsen, C.L., and M.G. McKinney. "El Paso—From war to depression." *Southwestern Historical Quarterly* 74 (Jan. 1971): 357–371.

"South Carolina's race war." *New Republic* 123 (11 Sept. 1950): 8–9.

"The South: Its dark side." *American Missionary Magazine* 13 (Oct. 1869): 230–231.

"Southern exposure." *Newsweek* 72 (25 Nov. 1968): 111–112.

"Southern reaction to the arrest of a klansman." *Nation* 174 (8 Marc 1952): 215.

Stagg, J.C.A. "The problem of Klan violence: The South Carolina up-country, 1868–1871." *Journal of American Studies* 8 (Dec. 1974): 303–318.

Stampp, Kenneth. *The Era of Reconstruction, 1865–1877.* New York: Alfred A. Knopf, 1965.

Stanton, Bill. *Klanwatch: Bringing the Ku Klux Klan to Justice.* New York: Grove Weidenfeld, 1991.

Stanton, E.F. *Christ and Other Klansmen or Lives of Love.* Kansas City: Stanton & Harper, 1924.

Stanton, Mary. *From Selma to Sorrow: The Life and Death of Viola Liuzzo.* Athens, GA: University of Georgia Press, 1998.

Stark, Rodney. *Police Riots.* Belmont, CA: Wadsworth, 1972.

Steinberg, Alfred. *The Bosses.* New York: Macmillan, 1972.

Stephens, Harold. "Mask and lash in Crenshaw." *North American Review* 225 (April 1928): 435–442.

Stern, Kenneth. *A Force Upon the Plain: The American Militia Movement and the Politics of Hate.* New York: Simon & Schuster, 1996.

_____. *Holocaust Denial.* New York: American Jewish Committee, 1993.

Stewart, John. *Ku Klux Klan Menace: The Cross Against People.* Durham, NC: The Author, 1980.

Stockbridge, Frank. "The Ku Klux Klan revival." *Current History* 14 (April 1921): 19–25.

Stone, Elizabeth. "KKK scum in Boston: 'Real issue is niggers." *Militant* 38 (18 Oct. 1974): 4.

"The strange invasion." *Newsweek* 49 (13 May 1957): 58.

"The strange invasion; British Klans." *Newsweek* 49 (13 May 1957): 58.

Suall, Irwin. "The Ku Klux Klan malady lingers on." *Civil Rights Quarterly Perspectives* 12 (Fall 1980-Winter 1980): 11–15.

Suall, Irwin, and David Lowe. "The hate movement today: A chronicle of violence and disarray." *Terrorism* 10 (1987): 345–364.

"Subpoena the Klan." *America* 96 (9 Feb. 1957): 520.

Sullivan, Mark. "Midsummer politics and primaries." *World's Work* 44 (July 1922): 296–302.

Swallow, Craig. "The Ku Klux Klan in Nevada during the 1920s." *Nevada Historical Society Quarterly* 24 (1981): 202–230.

Sweeney, Charles. "The great bigotry merger." *Nation* 115 (5 July 1922): 8–10.

Swertfeger, Jack Jr. "Anti-mask and anti-Klan laws." *Journal of Public Law* 1 (1952): 195–196.

"Talent rewarded: Mr. Justice Black." *Catholic World* 146 (Nov. 1937): 129–134.

Tannenbaum, Frank. "Books to cure clannishness." *World Tomorrow* 7 (March 1924): 94.

_____. *Darker Phases of the South.* New York: G.P. Putnam's Sons, 1924.

_____. "The Ku Klux Klan: Its social origin in the South." *Century* 105 (April 1923): 873–882.

Tarrants, Thomas. *The Conversion of a Klansman: The Story of a Former Ku Klux Klan Terrorist.* Garden City, NY: Doubleday, 1979.

Taylor, A.A. "The Negro in South Carolina: Opposition to Reconstruction." *Journal of Negro History* 9 (July 1924): 442–468.

Taylor, Alva. "Klan seen trying for a comeback." *Christian Century* 67 (1 Feb. 1950): 148, 150.

_____. "What the Klan did in Indiana." *New Republic* 52 (16 Nov. 1927): 330–332.

"Teachers' group plans to issue anti-Klan guide." *Jet* 60 (11 June 1981): 14.

Tenenbaum, Samuel. *Why Men Hate.* New York: Beechhurst Press, 1947.

"Tenn. Klansmen charged in gunning down black women." *Jet* 58 (8 May 1980): 6.

Tennessee General Assembly. *Report of Evidence Taken Before the Military Committee in Relation to Outrages Committed by the Ku Klux Klan in Middle and West Tennessee.* Nashville: S.C. Mercer, 1868.

"Terrorism today." *Christianity Today* 22 (22 Sept. 1978): 12–16.

Testimony for the Prosecution in the Case of United States versus Robert Hayes Mitchell. Cincinnati: Phonographic Institute, 1913.

"Then school bells rang." *Newsweek* 60 (17 Sept. 1962): 31–32, 34.

Theoharis, Athan. *Spying on Americans: Political Surveillance from Hoover to the Huston Plan.* Philadelphia: Temple University Press, 1978.

Thompson, Jerry. *My Life in the Klan: A True Story by the First Investigative Reporter to Infiltrate the Ku Klux Klan.* New York: Putnam, 1982.

Thornburgh, Emma. "Segregation in Indiana during the Klan era of the 1920s." *Mississippi Valley Historical Review* 47 (March 1961): 594–618.

Thornton, J. Mills III. "Alabama politics, J. Thomas Heflin, and the expulsion movement of 1929." *Alabama Review* 21 (April 1968): 83–112.

Toll, William. "Progress and piety: The Ku Klux Klan and social change in Tillamook, Oregon." *Pacific Northwest Quarterly* 69 (April 1978): 75–85.

Tourgee, Albion. *A Fool's Errand by One of the Fools: The Famous Romance of American History. The Invisible Empire: A Concise Review of the Epoch on Which the Tale is Based.* New York: Fords, Howard & Hulbert, 1879.

Toy, Eckard Jr. "The Ku Klux Klan in Tillamook, Oregon." *Pacific Northwest Quarterly* 53 (April 1962): 60–64.

"Trap for a terrorist." *Newsweek* 72 (15 July 1968): 31A.

Trelease, Allen. *White Terror: The Ku Klux Klan Conspiracy and Southern Reconstruction.* Westport, CT: Greenwood Press, 1971.

_____. "White terror." *New Republic* 165 (17 July 1971): 30.

"Tremors of bigotry that worry America." *U.S. News & World Report* 91 (13 July 1981): 48–49.

Trent, Willia. "A new South's view of Reconstruction." *Sewanee Review* 9 (Jan. 1901): 13–29.

"Trial by jury." *Newsweek* 66 (1 Nov. 1965): 36.

"Trouble at Charley's place." *Newsweek* 36 (11 Sept. 1950): 36–37.

Tourgee, Albion. *A Fool's Errand by One of the Fools.* New York: Fords, Howard & Hulbert, 1879.

Tucker, Richard. *Dragon and the Cross: The Rise and Fall of the Ku Klux Klan in Middle America.* North Haven, CT: Archon Books, 1991.

Tucker, Todd. *Notre Dame vs. the Klan: How the Fighting Irish Defeated the Ku Klux Klan.* Chicago: Loyola Press, 2004.

Tully, Andrew. *The FBI's Most Famous Cases.* New York: Dell, 1965.

Turner, William. *The Police Establishment.* New York: Tower, 1969.

_____. *Power on the Right.* Berkeley, CA: Ramparts Press, 1971.

Tyack, David. "Perils of pluralism" The background of the Pierce case." *American Historical Review* 74 (Oct. 1968): 74–98.

Tyler, Charles. *The KKK.* New York: Abbey Press, 1902.

"The ultimate white sale." *Mother Jones* 4 (April 1979): 8.

"Un-American Klan." *Economist* 215 (3 April 1965): 48, 50.

"Uncle Henry on the Klan komplex." *Collier's* 72 (27 Jan. 1923): 15–16.

"United against Ku Kluxism." *Messenger* 5 (Aug. 1923): 781–782.

"United front against the Ku Klux menace." *Messenger* 4 (Sept. 1922): 478–479.

United States Congress. *Joint Select Committee to Inquire into the Condition of Affairs in the Late Insurrectionary States.* 13 volumes. Washington, DC: Government Printing Office, 1872.

_____. *The Ku Klux Klan. Hearings Before the Committee on Rules, House of Representatives, 67th Congress, 1st Session.* Washington, DC: Government Printing Office, 1921.

_____. *Hearings Before Subcommittee on Privileges and Elections, United States Senate, 68th*

Congress, 1st Session, Pursuant to S. Res. 97 Authorizing the Investigation of Alleged Unlawful Practices in the Election of a Senator from Texas. Washington, DC: Government Printing Office, 1924.

_____. Report on the Alleged Outrages in the Southern States, by the Select Committee of the Senate. Washington, DC: Government Printing Office, 1871.

"University of Oklahoma and the Ku Klux Klan." *School and Society* 16 (7 Oct. 1922): 412–413.

"Unraveling secrets of the hooded Klan." *U.S. News and World Report* 59 (1 Nov. 1965): 12–13.

"Unsheeting the Klan." *Newsweek* 65 (12 April 1965): 29–30.

Van Der Veer, Virginia. "Hugo Black and the KKK." *American Heritage* 19 (April 1968): 60–64, 108–111.

"The various shady lives of the Ku Klux Klan." *Time* 85 (9 April 1965): 24–25.

Velie, Lester. "The Klan rides the South again." *Collier's* 122 (9 Oct. 1948): 13–15, 74–75.

"Verdict in Greensboro." *Progressive* 45 (Jan. 1981): 9–10.

"Victory in Gary." *Crisis* 35 (Jan. 1928): 13, 30.

"Vile bodies." *Economist* 264 (9 July 1977): 36–37.

"Violence erupts after jury acquits Klansmen in Chattanooga shooting." *Jet* 58 (7 Aug. 1980): 8.

"The violence trap." *Nation* 210 (9 March 1970): 261–262.

"The violent rebirth of the Ku Klux Klan." *Reader's Digest* 118 (March 1981): 118–121.

"A virulent Klan rearms." *Life* 4 (June 1981): 32–39.

Vollers, Maryanne. *Ghosts of Mississippi: The Murder of Medgar Evers, the Trials of Byron De La Beckwith, and the Haunting of the New South.* Boston: Little, Brown, 1995.

Von Vulcan, Joshua. *Brothers of the Robe: A Story of Unbridled Valor and Resistance to Racial Extinction.* Noxon, MT: Javelin Press, 1996.

Wald, Kenneth. "The visible empire: The Ku Klux Klan as an electoral movement." *Journal of Interdisciplinary History* 11 (Autumn 1980): 217–234.

Wallace, Max. *The American Axis: Henry Ford, Charles Lindbergh, and the Rise of the Third Reich.* New York: St. Martin's, 2003.

Wallace, Robert. "New forces in a broken land." *Life* 41 (10 Sept. 1956): 99.

Warnecke, Nancy, Kirk Loggins, and Susan Thomas. "'Just like the Scouts': The Klan Youth Corps." *Southern Exposure* 8 (Summer 1980): 91–92.

Waskow, Arthur. *From Race Riot to Sit-in.* New York: Doubleday, 1966.

"WBOX and the KKK." *Newsweek* 66 (16 Aug. 1965): 75–76.

"We stopped the Klan in Greensboro." *IFCO News* 7 (April 1980): 1, 4, 5, 11.

Weaver, Charles. *A Ku Klux Klan Raid, and What Became of It.* Durham, NC: The Author, 1897.

The Web of Hate: Extremists Exploit the Internet. New York: ADL, 1996.

Webb, Clive. *Fight Against Fear: Southern Jews and Black Civil Rights.* Athens, GA: University of Georgia Press, 1997.

"The week—KKK." *Nation* 6 (9 April 1968): 283.

Weir, Sally. "Reminiscences of the Ku Klux Klan." *Metropolitan Magazine* 26 (April 1907): 97–106.

Weller, Worth. *Under the Hood: Unmasking the Modern Ku Klux Klan.* North Manchester, IN: DeWitt Books, 1999.

Wells, James. *The Chisolm Massacre: A Picture of Home-Rule in Mississippi.* Washington, DC: Chisolm Monument Assn., 1878.

"'We're the future Klan.'" *NEA Reporter* 20 (June 1981): 9.

Wesberry, James. "KKK holds cross-burning near Atlanta." *Christian Century* 74 (9 Jan. 1957): 54.

West, Jerry. *The Reconstruction Ku Klux Klan in York County, South Carolina, 1865–1877.* Jefferson, NC: 2002.

Wetta, Frank. "Bulldozing the scalawags." *Louisiana History* 21 (Winter 1980): 43–58.

"What is wrong with the Klan?" *Nation* 118 (18 June 1924): 698–699.

"What the sit-ins are stirring up." *U.S. News & World Report* 48 (18 April 1960): 52–54.

Wheaton, Elizabeth. *Codename Greenkil: The 1979 Greensboro Killings.* Athens, GA: University of Georgia Press, 1987.

"When Carolina Indians went on the warpath." *U.S. News & World Report* 44 (31 Jan. 1958): 14–15.

White, Alma. *Heroes of the Fiery Cross.* Zarephath, NJ: Good Citizen, 1928.

_____. *Klansmen: Guardians of Liberty.* Zarephath, NJ: Good Citizen, 1926.

_____. *The Ku Klux Klan in Prophecy.* Zarephath, NJ: Good Citizen, 1925.

White, Arthur. "An American fascismo." *Forum* 72 (Nov. 1924): 636–642.

White, Walter. "Election by terror in Florida." *New Republic* 25 (12 Jan. 1921): 195–197.

_____. *A Man Called White: The Autobiography of Walter White.* New York: Viking Press, 1948.

_____. "Reviving the Ku Klux Klan." *Forum* 65 (April 1921): 426–434.

_____. *Rope and Faggot.* New York: Knopf, 1929.

White, William. "Annihilate the Klan!" *Nation* 120 (7 Jan. 1925): 7.

_____. "Patience and publicity." *World Tomorrow* 7 (March 1924): 87.

Whitehead, Don. *Attack on Terror: The FBI Against the Ku Klux Klan in Mississippi.* New York: Funk & Wagnalls, 1970.

_____. *The FBI Story.* New York: Random House, 1956.

"Whitewashing white racists: *Junior Scholastic* and the KKK." *Interracial Books for Children* 11 (1980): 3–6, 21.

"Why Kansas bans the Klan." *Literary Digest* 75 (11 Nov. 1922): 13–14.

"Why they join the Klan." *New Republic* 36 (21 Nov. 1923): 321–322.

Wieck, Agnes. "Ku Kluxing in the miners' country." *New Republic* 38 (26 March 1924): 122–124.

Wilayton, Phil. "Fighting the Klan in the military." *Southern Changes* 2 (Jan. 1980): 8–11.

Wilhoit, Francis. *The Politics of Massive Resistance.* New York: George Braziller, 1973.

"William Allen White's war on the Klan." *Literary Digest* 83 (11 Oct. 1924): 16–17.

Williams, Dennis, and William Cook. "Mistaken identity." *Newsweek* 88 (13 Dec. 1976): 35, 37.

Williams, Dennis, Eleanor Clift, and William Schmidt. "Klan also rises." *Newsweek* 87 (12 Jan. 1976): 33–34.

Williams, Dennis, and Lea Donosky. "The great white hope." *Newsweek* 90 (14 Nov. 1977): 45–46.

Williams, Donald. "Protest under the cross: The Ku Klux Klan presents its case to the public." *Southern Speech Journal* 27 (Fall 1961): 43–55.

Williams, Lou. *The Great South Carolina Ku Klux Klan Trials, 1871–1872.* Athens, GA: University of Georgia Press, 1996.

Williams, Robert. *Negroes with Guns.* New York: Marzani & Munsell, 1962.

Wilson, D.L. "The beginning of the Ku Klux Klan." *Southern Bivouac* 4 (Oct. 1885): 269–271.

_____. "The Ku Klux Klan, its origin, growth, and disbandment." *Century* 28 (July 1884): 398–410.

Wilson, Walter. "The Meridian massacre of 1871." *Crisis* 81 (Feb. 1974): 49–52.

Wilson, William. "Long, hot summer in Indiana, 1924." *American Heritage* 16 (2 Aug. 1965): 56–64.

Winter, Paul. *What Price Tolerance.* New York: All American Book, Lecture & Research Bureau, 1928.

"Wiping out Oregon's school law." *Literary Digest* 81 (26 April 1924): 33–34.

Witcher, Walter. *The Reign of Terror in Oklahoma.* Fort Worth, TX: The Author, 1923.

"With malice afore thought." *Time* 55 (13 March 1950): 24.

Wolf, Horace. "How shall we meet the Klan?" *World Tomorrow* 7 (March 1924): 85.

Wood, W.D. "The Ku Klux Klan." *Quarterly of the Texas State Historical Association* 9 (April 1906): 262–268.

Woodward, C. Vann. *Tom Watson, Agrarian Rebel.* New York: Macmillan, 1938.

Woolever, Harry. "Shall the Ku Klux Klan parade in the nation's capital?" *Southwest Christian Advocate* (30 July 1925): 601–602.

Wright, George. *Racial Violence in Kentucky, 1865–1940: Lynchings, Mob Rule, and "Legal Lynchings."* Baton Rouge: Louisiana State University Press, 1990.

Wright, Walter. *Religious and Patriotic Order of the Ku Klux Klan.* Waco, TX: The Author, 1926.

Young Nazi Killers: The Rising Skinhead Danger. New York: ADL, 1993.

"You're another." *New Republic* 183 (27 Sept. 1980): 7.

Zanden, James. "The Klan revival." *American Journal of Sociology* 65 (March 1960): 456–462.

Zeskind, Leonard. *The "Christian Identity" Movement: Analyzing Its Theological Rationalization for Racist and Anti-Semitic Violence.* Atlanta: Center for Democratic Renewal, 1986.

INDEX